MONTGOMERY CO
GERMANTOWN CAMPUS

POLITICAL REPRESSION
IN MODERN AMERICA

POLITICAL REPRESSION IN MODERN AMERICA
From 1870 to the Present

Robert Justin Goldstein

Schenkman Publishing Co., Inc.
Two Continents Publishing Group Ltd.
Cambridge/New York

Copyright © 1978

Schenkman Publishing Company, Inc.
3 Mt. Auburn Place
Cambridge, Massachusetts   02138

Distributed by Two Continents Publishing Group, Ltd.,
30 East 42nd Street, New York, New York 10017

GOLDSTEIN, ROBERT J.

   Political Repression in Modern American History
   Bibliography: p.
   Includes index.

   1. Civil rights—United States—History.   I. Title.   JC599.U5G58
323.4'0973   76-54842   ISBN 0-8467-0301-7

Printed in the United States of America.

ALL RIGHTS RESERVED. THIS BOOK, OR PARTS THEREOF, MAY NOT BE REPRODUCED IN ANY FORM WITHOUT THE WRITTEN PERMISSION OF THE PUBLISHERS.

For Renate

Acknowledgements

I am indebted to Professors Zolberg, Paul Peterson, and Peter Novick, for not repressing me, politically or otherwise, in this project. They were involved in an earlier stage of this book when they constituted a committee of the University of Chicago. I would like to thank Guy Williams, formerly a graduate student at San Diego State University, for undertaking the tedious task of compiling the index. I am grateful to all at Schenkman Publishing Company for their early seeing the importance of this project, and for their determination in getting this mammoth book to the press. I acknowledge the assistance of Production Editor Victoria Fraser in translating a mass of garbled pages into a final printed product. Above all, I am grateful to Libby Koponen, my editor, for letting this project invade her life for what must have seemed, to her as to me, years, for her good humor and enthusiasm, and for her apt suggestions and deft corrections which have immensely improved this book.

As usual, the author alone must take responsibility for any errors in this book. I would greatly appreciate it if readers who find errors either of commission or of omission would contact me so that future editions may benefit.

POLITICAL REPRESSION IN MODERN AMERICA is dedicated to a young East German woman who escaped from her country to Western Europe, knowing that she risked a year in jail in East Germany if she failed in her attempt. Her courage and her being illumined my life during the weeks in Europe that I knew her. Her story also served to remind me that political repression is a disease of the world, and not of any one country — and also that political repression unchecked can convert an entire society into a prison, complete with walls and barbed wire.

February, 1977
Rochester, Michigan

Table of Contents

INTRODUCTION	ix
The Consensus Approach	x
The Neglect of Political Repression	xiii
Towards a Definition of Political Repression	xvi
Some Warnings	xxi
1. THE REPRESSION OF LABOR: 1873-1937	**1**
The Power of Business in Post-Civil War America	6
The Techniques of Labor Repression	9
2. THE DEVELOPMENT OF REPRESSIVE TECHNIQUES, 1873-1900	**21**
The Red Scare of 1873-1878	24
The Communist-Anarchist-Labor Scare of 1886	34
The Communist-Anarchist-Labor Scare of 1892-1896	44
3. THE PROGRESSIVE ERA	**61**
The Anarchist Scare of 1901-1903	66
The Repression of the Western Federation of Miners, 1903-1907	70
The Anarchist-Labor Scare of 1907-1909	76
The Rise of Class Tensions, 1910-1917	80
Patterns of Repression, 1910-1913	84
The Crisis of 1914-1916	93
4. WORLD WAR I: WILSON'S NEW FREEDOM	**103**
The Strength of the Anti-War Movement	105
Federal Repression of the Anti-War Movement	107
The "Labor Deal"	121
State and Local Repression of the Anti-War Movement	125
The Effects of World War I Repression	131
5. THE GREAT RED SCARE OF 1919-1920	**137**
Radical Strength in 1919	139
Early Development of the Red Scare	144
Intensification of the Red Scare	151
Climax of the Red Scare—The Palmer Raids	154
Decline of the Red Scare	158

6. THE 1920s: CONFORMITY FOR THE MASSES, REPRESSION FOR THE FEW — 165

Repression and Conformity in the Twenties — 171
Repression of Labor — 183

7. THE GREAT DEPRESSION AND THE NEW DEAL — 193

The Hoover Administration: Depression and Repression, 1929-1932 — 195
State and Local Repression, 1929-1932 — 201
Reforms and Resistance to Repression, 1929-1932 — 206
A New Deal and a New Mood — 209
The Abortive Red Scare of 1934-1935 — 213
State and Local Repression, 1933-1938 — 217
The Failure of Repression in the Mid-Thirties — 233

8. THE COMING OF THE NEW WAR — 237

The Repressive Deal, 1938-1941 — 239
State and Local Repression, 1938-1941 — 255
World War II — The Good War? — 262
State and Local Repression During World War II — 281
An Assessment of the "Good" War — 283

9. TRUMAN-McCARTHYISM, 1946-1954 — 285

New Pressures for Repression, 1945-1947 — 287
Initiation of the Domestic Cold War, 1947-1950 — 298
The Rise of McCarthy, 1950-1952 — 320
The Eisenhower Administration, 1952-1954 — 334
The Role of Congress, 1950-1954 — 343
State and Local Repression, 1947-1954 — 348
The Collapse of the Liberals, 1947-1954 — 360
The Long-Term Effects of Truman-McCarthyism — 369

10. AN INTERLUDE BETWEEN THE WARS, 1954-1964 — 397

Less Repression, Even Less Dissent: 1954-1960 — 399
The Kennedy Era: A New Frontier in Civil Liberties? — 412

11. THE VIETNAM WAR ERA, 1965-1975 — 427

The Social Setting for Political Repression, 1965-1975 — 429
Johnson and the Great Society — 432
The "Law and Order" Nixon Administration — 461
State and Local Repression, 1965-1975 — 504
Repression on the Campus — 518
Joint Federal-Local Repression of the Black Panthers — 523
The Significance of Political Repression in the Vietnam War Era — 530
The Prospects for Political Freedom in the United States — 537

CONCLUSION — 547
The Significance of Political Repression — 547
Variables Associated With Changing Levels of Political Repression — 558
Closing Words — 574
Notes — 575
Bibliography — 653
Index — 663

Introduction

The conceptual heart of democratic theory is the free and open circulation of all ideas, no matter how abhorrent they may be to some or all segments of the population. The free market of ideas is the essence of a democratic society. Without the truly free exchange of ideas, the citizens of a society are denied the right to decide for themselves, for they are denied access to all possible alternatives. Suppression of ideas does not merely violate "abstract" theories concerned with democracy; it may well deprive an entire society of the opportunity to find out vital information, to correct widely believed mistruths and to consider new ways of solving previously unsolvable problems.[1] It is not a coincidence that after medieval religious authorities in Italy forbade Galileo to espouse his belief that the sun and not the earth was the center of the solar system, the center of scientific progress in Europe shifted to other countries.

The purpose of this study is to demonstrate that political repression (defined later in this chapter) has frequently interfered with the free market of ideas in modern American history (defined as beginning in 1870)[2] and has been a significant factor in shaping the development of crucial aspects of modern American politics and society. The holders of *certain* ideas in the United States have been systematically and gravely discriminated against and subjected to extraordinary treatment by governmental authorities, such as physical assaults, denials of freedom of speech and assembly, political deportations and firings, dubious and discriminatory arrests, intense police surveillance, and illegal burglaries, wiretaps and interception of mail. Such political repression has had a number of important effects upon American life. This book demonstrates that political repression has contributed significantly to the following:

- The failure of American labor to achieve major power until the 1930's.
- The destruction of radical labor movements.
- The destruction of radical political movements.
- The self-censorship which Americans have imposed upon their own exercise of basic political freedoms.

Given the obvious importance of the free circulation of ideas for democratic theory and practice, the lack of attention devoted to the possible importance of political repression in modern American history by social scientists is striking; this is partcularly so because the spectrum of what might be termed "acceptable" political opinion in the United States, especially with regard to radical labor or explicitly socialist ideologies, is and has been narrower than that of perhaps any other industrialized democracy. In the words of historian Richard Hofstader:

> The fierceness of the [American] political struggles has often been misleading; for the range of vision embraced by the primary contestants in the major parties has always been bounded by the horizons of property and enterprise. However much at odds, on specific issues, the major political traditions have shared a belief in the rights of property, the philosophy of economic individualism, the economic value of competition; they have accepted the economic virtues of capitalist culture as the necessary qualities of man ... The business of politics — so the creed runs — is to protect this competitive world, to foster it on occasion, to patch up its incidental abuses but not to cripple it with a plan for common collective action.[3]

American social scientists have not seriously considered political repression as one important factor which helps explain the narrowness of the American political spectrum, but there is certainly no reason to exclude the possibility that it has helped to shape this narrow "range of vision." The forced suicide of Socrates, the burning at the stake of medieval heretics, the forced recantation of Galileo, the expulsion of Roger Williams from Massachusetts Bay Colony, the attempted supression of the Jeffersonians during the Alien and Sedition Act crisis and the modern experience with totalitarian fascism and communism remind us that a wide variety of governments throughout history have responded with repression to the expression of ideas which were viewed as threatening. As political scientist Robert Dahl has pointed out, "Governments have usually tried to prevent the development of opposition . . . without question the most commonplace way for a government to deal with its opponents is to employ violence."[4]

The Consensus Approach

The standard explanation for the striking narrowness of the American political spectrum offered by American historians is that for various reasons conditions in America were so good that the social climate simply was not conducive to the development of radical ideas. Thus, America's wealth, her lack of a feudal background with its attendant class tensions, the existence of a frontier "safety valve" to provide an outlet for discontented urban workers, the relative ease of social mobility, the responsiveness of the political system and the tradition of strong individualism as opposed to collective action have all been cited frequently as factors which allegedly operated to prevent radical dissenters from gaining a strong foothold.[5] By tacit omission (and sometimes by commission) American social scientists have rejected the idea that political repression has been a major factor in shaping the American "consensus," and other important aspects of American society and politics.

The concepts in the preceding paragraphs, known as the "consensus" school of American historiography, have thoroughly penetrated the political science discipline.[6] Thus Grant McConnell writes:

> American politics has been largely free of class divisions and American political thought has had little to offer on this subject. This lack is the consequence, as Louis Hartz has said (echoing Tocqueville) of the fact that Americans were "born equal" without having had to become so. There has been a profound consensus on the large issues that in other countries have been subject to the overriding fact of class conflict.[7]

Robert Dahl also finds an "astonishing unity of views" in America over basic political and economic questions. Among the factors to which Dahl attributes this are a common English political tradition, and a lack of class consciousness, resulting from the "equality of conditions" arising from the "vast supply of cheap land," which in turn created a nation of landholders to whom "the virtues of private property were obvious" and who therefore developed a "strong emphasis on individual achievement." The main tenets of American social, economic, and political life have therefore enjoyed "an immunity from comprehensive criticism."[8]

The pervasive influence of the "consensus" school on political scientists can be demonstrated by a selection from a recently published textbook, designed for use in college courses in American government. Thomas R. Dye and L. Harmon Zeigler in *The Irony of Democracy*, a widely adopted text, write:

> The explanation for the broad popular consensus in America rests ultimately in the fact that capitalism as an economic system has been extremely successful. The very success of the economic system has helped to smother class differences, which in any case have never been as strong in America as in most other Western democracies. The absence in America of a feudal past and a European-type aristocracy, the vast opportunities provided by the frontier and relative economic abundance have combined to make Americans a "people of plenty."[9]

Given this explanation by American social scientists for a general lack of radical dissent, it is not surprising that similar answers are given when the inquiry is focused specifically on the failure of strong radical (i.e. anticapitalist) labor movements and strong radical (especially socialist and communist) political parties to develop in the United States. The usual answer is that such groups did not develop strength because social conditions were too good to allow them to do so.

It is a commonplace observation that one of the distinguishing characteristics of the mainstream of the American labor movement is its acceptance of the capitalist order and its concentration on narrow, bread-and-butter goals such as improvements in wages, hours, and working conditions — goals which make no attempt to change the clearly subordinate role of the worker in terms of ownership and management. Labor movements in most other industrialized countries have sought to achieve considerably more fundamental reforms in society.[10] As labor economist Everett Kassalow has commented:

> American unions were almost inevitably exclusionist in nature — their overwhelming concentration was on winning and defending benefits for members only, without great concern for the social order as such . . . On the other hand, European unions were part of a wider social movement aimed at changing the whole society on behalf of *all* workers — not just union members . . . Plans for socialization of the means of production, the liquidation of capitalism and the substitution of a society producing for social rather than private gain highlighted all these movements.[11]

In seeking to explain this deviation of the American labor movement from the pattern of other labor movements, most American scholars have stressed that conditions were so "good" in the United States that the social base for a radical labor movement simply did not exist. The dominant interpretation of the American labor movement has remained that first established fifty years ago by labor historians John R. Commons and Selig Perlman, sometimes known as the "Wisconsin theory." According to Commons, American labor rejected class consciousness largely due to the "wide expanse of free land," which provided an "escape" for oppressed workers. Commons also pointed to the fact that American workers won the ballot before the labor movement was even organized as another factor which tended to deradicalize the American labor movement; in contrast, the struggle for the right to vote had served as a great focal point for class consciousness in other labor movements. These conditions, together with other factors such as the difficulty of organizing many different races and nationalities, eventually led the American labor movement to adopt the conservative philosophy of the American Federation of Labor by "a kind of natural selection."[12]

Commons' disciple, Selig Perlman, expanded upon Commons' theory in his book, *The Theory of the Labor Movement*, which remains the single most influential analysis of the development of the American labor movement. According to Perlman, "The overshadowing problem of the American labor movement has always been the problem of staying organized," resulting primarily from the "lack of class consciousness in American labor." The American Federation of Labor survived and prospered because it "fitted" the American environment in recognizing the "virtually inalterable conservatism of the American community as regards private property and private initiative in economic life," the "limitations" of political action and because "it was under no deluson as to the true psychology of the workingman in general and the American workingman in particular." The lack of class consciousness is again attributed to the excellent economic opportunities available in America, especially social and geographic mobility arising from the availability of western land and the early obtaining of the ballot.[13]

The Perlman-Commons theory continues to dominate interpretation of the American labor movement. Thus, one recent review of the "new" labor history concluded that "as yet the new labor historians have posited no synthesis that would supplant Perlman's *Theory*, . . . or other commonly held reasons for American labor's failure to opt for socialism."[14] Similar interpretations have been advanced by most American social scientists seeking to account for the failure of radical political parties to gain major influence in modern American history.

The classic interpretation is that of the German writer Werner Sombart, who wrote in 1906 that socialism in the United States foundered due to the prosperity of the country. "All socialist utopias have come to grief on roast beef and apple pie," he concluded.[15] The leading modern historian of American socialism, David Shannon, follows along the lines laid down by Sombart and the consensus historians. Shannon attributes the lack of class consciousness in America, and the resultant failure of the Socialist Party, to American prosperity, the lack of feudal traditions, the heterogeneity of the working force, the relatively high degree of class mobility, and the individualistic and pragmatic traditions of the American people.[16]

Most studies which have not directly analyzed the failure of socialist and communist parties in terms of America's "goodness" have done so indirectly by stressing the ideological rigidities of the radical parties, especially their alleged unwillingness or inability to adapt Marxist ideologies to fit American conditions. Thus, Daniel Bell refers to the "set of ideological blinders" which "prevented the American Socialist Party from understanding the society," and the "psychological distance" which the Communist Party insisted on maintaining from American society.[17] Students of the Communist Party have emphasized the deleterious effects on the party's ideological flexibility of the strong influence which the Russian Communist Party exerted over American Communist Party policy.[18]

The Neglect of Political Repression

The purpose of this study is not to directly confront the "consensus" social scientists. It is a reasonable proposition that there has been *less* radical dissent in the United States than in most western industrialized democracies, and that *some* of the factors cited by consensus scholars have *some* explanatory power. My major contention is that the consensus school has overlooked an additional factor which has also been highly important in undermining radical dissent in the U.S.: the role of political authorities in repeatedly subjecting radical dissenters to severe penalties and harassment not faced by other, less "objectionable," persons, i.e. political repression.

In seeking to explain the development of various types of collective behavior, including social movements, sociologist Neil Smelser has suggested that a number of factors need to be taken into account, including general conditions in the society, the spread of ideologies, the behavior of movement leaders *and* "the operation of social control" or "those counter determinants which prevent, interrupt, deflect or inhibit" other factors which may lead to the growth of social movements.[19] The problem with the consensus scholars is that they have largely overlooked one of the major elements of "social control," i.e. the possibly repressive response of political authorities. These social scientists have looked back at American history, and, seeing little dissent, have concluded that everyone was happy. However, the result would have been the same had people been too frightened by political repression to join radical movements.[20] Political scientist Richard Rose makes this point very clearly:

> Both Hungary and New Zealand . . . have regimes that obtain compliance from their subjects. Yet, judging by the security measures of the former and their absence in the latter, the two differ greatly in the degree of popular support enjoyed. One gains compliance because it is coercive, and the other because popular attitudes diffusely favor the regime. . . . The effectiveness of a regime is . . . not synonomous with its type of authority. Both coercive and fully legitimate regimes may make claim to effective action. . . . In approaching the study of particular regimes, one should give at least as much attention to movement in the direction of repudiation and coercion as to movement towards full legitimacy. Unfortunately much social science writing concentrates exclusively upon the restricted problem of making or maintaining fully legitimate regimes.[21]

Similarly, Robert Dahl comments, "The element of coercion, the requirement for a limited preponderance of coercive potential, is worth stressing because it is not uncommon to understate the importance of violence and coercion in the evolution of democratic institutions." Dahl also suggests, on an impressionistic basis, that compared to nine European democracies, the U.S. has imposed the most severe legal and social "obstacles to political dissent."[22]

Other authors have also suggested, on a largely impressionistic basis, that political repression may wield important explanatory power in American history. For example, historian William Preston writes:

> The vast majority of workers joined neither the A.F. of L. nor radical unions, which proves nothing about the way they felt. If only 5% were A.F. of L. members does one conclude that 95% opposed [AFL President Samuel] Gomper's pragmatic conservatism and class collaboration? It does suggest that union identity was difficult, if not dangerous, and that the powers in control had the wherewithal to turn the heat on if unionism gained a significant degree of influence . . . leaving historians to argue fruitlessly about the meaning of the paltry few surface manifestations that resisted repression.[23]

Clearly then, not all American social scientists have ignored the possible significance of political repression. In fact, there are many good studies of particular periods of severe political repression in the United States, such as World War I, the Red Scare of 1919, and the so-called "McCarthy period," and many good studies of individual groups which have been subjected to severe political repression, such as the Industrial

Workers of the World and the Communist Party. However the most influential social scientists have systematically downplayed the importance of political repression, and no one has systematically studied and analyzed political repression's importance in American history over an extended period of time. Thus, there is no single study of *all* of the different periods and major groups affected by political repression. Nor is there a study which analyzes American political repression in a systematic manner, and assesses its significance for the American political system.

In order to understand the effect political repression has had on the course of modern American history, it is necessary to have a comprehensive chronological account of the repressive actions undertaken by American political authorities. This book provides the only comprehensive history of modern American political repression.

In the course of constructing this history, it became apparent that political repression reached "higher" levels during certain periods and "lower" levels during other periods. Along with an analysis of the significance of political repression in modern American history, the Conclusion of this book contains an analysis of the reasons political repression increases and decreases.

Certain variables which have regularly been associated with changes in the level of political repression are identified. The most important, and the *only* variable which *must* change for levels of political repression to change, is the attitude of policy-making authorities with regard to political dissidents.

There are other variables which do not in themselves directly affect levels of political repression, but are influential in changing the attitudes of political authorities. Increased levels of strain and tension in society and increased levels of dissent (which frequently, but not always, occur together) have been the most important factors disposing political authorities to increase political repression; decreased levels of strain and tension and decreased dissent have been the most important factors disposing political authorities to decrease political repression. Two other variables have played a somewhat less important role, largely limited to either spur on or rein in political authorities already embarked on a policy of repression. The existence of elements in society which can easily be made scapegoats and lack of opposition to repression by key elites tends to facilitate an expansion of repressive politics, while the lack of suitable scapegoats and significant opposition to repression by key elites tends to hinder the expansion and continuation of such policies.

Given the great length of the historical section, many readers may find it helpful to *first* read the Conclusion and to use the generalizations on significance and variables contained there as an analytical guide to the historical chronology. Readers who prefer to accompany the author on the arduous task of first collecting the evidence and then reaching conclusions will want to read the book in the sequence in which it is arranged.

Towards a Definition of Political Repression

"Political repression" or "repression" used in a clearly political sense is a term frequently used in the social science literature, but almost never clearly defined.[24] As a result of this lack of adequate definition, this term, along with similar phrases such as "coercion" or "supression" has been used in many ways by many different scholars, leading to considerable confusion in the literature.[25] The definition that will be used throughout this book is: **Political repression consists of government action which grossly discriminates against persons or organizations viewed as presenting a fundamental challenge to existing power relationships or key governmental policies, because of their perceived political beliefs.**

In order to elucidate this definition, it will be useful to analyze the *only* attempted definition of political repression that was found in the course of reading hundreds of books and articles related to this subject. Political scientist Alan Wolfe defines repression as "a process by which those in power try to keep themselves in power by consciously attempting to destroy or render harmless organizations and ideologies that threaten their power."[26]

The first problem with Wolfe's definition is that it does not differentiate between governmental and non-governmental power holders in any way. The definition suggested here applies *only* to governmental officials, in recognition of their unique monopoly of the legitimate application of law and legal force. Other groups may "grossly discriminate" against those who disagree with them, but the character of such action changes so drastically when political authorities become involved that a clear conceptual difference can easily be drawn.

Another problem with Wolfe's definition is that the categories are far too broad. Virtually any governmental or private activity which seeks to promote its own programs and thus "render harmless" the opposition qualifies as repression under Wolfe's definition. Wolfe includes the activities of the United States Information Agency and anti-labor propaganda issued by private corporations as examples of repression. At one point, he writes that "the chief importance of the family is in indirect repression, teaching values that support the political consensus rather than inculcating any specific politics."[27] If this is political repression, what is not!

My definition limits political repression to governmental actions which grossly discriminate against persons or organizations viewed as presenting a fundamental challenge to existing power relationships or key governmental policies, because of their perceived political beliefs. Any government faces many different instances of possible violations of law or expressions of opposition to various laws and policies. However, governmental authorities differentiate between what might be termed "ordinary criminal" or "anti-social" behavior such as violations of traffic laws and violations of or opposition to what Richard Rose terms "basic political laws."[28]

Those who are guilty of ordinary criminal violations are not normally regarded as dangers to the state itself, while those who challenge fundamental political structures or policies may be regarded as "subversives committing a crime against the state,"[29] and subjected to political repression, as opposed to ordinary criminal procedures. Of course, as Richard Rose has noted:

> As a regime moves toward totalitarianism, there is a great increase in the proportion of social activities defined as violations of basic political laws. Even drunkenness or abstract painting [or, in the United States, the waving of red flags or the burning of red, white and blue flags] can be considered anti-regime activity.[30]

The use of violence or any particular technique by dissenters is not what makes an act a political challenge in the eyes of the authorities; indeed, an act of mass violence, such as drunken rioting in celebration of a football victory, is generally not regarded as a political threat and is frequently treated with tolerance by political authorities, while a more peaceful but clearly anti-regime activity, such as a student demonstration *is* often considered a threat and is treated with repression. A good example of this point can be drawn from changing governmental responses to the labor movement. From 1870 to 1935, the entire labor movement was treated by government as an outlaw movement challenging the basic political and social structure of the state. The massive restrictions on the right to peacefully assemble, organize, strike, boycott and picket which existed before 1935 constituted political repression which was clearly aimed at destroying the labor movement. The radical (i.e. anti-capitalist) wing of the labor movement was defined by political authorities as especially threatening and subjected to especially repressive responses. After 1935, the mainstream of the labor movement was redefined by political authorities as non-threatening to the basic structure of power and was, with a few exceptions, subjected only to restrictions (similar to regulatory legislation placed on the business community), aimed at regulation of certain aspects of labor activities, and not at all at the repression or destruction of the movement. However, the radical labor movement continued to be considered threatening by political authorities, and was subjected to severe political repression, aimed at its complete destruction, even after 1935.

Any action by political authorities which interferes with or grossly discriminates against individuals or groups merely for the perceived holding or expression of political *beliefs* constitutes political repression; government activity which hampers or prohibits *action* can in some cases be differentiated as guarding against a "clear and present danger" to social order. As Thomas Emerson has written, "The central idea of a system of freedom of expression is that a fundamental distinction must be drawn between conduct which consists of 'expression' and conduct which consists of 'action.'"[31] Thus, the right to *advocate* the overthrow of the government must be protected if political freedom is to exist, and prosecution of such advocacy constitutes political repression; but overt *action* such as throwing rocks through windows, breaking into government offices or attacking police goes far beyond expression and prosecution of such offenses does not constitute political repression. Or, to give another example, a general ban on strikes, picketing, boycotts or other types of massive, general restrictions on labor constitutes political repression. On the other hand, carefully drawn and selective attempts to *regulate* specific union activities, (rather than *destroy* unions) such as strikes in basic industries which involve the "national health or safety," fall within the clear and present danger category, and thus do not constitute political repression.

By stressing the concept of overt, hostile action ("gross discrimination") by governmental authorities in my definition of political repression, the concept of "repressive tolerance" developed by Herbert Marcuse and others is deliberately excluded. The idea of "repressive tolerance" involves the granting of minor reforms by political authorities to deflect basic criticisms of the regime. Both repressive tolerance and political repression are designed to minimize dissent; but concessions (repressive tolerance) and hostile action (political repression) are clearly two different types of governmental activities aimed at social control.

The government can implement repression following "legal" procedures. For example, opposition parties can be legally outlawed, and penalties, including death, can be legally established for violation of repressive laws. As Franz Neuman has written, "there can be a legal system that is nothing more than a means of terrorizing people."[32] Conversely, political authorities may carry out repressive activities that are illegal under the official laws of the country: the constitution of the Soviet Union guarantees many civil liberties which are completely disregarded by Soviet authorities. Recent American examples of "illegal" political repression are police attacks on peaceful demonstrations, governmental wiretapping, burglaries and interception of first class mail.

Political repression is viewed in the definition as a policy, reflected in specific actions, undertaken by political authorities. Repression as used here is a technical and neutral term classifying, and not judging, government action. When this action grossly discriminates against the holders of certain beliefs, it is categorized as political repression, whether it succeeds or fails, is "justified" or "unjustified."

The only effective way of indicating exactly what is meant by the terms "gross discrimination" and "political beliefs" in the definition is to give concrete examples. The focus is on violation of first amendment-type rights and violation of due process in the enforcement and adjudication of law, related to the perceived political views of the targets of such violations. First amendment-type rights included are:

- Freedom of speech, assembly and travel, and freedom of the press up to the clear and present danger point very narrowly defined, regardless of the views communicated.
- Freedom of association and belief without suffering from governmental re-

prisals, obloquy or investigation unless clearly connected with possible violations of existing laws or investigation of the need for future laws that do not violate clear and present danger guidelines.
- The general freedom to boycott, peacefully picket or strike without suffering criminal or civil penalties.

Due process violations would essentially involve violations of generally accepted standards of police action and judicial and administrative behavior related to the political beliefs of the person involved.[33] That such violations are frequently linked to the alleged political beliefs of citizens has long been recognized; for example, Cardinal Richelieu stated:

> In normal affairs, the administration of justice requires authentic proofs; but it is not the same in affairs of state.... There urgent conjecture must sometimes take the place of proof; the loss of the particular is not comparable with the salvation of the state.[34]

Excluded from consideration under the definition suggested herein is material related to repression of dissent within the military, in view of the fact that even ardent civil libertarians have argued that the military system is "outside the civil system of freedom of expression and is subject to different rules," a position recently adopted by the Supreme Court.[35]

Some specific examples of what would be included as political repression are the following:
- All laws which directly infringe upon freedom of speech, without being tightly drawn so as to include only clear and present danger violations, for example, the federal Smith (sedition) Act, laws barring advocating violation of the selective service laws, and most state sedition, criminal syndicalism and criminal anarchy laws.
- Laws which place special burdens on individuals and groups alleged to hold certain political views, without trial and without relationship to actual violations of laws meeting clear and present danger standards, such as communist registration and ballot exclusion laws and laws depriving such politically designated persons and groups of benefits such as obtaining passports, living in public housing, or obtaining public employment. Also laws which require under any circumstances compulsory disavowal of political beliefs and affiliations which do not involve actual violations of laws meeting clear and present danger standards (i.e. negative loyalty oaths).
- Laws requiring mandatory affirmations of belief from non-voluntarily selected groups (i.e. mandatory flag saluting required of children compelled to attend public or private schools).
- Laws imposing additional penalties on already existing criminal conduct which tend to have a chilling effect on free speech through their vagueness, such as the 1968 Federal Anti-Riot Law, banning crossing state lines with intent to incite a riot, although inciting a riot is itself a prosecutable offense, and laws banning financial aid to students involved in campus disruptions, although disruptive campus activity is already subject to penalty.

- Laws banning "action" which clearly is symbolic exercise of freedom of speech, i.e. red flag laws, laws banning draft card or flag burning, laws unreasonably restricting picketing, or the right to strike or boycott.
- Administrative actions which discriminate, for political reasons, against groups and individuals or hold them up to public obloquy without trial or relationship to violations of laws; i.e. restrictions on passports, immigration and travel, the Attorney General's list of subversive organizations, discrimination in approval of various benefits, such as denial of equal access to use of public buildings.
- Administrative actions and programs which through their vagueness and overbreadth tend to have a chilling effect on freedom of speech and association, such as loyalty programs applying to all government employees, regardless of their access to "national security" information, and which are essentially concerned with potential future "disloyalty" and present and past thoughts and affiliations rather than actual harmful conduct.
- Excessive police violence used against political dissidents; failure to afford police protection to uphold the rights of political dissidents.
- Violations of due process procedures, such as illegal searches and seizures, biased judges and juries, etc., in cases involving political dissidents.
- Use of government informers and infiltrators and government surveillance techniques such as wiretapping, opening mail, and burglaries, without adequate judicial supervision to insure that target groups present a clear and present danger of violating laws that meet the guidelines suggested herein; use of government *agents provocateur* under any circumstances.
- Legislative investigations which tend to harass and hold up to public obloquy persons and organizations for their political views without any clearly legitimate legislative purpose.

Examples of what would *not* be included as political repression would include the following:
- Laws which apply to all persons regardless of political beliefs and affiliations which are drawn with clear and present danger standards, i.e. laws against theft, murder, assault, direct incitement of riots, bombing, destruction of governmental property which clearly involves interference with governmental functions (i.e. draft board raids, but not individual draft card burning). Thus political repression would *not* be involved in trials of political dissidents carried out in "good faith" and with observance of due process procedures for violations of laws applying to all persons and enforced against all persons; e.g. political asassinations, draft board raids, sit-ins, destruction of property, etc. However, trials for such crimes which involve due process violations (Sacco-Vanzetti),[36] or perjured testimony (Mooney-Billings)[37] *are* regarded as involving political repression even when resulting in *guilty*

verdicts; trials for such crimes which result in verdicts of *innocent* are regarded as *prima facie* involving political repression (Steunenberg, Ettor-Giovanetti, Berrigan).[38]

- Affirmative loyalty oaths for those voluntarily choosing governmental employment which are narrowly drawn; i.e. pledging to uphold the constitution and faithfully execute the duties of the office involved.
- Discrimination based on factors *other* than political belief; e.g. sex, skin color, national origins, sexual preferences.
- Laws related to first amendment freedoms which are not substantially concerned with political dissent, i.e. obscenity laws, slander laws, and personal libel laws (as opposed to sedition or criminal libel laws).

Given the complexity and subtlety of the concepts connected with "political repression," this section should be considered a working definition for my readers and not the final and definitive word. My aim is to provide a contribution towards a definition — a substantial theoretical basis for studies of political repression in the United States and other societies.

Some Warnings

At this point, it is necessary to make certain explanations regarding what I am and am not attempting in this book. This is simply to warn the reader what can (and can not!) be expected of POLITICAL REPRESSION IN MODERN AMERICA.

I am not saying that political repression in America has been similar in nature or degree to political repression in Nazi Germany, Stalinist Russia or Diemist South Vietnam. There is a great need for comparative studies in political repression, but that is outside the realm of this book. The smattering of evidence available on this topic clearly suggests that the level of political repression in the United States has been far below that of most other countries. For example, a study based on the 1948-1960 period placed the United States among the nine most "highly permissive" regimes among eighty-four nations categorized on a scale measuring "coerciveness."[39] In 1964, a study of the 113 members of the United Nations indicated that only 30 countries had political systems in which "full legal opposition among organized political parties had existed throughout the preceding decade."[40] In February, 1975, Freedom House, a private (and strongly anti-communist) research organization, placed the United States among the 17 freest countries in the world, among 152 nations studied.[41] Constitutional law expert Ivo Duchacek comments:

> The freedom of expression, however incomplete it may be in the United States, Britain, Canada, Australia, New Zealand and most European countries, is still separated by an abyss in comparison to the complete suppression of free speech in most of the modern world.[42]

This should be kept in mind as a different perspective on the material presented here, but it does not contradict my argument. Political repression may be *less* in the United States than in some other countries, but it is still an important and neglected factor in modern American history. When comparative materials are introduced in this study, they are brought in for the purpose of pointing out something about *American* repression.

This book does not attempt to give a balanced account of modern American history; it is a history and analysis of political repression, so naturally it stresses events relevant to this subject. I see no need to balance off each incident of political repression with an incident of non-political repression, as these can easily be found by consulting any standard American history text. David B. Davis makes this point in the introduction to his book on "Images of Un-American Subversion," which he says, "provides an opportunity to view the major events of American history through a special and highly distorted lens. Like other unusual lenses, this one enables the viewer to see configurations that are hidden from normal vision."[43] In constructing *this* view of American history, secondary sources only have been relied on, with the exception of the period since 1960, for which adequate secondary sources do not exist. Given the scope of the subject matter, the decision to rely essentially on secondary sources, rather than primary sources, was simply a practical necessity. It was reassuring to read the statement of the authors of the leading history of political repression in America during World War I, that "it would be impossible in one lifetime to personally examine or study all of the material relating to the subject under consideration."[44] This book covers over one hundred years, as opposed to the period of less than two years discussed in the account of World War I repression.

In selecting secondary sources, reliance has been placed on books and journals published by established and reputable scholars and publishers. In some cases journalistic or semi-journalistic accounts have been used when they have been generally accepted as reliable by scholars. Material published by parties directly involved in alleged cases of political repression have been excluded as sources, as have all other obviously slanted or unreliable sources. With a few clearly identifiable exceptions, all autobiographical material has also been excluded as too subject to distortion. For the period since 1960, when primary materials have been relied on, established sources such as the *New York Times,* the *Los Angeles Times* and the American Civil Liberties Union have been used. A particular attempt has been made to be as comprehensive as possible about events since 1960, since there are virtually no good secondary sources available for this period. Thus, the fact that more space is devoted to repression during the Vietnam War era than to repression during the World War I period should not be taken to necessarily mean that there was more repressive activity occurring.

This book is the most comprehensive work available on political repression in modern American history. It therefore contains some material which does not fall within any of the patterns discussed in the Conclusion — indeed some material may even contradict them. This is inevitably the case in a study of this historical scope, because history, being a science that deals with men rather than the stars, has a messy habit of rarely being predictable — of not always conforming to rules. Hopefully, the comprehensiveness of this study will provide source materials for other scholars and will give my readers a new view of modern American history.

1

The Repression of Labor, 1873-1937

From approximately 1873, the date which marks the peak of the post-Civil War revival of the American labor movement, until 1937, when the United States Supreme Court upheld the constitutionality of the Wagner Act, American labor suffered governmental repression that was probably as severe or more severe than that suffered by any labor movement in any other Western industrialized democracy.

According to the foremost historians of American labor violence, the U.S. has had the "bloodiest and most violent labor history of any industrial nation in the world."[1] An admittedly grossly underestimated tabulation of the number of casualties in labor disputes indicates over seven hundred deaths and thousands of serious injuries, almost all of which occurred in the 1873-1937 period.[2]

American labor history was punctuated by large amounts of violence initiated by both sides — labor on one side, and business and government, usually acting together, on the other.[3] However, the nature of the violence initiated by the two sides was, on the whole, of a very different character. Labor-initiated violence usually involved attacks on property, rather than people, and usually reflected in its intensity the intolerability of particular living and working conditions (which frequently included denials of freedom to orgnaze and assemble) or some specific provocation in a strike situation, such as the introduction of strikebreakers and/or armed private or public police forces, which frequently involved violent attacks on strikers. Violence originating with business, usually in the form of private police, or with government, usually in the form of local police, state militia and federal troops, was generally characterized by attacks on individuals (the great bulk of violence leading to deaths and injuries was initiated by business and government and the great majority of casualties in labor disputes were suffered by workers) and frequently, although not always, there was no apparent relationship between the degree of violence employed and provocations from workers.[4] Another difference between labor violence and government-business violence was that government attempted to seek direct reprisals against workers involved in violence, by arrests, jailings, beatings, and sometimes shootings, while almost invariably those in business or government responsible for violence suffered no legal or other reprisals.

These generalizations have their exceptions; for example, there are a number of cases in which workers did attack people as well as property, usually in cases involving the introduction of strikebreakers, with the most notorious example the slaughter of eighteen strikebreakers by striking coal miners at Herrin, Illinois, in 1922.

What is particularly striking about both the amount of American labor violence and, at least in terms of casualties, its general impetus at the hands of private and governmental police agents, is that American labor is generally regarded historically as among the least ideologically militant labor movements in the industrialized world. As Richard Hofstader has written:

> The rate of industrial violence in America is striking in light of the fact that no major American labor organization has ever advocated violence as a policy, that extremely militant class conflict philosophies have not prevailed here, and that the percentage of the American labor force organized in unions has always been (and is now) lower than in most advanced industrial countries. With a minimum of ideologically motivated class conflict, the United States has somehow had a maximum of industrial violence.[5]

Throughout the period under consideration here, the governmental apparatus in most localities acted as a handmaiden to business and acted to put down the labor movement in a manner which repeatedly violated the most elementary freedoms of working men, either through direct repression or through failure to protect labor's rights against massive private infringement upon them. Thus, according to a leading historian of the American Federation of Labor, with the possible exception of the metal and machines trades of France, employers in no other country "have so persistently, vigorously, at such costs and with such a conviction of serving a cause fought trade unions as the American employing class" and in no other Western democracy "have employers been so much aided in their opposition to unions by the civil authorities, the armed forces of government and their courts."[6]

In contrasting the combined private-government offensive against American labor, compared to the resistance faced by French labor, Val. R. Lorwin states:

> American workers had to fight bloodier industrial battles than the French for the right of unions to exist and to function. Their political history knew nothing like the "June Days" of the Commune. But the rail strikes of 1877, the pitched battle of Homestead, the Ludlow massacre were bloodier than Fourmies and Draveil and Villeneuve-Sainte-Georges. The 1919 steel strike was more brutally suppressed than the French general strike of 1920. "Bloody Harlan" had no rival in the coal country of France. France had nothing like the private armies, factory arsenals and industrial espionage services exposed by the La Follette Committee; nothing like South Chicago's "Memorial Day Massacre" as late as 1937.[7]

Similarly, Stuart Jamieson, in contrasting Canadian labor history to that in the U.S., states:

The use of professional strike-breakers, labor spies, "goon squads," "vigilante" groups, armed militia and other spectacular features of industrial warfare in the United States in previous decades have been absent from the Canadian scene . . . with several notable exceptions.[8]

The fundamental explanation for the government-business alliance against labor during this period lies in the fact of business' tremendous power in American society, and the corresponding lack of countervailing power on the part of labor. Especially during the periods 1873-1900 and 1919-1932, big business in America functioned effectively as a state within a state, controlling governmental policy, reaping the benefits of governmental largesse and usurping governmental functions for its own ends. Just as the amalgamation of church and state in colonial America made religious dissent in effect a political challenge to state authority, calling for state repression, so during most of the 1873-1937 period did the challenge posed to American capitalism by labor become transformed by the state-business amalgamation into a challenge to the ruling orthodoxy of the state, and it similarly faced frequent and harsh state repression.

It should be pointed out that there were some exceptions to the norm of governmental repressive responses to labor. In a number of small towns, workers were the dominant political force, and occassionally anti-business forces were able to gain control of state governments. Thus, it is possible to uncover some instances in which governmental officials intervened on the side of labor. For example, following outbreaks of industrial violence, Governor David Waite used the Colorado national guard to aid labor at a coal strike at Cripple Creek in 1894, and Governor John B. Tanner used state troops to prevent strikebreakers from arriving at Virden, Illinois during a coal strike there in 1898.[9] On the federal level, Presidents Theodore Roosevelt and Woodrow Wilson occasionally lent assistance to the conservative wing of the labor movement. However, it was not until the administration of Franklin Roosevelt and the passage of the Wagner Act that a major and long-term shift in the attitude of government towards labor occurred, and only when labor was offered governmental benevolence and aid of the type so frequently extended to business was labor able to make major gains and become a strong force in American society. Until the New Deal, the face of government that labor saw most often was that of the club, the gun, the injunction and the courtroom, and its progress was very meagre.

By the time of the effective "legalization" of the labor movement by the passage of the Wagner Act, all of the major radical (i.e. anti-capitalist) labor movements that had developed had disintegrated, largely as a result of governmental repression; thus the labor movement that was government accepted in the 1930's was perfectly willing to accept the existing capitalist system. Even during and after the New Deal, moreover, the fragments of radical labor that did manage to survive were faced with repression at every turn and every strike.

In short, the argument of this study with regard to governmental treatment of labor in modern American history is that repression was a major factor in retarding the progress of the labor movement from 1873 to 1937, in effect helping to postpone the emergence of labor as a major force for forty to sixty years; and, that a major explanation for the lack of a radical labor movement in the U.S. is that whenever such a movement has emerged it has faced strong, continuous and brutal repression at the hands of governmental authorities.

The Power of Business in Post-Civil War America

It is impossible to understand why American labor history developed as it did after the Civil War without understanding the tremendous power of American business during this period. As the so-called presidential election compromise of 1877 demonstrated, the real winner of the Civil War was not the black man, but the business man.[10] With representatives from the predominantly agrarian south absent from Congress during the war, a business-oriented Republican Congress adopted policy after policy designed to benefit the capitalists, such as a high protective tariff, and favorable immigration, currency and land policies.[11] Huge industrial fortunes were created during the war, and in the years afterwards, governmental units on the national, state and local levels continued to follow policies highly favorable to business, and especially to America's most important and powerful industry, the railroads. As incentives for the railroads to build, Congress between 1862 and 1872 chartered to the railroads two hundred million acres of land, of which slightly more than half actually came into the possession of the roads. States, towns and counties also vied to attract railroad builders, until by the late nineteenth century nearly one-tenth of all of the land in the U.S. had been turned over to them, including one-fourth of the territories of Minnesota and Washington, one-fifth of Wisconsin, Iowa, Kansas, North Dakota and Montana, one-seventh of Nebraska, one-eighth of California and one-ninth of Louisiana.[12]

While the Republican Party emerged from the war unabashedly an organ through which big business made its views known, the Democratic Party, until the nomination of William Jennings Bryan for president in 1896, also was under big business control. The policies followed by southern states under the control of "redeemer" Democrats during the post-Reconstruction period, and the dominant philosophy of "Bourbon" Democrats in the mid-west and elsewhere was virtually identical with the Republican Party, reflecting the belief that "the main purpose of government was to protect and promote the interests of property."[13] If there was any question as to the Democratic Party's subservience to business interests, they were settled during the two administrations of Grover Cleveland, the only Democrat to serve as President until Woodrow Wilson in 1912. Cleveland's policies with respect to labor and business were virtually indistinguishable from those of the Republicans. While Cleveland had no objection to pursuing tax and currency policies that favored the rich, when Congress in 1887 appropriated a paltry $10,000 to help drought sufferers buy new seed grain, he vetoed the measure, declaring that "though the people support the Government, the Government should not support the people."[14] During his second administration, from 1893-97, while a rising tide of agrarian and labor discontent shook the nation, Cleveland's cabinet did not have a single representative of the agrarian wing of his party, nor a single man who even "remotely sympathized" with labor.[15]

While businessmen could normally count on a friendly ear from both major parties, they could also use their huge fortunes to grease the appropriate palms in case of need. Railroad men were the richest and the most powerful, and through bribery, corruption and simple identification of interest easily dominated entire legislatures, especially in the middle and far west.[16] To a large extent, the railroads acted as "the governments within the government, the owners of executives, legislators and judges, the leviers of taxes, the arbiters of the destinies of cities, counties, states, industries and farms."[17] Sometimes the maintenance of such dominance required large expenditures. For example, the Central Pacific spent $500,000 yearly on graft between 1875 and 1885, while the LaCrosse and Milwaukee Railroad in Wisconsin admitted that during one year in the 1870's, it spent $872,000 for influence, including $50,000 for a governor, $10,000 for a state controller, $125,000 for thirteen legislators, etc.[18] John Hope Franklin's wry comment that northern industrialists were "bribing officials with greater regularity than they paid their employees," has more than a little truth in it.[19] But such expenditures for bribery were a small price for the larger companies to pay; during the late 1880's, the annual gross income of the railroads in California was five times that of the state itself.[20] The control of Standard Oil over the state of Pennsylvania was so obvious that Henry Demarest Lloyd observed that the company "has done everything with the Pennsylvania legislature except to refine it."[21]

Under such circumstances, as Louis Adamic has suggested, an honest politician "was one who stayed sold to one group of interests."[22] Government officials seemed to be mere lap dogs "increasingly housebroken" by businessmen.[23] United States Senators seemed to represent not states, but various business interest. Thus William Allen White wrote in 1889 that one Senator represented the Union Pacific, another the New York Central, another New York and New Jersey insurance interests, that coal and iron controlled a coterie of Senators from middle and eastern seaport states and that cotton had half a dozen senators.[24] Historian Brooks Adams commented, in the late nineteenth century, "the only question which occupies the ruling class is whether it is cheaper to coerce or to bribe."[25]

While the federal, state and local governments, especially in the late nineteenth century, restricted their functions to "the restraint of the crowd and its agitators and the protection of property and its gatherers,"[26] the power and wealth of the great corporations expanded until they effectively operated as private governments within the United States. "About the only things that Standard Oil, the Southern Pacific Railroad, the American Sugar

Refining Company or Carnegie Steel did not do was issue postage stamps."[27] Business control extended throughout all of the major power centers of American society. Thus, by the end of the century, Charles and Mary Beard wrote, "The roster of American trustees of higher learning reads like a corporate directory."[28]

The power of big business during this period led to severe distortions in virtually all aspects of American life, especially in the legal structure and the distribution of wealth. Business was free to carry out its operations virtually without governmental regulation, including the untrammeled use of yellow-dog contracts, blacklisting, the hiring of spies and private armies to disrupt labor organizations, and the consolidation into huge corporations which wielded immense power. Labor faced arrests, jailings and frequent beatings and shootings at the hands of the courts, the police and federal and state troops if it also attempted organization. While many laws were passed in the late nineteenth century for the protection of labor, they were either not enforced, had such huge loopholes that they were easily evaded, or were declared unconstitutional. The fourteenth amendment, which had been passed ostensibly to protect the rights of former slaves, became an instrument used by the courts to protect business against state regulation, while the Sherman Anti-Trust Act of 1890, apparently passed to prevent business combinations in restraint of trade became instead an effective tool to combat labor organizations.[29] In John Roche's words, the courts established a system of "free enterprise" which guaranteed the "freedom of the entrepreneur to follow his calling, and a governmental, constitutional protection of the entrepreneur from his institutional enemies, public and private. . . . The courts effectively sent the workers and the farmers into the boxing ring with the injunction that if they used their best punches on the corporations, it would be ruled a foul."[30] Under these conditions the only real legal freedom that most American workers enjoyed was to "work at the lowest wages and under the worst conditions acceptable to his hungriest rivals anywhere, or not to work at all."[31]

The courts, and most other organs of government, simply reflected the attitude of business toward labor, which was summed up by one manufacturer who used both dogs and men in his operations and preferred dogs because "they never go on strike for higher wages, have no labor unions, never get intoxicated and disorderly, never absent themselves from work without good cause, obey orders without growling, and are very reliable."[32]

The power of big business combined with the weakness of organized labor created a gulf between the rich and the poor previously unknown in American history. By 1900, 80 percent of all Americans were living on the margins of subsistence, while the remaining 20 percent controlled virtually all of the country's wealth. The top 1 percent owned half of all the property and 15 percent of all the income, while the average industrial worker was unable to earn enough money to support his family decently. This situation did not improve during the Progressive Era, and improved only marginally during the prosperity of the 1920's, before the great depression again placed the great majority of Americans in poverty.

Workers were faced not only with the problem of inadequate wages, but also of inadequate employment levels and abominable housing and sanitary conditions. During the late nineteenth century, about 25 percent of urban workers were unemployed for part of each year. Decent housing was unavailable for unskilled workers in the larger cities, while epidemics periodically swept slums which were among the most crowded on earth.[33] In Chicago, in the 1870's, "half of the children . . . died before they were five, and it is not clear which half were the luckier."[34] The typical employer-employee relationship during the 1873-1937 period was all too often one in which

> the employer made the money, while the toilers either went about their tasks half-starved or else procured further sustenance from almost equally impoverished relatives, or, in the form of charity from society, which in this way showed its benevolence to the sweatshop manager. A great deal has been said about the charity of the rich to the poor; this was a case of charity of the poor to the rich.[35]

Given these conditions of social dynamite, it is not surprising that the fear of class warfare dominated the thinking of wealthy Americans during much of the late nineteenth century. As one Englishmen who knew many wealthy Americans wrote, they were "pervaded by an uneasy feeling that they were living over a mine of social and industrial discontent, with which the power of government, under American institutions, was wholly inadequate to deal; and that some day this mine would explode and blow society into the air."[36]

The Techniques of Labor Repression, 1873-1937

It is only within the context of big business power that the repression of labor from 1873 to 1937 can be fully understood. For one of the major methods by which capital repressed labor was through the simple usurpation or voiding of what are normally thought of as governmental functions and guarantees — the ownership or effective domination of entire communities, the denial by fiat of the right of workers to freedom of speech, freedom of assembly, freedom of organization, and even freedom to read and to buy goods where one wished, and the employment of private police answerable to no one but themselves to enforce "their" laws. The struggle for the right of unions to organize during the 1873-1937 period was above all a struggle against political repression, and the Wagner Act of 1935 was above all a civil liberties measure. As Jerold Auerbach notes:

> Union organization depended on the constitutional freedoms of speech, press and assembly, but employers consistently abridged these rights. Their reliance on espionage, black-listing, strikebreakers, private police, and, ultimately armed violence, nullified the Bill of Rights for those workers who had the temerity to resist their employers' unilateral exercise of power . . . The

Wagner Act, by prohibiting interference with the right to organize, extended First Amendment guarantees . . . to workers who had enjoyed civil liberties, if they did at all, solely on their employers' sufferance.[37]

The Company Town

One of the most important and widespread, and least studied, of the means by which corporations repressed workers with governmental acquiescence was the "company town." In its pure form, such as Pullman, Illinois, and many cotton textile towns in the south, companies simply *owned* entire communities adjacent to their mines, mills or factories, and exercised complete control over the inhabitants as a matter of "law," including the ownership and building of churches and schools, the hiring of teachers, ministers and policemen, and the establishment of all town rules and regulations. In its impure form, the company town consisted of areas which were dominated economically, but not legally owned, by major corporations. In such areas, the companies often exercised complete control in fact, if not by law, usually operating through officials whose election, appointment and administration they supervised. The extent of "pure" and "impure" company towns was extremely widespread, especially in lumber, textile and coal mining areas in the south, coal and steel areas in the east and midwest, metal and coal mining areas in the mountain west, and lumber, copper and agricultural areas in the far west.[38]

The general atmosphere in such areas "might be described as the complete saturation by the company of the town, its inhabitants, and all its surroundings — the complete dominance of the business of the company in everything that is seen or talked about."[39] As a matter of course in many company towns, union organizers were barred or expelled and labor spokesmen were unable to hire halls or speak in public areas. In the steel town of Duquesne, Pennsylvania, a speaker sent by the federal government to speak about Abraham Lincoln during World War I was arrested and jailed for three days. During the 1919 steel strike, the Mayor of Duquesne boasted that "Jesus Christ could not hold a meeting in Duquesne," let alone a representative of the American Federation of Labor.[40] In many company towns, miners could only read newspapers which passed company censorship, were forced to live in company-owned homes, and were forced to buy goods at company-owned stores at which prices were considerably higher than at other stores.

In Harlan County, Kentucky, coal miners "entertained guests, traversed public highways and used the federal mails at the whim of management."[41] In towns owned by the U.S. Steel Corporation, "housing, gas, electricity and water became instruments of labor policy."[42] The company superintendent of cotton mill villages in the south included among his functions the exercising of "supervision over ownership of dogs by his workers, prohibit[ing] drunkenness, gambling and immorality, and dominat[ing] all other aspects of life."[43]

Under such circumstances, constitutional liberties became a mockery for millions of Americans.[44] The Commission on Industrial Relations reported in 1915 that towns either owned or controlled by corporations presented "every aspect of feudalism except the recognition of special duties on the part of the employer" and that the rights of free speech and assembly were seriously abridged in such areas.[45] A staff report of the Commission added that "industrial feudalism" was the "rule rather than the exception" in areas where labor was unorganized.[46] Twenty-five years later, the Senate LaFollette Committee termed the company town "an autocracy within a democracy. . . . It is an offense against duly constituted authorities."[47]

The power of the corporations was particularly marked in company towns when attempts at labor organizing or strikes were undertaken. In "impure" company towns, such as steel towns in Ohio, Pennsylvania and Indiana, local officials completely barred mass meetings, picketing and parading, and deported, jailed or beat union organizers. In "pure" company towns, the corporations could evict tenants, cut off credit, close meeting halls, arrest strikers with their own police, censor the mails and ban all outside forces from entering the area.

Private Police, Espionage and Arsenals

Major corporations frequently hired private police, used private espionage forces and accumulated private arsenals to fight labor organizing. The use of private police and private armies occurred only in the United States, and led to countless abuses of workers' rights. Although supposedly limited in their functions to the protection of company property, private police forces frequently roamed into nearby towns and took the law into their own hands, generally without any legal reprisal.[48] For example, during a 1935 strike in Canton, Ohio, Republic Steel police left company grounds, entered the city and indiscriminately attacked strikers, bystanders, women and children.[49] During a 1912-13 coal strike in West Virginia, according to a report of a citizen's committee appointed by the governor, company guards were guilty of "denials of the right of peaceable assembly, free speech" and "many and grievous assaults on unarmed miners," and their "main purpose was to overawe the miners and their adherents, and if necessary beat and cudgel them into submission."[50]

In numerous cases, private police forces shot and killed or seriously wounded strikers, but they were rarely prosecuted. For example, during a 1912 copper strike at Ely, Nevada, private guards shot and killed two strikers and wounded another who had gathered around the gates of a mine in an attempt to dissuade a struck company from bringing in strikebreakers. Although union officials obtained warrants for the arrests of two company officials for murder, the governor of Nevada declared martial law and refused to allow the warrants to be served. Later a coroner's jury concluded that the deaths of the two strikers was "unnecessary" and recommended a thorough grand jury investigation. Although twenty-one mine-guards were then arrested, charged with murder and held for the grand jury, the jury refused to return any indictments. Subsequent attempts to have the case re-submitted to a grand jury were blocked by a judge. This case was unusual in that some legal procedures were instituted; in scores of cases involving assaults and murders by private police no legal processes at all were undertaken.[51] It was indicative of the general power relationship that existed in the United States during the late nineteenth century that during this period the Pinkerton Detective Agency, the most notorious private police force available for hire, had more men than did the U.S. Army.[52]

In contrasting the widespread use of private police forces in American labor history to that of European labor history, H. M. Gitelman comments that in Europe:

> Nothing remotely equivalent to vigilante activity or to the role of company guards in American disputes appears to have occurred. On those occasions when armed men were deployed — and the incidence of this seems to have been very much lower — the men were almost always disciplined army regulars or nationally controlled police forces acting under orders . . . armed men rarely initiated violence in European labor disputes unless they had been specifically ordered to do so.[53]

Complementing the private police and private armies were the accumulation of huge arsenals by corporations and their extensive use of private espionage agents to disrupt labor unions. During 1933-37, four major American steel companies each purchased more tear gas equipment than any law enforcement agency in the country. Republic Steel, which had fifty-two thousand employees, bought over ten times as many gas guns and over twenty-six times as many gas shells as the Chicago police department. Republic's arsenal included over 500 revolvers, 64 rifles, 245 shotguns, 143 gas guns, over 4000 gas projectiles and over 2700 gas grenades.[54]

The LaFollette Committee found that the use of private spies by employers to infiltrate and disrupt labor unions was a "common, almost universal practice in American industry."[55] For example, General Motors alone paid over $800 thousand to labor detective agencies during the 1934-36 period. In one case, a Pinkerton agent told the LaFollette Committee, the activities of spies had been so effective that a union organization contained five officers and no members, with the officers all Pinkerton detectives.[56] The LaFollette Committee concluded that through the use of private detectives "private corporations dominate their employees, deny them their constitutional rights, promote disorder and disharmony and even set at naught the power of the government itself."[57]

Where private police, private arsenals and private espionage systems were introduced into company towns, workers knew no other authority than that of the company. Instead of American democracy, they knew only "industrial peonage."[58]

Local Police, State Militia, and Federal Troops

When a company's own resources failed to break union organizational efforts or strikes, corporations could often rely upon intervention by local police, state militia or federal troops, especially in major disputes. The first line of defense was local police and county sheriff's deputies, who, especially in areas under the economic domination of major industries, could usually be counted on to aid in breaking strike efforts. For example, in Chicago, the local police "could not have acted with more concern for the interests of the businessmen and manufacturers if they were hired Pinkertons."[59] In Harlan County, Kentucky, an area under the economic domination of major coal interests, the local sheriff "apparently selected his deputies for their criminal record."[60] Among sheriff's deputies serving in Harlan County in the 1930's were thirty-seven who had been convicted of felonies, including eight who had served time for manslaughter, and three who had been convicted of murder.

In scores of labor disputes, local police and sheriffs deputized company employees, who thus became official law officers. In many such cases, the deputized company employees continued to be paid by the companies. This practice merely institutionalized the convergence of business and government interests during the 1873-1937 period.[61] Thus, in company coal towns in the south, law officers were "always against the strikers since most officers in a mining region are paid by the companies and given a badge by the sheriff."[62] In Pennsylvania steel towns, company employees were deputized routinely during major labor disputes; thus, during the 1919 steel strike, twenty-five thousand men chosen, paid by and armed by the major steel corporations were deputized.[63]

In three states — Pennsylvania, Maryland and South Carolina — legislation specifically authorized the deputization of privately paid police.[64] The operation of the Pennsylvania Coal and Iron Police, in particular, became a national scandal. Paid and armed by employing companies, the Coal and Iron Police operated without regulation, supervision or responsibility on the part of the state of Pennsylvania, "which had literally created 'islands' of police power which were free to float as the employers saw fit."[65] The Coal and Iron Police were notoriously poorly chosen and trained, and frequently delighted in general brutality. During a 1927 coal strike, the Pittsburgh Coal Company alone paid $800 thousand for Coal and Iron Police; subsequently a Senate committee reported that during the strike

> No effort was made to invoke law and order or to maintain police protection, except through the Coal and Iron Police, and they were found to be the outstanding ones who showed little regard for law and order or the improvement of morality.[66]

When companies were unable to suppress labor disturbances through the use of their own resources or local police, they rarely encountered difficulty in obtaining the use of the state militia. Between 1873 and 1937, the national guard was called out a minimum of 250-300 times in labor disputes.[67] Almost invariably, the state militia acted as strikebreakers; indeed strikebreaking became the militia's "main function."[68] The state militia was reinvigorated following the civil war largely as a result of the nationwide railroad strike of 1877, and thereafter state appropriations for the militia bore a close relationship to the degree of labor disturbances experienced by each state. That the militia so frequently acted on behalf of employers' interests partially reflected the heavy preponderance of business elements in the militia leadership.[69] Thus, in one instance in Washington territory, a national guard colonel who was the attorney for a struck company sent two companies of troops to the scene of a labor disturbance involving the company, without any authorization from the governor.[70]

During extremely serious strikes, such as the 1877 railroad strikes and the 1894 Pullman strike, or when state troops were committed because of wars, such as during the 1899 Coeur d'Alene strike and World War I strikes, federal troops intervened during labor disturbances. Almost invariably, federal troops also served largely as strikebreakers; with the decline in Indian wars in the last quarter of the nineteenth century, strike-duty became the "most conspicuous function of the regular army."[71]

Not all uses of local police, state militia and federal troops in connection with strikes can be considered repressive. In some cases, serious disturbances that had broken out during labor disputes required the intervention of outside forces, and in many cases such forces limited themselves to the protection of men who wished to continue working. However, in all too many cases, police militia and federal troops acted so brutally and one-sidedly in restoring "order" that they clearly acted as handservants of the companies involved.

One technique often used to break strikes was the massive and indiscriminate arrests of strikers and strike sympathizers, often on the flimsiest charges. Thus, during labor disturbances at Coeur d'Alene, Idaho, in 1892, and again in 1899 federal troop intervention may well have been justified in that serious violence had occurred. However, instead of simply bringing peace to the area, the troops imposed martial law, jailed hundreds of men in make-shift bull pens and in effect barred union men from re-employment in the mines. During the 1913 textile strike at Patterson, New Jersey, local police arrested over two thousand. During the New York garment strike of 1926, seventy-five hundred were arrested in fifteen weeks. In the 1928 New Bedford textile strike, two thousand were arrested. Over twelve hundred were arrested in the Elizabethton, North Carolina textile strike of 1929. During the 1934-36 period, eighteen thousand strikers were arrested.[72]

Frequently, arrests were made for simple picketing, or on charges such as "intimidation," "inciting to riot," "obstructing the streets" and "trespass."[73] During a lumber strike in Minnesota in early 1917, members of the radical Industrial Workers of the World were arrested for "lurking and lying in wait with intent to do mischief" and for taking part in a "disturbance of the public peace by speaking . . . the following words (sic), to wit, 'Scab.' "[74] A man and his wife were arrested in Pittston, Pennsylvania, in 1928 on a charge of "rioting" after walking in front of a hall where a labor meeting had been banned while wearing black arm bands which stated, "We Mourn Free Speech."[75] The Commission on Industrial Relations reported in 1915 that it had

> been furnished with evidence showing that in a number of recent strikes large numbers of strikers were arrested, but that only a small number were brought to trial and relatively few were convicted of any serious offense . . . were as a rule required to give heavy bail . . . or detained without trial until their effectiveness as strikers was destroyed. . . . In each of the strikes investigated the charges as made were in essentials substantiated.[76]

In many cases, local police and state militia indiscriminately shot and killed strikers. For example, during a strike for an eight-hour day in Milwaukee in 1866, state militia opened fire without provocation on a crowd of demonstrators, killing five and breaking the back of the strike. In 1891, state militia in Pennsylvania fired on fleeing coke strikers, killing ten and wounding fifty. In 1897, unarmed striking miners near Hazleton, Pennsylvania were fired on by sheriff's deputies, with twenty-one killed and forty wounded. Colorado militia in 1914 attacked a tent colony set up by striking miners, first killing five men and a boy with rifle and machine gun fire, then firing the tents and in the process killing thirteen women and children. Colorado state police in 1927 shot to death six unarmed demonstrators who refused their orders to stop marching towards a mine. Sheriff's deputies in Marion, North Carolina shot and killed six strikers and seriously wounded twenty-five in 1929 after a sixty-eight-year-old man, lame with rheumatism, struck the sheriff with his cane. The last major incident of American labor violence occurred in Chicago in 1937, when police fired on a crowd of demonstrators during a steel strike, killing ten.[77]

In a number of cases, state or federal troops were sent to areas of labor disputes and broke strikes that originated because strikers were protesting company violations of state laws. Thus, labor violence broke out at Couer d'Alene in 1892 only after mineowners brought in strikebreakers from out of state under armed guard, even though it was against state law to bring men into the state under arms. Violence returned to the area in 1899 after the dominant mining company, in violation of state law, refused to hire union men. Disturbances in the Anderson County, Tennessee, coal mines in 1891, which led to the repeated intervention of state troops, broke out only after the Tennessee Coal Mine Company brought in convict labor to replace workers who refused to sign a contract which would have relinquished rights guaranteed to them by state law. In 1892, state militia in New York broke a strike of railroad switchmen at Buffalo who demanded only that they be allowed to work the ten hour day provided by New York law, instead of the twelve-to-fourteen-hour days they were working. In

1903, federal troops were used to break a strike at Morenci, Arizona, when miners demanded that mineowners honor the eight-hour law passed by the territorial legislature. Many of the major demands in the 1913-14 Colorado coal strike were simply requests that mineowners cease their blatant violations of numerous state laws.[78]

Although in most of the above cases, disturbances of varying severity had occurred before the introduction of state and federal troops, in many cases such forces were sent to strike areas that had experienced no disturbances or had suffered only disorders of a trivial nature. Almost invariably, the result of such action was to intimidate the workers involved into calling off the strike. Thus, in June, 1877, state troops were sent to Buffalo and Rochester *in advance* of a threatened strike on the Erie Railroad; the strike was subsequently called off.[79] One of the earliest miners' unions that was organized struck in Leadville, Colorado, in 1880; the most serious disorder that occurred came when a deputy sheriff opened fire on a group of strikers and injured three of them. When strikers were not intimidated by a vigilante citizens organization that was supplied with guns and ammunition by the state governor, state troops were sent and martial law was declared. The strike ended within two days, as "the fledgling union could not survive the appearance of the state militia."[80] State militia were sent and federal troops were alerted during an 1880 strike at the largest smelting works in the country at Omaha, Nebraska. There had been absolutely no disorders during the strike, and troops were sent at the request of the plant managers without consultation with local officials; the strike quickly collapsed. In 1882, both federal and state troops were sent to Omaha after a smelting strike by railroad workers resulted in minor violence. Although the only casualty in the strike occurred when a soldier bayonetted to death a man who tried to cross military lines, a number of strike leaders were arrested for "assault with intent to kill" as a result of an attack which strikers had made on strikebreakers. Louisiana state militia broke a strike of sugar workers in 1880 by arresting strike leaders, although little serious violence appears to have occurred.[81]

In at least three cases in 1893-94, Illinois and Indiana militia were sent to strike areas where no violence had occurred; in the Indiana case the "sending of troops was evidently based on rumor or on hope that the presence of troops would intimidate the strikers."[82] During an IWW strike at Goldfield, Nevada, in 1907, federal troops were sent without any investigation upon the request of the governor, and remained for months although federal investigators reported the troops were not needed and had been secured so that mineowners could break the union. During the 1922 coal strike, federal or state troops were sent in apparent anticipation of disorders to thirteen states. There was little or no violence in any of the states to which troops had been sent, and even with military protection coal operators were unable to reopen since they could not find enough nonstrikers to work the mines.[83]

Conspiracy Prosecutions and Labor Injunctions

In 1842, a Boston municipal judge declared in *Commonwealth v. Hunt* that combinations of workers were legal and that the refusal of a group of Boston bootmakers to work alongside non-union members in an attempt to impose a closed shop was also legal. Prior to this decision, courts had generally held that labor unions were criminal conspiracies per se. *Commonwealth v. Hunt* has therefore long been regarded as a landmark in U.S. legal history, and has sometimes been interpreted as effectively spelling the end of conspiracy prosecutions against labor unions.[84] Although between 1842 and the Civil War, labor was not seriously hampered by judicial hostility, as labor revived after the war and class conflict increased, conspiracy laws and conspiracy prosecutions were revived, finally re-emerging in the even more deadly form of the labor injunction. As David Montgomery suggests, it was not the court decision of 1842 "that made conspiracy indictments of unions subside during the next two decades, but the absence of union activity."[85]

While conspiracy cases that arose after the civil war did not involve the legal status of labor unions per se, the concept of conspiracy was used to restrain many union activities, and, in the form of the injunction, was eventually used to effectively outlaw the organized boycott and organized picketing. It was characteristic of each major period of increased tensions arising from labor conflicts that labor came under increasing legal attack from state legislatures and the courts. Conspiracy prosecutions and laws were first revived by the courts and state legislatures in a major way in the wake of the 1877 railroad riot. The riots also led to the development of an early predecessor of the labor injunction, when two federal judges issued "writs of assistance" ordering the arrest of any person interfering with railroads under federal receivership. While such interference would have been a criminal act in any case, the advantage of the writ procedure was that it was issued by a court of equity and thus violators could be tried for contempt without a jury, even though they had never received notice of such writs. In the aftermath of the railroad riots, six states passed laws which effectively outlawed railroad strikes altogether, and, by 1886, in twenty-five states the activities of workers in combination were subject to limitations imposed by conspiracy statutes or by judicial applications of the English common law governing combinations.[86]

With the easing of tensions during the early 1880's, the application of such repressive laws and judicial constructions eased considerably but the return of labor strife and class tensions during the middle 1880's brought a revival and extension of such techniques. By 1886, the courts were beginning to punish boycotters and to make wholesale convictions of union members on vague charges of "boycotts, conspiracy, intimidation and rioting."[87] Conspiracy doctrines were especially rejuvenated immediately after the Haymarket Riot of 1886, when there "seem to have been more conspiracy cases than during all the rest of the century."[88] Conspiracy statutes were interpreted so loosely by the courts that even if no interference with the right to work occurred as a result of union action, "the mere inducing of workers to break their contract" or the "mere presence of large numbers of strikers outside a mine or factory" frequently led to conspiracy convictions.[89] Following the Haymarket Affair, state legislatures again leapt to the aid of the courts by strengthening conspiracy laws. Thus, Illinois in 1887 made the boycott an illegal conspiracy, and at least five other states passed legislation either broadening the definition of conspiracy or delimiting collective working class action.[90]

During the 1880's and early 1890's the technique of the labor injunction began to reach full flower.[91] The labor injunction was a marriage of the doctrine of considering certain labor activities as criminal conspiracies together with the ancient power of courts of equity to enjoin a nuisance and prevent irreparable injuries to property. From the standpoint of employers, the problem with conspiracy prosecutions was that they could be brought only after the damage had been done, involved cumbersome legal processes, and in the case of large numbers of strikers, were impracticable. Also, in towns with large concentrations of workers, juries could not always be relied upon to deliver convictions. The problem with the use of equity injunctions was that traditionally such injunctions had been issued only to prevent irreparable injuries to tangible property that also constituted criminal acts — i.e. physical destruction. However, during the 1880's and 1890's strikes and boycotts initiated to compel union recognition were increasingly held as criminal conspiracies by courts even though the only damage they did was to intangibles, i.e. "probable expectancies" as to the future business of an employer. Gradually, the theory of damage to "probable expectancies" of future business was incorporated into the traditional concept of equity injunctions, creating a situation in which courts began to hand down injunctions which barred labor unions *in advance* from carrying out activities which frequently violated no statutory laws and posed no immediate threat to physical property. A further benefit of injunctions was that violators could be arrested summarily and tried before a judge without a jury for contempt. The Supreme Court upheld the use of the injunction for the first time in 1894, in a case (In Re *Debs*) involving Pullman strike injunctions which were so broad that they effectively outlawed any union activity whatsoever in furtherance of a nationwide railroad strike. Subsequently, the federal courts upheld "blanket" injunctions which applied to all persons who had notice of them whether or not specifically directed to them, (In Re *Lennon*, 1897) and upheld injunctions that in effect held that the boycott was a criminal conspiracy (*Gompers v. Bucks Stove and Range Company*, 1908) and *Loewe v. Lawlor*, commonly known as the Danbury Hatter's case, 1908); outlawed the secondary boycott (*Duplex Printing Co. v. Deering*, 1921); barred all picketing in excess of one picket per plant gate (*American Steel Foundries v. Tri-City Central Trades Council*, 1921); barred attempts to organize men who had signed yellow-dog contracts (*Hitchman Coal &*

Coke Co. v. *Mitchell*, 1917); and barred strikes for the purpose of organizing the unorganized segments of an industry (the "Coronado" cases, 1925).[92]

The courts became particularly adept at using the Sherman Anti-Trust Act of 1890, which had been passed supposedly to regulate business combinations in restraint of interstate commerce, as a tool to severely hinder the labor movement, even while business monopolies were multiplying. Until the strike injunction was effectively outlawed by the Norris-Laguardia Act of 1931, the courts steadily became more and more ingenious in applying the injunction to more and more disputes. A total of 1845 strike injunctions were issued by federal and state courts between 1880 and 1930, of which 921 were issued during the 1920-30 period.[93] By the late 1920's, the injunction, which had once been viewed as an extraordinary remedy to be utilized only in an emergency characterized by immediate danger of irreparable injury to physical property, had become the "ordinary legal remedy" for use during labor disputes.[94] Temporary restraining orders were customarily issued by judges upon the application of company attorneys without notice or hearing for the union, and by threatening violators with immediate arrest, generally sufficed to break strikes. If the strike continued, temporary and then permanent injunctions could be issued. Most injunctions barred such activities as the use of coercion and intimidation, prevented or regulated picketing, and barred boycotts, trespassing, the use of the word "scab" and the payment of strike benefits. Some injunctions completely barred strikes and union meetings, and occasionally injunctions incorporated such absurdities as barring striking clothing workers in New York City from "standing in the street within ten blocks . . . of the plaintiff's business" although this area was the center of the New York City men's clothing industry and included the strikers' headquarters.[95]

Like the use of private police, the labor injunction was a feature of American labor history unknown in other countries.[96] By the late 1920's, leading students of labor law were increasingly viewing the injunction, particularly as applied in the *Hitchman* case, as posing "a peril to the survival of trade unionism in the United States."[97]

2

The Development of Repressive Techniques, 1870-1900

During the 1870-1900 period, all of the various techniques used to repress labor were gradually developed and institutionalized by business and governmental elites: the company town, the use of private police, private arsenals and private detectives, the deputization of private police, the manipulation of governmental police agencies, the revival of conspiracy doctrine and the labor injunction. While the entire period was characterized by increasing fears about and use of repressive techniques on the part of business and governmental elites to meet the threat posed by labor organizations, three "peaks" of repression may be identified: approximately 1873-78, 1886-87, and 1892-97. Although each of these periods had its own unique characteristics, several themes are common to all of them. Each peak of repression occurred during a period of severe economic distress, which led to high unemployment and severe wage cuts for many workers. Each period saw a high degree of militant activity on the part of labor. Each period was dominated by fears on the part of conservative elites that American workers were becoming infected by foreign subversive theories.

The general characteristics of American society during the 1873-1900 period helped to create a climate which facilitated a repressive response on the part of ruling elites during periods of increased stress. In general, the period was a time of severe economic fluctuations and repeated depressions which largely reflected the fact that workers were not paid high enough wages to allow them to buy the goods that the economy was capable of producing. The period was one of tremendous social change, especially marked by massive industrialization, urbanization and immigration. Unlike the Progressive Era, this period was characterized by the lack of any strongly organized middle class reform elements which were inclined to ameliorate labor discontents and to oppose the use of repressive methods *only* in response to labor disorders.[1] The effect of the first two characteristics was to create a general climate of continuing uncertainty and fear among conservative elites in American society. The effect of the third characteristic was that there was no organized force available to soften the clash between labor and capital during periods of severe stress. The immediate inclination of capital during such times was to raise the "standard of suppression"[2] and no body of articulate public opinion existed to suggest any other solution. While in many smaller towns the forces of developing industrialism had not yet taken hold and face-to-face contact between social classes remained frequent, in the developing power centers of American society, the major cities, there "was almost no sympathy for city workers among the middle and upper classes."[3] Even among the so-called "liberal reformers," a devotion to the principles of laissez-faire, Social Darwinism and private property, and a fear of uprisings from the "dangerous classes" almost invariably led to support for repression, but little support for significant reforms. As Joan G. Sproat has written:

> Liberal reformers became deathly afraid of the poor and the unfortunate, afraid that the underprivileged masses would rise up and strike down property and all that was decent and respectable in life. . . . Liberals claimed to detest the crude businessmen who ran most of the giant corporations in postwar America. Yet they ultimately became staunch supporters of these same men; for, no matter how corrupt or unscrupulous or cruel a businessman was in his daily affairs, he stood for property. . . . For all their vaunted concern for the individual, liberal reformers readily and repeatedly set aside human rights whenever the rights of property came under attack. Much as they deplored outbursts of human passion and pleaded for reasoned solutions to human problems, most liberals agreed that the only sure method for dealing with violence among strikers was to shoot the offenders. . . . But with dogged consistency [they] opposed meaningful proposals to provide workers and their families with the means, the opportunity and the incentive to acquire good taste and enlightenment.[4]

The Red Scare of 1873-78

At least five elements came together during the 1873-78 period to precipitate the first major "red scare" in the United States history: the Paris Commune of 1871 created a severe fright among conservative Americans; until the 1873 depression began American workers and farmers showed increasing organizational gains and emitted increasingly threatening noises that appeared to pose severe challenges to the developing ascendancy of big business; Marxist parties appeared for the first time on the American scene and were increasing in strength; the 1873 depression caused unprecedented mass demonstrations by American workers for public works and relief; and the Molly Maguire affair and the 1877 railroad strikes seemed to confirm the growing belief among businessmen and government officials that American labor was turning increasingly radical, violent and subversive, and could only be put down with the club and the gun.

There is little doubt that the Paris Commune created as much fear among American ruling circles as it did in Europe; it was the Commune, more than any other single event except the French Revolution of 1789, which originated the fear of foreign radical subversion which has been a constant theme in American history. The immediate reaction of the American press to the Commune was severe hostility, and it was a frequent comment that American workers might well pose a similar threat to American society. The term "communism" quickly became an all-purpose epithet applied by conservatives to anyone or anything found distasteful.[5] Thus, Professor Hitchcock of Union Theological Seminary wrote in the late 1870's that "today there is not in our language, nor in any language a more hateful word than communism."[6] Friedrich Sorge, the leading representative of the First International in America, wrote to the International's General Council in London that the American ruling classes "have the Commune on the brain."[7] During the last part of the nineteenth century the appellation of "communism" was freely applied to virtually all labor activities, to proposals for regulating railroads or limiting hours or work, to farmers' pleas for reforms, and even to the Democrats' investigations of irregularities in the 1876 presidential election. As tensions rose in the 1870's, so did the fear of communist subversion. Thus, in 1875 Chicago businessman Joseph Medill declared, "Every lamp-post in Chicago will be decorated with a communistic carcass if necessary to prevent wholesale incendiarism."[8] Fears of communism were by no means restricted to the more industrialized areas of the country; thus, in 1879 an Alabama newspaper welcomed immigrant workers to the area "provided you are not tramps, strikers, communists nor Mollie Maguires."[9] Charges of communist influence were hurled not only by businessmen:

> In rationalizing their stand against unions and strikers, many employers and other conservative groups who usually shared industry's point of view . . . i.e., politicians, newspapermen, clergymen, jurists, lawyers and educators, engaged in substantial red baiting. Regardless of the merits of the individual case, employers and their sympathizers found charges of socialism, communism, anarchism and radicalism against workers to be particularly effective.[10]

A second factor lending intensity to the fears of radical subversion during the 1870's was the rapid growth of workers' and farmers' movements which appeared to threaten conservative hegemony. The labor movement had suffered severely from the post-civil war recession of 1866-68 and an employers' anti-union offensive, but with the return of prosperity in 1869 the unions experienced a strong revival.[11] Between 1868 and 1873 fourteen new national unions were organized, and by 1873 the union movement reached a peak of three hundred thousand members. Spearheading the labor revival was the National Labor Union (NLU), the first important national labor organization. The leader of the NLU, until his death in 1869, was William H. Sylvis, whose primary goal was the "abolition of an impersonal and degrading wage system, which would be replaced by a cooperative society based on the dominance of the small individual producer."[12] This philosophy permeated the NLU leadership, which wished to destroy the increasing power of the big corporations and to return to workers a greater share of the national wealth.

Although the NLU itself began to disintegrate as a result of factional disputes after Sylvis' death, the spirit of labor militancy did not disappear. The period from 1868 to 1872 was marked by a series of major strikes over the eight-hour issue, with the most spectacular strikes occurring in New York City, where one hundred thousand walked off their jobs in 1872 in an effort to force employers to comply with New York State's eight-hour law. About fifteen thousand strikers won their demands before the movement was halted when police began to direct "their clubs at workingmen's heads with utter abandon" and employers and the press helped bring about splits in the workers' ranks by claiming that "communists" were behind all of the trouble.[13] A number of other eight-hour strikes were more successful; on the eve of the 1873 depression trade unions had enrolled a greater proportion of the work force than ever before in American history, and it appeared that the eight-hour day "was well on its way to becoming the national standard."[14]

By the mid-1870's, farmers were also beginning to stir themselves. The Granger movement achieved a peak strength of eight hundred fifty thousand members in early 1875 (including two hundred fifty thousand in the south), and succeeded in pushing railroad regulation bills through the legislatures of five midwestern states. While these laws were soon repealed or pecked to death by railroad sniping, the Granger movement added to the general fears of businessmen — and of course added to the frequent cries of "communism" echoed throughout the country.[15]

Another development causing unease among conservative circles was the appearance of a small but vocal and growing Marxist political faction. While communist organizations had been in existence in the U.S. since 1857, the first significant Marxist groups arose during the late 1860's and early 1870's. The NLU had voted to join the First International in 1870; while such a relationship was never consummated, by early 1870 three sections of the International had been formed in the U.S. From 1871 to 1873, the International made slow but steady gains, especially in cities with large German populations such as New York, Milwaukee, St. Louis, Cincinnati, and Detroit. Marx's writings were widely circulated in the U.S. beginning in 1871. Many workers openly avowed their support for the Commune; for example, twenty thousand workers demonstrating for the eight-hour day in New York in September, 1871, greeted marching sections of the International with shouts of "Vive La Commune," and meetings and demonstrations were held in the larger cities to commemorate the Commune's founding and raise money for exiles. By 1876, when various Marxist-oriented groups merged to form the Workingmen's Party of the U.S. (WPUS), later renamed the Socialist Labor Party (SLP), about twenty-five hundred members were affiliated. Although this was a very small number, the movement was very active and received a great deal of attention in the press.[16]

Another factor contributing to the red scare of the 1870's was the massive dislocation resulting from the depression of 1873-78 and the mass demonstrations of unemployed workers for relief which resulted.[17]

By any measure, the distress caused by the depression was enormous. Most estimates indicate that during the first winter of the depression, 1873-

74, unemployment rose to at least 25 percent of urban workers. In New York City, fourteen thousand workers lacking housing slept in police station houses each night, while another two thousand were turned away for lack of space. During the last months of 1873, unemployment demonstrations were held in Boston, Chicago, New York, Cincinnati, Detroit, Philadelphia and many other cities; in Indianapolis and Chicago, the largest labor meetings in the cities' history occurred. Coming so soon after the Commune, these demonstrations "conjured images of enormous potential violence and destruction" among the more well-to-do. The movement was repeatedly red-baited by the press, which generally viewed it as a foreign subversive conspiracy aimed at overturning American institutions.[18] Thus, The *Chicago Times* asked, after a worker demonstration: "Is Chicago in the hands of 'La Commune'?" and warned that if such was the case then, "'La Commune' and not Chicago must perish."[19] The development of a large tramp movement during the depression also proved particularly alarming to the middle classes. Many legislatures increased their penalties for vagrancy, while some newspapers suggested the problem be halted by feeding tramps a "leaden" diet or putting poison in their food.[20]

Police action to break up unemployment demonstrations was a common occurrence during the depression. For example, many persons were hurt in St. Louis in January, 1874, when police attacked a socialist demonstration, and in Chicago in 1875 police dispersed crowds of destitute unemployed who were begging relief from charitable organizations. Destitute strikers at Fall River, Massachusetts who sought to demand bread for their starving children were barred from presenting their demands to City Hall in September, 1875 by state militia and local police.[21]

The most important example of police repression of the unemployed occurred in New York City on January 13, 1874, when police brutally attacked over seven thousand demonstrators at Tompkins Square. The unemployed movement in New York was the strongest in the country. By early 1874, factionalism within the movement and resistance from without had killed the organized efforts of the unemployed in other cities, but in New York, socialists, anti-monopolists and trade unionists had built a strong movement which included ward organizations. A rally permit which had been granted for the Tompkins Square meeting was suddenly cancelled the night before the rally; demonstrators had been given virtually no notice of the cancellation and were given no real warning before police attacked them with clubs and horses. After the Tompkins Square debacle, the New York unemployment movement fell apart.[22]

In the aftermath of Tompkins Square, New York officials and the press charged repeatedly that the entire affair was the work of foreign communists. New York police even claimed that the "communists" among the "revolutionaries" who had organized the demonstration had smuggled diamonds and precious gems stolen from churches by leaders of the Commune into New York to buy ammunition and bombs. Police agents began attending labor and socialist meetings, thereby intimidating workers who wished to attend them. The *Philadelphia Inquirer* boasted that the "American commune" had met its master and advised that if a similar spirit should arise again public officials in New York should "club it to death at the hands of the police or shoot it to death at the hands of the militia."[23]

Strikers as well as unemployment demonstrators were frequently the victim of governmental repression during the depression. During 1873-74, the mayor of Philadelphia barred the leader of striking weavers from speaking in the streets and New York police barred cigar workers from gathering in front of a factory to protest the firing of six union members. In Pittsburgh, seventy union members were held on a charge of "conspiracy" during a newspaper printers strike; they were released after the strike collapsed. Cleveland coal strikers were faced with Ohio national guardsmen and the arrest of several strike leaders, although they maintained order. While the Cleveland strikers won their fight, coal strikers in Ohio's Hocking Valley were beaten when the militia was mobilized and strikebreakers were deputized and armed by state officials, despite the lack of any violence. The thirty-five thousand member National Miners Association was destroyed by 1875 by incessant striking coupled with the arrest of two of its leaders for "conspiracy." In a related "riot and conspiracy" case, the judge, in pronouncing sentence, said, "I find you, Joyce, to be the president of the Union, and you, Maloney, to be secretary, and therefore I sentence you to one year's imprisonment." A planned strike of railroad workers in New York in June, 1877, was called off when state militia were mobilized. State militia were used during strikes in Indiana, Pennsylvania, Kentucky, Michigan, Colorado, Louisiana and Illinois during 1873-74 alone.[24]

A final element in the development of the 1873-78 red scare was the actual occurrence of violence in labor disputes. While the Molly Maguire affair and the 1877 railroad strike were the most serious disorders, there were other incidents of violence during this period which developed out of strikes. For example, in 1873 and 1874 there was a series of railroad strikes during which railroad workers reacted to wage cuts and firings by disabling freight cars, tearing up tracks, cutting telegraph lines and stopping trains. Most of these strikes occurred in small railroad towns and isolated semi-rural areas; what was particularly frightening to big businessmen about the strikes was that strikers frequently obtained significant support from the local populations and in some cases from local officials who depended on workers for business patronage and electoral support. For example, at Susquehanna Depot, Pennsylvania, when strikers seized control of the railroad repair shops, the local sheriff gave them his weapons and refused to allow strikebreakers to enter the town. Eventually eighteen hundred state troops occupied the town of eight thousand residents, set up thirty pieces of cannon and proclaimed martial law.[25]

The impact of these strikes was insignificant, however, compared with that of the Molly Maguire affair. The Maguire story is a confusing one and the full truth about it will probably never be known. The setting was the anthracite coal fields of eastern Pennsylvania, an area noted for grimy company towns, abominable working conditions and constant and often random violence, which apparently resulted from a mix of religious, ethnic and class tensions. There had been major outbreaks of violence in the area, including numerous murders, during the mid-1860's, and again during the middle 1870's, following the crushing — largely through starvation — of the miners' Workingmen's Benevolent Association (WBA) in the so-called "long strike" of 1875. Many of the victims of violence were mine officials; many were not. As Fred Shannon has suggested, there is considerable evidence to suggest that the lawlessness in the coal fields was less the result of a labor conspiracy than of "just plain, low-down orneriness."[26]

At about the same time Franklin P. Gowen, president of the dominant economic force in the area, the Philadelphia and Reading Railroad, was crushing the WBA, he began to hire Pinkerton detectives to infiltrate an alleged secret ring of miners known as "Molly Maguires" who supposedly were coordinating violence against mine officials. Largely on the basis of reports of Pinkerton agent James McPharlan, who claimed to have infiltrated the Maguires, a number of men were arrested in late 1875. In trials which lasted until late 1876, twenty-four alleged Mollies were convicted of various murders and other crimes, and ten were sentenced to death, on the basis of testimony by McPharlan and alleged Mollies who gained immunity from prosecution. Several defense witnesses were prosecuted for perjury. While some of those convicted were probably guilty, almost just as surely others were not. In later trials, ten more alleged Mollies were sentenced to death.

The Maguire suspects had been arrested by the Coal and Iron Police, who served Gowen's interests, while Gowen himself acted as prosecutor in some of the trials. While no evidence was ever introduced linking the Mollies with union activities, Gowen insinuated that this was the case. There have been frequent charges that the entire affair was instigated by Gowen in order to destroy the last vestiges of unionism in the area, and there is some evidence supporting this charge. In 1947 it was revealed that the coal operators had instigated some of the attacks on the mines that were later attributed to the Mollies in order to provide an excuse for crushing both the Mollies and the WBA.[27] McPharlan's own performance in another union trial thirty years later (the Steunenberg case) does not add much weight to his credibility. At any rate, as Joseph Rayback has written:

> Whoever was responsible for the Molly Maguire Riots, labor was their victim.... The trial temporarily destroyed the last vestiges of labor unionism in the anthracite area. More important, it gave the public the impression that miners in general inclined to riot, sabotage, arson, pillage, assault, robbery and murder.... The impression became the foundation of the anti-labor attitude held by a large portion of the nation to the present day.[28]

Thereafter, any union that tried to organize in the area

> would find itself soaked in the brew of Molly Maguireism. . . . Though "communist" was also vying for position as a favorite epithet, the words "Molly Maguire" were still good for calling up stereotyped prejudices for most of the rest of the nineteenth century, particularly in the Pennsylvania hard-coal fields.[29]

Another long term effect of the affair was to demonstrate how private detectives might be used to spy on and disrupt union activities; Gowen's effective use of the Coal and Iron Police suggested yet another useful tactic to other employers. In the aftermath of the Molly affair, American employers began to adopt systems of private espionage and private police on a widespread scale for the first time.[30] As Harold Aurand has written, the widespread use of private resources to attain the supposedly public ends of justice in the Molly affair constituted

> one of the most astounding surrenders of sovereignty in American history. A private corporation initiated the investigation through a private detective agency; a private police force arrested the alleged offenders; the coal company attorneys prosecuted them. The state provided only the courtroom and the hangman.[31]

The climactic event in the 1873-78 red scare was the great railroad strike of 1877. Precipitated by repeated wage cuts and grievances over working conditions, spontaneous strikes broke out on railroad lines throughout the country in mid-July, about a month after ten "Mollies" had been hung on June 21, 1877. Of the nation's seventy-five thousand miles of track, about two-thirds lay in areas affected by the strike; most freight trains and some passenger trains stopped running on virtually all lines outside of New England and the South. While in many areas, trains stopped running simply because the strike was effective, in numerous cases crowds sympathetic to the strikers blocked tracks, seized railroad facilities and disabled railroad cars.[32]

In city after city, the striking railroad workers received massive support from large numbers of other workers and from urban "mobs" which had developed during the depression. In many cities, other workers went out on strike in support of the rail strikers. General strike movements developed in a number of cities, including Buffalo, Harrisburg, Columbus, Chicago, Louisville and St. Louis. The spirit of the strikers and their supporters was aptly characterized by one militiaman sent to Pittsburgh, who reported, "I talked to all the strikers I could get my hands on, and I could find but one spirit and one purpose among them: that they were justified in resorting to any means to break down the power of corporations."[33] With the memory of the Commune fresh in conservative minds, business interests and the press throughout the country quickly took up the cry of "communism" and "revolution." In fact, the strikes were generally completely spontaneous and uncoordinated, and represented a gesture of des-

Development of Repressive Techniques 31

peration rather than a plan to overthrow the government. While the Marxist-oriented WPUS was active in strike activities in a number of cities, only in St. Louis, where the WPUS led a virtually complete and peaceful general strike, did communists exercise a significant role. Everywhere the WPUS was active, moreover "its influence in the 1877 strike was . . . a moderating one."[34]

The strikes were eventually broken by the massive use of federal and state troops along with local volunteer "citizens militia" groups. Federal troops were sent into seven states and the state militia were called out in many areas. Altogether forty-five thousand militiamen and two thousand federal troops saw service. While the use of troops was unquestionably needed in some areas due to severe breakdowns of law and order, in some cases they were sent with little apparent need. Thus, federal troops were ordered sent to Chicago, St. Louis, Philadelphia and Indianapolis before any serious disturbances occurred. At one point, President Hayes threatened to declare martial law throughout the country and occupy all disturbed areas with federal troops. In many cases the state militia in particular acted in a heavy-handed and trigger-happy manner. The most serious disorders of the strike occurred in Baltimore and Pittsburgh after state militia indiscriminately opened fire on crowds that had thrown stones and brickbats at them; militia fire in the two cities killed twenty to thirty people and injured scores. In the aftermath of the Pittsburgh shooting, mobs destroyed over twenty-two hundred railroad cars and burned over eighty buildings. Heavy casualties also occurred during clashes with militia in Chicago; Cumberland, Maryland; and Reading, Pennsylvania. Altogether, at least ninety deaths occurred during the railroad strike, the vast majority at the hands of police and militia. The heavy bloodletting undoubtedly partly resulted from the fact that businessmen volunteers often served as militiamen. The strikes were marked by numerous other violations of basic freedoms, some perhaps understandable under the circumstances, others simply reflecting the intense panic which seized government officials and the propertied classes. Strikers and strike leaders were arrested, generally indiscriminately, in many areas, including Martinsburg, West Virginia, and strike areas in Maryland and Pennsylvania, Toledo, and Albany. The St. Louis general strike, which had been so peaceful that the only serious casualty occurred when a militiaman scratched himself with his own bayonet, was broken when police and militia raided WPUS headquarters and arrested everyone in sight. In Chicago, police attacked a peaceful WPUS rally, while in Philadelphia, despite a lack of serious disorders, over four thousand special police and federal troops were deployed and kept themselves busy using nightsticks to disperse even small gatherings of men, tearing down all notices of meetings of any kind, and attacking all attempts of workers to hold meetings, with one death and many injuries resulting. Philadelphia police arrested one WPUS leader for inciting to riot when he persisted in attempting to address one peaceful gathering, and confiscated all copies they could of a WPUS newspaper. Pennsylvania railroad president Tom Scott closely cooperated with Philadelphia and federal authorities, furnishing supplies to federal troops and feeding city police free of charge.[35]

The real long-term result of the strikes was that they crystallized the fear of communist revolution and foreign radicals which had been building since 1871 in the minds of American elites. Throughout the strike, the newspapers were full of references to alien agitators, the Commune and red revolutionaries.[36] Thus, the *Brooklyn Daily Eagle* termed the strikes the "nearest approach we have yet had to Communism in America" and urged that "our authorities must act with unmistakable rigor in the present emergency" to save the country from "the darker horrors of that system."[37] The *Independent,* a religious periodical, suggested:

> If the club of the policeman, knocking out the brains of the rioter, will answer, then well and good; but if it does not promptly meet the exigency, then bullets and bayonets, canister and grape . . . constitute the one remedy and the one duty of the hour. . . . Napoleon was right when he said that the way to deal with a mob is to exterminate it.[38]

The entire labor movement was more than ever looked upon as a species of violent subversive beast. As Joseph Rayback has written:

> Not since slaveholders had ceased to be haunted by dreams of a slave uprising had the propertied elements been so terrified. They became convinced that not only coal miners but railway workers and other laborers were inherently criminal. They were likewise convinced that immediate steps had to be taken to ensure law and order in the future.[39]

After the strikes were broken, the states began to hastily improve their weapons and defenses against labor agitation. Many states passed new anti-labor conspiracy laws, while the old common law doctrine of malicious conspiracy was revived by some judges. Hundreds of strikers were arrested for their role in the disorders, although few were ever convicted. The state militia, which had been allowed to wither away in many states, experienced a major revival and armories sprang up in major cities across the country. In many cases the militia was privately subsidized by businessmen, and the leadership in militia companies generally represented the upper strata of society.[40] Thus, at the 1881 convention of the National Guard Association, an Illinois colonel reported:

> We have a battalion of five companies of cavalry, all located in the city of Chicago. It grew out of our riots of 1877, previous to which time we had no cavalry in the state. During the riots it was found necessary to have cavalry, and we hastily organized a battalion of cavalry among our businessmen who had seen cavalry service during the war. Our cavalry was not equipped by the state. It belongs to the National Guard, but was equipped and uniformed completely by the Citizens' Association of the City of Chicago. This association is composed of businessmen, who look after the best interests of our city.[41]

After about 1878, a number of factors brought about a reduction in tensions in American society. The crushing of the 1877 strikes and the effects of the depression had devastated the American labor movement. The number of national trade unions had declined from thirty in 1873 to nine by 1878, while total union membership had dropped from three hundred thousand to about fifty thousand.[42] The return of prosperity in 1879 put a damper on labor discontent, while the lack of additional spectacular strikes eased the fears of conservatives. Yet a deep strain of terror had become indelibly imbedded in the more fortunate. Thus, at Harvard University's commencement exercises in 1881, senior Curtis Guild compared the United States to Rome during the years of the downfall of the Republic; the modern counterpart to the plebians was the "ignorant mob misled by crafty demagogues, . . . Irish Molly Maguires, German Socialists, French Communists, and Russian Nihilists."[43] A contributor to the *Atlantic Monthly* wrote in 1882:

> Our era of prosperity and of happy immunity from those social diseases which are the danger and the humiliation of Europe is passing away. Optimistic as we are, we cannot fail to know that the increasing proportion of the incapable among us is repeating here the social problems of the Old World. . . . Every year brings the conditions of American labor into closer likeness to those of the Old World. An American species of socialism is inevitable.[44]

In the aftermath of the 1877 riots, the most innocuous proposals for reforming the conditions of labor to prevent further outbreaks were met with cries of "un-American" and "communist" in the press, and the myth attributing the disturbances to an international communist conspiracy was firmly enshrined in contemporary American histories.[45]

How to combat the pernicious influences of communism and labor radicalism became one of the major topics of the day among middle class elites and government officials, many of whom saw a way of bolstering the importance of their own organizations in fighting the menace. Thus, in 1878, the Rev. Joseph Cook proclaimed that the Church was "the chief barrier against communistic and socialistic inroads from the howling sea of an ignorant and unprincipled population."[46] The national commissioner of education, John Eaton, asserted that the public schools "could train the child to resist the evils of strikes and violence," and urged business to "weigh the cost of the mob and the tramp against the expense of universal and sufficient education."[47] The president of the National Education Association told the NEA convention in 1881 that the public schools would eliminate the threat of communism.[48] The increasing distrust of foreigners was reflected in the federal immigration law of August, 1882, which barred from the U.S. convicts, lunatics, idiots and those liable to become a public charge.[49]

While the impact of the Molly Maguires and the railroad strike upon the middle and upper classes is easy to document, it is much more difficult to be sure what effect they had on workers. However, workers, especially those considering joining unions, would have been less than alert if they did not conclude that any militant labor activity greatly increased their chances of being arrested, shot or even hung. Just to remind them, the use of state militia remained frequent during strikes after 1877, and while the application of conspiracy laws did ease somewhat in the early 1880's they too were enforced occasionally. The early 1880's also saw the issuance of what were probably the first labor injunctions, with courts ordering laborers working under contracts to refrain from striking.[50]

The Communist Anarchist-Labor Scare of 1886

Following the 1873-78 red scare, the next major period of repression in American history was the communist-anarchist-labor scare which centered around 1886. The 1886 scare had its roots in four major developments: the distress and discontent caused among workers by the depression of 1882-86; the general revival of the labor movement, which was particularly marked beginning in about 1885, and the radical rhetoric and goals of the dominant force in that revival, the Knights of Labor; the increasing strength of radical political parties, in particular the rapidly growing influence of the violence-advocating communist-anarchist movement, especially among workers in Chicago; and, the culminating incident, which played a role similar to that of 1877 railroad strikes, namely the mass eight-hour day movement of 1886 and the Haymarket affair. The depression of 1882-86 was not nearly as acute as the 1873-78 depression, but it still caused serious distress.[51] Business activities in six key segments of the economy declined by about one-fourth, unemployment averaged about 13 percent in the fall of 1884, and wage reductions were estimated to be about 20-30 percent. While no mass unemployment demonstrations arose during this period, there was an outburst of "almost hopeless strikes" which mounted steadily.[52] Business reaction to the increasing distress and to the accompanying revival of the labor movement was to increasingly identify the unrest with foreign influence, as memories of 1877 returned.[53]

The second factor involved in the 1886 scare was the revival of the labor movement and the radical rhetoric and approach of its dominant element, the Knights of Labor.[54] The growth of the Knights and the increasing use of the strike as a tactic during this period are easily documented:

	Membership in the Knights of Labor[55]	Workers Involved in Strikes[56] (1000)
1881	19,422	130
1882	42,517	159
1883	51,914	170
1884	71,326	165
1885	111,395	258
1886	729,677	610
1887	548,239	439

Both Knights membership and workers involved in strikes increased from rather small figures in 1881 and reached a peak in 1886-87, which, not coincidentally, was also the peak of repression in the 1880's. There were two elements about the Knights of Labor which appeared particularly frightening to business and government elites: their success and their goals and rhetoric. The massive membership jump which occurred from 1881-86, and especially in 1885-86 reflected Knights' victories in a number of important strikes. During the winter of 1883-84, the Knights won several strikes while walkouts led by other unions were lost. In the autumn of 1884 they won a major strike against the Union Pacific railroad, and in 1885 the Knights won two tremendous victories against railroad systems operated by tycoon Jay Gould.

It was particularly after the victories against the Gould line and the massive increase in Knights membership in 1885-86 that conservative hysteria began to mount. Elements in the press began to estimate Knights membership in the millions and suggested that the five-man executive board of the organization had the power to stop all industry in the nation, name the next president or overthrow the entire social system.[57]

These fears were accentuated by organizational structure, the announced goals and the rhetoric of the Knights. Unlike most unions in American history until that time, the Knights were open to workers in all occupations, of all nationalities and races, and of both sexes. As many as 10 percent of the Knights were black, and the great majority of members were unskilled workers who had never before been organized into unions. Thus, the Knights presented the spectre of a unified organization of the working class. Furthermore, the Knights openly called for abolition of what they termed "wage slavery" and its replacement by a system based on producers' cooperatives; they also championed government ownership of the railroads, telegraphs and telephones. The leader of the Knights, Terence Powderly, was rather fond of radical bombast; for example, in 1884, he declared that the Knights should "strike a powerful, telling blow at the base of the system which makes the laborer the slave of his master. . . . So long as a pernicious system leaves one man at the mercy of another, so long will labor and capital be at war."[58]

The fears aroused by the Knights were, in fact, grossly misplaced. Powderly, as Norman Ware has written, was mostly a "windbag"[59] whose incompetence gravely crippled the organization. While talking tough, he personally abhorred the only weapon the Knights had — the strike — and constantly undercut efforts by workers to make any attempt to realistically achieve any of their goals. It was typical of Powderly that when the eight-hour issue arose in 1886, he opposed any action by the Knights to support the nation-wide strike scheduled for May 1, instead suggesting that members of the order "write short essays" on the question. He also urged Knights to fight the depression by smashing their beer bottles so as to provide increased employment for glass workers.[60] In sum, the Knights under Powderly was an organization with a class struggle ideology, but no willingness to actually undertake the struggle.

If the Knights were a paper tiger, the same cannot be said of the growing and violently anti-capitalist communist-anarchist movement, organized officially as the International Working People's Association (IWPA).[61] The IWPA was a splinter group of the Socialist Labor Party (SLP), formerly the WPUS. What distinguished it from the SLP was the IWPA's open advocacy of force and "the destruction of existing class rule, by all means, i.e. by energetic, relentless, revolutionary and international action."[62] The single most influential figure in the development of the IWPA was Johann Most, a German immigrant, whose greatest literary contribution was a pamphlet entitled *Science of Revolutionary Warfare: A Manual of Instruction in the Use and Preparation of Nitroglycerine, Dynamite, Gun-Cotton, Fulminant Mercury Bombs, Fuses, Poisons, etc.*

After two years of existence, the IWPA had about seven thousand members in 1885, a figure which outstripped the parent SLP by over two thousand.[63] The two major centers of IWPA strength were Chicago and New York. The New York branch was dominated by Most and largely concentrated on the "purely practical aspects of insurrectional methods,"[64] while the far more vital Chicago movement worked on developing strong ties with the local labor movement. By 1885, the Chicago IWPA had attained a major or even dominant influence among organized Chicago workers. The Chicago Central Labor Union, organized under strong IWPA influence in 1884 to counter the Amalgamated Trades and Labor Assembly, quickly developed major strength; among the unions belonging to it were the eleven largest unions in the city. In 1885 the Chicago IWPA had about two thousand members and published five newspapers with a combined circulation of over thirty thousand.[65] Like other branches of the IWPA, the Chicago movement advocated the use of violence, with a particular emphasis on the purely practical aspects of using weapons. However, most members of the group "would have found the execution of what they advised wholly impossible" and "contemplated nothing more dangerous than violent accusation and denunciation."[66]

The increasing tension which developed as a result of the depression and the rise of the Knights and the IWPA was brought to a head by the nation-wide rash of strikes which developed in 1886, a year which various historians have termed a "revolutionary year," the "year of the great uprising of labor" and the "great upheaval."[67] According to the leading history of American labor, the strike movement of this year

> rising as an elemental protest against oppression and degradation.... bore in every way the aspect of a social war. A frenzied hatred of labour for capital was shown in every important strike.... Extreme bitterness towards capital manifested itself in all the actions of the Knights of Labor, and wherever the leaders undertook to hold it within bounds they were generally discarded by their followers and others who would lead as directed were placed in charge.[68]

The first major upheaval of the year was another Knights-led strike against Jay Gould's railroad system in the southwest. While Gould had been conciliatory in 1885, now he was determined to break the power of the Knights, and the strike was fought with few holds barred on either side. Strikers resorted to sabotaging railroad tracks and cars, while Gould succeeded in obtaining numerous court injunctions which placed strikers in contempt of court. Large numbers of special police paid by the railroads and special deputies chosen by the railroads were hired to fight the strike. In East St. Louis on April 9 a group of deputies fired into a crowd, killing seven people and wounding many others, and setting off a riot in which $75,000 worth of railroad property was destroyed before the Illinois militia restored order. Another incident which indicates the savagery with which the strike was fought was the arrest of nine men recruited by the struck railroads who came from Louisiana to Texas after being assured that there was no strike in progress. They were sworn in as deputy U.S. marshals with the job of protecting company property; when they found out about the strike and quit work, they were sentenced to three to four months in jail for contempt, intimidation and defrauding the company. In the aftermath of the strike, which collapsed in May, there were over four hundred arrests, mostly for contempt of court, but few convictions.[69]

While the Gould strike was collapsing, agitation across the country was growing on the eight-hour day issue. The climax of eight-hour agitation was scheduled for May 1, 1886, when workers across the country threatened to go out on strike. While the IWPA in Chicago had at first shunned the issue as too reformist, they later assumed a leading role in organizing around the eight-hour demand. As the May 1 date approached, Chicago's citizens and press were "in the grip of a deep terror," while anarchist scares developed in San Francisco, Pittsburgh and Denver.[70] The Knights of Labor, although officially not connected with the eight-hour agitation, were increasingly interpreted by conservative elites as "disciplined mass sedition," while "references to an American Reign of Terror and a domestic version of the Paris Commune were now heard everywhere."[71]

The May 1 strike turnout was something of a disappointment to labor but was still by far the largest nationwide strike movement in American history. About one hundred and fifty thousand workers were granted shorter hours without striking, while one hundred and ninety thousand workers walked out, of whom forty thousand gained shorter hours. The center of the strike movement was Chicago, where eighty thousand struck. In Milwaukee, a growing strike movement which had shut down most shops and factories in the city was broken on May 5 when the Wisconsin national guard opened fire on a peaceful group of strikers, killing five, and dispersed groups of strikers in the streets of Milwaukee.[72] In the aftermath of the militia actions, which broke "labor's most serious challenge to management in the city's history,"[73] a coroner's jury absolved the militia of any responsibility for the five deaths (one of whom was a sixty-eight year-old man killed by a stray bullet while feeding chickens in his backyard), while thirty-seven of the most radical strike leaders were arrested and convicted for fomenting riots; these charges apparently developed out of minor scuffling between strikers and national guardsmen on May 4, the day before the shooting, in which some strikers threw rocks and bricks at the guard. The leading radical strike leader, Paul Grottkau, who earlier in 1886 had formed the Central Labor Union, the first group in Milwaukee's history which attempted to actively recruit and organize unskilled workers on a large scale, was sentenced to a year in jail, although he eventually served only six weeks.

The events in Milwaukee were completely overshadowed by virtually simultaneous disturbances which occurred in Chicago and reached their climax in the Haymarket bombing on May 4.[74] The Haymarket incident in Chicago took place against the background of increasing IWPA agitation and success in that city, and of endemic clashes between police and workers. The Chicago police force operated as though it were a "private police force in the services of the employers."[75] Since February, 1886, the focus of worker-police conflict centered around a lockout and strike at the McCormick Harvester factory. During the months of the strike, the police regularly attacked gatherings of workers and strikers with clubs and horses. The widespread and uncontrolled use of Pinkerton operatives by Chicago employers was another source of irritation to Chicago workers. In his 1893 message pardoning the surviving defendants in the Haymarket bombing, Illinois Gov. John Peter Altgeld wrote that before the bombing

> in several cases a number of laboring people, guilty of no offense, had been shot down in cold blood by Pinkerton men and none of the murderers were brought to justice. The evidence taken at coroners' inquests and presented here shows that in at least two cases men were fired on and killed when they were running away and there was consequently no occasion to shoot yet nobody was punished; that in Chicago there had been a number of strikes in which some of the police not only took sides against the men, but without any authority of law invaded and broke up peaceable meetings, and in scores of cases brutally clubbed people who were guilty of no offense whatever.[76]

While May 1 passed peacefully in Chicago, on May 3 Chicago police fired on a crowd of McCormick strikers who had attacked strikebreakers leaving the plant. Police gunfire killed one striker and seriously wounded five or six others. On the evening of May 4, the IWPA sponsored a meeting to protest police brutality at the Haymarket Square. The meeting was completely peaceful, but just as the meeting was about to adjourn, one hundred and eighty Chicago police appeared and demanded that the few hundred persons still attending disperse. Suddenly a bomb was thrown into police ranks, and police responded by shooting into the crowd. According to some accounts, there was return fire from the crowd. The casualties from the bomb and the shooting amounted to seven policemen killed and about seventy wounded, and an undetermined number of civilian dead and wounded.

The aftermath of the bombing was a wave of hysteria directed against labor and radicals which convulsed the country. Without any evidence whatsoever, the press throughout the country identified the Chicago IWPA as the villains, and screamed for revenge. Police in Chicago opened up a reign of terror against radicals, making mass raids and arrests. The mayor of Chicago confessed later that to obtain evidence he had "utilized the extreme force of my office in a way which, if done by police in London would have upset the throne of Victoria and which could be done in no monarchical country with safety."[77] In general, as Henry David has suggested, the Chicago police department attempted to compensate "by a raging fury of activity" for "what it lacked in intelligence and skill."[78] Meanwhile, a general roundup of anarchists and suspected anarchist followers was undertaken throughout the country. In Cincinnati, where twelve thousand workers had struck on May 4, the lack of any violence proved no barrier to a decision by local authorities to swear in one thousand special police and to call out the National Guard; these actions apparently resulted from fears of Socialist-inspired violence and the fact that IWPA leader Johann Most had been seen in town, although he was only changing trains on the way to Chicago. On May 8, a planned Socialist meeting was forbidden in Cincinnati and police "advised" the proprietor of the meeting hall not to permit the gathering.[79]

By May 7 Chicago police had arrested about one hundred fifty persons, most of whom were arrested without warrant and held for hours without charges. The police claimed to have discovered bombs all over the city although in fact most of them were "either non-existent or had been planted by the police."[80] The chief of the Chicago police later testified that the police captain in charge of the investigation, Michael J. Schaack, "wanted to keep things stirring. He wanted bombs to be found here, there all around, everywhere. . . . After we got the anarchist societies broken up, Schaak wanted to sent out men to organize new societies right away."[81] One of the major anarchist papers in Chicago was shut down for three days and allowed to appear again only on the understanding it would be shut down if it carried inflammatory articles.

Ultimately thirty-one persons were indicted in connection with the bombing, although only eight were tried, on charges of conspiracy to commit murder. The only item common to the "Chicago eight" of 1886 was their membership in the IWPA; like the "Chicago eight" of 1968, some of the defendants did not even know each other.[82] The trial was a judicial farce, with persons admittedly prejudiced against the defendants placed on the jury and the judge displaying notorious bias against the defense throughout the case. No credible evidence was ever introduced linking the defendants to the bombing — the most well-known defendant, Albert Parsons, had voluntarily surrendered to the police and had brought his wife and child to the May 4 meeting — but the judge took care of this problem in his charge to the jury. The judge in effect told the jury the defendants could be held responsible for the bombing if it could be shown that they had advocated the commission of murder, even without reference to time, place or manner, and that murder had subsequently taken place as a result of this advice, even though the murderer could not be identified! (Strangely enough, this doctrine was never applied to newspaper editorial writers and businessmen who regularly advocated the shooting of unruly workers after police and private detectives committed such shootings. As Fred Shannon has pointed out, railroad tycoon Tom Scott and upcoming politician Theodore Roosevelt advocated such measures, and were not arrested, but they "were not anarchists and this apparently made all the difference in the world."[83]) This meant that police agents could effectively eliminate violence-advocating radicals by simply hiring *agents provocateur* to carry out the most extreme actions advocated by such groups.

During the trial, the prosecution introduced masses of extraneous evidence which demonstrated what was well known — that some of the defendants had advocated the use of violence to overthrow the existing system. The major theme of the state was that the case was not a murder trial at all but a contest between the good of a well-ordered society and the evil of anarchy. Thus, the state's attorney, in his address to the jury, stated:

> Law is on trial, anarchy is on trial. These men have been selected, picked out by the grand jury and indicted because they were leaders. They are no more guilty than the thousands who follow them. Gentlemen of the jury; convict these men, make examples of them; hang them and you save our institutions, our society.[84]

All of the defendants were found guilty and sentenced to hang, with the exception of one man (Neebe) who was given fifteen years.

It is difficult to adequately convey the surging wave of horror and hysteria which swept the "respectable" citizens of the nation in the wake of Haymarket. The killing of seven workers in East St. Louis on April 9 by deputies and the killing of the six Milwaukee strikers by militia aroused little concern, but the killing of seven police at the Haymarket Square as the result of a bomb thrown by an unknown hand catapulted all of the forces of "law and order" into a massive campaign to put down all radical, labor and alien doctrines. Because of the heavily immigrant composition of the IWPA, the bombing strengthened the public identification of aliens with radicalism and violence; indeed the Haymarket affair was the "single most important incident in late nineteenth century nativism."[85] The bombing also seemed to be the climax of years of labor-associated violence, confirming the lessons of the Maguires and the 1877 railroad strike that all laborers were "inherently criminal in character, inclined to riot, arson, pillage, assault and murder."[86] Indeed so perfectly did the Haymarket bombing bring together all of the fears of the conservatives — the fear of labor, of radicalism, of violence, of aliens — that had Haymarket not occurred it would have been necessary to invent it — which judging from the later actions of the Chicago police cannot be totally excluded from the realm of possibility. In the perspective of history, it is clear that the Haymarket defendants were convicted solely for their opinions by a public caught up in the grip of hysterical fears that society was in the process of disintegration.

For months and years after Haymarket, the press was filled with imprecations damning immigrants and labor unions with the stain of violence.[87] Newspapers vied with each other crying for vengeance and denunciations of anarchism; it was during this period that the stereotype was created of the anarchist as a "ragged, unwashed, long-haired, wild-eyed fiend, armed with smoking revolver and bomb — to say nothing of the dagger he sometimes carried between his teeth."[88] Anarchists and immigrants were variously referred to as "the very scum and offal of Europe," "venomous reptiles," "Europe's human and inhuman rubbish," and "that class of heartless and revolutionary agitators" who had come "to terrorize the community and to exalt the red flag of the commune above the stars and stripes."[89]

A new wave of anti-labor legislation soon made its way through state legislatures. Many states strengthened the application of common law doctrines of conspiracy to labor disputes, and many participants in strikes and boycotts were convicted of conspiracy, especially during 1886-87. Union members were convicted wholesale of charges such as "intimidation," "inciting to riot," "obstructing the streets," and "trespass." In Chicago, New York and elsewhere, police attacked strikers even more savagely than before. Thus, in New York, police attacked a peaceful crowd of about ten thousand with clubs flailing during a June, 1886, street car strike; assaulted a September, 1886, reception held in honor of arriving German socialists (including the daughter of Karl Marx); and within a two-month period arrested one hundred strikers and boycotters for "conspiracy."[90] Over twenty workers were sentenced to jail terms in New York City for boycott activity by judges and juries who were "swept along by the panic and outrage following the Haymarket Square riot."[91] Thus, New York City Judge George C. Barrett referred to boycotts as "socialistic crimes" and instructed juries trying boycott cases that picketing, distributing handbills or otherwise encouraging the public to boycott certain products or stores amounted to intimidation even if no violence or direct threats were used.[92]

Meanwhile, new efforts began to strengthen local police, militia and U.S. army forces, and wealthy citizens contributed money to build and equip more armories and military bases. The first increase in Congressional appropriations to aid the state militia since 1808 was passed in 1887. Appropriations for the militia by state in 1891 correlated .59 with numbers of workers involved in strike activity during 1881-86, an exceptionally high correlation, considering all of the influences which might affect state militia appropriations.[93]

The net impact of the public reaction to Haymarket and these examples of governmental repression was to severely damage the anarchist and radical labor movement in the U.S. and to set back the labor movement in general for about ten to fifteen years. While the anarchist movement did not completely collapse, it lost its top leadership in Chicago, toned down its talk of violence, lost its influence in the labor movement and disappeared as an effective political force. The movement did retain some vigor in Chicago for a short time, but faced continuous harassment, arrests and raids by the police who were continually discovering new plots and keeping the city alive with rumors that the anarchists were planning to destroy Chicago. There is considerable evidence that Chicago police deliberately strove to keep the anarchist menace alive; in the five years after Haymarket local businessmen contributed almost $500,000 to supplement policemen's salaries to combat the anarchist menace. When the businessmen cut off the money in 1891 police immediately began to make new raids to show that the danger still existed.[94]

The effect on the general labor movement was more significant in the long run. The combined effects of the Haymarket affair, the loss of the Gould strike, the incompetent leadership of Powderly and increasing factional disputes with the single-craft trade unions led to a drastic loss in Knights' membership beginning in 1886. While the exact extent of the influence of the post-Haymarket repression in causing this membership loss is difficult to determine — and is a matter of some dispute among historians — for thousands of Knights the lesson of Haymarket was probably that affiliation with a radical union might very well lead to their jailing or even hanging even if they had no connection with violent disorders.[95]

Certainly as far as ideas were concerned, the impact of Haymarket was to drive American labor to the right. The threat of further repression was so great that labor felt it essential to demonstrate that it was "opposed to lawlessness, that it was the sworn enemy of the communist and the anarchist, and that it was a pillar of strength in the perpetuation of the constitution and the flag."[96] The Knights of Labor, in particular, worked assiduously to keep radicals and workers separated in the public mind, by issuing the strongest denunciations of anarchism. Powderly even ordered Knights to cease collecting money for the legal defense of the condemned men, declaring, "Better that seven times seven men hang than to hang the millstone of odium around the standard of this order in affiliating in any way with this element of destruction."[97] According to Daniel Bell, Haymarket "did more to induce the rank and file of trade unions to reject all associations with revolutionary ideas than perhaps all other things together."[98]

While the Knights began a rapid collapse, the conservative and business-union-oriented American Federation of Labor, which organized only among the skilled trades, began a slow but steady pattern of growth, climbing from one hundred eighty-six thousand in 1886 to two hundred fifty thousand in 1892, and surpassing the Knights as the dominant force in American labor by 1890. The strategy of the AFL was to "gather the elect of the labor movement together, retreat to a safe and sane position, and weather the storm."[99] In contrast to the radical philosophy of the Knights, the dominant philosophy of the AFL in the 1880's as expressed by one of its future leaders, Adolph Strasser, in 1883, was to fully accept the existing system and concentrate only on working conditions. Appearing before a congressional committee, Strasser, the president of the Cigarmakers, was asked, "Do you not contemplate in the end the participation of all labor and of all men in the benefits of trades unions?" Strasser replied, "Our organization does not consist of idealists. . . . We do not control the production of the world. That is controlled by the employers. . . . I look first to cigars. . . . We have no ultimate ends."[100]

Strike activity fell drastically in the last years of the 1880's, as did labor militancy. The Illinois Bureau of Labor Statistics reported that the bomb "abruptly ended" the eight-hour movement; it explained that, "Men who would have ventured far in behalf of the principle underlying the demonstration shrank from any assertion of that principle under conditions which could hardly fail to involve misinterpretation." Similarly, the Wisconsin Bureau of Labor observed in 1887 that "everywhere the life and spirit of 1886 have departed."[101] Meeting in July, 1886, the Illinois State Federation of Labor refused to even deliberate upon a resolution which condemned anarchists, capitalists and corporations after the committee on resolutions deemed it "unwise to pass or even discuss any such resolution on account of the already excited state of the public mind." It was not until 1889 that the ISFL deemed it politic to publicly declare the men had not received a fair trial.[102]

The pattern of growing labor militancy, followed by repression and then a swing of labor to the right, would be repeated again at critical points in American labor history — especially in 1894 and in 1919.

Knights of Labor membership[103]	Workers in Strikes (1,000)[104]
1886	729,677	610
1887	548,239	439
1888	259,518	163
1889	220,607	260

With the return of prosperity after 1886, the weakening of the Knights and the anarchists and the decline in strike activity, a period of comparative calm and easing of repression could be observed in the country in the late 1880's.[105] Yet militant labor activity was still likely to lead to repression. For example, one of the few areas where the Knights continued to grow and demonstrate strength after 1886 was in the rural south. In 1887 the Knights tried to organize black laborers in South Carolina and black and white sugar field workers in Louisiana. In both states the organization met severe repression; in South Carolina, vigilante groups intimidated Knights organizers, while in Louisiana, the state militia was sent into Lafourche Parish on the first day of what turned out to be one of the most significant strikes of the decade, when nine thousand black and one thousand white sugar plantation workers peacefully walked out. Militiamen shot and killed four strikers, and turned some prisoners over to local officials, who shot them. Strikers were arrested on charges such as "resisting Parish officials" and making "incendiary threats" and were evicted from planter-provided cabins all over the sugar region. At Thibodaux, Louisiana, the state militia suddenly withdrew one evening, leaving the town under the control of armed local whites, who went on a rampage against black strikers who had taken refuge in the town after being evicted from their homes. On November 22, 1887, the white vigilantes began invading houses and shooting at every black they saw. Most accounts indicate thirty blacks were killed and hundreds were injured. Two strike leaders were taken from the Thibadaux jail and lynched. After the massacre was over, the militia returned, deputized local whites, and continued martial law. The strike was completely broken: those who persisted in holding membership in the Knights became the target of blacklists and frequent vigilante action.[106]

One of the few other major strikes in the late 1880's was the strike of engineers and firemen against the Burlington railroad in 1888. When the striking brotherhoods instituted a boycott against the handling of Burlington cars and Burlington-originated freight on connecting railroads, the company obtained federal injunctions against the boycott under the Interstate Commerce Act, which supposedly had been passed in 1887 to regulate the abuses of big business. Together with the use of strikebreakers, private detectives and the failure of other rail unions to support the strike, the injunctions helped to smash the strike and virtually eliminated the striking unions from the Burlington.[107]

The Communist-Anarchist-Labor Scare of 1892-96

The next major period of repression in American history was concentrated around 1892-96. The communist-anarchist-labor scare of this period resulted primarily from four developments: the revitalization of the American labor movement, together with new signs of radicalism among farmers and among the general populace; the attempted assassination of American capitalist Henry Frick in 1892 by a foreign-born anarchist, which coupled with a series of contemporaneous anarchist outrages in Europe, revived the fears of anarchism associated with Haymarket; the severe distress resulting from the 1893-97 depression, with the associated worker protests; and the culminating developments, a massive upsurge in labor radicalism in 1893-94, manifesting itself by increasing socialist influence in the AFL and a tremendous strike wave, which reached a climax in the Pullman strike of 1894.

Despite the collapse of the Knights of Labor, by 1890 the American labor movement was showing clear signs of revival. The number of workers involved in strikes, which had declined sharply after 1886, began to rise again beginning in 1889. The AFL made slow but steady membership gains, reaching two hundred fifty thousand by 1892. The general lull in union activities had been first broken when the AFL declared in December,

1888, that a general demand should be made for the eight-hour day on May 1, 1890. Although these plans ultimately fell through, some AFL unions did make major gains. Thus, fifty-five thousand carpenters won the eight-hour day in 1890, and as a result of an 1889 strike the Amalgamated Association of Iron, Steel and Tin Workers(AAISTW) was recognized by the Carnegie Steel Co., thereby establishing itself as the largest, richest and most powerful trade union in the United States.[108]

Number of Workers In Strikes (1,000)[109]	
1886	610
1887	439
1888	163
1889	260
1890	373
1891	330
1892	239
1893	288
1894	690

Even before 1892, all was not smooth sailing for unions, of course. In an 1890 strike in the Pennsylvania coal fields, Pinkertons, hundreds of sheriff's deputies and the Pennsylvania militia occupied the strike area for two months, beating the strike, and in the words of the governor, "had a very salutary effect on turbulent strikers."[110] During the same year, private detectives killed five people during a strike on the New York Central Railroad.[111] In 1891 Pennsylvania militia fired on fleeing strikers, killing ten and wounding fifty.[112]

By 1892, signs of increasing class conflict and repression were becoming obvious. Five major strikes in widely varying areas of the country — mining centers in the west and south, urban areas in the south and east, and a steel town in the east — were all partially or completely beaten by the use or threatened use of troops.

The first and most significant of these strikes began in late June at the Homestead, Pennsylvania Carnegie Steel Works, the site of the largest and most modern steel plant in the country, and the center of the power of the AAISTW. The strike was precipitated by the determination of Andrew Carnegie, and his plant manager, Henry Frick, to destroy the AAISTW, which at that time had 10 percent of the total membership of the AFL. Even before negotiations had broken off, Frick built a fence around the steel works, fully equipped with barbed wire, searchlights, hoses capable of shooting streams of pressurized water, and two hundred three-inch holes to allow the emplacement of rifles.[113]

After the strike (actually a lockout) began, the strikers effectively seized control of the town of Homestead and the steel works, deployed guards to protect the plant machinery, closed saloons to prevent drunkenness and barred unfriendly newsmen. Although only seven hundred fifty of the thirty-eight hundred plant employees were AAISTW members (since the organization, like most AFL unions only recruited among skilled workers) all of the workers participated in the strike. On July 6, strikers confronted three hundred Pinkertons who tried to land from barges on the Monongahela River in order to act as a strikebreaking force. During an ensuing gunfight (and later savage beating of the detectives after they had surrendered to strikers), nine strikers and seven detectives were killed, scores were shot, and nearly all of the detectives beaten. Although peace returned to Homestead after this bloody episode, about a week later the state militia was sent to Homestead. The militia guarded strikebreakers and the militia staff was housed in company cottages.

The strike was ultimately broken not only by the militia, but by extensive prosecutions brought against union leaders by the steel company and the state of Pennsylvania. On July 18, warrants were issued against seven members of the strike steering committee for murder on the basis of company complaints; on September 22 a grand jury returned 167 indictments against strikers on charges ranging from murder to aggravated riot; and on September 30 the crowning blow came when a grand jury issued warrants against thirty-five union members, including the entire steering committee, for treason under an 1860 statute which defined this offense as levying war against or aiding the "enemies" of the state of Pennsylvania. Although none of these charges ever led to convictions, they succeeded in temporarily decapitating the strike leadership and exhausting the AAISTW treasury through constant demands for bail money and legal assistance. There were no indictments by the state against the steel company or against the Pinkertons, even though the detectives had only technically avoided violating the law by bringing their arms across state lines separately instead of carrying the arms on their persons. The militia and the indictments broke the strike and the power of the AAISTW, who were perhaps guilty of "treason" after all, since given the business-government alliance, to rebel against the power of Carnegie Steel was virtually tantamount to rebellion against the state. The commander of the state militia reported "Pennsylvanians can hardly appreciate the actual communism of these people. They believe the works are theirs quite as much as Carnegie's."[114]

In July, 1892, almost simultaneously with the Homestead outbreak, a major strike broke out in the silver mine Coeur d'Alene district of Idaho. As the Homestead strike had followed on the heels of the rise of the AAISTW, the Coeur d'Alene strike came closely on the heels of a union strike victory in 1890 and amidst general signs of increasing labor strength. The 1892 strike followed attempts by mine owners to reduce wages and to import strikebreakers and armed guards, in violation of Idaho law which barred bringing armed forces into the state. When strikers sought to persuade the strikebreakers to leave the area, sometimes peacefully, and sometimes forcibly, mine owners secured an injunction which barred interference with the procurement of men. Fighting broke out between strikers and mine guards on July 11, during which one mine was dynamited, two mines were seized by strikers and six strikers and one mine guard were killed before strikebreakers surrendered and agreed to leave the area. Subsequently, Idaho's governor declared martial law, called out the national guard and obtained federal troops. State officials then removed local officials who had been elected by miners' votes, reintroduced the expelled strikebreakers and made mass arrests of union men, altogther jailing nearly six hundred persons in makeshift detention centers. Many of the men were jailed for months and were starved and mistreated. The military commander ordered mineowners to refuse to hire union men. On August 20, two mines which had been operating with union men were closed by military officials on the grounds that the mines were union meeting places. State and federal officials offered the jailed men their freedom only if they would implicate the union in the July 11 violence. None of those arrested were ever found guilty of any criminal offense. Some were found guilty of violating the injunction, but the Supreme Court reversed their convictions. Martial law was continued in the area until November, 1892.[115]

The third major conflict of 1892 was a strike at the Buffalo railway yards in August over the failure of New York to enforce its own eight-hour law for railway men. The strike was broken when six thousand state troops were sent to the scene and prevented effective picketing.[116]

The fourth major strike of 1892 occurred at about the same time as the Buffalo conflict, although its roots went back to 1891. Strife in the coal mines of Anderson County, Tennessee had been endemic since July, 1891 when the Tennessee Coal Co. had brought in convict labor to replace miners who had refused to sign iron-clad contracts which included provisions signing away rights guaranteed to miners under state law. Twice in July, 1891, miners had massed at convict stockades and, without using violence, persuaded or intimidated guards into allowing them to seize the convicts and place them on trains headed out of the area. The governor of Tennessee returned the convicts under the protection of the state militia, but declined to answer when miners asked him if he would send the militia so quickly to enforce state mine laws. When the state legislature refused to end the convict lease system, instead beefing up the state militia, miners again forced the release of the convicts in October, 1891. Miners destroyed mine property this time and allowed the convicts to flee. When convicts were again returned under militia guard, miners in Anderson and Grundy counties destroyed mine properties and forced the release of convicts once more in August, 1892. Virtual guerrilla warfare broke out at Coal Creek, where militia had established a fort to protect convicts. Subsequently, five hundred militia began mass roundups of miners and about two hundred were indicted on various charges. Only two were ever sent to jail however, since local juries would not convict. The convicts were again returned and served as an effective anti-labor force until the convict lease system was abolished in Tennessee in 1896.[117]

The final, and in many ways, the most remarkable major labor conflict of 1892 was the New Orleans general strike, which came as the climax to the "strongest labor movement in the south" during the nineteenth century. New Orleans had been the site of a major and overwhelmingly successful AFL organizing drive; by 1892 the southern city was as well organized as any city in the country, with a total of ninety-five unions coordinated by a Workingman's Amalagmated Council (WAC), which represented twenty thousand workers. In May, 1892, a strike of street car drivers had led to the arrest of union leaders under a reconstruction conspiracy law, but the strikers won the preferential closed shop they had been demanding. In November, the WAC called a general strike in support of a strike by teamsters, scalemen and packers. The supporting unions added to the original strike demands their own demands for recognition and the closed shop. The strike virtually paralyzed New Orleans. Although no disorders occurred, the press and business interest screamed about the dangers of anarchy. After three days, the governor of Louisiana in effect declared martial law and warned that the militia would be sent in if the strike continued. In the face of the governor's actions, the strike was called off; while some gains were made in terms of working conditions, no unions won recognition or the closed shop.[118]

Subsequently, in March, 1893, the federal government obtained an injunction under the 1890 Sherman Anti-trust Act against the WAC on the grounds that trade in New Orleans was being restrained by an illegal conspiracy. Forty-four union leaders were indicted, but the cases against them were later dropped.[119] The failure of the New Orleans strike was a major blow; its success would have marked "the greatest victory of the AFL in its early career, made New Orleans a city of the closed shop and raised up urban allies for the rural Louisiana populists."[120]

The fears aroused by the resurgence of the labor movement in the early 1890's were exacerbated by the development of a powerful and virulently anti-big business movement among farmers. After the decline of the Granger movement, farm groups calling themselves "alliances" had sprung up in the east, south and west. By 1890, they had consolidated into the Southern Alliance and the Northwestern Alliance and had entered the political arena, usually as third parties in the midwest and through the Democratic Party in the south. The platform of the alliances included demands for government ownership and regulation of railroads, cheap money, tax reforms, tariff reductions, antimonopoly laws and other proposals guaranteed to arouse severe opposition from the large corporations. During the 1890 elections, the alliances gained control of about ten state legislatures, and elected about fifty congressmen, along with several senators and governors.[121]

In 1892 the Southern and Northwestern Alliances amalgamated to form a new political party, the People's Party (Populists). The party's platform called for a "permanent and perpetual" union of farmers and workers, inflation of the currency, a graduated income tax, abolition of all land ownership by corporations "in excess of their actual needs" and government ownership and operation of the railroads, the telegraphs and telephones. The populists were *not* socialists, for they firmly believed in individual ownership of land, but they did represent a radical rejection of the trend towards increasing consolidation of power in the hands of fewer and fewer big capitalists. Their platform proclaimed:

> We meet in the midst of a nation brought to the verge of moral, political and material ruin. Corruption dominates the ballot-box, the legislatures, the Congress and touches even the ermine of the bench. . . . The newspapers are largely subsidized or muzzled; public opinion silenced; business prostrated; our homes covered with mortgages; labor impoverished; and the land concentrating in the hands of the capitalists. The urban workmen are denied the right of organization for self-protection; imported pauperized labor beats down their wages; a hireling standing army, unrecognized by our laws, is established to shoot them down, and they are rapidly degenerating into European conditions. The fruits of the toil of millions are boldly stolen to build up colossal fortunes for the few. . . . From the same prolific womb of governmental injustice we breed the two great classes — tramps and millionaires.[122]

In the 1892 election, the Populist presidential candidate gained over a million votes, carrying the electoral vote of five states. The Populists elected five senators, ten congressmen and three governors, along with over fifteen hundred local and state officials. This election was notable in that for the first time in post-reconstruction history it was marked by widespread governmental repressive efforts directed against a political party on the basis of its ideology. During the 1870's and 1880's radical political parties like the SLP, the Greenback and the Greenback Labor parties, and various labor parties had never faced governmental repression, perhaps because they had never developed signs of major strength and stability over any significant period of time. By 1892, however, the populists had developed a strength that far exceeded any other such party since the war. They were especially viewed as a threat by the dominant conservative forces in the south, where for the first time since reconstruction "two parties of anything approaching equal strength had contested an election."[123] Throughout the south Populists were attacked by mobs, threatened and in some cases killed during the campaign; when election day came, Democrats who controlled the election machinery

> set about the task of counting the challengers out of every election, protected by majorities in the state legislatures and a friendly judiciary. Republicans to a lesser degree used the same techniques in the West. Although voting frauds permeated politics in the late nineteenth century . . . the grim methodical work of the nineties belonged in another category. Exemplars of community virtue joined hands with hacks to prostitute the democratic process in the name of a higher civilization, claiming as so many did during those years that however sordid the means the end would glorify them. Above all else, the crisis mentality demanded results.[124]

Signs of increasing discontent were not limited to organized movements of workers and farmers. Thirty-five utopian novels were published between 1888 and 1895, of which the most widely read was Edward Bellamy's *Looking Backward,* published in 1888. This book sold almost one million copies by 1892, more than any American novel since *Uncle Tom's Cabin.* Bellamy's utopian vision of a completely state-owned productive system inspired a nationwide organization of Nationalist Clubs, which attracted many middle class professionals, who while shunning the labor movement or class struggle doctrines, were becoming "visibly alarmed at the grasping tycoons of finance and industry."[125] At its height in 1891, 165 Nationalist clubs were organized in over twenty-five states. The late 1880's and early 1890's also saw the development of a Christian Socialist movement among a small but active segment of the Protestant clergy, a group hitherto known for its rigid conservatism.[126]

The fears aroused by the general upsurge in labor and farmer militancy and the increasing acceptance of radical doctrines were greatly exacerbated by the 1893 depression, and by the development of a new anarchist scare. The 1893-97 depression was of great severity, with estimated unemployment ranging up to three million, or as much as 20 percent of the work force at times. Those fortunate enough to still have work often had their wages slashed severely. Armies of tramps began appearing across the American countryside, desperately searching for work. Many localities passed special anti-tramp laws, which according to a professor who studied them, nearly all had a "panicky look which suggested a pressing evil, real or imaginary."[127] Fears of anarchy and radical ideas began to convulse business and government circles. Thus, the governor of New York, in rejecting demands for public works in 1893, declared that

> it is not the province of the government to support the people. . . . The security of democratic government is purity and simplicity. Break down those safeguards and you invite corruption, socialism and anarchy.[128]

Meanwhile, a new anarchist scare had been touched off by the attempt of a Russian-born anarchist, Alexander Berkman, to assassinate Henry Frick during the 1892 Homestead strike. In the aftermath of Berkman's action, scores of alleged anarchists were arrested in major cities across the nation. Berkman was ultimately sentenced to twenty-two years for his deed after a farcical trial. He was not told the date of his trial until the morning it began, and arrived in court to find the jury already chosen. The jury convicted him without bothering to leave the courtroom to deliberate. Two other anarchists were convicted in connection with the shooting, although one of the accused detested Berkman, and suspected him of being a spy.[129]

The scare touched off by the Berkman shooting was heightened by the 1893 depression and by a series of anarchist outrages in Europe. The last decade of the nineteenth century saw repeated anarchist bombings and murders in Europe. From 1892 to 1894 alone, there were eleven major explosions in Paris, culminating in the execution of the notorious Ravachol in 1892 and the sensational trial of thirty Frenchmen for criminal conspiracy in 1894. The Berkman affair and the European outrages were quickly reflected in heightened fear of and harassment of American anarchists. Thus, in 1893 Chicago authorities banned a national convention of anarchists, and Berkman's close friend Emma Goldman was sentenced to a year in jail as the result of a speech delivered to a meeting of the unemployed in New York.[130] When Gov. Altgeld of Illinois pardoned the three surviving Haymarket defendants in June, 1893, he was hotly denounced in the press and by conservatives as a socialist, an alien and an anarchist.[131]

The effect of the 1893 depression on workers, meanwhile, was to greatly increase discontent and militancy. Even within the staid confines of the AFL, which restricted itself to the "upper class" of American labor, socialist doctrines made strong headway. In 1892, the AFL convention had endorsed government ownership of the telegraph and telephone systems; in 1893 the convention accepted and recommended for consideration by individual unions the entire socialist political platform, including "the collective ownership by the people of all means of production and distribution." During 1894, this program was endorsed by virtually all of the various craft unions, state labor federations and city central labor unions affiliated with the AFL. Only one union — the baker's — rejected it in its entirety, while hundreds of unions acted on the program and entered the political arena, often in close cooperation with populists and socialists.[132]

In 1894, a huge strike wave convulsed the country, exceeding even the strike wave of 1886. This strike wave affected all parts of the country, including the south, where state troops were called out in Alabama, Louisiana and Virginia.[133] One of the most important strikes, that of the United Mine Workers, brought out one hundred twenty-five thousand miners although union membership numbered only twenty thousand. The strike was characterized by widespread violence on both sides, with miners resorting to virtual guerrilla warfare, attacking coal mines, and blocking and sabotaging railroad tracks. Deputies in Pennsylvania shot and killed four strikers, while federal troops called out in connection with the Pullman strike shot and killed two miners at Spring Valley, Illinois, after the miners had stoned a troop train.[134] Guerrilla warfare also broke out in the metal mines at Cripple Creek, Colorado, where officials of El Paso County accepted the offer of mine owners to supply arms and money in return for the commissioning of a large force of deputies to protect the re-opening of mines with strikebreakers. Miners then organized their own military force, and skirmishes broke out between the two armies. In one of the few cases where the state militia intervened on the side of labor, Populist Gov. David Waite sent troops into the areas to disperse both groups and brought about a settlement which granted the union demands.[135]

By late 1893 and early 1894, growing signs of panic among conservatives — and increasing defections among moderates who had temporarily stressed reform over reaction — were becoming increasingly apparent, as the fear of revolution hung like a pall over the country. Signs of mounting tension were everywhere apparent. Middle class reformers suddenly began to revert to a position stressing repression.[136]

Farmers and wage earners, dissenting ministers and angry editors, immigrants and ideologists, peaceful petitioners and armed strikers, all blurred into visions of a society unhinged. The wells of panic, once tapped, flowed continuously. . . . Later people would realize that the nineties had remained surprisingly free from violence At the time, men who were so certain of an eruption saw volcanoes under each puff of smoke.[137]

The fear of disintegration led to a surge of superpatriotism and nativism among the fearful. Patriotic organizations like the Grand Army of the Republic, the Daughters of the American Revolution and the Sons of the American Revolution, stepped up their campaign which had begun after Haymarket to foster patriotism through worship in the schools of the Constitution, the flag and American heroes. Many states responded by passing state laws requiring the teaching of patriotism.[138] The anti-Catholic American Protective Association, which had been founded in 1887, and did not exceed seventy thousand members in 1893, suddenly jumped to a membership of half a million in 1894. Rumors in late 1893 that a Catholic uprising was imminent caused widespread panic.[139] Certainly it was no coincidence that it was in 1894 that the first major *cause celebre* involving academic freedom at a publicly supported university in the post-civil war period occurred and that it involved one of the leading academic liberals; this was the "trial" of Richard T. Ely, professor of economics at the University of Wisconsin, for believing in "strikes and boycotts, justifying and encouraging the one while practicing the other." While Ely was exonerated and retained, and the University regents issued a statement which was generally hailed as a "Magna Carta" for academic freedom, it could hardly escape the attention of other teachers that the alleged holding of "radical" opinions could lead to problems and that Ely himself denied the charges against him and said that had they been true they would "unquestionably unfit me to occupy a responsible position as an instructor of youth in a great University."[140]

The rapidly developing panic among the propertied elements reached its culmination in 1894 as a result of the "unemployed army" movement and the Pullman strike. The "unemployed army" movement developed spontaneously out of the numerous meetings of the unemployed held during the winter of 1894; the idea arose in many areas for the unemployed to band together and march to Washington to demand relief or employment. A total of seventeen "armies" set out for Washington during 1894, comprising perhaps ten thousand men altogether. These armies generally received highly sympathetic welcomes from labor and populist forces along their march route, and for the most part conducted themselves with strict discipline. However, conservative forces were highly alarmed at their popular reception, and especially at the common tactic used by "armies" in the west of boarding or "stealing" trains without paying for passage. Altogether the "armies" stole or "borrowed" about forty trains, mostly during May and early June. The federal government responded to the train stealing with a hard line, obtaining federal court injunctions barring interference with trains, and using federal marshals or troops to enforce these orders in fourteen states. Many "army" members were arrested and jailed for contempt of court as a result of the injunctions.[141]

In areas where Populist officials held office, the armies could count on a friendly reception from local authorities, but in other areas, their welcome was not so kind. Thus, members of the "armies" were arrested for vagrancy or other vague charges in Allegheny, Pennsylvania; Wilmington, Delaware; Washington, D.C.; El Paso, Texas; Oakland, California; Louisville, Kentucky; Wheeling, West Virginia; La Porte, Indiana; and other cities. In some areas the armies were barred from entrance or prohibited from parading.

The most well-known "army" was organized by Jacob S. Coxey, a wealthy businessman from Massillon, Ohio. After leading about five hundred marchers from Massillon, Coxey arrived in Washington on April 29, 1894. When the marchers tried to reach the capital grounds on May 1, they were greeted with masses of police and troops who barred their entrance to the grounds. Coxey and two supporters walked through police lines and tried to speak from the Capitol steps, whereupon they were arrested for walking on the grass and carrying banners on the Capitol grounds. When a shout of anger went up from the crowd, police began to wantonly attack the crowd with clubs and horses, beating or trampling fifty or more people. Coxey and the two other arrested persons were given twenty days in jail and a $5 fine. The arrests broke the back of the movement. The remnants of Coxey's followers were forced out of Washington, and their camp in Maryland was broken up by police in early August.

The excitement over Coxey's army had hardly died down when the Pullman strike broke out. Because the Pullman strike involved the attempt of the largest union in the country to create an industrial union appealing to workers of all skill levels in the most important industry in the American economy — the railroads — it was beyond any doubt the most important strike in American history until that time. It would remain the most important strike until a similar effort was launched in the steel industry in 1919. It was no coincidence that both the Pullman strike and the 1919 steel strike were substantially beaten by governmental repression.[142]

The Pullman strike grew out of increasing discontent among the workers of the company town of Pullman, Illinois, headquarters of the Pullman Palace Car Company. The major item of discontent was the Pullman Company's policy of reducing wages during the depression while maintaining rents on company housing (and maintaining dividends). After a strike broke out over the wage issue at the Pullman works in May, 1894, the American Railway Union (ARU) called a sympathetic boycott for June 26, instructing its members on all lines to refuse to handle Pullman sleeping cars.

The ARU had been founded only a year earlier, in June, 1893, but had quickly become the largest and most powerful union in American labor history. Following a major victory against the Great Northern Railroad in the early spring of 1894, ARU membership had soared to one hundred fifty thousand, at a time was the entire AFL membership was less than three hundred thousand and when the conservative railroad brotherhoods, which were open only to highly skilled workers, had a membership of under one hundred thousand. What particularly distinguished the ARU from both the AFL and the brotherhoods was its appeal to all railroad workers to join together, regardless of skill classifications, in one industrially organized union. It was this appeal and the response it provoked which particularly frightened the railroad managers and made them determined to smash the ARU. The ARU program stressed only wages and working conditions, but ARU president Eugene Debs, later to become the leading figure in the Socialist Party, publicly advocated government ownership of the railroads and the ARU indirectly endorsed the Populists.

The ARU sympathy strike was extraordinarily effective, tying up rail lines in twenty-seven states and territories, and paralyzing all transcontinental rail lines except for one. By June 29, one hundred twenty-five thousand men were supporting the boycott. The ARU leadership urged its membership to use peaceful methods only, and this advice was uniformly heeded. However, in some cities overzealous supporters of the strike resorted to forcible interference with trains and destruction of railroad equipment. Until the federal government intervened on a massive scale to smash the strike, total damage was relatively minor — less than $6,000 by July 5 — and the great majority of trains that had ceased operation were not running simply because they could get no operating crews.

From the very beginning of the strike however, the General Managers Association (GMA) of the railroads was determined to involve the federal government in breaking the strike. It found avid support for this policy from Attorney General Richard Olney, a former corporation attorney with close ties to the railroads (he was on the board of directors of one of the lines involved in the strike). Before any serious violence had occurred, Olney appointed as his special representative in Chicago, the heart of the strike, Edwin Walker, a leading corporation lawyer then serving as attorney for one of the affected roads and for the GMA. Olney wired Walker on the day of appointment, June 30:

> It has seemed to me that if the rights of the United States were vigorously asserted in Chicago, the origin and centre of the demonstration, the result would be to make it a failure everywhere else. . . . I feel that the true way of dealing with the matter is by a force which is overwhelming and prevents any attempt at resistance.[143]

Although the alleged justification for federal intervention in the strike was to protect property and prevent interference with the mails, in fact, every step taken by Olney was calculated to break the ARU.

The strategy adopted by Olney was to blanket the country with injunctions which while technically not outlawing the strike, in fact barred the ARU from taking any actions to further the strike, including peaceful persuasion of workers to cease work. Such injunctions were obtained in federal courts throughout the country, beginning on July 2; at the slightest sign of their being flaunted, federal troops were dispatched or federal marshals sworn in to enforce the injunctions. As the leading historian of the Pullman strike has written, the injunctions "were so sweeping and all-inclusive that the union leaders could not move without running afoul of it. The purpose of the writ was designed not so much to protect property as to crush the strike."[144] Troops and marshals were promiscuously dispatched throughout the country, frequently over the protests of state governors and other officials. In the most flagrant case, five thousand federal marshals, most of whom were chosen by and responsible to the railroads, were sworn in, and two thousand federal troops were sent to Chicago on July 2 and 3, although the only violence in the area had been some relatively minor disturbances in the Chicago suburb of Blue Island and no request for aid had been made by state or local officials. Many of the marshals were of notoriously poor character — the Chicago police chief described them as "thugs, thieves and ex-convicts"[145] — who made unnecessary arrests and in some cases destroyed railroad property. After the arrival of the marshals and troops, serious disorders and protests broke out in Chicago, with $340,000 worth of railroad equipment detroyed in riots on July 6.

Federal troops were also sent to Los Angeles; Sacramento; Ogden, Utah; Raton, New Mexico, and many other areas, especially in the west, often on the thinnest of excuses. Altogether sixteen thousand federal troops were made available to fight the strike. In a number of cases the actions of the troops were so reckless that local officials protested bitterly. Thus, the Sacramento Board of City Trustees adopted a resolution condemning the "tyranny and brutality which has characterized the conduct of the U.S. soldiers who have wounded and assaulted unoffending persons upon the streets," and condemned troops for "free and unprovoked use of their bayonets and guns and for the reckless wounding of innocent citizens."[146] After federal troops sent to Hammond, Indiana, without request from the governor, indiscriminately opened fire on citizens near the railroad tracks, the Mayor protested, "I would like to know by what authority U.S. troops come in here and shoot our citizens without the slightest warning."[147] Similarly, Populist Gov. David Waite, of Colorado, protested after troops and marshals were sent to his state without consulting him, that the federal government was "waging an active war in Colorado without any declaration thereof by the United States, or notice or knowledge thereof by the state authorities, and utterly in violation of law."[148] Gov. William Stone of Missouri protested that the deputy marshals had done more to provoke riots than anything else.[149]

State militia were called up in twenty states, in at least some cases with little justification. Thus, after the Governor of Michigan called up the militia, the United Press reported from Battle Creek, that, "the railroad company has no men here that it can use to pull the trains if there were one million soldiers here, and it is esteemed unwarranted. Then again, the men have done nothing to prevent the company from moving its trains."[150]

Altogether, thirty-four people were killed during the strike, most of whom appear to have been victims of state militia or federal troops and marshals.

When the use of federal and state troops, marshals and injunctions failed to break the strike, the federal government began to arrest ARU leaders. On July 10, Debs and three other ARU officials were indicted in Chicago for conspiracy to obstruct mails, interrupt interstate commerce and intimidate citizens in the free exercise of their rights under the constitution. On July 17, the same four were re-arrested for contempt of court, and on July 19, sixty-nine persons, including the same ARU officials, were indicted for violating a series of federal statutes. Meanwhile, throughout the country, similar indictments were being handed down by federal grand juries, and local officials were making arrests of strikers. Altogether, 190 strikers were indicted under federal statutes and 515 others arrested for local offenses. While most of these arrests could not stand up in court, they served their purpose of spreading fear and demoralization among strikers, and, in the case of the Chicago indictments, completely disrupting ARU communications. By late July, the strike was in tatters, beaten by the weight of injunctions, troops and arrests. The ARU rapidly collapsed shortly thereafter.

The conspiracy indictments against Debs and the other ARU leaders were eventually dropped, but Debs was convicted for contempt of court for violating the strike injunction, which was upheld under the Sherman and Interstate Commerce Acts. The Supreme Court upheld his conviction in 1895, thus for the first time putting the stamp of the nation's highest legal authority upon the doctrine that labor unions were illegal and enjoinable conspiracies in at least certain circumstances — which seemed to be when they posed a clear and present threat to the status quo.

Throughout the Pullman strike, the newspapers were filled with hysterical charges that Debs was seeking to make himself a "dictator" and that the Pullman dispute was not a strike at all, but instead an attempted revolution. The federal government's actions in suppressing the strike were lauded by conservatives everywhere; thus in July both houses of Congress passed resolutions fully backing President Cleveland's actions, all segments of the legal profession lauded the use of troops to smash the strike, and businessmen flooded Cleveland with congratulatory telegrams.

It is difficult to overestimate the importance of the repression of the Pullman strike for the history of the American labor movement. While the strike might have failed without federal intervention, given the large labor pool existing due to the depression, there is little doubt that in the historic event the federal role was crucial. As Ray Ginger has written, "The ARU was a corpse, killed by one strike and the federal government."[151] Had the strike succeeded and the power of an industrial union been demonstrated in the most important American industry, there is little doubt that similar movements would have sprung up in the other mass industries whose unskilled workers the AFL had largely ignored — for example, in textiles, steel and food processing. Had such organization occurred and succeeded,

Development of Repressive Techniques 57

American labor might well have achieved by about 1900 the power that it gained only about forty years later.

The potential threat that a militant industrial union posed was recognized both by the railroads and the federal government. While the railroads had a deep hostility towards the ARU, they felt no such antipathy towards the conservative railroad brotherhoods who "did not constitute a serious threat"[152] because they attempted to organize only the most highly skilled workers and therefore could be (and were) easily bought off without making concessions to the mass of workers. Similarly, after the ARU had been crushed, Olney intervened in a federal case to uphold the right of the conservative Brotherhood of Railway Trainmen to organize. Olney told the court that the Trainmen's Union served a very laudable purpose and characterized its policy on strikes as "eminently conservative."[153]

Aside from the destruction of the ARU, the federal role in the Pullman strike also had an important aftermath in frightening the AFL leadership away from the radical stance which the AFL had been drifting towards during the early 1890's. At its 1893 convention, it will be recalled, the AFL voted to submit for consideration by constituent unions the socialist political platform. During the 1893 convention, this platform had received "more than passive support" from AFL President Samuel Gompers, and afterwards had received overwhelming endorsement from affiliated unions.[154] However, when the next AFL convention met in December, 1894, Gompers pulled out all the parliamentary tricks he could muster and succeeded in preventing the convention from endorsing the platform, especially concentrating on the key plank calling for socialization of all means of production and distribution.[155]

In between these two conventions had come the Pullman strike. It is difficult to read a man's mind, but the most obvious explanation for Gomper's reversal in 1894 was that he feared militant labor postures might well lead to severe repression. Gompers had been thoroughly alarmed by the outcomes of the strikes at Pullman, Homestead, Buffalo and Couer d'Alene; thus he concluded that the only course open to the AFL was to adopt "a conciliatory policy towards the employers."[156] There is evidence to support this interpretation in Gomper's history. He had been present at the Tompkins Square riot of 1874, and had barely escaped being clubbed by a policeman. The repression of the meeting appears to have left a deep impression on him, for he wrote in his autobiography:

> I saw how professions of radicalism and sensationalism concentrated all the forces of organized society against a labor movement and nullified in advance normal, necessary activity. . . . I saw the danger of entangling alliances with intellectuals who did not understand that to experiment with the labor movement was to experiment with human life.[157]

In 1879 Gompers was jailed for talking to a picket. He wrote later about his experience, "That was one of the most uncomfortable days I ever spent, sitting there in the dirt and filth and vermin surrounded by men of unclean bodies and mind who used vile language. Fortunately for the effect on me, there was only one day of it."[158] The very thought of worker militancy and the potentially repressive reaction of political authorities appears to have haunted Gompers. Thus, in 1893, he was deeply frightened when he delivered a speech attacking capitalism that brought a meeting called to discuss unemployment to its feet, cheering and shouting. He wrote later, "The responsibility of my utterance haunted me not only that night but for many a day after."[159] Gompers was dominated by the desire to obtain "respectability" for himself and the labor movement. Thus, it was not surprising that when the ARU appealed to the AFL to call a general strike in support of the Pullman strike, the reply of the AFL executive committee, which was dominated by Gompers, turned down the request and indicated a fear of being viewed as not "respectable" had the request been acceded to:

> The public press, ever alive to the interests of corporate wealth, have, with few exceptions, so maliciously misrepresented matters that in the public mind the working classes are now arrayed in open hostility to Federal authority. This is a position we do not wish to be placed in.... We declare it to be the sense of this conference that a general strike at this time is inexpedient, unwise and contrary to the best interests of the working people.[160]

With a brief exception in 1919, at which time the AFL again ran into severe governmental repression and again reversed course, after the Pullman strike the organization "putting behind its radical days, began a long retreat in which it sacrificed both unskilled workers and consumers to win meagre gains for its own members."[161] The rejection of the socialist political platform meant also the rejection of the formation of an independent political party, as occurred in Great Britain. Instead, the AFL adopted the policy of voting for major party candidates who supposedly best represented labor's interests; but all too often this meant workers were left "with little choice other than to vote for labor-baiter Tweedledum or for anti-labor Tweedledee."[162]

The fear of radicalism was also influential in keeping the AFL away from serious attempts to organize immigrant groups and the mass industries, which were generally regarded as being more radical than native American skilled workers. Thus, Melvyn Dubofsky writes that immigrants "had few supporters within the ranks of the AFL" because AFL leaders "were unwilling to damage their hard-earned reputation by associating with alien groups bearing the taint of European radicalism."[163] In a book published in 1914, Gompers spelled out his views as to the general philosophy of the AFL:

> It is guided by the history of the past, drawing its lessons from history. It knows the conditions by which working people are surrounded. It works along the lines of *least resistance* and endeavors to accomplish the best results....[164]

The repressive spirit which was so clearly manifested in the government's response to the Pullman strike began to disintegrate after 1894, and especially after 1896.[165] At least five reasons may be cited for the relaxation of fears after 1894. First, the AFL withdrew from its flirtation with socialism and direct political action, and the number of strikes and workers participating in strikes dropped sharply after 1894.

	Number of strikes[166]	Workers involved in strikes (1,000)[167]
1894	1404	690
1895	1255	407
1896	1066	249
1897	1110	416
1898	1098	263
1899	1838	432
1900	1839	568

A second factor calming conservative fears after 1894 was the reassuring nature of Supreme Court decisions, symbolized by three extraordinary decisions in 1895 that made it unmistakably clear that the Court would stand as a bulwark of capitalism against labor, even if the other branches of government got "out of hand."[168] In In Re *Debs* the court upheld the Pullman strike injunctions; in *U.S. v. E. C. Knight Co.*, the court threw out a government suit brought under the Sherman Anti-Trust Act against the American Sugar Refining Company, which controlled over 90 percent of the sugar refining capacity in the country, on the specious grounds that the Sugar trust had a monopoly of manufacturing, and the Sherman Act was only directed against monopolies of commerce; and in *Pollock v. Farmers Loan and Trust Co.* the court declared unconstitutional the minimally progressive income tax of 1894, which had been widely denounced as "communistic." In an opinion related to the income tax case, Justice Field warned that the tax was only the beginning of an "assault upon capital" that "will become a war of the poor against the rich."[169] In 1896 William Jennings Bryan, the Democratic candidate who received Populist support, was defeated by Republican William McKinley, the candidate of conservatives and big business.[170] Bryan campaigned on a platform calling for free silver and an income tax, and which condemned the government's action in the Pullman strike and "government by injunction." Republicans and conservatives generally regarded Bryan as representing "the forces of anarchy and mob rule."[171] To defeat Bryan, Republicans raised a war chest estimated at from $3 to $10 million from leading corporations and banks, while the Democrats financed their campaign on a paltry $300,000. The campaign was among the bitterest in American history, with Bryan accused of socialism and communism; business firms "predicted that ruin would follow Bryan's election and hinted that ruin might be artificially induced if it failed spontaneously to materialize."[172] According to Russell Nye:

> If Bryan won, said the manufacturers, wages would fall, shops close, and industry stop dead in its tracks. Bankers threatened to call in loans if Bryan were elected, and every farm mortgage would be called in as soon as it

fell due. . . . John Hay reported that many of his friends were preparing to buy homes in Paris if Bryan won, fearing actual personal harm at the hands of mobs. "Probably no man in civic life," said the *Nation* later, "succeeded in inspiring so much terror, without taking life, as Bryan."[173]

The defeat of Bryan thus came as an immense relief to conservatives, and greatly eased their fears. At the same time, the defeat led to the collapse of the Populists and the demoralization of reformers and radicals, a number of whom "looked sideward with a sudden interest in a few, short-lived experiments in cooperative community living, an almost pathetic reversion from macrocosm to microcosm."[174]

A fourth factor leading to an easing of class tensions and repressive fervor was the return of prosperity in 1897; thus as early as December, 1897 the *Commercial and Financial Chronicle* exulted that "no one can study the industrial conditions of today in America without a feeling of elation."[175]

Finally, the Spanish-American war helped to divert attention away from domestic problems and led to a general joining together to fight against a foreign foe. "Concern over internal dissension was engulfed in a joyous consciousness of national unity," according to John Higham.[176] In fact, a number of leading conservatives had argued for a foreign war before 1898 precisely because they hoped it would lead to diverting attention from domestic ills, while reformers argued against entry into the war because they feared the same result.[177] From the standpoint of political repression, clearly the most remarkable aspect of the war and, especially, its aftermath — the brutal American suppression of the Filipino insurrection — was that protests against American war policies met virtually no suppression, marking the last time in American history that a major foreign conflict was not accompanied by severe domestic repression. Thus, anarchist Emma Goldman and socialist leader Eugene Debs delivered speeches against American foreign policy during the Spanish-American War and the suppression of the Filipino revolt without reprisal in 1898; twenty years later, for saying virtually the same things in opposition to World War I, Debs was sent to jail and Goldman was arrested and then deported.[178] The only noteworthy incident of repression during the entire period was the seizure and withholding from the mail of anti-war leaflets sent to prominent American officials serving in the Phillipines.[179]

3

The Progressive Era

From the standpoint of governmental repression, the Progressive Era is one of the most complex periods in American history. On one hand, there can be little doubt that the general position of labor, especially in terms of its treatment by the executive and legislative branches of the federal government improved considerably during this period, at least in terms of symbolic recognition and symbolic legislation. However, this relatively favorable treatment was not extended by many of the states, especially when major strikes developed, and it was most assuredly not extended by any branch of government at any level when the unions involved were militantly anti-capitalist unions rather than business unions such as the AFL which accepted the basic tenets of American capitalism.

In very broad outlines, what occurred during the 1900-17 period was an experiment which was later adopted as the American solution to the "labor problem": unions willing to accept American capitalism, and thus a subordinate place in the economy, were granted limited accommodation and acceptability, while radical anti-capitalist unions were ruthlessly repressed. Symbolic of the general shift in power from business corporations per se to the federal government that marked the Progressive Era was the fact that the era began with a "deal" between the AFL and powerful business corporations represented in the National Civic Federation, and ended with a similar "deal" between the AFL and the federal government during World War I. In both of these agreements, the two partners in effect pledged to scratch each other's back, while joining to smash their common enemy — the radical unions. The World War I agreement broke down after the war, however, when the government and powerful business firms concluded the AFL was not living up to its agreement — i.e. it had not stamped out labor radicalism and had failed to stem the rising tide of radicalism in society. It was only after the last vestiges of anti-capitalist labor radicalism were stamped out during the post-war Red Scare and the 1920's that the deal was resumed, culminating in the legalization of the labor movement in the 1935 Wagner Act.

While on the whole the general trend within the Progressive Era was towards less wholesale repression of the labor movement, the same was not true with regard to repression of political radicals. During the Progressive Era, as federal and state governments expanded their powers in a variety of fields, laws were passed for the first time which punished the abstract advocacy of "harmful doctrines" and punished mere membership in allegedly pernicious organizations. While anarchists and members of the radical labor movement were the primary targets of such laws during the 1900-17 period, these laws set the pattern for the general repression of political dissent which occurred during and after World War I.

Most American historians have tended to paint the Progressive Era generally as a period of buoyant optimism in which Americans joined together to cleanse the society of its ills. The defeat of Bryan in 1896, the return of prosperity in 1897, and the "splendid little war" against Spain are pointed to as explanations for the claimed marked change from the climate of class division and hatred which had wracked American society in the latter part of the nineteenth century. This picture of unity and optimism is particularly common in descriptions of American society at the turn of the century. Thus, Harold Faulkner writes:

> Most Americans faced the new century with exuberant optimism. The victory over Spain and the acquisition of Puerto Rico, Hawaii, and the Phillippines; the return of prosperity; the unprecedented material growth of the country in the past thirty-five years — all heralded America's coming of age. . . . Success, progress and prosperity were the dominant notes; the future was bright, and to many the new century held dreams of greatness and glory beyond any yet achieved.[1]

There is a good deal of truth in this picture of a marked change in the American mood; indeed it is impossible to explain the reforms of the Progressive Era without taking into account such a change. But this picture of black changing into white has been clearly overdrawn, and it is similarly impossible to understand the repeated episodes of panic and terror which swept the middle and upper classes during the period unless it is realized that underneath the surface optimism and buoyancy the same old fears were churning away. As Samuel Hays has pointed out, "memory of the social upheavals of the eighties and nineties hung like a pall over the minds of the articulate public" during the Progressive Era.[2] Each time a new anarchist "outrage" occurred or an economic slump set off new signs of worker unrest, or when radicals showed signs of increasing strength, the mood of the country changed from reform to repression. The latter half of the progressive period, from approximately 1907 on, was marked by a steadily darkening mood among businessmen and members of the middle class as radical agitation seemed to increase yearly. During the war the AFL was temporarily bought off as a progressive administration went after the socialists and the radical unionists, but after the war even the conservative unions bore the brunt of repression.

The failure of the progressives to blunt radical dissent and their repressive reaction to this failure was inherent in their approach to American social problems.[3] The progressives, simply put, did not really have a major quarrel with the basic structure of American society. Their major concern was to eliminate the worst abuses of the capitalist system, including those types of brutal exploitation of workers that in the past had brought about periodic rebellions. Part of their motivation was humanitarian, but to a great extent the progressives were motivated by fear of eruptions from the lower class. In effect, they sought a "peaceful, legal substitute for Gatling guns and bayonets."[4] Many of the progressives particularly feared the rise to power of the socialists; thus many progressive reforms, which sometimes aped socialist proposals, were directed at blunting the socialist appeal. Many of the progressives viewed the reactionary capitalists as enemies, not so much because of moral objections, but because the capitalists' intransigence threatened to provoke the lower classes into greater extremism. The fear of socialism and radicalism was particularly evident in the case of Theodore Roosevelt. In 1905, Roosevelt wrote that the growth of socialism was "far more ominous than any populist or similar movement in the past." A year later he wrote to William Howard Taft, "The dull, purblind folly of the very rich men; their greed and arrogance and the corruption in business and politics, have tended to produce a very unhealthy condition of excitement and irritation in the popular mind, which shows itself in the great increase in socialistic propaganda."[5]

The progressives' attitude toward labor was only slightly more friendly than their attitude towards socialism. The balance of power at the beginning of the Progressive Era was so overwhelmingly weighted on the side of business that on the surface progressives seemed to be pro-labor. In fact, the progressives looked upon labor as a "poor relation"[6] which could be tolerated only as long as its power was small and its demands moderate. Labor was treated with kindness only when it was willing to accept a subordinate role, not only in American society as a whole, but in the progressive movement. Independent political action by labor was regarded with horror by most progressives; labor was to accept a junior and filial role in the progressive coalition. Labor radicals were generally regarded by the progressives as pariahs. The progressive dream was the elimination of the concept of class struggle from American society, just as their nightmare was a renewal of labor upheavals of the past. For radicals such as the Industrial Workers of the World "to expose the class struggle rather than let it be obscured" was, as William Preston notes, a "supreme offense."[7]

Neither the good will nor the fear of the progressives succeeded in stopping the radical tide in America; the repression of 1917-20 finally accomplished this task. The progressive's failure to damp radicalism was rooted in their basic desire to uphold the existing system. The most obvious failure of the progressives was a complete unwillingness or inability to affect the gross maldistribution of income. National wealth increased from $88 million in 1900 to $350 million in 1917, yet the best evidence is that increasing industrial production resulted in no substantial addition to the real income of workers — in fact, according to some sources, real income actually declined during this period.[8] Maldistribution clearly increased; in 1910 the highest 10 percent of income earners received 34 percent of all income, while the lowest 60 percent received 35. In 1921, the comparable figures were 38 percent and 30 percent.[9] In the middle of the first decade of the twentieth century, after ten years of prosperity, the poorer half of the urban working class had average earnings of

> less than $600 a year at a time when even conservative social workers estimated that $800 was an absolute minimum for a family of five if it were to get enough to eat and wear — and to burn for fuel in a precarious stove. That is what hurt — for half the working people, the same poverty in a time of visible affluence as had been their lot in the earlier years of obvious want.[10]

In 1913, twenty-five thousand persons were killed in industrial accidents, while injuries reached nearly one million. There is little evidence that the highly vaunted progressive reforms in such areas as workers' safety, hours and minimum wages had significant effect on the life of the average worker. As Cochran and Miller note:

> To placate aroused and enlightened voters, legislators had to enact laws that were anathema to themselves and their business supporters. They did not, however, have to enforce such laws. And though the Progressive statutes steadily improved in quality and scope, appropriations for their enforcement remained as inadequate as ever, inspectors as venal as before, the courts as unsympathetic as old men could be who had been nurtured on the harsh and inadequate doctrine of Spencerian laissez faire.[11]

In summary, the Progressive Era was a period in which forces for reform and for repression were constantly in tension. In comparison with the late nineteenth century, the forces for reform were considerably more in the ascendent, but whenever a crisis appeared to be developing, strong pressures for repression invariably developed. While both reactionary businessmen and labor were viewed as potential threats by the progressives, when push came to shove, business and the forces of "law and order" got the nod. Furthermore, even in non-crisis time, reforms were extended only to those who showed signs of being worthy of rehabilitation, i.e. those willing to accept the basic structure of American society. Anarchists and labor radicals need not apply, except to receive the mailed fist.

The Anarchist Scare of 1901-03

Fear of anarchism had never died out in the U.S., and the many anarchist outrages in Europe during the 1890's had kept many Americans on edge. In 1900 King Umberto of Italy had been murdered by an Italian member of an anarchist group headquartered in Paterson, New Jersey. When Chicago anarchists rallied to celebrate this deed in Chicago in August, 1900, Chicago police demonstrated their anarchist-fighting trim was in good shape by precipitating a riot which led to the injury of thirty persons including ten children.[12]

These fears were reinvigorated on September 6, 1901, when Leon F. Czolgosz assassinated President William McKinley. Czolgosz was a native-born American, and it is by no means clear whether he was in fact an anarchist, a lunatic, or both, but his foreign-sounding name and claim of anarchistic affiliations were enough to set off a new anarchist scare. The Czolgosz affair revived the identification of all anarchists with images of murder and bombings which had been burned into the American psyche by the Haymarket and Berkman incidents, although in fact by the early twentieth century the few thousand remaining anarchists had largely toned down any talk of violence and were devoting themselves mostly to philosophical attacks on the evil of all governments. Thus, a survey of anarchism in the U.S. in 1908 disclosed that there were only half a dozen anarchist newspapers, of which only one advocated violence, and that "violence and terrorism" were not generally found in written or oral anarchist propaganda.[13]

Following the McKinley assassination, anarchists were arrested in Chicago, Buffalo, New Mexico, and Pittsburgh, then released for lack of evidence. Johann Most was arrested three times in New York; he eventually was sentenced to a year in jail for having had the misfortune to publish in a newspaper printed a few hours before the assassination extracts from an article published originally in 1849 which praised tyrannicide. Most had ordered withdrawal of the paper from circulation after the shooting, and the only copy sold was to a policeman, but this did not save him from jail. The newspaper of an anarchist colony in Spring Valley, Illinois, was forced to cease publication after a federal marshal arrested the editor for violating postal regulations by publishing lottery advertisements. Three members of the Home, Washington, anarchist colony were arrested by federal officials for publishing "obscene" material in their newspapers. Subsequently the federal government closed the post office of the Home colony, forcing the Home newspaper to cease publication for a year. In Newark, New Jersey, the local liquor board decided to revoke the licenses of any establishment allowing anarchists to congregate and demonstrate against the government. Mobs assaulted anarchists in Pennsylvania, New York and New Jersey.

While the immediate hysteria died down rather quickly — as John Higham writes, the response was "gentle and temperate" compared with the reaction to Haymarket[14] — the scare left behind a lasting and dangerous legacy in the passage of federal and state laws that for the first time since the Alien and Sedition laws penalized persons solely on the basis of opinions, affiliations and advocacy, rather than on the commission of what would normally be considered a crime.

The leading influence behind this development was the new President, Theodore Roosevelt. As pressures built up for federal action against anarchy, with proposals ranging from deporting anarchists to an American Devil's Island to lynching them, Roosevelt, in his first message to Congress, called for the waging of "war" against anarchists and "all active and passive sympathizers with anarchists."[15] The eventual outcome of agitation by Roosevelt and others was the passage in March, 1903, of a law which barred from the U.S. immigrants who "believe in or advocate the overthrow by force and violence" of the U.S. government, or all governments, or all forms of law, or the assassination of public officials; also excluded were persons who "disbelieve in" or opposed all organized government or were affiliated with organizations which entertained and taught such views. Such persons already present in the country were barred from naturalization and subject to deportation for up to three years, while any individual developing such views after arriving in the U.S. was also deportable within three years of entry.[16]

Meanwhile, four states passed legislation to outlaw the advocacy of anarchy in 1902 and 1903. The New York law, passed in April, 1902, later became the model for criminal syndicalism laws passed to outlaw the Industrial Workers of the World (IWW) in 1917-20. The law defined criminal anarchy as the doctrine that organized government should be "overthrown by force or violence or by assassination of the executive head or of any of the executive officials of government, or by any unlawful means." Persons who advocated such doctrines orally or in writing, who helped disseminate such doctrines, or who organized, joined or "voluntarily" assembled with any group advocating such doctrines faced up to ten years in jail and a fine of $5000. Also, any assemblage of two or more persons for the purpose of advocating such doctrines was outlawed, and any person knowingly allowing such meetings on their property, including janitors, also faced arrest.[17]

The federal statute was first enforced in October, 1903, when the English anarchist and trade unionist John Turner was arrested after his arrival in New York and ordered deported by the Secretary of Commerce and Labor after a secret hearing during which Turner was denied a lawyer. While the case was appealed, Turner was held in a nine by six foot cage. In April, 1904, the Supreme Court upheld the 1903 law, declaring it would be constitutional even if Turner were only a philosophical anarchist, since it was to be presumed Congress felt the advocacy of such views "is so dangerous to the public weal that aliens who hold and advocate them would be undesirable."[18]

The federal law saw little other use at first — from 1903 until 1921 there were only thirty-eight exclusions and from 1908 until 1917 there was not a single deportation under the law.[19] The state laws also saw little use — for example New York's law lay essentially dormant until it was used against the Communist Party in 1919.

Despite the lack of immediate use, the federal and state anarchist laws of 1902-03 are of immense significance in the history of American political repression, for a number of reasons. First, the passage of the laws reflected a greater role of government generally in society, which in terms of political repression meant an increasingly direct and immediate involvement of government, and a declining direct and immediate involvement of the private sector. Increasingly during the twentieth century, government tended to lead the way in political repression, until by the so-called McCarthy period, the role of private business (and labor) was largely limited to firing and excluding persons whom the government had already specified as "undesirable." Until the passage of the anarchist laws, direct government involvement in political repression usually occurred only when business was not able to handle the situation by itself, and therefore called in local, state and federal police and courts.

Secondly, the fact that the federal government passed an anarchist law reflected the increasing power of the federal government in particular in society,[20] which in terms of political repression meant that during the twentieth century (for example during World Wars I and II, the 1947-54 and Vietnam War eras) it was the federal government that dominated public attention in terms of both fostering periods of repression and fashioning means to implement repression, whereas in the 1870-1900 period the federal government usually entered the stage only on the tail end of local disturbances that could not be handled on the state and local level, such as the 1877 and 1894 railroad strikes. In other words, direct government repression tended to originate from below and work "upwards" before 1900; clearly after World War I repression frequently was "managed" by the federal government, even if still implemented often by state and local government agents.

Thirdly, the 1902-03 laws are significant in reflecting a general shift in the targets for political repression. Before these laws were passed, the overwhelming majority of repressive measures were directed against the labor movement, usually in the context of strikes or active organizational activity. Persons were rarely, if ever, prosecuted simply for advocating "bad" ideas or belonging to groups or political parties which advocated them (one major exception was the vote-stealing and intimidation directed against the Populists). Although repression against labor persisted in major ways until the 1930's, after the passage of the anarchist laws, repression was increasingly directed against those who advocated or belonged to groups which advocated "bad" ideas, including legal political parties such as the Socialist and Communist Parties. The anarchist laws were the first sedition laws in American history since 1798, and the first laws in American history to provide penalties for simply belonging to a group (what later became known as "guilt by association"). They became the models for later legislation directed at other targets — for example, the criminal syndicalism laws passed by many states in 1917-20 to outlaw the Industrial Workers of the World and again in 1947-54 to outlaw the Communist Party; the 1917-18 Federal wartime Espionage and Sedition Acts, which virtually outlawed all criticism of the government and were used to harass the Socialist Party; the 1917, 1918, 1920, 1940, 1950, and 1952 immigration laws used to exclude and deport members of the IWW and CP; and the 1940 Smith Act, outlawing advocating or belonging to groups advocating overthrow of the government, for all citizens, even in peacetime.

A final significance to the 1903 Federal law was that it ended America's history as an "asylum" for all persons, regardless of their political beliefs.

Together with later immigration laws, the anarchist exclusion and deportation measures also signalled the start of a new means of assault on American radicals — an attempt to destroy them by completely cutting off their foreign sources of recruitment. The implications of such measures for the history of American radicalism are difficult to assess precisely, but certainly were of major importance.

The Repression of the Western Federation of Miners, 1903-07

If the McKinley anarchist scare reflected fears of political radicals that lay not far from the surface of the American mind at the turn of the century, the brutal suppression of the Western Federation of Miners (WFM) during the 1903-07 period reflected a fear of labor radicals that was just as strong. The WFM had become, at the turn of the century, the first strong, militant and realistic (unlike the Knights of Labor) anti-capitalist union in American history, at least since the demise of the Haymarket anarchists. The radicalism of the WFM was a reflection of the repressive conditions in the hard-rock mining country of the mountain west, where the state governments were generally dominated by the mining companies and the militia was regularly and promiscuously sent to break strikes.[21]

The WFM was not an angelically non-violent organization. Its members were responsible for "plenty of murders, floggings, destruction of property and petty harassments"[22] but after years of observing that justice seemed to be "synonomous with injunctions, martial law and the bull pen" they "were absolutely correct in believing they had no peaceful, orderly recourse."[23] The WFM had been organized in the aftermath of the suppression of the 1892 Coeur d'Alene strike as an industrial union which would unite mine workers of all skills throughout the western mining region. Thus, like the ARU, the WFM was a challenge both to the craft structure of the AFL and to the industrial hegemony of the corporations. For the first few years of its existence, the WFM espoused only typical business-union goals, but repeated repression drove the WFM towards increasingly revolutionary postures. The first major WFM strike had been the Cripple Creek affair of 1894, in which Populist Governor David Waite had intervened to stop incipient guerrilla warfare.

Then, in 1896, a new Republican governor suppressed a WFM strike at Leadville, Colorado, a leading area for the production of lead silver ores. Strikers had been patrolling all points of entry to Leadville, sometimes peacefully and sometimes forcibly discouraging strikebreakers from entering. State troops were sent to the area in September following an outbreak of violence during which a mob set fire to one mine and tried to attack a second mine. While the governor conspired to remove the local pro-union sheriff and replace him with a less sympathetic sheriff, the troops broke the strike by preventing strikers from even talking to incoming strikebreakers. The WFM in Leadville was destroyed as a result of the defeat.[24]

The Leadville defeat caused the WFM to move towards an increasingly radical critique of American society. In 1897 the WFM withdrew from the AFL, and in 1898 transformed itself into the Western Labor Union (WLU), designed to embrace all workers in the west regardless of industry or skill. At the 1897 WFM convention, President Edward Boyce advocated miners' ownership of the mines, advised all unions to form rifle clubs, and added, "I strongly advise you to provide every member with the latest improved rifle . . . so that in two years we can hear the inspiring music of the martial tread of twenty-five thousand armed men in the ranks of labor."[25] Clearly, by 1898, the WFM was the nation's most militant labor organization.

The first conflict the WFM became involved in following its adoption of a more militant course was at Coeur d'Alene again in 1899. The key grievance was the refusal of the dominant mine company, the Bunker Hill and Sullivan, to hire union miners, a blatant violation of Colorado's 1893 law outlawing yellow dog contracts. Federal troops were sent to Coeur d'Alene after an incident on April 29 during which a group of several hundred miners dynamited a Bunker Hill & Sullivan concentrator, burned mine buildings and engaged in a fight which led to the death of two men. While the dispatch of troops may have been justified, the subsequent actions of federal troops amounted to imposition of a reign of terror. Martial law was proclaimed, and virtually any male remaining in the district became subject to arbitrary arrest and incarceration in box cars or bullpens. Boyce himself was arrested, along with a large number of Populist party leaders, including a local deputy sheriff. The Populist county sheriff and three Populist county commissioners were removed from office. No miner was allowed to return to work in the area unless he agreed to renounce allegiance to the WFM. While hundreds of miners were arrested, only fourteen were ever convicted of any crime. The repression of the strike broke the WFM in the area, and unionism remained insignificant in the area for years.[26]

Despite the crushing of the Couer d'Alene strike the WFM continued to grow in both numbers and militancy. From 1899 to 1903, the organization made rapid gains, reaching perhaps fifty thousand members. By 1903, the WFM openly espoused socialism and demanded a "complete revolution of present social and economic conditions."[27] The WFM's growth and pronouncements succeeded in throwing a tremendous scare into conservatives in the west, who determined to destroy the union. That active state intervention would be needed to accomplish this purpose became evident during a 1901 WFM strike at Telluride, Colorado. Armed miners at Telluride engaged in gun fights with local officials trying to protect strikebreakers, seized a mine and forced the scabs to leave.[28]

By 1903 the WFM was at peak strength, and had become "the most powerful labor organization in the West."[29] The heart of its power was in

Colorado, where it was secure in its control of most mining regions and was ready to begin a campaign to increase its membership among mill and smelter workers. One of the major grievances in the 1903 Colorado campaign was the WFM demand for an eight-hour day. In 1902, Colorado voters had mandated the legislature to pass an eight-hour law, but business interests had blocked the legislation.

As the WFM girded for new struggles, so did Colorado's business interests, who formed a state-wide association of anti-union organizations with close ties to Colorado's conservative Governor James Peabody. As strikes broke out over the eight-hour day and other issues in Idaho Springs, Colorado Springs, Cripple Creek and Telluride, businessmen succeeded in getting Peabody to adopt as state policy the smashing of the power of the WFM in Colorado.[30]

The subsequent repression of the WFM exceeded in ferocity and brutality anything in American labor history up to that time. State militia were sent repeatedly into strike areas around the state without cause and without investigation, were paid for by the mine companies and were housed in mine company quarters. Over 175 WFM members were arbitrarily thrown into local bull pens, and more than 400 union miners were forcibly deported from Colorado by troops who refused to obey habeas corpus orders from the courts. WFM President Charles Moyer and Secretary General William Haywood were arrested for flag desecration as a result of WFM flyers which protested the strike repression against the background of an American flag. Moyer was held as a military prisoner for almost three months. A labor newspaper was raided by the militia and five employees were arrested. The general attitude of the state militia was summed up by Gen. Sherman Bell, who declared, "I came to do up this damned anarchistic federation." When a lawyer sought to obtain a habeas corpus writ for his clients, Bell replied, "Habeas corpus, hell! — We'll give 'em post mortems!" Militia Lt. McClelland, told that the military was violating the constitution, proclaimed, "To hell with the constitution; we aren't going by the constitution."[31]

The use of the militia, the declaration of martial law in numerous areas of Colorado and the mass deportations broke the power of the WFM, and, according to George C. Suggs, the leading historian of the "Colorado labor war," "in doing so, altered the industrial history of Colorado and the West."[32] Suggs adds that during the 1903-04 period, Governor Peabody made "law and order . . . synonymous with the destruction of the WFM." Above all, he notes, it was the "industrial character of the WFM, its radical leadership, its tendency towards socialism and power" which led Peabody to "war against a labor union which dared to challenge the supremacy of the class and the values he represented." Ironically, Suggs notes, despite its reputation for violence, "At no time did the WFM engage in armed resistance against the constituted authorities even when their extreme harassment and provocation might have justified it."[33]

Repression of the WFM did not stop with the Colorado events. After the destruction of the Colorado WFM, union officials decided that the organization could not stand alone against the concentrated power of the state and big business. In 1905, the WFM became the main organization behind the founding of the Industrial Workers of the World (IWW), a militant industrial union open to all workers in the country. The IWW was dedicated to the proposition that the "working class and the employing class have nothing in common," and "between these two classes a struggle must go on until the workers of the world organize as a class, take possession of the earth and the machinery of production, and abolish the wage system."[34]

The IWW had hardly organized before it was dealt a crushing blow. On December 30, 1905, Frank Steunenberg, who had been governor of Idaho during the crushing of the 1899 Coeur d'Alene strike, was killed by a bomb explosion in Caldwell, Idaho. Subsequently, a man named Harry Orchard was arrested, and the state of Idaho hired Pinkerton detective James McPharland (of Molly Maguire fame) for the purpose of linking the killing to the WFM-IWW. After talking to Orchard at length, suggesting to him that the WFM was responsible for the crime and telling Orchard the story of how one person involved in the Maguire trials had gone free after turning state's evidence, McPharland obtained a statement from Orchard which implicated the WFM in virtually every major incident of labor violence in the West, including over twenty other murders.[35]

After Orchard's "confession," officials of Colorado and Idaho collaborated in February, 1906, to effect what amounted to the kidnapping from Denver to Idaho of Moyers, Haywood and George Pettibone, a former WFM leader. The arrest of the three men, and especially their manner of removal to Idaho, stirred major and strident protest throughout the country. (Indeed had the WFM officials been convicted, the Steunenberg case would today be as well known as the Sacco-Vanzetti case). Socialist Party leader Debs declared, "If they attempt to murder Moyer, Haywood and their brothers, a million revolutionists at least will meet them with guns."[36] On the eve of the trial, President Roosevelt termed Haywood, Moyer and Debs "undesirable citizens."[37]

After being held in jail for one and a half to two years, the three men were acquitted or released. Although Orchard stuck to his story throughout the trials, and supplied many corroborating details about his confessed acts, his trial testimony also included confessions to acts of violence he could not have committed, and demonstrated that at least once in his long career of arson, theft, bigamy and murder he had worked as an *agent provocateur* for the Pinkerton Agency. In fact, the only incident of mysterious "labor" violence in Colorado which appears to have been solved during this period was attributable to the mining companies.[38]

Coming on the heels of the Colorado events and right after the formation of the IWW, the Steunenberg trial had a shattering effect on both the WFM and the IWW. The affair badly frightened WFM leaders, who feared that unless the union moderated its position it would face continuing repression. More than any other incident the Steunenberg trial led the WFM to withdraw from the IWW in 1908, which dealt the latter organization a severe blow and delivered it into the hands of leaders who lacked the stabilizing experience of having actually done serious union organizing.[39] The trial was especially marked in its effect on WFM President Moyers, who had come into office espousing standard WFM rhetoric in 1904 and then quickly found himself arrested during the Colorado events and again in the Steunenberg trial. The fear of further repression was a rather abstract matter to many WFM leaders, but it was not to Moyer, who commented that "if to be conservative meant to stay out of prison, he was going to be conservative."[40] By 1911 the WFM had become so conservative that it rejoined the AFL, while the IWW was gravely weakened by the WFM defection and by the absence of the stabilizing influence of Moyer and Haywood during its formative years.[41]

As the WFM was being destroyed, important business corporations and the federal government were displaying a totally different attitude towards the more "responsible" unionism represented by the AFL. The first major step towards a coalition of the more "responsible" business and union leaders was the formation of the National Civic Federation (NCF) in 1900. While clearly dominated by big businessmen, the NCF included representatives of both the corporate giants and the more conservative unions, including AFL President Gompers, United Mine Workers (UMW) President John Mitchell, and representatives of the railroad brotherhoods. The NCF was essentially an effort by large corporations and conservative unions to fight both "reactionary" businessmen whose virulent anti-unionism might lead to increasing radicalism, and the growing threat of radical unions and the Socialist Party. The NCF was a coalition of the center against both the right and the left, although it was really the threat from the left that most worried business.[42]

President Roosevelt took up the cue during the UMW's Pennsylvania anthracite strike of 1902. Roosevelt refused mine owners' demands for court injunctions, and threatened to use the army to seize the mines and operate them unless mine owners agreed to arbitrate the strike. The combination of the UMW's conservative strike leadership, the refusal of the mine owners to bargain and the President's pressure combined to win the strikers the support of large segments of the public.[43] As one labor historian has written, the strike was the "most important single event in the history of American trade unionism," because "for the first time a labor organization tied up for months a strategic industry and caused wide suffering and discomfort to the public without being condemned as a revolutionary menace to the existing social order calling for suppression by the government."[44]

With the NCF actively urging businessmen to sign contracts with "responsible unions" and with the federal government displaying a friendly attitude towards such unions, the AFL made huge membership gains, jumping from less than one million in 1900 to over two million by 1904.[45]

Indeed, this period witnessed such friendly relations between conservative labor, big business and the government, that the leading labor historians have termed the 1898-1904 era a "honeymoon period of capital and labor."[46]

Obviously, however, the honeymoon was consummated only with blood in the case of the WFM. In fact, the huge AFL gains and good relations between some companies and some unions have obscured an incredible amount of violence that occurred during this period. According to one estimate, during 1902-04 alone, casualties in labor disputes included 180 union men dead, 1651 injured and over 5,000 arrested.[47]

In many areas, even relatively conservative unions faced severe repression. In the summer of 1901, when fifteen thousand workers walked out in San Francisco in support of the locked-out teamsters union, special police paid for by employers were hired, officers clubbed and arrested hundreds of pickets and a court injunction was obtained barring union members from using the word "unfair" and intimidating restaurant employees and patrons.[48] Teamsters retaliated by mercilessly assaulting drivers who tried to work through the strike. While the strike was lost, San Francisco labor subsequently organized the Union Labor Party and elected its own candidate for Mayor in November, 1901, largely as "an angry protest against the brutal treatment of pickets by the police and against the widely believed partisanship of the city authorities."[49] Under the pro-labor (and notoriously corrupt) administration which followed, San Francisco became one of the strongest labor bastions in the country.

A 1902 strike by the conservative UMW in West Virginia was ruthlessly crushed by the massive use of injunctions, the arrest of strike leaders and the sending of the national guard. In issuing a strike injunction, a West Virginia judge declared:

> No publicist or statesman loyal to this country ever claimed that free speech gave the right to one to advocate and defend treason to his country, or destruction to its institutions. . . . Are communism and anarchy, and all the dire evils which follow in the train of such people . . . who are preaching the most destructive heresies and doctrines to be protected by the Constitution? . . . Never, never, never.[50]

While the WFM was being destroyed in Colorado in 1903, UMW coal miners in that state were also being beaten by the declaration of martial law and the deportation of over four hundred strikers by state troopers.[51] When one of the militia commanders was asked if there was any specific charge against the deported men, he replied, "No, but I believe their absence is better for the people than their presence."[52] During a simultaneous strike by coal miners in Carbon County, Utah, the Utah National Guard was sent in following minor incidents of intimidation on the part of both strikers and deputized company guards who were paid and housed by the Utah Fuel company. Although the company guards "were as guilty, if not more so, of violence and intimidation than the strikers" not a single company employee or supporter was arrested before the strike collapsed; meanwhile strikers were denied the right of freedom of speech and assembly, and over one hundred fifty strikers and strike supporters, including most of the leading union organizers, were arrested on charges such as vagrancy, disturbing the peace, conspiracy and criminal libel.[53]

State troops were sent to Paterson, New Jersey, during a peaceful general strike of silk workers in 1902, and were also dispatched that year to Pawtucket, Rhode Island, where martial law was declared after deputy sheriffs opened fire on missile-throwing crowds. Troops were also sent to New Orleans in 1902 and to Waterbury, Connecticut in 1903 to suppress disorders during street car strikes. Eight strikers were acquitted in Waterbury for the killing of a special policeman during the dispute there.[54]

If there ever was a "honeymoon," it was over by 1904 as the reactionary wing of American business organized a nation-wide "open shop" offensive to combat the growing labor movement. With the aid of court injunctions and conspiracy indictments, along with such standard techniques as the use of spies, blacklists and yellow dog contracts, the anti-labor offensive brought the growth of the labor movement to a halt between 1904 and 1910.[55] Typical of the use of the courts by employers was the obtaining of an injunction against a teamster's boycott against the Kellogg Switchboard and Supply Co. of Illinois in May, 1903, followed by successful contempt proceedings against all of the union leaders save one; and the injunction issued by a Chicago judge in 1905 barring the use of "peaceful picketing" or "any moral suasion whatever" during a strike by the Chicago Typographical Union, followed by the jailing for contempt of two union officers and a fine of $1,500 levied against the union.[56] One of the most violent strikes in American history during this period destroyed the powerful teamsters' union in Chicago. Open warfare broke out in the streets of Chicago during the 1905 strike, with twenty-one persons killed, over four hundred injured and over eleven hundred arrested, of whom over nine hundred were strikers. Over forty-one hundred unpaid deputies, mostly recruited from the business community, were employed during the strike, along with over twenty-five hundred extra police and paid deputies.[57] Throughout the 1905-14 period Los Angeles business forces, allied in the anti-union Merchants and Manufacturers Association, (M & M) functioned as "part of the Los Angeles city government," supplying special deputies to be sworn as city police while remaining under the pay of the M & M whenever labor difficulties arose.[58]

The Anarchist-Labor Scare of 1908-09

While the anti-labor, and especially the anti-radical offensive clearly had never really died down in many areas during the 1900-07 period, it was not until the panic set off by the 1907 depression and a series of alleged anarchist "outrages" in 1908 that a *nationwide* scare, aided and abetted by the federal government, developed again.

All the old fears of anarchism, radicalism and labor that always lay just beneath the surface during the Progressive Era burst out again in the aftermath of the depression set off by the failure of the Knickerbocker Trust Company in New York in 1907. The depression, which lasted until 1909, was a very severe one; iron production during the first half of 1908 was 50 percent below 1907, prices on the stock market dropped by one-third, and overall unemployment, which had been 1.8 percent in 1907, rose to 8.5 percent in 1908.[59]

By the beginning of 1908, severe hardships caused by the depression were causing increasing unrest and militancy among workers and increasing fears among the more well off that a "catastrophe" comparable to the labor strife of the 1890's would come again. During January, 1908, unemployed workers demonstrated for relief in St. Louis, Boston, Seattle, and Detroit. In Muncie, Indiana, state troops established martial law in January after the local sheriff was unable to find any members of the community willing to serve as deputies after riots broke out during a street car strike. In New York City, a widespread rent-strike movement erupted into violence on January 5 when police freely clubbed tenants who resisted their demands to disperse meetings and take down red flags and protest signs they had hung on the front of their buildings. On January 23, club-swinging police in Chicago dispersed a peaceful unemployment demonstration. On February 20, an unemployment demonstration in Philadelphia ended in a riot during which three police were shot and slightly wounded and fourteen protesters arrested after being clubbed so severely that they had to be hospitalized.[60]

A clear sign of the increasing fear of radicalism and labor unrest was President Roosevelt's precipitous sending of federal troops to the mining town of Goldfield, Nevada, on December 5, 1907, during a peaceful IWW strike. Partly as a result of the S'~unenberg affair, the IWW had been racked with severe internal dissension during its first two years, but had achieved great strength at Goldfield. When the governor of Nevada requested troops, without consultation with local officials, after a committee of mineowners had asked him to do so, Roosevelt immediately sent the forces without making any investigation. The troops remained in Goldfield for three months, although Roosevelt's belatedly initiated investigation revealed as early as December 20 that there had been no need for troops and that local officials could have maintained order. Under the cover of the troops, local mineowners succeeded in destroying the IWW, and for good measure obtained a federal court injunction which barred IWW interference in any way with operation of the mines, and upheld the use of a "card" system to screen out hiring of union men, despite a 1903 Nevada law barring such tactics.[61]

The federal courts also showed severe signs of unease at manifestations of labor strength, dealing labor four blows between December 1907 and March 1908. The Supreme Court declared unconstitutional the portion the 1898 Erdman Act which barred yellow dog contracts on interstate railroads, and in the Danbury Hatters' case (*Lawlor* v. *Loewe*) it ruled a nationwide boycott of a Connecticut firm by an AFL union constituted a violation of the Sherman Anti-trust Act for which individual union members were liable. By the time the Supreme Court finally upheld a judgement of over $250,000 against individual members of the Hatters' union in Danbury, Connecticut, after fourteen years of legal wrangling, this case alone cost the labor movement over $420,000 in legal fees and fines; as a result of it "workers became wary of joining unions for fear of being sued."[62] Meanwhile, lower federal courts barred the UMW from trying to organize the West Virginia coal industry, and in the Buck's Stove case (*Gompers v. Buck's Stove and Range Co.*) prohibited the AFL from placing a struck company on its "We Don't Patronize List," and from even discussing the case. This case ended the use of the boycott by the AFL, and would have sent Gompers to jail except for a technicality. Taken together, the 1907-08 court decisions raised the threat that virtually all union activities would be outlawed as illegal conspiracies. The AFL, still suffering from "honeymoon" delusions, awoke with a shock since it had begun to assume that "as a respectable junior partner of industry" it was "immune from hostile governmental action."[63]

As signs of mounting labor distress and repression of labor were becoming increasingly obvious, a series of three alleged anarchist "outrages" set off a brief but severe anarchist scare. On February 23, 1908, an Italian immigrant who claimed to be anarchist murdered a Catholic Priest as the latter was administering holy communion in a Denver church; on March 2, Chicago's police chief suffered a superficial stab wound and the chief's son and driver were shot by what Chicago police claimed was an anarchist bent on assassination; and on March 28 a man fatally injured himself and blew up a bystander in an abortive attempt to throw a bomb into police ranks in New York City. In each case, local police immediately proclaimed that anarchist conspiracies were behind the "outrages," but such conspiracies were never proved. The New York bomb thrower was the only individual involved in these events ever proved to belong to an anarchist organization and there are severe doubts as to whether the Chicago affair really involved an assassination attempt rather than a tragic misunderstanding.[64]

Whatever the reality, however, public opinion was ready to believe the worst. Persecution of anarchists had never really ended — for example on at least eight occassions in 1906 and 1907 police in Philadelphia and New York City barred anarchist meetings or meetings called to discuss anarchism, sometimes arresting speakers and clubbing protesters in the process. Anti-anarchist agitation took on a new and frenzied tone during March and April, 1908, however. While the press demanded strong action to deport or incarcerate anarchists (the *Washington Post* advocated death for all anarchists, whether or not they had committed any crime since "an avowal of anarchy has been found to be equivalent to an intention to commit murder" and therefore "an anarchist, is in fact, a murderer, even before he has done the deed"), anarchist and other radical gatherings were banned in Chicago; Rochester; Philadelphia; Worcester, Massachusetts; New York City; and Paterson, New Jersey. (The New York City bomb attempt on March 28 came after police had brutally broken up a planned Socialist unemployment rally.) Alleged radicals and anarchists were arrested in Chicago, Los Angeles, San Francisco and New York.

The federal government played a leading role in fostering the 1908 anti-anarchist hysteria. The Department of Commerce and Labor announced a major campaign to deport alien anarchists (which produced no results because there were no anarchists to be found who had been in the U.S. less than three years and therefore were deportable). The secret service and Post Office suppressed or banned from the mails, without any legal authority, two anarchist newspapers.

President Roosevelt sent a special message to Congress which declared that "compared with the suppression of anarchy, every other question sinks into insignificance" and asked for legal authority to ban all materials from the mails which propagated "anarchistic opinions." The first government loyalty program since the civil war was quietly instituted to weed out potential anarchist infiltrators, and federal troops scheduled to be sent to the Phillipines were kept at home for fear that labor and anarchist rioting would develop. On May 26, Roosevelt signed into law a measure barring from the mails "matter of a character tending to incite arson, murder or assassination," the first time in American history that political criteria were established to exclude matter from the mails. An army private was sentenced to three years in jail after being court-martialled for publicly shaking hands while in uniform with anarchist leader Emma Goldman. Miss Goldman was the major victim of the scare; the federal government denaturalized her ex-husband in a futile attempt to make her eligible for deportation, and even after the hysteria died away after the spring of 1908, she had continual trouble in attempting to give public addresses. Thus, she was barred from speaking in eleven different places in May, 1909.

While anti-anarchism soon died down, labor continued to suffer from the hangover of fears. In July, 1908, the UMW, which had organized about 65 percent of Alabama coal miners into bi-racial unions, struck in that state to protest wage cuts. Violence broke out as strikers fought pitched battles with guards seeking to protect strikebreakers. Hundreds of strikers were jailed and mistreated by local police. The UMW in Alabama and the strike were finally crushed when "reform" governor Braxton Comer barred public meetings, threatened to arrest pickets and had the state militia cut down tent camps the miners had thrown up after being evicted from company houses.[65]

The International Ladies Garment Workers Union won a major victory in the dress and waist industry in New York City during a 1909 strike, despite the use and toleration of extraordinary brutality by the local police and courts. Company-hired thugs brutally beat adolescent girl strikers during the dispute, the police arrested over seven hundred pickets, and the courts regularly "ordered bruised and bleeding girls to prison while exonerating their assailants."[66]

The second major IWW strike, at the Pressed Steel Car Company at McKees Rock, Pennsylvania, in 1909, met severe repression. This strike, which the IWW entered after it had broken out, was the *only* strike the IWW was ever involved in which involved serious violence on the part of labor. Repeated battles broke out between strikers and deputy sheriffs and state police who sought to evict strikers from company houses and to protect strikebreakers. The climax of the strike came on August 22 when a gun battle broke out between troops and strikers during which twelve men were killed (eight of them strikers), and forty strikers were injured. Many strikers were arrested and dragged down the street behind state troopers' horses. Further IWW organizing efforts in Pennsylvania led to the jailing of the entire staff of the IWW publication *Solidarity*.[67]

The Rise of Class Tension, 1910-1917

If the early years of the Progressive Era were a time of relative class harmony, the crisis of 1908-09 marked a turning point. This is not to say that the progressive movement ended in 1908 — in fact most of the progressive reforms were passed during the 1910-17 period — but merely that the middle and upper classes never recovered from the crisis of 1908-09. As Robert Wiebe has written:

> Around 1908 a qualitative shift in outlook occurred among large numbers of ... men of authority, a shift roughly comparable to the one during the mid-eighties. Once again irritants became anxieties, a context of threat replaced isolated reactions, and responses acquired that cumulative, self-accelerating character which created an increasingly urgent movement to discipline an unruly society. ... Critics who had only grumbled about national reform earlier now cried 'socialism' and 'communism.' Organized labor received particularly heavy abuse, with each hint of violence reported as the first gun of civil war. ... When the pace of reform quickened after the panic of 1907, large numbers of new middle-class businessmen drew back. Progressivism run riot promised exactly the kind of turmoil they had always dreaded.[68]

Aside from bad memories from past periods of tumult, there were at least four factors which underlay the increased tensions and fear that led to gradually increasing repression in the latter half of the Progressive Era: 1) continuing economic uncertainty; 2) the rise of the Socialist Party of America (SPA); 3) the rise of and tremendous publicity given to the IWW; and 4) a general revival of the labor movement after 1910, marked by signs of increasing radical influence in the AFL.

The 1907 panic proved to be a turning point in the economic history of the progressive period. From that year until war prosperity revived the economy in 1915, American economic history "was largely one of brief spurts and recessions," with an upsurge in 1909, a minor depression in

1910-11, another upswing in 1912 and a recession in 1913 that turned into a serious depression by 1914.[69]

The rapid rise of the SPA during the progressive period was the single most important factor in creating increasing unease among leading politicians and businessmen, at least until the bursting into prominence of the IWW during the 1912 Lawrence strike. First organized as the Social Democratic Party in 1898, the SPA vote jumped from less than one hundred thousand in 1900 to almost nine hundred thousand in 1912 (about 6 percent of the popular vote), while SPA membership increased from about ten thousand to almost one hundred twenty thousand during the same period. By 1912 SPA members held 1200 local offices in 340 cities throughout the country, including seventy-nine mayors in twenty-four states — among them a few major cities like Milwaukee, Berkeley, Butte, and Schenectady. During 1912-13 the party published 323 periodicals with a circulation that probably exceeded two million.[70]

What was particularly striking — and to the conservatives frightening — about the SPA was its tremendous strength among native born and rural Americans; unlike previous Marxist parties which had largely appealed to German immigrants in the urban areas and had cut themselves off from native workers and rural Americans, the SPA had deep roots in the native radical tradition stretching back to the Grangers, the Populists and the Bellamyites. The party got its strongest support in the 1912 election in Oklahoma, Nevada, Montana, Washington, California, Idaho, Florida, Arizona, Ohio, Wisconsin, Texas, Minnesota, and Utah. In 1912, only 13 percent of the party membership belonged to the SPA's foreign language federations.[71]

Although SPA strength levelled off after 1912, it is not true, as some writers have suggested,[72] that the party began a major and irreversible decline in 1912. As James Weinstein has suggested:

> In general, in the years from 1912 to 1917, Socialist strength and organization seem to have remained stable. Gains were made in some areas, losses suffered in others, but no substantial downward trend is observable.[73]

Socialist activity and strength in unions such as the International Association of Machinists, the United Mine Workers, the Brewery Workers and Typographers remained considerable (although declining somewhat in the case of the Machinists and UMW) and the SPA gained control of the Ladies' Garment Workers Union, the third largest in the AFL, and organized the Amalgamated Clothing Workers Union in 1914.[74] The SPA press remained strong and party strength as measured by electing members of state legislatures increased. While membership declined to about eighty thousand by 1917, the party remained potent and continued to grow especially in the west and mid-west where the SPA had its strongest American roots; losses which did occur were mostly confined to eastern industrial states. The overall SPA presidential vote did decline markedly in 1916 but this partly resulted from the fact that for the first time Debs was replaced as SPA presidential candidate by a relative unknown. The SPA also suffered a decline in the number of locally elected officials, but in many cases this resulted from changes in local election procedures which meant the party might increase its vote yet decrease the number of candidates elected. Thus, in some areas, the major parties put up fusion candidates who succeeded in rending futile increases in the SPA vote, and in many areas the adoption of the commission-manager form of city government to replace the ward system led to the elimination of minor parties. For example, in Milwaukee the SPA elected a mayor with about one-third of the vote in 1910, but lost to fusion candidates despite an increased vote in 1912 and 1914, and in Dayton, Ohio, the SPA elected five city officials in 1912 with 25 percent of the vote, but after the adoption of city-manager government elected no one with 44 percent in 1917. Despite the decline in total number of locally elected officials, the SPA continued to win control of some important cities. Thus, in 1916, the SPA won the mayoralty in both Milwaukee and Minneapolis.

In addition to economic uncertainty and the rise of the SPA, the rise of the IWW to national consciousness was a third major factor heightening class tensions in the 1909-17 period. The IWW first began to gain significant national publicity during the "free speech" fights of 1909-13, and with its tremendous victory in the Lawrence strike of 1912 it became an object of hostility and fear unparalled in American history since the Chicago anarchists of the Haymarket period. The general impression created of the IWW in the American press at the time and by many American historians since is that the organization consisted of a band of reckless and dangerous men who spent their time destroying machinery, burning wheat fields and constantly preaching the most extreme forms of violence. Thus the "liberal" historian John Roche refers to the IWW as akin to European fascist movements, characterized by a "romanticization of violence . . . which often in practice amounted to an endorsement of revolutionary terrorism" and blandly terms Haywood responsible for the assassination of Steunenberg even though he was acquitted![75]

The facts about the IWW and violence are considerably more complex and considerably less sensational. There is no doubt that at *some* times *some* members of the IWW *preached* violence, and that at times the organization regularly urged the commission of "sabotage." However, IWW spokesmen repeatedly explained that sabotage meant such tactics as a work slowdown and giving poor service as well as disabling machinery, and there is no serious evidence that IWW members ever *practiced* violence or destruction of machinery on more than an extremely minor scale. As Rudolph Katz of the SLP pointed out in 1913, "The AFL does not preach sabotage but it practices it: and the Chicago IWW preaches sabotage but does not practice it."[76] Despite the ferocious campaign of extermination mounted against the organization, which regularly included the most absurd and trumped up charges, not a single member of the IWW was ever convicted of *practicing* sabtotage.[77] On the other hand, there is not the slightest doubt that the IWW was the constant *target* of both preaching and practicing of violence, by a broad spectrum of political forces in American society, culminating in its savage repression by the "progressive" Wilson administration.

Why did the IWW face such savage repression in comparison with the AFL during the latter part of the progressive period and during World War I, even though the AFL was responsible for many more strikes and far more violence? The answer is that the IWW, unlike the AFL, had "bad" *ideas;* the IWW advocated an openly revolutionary and class conscious philosophy that urged the complete overthrow of capitalism — preferably through a complete and peaceful general strike — and its replacement by a workers' state. It was this *philosophy* rather than any *action* taken by the IWW which elicited the following typical reaction from a small town sheriff: "When a Wobby [IWW member] comes to town, I just knock him over the head with a nightstick and throw him in the River. When he comes up, he beats it out of town."[78] Or as the *San Diego Tribune* put it:

> Hanging is none too good for them. They would be much better dead for they are absolutely useless in the human economy. They are the waste matter of creation and should be drained off into the sewer of oblivion, there to rot in cold obstruction like any other excrement.[79]

A final factor underlying the rise in class tensions after 1908 were signs of increasing radical penetration and influence within the AFL and the general revival of the labor movement. During 1911-14, the UMW and the carpenters both passed resolutions making NCF membership cause for expulsion, socialists were elected to the presidencies of the state federations of labor in Pennsylvania and Illinois, the Amalgamated Clothing Workers were organized under socialist influence, and socialists were elected to the presidencies of the machinists' union and Gompers' own cigarmakers union. In 1912, a socialist candidate running for president of the AFL against Gompers received one-third of the vote, and the years after 1912 were marked by the passage of many progressive resolutions by AFL conventions which reflected socialist influence.[80]

After the 1904-10 hiatus, the AFL as a whole began to grow rapidly, jumping from a membership of about one and a half million in 1910 to almost two and a half million in 1917. Another development frightening to conservatives and many progressives was the AFL's increasing political activity in the wake of the 1907-08 court decisions. The organization began a large-scale lobbying effort for pro-labor legislation, demanded that the major parties support its political demands and openly supported candidates deemed to be pro-labor. During the later years of the progressive period, and particularly during the Wilson administration, the AFL appeared to be wielding more and more political clout. In addition to the widespread passage of bills in state legislatures dealing with such questions as child labor, women's hours, workmen's compensation and safety conditions, the AFL was able to point with pride to the LaFollette's Seaman's Act of 1915, which reformed many of the most glaring abuses in the merchant marine; the formation of a Department of Labor as separate from the Commerce Department in 1913; the 1916 Adamson Act, which granted railroad workers an eight-hour day; and the 1914 Clayton Act, which, before the Supreme Court gutted it after World War I, appeared to outlaw the use of the Sherman Act and the granting of injunctions in labor disputes. Symbolic recognition of labor's new status was also granted when President Wilson officiated at the dedication of the AFL's new headquarters building in July, 1916 and when beginning early in 1916, a series of joint luncheon meetings were begun between Wilson's cabinet and the AFL executive council. With the appointment of AFL President Gompers to the Advisory Committee of the Council on National Defense in August, 1916, Gompers and Wilson seemed to have reached a close working alliance.[81] However, as John S. Smith has noted, the friendliness of the Wilson administration was contingent on the continued conservative character of the AFL. He notes that the alliance of Gompers and Wilson

> was compounded of various elements, but perhaps the most significant was Woodrow Wilson's appreciation of Gompers' basic conservatism in his approach to the labor problem. By supporting Gompers and the AFL, Wilson was identifying himself with the most sober segments of the organized labor movement, at a time when there were many indications of how radical such a movement might become.[82]

Patterns of Repression, 1910-1913

By 1910, increasing conservative opposition to progressivism coupled with the increasing appeal of radical doctrines to American workers was creating conditions of class tension that were "faintly reminiscent" of those in the 1880's. While the "profound anxieties of the earlier period were muted by the continuing vitality of the progressive impulse . . . some who found the pace of change too rapid, and others for whom it was too slow, drifted uneasily toward the psychology of the late nineteenth century, with its fears for the survival of the social order."[83]

The most important strikes of 1910 all met severe repression. By 1910 unionism had been virtually destroyed in the steel industry, but the possibility of a revival appeared when a spontaneous strike broke out at the Bethlehem Steel plant in South Bethlehem, Pennsylvania.[84] AFL organizers quickly moved in and recruited thirty-five hundred workers within a week into the Amalgamated Machinists' Union. However, strikers were soon faced with denial of the use of the town hall, the banning of IWW spokesmen, and massive beatings and in some cases shootings by the recently formed Pennsylvania state police. Even the Bethlehem police chief agreed with workers that the state police were responsible for whatever violence occurred during the strike, as a result of their "high-handed and cowardly attacks upon innocent people."[85] While on strike duty, the state police established their headquarters on company property, ate in company buildings, bought provisions from the company and detained prisoners on company grounds. The strike ended with disintegration of the union. Ironically, the state police had been created in Pennsylvania as a result of labor protests over the abuses of the Coal and Iron police, but the Bethlehem experience showed that "in place of its expensive and quasi-legal private regiments, capital had gained an efficient military force, financed by taxes and invested with public authority."[86]

A second major strike in 1910 brought out sixty thousand workers in the cloak makers' industry in New York City. The strike involved major violence on both sides, with the strikers forced to accept a settlement after a local judge issued a sweeping injunction which held that the strike's goal of a closed shop was illegal. The injunction barred all picketing, however peaceful, in pursuit of the closed shop; eighty-five pickets were arrested for ignoring it. The strikers won major concessions, but did not win the closed shop. Another strike of clothing workers in 1910 brought out virtually all of the forty thousand workers in the Chicago industry. Despite police attacks on picket lines, the strikers won a generally favorable settlement, but only after eight hundred seventy-four persons, mostly pickets and sympathizers, had been arrested, and seven persons killed.[87]

Another important strike in 1910 turned out to be a major disaster for the AFL. In order to break a series of major strikes in Los Angeles, "probably the most notorious open shop city in the country,"[88] the business-dominated city council completely outlawed picketing. Los Angeles police arrested four to five hundred pickets and broke up union parades with guns and clubs. On October 1, 1910, an explosion destroyed the building housing the *Los Angeles Times,* which was the dominant force among anti-union business in the city. Twenty persons were killed and scores were injured in the explosion.[89]

Subsequently, John J. McNamara, secretary treasurer of the AFL International Association of Bridge and Structural Iron Workers (IABSIW) and his brother James were arrested by private detective William Burns, and effectively kidnapped from Illinois and Indiana to stand trial in California. The IABSIW had been engaged in a long and violent struggle with employers — in the last four years anti-union construction companies had suffered seventy dynamite attacks — but the case had so many similarities to the Steunenberg affair, especially in the illegal extradition of the principals, that the entire labor movement regarded it as a frame-up. Gompers and the AFL spearheaded the defense effort, while thousands of workers demonstrated in protest across the country.

Meanwhile, in Los Angeles the case became entangled in the public mind with the concurrent socialist attempt to elect a mayor. In the 1911 primary, the SPA candidate had won a plurality of the vote, and was subsequently even endorsed by Gompers. Panic swept conservative business elements and progressives in Los Angeles, who united to try to defeat the SPA. On the eve of the election, the McNamaras confessed their guilt as part of an agreement which defense lawyer Clarence Darrow negotiated with a group of powerful city industrialists. In the aftermath of the confession, the SPA was decisively defeated in the mayoral election, while the AFL was dealt a severe blow in its efforts to convince public opinion that the labor movement was now a "respectable" force in American society.

The McNamara case is obviously not an instance of repression, since the evidence indicates their clear guilt, but it was important in increasing tensions in American society. Thus, when the December, 1911 issue of *Survey*, an influential progressive magazine, devoted an issue to the case, oustanding intellectuals, businessmen, labor leaders and correspondents all "appeared convinced that America was verging dangerously on a violent social upheaval. Over and over again they used the word 'war' to describe the country's plight."[90]

While the AFL faced repression mainly during its more spectacular strikes during the Progressive Era, the IWW met the club and the gun as a routine occurrence virtually every time it stuck its head out. The IWW first rose to prominence during the 1909-13 free speech fights. The pattern of these efforts in over twenty cities was about the same in each town. Wobblies attempting to speak on the streets in order to organize workers would be faced with local ordinances suddenly passed to bar street speaking; they would defy the ban and urge other Wobblies to come to the affected city to try to fill up the jails and bog down the courts; mass arrests would ensue; and in most cases the authorities would eventually give up and concede the right of free speech. These fights were not struggles over abstract questions of civil liberties, but involved the right of the IWW to conduct organizing campaigns in the areas where the greatest concentration of migratory and down-trodden labor existed — the streets of cities such as Spokane, San Diego and Fresno, which served as commercial hubs for the agricultural, mining and logging industries of the west.[91]

Since the IWW maintained a singular posture of non-violence throughout these struggles, the main variant was how much repression was exerted by local authorities. In Spokane, over six hundred were arrested, and in some cases fed on bread and water, housed in an unheated school house and moved back and forth between steaming hot and ice-cold cells. Spokane police raided the IWW headquarters, arrested the editors of the IWW paper and even arrested newsboys who peddled copies which they were not able to confiscate. In Fresno, the principal city of California's San Joaquin Valley, a major agricultural center, a ban on IWW street-speaking was lifted in March, 1911, after more than one hundred Wobblies had been arrested; when jailed Wobblies refused to stop singing and shouting one evening in December, 1910, they were blasted with one hundred fifty-pound pressure firehoses and left standing in knee-deep icy water all night. In Aberdeen, Washington, a lumber center for the Pacific northwest, police firehosed and arrested IWW members and supporters who defied street-speaking restrictions; when IWW activity continued, the mayor deputized hundreds of "citizen police" who on November 27, 1911, blocked the entrance to a scheduled IWW meeting, raided and ransacked the IWW hall, arrested forty men, including all local IWW leaders, and escorted the arrested Wobblies out of town. San Diego authorities arrested over 200 Wobblies in February and March, 1912 ("I am going to charge some with disturbing the peace and others with offenses which I shall figure out tomorrow," announced the police chief,)[92] and turned fire hoses on a crowd of five thousand persons who had gathered to hear IWW members protest jail conditions. The height of San Diego's repression came on April 5, 1912, when the local police chief solved the problem of overcrowded jails by turning IWW prisoners over to vigilantes who escorted the Wobblies to the county line, beat them with pickaxes and sent them on their way. Conditions in San Diego became so scandalous that Gov. Hiram Johnson sent an investigator who reported that police brutality was so bad in the city it was difficult to believe he was not "sojourning in Russia . . . instead of in the alleged 'land of the free and home of the brave.'"[93] In Minot, North Dakota, police jailed all those who encouraged or supported the IWW, fire-hosed protesters, raided hobo "jungles" and deported all of their inhabitants, wrecked an IWW camp, and deported incoming transients.

IWW strike activity during this period also met savage repression, whether conducted in the east, the west or the south. In Louisiana, the IWW became involved in the most important organizational effort attempted in the south since the smashing of the 1908 UMW strike in Alabama. Despite the efforts of lumber companies who controlled local police in Louisiana lumber towns, and arranged to have deputized company guards and gunmen suppress freedom of speech, press and assembly in lumber areas, an organization known as the Brotherhood of Timber Workers (BTW) met phenomenal success in organizing southern lumber workers. The BTW had been formed in 1910, and by 1912 had a bi-racial membership estimated at 18,000 to 35,000. As a result of a strong company counter offensive, replete with charges of anarchy and communism, and including the use of anti-union blacklists which violated Louisiana law, the BTW affiliated with the IWW in May of 1912. On July 7, 1912, striking BTW members meeting near the Galloway Lumber Company at Grabow, Louisiana, were fired on from the mill office. BTW members returned the fire. Casualties were four dead, including three BTW members, and forty wounded, almost all union men. Subsequently a grand jury cleared mill officials, but indicted sixty-five BTW members. An attorney hired by the lumber operators dominated the resulting trial, while over one hundred detectives hired by the operators searched for clues to convict the union men, resorting to such tactics as mailing threatening literature to the jurors which supposedly came from the IWW. All of the BTW men were eventually acquitted or released, but the trial paralyzed the organization for months, drained its treasury and exhausted its resources. The Grabow affair was followed by a strike in November, 1912 at Merryville,

Louisiana, during which strikebreakers brought into the area under false pretenses were locked in mill stockades and kept under armed guard, state troops were sent without justification, and deputized company gunmen beat and threatened strikers. The Merryville strike collapsed in February, 1913 when a mob of townspeople and company gunmen raided and wrecked union buildings, and created such a reign of terror that most strikers were forced to flee for their lives. That was the end of the BTW and the southern lumber drive.[94]

An IWW strike at Little Falls, New York, in 1912 led to mass arrests of pickets and eventual outlawing of all forms of agitation, including open-air meetings and parades. A strike the same year at a Seattle tailor shop led to a strike injunction which barred picketing and the subsequent arrest of one hundred pickets. IWW strikers who paralyzed the sawmills of southwest Washington in 1912 were met with trumped-up arrests, and vigilante beatings, kidnappings and deportations. Newspaper editor Albert Johnson, who led the armed citizen movement which broke the strike, rode anti-IWW sentiment into a seat in Congress after a campaign which turned into "a holy war against radicalism and for immigration restriction, raging at the IWW as a flag-hating foreign conspiracy out to wreck the country."[95] Antagonism to radical groups appears to have been particularly strong in the Pacific northwest. Thus, during 1912-13 federal officials in the area defined the IWW as a group teaching disbelief in and opposition to organized government, and thus all IWW members were barred from naturalization under the terms of the Anarchist Exclusion Act, even though federal officials in Washington and other areas of the country did not follow this policy. In July, 1913, a party of U.S. marines, with the tacit acquiesence of Seattle police, raided SPA and IWW headquarters in that city.[96]

The strike that really brought the IWW to the nation's attention and created the image of IWW as bogeyman was the 1912 strike at Lawrence, Massachusetts, a major center of woolen worsted products and home of the largest firm in the industry.[97] The unique features of the strike were the use of picketing on a massive scale and the IWW's ability to organize into an effective force masses of unskilled immigrants — exactly the type of worker the AFL had shunned as unorganizable. The IWW entered the strike after spontaneous walkouts had begun over wage reductions. Minor violence had occurred at the beginning of the strike when mill workers broke mill windows and damaged some property, but violence diminished on the part of strikers after the IWW arrival on the scene, while increasing on the part of local police and the twenty-five hundred state militia sent to the scene. Over twenty thousand workers were on strike at the height of the dispute.

While arrests and assaults on pickets occurred during the earliest days of the strike, severe police repression began on January 29 after a woman striker was killed during clashes resulting from police attempts to halt a strikers' parade. The next day, a militiaman bayonetted to death a fifteen-year-old boy, and martial law was declared, making all public meetings illegal.

Subsequently police arrested the two major IWW strike leaders, Arturo Giovannitti and Joseph Ettor, in connection with the woman's death, even though they were three miles away at the time of the incident. They were held in jail, without bail, for ten months in a fruitless attempt to break the strike.

After strikers began sending children out of Lawrence so they could be better cared for, the Lawrence city marshal announced that no more children would be allowed to leave. On February 24, when strikers attempted to place additional children aboard a train for New York, police beat and clubbed the children and their mothers, arrested over thirty persons for "congregation" and had fourteen children committed by juvenile courts to the city farm. Public reaction to this action was so strong that the companies completely acceded to strike demands in March. During the course of the strike 355 strikers had been arrested, with 54 given jail terms. One group of 34 strikers was given a year in jail each after five to ten minute trials. Although their sentences were later commuted to small fines on appeal, the IWW had to raise $27,000 for bail.

When the trial of Ettor and Giovannitti began in late September the two defendants were kept in metal cages in the courtroom; protesting strikers were brutally clubbed by police outside the courtroom. Massachusetts authorities indicted the entire defense committee on charges of conspiring to intimidate workers. Ettor and Giovannitti were acquitted in November. In the meantime, it had been revealed that the president of the major mill in Lawrence had paid a man at the beginning of the strike to plant dynamite in locations that would implicate the strikers; the dynamite planter was fined $500 while the textile executive went free.

In the aftermath of the Lawrence strike, the IWW replaced the SPA as the gravest menace to the American system in the eyes of conservatives.[98] In the late summer of 1912, at the request of Republicans in California, President Taft ordered a federal investigation of the IWW and urged his attorney general to "go in and show the strong hand of the United States" to put down the IWW in California. However, the Justice Department was unable to come up with any evidence that the IWW had violated any federal laws.[99]

The IWW victory at Lawrence was followed by increased activity — and increased repression. In 1912, IWW strikes at Paterson, New Jersey, and nearby Passaic and Garfield ran into run-of-the-mill repression of the sort the IWW encountered virtually everywhere — some police clubbing of strikers, occasional arrests and banning of IWW speakers, and arbitrary arrests and shooting at pickets on a minor scale. By 1913, however, authorities at Paterson, the nation's leading center of silk production, had prepared a truly repressive welcome for the IWW. After spontaneous strikes broke out at Paterson in January, 1913, IWW organizers moved in and shut down the entire silk industry by pulling twenty-five thousand workers out on strike. Police responded by arresting IWW leaders on trumped-up charges, closing every hall in town to the strikers, constantly interfering with strike meetings, confiscating strike literature and arresting strikers by the score — over two thousand altogether.[100]

When the New Jersey SPA state secretary tried to read the free speech clause of the New Jersey constitution to a meeting, police arrested him after reading the ancient riot act, including the final phrase, "God save the king."[101] When a socialist newspaper editor protested civil liberties violations in Paterson, police raided SPA headquarters, confiscated five thousand copies of the paper and arrested him for criminal anarchy. When the socialist mayor of nearby Haledon allowed strikers to meet there, Paterson police instigated a riot in Haledon and then arrested the mayor for "unlawful assemblage and malfeasance in office."[102] The Paterson strike collapsed by July, 1913, a complete failure. Investigators for the Federal Commission on Industrial Relations concluded later that during the strike "the police authority of the state was in effect, turned over to the mill owners" and the strike failed because of the complete violation of the strikers' fundamental rights. They concluded that all violence which occurred during the strike — which included the killing of two workers by private detectives — "was found on the part of the police officials and the inferior courts, who trespassed every natural right and constitutional guarantee of the citizens."[103]

In February, 1913, the IWW brought out about fifteen thousand rubber workers in Akron, Ohio, and shut down the city's major rubber plants. Police and vigilante groups broke the strike by attacking, beating and arresting scores of strikers. The strike defeat ended attempts to organize the Akron rubber plants until the 1930's. An IWW loggers' strike in Coos Bay, Oregon, in May, 1913, was defeated by vigilante raids, beatings, arrests and deportations. A poorly organized IWW strike of six thousand Studebaker workers at Detroit in June, 1913 — the first major automobile strike in American history — was lost partly as a result of a ban on parades and mass picketing and a police attack on peaceful strikers who were seeking to get other auto workers to join them.[104]

Aside from Paterson, the major IWW cause celebre of 1913 was the so-called Wheatland riot.[105] In the aftermath of the 1912 San Diego free speech fight IWW activity in California had expanded to the point where there were about five thousand members, including about 8 percent of migratory workers. In 1913, the IWW began one of the earliest major efforts in American history to organize agricultural workers, with efforts centering at the Durst ranch in Wheatland, the largest single employer of agricultural labor in the state. On August 3, 1913, a mass meeting of two thousand workers under IWW leadership was in progress when local police officers tried to disrupt the meeting and arrest IWW leader Richard Ford. A melee broke out when a deputy on the fringe of the crowd fired a shot; during the battle two workers, the local district attorney and a deputy sheriff were killed.

"Progressive" Governor Hiram Johnson immediately sent the national guard to Wheatland, while panic-stricken state authorities sent Burns agency detectives throughout the state and into Arizona, where they initiated a reign of terror. Hundreds of persons were arrested, held incommunicado and, in many cases, brutally beaten. In one case, a Burns' detective was given a year in jail and fined $1000 for his beating of a Wheatland suspect. Eventually Ford and another IWW organizer, Herman Suhr, were given life sentences for second degree murder, even though they had constantly advocated non-violence and no evidence was ever introduced that they had ever attacked anyone. Ford and Suhr were paroled after serving over ten years in jail.

The IWW was not alone in facing severe repression during these years. During 1912-13, the UMW engaged in one of the most savage strikes in American history in West Virginia.[106] Repeated clashes between private mine guards and strikers led to the deaths of about 25 people (with casualties about evenly divided), the repeated imposition of martial law, wholesale arrests of miners, and trials and sentences by military courts. All socialist organizers in the area were arrested by order of the governor, including two socialist constables. The miners accepted a compromise settlement after the governor apparently gave a miners' convention the choice between accepting his terms or the deportation of "idle troublemakers" from the strike area.[107] When two socialist papers agitated against acceptance of the governor's terms, the editors were arrested and national guard troops wrecked the offices and plant of one of the papers, which was located eighty miles away from the martial law zone. The UMW subsequently collapsed in the area, largely because the settlement did not include union recognition.

The WFM once again faced repression in 1913-14 during a strike at the lucrative copper mines in Calumet, Michigan.[108] Fifteen thousand miners came out beginning in July. The Houghton County sheriff swore in seventeen hundred deputies, including many company employees, and the entire Michigan national guard was sent to the area following some minor incidents in which strikers attacked or otherwise intimidated strikebreakers. Some of the deputies were out-of-state armed guards, who were deputized in violation of the Michigan law barring the swearing-in of out-of-state residents. On August 13, deputies shot and killed two strikers, leading to the eventual conviction of four of the gunmen for manslaughter. When workers attending the funeral procession cursed watching deputies, they were fired upon, with one woman suffering a gunshot wound. In September, a sweeping injunction was handed down which barred the WFM from a wide range of activities; two hundred strikers were subsequently given suspended sentences for violation of the injunction, and were warned not to picket or call men scabs.

On December 7, three strikebreakers were murdered at Painesdale, Michigan, under circumstances which suggest that mine guards had committed the atrocity to stir up resentment against the WFM. Subsequently vigilante groups raided WFM headquarters and rounded up union sympathizers in Painesdale. On December 4, seventy-two persons, mostly children, were killed when an unknown person set off a panic by shouting "Fire" in the hall where a Christmas party was being held for strikers' children. On December 26 WFM President Moyers was shot and deported by vigilantes and deputies at Hancock, Michigan. By the time the WFM gave up in April, 1914, the organization was "at the end of its ropes."[109]

The worst atrocity of 1913-14 was yet to come. In the fall of 1913, the UMW once more attempted to organize the Colorado coal fields, an area of virtually complete company despotism.[110] Civil liberties simply did not exist in the coal fields, where the coal companies owned the school buildings, chose the teachers, censored books and movies, and controlled elections by gerrymandering precincts, banning political meetings and barring "undesirables" from company camps and from polling places, which were located on company property. Five of the seven demands made by the UMW during the 1913-14 Colorado strike simply called for compliance by the coal companies with state laws.

As soon as the UMW began organizing in the area, over three hundred men employed, armed and paid by the coal companies were sworn as deputy sheriffs. After a strike began in September, 1913, gun battles erupted between strikers and police, with deaths on both sides. The entire Colorado national guard was sent into the area. Although at first the guard acted fairly impartially, guardsmen soon began arbitrary arrests and harassment of strikers, established martial law, and held strikers without charges for long periods of time. The militia was quartered by the coal companies and supplied by company stores, and became steadily infiltrated by mine guards. By late December, the militia was bringing in strikebreakers from outside of the state, in violation of Colorado law, and in some cases was forcibly detaining strikebreakers at the mines. In March, 1914, a militia detachment attacked a miners' tent colony and drove strikers into a mountain snowstorm. The climax of repression came on April 20 when state militia attacked and burned the miners' tent colony at Ludlow, thereby asphyxiating eleven children and two women. Three strikers who were taken prisoner were shot while unarmed and under guard.

In the wake of the Ludlow massacre, miners armed themselves and began attacking and burning mines and shooting mine guards throughout the state of Colorado. Altogether seventy-four persons were killed during the Colorado disorders before federal troops finally restored order. Over three hundred miners were subsequently indicted for murder or other crimes. Several strike leaders were convicted of first degree murder and sentenced to life imprisonment, but later released on appeal. The few mine guards or militia who were tried or court-martialled were acquitted, with one exception.

The Ludlow massacre caused great outrage among both labor and progressive circles across the country, but its immediate result was only more repression. Picketers outside the offices of John D. Rockefeller (who owned the major coal company in Colorado involved in the dispute) in New York and outside his estate in Tarrytown, New York were arrested. A socialist minister who challenged the minister of Rockefeller's church to a debate was dragged from the church by police and given six months in jail for disorderly conduct.[111]

The Crisis of 1914-1916

By the time of the Ludlow Massacre, class tensions were being further exacerbated by serious economic difficulties. A recession which began during the summer and fall of 1913 had turned into a serious depression by 1914. Unemployment, which had been 4.4 percent in 1913, jumped to 8.0 percent in 1914 and 9.7 percent in 1915 before allied war orders restored prosperity towards the end of 1915.[112] Unemployment demonstrations, generally under the organization of the IWW, became increasingly common, and frequently met stiff police resistance. Such demonstrations were attacked by or dispersed by police in Los Angeles, Boston, Detroit, New York and Sacramento in the winter of 1913-14; in Chicago in January, 1915; and at Salt Lake City, in November, 1915.[113] The most spectacular incidents occurred in Sacramento and New York City. The Sacramento affair involved "Kelley's Army," two thousand unemployed men who patterned themselves after Coxey's Army of 1894 (Coxey himself marched on Washington again, undisturbed, in the spring of 1914 to protest economic conditions). When Kelley's army attempted to march on the state capitol in Sacramento on March 9, 1914, "a rival 'army,' of eight hundred special deputy sheriffs, arrived with pick handles and drove them across the river, burned their blankets and equipment, and mounted an armed guard across the bridge to keep them out."[114] In New York, unemployment demonstrators who invaded churches during the early months of 1914 to seek food and shelter were tolerated at first, then arrested and jailed. Police subsequently pressured hall owners not to rent to the IWW and began regular attacks and arrests during IWW meetings. The leader of the New York church demonstrations, Frank Tannenbaum (later to become a professor and authority on Latin America) was given a year in jail; eight others were given three to sixty days in jail, while 180 others arrested for the church invasions were released.[115]

An IWW "idle army" of the unemployed in Oregon was hospitably received in some cities, but forced out of Woodburn and Albany. Wobbly speakers were banned from a number of cities, including Everett, Washington; Salt Lake City; Kansas City; Sioux City; and Des Moines. In the latter three cities, the IWW fought and won free speech fights.[116]

Further exacerbating the rapidly worsening climate was the development of another anarchist scare during the 1914-16 period.[117] A number of "outrages" led to the new scare: the July, 1914 explosion in a New York tenement house which killed three anarchists, which was attributed by police to a misfired plot to blow up John D. Rockefeller; the October, 1914, attempted bombing of St. Patrick's Cathedral in New York City, blamed by police on anarchists and the IWW, but later discovered to be the work of two illiterate anarchists inspired by a police *agent provocateur;* the

November, 1914, attempted bombing of the New York City courthouse on the twenty-seventh anniversary of the Haymarket execution; an abortive attempt in the spring of 1916 by an apparently anarchistic cook's helper to poison the guests at a dinner honoring Chicago's archbishop; and the shooting of two policemen in 1915-16 in San Francisco by Russian anarchists. In the aftermath of these developments, federal agents announced their intention of arresting every known anarchist in a number of cities across the country. Emma Goldman was arrested twice in 1915 and 1916 (for the first time since the 1908-09 scare) allegedly for her activities in behalf of birth control, and the post office, by the spring of 1916, banned three anarchist newspapers from the mails, again allegedly for their advocacy of birth control. U.S. immigration officials in the San Francisco area began attending radical meetings to gather information for possible deportations, while the San Francisco police chief announced that an armored car, perhaps furnished with machine guns, would be purchased for use against anarchist desperadoes. In 1916, an anarchist meeting in Milford, Massachusetts was broken up by police and the speakers arrested on the grounds that they did not have a police permit; among those arrested was an Italian immigrant named Nicola Sacco, later of Sacco-Vanzetti fame. Until a new police commissioner took office in the summer of 1914, New York City police habitually dispersed anarchist meetings.

During the last few years of the Progressive Era — i.e. after the depression of 1913-15 had begun — the fabric of American society was strained to the breaking point. Signs of increasing hysteria were everywhere. Nativism, which had been growing steadily since about 1905, by 1914 had reached a level of hysteria and violence "that had been rare or nonexistent since the 1890's."[118] Anti-Catholicism was increasing by leaps and bounds; in Georgia Tom Watson was agitating anti-Semitism in the Leo Frank case; and in 1915 the post-reconstruction Ku Klux Klan was organized. In 1913 and again in 1915, Congress, for the first time since 1897 passed immigration bills which contained a literacy test provision; the bills also contained a provision aimed at the IWW which would allow the deportation of any alien "advocating or teaching the unlawful destruction of property." Both bills were vetoed by President Wilson.[119] In 1913 and 1914 three states passed laws banning the display of red flags.[120] In 1914, the Montana board of education warned school teachers that "turmoil, agitation and intemperate discussion of public questions is inimical to the well-being, growth and success of the various educational institutions of this state."[121] In late 1915, the governors of four western states urged President Wilson to investigate the IWW immediately with a view toward federal prosecution. Wilson agreed to the proposal but the Justice Department was again unable to discover any violation of federal criminal laws.[122]

Violence in labor disputes, almost invariably originating with employers and police officials, became endemic during the 1913-16 period, with both radical and non-radical unionists bearing the brunt of innumerable shootings, beatings and arrests. For example, during 1913 local police and sheriffs deputies killed two strikers and wounded many others by firing into picket lines at Ipswich, Massachusetts, and Rankin, Pennsylvania, while private guards killed five and wounded many by firing into a group of strikers at Metuchen, New Jersey. In the latter case, nine guards were convicted for manslaughter.[123]

At Stockton, California, in 1914, strikebreakers armed with guns and blackjacks were deputized during labor strife, while Stockton employers tried to plant dynamite to implicate union members.[124] State troops placed Butte, Montana, under martial law in September of 1914, after considerable violence developed as a result of an interunion struggle between a conservative mine union and a more radical IWW-oriented union. While in this case the use of troops may have been justified — radical unionists had wrecked the moderate union's headquarters and then blown it up with dynamite — the methods of the state troops were extremely repressive. All street meetings save those of the Salvation Army were banned, local papers were censored, the socialist press was suppressed, and militant union leaders were arrested, held incommunicado and without bail, and tried by military courts without a hint of due process. The state troops totally crushed the radicals and left Butte under the complete domination of the mine companies.[125]

During a 1915 strike by the Amalgamated Clothing Workers in Chicago, all parades and demonstrations were banned, and motorcycle and mounted police drove into groups of strikers. Police brutality and favoritism to the employers was so notorious that the city council's Committee on Police censured the police department's activities.[126]

Scores of IWW agricultural organizers and farm workers were arrested in the midwest during a major Wobbly attempt to organize in the fields beginning in 1915. At Yakima, Washington, a major agricultural fruit and hop center, police promptly closed an IWW hall which was opened in the fall of 1916, arrested its inhabitants and barred Wobblies from holding street meetings.[127]

During June, 1915, 6 strikers at the Standard Oil plant at Bayonne, New Jersey were shot and killed by private guards, 129 of whom were arrested; a year later at the same plant, police and deputies swept through workers' residential areas after six policemen and strikebreakers were wounded by gunfire during a strike, killing four persons as they clubbed and shot at strikers and wrecked strikers' saloons.[128]

Riots broke out at East Youngstown, Ohio, and at Braddock, Pennsylvania during 1916 when private guards fired at strikers, killing four and wounding many. In both cases state troops had to be called in to restore order. During the same year, Pennsylvania state troops broke up a strike of IWW coal miners by the simple technique of raiding a union meeting and arresting all 250 miners present.[129]

During the 1916 strike by immigrants on the Mesabi iron ore range in Minnesota, IWW organizers brought out an estimated seven to twenty thousand miners.[130] Four hundred mine guards were deputized even after they had shot and killed one striker and wounded two others. The deputized guards dispersed parading strikers, arrested IWW organizers without cause, and generally established a reign of terror in the area. The climax of the Mesabi violence came when several of the deputized guards forced themselves without warrant into the home of a miner, allegedly to make an arrest for a liquor law violation; in the subsequent melee a deputy was killed along with a nearby soft drink peddler. All of the miners present were jailed on charges of first degree murder, along with IWW leaders who had not even been in the area. Eventually a settlement was reached in which the IWW leaders were released, while three miners pled guilty to manslaughter. They received sentences of up to twenty years, but were freed by executive clemency shortly after. While both sides in the Mesabi strike were responsible for acts of violence, federal and state investigating agencies placed the major share of the blame on the mining companies and the police. A report to the U.S. Commission on Industrial Relations found that the miners endured the "abuse and violence of beating up, shooting, jailing and terrorizing."[131] The Mesabi strike eventually collapsed due to the miners' exhaustion.

An IWW strike in December 1916 and January 1917 which crippled logging operations in northern Minnesota and severely hampered the operations of the largest white pine mill in the world at Virginia, Minnesota, was broken up by a reign of terror instituted by police and deputized lumber company officials. The police and deputies dispersed picket lines, banned leaflet distribution, arrested strikers and IWW leaders for offenses such as using the word "scab," and "lurking and lying in wait with intent to do mischief," raided and closed IWW halls, and finally simply ordered IWW members to either leave the strike areas or face arrest.[132]

While violence in labor disputes thus was almost a daily occurrence during the 1913-16 period and added greatly to increasing fears and tensions, there were three major "cause celebres" which had an unusual degree of importance in both reflecting and increasing the sense of division in American society: the Joe Hill case, the Tom Mooney Case and the so-called "Everett Massacre."

The Joe Hill case arose out of the murder of a grocer and his son in Salt Lake City on January 10, 1914.[133] Subsequently, Hill, perhaps the most well-known IWW folk-song composer, was arrested. Ultimately the entire case against Hill rested on the fact that he had been shot on the night of the murder, but no conclusive proof was ever shown that the grocer's gun had been fired that night. Although several witnesses said someone resembling Hill had been in the vicinity of the grocery, none could positively identify him.

Even those who have studied the case and concluded Hill was guilty have conceded he did not get a fair trial and that his execution was heavily influenced by hatred for the IWW. Like the later Mooney and Sacco-Vanzetti cases, the affair soon became an issue of whether "law and order" would be upheld in Utah rather than the guilt or innocence of the accused. Hill was executed on November 9, 1915, despite a plea from President Wilson for reconsideration of the case, and despite widespread protests in the U.S. and abroad. In the aftermath of the case, the University of Utah fired a professor who had been active in Hill's behalf, and Hill's attorney was disbarred in Utah for criticizing the state's justice.

The Mooney case had its origins in the bombing of the July 22, 1916 World War I "preparedness" parade in San Francisco, which resulted in the killing of ten and the injuring of forty others.[134] Subsequently two labor radicals, Tom Mooney and Warren K. Billings, together with three of their acquaintances, were arrested, largely because a private detective who had long been engaged in a personal vendetta against Mooney suggested their guilt to the district attorney. At the time of their warrantless arrest, there was absolutely no evidence to suggest their guilt, so they were held incommunicado for three to five days without charges, and repeatedly denied the right to a lawyer while their homes were illegally searched in a vain attempt to develop some evidence to justify their arrests.

Once Mooney and Billings had been arrested, San Francisco officials completely abandoned any other lines of inquiry into the bombing. Throughout the pre-trial period and during the trial itself, prosecutors repeatedly made the wildest charges connecting Mooney and the others with anarchism, radicalism and violence — even charging a plot to assassinate the governor of California and to overthrow the state government. While the prosecution was able to satisfy juries that Mooney and Billings were guilty, subsequent developments showed conclusively that the most crucial testimony against them had been perjured. The three other persons arrested with them were either acquitted or freed following the perjury revelations, but the district attorney refused to concede error in the Mooney-Billings case, which had become a symbol of "American capitalist oppression of militant labor" or of the "radical threat to patriotism and to law and order," depending on one's viewpoint. Mooney was finally fully pardoned in 1939; Billings was released from prison shortly thereafter, although due to a technicality he was not fully pardoned until 1961.

The "Everett Massacre" of November 4, 1916, developed out of attempts by the IWW to organize in Everett, Washington, a regional stronghold of organized labor in the Pacific northwest, and a major center of the shingle mill industry.[135] IWW organizers who attempted to come into Everett beginning in July, 1916, faced repeated arrests, brutal beatings and deportations by the local "progressive" sheriff and deputized members of the business community. During October, 1916 alone about five hundred Wobblies trying to enter the city were deported by local police. On October 30, forty-one Wobblies trying to enter Everett were beaten by deputies with saps, clubs, rifles and fists; during the melee one deputy split the scalp of another by hitting him on the head with a gun barrel.

The climax of the Everett affair came on November 4 when two hundred fifty Wobblies trying to land by boat were met at the dock by armed, and, in many cases, drunken deputies who tried to prevent their disembarkation. During a subsequent gun battle five wobblies and two deputies were killed and scores were wounded. Although the source of the first shot has never been determined, seventy-four Wobblies were arrested. No action was taken against the deputies, although it seems likely that most of the deputies' casualties resulted from gunfire from other deputies. The arrested Wobblies were all released after the first man tried was acquitted.

In 1915 and 1916, as the effects of the depression were being overcome in the economic sphere, three new developments added new fuel to the fires of repression: the rapidly increasing strength of the IWW; the emergence of a powerful new radical farmers' group, the Non-Partisan League (NPL); and the war-time atmosphere that began to envelop the country, especially after President Wilson joined the "preparedness" forces.

There is a persistent myth which has been fostered by many American historians to the effect that the IWW reached its peak during the Lawrence strike of 1912, and declined thereafter.[136] The fact is, however, that the IWW reached its pinnacle of power in 1917, exactly when the federal government began a concentrated and successful effort to smash the organization amidst war-time hysteria.

The IWW did suffer severely from the aftermath of the Patérson strike and other defeats in 1913, plus the 1913-15 depression. Between 1912 and 1914, IWW membership dropped from eighteen thousand to eleven thousand.[137] However, beginning in 1915, the IWW began a phenomenal rejuvenation as the result of the formation of the Agricultural Workers Organization (AWO), which began a concentrated organizational effort among midwestern farm workers.[138] The IWW has been repeatedly criticized by historians for being unable to create stable unions and for putting revolutionary rhetoric ahead of day-to-day organizing; with the formation of the AWO, the IWW began to show clear signs of concentrating exactly on organizing, and of becoming a stable organization for the first time in its history.

The heart of the AWO's phenomenal success was the "job delegate" system, in which AWO workers signed harvest workers upon the job, and were paid $.50 for each new recruit. By October, 1916, the AWO had recruited eighteen thousand members. Largely as a result of AWO efforts, IWW income for the year ending August, 1916, was almost $50,000, compared to $9,000 in the previous year. During the year ending August, 1916, the IWW issued 116 local charters, the largest number ever issued in a comparable period. At its 1916 convention, the IWW, for the first time in its history, was able to provide decent salaries for its national organizers and officers. In 1916 and 1917 the rejuvenated IWW began major organizing campaigns in the western copper and lumber industries. In both cases, the organization made rapid gains. By 1917, IWW membership reached about one hundred thousand, compared to eighteen thousand at the time of the Lawrence strike and forty thousand in 1916.

Thus, by 1917, the IWW

> for the first time in its history . . . was functioning regularly as a labor organization. It was using its finances and many new recruits to organize slowly and systematically some of the industrial areas it had staked out for itself. . . . Its shift away from the resultless, even though dramatic free speech fights and its concentration upon organization of the unorganized seemed to hold promise that it would be able to sink roots in some of the industries employing a large complement of unskilled labor.[139]

Had not the government smashed the IWW during and after World War I, there is good reason to believe that it might have become a "powerful economic organization of unskilled and semi-skilled workers."[140]

Yet another threat to conservatives came from the NPL, an organization of small farmers established in North Dakota in 1915.[141] The NPL did not advocate socialism of farm lands, but its program of state ownership of grain elevators, flour mills, packing houses and cold storage plants, state hail insurance and the operation of rural credit banks at cost was enough to send a shiver of fear through the main targets of NPL agitation — the grain, banking and railroad interests centered in Minneapolis-St. Paul. These interests held the fate of the small farmers in their hands, and treated them as ruthlessly as many large corporations treated their employees. Despite severe and ruthless attacks from conservative press and business interests, who accused the NPL of favoring everything from socialism to dynamite and free love, the NPL quickly achieved tremendous support in North Dakota.

In 1916, the NPL swept the governorship and the lower house of the North Dakota legislature, and thereby "aroused the fears of conservatives everywhere."[142] In early 1917, the NPL began organizational work in Minnesota, where winning similar gains would mean a virtual revolution in the organization and financial structure of midwestern farming. By March, 1917, the NPL claimed twelve thousand members in Minnesota.

A final ingredient in the recipe of increasing tensions and repression in 1915-17 was the controversy over the question of American preparation for possible war, which frequently broke on ethnic and class lines. Preparedness agitation, which began in an organized way in December, 1914, was greeted with bitter antagonism at first by President Wilson and most progressives, pacifists, socialists and labor groups, while gaining the support of important financial and industrial interests.[143]

As the controversy developed, American nerves were further set on edge by the revelation in 1915 of German sabotage and espionage operations in the U.S., and in 1916 and 1917 by mysterious explosions at major military munitions plants.[144] Before long, German-Americans were increasingly regarded as inherently disloyal, "riddled with treason and conspiring under orders from Berlin.[145] Following the sinking of the *Lusitania* in the spring of 1915, "wild rumors circulated that several thousand German-Americans living in the New York area intended to seize the city in the name of the Fatherland" and other reports alleged that German-Americans "were preparing for a German invasion by secretly constructing concrete foundations for German artillery installations" in major American cities.[146]

In mid-1915, President Wilson joined the preparedness forces, although most progressive, labor and farm organizations still opposed preparedness. From late 1915 on, Wilson actively fostered a national defense mentality which greatly added to the increasing fears being expressed about the patriotism and loyalty of labor, radicals and anti-preparedness ethnic factions.[147] In the fall of 1915, for example, Wilson publicly expressed alarm at voices speaking with "alien sympathies" and called for a division into "men who are thinking first of other countries . . . and all those that are for America, first, last and all the time."[148] In his State of the Union Message to Congress in December, 1915, Wilson stressed the need for rearmament and the need for legislation to suppress disloyal activities. Just as Sen. Joseph McCarthy, thirty years later, would stress the internal threat to American security at a time when the only real threat came from abroad, Wilson told Congress that "the gravest threats against our national peace and safety have been uttered within our borders. There are citizens of the United States, I blush to admit, born under other flags, but welcomed by our generous nationalization laws . . . who have poured the poison of disloyalty into the very arteries of our national life." He called for legislation which would allow "such creatures of passion, disloyalty and anarchy" to be "crushed out."[149] Wilson thus lent support to the most extreme preparedness forces, who had already "reidentified hyphenism and radicalism"[150] in the public mind.

In the 1916 Presidential campaign, Wilson instructed the Democratic Convention to make "Americanism" the keynote of its activities, and he repeatedly attacked anti-preparedness forces and cast doubts upon their loyalty — and indeed upon the loyalty of all persons who expressed dissenting opinions. Mammoth preparedness parades were organized in a number of cities; in New York, one hundred twenty-five thousand persons marched past a huge electric sign which proclaimed, "Absolute and Unqualified Loyalty to Our Country." On Flag Day, June 14, 1916, Wilson said "disloyalty" in the country "must be absolutely crushed" and predicted the nation would turn "with a might and triumph of sentiment" against ethnic political action and would "teach these gentlemen once for all that loyalty to his flag is the first test of tolerance in the United States."[151] In September, 1916, Wilson attacked "certain groups and combinations of men amongst us who were born under foreign flags" and suggested such men had "injected the poison of disloyalty into our own most critical affairs, laid violent hands upon many of our industries and subjected us to the shame of divisions of sentiment and purpose in which America was condemned and forgotten."[152]

By early 1917, the increasing strength of radicals, the severe divisions over the preparedness question, and unresolved fears and tensions over labor conflicts, immigrants and the continuation of progressivism was reflected in a number of developments which demonstrate clearly that "World War I repression" began even before the war. On February 5, Congress passed, over Wilson's veto, an immigration law which for the first time imposed a literacy test on entering aliens, and which provided for the deportation of any alien who at "any time after entry shall be found advocating or teaching the unlawful destruction of property or advocating or teaching anarchy or the overthrow by force or violence of the government of the United States or of all forms of law or the assassination of public officials." The new features of this law were: 1) the elimination of any time limit for the deportation of aliens for political reasons after their entry into the U.S.; and 2) the new provision related to advocacy of "unlawful destruction of property," which was aimed squarely at the IWW.[153]

On February 14, the Congress made threatening the life of or bodily harm to the President a crime for the first time in American history.[154] During the same month a measure was introduced in the Senate with the support of the War Department which would have barred unauthorized persons during wartime from collecting or communicating certain types of military information or publishing statements that were false or "likely or intended to cause disaffection in, or to interfere with the success" of American armed forces.[155]

On March 14, Idaho passed the first "criminal syndicalism" law, which was in effect a criminal anarchy law of the type passed by New York in 1902, slightly modified to outlaw the IWW by banning the personal or organizational advocacy or the membership in a group which advocated "crime, sabotage, violence or other unlawful methods of terrorism as a means of accomplishing industrial or political ends." Passage of the Idaho bill followed increasing IWW organizational and strike activity in Idaho's lumber industry, and reflected pressure for action by business interests in the state.[156] Also in March, the Justice Department prepared lists of aliens who were to be arrested immediately in the event that war was declared. On March 27, the Justice Department sent letters to local police chiefs and federal marshals urging vigilance, and asking them to keep track of arms and ammunition accessible to enemy aliens, to watch their meeting places, and to see that "especially pernicious agitators" were restrained "insofar as the law will permit." The army, meanwhile was authorized to "sternly suppress acts committed with seditious intent" and to protect "public utilities" essential to war preparations."[157]

4

World War I: Wilson's New Freedom

The Strength of the Anti-War Movement

When the United States declared war against Germany on April 6, 1917, the radical movement, as represented by the SPA, the IWW and the NPL was at its post-Civil War peak, in terms of overall organizational effectiveness, stability and grass roots appeal. Radical currents were influencing a large segment of the American labor movement through the IWW and through socialist penetration of the AFL, while the SPA and the NPL were making a sizable impact on the electoral process. By 1917 the IWW was demonstrating a combination of radical utopian goals and effective and pragmatic day to day organizing that had eluded the Knights of Labor, and it was generating a strong appeal to native American unskilled workers who had been ignored by the AFL. The SPA was demonstrating a strength and staying power that previous radical political parties such as the Populists and the SLP had never shown, and an appeal to native Americans that socialist political parties had failed to develop hitherto.

Given the strength of the radical movement in 1917, it is not surprising that opposition to American participation in the war was enormous. There is a tenacious myth that anti-war feelings during World War I were neglible after American entry,[1] but such a position is simply not supported by the facts. Although the Wilson administration eventually succeeded in generating a considerable amount of war hysteria through its propaganda agency, the Committee on Public Information (CPI),[2] when the U.S. first entered the war, "throughout the country, and especially in the middle west, influential groups of people were apathetic if not actually hostile to fighting."[3] Fifty-six congressmen voted against the declaration of war, compared with only one such vote against entry into World War II.[4]

Organizations which identified themselves as against the war, or which were identified as such in the public mind, made strong gains during 1917, despite the opening of a vicious campaign of repression against them on the part of the federal, state and local governments. Thus, the IWW recruited over thirty thousand new members between April 1, 1917 and September, 1917. During this five-month period alone, IWW income reached over $275,000, compared to a total income of about $50,000 for the entire year ending August 31, 1916.[5]

While the IWW took no formal stand on the war, there can be no question that the SPA's enormous gains during 1917 were a direct reflection of its strong anti-war stand. Shortly after American entry into the war, a special convention of the SPA overwhelmingly adopted a position of "unalterable opposition" to American entry and called for a program of "continuous, active and public opposition to the war, through demonstrations, mass petitions and all other means within our power," including opposition to conscription and opposition to raising money to pay for the war. This program was ratified by an SPA membership vote of over twenty-one thousand to less than three thousand.[6]

In the two months following adoption of this position, which President Wilson referred to in his private correspondence as "almost treasonable", SPA membership jumped more than twelve thousand.[7] In the fall, 1917, municipal elections, the party's vote reached what even an extremely hostile historian has conceded were "new spectacular heights."[8] A survey of the party's vote in fourteen cities showed the SPA polled an average of 21.6 percent of the vote, a total which if projected nationally would have meant four million votes, compared with the previous high of less than one million votes in a presidential election. In city after city the party registered remarkable gains, frequently increasing its vote five-fold compared with the last previous election in the various cities. In New York City, the SPA mayoral candidate received 21.7 percent, while the party elected aldermanic candidates for the first time and elected ten state assemblymen, compared to a previous high of two. In Chicago, the SPA got nearly 34 percent of the vote; in Buffalo 25 percent; in Dayton 44 percent; in Toledo 35 percent. Altogether the party received from 20 percent to 50 percent of the vote in a dozen of the largest cities in Ohio, in ten towns and cities in Pennsylvania, in six cities in Indiana, and in four in New York. SPA support was heaviest in working class districts, including both immigrant areas and areas dominated by native workers.[9]

Despite repeated attacks upon its patriotism, the NPL also continued to gain support during 1917. While the NPL formally backed the war effort, it did not hesitate to criticize many local and federal governmental policies. For example, the League called for the "conscription of wealth" to finance the war, and urged the federal government to nationalize basic elements of the economy. Despite this position and severe repression, the NPL continued to make gains in Minnesota and elsewhere.[10]

The People's Council of America for Peace and Democracy, an umbrella anti-war organization, organized in May, 1917, also gained a large public following. Thousands of persons attended rallies called by the Council across the country, even in small towns like Moline and Rock Island, Illinois.[11] In August, 1917, Ralph Easley of the NCF wrote that "how to neutralize the campaign being waged through the country in the interest of 'an early peace' under the guise of the so-called People's Council" was the question of the day; he lamented that "mass meetings are held nightly and are enthusiastically attended in the big industrial centers from Maine to California."[12]

Opposition to the war was by no means confined to organized groups of radicals, however. A total of over three hundred thirty thousand draft evaders or delinquents were reported during the war. The draft was immensely unpopular everywhere; as many as 60 percent of those registering requested exemptions.[13]

Charles S. Barrett, president of the Farmers Educational and Cooperative Union, told the pro-war League for National Unity in September, 1917, that anti-war sentiment was prevalent among southern farmers. In November, George Creel, chairman of the CPI, reported that, "You will find in Georgia and parts of South Carolina, you will find in Arkansas; you will find in many parts of the West, an indifference that is turned into a very active irritation that borders on disloyalty. . . . We must take on the whole country."[14]

Federal Repression of the Anti-War Movement

Given the tremendous amount of opposition to American participation in the war, the severe governmental repression which developed did not constitute an irrational response. Anti-war sentiment did not pose a threat of revolution or violence, but it did pose a threat of spreading disaffection which could paralyze the war effort. Thus the "progressive" Wilson administration quickly embarked upon a program of repression that matched or exceeded wartime repression even in clearly totalitarian countries such as Germany and Russia, and which clearly exceeded the degree of repression experienced by America's Anglo-Saxon partner, Great Britain.[15] Thus in many cases during World War I American citizens were sent to jail for up to twenty years for mere verbal opposition to the war, offenses "which at the most would have drawn from any English court a sentence of a few months in jail or a medium-sized fine."[16]

The general climate of repression which quickly enveloped the country was set up by the very highest levels of the federal government. Addressing the Congress on April 2, 1917 to ask for a declaration of war, Wilson warned that Germany had "filled our unsuspecting communities and even our offices of government with spies and set criminal intrigues everywhere afoot against our national unity of counsel, our peace within and without, our industries and our commerce." He warned, "If there should be disloyalty it will be dealt with a firm hand of stern repression."[17] In June, 1917, Wilson warned that "the masters of Germany" were using "liberals, . . . socialists, the leaders of labor" to "carry out their designs" and that "it is only friends and partisans of the German government whom we have already identified who utter these thinly disguised disloyalties. . . . Woe be to the man or group of men that seeks to stand in our way in this day of high resolution."[18] Attorney General Thomas Gregory, referring to war opponents in November, 1917, stated, "May God have mercy on them, for they need expect none from an outraged people and an avenging government."[19]

The two major legislative weapons of repression wielded by the federal government were the Espionage Act of June 15, 1917 and the Sedition Act of May 16, 1918. The Espionage Act, which consisted of an amalgamation of various bills prepared in the Attorney General's office, provided for punishment of up to twenty years in jail and a $10,000 fine for those who during wartime "wilfully" made false statements with "intent to interfere with the operation or success of the military or naval forces or to promote the success of its enemies" or who "wilfully" caused or attempted to cause "insubordination, disloyalty, mutiny or refusal of duty" in the armed forces or "wilfully" obstructed armed forces recruitment or enlistment. Another provision of the bill provided that the Post Office could exclude from the mails any matter violating provisions of the act or "advocating or urging treason, insurrection or resistance to any law of the U.S." Despite strenuous efforts by President Wilson, Congress defeated another proposed section of the act which would have provided authority to directly censor the press.[20]

The Sedition Act, also passed with the support of the Wilson administration, outlawed virtually all criticism of the war or the government. Among the types of activities outlawed by it were making statements or performing acts favoring the cause of any country at war with the U.S. or opposing the cause of the U.S. therein; making false statements that would obstruct the sale of war bonds, incite disloyalty or obstruct enlistment; and uttering, printing or publishing any "disloyal, profane, scurrilous or abusive language about the form of government of the U.S. or the constitution of the U.S., or the military or naval forces of the U.S. or the flag of the U.S. or the uniform of the army or navy" or any language intended to bring these institutions into "contempt, scorn, contumely or disrepute."[21]

The federal government also had a whole arsenal of other weapons to silence dissenters. On April 6, 1917, Wilson issued a proclamation establishing regulations for the conduct and control of enemy aliens, under the Alien Enemies Act of 1798, a law passed during the Alien and Sedition era. This proclamation made all enemy aliens subject to summary arrest. At the same time, the Attorney General approved publication of a statement assuring German aliens that they had nothing to fear so long as they were not implicated in plots against American interests and they agreed to obey the law and "keep your mouth shut."[22] As hysteria about potential German spies escalated, Wilson issued new orders in the fall of 1917 requiring all German aliens fourteen years of age and older to register with the government, and barred all such persons from a variety of places deemed to be of military importance, expelled them from Washington, D.C., required them to get permission to travel within the U.S. or to change their place of residence, and barred access to all ships and boats except public ferries. Altogether these regulations affected about six hundred thousand German-Americans, and led to the arrest of sixty-three hundred enemy aliens and the internment in concentration camps of twenty-three hundred who were alleged to be dangerous to the national security. Perhaps the most famous internee under this program was Dr. Carl Muck, conductor of the Boston Symphony Orchestra, whose main crimes appear to have been declining for a time to play the national anthem at the beginning of concerts and associating with German diplomats in the U.S. He was arrested and interned in March, 1918, just in time to prevent him from conducting Bach's *Passion According to Saint Matthew*.[23]

Under the February, 1917, law barring threats against the President, sixty cases were brought by June, 1918. Many of these cases were clearly ludicrous. For example, one man was sent to jail for saying, "I wish Wilson was in hell, and if I had the power, I would put him there." The judge in this case reasoned that Wilson "could not be in the state called hell until life was terminated," and thus this statement constituted a threat against the President's life.[24]

On April 7, 1917, Wilson instituted a program for the summary removal of any employee of the federal government deemed "inimical to the public welfare by reason of his conduct, sympathies or utterances, or because of other reasons growing out of the war." Further, the Civil Service Commission (CSC) was authorized to refuse all applications for employment if there was a "reasonable belief" that such employment would be "inimical to the public interest owing to . . . lack of loyalty."[25] While no dismissal figures are available, the *New York Times* reported in July, 1917 that firings under this provision had been "frequent." Thus, one postal clerk was reportedly fired for making statements such as, "To Hell with the Allies." The CSC barred almost nine hundred persons from taking entrance examinations on grounds of questionable loyalty from 1917 to 1921.[26]

Under the Trading with the Enemy Act of October 6, 1917, foreign language newspapers were required to submit to the Post Office for approval, before mailing, translations of all material concerning the government and the war; newspapers which satisfied the President as to their loyalty could be exempted, however. As a result of the financial and editorial problems posed by such delays, by mid-1918, "practically every one of the German newspapers . . . was forced to either adopt a pro-government editorial policy or to maintain a judicious silence on war questions."[27] Scores of German-language newspapers ceased operations altogether as a result of the law. The combined effects of the Trading with the Enemy Act and the general hostility in the country to things German-American reduced the German-American press by 47 percent by the end of 1919; the number of German-language dailies dropped to twenty-six, less than half the prewar figure, and their circulation dropped by two-thirds to about two hundred fifty thousand. In states with a small German ethnic population, the destruction of the German language press was usually total.[28]

On October 16, 1918, Congress completed the legislative arsenal of repression by passing an immigration law which extended the concept of guilt by association, first introduced for the purpose of excluding and deporting individual anarchists and advocates of violence to cover all persons who were *members* of organizations which advocated unlawful destruction of property, or the forceful or violent overthrow of the government — a provision aimed squarely at the IWW. Under this law, and the provisions of the immigration law of February, 1917, a total of 687 persons were arrested for deportation by the end of the war. Of these, about 60 had been deported by November 1, 1918, another 88 were under deportation orders, and 162 had had their orders cancelled.[29] While aliens were the major target of action under the immigration laws, in some cases steps were taken to denaturalize naturalized citizens, also. For example, a German immigrant who had been naturalized in 1882 had his citizenship cancelled in 1917 after he refused to contribute to the Red Cross and the Young Men's Christian Association because he refused to do anything to harm his native land. The revocation was based on the contention that he had taken his oath of renunciation in 1882 with a mental reservation.[30]

The strength and scope of various "internal security" agencies was greatly increased during the war. As noted earlier, beginning in March, 1917, the War Department authorized local army officers to "sternly repress acts committed with seditious intent" and to protect "public utilities" essential to the war, criteria which were vague enough to soon cover the smashing of IWW strikes.[31] Military intelligence forces expanded from two officers in early 1917 to thirteen hundred officers and civilian employees by the end of the war, and similar increases occurred in the security agencies of the Justice, Post Office and Treasury Departments.[32] Military intelligence agents participated in a wide range of dubious activities, which involved a wholesale system of spying on civilians that would be unmatched in scope until the late 1960's. Military intelligence activities included surveillance of the IWW, the SPA, the pacifist Fellowship of Reconciliation and the National Civil Liberties Bureau, forerunner of the American Civil Liberties Union. In some cases, military intelligence infiltrated the ranks of groups under surveillance and participated in raids and arrests of radical organizations. Military intelligence investigated one southern governor for his alleged "radical" leanings, and broke one strike in Butte, Montana by an illegal raid and jailing without charges of over seventy IWW members. Later, it turned out that the Butte strike had apparently been provoked by undercover military intelligence officers working with Anaconda copper company detectives. One military intelligence officer recommended that a federal judge be replaced by a man who would be a "500 percent American."[33]

Certainly the most novel security force organized by the Wilson administration during the war was the American Protective League (APL), a privately-funded volunteer organization which operated with the endorsement of the Justice Department.[34] The official purpose of the APL, which numbered three hundred fifty thousand persons by the end of the war, was to help the government with such matters as food rationing and putting the conscription machinery into operation, along with specific intelligence operations such as investigating the loyalty of soldiers and governmental personnel and (when for the first time in American history passports were introduced in 1917) investigating the loyalty of Americans who wished to leave the country for any reason. However, the organization quickly became a largely out-of-control quasi-governmental, quasi-vigilante agency which established a massive spy network across the land. The relationship between the APL and the Justice Department and whether or not APL members had the right to make arrests was deliberately left vague, allowing APL operatives to claim they were an arm of the government and had the right to make arrests. Along with illegal arrests and detentions, APL agents instigated attacks on radicals and disrupted meetings of unions and socialists. Some APL members infiltrated radical organizations, and some burglarized, wiretapped, bugged and opened the mail of such groups. Beginning in January, 1918, APL operatives began to collect information "on all rumors current in their communities which they considered to be harmful to the interests of the United States in the prosecution of the war;" as a result by the autumn of that year "there were few actions or attitudes of American people which were not duly noted by the APL and referred either to the Justice Department or to the War Department."[35] The Justice Department did not impose even minimal controls on APL activity until late 1918.

The APL tended to be composed of the "upper social, economic and political crust of each community"[36] and this was frequently reflected in both its legal and illegal activities. Thus, the head of the APL urged his chief lieutenants to obtain financial support from leading businessmen "who usually are the ones benefited in a property sense by the protection afforded by our organization."[37] Some APL operatives acted as labor spies for employers, while others pressured colleges to fire radical professors and librarians to take suspect material off the shelves. John Roche's characterization of the APL as a "government-sponsored lynch-mob which proudly took the law into its own hands in summary and brutal fashion"[38] was accurate all too often.

APL members were active, along with Justice Department agents, local police and federal troops in so-called "slacker raids" which took part in many American cities between April and September, 1918.[39] During these raids, which were designed to detect persons who had failed to register for the draft, thousands of wholly innocent people were seized and often detained in jail cells overnight if they could not produce draft cards. Men were seized from street corners, railroad stations, hotels, theatres, streetcars, saloons, pool rooms and dance halls. Thus, in Chicago during three days of raids in July, 1918, an estimated one hundred fifty thousand men were interrogated and sixteen thousand were arrested on suspicion of being slackers, of whom twelve hundred (about 8 percent of those arrested) were found to be evaders and two hundred sixty-five (about 2 percent of those arrested) were found to be deserters. The most notorious slacker raids occurred in New York City in September, 1918. Over ten thousand persons (according to some reports, twenty thousand to forty thousand persons) were arrested during the raids; in one case the exists to a theatre were blocked and all playgoers who could not produce draft cards were arrested. Troops had to be called in to disperse crowds of anxious relatives gathered before an armory where some of the arrested men were held. Less than 1 percent of those arrested turned out to be draft dodgers. The New York raids caused an immense storm of criticism in the Senate. Sen. Albert Fall, a conservative who later went to jail during the Teapot Dome scandals, commented about the slacker raids, "Never in the history of any civilized country under the heavens, except in the history of Russia, could such acts have been committed."[40] Attorney General Gregory later said his orders against the use of APL men and military men making actual arrests had been ignored, but otherwise defended the raids; at the same time, for the first time the Justice Department clearly told APL members that they did not have arrest powers. APL slacker raids continued, using federal or local police to make the actual arrests. By the end of the war APL raids had netted about forty thousand "slackers," a figure suggesting that over four hundred thousand men were arrested in the course of the raids, since most of those arrested were later released.

Unauthorized and illegal activities by military intelligence and the APL were not unusual during the war, but even Justice Department agents, presumably under the direct control of Gregory, sometimes acted on their own. Thus, in September, 1918 Justice Department agents acting without Gregory's approval sacked the offices of the NCLB.[41]

Gregory's inability to control his subordinates was a common experience among high-ranking federal officials during the war. Secretary of Labor William B. Wilson repeatedly instructed officials of the Bureau of Immigration that aliens could not be arrested for deportation solely for IWW membership, but immigration officials, particularly in the Seattle area, continually violated these instructions.[42] Secretary of War Newton D. Baker took an extremely generous and lenient view on the treatment of conscientous objectors, but lower ranking military commanders repeatedly ignored his instructions and treated objectors with extreme brutality. CO's were sometimes severely beaten, placed in solitary confinement, handcuffed for hours to cell bars, fed only bread and water, pricked with bayonets and/or immersed head first in the filth of camp latrines. Pressure on the conscientous objectors at military camps was so severe that although 20,873 men arrived at camps with draft board certificates supporting their claims, eventually only 3,989 refused to accept any kind of military duty. Senator George W. Norris commented that if the reports he had received about treatment of the CO's were "anywhere near the truth . . . we are more barbarous in the treatment of these unfortunate men, than were the men of the Dark Ages in the treatment of their prisoners." Eventually, 540 objectors were court-martialled, while in England such persons received sentences which did not exceed two years. In the U.S. 17 were sentenced to death, 142 to life in prison, and 345 to jail terms averaging sixteen and one-half years. With the quick termination of the war, none of the death sentences or lengthy prison terms were carried out.[43]

While the APL, military intelligence, deportation arrests and summary internment of enemy aliens were widely used to suppress dissent, the Espionage and Sedition Acts and the use of federal troops were probably the most important federal weapons of repression. The application of the Espionage and Sedition Acts was a combination of random terror, and carefully directed prosecutions designed to destroy the IWW and the SPA. The random terror resulted from the fact that the Justice Department made no serious attempt until very late in the war to veto the attempts of overzealous local U.S. district attorneys to prosecute in questionable cases. Thus, prosecutions were highly related to the character of federal attorneys and varied greatly from area to area, with prosecutions in thirteen of the eighty-seven federal districts accounting for almost half of the total number of prosecutions.[44] In October 1918, President Wilson expressed concern to Attorney General Gregory that the failure to control local district attorneys had created the "danger of playing into the hands of some violently and maliciously partisan Republicans."[45] After the November, 1918, Congressional elections, in which Democrats lost heavily, CPI Director Greel wrote to Wilson that the election had turned out as it did because:

> All the radical or liberal friends of your anti-imperialist war policy were either silenced or intimidated. The Department of Justice and the Post Office were allowed to silence and intimidate them. There was no voice to argue for your sort of peace.[46]

Altogether, over twenty-one hundred were indicted under the Espionage and Sedition laws, invariably for statements of opposition to the war rather than for any overt acts, and over one thousand persons were convicted. Over one hundred persons were sentenced to jail terms of ten years or more. Not a single person was ever convicted for actual spy activities.[47]

Many espionage and sedition indictments were brought for making statements of a clearly innocuous nature, and in some cases prosecutions were brought as a result of statements made in private conversations. Men were prosecuted for making statements such as the following: "We must make the world safe for democracy, even if we have to bean the goddess of liberty to do it;" "Men conscripted to Europe are virtually condemned to death and everyone knows it;" "I am for the people and the government is for the profiteers." One man was sentenced to twenty years in prison for stating in a private conversation that atrocity stories were lies, that the war was "a rich man's war and the U.S. is simply fighting for money" and that he hoped the "government goes to hell so it will be of no value." Another man got twenty years for circulating a pamphlet urging the re-election of a Congressman who had voted against conscription. In Louisiana, a state senator was indicted for writing that profiteers would take advantage of the war to establish financial slavery. A northerner with a German name who exclaimed, "Damn such a country as this," when he found Florida's weather unexpectedly chilly was arrested for violating the Espionage Act, as was a Mennonite farmer whose religious principles would not permit him to support the war, on the grounds that he had desecrated the flag after a mob seized him and trampled on a flag which had been thrust into his hand and had fallen to the ground.[48]

The producer of a movie called "The Spirit of '76" was given ten years in jail after it was alleged that by showing British atrocities during the American Revolution he tended to raise questions about the good faith of America's war-time ally. Probably the single most incredible case was that of Walter Matthey of Iowa, who was sentenced to a year in jail, for, according to Attorney General Gregory, "attending a meeting, listening to an address in which disloyal utterances were made, applauding some of the statements made by the speaker claimed to be disloyal, their exact nature not being known and contributing 25¢."[49]

Many of the actions of the Post Office Department in denying the use of the mails to newspapers and other publications also smacked of random terrorism. The first newspaper Attorney General Albert Burleson removed from the mails (even before Wilson signed the Espionage Act) was the Halletsville, Texas, *Rebel*, which, coincidentally, had exposed the eviction of tenant farmers and their replacement by unpaid tenant labor in land Burleson owned.[50] Other publications that were barred including Lenin's *Soviets at Work*; an issue of *The Public*, for urging that more of the wartime budget be raised by taxation and less by loan; the *Freeman's Journal and Catholic Register*, for reprinting Jefferson's opinion that Ireland should be free; the *Irish World*, for stating that Palestine would be retained by Great Britain on the same footing as Egypt, and that the trend of French life and ideals for a century had been toward materialism; and NCLB pamphlets deploring mob violence and explaining the beliefs of conscientious objectors.[51] Altogether seventy-five papers were interfered with in one way or another.[52]

If much of the government's repressive activity seemed to be random terrorism, much of it was not. It was certainly not just happenstance that the two major anarchist publications, *Mother Earth*, and *Blast*, were quickly banned from the mails and that anarchist leaders Goldman and Berkman were jailed for conspiracy to violate the conspiracy act; that the editors of the *Messenger*, one of the few black publications that refused to back the war all-out were jailed and the paper banned from the mails; that the *Jeffersonian*, a paper published by the former Georgia populist leader Tom Watson was banned from the mails after receiving over $100,-000 in contributions to challenge the constitutionality of the conscription act; and that in raids and arrests throughout the country the entire executive committee of the Jehovah's Witnesses was convicted for their published opposition to the killing of any human being.[53]

Even the seemingly random prosecutions had a pattern behind them however; persons or publications "who had assured economic and social status, did not question the basis of our economic system, accepted the war as a holy crusade and expressed their views in somewhat temperate language" were allowed to criticize the government; those who suffered were "those whose views on the war were derived from some objectionable economic or social doctrines . . . regardless of their attitude towards Germany" along with obscure individuals who used "indiscreet or impolite, sometimes vulgar language to express their views."[54] Certainly the strong attacks made by many congressmen and leading newspapers about arms and ammunition shortages and inadequate housing in the army was bound to depress morale in the armed forces more than private statements made in opposition to the war, but somehow prominent newspapers and members of the two major parties never suffered at the hands of the Post Office and Justice Departments.[55]

The bias of federal repression was most clearly shown in the campaign of the federal government to destroy the IWW and the SPA. The power of the IWW became evident first, and the government made the IWW its first major target. IWW workers in the northwest lumber industry had organized close to 90 percent of the industry in many areas. A strike under IWW leadership, but with AFL support, paralyzed more than 75 percent of the lumber industry in western Washington in 1917, threatening the production of wood for airplanes and military construction. The lumber strike also affected areas of Oregon, Idaho and Montana, constituting the "most spectacular and widespread lumber strike ever to occur in the U.S."[56] At about the same time IWW organizers had achieved major strength in Arizona's copper mining areas and in the Butte, Montana, copper mines; strikes at these locations in June and July, 1917 severely threatened copper production.[57] Both the copper and lumber strikes were quickly blamed by the press and local officials on the alleged pro-German sympathies or domination of the IWW. In fact, there is absolutely no evidence that the strikes were part of an anti-war effort on the part of the IWW; instead, as President Wilson's own investigators reported, they resulted from "unremedied and remediable industrial disorders" which had their origins in the intransigent attitudes of employers.

While federal troops had been authorized as early as March to suppress acts "committed with seditious intent", they had also been instructed to confine their activities to preserving "law and order" and to protecting "life and property."[58] However, during the IWW strikes in the west, federal troops began a massive program of strike-breaking, including raids on IWW headquarters, breaking up meetings, arresting and detaining hundreds of strikers under military authority without any declaration of military law, and instituting a general reign of terror against the IWW. By July, federal troops were patrolling the mining regions of Arizona and Montana, agricultural areas in Eastern Washington and lumber districts in Washington and Oregon, although aside from vigilante and official violence against the IWW there had been no disorders in any of these areas. Federal troops remained in the Arizona and Montana copper camps until 1920 and 1921, breaking up attempted strikes and demonstrations, raiding union and IWW halls and illegally arresting and detaining miners. Federal troops under the command of Gen. Omar Bradley were particularly vicious in beating and arresting workers in Butte. By September, 1920, the army had put down twenty-nine domestic "disorders" without any resort to constitutional procedures.[59]

Despite the massive use of federal troops and arrests in the Pacific Northwest in 1917, lumber production essential for the production of airplanes remained stymied when IWW-influenced workers resorted to a "strike on the job," showing up for work but spending most of the time loafing and feigning ignorance of production methods. The IWW grievances, which were joined by a relatively weak AFL union, centered around demands for an eight-hour day and improvement in working conditions, which might be politely described as "primitive." Since the lumber operators absolutely refused to negotiate with the IWW or to budge on the eight-hour day issue, in order to restore lumber production, the federal government resorted to perhaps the most extraordinary experiment in American labor history — the creation of a government "union," known as the "Loyal Legion of Loggers and Lumbermen."[60] Centered around a core of thirty thousand soldiers, the Legion eventually enrolled about one hundred thousand lumberworkers and succeeded in restoring lumber production. The secret of the Legion was government coercion of both employers and employees. Only employers who agreed to work with the Legion were awarded government contracts, but in order to work with the Legion employers had to grant the eight-hour day and most of the other demands that had brought on the strike in the first place. On the other hand, in order to join the Legion, which meant in effect in order to work, lumbermen had to pledge their support of the War and to promise to "stamp out any sedition or acts of hostility against the United States Government which may come within my knowledge."[61] Wobblies who "behaved" were allowed to join the Legion, but recalcitrant radicals were barred from employment and frequently quickly drafted as a result of intensive intelligence activities by Army intelligence and close cooperation with local draft boards, which were closely linked with the APL. By the end of the war, the IWW in the Pacific Northwest had been severely disrupted while the Legion lumberworkers "gained entrance into the twentieth century, so far as working conditions were concerned."[62]

In the meantime, federal officials in Washington were planning "legal" maneuvers to destroy the rest of the IWW.[63] Postal authorities banned virtually all IWW literature from the mails, while the Justice Department, in July, 1917, began an intensive investigation looking towards prosecution of the IWW. On September 5, 1917, Justice Department agents and local police raided IWW headquarters in Chicago and forty-eight local halls along with IWW homes across the nation. Operating under "perhaps the broadest search warrant ever issued by the American judiciary,"[64] agents seized tons of material ranging from IWW mailing lists to rubber bands, love letters and pictures of Frank Little, an IWW organizer who had been lynched in Butte by vigilantes in July, 1917. Agents even seized several empty beer bottles when IWW Ralph Chapin convinced them the bottles were evidence of German influence. Raiding Chapin's home, they seized a number of dress patterns, explaining to his astonished wife that they suspected code messages in the perforation.

The raid itself paralyzed the organization for weeks, since IWW officials lacked the equipment necessary to carry out even routine operations, but the real blow fell three weeks later when a federal grand jury indicted over 166 IWW members on a five-count charge, which essentially amounted to the contention that the IWW strikes were a criminal conspiracy to interfere with the war effort and that IWW members had conspired to obstruct the draft and violate the espionage act. Subsequently, another 27 Wobblies in Kansas and Oklahoma, 46 in California and 64 in Nebraska were indicted on similar charges. The Kansas and Oklahoma arrests followed IWW organizational gains among local farmworkers and oil-field workers. Although the U.S. attorney for Kansas who was responsible for the arrests conceded to a Justice Department official that the arrests had been designed "largely as a preventative matter to prevent possible violence" Justice Department officials pressed the prosecution, eventually trying the men after they had been held in jail for two years under conditions that became a national scandal — one Justice Department inspector denounced the Wichita jail, where some of the defendants were held, as "unfit for an animal, let alone any human beings."[65] One reason the defendants were held so long was that the first two indictments drawn up by government officials were discarded or quashed; one Justice Department attorney conceded "it looks pretty bad to hold men in jail two years principally because the Government's attorneys are not capable of drawing up a good indictment."[66] Many of the California defendants were arrested during widespread round-ups of Wobblies in that state following a bomb explosion at the mansion of California's governor on December 17, 1917. A Justice Department investigation was unable to find any evidence connecting the IWW to the crime, and later federal officials discovered the bombing had been arranged by the San Francisco district attorney involved in the Mooney case who was seeking to keep the anti-radical issue boiling because he faced a recall election on the day after the bombing.[67] The arrested Wobblies were prosecuted nonetheless, after being held in jail for a year, during which time four defendants died from a nationwide flu epidemic. Although the Nebraska indictments were dropped after a year and a half, over 170 Wobblies were eventually convicted in the other cases, with many given jail terms of over ten years. By the end of the war, virtually all persons who had played any important part in IWW affairs had been arrested — not only the top leaders, but also second and third string leaders. Raids on IWW halls and arrests of Wobblies continued throughout the war.

The IWW trials were little short of farcical. Although the IWW as an organization was not officially on trial — only individual members charged with specific "crimes" of conspiracy — the only evidence against many defendants was their IWW membership. Thus, most of the Kansas and Oklahoma defendants were not even mentioned by name during their trial. While ultimately the charges hung on the contention that IWW activity was part of an anti-war conspiracy, virtually all of the defendants who were eligible for the draft had registered. Further, after American entry into the war, the IWW had toned down some of its more extreme propaganda concerning sabotage and direct action. The IWW as such had taken no position at all on the war, instead concentrating on organizational work. As Peterson and Fite have put it, "They simply had no interest in this particular war. They preferred to devote all their effort to the private war being carried on against employers."[68] The real reason for the repression of the IWW was not that it had opposed the war, but that it had "bad ideas" — the war merely served as excuse to smash an organization which was unwilling to accept the progressives' dream of class harmony.

The mass trial of 101 Wobblies in Chicago in May, 1918 was typical of other federal and state trials of the IWW during the war. Most of the evidence introduced in the trial concerned statements made by IWW officials, often dating back years before the commencement of the war.[69] One of the men convicted at Chicago, Vincent St. John, had had no connection with the IWW since 1915; another had been in jail for nine days prior to the passage of the espionage act and continuously thereafter. The jury eventually found each of the defendants guilty on four different counts after deliberating for less than an hour, or about nine seconds per count.

If the IWW was denied a fair trial inside the courtroom, federal repression of defense activities outside the courtroom was so severe that defense efforts were virtually paralyzed. IWW defense material was banned from the mails (including appeals for contributions), IWW defense offices were repeatedly raided, defense meetings were broken up and defense workers were arrested. In the northwest, immigration officials detained for deportation IWW aliens active in defense efforts. Several persons active in defense efforts in California were themselves indicted, while a man in Montana who expressed the belief that the IWW would win its case in Chicago was convicted for sedition, before being freed on appeal. When the *New Republic* carried an advertisement calling for a fair trial for the IWW, Justice Department agents told the magazine not to reprint it under threat of getting into difficulty with the law; the ad did not appear again. It was symptomatic of the government's campaign against the IWW that an IWW resolution *against* sabotage was barred from the mails because it used the word "sabotage."[70]

The IWW was not the only organization to suffer severely from federal repression. Shortly after the espionage act was passed in June, Postmaster General Burleson began to ban major socialist papers such as *The American Socialist, Masses* and the *Milwaukee Leader* from the mails. In September, the SPA national headquarters in Chicago was raided and occupied by federal agents for three days, and many crucial files were confiscated. A number of important socialist figures were arrested and jailed before the November, 1917 elections — arrests which frequently served to highly disrupt election activity and in some cases to actually incarcerate SPA candidates. Those arrested and in some cases jailed before November, 1917, included the state secretary of the SPA in West Virginia; the general secretary of the party in Philadelphia; the three top SPA leaders in Ohio, including Charles E. Ruthenberg, candidate for mayor of Cleveland; Kate Richards O'Hare, former national SPA secretary; a former SPA candidate for governor of South Dakota; a SPA candidate for congress in Oklahoma and the SPA candidate for governor of New Jersey.[71]

Truly severe repression of the SPA by the federal governments only began after the tremendous socialist gains recorded in the November, 1917 elections, however.[72] In the months after the election sedition indictments were returned against virtually every major SPA leader, except for Morris Hillquit, who had been hospitalized for tuberculosis. The most important case was the indictment of five national SPA leaders in February, 1918, including Victor Berger, head of the strong SPA machine in Milwaukee and then a candidate for the U.S. Senate; party secretary Adolph Germer; Louis Engdahl, editor of the official SPA newspaper; William Kruse, secretary of the Young People's Socialist League; and Irwin St. John Tucker, a major SPA pamphleteer. They were sentenced to twenty years each before being freed by the Supreme Court in 1921. Other major socialists indicted after the elections included former socialist candidates for governor and senator in Minnesota; Socialist leader Scott Nearing and the American Socialist Society, for publication of an anti-war pamphlet; the state secretary of the Washington State SPA, given ten years after appearing as a defense witness for another socialist; Socialist leader Rose Pastor Stokes, who made the error of rejoining the party after quitting it earlier in disagreement with its anti-war stand; and the single most well-known SPA leader, Eugene Debs, given ten years for making an anti-war speech.[73]

Meanwhile, the post office campaign against the socialist press continued, until by the end of the war virtually the entire socialist press had been banned from the mails. In August, 1918, the SPA ordered a halt to the printing of a handbook, because, Hillquit wrote, "The mails are so suppressed I don't believe it is worth the money."[74] The editor of the Otter Valley, Oklahoma, *Socialist,* which came under federal investigation and was the victim of an unexplained fire, concluded that it was "quite useless to expect reasonableness during the present crisis"; terming the 1918 Sedition law the most "drastic piece of legislation since . . . even the ancient code of Hammurabi," he advised "each and all to remain silent upon the matters of war" if "your opinions" are "at variance with the now established ideas."[75]

Fear of government repression led to the total collapse of the SPA in Oklahoma, where the party had one of its strongest branches. Oklahoma had been the scene in August, 1917, of the so-called "Green Corn Rebellion," the only major incident during the war of an attempted armed rebellion against American war policy. The "rebellion" involved a pathetic and bungled attempt by a group of bewildered farmers to blow up bridges and march to Washington. The revolt's leaders were sentenced to three to ten years in prison after trials in which all socialists were barred from the juries. Although the SPA itself was not involved in the affair, an emergency convention of the Oklahoma state party decided to dissolve the party after the indictment of Berger and other national party leaders, for fear that the federal government would seek to establish a connection between the SPA's anti-war stand and the rebellion.[76]

In at least two cases, Federal repression of the SPA backfired on the Wilson administration. As a result of the Russian Revolution of November, 1917, the German attack on Russia in February, 1918, and the announcement of Wilson's Fourteen Points in January, 1918 — and also no doubt as a result of repression — many SPA members had begun to moderate their opposition to the war by early 1918. Serious consideration was even given to holding a convention of the party to reconsider SPA war policies; however, this convention was never held because the administration was then stepping up its repression and it was decided that any attempt to hold a convention or a referendum would run into opposition from the Wilson administration.[77]

Another example of backfiring repression was the Wilson administration's refusal to grant passports to allow SPA members to attend the proposed Stockholm conference of allied socialist parties scheduled for the fall of 1917. The conference was never held, because other allied governments followed Wilson's lead and also withheld passports. The result was that the moderate socialist forces that would have been represented at Stockholm were weakened and unable to present a united and moderate peace position, which would have come close to Wilson's own position, while the extreme right-wing forces among the allies who opposed any compromise peace and the extreme left-wing socialists who would have boycotted the conference were both strengthened. The strengthening of the left in Russia helped bring about the Bolshevik revolution.[78] As Merle Fainsod has explained:

One of the reasons for the failure of the Provisional Government in Russia was its inability or unwillingness to bring peace to a war-weary people. The Stockholm Conference represented a step in this direction. . . . The refusal of the Allied Powers to permit this conference to assemble and the supine acquiesence of the Provisional Government in this refusal drove the peace-hungry masses toward the extreme Left, which whatever its political or economic views, at least promised an immediate end to the bloodshed. The failure of the Stockholm conference to assemble thus combined with other domestic factors to lift the Bolsheviks into a position of supremacy.[79]

Aside from the IWW and the SPA, another organization which felt the force of federal repression was the People's Council. Council propaganda was banned from the mails almost immediately. At one point, the council published a facsimile of a Russian peace appeal, along with the note: "The original copy of the Bulletin from which this reproduction is made was smuggled over to this country — though not as in the old days — smuggled *out of* Russia, but as in these strange new days — smuggled *into* America!"[80] CPI chairman Creel worked behind the scenes to have pro-war organizations pass resolutions condemning the People's Council as pro-German and disloyal, while Justice Department agents regularly attended its meetings to prosecute seditious speakers. Thus, at a rally in San Francisco in August, 1917, the city attorney was arrested by federal agents for sedition. A pacifist soldier caught distributing Council propaganda in the army was charged under the espionage act. In October, 1917, Council headquarters were raided by federal agents. By April, 1918 the Council's executive secretary complained that federal censorship of the mails was so complete that he could scarcely mail a single letter; as a result of the censorship and federal and local harassment, the Council abandoned its activities shortly before the end of the war.[81]

The "Labor Deal"

While the federal government was busy suppressing those organizations which threatened to inject the labor movement with radical ideas, it was busy rubbing elbows with the AFL.[82] The federal government and the AFL in effect worked out an agreement during the war, by which the AFL agreed to support the government's war policies, the government agreed to support pro-AFL labor policies, and both joined together "into an alliance to crush radical labor groups such as the IWW."[83] The AFL was motivated by fear of repression if it did not back the government and hopes for government aid if it did.

Before and even after the outbreak of the War in Europe, Gompers had been a pacifist, and while the Wilson administration maintained a policy of neutrality the AFL likewise maintained that position. Gompers condemned the war as a conflict of "aggrandizement and conquest"[84] whose only aim was to divert the attention of people from domestic problems and demoralize organized labor so it would no longer be a threat to entrenched powers. However, in January, 1916, one month after Wilson had stressed the need for preparedness and the suppression of disloyalty in his state of the union message, Gompers suddenly became a public advocate of preparedness. In October, 1916, Gompers accepted a position as labor representative to an advisory commission of the major government preparedness organ, the Council on National Defense. In February, 1917, Gompers told the AFL executive council that if the AFL did not back the administration's war policies, the government might "as a consequence" have to impose its will on workers and plans for organized workers would be composed by men "out of touch with the labor movement and out of sympathy with the needs and ideals of workers."[85] Put more plainly, Gompers feared that if labor attempted to obstruct the war, "the results would be disastrous for the AFL."[86] In March, 1917, a special conference of the AFL and some independent unions, the "result of a collusive arrangement between leaders of the AFL and elements in the Wilson administration for the specific purposes of stemming the growing tide of opposition to a foreign policy that might involve the U.S. in the European conflict, and at the same time, solidly aligning labor with any policy pursued by the Administration in Washington,"[87] adopted a position of full support of the government in case of war, but in turn requested a number of concessions from the government to the labor movement — most of which were granted after entry into the war. Since there were widespread fears among government and business leaders over the loyalty of organized labor, the AFL declaration reassured these leaders "at a critical time" and "considerably increased" Gomper's prestige, "a fact which gave great pleasure to the AF of L leader, who throve on social approval."[88] After U.S. entry into the war, Gompers termed the conflict "the most wonderful crusade ever entered upon by men in the whole history of the world" and "the greatest event in human history since the creation."[89]

After U.S. entry into the war, AFL representatives were included on many wartime committees, and the conservative labor movement was granted by the federal government concessions unknown before in American history. In return for an AFL no-strike policy, by April, 1918, labor had been granted the right to organize into trade unions and bargain collectively through its elective representatives, business was barred from firing workers for union membership and activities, and the right of all workers to an eight-hour day where feasable and to a "living wage" was recognized. These concessions "marked the greatest advance unions had made so far in gaining acceptance on the American scene."[90] By September, 1918, the *New Republic* was reporting that "no important measure vitally affecting labor is now taken without consultation" with Gompers.[91] At the same time, the AFL, by agreeing to the no-strike policy, by foregoing any demand for the closed or union shop and by adhering to a tacit agreement with the Wilson administration not to attempt major organizing drives in unorganized industries, such as steel, failed in many cases to "obtain better working conditions for their membership when their economic power would easily have enabled them to do so . . . with the result that the federation became more of an agency for the government than an advocate of the working class."[92]

The Wilson administration repeatedly and publicly expressed its backing for the AFL — for example, Wilson became the first president to speak at an AFL convention in 1917, and in his speech praised Gomper's "patriotic courage, his large vision and his statesmanlike sense of what has to be done." At the same time, Gompers cleverly played on the administration's fear of growing radical influence in the labor movement by "raising the terrifying possibility that, if concessions were not made to him, his influence would be greatly diminished and his following would gradually drift into the camp of the pacifists and socialists."[93] Thus, in August 1917, Gompers wrote to Wilson that the government and employers would have to "deal with the representative of the bona fide organized constructive labor movement of the country or they will have the alternative of being forced to take the consequences of the so-called IWW with all that implies."[94] In May, 1918, Gompers proclaimed that "if it had not been for the AF of L during the war, you would have had the Bolsheviki in the U.S."[95]

Because most of socialist-dominated unions in the AFL backed the war effort, the war seriously disrupted socialist influence in the labor movement, but as in the case of the AFL as a whole, there is strong evidence that the stand of the socialist-dominated unions partly reflected fear of repression if the war was opposed and guarantees of government help if the war was supported. Thus, "it was particularly difficult, for instance, for the Machinists' Union to maintain its radical stand, since it occupied an important place in the armaments industry and was fearful of being considered disloyal"[96] while the heavily German-American Brewers' Union became considerably more conservative from 1917 to 1920 "when the German-American community was under tremendous pressure to conform to accepted American values" and after the editor of the union paper was almost arrested for criticism of the conduct of the war.[97] Officials of the Amalgamated Clothing Workers took steps to curb the expression of anti-war views after reports circulated that the union newspaper was being investigated by postal authorities due to its anti-war stand. Thus, union executive Frank Rosenblum wrote that there were "enough forces in and out of the labor movement seeking to destroy the Amalgamated without getting the U.S. Government on the job to assist them."[98] Further criticism of the war effort by the ACW ceased and "as a result, it got an official agreement which afforded the union its great opportunity to complete organization of the men's clothing industry."[99]

Throughout the entire period of the war, the AFL prospered as a result of favorable governmental policies and its support of the war, while the IWW was devastated by governmental repression. Although there were hundreds of AFL strikes including many in war-related industries, somehow the AFL was never accused of being disloyal and was never subjected to mass raids and arrests, while the radical IWW, responsible for far fewer strikes, was subjected to savage repression. AFL membership rose from 2.4 million in January, 1917, to 3.3 million, in January, 1919. Not once did the AFL protest the treatment of the IWW, its prime rival for the loyalties of American labor. In fact, the AFL even endorsed the Espionage and Sedition acts. In California, scene of some of the most vicious repression of the IWW, the state federation of labor publicly condemned the IWW and recommended the expulsion of all IWW members from AFL unions. The AFL representative on the Washington state council of defense favored the use of federal troops against the IWW, which had proved embarassingly more attractive to lumber workers in that state than had the AFL.[100]

Evidence of the AFL-federal coalition against the IWW is clearly demonstrated in a number of unusual developments during the war. Following federal raids on IWW halls, Justice Department officials furnished the AFL with IWW membership lists to help the AFL weed out radicals from its ranks; in turn Gompers placed AFL men on the Justice Department payroll to act as agents and informers to help the government ferret out "subversives."[101] When *The Nation* criticized Gompers in one of its issues, it was barred from the mails until President Wilson personally intervened; Solicitor Gerald W. H. Lamar told the *Nation's* editors that Gompers had rendered "inestimable service to this government during this war in holding labor in line" and "we are not going to allow any newspaper in this country to attack him."[102] The President's Mediation Commission report on the 1917 copper strikes in Arizona, which had involved both AFL and IWW unions, concluded that the strikes were not a result of seditious sentiment but resulted from increased living costs and managements' attempts to speed-up production. Nevertheless, the commission's settlement barred the rehiring of any miner who spoke disloyally against the government or who belonged to an organization which refused to recognize time contracts — i.e. the IWW. A federal representative in Washington state similarly openly sought to bolster AFL organizing while blocking the IWW.[103]

The culmination of the government-AFL alliance against radicalism was the formation of the American Alliance for Labor and Democracy (AALD), an organization formed by the AFL with the financial support of and under the direction of CPI chairman George Creel, for the purpose of counteracting the alarming rise of anti-war sentiment among American workers and fighting Gomper's foes within the labor movement. While the public was led to believe that Administration support of the AALD was limited only to funding, in fact Creel controlled the entire organization and personally suggested AALD resolutions and approved its literature. The AALD was in effect a "government front" group in which federal funds were used "to support a particular trade union and its philosophy against its opponents."[104] Acting behind the AALD shield, Creel put out resolutions and literature which left no phrase unturned to "point out to the laborer a golden opportunity to ingratiate himself with the nation" and promising "golden days for men who toil" in response to labor backing of the war, while terming anti-war forces "disloyal" and "un-American" as well as "attempting to incite sedition," abusing "the rights of free speech, free assemblage and a free press" and rendering "every possible aid and comfort to the brutal Prussian autocracy."[105] Using government funds, AALD even attempted to prevent the People's Council from meeting in Minneapolis by renting all available halls.[106]

State and Local Repression of the Anti-War Movement

While repression on the federal level was severely debilitating for anti-war groups and individuals, dissidents also faced savage repression on the local and state level. In many cases, such repression took the form of mob attacks — the NCLB listed 164 such attacks during a two-year period beginning April 1, 1917.[107] While such mob attacks cannot be termed governmental repression per se, in many such incidents local officials either participated or stood by while violence occurred. The major targets of state and local repression and of vigilante activities were German-Americans, the IWW, the SPA, the People's Council and the NPL. There were scores of incidents throughout the country in which German-Americans were coerced into buying liberty bonds, forced to kiss the American flag, and/or beaten, whipped or humiliated.

In one notorious incident, Robert Prager, a German immigrant who had sought, unsuccessfully, to enlist in the U.S. Navy, was lynched at Collinsville, Illinois on April 5, 1918. German churches and the homes of German-Americans were vandalized and several German parochial schools were destroyed by fire and dynamite. In Yankton County, South Dakota, when the local Liberty Loan Committee was dissatisfied with the liberty loan contribution of $30,000 made by a colony of Hutterites, a squad of patriots invaded the colony, seized twelve hundred steer and sheep and sold them for $16,000 which was used to buy bonds in the name of the Hutterites. In scores of communities, German names for streets, parks and schools were changed, German music was banned, and teaching of the German language was forbidden in the schools. In some communities, German language books were burned, and in dozens of areas and in the entire state of Louisiana the use of the German language was forbidden in public.[108]

Among radical organizations, the IWW was the single greatest target of state and local repression, suffering deportations, trumped-up arrests, and beatings at official and unofficial hands throughout the country.[109] To give only a few examples, IWW members were forcibly deported from the towns of Ray, Bisbee, Jerome, Kingman, Ash Fork, Choloride, Galconda, Mineral, and Tucson, Arizona; Gallup, New Mexico; Aberdeen, South Dakota; River Rouge, Michigan; Fairbury and Lincoln, Nebraska; and Bemidji, Minnesota, during the summer of 1917 alone. On August 29, 1917, an IWW organizer was hung to a tree until he was unconscious in Franklin, New Jersey by the chief of police and a mob of businessmen.[110] On February 12, 1918, a mob tarred and feathered two suspected IWW sympathizers at Staunton, Illinois and then dragged suspected pro-Germans from their beds and forced them to kiss the flag. The chief of police at Staunton stated that all patrolmen were busy looking for chicken thieves and none were available to stop the mobs.[111] On November 7, 1917, seventeen alleged IWW members who had been convicted on trumped-up charges in Tulsa, Oklahoma, were handed over by police to a mob which stripped, beat and tarred and feathered them.[112] IWW defense activities were frequently the target of repression from local authorities. Thus, the defense office in San Francisco was raided seven times in six months, and its secretary, a paid employee, was arrested fifteen times in four months on vagrancy charges.[113]

Probably the most spectacular acts of local repression were the deportation of about sixty IWW strikers from the copper town of Jerome, Arizona, on July 10, 1917 by local vigilantes, and the deportation of twelve hundred peaceful strikers, including hundreds of both AFL and IWW members, from the copper town of Bisbee, Arizona, two days later. The Bisbee deportation was organized by the local sheriff, and carried out by about one thousand deputized citizens. Deportations from the Bisbee area continued until November, 1917; deportees trying to return were either deported again or arrested for vagrancy. Many of those deported had bought liberty bonds and were registered with the draft. The Arizona repression destroyed unionism in the copper mines there until the New Deal.[114] IWW strikes in Clearwater and Latah Counties, Idaho, and IWW organizational activity throughout North Dakota were broken when local authorities simply rounded up and arrested IWW members. In Fargo, North Dakota, nationally known journalist and IWW organizer Max Eastman's planned street meeting was disrupted by the North Dakota National Guard; when Eastman moved his meeting inside, the guard stormed into the hall and again silenced him as he was speaking to a packed house.[115]

The Socialist Party was also a frequent target of severe local repression and vigilante activity. Socialist speakers in many places had difficulty renting halls for meetings, had meetings broken up by local police and met physical violence from vigilantes. Perhaps the most publicized vigilante incident involving the SPA was the kidnapping and severe beating of Rev. Herbert S. Bigelow, a prominent clergyman and progressive, shortly before he was to address a Socialist anti-war meeting in Newport, Kentucky, in October, 1917. Three weeks before the kidnapping, Justice Department agents had raided Bigelow's church in Cincinnati looking for subversive materials.[116] The effects of official and vigilante harassment were most severe on SPA locals in smaller cities and towns that were particularly exposed and tended to have the strongest roots among native Americans. At a joint meeting of state secretaries of the party and the National Executive Committee in August, 1918, the state secretaries reported one long tale of disasters as a result of local repression, with reports from parties in the southern and western states indicating it was practically impossible for locals to function. Thus the state secretaries in Colorado and Arkansas both reported they were too scared to distribute literature and similar tales were reported from other states.[117]

Socialist meetings were banned in most counties of Minnesota by the governor, while all Socialist anti-war meetings were banned in Philadelphia. State and local police raided the state headquarters of the SPA in Indiana, Ohio and other states, and broke up the state convention in South Dakota. Three elected members of the Cleveland city council were expelled when they refused to pledge support for the war.[118]

The People's Council also ran into severe local repression. The governor of Minnesota refused to allow the Council to meet anywhere in the state, the governor of Wisconsin ordered the Council barred from meeting in Milwaukee, Washington, D.C. police barred the Council from meeting in the streets of the nation's capital, and when the mayor of Chicago invited the Council to meet there, the Governor of Illinois sent troops to disperse the meeting. However, by the time the troops burst into the auditorium where the Council had been meeting, they discovered only a wedding party, as Council members had concluded their meeting for the day and subsequently met in private. Similar difficulties were encountered in many other areas by the Council. Thus, the Board of Regents of the University of Texas voted unanimously in July, 1917, to fire a political scientist who had helped to found the Council.[119]

Non-affiliated radicals and supporters of civil liberties also frequently ran into governmental repression. Thus, the University of Virginia fired a journalism professor for making a pacifist speech. The teaching certificate of an Oklahoma teacher was revoked when an IWW songbook was found in her classroom. A college teacher at Southwestern College in Oklahoma was fired for holding allegedly pro-German sentiments, then reinstated when it was discovered that the reports had originated with students who were disgruntled with their grades. A number of teachers were fired in New York City and elsewhere in the state for alleged disloyalty. In Montana, a state judge was impeached and convicted by the state legislature after testifying in defense of a man charged under the federal espionage act. Individuals suspected of anti-war sentiments were the targets of mob attacks throughout the country.[120]

While for the most part state and local repression of anti-war forces took place without the benefit of any legal process whatsoever, aside from trumped-up charges such as vagrancy and disorderly conduct, many states and localities did pass special laws for use against anti-war forces. During 1917-18, seven states and territories passed criminal syndicalism or sedition laws, aimed primarily at silencing the IWW, while eleven states passed laws which specifically barred various types of opposition to the war. These laws were particularly common in western states which were the targets of IWW and NPL activity. In seven states and territories such laws were passed before Congress passed the 1917 Espionage Act.[121]

The criminal syndicalism and sedition laws tended to be modelled after Idaho's March, 1917 law while the war opposition statutes outlawed activities ranging from speaking against the war to attempting to persuade people not to work in war-related industries and not to enlist in the army. Under Minnesota's law, which barred statements opposing enlistment in the armed forces or opposing aid to the U.S. during the war, it was held to be a crime to discourage women from knitting by making the remark, "No soldier ever sees these socks."[122]

Many cities passed their own laws to suppress criticism of the war. About half of the cities in Oklahoma passed anti-sedition laws, as did the city council in Kalispell, Montana. Portland, Oregon, passed a law barring display of the red flag, while Spokane, Washington, passed its own criminal syndicalism law. The city council in Duluth, Montana passed a law which defined vagrancy as "advocating the duty, necessity or propriety of crime or violence as a means of accomplishing industrial or political ends."[123] The city councils in Nampa and Pocatello, Idaho passed ordinances which either completely forbade street assemblies or permitted public assemblies only with the city's consent; similar laws were passed in other Idaho towns and the ordinances "generally were enforced and succeeded in stifling much of the anti-war 'agitation' to which so many Idahoans objected."[124]

The total of arrests and convictions under state and local anti-radical laws is not known, but clearly reached into the many hundreds, if not thousands. In the eight months following the passage of criminal syndicalism and sedition laws by Montana in February, 1918, there were 134 arrests and 52 convictions.[125] In Idaho, there were over 200 arrests and 31 convictions during 1917-18 under the criminal syndicalism law passed there in March, 1917; the law there "played a crucial role in encouraging repression of radical and sometimes not so radical activity and rhetoric."[126]

The motivation behind the passage of the criminal syndicalism and other state and local repressive laws (as well as behind the federal Espionage and Sedition legislation) was clearly to provide a means of incarcerating people who had "bad" ideas but who could never be found actually doing anything that would normally be considered criminal. Thus, in discussing Michigan' criminal syndicalism law (passed during the 1919 Red Scare), Robert J. Mowitz notes:

> The initial reaction of law enforcement officials to the criminal syndicalism law was one of quiet satisfaction that these foreign menaces might now be controlled. Previously there had been a puzzling inability to detain the evil fellows. Apparently everyone knew that they were dangerous to American democracy. But, unfortunately, it rarely seemed possible to prove that they ever did anything. They merely talked — or, in the words of the statute, "advocated" and "taught" their beliefs. If they had moved from expressing an opinion to acting upon it, the police would have been amply armed by law to deal with them. The rascals stubbornly failed to behave criminally.[127]

Probably the single most effective instrument of anti-radical repression on the state and local levels were the so-called councils of defense. Organized on the state, county and town level under the direction of the federal Council on National Defense (CND), the councils of defense constituted a network of officially sponsored patriotic organizations that covered the entire country. While some of the councils had statutory authority received from the state legislature, most of them were simply created by appointment of the state governor. Especially in the west, many of the state councils had wide discretionary powers, which in some states, such as Minnesota and Montana, amounted practically to the establishment of a dictatorship consisting of a handful of men. Invariably, the makeup of the state and local councils of defense reflected the most well-to-do and conservative segments of the community — for example the Oregon state council was dominated by lumbermen, while the North Carolina and Oklahoma state and local councils were dominated by lawyers, bankers, doctors and businessmen. The councils' makeup was generally similar to that of the APL, and frequently the two groups cooperated or overlapped.[128]

While supposedly non-partisan and operating under the general supervision of the CND, the councils were in fact controlled by the party in power in each state, and frequently exercised complete autonomy, sometimes even working at cross purposes with the national administration. The North Carolina council's cooperation was generous and unreserved with policies which reinforced rather than altered the existing social order, but federal reforms in areas such as child labor or racial areas met resistance. In Wisconsin, the state council was so clearly under Republican control that Wilson ordered the CPI to work instead with a patriotic organization set up by Wisconsin Democrats. In Minnesota the council banned NPL speakers, including those sponsored by the CPI, at a time when the Wilson administration was seeking to forge a political alliance with the NPL. While the CND and the CPI encouraged the use of the German language to reach those Americans who could not understand English, many state councils demanded the suppression of the German language press or the banning of the use of German. The Connecticut council condemned any peace negotiations except on the basis of unconditional surrender at a time when Wilson was negotiating with Germany over possible peace terms in the fall of 1918.[129]

Many of the state and local councils embarked on repressive programs of the most dubious legality. The Minnesota and South Dakota councils suggested that persons who had refused to buy enough liberty bonds be subpoenaed and investigated. The Montana State Council ordered public schools in that state to cease using a textbook which allegedly depicted German tribes prior to the year 812 A.D. in too favorable a light; at the time of this action the textbook's author was helping the CPI. The Cleveland County, Oklahoma, council erected a "slacker pen" and announced that those who "failed to do their duty" during a war stamp drive would be thrown in it and held until they changed their minds. The Fairview, Oklahoma, Council sold the car of a "bond slacker" and then gave the owner thirty days to either claim the bonds or see them given to the Red Cross. The Washington and Montana Councils organized secret service systems while the Minnesota Council organized a private military force of fifty thousand men who led a vigilante campaign against Wobblies and other non-conformists. The Nevada council kept a tight reign on IWW and NPL members by strictly enforcing an order which barred citizens from joining "disloyal" organizations. Some Idaho county councils attempted to create card index files for the entire population; scores of persons subsequently classified as "disloyal" were required by the councils to apologize for their behavior, purchase generous amounts of Liberty bonds and make large donations to the Red Cross or similar agencies. The Nebraska council demanded that twelve professors at the University of Nebraska be fired for their attitudes towards the war; three of them eventually were. State and/or local councils in Minnesota, Iowa and Wisconsin demanded that the U.S. Senate expel Robert LaFollette for his alleged disloyalty. The Montana council publicly opposed the reappointment of U.S. District Attorney Burton K. Wheeler as a result of his alleged "softness" towards anti-war forces and conducted a lengthy public hearing designed to intimidate Wheeler and the editors of a pro-labor newspaper published in Butte. The North Dakota Council virtually outlawed strikes and IWW organizational activity by promulgating "work-or-fight" rules which required every man between eighteen and fifty to be either employed or registered with an employment agency; local law officials enforced the rules by arresting men who refused jobs for vagrancy.[130]

Probably abuses of the state councils were the most notorious and state and local repression was most severe in Minnesota. This was no coincidence — Minnesota lumber and mining areas had been a prime target of IWW organizers and Minnesota was the key target of NPL organizers during the war.[131] It is no exaggeration to state that Minnesota held the key to the future of the NPL, due to its critical role in the financial structure of midwestern agriculture.

The Minnesota version of the state council, the Commission on Public Safety (CPS) exercised virtually dictatorial powers and together with its subordinate bodies instituted a literal reign of terror against the NPL. Although the NPL had publicly passed resolutions supporting the war during May and June, 1917, and the NPL-controlled state of North Dakota was the first state to oversubscribe its Liberty bond quota, the CPS publicly suggested that the NPL was disloyal, along with socialists, pro-Germans and members of the People's Council. Conservative forces in Minnesota, who were well represented on the CPS, particularly feared that an NPL victory in the 1918 state elections might duplicate the situation in North Dakota. More than one NPL meeting was broken up by the CPS military force, the Home Guard, while NPL meetings were completely banned in twenty-one Minnesota counties, usually by the local PSC, although in some cases by regularly constituted local officials. The

Faribault Country PSC threatened to burn the building the NPL had rented for a meeting. Under pressure from the PSC, an allegedly disloyal political science professor was fired from the University of Minnesota, and the mayor and city attorney of New Ulm were removed by the governor after they permitted an anti-war meeting.[132]

In March, 1918, four of the NPL's best organizers, including NPL president A.C. Townely were indicted for offenses ranging from unlawful assembly to conspiracy to violate the Minnesota sedition act. Mob violence in Minnesota, unrestrained by state and local officials, repeatedly made NPL spokesmen its target; on one occasion a defense witness in an NPL trial was kidnapped by a mob at gunpoint. The NPL candidate for governor, Charles Lindbergh, father of the famed aviator, was dragged from the speaker's platform by mobs several times, and was indicted for violation of the state sedition law two weeks before the primary election. Although the NPL did win many legislative races in Minnesota, the defeat of Lindbergh in the Republican primary by a vote of about two hundred thousand to one hundred fifty thousand, together with the loss of all NPL state-wide candidates, dealt the NPL a blow from which it never recovered.[133] According to a recent study of the NPL, in "any ordinary year" Lindbergh would have won "a decisive victory."[134]

The NPL suffered lesser, but sometimes severe, harassment in other states. In Nebraska, where the NPL had picked up fifteen to twenty thousand members by 1918, the State Council of Defense attempted to destroy the organization, declaring the NPL was not "in harmony with the government's purpose." Several Nebraska county councils banned NPL meetings and ordered NPL organizers to "get out," and after Nebraska's attorney general declared NPL organizers were "not engaged in useful occupations" NPL workers were subject to arrest.[135] In July, 1918, the Nebraska NPL reached an agreement with the state council allowing them to pursue electoral activities, but only if the NPL withdrew out-of-state organizers and ended circulation of all NPL propaganda, including President Wilson's *New Freedom*. According to recent studies of the NPL in Nebraska, the actions of the state and local councils caused "irreparable damage" to the "NPL's work and its image"[136] and had a "determinant effect upon the fortunes of the league."[137] NPL members also occasionally suffered from trumped-up arrests, mob attacks, meeting bans and other forms of legal and extra-legal harassment in Iowa, Texas, Montana, South Dakota, Washington, Colorado and Idaho.[138]

Effects of World War I Repression

The repression of the NPL during World War I was by no means the only reason for its rapid decline after 1918, but it was probably the most crucial reason.[139] Had the NPL won the state of Minnesota in 1918, as it appeared likely to do, it seems fair to say that the entire history of the agricultural midwest might have been very different. With control of both Minnesota and North Dakota, the NPL would likely have continued to expand throughout the midwest, and, possibly, recapitulating the days of the southern-middle western Populist alliance, into the south as well. But the defeat in the 1918 primary proved crucial, and the NPL never recovered from it. As Russell Nye has written "the war killed the League" and by 1920 it was "no longer a major force in Northwest politics."[140]

By the end of the war, the IWW was similarly dead as an effective factor in American society. At the beginning of the war the IWW was a flourishing and vigorous labor organization; by the end of the war it had been transformed into little more than a defense committee, "combating writs, government lawyers and judges" rather than "lumber barons, mine owners, and wheat farmers."[141] The attack of the federal and local governments, along with those of vigilantes, totally disrupted the IWW leadership, dispersed its membership and destroyed IWW locals. By the end of the war, the strong organizations that had been built up in the northwestern lumber industry and the Arizona and Montana copper mines were no more. The few remnants of the IWW that remained — largely in California and Washington — would continue to suffer severe repression after the war ended. But the spirit of the IWW had already been crushed, the "victim of the most systematic campaign of extermination in American history."[142]

The SPA was not dead at the end of the war, but it had been severely weakened and its geographical and national composition had been severely distorted. Some writers have persisted in stating or implying that the party's anti-war stand led to a lessened popularity with the American people,[143] while the facts clearly show that the party gained in strength and popularity as a result of its anti-war stand, until the campaigns of repression against it by mobs and the federal and local government became too strong. The party did decline in 1918, from a membership of about one hundred thousand in March to eighty-three thousand in August, and the party press was in an almost complete state of collapse, due to the arrests, mob attacks and suppression of the press.[144] As David Shannon has concluded, "It was not until the mob persecution, the governmental prosecutions and the suppression of socialist newspapers in 1918 that the party began to wane."[145]

As Gabriel Kolko notes, "At the very moment American Socialism appeared on the verge of significant organizational and political success, it was attacked by the combined resources of the Federal and various state governments."[146] While many American historians have suggested the party failed because it refused to adapt its radical ideology to American realities, Kolko suggests that the party suffered because it naively believed that it would be treated fairly by the political authorities if it played by the democratic rules. "American radicals accepted this mythology and tried to play the game according to rules that were quite irrelevent to social and political reality, a reality that was obscured until the exercise of nominal political rights threatened to become unmanageable."[147]

Even more serious in the long run than the general weakening of the SPA was the pattern of this weakening. Mob assaults and local repression and the suppression of the party press all took their greatest toll in smaller cities and towns and rural areas where party locals were most vulnerable, most dependent on the press for contacts with the national organization, and also most heavily concentrated among native Americans and therefore most squarely in the tradition of indigenous American radicalism. Of the five thousand SPA party locals existing in 1917, about fifteen hundred were destroyed by wartime attacks, and most of these were in the rural and mining states between the Mississippi and the Rockies, where the party had had one of its strongest pre-war bases. The party in these areas, which had been laboriously built up over a period of twenty years, and which had traditionally served as an adhesive in the long-standing left-right split in the party, now were in about the same weak and disorganized condition as they had been at the turn of the century. The party retained significant strength only in eastern and midwestern industrial centers where its base consisted heavily of recent immigrants who tended to interpret the United States in European terms and who had the least understanding of American politics. In sum, the SPA was not dead at the end of the war, but its press had been severely damaged, many of its leaders were in jail or under indictment, the rural midwestern and western heart of the party, which constituted its ideological middle, had been virtually cut out, and the portion of native Americans in the party was sharply lower than it had been before the war.[148]

Given the severe repression faced by the SPA during the war, what is particularly surprising is the strength the party still showed in those areas where repression had been relatively slight or where the party organization had been strong enough to withstand repression. Thus, in Wisconsin, where the Socialists had a strong machine and a sitting mayor in Milwaukee, Daniel W. Hoan, who resisted repressive measures during the war, the party elected the county ticket in Milwaukee in the November, 1918 elections, elected a congressmen and increased the number of SPA state legislators from thirteen to twenty-two. In Reading, Pennsylvania, repression was slight, the SPA machine remained intact, and eventually the party came to power there in 1927. The party also did well in the 1918 elections in parts of Iowa, Michigan, South Dakota, and even in Minnesota, where the SPA increased its number of aldermen in Minneapolis from three to seven and elected four members of the state legislature.[149] In sum, the SPA "held its own or gained in those areas where its organization was still intact," but in many cities "the wartime attacks had taken their toll, and even where the locals had not been entirely disrupted, their energies were often dissipated in defending their right to exist."[150]

Aside from the destruction of the People's Council and the IWW and the grave weakening of the NPL and the SPA, governmental repression during World War I completed the demise of the anarchist movement. The banning of anarchist literature from the mails and the arrest and later deportation of Goldman and Berkman spelled the virtual end of organized anarchist agitation in the U.S.[151]

There are some obvious reasons why repression became so severe during World War I — for example, the fear created in governmental and business circles by the growth of a strong radical movement, the strong anti-war feelings evident throughout the country, and the general war-time hysteria fostered by the Wilson administration. One more subtle reason was the virtual complete collapse of support for concepts of civil liberties among almost all segments of the population except for those groups that came under direct attack. As has been already pointed out, the AFL showed no concern for civil liberties so long as it was receiving help from the government and the target of the government attack was its enemy, the IWW. But the AFL was by no means the only organization which might well have been expected to support freedom of speech yet failed to do so. A number of prominent socialists who left the SPA as a result of its anti-war stand led the campaign for suppression of the SPA.[152] The academic community was caught up in the same hysteria that infected the rest of society. The Committee on Academic Freedom in Wartime of the American Association of University Professors declared that professors could be legitimately dismissed not only for violation of laws or executive orders related to the war, but also for "propaganda" tending to lead to draft resistance, for action designed to "dissuade others from rendering voluntary assistance" to the government, and in the case of professors of Teutonic extraction and sympathy, for violating the obligation to "refrain from public discussion of the war; and in their private intercourse . . . to avoid all hostile or offensive expressions concerning the United States or its government."[153]

The *New Republic* applauded the persecution of the IWW, and along with liberal publications such as *The Outlook* and the *Atlantic Monthly* refused to carry advertisements for espionage act defense cases. Prominent liberals and middle class reformers like Louis Post, Jane Addams and Lillian Wald refused to associate in any way with organizations which included pacifists or pro-Germans. One of the few well-known anti-war intellectuals, Randolph Bourne, found himself unable to get his articles published in his regular outlets, such as *The Atlantic* and *The New Republic*. Even the NPL refused to help the IWW defense, although it was suffering severely from the same types of repression visited upon the IWW.[154]

Judges, prosecutors, and juries were for the most part caught up in the same hysteria which infected the rest of the country. Although some public officials such as Federal District Judge George M. Bourquin of Montana and federal district attorneys Burton K. Wheeler of Montana and George W. Anderson of Massachusetts strongly upheld concepts of civil liberties, most judges and prosecutors made no attempt to check excesses. Thus, during the Berkman-Goldman trial, the judge required everyone in the courtroom except for the defendants to stand up when the strains of the national anthem entered the room from a liberty bond band that was playing outside; those who refused to do so were forcibly ejected. When a challenge was made to the constitutionality of the draft before the Supreme Court, the chief justice rebuked an attorney who charged that conscription had required men to take part in a war that had never received popular approval, terming this a "very unpatriotic statement." One federal judge in Texas declared that six allegedly anti-war senators should be shot; another federal judge, in an espionage act case, declared that "all men and women who are not traitors at heart are sacrificing their time and their hard-earned money in defense of the flag." In reviewing espionage act cases after the war, Justice Department officials concluded that in many cases justices imposed severe sentences in order to foster unity and bolster morale. There is also evidence that juries convicted even in the most dubious cases out of both patriotism and fear that their loyalties otherwise would be impugned. Thus, in one IWW trial, the jury foreman delivered a guilty verdict, and then declared, "Now no one can say we're not loyal."[155]

5

The Great Red Scare of 1919-1920

Radical Strength in 1919

By the end of World War I, the IWW had been effectively destroyed, the momentum of the NPL had been stopped and the SPA had been severely damaged. Yet the eighteen months following the end of the war in November, 1918, were to witness a red scare and a period of repression that was of comparable intensity to the repression of World War I. In attempting to explain why the American red scare of 1919 occurred, most historians have pointed to a carrying over of war-time hatreds and tensions, coupled with the fears engendered by the Russian revolution and the apparent spread of communism in Europe, all complicated by domestic tensions resulting from problems of post-war dislocation, such as the severe inflation which characterized 1919. While historians have also pointed to signs of labor and radical ferment in the U.S. during 1919 as another major factor in creating the scare, most have tended to downplay the radical and labor threat and thus have painted the red scare as an essentially irrational manifestation of general fears and tensions in American society.[1]

Insofar as there were strong fears about a possible radical revolution breaking out in the U.S., such fears were irrational, but by downplaying the labor and radical threat — often to make the valid point of the absurdity of the scare's excesses — most historians have obscured the fact that there *was* a tremendous upsurge in radicalism both within and without the labor movement in 1919. Before the full force of federal and local repression made itself felt in late 1919 and early 1920, the SPA and radicals within the AFL and the labor movement as a whole were making extremely strong gains and proposing programs that challenged the very structure of American capitalism. Seen in this light, the red scare of 1919 was a very rational response on the part of government and business elites who accurately perceived that extremely serious threats to the status quo were developing. The effect of the red scare was to destroy these developing forces of radicalism — and when this destruction had been substantially achieved the red scare ended. The red scare of 1919, then, was no more irrational than was the government's response to the Pullman strike or to the developing power of the IWW and the Socialist Party during World War I.

Radical gains in late 1918 and early 1919 came, not coincidentally, at the same time as repression appeared to be sharply easing, especially on the federal level. Although some major prosecutions initiated during the war continued — notably the trial of Victor Berger and the other top SPA leaders, and the Kansas and California IWW prosecutions — in the half year following the end of the war, the federal government abandoned hundreds of pending Espionage Act cases, including the prosecution of 64 Wobblies arrested in Nebraska; granted clemency to about 100 of the 239 persons then in prison as a result of the Espionage Act convictions; lifted parole restrictions on enemy aliens, and freed all interned enemy aliens (with the exception of 150 who had been convicted for violation of war-time laws and 500 German seamen who refused repatriation); freed many jailed conscientious objectors and drastically reduced the sentences of others; and, partly as a result of court orders, released most of the IWW members being held for possible deportation. In December, 1918, Attorney General Gregory ordered the dissolution of the APL and a reduction of Bureau of Investigation agents to pre-war levels. In December, 1918 Military Intelligence began to reduce its operations, and on January 24, 1919 all military intelligence officers were ordered to abandon investigations of civilians and to stay on military reservations, although they were still permitted to receive information from individuals not connected with Military Intelligence. In November, 1918, a Senate committee voted to dismiss disloyalty charges that had been brought against Sen. Robert La-Follette, and in December, 1918, the House began an investigation of the National Security League, which had accused a number of Congressmen of disloyalty.[2]

During this same period, strong signs of radical rejuvenation appeared everywhere. The SPA experienced a strong resurgence during the months following the end of the war, jumping from eighty-three thousand members in August, 1918, to almost one hundred ten thousand in the summer of 1919. However, most of these gains were from recent immigrants, especially Russian-oriented Eastern Europeans who tended to view the situation in the United States as equivalent to the situation in Russia before 1917. Whereas in 1917, the foreign language composition of the SPA had been about 35 percent, by 1919, due to the war-time destruction of the heavily native rural and small town locals, and the heavy membership increases among immigrants after the war, the foreign language composition reached 53 percent. The result was that a major faction within the SPA became increasingly Euporean oriented and enmeshed in dreams of imminent revolution, whereas the general character of the pre-war party had been moderate and oriented to the situation in the United States. Before the war, the rural and small town locals had played the ideological middle ground between left and right wing factions within the party, but with their destruction the SPA in 1919 rapidly split into two sharply divided wings. In September, the Communist Party (CP) and the Communist Labor Party (CLP) were formed as left-wing splits from the SPA. The split severely damaged the radical movement, but even after the division about eighty thousand persons remained in the three parties, and the radical movement retained considerable vitality. For example, shortly after the split, about fifty domestic communist publications sprang up, published in twenty-six different languages.[3]

Signs of increasing radical influence were evident far beyond the formal framework of radical parties. At the end of the war, "scores and scores of Americans entered the Armistice yearning for and expecting an upsurge of reform and progress."[4] Talk of a major "reconstruction" of American society was commonplace, and support for major and fundamental reforms was widespread among progressives, labor, clergymen, social workers and intellectuals. Many organizations held special conferences on the subject of "reconstruction." Thus, in November, 1918, the National Municipal League, during a "Conference on American Reconstruction Problems," called for continuation of most war-time federal economic controls, such as federal housing for industrial workers, the U.S. Employment Service and the Food and Fuel Administration. During the same month a Conference on Social Agencies and Reconstruction called for broad new federal legislation affecting education, civil rights, insurance, labor, housing and many other aspects of American life. The National Catholic War Council's Reconstruction and After-War Activities Committee called in February, 1919 for a living wage and stressed the identity of interests between "true religion" and "economic democracy" while urging the maintenance of war-time economic controls, enactment of minimum wage laws and provisions for comprehensive insurance against illness, unemployment and old age. Major segments of the progressive movement, including liberal magazines such as the *New Republic* and the *Nation* urged a new coalition with labor, advocated continued use of government economic planning, and urged some form of democratic control and ownership of industry. In a number of American cities, such as Butte, Portland, Seattle, Toledo and Denver, Soldiers, Sailors and Workers' Councils were formed in conscious imitation of the Russian soviets, while thousands attended meetings in cities such as Denver, San Francisco, Seattle and Washington, D.C. to demand recognition of Bolshevik Russia, the freeing of political prisoners and withdrawal of American troops from Russia.[5]

Even more ominous in the eyes of conservatives was the clearly increasing strength of radicalism within the labor movement.[6] The growing power of the AFL during World War I, the emphasis on the need to make the world "safe for democracy" and the impact of the Nottingham Program of the British Labor Party, with its demand for nationalization of basic industries, combined to whet the appetite of even the "conservative" labor movement — i.e. the AFL and the railroad brotherhoods. Organized labor, at the very least, was determined to hold onto its war-time gains, while big business was determined to stem increasing power of labor and to reverse the trend toward government regulation of the economy evident during the war, thus setting the stage for a major power clash. A substantial portion of the labor movement, highly influenced by the Nottingham Program, was determined to go far beyond merely maintaining war-time gains; "at the least they insisted upon such things as industrial unionization, comprehensive social insurance, the nationalization of part of the economy, and the creation of a political party through which these objectives could be achieved."[7]

The first major sign of increasing radicalism in the AFL was the adoption by the AFL Executive Council in December, 1918, of a post-war "reconstruction" program which called for a whole series of reforms, such as government ownership, operation or regulation of public utilities, increased government regulation of corporations, and government financing and building of low-cost housing for workers. The program included the demand that workers have a voice in determining "the laws within industry and commerce which affect them, equivalent to the voice which they have as citizens in determining the legislative enactments which shall govern them."[8] This last demand seemed to be endorsed by President Wilson, who called in May, 1919 for a "genuine democraticization of industry," a "cooperation and partnership based upon a real community of interest and participation in control."[9]

Other evidences of labor radicalism were manifold. The California Federation of Labor called for "common ownership of the means of production," while the Ohio Federation of Labor demanded nationalization of the railways, telegraph and telephone systems, the coal mines, oil production system, the merchant marine and all metallurgical mines. The UMW called for nationalization of the mines, while the conservative railroad brotherhoods called for government operation of the rail system. This latter demand was endorsed by the AFL at its 1919 convention, along with a proposal urging withdrawal of American troops from Russia. The AFL and the California Federation of Labor, which had both backed wartime repression of radicals, passed resolutions in 1919 calling for a repeal of repressive legislation and the release or shortening of the terms of political prisoners. Under the direction of John Fitzpatrick, president of the Chicago Federation of Labor, (who declared, "We are going to socialize the basic industries of the U.S.") a movement was begun in November, 1918, to create an independent labor party. During the first half of 1919, central labor organizations in over forty-five cities across the country organized local labor parties, and in November, 1919, the National Labor Party was organized in Chicago, with over half of the unions affiliated with the AFL represented despite the opposition of the AFL leadership.[10]

One index of labor radicalism on the eve of the red scare was the attendance at the January, 1919, "Mooney Congress," called to consider a national strike to protest the continued imprisonment of Tom Mooney. While the congress was ignored or condemned by the AFL leadership and most state federations, representatives of about twelve hundred labor organizations in thirty-seven states attended, including 8 state federations, 7 international unions, and 114 city central federations (compared to 143 city centrals represented at the AFL's June convention) — altogether indicating that radical ideas had penetrated perhaps one-third or one-fourth of the organized labor movement. An even better indication of labor militancy was the tremendous wave of strikes which developed during 1919 — thirty-six hundred strikes involving four million workers. The enormity of this strike wave and the severe effect that repression had upon the labor movement can be seen from the fact that more workers struck during 1919 than were to strike for the next six years or for the entire 1923-32 period. One of every five workers was involved in a strike during 1919, a record that has never been surpassed. Especially during the early part of 1919, unionism was making strong gains, with major victories in the men's clothing industries, in textiles, among the railroad shop crafts, and in preliminary attempts to organize the steel industry.[11]

Neither the AFL nor any significant sector of the labor movement was infected with communistic or revolutionary ideas — in fact under Gomper's leadership the AFL remained one of the major red-baiting forces in 1919 in a desperate attempt to keep the red stigma off the AFL. Nevertheless, conservative forces in the press and in industry — and eventually supposedly "progressive" forces in the government — constantly raised a hue and cry about communism and revolution virtually every time a major strike developed. While there may have been some sincere fears about communist influence in the labor movement, the alleged red menace was soon being deliberately used by business forces to smash unions and by politicians to foster their own political careers.[12]

The rising tide of radicalism and militant unionism was certainly not the only cause of the 1919 red hysteria. In general, 1919 was a year of severe frustration for Americans. As George Mowry has written, "Probably no other responsible government and certainly none of America's associates in the war was so reckless in making promises to its people"[13] during the war; the desire for a return to "normalcy" afterwards was frustrated not only by the great strike wave, but by widespread dissatisfaction with the Versailles treaty and its seeming threat of keeping the U.S. embroiled in European affairs. Further aggravating Americans was a wave of race riots in the summer of 1919, a rampant inflation which had pushed prices to a level 99 percent above what they had been in 1914 and caused a decline in real wages of more than 10 percent in 1919, a crime wave which pushed the homicide rate to double the pre-war rate, a severe flu epidemic and a brief but sharp economic recession in late 1918 and early 1919 which caused severe unemployment problems for returning servicemen before recovery occurred in the second quarter of 1919.[14]

Abroad, the threat posed by triumphant communism in Russia seemed to be rapidly engulfing Europe. At the end of 1918 and during early 1919, Bolshevism seemed to be sweeping Austria and Germany, serious disorders had broken out in many European countries and socialist parties throughout Europe were being driven to the extreme left. In March, 1919, the establishment of the Communist International and the coming to power of Bolshevik regimes in Hungary and parts of Germany created a wave of fear among conservative circles in America like that set off earlier by the French Revolution and the Paris Commune. Meanwhile, American troops remained stationed in Russia; while they were supposedly instructed not to intervene in Russian domestic affairs, their continued presence after the end of World War I was an obvious expression of American anti-Bolshevism. Because Russia had withdrawn from the war after the Bolshevik revolution, many Americans equated communism with Germany. Thus, war-time hatreds and passions which had been whipped up against Germany were easily transferred to those who espoused the cause of revolutionary Russia or to those accused of being communistic. This false identification of revolutionary Russia with Germany had been fostered during the war by government circulation of the fraudulent Sisson documents, and after the war by statements of high government officials.[15]

Early Development of the Red Scare

Amidst all of these festering tensions, a whole series of spectacular "incidents" occurred during 1919 which fueled the red scare and led up to its climax — the notorious Palmer raids. The first of these incidents was the Seattle general strike of February, 1919. The union movement in Seattle represented the extreme left wing of the AFL, openly supporting the Bolshevik revolution and favoring nationalization of key industries, organization of the unskilled and semi-skilled, and militant industrial unionism. Seattle was one of the strongest union towns in the country. About 50 percent of Seattle's workers were organized, and the labor movement operated many stores, a worker's college and the only labor-owned daily paper in the nation.[16]

The Seattle general strike developed in support of wage and hours demands made by Seattle shipyard workers which had been vigorously opposed by the government-run Emergency Fleet Corporation (EFC), a relic of the war. The strike was completely peaceful — not a single arrest was made in connection with it — and involved no revolutionary demands. However, the spectre of sixty thousand militant workers striking was enough to suggest the arrival of a Russian Soviet to many Americans. A campaign suggesting that a communist revolutionary plot was behind the Seattle strike was quickly developed by Mayor Ole Hanson, the conservative press and some federal officials. On the morning the strike was scheduled to begin federal troops were escorted into Seattle by Hanson, who had a huge American flag draped over the top of his car. Altogether almost one thousand federal troops were stationed in the city, while Hanson swore in three thousand extra police, placed machine guns at strategic downtown locations and placed troops with live ammunition at power plants. Hanson termed the strike a "revolution" and threatened to shoot on sight anyone causing disorders and to declare martial law and use troops to break the strike. Military intelligence operatives kept close tabs on the situation, while the U.S. attorney in the area reported to Washington that the strike was a "revolution led by extreme elements openly advocating overthrow of the government." As a result of Hanson's threats and pressures from national AFL unions, the strike was called off within four days, with the resultant collapse of the union movement in Seattle.[17]

The second major incident of the red scare was the bomb scare of late April. On April 28, a bomb was discovered in Hanson's mail before it did any harm, but the next day a bomb sent to former Senator Hardwick of Georgia blew off both hands of Hardwick's maid and caused painful burns to Mrs. Hardwick. Subsequently thirty-four other bomb packages were discovered by the Post Office before they were delivered. Many of them were addressed to prominent public officials who were notorious anti-radicals, but others were sent to persons generally regarded as liberals.[18]

The next major incident was the so-called May Day Riots, which in fact were attacks by police and bystanders upon radicals who were peacefully celebrating the traditional labor holiday. In Boston, New York, Cleveland, Chicago, Detroit, Los Angeles and elsewhere, police, soldiers and mobs attacked radical gatherings, parades and meeting halls. The worst disorders occurred in Cleveland, where police and soldiers drove army trucks, tanks and police cars into crowds to break up rioters, and two persons were killed and one hundred shot or badly beaten. Cleveland police arrested 125 socialists, but not a single anti-radical, although the disorders started when soldiers and civilians attacked socialist paraders, and before the day was over, crowds sacked two socialist offices. A similarly unbalanced arrest record was effected in Boston.[19] Although in each case, the disturbances were touched off by "solid patriotic citizens who supposedly championed law and order and abhorred violence" the press blamed the "riots" on the radicals.[20]

The May Day disorders were followed by bomb explosions which occurred in eight different cities within the same hour on June 2. The bombs were placed at the homes of public officials and private businessmen. The most widely publicized and ultimately most significant of these was an attempt to dynamite the home of Attorney General A. Mitchell Palmer. Palmer and his family were unhurt, but the bomb thrower was killed in the explosion. Palmer had taken a rather moderate course with regard to radicals until the attempt to kill him; it was after this incident that Palmer began to plan a coordinated federal campaign against the "reds." The June bombings also led to increased hysterical demands to smash radicals in the general press.[21]

While the federal government had been relatively inactive until June of 1919, it is important to note that clear signs of a serious red scare were already evident in many parts of the country, especially in California,

Oregon, Montana and Washington, where the IWW still had some strength, and in New York, where the socialists and other radicals were particularly strong. The Seattle strike appears to have been the immediate impetus for the early outbreak of the red scare in Washington and Oregon. In January, while the strike was being discussed, Washington passed a criminal syndicalism law; the months after the strike were marked by police raids on IWW halls and a general round-up of Wobblies and other radicals. Eventually twenty-seven men were arrested for criminal syndicalism as a result of the strike, but the cases were lost, dropped or thrown out of court. About twenty cities in Washington passed their own laws banning sedition, criminal syndicalism or unauthorized meetings or literature distribution. During the thirteen years following passage of the Washington law, a total of eight-six persons were convicted under it.[22]

Oregon passed a criminal syndicalism law in February, the month of the Seattle strike. Police immediately began raiding IWW halls and arresting Wobblies, although most of the victims were eventually turned over to local courts for prosecution for vagrancy or disorderly conduct.[23] In Montana, when labor radical William F. Dunne, a member of the Montana legislature who had been convicted of sedition, won the Democratic primary for Mayor of Butte in April, 1919, he was simply counted out in a massive electoral fraud. Former U.S. Attorney and later U.S. Senator Burton W. Wheeler commented, "You might as well throw your law books away and use them for fuel, they are no longer of any use in Montana."[24]

The early development of the red scare in California appears to have resulted largely from continuing fears of IWW activity left over from the war. In January, 1919, forty-six Wobblies were convicted for wartime violations of the espionage act in a trial held at the state capital at Sacramento. In February, a wave of IWW strike activity in the citrus region of southern California was broken by numerous arrests of strikers and a mob deportation of thirty-five strike leaders, together with the refusal of state and local authorities to give charity to the strikers, thereby ending labor agitation in the California citrus belt for over a decade. The California state legislature passed a criminal syndicalism bill in April; shortly after police began breaking up radical meetings, and raiding and arresting IWW members and other radicals for criminal syndicalism or vagrancy. By the fall of 1919, about sixty Californians had been arrested for criminal syndicalism, although only four of them were tried on this charge.[25]

In New York, the early red scare appears to have resulted especially from the continuing strength of various radical movements, which had picked up many recruits among recent immigrants to New York City. In the early months of 1919 New York City police put strong pressure on hall owners to bar radical meetings, the state legislature passed a red flag law and New York city police raided the Chinese branch of the IWW and the Union of Russian Workers (URW). Over 160 persons were arrested in the URW raid, although the organization functioned largely as a social club for Russian immigrants. A number of public school teachers in New York state were fired for teaching allegedly radical doctrines beginning in January of 1919, and in April, 1919, the New York City Board of Education published a list of persons banned from speaking in the New York schools. At about the same time, the school board issued a questionnaire designed to test students' knowledge of socialism; students were graded from zero to one hundred, with those persons having no knowledge at all graded the highest.[26]

In March, 1919, the New York state legislature created the so-called Lusk Committee, which was empowered to investigate the "scope, tendencies and ramifications" of "seditious activities" in the state. The committee soon became notorious for its rabid publicity-seeking, its repeated irresponsible suggestions of subversive influence among blacks, trade unions and many prominent American persons and organizations such as the ACLU, Roger Baldwin and Jane Addams, and especially for its extraordinary assumption of executive power in making its own raids on radical groups in conjunction with local police officials. In June, the committee conducted raids on the Russian Soviet Bureau, an agency of the Russian government; on the socialist-run Rand School of Social Science; on the left wing of the SPA; and on the IWW. Partly as a result of the Lusk raids, criminal anarchy charges were brought against five radicals, with two convicted and three eventually deported.[27]

While the red scares in Washington, Montana, Oregon, California and New York during the first half of 1919 appear to have been the most intense, considerable grass roots hysteria was in evidence throughout much of the country before it had a significant impact on the federal government. During 1919, a total of twenty-seven states passed red flag laws, sixteen states passed criminal syndicalism laws and twelve states passed anarchy and sedition laws. These laws were passed in many states during the early part of 1919 even in the absence of severe local scares. According to the best estimate available, during 1919-20 about fourteen hundred persons were arrested under these state laws with about three hundred ultimately convicted.[28] According to the most extensive study which has been made of criminal syndicalism laws, business and industrial interest groups were connected with the enactment of such measures in every state. In most states they passed with overwhelming support — thus among the states that passed such laws in 1919, the bills passed without a single vote of opposition in six states and with less than ten votes against them in each house in another nine states.[29]

The federal government was not entirely absent from the red scare scene during the first half of the year. Federal troops had been sent to Seattle despite the lack of violence. After the strike had been broken, the editor and staff of the Seattle labor newspaper were arrested under the war-time sedition law; they were later released. In January, Secretary of Labor Wilson announced that he was planning to round up and deport all aliens who fell within the 1918 immigration law, and in February and March he declared that the Seattle strike and other recent strikes had represented an attempt to "create a social and political revolution that would establish the soviet form of government in the U.S. and put into effect the economic theories of the Bolsheviki of Russia." In February, a few days after French Premier Clemenceau was wounded in an assassination attempt, secret service agents arrested fourteen Wobblies in New York, leading to speculation that they were involved in a world-wide plot to kill Allied and American officials. In April the Justice Department disclosed an alleged conspiracy by Pittsburgh anarchists to blow up Pittsburgh and announced that eleven anarchists had been arrested.[30]

The senate also made some anti-radical noises early in the year. In February, a Senate committee which had been investigating German propaganda was also authorized to investigate Bolshevik propaganda, along with any effort to incite the overthrow of the government, destruction of life or property, or the general cessation of industry. The committee, chaired by Sen. Lee Overman, spent a month in February and March listening to wild tales of free love, nationalization of women and atrocities alleged to be occurring in Russia, along with occasional unsubstantiated and irresponsible attacks on the patriotism of prominent Americans. Former Justice Department agent Archibald Stevenson, who later became an aide to the Lusk Committee, attacked, among others, social workers Jane Addams and Lillian Wald, federal Commissioner of Immigration Frederick C. Howe, and Oswald Villard, editor of *The Nation*. A list of sixty-two purportedly "dangerous radicals" compiled by military intelligence somehow leaked out during the hearings; among those listed was James Maurer, the socialist president of the Pennsylvania Federation of Labor. A. Bruce Bielski, chief of the Justice Department's Bureau of Investigation, forerunner of the FBI, said Roger Baldwin of the NCLB had been "actively disloyal." Another witness termed the NCLB sympathetic to Bolshevism, but when the NCLB requested the right to reply, it was not allowed to send a spokesman. In its report the Overman committee concluded that Bolshevism was the greatest danger facing America, recommended more stringent sedition legislation and urged strict enforcement of immigration laws.[31]

As the red scare heated up, Congress reflected the increasing fears of the business community by dismantling most progressive war-time economic measures. Congress abolished the U.S. Employment Service, drastically cut back government housing projects, returned the railroads to private ownership, killed a proposal to help veterans settle and develop unused farm lands, and allowed other war-time agencies, such as the Food and Fuel Administration, to expire. The reactionary trend in Congress was aided by President Wilson's preoccupation with foreign policy and his apparent disinterest in the reconstruction problem.[32]

Meanwhile, the Supreme Court was making a notable contribution to the development of red hysteria. In three rulings in March of 1919, the court unanimously upheld convictions under the war-time espionage act, all based on speeches or newspaper articles expressing opposition to the war. Later, after the red scare was well under way, the court, during the winter of 1919-20, upheld three more convictions. In one of these cases the court declared in effect that the allegation that the war had economic causes, made in a pamphlet that led to prosecution, was false, although President Wilson had recently stated that the conflict had been a "commercial and industrial war."[33]

It was only after the June bombing of Palmer's house that the federal government began to embark on a concerted anti-radical campaign, and that the red scare began to become a national scare, rather than a series of local affairs. Shortly after the bombing, Palmer announced the appointment of William J. Flynn, whom Palmer termed the "greatest anarchist expert in the U.S." as head of the Bureau of Investigation, along with the appointment of Francis P. Garman, a well-known detective, as Assistant Attorney General to head all radical prosecutions and investigations. On June 12, Palmer asked Congress to appropriate $500,000 to fight radicals, and announced that the Justice Department had "almost" accepted as a fact reports that "on a certain day in the future" there would be an attempt to "rise up and destroy the government at one fell swoop." Garman claimed that "the Russian Bolsheviki" were pouring money into the U.S., while Flynn stated that the recent bombings had been "connected with Russian Bolshevism, aided by Hun money."[34] At about the same time, Military Intelligence also asked Congress for $500,000 to continue its work, and some military intelligence offices began to actively solicit information on radical actvities from civilian informants, including former APL members, (who, in some cases had continued to operate in private superpatriotic groups, and were still claiming government sponsorship).[35]

Justice Department spokesmen broadly hinted that Bolshevik agents planned to make July 4, 1919, a day of terror or perhaps of revolution. July 4 was apparently seized upon because it had been set as the day of a nation-wide strike by labor radicals concerned with the Mooney case. In preparation for the feared day, Flynn met with police chiefs from a number of eastern and midwestern cities June 29 to prepare a response. As a result, on July 4, police and in some cases state troops were out in full force in many cities across the country. However, nothing occurred aside from "a bloody case of mayhem in Toledo, Ohio, where Jack Dempsey beat Jess Willard to a pulp to win the heavyweight boxing championship."[36]

It was a measure of the fear of radicalism which had become engrained in the American psyche by July that this fear survived the July 4 fiasco without diminishing. On July 19, Congress appropriated special funds for the Justice Department for prosecuting radicals, and on August 1 Palmer announced the creation of the General Intelligence Division (GID), which had the sole function of collecting information on radical activities. Under the leadership of a twenty-four-year old graduate of

Georgetown University Law School named J. Edgar Hoover, the GID soon began a program of collecting information on radicals from private, local, state and military authorities, set up index files on hundreds of thousands of alleged radicals, began to heavily infiltrate radical organizations, and became a major agent fostering the red scare through its practice of sending out sensationalized charges against radicals to major organs of the media, including charges that strikes and race riots had connections with communist activity.[37] The GID's program of general surveillance of radical activity was entirely without congressional authorization, since money appropriated could only be used for the "detection and prosecution of crimes" but the Justice Department got around this problem by authorizing the GID to secure evidence which might be of use under legislation "which may hereafter be enacted.[38] Palmer relied heavily on Hoover, Flynn and Garman for his information about the intentions and strength of radical groups; unfortunately for Palmer, as Stanley Coben has delicately put it, these men "were extraordinarily susceptible to the fear and extravagant patriotism so prevalent in 1919."[39] There is some evidence that Hoover and Flynn deliberately exploited the radical issue to enhance the power and prestige of the Bureau of Investigation and the GID, a tactic which Hoover would frequently use throughout his career.[40]

The red scare was temporarily displaced from the front pages during the summer by a series of race riots, which gave the summer of 1919 the name, "red summer" because of the amount of blood shed during seven major and eighteen minor disorders. A minor theme during the riots was suggestions by newspapers, the Lusk Committee, Secretary of War Baker, and J. Edgar Hoover that the riots were somehow connected with "radical" agitation among blacks.[41] Hoover charged in a report presented to Congress by Palmer in November that there was a "well-concerted movement among a certain class of Negro leaders . . . to constitute themselves a determined and persistent source of radical opposition to the government and to established rules of law and order." He complained these leaders had shown "an outspoken advocacy of the Bolsheviki or Soviet doctrines," had been "openly, defiantly assertive" of their "own equality or even superiority" and had demanded "social equality."[42] Both the Justice Department and Army intelligence conducted extensive investigations of the racial disorders of 1919 in order to determine if there were connections with radical groups. According to a recent study of Army intelligence during this period — which extended to moderate groups such as the Urban League — army investigators "collected a treasure trove of largely useless data, much of which was distorted or in error."[43]

One of the "race riots" of 1919, the so-called "Elaine Massacre," should in fact be treated as an instance of repression of attempts to organize agricultural labor. Black tenants in Phillips County, Arkansas, had been organizing a semi-secret fraternal order to advance economic demands against their landlords — demands which in rural Arkansas were virtually revolutionary in nature. During a meeting in a black church of black sharecroppers at Elaine on September 30, shooting broke out between the blacks and local deputy sheriffs, during which a deputy sheriff was killed. While the details of the September 30 shootout are unclear, what happened subsequently is crystal clear — a reign of terror broke out in the area, during which mobs of whites assaulted blacks and an estimated five whites and scores of blacks were killed. Federal troops were sent into the area, and arrested several hundred blacks. During subsequent trials, held in an atmosphere of hysteria, twelve Negro farmers were sentenced to death and over fifty others given long jail terms. These sentences were later nullified by the Supreme Court, but in the meantime the attempt to organize black sharecroppers had been smashed.[44]

Intensification of the Red Scare

While the Elaine disorders marked the last of the "race riots," by September, fear of radicalism and especially radical labor, was on the rise again. In the fall of 1919, two AFL unions tried to organize employees of the Great Southern Lumber Company of Bogalusa, Louisiana, the world's largest lumber manufacturer. After meeting with considerable success, the organizing drive was smashed when pro-company vigilantes, some of whom were deputized, harassed union members, pillaged the house of the union vice-president, and apparently killed the president of the union and three union men (they were acquitted, but given the company domination of the town and the known actions of the vigilantes, the justice of the verdict is open to question).[45] The first "major" incident of the fall that revived fear of communism was the Boston police strike which began on September 9.[46] The strike was based purely on police demands for a union, but the press and conservative forces quickly branded the strike a communist plot. Although the amount of damage that resulted from minor looting and rioting that occurred before order was restored by state troops and a volunteer police force was not great, the general impression that swept the country was that the city was "in the hands of Bolshevik mobs."[47] Governor Calvin Coolidge of Massachusetts joined Mayor Hanson of Seattle as an American hero when he stated that there is "no right to strike against the public safety by anybody, anywhere, anytime."[48] In the course of planning for the possible sending of federal troops, military intelligence, newly fortified with a congressional appropriation of $400,000, began to reestablish itself as a general intelligence agency; by the end of September "all large cities had resurgent Military Intelligence units."[49]

Following shortly on the heels of the Boston police strike was the great steel strike of September 22, 1919. Because of the crucial nature that steel played in the American economy in 1919 — it had replaced the railroads as the single most important industry — and the fact that, like most mass production industries, steel employed large numbers of unorganized unskilled and semi-skilled laborers, the steel strike was undoubtedly the single most important strike in American history between the Pullman strike of 1894 and the automobile sit-down strikes of 1937. As David Brody has noted, if steel could be organized, other unorganized mass production industries such as rubber, electrical equipment and food processing "could be swept into the labor fold."[50]

While governmental repression was not the only reason for the failure of the steel strike — poor planning and inadequate financial and organizational support on the part of participating AFL unions were also a major factor — repression played a crucial role and probably would have been enough by itself to break the strike. The heart of the steel industry was in the Pittsburgh-western Pennsylvania area. Even under normal conditions, steel company-dominated towns barred entry to labor organizers or arranged to have them jailed or attacked by mobs. During the steel strike, such repression grew to monumental proportions. Twenty-five thousand men, picked by, paid for and armed by the steel companies were deputized in the Pittsburgh area, strike meetings were banned throughout the entire area, and workers were regularly clubbed, robbed, shot and ridden down by mounted police and deputies. Many strikers were arrested without cause and held without charges. In Gary, Indiana, another crucial steel center, federal and state troops brutally broke strike efforts after rioting broke out when steel companies attempted to break the strike with imported black workers. Federal troops and military intelligence agents under General Leonard Wood placed Gary under "modified martial law," barred public assemblies, and regularly raided homes of alleged "Reds" in the middle of the night. Scores of alleged radicals were arrested. In Youngstown, Ohio, union organizers were arrested on criminal syndicalism charges and meetings were outlawed. At Pueblo, Colorado, after an unknown assailant shot at a steel-plant superintendent, the state militia was called in and picketing was barred.[51]

Meanwhile, the press and business interests began a major campaign branding the entire strike part of a communist revolutionary plot. These charges, which had no basis whatsoever, were supported by federal officials. Army intelligence units in Gary claimed they had uncovered evidence of bomb plots and radical domination, along with a plan to overthrow the state and establish a "dictatorship of the workers," while a Senate committee charged that "behind this strike is massed a considerable element of IWW's, anarchists, revolutionists and Russian soviets."[52] Justice Department agents detained hundreds of alien strikers for possible deportation.

Faced with massive public and press denunciation as a result of these charges, unable to effectively organize in the Pittsburgh and Gary areas — or even to penetrate these areas to combat false press stories which branded the strike a failure although over three hundred thousand steel workers had walked out — and essentially deserted by many of the AFL unions which had supposedly organized the strike, the steel walkout petered out by January, 1920. Altogether, twenty strikers had been killed and many hundreds injured at the hands of police. Hundreds, and perhaps thousands, of strikers had been arrested on charges such as "cursing," "going out of his house before daylight," "laughing at the police" and "smiling at the state police."[53] One investigator for the Interworld Church Movement concluded that the effectiveness of the strike in each area had been "proportional to the amount of civil liberty permitted."[54]

As Foster Rhea Dulles has written, had the strike been won, "the whole labor history of the 1920's would have followed a completely different course."[55] Oscar Handlin notes the defeat dealt labor "a blow from which it did not recover for fourteen years."[56]

Governmental repression of the great steel strike was quickly followed by repression of the nationwide coal strike called by the UMW for November 1, 1919. Coal operators and the press termed the strike an insurectionary plot, while President Wilson termed it "unlawful" and a "grave moral and legal wrong."[57] Palmer, after consulting Wilson, obtained a federal court restraining order on October 30 banning the strike. Despite the injunction, which was based on a war-time law passed only after the AFL had been assured that it would never be applied to labor, and despite the sending of federal troops to coal fields in five states, almost four hundred thousand miners walked out on November 1. Over eighty UMW officials were cited for contempt of court when thousands of miners refused to obey their orders to return to work. The strike ended on December 10 when miners accepted President Wilson's arbitration plan.[58] A strike originally planned for November 1 by the railroad brotherhoods and later rescheduled for February, 1920 was called off twice after union leaders were informed that the federal government would break the strike.[59]

The net impact of the Seattle general strike, the Boston police strike, the coal and steel strikes and the abortive rail strikes, coupled with the constant red-baiting of unions in the press and by businessmen was to create an atmosphere by the fall of 1919 in which much of the public began to view all unions and strikes as revolutionary conspiracies, while workers were growing increasingly reluctant to strike for fear of repression. By December, 1919, the number of monthly strikes had dropped to a six-year low, and the union movement had been sapped of much of its strength and vigor. The combination of the red scare and the SPA split virtually eliminated what was left of socialist influence among trade unions after World War I.[60]

The public mood by late 1919 was increasingly hysterical over the red menace. In October, 1919, a West Virginia businessman wrote to the Justice Department, "There is hardly a respectable citizen of my acquaintance who does not believe that we are on the verge of armed conflict in this country."[61] A British journalist wrote later:

> No one who was in the United States as I chanced to be in the autumn of 1919 will forget the feverish condition of the public mind at that time. It was hag-ridden by the spectre of Bolshevism. It was like a sleeper in a nightmare, enveloped by a thousand phantoms of destruction. Property was

in an agony of fear, and the horrid name "Radical" covered the most innocent departure from conventional thought with a suspicion of desperate purpose. "America," as one wit of the time said, "is the land of liberty — liberty to keep in step."[62]

The effects of repression were everywhere evident in American society. By late 1919, not only workers, but liberals in all areas of life — education, the clergy, even the government itself, were coming under attack from superpatriots for alleged radical leanings. While teachers theoretically still had freedom of speech, "they were abject fools if they exercised it;" the liberal clergy "sank into the cowardice of noncomittment," while the average citizen was led "to think twice" before letting it be known that he subscribed to such subversive publications as *The Nation, The New Republic, Dial, The Public* and *Survey*.[63]

Climax of the Red Scare — The Palmer Raids

Pressures on Attorney General Palmer to take strong steps against radicals steadily mounted. The heavily alien component of the newly-formed communist parties, and the strong support for the steel strike among immigrant workers, together with the traditional identification of radicalism with aliens, combined to make a strong demand for the deportation of alien radicals.[64] On October 19, the Senate unanimously adopted a resolution asking Palmer to report what actions he had taken against those who were preaching anarchy, sedition, defiance of the law and destruction of property; it pointedly requested that if Palmer had taken no action against such persons he report to the Senate "why not."[65] Palmer later recalled that during this period

> I was shouted at from every editorial sanctum in America from sea to sea; I was preached upon from every pulpit; I was urged — I could feel it dinned into my ears — throughout the country to do something and do it now and do it quickly, and do it in a way that would bring results to stop this sort of thing in the U.S.[66]

Acting under this pressure, Palmer, who had strong presidential ambitions, and feared appearing "soft" on communism, expedited the plans which had been laid in June to deport aliens subject to the 1918 law. Since he was reluctant to use the war-time sedition act, the deportation laws were the only federal weapon which could be used against radicals; however they had the advantage of avoiding the need for courtroom procedures, since deportation had been held by the Supreme Court to be a purely administrative matter. Further, the deportation laws allowed action based solely on membership in certain types of organization, thus avoiding the need for proving any unlawful behavior.

The first roundup of aliens occurred on November 7, as federal agents raided the offices of the Union of Russian Workers (URW) in twelve cities across the country. While the URW openly advocated revolution in its literature, the organization served largely as a social and educational center for Russian immigrants. No evidence of criminal activities were ever traced to the group. Arrests were made without warrant throughout the country; thus in New York City, 650 persons were arrested, although the Justice Department had obtained only twenty-seven arrest warrants. Many of those arrested were neither radicals nor aliens, but merely happened to be in the vicinity of the URW building, or were attending URW-sponsored classes. Many persons were severely beaten by police in the New York City raids. A number of alleged URW members arrested in Hartford were jailed for months before being given a hearing to determine their deportability. Additional raids against the URW continued until November 10, with 250 persons arrested in Detroit on November 8. The URW was raided again in New York City on November 25.[67]

On November 10, socialist congressman Victor Berger, then appealing his Espionage Act conviction, was barred from taking his elected seat in the House of Representatives by a vote of 311 to 1.[68] On November 14, Palmer reported to the Senate in answer to its October resolution. Palmer pointed with pride to the URW raids, and requested a peacetime sedition law to deal with citizen radicals. This request was endorsed by President Wilson in his December State of the Union address. On December 21, 242 alleged radical aliens, including Goldman and Berkman, were deported. Most of those aboard *The Buford* (quickly christened the "Soviet Ark") as it steamed from New York's harbor were bewildered members of the URW who posed no threat to any society and had only the haziest acquaintance with URW doctrines. About 50 of the deportees were alleged to be anarchists. Secretary of Labor Wilson's order that men with families not be sent on *The Buford* was ignored by New York immigration officials.[69]

The step up in federal repression inspired new action by state and local officials. On November 8, the day after the first URW raids, the Lusk Committee, with the cooperation of New York City police and federal officials, made its first raids in five months, breaking into seventy-three branches of the communist parties along with the offices of fifty radical publications. The committee seized twenty-five tons of documents, and arrested about one thousand persons. Of those arrested, thirty-five citizens were detained without bail on a charge of criminal anarchy, while a number of aliens were turned over to federal authorities for possible deportation. Eventually twelve of those arrested — the native leadership of the New York communist parties — were convicted and given up to ten years. As a result of the raids, the New York communists became the first to go underground.[70] Two socialists elected to municipal offices in New York City in November were barred from taking office through a process of "masterly inactivity and other dubious ruses" until two years later, shortly before their terms were to expire.[71]

On November 11, the so-called "Centralia Massacre" occurred. The IWW had been driven out of Centralia, Washington, by a mob attack in March, 1918, but had re-established a hall there in September, 1919. During a November 11 armistice parade, a group of American Legion members attacked the hall, and were fired upon by Wobblies who had armed themselves as a result of widespread rumors of an impending assault. Three legionnaires were killed in the battle; an IWW named Wesley Everest who was arrested was turned over to a mob by jail guards that night and lynched. The Centralia incident set off a true reign of terror in Washington; hysterical mobs assaulted Wobblies, and ransacked IWW headquarters, while police arrested at least one thousand alleged IWW's. The "white terror" decimated what was left of the IWW in the state. When the Seattle *Union Record* asked that judgment be suspended until the facts about Centralia became known, federal agents seized the press plant, banned the issue from the mails and arrested several of the editors under the war-time sedition law.[72]

Following the Centralia incident, Idaho officials instructed local police to arrest all IWW members and organizers, and the governor of Idaho asked each of the seventy-two American Legion posts in the state to designate ten men that could be deputized "to gather information, to assist in raids on known radical offices and to pick up men of anarchistic tendency."[73] Raids and arrests also occurred following the Centralia incident in Denver and Pueblo, Colorado, and in Los Angeles, Oakland and other cities in California. By the end of 1919, 108 persons had been indicted for criminal syndicalism in California, with the most notable victims the top leadership of the California Labor Party. Although only three of the thirteen CLP leaders arrested were eventually convicted, the raids and arrests succeeded in driving the California CLP underground and decimating it.[74] All IWW meetings were banned in Los Angeles on the grounds that public sentiment made it "unsafe for enemies of peace and government to gather in public."[75]

The climactic event of the red scare occurred on January 2, 1920, when federal agents under the direction of Hoover and Palmer swooped down on radical hangouts in over thirty cities across the country and arrested somewhere between five and ten thousand persons believed to be alien members of the CLP and the CP. Those arrested included virtually every local or national leader of the parties, and the raids disrupted the activities of practically every local communist organization in the country. Although only aliens were supposed to be arrested, thousands of American citizens were caught in the general dragnet. Thus, of over one thousand arrested at Detroit, four hundred turned out to be citizens. While many citizens were turned over to local authorities for prosecution under criminal syndicalism laws, thousands were quickly freed for lack of any evidence against them. The majority of arrests and break-ins were made without either search or arrest warrants. Thus, of five thousand arrest warrants which had been authorized, only three thousand were served, indicating about two to seven thousand arrests made without warrants.[76]

The general procedure of the raids was to make wholesale arrests of persons in bowling alleys, pool halls, cafes or other places believed to be radical hangouts. According to a Seattle immigration inspector, federal agents "went to various pool rooms, etc., in which foreigners congregated, and they simply sent up in trucks all of them that happened to be there."[77] In Lynn, Massachusetts, thirty-nine bakers were arrested as they met to discuss establishing a cooperative bakery. In other raids the cast and spectators at a theatrical performance put on by a Ukranian group were arrested; an orchestra and all male dancers at an alleged left-wing dance were arrested; and police broke down the door of an alleged CP meeting only to discover an accordian concert in progress. Many arrested in Detroit and Philadelphia were attending classes.

One man who had resigned from the CP was arrested while eating at a cooperative restaurant located in a CP building; his sister explained "he didn't believe in force but the restaurant has better meals at cheaper prices than any place around there."[78] In New Jersey, several "bombs" were seized which turned out to be iron bowling balls. Throughout the country, only three pistols were seized in raids on what were believed to be dangerous radicals actively plotting a revolution.[79]

The massive arrests completely overwhelmed detention facilities in many areas. In Detroit, eight hundred persons were detained for up to six days in a dark, windowless, narrow corridor in the city's federal building; they had access to one toilet and were denied food for twenty-four hours. Eventually conditions in Detroit were termed a "menace to the health of the city" by the local health commission.[80] Many of those arrested were beaten or threatened while in detention; in some cases persons coming to visit or bail out those arrested were themselves seized on suspicion of being communists. Palmer explained such persons were "practically the same as a person found in an active meeting of the organization."[81]

The January 2 raids were followed by minor sweeping-up operations in various parts of the country during the next six weeks, with the last major raid made in Seattle on January 20. On January 10, the Senate passed a peacetime sedition bill, while on the same day, Victor Berger, who had been re-elected to the House in a special election after his exclusion in November, 1919, was again barred from taking his seat.[82] The January 2 raids were preceded in Chicago on New Year's Day by local officials reluctant to see Palmer get all the glory; about seventy radical gatherings were raided there and about one hundred fifty to two hundred persons arrested. Subsequently, over one hundred twenty native communists were indicted in Chicago; over one hundred of them were sentenced to up to ten years in jail under Illinois' Sedition Act.[83] On January 3, the Lusk Committee confiscated the entire current editions of four radical newspapers, and confiscated five tons of material, including mailing lists, metal type and oil paintings of Lenin and Trotsky. On April 1, five elected socialist members of the New York legislature, who had been temporarily excluded since January 7, were permanently barred from taking their seats.[84]

During a strike of twenty-five thousand railroad workers in April, the

Justice Department arrested thirty-eight strike leaders on charges of violating the war-time Lever Act and interfering with transportation of the mails. Palmer, Garman and Hoover charged the strike had been instigated by IWW's and Communists. In May, 1920, Palmer lumped together the coal, steel and rail strikes as "three signal failures to promote economic and social revolution."[85] Meanwhile, the War Department and Military Intelligence, estimating that the radical danger was likely to be "present as a permanent feature to be reckoned with" prepared "War Plans White," a lengthy plan to deal with minor and major emergencies arising out of labor and radical unrest.[86]

Spurred on by the examples of Palmer and the Justice Department, many employers and local public officials used particularly brutal methods to break strikes in 1920. In April, 1920, mine guards killed one striker and wounded fourteen others during an IWW strike at Butte, Montana. A labor newspaper which reported on the strike was promptly suppressed. In Denver, federal troops were called in to restore order after rioting broke out during a street car strike; before the troops arrived, two persons had been killed in rioting and five had been shot to death and twenty-five injured when strikebreakers fired on a crowd. A strike of four thousand cotton field workers in Arizona was broken when scores of workers were arrested and the leaders were deported.[87]

In June, Congress passed a new immigration act which provided for the deportation of all aliens convicted under the espionage and sedition acts, and which defined the "giving, loaning or promising money or anything of value" to organizations falling within the 1918 Immigration law as well as possession of their literature as constituting affiliation for the purposes of deportation.[88] This law was clearly designed to reach not only all alien members of radical groups, but also to reach the "alien sympathizer and the non-member who supported the financial drives of such organizations."[89] However, with the waning of the Red Scare after mid-1920, the law was never applied in deportation proceedings.

Decline of the Red Scare

In the weeks and months after the January 2 raids, Palmer and GID officials continued to agitate the red issue, sending huge amounts of antiradical propaganda to the news media, stepping up the drive for peacetime sedition legislation, and promising thousands more deportations and more "Soviet Arks."[90] In one circular letter sent to the editors of leading magazines, Palmer referred to "the real menace of evil-thinking which is the foundation of the Red movement."[91] In other public statements made in January and February, Palmer referred to the "alien filth" captured in the raids, typified by "sly and crafty eyes . . . lopsided faces, sloping brows and misshapen features" which sheltered "cupidity, cruelty, insanity and crime.'" He claimed that before the raids, "the blaze of revolution . . . was eating its way into the homes of the American workingman, its sharp tongues of revolutionary heat were licking the altars of churches, leaping into the belfry of the school bell, crawling into the sacred corners of American homes, seeking to replace marriage vows with libertine laws, burning up the foundations of society."[92]

But as Palmer and the GID tried to maintain fear of radicals, a variety of factors brought the worst excesses of the red scare to a halt after January, 1920. The most important of these were: 1) increasing opposition on the part of influential elites in the government, the press and other prominent sectors of public life; 2) developments in the red scare which proved embarassing to the proponents of repression; 3) the decline of the apparent threat of spreading communism abroad, and a general decline in domestic tensions, and 4) the fact that the destruction of the radical movement in the U.S. had been essentially completed, and that the unions were lying low.

While there was a noticeable lack of opposition to excesses of the red scare before January, 1920,[93] there were increasingly vocal and negative reactions expressed to the scare after this date. On January 12, Francis F. Kane, the U.S. Attorney for the eastern district of Pennsylvania resigned in protest over Palmer's policies. Beginning in January, the major elements of the nation's press began to express strong opposition to Palmer's and other congressional proposals for peacetime sedition legislation. Similar opposition was expressed by a number of prominent lawyers and clergymen, by the AFL, and inferentially by Supreme Court Justice Oliver Wendell Holmes. Sedition legislation which had passed the Senate on January 10 was dead in the house by February. Important business executives, some of whom had been largely responsible for creating the red scare hysteria, began to attack Palmer' policies; labor unrest had faded and radicals had been virtually wiped out, and they feared that continuing anti-radical nativism could cut off their source of cheap labor. In California, the conviction for criminal syndicalism of prominent suffragist and social worker Charlotte Anita Whitney aroused tremendous protest from a broad spectrum of prominent civic, business, church and educational leaders.[94]

On May 28, 1920, an extremely influential pamphlet attacking Palmer was issued by twelve of the nation's leading lawyers including Kane, Felix Frankfurter (who had played a major role in repressing the IWW during the war),[95] Zechariah Chafee, Roscoe Pound, Ernst Freund, and Frank P. Walsh (who had been associated with the AALD).[96] This report charged that the wholesale arrests of the Palmer raids were without justification, that searches and seizures had been made unlawfully, that prisoners had been illegally treated while in captivity and that *agents provocateurs* had enticed many innocent persons into traps. This pamphlet, in turn, persuaded other influential persons to speak out against Palmer.[97]

Several important court decisions also helped to stem the red hysteria. A Supreme Court case decided in January ruled out the use of illegally seized papers in criminal cases; shortly afterwards this principle was applied by Montana federal district court Judge Bourquin, who had been attacked for being "soft" on radicals during World War I, to free an alien held for deportation. Bourquin used his decision to blast the behavior of federal troops in Butte, Montana, from August 1918 to February, 1919. Bourquin declared the troops had "perpetrated a reign of terror, violence, and crime against citizen and alien alike . . . whose only offense seems to have been peaceable insistence upon and exercise of a clear legal right."[98] In June, another district court judge, George Anderson of Massachusetts, sharply denounced the actions of the Justice Department and released a number of CP members being held for deportation on the ground that they had been ruled subject to deportation on the basis of CP declarations which in some instances had been written by Justice Department agents who had infiltrated the party. Andersen stated, "A mob is a mob whether made up of government officials acting under instructions from the Department of Justice or of criminals, loafers and the vicious classes."[99]

Many writers on the red scare have termed the reaction to the expulsion by the New York legislature of the five elected socialists as perhaps the single incident most responsible for breaking the hysteria. The action was attacked by most of the nation's press, and by noticeably non-radical groups and figures, such as the New York City Bar Association, Charles Evans Hughes, Gov. Alfred E. Smith of New York, the New York Federation of Labor, Roscoe Pound, Sen. Warren Harding, Henry L. Stimson and William Allen White.[100]

Certainly the most important acts of opposition to the red scare were taken by officials in the Labor Department, who were ultimately responsible for making deportation decisions. Although Secretary of Labor Wilson decided in January that CP membership was a deportable offense, in May, Wilson decided that membership in the CLP was not a deportable offense. There was little difference between the parties; the later decision simply reflected the easing of the scare. The most important role was played by Assistant Secretary of Labor Post, who became acting secretary in March when Wilson became ill. Post began a careful review of all of the cases and soon discovered that there was no basis for most of the arrests. Working day and night, seven days a week, Post cancelled thousands of deportation warrants, with the result that only 556 persons were eventually ordered deported. Post's action soon aroused the vigorous opposition of Palmer, Hoover and congressional conservatives, which eventually led to a House investigation to determine if Post should be impeached. Post gave such an impressive performance before a House committee that the impeachment issue was quickly dropped. Appearing before the same committee, Palmer accused Post and certain others of "tender solicitude for social revolution and perverted sympathy for the criminal anarchists of the country." Hoover, meanwhile, searched military intelligence and seized IWW files for evidence that Post and other critics of the Justice Department had radical affiliations.[101]

The expulsion of the New York socialists and the excesses of the Palmer raids were not the only red scare developments which soon became an embarassment to the perpetrators of repression. On May 3, an Italian immigrant namd Andrea Salsedo plunged to his death while under detention by Justice Department agents in New York City. It was subsequently revealed that Salsedo and another alien had been detained — voluntarily the Justice Department claimed — for eight weeks without a warrant on charges for interrogation in connection with the 1919 bombings.[102]

Even more embarassing was the May Day fiasco of 1920. For days before May 1, the Justice Department issued warning that radicals were planning a major uprising. As a result some state militia were called up, federal troops were mobilized and heavy police reinforcements guarded public buildings and public officials in many cities. When nothing happened, Palmer was hotly denounced for suffering hallucinations and crying "wolf."[103]

Another factor in the decline of the red scare was the lessened threat of communist expansion abroad and a general decline in domestic tensions. The soviets that had been declared in 1919 in Hungary and Germany had been overthrown, and by mid-1920 it was evident that Europe was at least temporarily safe from Bolshevism. At home, labor strife had virtually vanished from America's major industries, prosperity appeared to have returned for good and the cost of living had stabilized.[104]

Perhaps the most important factor leading to the decline of the red scare after early 1920 was simply that it had accomplished its purpose — the intimidation of the labor movement and the decimation of the radical movement in the U.S. As Robert Wiebe has summed up, "When the rabble seemed quiet, the violence abated."[105] By the time of the 1920 presidential elections, "Warren Harding's quiet promises of serenity were far more appealing than the continued frenzy of Attorney General Palmer,"[106] who lost the Democratic nomination to Governor James Cox of Ohio after running second in the convention balloting.

On the individual level, by mid-1920, most liberals and social reformers had been thoroughly intimidated. But the more lasting significance of the red scare (and the World War I repression) was its devastation of all the organizations that had been built up so laboriously for twenty years which were capable of providing leadership for any sort of radical political or labor movement — the SPA, the IWW, the NPL, the CP and the CLP. The general lack of a radical labor or political movement in the United States during the 1920's was certainly partly due to the prosperity of the times, and partly due to the split in the SPA, but the most important reason was that the repression of 1917-20 had destroyed the radicals' organizational base. The general climate of repression that prevailed throughout the twenties made it extremely difficult for any rebuilding to occur.

The 1919-20 repression effectively finished off what had been left of the IWW, except in some areas of California. As a result of further defections to the communist parties and the prevailing climate in American society in the early 1920's, the SPA, which had about forty thousand members after the September, 1919 split, declined to about eleven thousand members by 1922. The role of repression in destroying the fledgling communist parties is perhaps the clearest. After the 1919 split, the CP and CLP had about forty thousand members. Following the Palmer raids, both communist sources and the FBI indicate membership plummetted to about ten thousand. The effects of the raids can be seen from the following monthly CP dues figures for October, 1919 through April, 1920:[107]

October, 1919	27,341
November, 1919	20,261
December, 1919	23,624
January, 1920	1,714
February, 1920	2,296
March, 1920	4,517
April, 1920	8,223

The raids drove both communist parties underground, scared away most of the English speaking members, and led party members to develop a semi-fantasy world which glorified underground life. Given the Palmer raids and massive infestation of government spies even into their underground ranks, party members not surprisingly began to view themselves as romantic revolutionaries in the Russian tradition facing a government as tyrannical as the czar's. The government persecution drove the more moderate members out of the party, and left behind those most inclined to conspirational activities and those who believed that in order to survive the party had to become ideologically purified for the forthcoming revolutionary struggles. These members viewed purges as a casting off of the impure, and viewed their present state of weakness and isolation as a normal condition of true revolutionaries. As Burl Noggle notes:

> The more doctrinaire American communists . . . had never favored any compromise with capitalism or support for moderate tactics, such as voting in elections or organizing into trade unions. Instead they insisted upon direct action, violence, overthrow and seizure of power. The Palmer Raids simply confirmed these communists in their belief that they were the American counterparts of the pre-1917 Bolsheviks in Russia. Just as the latter had worked against czardom, so now Communists in America must plot in underground isolation against the system in America.[108]

Adrift in the underground, the party became increasingly isolated from what most persons perceived as realities of American life, and increasingly looked towards the only source of radical strength that appeared to remain in the world — the Communist Party of the Soviet Union. The Russian influence in the Communist parties was strong even before the Palmer raids but during 1919 communication with Russia was spasmodic; the left had to think for itself and was by no means under Russian domination. After the raids, the communists, in their pitifully weak state, welcomed Russian control, which was formally established only in 1921 when the CP and CLP were united. The party stayed underground for about two years, as membership declined to about five thousand under the severe tensions of underground life. Virtually all of the party's leaders were in jail or under indictment, living in a maze of trials, defense committees, appeals, sentences, and prisons. Thus, Communist leader Charles E. Ruthenberg, who had the singular distinction of being arrested under criminal syndicalism or criminal anarchy laws in three separate states in 1919, (and in one more state in 1922), never spent a day free from appeals of various sentences until his death in 1927.[109]

All of these aspects of American communism — its isolation from American life, its conspiratorial nature, its heavy base among non-English speakers and its heavy dependence on Moscow — stayed with the party for decades and crippled the party's appeal to most Americans throughout its existence. It would be naive to suggest that none of these tendencies were present in American communism at its creation, but American repression greatly reinforced these tendencies. American communism has frequently acted as if it faced repression similar to that in czarist Russia; the fact is that save for the lack of summary executions, communism in America in 1919-20 faced repression that *was* like that of Russia — except that in America it was more effective.

6

The 1920's: Conformity for the Masses, Repression for the Few

The long-term significance of the 1917-20 period of intense overt repression can be most clearly seen by studying the 1920's.[1] Characteristic of the 1920's were the following: 1) the lingering on among the general public and government officials of war-time and post-war feelings of extreme hostility towards new ideas, radicals and aliens, and the continuation of a general attitude stressing conformity, business supremacy and "100 percent Americanism;" and 2), the repudiation of progressive political ideals and active reformist agitation on the part of large segments of the middle class, coupled with the absence of any significant radical political opposition or militant labor movement. Together, these two developments, both largely traceable to the 1917-20 repression, created a situation in which business supremacy ruled without any significant opposition. As a result, during the entire decade extremely serious social problems were virtually entirely neglected. The decade was instead characterized by "massive public apathy"[2] towards such problems as income redistribution, industrial democracy, and the plight of farmers and sick industries. As Russell Nye has grimly but accurately stated, "If a survey had been made of all the issues and problems current in American life during the period of 1920 to 1929, it would have concluded that not a single one was handled, if at all, with any energy or efficiency."[3]

In 1920, Sen. Hiram Johnson told newspapermen:

> The war has set back the people for a generation. They have bowed to a hundred repressive acts. They have become slaves to the government. They are frightened at the excesses in Russia. They are docile; and they will not recover from being so for many years. The interests which control the Republican Party will make the most of their docility.[4]

Johnson's prophecy proved frighteningly accurate, but he failed to add that a continuation of the wartime habit of conformity would be joined by the continuation of wartime hatreds of radicals, aliens and other "deviants." As Robert Murray has noted, "There was a high degree of scare-inspired psychology at work on public opinion down to 1924-25" and "the whole pattern of thought and action common to the 1920's was in part at least traceable to the red scare."[5] Particularly clear lines can be drawn between the red scare psychology and the fluorishing of superpatriotic private organizations during the 1920's, such as the Ku Klux Klan, the American Legion, the National Security League and many other such groups, who spent much of their time labelling any proposals for reform as "communist" and "radical" and were able to support themselves financially by exploiting the tide of opinion created largely by the government during 1917-20.[6]

Fear of alien radicals and general nativistic feelings which had reached new heights during 1917-20 were reflected after the war in the immigration legislation of 1924, which for the first time established as permanent policy a limit to the number of immigrants who would be accepted per year in the country, as well as establishing a quota system which discriminated against the culturally "suspect" immigrants of eastern and southern Europe.[7] American businessmen took advantage of the war-time attitudes to campaign for the open-shop under the slogan, "American Plan," which suggested, not so subtly, that unionization and anti-business attitudes were somehow "un-American."[8] The Ku Klux Klan reached stupendous heights during the mid-twenties by attacking blacks, Catholics, Jews, radicals, immigrants, and others who did not fit the model of the 100 percent white, conformist, Anglo-Saxon American.[9] When a reform government took power in Mexico and threatened American oil interests, the American press demanded intervention to stop the spread of Bolshevism. And when the U.S. sent armed forces into Nicaragua in 1927, the public justification offered centered largely around the danger of a communist uprising. Referring to reports that Mexican communists were stirring up unrest in Nicaragua, President Coolidge stated, (in terms similar to those Harry Truman would use twenty years later), that the U.S. could not ignore "any serious threat to stability and constitutional government in Nicaragua tending towards anarchy and jeopardizing American interest, especially if such state of affairs is contributed to or brought about by outside influence or any foreign power."[10]

The Sacco-Vanzetti case perhaps best typified the continuation of war-time hatreds and fears.[11] Sacco and Vanzetti were two Italian anarchists who were arrested in May, 1920, during the red scare, for a robbery and double murder which had occurred at South Braintree, Massachusetts. The guilt or innocence of the pair will probably never be conclusively established, but it is certain that they did not receive a fair trial, were tried by a biased judge and suffered heavily from the general anti-alien and anti-radical tenor of the times. As the case dragged its way through the appeals process and the immediate days of the red scare faded, increasing support developed for the pair among "respectable" elements of society. This, in turn, set off a new scare as the date set for the execution approached in 1927. For while some "respectable" elements now urged clemency, the majority of the "respectables" in Massachusetts and elsewhere increasingly came to regard the entire issue as involving the attempts of radicals to "pry apart the foundations of law and order" and "adopted the view that Sacco and Vanzetti had become a challenge to society that could be answered only by their deaths."[12] Justice Department agents infiltrated the Sacco-Vanzetti Defense Committee (one of them became a fund-raiser and kept most of the money for himself), were planted in the Dedham, Massachusetts jail where the pair were held, and attempted to gain evidence to deport Sacco and Vanzetti in case they were freed from the murder charge.

Police in New York City "won the day" during a massive protest demonstration over the Sacco-Vanzetti case in July, 1927, "by the simple expedient of hitting everybody."[13] When six bombings in three different cities occurred on August 6, four days before the scheduled execution, it appeared as though another full-fledged red scare would develop. Federal buildings were placed under guard, troops were alerted to protect the Capitol in Washington, and Boston police prepared an arsenal including twelve submachine guns and fifteen thousand rounds of ammunition. Shortly afterwards, police broke up protests in New York and Chicago. In one incident, a detective suffered a fractured skull when a uniformed patrolman failed to recognize him and therefore gave him the standard treatment meted out to radicals. State troopers attacked a picnic demonstration at Cheswick, Pennsylvania, shedding much blood among the gathered men, women and children, and suffering one fatality during the melee. On the night of the execution, which finally occurred on August 23, 1927, police arrested scores of persons who were picketing the state house in Massachusetts. Repression did not end even with the death of Sacco and Vanzetti, as police brutally attacked the funeral procession and innocent bystanders at the cemetery. In November, 1928, a CP member was arrested for criminal libel and given a year in jail for carrying a public banner branding the Governor of Massachusetts a murderer for failing to halt the executions.[14]

Even more important than the continuation of war-time hatreds and fears during the twenties was the general paralysis that the 1917-20 repression created among radical and even liberal reform movements and sentiments, with the result that business rule was virtually unchecked throughout the decade. As Irving Bernstein has written:

> At no period in the twentieth century, at least, were employers as a class so free of the countervailing restraints of a pluralistic society as during the twenties. Labor organizations were deplorably weak and government was dedicated to fostering the employer's freedom. The businessman rode high, his voice the decisive one in a business society dominated by business interests.[15]

Much as had occurred during the 1870-1900 period, without the opposition of middle class reformers and strong radical political and labor groups, governmental power was simply handed over lock, stock and barrel to business interests. Business became virtually a national religion, sanctified by President Coolidge, who announced that "the man who builds a factory builds a temple, the man who works there worships there."[16] *The Wall Street Journal* commented, "Never before, here or anywhere else, has a government been so completely fused with business."[17]

Under the Republicans in the twenties, entire branches of the government, especially the Commerce Department, functioned as "arms of business within government;"[18] the regulatory agencies were packed with pro-business representatives; business concentration proceeded apace while anti-trust laws were enforced stringently against labor; and Secretary of the Treasury Andrew Mellon, one of the richest men in America, devoted much of his time to reducing taxes in the highest brackets, thereby succeeding in aiding his own companies to the tune of several million dollars.[19] The most fraudulent and illegal business practices went unchecked; thus new securities were manufactured "almost like cakes of soap, for little better reason than that there was gain to be made."[20]

With the power of business unrestrained, the voices of protest emasculated and an illusive prosperity placing a chicken in at least every other pot, the country was dominated by apathy and complacency with regard to social and economic problems. Thus, the drive for universal compulsory health insurance, which had made considerable headway during the 1915-17 period, "died in the quiet of the 1920's."[21] A major advertising point made on behalf of the Columbia Six automobile was that it had "no bolshevistic tendencies."[22] Typical of the general mood was President Coolidge's statement to Congress in 1928 that "no Congress of the United States ever assembled, on surveying the state of the nation, has met with a more pleasing prospect than that which appears at the present time."[23]

Coolidge's complacency reflected the general feeling in the 1920's that true "Americanism" consisted of unswerving loyalty and obeisance to the *status quo*. Under this philosophy the U.S.

> was regarded as having been always right in the past and bound to be always right in the future. American government and American institutions surpassed all others in excellence. America was conceived, not as a process, a development, but as a finished and perfect product, not to be changed, not to be criticized. . . . However disguised such an Americanism might be under glittering generalities about freedom, democracy and justice, it actually identified loyalty to the nation with support of the dominant economic system.[24]

The 1920's are generally thought of as a period of general prosperity. While it is true that the average real earnings of employed workers advanced during the decade — from about 8 percent above the 1914 level in 1921 to 32 percent above the 1914 level in 1928 — workers did not receive a fair share of increasing prosperity. The leading beneficiaries of the economic advance were those who received income from dividends, interest and rent, rather than the wage earner. Thus, between 1923 and 1929, workers' income increased 11 percent, but corporate profits and dividends increased over 60 percent. The best studies available indicate that in 1929, at the end of the "prosperity decade," about 60 to 70 percent of all American families were not earning enough to provide a decent standard of living. In 1929, the top 1 percent of all Americans earned as much as the bottom 42 percent. The entire period was characterized by chronically high unemployment levels, ranging at 10 percent or over during most of the decade, and amidst the general prosperity there were many "sick" industries, such as agriculture, coal, textiles, leathers, shipbuilding and railroading which never shared any of the benefits of prosperity.[25]

The worker and the farmer not only failed to benefit proportionately from the increases in productivity in terms of wages, but they also failed to benefit from price reductions that would have occurred in a society really characterized by free enterprise. Instead, increasing monopolization of production, high tariffs, and rigidities in the market unchecked by government regulation kept prices at artificially high levels. Like so many other features of the twenties, all of these developments were partially a reflection of the destruction of the labor and radical movement during 1917-20 and their resultant lack of influence on government policies and in the market.

The end result of the distorted economic structure which literally ran riot during the 1920's was that the rich accumulated more and more wealth, the corporations maintained inflated prices, and income was so poorly distributed that the majority of the people could not afford to buy goods in sufficient quantities to maintain the economy. In 1929, all of this ended in the greatest depression in American history — a depression which was at least partially a direct result of the 1917-20 repression. The federal government, "seeing all problems from the viewpoint of business . . . had mistaken the class interest for the national interest. The result was both class and national disaster."[26]

Repression and Conformity in the Twenties

Compared to the wave of severe repression that swept the country during 1917-20, there was a marked decline in the degree of overt repression exerted by governmental bodies during the 1920's, and a marked increase in the tolerance accorded dissenting speech. The climate during the twenties, however, was not favorable to civil liberties. The increased "tolerance" was mostly a reflection of the fact that radical political parties and militant labor and farm organizations had been so thoroughly shattered by the 1917-20 repression that the dissent of malcontents no longer seemed very threatening. "The idea that those who might criticize or assault the system posed a serious danger casually slipped into the background."[27] However, when dissent did arise in ways which seemed to pose a real threat — as in major strikes, especially strikes in crucial industries and those led by remnants of radical groups — the iron hand of repression appeared in as naked a form as ever. Just in case, the great bulk of repressive legislation, such as criminal syndicalism laws, remained on the books, and could be reactivated in time of need. The situation in the twenties was perhaps best summed up by the American Civil Liberties Union, which in its report for 1927-28 reported, "The reason for the decrease in repression is that there is little to repress" but that "wherever labor is militant or radicals active the forces of repression are aroused."[28]

The signs of a relative "thaw" in the domestic war against radicals were numerous throughout the decade. No additional criminal syndicalism laws were passed during the twenties, and except for a few states such as Pennsylvania, California and Oregon where industrial conflict remained intense, syndicalism laws essentially became dead letters after about 1921. With the inauguration of a less crusading and ideological Republican administration in 1920, war-time restrictions on the press were finally lifted and remaining war-time prisoners were released. While Wilson's Postmaster General Albert Burleson had refused even after the end of the war to restore second-class mailing privileges to periodicals which had lost them during the war, Harding's Postmaster General quickly restored those privileges in 1921. After a long and well-organized campaign to gain the release of war-time political prisoners, the last of those convicted under the Espionage and Sedition acts had their sentences commuted by President Coolidge in 1923.[29]

There were other commutations from state officials. In 1923, Benjamin Gitlow and other leading New York communists were released by New York Gov. Al Smith. Governor Len Small of Illinois pardoned William Bross Lloyd and other leaders of the Illinois Communist Labor Party shortly after their convictions were upheld in 1922. Governor C. C. Young of California pardoned Charlotte Whitney after the Supreme Court upheld her criminal syndicalism conviction in 1927.[30]

The Federal sedition act was repealed March 3, 1921, while the espionage act became inapplicable with the formal ending of the war with Germany in July, 1921. Deportations for political reasons dropped drastically after the leftovers from the Palmer Raids were dispatched in the early 1920's. Three New York socialists were seated without protest in the state legislature in 1921, while Victor Berger regained his seat in the House of Representatives without protest in 1923. (He had been elected again in 1922 after the Supreme Court in 1921 had overturned his espionage act conviction on a technicality.) In general, the 1922 elections resulted in notable successes by liberals and pro-civil libertarians, including the election of Al Smith as Governor of New York, who had run on a pledge to get rid of the "anti-subversive" Lusk Laws (which were repealed in 1923). Criminal syndicalism cases arising after 1920 were increasingly marked by acquittals, hung juries, untried cases and reversals on appeal. By 1923, the Communist Party formed by a fusion of the former CP and CLP under orders from the Comintern, felt secure enough to finally emerge from the underground. In 1928, the unified CP functioned for the first time on a more or less national scale. Most major civil liberties fights during the twenties involved a fair number of "respectable" citizens standing up for the rights of radicals and labor, spearheaded by the American Civil Liberties Union, formally organized at the height of the red scare in January, 1920.[31]

	Political Deportations[32]	Prisoners held under political offenses[33]	
		Federal	State
1920	314		
1921	446		
1922	64		
1923	13	0	122
1924	81	0	98
1925	22	0	77
1926	4	0	17
1927	9	0	7
1928	1	0	0

Unfortunately, the picture presented thus far is a far from complete portrait of the state of civil liberties in the twenties. While the degree of overt repression did decrease considerably, there remained in the minds of the public and governmental officials a strong carryover of 1917-20 hatreds and prejudices, and in the minds of "malcontents" a strong reminder of the way dissent had been treated in those years. This created, on the one hand, continued harassment of the remaining fragments of dissident thought, and on the other hand, a strong tendency towards either self-censorship or total avoidance of controversy on the part of dissidents. During the 1920's,

> Repression no longer manifested itself in the dragnet roundups, the group prosecutions and the mass deportations of radicals typical of the war and postwar years; but the federal government had not lost all interest in the problem. Convinced that the class war was a continuing threat to America, the Republican administrations of the 1920's remained on the alert, and, in some areas, on the offensive. . . . The concerted war-time attack was over, but fear and hatred of left-wing beliefs endured as an influence on official policy.[34]

Although with the repeal of the Sedition act and the expiration of the Espionage act in 1921, the Federal government had absolutely no legal authority to act against citizen radicals,[35] the Justice Department and the War Department along with leading administration officials, continued to keep a watchful eye on radical activities, and to agitate the radical menace. Thus, in October, 1922, military intelligence in the state of Washington asked leading lumber corporations to keep the military informed about the activities and membership of "radical groups" such as the IWW,

CP and CLP and "such semi-radical organizations as the Socialists, Non-Partisan League, Big Four (railroad) Brotherhoods, and American Federation of Labor."[36] Major Gen. Amos H. Fries, head of the Chemical Warfare Service (CWS) of the War Department, (whose wife was publicity chairman of the Daughters of the American Revolution), declared in December, 1922, that the National Council for the Prevention of War, a leading pacifist group, was "financed, inspired and directed from Moscow" and proposed to "establish communism in America."[37] With Fries' blessing and encouragement, the CWS librarian prepared a "Spider Web Chart" which purported to prove that American pacifist organizations were a "fundamental and integral part of international socialism." Among the groups branded as "red" by this chart, which was widely circulated among women's groups, were the League of Women Voters, the Women's Christian Temperance Union and the American Home Economic Association. Although the chart was later repudiated by Secretary of War John W. Weeks, it was repeatedly cited during the twenties as proofs of subversive influence among pacifist groups. Similar charges against pacifist groups and anti-ROTC protesters were made by Defense Department spokesmen throughout the decade.[38]

Vice-President Coolidge added to fears of the "red" menace by publishing a series of red-baiting articles in the *Delineator,* a women's magazine, in the summer of 1921. Coolidge especially stressed the threat of radical infiltration of women's colleges. He ominously noted that Professor Mary Calkins of Wellesley was "said to have voted for Debs for President at the recent election."[39] Harding's Commissioner of Education declared there is "altogether too much preaching of these damnable doctrines of Bolshevism, Anarchy, Communism and Socialism" and avowed that "if I had it in my power I would not only imprison but would expatriate all advocates of these dangerous un-American doctrines. I would even execute every one of them — and do it joyfully."[40]

Attorney General Daugherty declared in 1921 that agitation for release of war-time prisoners was being led by "persons mainly hostile to American institutions. . . . Socialists, IWW, and anarchists, whether they be natives of this country, or as most of them are, importations from the Old World." Daugherty viewed the 1922 railroad strike as a communist plot, and after being forced from office in 1924 by a group of senators led by Burton K. Wheeler, declared that Wheeler was the "communist leader in the Senate." He termed the Senate committee which had investigated him "the Red Triumvirate."[41]

The chief government red-baiter was William J. Burns, who had been appointed as head of the Bureau of Investigation in 1921. Burns had been head of the Burns Detective agency, and he did not hesitate to stir up business for his company by warning about the growing threat of bolshevism. Although the communist "menace" was virtually non-existent in the early 1920's, year after year Burns told congressional committees and the public that the danger was increasing. Thus, he declared that the 1922 coal strike was a result of Comintern inspiration, and stated his goal was to "drive every radical out of the country and bring the parlor Bolsheviks to their senses."[42] In 1924, Burns told Congress:

> Radicalism is becoming stronger every day in this country. These parlor Bolsheviks have sprung up everywhere, as evidenced by this ACLU in New York. . . . Unless the country becomes thoroughly aroused concerning the danger of this radical element in this country we will have a serious situation.[43]

Under Burns' administration, the Justice Department knew "what every radical organization in the country was doing"[44] as Bureau agents kept close tabs on a variety of organizations ranging from the CP to the ACLU and the NAACP. Thus, Bureau agents attended all speeches given by ACLU head Roger Baldwin and kept close tabs on ACLU literature, mailing lists and minutes. Justice Department agents also closely cooperated with local and state officials to help develop criminal syndicalism cases. In at least one case, Burns authorized Justice Department agents to cooperate with Burns Agency detectives who had been hired to spy on union activities in the Arizona copper mines. Right-wing organizations were routinely leaked material from Bureau files.[45]

With the revelation of the Teapot Dome scandals and the alleged failure of the Bureau of Investigation to look into certain business fraud cases related to the war, the Department of Justice came under increasing congressional fire during 1922-24. The chief antagonist of the Bureau was Sen. Burton K. Wheeler of Montana. The Bureau retaliated against its critics with an early version of Watergate. As the result of a Congressional inquiry, it became widely known that Bureau agents "wiretapped, broke into offices, and shuffled through personal files, and kept tabs on people's private lives,"[46] especially if they were persons, including Congressmen, who criticized the Department of Justice and the Bureau of Investigation. Bureau agents subjected Wheeler to "harassment, threats, espionage and villification;"[47] they "hid in the bushes outside Wheeler's . . . home to spy on him, ransacked his Capitol Hill office, and tried to lure him into a compromising situation with a woman in an Ohio hotel room."[48] Wheeler was indicted on a trumped-up bribery charge in an attempt by the Department of Justice to intimidate him, but was quickly acquitted in court and exonerated by a Senate investigation.

As a result of the Teapot Dome scandals and the revelation of Bureau spying on Congressmen, pressure for a clean-up in the Justice Department became so strong that Attorney General Harry Daugherty was replaced as Attorney General in March, 1924 by Harlan F. Stone. Stone quickly replaced Burns as head of the Bureau of Investigation, installing in his place J. Edgar Hoover. On May 14, 1924, Stone issued a public statement which indicated that the activities of the Justice Department in spying on American citizens due to their political beliefs and affiliations had come to an end. He declared:

> There is always the possibility that a secret police may become a menace to free government and free institutions because it carries with it the possibility of abuses of power which are not always quickly apprehended or understood. . . . It is important that (the Bureau's) activities be strictly limited to those functions for which it was created and that its agents themselves be not above the law or beyond its reach. . . . The Bureau of Investigation is not concerned with political or other opinions of individuals. It is concerned only with their conduct and then only with such conduct as is forbidden by the laws of the United States. When a police system passes beyond these limits, it is dangerous to the proper administration of justice and to human liberty, which it should be our first concern to cherish.[49]

Stone terminated the anti-radical division of the Bureau (the GID), and ended its link with private detective agencies, its dissemination of anti-radical propaganda, its undercover espionage into labor and radical groups, its encouragement of state anti-radical prosecutions and its illegal searches, seizures and wiretappings.[50] According to an internal FBI history made public by the Senate Intelligence Committee in March, 1976, until Franklin D. Roosevelt reactivated the FBI as a political intelligence agency in the mid-1930's, Justice Department and Bureau policy "was to not engage in general domestic security intelligence operations" although the FBI did conduct "general domestic radical investigations where the activity indicated a violation of Federal laws" or "where investigations were specifically requested by (the) State Department;" otherwise the Bureau "obtained such intelligence-type information only when volunteered by some outside source."[51]

Hoover, voicing the new Justice Department line, tacitly admitted the Bureau had been violating the law in its previous anti-radical investigations; thus, in a memorandum to Assistant Attorney General William J. Donovan in October, 1924, he stated that:

> The activities of the Communists and other ultra-radicals have not up to the present time constituted a violation of the Federal statutes, and consequently the Department of Justice, theoretically, has no right to investigate such activities as there has been no violation of the Federal laws.[52]

ACLU head Roger Baldwin was highly impressed in a talk with Hoover in August, 1924, and soon the ACLU became one of Hoover's staunchest backers.[53] That confidence appears to have been well placed at first, as Hoover repeatedly resisted pressure from Congress and other sources to initiate general intelligence activities until President Roosevelt asked him to investigate fascist organizations in the U.S. in 1934 and to expand FBI intelligence activities to include communist groups in 1936. Thus, in January, 1932, Hoover, in a memorandum to the Attorney General concerning proposed legislation which would direct the FBI to investigate "the revolutionary propoganda and activities of communists" and others who "teach or advocate the overthrow by force and violence" of the government, wrote that if the FBI were to investigate such activities it would be investigating "conditions, which from a Federal standpoint, have not been declared illegal and in connection with which no prosecution might be instituted." Thus,

> the Department and the Bureau would undoubtedly be subject to charges in the matter of alleged secret and undesirable methods in connection with investigative activities, as well as to allegations involving charges of the use of "Agents Provocateur."[54]

At about the same time that the FBI terminated its general anti-radical investigations in 1924, Military Intelligence also closed down its anti-radical operations.[55]

The executive branch of the federal government more or less got out of the business of repression of political radicals after about 1924, but the judicial branches of both the federal and state governments maintained a hard line throughout the decade. With the exception of the New Mexico Supreme Court, criminal syndicalism laws were repeatedly upheld by the state courts and the Supreme Court.[56] Although in the 1919 *Schenck* case the Supreme Court had laid down the "clear and present danger" test for determining the legality of laws punishing political dissent and for convictions under such laws, in practice the courts "could not refrain from holding that ideological nonconformity, even though no criminal act was involved, constituted in itself a clear and present danger."[57]

Repression of Free Speech by Local Police 1921-28[58]

	Meetings Broken Up	Arrests
1921	82	289
1922	28	846
1923	58	340
1924	24	235
1925	22	352
1926	28	52*
1927	14	46*
1928	54	418

*Arrest data for 1926 and 1927 exclude cases arising out of labor disputes

Although the executive branch of the federal government relaxed its anti-radical vigilance after 1924, local police officials continued to harass radicals throughout the decade. The major target was the CP, although the SPA suffered somewhat also. While the CP gradually emerged into the sunlight during the twenties, its activities were constantly interfered with by governmental infiltration and persecutions, even though CP membership generally remained below ten thousand. Especially in the early years of the decade, the CP was riddled with government spies. In one episode, a government spy charged that a leading CP member, Louis Fraina, was a government agent; as a result of these charges Fraina was "tried" and "cleared" by the party. His defense counsel later turned out to be yet another government spy. Partly as a result of the phony charges, Fraina was eventually repudiated by the party, and left the communist movement.[59]

In another episode, a government spy, Francis A. Morrow, who had founded a CP unit in New Jersey and became secretary of the Camden district of the party, cast the key vote in which the party voted twenty-three to tweny-two during a secret convention in 1922 at Bridgman, Michigan, to place stress on underground work. Subsequently, Federal and state agents who had been tipped off by Morrow raided the Bridgman convention, and eventually a number of leading communists were arrested under Michigan's criminal syndicalism law. When the trials began, the government introduced as evidence against the party the decision which Morrow had been instrumental in bringing about! During the Michigan trials, CP leader Charles Ruthenberg was sentenced to five years; William Z. Foster had a hung jury; and the other cases were eventually dismissed.[60]

The party suffered moderate repression throughout the decade in its political activities, and severe repression in its attempts to organize trade unions. In 1922, Foster, visiting Denver to fulfill a speaking engagement, was arrested, driven into Wyoming, dumped into the desert and told never to return. CP speakers and party workers faced occasional arrests, and CP headquarters and meetings were the targets of police raids. Thus, in 1927 four CP members were sentenced to twenty days in Brooklyn for "conspiracy to undermine respect for the courts of law" for distributing handbills protesting the issuance of labor injunctions.[61] During the 1928 election campaign, the party "won considerable publicity through the frequent arrests of its candidates and campaigners."[62] For example, the CP candidate for governor of Arizona was arrested and beaten while in jail, and presidential candidate Foster was arrested in Delaware on the charge of using an "inflammatory slogan" by advertising his meeting with a leaflet proclaiming "abolish lynching."[63] Five CP workers were arrested for criminal syndicalism in July and August, 1929 after distributing party literature and attempting to address small groups in Martins Ferry, Ohio; the convictions of all five defendants were eventually overturned on appeal.[64]

The SPA remained extremely weak throughout the 1920's — its membership was below eight thousand in 1928 — and it was even less active than the CP. Indeed, the SPA was "all but completely dormant" during the Coolidge period.[65] Even SPA workers ran into occasional harassment, however. For example, in 1923 two SPA speakers who tried to speak in Old Forge, Pennsylvania, were kidnapped by policemen and deported from the county; when they tried to come back and speak they were arrested. In 1924, an SPA peace meeting called for Defense Day was banned in Boston, and in 1928 a party member was arrested for "obstructing a public highway" after the city council had voted to allow street speaking, but the mayor had banned such activities.[66]

The 1920 and 1924 elections both demonstrated that there were hundreds of thousands of radicals who had not foresworn their beliefs, but were only willing to express them inside the secrecy of a polling place in the climate of the 1920's. In the 1920 election, SPA candidate Eugene Debs received over nine hundred thousand votes even though he was in prison, while Parley P. Christensen, candidate of the Farmer-Labor Party, whose platform was similar to that of the SPA, received another two hundred ninety thousand votes.[67] While the SPA substantially outpolled its record 1912 vote in the few areas where its machinery was still intact, in 1920 it had effective organizations left in only nine states, and thus its remaining "pockets of strength tended to become isolated islands, rather than parts of a national movement."[68]

In terms of electoral politics, the high point of radicalism in the 1920's was the 1924 presidential election campaign of the Progressive Party, headed by Sen. Robert LaFollette.[69] LaFollette was backed by an extremely loose and disorganized coalition which included the Socialist Party, the AFL, the independent railroad unions, and remnants of a variety of liberal and radical movements, including the NPL, the 1912 Progressive Party and the 1920 Farmer-Labor Party. The Progressive platform declared that the great issue of the day was "control of government and industry by private monopoly" and called for government ownership of the railroads and water power, an end to labor injunctions, the right of labor to organize and a curb on the power of the Supreme Court. LaFollette received almost five million votes (17 percent) out of about twenty-nine million votes which remains one of the best third party showings in American history. Although the vote clearly demonstrated that "even in the palmiest days of Coolidge prosperity, a vast reservoir of liberal thought and opinion, a reservoir merely concealed and not obliterated by the political successes of the reactionaries and the economic sedatives of the twenties"[70] remained, the Progressive Party disintegrated after the election.

A number of points are worth making about the 1924 Progressive campaign. First, the 17 percent vote received by the party suggests that the destructive effects of the 1917-20 period and its intimidating aftereffects created the paradox of shattered radical organizations alongside a large radical or semi-radical constituency. Secondly, the main issue used against LaFollette by the Republicans was the "red" issue, even though LaFollette had spurned the support of the 1924 Farmer-Labor Party precisely to avoid being red-baited and had stationed "one hundred husky sergeants-at-arms" at the doors of his nominating convention to "prevent any possible intrusion from Moscow."[71] Nevertheless, according to Republican Vice-Presidential Candidate Charles Dawes, the issue in the election was "whether you stand on the rock of common sense with Calvin Coolidge or upon the sinking sands of socialism with Robert M. LaFollette."[72] Dawes referred to the Progressive Party as a "heterogeneous collection of those opposed to the existing order of things, the greatest section of which, the Socialists, flies the Red Flag."[73] Republican supporters also made much of LaFollette's anti-war stand during World War I and occasionally insinuated his cause was being financed with Russian money.

Thirdly, the Progressive Party suffered in many cases from obstruction or banning of party rallies and in some cases from physical assault. Thus, in Darien, Connecticut, a Progressive spokesman was removed from his speaking platform by police, hauled before a judge, lectured for "insulting the people of the United States" and ordered to leave town.[74] In Pasco, Washington, a Socialist was arrested and fined for speaking on behalf of LaFollette.

Finally, one major reason why LaFollette did less well than he might have was that despite its formal support for him, the AFL held back from real financial or organizational support, apparently for fear of being tinged with the "red" issue. By the end of the campaign, the AFL "was almost openly apologizing for its association with LaFollette."[75]

Unorganized radicals during the twenties faced not so much the threat of overt repression but the general pall of conformity which hung over the land. Many intellectuals simply avoided politics altogether, partly as a result of intimidation, partly from a distrust in the power of the state and in the entire concept of democracy, progress and rationality in the aftermath of 1917-20.[76] Some intellectuals fled physically, escaping to the bohemian refuge of Greenwich Village or to Europe, while others escaped emotionally, like the political dissenter in *Middletown* who, forced into conformity by the pressure of public opinion, said, "I just ran away from it all to my books."[77] F. Scott Fitzgerald summed up the position of many intellectuals when he noted, "It was characteristic of the jazz age that it had no interest in politics at all."[78]

Most teachers were shrewd enough judges of the political situation to simply avoid any mention of controversial political activities whatsoever. The business influence on the schools, as in the rest of society, was pervasive, and the pressure on teachers to conform was extremely high. About twenty states passed "positive" teacher loyalty oaths during the twenties, and in many cases textbooks that were deemed insufficiently patriotic were banned from the schools. Many states also passed laws requiring the teaching of courses in American history and observance of patriotic holidays. In 1921 the Massachusetts Senate passed a bill to ban a particular book from the schools, but the measure died in the house. Several states passed legislation which banned "disloyal" teachers from employment, and Congress in 1925 passed a bill barring payment of any teachers in Washington, D.C. who taught "that ours is an inferior form of government." Oregon and Wisconsin both passed legislation which barred textbooks which disparaged America's founding fathers. In a number of cases, teachers who still failed to get the message were fired. Thus, a journalism professor was fired from Ohio State University for treating a coal strike favorably, while two members of the University of Illinois staff were bounced for criticizing the zinc smelting industry.[79]

Civil liberties, radical and peace groups found the campus an unfriendly place during the 1920's. Thus, the ACLU fought for two years, from 1926 to 1928, before it was allowed to use public school facilities for a meeting on the subject of "free speech;" the New York City Board of Education declared use of school facilities for such a purpose might lead its "principles of Americanization" to be "nullified and flaunted in the faces of the maturing citizenship."[80] Students found the twenties to be "characterized by substantial repression; students with radical inclinations were often expelled from colleges, student newspapers were censored and administrators often acted in a heavy-handed manner."[81] Thus, the Intercollegiate Socialist Society, a college-student socialist group "found it difficult to sponsor liberal pacifist and radical speakers on campuses because of the reluctance of college administrations to have them."[82] Pacifist leader Nevin Sayre was barred from speaking at the University of Oklahoma. When the faculty at Ohio State University expressed a preference for making ROTC drill optional, a local ROTC officer accused them of disloyalty, and under administrative pressure the faculty quickly reversed themselves.[83]

While pitifully weak left-wing organizations and individuals suffered persistent harassment during the twenties, scores of superpatriotic, nativist, racist and anti-Semitic extreme right-wing groups flourished during the decade untouched by official reprisals.[84] The one exception to this generalization was the Ku Klux Klan, which at its height in the early part of the decade had a membership variously estimated at from two to six million, and which at times dominated a number of state governments, including those of Oregon, Indiana, Colorado and Texas.[85] The Klan, which fostered "100 percent Americanism" and which opposed radicals, blacks, Jews, Catholics and the "immoral," was accurately described by one journalist as "the most vigorous, active and effective force in American life, outside business."[86] There is no question that in many areas the KKK was subjected to official reprisals that must be termed political repression, but it is important to point out that, unlike left-wing groups, the KKK was responsible for the actual *commission* of acts of violence, rather than alleged *advocacy* of such deeds; according to various accounts the KKK was responsible for at least six murders, and thousands of assaults. Thus, many of the scores of investigations and arrests directed against the Klan clearly cannot be reasonably construed as political repression. However, just as clearly some of the actions directed against the Klan do fall into the category of political repression, especially since many of these actions were directed against the Klan as an organization, rather than against individuals; despite the general aura of violence which surrounded the Klan, the vast majority of members never engaged in any form of violence, but instead concerned themselves with electoral politics, picnics, and even charitable enterprises. In fact, outside the South, Klansmen were engaged in relatively few acts of violence and were frequently "more often the victims than the instigators of foul play."[87]

The most common form of repressive anti-Klan activity involved the passage of laws barring the wearing of masks in public by a number of states, including New York, Michigan, Illinois, Texas, Arizona, and California. Similar bans on masked Klan activity were ordered by the mayors or municipal governments of many cities, such as Atlanta, Memphis, Indianapolis, Minneapolis and Los Angeles.[88] In Salt Lake City, the local Klan retaliated against an anti-mask law "by getting all bewhiskered Santa Clauses banned at Christmas time."[89] Anti-mask laws were certainly a mild — perhaps even a borderline — type of repression, but the Klan suffered far more severely in many areas. Thus KKK members were ordered fired from public employment in Dallas, Minneapolis, Los Angeles and Fresno, jury duty was denied Ku Kluxers in Chicago and Minneapolis, the sale of Klan literature was barred in Louisville and Indianapolis and Klan meetings were completely forbidden in Boston, Louisville and Atlantic City. The mayors of Cleveland and New York, and the city council of Chicago, directed that the Klan be driven from their communities. State laws requiring the registration of all Klan members were passed in New York and Louisiana, while the Klan was barred from doing business in the state of Kansas by the refusal of state officials to grant it a charter. In Harrison, New Jersey, being a member of the Klan subjected one to arrest, while in Springfield, Ohio, a Klan funeral procession was charged with disorderly conduct.[90] The strongest actions directed against the Klan occurred in Oklahoma, where Governor Jack Walton reacted to hundreds of Klan assaults by instituting martial law, censoring Tulsa's leading newspaper, banning Klan meetings, using military courts to try alleged Klan vigilantes, and, finally, by using troops to block an attempted grand jury investigation of his administration and an attempt by the state legislature to meet. Eventually, the Oklahoma courts ordered an election to authorize a special session of the legislature without waiting for Walton to convene it. The legislature succeeded in meeting, impeached and removed Walton from office and passed an anti-mask bill directed at the Klan.[91]

By the second half of the twenties the Klan was in a state of general collapse across the country, and by 1930 had fallen to a membership of no more than one hundred thousand. There can be little doubt that the repeated investigations, dubious arrests and general harassment of the Klan played a role in its decline, but more important factors were repeated squabbles within the Klan leadership, the Klan's inability to maintain the high pitch of emotional fervor which marked its rise in the early twenties, and a general public revulsion against the very real acts of violence committed by KKK members. Perhaps another reason for the decline of the Klan was the fact that many of its basic ideas, such as immigration restriction, "100 percent Americanism" and vigilant anti-radicalism, were accepted and enforced, without the need for illegal violence, by the established authorities.

Repression of Labor

With radical political groups pitifully weak during the twenties and most intellectuals intimidated into silence or simply not interested in politics, the only real threat to the status quo that arose during the decade came from labor. Not coincidentally it was labor, and particularly radical labor, that suffered the bulk of repressive governmental activity during the twenties. In fact, labor was probably repressed more consistently during the twenties than during any other decade in American history.

The major weapons by which labor suffered at the hands of the government were the injunction and other unfavorable court decisions, and the militia. Because business and a business mentality thoroughly dominated not only the federal government, but also most state governments, virtually all labor activity was viewed and treated as somewhat subversive by most governmental agencies, especially the courts. The twenties were the high-tide of the labor injunction. Over nine hundred injunctions were issued by federal and state courts from 1920 to 1930, about half of the total number of injunctions issued during the entire 1880-1930 period. The power of the strike injunction was especially severe when coupled with the so-called Hitchman doctrine. The Supreme Court ruled in 1917, in the case of *Hitchman Coal & Coke Co.* vs. *Mitchell,* that injunctions could be issued to enjoin unions from even attempting to organize workers who had signed yellow-dog contracts, on the grounds that such activity would be inducing a breach of contract. Previously, yellow-dog contracts could not be legally enforced, but under the Hitchman doctrine employers were promised full protection of the law in prosecuting unions who sought to organize their workers after employees had been induced to sign such contracts. By the end of the decade, more than sixty injunctions had been issued under the Hitchman doctrine and about 1.25 million workers were covered by yellow-dog contracts. Some of the Hitchman injunctions covered large segments of major industries. The most noted of these injunctions was the so-called "Red Jacket" injunction issued in 1927 which barred the UMW from organizing in 316 coal companies with over forty thousand employees in the critical West Virginia coal regions. Between 1924 and 1928 the UMW spent over eight million dollars in fruitless litigation fighting in the Red Jacket and related cases.[92]

Aside from the issuance of strike injunctions, the state and federal courts, and the Supreme Court in particular, consistently ruled during the twenties in ways which hampered labor activities and its free exercise of civil liberties. William Howard Taft, who became chief justice in 1921, was notoriously biased against labor. The most important of the court's anti-labor decisions included: 1) *Duplex Printing Press* v. *Deering* (1921), holding that a nationwide boycott imposed by a labor union upon the installation of printing presses manufactured in a non-union shop, for the purpose of unionizing the shop, was in violation of the Sherman and Clayton Acts — in effect declaring secondary boycotts illegal and voiding the Clayton Act provision barring injunctions "unless necessary to prevent irreparable injury to property or to a property right;" 2) *Bedford Cut Stone* v. *Journeyman* (1927), holding that an order by a union to its members to refuse to handle limestone produced by a non-union mine, for the purpose of unionizing the mine, was illegal under the Sherman Act; 3) *American Steel Foundries* v. *Tri-City Central Trades Council* (1921), which in effect outlawed peaceful picketing that exceeded one picket at each plant gate, thus making effective picketing impossible; 4) *Truax* v. *Corrigan* (1921), declaring unconstitutional Arizona's anti-labor injunction law; and 5) the Coronado Coal cases (1925), which held that unions which struck for the purpose of organizing the unorganized segment of an industry, would, by obstructing production, violate the Sherman Act, in effect making it impossible for any union to attempt to achieve a nationwide closed shop for the purpose of protecting union standards and wages.[93]

While the court was chiseling away at labor's rights, it was throwing out labor reform laws, winking at the activities of big business, and emasculating regulatory agencies like the Federal Trade Commission. "In the eyes of the court, interstate commerce was an india-rubber concept, one that would stretch to prohibit activities by unions and relax to permit similar activities by employers."[94] The court's concept of liberty was equally strange, since:

> In virtually every case in which labor was involved the liberty guaranteed was of the nature to make labor's demands and hopes ineffectual, especially those seeking concessions in the form of better hours, wages and working conditions, while in virtually every case in which business prerogatives threatened the public welfare, the liberty on whose side the Court came up was liberty of business to continue its practices and the liberty of the public to accept and adjust to them on business's terms.

At the same time, the court showed a "callous unwillingness to protect the freedoms and liberties of the dissenters and have-nots within American society against whom the Court had little difficulty in upholding and enforcing state authorized proscriptions and inhibitions."[95]

The twenties also saw the frequent use of the state militia during strikes, especially during the first five years of the decade, before strike activity dropped off drastically. During 1920-24, about 90 percent of all national guard active duty was related to strikes. In a high percentage of cases in which troops were sent, there had been no violence.[96] The combined effect of the massive use of troops and injunctions, and the various hostile court decisions, was that union membership and strike activity crumbled as the decade proceeded. By 1926-30, the annual number of strikes had shrunk to 24 percent of that during the 1916-21 period, and the number of workers involved was 13 percent of the earlier period. In 1928, the number of strikes was lower than any year since 1884.[97] Union

The 1920's: Conformity and Repression   185

membership declined from over 5 million in 1920 to about 3.4 million in

	Union Membership (in thousands)[98]	No. of Strikes[99]	Nat'l. Guard Use in Labor Disputes[100]
1920	5,048	3,411	5
1921	4,781	2,385	9
1922	4,027	1,112	24
1923	3,622	1,553	8
1924	3,536	1,249	5
1925	3,519	1,301	4
1926	3,502	1,035	3
1927	3,546	666	6
1928	3,430	620	1
1929	3,443	924	3

1929. There were other factors involved in this decline in union membership and strikes — the general rise in the standard of living, the adoption of "welfare capitalism" and company union plans by many businessmen, the generally hostile climate with regard to labor, the timid attitude of the AFL and the development of the massive anti-union employer campaign known as the "American Plan." However, many of these factors may be indirectly traced also to the effects of the 1917-20 repression and the generally repressive climate of the twenties.

The IWW and the CP were the most consistent victims of repression directed against labor activity. The IWW was involved in major strike activities only in 1922-23 and 1927, but in each case it faced savage repression. The use of the criminal syndicalism law in California had never quite died out — there were twenty-eight indictments under the law in 1920 and forty-nine in 1921, almost all directed against IWW members — but it was not until the IWW in California showed strong signs of revival in 1922 that massive use of the law began again. In October 1922, the IWW led a strike of seventeen hundred workers at the Hetch-Hetchy acqueduct project in southern California, which eventually spread to and tied up a major power project of the Southern California Edison Co. Subsequently, in the spring of 1923, three thousand maritime workers in the rapidly growing IWW Maritime Transport Workers Union completely tied up the port of San Pedro, near Los Angeles. In each of these strikes, strikers were met with mass arrests, denials of free access to the strike areas, deportations and raids on strike meetings. On one day alone, four hundred men were arrested on various charges of vagrancy, traffic violation and criminal syndicalism. The high (or low) point of the San Pedro strike came when Upton Sinclair and three companions were arrested for inciting a riot and addressing an unlawful assemblage as they tried to read the Bill of Rights at a meeting held on private property.[101] Altogether, during a fifteen-month period of 1922-23, 265 arrests were made in California for criminal syndicalism, and during a six month period 772 arrests were made in connection with the San Pedro strike. In August, 1923, California authorities obtained a court injunction which in effect outlawed the IWW entirely. Over two hundred cases were brought in 1923-24 for violation of the injunction. Criminal syndicalism prosecutions against the IWW in California ceased after 1924, apparently because the effect of the injunction and prosecutions was to effectively destroy what was left of the organization. By then, a total of 531 persons had been arrested for criminal syndicalism since the passage of California's law in 1919, of whom 264 were eventually tried and 109 ultimately convicted after appeals.

During the 1922-23 IWW revival the organization also suffered in other states. In 1922, North Dakota's attorney general directed all state attorneys to do everything possible to prevent harvest workers from coming into contact with IWW organizers. The last remnants of the IWW in North Dakota were destroyed in 1925 when police in Fargo rounded up two hundred men in raids on the IWW hall and "hobo jungles," then forced the men to run a gauntlet across the bridge crossing the Red River to Moorhead, Minnesota between a double line of men armed with clubs; guards were posted at the bridge to prevent a return to Fargo. IWW maritime workers who led a strike in Portland, Oregon, in October, 1922 were met with massive arrests — over four hundred altogether. Criminal syndicalism charges were brought in 1923 to break up IWW activity in the lumber and mining districts of Idaho, and two IWW organizers were convicted for criminal syndicalism in Oklahoma during the same year. In the spring of 1923, Mobile, Alabama police raided IWW maritime workers' headquarters, but failed to gain convictions for arrests under state vagrancy, anti-boycott and criminal anarchy laws. By 1924, criminal syndicalism prosecutions virtually ceased across the country, due to the destruction of the IWW and increasing difficulty in getting convicttions due to juror resistance.[102]

The last major IWW strike during the 1920's came in the Colorado coal fields in 1927. This strike featured the closing of strikers' meeting places, vigilante and police raids on IWW halls, mass arrests of picketers and strike leaders, detentions without charges and in *incommunicado* conditions, the banning of public meetings and demonstrations, and kidnapping and beating of strike leaders by national guardsmen. The climax of the Colorado strike came on November 21, 1927, when Colorado state police fired on a group of peaceful and unarmed marchers who had ignored police orders to cease marching on a mine where they had previously been allowed to march without hindrance. Six persons were killed and twenty-three wounded by the police fire. Although the strike collapsed under the weight of state repression, the miners eventually won a favorable wage settlement, but it was the UMW, not the IWW, that gained recognition.[103]

The CP had little better luck than the IWW during the few strikes it organized during the twenties. In 1926, the first major strike led entirely by the CP was called at the Passaic, New Jersey textile mills. The CP succeeded in bringing out sixteen thousand mill workers, mainly unskilled employees who had been ignored by the AFL's United Textile Workers (UTW), which had organized less than 5 percent of the textile industry. The Passaic strikers faced attacks by police and deputy sheriffs who used clubs, icy streams of water from fire hoses, tear gas bomb and guns. The police broke up picket lines and union meetings, raided and closed union halls and made about one thousand arrests. Picketing was eventually banned and the key CP strike leader was arrested for criminal anarchy and held in jail on $50,000 bond in an attempt to break the strike. Passaic authorities even broke the cameras of newsmen covering the strike. Eventually the press corp took to wearing steel helmets and covering the strike from low-flying planes or automobiles which resembled tanks. When Socialist Party Chairman Norman Thomas tried to speak in a vacant lot in nearby Garfield, New Jersey, sheriff's deputies attacked the crowd that had gathered to hear him and arrested Thomas for disorderly conduct. Eventually an injunction was obtained barring local authorities from interfering with meetings or peaceful picketing, but the strike was completely lost.[104]

Other communist strikes in the twenties also met fierce resistance. In the unsuccessful New York garment workers strike of 1926, seventy-five hundred were arrested in fifteen weeks, and in the successful fur workers' strike of the same year, almost nine hundred were arrested.[105]

The CP tried again to crack the textile industry in a 1928 strike at New Bedford, Massachusetts. The CP succeeded in calling out twenty-seven thousand workers. The police and national guard were called in and arrested over two thousand strikers. Although mass picketing continued, many strikers were "savagely mauled by the police and then punished still further by severe penalties in court." The strike was lost after about six months.[106]

The CP tried once again to organize textile workers during a 1929 strike at Gastonia, North Carolina. Gastonia was the leading textile center in the entire country and the home of the largest textile mill in the world under one roof, the Loray Mill. On April 1, 1929, 80 percent of the twenty-two hundred employees of the Loray Mill walked out under communist leadership. After a minor picket line scuffle, five companies of national guard troops were sent to Gastonia. A Department of Labor conciliator quickly branded the strike as "communistic" and a "form of revolution"; numerous arrests and the recruitment of strikebreakers under national guard protection broke the back of the strike by mid-April.[107]

However, rougher treatment was deemed necessary to completely destroy the remnants of the CP organization. Picketing and parading were barred in Gastonia and dozens of strikers arrested for defying the order. On April 18, a mob of masked men destroyed union strike headquarters and burned the contents of a strike relief store while national guard units stationed nearby failed to stir until the mob had dispersed, whereupon they arrested a number of strikers on the theory that they had destroyed their own equipment in order to gain public sympathy. Although strike parades were regularly broken up with considerable violence, only one policeman was ever arrested for unnecessary brutality; he had had the misfortune to beat a newspaper reporter unconscious.

On June 7, gunfire broke out between police officers who sought to invade the CP tent headquarters and strikers. The local police chief was killed, and three policemen and one striker wounded. At least two of the policemen had been drinking heavily, and it is not improbable that some of the police shot each other. Subsequently, mobs raided the tent colony and the homes of strikers, and fifteen strikers were arrested for conspiracy leading to murder. When the case ended in a mistrial on September 9, mob violence again convulsed the area. Mobs singing "Praise God from Whom All Blessings Flow," again destroyed CP headquarters, beat CP organizers, and shot and killed a striker. Freedom of assembly was completely supressed in the area for ten days. The reign of terror finally ended when the CP completely ended all organizational activities at Gastonia on September 20. Not a single person was ever convicted for the assaults on strikers; however, while the state was completely unable to prove the source of the shots that killed the police chief on June 7, seven strikers were sentenced to from five to twenty years in jail for the slaying in a second trial. The Gastonia terror completely smashed the first major CP organizational drive in the South.[108]

Radical unions were not the only labor organizations to face repression during the twenties. Conservative railroad unions and AFL affiliates also met injunctions, troops and arrests if they attempted to organize in crucial industries.

The single most important strike of the twenties was the 1922 railroad shopcrafts strike.[109] After President Harding's pro-business packed Railroad Labor Board had approved two major wage reductions during 1921-22, four hundred thousand organized shop craft workers walked out on July 1, 1922. State militia were sent to railroad centers in six states. After the railroads began recruiting strikebreakers, widespread violence broke out, leading to the deaths of nineteen persons, almost all strikebreakers, guards or railroad watchman.

Attorney General Daugherty, convinced that the strike was a communist plot to seize the government, on September 1 obtained a restraining order from a federal judge which in effect made it illegal for anyone connected with the shop crafts to do or say anything in furtherance of the strike, including attempts to persuade shop men to strike, "in any manner, by letters, printed or other circulars, telegrams, word of mouth, oral persuasion or suggestion or through interviews to be published in newspapers or in any manner whatsoever." Daugherty announced, "I will use the powers of the government to prevent the labor unions of this country from destroying the open shop." Under the impact of the Chicago injunction and similar injunctions issued by three hundred local courts across the country, the railroad unions scrambled to settle the strike in as beneficial a way as they could. The shop crafts were able to reach agreements with a number of rail systems and maintain the union status of two hundred twenty-five thousand shop men, but other roads refused to arbitrate and established open shops, with a resultant loss of one hundred seventy-five thousand union members. About twelve hundred strikers were convicted for contempt of the injunctions, although the Justice Department was unable to come up with any evidence of communist influence despite a massive investigation.

Injunctions and the arrests of three hundred pickets for vagrancy helped to break the 1921 strike of the International Seaman's Union (ISU), which tied up all American shipping from Maine to Texas in the largest seafarer's strike in history. Within two years the ISU fell from one hundred thousand members to eighteen thousand.[109a]

The UMW in 1920 was the largest and most powerful union in the country, with more than half a million members. By the end of the decade, the UMW was in ruins. There were many causes for the decline of the UMW, including the generally sick state of the coal industry and vicious interunion quarrels, but the role of governmental repression, especially in the key West Virginia and Pennsylvania fields, was also a major factor.

In 1920, the UMW began a major organizational campaign in Mingo and Logan counties, West Virginia, where 80 percent of the miners lived in "company-owned, company-financed and company-dominated towns carefully monitored by local authorities subservient to the mine owners."[110] Union organizers in these areas were barred from entering miners' homes, barred from holding public meetings and regularly arrested and deported by deputy sheriffs on company payrolls. Federal troops were sent into West Virginia in the summer of 1920 after virtual civil war broke out in the coal areas, including gun fights between union men, private detectives and deputies which led to the deaths of sixteen men. The coal companies thereupon obtained injunctions under the *Hitchman* doctrine to bar further union organizing; after Federal troops were withdrawn, martial law was declared and state troops were used to break up union meetings, suppress the local UMW newspaper, raid the UMW hall and arrest union leaders for unlawful assemblage. President Harding sent federal troops to West Virginia again in 1921 when thousands of miners who had been fired and evicted from company-owned property threatened to invade Logan County after a pro-UMW police official and a union officer were shot on the courthouse steps in Welch, Logan County, by a private detective. West Virginia grand juries returned eighteen hundred indictments charging UMW officials and strikers with treason, conspiracy to incite riot and other offenses. Although acquittals were eventually won in all of the cases, the union drive in West Virginia had been destroyed. As noted earlier, in 1927, a federal judge barred the UMW from further attempts to organize the West Virginia coal industry under the *Hitchman* doctrine.

In 1922, more coal miners went on strike than ever before in U.S. history, with both anthracite and bituminous fields striking at the same time. Although the strikes were generally free of violence, with the exception of the notorious incident at Herrin, Illinois, in which eighteen strikebreakers were massacred by strikers, state and federal troops were sent to coal fields in over ten states. The Pennsylvania Coal and Iron Police acted with their customary brutality, riding down men, women and children, shooting up tent colonies, and torturing arrested strikers. Even with military protection, the mine owners were unable to secure enough workers to resume productions, and were forced to bargain with the UMW.[111]

The single most important point of UMW strength was the Pittsburgh Coal Co. of Western Pennsylvania, the largest producer in the nation. In 1925, the UMW struck to protest Pittsburgh's violation of an earlier contract agreement. The company succeeded in smashing the UMW through a combination of armed power and starvation. A newspaper reporter who visited the area wrote that in visiting the area:

> We unearthed a system of despotic tyranny reminiscent of Czar-ridden Siberia at its worst. We found police brutality and industrial slavery. We discovered the weirdest flock of injunctions that ever emanated from American temples of justice.[112]

A 1927 coal strike in Pennsylvania and Ohio was met with such vicious police repression that the UMW called off the strike "to spare the worker further brutality."[113] The Pittsburgh Coal Co. spent $800,000 to pay the Coal and Iron Police to suppress the 1927 strike. A Senate committee report on the strike concluded that the Coal and Iron Police "were found to be the outstanding ones who showed little regard for law and order."[114]

The only major agriculural strike of the decade, which brought out hundreds of Mexican cantelope pickers in California's Imperial Valley in 1928, was broken by the arrests of strikers, the banning of strike meetings, red-baiting, the deputizing of field bosses, and threats of deportation. Many arrested strikers were released only when they promised to return to work.[115]

With the exception of the UMW, the AFL spent much of the twenties in a torpor, with most of its energies devoted to proving its respectability through red-baiting. Having seen the treatment given to radical unions and to its own unions in 1919 and afterwards who had shown signs of militancy, the AFL chose to avoid any taint of radicalism, which meant in effect to virtually cease organizational activity. Throughout the decade, the AFL "advertised itself both as a proponent and a bastion of the existing order of society, an enthusiastic admirer of capitalism and a staunch enemy of Bolshevism."[116] No attempt was made to organize the unskilled or to penetrate mass industries. Instead the AFL leadership spent its time fighting and purging communists from its unions and taking advantage of the general climate to tag the most progressive elements within the AFL — those groups which favored industrial unionism and organization of the unskilled — as communist. The AFL leadership attack destroyed these elements, even though the progressives had themselves supported the purge of the communists. It was typical of the AFL during the twenties that its spokesmen even red-baited the ACLU, which was doing more than any other organization to fight for labor's civil liberties.[117]

The single effort the AFL made during the twenties to organize in new areas merely reaffirmed the group's caution. In 1929, the organization opened up a campaign to organize the southern textile industry but found that conservative unionism was no more welcome than communist unionism. An AFL strike at Elizabethton, Tennessee, in March, 1929 was met by sweeping injunctions, vigilante deportations of AFL organizers, the sending of eight hundred state police and deputy sheriffs and the arrest of over twelve hundred strikers for picketing in violation of strike injunctions. The strike ended in a disastrous defeat for the AFL.

The AFL tried again at Marion, North Carolina, in July, 1929. State troops were sent in and arrested 148 strikers for "insurrection against the state," rioting and resisting an officer when they removed the furniture of a strikebreaker who had moved into a house from which a striker had been evicted. On October 2, after the original strike had been called off due to the military occupation, a new dispute broke out. Strikers who gathered outside the Baldwin mill in Marion that morning to inform the day shift of the new strike were fired on by sheriff's deputies, half of whom were paid by the mill, after a sixty-eight-year-old man, lame with rheumatism, struck the sheriff with his cane. The man and five others were fatally wounded, and twenty-five were seriously wounded. The strike collapsed. Six strikers were eventually convicted of rioting in connection with the furniture incident, while the sheriff's deputies were acquitted of murder by a jury on December 22, 1929, so they could "go home for Christmas," according to a juryman.[118]

During the three major southern textile strikes of 1929 — Gastonia, Marion, and Elizabethton — eight people were slain, including seven strikers, thousands of strikers were arrested, and at Gastonia, mobs ran roughshod over strikers' liberties. The only convictions obtained were those of strikers for strike activities and for the death of the Gastonia police chief. Not a single conviction was obtained for the violation of strikers' rights, or for the cold-blooded murder of seven strikers.

7

The Great Depression and The New Deal

The Hoover Administration: Depression and Repression, 1929-1932

Most historians who have studied the early (Hoover) years of the Great Depression have stressed how little radical protest occurred and have concluded from the seeming inability of revolutionary movements to make major inroads that most Americans were either apathetic or did not desire fundamental social change. Thus, the most disinguished scholar of labor history during the early depression writes:

> Melancholia and defeat had overwhelmed not only the jobless but also those who sought to infuse spirit into them. Workers on the way down were in no mood to improve, far less to reorganize society. . . . Their obsession with survival made them bad material for revolution.[1]

Similarly Bernard Sternsher states that "the regime was in no real danger" because most Americans "*believed* in the 'system' or the 'American way of life,'" and that "the active protesters comprised only a small minority of the adult population."[2]

What most American historians have ignored is the possibility that many more Americans would have protested openly or joined radical organizations had not there been extremely severe repression of those who *did* take such action. The fact is that as the scope of the depression became clear, as protests *did* increase and as radical parties (e.g. the Communist Party) *did* step up their activities and did make significant gains, an extraordinary reign of repression swept the country. The ACLU report for 1932-33 concluded that "those who have borne the brunt of the depression have not responded by widespread movements of protest nor by strong class organization," but it also noted that "such opposition or protest movements as have developed among workers or farmers have been pretty generally attacked."[3] While the ACLU failed to make any connection between these two facts, there clearly was a relationship. Thus, John A. Garraty, in his study of radicalism during the depression, notes that American authorities frequently reacted to protests with "brutal repression" and suggests that with "so many unemployed, those who still held jobs were afraid of losing them and were thus unlikely to give tongue to criticism of the system, whatever their beliefs."[4] Radical writer Matthew Josephson found most unemployed men in New York City to be resigned and ashamed rather than angry, but his evidence suggests that such feelings arose out of fear as much as lack of interest in radical change. Thus, when he asked residents of a dreadful municipal shelter why they didn't protest about their conditions, the men replied: "We don't dare complain about anything. We're afraid of being kicked out."[5]

In light of the severe repression which occurred, what is perhaps really remarkable are the striking gains that radical groups did make during the early depression. Thus, the SPA, which had been practically moribund during the late 1920's, showed signs of a marked revival shortly after the Wall Street crash. The SPA vote increased significantly in a number of local and state elections, and organizational work greatly increased. Between 1928 and 1932, SPA membership increased from eight thousand to thirteen thousand, while SPA presidential votes leaped from two hundred sixty-seven thousand to eight hundred eighty-four thousand.[6] The CP also made major gains, with membership jumping from about seventy-five hundred in 1930 to over twenty-three thousand by 1934, and its presidential vote jumping from forty-seven thousand to over one hundred thousand between 1928 and 1932.[7] Even more threatening than these membership and electoral gains, however, were striking CP organizational successes among unemployed workers, mine workers in Kentucky, and agricultural workers in California, and the beginning of a major CP campaign to organize blacks and whites in the south. The unemployment movement which developed largely under CP leadership, during the early depression, was "the largest movement of the unemployed in the history of this country,"[8] and by 1932, "communism had filtered through a large part of the labor world as the only hope in the midst of despair."[9] According to one leading study of the political left during the depression "literally tens and maybe hundreds of thousands of American workers . . . became sympathizers" of the CP unemployment movement and similar movements sponsored by other radical groups.[10] One survey of unemployed workers revealed that nearly 25 percent felt that "a revolution might be a very good thing for this country."[11] How much greater gains would have been made by radical political and trade union organizations during the depression had not their organizational substructure been destroyed during the 1917-20 repression can only be imagined.

The result of the depression and the growing signs of radical discontent was a striking increase in the fear of an impending revolution on the part of important segments of American elites, especially businessmen, the Hoover administration and many state and local governments. As David Shannon has written, much of the politics of the early 1920's "can be understood fully only by viewing political events against the background of anxiety about violent revolution."[12] Constant red-baiting of virtually all protest activity coupled with appeals for "law and order" were recurrent themes.[13]

Warnings about the possibility of violent revolution came with increasing frequency — even from moderate elements of the population. AFL President William Green told the 1931 convention, "I warn the people who are exploiting the workers that they can drive them only so far before they will turn on them and destroy them." Chicago lawyer Donald Richberg told a Senate committee in 1932, "There are many signs that if the lawfully constituted leadership does not soon substitute action for words, a new leadership perhaps unlawfully constituted will arise and act." Mayor Anton Cermak of Chicago warned that the choice facing the government was either to provide relief or "call out the troops."[14] Gov. Theodore Bilbo of Mississippi told reporters:

> Folks are getting restless. Communism is getting a foothold right here in Mississippi. Some people are about ready to lead a mob. In fact I'm getting a little pink myself.[15]

As unrest increased, reports spread of wealthy persons stocking their country homes with canned goods, arms and ammunition in anticipation of serious disorders. The mood of the well-to-do was caricatured in a cartoon in the *New Yorker*, in which a young heiress was shown pleading with her mother, "Well then, can I come out *after* the revolution?"[16]

As signs of discontent and militancy mounted, the fear of impending revolution increasingly dominated influential elements within the Hoover administration. The most recent and comprehensive study of Hoover's own attitude towards dissent presents convincing evidence that Hoover himself, until the Bonus Army episode of July, 1932, upheld the right of even revolutionary agitators to express their views and consistently resisted pressure to support repressive measures such as outlawing the Communist Party.[17] However, there is overwhelming evidence that many important elements in the Hoover administration did not share Hoover's approach and implemented repressive policies which Hoover was either unaware of or did nothing to overrule. Thus, deportations for political reasons, which had virtually ended during the late twenties, jumped sharply after the beginning of the depression. The deportation weapon was especially wielded against aliens involved in left-wing strikes and against left-wing union organizers, and the frequent and publicized presence of Immigration Service agents at left-wing strikes inevitably must have had a "chilling effect" on the willingness of aliens to participate in such events.[18] Beginning in 1930-31, postal officials began to bar radical papers from the mails for the

Political Deportations[19]	
1929	1
1930	1
1931	18
1932	51
1933	74

first time since the Wilson administration.[20] During the prosperity of early 1929, the Pardon Office in the Justice Department recommended a general pardon (i.e. restoration of all citizenship rights) for World War I political prisoners; after the crash the Pardon Office reversed itself for fear such actions would encourage the radical movement.[21] In 1931, a representative of the Labor Department publicly urged Texas to pass a criminal syndicalism bill and suggested the bill specifically outlaw the Texas CP, and in 1933 a representative of the Immigration Service opposed repeal of Oregon's Criminal Syndicalism law.[22] Hoover administration officials participating in a 1931 disarmament conference opposed reductions in the Army ground forces because it would lessen the country's ability to maintain "domestic peace and order."[23]

Although Hoover took a benign view of protests in Washington, D.C. — when communist pickets were arrested in December, 1929 after they "stormed" the White House he ordered their immediate release and publicly stated such treatment merely created needless martyrs — his attitudes were often not reflected by Washingon police and by military and intelligence agencies.[24]

In March, 1930, CP-led unemployment demonstrators were greeted with tear gas, and in December, 1930, communists protesting restrictions on immigration who tried to march on the Capitol were met with tear gas and clubs by police.[25] In October, 1931, the CP announced plans for a national hunger march on Washington for the end of the year, but despite this announcement, the Secret Service gained front page coverage by announcing at the end of November the "uncovering" of a communist plot to come to Washington and subvert the government. Although Hoover ordered the demonstrators be provided with tents, blankets, kitchen equipment, medical assistance and campsites, an advance contingent of fourteen communists were arrested and fined $100 in late November for demonstrating in front of the White House, and when the main contingent reached Washington, the number of police on duty and on reserve outnumbered the sixteen hundred marchers. When the group marched to the Capitol under police escort on December 3, they were met on the Capitol ramps by police armed with rifles, riot guns and tear gas pistols, and by machine gun nests installed above the Capitol steps.[26]

The turning point in Hoover's attitude toward protesters was the Bonus Army episode.[27] The Bonus Army, often known as the Bonus Expeditionary Force (BEF) consisted of unemployed veterans who gathered in Washington in the spring of 1932 to demand immediate payment of their World War I bonuses, which were not scheduled to mature until 1945. Hoover's initial attitude towards the BEF was at first most tolerant; he secretly cooperated with Washington Police Chief Pelham Glassford to provide the BEF with campsites, food, bedding equipment and medical aid and resisted pressure from elements within the military and the Congress to disperse the veterans. However, the attitude of military and police and local governmental officials grew increasingly jittery after about ten thousand of the original total of over twenty thousand veterans remained in Washington after the Senate defeated the Bonus proposal on June 17. Several attempts by veterans to demonstrate near the White House and Capitol were forcibly broken up by police in July, and in late July, federal and local officials, with Hoover's approval, ordered veterans to clear out of some abandoned government buildings in the downtown area which they had earlier occupied with permission. During the morning of July 28, one of the buildings was cleared by police without incident, but in the early afternoon two clashes broke out between police and BEF members, during which two veterans were fatally wounded by a policeman, three police were injured seriously enough to require hospitalization, and many other persons were injured. When reports of these clashes reached the White House, Hoover authorized Army troops to move in and clear the veterans out of the downtown buildings. Subsequently, six hundred troops armed with sabers, bayonets, tanks, machine guns and tear gas bombs cleared the buildings, burned and destroyed other campsites in the downtown area, and then dispersed veterans from and destroyed the main encampment at Anacostia Flats, which was separated from the downtown area. During the operation, Army troops indiscriminately tear-gassed and attacked veterans, their families and innocent bystanders; altogether over one thousand persons were tear-gassed, and over fifty were treated for injuries, including a seven-year old boy who was bayonneted while trying to rescue a pet rabbit.

The rout of the BEF was led by Army Chief of Staff General Douglas MacArthur, who apparently was partially influenced by an Army Intelligence report which claimed that "the first bloodshed by the Bonus Army at Washington is to be the signal for a communist uprising in all large cities, thus initiating a revolution."[28] Army intelligence operations during this period involved large scale domestic intelligence activities for the first time since the mid-twenties; all Army Corps Area commanders throughout the country were asked to report on Bonus Army marchers passing through their region, "indicating presence, if any, of communistic elements and names of leaders of known communistic leanings."[29] By driving the veterans out of Anacostia Flats, MacArthur ignored direct orders from President Hoover, who had ordered that the veterans in the downtown buildings *only* be surrounded and turned over to local police and that the troops *not* cross the drawbridge leading into the Anacostia Flats area. However, instead of repudiating MacArthur's actions, Hoover defended them, and administration spokesmen, including Hoover, repeatedly issued statements labelling the BEF as consisting largely of communists and criminals, and suggesting that the BEF was part of a planned communist insurrection.

In fact, the BEF leadership and the overwhelming majority of the membership was fervently anti-Communist, and throughout the two-month stay of the BEF in Washington, only twelve arrests had been made for violations more serious than vagrancy and liquor. One of the main sports of the BEF's own police force had been beating up CP veterans, and Washington police frequently turned their backs on such activities along with generally harassing the few CP members who were in Washington as part of the protest. After the Bonus Army was routed and Hoover had publicly committed himself to the communist-criminal conspiracy theory, local and Federal officials embarked on a flurry of activity to prove the subversive aspects of the BEF affair, but could come up with nothing. On July 29, Washington police arrested forty alleged Communists and radicals, including the CP vice-presidential nominee, but had to release them since there was no basis for a charge. Subsequently a grand jury investigated the BEF, but despite the best efforts of the Secret Service, the Washington police, the FBI, the Immigration Bureau, the Veterans Adminisration, Military Intelligence and the Attorney General's office, no evidence of a communist plot could be uncovered.

After the Bonus Army affair, and the avalanche of criticism which it brought about, Hoover became increasingly intolerant of dissent and convinced that subversive conspiracies were threatening the republic. When Congress voted a 10 percent cut for government employees, Hoover sent Congress a secret message urging an exception for armed forces enlisted personnel because in case of internal trouble he did not want to have to rely on disgruntled troops. Towards the end of the Hoover administration, Secretary of War Patrick Hurley began concentrating troops around major cities because of what "reds and possible communists" might do.[30] Communist hunger marchers were met on the outskirts of Washington in December, 1932, by police who herded them into a makeshift concentration camp, where they were held for three days, forced to sleep in the open without shelter in a freezing wind, and for a period were denied food, water, medical attention and the right to dig a latrine. Finally, congressional protests led to their being allowed to march to the Capitol under the escort of armed police and tanks.[31]

Hoover's changed attitude was readily apparent during the 1932 presidential campaign. Hoover charged that Democratic candidate Franklin D. Roosevelt was proposing changes that would "destroy the very foundations of our American system" and that the Democratic philosophy was the "same philosophy of government which has poisoned all Europe . . . the fumes of the witches' caldron which boiled in Russia." Perhaps most revealing of Hoover's state of mind was his extemporaneous outburst in one speech: "Thank God you still have a government in Washington that knows how to quell a mob."[32]

Hoover and other officials in the executive branch were not the only governmental sources which fostered a climate of repression during the 1929-33 period. The 1930 Smoot-Hawley Tariff Act included a provision which allowed the courts to confiscate any imported material which advocated or urged "treason, insurrection or forcible resistance to any law of the U.S."[33] In the spring of 1930, following massive communist-led unemployment demonstrations and charges by New York City Police Commissioner Grover Whalen that a New York trading corporation was disseminating Communist propaganda, the House of Representatives voted two hundred ten to eighteen to authorize a committee investigation of all groups or individuals "alleged to advise, teach or advocate the overthrow by force or violence of the government of the United States or attempt to undermine our republican form of government by inciting riots, sabotage or revolutionary disorders."[34] The vagueness of this resolution was perhaps best indicated during the House debate when one representative asked if it would cover fascism; the chairman of the House Rules Committee replied that he did not know what fascism was but he guessed the resolution covered it "if it is something wrong."[35]

The committee was chaired by Rep. Hamilton Fish, who implied at the outset that American economic troubles would disappear when the communists were driven from the U.S. The Fish Committee held hearings for about six months in different parts of the country, beginning in June of 1930. The hearings were dominated by representatives of superpatriotic organizations who regaled the congressmen with tales that ranged from "responsible to fantastic allegations of communist deceit and treachery."[36] In general, the hearings served as a "display case for all sorts of foolishness" during which Fish showed he was "equal to any man in the house in his ignorance of the subject he was investigating."[37] The Fish Committee was unable to come up with any real evidence of dangerous communist activities, but it did succeed in "stirring up prejudice, breaking up meetings and causing arrests" as it travelled around the country.[38] The committee's final report amounted to a recommendation that the CP be suppressed "root, lock, stock and barrel."[39] Included among the recommendations were proposals to deport alien communists, ban communist literature from the mail, outlaw the CP and other parties advocating forcible overthrow of the government, and to send treasury agents to Russia — a country the U.S. did not recognize — to study the use of forced labor in the Russian lumber industry in order to determine whether such products should be barred from the U.S. Although a flood of bills were introduced in 1931 to combat the red menace, the only bill passing even one house was a measure to deport alien communists.[40]

State and Local Repression, 1929-1932

While the Hoover administration and the Fish Committee bear a major responsibility for setting a repressive tone in the country from 1929 to 1933, the great bulk of actual repression was carried out on the local level. As protest activity among the unemployed and left-wing forces increased, police repression soared to heights unmatched for years. Thus, in May, 1930, the ACLU reported that early months of that year alone had "produced a larger crop of court cases involving civil liberty than any entire year since the war . . . due to a wave of suppression by officials of the militant activities of the Communist Party and left-wing strikes."[41] During the first three months of 1930, the ACLU reported a total of 930 arrests involving free speech cases, exceeding the total for any entire year from 1921 to 1929. During the entire year of 1930, the number of free speech prosecutions exceeded the entire period 1924-29, while the number of meetings broken up by police exceeded by far the total for any year during the 1921-29 period, as in "one local community after another, police used disorderly-conduct and disturbing-the-peace statutes to disrupt radical meetings and disband picket lines."[42] After 1930 the ACLU stopped keeping a yearly count of free speech prosecutions and interferences with meetings, but the annual ACLU reports indicate the continuation of an extraordinarily high number of such cases.

Repression of Free Speech by Local Police 1928-30[43]

	Meetings Broken Up	Arrests*
1928	54	418
1929	52	228
1930	121	1630

*arrests exclude cases arising out of strikes.

In order to keep up with radical activity, state and local political intelligence activity was stepped up in many areas. Thus, police in Portland, Oregon, placed a spy inside local communist organizations following a March, 1930 conference with local officials and a federal immigration official. State national guard military intelligence officials were soon collecting information on, among other things, communist activity in Birmingham, Alabama, and "radical activity" at the University of Illinois in Champaign-Urbana.[44] A member of the Michigan state police wrote "confidentially" to Washington, D.C. police during the Bonus Army episode that "we had a little trouble here in Lansing wich (sic) the reds but on the second visit a few of the boys took the leader for a short ride, they have not returned."[45]

Another clear indication of increasing local repression was an extraordinary upsurge in the use of criminal syndicalism, sedition and insurrection laws, which had generally lain unused after 1924. During the 1929-33 period, prosecutions under such laws occurred in New Jersey, Pennsylvania, Oregon, Georgia, California, Michigan, Ohio, Kentucky and Illinois.[46]

Many of the free speech and criminal syndicalism arrests arose out of circumstances reminiscent of some of the worst cases arising during 1917-20. For example, a book-salesman was arrested and held for forty-eight hours in Memphis, Tennessee for inquiring at police headquarters where the CP office was located. Six young radicals who raced around the stadium wearing "Free Tom Mooney" signs at the 1932 Olympics at Los

Angeles were arrested for suspicion of criminal syndicalism and eventually given nine months in jail for disturbing the peace. In Akron, Ohio, a man was arrested for criminal syndicalism on the basis of remarks made in private conversation, before being freed by a judge. Two young women who ran a communist youth camp were convicted of desecrating the flag by refusing to run one up on the order of a mob, and sentenced to three months in jail. Over 130 persons were arrested in Los Angeles during 1932 for "suspicion of criminal syndicalism."[47]

Many of the most outrageous violations of free speech and assembly involved police attacks on peaceful demonstrations of unemployed workers, usually conducted under CP auspices. Such attacks, which frequently featured the use of tear gas and clubs, occurred in Philadelphia, Chicago and Los Angeles in February, 1930; in many cities across the country during CP-led demonstrations which brought out about one million persons on March 6, 1930; in New York in April 1931; in Detroit, in November, 1931; in Dearborn, Michigan, in March, 1932; in Philadelphia and Birmingham, in May, 1932; in St. Louis, in July, and repeatedly in the Chicago area during 1932-33.[48] During one unemployment demonstration in Richmond, Virginia, the mayor instructed the police chief to respond to a delegation of jobless who had come to call on him: "Take these men by the scruff of the neck and the seat of the pants and throw them out." When John P. O'Brien was elected mayor of New York City in 1932 he pledged to "preserve the metropolis from the Red Army."[49]

In many cases police repression of demonstrations was of an extraordinarily vicious nature. Thus, during the New York City unemployment demonstration of March 6, 1930 the *New York Times* reported:

> Hundreds of policemen and detectives, swinging nightsticks, blackjacks and bare fists, rushed into the crowd, hitting at all with whom they came in contact. . . . A score of men with bloody heads and faces sprawled over the square with policemen over them.[50]

During one demonstration in Seattle, police evicted demonstrators who squatted in the County-City building with fire hoses, and during a Chicago demonsration, police clubbed unpaid teachers, "two of them holding one middle-aged woman while a third smashed her face."[51]

In a number of cases, protesters were shot and wounded or killed during police attacks. On August 3, 1931, after several Chicago police had been roughed up by a crowd resisting an attempt to evict a black family, officers fired point blank into the crowd, killing three and wounded many more.[52] At Dearborn, Michigan on March 7, 1932, police fired into a crowd of communist-led unemployed demonstrators after the protesters had refused to turn back at the Dearborn city line and had responded to police tear gas and freezing streams of water by throwing rocks and debris. The police fire killed four persons and wounded two dozen others. Subsequently police in the Detroit area began raiding radical groups and arrested thirty-five persons, none of whom were ever tried, while the police were cleared by a grand jury.[53] In May, 1932 police in Melrose Park, Illinois, broke up an attempt to hold an unemployment rally, then lined up protesters against a wall and opened up with machine guns, wounding eight. Subsequently fifty-eight protesters were arrested; all were acquitted.[54] Police fired into a crowd of unemployment demonstrators in St. Louis in July, 1932, wounding four.[55] On October 6, 1932, a violent police attack on an unemployment demonstration in Chicago ended with the police killing of a demonstrator after an attempt had been made to disarm a policeman.[56]

The Communist Party was throughout the early depression "frequently the only ones who were attempting to do something immediately about jobs, relief and general welfare,"[57] and, not surprisingly, it was the CP which bore the brunt of local repression. For example, between January 1929 and November, 1930, 167 persons indentified as "communists" were arrested in Boston on such charges as "violation of park rules," "disturbing the peace," "violation of city ordinance," and, in one case, "larceny of the captain's short club."[58] Between November, 1929 and March, 1930, CP leader Eugene Dennis was arrested five separate times in Los Angeles for charges such as "suspicion of criminal syndicalism," speaking without a permit, rioting and resisting police officers.[59] Caesar J. Scarvada, Chief of Police in Flint, Michigan, told the Fish committee in July, 1930, how he arrested the leaders of a CP-led unemployment demonstration:

> Mr. Nelson: What charge did you make against them that you might arrest them?
> Mr. Scarvada: There was not any charge.
> Mr. Nelson: You just arrested them.
> Mr. Scarvada: That is all.
> Mr. Bachman Why, you arrest them for disorderly conduct, do you not?
> Mr. Scarvada: Well, possibly that would be a good excuse. There is not any particular law we can act on.[60]

Of fifty-two meetings broken up by police across the country during the first three months of 1930, forty-three of them were conducted under communist sponsorship.[61] In Oklahoma alone, the CP organized thirty thousand persons into unemployment councils by 1933, but the organizations were "soon disrupted by the arrest and conviction of their most active leaders, after violent demonstrations and clashes with police."[62]

While the CP met severe repression throughout the country, nowhere did it face greater obstacles than in its campaign to organize among poor whites and blacks in the south. As Wilson Record has noted, "Local law enforcement officials and business interests in southern communities reacted on a hysterical basis to even the slightest manifestations of mass discontent."[63] In Dallas, two CP organizers were jailed for vagrancy in 1931, then kidnapped from jail "under circumstances which strongly suggest collusion between police and kidnappers, taken into the country, flogged and left unconscious."[64] In Atlanta, CP workers were arrested in 1930 and again in 1932 for "insurrection," a charge carrying a possible death penalty, as a result of their attempts to organize blacks and unemployed whites. Other party workers were arrested in Chattanooga and New Orleans. In Tampa, Florida, and Greenville, South Carolina, CP organizational work among the unemployed and labor unions was stifled by physical attacks from police and local vigilante groups working hand-in-glove.

The most serious and sustained CP organizational effort in the deep south was in Birmingham, Alabama, and among black sharecroppers in the rural southern and eastern areas of Alabama. The CP made its greatest organizational gains in these areas, and also faced the most severe repression it met anywhere in the south. After the CP became prominently identified with the defense in the Scottsboro case in 1931, the party became a focal point for racial hatreds in Alabama as well as bearing the normal burden of its radicalism. CP organizers in the Birmingham area and other cities in Alabama faced constant police harassment, culminating in the 1933 passage of city ordinances in Bessemer and Birmingham, which barred the possession of more than one copy of any kind of literature "advocating the overthrow of organized government by force or any unlawful means." Over sixty persons were arrested for violation of the Birmingham law. In May, 1933, Montgomery, Alabama chimed in with its own criminal anarchy ordinance, barring the teaching of any doctrine "advocating the overthrow of organized government."[65]

CP efforts to organize black sharecroppers in Alabama met a reign of terror from police officials and vigilante groups; hundreds of blacks were beaten, scores were arrested and at least six were shot and killed by police in 1931 and 1932. Eventually, the Alabama Sharecroppers Union (ASU) was forced to go underground to survive, but it grew steadily, claiming over five thousand members by the fall of 1933. As Wilson Record has pointed out, the fact that the ASU made any headway whatsoever against the face of "illegal violence systematically employed against it . . . reflected the desperate plight of Negro sharecroppers and laborers in the rural south."[66]

In the upper south, the greatest CP gains were made in organizing coal miners in Harlan County, Kentucky and repression was no less severe there.[67] Over eleven thousand miners had walked out under UMW leadership in March, 1931, in Harlan County, an area notorious for mineowner domination. Violence broke out on both sides shortly after the walkout began, with strikers looting stores, coal operators evicting strikers and deputized mine guards assaulting strikers. Following a gun fight between strikers and deputies on May 4, 1931, in which three deputies and a miner were killed, the National Guard was sent in, UMW headquarters were raided and thirty UMW leaders arrested and charged with murder and criminal syndicalism.

Faced with this onslaught, the UMW withdrew from the strike area, and the communist-led National Miners Union (NMU) moved in and quickly organized about four thousand miners. At this point, an officially sponsored reign of terror began, with scores of arrests for criminal syndicalism, raids on strike meetings and private homes, shootings, beatings and deportations of strikers and sympathizers. About twelve persons were killed between May and September, 1931, almost all of whom were strike supporters. Outside groups which tried to enter Harlan County to investigate the situation were either arrested, deported or beaten; thus, author Theodore Dreiser faced arrest for adultery and criminal syndicalism after his visit to the area. Authorities in Harlan County barred the distribution and possession of radical papers, and miners were arrested for possessing copies of the *Daily Worker*. In March, 1932, the strike was called off, with the NMU completely driven from the area. Seven miners were eventually sentenced to life imprisonment for their role in the disorders, but all were released or pardoned by 1941.

Aside from its work among the unemployed in urban areas, in the south and in Harlan County, the major area of CP success, and the inevitable resultant repression, was among agricultural workers in California. Growers completely dominated California's agricultural areas and were often deputized by sheriffs during labor disputes, while agricultural workers were completely bereft of political power. The result was that the record of attempts to organize agricultural workers was generally one of "turmoil, violence, illegality and infringement of civil liberties."[68] During the 1930-32 period, the CP organized a number of agricultural strikes in California. Following strikes by Mexican laborers in the lush Imperial Valley in January and February, 1930, residences and public-meeting places throughout the Valley were raided by authorities in mid-April, shortly before a planned conference of all agricultural workers. Over one hundred workers were arrested and eight union leaders were subsequently convicted of criminal syndicalism. An aggressive CP-led strike in Santa Clara County in July, 1931, was broken when meetings and parades were broken up by police and many strikers were arrested.[69]

The CP was not the only organization to face repression during the relatively few strikes which occurred during the Hoover period of the depression. The AFL's southern textile organizing campaign finally collapsed in January, 1931 when a strike at the Riverside & Dan River Mills Co. in Danville, Virginia, the largest textile firm in the south, was met with a strike injunction, the national guard and the eviction of strikers from company homes.[70] A strike of beet workers in Colorado in May, 1932, collapsed in the wake of denials of relief to strikers, police arrests of dozens of pickets for "vagrancy," "intimidation" or "attempting to persuade workers to leave their jobs," and deportations of militant Mexican strikers.[71]

Reforms and Resistance to Repression, 1929-1932

The picture which has been painted thus far of the state of civil liberties during the early depression has been unreservedly bleak. However, this is not the entire picture. What distinguished the 1929-33 period of repression from more severe periods of repression, such as 1917-20 and 1947-54 was: 1) unlike these other two periods, in which all three branches of government at virtually all levels of government were united in a policy of repression, during the 1929-33 period many local and state governments and strong elements in the legislative and judicial branches of the federal government adopted a policy which stressed reform over repression; and 2) unlike the other two periods, when eventually the forces of repression were so strong that resistance virtually collapsed, during the 1929-33 period, there was constant and strong public opposition to repressive measures from influential groups, and this opposition undoubtedly helped to curtail the degree of repression which occurred.

While the discontents and protests aroused by the depression often elicited repression, there were also many examples of attempts at reform. This was particularly true in the midwestern farm belt, where milk and wheat farmers staged massive protests, physically blocking highways, marching on state legislatures, intimidating foreclosure officials into selling mortgaged farms back to their former owners for prices as low as five cents, and in many cases simply blocking foreclosure proceedings. In the first two months of 1933 alone, farmers in fourteen states halted at least eighty foreclosures. For the most part, the reaction of public officials in the midwest to these grossly illegal activities was highly conciliatory. By March, 1933, nine states had established a two-year moratorium on foreclosures; in Nebraska such a bill became law shortly after three thousand farmers marched through the state capitol building. Governor William Langer of North Dakota mobilized the state militia to *prevent* foreclosures.[72]

Similar conciliation was not limited to the midwest. In San Francisco, Mayor Rolph greeted unemployment demonstrators at the steps of city hall, while other mayors were responding with clubs. Mayor Frank Murphy of Detroit invited unemployment demonstrators into his office and insisted that their rights be respected. The governor of North Carolina intervened in a 1932 hosiery strike to protect the wages of strikers. In Pennsylvania, officials, courts and juries winked as a $30 million annual industry developed in the illegal bootlegging of coal. By March, 1933, most states had created emergency relief administrations, and a number of states had passed old age pension laws, anti-labor injunction bills and laws barring yellow-dog contracts.[73]

A sympathetic attitude towards labor and civil liberties was also manifested in some of the actions of the Supreme Court and the Congress. In 1930, the Supreme Court upheld a provision of the 1926 Railway Labor Act which in effect outlawed company unions on the railroads. In 1931, the court declared California's red flag law unconstitutionally vague, and in 1932 the court reversed Alabama convictions in the Scottsboro case, despite the fact that the case had become prominently identified with the Communist Party.[74]

In the Congress, dozens of bills were introduced during the early years of the depression aimed at labor reform and the alleviation of labor's distress. In 1932 both houses passed by overwhelming margins the landmark Norris-LaGuardia bill, which banned federal courts from issuing injunctions in labor disputes except under extremely narrowly defined conditions. Injunctions were specifically barred in cases regarding yellow-dog contracts, strike prevention bans on unions and use of union funds to pay strikers, and prevention of peaceable assemblies. The bill also established as public policy the right of the workers to "full freedom of association, self-organization and designation of representatives of his own choosing to negotiate the terms and conditions of his employment and that he . . . be free from the interference, restraint or coercion of employers . . . in his activities for the purpose of collective bargaining or other mutual aid or protection."[75]

Another incident reflecting the increased pro-labor feeling in the Congress was the Senate's rejection in May, 1930, of Hoover's nomination of Federal Judge John J. Parker to the Supreme Court. Parker had issued the notorious "Red Jacket" injunction in 1927, and the AFL stressed this in its campaign against him.[76] Another instance was the tremendous outcry which arose when Hoover nominated Judge James H. Wilkerson of Chicago to the Seventh Circuit Court of Appeals in January, 1932. Wilkerson had issued the original 1922 railroad strike injunction. Public opposition to him was so strong that Hoover eventually was forced to withdraw the nomination.[77]

While Hoover and some local and state officials maintained a rigid repressive posture, there is little doubt that the general mood of the country swung to the left under the impact of the depression, and this created a general climate in which repression directed largely against the left lost much of its previous appeal. Thus, in the November, 1930 election, the Democrats picked up 10 seats in the Senate and 105 seats in the House in an election in which the AFL made the Norris-LaGuardia and Parker issues a major theme.[78]

Examples of public resistance to repression during the early depression are very numerous. Sixty-two prominent Atlantans signed a protest statement over the 1930 "insurrection" arrests of CP members. About sixty thousand attended the funeral of the three persons killed by police in Chicago during the August, 1931, eviction riot, while forty thousand attended the funeral of the four slain by police at Dearborn, Michigan in March, 1932. In February, 1933, a crowd of protesters freed from police demonstrators who had been arrested during an invasion of the city-county building in Seattle. When officials in Council Bluffs, Iowa, arrested fifty-five pickets during farm protests, one thousand farmers threatened to storm the jail and obtained their release on bail. In Detroit, two families that shot a landlord who was trying to evict them were acquitted of murder by sympathetic juries. An unusually high number of free speech arrests, including those of communists, ended in acquittals or the dropping of charges: thus, in Chicago, unemployed demonstrators who had been arrested were repeatedly acquitted by juries. Hoover's routing of the Bonus Army was an extraordinarily unpopular action. While the Fish Committee did stir up increased repression in many areas, there was a great deal of hostile reaction to it not only from liberals but among large segments of conservative opinion also. Even the American Legion's Americanism committee recommended that the committee's legislative proposals be tabled. A final indication of strong public resistance to repression is that protest activity was significantly increasing in 1932, despite the increasing violence of official response to protests.[79]

What explains the failure of repression to crush dissent during the early years of the depression and the lack of a unified policy of repression among ruling elites, especially as compared with the 1917-20 and 1947-54 periods? Fundamentally, what explains these differences is the massive reality and magnitude of the problems facing the country during the depression. Many political leaders realized that these problems simply could not be eliminated by scapegoating and smashing dissenters. On the other hand, from the viewpoint of most Americans, including many who did not actively protest, the government had been discredited by its failure to solve the economic problem. Further, while repression had been constantly directed against the left, it was clear to most Americans that it was not the left that had failed — it was the business system that had collapsed. By late 1932, "public hatred and contempt for Herbert Hoover had reached proportions possibly unique in the history of the republic's opinions of its presidents,"[80] while the businessman, who "had been thought of as a magic-maker who could master the forces of a complex industrial society which the common man viewed with awe" had "lost his magic and was as discredited as a Hopi rainmaker in a prolonged draught."[81] It was typical of the general climate that Carter Glass, the conservative senator from Virginia, was heard to remark, "one banker in my state attempted to marry a white woman and they lynched him."[82]

In short, the ruling segments of society — the Republican administration and the business community — had been in effect delegitimized in the eyes of a majority of the population. Under such circumstances, while repression could still serve to intimidate, it only further eroded governmental legitimacy in the eyes of many. Further, a majority of people essentially identified with at least the general trend of proposals put forward by the left instead of viewing the left as a threat to society as was the case in 1917-20 and 1947-54. The government wished to suppress the left, in other words, but the people would have preferred to suppress the right — the business community. Franklin D. Roosevelt understood this fundamental fact, and much of his popularity flowed from this understanding.

A New Deal and a New Mood

With the inauguration of Franklin D. Roosevelt as president in March, 1933, a drastic change occurred both in the general mood of the country and in the civil liberties climate, fostered by the federal government. Where Hoover seemed to represent rigidity, reaction and repression, Roosevelt conveyed an atmosphere of optimism and experimentation.[83]

Roosevelt clearly displayed his commitment to reform rather than to repression in both symbolic and substantive actions. As President-elect, Roosevelt agreed to see Tom Mooney's mother and forward her appeal for clemency for her son to the governor of California; President Hoover had refused to see her (although the decision was made by Hoover's secretary without his knowledge and Hoover was angered by the action). While President-elect and again after his inauguration, Roosevelt personally received communist protesters; he also issued orders that peaceful communist demonstrations be allowed in Washington. When a second bonus army visited Washington in May, 1933, Roosevelt greeted them with meals and coffee, free medical care and the use of Army housing facilities (located fifteen miles from Washington), and provided all those who wanted jobs with employment in the Civilian Conservation Corps. Roosevelt personally met with their leaders, while his wife waded through ankle-deep mud to greet the veterans at their camp. As one veteran put it, "Hoover sent the army, Roosevelt sent his wife." In November, 1933 the United States became the last major world power to recognize Soviet Russia. On Christmas Day, 1933 the U.S. became the last world power to grant World War I political prisoners a full pardon. Exclusion of radical papers from the mails was ended, while radical aliens were permitted to enter the U.S. as visitors for the first time in over ten years. Thus, Emma Goldman was allowed to reenter the U.S. to give a lecture tour for the first time since her deportation (she was kept under close surveilance by J. Edgar Hoover, however).[84]

While President Hoover had resorted to red-baiting, FDR stressed business-baiting. In his inaugural address, he referred to the "money changers who have fled from their high seats in the temples of our civilization" and called for an end "to a conduct in banking and in business which too often has given to a sacred trust the likeness of callous and selfish wrongdoing."[85] Roosevelt issued similar remarks periodically throughout his first two terms. In his January, 1936, State of the Union address, FDR said that the forces of "entrenched greed" were seeking "the restoration of their selfish power." He added:

> They steal the livery of great national constitutional ideals to serve discredited special interests . . . they engage in vast propaganda to spread fear and discord among the people — they would "gang up" against the people's liberties. The principle that they would instill into government if they succeeded in seizing power is well known by the principles which many of them have instilled in their own affairs; autocracy toward labor, toward stockholders, toward consumers, toward public sentiment.[86]

During the 1936 campaign, Roosevelt referred to "economic royalists" and termed some opponents of social security legislation as "aliens to the spirit of American democracy" who should "emigrate and try their lot under some foreign flag in which they have more confidence." The forces of "organized money" were "unanimous in their hate for me," said Roosevelt, "and I welcome their hatred."[87]

Roosevelt's switch from repression to reform was not limited merely to symbolic actions and speeches. The New Deal reforms, while essentially an attempt to preserve American capitalism, represented a drastic departure from the business rule of the twenties and brought American labor into the accepted circles of power for the first time in American history. Massive public works legislation, hours and wages legislation, social security and a host of other measures made the worker a beneficiary of government favor on a scale unprecedented in American history. From the standpoint of civil liberties, the most important measures by far were section 7(a) of the 1933 National Industrial Recovery Act, (NIRA) and the 1935 Wagner Act. Section 7(a), passed with the full backing of the Roosevelt administration, required that all codes of business competition worked out under NIRA include provisions that employees "have the right to organize and bargain collectively through representatives of their own choosing, and shall be free from the interference, restraint or coercion of employers of labor" in such activities.[88]

While 7(a) provided a major impetus to a massive upsurge in labor organization and strike activity in 1933-34, the lack of any adequate enforcement machinery, the failure of 7(a) to ban company unions, employee resistance and the voiding of NIRA in 1935 by the Supreme Court led Senator Robert Wagner to push strongly for his National Labor Relations Act. The Wagner Act, which gained belated support from Roosevelt, remains the single most important act of labor legislation in American history, and in all of its ramifications "perhaps the single most important civil liberties statute on the sufferance of their employers."[89]

The Wagner Act again asserted the principles set out in 7(a) of the NIRA, further provided that the majority of workers in a bargaining unit should have the right to represent all such workers, and specifically barred a series of "unfair" employer practices such as support of company unions, refusal to bargain collectively with employees' representatives, and interference with employees in the exercise of guaranteed rights. Finally, the Wagner Act established the National Labor Relations Board (NLRB) to supervise and enforce the principles enunciated in the bill and to carry out elections to determine who represented the majority of workers in various bargaining units. As interpreted by the NLRB and upheld by the courts, the Wagner Act outlawed such historic anti-union practices as industrial espionage, yellow-dog contracts, black lists, employment of *provocateurs*, strikebreaking, private police, and the creation of private arms stockpiles, which together had made the civil liberties of workers a mockery. Following the upholding of the Wagner Act by the Supreme Court in 1937, most employers gave up these practices without a struggle and the amount of violence in American labor relations diminished markedly.[90]

In addition to passing New Deal legislation, including the NIRA and the Wagner Act, the Senate made a notable contribution to the cause of labor and civil liberties generally by authorizing in 1936 a committee investigation of "violations of the rights of free speech and assembly and undue interference with the right of labor to organize and bargain collectively." This committee, known as the LaFollette committee after its chairman, Sen. Robert M. LaFollette, was the first committee in congressional history devoted exclusively to investigating violations of civil liberties. It performed invaluable service during its days of glory in 1936 and 1937 in exposing company towns, the massive use of detectives to infiltrate and disrupt unions, the creation of private armies and arms stockpiles by private business, and massive violations of the right of free speech, free assembly and freedom of organization which workers had suffered for many decades and in many areas across the country. In some cases, as in the drive by the newly formed Congress of Industrial Organization (CIO) to organize the Detroit automotive industry, the LaFollette Committee went beyond the bounds of mere investigation and actively aided union organizing attempts. In some cases, LaFollette Committee hearings led employers to abandon the use of industrial espionage and anti-union violence and contributed to favorable strike settlements, as well as adding immeasurably to the growth of pro-union sentiment. In a sense the LaFollette Committee exposures only repeated some of the same findings that the Indusrial Relations Commission of 1913 and the Interchurch World Movement report on the 1919 steel strike had revealed, but "the committee luxuriated, as its predecessors had not, in a climate of union and government opinion warmly sympathetic to its efforts."[91]

While the Supreme Court, until 1937, was conservative in its rulings on many New Deal reform measures, on civil liberties cases the court maintained a strong libertarian position throughout the thirties. The most important cases were a 1935 decision again upsetting convictions in the Scottsboro cases, the 1937 ruling upholding the Wagner Act, and 1937 decisions throwing out a Georgia conviction for "insurrection" and declaring the law involved unconstitutionally vague as applied in the case of a black CP organizer (*Herndon* v. *Lowry*), and declaring Oregon's criminal syndicalism law unconstitutional as applied to a CP member who had been charged as a result of attending a peaceful meeting of the party (*DeJonge* v. *Oregon*).[92]

Taken together, the actions of the Roosevelt administration, the passage of the Wagner Act, the creation of the LaFollette Committee and the rulings of the Supreme Court during the 1933-37 period created a true "revolution in labor law,"[93] and a revolutionary reconstruction in the concept of the federal government's role in the area of civil liberties. Until the 1930's, the major role of the federal government when it intervened at all in questions concerning civil liberties, such as during the Alien and Sedition hysteria, the Civil War and World War I, had been a highly repressive one. Now, for the first time, the federal government intervened to *protect* civil liberties against local abuses. Civil liberties, once privileges granted by a community to its members, became rights enforceable against local majorities. By assuming responsibility for protecting civil liberties, the federal government made certain rights inalienable, empirically rather than metaphysically.[94]

The Abortive Red Scare of 1934-35

The first major target of repressive forces at the federal level during the New Deal was not the left but the right wing. The rise of Hitler and the subsequent growth of pro-Nazi groups in the United States, the most important of which, the Friends of the New Germany, had a membership of around five thousand during the 1933-35 period, led to increasing concern among many liberals and especially among American Jews.[95] Following the so-called "Spanknobel Affair," in September, 1933, in which Heinz Spanknobel, a German emissary of the Nazi party who had been designated to lead Nazi groups in America, used bullying tactics to gain influence in New York's German-American community, American Nazis began to receive press attention far out of proportion to their influence. A New York grand jury and the Justice Department began investigations of the Friends of the New Germany, Spanknobel fled the U.S. after being indicted under an obscure Federal law requiring registration of foreign agents, and Rep. Samuel Dickstein began a preliminary investigation of Nazi groups in his capacity as chairman of the House Committee on Immigration and Naturalization. In March, 1934, Dickstein convinced the House to create a special committee to investigate "Nazi propaganda activities" and the diffusion of "subversive propaganda that is instigated from foreign countries and attacks the principle of the form of government as guaranteed by the constitution."

The committee was placed under the chairmanship of Rep. John McCormack, with Dickstein made vice-chairman.[96] While McCormack conducted the hearings on a generally high plane, Dickstein, who had publicly stated his hope that the hearings would eradicate all traces of Nazi influence in the United States, demonstrated undisguised contempt for the Nazi witnesses who appeared before him and "not only intimidated several witnesses but also accused them of treasonous activities."[97] The committee's final report and recommendations were very restrained, at least in comparison to those of the Fish Committee. The committee demonstrated the financial and ideological ties between Germany and American Nazidom, but concluded that fascism and communism were making little headway in the United States. The committee did create one grave precedent in submitting a list of organizations to the Congress that it deemed "subversive," an extraordinary course of action seemingly unrelated to any authority granted the committee and amounting to an official condemnation of organizations without any trial or specified charges.

At the same time as the McCormack-Dickstein hearings, President Roosevelt reactivated the FBI as a political spying agency by asking it to undertake an investigation of the Nazi movement in the United States, concentrating on the relationship of the movement to German diplomatic officials in the U.S. On May 10, 1934, instructions were sent to all FBI field offices directing that an intensive investigation begin of the Nazi movement "with particular reference to anti-racial and anti-American activities having any possible connection with official representatives of the German government in the United States." According to an internal FBI history, Roosevelt's directive "was not a sweeping and general assignment to conduct domestic security intelligence investigations" but it resulted in the FBI departing from "past statutory practice" and beginning an "intelligence investigation, which by necessity, involved aliens and United States citizens and was conducted for the primary purpose of informing the Attorney General and the President as to the general activities of the movement."[98]

As a result of the McCormack-Dickstein hearings, the consistently hostile press received by Friends of the New Germany, and internal bickering within the Nazi group, in November, 1935, the German government forbade all German nationals and Germans seeking naturalization from joining the group and cut off financial aid in the hope of bringing about the collapse of the Friends. However, no federal action was taken against the Friends, since no evidence was ever uncovered indicating any law violations.

The flurry about Nazi activities proved to be only a temporary diversion from the more traditional target of repressive forces, the American left. While the general trend of the early New Deal years was clearly in the direction of reform as opposed to repression on the federal level, the "red" issue never wholly disappeared and at times both the Roosevelt administration and the Congress took actions which fed the forces of repression. New deal measures such as the Agricultural Adjustment Bill, direct federal relief, deficit financing, the Tennessee Valley Authority, the Civilian Conservation Corps, and even pure food and drug legislation were all attacked as being communistically inclined or inspired. The fear of communism was in some cases used by Roosevelt and other New Dealers to support their own proposals. Thus, Roosevelt warned coal mine owners that if they did not agree on a code for the coal industry, they would only be helping communism, and proponents of the Wagner Act similarly argued that it would head off communism.[99]

As early as 1934, a coordinated assault was launched on the Roosevelt administration charging that it was under communist domination or influence. In April, 1934, a House committee dignified these charges by holding hearings into the claims of Gary, Indiana's superintendent of schools, Dr. William A. Wirt, that Roosevelt's brain trusters viewed FDR as "the Kerensky" preparing the way for a "Stalin." Although the Wirt charges turned out to be based on nothing at all, they helped to create the stereotype of the New Deal as a communist plot.[100]

The McCormack Commitee also touched briefly on the communist threat, stating the CP posed little threat to American institutions at the moment but that its growth presented a definite danger to the country. By the summer and fall of 1934, right-wing charges of communist influence in the Roosevelt administration reached flood-tide proportions. Under the leadership of the Hearst newspapers and the business-dominated American Liberty League, a steady crescendo of claims was made that FDR was determined to turn the U.S. into a totalitarian dictatorship.[101] In November, 1934, the Hearst press began a determined campaign to paint the nation's colleges as a hot bed of communism, although, as Arthur Schlesinger has written, Hearst's primary object was "evidently less to uncover genuine communists than to frighten liberals out of expressing opinions on public affairs."[102] Hearst attacked as subversive a variety of people ranging from Prof. Sidney Hook to Nicholas Murray Butler and Rep. John McSwain, the conservative chairman of the House Military Affairs committee. At about the same time, Elizabeth Dilling published a book entitled *The Red Network* which listed about five hundred organizations and thirteen hundred persons who were allegedly involved in a subversive communist conspiracy, ranging from Sen. Borah to Eleanor Roosevelt, Mahatma Gandhi, and Chiang Kai-Shek.[103]

While the major impact of the Hearst-Dilling inspired scare was felt at the local level, the Roosevelt administration made some concessions to the spirit of repression fostered by the red-baiters. In August, 1936, Roosevelt asked FBI chief J. Edgar Hoover to broaden his political intelligence activity which had been revived in 1934 to study Nazi and fascist groups to include communist groups, also. According to Hoover's notes of the meeting, Roosevelt told him that "he was interested in . . . obtaining a broad picture of the general movement and its activities as may affect the economic and political life of the country as a whole." Don Whitehead's "authorized" study of the FBI states that at the meeting Hoover and Roosevelt agreed that the investigation was to be "for intelligence purposes only and not the type of investigation required in collecting evidence to be presented to a court."[104] On September 5, 1936, Hoover notified FBI offices across the country:

> The Bureau desires to obtain from all possible sources information concerning subversive activities being conducted in the United States by Communists, Fascists and representatives or advocates of other organizations or groups advocating the overthrow or replacement of the government of the United States by illegal methods.[105]

At Roosevelt's request, Hoover also agreed to coordinate his information with State Department and Military Intelligence agencies. Meanwhile, political deportations, which had dropped sharply during the first years of the New Deal, jumped sharply in 1936, reflecting proceedings initiated during 1935, the high point of the Hearst-Dilling scare. Roosevelt took a personal interest in the initiation of deportation proceedings against left-wing union leader Harry Bridges and against California CP leader Sam Darcy in the aftermath of the 1934 San Francisco

Political Deportations[106]

1933	74
1934	29
1935	17
1936	47
1937	17
1938	8

general strike.[107] Emma Goldman, who had been allowed to enter the U.S. in February, 1934, was barred from re-entry in the fall of 1934, because, Secretary of Labor Perkins admitted privately, "she could not risk it because of the San Francisco General Strike, the mounting anti-radical, anti-alien attack of the Hearst newspapers and the *Chicago Tribune* and the general worsening of the public attitude towards aliens."[108] In a number of cases the Labor Department arrested aliens involved in strike activity for possible deportation.[109]

In March, 1935, the War and Navy departments supported one of the bills proposed by the McCormack Committee, which would have made it illegal to attempt to incite members of the armed forces to "insubordination, disloyalty, mutiny or refusal of duty." No evidence of any serious subversive penetration of the armed forces was presented, and statutes regarding attempts to cause disaffection in the services already existed. The proposed bill was so broadly written that "it might be used against the recent Methodist manifestoes of pacifism or to punish civilians objecting to the use of troops in a strike." The bill passed the Senate but died in the House.[110]

Secretary of Commerce Henry Wallace also contributed to the red scare. In March, 1935, he voiced disapproval of activities by "communist and socialist agitators" in the south who were attempting to organize sharecroppers in Arkansas who had been severely exploited by landlords and were the targets of severe repression by local police officials.[111] Secretary of the Interior Harold Ickes spoke out against the scare, but he noted in his diary in March, 1935, that FDR was "anxious just now not to do anything to stir up William Randolph Hearst."[112]

The only legislative product of the 1934-35 red scare at the federal level was a bill passed by Congress in 1935 which barred the payment of salaries to any teacher in the Washington, D.C. public schools who was "teaching or advocating communism." This provision was repealed in February, 1937, after the red scare had died down, although Congress was careful to include in the 1937 law that "nothing herein shall be construed as permitting the advocacy of communism."[113]

The mid-thirties' red scare met a decisive rebuff at the polls in the 1936 election. In December, 1935 the Republican National Committee had declared that the election would determine "whether we hold to the

American system of government or whether we shall sit idly by and allow it to be replaced by a socialistic state honeycombed with waste and extravagance and ruled by a dictatorship that mocks at the rights of the States and the liberty of the citizen."[114] Such charges become common currency in 1936 from Republicans, Liberty Leaguers, and disaffected former Democrats such as John W. Davis and Al Smith as well as crackpots like Gerald L. K. Smith.[115] Thus, Republican Vice-presidential candidate Frank Knox declared that the Democratic Party had been "seized by alien and un-American elements" and that FDR "has been leading us towards Moscow."[116] Presidential Candidate Alf Landon declared that FDR had started the nation on the road to dictatorship, that New Deal policies would lead to the guillotine and that, "If we are to preserve our American form of government this administration must be defeated."[117] The Republican National Committee declared that Roosevelt was "the Kerensky of the American Revolutionary movement."[118] These charges were taken so seriously by the White House that a special rebuttal statement was issued in September, 1936, and FDR personally addressed the issue in a speech on September 29, declaring that the Democrats were fighting communism by tackling the causes of social unrest, while the Republicans were fostering communism by rejecting the obligations of social justice. FDR declared, "I have not sought, do not seek, I repudiate the support of any advocate of Communism or of any other alien 'ism' which would by fair means or foul change our American Democracy."[119] Roosevelt's supporters also devoted special efforts to combatting the "red" charges. Thus Democratic vice-presidential candidate John Nance Garner declared piously, "You might as well suspect atheism in a cathedral as communism in the environment of Hyde Park."[120]

Communism had thus become a major issue for the first time in American history as a charge levelled by one major party against another in a presidential campaign. The American people responded by awarding Roosevelt a decisive victory — the largest presidential vote in history, the largest presidential plurality, and the largest congressional majority in about seventy years. In 1937, civil liberties seemed to be riding at high tide on the federal level as Congress repealed the Washington, D.C. teachers' provision, the Supreme Court issued rulings favorable to civil liberties and the LaFollette Committee exposed the widespread suppression of the rights of labor.

State and Local Repression, 1933-38

While the dominant tone set by the federal government during the 1933-38 period was favorable to the exercise of civil liberties, this was not the case in many localities around the country which faced militant labor activity. Labor unions *were* able to make major gains in many important industries across the country, particularly in the clothing, coal mining, rubber, electrical and hotel workers industries, under the impact of 7(a), the

Wagner Act and the climate favorable to union activity fostered by the federal government. In many cases, major union gains were achieved with surprising lack of resistance. For example, the UMW won a major victory in the soft coal industry in 1933 that gained without violence "all the things that deputy sheriffs usually shoot people for demanding," as a New York newspaper reporter put it.[121]

However, until the Wagner Act was upheld in 1937, as labor membership and strike activity increased dramatically, the use of the militia and the traditional repressive apparatus of police assaults and arrests, deputized private armies and wholesale violations of civil liberties increased sharply. A total of eighteen thousand strikers were arrested from 1934 to 1936, and over 100 strikers were killed during labor disputes from 1933 to 1936.[122]

Labor repression during the mid-thirties was generally a cooperative effort between local and state governments and businessmen, who had never before "hired so many private police, strikebreakers, thugs, spies and agents provocateurs" and never before "laid up such stores of tear gas, machine guns and firearms."[123]

	Labor Union Membership[124] (in thousands)	Workers on on Strike[125] (in thousands)	Nat'l. Guard Use[126]
1932	3144	325	2
1933	2689	1144	9
1934	3088	1480	24
1935	3584	1102	19
1936	3989	710	11
1937	7001	1950	8
1938	8034	688	2

The repression of labor during the mid-thirties was most consistent and vicious in the south and in agricultural areas. Repression was strong in these areas because radical groups were frequently involved in such labor agitation and because labor unions were so weak in these areas that businessmen and local officials, never having experienced the actual conservatism of most established unions, were frightened to death of unionism on the one hand, and, on the other hand, correctly perceived that any challenge to their power was in fact somewhat revolutionary because existing power relationships in these areas were so imbalanced.

The greatest revolt in southern labor history occurred during the mid-thirties, with over four hundred fifty thousand southern workers striking between 1933 and 1936. Although labor did make major gains in the south during this period, especially after the passage of the Wagner Act, throughout the region unions often had to deal with local and state police who were ready to do management's bidding, repressive legislation adopted by local authorities (for example, Macon, Georgia barred the distribution of "any handbill, circular, pamphlet, posters, postcard or literature of any kind"), arbitrary police arrests and beatings, vigilante assaults, which frequently included kidnappings and beatings of union organizers often in cooperation with the police. As elsewhere, southern companies made major investments in labor spies and in private arms stockpiles. Communist organizers were a particular target of police and vigilante abuses in the south. In June, 1935, three left-wing writers who journeyed to Birmingham to protest the 1933 ordinance barring possession of more than one copy of "seditious" literature were pushed around by detectives, then fingerprinted, photographed and ordered out of town. Several shots were subsequently fired into their car, but investigating police declared that they were fired by the writers themselves. In the summer of 1936, police in Bessemer, Alabama, arrested Jack Barton, the local CP secretary, under Bessemer's 1933 seditious literature law, basing the arrest on his possession of communist party material as well as such publications as *The Nation* and *The New Republic*. He was sentenced to 180 days at hard labor and a $100 fine by a judge who refused to examine the materials involved in the case; the judge simply declared, "It is all communist stuff and you can not have it in Bessemer." Barton was arrested three other times on similarly flimsy charges in a period of eighteen months. In the Birmingham area, the dominant Tennessee Coal and Iron Company regularly hired special guards through the county sheriff; the sheriff was given a bonus by the company for each man so hired and in return he deputized the guards during periods of labor strife. The Birmingham police set up a special red squad which regularly raided the homes of active union men and suspected communists and terrorized and intimidated their victims.[127]

During the 1934 cotton textile strike — the largest single strike until then in American labor history, during which about four hundred thousand workers walked out from Maine to Georgia — the national guard was called out in Alabama, Georgia, Mississippi and the Carolinas. Altogether a total of twenty-five thousand national guard and armed deputies were mobilized to fight the strike in the south. Strike organizers were beaten and arrested throughout the strike area. Partial martial law and a state of "insurrection" were declared in South Carolina, where police and deputized workers shot and killed seven pickets. The governor of Georgia declared martial law in strike areas and put two thousand strikers in a concentration camp after mass arrests by the National Guard. Thirty-four key strike leaders were arrested and held incommunicado in Georgia, thus crippling strike relief efforts. Entire towns in Alabama were closed to union organizers, while the Alabama relief administrator, who was an official of the dominant industrial corporation in the state, cut off relief, although announced federal policy was that strikers were entitled to relief. Officials of the West Point Manufacturing Company in Chambers County, Alabama purchased $1700 worth of tear gas and obtained seven machine guns to fight the strike. They were immediately deputized by local officials and thereupon barricaded public roads and assaulted union sympathizers. The strike ended in a complete defeat for the cotton textile workers.[128]

Harlan County, Kentucky, remained a major site of repression through the mid-thirties. UMW attempts to organize there collapsed in the face of repeated use of the militia, assassinations and kidnappings of union organizers and sympathetic law-enforcement officials, and the regular deputizing of thugs and murderers by the local sheriff. A special commissioner appointed by the governor of Kentucky reported in 1935:

> It is almost unbelievable that anywhere in a free and democratic nation . . . conditions can be found as bad as they are in Harlan County. There exists a virtual reign of terror.

Harlan County was finally cracked by the UMW in 1938 following public hearings by the LaFollette Committee and federal indictments against forty-seven company officials and deputies and twenty-two coal mining companies for conspiracy to violate the Wagner Act.[129] In other labor disputes in the south, over twenty persons were killed between 1933 and 1937, almost all of whom were strikers, and scores of strikers were shot.[130]

Agricultural workers throughout the nation faced repression which was even more consistently vicious than that faced by workers in the south. As Stuart Jamieson has pointed out, "Suppression of many kinds could be employed safely against an occupational group which was heterogeneous in composition, low in social status, weak in bargaining power, poorly paid, lacking in political influence, and denied the benefits of protective labor legislation (including the Wagner Act)."[131]

As agricultural strikes increased, so did repressive activity. Such activity was particularly frequent where strikes affecting particular industries and crops were large, numerous, and long-sustained, or where they affected highly perishable crops — which is to say when strikes were particularly threatening.[132]

California remained the major center of agricultural union activity and was also the major center of repression of farm workers. During 1933, a record wave of sixty-one agricultural strikes involving almost fifty thousand farm workers swept California. Growers and police officials responded with arrests of strikers and strike leaders, raids on union headquarters, assaults on pickets by armed deputies, driving cars into crowds of strikers, patrolling strike areas with shotguns and tear gas bombs, shootings, denials of relief assistance, efforts to deport aliens and widespread red-baiting.[133]

Typical of the attitudes of California public officials were the following comments, the first by a justice of the peace who heard some of the strikers' cases, and the second by an undersheriff:

> These men are nothing but a bunch of rats, Russian anarchists, cutthroats and sweepings of creations. This defendant doesn't know when he is well

off if he wants a jury trial. In some places they would take him and his kind and hang them from the town hall. . . . This town may see a few hangings yet.

We protect our farmers here in Kern County. They are our best people. They are always with us. They keep the county going. They put us in here and they can put us out again, so we serve them. But the Mexicans are trash. They have no standard of living. We herd them like pigs.[134]

Most of the important strikes in California agriculture during the 1933-34 period were led by the Communist-dominated Cannery and Agricultural Workers' Industrial Union (CAIWU), partly because of the AFL's long-standing neglect of farm workers (as one AFL official in California said in 1935, "Only fanatics are willing to live in shacks or tents and get their heads broken in the interests of migratory labor").[135] The most important CAIWU walkout in 1933 brought out ten thousand cotton pickers in the San Joaquin Valley. During the strike, police rounded up workers and held them incommunicado in the Tulare County fairgrounds stockade, and armed ranchers shot fourteen strikers on October 10, killing three. By the time the strike collapsed, about fifty strikers had been shot and one hundred thirteen arrested. A special board created by the governor of California concluded, "Without question, civil rights of strikers have been violated."[136] Cotton growers and strikers eventually agreed to a compromise settlement in the face of pressure from federal and state authorities.

Number of Agricultural Strikers, 1930-39[137]

	California	Other
1930	7,300	1,305
1931	1,575	1,430
1932	2,497	665
1933	48,005	8,811
1934	19,882	10,666
1935	6,550	13,575
1936	13,659	4,053
1937	3,086	3,148
1938	5,469	5,604
1939	19,153	1,355

The growers declared they did so "in the interests of good American citizenship, law and order and in order to forestall the spread of communism and radicalism and to protest the harvesting of other crops."[138] The strikers had been aided significantly during the strike by the provision of relief by the California Emergency Relief Administration (CERA), probably the first time in American labor history that "a public agency under Federal direction provided public relief to workers actively involved in a large-scale strike."[139] However, CERA later cut off food relief to force strikers to accept the settlement.

The second major AWIU strike brought out Mexican farm workers in California's Imperial Valley in late 1933 and early 1934. As Irving Bernstein has noted, this dispute was, in truth, less a strike than a "proto-Fascist offensive by the grower-shippers and the corrupt local officials they dominated to suppress civil liberties in order to destroy unionism."[140] Police attacked strikers' meetings, made mass arrests and raided the strikers' desert camp, burning workers' shacks to the ground and driving inhabitants out with tear gas bombs, killing a baby in the process. Events in the Imperial Valley eventually led federal conciliator Pelham D. Glassford, who earlier labelled CAWIU leaders as "vile agitators"[141] to state publicly that the Valley:

> is governed . . . by a small group, which in advertising a war against communism is sponsoring terrorism, intimidation and injustice. . . . It is time the Imperial Valley awakens to the fact that it is part of the United States.[142]

Glassford's statement was too late to save the CAWIU.

The Imperial Valley repression had severely weakened the organization, and what was left of it was destroyed by massive repression in the spring and summer of 1934 which swept California under the prodding and aegis of the newly organized Associated Farmers, Inc., (AF), an organization of conservative farmers who worked closely with state and local authorities. On July 24, 1934, police armed with sawed-off shotguns, blackjacks, rubber hose, clubs and gas bombs, raided CAWIU headquarters in Sacramento and arrested seventeen top leaders for criminal syndicalism. Eight leaders were convicted and sent to jail in a trial heavily financed by the AF.[143] Although the eight were released in 1937, the trial completed the destruction of the union and by forcing "the most experienced and most militant agricultural union leaders out of the field"[144] deprived migratory workers of their best organizational allies.

Agricultural unionism in California never again reached 1933-34 levels during the decade, but repression did not cease. After 1934, the AF became a ready pool of deputies for local sheriffs during strike activities. By the late 30's over thirty of California's fifty-eight counties, and nineteen municipalities, covering a large proportion of all agricultural areas of the state, had passed stringent anti-picketing ordinances under AF pressure.[145] In eighteen counties, these laws barred picketing for the purpose of inducing others to quit work or not to seek employment, and in nine counties the laws followed the pattern of the San Joaquin County ordinance in barring "any derogatory, indecent, opprobrious epithets of language" or "any loud or unusual noise," any "loud or unusual tone," and even "any gesture" in order to induce persons to strike or boycott.[146] In 1939 and 1940, some of the ordinances were declared unconstitutional but they were "in full force during the 1930's and they operated to aid agricultural employers in their attempts to break unions and strike activities."[147]

Meanwhile, repression of agricultural strikes by more forceful methods continued. In August, 1935, during an apple strike in Santa Rosa, vigilantes raided a strike meeting and attacked workers, dragged five workers through the streets, and tarred, feathered and deported two of them. Tweny-three professionals and businessmen in the community were indicted in connection with the disorders, but quickly acquitted, and the general atmosphere of intimidation in Santa Rosa not only crushed the strike but frightened away so many workers that the fields were undermanned.[148] During a 1936 celery field workers' strike in Los Angeles County, fifteen hundred police and deputy sheriffs broke up strike parades and tossed tear gas bombs into strikers' homes. According to one account, "So many arrests were made that neither the police nor the union could keep a tally."[149] Shortly afterwards a strike of twenty-five hundred citrus workers in Orange County faced police disruption of parades and picket lines, the jailing of two hundred strikers in a stockade, and injury of many strikers when growers commissioned bands of armed men, armed with tear gas and shotguns to conduct "open private warfare against citrus strikers."[150] Another 1936 strike, that of four thousand lettuce-packers and their supporters in the Salinas Valley was checked by massive employer resistance coupled with what the NLRB termed "inexcusable police brutality, in many cases bordering on sadism."[151] In smashing the strike, local and state police operated effectively under the command of an army reserve officer employed by Associated Farmers. Twenty-five hundred men were mobilized, armed and deputized to fight the strike, with the local sheriff threatening to arrest any resident who failed to respond to a general mobilization of all male residents between the ages of eighteen and forty-five. Salinas became an armed camp, with machine guns placed on roofs, picket lines broken with tear gas assaults and the jail filled to capacity. The strike was completely crushed, bringing down with it a rapidly growing union of Salinas shed packers, the Fruit and Vegetable Workers Union, which had made strong gains in 1935 and 1936.[152]

During the most important agricultural strike in California in 1937, that of Stockton cannery workers, twelve hundred farmers were sworn in as deputies and armed by the Associated Farmers with clubs, rifles and shotguns. Acting under the command of the president of the Associated Farmers, the "deputies" assaulted pickets with tear gas bombs and gunfire. One of the only two important field workers' strikes in 1937 was broken by the arrests of pickets. Another strike was averted when the local sheriff swore in one hundred special deputies and warned workers either to continue work or face arrest for vagrancy. The most important strike of 1938, involving cotton pickers in Kern County, was broken by mass arrests of pickets and the denial of state relief.[153]

The LaFollette Committee concluded following hearings in 1939 and 1940 that the Associated Farmers in California had formed a conspiracy "designed to prevent the exercise of their civil liberties by oppressed wage laborers in agriculture, (which) was executed ruthlessly with every device of repression that anti-unionism could muster." Where the Associated Farmers had successfully implemented its policies, the committee concluded, "local fascism was the result."[154]

The repression of agricultural labor was not confined to California. In the summer and fall of 1933, the long-dormant IWW agricultural drive was renewed in strike efforts which marked the "most important farm labor dispute which the Yakima Valley (Washington) had experienced."[155] Peaceful IWW strikers and picketers were met with mass arrests, attacks by vigilantes armed with pick handles and pipe lengths, a ban on public meetings, the calling out of the National Guard and imposition of martial law. Guardsmen and state police raided and destroyed hobo jungles and suspected Wobbly camps, in one case giving inhabitants five minutes to leave the area. Federal immigration officials interrogated jailed strikers, apparently searching for deportable aliens. A total of between eighty and one hundred Wobblies were held in a hastily built wooden stockade, first under criminal syndicalism and later under vagrancy charges. Twelve men eventually pleaded guilty to vagrancy and agreed not to take civil action against the county, while non-resident IWWs promised to leave the county for at least one year; in return, Yakima authorities dropped all other charges. The Yakima repression "utterly smashed" the strike and agricultural unionism in the Valley, but the wooden stockade remained on the county courthouse grounds until 1943 as "a silent reminder to future malcontents that the spirit of 1933 remained alive in the region."[156]

A strike of three hundred cranberry workers in Massachusetts in 1933 was smashed by the arrest of strikers for trespassing and intimidation, and the arrest of union organizers for obtaining signatures and money "under false pretenses."[157] A growing communist-influenced radical movement among small farmers in central Nebraska was crushed in June, 1934, when vigilantes attacked a group of three hundred protesters with blackjacks and fists in front of the county courthouse at Loup City; subsequently nine of the victims were arrested and seven convicted for rioting on the grounds that public statements made during the protest showed "there was violent interference with the sheriff and his deputies in their duty to preserve order."[158]

Onion workers striking in Ohio in 1934 were met with an anti-picketing injunction which barred them from assembling in numbers "in excess of two," by tear gas attacks and by the kidnapping and beating of their strike leader, "Okey" Odell. Odell and eight other strikers were indicted on various charges, but the local grand jury refused to indict Odell's assailants. During a strike at the huge Seabrook Farms in New Jersey in 1934, vigilante farmers were deputized and over fifty strikers were arrested. At Bridgeton, New Jersey, union organizers were arrested under the terms of a city ordinance which required police permits for all public meetings, "if noisy," even if held in private homes. As a result of the strike the New

Jersey legislature appointed a committee to investigate communist activities in New Jersey.

A strike of cherry pickers in Wisconsin in 1935 was broken when police gave the strike leader a choice between six months in jail or leaving the county.[159] A strike of fifteen hundred pea pickers in Idaho in 1935 was smashed when the National Guard was sent in. According to the governor, "Deportation of about one hundred strike agitators . . . resulted in a return of the workers to their jobs and law and order prevailed again."[160] Striking hop pickers in the Yakima Valley of Washington were deported by state and county police in September, 1937. Police in Texas arrested over one thousand pickets on charges such as "blocking the sidewalks" and "congregating in unlawful assemblies" during a strike of six thousand pecan shellers in 1938.[161] During a 1938 strike of pea pickers in Idaho, the sheriff arrested strike leaders and members of the negotiating committee. He declared, "The growers of this county have put forth lots of effort in growing these peas and they are going to have the full protection of the law in getting them harvested and marketed."[162]

Aside from California, the most concerted effort to organize farm workers and the most concerted campaign of repression occurred in Arkansas where organizers under strong socialist influence created the Southern Tenant Farmers Union (STFU).[163] The STFU was a response to the wretched conditions of landless farm laborers in the south — they would have been called peasants in Europe — and their steadily deteriorating conditions under the impact of New Deal farm programs. One French visitor asserted, with considerable basis, that in none of the European democracies "is the lot of the agricultural tenant as wretched, his prospects as hopeless and his rights as unprotected as in the southern regions of America."[164] Beginning in July, 1934, thousands of black and white sharecroppers, tenant farmers and wage laborers flocked to join the STFU. Local growers and police officials replied with a campaign of terror similar to that familiar in the history of farm labor organizing in America — i.e. Wheatland, Elaine, rural Alabama and California.

Organizers were arrested on charges such as blasphemy, criminal anarchy, "disturbing the peace," "obtaining money under false pretenses" and "interfering with labor." Union meetings were assaulted and broken up by police and vigilante attacks, while individual union members were arrested, beaten and shot at. Outside "agitators" such as Norman Thomas were barred from speaking and sometimes assaulted and deported. STFU meeting places, including churches, were burned, vigilantes patrolled highways to prevent picketing, and during a 1936 cotton pickers strike, the militia was called in. At Marked Tree, Arkansas, the city fathers passed an ordinance making it illegal for any person to "deliver a public speech" at "any street, alley, park or other place" without prior permission from local authorities. The mayor explained, "Of course the law don't mean that church people can't hold speakin', just the radicals, that's all."[165]

While the STFU did not collapse it was gravely weakened by the severe repression. STFU membership continued to increase, reaching about thirty-one thousand members by the end of 1936, but the organization began to shy away from militant labor activity, instead stressing propaganda and pressure group activity. The STFU slowly disintegrated after 1937, largely as a result of a disastrous merger with the communist-dominated United Cannery, Agricultural, Packing and Allied Workers of America (ACAPAWA).

Agricultural labor and southern labor were not the only union forces to suffer severe repression during the 1933-38 period. Communist organizers and workers associated with the National Miners Union in the coal mines of Carbon County, Utah had achieved considerable success during the summer of 1933, until they were met with the National Guard, tear gas assaults on and mass arrests of pickets, deportation proceedings against aliens, raids on private homes and boardinghouses, bans on public meeting and criminal syndicalism arrests. On September 11, 1933, NMU members marched on the courthouse in Price, Utah to protest the jailing of pickets; when they refused to obey orders to halt the march, the National Guard assaulted them with firehoses, tear gas and rifle butts. Criminal syndicalism charges against the NMU organizers and riot charges against NMU members were dropped only when the organizers agreed to leave the county and the NMU drive had been crushed; in the meantime coal operators reached an agreement with the "safe" United Mineworkers, whose organizational efforts had been unobstructed — in fact had, for the first time, been aided — by local officials.[166]

During 1934, a massive wave of militant strike activity comparable only to that of 1877, 1886, 1894 and 1919 occurred, and it was met with a massive wave of repression. The response to the 1934 textile strike in the south and to agricultural organizing in California and Arkansas has already been discussed.[167] Other major strikes in 1934 that met severe repression included the San Francisco General Strike, the Toledo Auto-Lite Strike, and the Minneapolis Truckers' strike.

The most spectacular labor dispute of 1934, the San Francisco General Strike, grew out of a strike of West Coast longshoremen over demands which centered around union recognition and control over hiring.[168] The longshoremen strike was quickly joined by strikes of West Coast maritime unions and truckers. The heart of the strike was in San Francisco, where bloody clashes between pickets and strikebreakers and police were common occurrences. On July 3 and 5 serious rioting broke out in San Francisco's pier area when hundreds of police attempting to provide protection for the movement of freight from the docks by non-union workers clashed with thousands of pickets determined to block their efforts. Police using tear gas (paid for by shipowners), clubs and guns, killed two strikers and shot around thirty; pickets fought back with bricks, railroad spikes and rocks. Altogether over one hundred strikers and police were hospitalized. On July 5, the national guard was sent into San Francisco. Troops set up machine gun nests and barbed-wire barricades in the port area and freight movement resumed under military protection.

On July 16, all but essential services in San Francisco were shut down as one hundred thirty thousand workers under the direction of the AFL Central Labor Council (CLC) initiated a sympathetic general strike. Local newspapermen and businessmen quickly initiated a coordinated campaign to tag the general strike a communist insurrection, a charge supported by National Recovery Administrator Hugh Johnson, the mayor of San Francisco and the governor of California. Within a few days eighteen hundred police and forty-five hundred national guardsmen had transformed San Francisco into an armed fortress, although there was no labor-initiated violence during the general strike. On July 17, a week-long concerted campaign of police and vigilante terror was launched against over a dozen radical and union hangouts in the San Francisco area, including CP headquarters, the offices of left-wing unions and even private homes frequented by radicals and strikers. The invariable pattern of the assaults was that vigilantes would wreck the hangouts and beat the inhabitants, and police would then arrive and proceed to arrest the victims of the beatings. No vigilantes were apprehended.

The general strike began to collapse within a few days of its initiation due to the vigilante and police repression, the pressure from AFL President William Green, and the timidity of the CLC conservative leadership.

Although the general strike was called off on July 19, the longshoremen and maritime strike continued. Both sides finally agreed to arbitration by the federal National Longshoremen's Board, which on October 12, 1934, handed down what amounted to a "smashing victory" for the unions.

In another major strike of 1934, serious rioting broke out in Toledo, on May 23, during a strike effort called by an AFL union with the support of local unemployment groups at the Electric Auto-Lite Company, a major auto parts manufacturer.[169] Deputized company officials who were protecting strikebreakers inside the plant attacked a crowd of strikers and strike supporters with tear gas bombs, water hoses, iron bars and occasional gunfire, while the crowd responded with stones and bricks. National guardsmen sent to Toledo the next day attacked crowds who sought to invade the plant with tear gas, fixed bayonets and guns, killing two and wounding over fifteen. The strike was eventually settled with a major union victory.

The Minneapolis truckers' strike of May, 1934 was a result of efforts by teamsters to break the closed-shop tradition which had been imposed on Minneapolis by the virulently anti-labor Citizens' Alliance.[170] The Citizens' Alliance had dominated Minneapolis for years by resorting to "espionage, propaganda, placing stool pigeons in unions, hiring thugs to beat up labor leaders, and tampering with grand juries."[171] The strike by five thousand teamsters, which was supported by sympathetic walkouts of thirty-five thousand taxi drivers and building trades workers, threatened to collapse the economy of Minneapolis, which, as a major distribution center for the entire northwest, was highly dependent on trucking.

In response to the strike the Citizens' Alliance created a volunteer "citizens' army," many of whom were deputized as special police, to break the walkout. Widescale rioting broke out on May 21 and May 22 between strikers and the "citizens' army," during which two deputies were killed, and hundreds were injured on both sides. On July 20, police opened fire when a truck loaded with pickets tried to stop the movement of another truck in the central market area. The police fire killed two persons and wounded sixty-five others. A report commissioned by the governor of Minnesota subsequently concluded that the truck movement had been a "plant" arranged by police rather than an attempt to move merchandise, that the pickets had not threatened the police and that in general the police "did not act as an impartial police force to enforce law and order, but rather became an agency to break the strike."[172] After the shooting, the national guard was sent into Minneapolis, martial law was declared and both strikers' and Citizens' Army headquarters were raided. The final strike settlement was a major victory for the truckers.

During 1935 and 1936, the national guard was dispatched to quell labor disorders about twenty times, and about forty persons were killed in labor disorders, but none of the disputes had the spectacular character of the 1934 strikes.[173] Perhaps the most interesting dispute of 1935 was the general strike which shut down Terre Haute, Indiana, in support of seven hundred strikers at the Columbia Enameling and Stamping Co. The company brought in strikebreakers, and the strikers retaliated by inflicting $15,000 worth of damage on the plant facilities. Over twenty thousand workers in Terre Haute walked out on July 22 to support the Columbia strikers. The governor quickly declared martial law and sent in one thousand national guardsmen. The troops attacked pickets with clubs and tear gas and arrested almost two hundred strikers within a few days. When the AFL's district organizer announced the end of the strike, the military censored his radio announcement because he criticized the city administration. Martial law was continued in Terre Haute for over half a year.[174]

Martial law was imposed for six months at Gallup, New Mexico, during a peaceful 1935 strike of several thousand Mexican coal miners. Attempts to evict the miners from their shacks led to a bloody riot, which in turn resulted in the arrest of over one hundred miners. Authorities eventually abandoned plans to try the miners for criminal syndicalism, but one of their key leaders was deported to Mexico.[175]

An IWW strike of loggers in Idaho in July, 1936, was broken when the governor declared martial law "to control incipient violence" and troops deported a series of IWW strike committees while protecting imported strikebreakers.[176]

The year 1937 marked a major turning point in American labor history. On the heels of FDR's tremendous victory in the 1936 elections, the greatest strike wave in American history erupted involving almost two million workers in over forty-five hundred strikes. Almost five hundred sit-in strikes involved four hundred thousand strikers. Union membership jumped from about four million in 1936 to about seven million in 1937, by far the greatest one year increase in American labor history.[177] Clearly the single most important reason for labor's tremendous gains was the new benevolent outlook on the part of the federal government and many local governments. Only a handful of sit-in strikes were broken up by police, and even though they were clearly illegal and went far beyond "free speech" the national guard was called out only three times during the year.[178] "Neither state nor federal governments would employ force as they had so often in the past to break strikes."[179]

One of the greatest breakthroughs in labor history was scored by the CIO through the use of the sit-in at key automobile plants of the General Motors Company in Flint, Michigan.[180] Despite the issuance of a court injunction, Michigan Gov. Frank Murphy refused to send in state troops to break the strike. Under pressure from Murphy, the LaFollette Committee and President Roosevelt, GM capitulated. Shortly afterwards, Chrysler agreed to bargain with the CIO, leaving outside the fold only Ford, which responded to union organizing attempts with vicious assaults on union organizers and a system of espionage that was so pervasive that "conversation and even smiling became dangerous" among Ford employees.[181] However, under pressure from the NLRB, the courts and the governor of Michigan, even Ford had capitulated by 1941.[182]

Correctly sensing the climate of public opinion and the determination of the federal government to support the rights of unions to organize, the major steel companies agreed to bargain with CIO steel unions in 1937 even before a strike had been called.[183] By mid-1937 the CIO Steel Workers Organizing Committee (SWOC) had almost three hundred thousand members and bargaining agreements with most of the major steel firms. This development, truly incredible in the light of the long history of severe repression of labor in the steel industry, clearly was influenced by the adverse publicity for employers generated by the LaFollette Committee's investigation of industrial espionage and sabotage, the reluctance of state governors to call out troops in labor disputes and the general attitude of the Roosevelt administration on questions affecting labor. When a preliminary contract was signed on March 17 in the conference room of Carnegie-Illinois Steel between Benjamin Fairless of Carnegie-Illinois and Phillip Murray of the CIO, a picture of Henry Frick had been removed from the room. "Didn't think he could stand it," explained a Carnegie-Illinois official.[184]

The last major campaign of real terror launched against union organizational efforts in American history came during the 1937 "little steel" strike.[185] The minor steel companies had refused to join the majors in bargaining with the CIO, resulting in widespread strikes in the spring of 1937. To fight the SWOC, the little steel companies widely employed the so-called "Mohawk Valley formula," which in essence consisted of labelling the strikes subversive assaults on law and order, creating vigilante groups of citizens to oppose the strikes, and mobilizing local police forces to aid in assaults on strikers and to furnish protection to strikebreakers. The LaFollette Committee concluded that the widespread formation of citizens' "law and order" committees by steel companies during the strike was an effort by industrialists to create an organization "to do to labor on industry's behalf what the individual employer could no longer do legally" because of the Wagner Act. The Committee said such groups had become an "invisible super-government" in many communities, which under the "law and order" cloak had aroused or cooperated with a spirit of vigilantism that suppressed workers' constitutional and statutory rights.[186]

Repression was widespread during the little steel strike. A total of $141,000 worth of private munitions were stockpiled for use by companies during the strike, while seven thousand private guards, police, deputy sheriffs and national guardsmen were mobilized to fight the strikers in Illinois, Ohio, Michigan and Pennsylvania. At Canton, Ohio, private police and non-striking employees assaulted pickets, while the national guard dispersed pickets and arrested union leaders. At Massillon, Ohio, special deputies and city police raided CIO headquarters, killing three strikers and arresting 165 people while wrecking the building. At Monroe, Michigan, the mayor recruited a private police force armed and financed by Republic Steel, and assaulted picketers with clubs and baseball bats. Republic police, meanwhile set fire to SWOC headquarters. At Johnstown, Pennsylvania, the mayor deputized over six hundred "untrained, emotionally involved" vigilantes, while Bethlehem Steel purchased munitions for the city government and provided the mayor with over $30,000 for the purpose of "maintaining law and order," which somehow was converted to the mayor's personal use. The Johnstown strike was marked by violence on both sides, and by a brief attempt by the governor of Pennsylvania to aid the strikers by declaring martial law and forcing the Bethlehem steel works to shut down.[187] At Youngstown, Ohio, employees of the steel companies were sworn in as deputy sheriffs and special police, and two hundred persons were arrested.

The most outrageous instance of repression during the little steel strike occurred in Chicago, where Republic Steel had been struck. Chicago police had repeatedly interfered with attempts to picket at the South Chicago Mill of the Republic corporation, clubbing and arresting recalcitrant strikers. On May 30, 1937, about fifteen hundred strike supporters attended a meeting in a field outside strike headquarters to protest police repression. When the crowd began to march towards the Republic plant, three hundred Chicago policemen blocked their path and ordered them to disperse. When a club and several stones were thrown at the police, the law officers suddenly opened fire at the marchers with tear gas and bullets, and then began savagely clubbing the fleeing demonstrators. Police gunfire killed ten demonstrators, six of whom were shot in the back, while thirty were wounded by gun shots and twenty-eight others were hospitalized. Sixteen police were injured, three seriously enough to require hospitalization.[188]

The police and the Chicago press quickly blamed the incident — which has become known as the Memorial Day Massacre — on outside agitators and communists. They claimed the crowd was intent on disarming and attacking the police and that members of the crowd had opened fire first. Although all of these police charges were later shown to be "thoroughly transparent, if not patently absurd,"[189] a coroner's jury found the killings "justifiable homicide" and the only legal result was that fifty demonstrators were fined $10. A movie which clearly demonstrated that the police had fired without cause and then brutally beaten demonstrators was withheld for over a month by Paramount Pictures, and then banned from viewing in Chicago after it was released.

The "little steel" strike ended in a complete defeat for the SWOC, largely due to ability of the steel companies to foster repression and control public opinion in the steel towns. A total of 16 persons had been killed and 267 injured in the strike. However, in 1941, the "little steel" companies were forced to accept NLRB-supervised elections, and the SWOC quickly won bargaining rights at all of the affected companies.

Labor unions were not the only victims of local and state political repression during the 1933-37 period. Radical political parties, militant students and the unemployed also were targets of policemen's clubs, meeting bans, and in some cases repressive legislation. The curve of political repression as applied to such targets was similar in development to the pattern of repression faced by labor, peaking in 1934-35, and then steadily improving until 1937, at which point considerable tolerance was accorded political radicals. Considering the overall dimensions of political repression in 1934-35 the ACLU reported that this period "recorded a greater variety and number of serious violations of civil liberties than any year since the war."[190]

During the 1933-35 period, criminal syndicalism prosecutions were brought in eleven states, generally on the basis of radical speeches or the distribution of literature; in 1936 and 1937 such charges were brought in only three states. Similarly, attacks on or bans against unemployment demonstrations and communist meetings were frequent from 1933-1935, but then dropped sharply, with the exception of some rather severe harassment of Communist Party candidates in the 1936 campaign.[191]

The major targets of repression in 1934-35 were radical students and faculty, largely because they were depicted as the major threat by the Hearst newspapers' campaign to whip up a red scare. Drawing a contrast between radicals in the schools as "villains" in contrast to past assaults on immigrants, University of Chicago President Robert Hutchins commented sarcastically in February, 1935:

> We are being treated to one of the red scares which we have every once in a while. The only new aspect of this one is that the reds are now in college. They used to be impoverished foreigners.[192]

Six states passed laws in 1934-35 which required teachers to pledge their loyalty, while legislative committees in Illinois, Wisconsin and Arkansas investigated possible subversion in colleges. Illinois' investigation of the University of Chicago was unable to come up with anything, but legislators in Wisconsin hinted darkly at sex orgies at the University of Wisconsin and termed the school an "ultra liberal institution in which communistic teachings were encouraged and where avowed communists were welcome." Legislative sleuths in Arkansas urged that "a close check" be kept on Commonwealth College. By 1936, however, such investigations had become so out-of-favor that a New York legislative committee authorized to investigate "seditious and treasonable" propaganda in the state's schools did not even bother to hold hearings.[193]

College student activists during the 1934-35 period frequently "were dismissed, their meetings were prohibited, they were arrested for distributing handbills, and on several occasions, attacked and beaten."[194] In October, 1934, five students were suspended at UCLA for alleged Communistic activities, largely because they had held an illegal meeting to discuss the state elections; subsequently UCLA Provost Ernest Moore termed his campus "one of the worst hotbeds of Communism in America" and allowed 150 athletes to form a vigilante committee to rid the campus of "all students holding extreme political views."[195] Eighteen students at Berkeley were arrested, and then released, when they distributed leaflets advertising the massive anti-war strike of 1935. In New York, radical students were expelled and suspended by the city's public high schools and colleges. While harassment of college and high school students declined after 1935, young Jehovah's Witnesses who refused to salute the flag in school were expelled from public schools on a regular basis. By 1939, 200 children in thirteen states had been expelled for this crime.[196]

Aside from the expulsion of the Witnesses, the passage of the teachers' loyalty oath bills, and the 1935 passage of a bill by the California legislature barring groups which advocated the overthrow of the government by unlawful means from the use of public school buildings, the 1934-35 red scare left a few more ugly legacies. In 1935, four states passed laws utterly without precedent in American history: Tennessee, Arkansas, Indiana and Delaware barred from the ballot political parties which advocated the forceful overthrow of the government, thus making it impossible for such parties to achieve power in any other way than forcefully overthrowing the government! Also in 1935, Michigan passed a sedition bill, the only such legislation passed in any state since 1920, with the exception of a similar bill passed in Delaware in 1931, during the Hoover depression scare. Michigan seems to have been particularly jittery in 1935, since during this same year the state supreme court upheld the state's 1931 Red Flag law on the grounds that display of the red flag would inevitably "cause a breach of public peace and endanger the lives and property of citizens generally."[197]

Despite the aberrations of 1934-35, by late 1937 and early 1938 the state of civil liberties in America looked better than it had for over twenty years. In its report for 1937-38, the ACLU reported that the only large community in the U.S. where practically all meeting places were closed to organizations opposed by the authorities was Jersey City, New Jersey — a situation rectified by the 1939 Supreme Court Decision in *Hague* v. *CIO* enjoining Jersey City officials from interfering with CIO organizing efforts. In the same ACLU report, it was noted that 1937-38 had not seen a single new prosecution involving the Communist Party; that the Supreme Court had just upheld the Wagner Act; that Washington and Oregon had actually repealed their criminal syndicalism acts; that Congress had repealed the Washington, D.C. teacher appropriation rider; that the LaFollette Committee was making a major contribution to the cause of civil liberties; that California's Supreme Court had freed the communists arrested for criminal syndicalism in the 1934 agricultural strikes; that a federal court had held CP membership alone could not justify deportation; and that in New York the borough president of Manhattan had rejected demands that he fire a CP member he had appointed as an aide. In 1938, the University of Minnesota publicly reinstated a professor it had fired for disloyalty in 1918. In 1937, Pennsylvania created a state civil liberties bureau, while in 1938 the conservative American Bar Association set up a committee on the Bill of Rights to head off the threat posed by a rival liberal organization, the National Lawyers Guild.[198]

By early 1938, the CP had achieved a tolerance and a following unprecedented in its history. In 1937, a regional CP conference was conducted without harassment in Chattanooga. At the University of California at Berkeley, the Young Communist League operated as actively and openly as the Young Republicans. CP leader Earl Browder was invited to speak at the University of Virginia, spoke on nationwide radio broadcasts for the first time, and had his speeches reproduced in college textbooks on public speaking. Among those present at the twentieth anniversary celebration of the Bolshevik Revolution at the Soviet Embassy was the president-general of the Daughters of the American Revolution. CP membership jumped from twenty-four thousand in 1934 to fifty-five thousand in January 1938, while party "front" groups gained followings that reached into the hundreds of thousands. Some of the "front" groups exercised considerable influence on American political life; thus the American Youth Congress was repeatedly consulted by federal officials as the "voice of youth" and developed a close relationship with Mrs. Franklin Roosevelt. The CP also made major gains in the CIO, controlling a number of important unions and establishing strong bases in others.[199]

The Failure of Repression in the Mid-Thirties

What explains the development and ultimate failure of the 1934-35 red scare, and the subsequent highly favorable developments in the civil liberties fields?

The development of the 1934-35 scare was clearly a transparent effort on the part of conservative interests, as represented by the Hearst press, to turn back what was seen as a tide of increasing radicalism that threatened their wealth and their status. The anti-business rhetoric and pro-labor actions of the Roosevelt administration, coupled with the upsurge in labor activity severely frightened business interests.

Even more threatening were the development and increasing popularity of more radical political movements. Huey Long, before his assassination in 1935, had attracted a following of millions with his plan to "Share Our Wealth." (In fact Long's popularity was growing so rapidly that FDR feared Long would run for president in 1936 and pose a serious threat to him; thus Roosevelt cut off Long's patronage and sent an army of Internal Revenue Service Agents into Louisiana to search for possible income-tax violations on Long's part.)[200] In California, Upton Sinclair was almost elected governor in 1934 on a pledge to "End Poverty In California" (EPIC) by replacing "production-for-profit" under capitalism with "production-for-use" under a system of semisocialistic workers' cooperatives.[201] Sinclair was defeated by a vicious campaign of distortion and red-baiting, and did not receive any help from FDR, even though Sinclair had won the Democratic primary. "The propertied classes saw in EPIC the threat of social revolution by a rabble of crazed bankrupts and paupers — a horrid upheaval from below led by a Peter the Hermit, which could only end in driving all wealth and respectability from the state."[202]

In Wisconsin, Phillip LaFollette was elected governor on a third party ticket in 1934; he called for a national "real leftist party" and denounced liberalism as "milk-and-water tolerance" that would only obscure the need for a "cooperative society." In Minnesota, Gov. Floyd Olson, who had been elected in 1930, publicly called for nationalization of "key industries," and declared that if capitalism could not prevent depressions, "I hope the present system of government goes right down to hell."[203] The 1934 congressional elections virtually wiped out the Republican Party as a national force, and sent to Washington so many Democrats elected on platforms of public ownership or "production for use" that the Congress threatened to push Roosevelt "in a direction far more radical than any he had originally contemplated."[204]

Radical sentiment was widespread among the general population. The largest student movement in American history arose on college campuses in the thirties, largely centered around the issue of peace and largely under the influence of the socialist and communist parties. About 81 percent of sixty-five thousand college students polled in 1935 said they would not bear arms if the U.S. invaded another country while over 15 percent said they would not fight even if the U.S. were invaded. About one hundred seventy-five thousand students struck for peace in 1935. A poll of over twenty thousand clergymen in 1934 reevaled that 95 percent felt a "cooperative commonwealth" was more consistent with the ideals of Jesus than was capitalism.[205]

The failure of the 1934-35 red scare is partially explainable in terms of the reasons for its development. During previous red scares, radicals and liberals had represented either a *relatively* small proportion of the population (as in World War I) or else had been highly disorganized (as in 1877), while conservative forces had dominated the organized institutions of society. Further, in previous red scares, the victims could be targeted as the "cause" of societal disruptions with at least a surface degree of truth, since they were "responsible" for strikes or for opposition to American foreign policy which threatened the stability of American society. But in the mid-thirties, the forces of radicalism and liberalism were both extremely strong and organized, while the businessmen were most clearly the "cause" of the nation's troubles — the depression.

Further, previous successful red scares had been marked by a general lack of strong organized opposition to repression on the part of those not directly involved. The 1930's, however, witnessed the development of a strong civil liberties "lobby" which brought together such groups as the ACLU, the National Farmers' Union, the Federal Council of Churches, the National Catholic Welfare Conference, and the Central Conference of American Rabbis, as *well* as victims of repression such as the CP and the AFL.[206] Even teachers responded to the academic red scare of 1934-35, on the whole with "frequent, vigorous and often successful protests against violations of freedom."[207]

Perhaps most importantly, the federal government, while throwing a few bones to the repressors in 1935, did not waver in its reform efforts. In fact, 1935 saw Roosevelt's so-called "second hundred days," in which the Congress passed social security, the Wagner Act, the Public Utilities Holding Company Act, and other reform legislation.[208]

There are other reasons for the failure of the 1934-35 scare and the development of increasing toleration in the years immediately afterward. Because public sentiment was so strongly reformist and because the red-baiters were so reckless in their charges of communism, red-baiting became severely discredited for at least a few years. In effect, the reaction that had set in after the expulsion of the New York socialists in 1920 and the 1920 May Day fiasco set in 1934-35 even before any serious damage had been done. "Where nearly everybody to the left of Herbert Hoover seemed a 'Red' in the eyes of the Hearst press — then few could take such charges seriously, even when they happened to be true."[209]

Finally, the red scare was over after 1935 because most Americans felt that neither the Roosevelt administration, the Communist Party nor the labor movement really sought revolutionary change in American society. FDR was a profoundly conservative man, who like the pre-war progressives, fundamentally sought to reform capitalism in order to save it. Thus, FDR told an emissary of Hearst in May, 1935:

> I am fighting Communism, Huey Longism, Coughlinism, Townsendism. I want to save our system — the capitalistic system; to save it is to give some heed to world thought of today . . . it may be necessary to throw to the wolves the forty-six men who are reported to have income in excess of one million dollars a year.[210]

The CP, which had adopted a militantly anti-capitalist and anti-Roosevelt stance during the early years of the New Deal, suddenly did an about-face in 1935, and began pushing the policy of the "popular front" coalition with liberal and progressive groups.[211] Adopting the slogan, "Communism is Twentieth Century Americanism," the CP moderated its rhetoric, clothed itself in the American flag rather than the red flag, and began a program of "fellow travelling" with the Roosevelt Administration. The CP about-face, which reflected Russian desires to forge an anti-Hitler coalition, was beyond question a fraudulent and short-term tactical device ("The communists were the fellow travellers and their efforts to identify communism and liberalism was as fraudulent as were the efforts among the Roosevelt-haters on the other side, to identify liberalism with communism"[212]), but on the surface the CP position eliminated the only powerful source of truly revolutionary opposition to the government.[213]

Finally, most Americans realized that the American labor movement had no revolutionary aspirations in the thirties, but only wanted a "piece of the pie." This reflected the fact that the IWW had been destroyed and that organizational efforts by the CP, when it was in its revolutionary phase, had met consistently violent repression. By the time the Wagner Act was passed, revolutionary unionism had been essentially destroyed by governmental repression, so only moderate unionism was left. The CIO did represent industrial unionism, but it was an industrial unionism that was a far cry from the IWW. CIO leaders, including John L. Lewis, who dominated the organization, openly proclaimed that industrial unionism was the *alternative* to radical unionism, and presented itself to management as a system for "disciplining the work force, managing workers' discontent and protecting 'against sit-downs, lie-downs, or any other kind of strike.'"[214] The CIO in short

> did not in actual fact differ very much from the A.F. of L. In spite of attacks made upon it, and the charges that it was fostering communism, it was no less conservative in its basic principles than the parent organization. . . . The CIO was wholly committed to advancing the interests of the wage earners through collective bargaining within the existing structure of democratic capitalism. . . . There was no reflection of a radical or revolutionary demand for any change in our political system.[215]

The CP presence within the CIO did present a *potential* future threat to the government and vested interests. Not coincidentally, when the CP-line *changed* after World War II, the communist-dominated unions in the CIO faced a campaign of concerted government-conservative union repression similar to that faced by the IWW during World War I.

8

The Coming of The New War

The Repressive Deal, 1938-1941

Beginning in 1938, and increasing in intensity until American entry into World War II, a new wave of anti-radical, and to a lesser extent, anti-labor repression swept the country. The development of a new period of repression during this period has a bittersweet irony, because the developments of 1935-37 had been so hopeful that a new era of tolerance and respect for civil liberties appeared to have arrived. Thus, the ACLU, in its 1938-39 report (before the dimensions of the new repression had become fully apparent) stated that "for the first time in its existence" the first item in its program was "popular education in the meaning and practice of civil liberty" because of the "decline in court cases and the emergence of propaganda as the major force making for repression."[1] In other words, the ACLU viewed the main threat to civil liberties in June, 1939, when this report was issued, as "bad ideas," because so little actual repression was occurring.

What accounts for the drastic change in the mood of the country after 1937? Three developments in 1937 helped to create a new climate of public frustration and anger and to focus this anger on labor, liberals and radicals: FDR's fight to pack the Supreme Court alienated large segments of the public and gave anti-New Deal southern Democrats an issue around which they could precipitate an open break with what they viewed as increasingly radical New Deal policies; the massive wave of sit-in strikes in 1937 and the extensive violence associated with the "little steel" strike increasingly alienated the public from labor and especially militant labor tactics; and the severe recession which began in 1937 wiped out all of the economic gains made since 1933 and eroded FDR's public image as an economic magician. Aside from these particular developments of 1937, which created a new climate of surliness and tension, three continuing developments after 1937 constantly agitated and aggravated Americans. First, the increasingly serious situation in Europe threatened to involve the western world and the United States in a major war. Secondly, at home, both the Communist Party and various pro-Nazi and fascist groups were gaining increasing influence (by 1939 the CP was claiming a membership of one hundred thousand, while the German-American Bund, successor to the Friends of the New Germany, had from fifteen thousand to twenty-five thousand members, at its height in 1938). After the signing of the Nazi-Soviet Non-Agression Pact in August, 1939, the American CP was deprived of much of the tolerance that it had gained and the Bund and the CP were seen as part of a general alien totalitarian threat. The Nazi-Soviet invasion of Poland in September, 1939, which brought on the outbreak of World War II, further confirmed this view and inflamed the fears of American involvement in a European war. A third major continuing development which fostered a repressive climate was the creation of the House Committee on Un-American Activities (Dies Committee) in May, 1938; its subsequent continual and irresponsible charges of widespread subversion in the country at large, and particularly within the federal government, greatly added to a growing climate of hysteria. It is indicative of the increasing fears and tensions already apparent in American society by the fall of 1938 that a radio broadcast of H. G. Wells' "War of the Worlds" on October 30, 1938, shortly after the Munich crisis, set off a large scale public panic.[2]

It is unusually easy to trace the institutional path of political repression during the 1938-41 period. The repressive infection gripped the Congress by mid-1938, infiltrated the executive branch by late 1938 and conquered the Supreme Court in 1940. In its early stages — until the outbreak of war in Europe in 1939 — the disease had relatively mild effects and was difficult to even diagnose, as is evident from the already-quoted ACLU statement of June, 1939. In its later stages, particularly after the Nazi invasion of France and the low countries in June, 1940, repression reached monumental proportions. In its report covering 1939-40, dated June, 1940, the ACLU reported that "at no period in the twenty years of its existence" had it "been confronted with such an array of threatened measures of repression."[3]

The 1938-41 period of repression can be conveniently dated as beginning with the creation, in May, 1938, of a House committee to investigate:

> 1) the extent, character and objects of un-American propaganda activities in the U.S., 2) the diffusion within the United States of subversive and un-American propaganda that is instigated from foreign countries or of a domestic origin and attacks the principle of the form of government as guaranteed by the Constitution, and 3) all other questions in relation thereto that would aid Congress in any necessary remedial legislation.[4]

Just a year earlier, in April, 1937, a similar proposal sponsored by Rep. Samuel Dickstein, who had made himself rather unpopular in the House with his continual campaign against "Nazi rats, spies and agents," had been defeated by a vote of 184-38. However, in the increasingly anxious atmosphere created by the Nazi occupation of Austria, the beginnings of the Sudeten crisis, and increasing activities on the part of communist and pro-Nazi groups, the 1938 resolution, sponsored by Rep. Martin Dies with the backing of Vice-President Garner, Speaker Bankhead, and majority leader Rayburn, passed 191-41.[5]

A number of liberal groups, including the American League for Peace and Democracy (ALPD), which would later be attacked by the Committee as a communist front, actively backed the creation of the Committee because they understood the investigation would be directed against right-wing groups, especially the German-American Bund, which under the leadership of Fritz Kuhn had gained membership and publicity in the 1936-38 period. While the Bund's predecessor, Friends of the New Germany, had seemed on the brink of collapse in 1935-36, under Kuhn's leadership the Bund enjoyed internal stability and financial success for the first time in the history of American pro-Nazi groups. Ironically, the establishment of the Dies Committee in May, 1938, followed by less than five months a public announcement by the FBI in January, 1938, that it had been unable to find any evidence of federal law violations by the Bund, and a public (and accurate) announcement by Nazi Germany on March 1, 1938 that the Nazi government was completely cutting all ties with the Bund, again ordering German nationals out of the organization and even forbidding the Bund's use of Nazi insignia. Despite the public impression that the Bund was merely a German front, after March, 1938, the group received no financial or significant other support from Nazi Germany and was regarded by the German government as an unfortunate embarassment. However, the continued military posturing and aggression of the German government, the shock in the United States resulting from the Jewish pogrom throughout Nazi Germany carried out on November 10, 1938 (known as the *Kristallnacht* or "Night of Broken Glass" as a result of the desecration of Jewish synagogues) and the continued and highly publicized activities of the Bund, climaxing in a rally at Madison Square Garden on February 20, 1939, attended by thirty-two thousand Bundists and sympathizers, kept public opinion at a feverish anti-Bundist pitch.[6]

The Dies Committee concentrated most of its fire on left-wing groups, but it did investigate the Bund, as well as other pro-fascist groups such as the Silver Shirts, which resulted in increasing pressure against the Bund. Dies publicly accused the Bund of carrying out "treasonable work," asked the FBI to look into the activities of Bundists working in the navy yards and airplane factories, and labelled the Bund a conspiratorial, subversive, and un-American threat to the U.S. In 1938, the Justice Department began a new study to determine if the Bund was in violation of any Federal laws and to see if Bund leaders could be denaturalized. In 1939, the first major Bund leader was denaturalized, and many other top alien Bundists fled to Germany in fear of Federal action, thereby contributing to a major breakdown in the Bund's organizational structure. By 1939, more than half of the people on a list of top Bund leaders composed by Dies had returned to Germany.[7]

The major target of the Dies committee was the left-wing; most of its fire was concentrated on the CP, the CIO and the Roosevelt administration. The Dies Committee essentially engaged in a wholesale vendetta against the left, and sought to portray the New Deal as part of a vast communist conspiracy. As U.S. entry into the war approached, Dies increasingly focused on charges of communist influence and infiltration in the Roosevelt administration.

In hearings held on the eve of the 1938 congressional elections, the Dies Committee heard testimony which suggested that pro-New Deal Democratic candidates in California and Minnesota were consorting with communists, and that Gov. Frank Murphy of Michigan had committed "treasonable" action by not calling out troops to break the General Motors sit-in.[8] Shortly after the elections, Dies called for the resignation of Secretary of the Interior Harold Ickes, Secretary of Labor Frances Perkins and Works Progress Administrator (WPA) Harry Hopkins along with their "many radical associates" who "range in political insanity from Socialist to Communist, with the common garden variety of 'crackpots' preponderating."[9] In his book, *The Trojan Horse in America,* issued on the eve of the 1940 elections, Dies declared that Mrs. Roosevelt "has been one of the most valuable assets which the Trojan Horse organizations of the Communist Party possess," and termed the WPA "the greatest financial boon which ever came to the Communists in the United States."[10] Dies repeatedly made highly inflammatory charges of communist infiltration of the government, which could only have the effect of gravely heightening fears and tensions which had already reached dangerous levels. Thus, in October, 1939, he referred to "thousands of members of the communist controlled organizations scattered throughout" the federal government, and during the same month the Dies Committee released a list of alleged members of the Washington chapter of the ALPD, including the names of over five hundred federal employees.[11] Since the committee had listed the ALPD as a communist-front earlier, the implication was that all of those listed were involved in some sort of subversive activity. In fact, it was never made clear whether the list released was a membership list or just a mailing list, and in any case by definition a "communist front" group was considered to be an organization dominated by communists but including many non-communists. In October, 1941, Dies submitted a list of 1,121 federal employees to the Attorney General whom he claimed were either "communists or affiliates of subversive organizations."[12]

Dies was not the only member of the committee to make such charges. Congressman Noah Mason attacked high-ranking government officials in November, 1938, for sponsoring what he termed forums organized by communist-front organizations. Committee member J. Parnell Thomas, in June, 1940, said that in some respects the fifth column "is synonymous to the New Deal, so the surest way to removing the fifth column from our shores is to remove the New Deal from the seat of government." Thomas earlier had led a committee crusade against the Federal Theatre Project, declaring that, "practically every play presented under the auspices of the Project is sheer propaganda for communism or the New Deal."[13] A committee investigation into the Federal Theatre Project and the Federal Writers Project in 1938, which featured "one of the weirdest collections of evidence ever permitted before the committee"[14] was largely responsible for the Congressional gutting of the Federal Theatre and concomitant elimination of federal support for the Federal Writers Project in the summer of 1939.[15] While the Dies hearings had suggested the Federal Theatre Project was infested with communists and communist propaganda, in fact only 2 percent of the plays presented even dealt with controversial themes, with productions such as *Macbeth*, *Pinocchio* and *Dr. Faustus* far more typical. The most subversive play ever presented, the Federal Theatre's historian, Jane Matthews, reports, was a production entitled "Revolt of the Beavers." This play, designed for children, was about a country run by a cruel beaver chief who refused to grant working beavers their fair share of the country's production and was overthrown by a beaver who disguised himself as a polar bear and organized other beavers to overthrow the cruel chief. It was during the Federal Theatre hearings that Dies Committee member Joe Starnes achieved a certain type of immortality by inquiring, when the name of Christopher Marlowe was mentioned, "Is he a communist?"[16] During the investigation of the Federal Writers Project, Dies charged the state guidebooks produced by the project, now regarded as a legacy of incalculable value, had been infiltrated with "communist phraseology" and material "along lines of class struggle and class hatred."[17] While the Federal Writers Project survived the Dies assault, unlike the Federal Theatre, the continuing charges of communist infiltration sapped the morale of the project and led project directors to institute measures of self-censorship to avoid further charges; thus Writers Project Director Henry G. Alsberg told Dies that nothing "inimical" and nothing which seemed "offensive, unfair, prejudiced, or partisan, or from a class angle" would be included in the state guidebooks.[18]

The Dies Committee hearings were repeatedly marked by the most extreme forms of irresponsibility. Thus, in August, 1938, the committee heard John P. Frey, president of the Metal Trades Department of the AFL, level a sweeping indictment of the CIO as communist-controlled. A few days later, Walter Steele, a representative of 114 patriotic organizations, named 640 organizations as communistic, and even suggested that the Boy Scouts and the Camp Fire Girls were serving subversive purposes. One witness before the committee even suggested that Shirley Temple had unwittingly served communist interests by sending greetings to a French communist newspaper. By the end of 1938, hundreds of organizations and hundreds or even thousands of individuals had been named before the Dies Committee, without any right of advance notice or rebuttal, as communists, or much more rarely, as Nazis. As Robert Griffith has written, "Martin Dies named more names in one single year than Joe McCarthy did in a life time."[19] Meanwhile, immense and largely uncritical newspaper publicity (during the four months of its existence in 1938, the committee "received more newspaper space than any other single institution in the nation")[20] gave the Dies Committee enormous impact upon the country.

The Dies Committee was not alone in Congress in expressing increasing anxiety in repressive forms. In June, 1938, Congress passed the Foreign Agents Registration Act, which required all persons acting as agents for foreign principals to register with the Secretary of State and to file information regarding their relationship to the foreign principal involved. While this law was perhaps not repressive per se — "the idea behind this was to avoid the coercive method of banning propaganda and yet to reduce its effect by exposure of its sources"[21] — it clearly reflected a repressive mood. In June, 1939, Congress passed a relief appropriation act which barred payment of funds to "any person who advocates, or who is a member of an organization that advocates the overthrow of the government of the United States through force or violence." This measure reflected increasing concern over communist infiltration of the WPA, which became a prominent subject of 1939 hearings of a House investigating committee. During these hearings, which again prominently featured the Federal Writers Project, manuscripts were seized from the New York City Writers Project office and scrutinized for "Red propaganda," and staff workers for the House committee planted Communist periodicals in the New York office in an attempt to produce photographs demonstrating that the Project was a hotbed of subversion.[22]

The principle expressed in the 1939 relief act was generalized in August, 1939, when Congress passed the Hatch Act. This law included the provision that no person who had "membership in any political party or organization which advocated the overthrow of our constitutional form of government in the United States" could obtain federal employment of any type. Thus, the principles of guilt by association and punishment for abstract advocacy of violence, which had formerly been applied only by the states in criminal anarchy and syndicalism laws, and by the federal government only in immigration laws, now were to be applied to all American citizens.[23] In March, 1940, Congress re-enacted the Espionage Act of 1917, severely increasing the penalties, and making some of its provisions applicable in peacetime.[24]

By June, 1940, the Nazi spring invasion of France and the lowlands had thrown both the country and the Congress into a state of true hysteria. Arthur Link notes, "It is difficult to describe the terror that swept over the American people as this blitzkrieg developed."[25] Thus, after a WPA official told a House Committee in 1940 that he had been unable to apply the 1939 relief law because he had been unable to discover a single organization then publicly advocating the overthrow of the government, the Congress sought to resolve this problem by specifically providing in the relief appropriation passed June 26, 1940, that "no alien, no communist and no member of any Nazi bund organization" could receive any federal employment under the relief program.[26]

This law also reflected the increasing nativism that was developing as tensions increased. In March, 1938, the House had passed a bill providing for the exclusion and deportation of any alien who advocated "any changes in the American form of government;"[27] in June, 1940, the House passed legislation providing for the deportation, by name, of left-wing labor leader Harry Bridges by a vote of 330-42.[28] In May, 1940, the Senate passed a bill which provided that no company engaged in interstate or foreign commerce could employ aliens in excess of 10 percent of its working force and that such companies could not employ "any Communist or member of any Nazi bund organization."[29]

In June, 1940, the War and Navy departments were authorized by Congress to summarily fire any employee when such action was "warranted by the demands of national security."[30] The culmination of the 1940 hysteria in the Congress came with the passage, on June 28, of the Alien Registration or Smith Act, the first peacetime sedition law in American history since 1798. This law made it illegal to "knowingly or wilfully advocate, abet, advise, or teach the duty, necessity, desirability or propriety of overthrowing or destroying any government in the United States by force or violence, or by the assassination of any officer of any such government" as well as outlawing participating in the printing, writing or circulation of matter advocating such doctrines or in the organization of groups with such purposes. Membership in such groups was also outlawed. In effect, this constituted the peacetime sedition law that even A. Mitchell Palmer had been unable to succeed in gaining from the Congress in 1920. The Smith Act also included the provisions first suggested in 1935 outlawing inciting disloyalty in the armed forces, added violation of the Smith Act itself as a cause for deportation, and provided that *past* beliefs or activities which qualified a person for deportation under the 1918 immigration law, even if discontinued or repudiated, still subjected aliens to deportation. This latter provision was included because in 1939 the Supreme Court had ruled in *Kessler* v. *Strecker* that past, but discontinued, Communist Party activity could not be used to justify deportation.[31]

It was indicative of the general atmosphere in the Congress at the time of the passage of the Smith Act that Rep. T. F. Ford remarked during the House debate:

> The mood of the House is such that if you brought in the Ten Commandments today and asked for their repeal and attached to that request an alien law, you could get it.[32]

At about the same time, FDR commented that alien-baiting bills were coming through the Congress at the rate of three a minute.[33]

The Smith Act was by no means the last of the repressive bills passed during this period. In the Selective Service Act passed in September, 1940 — the first peacetime draft bill in American history — a provision was inserted stating that "it is the expressed policy of this Congress that whenever a vacancy is caused in the employment rolls of any business or industry by reasons of induction into the service of the U.S." that such vacancies should not be filled "by any person who is a member of the Communist Party of the German-American Bund." The same law also included the standard provision making it illegal to knowingly counsel, aid or abet the evasion of the draft.[34]

The Nationality Act of October 14, 1940, provided for the denaturalization of former alien communists, and provided that no persons could thereafter be naturalized who had, within a ten-year period preceding their filing a naturalization petition, belonged to any organization advocating, or wrote or circulated material advocating, the violent overthrow of the government. The bill further provided that no persons could be naturalized unless they had been and still were "attached to the principles of the Constitution of the United States and well disposed to the good order and happiness of the United States."[35]

Under the so-called Voorhis Act of October 17, 1940, Congress required the registration of all organizations which had as one of their purposes the violent overthrow of any government, or which combined preparation for military activity with a purpose of forceful overthrow of the U.S. government, or which were subject to foreign control and engaged in preparation for military action, or had as a purpose the overthrow of the U.S. government. The required registration material included the names and addresses of all branches, officers, contributors and meeting places, copies of all publications, and a raft of other information which in short, "was a list of what the government wished to know about the Communist Party." The only effect of this law was that the CP dissolved its ties with the Comintern in November, 1940, and five organizations which had as their purpose the overthrow of Nazi Germany registered.[36]

By 1941, Congress had exhausted most of the repressive possibilities available. Action during that year included language in all appropriation bills barring payment to persons advocating or belonging to organizations advocating the overthrow of the government, and the appropriation of $100,000 to allow the FBI to investigate federal employees who belonged to "subversive organizations or advocate the overthrow of the federal government."[37]

Government officials abroad were authorized to refuse visas to aliens who were believed to be seeking to enter the U.S. "for the purpose of engaging in activities which will endanger the public safety."[38] Both houses passed legislation which specifically barred payment of federal moneys for a man named David Lasser who was suspected of subversive activities in connection with WPA.[39]

In reaction to the coal strike of 1941, the House passed on December 3, 1941, legislation banning all strikes in defense industries which grew out of disputes involving the closed shop or jurisdictional conflicts, and banning all strikes on any other issue unless approved by a majority of workers in a government supervised election following a thirty-day cooling-off period .This bill would also have denied benefits of the Wagner Act to unions with Communist or Bundist officers.[40]

Throughout the 1938-41 period, the House granted full and increasing support to the Dies Committee as measured by appropriations and votes on continuation of the committee.

	Appropriations[41]	Votes on creation (1938) and continuation of the Dies Committee[42]
1938	$ 25,000	191-41
1939	$100,000	-
1940	$110,000	344-21
1941	$150,000	354-6

By 1940, the committee had already received higher appropriations than ever had been granted to a special investigating committee in the experience of the chairman of the Committee on Accounts.[43]

The executive branch of the federal government was somewhat slower than the Congress in jumping onto the repressive bandwagon, but by late 1938, FDR had also begun to join the crusade. In November, 1938, Roosevelt met with FBI Director J. Edgar Hoover and informed Hoover that he approved a plan Hoover had submitted two weeks earlier to expand FBI intelligence investigations of "subversive" activities. Hoover's proposal included the suggestion that FBI intelligence activities be expanded "with the utmost secrecy in order to avoid criticism or objections which might be raised to such an expansion by either ill-informed persons or individuals having some ulterior motive." Hoover informed Roosevelt that the FBI had already created an index of twenty-five hundred names of persons "engaged in activities of Communism, Nazism and various types of foreign espionage," and that the FBI was coordinating its intelligence gathering with Military Intelligence and Naval Intelligence.[44]

Although the Justice Department notified various Federal department heads in February, 1939, that the FBI and Military Intelligence would investigate matters "relating to espionage and subversive activities," the FBI and the Justice Department complained to Roosevelt in June, 1939, about attempts by the State Department to create an interdepartmental committee to coordinate domestic intelligence. As a result, on June 26, 1939 Roosevelt issued a secret directive designating the FBI, Military Intelligence and Naval Intelligence as solely responsible for investigations of "espionage, counterespionage and sabotage matters."[45] When reports were subsequently received that local police authorities were forming "sabotage squads," Roosevelt, in response to FBI and Justice Department pressure, issued a public statement in September, 1939, shortly after the outbreak of World War II, announcing that he had asked the FBI to "take charge of espionage, sabotage and violations of the neutrality regulations" and that all law-enforcement officers were requested to turn over to the FBI "any information relative to espionage, counter-espionage, sabotage, subversive activities and violations of the neutrality laws." This public directive, which was substantially reissued by Roosevelt and Truman in 1943, 1950, and 1952, has subsequently repeatedly been cited by the FBI as the legal basis for its political intelligence activities.[46]

On December 6, 1939 Hoover sent a confidential letter to all FBI offices informing agents that the FBI was "preparing a list of individuals, both aliens and citizens of the United States, on whom there is information available to indicate that their presence at liberty in this country in time of war or national emergency would be dangerous to the public peace and the safety of the United States government."[47] Hoover publicly hinted at the existence of such a secret arrest list when he told a House subcommittee on January 5, 1940, that the FBI had revived the General Intelligence Division of the Palmer Days, had initiated "special investigations of persons reported upon as being active in any subversive activity or in movements detrimental to the internal security" and that the FBI had a "general index" which would "in the event of any greater emergency" allow the FBI "to locate immediately these various persons who may need to be the subject of further investigation."[48] FBI espionage investigations had increased from about thirty-five cases per year from 1933 to 1937 to two hundred fifty in 1938, and Hoover told the House subcommittee that he expected as many as seventy thousand espionage complaints in 1940.[49] (Subsequently, in July, 1943, Attorney General Francis Biddle informed Hoover that there was "no statutory authorization or other justification for keeping a 'custodial detention' list of citizens," that the classification system used by the FBI was "inherently unreliable" and that Hoover's list should "not be used for any purpose whatsoever." However, Hoover simply renamed the project "Security Matter" rather than "Custodial Detention" and informed FBI agents to continue to "prepare and maintain" lists of "dangerous and potentially dangerous individuals" under the rubric "Security Index." He cautioned this program "should at no time be mentioned or alluded to in investigative reports discussed with agencies or individuals outside the Bureau" except for Military and Naval Intelligence "and then only on a strictly confidential basis.")[50]

Beginning in late 1939, the Roosevelt administration began subjecting the CP and other left-wing groups to a campaign of severe harass ment and public villification. In December 1939 and March 1940, three cases were brought against alleged Russian agents for failing to register under the Foreign Agents Registration Act, a law which had gone completely unused for over a year.[51] In January, 1940, CP chairman Earl Browder was sentenced to four years in prison and a $2000 fine for a passport fraud committed years before "which during the Popular Front period the government had never got around to noticing."[52] In March, Communist leaders of the Fur Workers Union were indicted on antitrust charges, while in June charges were brought to take away the citizenship of California CP secretary William Schneiderman. Schneiderman had become a citizen in 1927, but suddenly the government discovered that he had not taken his naturalization oath in good faith.[53]

In January, 1940, FBI agents arrested seventeen members of the right-wing Christian Front Sports Club in Brooklyn on charges that they had been plotting the overthrow of the Federal government ("It took only twenty-three men to overthrow Russia," Hoover told the press), had stolen arms and ammunition from a national guard armory, had been making bombs and planned to institute a reign of terror and violence. The government case collapsed during the April, 1940 trial, when the key evidence in the case was provided by a government informer who had obtained guns and ammunition for the group with the cooperation of the National Guard.[54]

In February, 1940, FBI agents arrested twelve persons in Detroit and Milwaukee in pre-dawn raids on charges that they had violated federal laws barring recruitment of personnel for foreign armies during the Spanish Civil War. While technically this was perhaps not a case of repression, since in fact there is no doubt that a formally non-political law had been violated, given that the Spanish Civil War had been over for a year and that all of those arrested had fought for the loyalist (left) faction, the arrests took on repressive overtones. Criticism of the arrests was so strong that Attorney General Robert Jackson quashed the indictments.[55]

At about the same time, it was revealed that the FBI had been wiretapping in criminal cases in apparent flagrant violation of the Federal Communications Act of 1934 and Supreme Court decisions in 1937 and 1939. When Attorney General Jackson thereupon banned the use of FBI wiretaps, Roosevelt, in a secret May, 1940, memo to Jackson, referred to the danger of "sabotage, assassinations and 'fifth column' activities" and directed that the FBI be "at liberty to secure information by listening devices directed to the conversation or other communications of persons suspected of subversive activities directed against the Government of the United States;" Roosevelt directed that Jackson approve FBI use of such techniques "after investigation of the need in each case" and that such investigations be limited to "a minimum" and "insofar as possible to aliens."[56] This directive, issued in a pre-war situation, subsequently became the basis for all later FBI warrantless wiretaps, which were used in war and peace against "embassies, suspected spies, civil rights leaders, political groups and government officials and newspapermen."⁵⁷ Also in 1940, the FBI began a program of monitoring and opening first class mail for "national security" purposes that lasted, according to the FBI, until 1966. During the program, the FBI examined the outsides of millions of envelopes and opened and photographed at least one hundred and thirty thousand first class letters.⁵⁸

The Spanish loyalist arrests and the revelation of FBI wiretapping led to a storm of public criticism of the FBI in early 1940. In March, Roosevelt went out of his way to indicate his support of Hoover at a dinner of White House correspondents.⁵⁹ Subsequently, Hoover began a campaign of public speeches in which he villified critics of the FBI in terms so vicious as to be reminiscent of the Palmer days. In one speech, he termed the enemies of the FBI "the scum of the underworld, conspiring Communists, and goose-stepping bundsmen, their fellow travellers, mouthpieces and stooges." His speeches were filled with references to "anti-American forces," "un-American bodies," "cowardly, slithering" foreign "isms," "Communist termites," "pseudo-liberals," and "prattle-minded politicians."⁶⁰

By mid-1940, Roosevelt was becoming increasingly obsessed with the problem of fifth column activities and increasingly inclined to view opposition to his policies as representing an ominous threat to the United States. Beginning in May, 1940, Roosevelt began sending to the FBI hundreds of names and addresses of persons who had sent him messages indicating opposition to his foreign policy (Roosevelt later wrote Hoover to thank him for the "many interesting and valuable reports that you have made to me regarding the fast moving situations of the last few months").⁶¹ In July and October, 1940, Roosevelt asked the FBI to make loyalty checks on a number of persons, including his wife's social secretary. Apparently during this same period, Roosevelt ordered the FBI to wiretap the home phones of his closest aides.⁶² After his re-election in November, 1940, Roosevelt commented to his aides, "We seem to have averted a *putsch*."⁶³

Meanwhile, other government agencies were also moving against "subversives." In June, 1949, the Civil Service Commission announced — apparently because of the Hatch Act and the then-pending relief bill — that it would not certify for government employment any person found to be a "member of the Communist Party, the German Bund, or any other Communist or Fascist organization." At the same time, the CSC notified government agencies that they could dismiss present employees for disloyalty under regulations authorizing dismissal "for such cause as will promote the efficiency of the service."⁶⁴ In late 1940, the Post Office invoked a severely tortured interpretation of the Foreign Agents Registration Act to interfere with foreign propaganda sent into the United States that was not addressed to a registered foreign agent in the U.S. or that emanated from a foreign agent abroad not registered in the United States. Under this ruling the Post Office excluded and destroyed tons of material, somehow overlooking material emanating from friendly countries while destroying material coming from totalitarian regimes.[65]

Following his request that Congress support the Lend-Lease policy in early 1941, Roosevelt asked the FBI to investigate those who opposed Lend-Lease, according to William C. Sullivan, who served as a high-ranking FBI official for thirty years. According to Sullivan, Roosevelt "also had us look into the activities of others who opposed our entrance into World War II, just as later administrations had the FBI look into those opposing the conflict in Vietnam."[66] Publicly, the Roosevelt administration attempted to "identify all isolationists with the external forces threatening the national security."[67] Thus, in March, 1941, FDR condemned the America First Committee, which consisted of many sincere American isolationists as well as representatives of extreme pro-fascist forces (despite efforts of Committee leaders to exclude them) as "unwitting agents of Nazism." In April, 1941, the president labelled Charles Lindbergh, the leading spokesmen for the America First Committee, a "Copperhead" and "modern Vallandigham," referring to northerners who had opposed the Civil War, an attack which ignored the fact that the U.S. was not at war. When Sen. Burton K. Wheeler sent franked postcards to American soldiers and their families in July, 1941, urging them to petition the president to keep the country out of war, Secretary of War Stimson termed Wheeler's action "subversive . . . if not treason."[68]

In February, 1941, the Roosevelt administration initiated new deportation proceedings against Harry Bridges, even though as recently as December, 1939, a labor department examiner had concluded that Bridges was not a communist. The new proceedings were undertaken as a result of the passage of the Smith Act, which had included the provision that persons who had at any time since entering the country been affiliated with an organization believing in the violent overthrow of the government could be deported, even if they had long since severed such affiliation. In September, 1941, a new examiner ruled that Bridges had been affiliated with the CP and recommended his deportation.[69]

In June, 1941, after Congress had appropriated money to investigate "subversive" federal employees, the Attorney General ruled that "subversive" meant advocacy of the overthrow of the government, and that such a definition included the CP and its affiliates, some Communist fronts, and the German-American Bund. In September, 1941 the FBI distributed to its field offices a more complete list of organizations which the Justice Department — without a hearing or notice to the organizations involved — had declared subversive. The new list included the CP and the German-American Bund, as well as six "communist front" groups, including the American Youth Congress, which Mrs. Roosevelt had had close ties to.[70]

Although originally FBI investigations of federal employees accused of subversive activities or affiliations were to be made only at the request of the agency involved, in October the Attorney General ordered the

FBI to begin investigations upon receipt of complaints without notice to the employing agencies. However, as before, final disposition of the cases were left up to the agencies.[71]

On June 10, 1941, Roosevelt sent federal troops to break a communist-influenced strike of twelve thousand workers at the North American Aviation Plant near Los Angeles.[72] As part of their anti-war efforts, communist-influenced unions were involved in a number of strikes during this period, "particularly if war production were involved."[73] Roosevelt's action in sending troops followed a specific refusal by Congress to authorize the seizure of defense plants during strikes, and the only authority claimed for the action was that he was acting under the "Constitution and laws of the United States" to protect defense production. The troops proceeded to forbid picketing within a mile of the plant and in effect established martial law within this area. Meanwhile, Attorney General Jackson branded the strike the result of "disloyal men who have wormed their way into the labor movement" and were following the "Communist Party Line," while Selective Service Director Lewis Hershey told draft boards to reconsider the classification of all strikers "who have ceased to perform the jobs for which they were deferred and are by such failure, impeding the national defense program." Although the administration painted the dispute as a purely political strike rather than a legitimate labor disagreement, the strike settlement gained for the workers most of their demands, which would seem to indicate that real labor grievances were also involved.

On June 28, 1941, federal marshals raided the Minneapolis headquarters of the Socialist Workers Party (SWP), who had built the only truly radical labor bastion in the 1930's in the wake of the 1934 victory in the Minneapolis truckers strike. After the German invasion of Russia on June 22, the SWP was about the only left-wing group that still opposed Roosevelt's foreign policy. It also so happened that the SWP bastion among Minneapolis truckers was an increasing threat to the conservative teamsters leadership under Dan Tobin and Jimmy Hoffa, who were political allies of the Roosevelt administration. By 1938, the SWP faction of the teamsters union had organized two hundred fifty thousand men in eleven states in the northwest.[74]

In June, 1941, the SWP teamsters withdrew from the AFL and joined the CIO. Tobin complained to Roosevelt on June 13 about the switch, and referred to his own support of Roosevelt in 1940 and the "radical Trotskyite" nature of the CIO teamsters. He asked Roosevelt to move against "those disturbers who believe in the policies of foreign radical governments."[75] The White House press secretary shortly afterwards told the press that Roosevelt condemned the CIO for chartering the SWP group and had asked that the "government departments and agencies interested in this" be immediately notified. The June 28 raid followed, resulting in indictments of twenty-nine members of the SWP, including the top union leadership in Minneapolis, under the Smith Act.

Acting Attorney General Francis Biddle publicly termed the arrests the beginning of a nationwide drive against dangerous radicals and communists. Despite the fact that no evidence was ever presented indicating any "actual danger to either our government or our democratic way of life,"[76] eighteen SWP leaders were convicted and sent to jail for twelve to sixteen months. The trial succeeded in destroying the SWP in Minneapolis, and in the long run helped bring about the rise of Jimmy Hoffa instead of Trotskyites in the leadership of the Teamsters' Union.

By the time of American entry into World War II in December, 1941, the domestic intelligence capability of the FBI was fully mobilized and had been built up to levels resembling the 1917-1920 period. Operating under vague directives from President Roosevelt which called for general investigations of "Nazi," "fascist," "communist" and "subversive activities," the FBI steadily expanded its operations to cover a wide variety of completely legal activities of peaceful groups. In revealing for the first time some of the details of FBI activities during the pre-war period, a Senate Intelligence Committee staff report noted in 1976 that "factors of political belief and association, group membership and nationality affiliation became the criteria for intelligence investigations before the war," that the purpose of these investigations "was not to assist in the enforcement of criminal laws," but rather to supply top executive officials "with information believed to be of value for making decisions" and that such procedures "continued to be used through the Cold War period to the 1960's and 1970's."[77] While the focus of FBI investigations was on members of pro-fascist organizations such as the Bund, and on active communists, including communist speakers, writers, officers and candidates for public office, the scope of FBI intelligence collection went far beyond active members of allegedly "subversive" organizations. Thus, in September, 1939, FBI field officers were directed to investigate persons of German, Italian and communist "sympathies," to identify all members of German and Italian fraternal societies and other organizations, and to gather lists of subscribers and officers of German, Italian and communist foreign language newspapers. Hoover defined "subversive activities" in a memo to the Justice Department in August, 1940, as including:

> the holding of official positions in organizations such as the German-American Bund and Communist groups; the distribution of literature and propaganda favorable to a foreign power and opposed to the American way of life; agitators who are adherents of foreign ideologies who have for their purpose the stirring up of internal strike (sic), class hatreds and the development of activities which in time of war would be a serious handicap in a program of internal security and national defense.[78]

Using such criteria, the FBI by 1941 was gathering intelligence on such organizations as Father Charles Coughlin's Christian Mobilizers, the "America First" movement and the NAACP. The latter investigation continued for twenty-five years despite the fact that the FBI never uncovered any evidence of subversive domination of the NAACP. Perhaps indicative of the scope of FBI activities by 1941 was its study of a group called the League for Fair Play, which, the FBI reported, had been founded to further fair play, tolerance, adherance to the Constitution, liberty, justice, understanding and good will, and was found to have "no indications of Communist activities."[79]

As part of its general intelligence program, the FBI initiated many activities during the pre-war period which lasted for decades. An FBI program begun in 1940 of maintaining informants in defense plants to watch out for possible espionage lasted until 1969, and another FBI program begun in 1940 of using American legion members as confidential sources reporting on subversion and espionage lasted until 1954. The creation of lists of persons to be possibly incarcerated in case of war or national emergency, begun in 1939, lasted at least until 1973. Candidates for inclusion on such lists expanded along with general intelligence operations during the pre-war period, growing from persons with "strong" communist and Nazi "tendencies" in 1939, to persons with "Communistic, Fascist, Nazi or other nationalistic background" by 1940, and to members of the SWP or any "Communistic" organization or "'front' organization" and "pronouncedly pro-Japanese" individuals by 1941. FBI warrantless wiretapping of domestic "subversives" began in 1940 under Roosevelt's directive, and the FBI also began implanting "bugs" against domestic subversive targets in 1940 without any clear authority to do so. The FBI placed twelve taps and bugs in 1940, and ninety-two in 1941. While beginning in 1941 the FBI obtained approval in advance from the Attorney General before placing wiretaps (thus in 1941 Attorney General Biddle approved a tap on the Los Angeles Chamber of Commerce under the standard of "persons suspected of subversive activities" even though he told Hoover there was "no record of espionage" for the group), until at least the 1950's the FBI placed bugs without the explicit knowledge or advance approval of Justice Department officials. FBI use of warrantless bugs and wiretaps against domestic subversive targets continued at least until 1972, when a Supreme Court decision outlawed such practices. FBI mail-opening, begun in 1940, continued until 1966 without ever being authorized by the Justice Department or any official outside the FBI.[80]

While Congress and the executive branch had clearly succumbed to repressive forces by late 1938, the Supreme Court held out until the spring of 1940. In a series of cases from 1938 to 1940 concerning the rights of Jehovah's Witnesses to distribute literature and canvass from house to house without prior approval from city officials, the court consistently upheld the rights of the Witnesses who had come under extreme harassment because of their widely publicized refusal to salute the flag. The court also wrote a pro-civil liberties record during this period on virtually all cases involving labor, with the culminating decision *Thornhill* v. *Alabama* (1940). In *Thornhill,* the court invalidated a state law which barred peaceful picketing and for the first time clearly established that such activities were a form of free speech protected by the Constitution. The first sign of a shift in the court's sentiment came in *Minersville School District* v. *Gobitis*, in which the court held that school children could legally be expelled for refusing to salute the American flag. This decision, handed down in June, 1940, when the German spring offensive was overrunning France and the Low Countries and "American security was challenged as it had not been for one hundred twenty-five years" was followed by a massive upsurge in local and state harassment, beatings and arrests of Jehovah's Witnesses. The new trend of the court was confirmed in *Cox* v. *New Hampshire* (1941), when the court for the first time ruled against the Witnesses in a free speech case, and in *Milk Wagon Drivers Union* v. *Meadowmoor Dairies* (1941) when the court, backing away from the implications of *Thornhill*, declared that picketing could be enjoined in a labor dispute which had been marred by past violence.[81]

State and Local Repression, 1938-1941

Just as the repressive virus spread from the Congress to the executive branch and finally to the Supreme Court at the federal level in 1938-41, the same disease can also be observed gradually infecting the states, until by 1941 more states passed repressive legislation than in any year since 1919. The increase in repressive sentiment can be easily observed by studying developments in some of the states.

In 1936, a New York legislative committee authorized to investigate subversive activities in the schools had not even considered it worthwhile to meet, but in 1938 a legislative committee which had been authorized to look into the general administration and enforcement of the laws began to concentrate exclusively on subversion. In March, 1938, the New York legislature passed a bill excluding persons epousing forceful overthrow of the government from state employment only to have it vetoed, but in 1939 the legislature passed a similar provision which was now signed by the same governor who had vetoed it a year earlier.[82] In 1940, the New York legislature approved a committee investigation into school finances and other issues involving the public schools, including "the extent to which, if any, subversive activities have been permitted to be carried on."[83] This topic, which had been only one item among many topics suggested for the committee's attention, occupied the spotlight almost exclusively for two years of hearings by the so-called Rapp-Coudert Committee in 1940 and 1941 which led to the dismissal and resignation of over thirty New York City public college teachers as a result of their alleged Communist Party membership. Ironically, the only information presented during the hearings about the teachers' classroom performance pointed to "1) outstanding scholarship, 2) superior teaching, 3) absence of indoctrination in the classroom."[84] Under the pressure of the Rapp-Coudert committee, the New York City Board of Higher Education drastically changed its position on the employment of Communist teachers. In 1938, the chairman of the board said communist activity within the schools was well-known but "differences of opinion and attitude among faculty members are a wholesome sign of vitality and as this is reflected in the teaching, it supplies students with a useful cross section of the divergence of views of the community as a whole."[85] By 1941, however, the board was declaring that "members of any communist, fascist, or Nazi group" or of any group "which advocates, advises, teaches or practices subversive doctrines or acts" were not fit for employment.[86]

In the state of Washington, the governor and the board of trustees fired the president of Western Washington College of Education in 1939 as a result of charges alleging tolerance of subversive activities which had been made in 1936 and then found completely unsubstantiated. In 1938, the Washington Supreme Court ruled that the secretary of state had no authority to refuse to accept declarations of candidacy for public office just because the secretary believed the candidates ineligible, but in 1940 the state attorney general advised the secretary of state to bar CP petitions. The state supreme court overruled this action. In 1940, the Washington legislature refused to seat an elected state senator who had been a former CP member, the first time that an elected legislator had been excluded on political grounds in the United States in twenty years.[87]

In California, Gov. Culbert Olson had been elected in 1938 with communist support on a platform promising to free Mooney and Billings. Although Mooney and Billings were freed in 1938 and 1939, by 1940 Olson was asking the state legislature to ban the Communist Party from the ballot, a step taken in that year. In 1940, a state legislative committee chaired by Rep. Samuel Yorty became known as a "little Dies Committee" as a result of its charges of subversive infiltration of the State Relief Administration. During the same year, a teaching assistant was fired by the University of California at Berkeley for his CP membership and the University declared as a matter of policy that CP membership was incompatible with faculty status. Prof. Max Radin of the University of California Law School, nominated in the spring of 1940 by Gov. Olson to the California Supreme Court, was turned down by the state Commission on Qualifications after questions were raised about his alleged radical activities. In January, 1941 the California legislature established a "Fact Finding Committee on Un-American Activities" to investigate the CP, fascist organizations, the Nazi bund or any other organization believed to be interfering with California's defense effort or any state agencies.[88]

In Oklahoma, charges of communist influence at the University of Oklahoma raised in 1939 had little impact, but in 1940 fourteen CP leaders in Oklahoma City were arrested in the first criminal syndicalism proceedings in that state since 1923. Four of them were tried, convicted and sentenced to the maximum sentence of ten years in jail in trials during 1940 and 1941, with the main evidence submitted by the state, seven thousand books that had been seized in a raid on a CP bookstore and the membership of the accused in the CP. During one of the trials, a lawyer for the accused was arrested, held incommunicado and had his briefcase ransacked by Oklahoma State Highway Patrolmen. In 1943, when the United States and Russia were allied in the war, the convictions were overturned by a court of appeals and the cases against the other ten persons arrested were dropped. Meanwhile, in 1941 the Oklahoma legislature established a committee to investigate the Oklahoma CP and other subversive and un-American activities in the state. The Oklahoma committee spent most of its time investigating communist activities at the University of Oklahoma.[89] University President William Bizzell declared that there were no communists to be found on the faculty; he proclaimed, "I believe that the University faculty is as conservative as any in the country, and I believe the same applies to the student body."[90] When a suspect mathematics professor, W. C. Randels, appeared before the committee, state Representative Claud Thompson expressed interest in Randels' writings. After obtaining reprints of four published articles on higher mathematics, Thompson proclaimed:

> This stuff may be mathematics. I wouldn't know; it doesn't look like anything I ever studied; but I only went to the third grade. But even at that, I would be more than willing to leave him alone, if he will just confine his teaching to a thing like this. . . . What I still want to know is what he is doing as a mathematics teacher messing around with government?[91]

The final report of the Oklahoma committee cleared the University of Oklahoma, along with other organizations from the Highway Patrol to the American Legion and the Dies Committee. However, the report attacked the Oklahoma Federation for Constitutional Rights and suggested that "a large amount of communistic influence" had been detected among labor organizations in Oklahoma and that "there has been connected with the State University in the past active members of the Communist Party and unamerican liberal minded crackpots."[92] The general tenor of the final report combined anti-communist hysteria with an appeal to patriotism and Christianity; it also had the distinction of reaching a grammatical low that would not be matched again until the 1949 report of the Illinois (Broyles) Committee on Un-American Activities. The flavor of the report is suggested by the following excerpt:

> The time may come in the near future when this nation may be offered only 'blood, sweat and tears,' therefore let us all help to hoist high the stars and stripes and to it once again, renew our pledge of loyalty. . . . For the consecration of mankind to the cause of Christianity Jesus Christ the Savior allowed his blood to bathe the cross . . . when the young men of American unselfishly and patriotically, stand ready to bathe a million crosses in their blood, to say the least our citizenship can relieve them from the pain and burden of carrying the cross to their Calvary.[93]

A "little Dies" committee was authorized in Colorado in 1939. Arkansas finally succeeded in 1940 in closing down Commonwealth College, which had been the target of a 1935 legislative investigation.

The College folded after a state court seized its property to pay the fine resulting from a suit brought on a charge of anarchy, resulting from the school's alleged failure to fly the American flag during school hours, and its display of an "illegal emblem" (the hammer and sickle).[94]

During the 1940 elections, the CP was barred from the ballot on various pretenses in fifteen states, a new record. In four states, pressure from the Dies Committee led to convictions of CP petition circulators for fraud or misrepresentation. In Lewistown, Illinois, five communists were arrested for sedition while soliciting signatures to nominating petitions; these cases were eventually settled on minor charges resulting in the payment of fines. A high school teacher in Pennsylvania was fired in 1940 solely on the evidence that he had signed a CP petition, although he was a local Democratic committeeman; he was reinstated by the State Superintendant of Instruction. In West Virginia, a CP organizer was sentenced to six to fifteen years for "fraudulent solicitation of names" on the grounds that in soliciting signatures to be placed on the ballot, he had not orally told would-be signatories that he was a Communist; this sentence overlooked the fact that the petitions he had circulated had "Communist Party" placed across the top along with a half an inch high red hammer and sickle.[95]

While the CP was the major target of repression in states and localities, the German-American Bund also suffered severe harassment during the pre-World War II period. In November, 1937, the Bund purchased land for a camp-site in Southburg, Connecticut; when Bundists began to clear the land, local police arrested them under an old blue law barring work on Sunday, and suddenly the town council revised zoning regulations which forced the Bund to abandon the camp rather than face a fine of up to $250 a day if it continued the project. Following the creation of the Dies Committee in May, 1938, harassment of the Bund became open and intense, especially in New York and New Jersey, the two main centers of Bund strength. Bund locals and camps had their tax records frequently examined, their liquor licenses suspended and revoked, and their meetings subjected to open police surveillance. The New York legislature's McNaboe Committee held several days of sensational hearings on the Bund in June, 1938, and New Jersey passed a law barring the wearing of uniforms of a foreign nation and printing or distributing materials which could incite to violence. In 1938, six New York Bundists were convicted for failing to register as members of an oath-bound organization as required in a 1923 law directed against the Klan. In May, 1939, Bund leader Fritz Kuhn was indicted in New York and eventually sentenced to two and one half to five years in jail for alleged misuse of funds; the indictment followed New York Mayor LaGuardia's decision to put Kuhn behind bars on one pretext or another and an intense investigation of Bund financial records by New York State authorities. By September, 1939, the wearing of Bund uniforms had been outlawed in several states. In 1941, nine Bundists were convicted in New Jersey for alleged violation of that state's law against inciting racial or religious hatred. Bund headquarters in Chicago were raided to gather information for an Illinois tax suit against the organization. In 1941, the Bund came under investigation by state legislative committees in California and New York, and was effectively outlawed in California and Florida.[96] Vigilantes obstructed and harassed Bund meetings, until the Bund was no longer able to hold public meetings and "to avoid violence and harassment, local units often masqueraded as singing or gymnastic societies."[97]

The effect of the local and state repression, especially in New York and New Jersey, coupled with the hostile publicity emanating from the Dies Committee and leaks from FBI investigations was extremely debilitating for the Bund. The jailing of Bund leader Kuhn severely disrupted the organization, and the intense pressure and hostility directed against the organization caused thousands of Bundists and Bund sympathizers to withdraw their support. Merchants fearful of having their names associated with the Bund withdrew advertising from Bund publications, other right-wing groups declined to be publicly associated with the Bund, sympathizers asked that their names be removed from Bund mailing lists and many Bundists left the movement, which had fallen to about fifteen hundred to two thousand members by 1940. By the end of 1941, the Bund had been "harassed out of existence."[98] As Oscar Handlin notes, "the Bund lost the support of many German-Americans, fearful of another such period of persecutions as they had suffered during the first World War."[99] Perhaps the greatest irony was that the Bund was regarded as simply being an arm of Nazi Germany; yet there was no control exerted from Berlin and the organization was forced to rely on its own resources for financial support, managing to "break even each year until the expense of legal battles threw its finances into chaos."[100]

By 1941, the repressive atmosphere increasingly fostered by the Congress and the Roosevelt administration was becoming institutionalized by state legislatures. During that legislative year, nine states passed laws barring from the ballot organizations advocating unlawful overthrow of the government. Four of these state barred the Communist Party by name. Two states passed general sedition laws in 1941, while five states barred "subversives" from all state employment, following the example of the Hatch Act. Arkansas' law specifically excluded from public employment any "member of a Nazi, Fascist or Communist society."[101]

Another indication of the increasingly sour mood of the country in the 1938-41 period was the tendency of state legislatures to pass anti-labor legislation. The 1937 sit-ins, AFL charges of communist influence in the CIO, and a strike wave in 1941 combined to cause a severe reaction against labor, leading to the passage of anti-labor laws of varying severity in twenty-two states by the end of 1941. While most of these laws did not remove the fundamental gains of the Wagner Act, some of the laws did restrict picketing, and barred such techniques as jurisdictional strikes and secondary boycotts. The amount of violence used against labor, however, remained very small compared to previous times. State troops were called out only four times from 1938-41; deaths resulting from labor disputes were about twenty-five.[102]

Aside from FDR's suppression of the 1941 North American Aviation Strike, the most historically remarkable incident of labor repression during this period was the smashing of the 1938 lumber strike by the CIO International Woodworkers of America (IWA) at the Westwood, California operation of the Red River Lumber Company.[103] Westwood was a company town in every aspect, with the Red River Company owning all of the land, controlling all utilities and enforcing its will through deputized company law officers. When the IWA struck in July, 1938, company-organized vigilantes attacked strikers with pick and axe handles, high pressure fire hoses, rifles and shot guns, barricaded all roads in the area and deported over five hundred persons. Company deputies and state highway patrolmen either stood by during the vigilante assaults or actively cooperated in the violence. "Not until the 1942 deportation of the Japanese-Americans was there a larger forced migration of United States citizens."[104] Governor Merriam subsequently praised Westwood's efforts to "do away with the communistically led CIO."[105] The effect of the vigilante assault was to destroy the IWA local at Westwood, and to place union efforts at the company in the hands of a much more docile AFL union, which circulated propaganda portraying the CIO leadership as a communist conspiracy planning to overthrow the U.S. government.

The combination of radicalism and agricultural unionism in the south led to an interesting incident of repression in January, 1939, when over one thousand sharecroppers in southeast Missouri under the leadership of the STFU camped out along U.S. highways 60 and 61 to bring attention to their eviction by landlords. The governor of Missouri blamed the protest on "un-American and communist practices."[106] Outsiders who tried to enter the area and help the protesters were arrested. After a few days, the state health commissioner declared the tenants' camps a menace to public health, and police began to forcibly evict the protesters. About one hundred families were deposited by Missouri officials in a swampy area that had no sanitary facilities, suggesting that "the decision to move the croppers was determined more by a desire to get them out of the public eye than by the fear of a health menace."[107]

In some cases, the repressive spirit of 1938-41 was institutionalized at the local level. Thus, in 1941, Los Angeles amended its city charter to ban from public employment any person who advocated or was a member of a group advocating violent overthrow of the government, along with persons who had fallen within this category during the previous five years. The town of Bartow, Florida, banned all Communist or Bund meetings by ordinance, while other cities interfered with left-wing and right-wing meetings without the benefits of legality. Some cities even banned meetings of the isolationist America First Committee.[108]

Perhaps the best single indicator of the increasing hysteria noticeable everywhere in American society during the 1938-41 period was the reign of terror unleashed against the Jehovah's Witnesses. In addition to massive expulsions of Witness children from the schools for refusing to salute the flag, by early 1940 the Witnesses were subjected to vicious attacks and persecution by vigilantes and local officials. These attacks reached dramatic proportions after the Supreme Court decision of June 3, 1940, in the *Minersville* v. *Gobitis* case. In the period between June, 1940 and December, 1941, witnesses reported hundreds of assaults, many involving police officials, and hundreds of arrests.[109] In its report for 1940-41, dated June, 1941, the ACLU reported that "nothing in the record of attacks against communists, strikers or Negroes" was comparable to the wave of violence against the Witnesses during that year, and reported that no religious organization had suffered such persecutions "since the days of the Mormons."[110] The ACLU reported that between May and October, 1940, almost fifteen hundred Witnesses had been the victims of mob violence in three hundred thirty-five communities in forty-four states. The worst legal persecutions of the Witnesses took place at Connersville, Indiana, where seventy-five witnesses selling literature in April, 1941, were arrested, held incommunicado for nearly a week and then indicted for sedition.[111]

As in previous periods of severe repression, the 1938-41 period was marked by a general collapse of resistance to repression or tacit support of repression on the part of many groups which might be expected to be particularly vigilant in their opposition to such measures because of their own history as victims or supposed positions as defenders of free speech, freedom of association and academic freedom. The AFL practiced red-baiting of the CIO on a large scale during this period, and its 1939 convention instructed affiliated unions to "refrain from taking into membership any known member of the Communist Party or any sympathizer."[112] AFL unions dutifully began purging communists from leadership positions and in some cases expelling entire locals for "having come under Communist influence."[113] As a condition of his election as CIO president in 1940, Phillip Murray obtained a resolution condemning communism and all foreign ideologies, and subsequently demanded that all Communists be purged from CIO locals.[114]

Leading liberals such as Walter Lippman began giving the Dies Committee their support, while others such as Lewis Mumford, Dorothy Thompson, the *New Republic* and the *New Leader* urged extension of the Bill of Rights only to the "friends of democracy."[115] The American educational establishment, as usual in time of crisis, also reacted to the climate by instituting new measures of repression. Purges of suspected communist teachers spread from New York state across the nation, the National Education Association began a major campaign to expose subversive teachings, and the Chicago superintendant of schools had "teachers and principals comb textbooks and children's classics such as *Grimm's Fairy Tales, Robinson Crusoe* and *The Swiss Family Robinson* for evidence of subversion by long-dead fifth columnists."[116] Harvard, Dartmouth, Princeton and the University of Chicago banned CP chairman Earl Browder from their campuses, while the University of Michigan expelled twelve students for their pro-labor, civil rights and anti-war activities. Columbia President Nicholas Murray Butler told students in 1940 that:

> Before and above academic freedom of any sort comes university freedom, which is the right and the obligation of the university itself to pursue its high ideals, unhampered and unembarrassed by conduct on the part of any of its members which tends to damage its reputation.

When two thousand students demonstrated against the impending Selective Service Act at the University of California at Berkeley, President Robert Sproul warned that all of them would be expelled if such a demonstration were repeated once the act became law.[117]

Certainly the most incredible collapse in the face of repressive forces was the ACLU's decision in February, 1940, to bar from its governing committees or staff any person "who is a member of any political organization which supports totalitarian dictatorship in any country, or who by his public declarations indicates his support of such a principle."[118] The ACLU, which had long attacked the concept of guilt by association and persecution based on abstract advocacy, thus bowed to the temper of the times. Subsequently, the ACLU requested the resignation from its board of directors of Elizabeth Gurley Flynn, an open CP member, who had been unanimously reelected to the board before the signing of the Nazi-Soviet Pact with full knowledge of her CP membership. When she refused to resign, she was "tried," convicted and expelled from the board on three counts, one of which was based on her CP membership, and two of which, incredibly, were based on her public criticism of the ACLU. As Jerold Auerbach notes, "With the resurgence of anti-communism on the eve of World War II, the story of civil liberties in the Depression decade ended as it began: the right to dissent was reserved for those who repudiated Communism."[119]

World War II — The Good War?

World War II has been presented by most historians as having been, in John Roche's phrase, a "good war" from the standpoint of American civil liberties, with the exception of the forced evacuation of one hundred ten thousand Japanese-Americans, including over seventy thousand American citizens, from the west coast, and their incarceration in concentration camps.[120] Even the ACLU found little to criticize in the Roosevelt administration's war-time record; in its report for 1943-44, dated June, 1944, the ACLU referred to the "extraordinary and unexpected record of the first two years (of the war) in freedom of debate and dissent on all public issues and in the comparatively slight resort to war-time measures of control or repression of opinion."[121]

Two reasons which are often cited to explain this allegedly good civil liberties record are that there was hardly any opposition to the war ("Significant opposition... simply did not exist after the Pearl Harbor attack") and that the Roosevelt administration, particularly in the persons of FDR and Attorney General Biddle, was liberally inclined on civil liberties matters.[122]

There are two other reasons, rarely if ever mentioned, which also help to explain the common view that World War II was a "good" war for American civil liberties. First, the excesses of World War I appear to have been consciously or subconsciously used as a measuring stick by many, despite the fact that there was massive opposition to World War I, unlike World War II; thus in 1943, the ACLU commented on the "striking contrast between the state of civil liberty in the first eighteen months of World War II and in World War I," and noted that the "country in World War II is almost wholly free of those pressures which in the first World War resulted in mob violence against dissenters, hundreds of prosecutions for utterances; in the creation of a universal volunteer vigilante system, officially recognized, to report dissent to the FBI; in hysterical hatred of everything German; in savage sentences for private expressions of criticism; and in suppression of public debate of the issues of the war and the peace."[123] A second reason appears to be that most historians are liberally inclined, while the bulk of World War II repression was directed against right-wing forces, and thus has been consciously or subconsciously downplayed.

It is true that before and after U.S. entry into the war members of the Roosevelt administration did take certain actions and make certain statements intended to put a damper on hysterical repression of opposition forces. For example, in 1940, FDR, Attorney General Jackson and other administration officials urged a conference of the nation's governors and law enforcement officials to leave matters of internal security to federal officials. Roosevelt warned the conference against the "untrained policeman" and the "cruel stupidities of the vigilante" while Jackson cautioned that "amateur efforts or mob efforts almost invariably seize upon people who are merely queer or who hold opinions of an unpopular tinge, or who talk too much or otherwise give offense."[124] The meeting resulted in an almost completely unpublicized gentlemen's agreement in which state officials promised to restrain vigilantes and to let state sedition laws go unenforced so that the federal government could combat disloyalty with the Smith Act and other actions in a centralized manner. According to Biddle, similar meetings between state and federal officials designed to head off state excesses continued during the war.[125]

Attorneys General Biddle and Jackson and FBI Director Hoover publicly warned against vigilantism and privately turned down suggestions from private groups urging the revival of the APL. In September, 1941, Biddle pledged that civil liberties would be protected and that "we do not again fall into the disgraceful series of witchhunts, strike breakings and minority persecutions which were such a dark chapter in our record of the last world war."[126] Ten days after Pearl Harbor, Biddle told U.S. attorneys throughout the country that sedition prosecutions under the revived 1917 Espionage Act "must not be undertaken unless consent is first obtained from the Department of Justice." A few days later, Biddle ordered the dismissal of sedition complaints lodged against three men and stated that "free speech as such ought not to be restricted."[127]

With two major exceptions, the civil liberties record of the Roosevelt Administration was good for the first two months of the war. Beginning on December 7, 1941, allegedly dangerous enemy aliens were seized by federal authorities under the terms of the Alien Enemies Act of 1798, which authorized summary arrests on presidential warrant. During the first seventy-two hours after Pearl Harbor, the FBI arrested 3846 alien enemies. Internment of these aliens was conducted solely under executive order; in cases of doubt government policy was to play it "safe" and intern "even if conclusive evidence of subversive words or acts is lacking."[128] By the end of the war, about sixteen thousand enemy aliens had been arrested and about four thousand jailed. One concession which was made was the granting of hearings before Alien Enemy Hearing Boards, composed of citizens, a procedure which was not required by law. Many of those not interned were placed on parole.[129]

In addition to being subject to arbitrary arrest, all enemy aliens were subjected to certain restrictions on their travel, and were barred from using firearms, cameras, short wave radio sets, and invisible ink, among other regulations. It should be noted that the vast majority of German and Italian aliens did not suffer any severe deprivations; the case of the Japanese was considerably different. All restrictions on Italian aliens were lifted in October, 1942, and restrictions on Germans living on the west coast were removed two months later.

A considerably more serious early exercise of political repression was the establishment of martial law in Hawaii, which was continued for almost three years after Pearl Harbor. During this period, trial by jury, the writ of habeas corpus and other fundamental due process rights were suspended. "Never before in American history had citizens been subject to military rule for so prolonged a period."[130] Although there was no evidence of disloyal activities in Hawaii on the part of Japanese-Americans, this was the official rationale for the continuation of martial law. FDR favored going beyond martial law in Hawaii to evacuating all Japanese-Americans to the mainland or to some less strategic island, but protests that this would have catastrophic effect on the Hawaiian economy blunted this plan. Roosevelt explained:

> I do not worry about the constitutional question. The whole matter is one of immediate and present war emergency.[131]

Repression in Hawaii was so severe that martial law could not even be discussed in the mass media. During over twenty-two thousand military trials conducted in 1942, about 99 percent of defendants were found guilty; in some cases they were forced to give blood or purchase war bonds in addition to suffering jail sentences and fines.

Martial law was finally lifted in Hawaii in October, 1944, partially as a result of strong pressure brought to bear on FDR by Secretary of the Interior Harold Ickes and Attorney General Biddle, but mainly due to American military successes in the Pacific in 1943 and 1944.

The general civil liberties record of the Roosevelt Administration began to seriously disintegrate during the early months of 1942, when the battle situation appeared to be growing increasingly critical for the Allies. Whereas the outbreak of the war had led to a new mood of national unity, optimism, and almost exuberance ("People had been excited and even titilated by the war, as with a new fad"),[132] as the battlefield situation worsened a mood of querulousness, frustration, and anxiety increased and a search for scapegoats developed. Fears of invasion, bombardment, and enemy sabotage and espionage seized the minds of the public and government officials, and were reflected in increasing and hysterical demands for action against Japanese-Americans and other alleged pro-fascist forces. German U-Boats prowling off the East Coast, which in some cases attacked and sank ships near the shore in broad daylight added to invasion jitters; on February 24 a panic was set off in Los Angeles when a weather balloon strayed into the skies, and three persons were killed in stampedes and dozens injured when spent shell fragments of Army antiaircraft batteries fell back to earth.[133]

Because Russia and the U.S. were now allies, the Communist Party was fully in support of the war policies. Since the SWP had already been devastated, the only remaining war opposition came from extreme right-wing groups, who often were ideologically attuned to Nazi Germany. While previously left-wing groups had faced the greatest amount of repression, and radical and liberal groups had tended to form the backbone of civil liberties organizations, suddenly liberals and radicals began to lead the demand for repression of the pitifully weak anti-war opposition. Liberal and radical organizations and publications such as *The Nation, PM, The New York Post,* the New York American Labor Party, the Southern Conference on Human Welfare and the Michigan Civil Rights Federation demanded the suppression of the anti-war press and sedition indictments against anti-war spokesmen. *Life* magazine even thoughtfully printed a list of persons whom it thought should be arrested for spreading "subversive doctrines."[134]

Freda Kirchwey, editor of *The Nation,* contended that the traditional civil liberties position of giving all ideas an open hearing and trusting the people to determine the truth was no longer adequate since "the treason press in the U.S. is an integral part of the fascist offensive" and "should be exterminated exactly as if they were a machine gun nest in the Bataan jungle."[135] The ACLU announced that it would not intervene in cases in which "there are grounds for a belief that the defendant is cooperating with or acting on behalf of the enemy, even though the particular charge against the defendant might otherwise be appropriate for intervention" unless "the fundamentals of due process are denied."[136] In short, there was as little organized support for civil liberties during World War II as there was organized opposition to the war.

According to Biddle, the greatest source of pressure on him from *within* the administration for the taking of repressive action was President Roosevelt himself. Biddle wrote later:

> The president began to send me brief memoranda to which were attached some of the scurrilous attacks on his leadership, with a notation: "What about this?" or "What are you doing to stop this?" I explained to him my view of the unwisdom of bringing indictments for sedition except where there was evidence that recruitment was substantially being interfered with, or there was some connection between the speech and propaganda centers in Germany. . . . He was not much interested in the theory of sedition, or in the constitutional right to criticize the government in wartime. He wanted this anti-war talk stopped . . . he began to go for me in the Cabinet. . . . When my turn came, as he went around the table, his habitual affability dropped. . . . "When are you going to indict the seditionists?" he would ask; and the next week, and every week after that, until the indictment was found, he would repeat the same question. . . . I cannot remember any other instance of his putting pressure on me.[137]

That Biddle's account accurately reflects Roosevelt's views is evident from a letter written by FDR in October, 1942 to Morris Ernst of the ACLU. He wrote:

> I would raise the question as to whether freedom of the press is not essentially freedom to print correct news and freedom to criticize the news on the basis of factual truth. I think there is a big distinction between this and freedom to print untrue news.[138]

It is evident that FDR regarded material critical of him as "untrue news," if World War II sedition prosecutions are a guide.

By the late winter and early spring of 1942, whatever hopes there might have been of a "good" civil liberties record were irrevocably shattered. In February the Roosevelt administration decided to evacuate all Japanese-Americans from the west coast; in March and April the administration began to move against the handful of allegedly seditious speakers and publications; in March, Biddle announced a major campaign to denaturalize members of the German-American Bund; during the same month the Civil Service Commission (CSC), with presidential approval, issued new regulations providing that applicants for federal employment and present employees could be denied clearance or fired if there existed "reasonable doubt" as to their loyalty to the government; the Supreme Court handed down two important rulings against the Jehovah's Winesses; and a new wave of vigilante assaults against the Witnesses broke out.

The decision to evacuate Japanese-Americans from the west coast was approved by FDR on February 19, following severe pressure from California officials and representatives of the War Department stationed in the west.[139] Although ostensibly the pressure for deportation arose from fears of sabotage, other significant factors were traditional racism and jealousy on the part of the white establishment in California over the success of Japanese-Americans in their business and farming enterprises. General John DeWitt, the head of the Western Defense Command, in his final report recommending deportation on February 14, conceded that there had been "no sabotage" by Japanese-Americans, but argued this was simply "a disturbing and confirming indication that such action will be taken."[140] DeWitt had earlier reported, correctly, that "a tremendous volume of public opinion" was developing against the Japanese on the part of "the best people of California." Thus, California Attorney General Earl Warren, in supporting action against the Japanese, reported that:

> When we are dealing with the Caucasian race we have methods that will test the loyalty of them. . . . But when we deal with the Japanese we are in an entirely different field, and we cannot form any opinion that we believe to be sound.[141]

The deportation of the Japanese-Americans was undertaken under the terms of an executive order issued February 19, authorizing the Secretary of War and military commanders whom he might designate to prescribe military areas in their discretion, and to exclude any or all persons from such areas or to establish conditions under which any or all such persons could enter, remain in or leave such areas. On March 21 FDR signed into law a measure which provided statutory authority for his earlier order. Early in March the War Department ordered Japanese-Americans living in the western areas of California, Oregon and Washington to leave. At first, they were allowed to move freely in the interior, but after officials in other western states protested against serving as a "dumping grounds" for the Japanese and mob violence threatened, the Army began transporting the deportees to makeshift assembly centers and then to ten "relocation centers" in seven western states.

About one hundred ten thousand Japanese-Americans, including seventy thousand American citizens, were caught in the mass round up, making the program "the most widespread disregard of personal rights in the nation's history since the abolition of slavery."[142] Inside the "relocation centers" (which President Roosevelt inadvertently, but correctly referred to as "concentration camps"), reading material was censored, Japanese phonograph records were confiscated, and arbitrary searches and harassment were commonplace. A widescale program of releasing internees who were willing to swear their loyalty to the U.S. and repudiate Japan began in 1943. However, the exclusion order from the West Coast was not rescinded until December, 1944, and even then individuals could still be excluded by name by military order, and five thousand were in fact so excluded from returning to their homes. Meanwhile, the seven thousand internees who refused to swear loyalty to the U.S. were segregated in a maximum security camp at Tule Lake, California. Following disturbances at Tule Lake in November, 1943, the Army was sent in, placed two hundred people in a stockade and maintained martial law for two months.

Under the same authority used to exclude the Japanese-Americans from the west coast, another three hundred persons were excluded by military order from both east and west coasts. The military orders were issued in what the ACLU termed a "star chamber procedure" with no right to charges, witnesses or counsel to contest the orders. These proceedings were ended in 1943 due to reversals in lower federal courts and the refusal of the Justice Department to back up the War Department on appeal.[143]

Sedition prosecutions and harassment of the miniscule war opposition press began in the spring of 1942. During the first year of the war, twenty-three persons were jailed for sedition and indictments were returned against forty-six other persons under the Espionage Act of 1917 and for counselling draft opposition. A total of about two hundred persons were charged with such offenses during the course of the war.[144] In many cases, the offenses charged dated from before Pearl Harbor, but "a change in the climate" had made those "who were formerly dismissed as nuisances and cranks... viewed as menaces."[145] During the first year of the war, seventy newspapers and publications were barred from the mails under the Espionage Act, and in many cases all future issues were excluded from second class mailing privileges on the grounds that they no longer qualified as regular publications under the postal regulations. Postal officials were guided in their selection of materials to be suppressed by political scientist Harold Lasswell, who had worked out "an elaborate chart on means of which the patriotism of a publication could be scientifically measured."[146] Thus, a publication called *X-Ray* was found to be "65 percent subversive" and was banned from the mails. Virtually no new cases against individuals or publications were brought during the last two years of the war, probably because: by mid-1943, it was clear that the Allies were winning; there was no opposition press left and most opposition leaders were under indictment or in jail; and by 1943 and 1944 the Supreme Court had ruled against so many repressive actions of the Roosevelt Administration that further repression seemed a waste of time and money.

The most important publication barred from the mails was Father Charles Coughlin's *Social Justice*, excluded in April, 1942. *The Militant*, the SWP's weekly publication, was also excluded. Many of the other publications barred were incredibly obscure. For example, in May, 1942, an issue of the monthly monetary reform magazine, *Money*, was barred without any specification of the objectionable features or any hearing. The *Boise Valley Herald*, a weekly publication with a circulation of five hundred, which was Christian pacifist in orientation, had its second class privileges restored only after the ACLU intervened in its behalf.[147]

Neither of the two most important sedition prosecutions led to convictions. The most notorious political prosecution in American history since the IWW trials of World War I was initiated in July, 1942, against about thirty so-called "native fascists."[148] Although most of the defendants had nothing in common with each other aside from a hatred for Roosevelt, Jews and Communism and tendencies toward pro-fascism, they were charged with conspiring under the Espionage and Smith Acts. Before the case finally came to trial in April, 1944 (leaving the defendants in jail or under bail for two years), the government had twice revised its original indictment; the final charge was alleged conspiracy on behalf of the German government to undermine morale of the military, in violation of the Smith Act.

The defendants in the case have been variously described as "as queer a kettle of fish as was ever assembled by such means"[149] and "a grand rally of all the fanatic Roosevelt haters."[150] They ranged from fascist philosopher Lawrence Dennis, to anti-Semitic prophet Gerald L. K. Smith, from red-baiter Elizabeth Dilling, to German-American Bund Leader William Kunze. The Justice Department dragnet even included James True, who was the inventor of a billyclub he called the "kike killer" (U.S. Patent 2026077) which reportedly came in a special size for women.

When the case finally came to trial, it proved to be an embarassing fiasco, proceeding amidst scenes of "uproar approaching the dimension of a riot"[151] for eight months, during which five defense lawyers were cited for contempt of court, and the number of defendants dropped by four, due to death, illness and disruptive behavior. The case finally ended in a mistrial when the presiding judge died. Although the government case which had been presented was notably weak in showing any conspiracy or any intent to undermine the armed forces, the government proceeded to re-indict the "native fascists" in 1945. However, an appeals court threw the case out in November, 1946, as a travesty of justice. But, as Biddle notes, "the propaganda had long since ceased" and "in that sense, at least the prosecution had accomplished the purpose which the President had in mind."[152] William Preston notes that compared to the Japanese-American cases, the mass sedition trial "may look like a comic interlude" but in fact it

> invigorated widely held attitudes that threatened traditional liberties and forecast what would come to typify cold war repression. Applauded by almost the entire country, including the left and liberal leadership, the prosecution attacked the free speech then despised by the majority by means of dragnet conspiracy charges, using guilt by association and condemning the defendants for views that paralleled Nazi propaganda *before*

the outbreak of the war. The case thus made the "party line" and past associations the tests of loyalty and abandoned the standard of overt acts.[153]

In the other major sedition case, the Supreme Court in 1945 threw out the conviction of twenty-four leaders of the German-American Bund on the ground that the evidence offered could not sustain the charge of conspiring to counsel draft evasion.[154]

This was the only draft case which reached the Supreme Court. The Court also reversed the only Espionage Act case which reached it, in *Hartzel* v. *U.S.* (1944), involving a man who had written some articles in 1942 attacking American war policies, the Jews and President Roosevelt, and mailed them to Army officers and selective service registrees. The court reversed on the grounds that there was no proof Hartzel had wilfully sought to cause insubordination or disloyalty in the armed forces or to obstruct enlistment.[155]

Many of the other defendants in draft and espionage cases were as obscure as Hartzel, which reflected the lack of opposition to the war and the fact that the Roosevelt administration carried out a policy of severe repression considering the meagre opposition that existed. For example, in the fall of 1942, the government brought sedition charges against more than eighty members of black religious cults, such as the Peace Movement of Ethiopia and the Brotherhood of Liberty for the Black People of America, who had indicated an affinity for the Japanese as a fellow "dark" race. Other victims included George W. Christians, described by the ACLU as the leader of "a largely paper organization, the Crusader White Shirts;" two publishers of "a little periodical entitled Publicity"; Rudolph Fahl, "apparently connected with no organized movement, charged with seditious remarks in private conversation with army officers;" "a Wisconsin farmer charged with writing letters to a brother in the army urging him to seek a discharge;" and twelve members of Mankind United, "an obscure California pseudo-religious sect."[156]

The shortage of prosecutable defendants during World War II was so severe that two members of Friends of Progress, a California pro-Nazi group, found themselves charged in four separate state and federal prosecutions. Robert Noble and Ellis O. Jones were convicted under the Espionage Act; indicted in the "native fascist" conspiracy trial; charged with criminal libel by the state of California for remarks about General Douglas MacArthur; and convicted (until freed on appeal) under a 1941 California law which required subversive organizations to register with the state.[157]

German-American Bund leader Kunze was involved in three different trials. He was convicted and sentenced to fifteen years for conspiracy to send military secrets to Germany and Japan, and then was indicted in both the "native fascist" and Bund draft conspiracy cases.[158] William Dudley Pelley, leader of the pro-Nazi Silver Shirts, also suffered repeated harassment. In January, 1942, he had his parole revoked in a North Carolina fraud case dating back to 1935, after a judge had ordered a revocation hearing and denounced him for "seeking to overthrow and undermine our system of government." Two months later, the Post Office barred his newspaper from the mails, and a month after that Pelley was arrested and eventually sentenced to fifteen years in prison for seditious statements allegedly made in the newspaper. An associate was sentenced to five years and Pelley's press was fined $5000.[159]

Ironically, the single most well-known "native fascist," Father Coughlin, was never indicted for sedition. Although Biddle had *Social Justice* excluded from the mails, he was afraid to make Coughlin a martyr to his Catholic and isolationist followers. So instead, Biddle succeeded in having the Archbishop of Detroit, Caughlin's superior, order Coughlin to cease his propaganda or face being defrocked. As Biddle chortles in his book, "That was the end of Father Coughlin." Biddle adds that the president "was delighted."[160]

Post Office harassment and sedition and draft prosecutions were by no means the only weapons used by the Roosevelt Administration to harass alleged war opponents. Beginning in March, 1940, Biddle began a massive campaign to denaturalize members of German-American Bund and other allegedly disloyal naturalized citizens, on the grounds that their conduct proved they had initially obtained their citizenship under false pretenses. By December, 1940, forty-two citizens had been denaturalized under this campaign, three hundred suits were pending and over twenty-five hundred cases were under investigation.[161] However, the denaturalization campaign was derailed by Supreme Court decisions in *Schneiderman* v. *U.S.* (1943) and *Baumgartner* v. *U.S.* (1944). Schneiderman involved the California CP secretary who had been moved against during the 1945 campaign against the CP. The court ruled that in the absence of an overt act, mere membership in the CP did not establish fraudulent intent when Schneiderman had obtained his citizenship in 1927, and further that there was nothing in the party program that was necessarily incompatable with the Constitution.[162]

In *Baumgartner*, the court ruled that the government had failed to prove that a citizen naturalized in 1932 who one year later began public espousal of Nazi causes had had mental reservations when he became a citizen.[163] The Baumgartner decision led the Justice Department to drop scores of cases still pending, after having succeeded in denaturalizing a total of about 180 citizens.[164] Former Bund leader Fritz Kuhn was among those successfully denaturalized, and after the war ended he was deported to Germany on the grounds that he was an enemy alien and "dangerous to the public peace and safety of the United States." He was subsequently arrested by Bavarian de-Nazification officials and sentenced to ten years at hard labor on charges of having close ties with Hitler (which was not correct) and of trying to transplant Nazism to the U.S.

Kuhn successfully appealed the conviction and was freed in 1950, one year before he died.[165]

The Supreme Court frustrated the administration in its continuing attempt to deport Harry Bridges. After a special examiner had recommended Bridges be deported in September, 1941, the Board of Immigration Appeals ruled in Bridges' favor. However, Biddle reversed the board and ordered deportation in May, 1942. The court overturned Biddle's decision in 1945, ruling that there was no evidence showing Bridges had any connection with any organization advocating illegal overthrow of the government (i.e. the CP) except in "wholly lawful activities."[166]

Thus largely frustrated by the Court in its deportation and denaturalization attempts, the Roosevelt Administration reached back to an obscure provision of the Alien Enemy Act of 1798, which allowed for the deportation of enemy aliens without any legal rights to a hearing and without judicial review. A case using this approach was upheld in 1948 by a Supreme Court which had taken on a considerably more conservative cast than the World War II court.[166a]

Another war-time case lost by the Roosevelt administration was the prosecution of pro-Nazi propagandist George Sylvester Viereck under the Foreign Agents Registration Act. In 1943 the Supreme Court ruled that Viereck was required to report only those propaganda activities undertaken as a foreign agent — which he had — and not those undertaken on his own initiative. The court's decision in the Viereck case strongly criticized the highly emotional tone of the government's court case.[166b]

Yet another action taken by the administration was the confiscation of property of war opponents who were allegedly financed in part by enemy capital. Japanese newspapers published jointly by American citizens and Japanese were seized, as were the publications of the German-American Bund, although there is little evidence of strong financial links between the Bund and the German government. The Bund was perhaps the most well-known opposition group, and it suffered from virtually all of the tactics used by FDR to suppress opposition — property confiscation, draft and sedition prosecutions, denaturalizations and deportations.[167]

The FBI and military intelligence agencies greatly expanded their surveillance activities under the exigencies of war-time pressures, and continued some of the most dubious of these activities even after the war ended. Thus, the FBI began to engage in "surreptitious entries" (i.e. illegal break-ins) against various groups connected with foreign intelligence and espionage operations and against "domestic subversive targets." Such break-ins against domestic groups continued on a wide-scale until 1966. The "surreptitious entries" took two major forms: so-called "black bag jobs" in which FBI agents stole confidential material belonging to target groups, and entries made for the purpose of installing microphone "bugs." According to admittedly incomplete FBI records, about 240 "black bag jobs" were directed against at least fifteen "domestic subversive targets" from 1942 to 1968, with an additional three "domestic subversive targets" the subject of "numerous entries" after the war from 1952 to 1966. According to an FBI memo, these "black bag jobs" on "numerous occasions" obtained "material held highly secret and closely guarded by subversive groups and organizations which consisted of membership lists and mailing lists." Although the FBI has no figures for "surreptitious entries" aimed at placing "bugs" for the World War II period, over six hundred "bugs" were installed from 1942 to 1945, and many of them probably were implanted during break-ins. The FBI also placed over eighteen hundred wiretaps on phones during the war. While all wiretaps were placed on the authorization of Attorney Generals, there is no evidence that any official outside the FBI ever knew about the "black bag jobs." The placing of "bugs" by means of surreptitious entry or other techniques was not formally approved by an Attorney General until 1954, and did not require advance approval by Attorney Generals until 1965. FBI mail-opening continued during the war, without any knowledge outside the Bureau.[168]

Towards the very end of the war, when it was clear the United States and its allies, including the Soviet Union, would conquer its enemies, the FBI did begin to substantially limit its general intelligence investigations. Thus, in 1944 FBI field offices were told to limits their general intelligence investigation of communists to "key figures in the national or regional units" of the party, instead of investigating all members as had been the previous policy, and in 1945 similar restrictions were issued with regard to investigation of "fascist individuals" and "various foreign nationality groups." However, these restriction lasted only a short time before the FBI began to massively increase its political intelligence activities during the Cold War climate which began to develop within a short time after World War II ended.[169]

Military intelligence operations expanded during the war, and at least in one major area, continued after the war. Under wartime censorship laws, all international message traffic was made available to military censors, and copies of pertinent foreign messages were turned over to military intelligence. This program continued even after the war ended, when representatives of the Army Signal Security Agency convinced the major international communications companies in the autumn of 1945 to continue to turn over copies of messages sent by private citizens to and from foreign countries. This program was later taken over by the National Security Agency (NSA) when it was created in 1952, and continued until 1975 under the name Operation SHAMROCK. While the focus of the program was on the collection of "foreign intelligence" information, government monitors intercepted many messages involving domestic affairs, and, during the Vietnam War era, NSA deliberately concentrated on messages involving domestic dissidents. During the thirty-year post-war life of the program, millions of private messages of American citizens were intercepted, and NSA built up files containing the names of seventy-five thousand American citizens, largely based on the mere mention of a name in an intercepted communication. Towards the end of SHAMROCK, NSA was intercepting about one hundred fifty thousand messages a month in what a Senate Intelligence Committee staff report termed "probably the largest governmental interception program affecting Americans ever undertaken."[170]

The treatment of conscientious objectors in World War II was, on the whole, not as brutal as during World War I, but still left much to be desired.[171] A total of 6086 objectors, many of them Jehovah's Witnesses, were jailed, compared to 450 jailings in World War I of objectors. In the case of the Witnesses, the typical pattern was for draft boards to refuse to accept their request for objector status, and then for the Army to court-martial them for refusing to salute the flag. Sentences for jailed objectors averaged five years in the first years of the war, then declined to less than four years by 1945, but some offenders received up to life imprisonment. (In Great Britain, CO status was considerably easier to obtain, and jail sentences for those who refused to accept the government's finding in their case were usually for several months.) Jailed objectors were subjected in some cases to beatings, and to routine petty harassment; hundreds of Witnesses jailed at Fort Leavenworth, Kansas, were kept in solitary confinement for sixteen months, and were fed only bread and water for half of this period.

Persons whose request for CO status was upheld were placed in "Civilian Public Service" camps for noncombatant alternative service. About twelve thousand persons worked in these camps, which amounted to outdoor prison camps. In order to avoid the spectre of army control of the camps, the National Service Board for Religious Objectors (NSBRO), representing pacifist churches and organizations, agreed to absorb the cost of administering the camps. Objectors working in the camps were forced to work fifty hours a week without receiving any compensation on government-chosen work projects. During the war, they performed over eight million man-days of free work for the government, at a cost to the NSBRO of over seven million dollars. Selective service regulations provided that once in the camps, the CO ceased "to be a free agent" and was "accountable for all of his time, in camp and out, twenty-four hours a day," with "his movements, action and conduct" subject to "control and regulation." (By contrast, in Canada, CO's lived at home, did work chosen by the government, and were paid for their services.) The government-assigned work projects were almost entirely in the field of rural conservation, although many of the jailed objectors were highly educated and skilled men. Thus, Dr. Don DeVault, a research chemist and teacher at Stanford University who had ten published papers, was removed from the camps and jailed when he refused to dig ditches because he wished to continue research on penicillin. When CO's were retained in the camps beyond the expiration of the war, widespread work strikes broke out. Over fifty objectors were arrested, and twenty-two were convicted and given suspended sentences before the last of them were released from the camps in 1947, two years after the end of the war.

Throughout the war, the draft was frequently used as a means to insure conformity with administration policies and to punish those who displeased the administration. Thus, in January, 1943, Paul McNutt, head of the War Manpower Commission, issued a "work or fight" order which threatened the end of all deferments for persons, including men with children, working in unessential industries. Congressional action subsequently barred the drafting of fathers, however unimportant their work, before men without children, no matter how vital their work, but by the late summer of 1943 a quasi-coercive manpower system was established which in effect barred men from quitting defense-related employment without government approval.[172]

Since this system did not solve the problem of recruiting new defense workers or shifting men from non-defense to defense employment, in January, 1944, FDR asked Congress to enact a National Service Bill which would essentially place all citizens at the government's disposal for whatever job assignment was deemed necessary — a proposal which would in effect, be a devastating anti-strike weapon. Roosevelt himself said the bill "will prevent strikes, and with certain appropriate exceptions, will make available for war production or for any other essential services every able-bodied adult in this nation."[173] Although the proposal met heavy Congressional opposition, in December, 1944, under the impact of the brief crisis created by the threatened German breakthrough during the Battle of the Bulge, the House passed a diluted National Service Bill. The House version required every male registrant between eighteen and forty-five to work at an essential job, if so ordered; with civil penalties for violation rather than induction into the army as FDR had proposed. By the time the measure reached the Senate in March, 1945, the German offensive had been turned back, and the Senate substituted a version which thoroughly mutilated the bill. In the meantime, the administration, on its own authority, in December, 1944 issued a "work or fight" order providing for the drafting of men under age not working at essential jobs and assigning them to particular industries. The Army, however, balked at using the draft as a manpower sanction, and twelve thousand men drafted in this manner were never released to industry.[174]

The draft was used effectively as a political tool in a number of cases. For example, military intelligence agents determined that a man named Lomanitz employed at the University of California's Berkeley Radiation Laboratory was a menace to national security, and decided to have him drafted. When Lomanitz appealed his draft order, his local board sided with him, but Draft Director Lewis Hershey warned that if Lomanitz was not drafted he would abolish the state and local draft boards involved. Twice

Lomanitz secured draft-deferable jobs in private electronic plants, but twice the employers were persuaded to withdraw the job offers, and he was eventually drafted.[175]

During the 1943 coal strike, the government twice seized the coal mines and succeeded in gaining the miners' return to work only after combining patriotic appeals with threats to draft strikers. During the 1944 Philadelphia transit strike, which broke out when white workers walked out to protest the hiring of Negro trainees, the Army brought in eighty hundred soldiers to run the street cars, the FBI arrested strike leaders and selective service announced workers who did not return would either be drafted or denied unemployment benefits. The strike collapsed within forty-eight hours.[176]

The general state of government-labor relations during World War II was highly reminiscent of the World War I "deal" between the AFL and the Wilson Administration.[177] Organized labor — both AFL and CIO — agreed to refrain from striking, and in turn the government enforced the "maintenance of membership" principle under which new workers were not forced to join unions but present or future union members could resign from the union and keep their jobs only if they acted within fifteen days. This provision guaranteed unions against any substantial loss of membership, and in fact "amounted to a camouflaged closed shop"[178] which spurred union growth during the war from 10.5 million in December, 1941, to 14.75 million in June, 1945. The War Labor Board (WLB) was empowered to withdraw the maintenance of membership privilege from any union which struck or otherwise behaved "irresponsibly;" such sanctions were in fact imposed even for work stoppages which only lasted a few hours.

The WLB carried out its part of the bargain by strongly supporting labor's right to organize and bargain collectively, and resisting all threats to labor's position. In turn, labor unions discharged members who walked out on wildcat strikes, even though this meant that management would have to fire them under the maintenance of membership principle, and in turn this would make them liable to the draft.

The WLB explicitly recognized the elements of the World War II "deal" in a report issued in 1942:

> By and large the maintenance of a stable union membership makes for the maintenance of responsible union leadership and responsible union discipline. . . . If union leadership is responsible and cooperative, then irresponsible and uncooperative members cannot escape discipline by getting out of the union and thus disrupt relations and hamper production.[179]

Despite the best efforts of union leaders, thousands of wildcat strikes broke out — there were more strikes in 1944 than in any year in American history, and more strikes during the entire war period than in any comparable period in history. These strikes, and especially the 1943 coal strikes led by John L. Lewis' UMW, created a sharp increase in anti-labor sentiment among the public and the Congress. In June, 1943, Congress passed over FDR's veto the Smith-Connally Act, which authorized the president to seize any plant that was useful to the war effort and threatened with a halt in production, made it a crime to encourage strikes in such seized plants and required union officials to observe a thirty-day cooling off period and to obtain a majority vote from union members before striking in other plants. In overriding Roosevelt's veto, Congress ignored his suggestion that a substitute bill be passed authorizing the drafting of strikers up to age sixty-five as non-combatants. Most of the provisions of the Smith-Connally Act proved to have little effect, but FDR did use its authority to seize plants in fifty cases where labor and management could not agree on a settlement.[180]

The Smith-Connally Act was not the only instance in which repressive forces in the Congress pushed the Roosevelt administration farther than it wished to go. Congressional pressure for the firing of "disloyal" government employees was constant throughout the war, particularly on the part on Martin Dies. In October, 1941, Dies had submitted the names of 1,121 alleged subversives to the Attorney General, and the Attorney General had instructed the FBI to investigate all employees whose loyalty had been called into question. Resistance to the Dies Committee was extremely strong within the federal bureaucracy, which correctly perceived that Dies' real target was the New Deal rather than true subversion. In March, 1942, the CSC, in order to aid the federal departments in interpreting FBI reports and achieving a standardization of criteria, issued new regulations providing that applicants for federal employment would be denied clearance if there existed "reasonable doubt" concerning their loyalty "to the government of the United States." This same standard also applied to current government employees, but in fact throughout the war employing agencies appear to have relied upon the Hatch Act and appropriations act provisions, which provided for the firing only of those persons who were advocates of or members of organizations which advocated the overthrow of the government.[181]

In order to provide further centralization, in April, 1942, Biddle established an Interdepartmental Committee on Investigations to oversee the federal loyalty program and to advise employing agencies as to the character of various organizations accused of being communist "front" groups. On September 1, 1942, this committee reported to Biddle, and to the Congress, with Biddle's endorsement, that "sweeping charges of disloyalty in the federal service" had not been substantiated, urged discontinuance of any "broad personnel inquiry" and urged that investigations be restricted only "to those instances in which there is substantial reason for suspecting that there has been a violation of law requiring prosecution or dismissal from the federal service." The report indicated that of the 1,121 employees attacked by Dies, dismissal or disciplinary action had proven justified in only three cases, and that such action had been taken in a total of forty-six cases arising from thirty-five hundred complaints made by sources other than Dies. The Committee did recommend that a permanent interdepartmental board be set up to make advisory reviews in loyalty cases on the request of either the accused employee or the employing agency.[182]

Attorney General Biddle, in his letter to Congress accompanying the report, stated:

> It is inevitable that such sweeping investigations should take on an appearance of inquisitorial actions alien to our traditions. They create disturbance and unrest, hurt espirit de corps and produce a feeling of uneasiness and insecurity. This impression is heightened by the occasional complaint which has obviously been inspired by the jealousy or malice of a fellow employee who knows that his identity as an informant will remain undisclosed.[183]

Because the report of the committee was widely regarded in Congress as a whitewash, and because pressure from Dies and other congressmen for stern action continued, on February 5, 1943 Roosevelt created a new Interdepartmental Committee on Employer Investigations, with functions similar to those of the earlier committee. This committee, which concerned itself largely with the status of present employees, and the CSC, which was concerned with screening applicants for employment, both established guidelines which allowed employees and applicants to appeal adverse decisions, including the right to be represented by counsel at hearings. They both stressed the need for judicious investigations; for example the committee advised that membership in "fellow-travelling" organizations was not in itself sufficient cause for removal, while the CSC issued similar guidelines and cautioned its investigators against questioning applicants about such matters as their readership of radical periodicals, participation in union activities, or membership in such groups as the ACLU or Spanish loyalist organizations. However, the hearing procedures established essentially corresponded to standards later established by President Truman in 1947 that were thoroughly criticized for violating basic standards of due process, especially in failing to provide for revelation of the sources of charges to the accused and concomitant denial of the right of cross examination of such sources.[184]

Meanwhile, the Justice Department, acting under the mandate of the Hatch and appropriations acts, was busy creating a list of organizations in which membership would lead to automatic disbarment from federal employment. By September, 1943, a list of about twenty-five such organizations had been compiled, and later a secondary list was assembled of groups characterized as neither subversive nor non-subversive but requiring further investigation of individuals accused of membership. These lists were compiled without any notice or hearing for the groups involved. Although neither the names of the organizations (except for the CP, the Bund, and the Silver Shirts) nor any information about them was supposed to be made public, internal Justice Department memoranda on twelve groups listed as Communist fronts were obtained by Dies and published in the Congressional Record.[185] While lacking in important procedural guarantees, the World War II loyalty program appears to have been administered with considerable restraint. Thus, during the entire war-time period, only 175 federal employees were dismissed or subjected to disciplinary action on loyalty grounds, while 1300 were barred from entry to the federal service on such grounds.[186]

While the loyalty machinery ground away within the executive department, Dies continued to make charges of widespread subversion on the federal payrolls. In March, 1942, Dies attacked thirty-five members of the Board of Economic Warfare (BEW), leading to a response by Vice-President Henry Wallace, who chaired the BEW, that the effect on government employees' morale of Dies' charges "would be no less damaging if Mr. Dies were on the Hitler payroll."[187] The chief target of Dies' attack was an economist named Maurice Parmalee who had written a book entitled *Nudism in Modern Life*. Dies hopelessly confused one of his victims, an BEW official named David Vaughn, with another man named David Vaughn, leading to a lawsuit, for which the House paid the court costs. Undaunted, Dies named another nineteen government employees on September 4, 1942, and added thirty-nine more names on February 1, 1943.[188]

Dies' February, 1943 assault led to one of the most dismal episodes in the history of the Congress. Shortly after his speech an amendment was offered on the House floor to the pending Treasury and Post Office Appropriation bill barring the use of such funds to pay the salary of William Pickens, a Treasury Department employee, the only one of the thirty-nine named by Dies who worked for either the Post Office or the Treasury (a precedent of sorts had been set for this proposal by Congressional action in the Lasser case and in the House's action in January, 1942, specifically deleting the salary of psychologist Goodwin Watson from the Federal Communication Commission's appropriation after Watson had come under Dies' vigilant assault). The Pickens amendment was adopted 163-111 but then hastily rescinded when the shocking discovery was made that Pickens happened to be the only Negro named among the thirty-nine. In order to avoid appearing anti-Negro rather than anti-communist, the House instead set up a subcommittee to investigate the charges against all thirty-nine of the accused.[189]

The subcommittee eventually investigated only nine persons. It cleared six but announced that three of the suspects — Watson, William E. Dodd, Jr., and Robert Morse Lovett — were unfit for federal employment. None of the men were accused of any criminal activities or even with associations which would disqualify them under the Hatch or appropriations acts. When subcommittee chairman John H. Kerr was asked if his group had inquired into the competence of the three men, he replied, "Nobody asked us to see whether these men were conducting themselves properly."[190] During the subcommittee's hearings, the accused were not given any specific charges, were not allowed to examine material considered by the subcommittee as evidence against them, were not told the sources of such information, and were not confronted with any witnesses or allowed to present their own witnesses.

Ultimately, the House voted 317-62 on May 18, 1943, to delete the trio's salary from a deficiency appropriations bill, and refused to rescind its action although the Senate rejected the rider six times. Finally, the Senate agreed to a compromise which barred payment for their salaries after November 15, 1943, unless in the meantime their names had been submitted to the Senate by FDR and their appointments confirmed. Roosevelt signed the appropriations bill under protest. When the trio appealed the Congressional action to the Courts, Attorney General Biddle notified Congress that it would have to find a lawyer on its own since the Solicitor General was busy defending the plaintiffs. In June, 1946, the Supreme Court invalidated the Congressional action as a bill of attainder and ordered the men awarded back pay.

Robert Cushman has summed up this sorry tale:

> The record makes it amply clear that Lovett, Watson and Dodd were dismissed not because they were dangerous or subversive within any reasonable meaning of those words, but because they held and expressed political and economic views and belonged to organizations which members of the Kerr Committee and of the House did not like.[191]

While the White House and the Congress generally exercised pressure for repression during World War II, the Supreme Court on the whole exercised a liberalizing influence. To the extent that World War II was a good war for civil liberties, in fact, the court bears a good deal of the responsibility.[192] The court's decisions in *Hartzel*, the German-American Bund case, *Baumgartner*, *Schneiderman*, *Bridges* and *Viereck* have already been discussed. It should be noted that all of these cases came in 1943 or afterwards — i.e. when the tide of the war had turned towards the Allies.

In 1942, the most critical year of American participation, the court's record was not particularly good. In two cases involving the Jehovah's Witnesses (*Chaplinsky* v. *New Hampshire* and *Jones* v. *Opelika*), the court ruled against the Witnesses. But in 1943, the Court reversed itself in *Jones* v. *Opelika*, thus allowing Witnesses to sell religious materials door to door without paying license fees, and in the landmark case, *West Virginia State Board of Education* v. *Barnette*, the Court reversed its 1940 *Gobitis* decision, now holding that children could not be expelled from school for refusing to salute the flag.[193] Justice Jackson's opinion in *Barnette* remains one of the most eloquent expressions of the meaning of freedom of opinion:

Those who begin coercive elimination of dissent soon find themselves exterminating dissenters. Compulsory unification of opinion achieves only the unanimity of the graveyard. . . . If there is any fixed star in our constitutional constellation, it is that no official, high or petty, can prescribe what shall be orthodox in politics, nationalism, religion or other matters of opinion or force citizens to confess by word or act their faith therein.[194]

In *Thomas* v. *Collins* (1945) the court threw out a 1943 Texas law which required all labor union organizers to secure official cards from the secretary of state before soliciting union members. In *Duncan* v. *Kohonomoku* (1946), decided after the end of the war, the court ruled that martial law had been illegally applied in Hawaii during the war.[195]

The worst decision of the court during the war, from the standpoint of civil liberties — and perhaps the worst decision by the court since the Dred Scott case — came on the question of the treatment of the Japanese-Americans. After ducking the issue of the legality of the evacuation in 1943, the court in the 1944 case of *Korematsu* v. *U.S.* ruled that evacuation was a reasonable military precaution, and that the danger was so great that there was no time to set up procedures to consider the Japanese on an individual basis. In *Ex Parte Endo,* handed down the same day, the court did hold that the government had no right to detain loyal citizens in detention centers. This decision was handed down one day after the exclusion order had been rescinded, and well after the government had begun releasing "loyal" Japanese-Americans.[196]

As Eugene Rostow has suggested, the Japanese-American cases were a "disaster" from any standpoint concerned with civil liberties. Justice Jackson, who dissented in *Korematsu,* termed the principle established in these cases "a loaded weapon ready for the hand of any authority that can bring forward a plausible claim of an urgent need."[197] Clinton Rossiter concludes the lesson of *Korematsu* is that:

> The government of the United States, in a case of military necessity proclaimed by the president and *a fortiari* when Congress has registered agreement, can be just as much a dictatorship, after its own fashion, as any other government on earth. The Supreme Court of the United States will not and cannot be expected to get in the way of this power.[198]

State and Local Represson During World War II

The Roosevelt administration's efforts to centralize repression at the federal level undoubtedly helped to greatly curb local and state efforts designed to stifle dissent, but there were a number of such incidents. For example, school teachers and other public employees who were pacifists, and in some cases officially recognized conscientious objectors, were barred or fired in California, Kentucky and Florida. In two cases in California, teachers who refused to sell defense stamps to elementary school children were fired. Pacifist pickets associated with the People's Peace Now Committee who picketed in Washington in 1943 had their signs confiscated by the police and were prevented from continuing their activities.[199]

California's Committee on Un-American Activities harassed a number of right-wing anti-war groups, in one case invading a meeting of a group known as Friends of Progress and seizing membership records at request of the FBI. The committee also denounced alleged communist influence in California's public schools and universities. Thus, the committee termed a meeting of the Writer's Congress at the University of California at Los Angeles in 1943 communist-inspired, but UCLA refused to cancel the meeting and President Roosevelt sent the gathering a welcoming telegram.[200]

New Jersey authorities closed down the German-American Bund's Camp Nordlund shortly after Pearl Harbor and cooperated with the FBI in rounding up Bundists and members of other suspicious groups. Many mistaken arrests were made in the roundups, including two artists who were seized because the landscapes they were sketching happened to include defense installations.[201]

Repressive laws and prosecutions were relatively rare in the states during the war. Pennsylvania brought sedition charges against two persons for remarks made in private conversations; in one of these cases a naturalized citizen was acquitted after being arrested for making a barroom comment disparaging President Roosevelt and shouting "Viva Mussolini." Pennsylvania's legislature in 1943 barred subversives from receiving welfare and pension assistance, but thoughtfully excepted the blind from this provision. During the same year Illinois' legislature barred from the ballot organizations associated "directly or indirectly, with Communist, Fascist, Nazi or other un-American principles and ideals of foreign nations" or with the violent overthrow of the government. Indiana passed a similar bill in 1945. California required schools teaching foreign languages to obtain state licenses and required the denial of such licenses where it appeared instruction materially tended to cause disloyalty to the U.S. The California prosecution of Friends of Progress for failure to register under the 1941 state Subversive Activities Registration Act was overturned in the courts in 1945.[202]

Sedition laws were passed only in Mississippi and Louisiana. Mississippi's law made it illegal to encourage "by speech or in print disloyalty to the government, or to incite to racial distrust, disorder, prejudices or hatreds, or to create an attitude of refusal to salute the flag."[203] Within a few months after passage of the Mississippi law, over fifty members of the Jehovah's Witnesses were arrested, some for making statements such as, "It was wrong for our President to send our boys across in uniform to fight our enemies." In 1943, the Supreme Court reversed a test case under the law on the grounds that criminal sanctions could not be imposed in such cases without a showing of clear and present danger to American Institutions or of intent to incite subversion.[204]

The Witnesses faced harassment not only in Mississippi; indeed the brutal treatment they faced in many communities across the nation during the war makes it difficult to understand how some historians can suggest World War II did not see the vigilantism and mob action that marred World War I. Witnesses were subjected to forcible deportation, beatings by mobs, arbitrary arrests, tarring and feathering, and, in at least one case, castration. In many incidents local officials participated in the mob actions, either standing by and taking no action, or arresting Witnesses and then turning them over to mobs.[205]

Witnesses reported about three hundred incidents of all types and about two hundred arrests between December, 1941, and December, 1943. In about 20 percent of the incidents the flag-salute issue was specifically reported as a factor, but there is little doubt that the Witnesses' political views — including their refusal to salute the flag, their opposition to all wars and their general refusal to recognize the authority of the U.S. government — were involved in almost all of these incidents and characterize them as clear cases of political repression. It is true that the Witnesses were the only objects of vigilantism and wide-scale illegal police action during World War II, but this hardly indicates it was a "good" war, since the Witnesses were the only visible, organized opposition to the war that existed.

Persecution of the Witnesses declined significantly after May, 1942, largely because the Civil Rights Division of the federal Department of Justice, after long delays, began to threaten local officials with prosecution under federal statutes if they continued to interfere with the constitutional rights of American citizens.

In June, 1942, the Civil Rights Division brought an action which led to the conviction of two police officials in West Virginia who had turned a group of Witnesses over to American Legion members who forced them to drink castor oil, tied them together with police department rope and marched them out of town.[206]

Along with arbitrary arrests and vigilante attacks, the Witnesses continued to have their children thrown out of the schools in large numbers until the Supreme Court decision in *Barnette*. By June, 1943, a total of two thousand expulsions had taken place in forty-eight states since 1935, of which most had occurred since the war began. In several cases refusal of Witness' children to salute the flag led to attempts to take children away from their parents, or prosecutions of parents for delinquency or violation of school laws; most of these cases led to acquittals or were dismissed after the *Barnette* decision.[207]

An Assessment of the "Good" War

World War II may have been a "good" war in that it was unquestionably a "just" war, but to maintain that it was "good" for civil liberties is to indulge in the same sort of blindness demonstrated by superpatriots during the McCarthy period who maintained that *they* did not feel suppressed. As Geoffrey Perrett suggests, "America's left-liberals were blind to the real nature of what had occurred because they had not suffered, as many of them had in the earlier war."[208]

In fact, by virtually any measure, World War II was pretty much of a disaster for civil liberties. One measure might be simply the number of people affected by government repression:

> In the first World War the number of victims of mob attacks, the people suppressed under the Sedition Act, all of those arrested and ordered deported, all of those sent to prison for conscience, total (so far as it can be gauged) about eight to ten thousand. The interned Japanese and Nisei alone numbered one hundred twenty thousand [most sources say one hundred ten thousand] in 1942. The likelihood of a CO's being jailed, which was four times greater in this war, resulted in six thousand men being imprisoned for conscientous objection. The victims of mob violence ran into the thousands. And small anti-war cults . . . were vigorously suppressed, producing still more victims. Thus, for every person falling foul of official or spontaneous persecution in the First World War, there were more than ten times as many victims in the Second.[209]

Although this analysis grossly underestimated the victims of governmental repression during World War I (for example the one hundred fifty thousand or so falsely arrested in the slacker raids), clearly a very large number of people suffered severely from repression during World War II. The Japanese-American affair was *not* an exception (what it reflected was the depth of repressive fervor combined with a lack of any *real* war opposition), but even if it was an exception, it alone cancels any claim to a "good" civil liberties record.

Another measure of the "goodness" of the civil liberties record might be the "ratio" of repression to dissent. In these terms, there was probably more repression during World War II in *relation* to the amount of dissent voiced, than in any period in American history, with the possible exception of the 1950-54 period. Another measure might be the degree of support voiced during the war for concepts of political freedom by influential segments of American society. Once again, the record here was disastrous. Another measure might be the American record in comparison with similar countries. While Perrett's statement that, "compared with the other four English-speaking democracies fighting in the war, America unhappily had the worst civil liberties record,"[210] appears to be based only on impression, it does suggest that a comparative study might also cast doubt on the "goodness" of America's civil liberties record during the war. Perhaps the real question raised by the war, then, is why has it been treated as a "good" civil liberties war for so long?

9

Truman-McCarthyism, 1946-1954

New Pressures for Repression, 1945-1947

With the end of the war in 1945, the prospect for American civil liberties looked more favorable than at any time since 1937. Largely as a result of Supreme Court decisions and the favorable developments in the war, repression in 1944 and 1945 had been minimal. In July, 1945, the ACLU reported that its case load had "markedly declined" and that it foresaw its post-war activities as revolving much less around court cases that involved challenges to individual civil liberties. Instead it looked forward to building "institutional arrangements to protect civil liberties" such as fighting monopolistic practices in communications and promoting "the wider participation of faculties and students in educational control."[1] A similarly optimistic tone marked the ACLU report of July, 1946.[2] However, by August, 1947, the ACLU reported, "The national climate of opinion in which freedom of public debate and minority dissent functioned with few restraints during the war years and after, has undergone a sharply unfavorable change."[3]

What accounts for the apparent lack of a repressive climate in 1945-46 and the sharp change that is easily observable by 1947? Since pro-Nazi groups had been of extremely minor importance after 1939, the real measuring rod for the climate of civil liberties was the treatment of the Communist Party. During the war, Russia had been aligned with the U.S., and the American Communist Party had strongly backed the war effort. When the CP "party line" switched after the Nazi invasion of Russia in August, 1941, the American government's "party line" switched also. Suddenly the CP found itself for the most part a welcome partner in the American political spectrum. CP leader Earl Browder, who had been sent to jail in 1940 for passport fraud, was pardoned by President Roosevelt in the spring of 1942 in the interest of national unity. Similar actions were taken in the states. Thus, in North Carolina, CP leader Fred Beal, who had been jailed in connection with the slaying of the police chief of Gastonia in 1929, was pardoned by the governor in January, 1942. Left wingers sent to jail for contempt of California's Un-American Activities Committee in 1940 were pardoned in December, 1942. The Rapp-Coudert investigation of communism in the New York schools petered out after the German invasion of Russia, when red-baiting suddenly became considerably less popular.[4] Although Martin Dies continued his anti-communist campaign, appropriations and votes for his committee declined significantly in the House during the war years.

Support of the Dies Committee in the House, 1941-45

	Appropriations[5]	Votes for continuation[6]
1941	$150,000	354-6
1942	110,000	331-46
1945	82,000	302-94
1944	75,000	
1943	50,000	

In general, the American Communist Party and the Soviet Union were regarded more favorably in the United States during World War II than ever before. As John Lewis Gaddis has noted, "Through a curious kind of logic, the Russians' vigorously successful resistance to Hitler purified them ideologically in the eyes of Americans."[7] Spurred on to this belief by the dissolution of the Comintern in 1943, the transformation of the American CP into the "Communist Political Association" in 1944, and Browder's declaration that "we are ready to cooperate in making capitalism work effectively in the post-war period,"[8] the Soviet Union basked in admiration from virtually all segments of American society during World War II.

President Roosevelt told a radio audience in December, 1943, that Stalin represented the "heart and soul of Russia" and "I believe that we are going to get along very well with him and the Russian people — very well indeed."[9] In March, 1943, *Life* magazine devoted a special issue to the theme of "Soviet-American cooperation." It informed American readers that the Russians were "one hell of a people" who "look like Americans, dress like Americans and think like Americans;" the Russian secret police, the NKVD, it continued, were simply a "national police similar to the FBI."[10] The 1942 convention of the Daughters of the American Revolution praised Russia, as did numerous business executives, leading political and military figures, and the *Readers Digest*.[11]

Operating within this favorable climate of opinion, the American Communist Party made major organizational gains during the war.

CP membership, which had dropped drastically after the signing of the Nazi-Soviet pact in 1939 and under the impact of the 1938-41 repression, doubled during the war years, reaching about seventy-five thousand to eighty-five thousand members by May, 1945. CP gains were particularly marked among industrial workers; by the end of the war the CP dominated over 20 percent of the unions in the CIO and exercised important influence in the CIO national office and in several key state and city CIO councils. In 1943, the CP elected two city councilmen in New York City, and party candidates for mayor in New York and for the school board in Cleveland each received about fifty thousand votes.[12] By the end of the war, the party was "maneuvering with an unprecedented assurance and basking in unprecedented public acceptance," and had "widespread influence beyond its own boundaries."[13]

The growing CP influence and power led to an attempt to revive the domestic red scare in 1944. Dies concentrated on labelling the CIO's Political Action Committee (CIO-PAC) as communist dominated, while Republican spokesmen reasserted their support for Russia but at the same time launched a new attack on alleged domestic communist infiltration of the Democratic Party.[14] Thus, Republican presidential candidate Thomas Dewey declared that the "communists are seizing control of the New Deal, through which they aim to control the government of the United States," while vice-presidential hopeful John W. Bricker repeatedly charged that the Democratic Party had become the "Hillman-Browder Communistic Party with FDR at its front."[15] Roosevelt's victory seemed to dispose of this issue, however, as did the defeat of two members of the Dies Committee and Dies' own decision not to run for re-election due to strong CIO-PAC opposition in his home district.[16]

A number of factors were responsible for the drastic change in the civil liberties climate between 1945 and 1947. Among the most important of these were frustration and anger arising out of the strike wave and other economic dislocations which marked 1946; the disappointment of utopian hopes for post-war cooperation with Russia raised by the Roosevelt administration; a slowly developing obsession with the question of internal security and Soviet espionage; the continued agitation of the "red" issue by the Republican party; the development of a new "line" by the American Communist Party; and the increasing adoption of a hard-line against both foreign and domestic communists by the Truman administration, which crystallized in 1947 in the shape of the Truman Doctrine and a new government loyalty program.

In terms of both number of strikes and workers involved, the strike wave of 1946 surpassed all previous strike records in American history. The strikes themselves were marked by very little repression on the local level — only four persons were killed and no state troops were called out. However, the strikes did bring on a wave of anti-union sentiment, and led to a number of repressive actions on the part of the Truman administration. In October, 1945, Truman broke an oil workers' strike by ordering the Navy to seize half the refining capacity of the U.S., and in January, 1946 a packinghouse workers strike was broken when the packinghouses were seized on the grounds that the strike was impeding the war effort, even though the Japanese had surrendered four months earlier.[17]

In May, 1946, Truman seized the railroads to head off a nationwide strike. Truman then asked Congress to grant him emergency power to break strikes in any industry seized by the government, to induct strikers into the army and to jail union officers who refused to obey a back to work order. The settlement of the rail dispute blocked passage of this bill — which would have been the most repressive labor legislation in American history — but not before the House passed it, 306-13, within two hours of Truman's request.[18] The so-called Case bill, which would have imposed a number of restrictions on unions, including a ban on secondary boycotts and a sixty-day cooling off period before any strikes could be called, passed both houses but was vetoed by Truman.[19]

When John L. Lewis called out UMW coal miners in November, 1946, Truman obtained a court injunction barring the strike, partially under the terms of the war-time Smith-Connally Act. Faced with a contempt citation and a fine of $700,000 levied by the Supreme Court in March 1947 (despite the apparent ban on such strike injunctions under the Norris-LaGuardia Act), Lewis was forced to call the strike off.[20]

The 1946 congressional and state elections were a disaster for labor; in their aftermath state legislatures enacted "the largest number of anti-union laws since the Haymarket Riot."[21] About thirty states passed anti-union laws, with twenty-one states providing for strike notices and cooling off periods, sixteen states banning the closed shop, twelve states banning secondary boycotts and six states lowering bars against the use of injunctions during labor disputes.[22]

Anti-labor sentiment in the new Congress was also strong. Truman proposed barring jurisdictional strikes and certain types of secondary boycotts, but Congress brushed this aside in favor of the Taft-Hartley Act of 1947, which was designed to greatly "curb the power of labor and specifically to eliminate communist influence in the labor movement."[23] The Taft-Hartley Act, passed over Truman's veto, included a whole range of anti-labor restrictions, of which the most important were a ban on the closed shop, a provision for injunctions to bar strikes for eighty days in the case of disputes affecting the national welfare, and bans on secondary boycotts and jurisdictional strikes. The Taft-Hartley Act clearly had a dampening effect upon labor; strikes dropped 40 percent immediately after its passage and then dropped in 1949-50 to the lowest point since World War II.[24]

While the main thrust of Taft-Hartley was to *regulate* the labor movement in the interest of what was deemed the general welfare, with regard to communists in the labor movement the intent was *annihilation* rather than regulation. Many of the provisions of Taft-Hartley were clearly repressive, but the *overall* intent was to curb labor abuses rather than to destroy the labor movement or roll back the Wagner Act, much as the intent of anti-trust legislation was to curb business abuses rather than destroy capitalism. Labor's overall acceptance by the American polity was *not* reversed by the Taft-Hartley Act, but the acceptability of communist influence in labor was ruled out completely. One provision of the act provided that all benefits of the Wagner Act would be denied to labor organizations unless each officer of the organization and the officers of any affiliated national or international unit filed an affidavit stating that "he is not a member of the Communist Party, or affiliated with such party, and that he does not believe in or teach the overthrow of the United States government by force or by any illegal or unconstitutional means."[25] Thus, CP union officials had to either resign, perjure themselves or leave the CP to comply. Although at first there was considerable resistance to signing the oath among a wide spectrum of labor leaders, this resistance soon collapsed, especially after the October, 1947, ruling of the NLRB that while the top CIO leadership would not have to sign, the leaders of all constituent and local unions would have to sign the oath to use NLRB machinery. The NLRB announced that it would not process any case brought by unions whose officers did not comply, and ruled that such unions could not be placed on the ballot or certified as bargaining agents, thus making it impossible for them to win union shop authorization. Further, the NLRB refused to process unfair practice charges brought *by* non-complying unions, but processed charges brought *against* such unions.[26] As a result of these rulings, "non-communist leaders who originally objected to complying on principle later felt impelled to do so to save their unions from destruction."[27]

Post-war inflation also contributed to the increasingly surly mood of the country. By the end of 1946, living costs had risen an estimated 33 percent above pre-war levels. The year was also marked by a series of annoying economic shortages — nylons, clothing, automobiles, housing, even food.[28]

Another factor which added to an increasing national mood of bitterness and frustration was the seeming break-down in post-war cooperation between the United States and Russia. This frustration was similar in origin to the disappointment felt by many Americans in the aftermath of World War I. Wilson had promised to make the world "safe for democracy" and to bring peace and enlightenment to the world, but the world had seemingly betrayed American hopes. Similarly, Roosevelt had promised an era of post-war cooperation with Russia and an end to strife between nations. Thus, Secretary of State Cordell Hull had told Congress in 1944 that "there will no longer be need for spheres of influence, for alliances, for balances of power or any other of the special arrangements" of the "unhappy past."[29] After the Yalta conference, FDR told Congress that his talks with the Russians "ought to spell the end of the system of unilateral action, the exclusive alliances, the spheres of influence, the balance of power and all other expedients that have been tried for centuries — and have always failed."[30]

Such public statements and the constant reiteration during the war of the need for war-time and post-war cooperation with Russia had created a general expectation of continued good relations with the Soviets. When the Grand Alliance began to fall apart in 1946, many Americans reacted with deep feelings of frustration and anxiety, which could easily be harnessed in repressive directions.

Another major factor behind the forces developing in support of increased repression between 1945 and 1947 was a developing obsession over the question of internal security and the threat of Soviet espionage. In January, 1945, HUAC had been made a standing, rather than a special committee of the House, for the first time, although by the slim vote of 207 to 186.[31] At about the same time, the House Civil Service Committee was authorized to study loyalty among government employees, but no action was taken on the matter until July, 1946.[32]

While HUAC held a few days of hearings in 1945-46, its appropriations were limited and its investigations got little general attention.[33] Aside from Rep. John Rankins' charge that "loathsome paintings" by left-wing artists were hanging in the homes of Hollywood celebrities, and Rep. J. Parnell Thomas' suggestion that Frank Sinatra was "sort of a Mrs. Roosevelt in pants" because of his alleged left-wing activities, HUAC generated little during these years that was either newsworthy or amusing.[34]

Much more important in developing public fears about subversion were two major spy scares. The first of these, the so-called *Amerasia* affair, was generally regarded as a major espionage case but was in fact nothing of the kind. The *Amerasia* affair originated in February, 1945 when an Office of Strategic Services (OSS) officer discovered that *Amerasia*, a magazine specializing in Far Eastern affairs edited by Phillip Jaffe, an ardent left-wing activist, had printed an article clearly based on a classified OSS report. Subsequently, OSS and FBI agents embarked on a series of illegal break-ins into the *Amerasia* office and the homes of two suspects and discovered hundreds of classified documents. John Stewart Service, a long-time State Department China hand, became involved in the case when he loaned Jaffe personal copies of several reports he had filed from China, which were technically classified because Service had classified them. Service turned the documents over to Jaffe in the latter's hotel room, which had been bugged by the FBI. On June 6, 1945, Service, Jaffe and four others were arrested for conspiracy to violate the Espionage Act. However, there was no evidence whatsoever of espionage, since there were no indications that any of the material had been turned over to any foreign power.

In essence, what was involved in the *Amerasia* affair was the massive leak of documents related to Far Eastern affairs to a magazine concerned with this subject, which had used some of this material openly in the magazine. The government subsequently changed its charge to conspiracy to steal government documents, but even so a federal grand jury in the summer of 1945 refused to indict Service and two others of the original six. The Justice Department later dropped charges against one of the remaining three and hastily settled charges against the other two defendants for fines when it appeared the government case was about to completely collapse after one of the defendants learned about an illegal government entry into his apartment. Although congressional committees concluded in 1946 and 1950 and a federal grand jury concluded in 1950 that there had been no government "cover-up" of the *Amerasia* case, Republicans and the right-wing press periodically dredged up the affair to bolster their claims that a cover-up had occurred and American security was imperilled.[35]

The second major spy scare began in February, 1946 when Canadian officials announced the arrest of twenty-two persons on charges of trying to steal information on the atomic bomb for Russia. In June, 1946, this case was revived with the publication of a report on the affair by the Canadian Royal Commission, which disclosed widespread Russian espionage in Canada, and, according to a Russian informer, in the U.S. as well.[36]

Meanwhile, out of the public spotlight, FBI Director Hoover reported to President Truman in February, 1946, on alleged Soviet espionage operations in the U.S., based on statements made to the FBI by Elizabeth Bentley and Whittaker Chambers, who stated they had been members of an extensive Russian spy network that had reached into the government. Hoover reported that the FBI had "found it necessary to intensify its investigation of Communist Party activities and Soviet espionage cases," that the Bureau was "taking steps to list all members of the Communist Party and others who would be dangerous in the event" of a "serious crisis" with the Soviet Union, and that it might be necessary in such a crisis "to immediately detain a large number of American citizens." Truman ordered Hoover to give top priority to investigating possible communist espionage in the U.S., and especially within the federal government. Apparently as a result of the Hoover report and the

Amerasia and Canadian spy scares, Attorney General Tom Clark pressed Truman in the summer of 1946 to appoint a committee to investigate the loyalty of federal employees and to reapprove Roosevelt's 1940 directive authorizing the FBI to wiretap in cases involving "subversive activities." Truman postponed action on the first request, but on July 17, 1946, agreed with Clark's request to "concur" on Roosevelt's wiretap policy, apparently not being aware that in quoting from the 1940 authorization, Clark had omitted Roosevelt's request that taps be held to a "minimum" and limited "insofar as possible to aliens."[37]

While the FBI never ceased its political intelligence investigations, such activities became somewhat limited towards the end of World War II. The 1945-46 spy scares, the heating up of the Cold War, and Truman's authorization of wiretaps and order that the FBI give top priority to communist espionage investigations led to a sharp increase in FBI political intelligence activity. FBI reports that were disclosed during the Judith Coplon espionage trial in 1949 revealed that the Bureau was engaged in wide-ranging political intelligence that involved gathering information unrelated to any evidence of illegal activities. Thus, the reports indicated that the FBI was compiling a dossier on actor Frederic March and his wife because they were reported to have participated in activities of various organizations associated with the Wallace campaign of 1948 ,and had investigated a music student because he had visited the New Jersey headquarters of the CP and talked with his mother there. Another person was under FBI surveillance because he was connected with "some pro-Israel organization which was sending representatives to various parts of the world." One of the files revealed the reports of an informant that his neighbors entertained military officers "under suspicious circumstances," engaged in parties "which lasted throughout the night and sometimes into the following morning" and were observed "moving around the house in a nude state." Another report indicated the subject of surveillance had "many books in his library at home which the informant considered to be of a Communist character." Wiretap information contributed to fifteen of the twenty-eight dossiers that were made public at the Coplon trial, and the reports also indicated that the FBI had intercepted and opened private mail, and, in at least three cases, searched and entered homes without warrants.[38] Later revelations indicated that the FBI, during the immediate post-war period, investigated a New York City child care center which was found to be "apparently dominated and run by members of the Communist Party," and the Independent Voters of Illinois, which the FBI report indicated was formed in 1944 "for the purpose of developing neighborhood political units to help in the re-election of President Roosevelt and the election of progressive congressmen," and which allegedly had a "very liberal" chairman and Communist involvement among 10 percent of its membership.[39]

The *Amerasia* and Canadian spy affairs and the heating up of the cold war led to a major public revival of interest in the domestic communist issue for the first time since 1938-1941. On July 2, 1946, the House Civil Service Committee appointed a subcomittee to investigate the government's loyalty program. After about two weeks of hearings, the subcomittee concluded there was an "immediate necessity" for action, and recommended the establishment of a government commission to establish a "complete and unified program" to protect the government "against individuals whose primary loyalty is to governments other than our own."[40] Meanwhile, on July 5, Congress extended the power of summary dismissal of government employees, previously restricted to the military, to include the State Department. In August, the act establishing the Atomic Energy Commission (AEC) included a provision providing that all AEC employees undergo an FBI investigation of their "character, associations and loyalty."[41]

In October, 1946, the danger of communist infiltration was stressed in a highly publicized report issued by the U.S. Chamber of Commerce. The Chamber report, which was partially based on information leaked from secret FBI files, charged that communists or "fellow travelers" had made substantial inroads into governmental agencies, including the State Department, and non-governmental groups, especially unions. The report suggested a program to drive all "subversives" out of opinion-forming agencies such as the schools, radio, movies, television, newspapers and libraries.[42] As I. F. Stone has noted, "Much of what happened in the sphere of thought control was forecast and blueprinted in advance"[43] by the Chamber's report. Similar pressure for a tougher stance against domestic "subversives" came from other conservative elements, including the Catholic Church, segments of the press and conservative intellectuals and politicians.[44]

During the 1946 congressional elections, Republican candidates experimented with charges of communist infiltration in Washington on a major scale.[45] The communist issue was mixed in by Republicans with other issues that tapped popular frustration — strikes, economic dislocations, inflation — in a campaign that used as its theme "Had Enough?" In California, an obscure lawyer running for Congress named Richard Nixon stressed his opponent's ties with the "communist-dominated" CIO-PAC and warned about high government officials who "front for un-American elements."[46] An equally obscure senatorial candidate in Wisconsin named Joseph McCarthy also used the communist issue against his opponent in 1946, as did scores of other Republicans. Thus, in Washington state, a candidate for the state legislature named Albert Canwell, later to become chairman of that state's Un-American Activities Committee, declared that "if someone insists there is discrimination against Negroes in this country, or that there is inequality of wealth, there is every reason to believe that person is a communist."[47] In sum, while "the frequency and shrillness of the charges would increase in the years which followed," by 1946 charges of communism "were already a staple of Republican platform oratory."[48]

The new Republican-controlled Congress showed every sign of continuing to agitate the communist issue. Thus, in January, 1947, HUAC announced an eight-point program which included the exposing and "ferreting out" of communists and "communist sympathizers" in the federal government, as well as focusing on "outright" communist control of "some of the most vital" unions.[49] In February, House Speaker Joseph Martin pledged the new Congress would "ferret out" all those who sought to destroy the "American way of life."[50]

By early 1947, the Truman administration was on the horns of a serious dilemma, which was comprised of three parts. First, despite its increasing adoption of a hard-line anti-Soviet policy, the administration was being criticized by Republicans as being too "soft" on communism both at home and abroad. Secondly, a major segment of the left-wing of the Democratic Party as well as many independent spokesmen and the Communist Party were increasingly criticizing the administration for seemingly abandoning Roosevelt's policy of trying to reach an accomodation with Russia. Thirdly, the administration was discovering that it was unable to sell programs for the economic reconstruction of Europe, which it believed to be vital for American economic health, except on the basis of anti-Communism.

The first component of this problem has already been discussed. The second component, the extremely strong opposition to the development of a hard line against Russia which was apparent in the early days of the Cold War, has been an extremely neglected aspect of American history. As noted previously, the Roosevelt administration had repeatedly assured the American public that Russia and the United States would continue to have good relations after the war, and the Soviet Union was held in good stead by a majority of Americans during the war. Although the Truman Administration gradually drifted into a hard line anti-Soviet policy during 1946, many Americans remained firmly committed to a conciliatory approach. In 1945, for example, public opinion polls showed that 42 percent of Americans believed that U.S.-Soviet relations would improve, and only 19 percent felt they would worsen. Winston Churchill's "iron curtain" speech at Fulton, Missouri, in March, 1946, suggesting an Anglo-American anti-Soviet alliance, was greeted with a storm of adverse public reaction; polls showed that forty percent disapproved of the speech while only 18 percent approved.[51]

A new storm of adverse public reaction erupted in September, 1946, when Henry Wallace, who symbolized the new deal to many Democrats, was fired by Truman as Secretary of Commerce after delivery of a speech alleged to be too conciliatory to Russia. Increasing talk soon developed of the possibility of Wallace's running against Truman as a third party candidate, stressing increased domestic reforms and a return to Roosevelt's policy of conciliation towards Russia. In December, 1946 a poll showed that 24 percent of Democratic voters favored Wallace for president in 1948, compared to 48 percent favoring Truman. A major segment of the left wing of the Democratic Party began to rally around Wallace.[52]

Meanwhile, the "Communist Political Association" had by mid-1945 abandoned its policy of accomodation with capitalism, reconstituted itself as the Communist Party and adopted a program increasingly critical of American foreign policy. In 1946 the party had a membership of about seventy-three thousand, clearly not enough to pose any serious revolutionary threat, but just as clearly an organization which could and did pose a serious propaganda threat to the development of a hard-line anti-Soviet foreign policy. The party continued its pre-war policy of attempting to operate through "front" groups, which greatly expanded its influence and added to its financial resources. The most successful of the post-war front groups, the International Workers Order (IWO), which functioned primarily as a life insurance organization, had almost two hundred thousand policy holders in 1947 whose policies totalled over $100 million. The party conducted vigorous propaganda and fund-raising campaigns and showed signs of considerable vitality. Thus, in April, 1947, the CP made one hundred local radio broadcasts and two national network broadcasts; in March and April, 1947, the party distributed 4.5 million leaflets.[53]

The Wallace wing of the Democratic Party, which in 1946 and 1947 included many labor union members and officials disenchanted with Truman's 1946 labor policies, was joined in its criticism of Truman's new foreign policy direction not only by the CP but also by a large and divergent group of spokesmen who shared the belief that "reconciliation with the Soviet Union was possible without sacrificing the national interest, that American foreign policy and its misconceptions were helping to aggravate Soviet-American friction, that the Cold War should not be increasingly militarized and that the conflict threatened American institutions and cherished principles at home."[54] Among the spokesmen for such a viewpoint were Walter Lippmann, James Warburg, Albert Einstein, Fiorello LaGuardia, Joseph Davies, Elliot Roosevelt, Norman Thomas and Henry Morgenthau Jr.[55]

That left-wing opposition to Truman's foreign policy was a restraining and upsetting influence to the administration is well-documented. For example, Truman was sufficiently concerned over public opposition towards an open policy of outright hostility towards Russia such as was incorporated in the Truman Doctrine that he rejected taking strong public action before the 1946 Congressional elections for fear of alienating the Democratic left-wing.⁵⁶ Leading administration officials, including Truman, Attorney General Tom Clark, FBI Director J. Edgar Hoover and Secretary of the Navy James Forrestal are all known to have expressed their concern privately about the activities of American Communists in opposing American foreign policy and in the possibility of their aligning with other groups such as isolationists and pacifists and thus gaining broader public support.⁵⁷ Thus, after Wallace's speech of September, 1946, Truman wrote in his diary that "the Reds, phonies and 'parlor pinks' seem to be banded together and are becoming a national danger. I am afraid they are a sabotage front for Uncle Joe Stalin."⁵⁸

State Department Information Officer Joseph Jones complained later that the Truman administration's desire to aid Greece was severely hindered in the days prior to the statement of the Truman Doctrine "by the fact that incessant Communist propaganda, echoed by fellow travelers and misinformed liberals, had been widely successful" in portraying the Greek rebels as "patriotic rebels resisting corruption, fascism and monarchy" and that as a result "the president's program therefore ran into considerable opposition on the American left."⁵⁹ According to a recent account, "of the many domestic political restraints upon the Administration's foreign policies at the beginning of 1947, none was more important, in the eyes of the men around the President, than continuing public optimism that the world of U.S.-Soviet cooperation that Roosevelt had promised yet would be born."⁶⁰

In addition to right-wing pressure for stronger anti-Soviet policies abroad and stronger anti-communist policies at home, and left-wing pressure in the opposite direction, the third horn of the dilemma faced by the administration was its inability to persuade Congress and the American public to adopt policies directed towards the economic reconstruction of Europe, which top policy-makers believed was essential for continued American economic vitality, except on the basis of anti-communism. While Republican isolationists in Congress verbally urged tougher anti-communist policies, they were extremely reluctant to commit the U.S. to economic aid policies which they viewed as inextricably involving the country in the tangled affairs of Europe. For example, the administration was able to win approval for a $3.75 billion loan to Britain in the summer of 1946 only after several key congressional leaders stressed the anti-communist aspects of the proposal.⁶¹ This formula was consciously adopted in Truman's enunciation of the Truman Doctrine in March, 1947, after Republican Sen. Arthur Vandenberg advised Truman to "scare hell out of the country."⁶²

Initiation of the Domestic Cold War, 1947-1950

By March of 1947, the Truman administration had decided upon a policy which would meet all three aspects of the dilemma it faced. Announcement of a strongly anti-communist foreign policy (The Truman Doctrine) would be coupled with the beginning of a policy of stern repression at home which would picture all opposition to his foreign policy as stemming from communist or subversive sources. Thus, in two bold, coordinated strokes, Truman could: defuse the right-wing opposition by adopting their own policy; destroy the left-wing opposition by picturing it as a subversive plot and, if necessary, resorting to repressive measures; and sell policies which were based on American economic needs by stressing their anti-communist potentialities. Not only would such a program solve all three of the dilemmas, but the results of the 1946 congressional elections clearly indicated that the left-wing was weaker than had been thought, and that failure to adopt such policies would mean losing control of the anti-communist issue to the Republicans.[63]

The first major sign of the new policy was Truman's decision on November 25, 1946 — after the congressional elections had shown the potency of the anti-communist issue — to accept the recommendations of the House Civil Service Subcommittee and establish a Temporary Commission on Loyalty to study the issue of a government's loyalty program. The commission was given only two months in which to make its report, and it is evident that it *assumed* that there was a need for a major departure in existing government loyalty programs, rather than making a real study of the situation. In its report to Truman on February 20, 1947, the commission concluded "the employment of disloyal or subversive persons presents more than a speculative threat to our system of government" but admitted it was unable to state "how far-reaching that threat is." The commission solved this problem by accepting the formula originally suggested by Attorney General Tom Clark that the presence with the government or the attempt to obtain employment by "*any*" disloyal or subversive person "presents a problem of such importance that it must be dealt with vigorously and effectively."[64]

On March 11, 1947, Secretary of Labor Lewis Schwellenbach publicly suggested the outlawing of the Communist Party.[65] On March 12, Truman announced the Truman Doctrine, with its strongly anti-communist overtones. On March 21, Truman announced the establishment of a new government loyalty program based on the report of the temporary commission. Since the commission had reported to Truman on February 20, the timing of this announcement seems to have been part of a campaign to convince the country that the communist danger was both an external and internal one — in effect, it amounted to a "domestic Truman Doctrine."[66]

The announcement of Truman's executive order on government loyalty marks the real beginning of what has been called "McCarthyism." It was this program, more than any other single action, which set the tone and paved the way for the anti-communist hysteria which gripped the country from 1947 onwards. The executive order establishing the loyalty program accepted the reasoning of the temporary commission, stating that the "presence within the Government service of any disloyal or subversive person constitutes a threat to our democratic processes." Under the program, all present or prospective government employees were to undergo loyalty investigations, including checks of any information pertaining to them held by the FBI, CSC, military intelligence, HUAC, and local law enforcement officials. Whenever "derogatory" information was uncovered in such checks a "full field investigation" would be undertaken by the CSC or the FBI, and, when deemed necessary, hearings would then be held by boards set up within each agency or department (in the case of incumbent employees) or by CSC hearing boards (in the case of prospective employees). Adverse decisions could be appealed to a Loyalty Review Board (LRB) established by the CSC, which was to have advisory power to government agencies.

The standard for an adverse loyalty finding was to be that "reasonable grounds exist for belief that the person involved is disloyal" to the U.S. government. No definition of what constituted "disloyalty" was included in Truman's executive order; the only guidance given in the order for making such determinations was that six types of activities by employees or applicants could be considered: 1) sabotage, espionage and related activities; 2) treason or sedition; 3) advocacy of illegal overthrow of the government; 4) intentional and unauthorized disclosure of confidential information; 5) serving a foreign government in preference to the interests of the U.S.; and 6)

> Membership in, affiliation with or sympathetic association with any foreign or domestic organization, association, movement, group or combination of persons, designated by the Attorney General as totalitarian, Fascist, Communist or subversive, or as having adopted a policy of advocating or approving the commission of acts of force or violence to deny other persons their rights under the Constitution of the United States, or as seeking to alter the form of Government of the United States by unconstitutional means.[67]

Applicants and employees found to have "derogatory" information in their files and subsequently required to undergo hearings were entitled to have written notice of charges "stated as specifically and complete, as, in the discretion of the employing department or agency, security considerations permit" and were entitled to appear before hearing boards and present evidence and witnesses in their behalf. At the hearings, the investigating agency involved — which eventually meant the FBI in almost all cases — was authorized to "refuse to disclose the names of confidential informants" who had made charges or given information in the case "provided it furnishes sufficient information about such informants on the basis of which the requesting department or agency can make an adequate evaluation of the information furnished."[68]

All of the grave abuses which quickly developed under the Truman loyalty program flowed directly from the procedures established in the original executive order. The first five categories of activities which might be considered in making loyalty decisions were *already* grounds for criminal prosecution under existing laws and/or dismissal under civil service regulations allowing discharges for "such cause as will promote the efficiency of the service."[69] The sixth criterion, relating to membership, affiliation or "sympathetic association" with certain types of groups, was in fact the only new criterion outlined, and it was also the only criterion which focused on *beliefs* and *associations* rather than actual activities. Given the lack of definition as to what constituted disloyalty, and Truman's statement of November 14, 1947, that the program was designed to ferret out "potential subversives,"[70] it is clear that the real purpose of the loyalty program was to attempt to determine whether or not "disloyal" *thoughts* were being entertained in employees' or applicants' heads, which *might* at some future time lead to disloyal action.

Aside from this basic defect, which in effort required hearing boards to attempt to predict future actions on the basis of their perceptions of past and present thoughts and associations, the loyalty program suffered from the following grave procedural defects.

- The provision that specific charges might be omitted due to security considerations led to the filing of charges in case after case which made only vague allegations of general disloyalty or allegedly disloyal past or present affiliation, actions or statements without specifics of time, place or even activity.

- The provision that names of "confidential informants" could be denied to those charged meant that employees and applicants faced with grave allegations could not determine who their accuser was and were denied the right to confront and cross-examine their accuser.[71]

- No time limit was imposed upon those activities, associations and statements for which employees and applicants might be held responsible; persons could be charged on the basis of a "sympathetic association" with an organization which had occurred forty years previously.

- Because each agency had its own procedures and hearing boards (altogether there were five hundred loyalty boards scattered throughout the government, staffed by over two thousand men), employees might be cleared by one agency, yet faced with another hearing if transferring to another agency.

- As the political atmosphere deteriorated, loyalty standards were significantly altered and tightened in 1951 and 1953, with the result that many employees were repeatedly tried on the same charges under different standards; increasingly the loyalty boards tended to "measure (their) success by the numbers dismissed and to alter (their) rules to increase those numbers."[72] Thus, State Department "China hand" John Stewart Service was cleared seven times by a State Department board, and then was ordered fired by the LRB.

- Employees and applicants could be and repeatedly were charged with committing offenses that involved completely lawful activities.
- While in court proceedings, the judge hears only evidence offered in open court and during the actual trial, in loyalty hearings the agencies boards frequently immersed themselves in confidential papers related to the case before the accused person came before them, thus denying the accused the opportunity of rebuttal and frequently creating in the minds of the boards a grave bias against the accused before hearings began.
- While in court proceedings, the accused are considered innocent until proven guilty beyond a "reasonable doubt", in the loyalty program, the accused were considered guilty unless they could prove that no "reasonable grounds" existed for doubting their loyalty.
- Hearing boards had no power of subpoena to compel the attendance of those adverse witnesses who could be identified, and had no money to pay for the transportation costs of favorable witnesses.
- Final adjudication of loyalty cases frequently took six months or longer, during which period the accused lived in a twilight world of neither regular employment nor non-employment.
- Although loyalty proceedings were supposed to be kept confidential, word of accusations frequently leaked out, causing severe difficulties for the accused in his current position, and making future employment extremely difficult in the case of firing.

Because the loyalty criteria required hearing boards to attempt to predict future loyalty rather than determine if disloyal actions had actually been undertaken, the charges levied in loyalty proceedings and the questions asked at loyalty hearings took on the character of a medieval inquisition.

Among the formal charges issued were the following.[73]

"You have associated for a considerable time with persons who are known communists."

"It is known that you were at one time a subscriber to the Communist newsletter 'In Face' and you were a subscriber after this publication was exposed by the press as expressing the views of the Communist Party."

"You have during most of your life been under the influence of your father, who . . . was an active member of the Communist Party."

"Communist literature was observed in the book shelves and Communist art was seen on the walls of your residence."

"A confidential informant, stated to be of established reliability, who is acquainted with and who has associated with many known and admitted communists, is reported to have advised as of May, 1948, that the informant was present when the employee was engaged in conversations with other individuals at which time the employee advocated the Communist Party line, such as favoring peace and civil liberties. . . . Another informant . . . reportedly advised that while the informant did not have any concrete or specific pertinent information reflecting adversely on the employee's loyalty, informant is of the opinion that the employee's convictions concerning equal rights for all races and classes extend slightly beyond the normal feeling of the average individual and for this reason informant would be reluctant to vouch for the employee's loyalty."

"A former landlord of yours has reported that in 1943, after you moved from the premises . . . certain magazines and pamphlets which may have been left on the premises by you may have included a copy of the magazine *New Masses*."

Among the questions asked during loyalty hearings were the following.[74]

"What do you think of the third party formed by Henry Wallace?"

"To what do you attribute the recent swing to the 'left' in France?"

"Have you ever had Negroes in your homes?"

"There is a suspicion in the record that you are in sympathy with the underprivileged. Is this true?"

"Did you ever write a letter to the Red Cross about segregation of blood?"

"Do you read Howard Fast? Tom Paine? Upton Sinclair?"

"When you were in X's home, did X's wife dress conventionally when she received her guests?"

While these examples are admittedly taken out of context, such charges and questions were the inevitable result of a loyalty program which sought to root out *potential* rather than actual disloyalty, since such determinations could not even be attempted without a wide-ranging examination of a man's entire life. In the context of the developing cold war, moreover, the emphasis of the loyalty proceedings inevitably tended to stress discovery of the holding of unorthodox ideas in general; as Alan Barth has written, the program applied "a kind of intellectual means test under which only the indigent in ideas can qualify."[75] In one case, a security officer, when presented with a glowing recommendation for a prospective employee which stressed her intelligence, commented, "These intelligent people are very likely to be attracted to Communism." In another instance, a loyalty hearing board member commented privately, "Of course the fact that a person believes in racial equality doesn't *prove* that he's a communist, but it certainly makes you look twice, doesn't it?"[76]

In one study of eighty-five loyalty cases, not one case was found which involved charges of treason, sedition, espionage, sabotage or advocacy of illegal overthrow of the government; virtually all charges fell within the sixth category of the Truman order. Only about twenty of the cases involved charges of actual past or present membership in the CP or the Young Communist League. The most frequent single charge was association with another individual said to be subversively inclined; in many cases such charges involved associations with sisters, wives, mothers and fathers. Charges of reading communist literature occurred in ten of these cases, and possession of books on communism were involved in four cases.[77]

In another study of three hundred twenty six cases which were gathered in 1955, the most recent year of activity referred to in any charge was no later than 1945 in over half of the cases for which information was available. Questions about general political views other than communism were asked at hearings in about half of these cases, with questions about reading habits asked in over 10 percent. In twenty-four of these cases, the sole basis for the charge was the allegedly subversive activities of associates of the accused. In twenty cases, questions were asked regarding the signing of petitions by the accused.[78] Truman administration officials did not even claim that the loyalty program was catching any spies. Thus, in 1950, Seth Richardson, first chairman of the LRB, told a Senate committee that as a result of the loyalty program "not one single case or evidence directing toward a case of espionage" had been uncovered and that "all of these cases that we have had, have had to do with this question of association, affiliation, membership with organizations which have been certified by the Attorney General to be subversive."[79]

The best short description of the Truman loyalty program was given by Alan Barth in the early 1950's. He wrote:

> To enumerate the features of the loyalty program is to suggest the description of an authoritarian society. Any American hearing of a foreign country in which the police were authorized to search out the private lives of law-abiding citizens, in which a government official was authorized to proscribe lawful associations, in which administrative tribunals were authorized to condemn individuals by star-chamber proceedings on the basis of anonymous testimony, for beliefs and associations entailing no criminal conduct, would conclude without hesitation that the country was one in which tyranny prevailed.[80]

Thomas Emerson and David Helfeld, after studying government loyalty programs in Vichy France, Nazi Germany, and Fascist Italy, and under democratic regimes in France, Germany, Great Britain, Canada, Australia, Belgium, Switzerland, Norway, Sweden, New Zealand and Mexico, concluded in 1948:

> Despite conditions of political instability far exceeding those in the United States, other democratic nations have not found it necessary to impose loyalty tests going beyond the standard of active participation in a revolutionary party . . . or the transfer of Communist employees to "non-secret" government work, recently instituted in England. . . . No precedent is to be found in foreign experience, outside the totalitarian states, for a comprehensive, continuous system of loyalty surveillance similar to that instituted by the Loyalty Order in the United States.[81]

Had the institution of the loyalty program been the only repressive program initiated by the Truman administration during the period when Cold War policies were first formulated, it might simply be written off as an attempt to head off further Republican agitation of the "red" issue and to avoid an even more repressive loyalty program dictated by the Republican-controlled Congress. This interpretation was a common one at the time and has been reiterated since by a number of historians. For example, Republican House Speaker Martin commented on March 22, 1947 that it was "good" that Truman "has finally awakened to the truth of what we have been telling him for the last few years,"[82] while Walter Goodman terms the loyalty program "an effort by the executive to take the play away from Congress" and to put "the testing of loyalty into more responsible hands than those of the flag-waving legislators."[83] This interpretation, however, falls apart when the long list of other repressive actions taken by the Truman administration during the 1947-48 period is considered.

The context of these repressive actions must be kept in mind: the Truman administration was initiating a *major* shift in American foreign policy, one that committed the nation to fight communism all around the world by supporting "free peoples who are resisting attempted subjugation by armed minorities or by outside pressures."[84] When this policy was announced in the Truman Doctrine speech of March 12, 1947, opposition to such a major departure from Franklin D. Roosevelt's foreign policy and the generally isolationist thrust of American foreign policy in times of peace did not diminish but increased. Beginning in March, 1947, Henry Wallace began a major campaign of speeches opposing the Truman Doctrine and the loyalty program. The response that Wallace received during his speeches in 1947 was generally viewed as little short of amazing, and could not help but frighten Truman, especially in the light of his poor standing in the popular opinion polls and in view of increasing talk about formation of a third party with Wallace as its standard bearer. During his speaking tour across the U.S. in the spring and summer of 1947, Wallace addressed an estimated two hundred thousand persons who paid from sixty cents to over three dollars to hear him talk.[85]

A number of elections also showed strong support for left-wing political activity. For example, in May, 1947, an anti-Truman congressional candidate beat a Truman supporter in a special congressional primary before losing by a small margin in the June election to a Republican. In November, 1947, progressive candidates made a strong showing in the Cook County, Illinois, superior court elections, and communists made strong showings in several California elections. Despite increasing attacks which suggested that critics of American foreign policy were subversive and communist-dominated, the Progressive Citizens of America (PCA), which eventually became Wallace's presidential vehicle, increased in membership from seventeen thousand dues payers at its formation in May, 1947 to forty-seven thousand in September, and claimed one hundred thousand at the beginning of 1948, shortly after Wallace announced his presidential candidacy.[86]

In retrospect, the high point of the Progressive Party was reached in February, 1948. On February 17, a Progressive candidate was elected to Congress in a special election which featured American foreign policy as a major issue.[87] On February 24, the Progressive Party in California filed four hundred eighty-two thousand signatures to qualify for a position on the state ballot, an achievement which the California secretary of state responded to by noting, "When we wrote this law (requiring four hundred sixty-six thousand signatures) we thought no one would ever be able to do it."[88] Despite often severe requirements restricting the access of third parties to the ballot, the Progressives eventually succeeded in getting on the ballot in forty-four of the forty-eight states, and were excluded by flimsy or non-existent grounds in three other states.[89]

As signs of increasing opposition to Truman's new direction in American foreign policy developed throughout 1947 and early 1948, the Truman administration and the Republican-controlled Congress cooperated to institute a campaign of repression unmatched since World War I. Throughout the year, HUAC, which had in effect been given a sign of approval by the administrations' loyalty program conducted a series of highly publicized investigations into communist activities, funded with the highest appropriation it had been granted since 1942. Although several HUAC hearings were explicitly designed to embarrass the Democrats — one hearing attempted to show that Mrs. Roosevelt had helped a communist immigrant obtain favorable treatment in 1939 and the "Hollywood Ten" hearings were billed as proving that pressure from President Roosevelt had led Hollywood movie-makers to include pro-Russian propaganda in their films — the FBI and the Justice Department repeatedly aided the committee by providing it with secret government documents and files.[90] Attorney General Clark stated in April, 1947, that the Justice Department "will, as it has in the past, cooperate fully with the House Committee." In early 1948, Clark told HUAC that the Justice Department and the committee "work in neighboring vineyards" and that "the program of this committee in bringing into the spotlight of publicity the activities of individuals and groups can render real service to the American people."[91] In June, 1948, HUAC Chairman J. Parnell Thomas stated:

> The closest relationship exists between this committee and the FBI. . . . I think there is a very good understanding between us. It is something, however, that we cannot talk too much about it.[92]

FBI Director Hoover personally appeared before HUAC during the 1947 hearings, representing a reversal (over Hoover's protest) of Justice Department policy which had been established in 1940 barring Hoover from making such appearances. On March 26, Hoover publicly opposed proposals to outlaw the Communist Party; he also charged that "since the President called for aid to Greece and Turkey the Communists opposing the plan had been mobilizing, promoting mass meetings, sending telegrams and letters to exert pressure on Congress."[93] This was perhaps the first explicit public statement of what rapidly became the official administration line — that opposition to American foreign policy was communist inspired.

Even the most flagrant abuses on the part of HUAC drew no rebukes from the Truman administration in 1947. On July 21, 1947, Walter Steele, the superpatriot who had named hundreds of allegedly subversive persons and organizations before the Dies Committee in 1938, reappeared to point the finger at another huge list of persons and organizations. During the "Hollywood Ten" hearings in October, the committee heard testimony from often politically naive actors, writers, directors and producers who were encouraged to make charges of communist influence against their professional colleagues and competitors.[94] The testimony "ranged all the way from intelligent penetrating analysis of the communist influence in Hollywood, to the strange, the bitter and the stupid."[95] Thus, Gary Cooper told the committee that he didn't like communism, because "from what I hear, it isn't on the level;" he added . . . that he had turned down scripts tinged with communist ideas, but he could not name any of them "because most of the scripts I read at night."[96] The climax of the hearings was reached when ten witnesses refused to answer questions about their past and present political affiliations, were quickly "dismissed, hollering from the witness chair,"[97] then were publicly charged by the committee staff with being Communist Party members on the basis of FBI information, and eventually were sent to jail for contempt of Congress.

Subsequently, the Hollywood movie industry announced that it would not employ any persons accused of communism who did not deny such charges, thus setting the pattern for hundreds of future congressional hearings which were explicitly designed to bring about the firing of those persons accused before them. The blacklist reflected the HUAC philosophy that not only was

> communism a subversive doctrine, not only that communists in sensitive positions . . . threats to the nation but . . . the presence in this land of every individual communist and fellow traveler and former communist who would not purge himself was intolerable; that the just fate of every such creature was to be exposed in his community, routed from his job and driven into exile.[98]

This philosophy was tacitly endorsed by the Truman administration's cooperation with HUAC; indeed the entire concept of the blacklist was simply an imitation of the government loyalty program. The revival of HUAC as a major force in American life came only *after* the Truman administration had initiated its own anti-communist program.

Activities of the House Un-American Activities Committee, 1945-50

	Hearing Days[99]	Appropriations[100]
1945	8	$ 50,000
1946	3	$ 75,000
1947	27	$100,000
1948	35	$200,000
1949	38	$200,000
1950	77	$150,000

The initiation of the government loyalty program and cooperation with HUAC were by no means the only examples of Truman administration activities which fostered or bowed to the forces of repression. In mid-1947, after State Department spokesmen appearing before the Senate Appropriations Committee came under strong pressure to use the authority provided in 1946 to summarily dismiss security risks, ten department employees were suddenly fired without hearings, charges or evidence. Public protests proved to be so strong that eventually all ten of the men were allowed to resign without prejudice.[101] Probably the single most outrageous repressive activity initiated by the Truman Administration was the publication of the so-called Attorney General's List of Subversive Organizations, beginning in December of 1947 (shortly before Wallace announced his presidential candidacy).[102] While preparation of such a list was required by the sixth criterion of the Truman Loyalty Order, there was no requirement in the order that the list be publicized. Such lists had been compiled during World War II, but were kept confidential. Since the rationale for establishing the list was based solely on the needs of the government loyalty program there was clearly no necessity for publishing the list, aside from the intimidating effects it would have on critics of American policy. The Attorney General's list quickly became what amounted to an "official black list"[103] which came to have in the public mind "authority as *the* definitive report on subversive organizations" and became understood as a "proscription of the treasonable activity of the listed organizations" and "the litmus test for distinguishing between loyal and disloyal organizations and individuals."[104]

Those organizations listed had no hearings or notification before the list was published. With one or two exceptions, no dates were listed to indicate when the organizations had become "subversive;" in fact, some of the organizations that were listed had actually been endorsed by governmental officials during earlier periods. For example, the American Slav Congress, organized in 1942, had received messages of greetings from President Roosevelt and Secretary of State Hull during World War II, while the National Council for American-Soviet Friendship (NCASF) had been greeted or addressed during the war by leading American military officials including Generals Marshall, MacArthur, Eisenhower, Pershing and Clark.[105]

Many of the non-communist groups that were listed were defunct pro-Nazi or pro-Japanese organizations, while most of the still-existing organizations listed were in the category of "communist-front" groups. Thus, the evidence indicates that the real purpose of publication of the list was to discredit left-wing groups that were opposing or contributing to organizations that opposed American foreign policy. The Communist Party had staged a major campaign against aid to Greece and Turkey in the spring of 1947, and top ranking officials of the Truman administration were extremely concerned about the possible success of communist front groups in appealing to broader segments of the population. By the simple device of listing and publishing such groups in the Attorney General's list, the Truman administration could, without hearings or charges, effectively cripple organizations that were guilty of no crime whatsoever and at the same time suggest that all opposition to American foreign policy was "subversive" in nature.[106] As Richard Freeland suggests, the evidence clearly supports the conclusion that the publication of the Attorney General's list represented a "deliberate attempt by the Department of Justice to neutralize various political organizations that were, among other subversive things, impeding the Administration's efforts to win support for Cold War foreign policy" and was an attempt to "destroy the effectiveness of communist and communist-affiliated organizations without bringing legal sanctions against them."[107] Indeed Attorney General Tom Clark virtually admitted as much, referring to the listed groups as "those organizations that are engaged in propaganda activity of a subversive nature" and citing the list as part of a general effort "to isolate subversive movements in this country from effective interference with the body politic."[108]

The effect of being listed was clearly to seriously hinder or destroy the organizations involved. Membership and contributions usually dried up, the Treasury Department revoked the tax exempt status of at least sixteen organizations that were listed, meeting places suddenly became difficult to find, and the list was soon incorporated into state and local loyalty programs and became the basis for private blacklisting. In 1952, Congress banned members of listed organizations from eligibility for public housing (a law quickly declared unconstitutional) and barred veterans from using veterans benefits to enroll in listed educational institutions.[109]

While no general study of the effect of listing has thus far been made, the impact of listing on several organizations which have been studied support Emerson and Helfeld's conclusion that "in practical terms" listed organizations were "gravely stricken" and might "be forced out of existence."[110] For example, the day after being listed apparently because it had demonstrated against American intervention in Greece during the spring of 1947, the Connecticut State Youth Conference was barred from using hotel facilities in Hartford for its planned convention. The NCASF reported the listing caused the loss of numerous members, sponsors and considerable public support, the denial of meeting places and radio time and increasing difficulties in gaining acceptance of its materials in schools and elsewhere. After the Seattle Labor School was listed, the Seattle Central Labor Council disaffiliated from the school and most labor unions withdrew. The Southern Negro Youth Congress and the United Negro and Allied Veterans of America collapsed or were liquidated by the Communist Party shortly after their listing. Probably the greatest blow against the CP came when the State of New York revoked the charter of the International Workers Order (IWO) in 1950 after it was listed. The IWO was the largest CP-dominated group in the postwar period. The IWO was primarily a fraternal benefit society for immigrant workers which specialized in low-cost insurance.[111] Until its liquidation by New York state, the IWO had been repeatedly rated by New York authorities as giving excellent service to its policyholders, most of whom were "apolitical people ... who were in the IWO solely for its capitalistic insurance benefits."[112]

Undoubtedly the greatest effect of the Attorney General's list was not that on the organizations listed, however, but on the general climate of political dissent. The loyalty program directly affected only federal employees, but the Attorney General's list affected all Americans who belonged to or contemplated belonging to or in any way associating with organizations. One minor but revealing incident was the decision in 1950 of the Institute of Pacific Relations, a scholarly organization concerned with the study of Far Eastern Affairs, which itself had come under attack by private individuals for alleged subversive leanings, to refuse to honor a previous commitment to publish material by a member of the Committee for a Democratic Far Eastern Policy, a group which supported the Chinese Communists and which had been listed by the Attorney General.[113] More generally, since the criteria for listing were unknown and new groups were constantly being added (the list grew from 87 in March, 1948 to 197 by November, 1950) all persons and especially government employees soon became extremely wary about joining organizations, since no one knew what group might be listed next, what group might in the future become a target for possible "subversives," or what group might be viewed as "subversive" if the political climate changed in the future. It was widely speculated in 1947, for example, that the PCA might soon be listed and it "would have been entirely reasonable to assume that active and consistent opposition to the Administration's foreign policy was sufficient to win a place on the list."[114] Under the circumstances prevailing in the United States after 1947, one scholar concluded in 1953 that the "only safe course is to refrain from joining."[115]

Clearly Alan Barth was close to the truth when he termed the power given the Attorney General with respect to the listings

> perhaps the most arbitrary and far-reaching power ever exercised by a single public official in the history of the United States. By virtue of it, the Attorney General may stigmatize, and in effect, proscribe any organization of which he disapproves.[116]

With the development of the Progressive Party campaign in 1948, the Truman administration resorted to new methods of repression. The State Department began to deny passports to Americans whose overseas travel was considered "not in the interests" of the U.S., while alien communists were barred from visiting the country except in the cases of diplomatic personnel. Under this program, Congressman Leo Isaacson, who had been elected with Progressive Party backing in a special congressional election in February, 1948, was barred from attending an international conference dealing with aid to Greece on the grounds that one of the participating groups had as its avowed purpose "the furnishing of material and moral assistance to the guerilla forces in Greece."[117] In 1950, Negro actor and singer Paul Robeson, who had been lionized by American society only five years earlier, was denied a passport for the purpose of giving a European concert tour. Blacklisted at home and unable to travel abroad, Robeson was reduced to giving concerts by overseas telephone until he won the right to a passport again as the result of a Supreme Court decision in 1958.[118]

Beginning in early 1948, the Truman administration added another string to its repressive bow with a series of highly publicized deportation arrests for subversive activities. Although few of the arrests led to immediate deportation, the large numbers involved — over one hundred arrests of alleged Communist aliens between February and May of 1948 — and the great publicity given them, amounted to a clear warning to aliens to stay out of "dubious" political activities and suggested once more that opposition to American foreign policy was "un-American." During the 1948 drive, deportation arrests were especially concentrated upon leaders of left-wing unions and those who actively opposed administration foreign policy or supported the Wallace campaign. Among those arrested were CP labor secretary John Williamson, who was seized shortly after publishing an article criticizing CIO president Phillip Murray for his support of the Marshall Plan, and Ferdinand Smith, Secretary of the CP-dominated National Maritime Union, who was arrested twenty-four hours after he had appeared on a speaker's platform with Wallace in support of Isaacson's congressional candidacy.[119]

On August 3, 1948, the Justice Department submitted to the FBI a plan providing for the "detention of dangerous individuals at the time of an emergency."[120] The plan, which could be activated at a time of "threatened invasion," as well as actual invasion or insurrection, called for the suspension of the Writ of Habeas Corpus, the arrest of all subjects listed on the FBI's Security Index, dating from 1939,[121] under "one master warrant of arrest executed by the Attorney General," hearings within forty-five days before special "Boards of Review" which would not be bound by legal rules of evidence, and no appeal except to the President.

Following the showing of Progressive Party strength in February, 1948, the Truman administration began a campaign to label the Progressive Party communist-dominated. In doing so, Truman was following advice which his aide, Clark Clifford, had given him in November, 1947. Noting that Truman had stolen the "thunder" of the Republicans on the communist issue by initiating the loyalty program, Clifford explained that Truman could defeat Wallace by making "every effort . . . jointly and at one and the same time — although of course by different groups — to dissuade him and also to identify him and isolate him in the public mind with the Communists."[122] Twice in February, after the Isaacson victory, Sen. J. Howard McGrath, chairman of the Democratic National Committee, linked Wallace with the communists. In mid-March, on the same day that Truman provoked what appears to have been an artificial war scare to bolster lagging support for the Marshall Plan, Truman announced that he was rejecting the "political support of Henry Wallace and his communists." On March 29, Truman suggested, in effect, that Wallace should go to Russia and "help them against his own country if that's the way he feels."[123]

On July 24, shortly before the Progressive Party convention, a grand jury which had been empanelled by the Truman Administration to investigate subversive activities handed down indictments against twelve top CP leaders for violating the Smith Act by conspiring to advocate and to organize a group which advocated the overthrow of the government. On September 23, Truman said the "fact that the communists are guiding and using the third party shows that this party does not represent American ideals."[124] Given the July indictments of the CP leaders, this statement in effect warned that anyone working to help the Wallace campaign might well face prosecution under the Smith Act. In October, federal grand juries began investigations into CP activities in Ohio, Colorado and California; in all three investigations CP leaders were cited for contempt when they refused to testify or produce records, and in two of the investigations they were denied bail until an appeals court directed their release on bail.[125]

The Wallace campaign faced severe harassment from many other sources aside from the executive branch of the federal government.[126] Liberal leaders and organizations such as Phillip Murray, the Americans for Democratic Action (ADA), the *Washington Post,* the *New York Post* and Walter Reuther were in the forefront of those who red-baited the Wallace campaign. ADA even paid for advertisements in major urban newspapers which listed the names of the Progressive Party's major contributors and the organizations on the Attorney General's list to which they belonged or had belonged, a tactic which was also used by HUAC in the Congressional Record with the cooperation of ADA. Progressive Party officials were called before two Congressional committees during the election campaign. Progressive party spokesmen were frequently subjected to harassing arrests, and in a number of cases were pelted with fruit, heckled into silence, assaulted, and in a couple of cases kidnapped. A Progressive Party worker was stabbed to death in Charleston, South Carolina, and Progressive workers were stabbed and injured in Calhoun Falls, South Carolina, and in Durham, North Carolina. In Illinois, the Progressive candidate for Senator was told by local police, after being stoned by a mob, "We don't like you any better than they do. Get out of town."[127] Progressive spokesmen were often banned from speaking in public facilities. Thus, Wallace and/or his vice-presidential running mate, Sen. Glen Taylor, were prohibited from speaking at the University of Cincinnati, the State University of Iowa, and the universities of Missouri, California and Michigan. As Curtis MacDougall has suggested, "To list the cities in which New Party leaders found it difficult or impossible to find adequate meeting places would mean to virtually compile a postal guide."[128]

On May 1, 1948, Progressive Party Vice-Presidential Candidate Sen. Glen Taylor was arrested in Birmingham, Alabama, for refusing to comply with city codes banning unsegregated meetings. Birmingham Police Commissioner Eugene "Bull" Connor, who would later become famous for using firehoses and police dogs on civil rights demonstrators in Birmingham in 1963, declared, "There's not enough room in town for Bull and the Commies."[129]

The repression and red-baiting suffered by the Progressive Party was not the only reason for its steady decline from the early part of

1948, when it was generally expected to receive about five million votes, to its final dismal showing of only 1.15 million votes in November.[130] Other important reasons included the Communist coup in Czechoslavakia in February, and the Berlin blockade of June, which undoubtedly increased support for Cold War policies; Truman's leftward shift on domestic policies, which cut heavily into Wallace's labor support; and internal squabbling and disorganization within the Progressive Party. But repression and red-baiting did take a serious toll.

Because the Progressive Party was never accused of any criminal activities, the degree of communist influence in it is irrelevant from the standpoint of the study of political repression.

While the exact degree of CP influence can probably never be determined, it is clear from both hostile and non-hostile sources that: 1) The CP played an important role in the Progressive Party; 2) many non-communists also supported the progressive party; 3) the formation of ADA as a liberal but vociferously anti-communist pressure group operating largely within the Democratic Party left opponents of Truman's foreign policy no place to go except for the Progressive Party; 4) the vicious red-baiting to which the Progressive Party was subjected, largely by liberals and the ADA, helped to lay the groundwork for McCarthyism, tended to identify all opposition to American foreign policy as subversive and tended to legitimize officially sponsored repression and vigilante assaults to which the Progressives were subjected; 5) the Truman administration's policy towards the progressives tended to intimidate the party's supporters and lead non-communist elements to leave the party and thus increase the CP influence; 6) by red-baiting the Progressives, the Democrats were largely able to avoid being red-baited themselves during the 1948 campaign; and 7) the net effect of the red-baiting and repression suffered by the Progressives was to stiffle any debate over American foreign policy and to seriously impair the party's chances of electoral success and survival.

The real casualty of the 1948 election campaign was not the Progressive Party but freedom of debate over foreign policy in America. The collapse of the Progressive Party meant "the collapse of the only movement that might conceivably have made a contribution in keeping alive a genuine discussion of foreign policy alternatives."[131] After 1948, the mere presentation of views contrary to the official foreign policy "line" moved "into the realm of treasonous or at least 'un-American' activity."[132] Thus, Richard Scandrett, an establishment lawyer from New York, lamented in his private correspondence in October, 1948, "Even to suggest in a whisper . . . nowadays that every Russian is not a cannibal is to invite incarceration for subversive activities."[133]

Despite the signs of increasing repression that were virtually omnipresent in American society by 1948, the victory of Truman in the elections that year ironically gave civil libertarians a faint ray of hope. Since Truman's repressive actions were viewed in many liberal quarters as mainly an attempt to head off Republican exploitation of the "red" issue, it appeared that his 1948 victory signalled that he had gained control of the issue and that further repression would not be necessary.

The Republicans had never ceased to agitate the "red" question, even after Truman had instituted the loyalty program and consistently stressed anti-communism in both his domestic and foreign policies. For example, during the 1947 congressional session, Republicans had pushed for congressional enactment of a loyalty program to substitute for Truman's program and had placed strong pressure on the State Department for the firing or transfer of allegedly disloyal employees. In 1948, a high-ranking State Department official resigned after Republican Congressman Fred Suseby of Illinois had attacked him on the grounds that he had an allegedly leftist second cousin. During the 1948 presidential election year, six different Republican-controlled congressional committees investigated communist influence in the government or in other areas of American life. In May, 1948, the House passed over administration opposition the so-called Mundt-Nixon bill which would have required the CP and "communist front" groups to register with the government and would have barred members of such groups from government employment.[134]

While Truman had cooperated fully with HUAC during the 1947 legislative session, as Republican use of the "red" issue increasingly focused on the issue of communist infiltration into government, Truman initiated an open break with HUAC. In March 1948, HUAC issued its first post-war attack on a major government official by releasing a report which termed Dr. Edward U. Condon, director of the National Bureau of Standards "one of the weakest links in our atomic security." The attack on Condon proved to be a malicious mixture of innuendos and irrelevancies — such as the fact that his wife was of Czechoslavakian descent — and the Truman administration came strongly to Condon's defense. Both the Commerce Department and the Atomic Energy Commission publicly announced that they had cleared Condon, and when the House voted 300-29 on April 22, 1948, to demand that it be given access to Condon's loyalty file, Truman refused to comply (earlier, on March 13, Truman had issued an executive order requiring that all loyalty files be kept confidential).[135] In September, 1948, Truman publicly shook hands with Condon at a meeting of the American Association for the Advancement of Science and warned that "reckless or unfair" attacks might drive America's scientists out of the laboratories and that scientific work might be made impossible "by the creation of an atmosphere in which no man feels safe against the public airing of unfounded rumors, gossip and villification."[136]

During the presidential campaign, Republican candidate Thomas E. Dewey suggested the Democrats had consciously employed communists in government, but did not lay major stress on the issue. However, Republican-controlled Congressional committees, especially HUAC and the Senate Committee on Expenditures in the Executive Branch, issued or heard sensational charges of communist infiltration of the executive branch. The most widely publicized of these charges came in testimony before HUAC by ex-communists Whittaker Chambers and Elizabeth Bentley, who claimed that there had been a number of communist cells operating within various government agencies before and during World War II.[137] HUAC Chairman Thomas later wrote that the Republican National Committee had urged him to hold these hearings to "keep the heat on Harry Truman."[138]

Truman and Attorney General Clark, who had both repeatedly agitated the "red" issue when it seemed to promise increasing yields in terms of support of administration foreign policy, suddenly became civil libertarians in response to the HUAC hearings. Truman suggested that the hearings had impeded and made "more difficult our effort to cope with communism" by having "recklessly cast a cloud of suspicion over the most loyal civil service in the world." He termed the charges a "red herring" and a "plain malicious lie." Clark challenged the Republicans to name "any communists now in the executive branch" and termed one of the congressional reports charging communist infiltration of the government a "mass of incorrect and misleading statements."[139]

Although Truman's own red-baiting of the Wallace campaign had largely succeeded in blunting the Republican use of the issue against him, his electoral victory was widely interpreted as indicating he had now gained control of the "red" issue and that it would die a natural death. For example, Washington saw general speculation shortly after the election that the new Democratic-controlled House would either abolish HUAC altogether or let it wither away. Truman even referred to HUAC at one point as a dead agency.[140]

But just as the "red" issue seemed about to go away, a series of sensational developments in late 1948 and 1949 caused a new escalation of anti-communist hysteria and took control of the issue away from Truman again. The first major development occurred when Whittaker Chambers suddenly changed his story about Alger Hiss, a former State Department official. In his testimony before HUAC and before a federal grand jury, Chambers had stated that Hiss had been a member of a CP cell while serving in the State Department, but had repeatedly denied that Hiss was involved in any espionage activities. However, on November 17, 1948, after Hiss had sued him for libel, Chambers suddenly produced State Department documents which he said Hiss had turned over to him in the 1930's. As a result of this new material, Hiss was indicted for perjury (the statute of limitations precluded espionage charges) on December 14, 1948, and was tried during the spring and summer of 1949 at the same time that the top CP leaders indicted in July, 1948 were being tried.[141]

Because Hiss became widely identified in the public mind as a representative of the New Deal, the Hiss case soon took on an overriding symbolic importance, as if the jury's determination in this single case would by itself prove or disprove Republican charges of communist influence or domination of the New Deal which had been made for fifteen years. Thus it was not surprising that when the jury in the Hiss case could not agree on a verdict, Republican Congressman Richard M. Nixon and three other members of HUAC accused the trial judge of bias and demanded that his fitness be investigated. Nixon further charged that the Truman administration was "extremely anxious that nothing bad happen" to Hiss for fear a guilty verdict would prove the truth of charges of communist infiltration of government "during the New Deal days."[142] Hiss was retried in the late autumn and early winter of 1949-50, and found guilty on January 21, 1950. The Hiss case has remained the subject of heated popular and scholarly debate, but no convincing evidence has yet been disclosed that would establish Hiss's innocence; therefore it must be regarded as important in fostering a climate which was conducive to political repression, rather than the result of political repression. In early 1976, the last of a long series of books on the Hiss case, by a journalist, proclaimed Hiss's innocence, while at the same time Smith College historian Allen Weinstein announced, after having studied fifteen thousand pages of FBI material on the case recently made public, that Hiss had "lied repeatedly" and people "who once believed in Alger Hiss" might be persuaded upon publication of his own book that Hiss "stole the documents in question and that Whittaker Chambers told the truth."[123]

While the Hiss case helped to keep the "red" issue alive throughout 1949, several other developments added fuel to the fires of hysteria. Another sensational spy case broke on March 6, 1949, when Judith Coplon, a Justice Department employee, was arrested for espionage. She was tried and convicted in the summer of 1949 on two counts of espionage, and then tried and convicted on an additional count in early 1950. Eventually her convictions were overturned after it was revealed that she had been subject to illegal FBI wiretapping and that the FBI had destroyed records of some of the taps in order to protect the repeated statements of FBI agents made in court that the agency had *not* wiretapped in the case.[144]

In addition to the Hiss and Coplon cases, the announcement on September 23, 1949, that the Soviet Union had exploded its first nuclear bomb, the conviction of the CP leaders tried under the Smith Act on October 14, 1949 and the final collapse of the Chinese Nationalist Government in December, 1949, all had a severely inflammatory effect in boosting anti-communist hysteria.[145]

One typical indicator of the climate of 1949 was the incident of "Hans and the thirty-two grams." On May 12, 1949 Rep. Sterling Cole of New York publicly charged that Hans Freistadt, a naturalized citizen and a communist, was studying at the University of North Carolina under an Atomic Energy Commission fellowship. A few days later the press reported that thirty-two grams of uranium used for atomic bomb production were missing from the Argonne Laboratory in Chicago. Virtually all of the missing uranium was quickly recovered, but in the meantime a major congressional campaign began to bar AEC fellowships to alleged "subversives," even though in the case of Freistadt and most other AEC fellowship recipients, only non-secret research was involved. On May 24, the University of North Carolina fired Freistadt; shortly afterwards the AEC announced that a loyalty oath and non-communist affidavit would be required of all fellows. However, even this action did not prove satisfactory; Congress passed legislation in the fall of 1949 requiring that AEC fellowships be barred to any person advocating or belonging to any organization advocating the overthrow of the government by force and violence or any persons of whom the AEC had reasonable grounds to believe was "disloyal by character or association." The end result of the affair was the virtual destruction of the AEC's fellowship program. On December 16, 1949, the AEC announced it had "drastically reduced" the number of research fellowships for 1950 "because of the opposition of many scientists and scholars to loyalty investigations of applicants in non-secret fields." Whereas the AEC had previously been awarding about five hundred such fellowships per year, the number of applicants declined so rapidly that only seventy-five new fellowships were granted for 1950 and only one hundred seventy-five existing fellowships were renewed.[146]

The Truman administration did little during 1949 to attempt to keep anti-communist hysteria under control. For example, Truman publicly labeled the CP leaders "traitors" during their trial, and along with Commissioner of Education Earl J. McGrath announced his support of the position of the National Education Association that all CP members should be fired from teaching positions.[147] In May, 1949, the federal government indicted Harry Bridges for perjury in connection with his testimony that he was not a Communist at his 1945 naturalization hearing (after the failure of the Roosevelt administration's attempt to deport him). Attorney General Clark publicly stated that a successful prosecution of Bridges might "break" a simultaneous strike in Hawaii led by Bridge's International Longshoremen's and Warehousemen's Union (ILWU) and noted that Hawaii "is the only spot at present where our domestic communist problem is serious." Two committees formed to defend Bridges were placed on the Attorney General's list. (Bridges' perjury conviction was overturned by the Supreme Court in 1953).[148] In late 1949, the scope of the federal loyalty program was vastly expanded when the Defense Department announced that private employees performing work for Defense Department contractors which involved access to classified information would be denied such access (and thus, in effect, private employment for such firms) for essentially the same reasons that would cast doubt on a government employee's loyalty. According to a Congressional committee estimate made in 1955, the number of private employees thus subjected to the government loyalty program under the Defense Department ruling, together with the much smaller number of private employees who had been subjected to an Atomic Energy Commission clearance program since 1946, amounted to close to three million persons.[149]

During HUAC hearings in 1949-50, the FBI resumed its open collaboration with the now-Democratically-controlled committee. In fact the major purpose of HUAC hearings during these years seemed to be that of "publicizing information in FBI files."[150] While HUAC procedures became somewhat more restrained, the committee's hearings continued to generate sensational scare headlines. In addition to putting pressure on left-wing factions in CIO unions, HUAC took aim at the Progressive Party and several alleged CP "front groups," and added considerably to fears of atomic espionage by publicizing charges already well known to Justice Department officials concerning alleged CP espionage at the University of California's Berkeley Radiation Laboratory during World War II.[151]

As anti-communist hysteria grew in 1949, the Republican Party increasingly moved to make the issue of communism-in-government their own once more. The Republican Party had fully expected to win the 1948 election; the Truman upset led to increasing frustration and desperation within the party, and a conviction that the election had been lost because Dewey had been too much of a "me-too" candidate and had exercised too much restraint on, among other items, the "red" issue. As the Chinese nationalists collapsed in 1949, a number of Republican leaders began to link the "loss of China" with the "reds in government issue." Thus, on April 15, 1949, Republican Senator Styles Bridges called for a congressional investigation of the State Department and suggested that Secretary of State Dean Acheson was guilty of "what might be called sabotage" of the Chinese Nationalists. A few days later, Senator William Knowland charged that "if ever a non-communist government in the world has reason to feel betrayed, that government is the Republic of China." In early 1950, Sen. Robert Taft charged "the State Department has been guided by a left-wing group who obviously have wanted to get rid of Chiang, and were willing to turn China over to the Communists for that purpose."[152]

The communism issue was stirred up to new fever heat by a rapid series of startling developments in early 1950. On January 21, Hiss was convicted in a second trial; a few days later Acheson said that as an old friend, "I do not intend to turn my back on Alger Hiss."[153] On January 31, Truman announced the U.S. had decided to build a hydrogen bomb. On February 3, it was revealed that the British had arrested Dr. Klaus

Fuchs, who had worked in the U.S. on the atom bomb project, on charges of giving atomic secrets to the Russians.[154]

The response of the Republican Party to these developments was to further agitate the communist issue. Sen. Homer Capehart asked:

> How much more are we going to have to take? Fuchs and Acheson and Hiss and hydrogen bombs threatening outside and New Dealism eating away the vitals of the nation. In the name of heaven, is this the best America can do?[155]

Rep. Robert Rich of Pennsylvania suggested that no one was "working with Joe Stalin" more than Secretary Acheson. On February 6, the Republican National Committee and the congressional party leadership issued a statement of principles which deplored the "dangerous degree to which Communists and their fellow travelers have been employed in important government posts" and termed the Truman administration "soft" on "government employees and officials who hold or support communist attitudes."[156] During Lincoln day speeches across the nation on February 9, 1950, Republican orators picked up this theme. Thus, Rep. Richard Nixon termed the Hiss case "a small part of the whole shocking story of communist espionage in the United States."[157] Another congressman who chose that day to stress the communist issue was a senator from Wisconsin named Joseph Raymond McCarthy.

The Rise of McCarthy, 1950-1952

By the time Sen. McCarthy came to public prominence in early 1950, anti-communism had already been established as a major issue by both the Truman administration and by the Republicans; the only real item of contention was who would control the issue. Truman had used the anti-communist issue to foster his foreign policies and to beat back left-wing opposition; the Republicans had used it as a battering ram against the Democrats. The personal role of McCarthy in fostering anti-communist hysteria has thus been considerably overemphasized in most accounts of what has come to be known as "McCarthyism." Even after his rise to public prominence in early 1950, "McCarthyism" cannot be understood without taking into account the following facts: 1) McCarthy received strong support for his charges by leading Republicans; 2) McCarthy's charges came during the same year that the Korean War broke out and that the Rosenberg atomic-espionage case developed; and 3) the response of the Truman administration to McCarthy's charges and increasing anti-communist hysteria was confused and inept, with Truman frequently mouthing libertarian sentiments, but more often acting in ways to further heighten the repression of dissent.

Although leading Republicans at first held back somewhat from endorsing McCarthy's initial charges of widespread communist infiltration of the State Department, as his charges gained increasing publicity and the issue became more overtly partisan, McCarthy soon picked up their support.[158] Thus, while Sen. Taft called McCarthy's initial Senate speech repeating his charges of widespread CP infiltration of the State Department a "perfectly reckless performance," within a short time he was telling McCarthy, "If one case doesn't work, try another."[159] After a Senate Republican Policy Committee meeting March 22, 1950, Taft announced that while support of McCarthy was not a party matter, Republican senators would in fact assist McCarthy.[160] As McCarthy repeated his charges and presented his case, beginning in March, to a rather clearly partisan Democratic-controlled subcommittee of the Senate Foreign Relations Committee, chaired by Sen. Millard Tydings, Republican leaders continued to aid him. Thus, Rep. Richard Nixon advised McCarthy and allowed McCarthy to use material from his personal files to bolster McCarthy's case. This Republican support was a crucial factor in the continued heavy publicity accorded to McCarthy, and, along with McCarthy's own genius for publicity, his ability to manipulate the press and his luck in tying the communists-in-government issue to the "loss of China" issue, helped obscure the fact that he was able to prove none of his charges.[161]

A series of events in 1950 greatly aided McCarthy and the Republicans in their exploitation of the anti-communist issue. During several primary elections in May, 1950, Republicans and Democrats alike used the "red" issue in successful campaigns. Beginning in May and continuing through the early fall of 1950, a series of nine arrests connected to what appeared to be a massive atomic espionage ring (the "Rosenberg case") occurred. Although only four or five of these arrests turned out to be linked to atomic espionage, the highly sensational treatment of these events by the press and the administration greatly heightened anti-communist hysteria in general and fear of communist infiltration of the government in particular. The outbreak of the Korean War in late June, and the rapid introduction of American troops was reflected in another drastic increase in anti-communist hysteria and a surge of repressive measures passed on both the local and national levels. The harsh and seemingly partisan attack on McCarthy issued by the Democratic majority on the Tydings Committee in July, and the subsequent adoption of this report by the Senate on a strict party-line vote demonstrated the Republican commitment to McCarthy and discredited Democratic opposition as seemingly only partisan in nature.[162]

The heightened anti-communist hysteria of late 1950 was reflected in three new federal laws. The so-called Mundt-Nixon or Internal Security Act had been passed by the House in 1948 and had been recommended for passage by the Senate Judiciary Committee in the spring of 1950 without making noticeable progress. In July, 1950, however, the Senate Republican Policy Committee placed a version of the Mundt-Nixon bill on its must list and in August, 1950, HUAC reported out a similar bill in the House. During the same month Truman sent a message to Congress which, while opposing the Mundt-Nixon bill, proposed several measures to expand existing espionage, foreign agents registration, and wiretap laws. Brushing aside Truman's proposals, both Houses passed the Mundt-Nixon bill by overwhelming majorities together with an amendment sponsored by "liberals" authorizing the use of concentration camps to detain suspected subversives in time of national emergency, and amendments sponsored by Sen. Pat McCarran tightening control of entering alien radicals.[163]

The major provisions of the Internal Security Act of 1950, passed over Truman's veto, included the following.[164] 1) It was declared illegal for any person to knowingly "combine, conspire or agree with any other persons to perform any act which would substantially contribute to the establishment within the United States of a totalitarian dictatorship" (aside from proposing constitutional amendments to this end). 2) "Communist-action organizations," (defined as organizations substantially controlled by the foreign government controlling the world communist movement, which operate "primarily to advance the objectives of such world Communist movement") and "communist front organizations," (defined as organizations controlled by a communist-action organization and operating for the purpose of aiding such, without directly engaging in the advancement of illegal communist objectives), were required to register with the Attorney General and report names of officers, sources of funds, and in the case of communist-action organizations, membership lists. 3) Organizations and members of organizations refusing to register voluntarily could have action brought by the Attorney General before a five-man Subversive Activities Control Board (SACB) which would be empowered to hold hearings and order registration of communist front and communist action organizations and members of communist-action organizations. 4) While holding office and membership in communist organizations was specifically declared to be lawful, members of registered organizations were barred from government employment or employment in private industries performing governmental defense work and barred from applying for or using passports. 5) Registered organizations were denied income tax exemptions and contributions to such organizations could not be deducted for income tax purposes. 6) Registered organizations were required to label their publications and broadcasts as originating from a "communist organization." 7) In event of invasion, declaration of war or insurrection, the President was authorized to declare an "internal security emergency" during which the Attorney General was empowered to detain all persons for whom there was "reasonable ground" for believing "probably will engage in, or probably will conspire with others to engage in, acts of espionage or sabotage," with provisions for administrative hearings, appeals and judicial review, but no court trial or confrontation and cross examination of adverse witnesses. 8) Aliens who had at any time been "members of or affiliated with" the "communist or other totalitarian party" of any country in the world or who advocated doctrines of any "form of totalitarianism" were barred from entry to the U.S. and made deportable, with no hearings required for such exclusions or deportations if information might be disclosed at such hearings which would be contrary to the best interests of the U.S. 9) Aliens seeking entry to the U.S. or engaging while in the U.S. in "activities prejudical to the public interest" or activities which would endanger the "welfare, safety or security" of the U.S. were subject to similar penalties. 10) Persons naturalized after January 1, 1951, who within the next five years became members of such organizations could be denaturalized. 11) Aliens who were members of communist-front organizations were barred from naturalization unless they could show that they had left such organizations within three months of the issuance of a registration order against such groups.

The Internal Security Act was clearly one of the most massive onslaughts against freedom of speech and association ever launched in American history. Much as criminal syndicalism laws had made it possible to repress the IWW without making it necessary to show any specific wrongdoing, the Internal Security Act was designed to make it impossible for organizations designated as communist-front and communist-action groups to function, simply by so designating them. The emergency detention provision of the bill provided legal authority for mass round-ups of dissidents and their indefinite detention without trial simply because the Attorney General believed that they "probably" would engage in future illegal conduct. Thus, the loyalty program's attempt to predict future illegal behavior and use this as a basis for severely punitive action was to be extended to the entire population during an "internal security emergency." The alien control provisions of the law followed the previous trend of such legislation towards providing penalties for increasingly vague activities, affiliations and beliefs. Now aliens could be barred or deported not merely for membership in the American CP but also for affiliations with foreign communist or "other totalitarian parties;" further they were put on notice not to engage in activities "prejudicial to the public interest," a phrase which any intelligent alien would have been correct in interpreting to mean no political activities of a controversial nature.

The passage of the emergency detention provisions of the Internal Security Act created, unknown to the Congress, a dilemma for the FBI, which had been maintaining a list of persons to arrest under the Justice Department's plan of August, 1948, which was considerably more flexible in its provisions, since it could be invoked in a time of "threatened invasion" against "dangerous" persons, suspended the writ of habeas corpus and barred legal rules of evidence and the possibility of judicial review. The FBI initiated a long series of meetings and correspondence with the Justice Department, inquiring whether the secret FBI arrest lists should be maintained under the 1948 plan or the more restrictive 1950 law, which the FBI told the Department would make it more difficult for the FBI to "discharge its responsibilities . . . effectively," and would force it to drop "many people" from its lists "whom we feel constitute a danger to the internal security of the country." Finally, the Justice Department informed the FBI in November, 1952, that it was the Department's intention to "proceed under the program" originally outlined in 1948.[165] At its peak in 1955, the FBI's Security Index list of persons to be arrested in a national emergency included twenty-six thousand individuals including educators, labor union organizers, journalists, lawyers, doctors, scientists and "individuals who could potentially furnish financial or material aid" to any enemy. The Security Index was reduced to about twelve thousand persons by 1958, and those dropped from the list were placed on a separate Reserve Index of persons who would not be arrested in a national emergency but would receive "priority investigation and/or action" following Security Index arrests since they were "in a position to influence others against the national interest or are likely to furnish material financial assistance to subversive elements due to their subversive associations and ideology." Among the persons listed on the Reserve Index, according to the Senate Intelligence Committee's report of April 1976, were author Norman Mailer and a professor "who merely praised the Soviet Union to his class." As late as 1962, ten thousand names were on the Reserve Index, and by the time the Internal Security Act was repealed in 1971, twelve thousand persons were still listed on the Security Index.[166]

Meanwhile, Congress was blissfully unaware of these developments, and assuming that the 1950 law would be followed by the Justice Department, appropriated $775,000 in 1952 to set up six detention camps in Arizona, Florida, Pennsylvania, Oklahoma and California, including Tule Lake, California, one of the major camps used to house Japanese-Americans during World War II.[167]

Congress supplemented the Internal Security Act with two other laws which reflected the increasing tide of repression in late 1950. In August, the so-called Magnusson Act was passed, authorizing the president to safeguard American ships and waterfront facilities from "sabotage and other subversive acts." President Truman soon issued an executive order to implement this bill which barred any person — whether in government or private employment — from seagoing employment or access to restricted waterfront areas unless the commandant of the Coast Guard "is satisfied that the character and habits of life of the applicant are such as to authorize the belief that the presence of such individual on board a vessel or within a waterfront facility would not be inimical to the security of the United States."[168]

Also in August, Congress extended the right of summary dismissal from government employment for security reasons which had previously been restricted to the secretary of state, the AEC, and the armed forces secretaries, to the secretaries of Defense, Commerce and the Treasury (for the Coast Guard), the Attorney General, the chairman of the National Security Resources Board, the director of the National Advisory Committee for Aeronautics and any other agency head designated by the President.[169]

As anti-communist hysteria increased in the wake of McCarthy's charges, the Korean War and the atomic espionage arrests, Republican charges reached a new pitch of irresponsibility. For example, Senate Republican Leader Kenneth Wherry charged that Secretary Acheson was stained with "the blood of our boys in Korea," Republican Sen. Andrew Schoeppel accused the Secretary of the Interior of pro-communist leanings, and Sen. William Jenner called Secretary of Defense George Marshall a "living lie," a "front man for traitors" and "either an unsuspecting stooge or an actual co-conspirator with the most treasonable array of political cutthroats ever turned loose in the Executive Branch." Sen. Taft asserted that the "greatest Kremlin asset in our history has been the pro-communist group in the State Department who promoted at every opportunity the Communist cause in China."[170]

If there was any doubt by late 1950 that "McCarthyism" had been fully embraced by the Republican Party, it was dispelled by the November elections. Taft announced that a Republican victory in the elections would remove those who had shown "continued sympathy for communism and socialism." McCarthy was the most sought after speaker by Republican hopefuls, receiving two thousand invitations to speak, more than all other Republican spokesmen combined. The head of the Republican House Campaign Committee stated that the Democratic Party was in the hands of "fuzzy minded pinks," while the Republican National Committee's election handbook for candidates had as its central thesis the idea that a dark conspiracy was at the root of America's international troubles.[171]

Although Republican gains in the election were quite modest — five seats picked up in the Senate and twenty-eight in the House, below Republican gains in the last three off-year elections — national attention was focused on several important races where Republicans who had particularly pinned the "soft on communism" label on their opponents were successful. Especial attention was given to the Senate race in Illinois, where Everett Dirksen whipped Democratic Senate Leader Scott Lucas; the Senate race in California, where Rep. Richard Nixon had followed the example of Sen. Helen Gaghagan Douglas' Democratic primary opponents and stressed her alleged repeated votes "against measures that are for the security of this country;" and in Maryland, where McCarthy personally campaigned in a successful effort to beat Sen. Tydings, whom even President Franklin Roosevelt had been unable to oust in his abortive purge of conservative Democrats in 1938.[172]

In retrospect, it is clear that the effect of the communist issue in the 1950 election was overrated, and that local issues and a general disaffection with the Truman administration were also extremely important. Further, a number of races where the "red" issue was stressed and yet Democratic candidates emerged victorious were somehow overlooked. For example, in Connecticut Sen. Brion McMahon held on to his seat despite McCarthy's personal intervention; in Missouri, Thomas Hennings won a Senate seat despite his strong support for civil liberties and a personal appearance by McCarthy; in New York, Sen. Herbert Lehman won re-election although he had vouched for Alger Hiss' loyalty; and in Washington Sen. Warren Magnusson won re-election despite a red-baiting campaign against him.[173] Nevertheless, in the atmosphere which prevailed in November, 1950, fearful men were inclined to see only that which fed their fears, and the net effect of the elections was to vastly increase both McCarthy's personal power and prestige and the support given to him by Republicans, and to decrease the willingness of Democratic senators and others to oppose him. In effect, an exaggerated perception of McCarthy's power "ultimately enlarged his power itself."[174]

Anti-communist hysteria and the forces of repression were fueled throughout 1951 and 1952 by continuing charges of communist influence made by McCarthy and other Republicans, extensive hearings held by HUAC and its newly-formed Senate rival, the Senate Internal Security Subcommittee (SISS), by the continuing war in Korea and by the Rosenberg trial in 1951, which ended in a guilty verdict and the handing down of a death sentence for Ethel and Julius Rosenberg.[175] (The Rosenberg case has been a subject of continuing controversy, including allegations that the government introduced forged evidence and that government witnesses were pressured by the FBI into concocting stories damaging to the defendants.[176] However, given the lack of any conclusive evidence along these lines, the case is not treated as an example of political repression *per se* herein; nevertheless it must be recognized that the general climate of the country during the trial was not conducive to a reasoned trying of the case and that the government's introduction of evidence about the left-wing affiliations of the Rosenbergs was prejudicial. Certainly the judge's accusation, made while pronouncing sentence, that the Rosenbergs were responsible for "the Communist aggression in Korea, with the resultant casualties exceeding fifty thousand"[177] was without any evidentiary basis. As Herbert Parmet has written, even if the Rosenbergs were clearly guilty, "it is impossible to disassociate the execution from the contemporary hysteria."[178] In November, 1975, the Justice Department released documents which included alleged statements by Julius Rosenberg confessing that he was an espionage agent to a cellmate who was an FBI informer.[179] Smith College historian Allen Weinstein stated in February, 1976, that based on an examination of thousands of pages of Justice Department material on the Rosenberg case, there was no "substantial evidence" that had "yet emerged" to indicate the Rosenbergs were the "victims of callous conspiracies designed by FBI officials and others highly placed in government.")[180]

The Republican identification with McCarthy was made clearer than ever during the 1952 election. Even before the Republican convention, presidential hopeful Dwight D. Eisenhower attacked the Truman administration for the "loss" of China and for weakness against communism abroad. Red-baiting of the Democrats was a major staple at the Republican convention, as Gen. Douglas MacArthur, Rep. Martin and Sen. McCarthy all gave speeches to the assembled Republicans. The Republican platform charged that Democrats had "shielded traitors to the Nation in high places" and had "so undermined the foundations of our Republic as to threaten its existence." As his vice-presidential candidate, Eisenhower selected Sen. Nixon, whose entire reputation had been based upon his role in the Hiss case.[181]

During the campaign, Eisenhower raised the "communist issue" in thirty speeches. He publicly appeared with Sen. Jenner and Sen. McCarthy, both of whom had viciously attacked Eisenhower's close friend, Secretary of Defense Marshall. In one famous incident, Eisenhower deleted a defense of Marshall from a speech to be given while campaigning in Wisconsin with McCarthy. While Eisenhower lauded Nixon as a man who had seen the threat of those "who plot against" the American system, Nixon blasted Truman as soft on communism and repeatedly attacked Democratic presidential contender Adlai Stevenson for testifying to Alger Hiss's good character in 1949. McCarthy himself campaigned widely during the election, and the general Republican victory coupled with his own re-election and the defeat of four Democratic incumbents he had campaigned against added to the legend of McCarthy's political power. Once again, however, it seems clear that the power of McCarthy was overrated — both in his Wisconsin senate race and in every non-southern state where he campaigned, the Democratic senatorial candidate ran ahead of the national ticket, indicating that it was Eisenhower who was the real power in the election.[182] But what counted was that McCarthy "was believed to be more powerful than ever, and because of this 'simple fact' he was."[183]

The response of the Truman administration to the Republican-McCarthyist assault in 1950-52 was confused and inept, and in the long run only fostered repression and hysteria. During the first months of McCarthy's charges, there were signs that Truman and the Democrats were planning a concerted campaign of opposition to him. A number of Democratic senators reacted angrily to McCarthy's initial charges and the Tydings Committee was set up in February, 1950, after the Senate Democratic Policy Committee decided that McCarthy had to be investigated and discredited. The Truman Administration actively cooperated with the Tydings Committee in this endeavor; for example Truman allowed the committee to examine secret loyalty files which disproved some of McCarthy's charges and personally met with members of the Tydings Committee to discuss how the communist issue could be defused.[184]

In the spring of 1950, Democrats opened up a wide-swinging public attack on McCarthy. Truman charged that the claims of McCarthy and other Republicans who attempted to "sabotage" American foreign policy were the Kremlin's "greatest asset;" Vice-President Alben Barkley denounced those who would "abridge our freedoms and sow rumors and suspicions among us;" and Secretary Acheson compared McCarthy to the mad slayer of Camden, New Jersey.[185] On April 25, Truman declared that the "internal security of the United States is not seriously menaced by the communists in this country," whom he termed a "noisy but small and universally despised group" that was proportionately weaker than "in any other large country on earth." On May 29, Truman wrote the commander-in-chief of the Veterans of Foreign Wars that

> all this howl about organizations a fellow belongs to gives me a pain in the neck. I'd be willing to bet my right eye that you yourself and I have joined some organization that we wish we hadn't. It hasn't hurt me any and I don't think it has hurt you any.[186]

Occasional flashes of resistance by Truman to McCarthyite pressures were also shown at other times in 1950-52. It clearly took considerable courage for Truman to veto the Internal Security Act, considering the atmosphere prevailing in September, 1950, and Truman stood up under comparable pressure in nominating Phillip Jessup to be a delegate to the United Nations General Assembly in September, 1951, after Jessup had come under strong attack from McCarthy.[187] In January, 1951, Truman established a bipartisan committee to investigate the question of "communist infiltration in the government" which he clearly hoped would head off McCarthy. At the first meeting of the commission, Truman told the group he was "anxious that this job be done in the manner that will stop witch-hunting and give us the facts." However, the operations of the commission were blocked by anti-administration senators who refused to exempt commission members from the application of certain conflict of interest statutes that were normally routinely waived for members of temporary commissions.[188]

In May, 1951 Truman sent a memo to his special counsel, Charles Murphy, stating that he had been "very much disturbed with the action of some of these (loyalty) boards and I want some way to put a stop to their un-American activities."[189] In July, 1951, Truman requested the Interdepartmental Committee on Internal Security of the National

Security Council to investigate the administration of the loyalty program; the report subsequently submitted in April, 1952, amounted to a severe condemnation of certain aspects of the program.[190] In August, 1951, Truman delivered a severe public attack on McCarthy to an American Legion audience. He referred to "this terrible business" of smear and accusation, attacked those who were "chipping away our basic freedoms" and "trying to divide and confuse us and tear up the bill of rights" by resorting to character assassination, and asserted that "real Americanism" meant protection for freedom of dissenters to speak "regardless of how much we may disagree with them." All Americans were in peril, Truman told the Legion, "when even one American — who has done nothing wrong — is forced by fear to shut his mind and close his mouth." In January, 1952, Truman referred to McCarthy as a "pathological liar" at a press conference. When he heard reports in mid-1952 that State Department official John Paton Davies might be indicted for perjury as a result of his testimony before a congressional committee, he wrote Attorney General James P. McGranery that this was "just another example of witchhunting" and told McGranery to check with him before any action was taken.[191]

The problem with the Truman administration's counterattack against McCarthy was that it was riddled with inconsistencies. While he was attacking McCarthy in the spring of 1950, Truman stressed how strongly his own administration was fighting and jailing communists.[192] While Truman downplayed the communist threat in April, 1950, in May, FBI Director J. Edgar Hoover stated that while the number of communists might not be large, this fact had been cited "by the ignorant and the apologists and appeasers of communism in our country as minimizing the danger of these subversives in our midst."[193] Meanwhile, Attorney General McGrath was warning that there were "many" communists in America and "they are everywhere — in factories, offices, butcher shops, on street corners, in private business — and each carries in himself the germs of death for society." On July 28, 1950, the Justice Department issued a statement warning that communists "utilize cleverly camouflaged movements, such as some peace groups and civil rights organizations, to achieve their sinister purposes."[194] In vetoing the Internal Security Act in September, 1950, Truman undercut the civil libertarian arguments which he made in his veto message by stressing above all that the bill as enacted would "help" communists instead of hurting them.[195] It is obvious that the effect of these examples of Truman administration rhetoric could only undermine any campaign to combat McCarthy, since it basically conceded many of McCarthy's arguments.

Even more damaging for American civil liberties than some of the administration's *rhetoric,* however, were continuing *actions* which added to the climate of repression. Despite Truman's misgivings over the operations of the loyalty program, in April, 1951, Truman changed the standard for loyalty firings from the existence of "reasonable grounds" for the belief that the employee involved was disloyal to "reasonable doubt" as to the loyalty of the individual. Whereas hearing boards previously had to establish reasonable grounds for belief in guilt, now all they had to do was establish reasonable doubt as to innocence, a complete reversal of normal American standards of justice.

As a result of this change in standards, the Loyalty Review Board (LRB) ordered that all cases decided prior to May 1, 1951, in which an adverse decision of a hearing board had been reversed by the LRB, all cases in which a favorable decision of a hearing board had been reviewed by the LRB, and all cases in which an individual cleared under the old standards had been given a new appointment be reopened. Furthermore, any case in which new information was developed was to be reassessed as a whole under the new standards. This policy led to the reopening of 565 cases that had previously been decided favorably for the employees involved. Subsequently, John Stewart Service, a State Department official who had been arrested and later cleared in the *Amerasia* affair and who had long been a prime target of McCarthy, was fired by the State Department on the recommendation of the LRB even though he had been repeatedly cleared by the State Department's Loyalty Board.[196]

Beginning in February, 1951, the State Department refused to issue passports to persons about whom it had information which gave it "reason to believe" the applicant was "knowingly a member of a Communist organization or that his conduct abroad is likely to be contrary to the best interest of the United States." Under these regulations three hundred persons were denied passports. In 1952 the State Department issued new regulations which denied passports to: 1) CP members or those who had recently terminated their support of the CP under conditions indicating that they continued to act "in furtherance of the interests and under the discipline of the Communist Party;" 2) persons whose activities supported the CP under circumstances suggesting communist direction; and 3) persons about whom there was "reason to believe" they were going abroad to knowingly and willfully "advance the communist movement." Under these guidelines — which punished individuals on the basis of predictions of future perfectly legal behavior, since it was not yet a crime to "advance the communist movement" — passports were denied to Dr. Linus Pauling (until he was awarded a Nobel prize) and to Dr. Otto Nathan, an internationally known economist. The State Department also stepped up its policy of barring even temporary entry into the U.S. to politically suspect aliens, with the result that some of the most distinguished scientists, artists and men of letters of the world were barred from the U.S. In several cases scientific congresses had to be cancelled due to State Department policies.[197] Among the most prominent persons barred from temporary entry by the State Department because of their alleged past or present political affiliations were Pablo Picasso and Joseph Krips, the conductor of the Vienna State Opera, who "was forbidden to fill a summer engagement with the Chicago Symphony Orchestra because he had previously conducted performances at Moscow and Leningrad."[198] Charles Chaplin also fell victim to the tightened up policies. Chaplin was a British subject who had been living in the U.S.; during one of his travels abroad in October, 1952, Attorney General McGranery announced that Chaplin would be barred from re-entry, and the film star subsequently surrendered his re-entry permit in April, 1953.[199]

Armed with the expanded authority granted in the Internal Security Act of 1950 to deport, denaturalize and exclude from permanent entry "subversive" aliens (authority which was essentially reconfirmed by the McCarran Walter Immigration Act of 1952, which eased somewhat the automatic ban on entry of aliens who had ever belonged to "totalitarian" parties of any country but added the provision that the President could ban any alien whose entry he deemed "detrimental to the interests of the United States"[200]), the Truman administration also stepped up its campaign of harassment directed against foreigners living in or seeking to live in the U.S. This campaign was later enthusiastically continued by the Eisenhower administration; by December 1953, fifteen editors of radical and foreign language newspapers, including Cedric Belfrage of the *National Guardian,* had been arrested for deportation, along with less well-known "subversives" such as Mr. and Mrs. Lars Berg, Swedish aliens in their late sixties who had been living in the United States since 1904.[201] In March, 1952, the Supreme Court upheld the deportation of an Italian who had come to the U.S. in 1920, joined the CP in 1923, and left in 1929, and the deportation of a mother of three children born in the U.S. who had been a dues paying member of the CP from 1919 to 1936 but had taken no active part in CP activities. In the latter case the court upheld a provision of the Internal Security Act which stated that alien communists could be held indefinitely without bail pending deportation proceedings.[202] In perhaps the most extraordinary case involving an alien, the Supreme Court also upheld in March, 1953, the Truman administration's imprisonment on Ellis Island of a man who had lived in the U.S. since 1923, travelled to Europe in 1948, then was excluded when he attempted to return to the U.S., deported and returned to the U.S. when no country which would accept him could be found. The exclusion, deportation and apparently indefinite confinement on Ellis Island were all based on confidential information alleging that the man was a danger to national security which the Attorney General refused to disclose.[203] Commenting on the case (*Shaugnessy* v. *U.S. ex rel Mezei*) constitutional law expert C. Herman Pritchett noted that "executive imprisonment" had "come to the United States out of the middle ages" and had condemned a man to the prospect of spending the rest of his life on Ellis Island "condemned to confinement without accusation of crime or judicial trial by an exercise of unreviewed and unreviewable executive discretion."[204] But the Court's decision merely reflected the general state of American society, which had created an "Ellis Island for ideas."[205]

Deportations for Political Reasons, 1946-1952[206]

Year	Number
1946	0
1947	3
1948	3
1949	4
1950	6
1951	18
1952	31

The Truman administration also initiated a major assault on Americans' freedom to read. Beginning in 1951, the government began to seize "foreign communist propaganda" entering the country, on the theory that persons abroad who sent such propaganda into the U.S. could be considered foreign agents who had failed to comply with provisions of the Foreign Agents Registration Act. This policy eventually led to the seizure by the Truman and Eisenhower administrations of such materials as *Pravda, Izvestia, The London Economist,* Lenin's *Selected Works* and a book entitled *The Happy Life, Children in the Rumanian People's Republic.* In one case the Post Office delayed shipment of seventy-five copies of Lenin's *State and Revolution* intended for use in a history class at Brown University until University officials explained the purpose of the order and promised to place restrictions on its accessability.[207]

Although Truman had vetoed the Internal Security Act, he lost little time in attempting to enforce it. The law made deportations and exclusions considerably easier, and both increased markedly. Truman appointed members of the SACB within a month of passage of the act, although it had taken him over half a year to appoint the LRB and thus set his own loyalty program in motion in 1947. Two months after passage of the act, on November 22, 1950, Attorney General McGrath asked the SACB to compel the CP to register as a communist-action organization, thus initiating fifteen years of fruitless litigation. Following the 1951 Supreme Court decision upholding the 1948 Smith Act convictions of the CP leaders, the Truman administration began to indict second-string CP leaders under the Smith Act. In 1951 and 1952 sixty-eight additional CP leaders were indicted, and reports circulated that twelve thousand Smith Act prosecutions were planned, no doubt fueled by FBI Director Hoover's 1950 statement that the FBI could round up twelve thousand communists at a moment's notice.[208]

Concessions by the Truman administration to McCarthyite pressure after the outbreak of the Korean War were particularly noticeable in areas connected with foreign policy. In addition to the purging of John Stewart Service, virtually the entire China desk of the State Department was dismantled. By 1952, out of about twenty China experts in the Department, only two were still assigned to their specialty, the others having been transferred to other areas.[209] There is considerable evidence that the Truman administration failed to prevent Gen. McArthur from advancing north of the 38th parallel in Korea for fear of appearing "soft" on communism, and there is no doubt that many of the Cold War policies initiated by Truman in the aftermath of the Korean War — such as continued aid to Formosa, sending the Seventh Fleet to the Formosa Strait, increased aid to the French in Indochina, and refusal to recognize Communist China — reflected similar motivations.[210] Before the outbreak of the Korean War, which led to increased Republican attacks on administration foreign policy, Truman had been moving towards a policy of abandoning Taiwan completely and towards some kind of accomodation with Communist China. However, in May, 1951, Assistant Secretary of State Dean Rusk announced that the communist regime was "not the government of China . . . It is not Chinese."[211]

Even in the closing days of the Truman administration, new concessions to right-wing pressure were made. In December, 1952, the Justice Department bowed to pressure from Sen. Pat McCarran and had Owen Lattimore, one of McCarthy's major targets, indicted for perjury based on testimony before McCarran's Internal Security Subcommittee in 1951, which had held hearings designed to show that American policy in China was influenced by pro-Communists within and without the State Department. The charges against Lattimore were so flimsy that some of them were thrown out of court and eventually the government dismissed the entire indictment.[212] At the very end of the Truman administration, a great hubbub arose over charges that persons regarded as "bad security risks" by the State Department were being employed by the U.N. In one of his last acts as president, Truman issued an executive order requiring the investigation of Americans employed or about to be employed by the U.N., even though U.N. employees were not officially responsible to the United States government. This policy soon led to the establishment of an FBI office on UN territory (until Dag Hammarskjold ordered the FBI off UN property) and the 1953 smearing and clearing of Nobel Prize winner Dr. Ralph Bunche, then a director of the UN Trusteeship Division. Bunche was cleared by the "International Organizations Employees Loyalty Board" established by President Eisenhower under Truman's guidelines, following accusations challenging his loyalty which were made by former communists Manning Johnson and

Leonard Patterson, who functioned as professional witnesses on the Justice Department payroll.[213]

In addition to American freedoms, another casualty of the increasing anti-communist fervor in the United States after 1950 was the Truman administration's increasing abandonment of "New Deal" domestic reform proposals. Before 1950, Truman had placed a heavy stress on such reforms; after 1950, facing increasingly irresponsible Republican attacks focussed on the communist issue, Truman decided to place party unity above all else and "quietly shelved most of his domestic legislative program and sought to bring the conservative wing of his party behind his military and defense policies."[214] Domestic programs were increasingly "soft-pedaled to near-invisibility" as executive agencies feared to push "plans that might be damned as 'socialistic.' "[215]

The Eisenhower Administration, 1952-54

A number of accounts of the Eisenhower-McCarthy relationship essentially present a picture of the Eisenhower administration desperately trying to appease McCarthy for about a year, and then finally turning on McCarthy in the Army-McCarthy affair after concluding that appeasement would not work.[216] Such an interpretation is far too simplistic. While in a number of cases the Eisenhower administration did go to all lengths to appease McCarthy, in some cases, even before the Army-McCarthy affair, it fought McCarthy and won; in other cases it took McCarthyite actions, not necessarily to appease the Senator from Wisconsin, but because the Eisenhower administration believed that appearing to fight communism was good politics. In other words, Eisenhower's actions cannot be explained merely by his general disdain for strong leadership or by his oft-quoted remark about McCarthy, "I will not get in the gutter with that guy;"[217] Eisenhower was *himself* a part and parcel of the whole trend of Republican politics in the early 1950's that supported McCarthyist tactics and objectives. As Herbert S. Parmet has suggested, "All the good reasons for acquiescence" to McCarthy in terms of politics, "were embellished by the lack of conviction that the battle was worth fighting."[218] Thus, it was not until McCarthy threatened to totally undermine the administration that Eisenhower took a decisive and consistent stand against him.

Incidents of obvious appeasement of McCarthyist forces during the first year or so of the Eisenhower administration are numerous. For example, when Republican Congressman Fred Buseby protested the proposed inclusion in the 1953 inaugural program of a musical selection by Aaron Copeland on the grounds that Copeland had lent his name to a number of leftist groups, the piece was immediately withdrawn. This was no one-time musical fluke; shortly afterwards, in response to a complaint from the Veterans of Foreign Wars, the Voice of America promised not to play the music of Roy Harris, who had committed the sin of dedicating a symphony to the Soviet Union in 1943, at a time when the U.S. and the Russians were war-time allies.[219]

Secretary of State John Foster Dulles was so afraid of McCarthy that he literally turned the department over to the Senator. As one writer puts it, Dulles, "cowered and did what he was told."[220] Perhaps fearful that he was particularly vulnerable because he had endorsed Alger Hiss as director of the Carnegie Endowment for International Peace and had offered to testify as to Hiss' character, Dulles' first step upon being named secretary of state was to ask for a full FBI investigation of his own loyalty. He then began his tour of duty by publicly demanding "positive loyalty" from State Department employees.[221] In February, 1953, Dulles gave John Carter Vincent, a long-time China hand and former director of the Office of Far Eastern Affairs, the choice of either resigning or being fired. Vincent had long been under attack by right-wing Republicans, including McCarthy, for alleged pro-communist leanings. He had been repeatedly cleared by the State Department Loyalty and Security Board, but in December, 1952, had been suspended upon recommendation of the LRB. Secretary Acheson had refused to accept this recommendation and with the consent of Truman had established a special five-man board to further review the case. On March 4, 1953, however, Dulles publicly announced that while Vincent was not a security risk and there was no reasonable doubt as to his loyalty, he had failed to "meet the standard which is demanded of a foreign service officer of his experience and responsibility."[222]

The appointment of Scott McLeod, a former FBI agent and close friend of McCarthy, as State Department chief security officer, was also generally interpreted as a concession to McCarthy, although McLeod's appointment seems to have been arranged by an undersecretary of state. Dulles was set to fire McLeod at one point, but quickly backed off for fear of stirring up the Republican right wing. McLeod quickly set up a squad of about twenty-five ex-FBI agents to clean house in the State Department. His men specialized in meticulous after-hours checks of desks and files in the department; one department official recalls an atmosphere reminiscent of a police-state. By November, 1953, McLeod had announced the firing of almost five hundred department employees for security reasons. None of them were given hearings, and no real evidence was ever presented to indicate any subversives had actually been unearthed.[223]

Undoubtedly the greatest and most humiliating surrender made by the State Department came during McCarthy's investigation of the Voice of America (VOA) and the International Information Administration (IIA).[224] McCarthy's hearings on VOA began in February, 1953; their major justification was the suggestion that a massive anti-American conspiracy was involved in a technical internal dispute within VOA over the location of two radio transmitters. As a result of the ruckus raised by the hearings, the transmitters were never installed, although there was not "one scintilla of evidence that the decision was in any way achieved through the influence of communists, pro-communists, fellow travelers, pinks or any of the other rubicund tones. The testimony failed in every respect to uphold the promise of the headlines that Marxist marplots were garbling the Voice of America by strangling its signals."[225]

During the course of the VOA hearings, McCarthy questioned author Howard Fast, who had never been employed by the VOA, on the grounds that his name had been mentioned in a memorandum issued to VOA and IIA staff on February 3, 1953; the document stated that authors "like Howard Fast" might be used in IIA programs if their works included materials "favorable to the United States" since this might give such otherwise politically dubious authors "special credibility among selected key audiences." When McCarthy's antagonism to this policy became apparent during his hostile questioning of Fast, a new policy was issued February 19 which banned the books, music and paintings of "any communists, fellow travelers, etc." As a result of this directive, IIA librarians overseas, unsure as to what "etc" meant, began pulling off the shelves works by such writers as Bert Andrews, head of the Washington Bureau of the *New York Herald Tribune;* Joseph Davies, former ambassador to Moscow; Vera Micheles, Dean of the Foreign Policy Association; Walter White, head of the NAACP; and Foster Rhea Dulles, a cousin of the secretary of state. When New York VOA chief Alfred H. Morton wired Washington that he would continue to "quote Stalin, Vishinsky, Gromyko and other communists to the extent that the use of such material advances our cause," he was suspended from his job, and then quickly reinstated. In June, Secretary Dulles admitted that at least eleven books had been burned by IIA librarians during the book purge.[226]

Meanwhile, McCarthy aides Roy Cohn and G. David Schine were barnstorming through Europe investigating the holdings of IIA libraries and succeeding in making the U.S. look utterly ridiculous in the eyes of the world. During their tour, Theodore Kaghan, public affairs officer of the U.S. High Commission for Germany, rather astutely described the pair as "junketeering gumshoes." He was soon called before McCarthy's committee for questioning about left-wing affiliations in 1935-40, including the fact that he had signed nominating petitions for a Communist candidate for New York City councilman. He was soon eased out of his job. Another casualty of the VOA hearings was VOA deputy administrator Reed Harris, who was allowed to resign after McCarthy questioned him about a book he had written twenty-one years earlier while a student at Columbia University, which had included some passages critical of American capitalism.[227]

Numerous other cases of attempted appeasement of McCarthy by the Eisenhower administration could be cited. In September, 1953, McCarthy berated the Army's chief intelligence officer, Major General Richard C. Partridge, as "completely imcompetent" for his job on the grounds that an Army intelligence document contained pro-communist propaganda and included the works of alleged communists in its bibliography. Shortly afterwards, Partridge was replaced and transferred to a post in Europe. For months, Secretary of the Army Robert Stevens tried to appease McCarthy in connection with the senator's investigations into subversion at Fort Monmouth, New Jersey, and in the Army generally, until finally the Eisenhower administration decided to take a firm stand.[228]

To view the Eisenhower administration's repressive actions as aimed only at trying to appease McCarthy is to see only one side of the coin, however. The fact is that Eisenhower shared many of the basic ideological elements of McCarthy's anti-communism, and further believed that anti-communism was good politics. In many cases, the administration took action that went above and beyond any need to appease McCarthy. For example, on March, 17, 1953, two months after Eisenhower's inauguration, Attorney General Brownell announced that ten thousand citizens were being investigated for denaturalization and twelve thousand aliens for deportation as "subversives."[229] Political deportations in 1953-54 reached the highest levels for any two-year period since 1933-34.

Political Deportations[230]	
1951	18
1952	31
1953	37
1954	61

In May, 1953, Eisenhower, flanked at a White House ceremony by chief congressional red-hunters, McCarthy, Velde and Jenner, announced a major revision of the existing loyalty program. Under Executive Order 10450, a new and more stringent loyalty standard was established under which "employment or retention in employment in the Federal service" must be "clearly consistent with the interests of national security." Further, all agencies were now given summary dismissal power, and were directed to reopen all cases where there had been a full field investigation under the Truman program, to determine if all cases previously cleared could meet the new standard. Moreover, the Truman program, which had distinguished between dismissals for "loyalty" problems and dismissals which could be made in a limited number of agencies for "security" grounds in cases which did not raise questions as to loyalty but did raise questions as to ability to handle security information with discretion, was replaced by a new program which allowed all agencies to make dismissals on "security" and "suitability" grounds for such offenses as drunkeness, sexual perverion and mental disorders as well as the criteria outlined in the original Truman order. All dismissals under the Eisenhower program were labelled as based on "security grounds" whether or not specific information indicating disloyalty was uncovered.[231]

> As a consequence, the norm and process of dismissal became easier, but the effect on the reputation of the dismissed remained the same. While the security chiefs found it easier psychologically to brand a man a security risk than a disloyal citizen, the public saw little difference.[232]

The most prominent victim of the Eisenhower loyalty-security order was John Paton Davies, one of the "old China hands," who, along with Service and Vincent, had served as major whipping boys of the McCarthyists. Davis had been cleared by loyalty boards under the Truman administration, but his case was reopened by the State Department in 1953, and Davies was fired in November, 1954, after Secretary Dulles upheld hearing board findings that while Davies was not a communist sympathizer, he was lacking in "judgement, discretion and reliability" and therefore his continued employment was not "clearly consistent with the national security."[233] As Davies was cashiered, he remarked bitterly, "I think a prudent young man would enter the Foreign Service knowing another trade."[234] By 1960, Davies was living in Lima, Peru, trying to support a wife and seven children by making furniture.

Shortly after the Eisenhower program was initiated, the White House began to play what became known as the "numbers game" to demonstrate its subversive-hunting prowess. Thus, in October, 1953, the White House announced that thus far 1,456 employees had left the government under the new system; two weeks later a White House spokesmen said 1,456 "subversives" had been kicked out. As the 1954 elections approached, the number of separations rose steadily. Three weeks before the election, Vice President Nixon got the Civil Service Commission to announce that almost seven thousand federal employees had been dismissed or had resigned under the Eisenhower program, and that over seventeen hundred of these had data in their files indicating subversive connections. Nixon announced that the administration was "kicking the communists and fellow travelers and security risks out of government . . . by the thousands."[235] After the 1954 elections, which led to the seating of a Democratically-controlled Congress and an investigation of the loyalty program by a congressional committee, the Eisenhower administration stopped issuing statistics on separations and in effect admitted its data had been misleading or false. The CSC admitted that more than

90 percent of these described as security risks had left the government by regular civil service procedures without hearings to test any security charges, and that only 342 had been dismissed under security procedures. Further, while the impression had been disseminated that the security separations had cleared out Democratic leftovers, it turned out that over 50 percent of the cases had involved persons hired during the Eisenhower administration.[236]

In many other ways the Eisenhower administration took highly repressive actions that went far beyond any need to appease McCarthy. The prosecution of second-string CP leaders under the Smith Act was continued, with forty-two communists indicted between 1953 and 1956. Acting under the Internal Security Act of 1950, Attorney General Herbert Brownell petitioned the SACB on April 22, 1953, two days after the SACB had ordered the CP to register as a communist-action organization, to order twelve organizations to register as communist-fronts.[237]

In February, 1953, the CIA, with the knowledge of postal officials, began a project involving examination of the outsides of envelopes carrying letters between the United States and the Soviet Union.[238] In May, 1954, Postmaster General Arthur Summerfield was briefed on the project. In early 1956, the CIA, without the knowledge of anyone outside the agency, began covertly opening and reading the correspondence, using kettles to steam open the mail. Although the purpose of the project was to obtain useful foreign intelligence and counterintelligence information, the project inevitably involved opening mail which had no relationship to these subjects, and during the Vietnam War era, the CIA specifically focussed on mail involving domestic dissidents.

The major focus of the mail-opening operation was at postal facilities in New York City, where mail was opened continually from 1956 until the project was ended in 1973. During this period CIA agents examined over 28 million pieces of mail, photographed 2.7 million envelopes and opened 215,820 pieces of mail. Mail to and from foreign countries was also opened in San Francisco from 1969 to 1971, in New Orleans in 1957 and in Hawaii in 1954 and 1955, involving a much smaller number of examinations and openings. Throughout the entire seventeen year life of the mail opening program, there is no clear evidence that a single Postmaster General, Attorney General or President was ever informed that the operation involved more than the examination of the outsides of envelopes.

Beginning in 1958, according to The Rockefeller Commission, the CIA informed the FBI of "mail project items which were of internal security interest" and the FBI began to provide the CIA with "watch lists of particular persons or matters in which the Bureau was interested." The number of names on the watch lists varied, but "on the average, the list included approximately three hundred names, including about one hundred furnished by the FBI." From 1958 until 1973, the FBI obtained copies of about fifty thousand letters from the CIA, while continuing its own program of opening domestic mail begun in 1940; according to the 1975 Rockefeller Commission report, the "primary purpose" of the CIA project eventually became "participation with the FBI in internal security functions."[239] In at least one case, over one hundred pieces of mail were removed from the postal service and not returned until they were discovered in the CIA three years later. Among those persons whose mail was intercepted and copied by the CIA were then presidential candidate Richard Nixon in 1968, Senators Frank Church, Edward Kennedy and Hubert Humphrey, Federal Reserve Board Chairman Arthur Burns, Martin Luther King and his wife Coretta, Rep. Bella Abzug, Harvard University and the Ford and Rockefeller Foundations.

In May, 1954, Attorney General Herbert Brownell authorized the FBI to implant microphones for surveillance purposes in cases involving "espionage agents, possible saboteurs and subversive persons." In a memo to FBI Director Hoover, Brownell noted that "not infrequently the question of trespass arises in connection with the installation of a microphone" but that the Justice Department "should adopt that interpretation which will permit microphone coverage by the FBI in a manner most conducive to our national interest" since "for the FBI to fulfill its important intelligence functions, considerations of national security and the national safety are paramount."[240] In fact, the FBI had been conducting illegal entries and using microphone surveillance since the 1940's; the Brownell memo simply served the FBI later as an alleged legal justification for the use of microphone surveillance.[241]

Also in 1954, the Eisenhower administration succeeded in prodding Congress to pass a new set of anti-subversive laws, which included the revocation of the citizenship of persons convicted under the Smith Act, required communist organizations to register all printing equipment, and made peacetime espionage a capital offense.[242] The major anti-communist law of 1954, the so-called Communist Control Act, was signed without protest by Eisenhower and quickly implemented by the administration.[243] This law declared as a matter of policy that the CP "should be outlawed" and provided that the CP and any successor organization was "not entitled to any of the rights, privileges and immunities attendant upon legal bodies created under the jurisdiction" of the laws of the U.S. or any political subdivisions.

While the meaning of these provisions has always remained obscure, and they have never been invoked in any major case, instead remaining on the statute books "as a monument to the incompetence, irresponsibility and hysteria of the 83rd Congress" or "possibly as a peg upon which to hang suppression in a future hysteria,"[244] one provision of the law was considerably more precise and repressive. This provision allowed the Attorney General to petition the SACB to declare that labor unions or other organizations were "communist-infiltrated," based on criteria related to the extent to which such organizations promoted the communist movement and were controlled by pro-communists, among others. Once a labor union or other organization was designated "communist-infiltrated" it lost all rights and privileges accorded labor unions under existing law, and its members were barred from employment in defense facilities, denied access to classified information and, along with members of communist-action and communist-front organizations ordered to register, barred from holding union office. The 1954 act specifically provided that any labor organization which was an affiliate in good standing of a "national federation or other labor organization whose policies and activities have been directed to opposing communist organization, any communist foreign government or the world communist movement" was to be presumed not to be a "communist-infiltrated" organization, thus exempting the CIO (which by then had purged its communist-controlled unions) and the AFL. The act further encouraged the ousting of communist leaders in the few communist-controlled unions still remaining by providing that 20 percent of the members of an organization determined to be communist-infiltrated could petition for an NLRB-sponsored election to choose a new bargaining representative. In 1955, the Eisenhower administration brought action to have two of the only three remaining communist-controlled unions with significant membership designated communist-infiltrated. The Eisenhower administration also prosecuted a number of left-wing union leaders for perjury in connection with taking the Taft-Hartley non-communist oath, (obtaining over twenty convictions by 1956) and tried once again — futilely — to have Harry Bridges deported.[245]

In retrospect, the climax of the Eisenhower-McCarthy repression was reached on June 29, 1954, when the Atomic Energy Commission (AEC) declared that J. Robert Oppenheimer, the so-called "father of the atomic bomb," was to be denied further access to classified AEC data on security grounds.[246] The Oppenheimer case symbolized the excesses of the loyalty program and the severe damage that repression was causing to the basic structure of American life by 1954. Based on the criteria of the Eisenhower loyalty program, there is no question that Oppenheimer *was* a "security risk;" during the 1930's he had been a "fellow traveler" with various CP causes, and his wife had been a CP member, as had his brother and his brother's wife. Yet during World War II, Oppenheimer had been in charge of the atomic bomb project, and had never been accused of mishandling classified information.

By the *criteria* of the loyalty program, Oppenheimer was a security risk, yet in *actuality* he had demonstrated that he was not. Further, Oppenheimer had been cleared by the AEC in 1947 on essentially the same charges which led to his clearance denial in 1954 under the more stringent criteria of the Eisenhower program and during a considerably more repressive political climate. The only charges brought against Oppenheimer in 1954 that were based on information unavailable in 1947, furthermore, concerned *policy* positions he had taken while chairman of the General

Advisory Committee of the AEC, in particular his opposition to the development of the hydrogen bomb. Aside from the loss of Oppenheimer's services to the government and the personal tragedy involved — Oppenheimer was denied access to papers that he had written while a government official and irrevocably and publicly smeared when his security clearance was withdrawn — the message of the Oppenheimer case was clearly that any policy position which deviated from the strongest possible anti-communist position might well lead to suggestions of disloyalty. In December, 1975, the *Washington Post* reported that the FBI had wiretapped and bugged conversations between Oppenheimer and his lawyers during the AEC hearings in 1954.[247]

A complete picture of the Eisenhower-McCarthyite relationship is not obtained solely by a portrait of appeasement and repression on the the part of the Eisenhower administration. Even before the climactic clash which began in March, 1954, as a result of McCarthy's attack on the Army, Eisenhower did fight McCarthy on a number of occasions, and in each case, he won. These incidents showed that Eisenhower could have stopped McCarthy long before he did had he taken a strong and consistent stand against him.

For example, in February, 1953 Eisenhower nominated Charles Bohlen, a distinguished career foreign service officer, as ambassador to Russia. Despite attacks on Bohlen led by McCarthy and other right-wing Senators, Eisenhower stood firm, and the nomination was confirmed 74-13. Yet the lesson learned by the Eisenhower administration was not that it could lick McCarthy but that it should not antagonize him. After Sen. Taft warned Eisenhower that there must be "no more Bohlens," the administration was careful to make no further nominations that would upset the Republican right-wing.[248]

In July, 1953, the administration took McCarthy on in a number of controversies and won in each case. On July 8, the IIA announced it was reverting to its previous policy of using books by communists and communist sympathizers in cases where this might serve the ends of democracy, and denounced book burning in the strongest terms. Despite strong attacks by McCarthy on this policy, the administration held firm.[249] At about the same time, Eisenhower issued a statement deploring "unjustifiable and deplorable" attacks on the American clergy and denouncing "generalized and irresponsible attacks that sweepingly condemn the whole of any group of citizens" shortly after McCarthy had announced the appointment of veteran red-baiter and ex-communist J. B. Matthews to head his subcommittee staff. Matthews had just written a magazine article which charged that the "largest single group supporting the communist apparatus in the United States today is composed of Protestant clergymen." Although McCarthy decided to fire Matthews as a result of pressure from within his subcommittee before Eisenhower's statement was issued, Vice-President Nixon managed to delay McCarthy's announcement of his decision until after the White House statement was released, thus suggesting to the public that Eisenhower had forced McCarthy's hand.[250] Also in July, 1953, after McCarthy announced he was planning to investigate the CIA, CIA Director Allen Dulles and Nixon convinced McCarthy not to press the probe.[251]

What these incidents demonstrate is that Eisenhower could have stopped McCarthy much earlier had he decided to do so, but that the will simply was not there. Eisenhower, in short, was a McCarthyite in his own way, and it was only when McCarthy threatened to totally undermine the administration with his attack on the Army and his humiliation of Secretary of the Army Stevens in early 1954 that Eisenhower finally took a firm and consistent stand against the Senator. When he did so, McCarthy's power crumbled quickly.

The Role of Congress, 1950-1954

The major pressures toward repression at the federal level during the 1950-1954 period were by no means confined to the actions taken by Senator McCarthy or Presidents Truman and Eisenhower. Along with the loyalty program, the major continuing institutional source of pressure for repression during this period came from congressional investigations of "subversion."[252] Such investigations reached heights unmatched in American history during this period.

Public Hearing Days of HUAC[253]		Number of Separate Congressional Investigations of Communism[254]
1945-1946	11	4
1947-1948	52	22
1949-1950	115	24
1951-1952	108	34
1953-1954	147	51

Although the most widely publicized hearings were those held by Senator McCarthy's Subcommittee on Investigations of the Committee on Government Operations, by HUAC and by the Senate Internal Security Subcommittee (SISS) of the Committee on the Judiciary, communist-hunting expeditions were also occasionally conducted by House committees on Education and Labor, Public Works, District of Columbia, Immigration and Naturalization, Military Affairs, Foreign Affairs and Veterans Affairs, and Senate committees on the Judiciary, Labor and Public Welfare, Expenditures in the Executive Departments and Interstate and Foreign Commerce.[255]

The effective functions of the Congressional committees were twofold: 1) "to define subversive or 'un-American' activity and thereby to set the standards of American thought and conduct with respect to orthodoxy and heresy in politics"; and 2) to enforce its standards by holding hearings which were a "device for condemning men without the formalities of due process" by the use of exposure to accomplish "what may not be done by legislation — that is, to punish men for associations and beliefs."[256] Just as the loyalty program in effect provided severe penalties for dissent without the type of due process guarantees that would have been provided in a courtroom, the congressional hearings led to the blackening of reputations and to hundreds of blacklistings and firings without trials or due process. Most of the congressional hearings which were supposedly investigating subversion had no serious legislative purpose but were designed to "expose" alleged Communists to the public with the obvious intent of inducing their employers to fire them. Persons accused of subversion before or subpoenaed to appear at congressional committees were "accused" of political beliefs and affiliations, often stretching back twenty years or more, that were not illegal, were denied the right to cross-examine their "accusers" and denied any formal due process procedures. Thus, SISS Chairman James Eastland announced at one hearing, that with regard to the ground rules of his hearings, "I will decide those as we go along and announce them when I desire."[257]

The net extended by various congressional committees in their investigations of communism extended into virtually all aspects of American life, including labor, education, the clergy, the press, governmental agencies and independent foundations and scholarly organizations. The field of education proved so politically attractive for congressional investigators that three different committees threatened to expose the "reds" in the schools in the winter of 1953. Eventually the Republican leadership tried to work out an arrangement to prevent the committees "from colliding as they snatched at star witnesses."[258] Cheered on by J. Edgar Hoover, who declared that, "Every Communist uprooted from our educational system is one more assurance that it will not degenerate into a medium of propaganda for Marixism,"[259] the congressional red-hunts in the schools during 1953-54 eventually led to the firing of hundreds of teachers from public schools and universities.[260] Just as the loyalty program spread a chill of fear throughout the Federal government, the congressional investigations spread fear throughout the whole of American society — fear not only of advocating communism, but of advocating virtually *any* dissenting or unpopular opinion, fear of joining radical or liberal organizations, fear of reading dissenting periodicals, and ultimately fear of thinking "bad" thoughts. The effects of the congressional investigations was to virtually create a status of "outlawry" in which citizens could be "effectively stigmatized though never convicted of any offense."[261] The lesson the congressional committees taught was that in order to avoid the possibility of investigation, the average citizen "had better not join anything, or lend his name to anything, or say anything, or do anything that may, after some change in the climate of opinion, be construed as unorthodox by a committee of Congress."[262]

Although sometimes overshadowed by SISS and Senator McCarthy, HUAC remained the most prolific subversive-hunting congressional committee carrying to an extreme the tactics and activities of other red-hunting committees.[263] From 1945 to 1957, HUAC alone heard over three thousand witnesses, and cited one hundred thirty-five witnesses for contempt, compared to a total of ninety-one witnesses cited for contempt by all other congressional committees combined during this period (by 1958, only thirty-seven of the HUAC contempt citations had led to court convictions which were upheld, while about eighty citations led to acquittals or were not prosecuted in the courts). HUAC was audacious enough to openly admit on occasion that its purpose was essentially the exposure and ruination of individuals. Thus, J. Parnell Thomas, chairman during 1947-1948, declared that the "chief function" of HUAC "has always been the exposure of un-American individuals and their un-American activities" based upon the "conviction that the American public will not tolerate efforts to subvert or destroy the American system of government once such efforts have been pointed out." Francis Walter, HUAC chairman from 1955 until 1963, declared that he hoped to expose "active Communists . . . before their neighbors and fellow workers" with the "confidence that the loyal Americans who work with them will do the rest of the job."[264]

HUAC's hearings left behind a trail of ruined reputations and wrecked careers. One study of sixty-four "unfriendly" witnesses appearing before the committee found that fifty lost their jobs.[265] Following hearings in May, 1954 in the home district of HUAC member Kit Clardy of Flint, Michigan, a number of "accused" persons were physically attacked by local vigilantes, leading Clardy to state, "This is the best kind of reaction there could have been to our hearings."[266]

One typical HUAC investigation looked into Communist activities in western Pennsylvania in 1950. The star witness before HUAC was Matthew Cvetic, an FBI agent who had infiltrated the CP. During his appearance before HUAC, Cvetic named three hundred persons as Communists or "Communist sympathizers." As a result of Cvetic's charges, nearly one hundred persons lost their jobs. In one case, a member of the Pittsburgh Symphony Orchestra was not only fired, but was also expelled from the American Federation of Musicians.

In many cases, AFL and CIO unions demanded that persons named by Cvetic either deny the charges or resign, and some unions invited Cvetic to look over their membership lists and pick out the "reds." A wave of firings occurred on every level of the Pittsburgh school system, and various civic organizations expelled members and officers. The state of Pennsylvania cut off from relief a mother named by Cvetic, along with her two children, on the ground she had violated an oath requiring relief recipients not to seek the overthrow of the government, while a judge dismissed a grand juror named by Cvetic. CP leaders named by Cvetic were indicted under the Pennsylvania sedition act.[267]

That HUAC was highly successful in gaining publicity for its members but not seriously interested in producing legislation was widely recognized in the House of Representatives. Thus, in 1953, 185 members of the House applied for membership on HUAC, yet anti-subversive bills were virtually never referred to HUAC for consideration. From 1951 to 1960, a total of 181 anti-subversive bills were referred to House committees, of which 31 were referred to HUAC. No legislative hearings were held on any of the 12 bills referred to HUAC between 1951 and 1958, and from 1945 to 1960, the committee was responsible for only one piece of legislation which became law — the 1950 Internal Security Act. The political benefits which HUAC offered to its members were increased by the committee's habit of travelling around the country to hold its investigations, travels which somehow increased during election years and were often held in the districts and states of its members. From 1952 to 1958, between January 1 and Election Day, a total of sixty-seven hearing days were held in the home states of HUAC members and twenty-five hearing days were held in the home districts during election years, amounting to 69 percent and 26 percent, respectively, of total hearings days spent away from Washington.[268]

In addition to its highly publicized hearings, HUAC also compiled massive files on "subversive" activities and published lists and reports on "subversive" organizations. Thus, in 1948 HUAC issued a report stating that it had "a collection of three hundred thousand card references to activities and affiliations of individuals" and that it had compiled lists of signers of CP election petitions "for various years in twenty States, showing 363,119 signatures." The report also stated that from January, 1947 to December, 1948, HUAC files had been consulted by 5,975 "accredited representatives of Government agencies."[269] HUAC reports describing various "subversive" organizations have been described by students of the committee as "marred by an unfastidious use of evidence, sloppy organization and writing, rampant emotionalism and wild charges" and as containing "so many obvious errors and grossly unfair attacks upon persons of undoubted non-Communist standing that it is often difficult to single out or evaluate the authentic information about Communists and Communist activity that they contain."[270] Aside from issuing reports on specific groups, HUAC also published lists of "subversive" organizations; thus in 1951, HUAC listed 624 subversive groups although the Attorney General had only been able to uncover 200 such organizations.[271]

One of the strangest developments of the Congressional hearings (and the Smith Act trials and various administrative communist-hunting bodies such as the SACB) was the development of the informer as a hero in American society.[272] Many of the informers were FBI agents who had so thoroughly penetrated the CP that FBI Director Hoover repeatedly informed Congress during the 1950's of what he claimed was the exact membership of the Party (24,796 in 1953, he reported) and Attorney General McGrath stated in May, 1950 that the FBI knew "every Communist in the United States."[273] Some of the FBI agents achieved high rank within the CP; thus during the 1949 Smith Act trial three FBI agents testified that they had served on CP recruiting committees. Under the Smith Act doctrine, the agents apparently were "actively inducing American citizens to become members of a conspiracy against the United States"[274] and, indeed, one of the agents testified that he had recruited friends and relatives to join the party and then turned over their names to the FBI.[275]

Altogether, according to a Justice Department statement issued in August, 1955, the government paid a total of forty-seven undercover informants $43,000 for fees and expenses from July, 1953 through April, 1955, with the highest paid informant receiving $16,000.[276] In some cases an FBI informer would surface at a hearing or trial and seldom be heard from again, such as the sixty-eight year old grandmother who named 120 names at a HUAC hearing into Communist activities in Los Angeles in 1953. But in other cases, the same informer would appear at many different hearings and trials and make his living as a "professional informer" off fees paid by congressional committees and the Justice Department and income earned by books, movies, lectures and magazine articles. Especially valued for their testimony were former Communists who had left the party and identified their old comrades — individuals the *Washington Star* once described as persons "whose only claim to credibility is that they used to belong to a society of liars."[277] In 1950, journalist I. F. Stone noted acidly:

> In an earlier America, a man had to be born in a log cabin to make his mark politically; today he needs to have acquired a Communist Party card in his youth. The "ex's" are not merely used as informers but are regarded as oracles; crowds shiver in expectation of their revelations. The longer they are out of the party the more they remember of frightful conspiracy and diabolic plot.[278]

While there is no doubt that FBI agents had thoroughly infiltrated the CP, there is severe doubt about the credibility of the informers the government relied upon the most. Thus, Matthew Cvetic was revealed in 1955 to have a long history of mental illness. The testimony of professional informers Manning Johnson and Leonard Patterson was rejected by the International Organizations Employees Loyalty Board in the Ralph Bunche case, and the same board rejected Elizabeth Bentley's charges against International Monetary Fund employee William Henry Taylor. The Senate rejected charges of former CP membership leveled against Assistant Secretary of Defense-nominee Anna Rosenberg by professional informer Ralph DeSola. Professional ex-communist Louis Budenz told a Senate Committee in 1950 that he had been "officially informed" by CP officers that John Hopkins University Professor Owen Lattimore was a CP member, yet in 1947 and 1949 he had specifically denied that Lattimore was a Communist and he had never mentioned Lattimore during repeated sessions with the FBI from 1946 to 1950. There is strong evidence that professional informer George Hewitt lied to a Washington state legislative committee, while professional informer Paul Crouch (who was admittedly a former Soviet agent and had been convicted for attempting to incite rebellion against the United States while a member of the armed forces) lost a libel suit resulting from one of his charges. The Justice Department admitted in a court document filed in 1956 that it had "serious reason" to doubt statements made in legal proceedings by professional informer Joseph Mazzei, while professional informer Harvey Matusow publicly stated in 1955 that he had repeatedly lied in various proceedings. In 1956, the Supreme Court remanded to the SACB its original order that the CP register after the Party made allegations which were uncontested by the government to the effect that Crouch, Johnson and Matusow had engaged in wholesale perjury.[279]

Repression on the State and Local Level, 1947-54

The pattern of state and local repression from 1947 to 1954 closely corresponds with that of the federal government, both in terms of steadily developing intensity and in terms of repressive institutions and laws. As during the World War I period, the federal government set a pattern, and the states and localities followed, sometimes going beyond the federal example.[280] In many cases, state legislatures, in particular, "responded almost slavishly to the force of federal law and precedent and to the anxieties aroused by national leaders."[281]

One excellent measure of the increasing pressures towards repression across the country during the 1947-54 period is a simple tabulation of states passing repressive laws of various type during each two-year period (since most state legislatures met every other year, usually during non-Congressional election years, this is a more accurate measure than an annual tabulation). Tabulating the number of states which in each two-year period passed the most common types of repressive laws — sedition laws, laws outlawing the CP or "subversive" organizations, (usually defined as organizations advocating the unlawful overthrow of the government), laws barring membership in the CP or "subversive" organizations, laws barring the CP or "subversive" organizations from the ballot or their membership from public employment or office, and laws requiring the swearing of various "negative" loyalty oaths to qualify for public employment or elective office, it is evident that severe repression on the local level developed only after the Truman administration began its repressive measures in 1947, and increased significantly after the rise of McCarthy, the outbreak of the Korean War, the atomic espionage arrests, and the passage of the Internal Security Act in 1950.

Number of States Passing Repressive Legislation, 1946-54[282]

	Total	Type A	Type B	Type C	Type D	Type E	Type F
1945-46	3	1				1	1
1947-48	4	1		1		2	1
1949-50	13	4	4	1		6	9
1951-52	17	3	6	4	4	11	12
1953-54	8	3	5	4	2	5	6

Type A: Sedition Laws
Type B: Laws outlawing membership in the CP or in "subversive" organizations.
Type C: Laws outlawing the CP or "subversive" organizations.
Type D: Laws requiring registration of the CP or "subversive" organizations.
Type E: Barring CP or "subversive" organizations or members of such organizations from the ballot or requiring disclaimer oaths for listing on the ballot.
Type F: Similar to type E, applying to public employment
Note: Totals vary from the sums of different types of legislation because many states passed more than one type of repressive law during the same legislative session.

Many of the state laws closely followed the pattern laid down by the federal government. For example, following the institution of the Truman loyalty program in 1947, almost thirty states passed laws between 1947 and 1954 designed to bar subversives from holding state employment. In nine states, communists were excluded by name from such employment. Although most states did not set up any machinery to enforce such laws, a number of states instituted full-scale loyalty programs to screen employees. Frequently the criteria used in the state laws to bar subversives was directly copied from the Truman loyalty program, requiring the exclusion from state employment of persons about whom there were "reasonable grounds" for suspicion of loyalty. When Pennsylvania passed its loyalty program in 1951 (the so-called Pechan Act), the federal revision of loyalty criteria was incorporated, requiring exclusion in cases of "reasonable doubt" as to loyalty of the person involved. In some cases, state loyalty programs provided more protection for accused employees or were less sweeping than the federal program. For example, the Washington state program and several other state loyalty programs provided specifically for the right of cross-examination and confrontation of adverse witnesses, and the right to judicial review, procedural guarantees lacking in the federal program. Whereas the federal program applied to all employees, including janitors and other laborers, the Louisiana program and that of several other states specifically exempted from its scope "laborers in any case in which the employing authority shall . . . specify the reason why the nature of the work to be performed is such that employment of persons as to whom there may be reasonable grounds to believe that they are subversive persons . . . will not be dangerous to the health or security of the citizens or the security of the state."

Following the passage of the 1950 Internal Security Act requiring registration of "communist-action" and "communist-front" organizations, nine states passed similar legislation from 1950 to 1954. In a number of cases, these states specifically required the registration of the Communist Party, a provision not found in the federal law. Some of these laws, as well as some of the state loyalty programs, incorporated by reference the Attorney General's list of subversive organizations. For example, the Delaware Act of 1953 required all "communists," members of the CP and members of "communist front" organizations to register with the state; a "communist front" organization was defined as "any organization which is listed as such by the Attorney General of the United States." Some of the registration provisions were obviously designed to make it impossible for registered organizations to continue to function. For example, the Texas law of 1951 required that officers of Communist Party and Communist front organizations furnish the names of officers and members, and financial statements, as well as the names of "any person who has attended its meetings in the state of Texas." The Montana law of 1951 and several others specifically required that all registration information be made public, thus subjecting the members of registered organizations to the possibility of severe reprisals.

Several states went beyond mere registration requirements and completely outlawed the CP (four did so between 1951 and 1954) or organizations advocating the unlawful overthrow of the government. During the 1951-54 period, four states made it a crime to belong to the CP, while many others outlawed belonging to organizations advocating the illegal overthrow of the government, even though such laws frequently duplicated earlier criminal syndicalism laws. About twenty states passed laws in 1947-54 barring members of the CP or seditious organizations from the ballot, or barring advocates of the illegal overthrow of the government from the ballot. Including all such laws passed since 1935, by 1958 thirty-five states barred advocates of violent overthrow from the ballot, with eighteen states barring the CP by name; such laws, of course, merely proved that advocates of violent overthrow could only achieve power through illegal means, since legal pathways were barred to them. Anti-subversive laws were frequently passed without serious debate or opposition in the state legislatures. Thus, Oklahoma passed a stringent loyalty oath bill in 1951 without a single vote of opposition in either house, and similarly lopsided votes were recorded when Maryland passed a strong anti-subversive bill in 1949, when California passed its public employee's oath bill in 1950 and when the Michigan legislature unanimously outlawed "subversion" in 1950.[283]

Writing in 1956, Robert Cushman lamented, "What appears to be going on ... is a sort of competition amongst many of the states as to which can pass the toughest legislation against communism."[284] Illustrative of Cushman's point was Indiana's law which declared it state policy to "exterminate communism and communists and any teaching of the same;" Texas' law outlawing any party which "entertained any thought or principle" contrary to the Constitution; Tennessee's law providing the death penalty for advocating the unlawful overthrow of the government; and Massachusetts' law banning persons taking the fifth amendment before congressional committees from appearing on educational television. Another unusual law was New York's 1949 "Feinberg Law" which required state education officials to compile a list of "subversive" organizations and provided that anyone belonging to such organizations would automatically be disqualified "for appointment to or retention in any office or position in the public schools."[285] In order to enforce the Feinberg Law, New York state established procedures requiring annual reports on the loyalty of all school employees. State Commissioner of Education Francis T. Spaulding informed school officials:

> The writing of articles, the distribution of pamphlets, endorsement of speeches made or articles written or acts performed by others, all may constitute subversive activity. Nor need such activity be confined to the classroom. Treasonable or subversive acts or statements outside the school are as much a basis for dismissal as are similar activities in school or in the presence of school children.[286]

As well as copying from the federal government, many states copied repressive legislation from each other. One particularly popular state law was Maryland's 1949 Ober Act, which was derived from the Smith Act, the Truman Loyalty Program, and the Mundt-Nixon Bill then pending in Congress. The Ober Act established a state loyalty program, outlawed "subversive" organizations, banned "subversives" from running for or holding public office and created a Special Assistant Attorney General in charge of Subversive Activities to enforce its provisions. Within a few years, the Ober Law was copied in part or whole by Florida, Georgia, New Hampshire, Ohio, Pennsylvania, Washington, Alabama, Louisiana, Michigan, and even Mississippi, which, according to FBI Director Hoover, had a CP consisting of one man.[287]

A virtual plague of loyalty oaths was a concomitant feature of much of the repressive state legislation passed during this period, "although it was generally acknowledged that no Communist really engaged in subversive activities would hesitate to sign."[288] Many states included in their laws requirements that candidates for elective office and applicants for public employment disavow membership in the CP or other "subversive" organizations and/or swear that they did not advocate the violent overthrow of the government. The swearing of loyalty oaths was also required to obtain permits to fish in New York City reservoirs, to become a public

352   Political Repression in Modern America

accountant in New York State, to sell insurance or pianos in Washington, D.C., to obtain unemployment compensation in Ohio, to box, wrestle, barber or sell junk in Indiana, to be licensed as a pharmacist in Texas or to become a veterinarian in the state of Washington.[289] The Texas legislature passed a bill requiring all faculty and students in state colleges to sign affidavits swearing loyalty and disclaiming membership in subversive organizations after being "irked by a voluble Communist student from the University of Texas who insisted on testifying before legislative committees."[290] (The student involved took the oath, which did not require a disavowal of communism per se.) Texas also passed a law banning the use of any books in the public schools unless the author filed an oath disclaiming communism; in the case of books whose authors were no longer living, such as Aristotle or Shakespeare, the book could be used only if the publisher filed an oath on the author's behalf. Alabama surpassed even Texas, requiring not only the filing of statements regarding the organizational affiliations of authors of books, but also with regard to the author of any book or writing *cited* in books used in the schools for collateral reading. The Alabama law was so extreme that it was declared unconstitutional by a state court. Alabama also required the taking of an oath disavowing belief in or affiliation with any group advocating unlawful overthrow of the government in order to *vote* in elections.[291]

The loyalty oath craze reached its height perhaps in California, where the legislature required oaths for all state employees, for residents living in public housing and for organizations seeking to qualify for tax exemptions, including churches. In Los Angeles County, a loyalty oath was incorporated into tax forms, so that it was impossible to pay taxes without swearing one's loyalty. When the University of California Board of Regents discovered that they were not covered by a communist-disavowal oath which they had required of all University of California employees "they immediately made a gala event of the sign-in and the society pages soon reported oath-signing parties as the rage."[292] Altogether, by 1956, forty-two states and over two thousand county and municipal subdivisions and state and local administrative commissions required loyalty oaths.[293]

There is little evidence that any spies or saboteurs were deterred from taking loyalty oaths, but in a number of cases persons of unquestioned loyalty who objected to taking the oaths on grounds of principle were dismissed from government employment. In addition to the widely publicized case of thirty-six University of California faculty who were fired or resigned, casualties of the oath mania included three Quakers in Maryland who refused to sign a subversive-disavowal oath for religious reasons and were fired from public employment, a Jehovah's witness fired by the Detroit city government under similar circumstances, and a parking meter maintenance employee who declined to sign the Oklahoma state oath because of religious reasons.[294]

Along with the passage of repressive legislation, many states imitated the federal government by establishing legislative committees to investigate "un-American" activities. Altogether, such committees functioned in at least twelve states between 1947 and 1955. By 1948, there were so many un-American activities committees functioning in state legislatures that an interstate conference of such committees was held in Los Angeles. Represented at the conference were the un-American activities committees of Washington, California, Arizona, and Illinois, along with representatives of the state governments of five other states. All representatives at the meeting publicly took an oath of allegiance, and then established a permanent interstate legislative conference on subversive activities.[295]

The most notorious (and most studied) of these committees were the Canwell Committee of Washington State, the Tenney Committee of California, and the Broyles Committee of Illinois.[296] From what is known of these committees, it seems likely that all of these groups followed the lead of HUAC in concentrating above all else on the exposure of alleged subversives, in featuring irresponsible and often irrelevant charges by witnesses and committee members, in denying accused persons the right to reply or to cross-examine their accusers, in accumulating huge files of alleged subversive individuals and organizations and in generally exacerbating the general atmosphere of hysteria.

The Tenney and Canwell committees were particularly notorious for viewing their prime function as exposure and for labelling their opponents as subversive. Thus, during a 1948 hearing, Chairman Albert Canwell of the Washington Committee declared:

> We feel and have felt at all times that Communists cannot function in the light of day. We feel that with the publicity given their activities during the course of this hearing, that the people of the state of Washington will properly and adequately take care of the communists.[297]

Chairman Tenney of the California committee generally viewed his critics as "spies, traitors and potential saboteurs," frequently denounced unfriendly witnesses as communists and even accused spectators whose reactions displeased him of being communist sympathizers.[298] In its 1949 report the Tenney Committee listed several hundred of what it called its "more notorious critics" who were "typical of the individuals within various Stalinist orbits;" among those listed were entertainers and actors such as Edward G. Robinson, Frederick March, Gregory Peck, Vincent Price, Katherine Hepburn and Frank Sinatra. The committee termed its report a

> challenge to the communists, the fellow travelers, the apologists, the pinks, confused liberals, innocents and dupes to read in this report from the sacred texts of Marxism-Leninism-Stalinism, what communism really believes in and promises to do; and then either stand out openly and honestly and unfurl the hammer and sickle Red flag of treachery and brutality or else to learn as the Whittaker Chamberses and Elizabeth Bentleys and

Louis Budenzes learned the sickening, bloodstained truth of the Stalinist betrayals of the socialist revolutionaries' dream.[299]

When a number of those persons named as "within various Stalinist orbits" protested their designations, the Tenney Committee issued a new report listing their alleged subversive affiliations.

Both the Canwell and Tenney Committees made a practice of collecting huge files listing the alleged subversive affiliations of thousands of Americans. The Canwell committee claimed in 1949 to have an index file of "approximately forty thousand subjects dealing with the communists, their front organizations and activities and related materials," while the Tenney committtee asserted in 1943 that it had fourteen thousand files on individuals.[300]

The Tenney Committee was particularly active in attempting to impose severe sanctions on those it viewed as subversive:

> Once it had established to its satisfaction that a particular individual was a Communist or fellow traveler . . . it sought literally to banish him from all community life. The objective was to quarantine him as though he were infected with smallpox. Efforts were made to prevent association with him, to forbid lawyers to defend him . . . and to cause his employer to discharge him and his union to expel him. People were warned that they should not rent him a hall for a meeting or join any group of which he was a member or read any book or attend any play or motion picture written by him, or even espouse any cause espoused by him.[301]

According to one student of the Tenney Committee, its hearings "devastated lives and ruined the careers of hundreds of innocent Californians."[302]

Subversion in the nation's public schools and colleges was a particularly attractive subject for many of the state investigating commitees. Following hearings before the Canwell committee in 1948 which featured charges of communist affiliations against a number of members of the University of Washington faculty, the University of Washington held its own hearings. In January, 1949, the University of Washington Board of Trustees, overruling the recommendations of the faculty senate's tenure committee, fired two professors solely for their present CP membership, and placed three other professors who admitted to past CP membership on "probation" for two years. This action by the University of Washington established a policy which was soon adopted by universities throughout the country; as hysteria increased in the early 1950's faculty firings soon became frequent not only for CP membership but also for exercising the constitutional right of taking the fifth amendment before legislative committees when asked about political activities.[303]

The Tenney committee specialized in investigating subversion in California's high schools and universities. In 1947, the Tenney Committee concluded that a sex-education class at a California high school was part of an overall "communist plan for the corruption of America's coming generation."[304] Partly in order to head off pressure from the Tenney Committee, the Board of Regents of the University of California in 1949 required all faculty members to take an anti-communist loyalty oath. The resulting eighteen-month controversy ripped apart the University of California community and eventually led to the firing of twenty-five members of the faculty senate who refused to sign the oath and the resignation of eleven others, none of whom were ever accused of subversive activities, and the firing of an additional eighty-four non-academic employees and academic employees who were not members of the faculty senate. In the aftermath of the controversy, the University lost three-fourths of its theoretical physicists and had to cancel fifty-five scheduled courses, and had offers of appointment refused by forty-seven scholars, including noted literary critics Robert Penn Warren and Howard Mumford Jones.[305] One dean at the University commented, "No conceivable damage to the university at the hands of the hypothetical Communists among us could have equalled the damage resulting from the unrest, ill will and suspicion engendered by this series of events."[306]

The California controversy had many ironies, including the facts that the Tenney proposals which helped cause the Regents to act in 1949 were defeated; that the faculty senate repeatedly endorsed the 1940 University policy of refusing to hire CP members (the controversy was over the required individual disclaimers); that the regents' oath was thrown out by the California Supreme Court in 1952 and the non-signers ordered reinstated upon signing an anti-subversive oath applying to all state employees passed by the California legislature in late 1950; and that the 1950 state oath, which was even more objectionable than the regents oath, was signed by virtually all of the previous non-signers without controversy. The 1950 state oath, which was endorsed in a public referendum in 1952, was declared unconstitutional by the Supreme Court in 1967.

A 1949 investigation of Communist activities at the University of Oklahoma was initiated by the Oklahoma legislature after members of the University community voiced opposition to a proposed loyalty oath for teachers and students.[307] This investigation collapsed after a few days, however, apparently due partially to the fact that one legislator pointed out that the proposed oath might bar an outstanding football player from playing at the University of Oklahoma, and partially because of the "half embarassing, half amusing" conduct of the committee chairman, Rep. D. C. Cantrell, who before the investigation began announced that opponents to the oath "show they are Communists" and who during the hearings "made himself famous for his colorful, if somewhat incorrect grammar, when he began the questioning of each witness with 'Where was you borned at?' "[308]

The Broyles Commission established by the Illinois legislature was also noted for its "colorful, if somewhat incorrect grammar" as well as its vindictive approach towards students and educators who dared to oppose its recommendations.[309] The Broyles Commission was created in 1947; unlike other legislative committees, it operated initially behind closed doors.

In 1949, the committee recommended a series of anti-communist measures in a final report that was ungrammatical almost to the point of illiteracy. Thus, the committee urged strong actions against communists since:

> Communist criminals are least entitled to refuge under our laws, than any other criminal who holds all moral, spiritualistic and patriotic concepts in contempt. May we further state that this Commission fearlessly and without any pretence of dealing with the subject matter of its investigation; without docility, are anxious to advocate legislation to absolutely curb their operations because of their violation of the basic principles of the very constitution which they seek to destroy, and so this Commission, strongly advocates the passing of nihilitory legislation so needed to treat them as the mongrel class of citizenry.[310]

When hearings were held on the committee's recommendations in February, 1949, students from the University of Chicago and Roosevelt University demonstrated against the proposals. This "subversive" activity led both houses of the Illinois legislature to authorize the Broyles Commission to investigate the two universities on the grounds that "it appears that these students are being indoctrinated with communistic and other subversive theories."[311]

The resulting hearings were similar to the Canwell hearings into subversion at the University of Washington, with the significant difference that whereas the University of Washington cooperated with the Canwell investigation, Roosevelt University and the University of Chicago strongly resisted the Broyles investigation. University of Chicago President Robert M. Hutchins made mincemeat out of Broyles Commission special investigator J. B. Matthews, an ex-communist and former staff aide to HUAC. Hutchins told the Commission:

> It would not be in the public interest to exclude students of communistic leaning. If we did, how would they ever learn better?[312]

When Matthews asked about one professor emeritus who had been accused of affiliations with suspect groups, Hutchins replied that the professor involved had "retired many years ago after confining her attention for a considerable number of years exclusively to mice."[313]

Although the Broyles investigation was unable to find any evidence of subversive activities, it called for extremely punitive legislation to deal with the threat of such activities, leading the Commission's historian to term the group "an anti-subversive agency which failed to find subversion yet lacked the good grace to say so."[314] Along with calling for severe sanctions against any school tolerating subversion, the majority report of the Broyles Commission denounced opposing voices as being "in the main" coming from "communists and their close fellow travelers ... those who have been duped or compromised by the Communists" and "those who are too naive to believe that there is a serious Communist menace to our way of life."[315]

While anti-communist hysteria was well advanced throughout the country by 1948-49, it is evident from studying repression on the state level that there was still considerable resistance to repression during these years that evaporated under the impact of the events of 1950. For example, three members of the Canwell Committee who ran for re-election in 1948 stressing their anti-communist activities were defeated, while the one committee member who did not make any particular issue of his role on the committee was re-elected. The 1949 Washington state legislature allowed the Canwell committee to expire and failed to pass any of its recommended anti-communist legislation; in 1951, however, Washington passed strong repressive legislation modelled on the 1949 Maryland Ober Act.[316]

In Oklahoma, a proposed loyalty oath for teachers and students did not pass in 1949, but similar legislation was approved in 1951. The potential opposition to such legislation was probably no less than in 1949, but by 1951 opponents apparently feared to make their positions known for fear of being "on the same side of a question with the communists."[317] Gov. Murray of Oklahoma declared in 1951 that there was a "minimum of communists in Oklahoma" but added, "I think the anti-communist bills should be passed to keep us in line with the thinking of the rest of the country." The loyalty oath eventually passed without a single vote of opposition in either house; the chairman of the Board of Regents of Oklahoma Agricultural and Mechanical College declared, "Any man who opposes the bills is nothing but a damned communist."[318]

The anti-communist proposals of the Tenney Committee and the Broyles Commission were both defeated in 1949. During that year the Broyles Commission was allowed to expire by the Illinois legislature, while Tenney was forced to step down as chairman of his committee due to increasing opposition to the excesses of the Tenney Committee from a broad spectrum of public opinion in California. After the defeat of the Tenney bills in the California State Assembly on June 29, 1949, all members of the assembly and others in the chamber publicly gave the pledge of allegiance to the flag to demonstrate their loyalty.[319]

The impact of the Korean War and the other events of 1950 in changing the civil liberties climate is particularly evident in California. Gov. Earl Warren, who had opposed the University of California Regents Oath before the outbreak of the Korean War, called an emergency session of the California legislature after the war erupted to consider legislation "relating to civil defense, disaster relief and subversive activities and civil and military service in connection therewith."[320] As one student of the California situation has noted, "The changed tenor of public opinion resulting from the situation in Korea and from the nationwide attacks upon alleged communists in government was reflected in a quite different approach by the legislature to the problem of regulating subversive activities than it had taken in 1949."[321] California now passed negative loyalty oath legislation applying to all public employees, including school and college teachers. The Korean situation also directly affected the University of California oath controversy. On July 21, shortly after the outbreak of the war, the regents accepted a compromise proposal under which faculty members who refused to sign the oath but answered questions before faculty committees about their political affiliations could be retained. However, a month later, with the war going badly for South Korean and American forces, the board reversed itself and called for the firing of all non-signers.[322]

The impact of the Korean War and other events of 1950 was also marked in producing the passage of repressive legislation and increasing administrative repression on the local level. Such laws and administrative actions were not unknown before 1950 — for example Los Angeles County and the city of Los Angeles initiated loyalty programs for public employees in 1947 and 1948, respectively — but there was a massive upsurge in local repression after the outbreak of the war.[323] The first major local repressive law was the Birmingham ordinance of July 18, 1950, which made it unlawful for CP members to remain "within the corporate limits" of the city within forty-eight hours after publication of the ordinance or else face a fine and 180 days in jail. The Birmingham law made CP membership presumed if a person was found "in any secret or non-public place in voluntary association or communication with any person or persons established to be or to have been" a CP member.[324] Many other cities quickly imitated Birmingham in passing anti-communist legislation; in most cases local laws either required Communists to register with the police or to leave town entirely. The Jacksonville, Florida, law created the presumption of CP membership and required the expulsion of any person who distributed "communist literature" or communicated with a present or former communist. The Bessemer, Alabama, law made it illegal for any CP member to enter the city without first notifying the chief of police of his intent to do so, furnishing full details of his planned activities upon arriving. Communists or other subversives were barred from meeting in Miami without giving the police ten days notice, or from distributing literature without advertising their material in the daily newspapers ten days prior to distribution. Cumberland, Maryland, completely banned the sale or distribution of communist literature. Cumberland, Miami, Los Angeles and McKeesport, Pennsylvania, among other cities, required CP members and/or members of other subversive groups to register. Two communists attending a meeting of the McKeesport City Council to protest the proposed ordinance were ejected, as the city mayor told them, "We are not going to give you an opportunity to broadcast your propaganda here. We are going to treat communists in McKeesport just as Americans would be treated in Moscow."[325] A number of the estimated one hundred fifty anti-subversive municipal ordinances adopted by 1951 were soon declared unconstitutional, including those of Birmingham, Miami, Los Angeles, Jacksonville and McKeesport.[326]

A number of cities, including Cincinnati, Knoxville, Oakland, Tacoma and Detroit, implemented local loyalty programs for public employees in the wake of the Korean War. In addition to the general anti-communist and loyalty legislation, many cities took action to deal with specific examples of perceived subversion. In many areas, publications viewed as dangerous were removed from public schools and libraries. Thus, the Los Angeles County Board of Supervisors voted to remove Communist books from the county library, and a controversial pamphlet published by a United Nation agency was removed from the Los Angeles school system. At Sapulpa, Oklahoma, school books criticized for their treatment of socialism and sex were burned with the approval of the vice-president of the board of education. All books written or edited by literary critic Mark Van Doren were temporarily removed from the library of a Jersey City junior college, a book containing material on Henry Wallace was removed from a high school library in Rochester, and the *New York Times* was banned from use in a school in upper New York State on the grounds that the *Times* had a "communist slant." The mayor of San Antonio and the city council of Burbank, California proposed that all public library books which were subversive be stamped to that effect. A member of the Indiana State Textbook Commission charged that there was a "Communist directive in education now to stress the story of Robin Hood" because "he robbed the rich and gave it to the poor," whereupon the Indiana State Superintendent of Education announced that he would reread Robin Hood to consider the charge.[327]

UCLA banned an art exhibit by Jose Clemente Orozco because he allegedly used communist symbols. In Houston, a man and his wife were detained by police for over fourteen hours after a man overheard them criticizing Chiang Kai-shek and reported to the police that the couple had been "talking communism." The city of Peoria banned Paul Robeson from singing in the city hall; the city of Indianapolis barred the ACLU from using the publicly supported war memorial to hear Paul Hoffman, chairman of the board of Studebaker-Packard, discuss the free enterprise system; and the Ohio State Fair banned a singing group known as the Weavers from appearing as scheduled since, as the Fair Board announced, "rather than support any act about which there was the slightest doubt it was decided that it would be better to eliminate it." The city of Providence, Rhode Island, declined to accept a statue of Thomas Paine, on the grounds that Paine was still a "controversial figure." A number of communists were arrested in Oklahoma City on a charge of disorderly conduct after police found them meeting in a field of sunflowers with anti-Korean War and anti-bomb literature. The police chief explained that they were arrested for disorderly conduct because, "the city has no ordinance forbidding such meetings." In August, 1950, opponents of the Korean War were denied a rally permit by New York City police, and then beaten and dispersed by police when they attempted to meet. At about the same time, a New York judge sentenced two persons to six month and twelve month jail terms for having painted the words "peace" and "no H-Bomb" on a Brooklyn park bench. Although the painting had occurred before the outbreak of the Korean War, the sentencing did not, and the judge accused the vandals of stabbing Americans fighting in Korea in the back.[328]

In comparison with World Wars I and II, there was little overt physical violence directed against dissenters during the Truman-McCarthy period, but there were some incidents marked by severe violence and usually accompanied by police indifference. Thus, on March 30, 1948, a mob broke into a house in Columbus, Ohio, being used by a Communist organizer and destroyed it. The curator of archeology at the Ohio State Museum was fired when it turned out his stepson had rented the house to the Communist, and the local police chief refused to provide protection, since as he put it, "Columbus is a peaceloving and churchgoing community and the city administration is not going to tolerate any Communist, Communist front or organization interfering with our way of living if it is humanly possible."[329] Perhaps the most notorious incidents of vigilante activity occurred at Peekskill, New York, in the summer of 1949.[330] A Communist Party concert featuring Paul Robeson was prevented on the night of August 28, 1949, when a mob attacked concert-goers with clubs, brass knuckles and rocks and burned chairs, the platform and songbooks. Police appeared only after the violence had ended and did not make any arrests. The concert was rescheduled and held as planned on September 4, 1949, but after the concert ended, the audience was attacked while leaving the concert by "American Legionnaires, Westchester police and local anti-communists"[331] with about one hundred fifty persons injured and scores of cars stoned or wrecked. In another relatively notorious incident, a group of blacklisted motion picture artists who attempted to make a movie in Grant County, New Mexico, were forced to pack up and leave by local vigilantes after Congressmen Donald Jackson charged that they were making a Communist movie. The Immigration Service began deportation proceedings against a Mexican actress who had the leading role in the movie, which was finally completed but was refused showing in all standard American movie theatres.[332]

The Collapse of the Liberals, 1947-54

From one standpoint, what occurred in American society from 1947 to 1954 was a steady rise in anti-communist hysteria and governmental repression; from another standpoint what occurred was a steady collapse in the support of civil liberties on the part of those segments of society that would presumably be most dedicated to freedom of expression and other fundamental liberties — i.e. the communications industry, labor unions, educators, lawyers, liberals and the Supreme Court. It is important to point out that this collapse was never complete. For example, McCarthyism was strongly opposed by influential segments of the press such as the *Washington Post*, the *New York Times* and the *St. Louis Post-Dispatch*; by a significant number of educators, represented most strongly by the American Association of University Professors, which never abandoned its position that teachers should not be fired solely for CP membership; and by a number of scientific organizations — for example, the American Association for the Advancement of Science which elected Edward Condon as president in 1952 despite repeated attacks on his loyalty by HUAC and others.[333]

But these examples were exceptions and occurred with diminishing frequency after 1950. The earliest and most complete collapse came in the communications industry. As early as 1946, a number of liberal radio commentators were fired following pressure from HUAC. In 1947, a blacklist was instituted in the movie industry following the "Hollywood ten" hearings. A similar blacklist was instituted in the radio and television industries in 1950 following the publication in June, 1950, of *Red Channels*, a listing of about one hundred fifty entertainers together with their alleged left-wing affiliations which was produced by a group of former FBI men. *Red Channels* quickly became a "bible" to the broadcasting industry. By 1953, the ACLU estimated that about two hundred fifty radio performers had been blacklisted; another two hundred fourteen workers were estimated in 1955 to be blacklisted by the movie industry. The communications industry blacklists did not break down until the 1960's; thus folk singer Pete Seeger (who was spared from serving a year in jail for contempt of HUAC by a federal appeals court in 1962) did not appear on network television from 1950 to 1967, and when he finally appeared, CBS executives refused to let him sing a song they interpreted as critical of American policy in Vietnam.[334]

A study of the content of Hollywood movies revealed that about 28 percent of all Hollywood films produced in 1947 were of a "serious social bent." However, after the blacklist was instituted, the percentage of films with such themes declined until by 1953 they represented only 9 percent. At the same time, Hollywood began grinding out a large number of films with simplistic anti-communist themes — over forty between 1948 and 1954. Many of these films were not commercial successes but were regarded by Hollywood studios as "being necessary for public relations."[335] In short, following widely publicized insinuations of rampant subversion in Hollywood, the motion picture industry set out to prove its loyalty by turning out a series of crude, propagandistic films that closely adhered to well-defined formulas of ideological purity. Hollywood's main contribution to the new war effort was thus to give dramatic, visual life to the fear-ridden currents and undercurrents of the age, thereby magnifying the fear and strengthening the hands of McCarthy and his followers.[336]

Perhaps the most ludicrous case involving the motion picture industry occurred when Monogram Studios dropped plans for a film about Hiawatha, because it feared that depicting the Indian chief's efforts for peace among the Indian Five Nations might be viewed as furthering Communist "peace propaganda."[337]

The print media was also affected by the aura of fear enveloping the country. Little, Brown suddenly stopped publishing the works of CP member Howard Fast, while Paul Robeson, perhaps the most prominent black American before and during World War II, was omitted from *Who's Who in America*, and the publishers of *American Sports Annual* rewrote history to eliminate the fact that Robeson had been designated an All-American football player at Rutgers University in 1917 and 1918. Despite its editorial opposition to McCarthyism, the *New York Times* refused to publish advertising protesting the verdict in the Rosenberg case, and every New York paper refused to print advertising for a mock "trial" of McCarthy held by radical groups in January, 1954. I. F. Stone's book critical of the "official" version of the Korean War, was turned down by twenty-eight American publishers — many of whom told Stone the book was excellent in quality but "too hot to handle" — before Stone found a socialist press willing to publish it. Employees of four New York and Los Angeles newspapers and of a wire service were fired for taking the fifth amendment before a congressional committee. Between 1945 and 1950, China specialists who later came under attack by right-wing forces reviewed twenty-two out of thirty books on China for the *New York Times* and thirty out of thirty-five books on China for the *New York Herald Tribune,* the most prestigious book review sections in the country. From 1952 to 1956, not a single one of the same writers was engaged to review a single book by either paper. Prominent Asian scholars such as John K. Fairbank and Owen Lattimore who had come under attack for alleged communist inclinations, were unable to publish through their normal outlets until the late 1960's.[338]

The first major indication of a collapse among American educators was the firing of two Communist Party members from the faculty of the University of Washington in January of 1949, solely for their CP membership. In July, 1949, the National Education Association adopted a policy of opposing employment of Communist Party members as teachers and banning communist teachers from NEA membership. In March, 1953, the Association of American Universities, which represented the heads of thirty-seven of the most prestigious American colleges, resolved that CP membership "extinguishes the right to a university position" and further declared that exercise of the constitutional right of taking the fifth amendment "places upon a professor a heavy burden of proof of his fitness to hold a teaching position and lays upon his university an obligation to re-examine his qualification for membership in its society."[339] Hundreds of public school and college teachers were fired by scores of institutions around the country during the 1949-54 period, generally on grounds of admitted or suspected CP membership or for the exercise of their fifth amendment rights. None of these cases appears to have involved any allegations of improper, incompetent or otherwise unsatisfactory teaching. Such firings occurred at many publicly supported institutions, including the universities of Washington, California, Colorado, Oklahoma, Vermont, Kansas City and Michigan; also at the New York City municipal colleges, San Diego State College, Rutgers University, Wayne University and Ohio State University.[340]

Most American institutions of higher learning showed eagerness to cooperate with congressional and state legislative committees hunting out educational subversives; thus in July, 1953, the SISS reported that "in all but a few of the cases before the subcommittee, the university officials and local authorities suspended the teachers who invoked their privilege against incrimination when asked about Communist Party membership."[341] The president of Southern Illinois University told the Broyles Commission that he felt "the advantages of our way of life ought to be set forth so persuasively that only the keenest minded students would be thinking over and above what they were taught about government."[342]

While most firings were in some way related to allegations of CP activity, this was not always the case. In one notorious instance, a professor was fired at Oregon State College for having defended the position of the controversial Russian geneticist Lysenko, thus clearly demonstrating that Russia was not the only country demanding scientific orthodoxy. In 1953, an assistant professor at Kansas State Teachers College at Emporia was suspended for signing a petition asking clemency for CP leaders convicted under the Smith Act.[343]

Large segments of the legal industry joined large numbers of educators and persons in the communications industry in demonstrating little concern for civil liberties. In many cases, persons involved in cases concerning allegations of communist activity found it virtually impossible to obtain legal counsel. Thus, in one of the "second string" CP indictments under the Smith Act, the defendants appealed in vain to over thirty lawyers to take the case, and in one Pennsylvania state sedition case the defendant was forced to represent himself after futile appeals to seven hundred lawyers.[344] In 1950, the American Bar Association urged that all lawyers be required to take anti-communist oaths before being admitted to the bar. In 1951 the ABA called for the expulsion from the organization of all CP members as well as all advocates of "Marxism-Leninism" and urged similar action by state and local bar associations, as well as the disbarment of all such persons. Subsequently, many state and local bar associations adopted various loyalty tests, and in several cases lawyers who refused to answer questions about their affiliations were denied entrance to the bar.[345]

The general political climate which made lawyers reluctant to get involved in controversial cases was considerably heightened by governmental activities. Lawyers who defended the top CP leaders in the 1948 Smith Act trial were sentenced for contempt of court and subjected to attempts to disbar them, and over two dozen lawyers involved in left-wing causes were summoned before HUAC in 1952. In August, 1953, Attorney General Brownell announced that he would seek to have the National Lawyers Guild, an organization which frequently was involved in controversial cases, listed on the subversive organizations list. Although the attempt to have the Guild listed was abandoned by the government in 1958, Brownell's statement alone was enough to severely stigmatize the organization.[346]

The collapse of labor (which given the traditionally superpatriotic stance of the AFL meant the CIO) came with the expulsion of communist-dominated unions from the CIO in 1949 and 1950. At the end of World War II, communist-controlled unions encompassed over 20 percent of the membership of the CIO. Beginning in 1947 the CIO came under extremely strong pressure from the government to purge itself of its communist elements. The passage of the Taft-Hartley Act in 1947 was followed by a 1948 directive from the Atomic Energy Commission which ordered General Electric not to recognize the communist-led United Electrical, Radio and Machine Workers of America (UE) as the bargaining representative of any persons to be employed at a new atomic laboratory in Schenectady, New York. Between 1948 and 1952, investigations of left-wing labor unions were conducted by HUAC, two subcommittees of the Senate Judiciary Committee and subcommittees of the House Committee on Education and Labor and the Senate Committee on Labor and Public Welfare.[347] Occasionally congressmen admitted that the intent of the hearings was to cause the unions involved to lose elections. Thus, one Senate subcommittee reported that its hope was that following its hearings "when the rank and file of the United Public Workers of America learn the truth concerning the Communist leadership of the organization, they will take effective action to rout such leadership."[348] During a 1948 dispute within the seventeen thousand member Pittsburgh chapter of the UE, anti-communist forces arranged to have HUAC subpoena the left-wing leaders of the chapter to question them about their communist backgrounds on the eve of a union election. The election resulted in the defeat of the left-wing slate.[349]

In November, 1949 the CIO convention made communists ineligible for CIO national offices and authorized the executive board to expel any unions whose policies were "consistently directed toward the achievement of the program or purpose of the Communist Party." Subsequently charges against all of the left-wing unions in the CIO were brought and "trials" held by the executive board (much on the pattern of the loyalty program hearings and congressional investigations). The CIO convention held in November, 1950 ratified the executive board's expulsions of the unions.[350]

It is obvious that the CIO did not expel unions with such a large proportion of its membership solely because the CIO leadership had suddenly become converted to the wisdom of staunch anti-communism. Adherance to the CP line had been standard fare for many of the left-wing unions for over ten years, and had never before been regarded as conflicting with their functions as labor unions; in any case their pro-CP line "was no more blatant than (CIO President) Murray's adherence to the Democratic party line."[351] The real explanation for the CIO actions was undoubtedly fear of further severe governmental repression if it continued to tolerate the presence of communists within its ranks, especially after the outbreak of the Korean War:

> Aside from the fact that many CIO leaders were themselves ideologically opposed to Communism, most of them were able to perceive that organizations accused of being either pro-Communist or Communist-dominated would face serious and increasing difficulties in post-war America. The final break came not because the CIO could tolerate no internal dissent from its official position on such largely peripheral issues as the Marshall Plan, the Atlantic Pact, the Greek Civil War, the Berlin airlift, etc., but because the communists and pro-communists within the CIO were making statements on such matters which could (and were) interpreted by the public to represent the official CIO position. Given the attitudes which prevailed in the country between 1948 and 1954, it would have been extremely difficult for an organization such as the CIO to refuse to take action against known and suspected communists within its ranks.[352]

By expelling the communist-dominated unions in November, 1950, "as the Korean War reached its critical stage, the CIO could claim a purity equal to that of the AFL and was able thereby to escape public indictment during the years when anti-communist hysteria in the nation reached its height."[353]

By 1954, forty unions with six million members barred communists from membership, while fifty-nine unions with ten million members (60 percent of total union membership) barred communists from holding office. By 1952, communists and "party-liners" were estimated to be a force in unions with less than 2 percent of all union membership, compared to over 20 percent only five years earlier. Nevertheless, the Eisenhower administration initiated a series of perjury prosecutions against the officers of the remaining remnants of the purged CIO unions in connection with their signing of Taft-Hartley affidavits. By 1956, twenty convictions had been obtained, and the fining, jailing and exhaustion of union legal defense funds had contributed to the demise of six of the ten expelled CIO unions by 1955. Despite this almost virtual collapse of the radical labor movement, Congress in 1954 included in the Communist Control Act provisions designed to totally cripple the remaining left wing unions. As noted previously, the 1954 act rewarded the anti-communist activities of the AFL and CIO by in effect excluding their constituent unions from its effects. In turn, when the AFL and CIO merged, in 1955, the new organization reciprocated by barring organizations dominated by communists, fascists or other totalitarians from membership, stressed its anti-communist principles and gave the executive council special powers to suspend affiliates (and members of the executive council itself) viewed as tainted with totalitarianism.[354]

The general collapse of American liberals in the face of rising anti-communist hysteria was presaged by the role of Americans for Democratic Action (ADA), an organization of Democratic liberals, in the 1948 election campaign.[355] Not content with supporting Truman's Cold War policies, ADA launched a vicious campaign of red-baiting against the Wallace movement and, along with Truman, was largely responsible for creating the equation between dissent and subversion which McCarthy was to use as a battering ram against the Democrats and liberals later. Undoubtedly part of ADA's motivation was to attempt to draw a distinction between liberalism and communism in an attempt to demonstrate its own patriotism, but the recklessness of its attacks forfeited any claim on its part to self-righteousness when similarly reckless attacks were launched against liberals in general.

Leading American liberals in Congress desperately attempted to prove their own patriotism during the height of the red scare. For example, when the Internal Security Act came up for debate in September, 1950, liberal senators such as Paul Douglas of Illinois proposed what later became the emergency detention provisions of the act as a substitute proposal for the Mundt-Nixon and alien control provisions of the pending bill. This proposal, which when passed legalized in advance the establishment of concentration camps and incarceration without trials of subversives during times of "internal security" emergencies, was drawn up with the aid of ACLU attorneys.[356] Senator Hubert Humphrey argued for the detention bill as a "tough bill" compared to the "cream-puff special" then on the floor.[357] When the proposed detention substitute was instead incorporated in the pending bill, many Senate liberals, including Douglas, Humphrey, Wayne Morse and Harley Kilgore, voted for the final version. This version was also backed by the entire Democratic congressional leadership, including Sen. Scott Lucas, Vice President Alben Barkley,

House Speaker Sam Rayburn and House Majority Leader John McCormack.

Throughout the peak of McCarthy's influence, Democratic liberals in the Congress, such as Sen. John F. Kennedy, displayed great reluctance to criticize McCarthy or take any actions to deprive him of his committee appropriations, despite repeated indications of McCarthy's personal financial finagling, unethical tactics in election campaigns and contempt and defiance of Senate investigating committees. When the 1954 Communist Control Act was debated, the Democratic congressional leadership pressed for a bill to outlaw the CP, and an amendment to make CP membership a crime was introduced by Humphrey and co-sponsored by Morse and Kennedy. This provision was passed by the Senate and taken out of the bill only after President Eisenhower indicated he would veto such a bill.[358]

The conduct of liberal congressmen throughout the 1950-54 period was caused by determination to prove their own anti-communism, no matter what the cost to their democratic principles. Thus, in 1950, Sen. Herbert Lehman's legislative assistant wrote to Lehman that the concentration camp proposal was a "very bad bill" with "profound" constitutional weaknesses, but it would "certainly impress the public with the fact that you are determined to act against communists." During the 1954 debate on the Communist Control act, Morse declared, "In the Senate there is no division of opinion among liberals, conservatives and those inbetween when it comes to our utter detestation of the communist conspiracy."[359]

Fear of being labelled "soft" on communism played a similar role in influencing the behavior of liberal public officials throughout the country. Thus, in Pennsylvania, during debate on the "Pechan" anti-communist act of 1951, Democratic Minority Leader Sen. John H. Dent declared that although he personally opposed the bill:

> I would be derelict in my duties to the Democratic Party if I did not vote for this piece of legislation today. . . . I cannot permit my party to be further stigmatized as a party friendly to un-American activities. . . . We are living in a day when men will hide behind the decent emblem of patriotism to do things that they would not do openly, but as a leader of my party, I must subscribe to the days that we live in.[360]

Similarly, during debate on Maryland's 1949 Ober Act, "few lawmakers were willing to incur the political risks involved in taking a stand that might be interpreted as a manifestation of sympathy toward communism."[361] During debate in California over the 1949 Tenney proposals (which were defeated), one member of the State Senate wrote to the League of Women Voters that while he opposed the bills:

> one hesitates to express his honest conviction in a public forum because the danger of being misunderstood and forever labelled as being a 'fellow traveler,' leftist, disloyal or some other derogatoy term, which may prejudice people against him and seriously handicap his further usefulness.[362]

The role of the ACLU during the height of the red scare brought it little credit. According to a recent student of the ACLU, the organization "wavered in its defense of freedom and contributed instead to the growing national hysteria."[363] In 1940, when anti-communist and anti-fascist sentiment had been rapidly growing, the ACLU had first adopted the theory of guilt by association and voted to exclude members of political organizations supporting totalitarian dictatorships from serving on its governing committees or staff. In 1951, the ACLU incorporated the 1940 policy into its constitution; in 1953 the ACLU Board of Directors established a new policy in which it rejected as *members* any persons whose "devotion to civil liberties" was "qualified by adherence to Communist, Fascist, KKK or other totalitarian doctrine." To further demonstrate its anti-communism, beginning in 1951 the ACLU included a statement of its opposition to Communism in all legal briefs filed in cases where Communism was an issue. In a number of controversial cases, the ACLU's participation was delayed or ambivalent when it was forthcoming at all. For example, the ACLU refused to become involved actively in the 1949 CP Smith Act trials.

Along with the collapse of most of the liberal institutions in American society that might be expected to defend first amendment freedoms during the 1947-54 period came the collapse of the Supreme Court.[364] With only a few exceptions, the Court, which up to about 1946 followed a policy strongly favorable to civil liberties, after 1948 began to refuse to review lower court decisions adverse to civil liberties or else took cases and handed down decisions which dealt the first amendment severe blows. As Walter Murphy has noted, the Vinson Court "managed to sidestep or to sustain almost every question of federal power" and in cases involving loyalty questions performed the function of "imparting the benediction of constitutional orthodoxy upon political decisions."[365]

The court avoided challenging the power of HUAC during 1948-50 by the simple device of refusing to grant *certiori* in appeals against lower court decisions which upheld HUAC's powers to make broad investigations into subversive activities and upheld contempt citations of persons who had refused to answer questions before HUAC on grounds related to the first amendment. The court also refused to review the convictions in the Hiss and Rosenberg cases. Even more damaging to civil liberties were those cases where the court ruled. The major cases included: *Bailey v. Richardson* (1950) upholding by a 4-4 vote a lower court decision ruling that federal employees could be dismissed in loyalty proceedings on the basis of unsworn secret evidence submitted by unnamed persons; *Dennis v. U.S.* (1951), upholding the constitutionality of the Smith Act in the 1949 CP trial *Gerende* v. *Board of Supervisors of Elections of Baltimore* (1951), upholding a modified version of Maryland's Ober Law; *Garner* v. *Board of Public Works of Los Angeles* (1951), upholding a Los Angeles loyalty oath required of public employees; *American Communications Association* v. *Douds* (1950), upholding the Taft-Hartley anti-communist oath; and *Adler v. Board of Education* (1952), upholding New York's Feinberg Law of 1949 which provided that teachers could be fired for mere membership in organizations listed by the New York State Board of Regents as advocating the teaching of the violent overthrow of the government. The court also upheld a whole series of extremely repressive laws and administrative measures with regard to allegedly subversive aliens, including deportations under the Smith Act for CP membership which had ended before passage of the act, deportations and exclusions without notice, hearings or judicial inquiry into the truth of allegations, and denial of bail to alleged subversives pending deportation hearings.

The Vinson court reached only two major decisions favorable to civil liberties during the 1947-54 period. In *Weiman v. Updegraff* the court threw out an Oklahoma loyalty oath for state employees on the grounds that it required disavowal of membership in various organizations without requiring that the membership have been held with knowledge of the organizations' allegedly subversive activities. In *Joint Anti-Fascist Refugee Committee v. McGrath* (1951), the court held that for the Attorney General to list organizations as subversive without hearings or notice was "patently arbitrary" and could not be allowed. After the federal government established hearing procedures for listing groups in compliance with the court decision, the Attorney General made no attempt to list any additional organizations. Further, in every case in which organizations already listed sought to challenge the listing, the Justice Department eventually abandoned the case. Few such challenges were brought however, since by the time hearing procedures were established in 1953, few of the listed organizations were still in existence. Thus, the Attorney General's list had caused untold damage to scores of organizations by a procedure later held to be totally illegal by the Supreme Court, and once procedures were established to bring the listing into compliance with legal requirements the Federal government was unable to sustain a single case.[366]

The Long-Term Effects of Truman-McCarthyism

Some of the long-term effects of the Truman-McCarthy period of political repression are quite easy to document, while others are difficult to conclusively demonstrate yet are clearly apparent from a serious study of the period and its immediate aftermath. The most dramatic and easily documentable effect of the Truman-McCarthy period was the virtual annihilation of the Communist Party, whose membership dropped from over seventy thousand in 1946 to less than twenty-five thousand in 1954.[367] Certainly many of these defections resulted from ideological fallings-out, but the Smith Act prosecutions of over one hundred top CP leaders, coupled with the incessant Congressional hearings, the government loyalty programs, private blacklistings and firings and the general atmosphere in the country were of major importance. Irving Howe and Lewis Coser, the leading (and highly critical) historians of the CP, maintain that even "if the party had not been harassed by government attack" it would have lost a large portion of its membership as a result of internal party policies; however, they concede that, "as it was, the party lost heavily, but often for reasons having less to do with genuine intellectual disenchantment than with personal fear."[368]

One of the clearest indicators of the effects of fear on the CP was the pattern of collapse in subscriptions to party newspapers. Subscriptions to the *Daily* and *Sunday Worker* held, respectively, at about twenty thousand and sixty-seven thousand from 1945 to 1950, well after the development of the Cold War should have caused the ideologically disenchanted to leave, but before the rise of McCarthyism and the high point of the repression. By 1953, subscriptions to the *Daily Worker* had dropped to ten thousand and subscriptions to the *Sunday Worker* to twenty-nine thousand.[369]

Those who chose to stay *in* the CP were as strongly affected by repression by those who left the party in fear. In 1949, following the first Smith Act prosecution, the CP went underground for the first time since the Palmer Raids, and with many of the same disastrous effects of underground life suffered earlier. The underground mentality led to an increasing isolation from the mainstream of American life and to an internal cannibalization and series of purges which resulted largely from the fear of government infiltration.[370] David Shannon notes:

> There is a bitter humor in the fact that the measures the party took to safeguard its 'internal security' against its enemies were in many ways similar to the measures that federal and state governments and American society in general took to protect itself against the Communists. Both instituted loyalty checks. Both became irrationally suspicious of behavior and thought that did not conform to its norms. Both expelled and ostracized suspected individuals. Both infringed freedom in the quest for security, although the party never had afforded freedom to its own members. Both injured innocent people — that is, those who were not actually working for the enemy.[371]

According to Joseph Starobin, foreign editor of the *Daily Worker* during the underground period, the underground existence took an "enormous political, financial and personal toll" as husbands and wives separated, children grew up without understanding what had happened to their parents, and "scores of nervous and mental breakdowns occurred." He adds, "The fact that government agents seemed to know all about it utterly undermined its credibility."[372] Howe and Coser write:

> Because everyone knew that the party was crawling with informers . . . the relationship among the members became poisoned with suspicion; and the tough policies of the leaders, though meant as a means of protecting the organization, actually contributed to this mood of pervasive mistrust. It would be hard to say which did more damage to the psychological security and intellectual morale of the average party member: the assaults of the government or the responses of the party leadership. Between the

two an unbearable tension was set up in the mind of the average comrade; for a year or two he might try to live with it; but then, unless he were one of the hardened veterans, he found himself, sometimes against his will, drifting away.[373]

Operating under the conditions which prevailed from 1950 to 1954, the CP had to abandon virtually all activity directed at promoting party growth and policies; instead "from 1949 on, the American communists were forced to spend a large part of their time, energy and money trying to stay out of prison and trying to maintain the legality of their organization."[374] The silencing of the CP during this period meant also the silencing of the most important organization which had maintained a constant criticism of American Cold War foreign policy, and reinforced the lesson which the Truman administration had been teaching since 1947 — that it was not "safe" to engage in such criticism.

The Communist Party was not the only organization which suffered severely during the 1947-54 period. Organizations which were listed by the Attorney General suffered major membership losses and were subjected to severe discrimination at the hands of governmental agencies, also. Other organizations suffered merely as a result of being mentioned unfavorably before Congressional or state subversive activities committees. For example, charges were made before the Canwell Committee of Washington State that the Seattle Repertory Playhouse, a local theatre group, was controlled by Communist Party members and was part of a CP plot to propagandize youth at the University of Washington. Subsequent to the first charges made against the playhouse in January, 1948, total gross income of the playhouse dropped from $40,000 in the 1946-47 season to $14,000 in the 1948-49 season, as the result of a sudden drop in attendance and cancellation of advance sales. In late 1950, the University of Washington purchased the playhouse theatre and the Seattle Repertory Playhouse went out of business.[375]

In a Cold War atmosphere in which any foreign policy position which did not advocate the strongest possible stand against communism appeared suspect, the American peace movement, which had shown signs of renewed vitality in the immediate aftermath of World War II, was virtually devastated by 1950. In 1952, a representative on the United States Commission of a United Nations agency commented, "I have found recently that to be an advocate of peace or world government is almost equivalent to advocating the overthrow of the United States Government by force." It was indicative of the general atmosphere that of twenty-three state legislatures that passed resolutions after World War II supporting world federation, sixteen states had repealed their resolutions by late 1951.[376]

Another indicator of the effects of fear was the fate of the *American Review of Soviet Medicine,* a journal founded in 1943 which published translations of scholarly articles which had previously appeared in Russian medical periodicals. When the Truman loyalty order was issued in March,

1947, the publishers of the journal, the American-Soviet Medical Society, had six hundred members in Washington, D.C.; within two years, this number had dropped to thirty. In Bethesda, Maryland, a Washington suburb, with many government health research installations, the journal had one hundred fifty subscriptions in March, 1947; by the time publication was suspended in October, 1948, not a single subscription remained in Bethesda. The American-Soviet Medical Society was never listed as a "subversive" organization, but in the climate of the times, as Walter Gellhorn has commented:

> In order to avoid doubt about their loyalty, federal medical scientists appear to have felt that they must remain ignorant of Soviet research that might very well possibly have furthered their own work.[377]

The effect of the loyalty hysteria, and the secrecy cult which accompanied it, upon scientific research generally in the United States cannot be measured with any accuracy, but clearly was adverse. In June, 1949, Dr. Arthur H. Compton, one of America's leading nuclear physicists, who had been intimately involved in the research leading to the development of the atomic bomb, stated:

> Many of our best scientists left Nazi Germany because science was not free, and the tenor of political thought today is leading many a scientist to ask himself whether this situation is not repeating itself in America, whether even in the United States thought can be free and humane motives be supreme.[378]

Some eminent scientists were in effect driven from the country as a result of charges made about their political beliefs and affiliations, some foreign scientists who could have contributed to American research progress were barred from entry to the U.S., some scientists were denied government appointments on the grounds that their loyalty was suspect, and thousands of scientists decided not to apply for government work or grants, or were delayed in their work because of the loyalty procedures.[379] The *New York Times* reported in June, 1949:

> Officials estimate that as many as twenty to fifty thousand technicians, engineers, scientists and other key industrial employees either are not working or have only interim clearance on their jobs pending their specific approval for handling classified processes or material. . . . The mounting accumulation of security investigations to be made of industrial workers threatens not only to be a drag on important defense contracts that should be completed promptly, officials believe, but also to be a staggering administrative task for the national military establishment.[380]

During the course of J. Robert Oppenheimer's security clearance hearing in 1954, Major General Leslie Richard Groves, who had been in charge of security for the atomic bomb development program that Oppenheimer headed during World War II, testified that he "would not clear" Oppenheimer on the basis of current security standards, largely because of

Oppenheimer's pre-war political and personal associations; had such standards existed during World War II and Oppenheimer been excluded from the program, the U.S. might have been considerably delayed in its atomic bomb program.[381] Since many scientists who dealt with classified materials would not have been able to work at all in their fields and many other scientists could not be hired by universities unless they had security clearances, the net effect of the Cold War loyalty fetish was to deter large numbers of scientists from becoming involved in virtually any political matters. As Walter Gellhorn wrote in 1950:

> No scientist who has confined his interests to his laboratory, his flower garden and his golf game has been touched by scandal. In the main, those to whom the Government has brought distressing embarassment were ones who became concerned, in a perfectly legal way, about racial discrimination or the Franco government or the importance of peaceful relations with the Soviet Union. Knowing this fact, many people now avoid the areas of non-professional debatability lest they jeopardize their professional futures.[382]

Scholarly and research organizations concerned with the social sciences were also severely adversely affected by the climate of the Cold War period. Perhaps the clearest victims in this area were the Institute of Pacific Relations (IPR) and the Fund for the Republic. IPR, a private organization founded in 1925 to coordinate research and information on Asia, had achieved by World War II, "pre-eminent status among Asian studies groups in the United States and abroad."[383] During the Cold War, IPR was subjected to repeated irresponsible and sensationalized charges to the effect that it was a Communist-dominated organization that was controlling American far eastern policy. Following the climax of these assaults, a highly publicized SISS investigation of IPR in 1951, foundation and corporate donations to IPR dried up and membership and membership contributions fell by two-thirds. In 1955, the Internal Revenue Service revoked IPR's tax exempt status on the grounds that IPR had "engaged in the dissemination of controversial and partisan propaganda" and had attempted to influence government officials. Although in 1960, a federal judge overruled the tax exempt revocation, declaring that the government did not produce a "scintilla of evidence" to support its allegations, IPR had been so gravely wounded that it dissolved in 1961. IPR was replaced as the leading organization for American scholars in the late 1950's by the Far Eastern Association (FEA); it was no coincidence that FEA, in both its journal and its other activities, carefully "stressed historical studies in preference to questions of current controversy."[384] According to IPR's historian, "it is likely that political pressures — or at least concern for political pressures by foundations and universities" account for the fact that even by the mid-seventies the leading scholarly journal devoted exclusively to modern China, *China Quarterly,* is published in London.[385]

The drying up of foundation money which helped to kill off IPR reflected the fact that in 1952 and again in 1954 House committees investigated the activities of American foundations. Although the foundations were given a clean bill in 1952, in late 1954 the Reece Committee charged that some large foundations were "directly supporting subversion," a charge which gave a clear warning to foundations to "stay away from grants which would give hostile congressmen an opening." The Reece report specifically cited foundation support of IPR — suggesting that this money somehow led to the "loss of China" and the Korean war — and attacked by name the largest and most prestigious private foundations in the United States, including the Carnegie, Rockefeller and Guggenheim foundations and a variety of scholarly organizations including the American Council of Learned Societies, the Social Science Research Council, the Foreign Policy Association and the Council on Foreign Relations. The report also attacked the Ford Foundation, which had financed the Fund for the Republic, and subsequently Congressman Reece named Fund President Robert M. Hutchins as having "clearly adopted a communist tactic."[386] Since its establishment in 1952, the Fund had been perhaps the leading private organization promoting research on problems of civil liberties arising from the Cold War atmosphere, and it had repeatedly honored other organizations and individuals who had opposed encroachments on American freedoms.[387] Faced with continuing attacks, including a HUAC investigation in 1956, and repeated harassment by the Internal Revenue Service, the Fund gradually drew in its horns and by the late 1950's transformed itself into a more self-contained and inner-directed study group concerned with an essentially abstract approach to the "study of the theory and practice of freedom," now known as the Center for the Study of Democratic Institutions.

The long-term effects of the Truman-McCarthy period of repression on individuals, as opposed to major organizations and sectors of American society, is particularly difficult to document but certainly was major. Ralph S. Brown, the author of the most comprehensive study of loyalty and security programs carried out by government and private organizations during this period, estimates that a total of 13.5 million Americans, out of a total labor force of 65 million, were subjected to such programs. Over 7 million government employees and employees of firms performing for defense agencies were subjected to such programs; among the 13.5 million were 7.2 million government employees and employees of private companies performing work for defense agencies and therefore subject to the federal loyalty program. At a cost to federal agencies from 1947 to 1957 of about $350 million, the federal government was unable to uncover a single spy, but did fire about thirty-nine hundred persons from federal employment and was responsible for the firing of another fifty-four hundred persons from private employers affected by the federal government; these figures indicate that about one-eighth of one percent of all employees affected by the Federal program were found to be not "loyal" and that the cost of firing such employees amounted to over $35,000 a piece. According to Brown, another one thousand state and local government employees were fired under loyalty programs and about twelve hundred persons were fired as a result of private programs and blacklists which imitated government programs. Brown's total figure of over eleven thousand firings as a result of government and private loyalty programs should be taken as an absolutely barebones minimum measure of how many persons had their lives *drastically* affected by the repressive climate of the period, to whom must be added the over one hundred persons prosecuted under the Smith Act and the one hundred thirty-five persons cited for contempt of HUAC.[388]

These firings had long range consequences. For example, one ex-Communist Party member was hired and fired from fourteen mediocre jobs within a six month period in 1957; in each case he was fired as soon as his background was discovered.[389] In some cases firings eventually resulted in the destruction of marriages; in one case, a professor who was fired from a Michigan university and moved to Canada because he could not get another job in the United States, reported that his dismissal

> had a relatively permanent effect on our eldest son, who was seven at the time. . . . He was subjected to a considerable amount of both verbal and physical abuse and has never forgotten it.[390]

In many cases, those fired or who resigned under pressure who were able to gain employment at all were forced to accept jobs far below their skill level. For example, Frank Oppenheimer, the brother of J. Robert Oppenheimer, who resigned as a physics professor at the University of Minnesota to avoid certain firing in 1949 when he appeared before HUAC and admitted to former CP membership, was unable to get a job teaching physics at the college level for ten years. In the meantime, he worked as a sheep rancher and high school teacher, all the time under constant and open surveillance from FBI agents.[391] Many entertainers who were blacklisted were totally unable to find work, and some left the country. Thus, the income of actor Frederic March, and his wife, actress Florence Eldridge, dropped from one of the highest in the country for an acting team to $2.58 in 1948 after attacks were made upon them by private groups and Mrs. March was called before California's Tenney Committee. Movie director Jules Dassin, unable to find employment after being "named" before HUAC, went to Europe, where he directed major movies, including "Never on Sunday" and "Topkapi." Film writer and producer Carl Foreman moved to Britain in 1952, after being called before HUAC, blacklisted and denied credit for producing the movie "High Noon." While in exile, Foreman produced major movies such as "The Bridge Over the River Kwai," and "The Guns of Navarone." Tap-dancer Paul Draper and his sidekick, harmonica player Larry Adler, who were among the most successful American entertainers in the late 1940's, earning $200,000 a year, also went to Europe following their blacklisting, they performed again for the first time in the U.S. in June, 1975. Composer Lan Adomian, who had fought with the Abraham Lincoln Brigade in the Spanish Civil War, was never involved in a public controversy, but was simply unable to find work; he returned to his native Mexico in 1952, and by 1975 had composed eight symphonies, an opera, thirty-three cantatas, chamber music pieces and other compositions. Whether the loss of these and other individuals was a greater tragedy for them or for the country is an open question.[392]

In addition to the eleven thousand persons actually fired as a result of loyalty investigations and blacklists, between 1947 and 1953 over twenty thousand other people were subjected to formal filing of charges in in the federal loyalty program alone. Another three thousand persons were called before HUAC alone, and additional thousands of persons were "named" as subversives before HUAC, other congressional committees, state committees and by individual congressmen.[393] Although McCarthy was never able to find a single communist in government employment and the hearings held by HUAC and SISS led to only two convictions of federal employees — Alger Hiss and William Remington, both convicted of perjury[394] — the total number of persons "'injured' by the committees, whose connection with anything associated with the Communist Party was, at best, peripheral and farfetched, would be very copious," and the "fear, however vague, of being called to testify, of being somehow 'named' or of joining an organization that might someday be cited, was an integral part of the impetus toward 'caution' so characteristic of the McCarthy era."[395]

As loyalty program expert Ralph Brown has suggested, even those subjected to loyalty charges but not fired or jailed suffered

> severe economic and emotional hardships. . . . For those who are brushed even lightly with security suspicions, the upshot is often a special kind of personal insecurity. If they have any kind of tenure in a job, they can probably hang onto it; but their ability to move either upward or outward is much lessened. A possible promotion or a different job are occasions for a formal review of the employee's record; they revive the old doubts and require a new decision whether those doubts are a barrier to the new position, though they are not to the old one.[396]

In some cases, being named before a Congressional committee led to severe physical reprisals. For example, in 1959, an FBI informer who had been identified before a committee by *another* informer as a Communist reported:

> My family and myself have been discriminated very badly and hurt, cut up to pieces because people pointed and thrown bricks and slapped me in the face and done everything imaginable because the neighborhood I lived in, there are no Communists and they can't stand a Communist.[397]

In some cases, there is poignant first-hand testimony as to the effect facing loyalty charges or undergoing loyalty hearings had on the individuals involved. For example, Melville Jacobs, a professor at the University of Washington who admitted former CP membership and was ultimately put on "probation" for two years by the University after facing dismissal proceedings in 1949, was asked if he might join the CP again if there was a threatened fascist resurgence. He replied:

> I have been through a lot, especially in recent months. . . . In my present state of mind, something would have to happen to some of the cells of my cerebrum before anybody could persuade me to ever touch politics with a ten-foot pole after what I have been through.[398]

Actress Judy Holliday, who was called before a congressional committee in 1952 for questioning about her support of the Wallace campaign of 1948, stated, "I don't say 'yes' to anything now except cancer, polio and cerebral palsy, and things like that."[399] One government employee who had been investigated and cleared several times, stated, "If the communists like apple pie and I do, I see no reason why I should stop eating it, but I would."[400]

The experience which many people had during the 1947-54 period appears to have drastically affected their basic view of human nature in an extremely negative way. Thus, one professor who was fired from a university stated:

> Having been treated almost like a pariah . . . I shall never again view friendship with anything but a cautious, even cynical eye. It isn't simply that people are self-interested . . . but that almost everyone lacks the simplest requirement of courage.[401]

Millard Lampell, a writer who was blacklisted for ten years recorded the following vignette in his journal:

> Walking down Broadway, someone catches my elbow from behind. It is R., whom I have known for fifteen years, and who recently appeared as a 'cooperative witness' before the Committee (HUAC). He asks plaintively why I passed him without saying hello, and I explain that I didn't see him. He shakes his head, 'No, no you stared right at me.' He grimaces. "I don't blame you. I'm disgusting. Do you think I'm disgusting?" I am not particularly proud of the fact that I nodded yes and walked away. Who appointed me his judge? He's as much a victim as the rest of us.[402]

Some persons accused of disloyalty reacted to the charges against them with a proclamation of their anti-communist and pro-American credentials that must have been a humiliating and self-degrading experience. For example, Phillip C. Jessup, a distinguished ambassador, made the following remarks before the Tydings Committee in 1950 to answer charges of pro-Communism made by McCarthy:

> An inquiry into my background would have shown that my ancestors came to this country from England in the seventeenth century. . . . My great-grandfather, Judge William Jessup of Montrose, Pennsylvania, was a dele-

gate to the Republican convention of 1860 which nominated Abraham Lincoln for the presidency. . . . In July, 1921, I married Lois Walcott Kellogg, whose ancestors were also of English and Dutch pioneer stock, and whose mother was a sister of the late Frederick C. Walcott, United States Senator from Connecticut . . . in Utica, I was also superintendent of the Sunday School of the First Presbyterian Church and commander of a local post of the American Legion. I am still a member of the American Legion.[403]

Appearing before HUAC in 1953, University of Chicago historian Daniel Boorstin, who had left the CP in 1939, told the Congressmen he had expressed his opposition to communism by "affirmative participation in religious activities, because I think religion is a bulwark against communism" and by writing and teaching about the virtues of democracy, including writing a book about Thomas Jefferson, "which, by the way, was bitterly attacked in the *Daily Worker* as something defending the ruling class in America."[404]

While the effects of the Truman-McCarthy period were especially marked upon those actually fired, jailed or accused of subversive activities, affiliations or beliefs, the most important effects of the period were probably in "chilling" the potential for dissent — or even thought — among those who had not *yet* been accused. The Navy, in a document entitled "Suggested Counsel to Employees" perhaps best summed up the message which the atmosphere of this time transmitted to the average citizen:

> A number of our citizens unwittingly expose themselves to unfavorable or suspicious appraisal which they can and should avoid. This may take the form of an indiscreet remark; an unwise selection of friends or associates; membership in an organization whose true objectives are concealed behind a popular and innocuous title; attendance at and participation in the meetings and functions of such organizations even though not an official member; or numerous other clever means designed to attract support under false colors or serving to impress an individual with his own importance. It is advisable to study and seek wise and mature counsel prior to association with persons or organizations of any political or civic nature, no matter what their apparent motives may be, in order to determine the true motives and purposes of the organization. . . . The existence of (rights and liberties under the Constitution) should encourage and inspire each one of us to so conduct ourselves that there cannot be the least concern on the part of our associates as to our adherence to the principles of this government, or as to our reliability.[405]

The none-too-subtle message of this Navy document, and of the loyalty program and legislative investigations, was that citizens should be careful about joining *any* organization, signing *any* document, saying *any* thing, or even thinking *any* thought if this might (to use the Navy's phrase) create the "least concern" about one's "reliability."

Concrete evidence as to the effect of Truman-McCarthyism on the "average" person is sketchy, and somewhat anecdotal, but it all points in one direction — that the chilling effect was very strong indeed. For example, in a number of experiments undertaken during the height of the repression, researchers found that 80 percent or more of persons stopped at random and asked to sign petitions consisting of quotes from the Declaration of Independence and the Bill of Rights refused to do so.[406] A series of interviews with seventy federal employees in the Washington, D.C. area, (a group particularly vulnerable to repressive pressures) in the early 1950's led two New York University researchers to conclude:

> The security issue has become part of the prevalent climate of thought, and underlies in the form of tacit assumptions many aspects of everyday behavior ... the hazards of *being investigated* — even if one is subsequently cleared — are so great that individuals are induced to limit their behavior by avoiding (or trying to avoid) anything that might conceivably arouse anyone's suspicion and thus lead to charges and an investigation.[407]

Among the specific "precautions" which many of the federal employees interviewed in this study reported taking were dropping membership or literature subscriptions from groups on the Attorney General's list, being careful in political conversations with strangers, not signing petitions without being convinced of bona fide sponsors and not reading in public communist publications. When asked what kind of people they thought might form the target for unfounded suspicions, the employees repeatedly mentioned persons who "belong to voluntary organizations with definite purposes," suggesting that a major effect of the political atmosphere was to make joining such organizations a less likely behavior.[408]

Two anecdotes from this study capture the effect of the climate upon at least some federal employees. One subject of the study

> told a joke against himself: he had a very good shortwave set, and in fiddling with the set he caught Radio Moscow. "I looked over my shoulder to see whether anybody was observing me, being scared for a moment," he said, laughing off his hysterical reaction.

Another respondent reported:

> A friend and I were riding on a streetcar and he read a newspaper reporting about the American Legion and began to mock it so that our immediate neighbors could hear him. I thought to myself: why doesn't he shut up before we are accused of being communists. Several friends have told me that they found themselves in similar situations and that they experienced feelings similar to mine.[409]

Other studies suggest that the pressures created by the loyalty program were so great that many federal employees suffered severe mental problems. Two suburban Washington psychiatrists wrote in 1955 that their observations of thirty patients suggested that "the effects of the security program may now or may soon be of sufficient scope to constitute a mental hygiene problem of national proportions."[410] Another Washington area psychiatrist wrote in 1953:

> Dismissal from government positions, demotions, transfers, interdiction of classified material, or even the ever-impending danger of such actions as

> the result of security investigations have the effect not only of posing grave threats to economic and social status but have actually brought about an appreciable number of symptomatic mental and emotional illnesses ranging in severity from anxiety and obsessive ruminative states to paranoid psychotic breaks. There are a number of factors which favor the development of paranoid states by characterologically predisposed people. These include the essentially secret, almost furtive nature of the proceedings, the difficulty in obtaining specific charges, the Kafkaesque feeling of isolation and helplessness of the indivdual confronted wth the vast and impersonal mass of government procedural machinery, the almost inevitable feelings of shame and guilt of even the most innocent, the anxious self-questioning, the doubts about friends and neighbors, and the impossibility of ever being faced with a specific personal accuser.[411]

More impressionistic studies of the effects of the federal loyalty program upon federal employees and employment report with monotonous regularity the author's feeling that the program tended to deter people from entering government employment, greatly lowered the morale of employees, led thousands of federal employees to exercise self-censorship of their political affiliations, activities, beliefs and reading matter, and in general severely stifled creativity and innovation in the executive branch. According to students of the federal program, "it spread a pall of fear through the ranks of the Federal bureaucracy, from file clerks to bureau heads," and caused the Federal employee to be "guarded in his utterances" and "ruthless in his associations" for fear of the consequences. Government workers were reported to "hesitate to join or support any new organization" and to resist signing "any petition, no matter how impeccable its backers."[412] Eleanor Bontecue noted:

> People both in and out of the government are aware that their books may be regarded as evidence against them and anyone renting his house to a stranger in the neighborhood of Washington is careful to censor his library before surrendering possession to his tenants.[413]

Attorneys defending accused Federal employees reportedly tried to picture their clients as "models of orthodoxy, limited intelligence and subservience"; in one case a lawyer advised one government employee who had been through one loyalty hearing and wanted to avoid another, "Drop your Negro friends and express no views whatsoever on any programs which are not generally accepted as conservative."[414]

The most extensive study of the effect of Truman-McCarthyism upon individuals was a series of interviews with 2541 social science teachers in 165 colleges (another group particularly vulnerable to repressive pressures), carried out by a research team headed by sociology professor Paul Lazarsfeld in the spring of 1955, shortly after the Senate's censure of McCarthy.[415] The Lazarsfeld study concluded that the climate of opinion had created "widespread apprehension among these social science teachers" and had placed a "noticeable damper on the activities and opinions of a sizable minority;" however, the study found that the effects were not of a "paralyzing nature." The study found that 46 percent of respondents exhibited "medium" or "high" apprehension about possible adverse repercussions to them as a result of their political beliefs and activities.[416]

Among some of the specific findings of the study were the following: about 40 percent were worried that their students may pass on "warped" versions of what they said or wondered if their political beliefs might become a "subject of gossip" in the community; about 35 percent reported their colleagues were less willing to express unpopular views in the community and their students were less willing to express such views in class as compared to "six or seven years ago;" 46 percent said students were less willing to form and join political organizations which advocated possibly unpopular political beliefs; 18 percent said they avoided bringing up certain topics with their colleagues; about one-third reported that they were less inclined to sponsor controversial student political groups; and over 40 percent reported that their colleagues were less willing to sponsor such groups.

Among the more apprehensive respondents, the Lazarfeld researchers reported that one ex-supporter of Wallace had stopped lecturing on Soviet geography, that some teachers stopped using the *Communist Manifesto* or material from the Soviet Embassy, that one teacher tape-recorded every session of his course on a "critical study of Marxism" to guard against any misquotations by his students, and that some teachers concluded the "only safe course is simply to shun all political participation." One teacher stated, "I habitually keep all my classes as confused as possible as to my own views." The study found that as a result of the political climate some teachers omitted certain topics from classroom discussions, and others slanted their presentations away from their real convictions, or else "balanced an intellectually preferred but controversial position with discussion of a more popular opposing viewpoint." The researchers concluded:

> It appears likely that for every teacher who was actually conscious of shifting his classroom stand there were more who unwittingly either drifted along with the times completely, or partially reoriented their position.

The only scientific study of the effects of the political climate upon a cross-section of the general population was a study conducted in the spring and summer of 1954 by a research team headed by Samuel Stouffer of almost five thousand citizens, plus an additional sample of fifteen hundred selected "local community leaders."[417] Among the cross-section of citizens 31 percent said "some people do not feel as free to say what they think as they used to" and 10 percent said "hardly anybody feels as free to say what he thinks as he used to." However, only 13 percent admitted to personally feeling not "as free." Among the community leaders, similar responses were made by 41 percent, 7 percent and 13 percent, respectively.

One of the clearest indicators of the long-term effects of the Truman-McCarthy period was the political lethargy of American college students throughout the 1950's, which earned them the appellation, "The Silent

Generation." The number of activist students during the entire decade—although increasing in the last two or three years of the 1950's — was miniscule, and most left-wing organizations on campus that had been active in the previous twenty years were virtually moribund.[418] In March, 1957, *The Nation* devoted an entire issue to reports from sixteen college campuses documenting the political apathy exhibited by most students. Stanley Kunitz, a poet and English professor at Queens College, wrote that students "matriculate cautious, wanting above all — so well-conditioned are they by the prevailing social climate — to buy security for themselves in the full knowledge that the price is conformity."[419] Jack Newfield wrote of his college experiences in the late 1950's that few of the three thousand undergraduates at Hunter College joined any campus organization, "a lesson absorbed from the 'Don't sign and don't join' McCarthy experience. We all remembered the State Department employee McCarthy pilloried because of editorials he had written for the *Columbia Spectator* and peitions he had signed twenty-five years before. When speakers like Norman Thomas came to the campus he addressed seventy-five students and hundreds of vacant auditorium seats."[420]

Cartoonist Jules Fieffer recalls that when lecturing at college campuses during the 1950's he would often make what he thought was a most provoking speech on contemporary issues, and then be greeted at the end with abysmal silence. Finally someone would ask a question like, "Where do you get your ideas?" or "What size drawing paper do you use?"[421] Aryeh Neier, president in 1957-58 of the Student League for Industrial Democracy, (SLID) one of the few even vaguely leftish groups still functioning on campuses, recalled later the reasons for SLID's near collapse:

> The fears engendered by the McCarthy headline hunting may not have resulted in mass hysteria on the college campus but they did result in a degree of overcautiousness on the part of the college student who decided to play it safe and never sign or join anything.[422]

College students were by no means the only Americans who remained "silent" during the decade; the 1950's in general (even after the censure of McCarthy and the easing of repression) exhibited characteristics of complacency, conformity and super-patriotism strangely reminiscent of the 1920's — which, not coincidentally, was an earlier period which had followed an era of intense repression. In 1959, Norman Mailer wrote:

> These have been the years of conformity and depression. A stench of fear has come out of every pore of American life, and we suffer from a collective failure of nerve. The only courage, with rare exceptions, that we have been witness to, has been the isolated courage of isolated people.[423]

The "lessons" of the Truman-McCarthy period were no more quickly forgotten than were the lessons of the 1917-20 repression. Further, the destruction of the leading organizations of radical dissent — the Progressive Party and the Communist Party — left dissenters with no organization to rally around, while the hangover effects of the repression made it extremely difficult to try to organize new vehicles of dissent. Like the 1920's, again, domestic prosperity and a desire for a return to "normalcy," added to the factors which dampened dissent during this period, but fear of being brought before a Congressional committee, spied on by the FBI, tried for sedition, fired from one's job, or simply being accused of being a "subversive" remained a potent disincentive to dissent. While it cannot be proved with any certainty or specificity, the overwhelming impressionistic evidence is that, as many scholars of the McCarthy period have suggested, millions of American citizens severely censored themselves in their speech, associations, reading materials, and even thoughts. Alert citizens "noted that one enters the zone of suspicion as soon as one moves any distance from the most orthodox of political or civic involvement" and "deciding that discretion was the better part of civic valor, avoided trouble by indulging in a kind of political prophylaxis."[424]

> Nearly everyone learned to be careful, to be anxious, to fear: not to sign a petition, not to join an organization, not to give money, not to be seen with certain books, not to speak your opinion lest someone misinterpret, accuse, inform. Americans were told every horror story of Soviet suppression of free expression, and everyone knew that Siberia was the cold and barren place where the Russians sent their dissidents for punishment. Yet all too few Americans realized they were generating their own Siberias in their minds.[425]

It seems likely that thousands of Americans were deterred from even entering certain professions for fear of the restrictions on their freedom that would have been entailed; certainly this was the case for those who took the poignant advice offered in 1954 by Albert Einstein, who had earlier fled the tyranny of Nazi Germany:

> If I would be a young man again and I had to decide how to make my living, I would not try to become a scientist or scholar or teacher. I would rather choose to be a plumber or a peddler in the hope to find that modest degree of independence still available under present circumstances.[426]

During the 1950's (again, as during the 1920's) proposals for serious domestic reform were likely to be attacked as "communistic" or "socialistic" when they were made and discussed at all, which was increasingly infrequently. Indeed, one of the major virtues of the "anti-communist" fever was, as Carey McWilliams has pointed out, like most heresy-hunts, anti-communism proved to be a "highly versatile weapon to catch heretics," with the targets of the hunt gradually swelling from "Communists to former Communists, anyone accused of being a Communist, socialists, liberals, New Dealers and Democrats in general."[427] The anti-communist argument was used to fight government programs of health care, fluoridation of water, the admission of Hawaii to the union, and even the unrestricted sale of oleomargarine.[428] Historian Henry Steele Commager pointed out the "new loyalty" was above all, conformity. It is the uncritical and unquestioning acceptance of America as it is — the political institutions, the social relationships, the economic practices. It rejects inquiry into the race question or socialized medicine, or public housing, or into the wisdom of our foreign policy. It regards as particularly heinous any challenge to what is called "the system of private enterprise" identifying that system with Americanism. It regards America as a finished product, perfect and complete.[429]

The Democratic Party, throughout the 1950's, remained "three parts loyal and only one part opposition,"[430] while, as John Caughey wrote in 1958:

> Reform and liberalism in general have been intimidated. Many a liberal organization has felt it so necessary to prove that it harbors no communists that it has had little energy left to do anything else.[431]

While charging a program was "communistic" or "socialistic" was one of the easiest ways to defeat a proposal without bothering to discuss its merits, conversely, claiming a program would help to "fight" communism was of considerable aid in fostering proposals. Thus, as early as 1950, Walter Lippman lamented that America's obsession with communism "had gotten to the point where we can hardly send milk to babies abroad without explaining that this is an important action in our cold war against communism," while as late as 1962, New York Times Columnist James Reston complained, "It has got so you can't get money for a school or road from Congress without arguing that failure to build them will mean the triumph of communism."[432]

While liberals tried to use anti-communist rhetoric to further their goals, in general conservative and business groups were far more successful in riding the anti-communist wave in order to further and consolidate their power and influence. Writing in 1972, Richard Barnett commented:

> The successful effort to make all challenges to the anti-communist business creed look treasonous deserves some of the credit for the strange disappearance of the issues of fair distribution and concentration of corporate power during most of the postwar period. It was not easy during this period to admit the existence of a class conflict without running the risk of being labeled a "crypto" or "creeping" subversive. Business groups devoted considerable resources to blunderbuss attacks on leftists and radicals who raised such issues. Big business, the principal target of the Depression Era, became a prime mover in forging a patriotic consensus in which the legitimacy of its own rapidly expanding power was never questioned. The effect has been to eliminate serious economic and social criticism of the basic institutions of American life for two decades and to make the business creed the official standard for defining the national interest.[433]

The disappearance of domestic reform as a serious issue in American politics (at least until the Kennedy administration) was complemented by a lack of any serious challenge to or even serious debate about American foreign policy, until the massive escalation of the Vietnam War in 1965. If the "lessons" of the 1947-54 period with regard to domestic issues were that dissent might be viewed as subversive, the clear lesson with regard to foreign policy was that any dissent from a "hard-line" anti-communist stance was little short of treasonous. As William O'Neill suggests:

> People supported the government . . . more out of fear than confidence, partly also from habit. The Cold War had inspired a reflexive patriotism that turned blunders abroad into votes at home. Among those who did criticize the government's politicies, few were liberal or left wing. For one thing, there were hardly any leftists by (the early 1960's). . . . Most liberals . . . had been conditioned to accept the government line on foreign policy. What thought they gave it was mainly devotional. . . . This meant that attacks on government policy came mainly from the right.[434]

One clear indicator of the lack of debate over the orientation of American foreign policy was the passage by Congress in two days, with only two dissenting votes, of the so-called Gulf of Tonkin resolution in August, 1964, which in effect gave President Johnson a blank check in Vietnam to "take all necessary measures to repel any armed attack against the forces of the United States and to prevent further aggression."[435]

The main effect of "Truman-McCarthyism" on American foreign policy had a different character than did the effect on domestic policy, although in both cases the impact was to stifle debate. On domestic issues, the most important effect of the 1947-54 era was to dampen dissent in the society generally; on foreign policy issues, the most important effect was to freeze American policy *within* the executive branch, where foreign policy is essentially determined. In other words, the main effect of the repression with regard to domestic issues was on the general society; in foreign policy the main effect was to repress the policymakers themselves.

This process proceeded in essentially two ways: 1) within the State Department and the federal bureaucracy generally, officials who were regarded as "suspect" (i.e. not dedicated to a hardline anti-communist policy which viewed international communism as a monolithic conspiracy) were purged or reassigned out of their areas of speciality, and in general the message was clearly transmitted that any serious consideration of America's basic foreign policy orientation was not welcome. 2) Within the White House itself, the fear of a political backlash similar to that following the "loss" of China froze American presidents into a posture of responding to any alleged "communist" threat with the use of American armed forces or military aid, to the virtual exclusion of considering any other reaction.

The effects of the Truman-McCarthy period upon the State Department have been well documented. Virtually the entire China section of the department was purged by 1952, in most cases essentially for having correctly predicted that Chiang Kai-shek was fighting a losing struggle against the Chinese Communists. The general attack of the Republicans upon the State Department as a hotbed of subversion so paralyzed the department and discouraged applicants that not a single junior foreign service officer was appointed between 1952 and 1954.[436] In January, 1954, five veteran diplomats wrote in a letter to the *New York Times* that attacks upon the department had created a situation in which

The conclusion has become inescapable, for instance, that a foreign service officer who reports on persons and events to the very best of his ability and who makes recommendations which at the time he conscientiously believes to be in the interest of the United States may subsequently find his loyalty and integrity challenged. . . . It is not long before accuracy and initiative have been sacrificed to acceptability and conformity.[437]

In May, 1954, a committee appointed to study the problem of recruitment in the State Department reported to Secretary Dulles that a survey of forty-three chiefs of mission had led to thirty-three replies that morale within the Department was either low or "very low."[438] According to the leading expert on the fate of the "China hands," by the mid-fifties, "any mention at State of China in words that did not emanate from the lips of the Generalissimo (Chiang Kai-Shek) himself was regarded with suspicion."[439]

The problems of low morale and enforced conformity lasted within the Department well after the censure of McCarthy. According to another expert on the effects of the great Red hunt on the State Department writing in 1960, as a "direct result of the treatment of the China specialists" there is "over-whelming evidence that American officials in foreign posts consistently fail to seek out, to recognize or to report the activities of political groups which are not acceptable in Washington."[440] Oliver E. Clubb, one of the "China hands," who was forced to resign in the face of loyalty charges, stated later that the effect of the State Department purges was to place surviving State Department officials in a state of "psychic preventive detention."[441] In 1975, Clubb stated:

> Most of the names of persons involved (in the purge of the foreign service) never hit the press, but it was well known in the Foreign Service what was going on, with severe effect on morale and a willingness for innovation. The deadening of the intellectual atmosphere became terrible. . . . Ignorance of Asia became a particularly important factor when you took the experts out of this formulation process, as you did under the impact of McCarthyism and the introduction of more of the military element into our national strategy by reason of the cold war philosophy. After the Korean War, our development of a new policy toward China remained in a peculiarly stagnant condition. There were no voices of criticism or suggestion for nearly two decades. Instead of the experts, who had been discredited, you had people in roles of responsibility who reacted to what they thought were political forces in Congress.[442]

When Averell Harriman was appointed Assistant Secretary of State for Far Eastern Affairs (the State Department branch which handled Vietnam policy) in 1961, he confided to friends that the branch was

> a wasteland. It's a disaster area filled with human wreckage. Perhaps a few can be saved. Some of them are so beaten down, they can't be saved.[443]

Similarly, James C. Thompson, who was involved in Vietnam policymaking from 1961 to 1966 as an East Asian specialist at the State Department and the White House wrote later:

In 1961, the U.S. government's East Asian establishment was undoubtedly the most rigid and doctrinaire of Washington's regional divisions in foreign affairs. This was especially true at the Department of State, where . . . the Bureau of Far Eastern Affairs . . . had been purged of its best China expertise, and of farsighted, dispassionate men, as a result of McCarthyism . . . the shadow of the "loss of China" distorted Vietnam reporting. Career officers in the Department, and especially those in the field, had not forgotten the fate of their World War II colleagues who wrote in frankness about China and were later pilloried by Senate committees for critical comments on the Chinese Nationalists. Candid reporting on the strengths of the Viet Cong and the weaknesses of the Diem government were inhibited by the memory . . . a recurrent and increasingly important factor in the decision-making process was the banishment of real expertise.[444]

The "loss of China" syndrome affected other elements of the bureaucracy besides the State Department. Daniel Ellsburg, who worked on Vietnam policy for the State and Defense Departments from 1964 to 1967, wrote later that he was assigned in 1964 to write a paper for the Defense Department considering the possibility that the U.S. might "lose Indochina." According to Ellsburg, Assistant Secretary of Defense John McNaughton told him several times:

> You should be clear that you could be signing the death warrant to your career by having anything to do with calculations and decisions like these. A lot of people were ruined for less.

Ellsburg states that he was told to discuss the project with no one but McNaughton and that he was not to use a secretary, but to type his reports himself.[445]

The effects of the "loss of China" upon American foreign policy-making were perhaps even greater upon the White House than upon the State Department, since it was President Truman who was the ultimate target of the China recriminations. These effects were apparent immediately upon the "loss of China." Until the end of 1949, the U.S. "displayed little, if any real interest in Indochina" aside from "mild and restrained" urging to the French that they grant independence to the area. However, following the collapse of the nationalist regime in China in mid-1949 and the rise of the "who lost China" issue, the Truman administration, which had previously viewed Vietnamese emperor Bao Dai as incapable of mobilizing substantial support suddenly began to "depict him as a staunch patriot, capable of successfully challenging Ho Chi Minh for the allegiance of the Vietnamese nationalists." The initial American commitment to the French cause in Indochina, made *before* the Korean War, was increased after that event. The decision to send Gen. McArthur north of the 38th parallel during the Korean War, and the Truman administration's abandonment of moves in the direction of accomodation with Communist China in the early 1950's appear to have been motivated by similar fears of appearing to look "soft" on Communism.[446]

The Eisenhower administration's policy on Vietnam was influenced by similar considerations. While armed intervention in Indochina was rejected (Eisenhower had been elected partly because of frustration with the Korean War), the administration feared that "the same wing of the Republican Party that was still defending Joe McCarthy, and a public that was anxious about the advance of 'international communism' would not tolerate the abdication of still more territory to the Reds, especially by a government that had come into power vowing a tougher policy after having attributed previous enemy gains to the Democrats."[447] Thus, the administration refused to sign the 1954 Geneva accords for fear it would be remembered some day as a Republican "Yalta" (Secretary of State Dulles refused to even shake hands at Geneva with Chinese Foreign Minister Chou En-lai) and subsequently began sending aid to South Vietnam in hopes of averting its "fall."[448]

When the Kennedy administration entered office in 1961, the fear of being viewed as "soft on communism" had not diminished; indeed with a Democratic administration in office once more, the political lessons of McCarthyism became perhaps even stronger. Thus, according to Kennedy aide Theodore Sorenson, when Kennedy inherited the plans for the Bay of Pigs invasion of Cuba from the Eisenhower administration, he "permitted his own deep feelings against Castro . . . and considerations of public opinion — specifically his concern that he would be assailed for calling off a plan to get rid of Castro — to overcome his innate suspicions."[449] Shortly after the Bay of Pigs debacle, according to Kennedy aide Arthur Schlesinger, Jr., Kennedy told his aide Walt Rostow, in explanation for placing troops on the alert during a crisis over Laos

> that Eisenhower could stand the political consequences of Dien Bien Phu and the expulsion of the West from Vietnam in 1954 because the blame fell on the French. "I can't take a 1954 defeat today."[450]

Schlesinger also says Kennedy told U.N. Ambassador Adlai Stevenson in 1961 that American policy attempting to exclude Communist China from the U.N. "really doesn't make sense" but Stevenson "must do anything you can to keep them out" until "after the (1962 congressional) election."[451] According to journalist David Halberstam, top-ranking officials in the Kennedy administration learned that

> China must be discussed in private, not even at the most secret meetings, for fear that the idea that the Administration was even *thinking* of China might somehow leak out to the press and arouse the primitives.[452]

A memorandum submitted to Kennedy by Secretaries of State and Defense Rusk and McNamara in November, 1961, urging increased aid to South Vietnam stated that its "loss"

> to Communism would not only destroy SEATO but would undermine the

credibility of American commitments elsewhere. Further, the loss of South Vietnam would stimulate bitter domestic controversies in the United States and would be seized upon by extreme elements to divide the country and harass the Administration.[453]

In 1963, according to White House aide Kenneth O'Donnell, Kennedy said during a conversation with Senator Mike Mansfield that he agreed with Mansfield that a complete withdrawal from Vietnam was needed. However, O'Donnell (who witnessed the conversation) reports, Kennedy added:

> "But I can't do it until 1965 — after I'm re-elected" . . . President Kennedy felt, and Mansfield agreed with him, that if he announced a total withdrawal of American military personnel from Vietnam before the 1964 election, there would be a wild conservative outcry against returning him to the presidency for a second term. After Mansfield left the office, the President told me that he had made up his mind and that after his re-election he would take the risk of unpopularity and make a complete withdrawal of American forces from Vietnam. "In 1965, I'll be damned as a Communist appeaser. But I don't care. If I tried to pull out completely now, we would have another Joe McCarthy red scare on our hands, but I can do it after I'm re-elected."[454]

Lyndon Johnson was no less affected by fears of a right-wing attack if Vietnam were "lost" during his administration. Thus, in his memoirs, Johnson led off his discussion of Vietnam by stating, "A divisive debate about 'who lost Vietnam' would be, in my judgment, even more destructive to our national life than the argument over China had been."[455]

Shortly after taking office, Johnson told U.S. ambassador to South Vietnam Henry Cabot Lodge:

> I am not going to lose Vietnam. I am not going to be the President who saw Southeast Asia go the way China went.[456]

In February, 1965, shortly before the U.S. began continuous bombing of North Vietnam, national security adviser McGeorge Bundy sent Johnson a memo recommending a "policy of sustained reprisal" even though such a policy might fail and its chances of success could not be estimated

> with any accuracy. . . . What we can say is that even if it fails, the policy will be worth it. At a minimum it will damp down the charge that we did not do all that we could have done, and this charge will be important in many countries, including our own.[457]

Fears of a right-wing backlash also appear to have been instrumental in Johnson's decision to invade the Dominican Republic to head off a feared Communist-led revolt in 1965. "With 'no more Castros' becoming a shibboleth governing dealings with Latin America," Johnson feared that "a successful Communist revolution in the Dominican Republic might well jeopardize the future of the Democratic Party in the United States, if not of American liberalism in general."[458] Thus, Johnson is quoted as stating during the Dominican crisis:

> When I do what I am about to do, there'll be a lot of people in this hemisphere I can't live with, but if I don't there'll be a lot of people in this country I can't live with.459

According to Sen. William Fulbright, commenting on the Dominican affair:

> The specter of a second Communist state in the hemisphere — and its probable repercussions within the United States and possible effects on the careers of those who might be held responsible — seems to have been the most important single factor in distorting the judgment of otherwise sensible and competent men.460

While the Nixon administration was able to eventually extricate the U.S. from Vietnam the process was apparently delayed considerably for fear of the repercussions at home of a rapid withdrawal. Thus, Secretary of State Kissinger is quoted as telling reporters at an off-the-record news briefing in January, 1971:

> If we had done in our first year what our loudest critics call on us to do, the 13 percent that voted for (George) Wallace would have grown to 35 or 40 percent; the first thing the President set out to do was to neutralize that faction.461

President Nixon repeatedly stated publicly that he would not be the first American president to preside over a "defeat" by a foreign power. In June, 1971, *The New York Times* reported that the administration was concerned "about the effects a major South Vietnamese military defeat in the spring of 1972 might have on Republican fortunes in the Presidential election in November."462 CIA intervention aimed at "destabilizing" the popularly elected government of Marxist President Salvatore Allende of Chile was presumably partially motivated by fears of the domestic reaction to another "Castro."

In December, 1975, it was widely reported in the press that President Ford was wary about making agreements with the People's Republic of China concerning the status of Taiwan because "facing a tough conservative Republic opponent in his bid for reelection, the President simply cannot, in the opinion of his top political advisors, afford to make himself vulnerable to the charge of 'selling out' yet another of America's anti-communist allies so soon after the fall of Vietnam, Laos and Cambodia."463

David Halberstam has summed up the pressure towards militaristic and simplistic thinking that Truman-McCarthyism embedded in the American foreign policy making process in contrasting the later careers of the China "experts" with that of Dean Rusk, who was assistant secretary of state under Truman, and later secretary of state under Kennedy:

> The best people, who had correctly predicted the fall of China, would see their careers destroyed, but Dean Rusk, who had failed to predict the Chinese entry into the Korean War, would see his career accelerate. There had

to be a moral for him here; if you are wrong on the hawkish side of an event you are all right; if you are accurate on the dovish side you are in trouble.[464]

The "hangover" effect of the Truman-McCarthy period is certainly not the only explanation for the lack of a foreign policy debate in the United States and within American administrations during the 1950-1965 period, and the rigidity of American policy and the repeated stress on military solutions to situations threatening "communist" gains around the world. However, the political lesson of the "fall of China" debate clearly was an important and underlying theme in the American foreign policy making process throughout this period that operated to put restraints on the flexibility and open-mindedness of the American public, and more importantly, of American foreign policy-makers. This ironic outcome of the political repression first initiated by the Truman administration suggests that repression, like the genie in the bottle, may be far easier to unleash than it is to control. In the case of Vietnam, a good argument can be made that fifty thousand American soldiers eventually paid the price of unleashing repression with their lives.

Aside from the effects of Truman-McCarthyism upon the freedom of individuals and organizations both inside and outside of government to think and function freely, the period left what was perhaps an even more insidious legacy behind in grossly distorting basic concepts of American constitutional law. Three major themes unite the myriad of repressive activities which occurred during the Cold War period: 1) the essential charge made against the victims of repression was "wrong thinking," and since thought could not be probed directly, investigations by the FBI, congressional committees and government loyalty boards concentrated on entirely legal actions, such as friendships, organizational membership, reading matter and expression of political opinions; 2) since it could not be shown that the "wrong thinkers" had actually done anything harmful, most of the statutory and administrative repressive actions, such as the loyalty program, the Smith Act trials, passport restrictions and the detention provisions of the 1950 Internal Security Act, were designed to prevent possible future wrongdoing; and 3) since it was so difficult to frame legislation with enough precision and with any possible constitutional basis to punish "wrong thinking" and possible *future* wrongdoing, the overwhelming bulk of repressive activities were carried out by administrative and legislative bodies which could try and punish people for "wrong thinking" without the bother of a formal trial which would offer the "accused" due process protections, such as the right to know the exact nature of charges, to subpoena witnesses in one's defense and to know and cross-examine one's accusers.

All of these constitutional aberrations ultimately stemmed from the essential concentration of the subversive hunters on the possibility that American citizens were thinking incorrect thoughts, especially thoughts associated with the word "communism." The Truman-McCarthy repression reflected, as Walter Millis has written, a governmental policy that "communism, as a belief, as a teaching, as a plan of action, as a moral ideal, should be extirpated from the American society."[465] But such a concentration on thought inevitably meant that to fight the menace, it was necessary to investigate all aspects of a person's life, since thought processes could not be probed directly but could only be inferred from the petitions one signed, the groups one joined, the books one read, the friendships one had, and the statements one made. That all of these actions were perfectly legal in the overwhelming number of cases was no barrier to the mind-probers; indeed it was precisely their *purpose* to deter American citizens who had "wrong" thoughts from exercising their constitutional rights, so that the "American mind in general could be protected from "pollution with ideas branded as dangerous."[466] The vagueness of the possible range of activities which one might participate in which could potentially brand one as "disloyal" further served the purpose of deterring millions of citizens who were not habitual "wrong thinkers" from even venturing out of the mainstream of American political life; "the common fear was the possibility of 'guilt' as a result of some scarcely remembered relatively trivial comment or action or personal association, reported by unknown sources, and judged by unseen figures."[467]

The concentration on "wrong thinking" as a target of repression created problems for the repressors. Since it was clearly constitutionally impermissable to clearly punish people by official action for thought only, many of the repressive activities were justified on the implicit or explicit grounds that the victim was *likely* to commit some illegal overt act in the *future* even if he had not already done so, a tendency which former Justice Department official John Lord O'Brien termed the development of "preventive law."[468] Thus, J. Malcolm Smith and Cornelius P. Cotter viewed American society in the 1950's as "characterized not so much by the mobilization of human energies toward attainment of positive social goals as it is by the precautionary exclusion of individuals and groups from various occupations and activities in an effort to prevent breaches of national security."[469]

Examples of "preventive" law and administrative action pervade the Truman-McCarthy period. Truman said the loyalty program was designed to catch "potential subversives;" the State Department denied passports to persons whose conduct abroad was "likely to be contrary to the best interest of the United States;" the Post Office seized "foreign communist propaganda" to avert the potential harm such material might cause to innocent American readers; and the Attorney General's list was designed to quarantine American society from the potential danger which the groups listed might cause. The height of "preventive law" was reached in the Smith Act trials and the emergency detention provisions of the 1950 Internal Security Act. The Smith Act prosecutions did *not* maintain that the Communist Party was actively planning a revolution, or even that the party was advocating the overthrow of the government; instead the charges were that the CP was *conspiring* to *advocate* the overthrow of the government and that the CP was *conspiring* to *organize* to *advocate* the overthrow of the government. The Smith Act was upheld by the Supreme Court in the 1951 *Dennis* decision, with the court ruling that that the clear and present danger test "cannot mean that before the Government may act, it must wait until the *putsch* is about to be executed, the plans have been laid and the signal is awaited;" instead the court adopted the following standard for prosecuting speech and organizational activity: "Whether the gravity of the 'evil,' discounted by its improbability, justifies such invasion of free speech as is necessary to avoid the danger."[470] In the less legal language of Zechariah Chafee, this decision said in effect that "Congress shall make no law abridging the freedom of speech and of the press unless Congress does make a law abridging the freedom of speech and of the press."[471]

The height of "preventive law" was unquestionably reached in the emergency detention provisions of the Internal Security Act, in which the Attorney General was authorized to round up and detain persons he believed would "probably" become involved in acts of espionage and sabotage during an "internal security emergency." Simply put, this law

> authorized an administratively determined finding of anticipated criminal guilt free of the normal evidential burdens relating to commission, conspiracy, indictment or attempt. Liberty, reputation, property or livelihood . . . could be lost without the constitutional protections afforded a common felon.[472]

The administrative rather than the judicial nature of the emergency detention provisions was characteristic of the general lack of judicial processes in most of the major techniques used to fight "wrong thinking" during the Truman-McCarthy period. The overwhelming mass of repressive activities — the legislative hearings, the loyalty programs, the passport and immigration controls, the provisions regarding the SACB, the Attorney General's list — were proceedings in which no criminal charges were brought, no legal trial was held, and thus no legal protections were afforded the accused. Of the thousands of persons severely and directly affected by the repression, and of the millions deterred from engaging in political activities, only the Smith Act victims (who, John Roche tastelessly said, were probably "about enough to fill Tom Mooney Hall")[473] and those cited for contempt of Congress, altogether amounting to less than three hundred persons, were afforded the legal protections associated with a criminal procedure. The stress on administrative and legislative tribunals once more reflected the fact that thought was the real target of the repression, and therefore too difficult to punish by normal legal processes:

> By the simple strategem of charging a man with disloyalty, instead of with treason or espionage or sabotage, it is possible to evade the constitutional

requirements that he be indicted by a grand jury, that he enjoy a speedy and public trial by an impartial petite jury, that he be informed of the nature and cause of the accusation and confronted with the witnesses against him, that he be accorded the benefit of compulsory process to obtain witnesses in his favor. He is indicted and tried and sentenced by congressional committee or administrative tribunal, with the same men acting as prosecutors, judges and jury.[474]

While the grossest abuses of the Truman-McCarthy period unquestionably eased after 1954, it is important to note that many of the repressive measures initiated during the period persisted for years. The government loyalty program still exists and is still characterized by many of the same abuses which marked the program from its inception;[475] it receives less attention now largely because it has become accepted as a matter of course, and few firings occur because the government "no longer finds communist associations in the backgrounds of job applicants, because a whole generation has been forcibly trained not to have any."[476] In mid-1969, it was revealed that the Department of Health, Education and Welfare still maintained a blacklist barring scientists from serving as HEW consultants for security reasons, even though the positions involved no secrets; at the same time it was revealed the Small Business Association was still refusing business loans to members of "subversive" organizations or persons who had taken the Fifth Amendment in declining to answer questions about subversive activities.[477] The emergency detention provisions of the Internal Security Act were not repealed by Congress until 1971, while the SACB set up in that act was not finally abolished until 1973, after the courts had frustrated twenty years of efforts by various presidents to keep the SACB alive and provide it with business. The Attorney General's list continued to be used by governmental officials until it was finally abolished in 1974. The CIA's interception of mail begun in 1953 continued until 1973. The Smith Act remains on the books, waiting for another crisis to lead to new prosecutions and more liberal court interpretations than those which whittled the measure down after 1956. The Supreme Court did not begin to outlaw state and local loyalty oaths until the 1960's, and it was not until the 1970's that the Supreme Court began throwing out state laws which banned "subversive" groups from the ballot.[478]

Probably the most dangerous institutional legacy of the Truman-McCarthy period was the tremendous expansion in the activities and power of the FBI.[479] By 1960, the FBI had opened over four hundred thirty-thousand files on individuals and groups concerning "subversive" matters, a category which embraced a huge number of political activities which were completely lawful and peaceful. As the Attorney General indicated publicly in his 1955 annual report, FBI investigations covered "the entire spectrum of the social and labor movement in the country." The purpose of most FBI investigations was general intelligence rather than investigation of possible lawbreaking; as the Attorney General said in his 1958 annual report, FBI investigations were designed to "fortify" the government against "subversive pressures."[480] The general operating rule of the FBI was stated in the Bureau's 1960 operating manual:

> Where there is doubt an individual may be a current threat to the internal security of the nation, the question should be resolved in the interest of security and investigation conducted.[481]

The most expansive FBI domestic intelligence program was carried out under the heading COMINFIL, or Communist Infiltration. Under this program, the FBI investigated Communist attempts to "influence" blacks, young people, women, veterans, religion, education, industry and other targets. As the Senate Intelligence Committee reported in 1976, although the COMINFIL investigations were supposed to focus on CP attempts to infiltrate various groups, "in practice the target often became the domestic groups themselves" and the COMINFIL investigations "reached into domestic groups in virtually every area of American political life."[482] In addition to the COMINFIL program, the FBI in the post-war period investigated "persons holding important positions who have shown sympathy for Communist objectives and policies;" members of "non-Stalinist" revolutionary groups who viewed Russia as the "center for world revolution;" persons who saw the Soviets as the "champion of a superior way of life;" persons whose membership in revolutionary groups was not proven but who had "anarchistic or revolutionary beliefs" and had committed past "acts of violence"; persons not currently engaged in "subversive" activity but who had done so "several years ago" and shown no "positive indication of disaffection" and persons who were "espousing the line" of "revolutionary movements." Other targets for investigation included violent "Klan-type" and "hate" groups, vocal anti-communists, prominent opponents of racial integration, and the entire civil rights movement, under the heading "general racial matters." Included subjects for investigation were "race riots," "civil demonstrations" and "similar developments" and "proposed or actual activities of individuals, officials, committees, legislatures, organizations, etc., in the racial field."[483]

The FBI investigated the black separatist Nation of Islam (Black Muslims) for over a decade in the 1950's and 1960's without ever finding any evidence of violation of federal laws, and maintained a wiretap on the group's leader, Elijah Muhammed, from 1957 until 1966. The FBI investigation of the NAACP, begun in 1941, continued until 1966. Although the FBI prepared massive reports on the NAACP, including information on the group's political and legislative plans, the Bureau never uncovered any evidence of subversive domination or sympathies. In 1957, the New York field office of the FBI prepared a 137-page report on NAACP activities during the previous year, based on information supplied by 151 informers or confidential sources. From 1946 to 1960, the FBI used about three thousand wiretaps and over eight hundred "bugs," and continued its practice of opening mail and using illegal entries to place "bugs" and obtain membership and financial records of dissident groups.[484]

In a number of cases the FBI furnished to Presidents Truman and Eisenhower politically sensitive information gathered in the course of intelligence investigations. Hoover sent Truman letters including information on such subjects as the negotiating position of a union, the activities of a former Roosevelt aide who was trying to influence Truman administration appointments, the publishing plans of journalists and plans of a lawyers group to denounce the FBI. Eisenhower was furnished with information on the political and social contacts with foreign officials of Bernard Baruch, Mrs. Eleanor Roosevelt and Supreme Court Justice William O. Douglas; was given FBI data on thirteen persons, including Linus Pauling and Bertrand Russell, who had filed suit to stop nuclear tests; was given information on the meetings of an NAACP delegation with Senators Paul Douglas and Everett Dirksen; and was provided with derogatory information on members of a group which criticized the FBI for allegedly practicing racial discrimination.[485]

As the FBI established its position as a leading anti-Communist savior of the nation, the Bureau's autonomy and political untouchability increased. The FBI carried out some of its programs, including its burglary and mail-opening programs without the knowledge of Justice Department officials, and in a number of cases deliberately withheld information from Attorney Generals, none of whom made any serious attempt to control the FBI or provide meaningful guidance for its domestic intelligence activities. As the Senate Intelligence Committee concluded in 1976, during the postwar period the full scope of FBI operations and programs were not "fully known by anyone outside of the Bureau."[486]

10

An Interlude Between the Wars, 1954-1964

Less Repression, Even Less Dissent, 1954-1960

At the beginning of 1954, Sen. McCarthy appeared to be unstoppable. The January, 1954, Gallup Poll revealed that for the first (and last) time, McCarthy was regarded favorably by 50 percent of the American people. On February 2, the Senate voted to appropriate $214,000 for McCarthy's Subcommittee on Government Investigations by a vote of eighty-five to one (the lone dissenter was Sen. William Fulbright).[1]

Beginning in late February however, "McCarthyism" began to come under increasing assault from powerful forces in American society, largely as a result of McCarthy's persistent assault on loyalty practices in the Army, which focused on the Army's promotion and subsequent honorable discharge of an obscure dentist named Irving Peress who had refused to answer questions about possible subversive activities and affiliations, an incident which in February, 1954, ultimately led McCarthy to denounce Brigadier General Ralph W. Zwicker as "unfit" to wear the uniform.[2]

On February 24, Eisenhower issued a statement asserting that he would never accede to Army personnel "being browbeaten or humiliated."[3] On March 2, Republican National Chairman Leonard Hall, who a week earlier praised McCarthy as a "great asset," emerged from a meeting with Eisenhower and criticized McCarthy's dispute with Army Secretary Stevens. On March 9, conservative Republican Sen. Ralph Flanders denounced McCarthy on the Senate floor, asserting that "the scalp of a pink Army dentist" appeared to represent the "depth and seriousness of the Communist penetration in this country at this time."[4] That same evening CBS television broadcast an enormously influential documentary narrated by Edward R. Murrow which amounted to a severe indictment of McCarthy.

On March 11, the Eisenhower administration, acting through the Army, officially declared war on McCarthy by issuing a detailed chronology which claimed that McCarthy had sought privileged treatment for his staff aide, G. David Schine, who had been drafted. On March 13, Vice-President Nixon delivered a television speech in which he criticized those whose efforts to expose communists "not only have diverted attention from the danger of communism but have diverted that attention to themselves" and who through "reckless talk and questionable methods" divided the Senate and diverted attention from the Eisenhower administration's programs.[5] During the Army-McCarthy hearings which dominated American attention in the spring of 1954, Eisenhower refused to accede to McCarthy's demand that discussions within the executive branch be revealed, while Attorney General Herbert Brownell suggested that by urging federal employees to ignore Eisenhower's decision, McCarthy was seeking to "set himself above the laws of our land."[6] At the conclusion of the hearings, both Republicans and Democrats on the hearing committee issued reports which, in varying degrees, rebuked McCarthy. On June 11, Sen. Flanders introduced a resolution in the Senate which ultimately led to the censure of McCarthy following a unanimous recommendation for such action by a select Senate committee dominated by moderate and conservative senators of both parties. McCarthy was censured by the Senate on December 1, 1954, by a vote of 67-22, with all Democrats voting against him, and the Republicans splitting 22-22.

Unquestionably the major immediate factor behind the censure and McCarthy's subsequent fall from influence was the decision of the Eisenhower administration and moderate Republican Senators to stand against him, but this decision reflected increasing opposition to McCarthy among influential individuals and groups that mushroomed during 1954. According to *Fortune,* business executives were becoming increasingly exasperated with McCarthy; thus, a banker from Wichita Falls, Texas, suggested that McCarthy had been hurting the Republicans so much he might even be "in the employ of the New Dealers."[7] Many of McCarthy's strongest critics during 1954 were members of the Committee for Economic Development, which included a number of presidents of major corporations. On Capitol Hill, a lobby known as the "Clearing House," which was funded largely by Paul Hoffman, a liberal Republican businessman, worked for McCarthy's censure with the support of the legislative directors of several large labor unions and Washington representatives of a number of liberal pressure groups, including ADA, the Anti-Defamation League, the National Farmers' Union and the American Veterans Committee. Newspapers also became increasingly critical of McCarthy.[8]

Republican leaders around the country wrote to Eisenhower and other influential Republicans in Washington warning that the party was being severely damaged by McCarthy. Thus, Republican Congressman George H. Bender wrote Eisenhower in May, 1954, that

> There is a growing impatience with the Republican Party. McCarthyism has become a synonym for witch-hunting, star-chamber methods and the denial of those civil liberties which have distinguished our country in its historical growth.[9]

A New Hampshire Republican national committeeman warned that if something wasn't done about McCarthy "we are going to lose a lot of votes," while Palmer Hoyt of the Denver *Post* called for the Republicans to repudiate McCarthy "before he drags them all to defeat." The chairman of the Republican National Finance Committee wrote to Sen. Karl Mundt:

> My own personal views coincide with the general run of Republicans who are engaged in fund-raising . . . that the McCarthy-Stevens hearings are a disgraceful affair and the sooner they finish the better for the party.[10]

McCarthy was brought down in the end not because he lost his hardcore support, even in the Republican Party (as the twenty-two Republican votes against censure demonstrated) but because he increasingly lost the active support of and eventually gained the active opposition of "moderates who had long tolerated McCarthy, despite of or in ignorance of his methods."[11]

The censure of McCarthy clearly inaugurated a period in which overt repression significantly declined, but the censure was not the only reason for this decline. In the November, 1954, elections, which preceded the censure vote, the American electorate clearly signalled that it had had enough of McCarthyite tactics. Vice-President Richard Nixon and many Republican candidates again attempted to use the "red" issue against the Democrats. For example, Nixon charged that liberal Democratic Senate candidates were "almost without exception members of the Democratic Party's left wing clique which . . . has tolerated the Communist conspiracy in the U.S."[12] In one case, Nixon used a Naval Intelligence report to charge that Democratic Congressman Robert L. Condon had been a member of the Communist Party. Although Condon was defeated, the Democrats scored heavy gains in the elections, picking up twenty seats in the House and two in the Senate and winning control of both houses of Congress. In many races, Democrats won despite the heavy use of the "red" issue by their opponents. For example, in Wyoming, Joseph O'Mahoney regained his Senate seat despite a campaign which turned heavily on the fact that he had served as an attorney for Owen Lattimore, a major McCarthyite target.[13]

Shortly after the censure of McCarthy and the 1954 elections, a number of incidents occurred which further put red-hunters on the defensive. In December, 1954, it was revealed that Wolf Ladejinsky, a State Department agricultural expert, had been barred by Secretary of Agriculture Ezra Taft Benson from employment in his department on security grounds, even though the State Department had cleared Ladejinsky on the same information which Benson found objectionable, and even though Ladejinsky had a history of anti-communist writings. The reason for Ladejinsky's bar from Agriculture turned out to be the fact that he had close relatives who lived in Russia, leading Benson to conclude Ladejinsky's anti-communist writings were only a Soviet plot directed from Moscow. Ladejinsky was eventually hired by another government agency for work in Indochina, as Benson stuck resolutely to his position. The Ladejinsky affair, like the Oppenheimer case, was a perfect example of the basic flaw in the concept of the loyalty program. If one accepted the principle that having relatives in Soviet-controlled countries made one subject to blackmail, then Ladejinsky *was* a security risk, yet his entire record in the government had been outstanding.[14]

In February, 1955, Harvey Matusow, one of the Justice Department's most frequently used professional ex-communist informers, publicly declared that he had lied in a series of cases in which he had testified for the government. Rather than re-open cases in which Matusow had appeared, the Justice Department had him sentenced for contempt of court for retracting his testimony in one case, while SISS held hearings in an attempt to prove Mutasow's recantation was just another communist plot. However, the Mutasow affair strongly discredited the cult of the professional informer.[15]

Perhaps most embarassing of all to the red-hunters, former Sen. Harry Cain, once an arch-conservative and then a member of the SACB, began in January, 1955 a year-long campaign of attacking the abuses of the government loyalty program. Cain maintained that the Truman and Eisenhower programs had not discovered a single disloyal citizen and that the entire system should be applied *only* to the small number of federal employees with access to national secrets. Cain's attack on the loyalty program had a tremendous impact because of his impeccable credentials as a Republican and an ardent anti-communist.[16]

Meanwhile, the Democrats, who now controlled Congress, began a full scale assault on the loyalty program. Several congressional committees began hearings clearly designed to expose the abuses of the system, and in April, 1955, the Senate authorized hearings into the need for legislation to safeguard freedoms guaranteed in the Bill of Rights.[17]

The decreasing hysteria that was evident in the country after 1954 also resulted from certain foreign developments, especially the decline in the tempo of the Cold War. Stalin had died in March, 1953, and the foreign policy adopted by Russia's new leaders appeared to be considerably more conciliatory. In July, 1953, an armistice had terminated the Korean conflict, and in May, 1955, the Soviet Union signed a treaty restoring the independence of Austria and agreeing to the withdrawal of Soviet troops from that country — the first time in the post-war period that Soviet troops had withdrawn from an area where they had gained a foothold. In July, 1955, Eisenhower met with Russian, French and British leaders at Geneva for the first summit conference since 1945. When McCarthy introduced a resolution in the Senate opposing the Geneva conference, it was defeated 77-4.[18]

By 1955, there were a number of clear signs that repression was easing on all levels of government. Between 1955 and 1960 the passage of repressive legislation practically disappeared on the state level. On the federal level, political deportations dropped sharply after 1954.

Passage of Repressive Laws by State Legislatures, 1955-60[19]
Number of States Passing Repressive Laws

1955-56	6
1957-58	2
1959-60	1

Political Deportations[20]

1954	61	1964	0
1955	30	1965	0
1956	16	1966	1
1957	12	1967	0
1958	6	1968	0
1959	7	1969	3
1960	12	1970	1
1961	4	1971	2
1962	2	1972	2
1963	4		

While the government loyalty program remained intact, its operation showed clear signs of improvement, apparently as a result of the wide spread attacks made on it. In March, 1955, Attorney General Brownell issued a memorandum stressing the need for greater caution in making loyalty determinations. In November, 1955, Secretary of Defense Charles Wilson announced a return to the pre-McCarthy policy of basing dishonorable discharges from the armed forces solely on the basis on military service records, rather than taking such action on the basis of pre-service activities or associations. This action came shortly after the publication of a privately-sponsored report on the operation of the loyalty program within the armed forces, which disclosed scores of cases in which soldiers had been branded disloyal because they had close associations with mothers, fathers, grandparents, siblings and in-laws who were allegedly of dubious loyalty.[21] The author of the report concluded that

> A careful study of the Army Military Personnel Security program ... makes it difficult to avoid the conclusion that the ideal draftee is an only child of spontaneous generation, who, despite a hermit childhood, has miraculously acquired the ability to read and write English but has never made use of these skills.[22]

After 1956, Congress lost interest in maintaining the detention camps authorized in the 1950 Internal Security Act, and the sites were leased, sold or given to state governments, or put to other use by the federal government.[23]

By 1956, the signals of a reaction to McCarthyism had gained sufficient clarity to allow the Supreme Court to suddenly leap into the lead of the battle against repression. The appointment of Earl Warren as Chief Justice in late 1953, when McCarthyism was at flood tide, had made little difference at first.[24] For example, in *Barsky* v. *Board* (1954), the court had upheld the suspension by New York State of a physician's license to practice medicine because he had refused to cooperate with a congressional investigation; and in *Galvan* v. *Press* (1954) the Court had allowed the deportation of an alien whose CP membership had terminated in 1946, and held that under the 1950 Internal Security Act the mere joining of the CP, even without knowledge of its aims, justified deportation.

The first sign of a new direction in the Supreme Court came in *Peters* v. *Hobby* (1955), which reversed a loyalty firing on technical grounds. In 1956, the Court began a major assault on repressive policies initiated under the guise of national security. The major cases included *Slochower* v. *Board* (1956), reversing the firing of a New York City college professor solely for invoking the fifth amendment before a congressional committee; *Cole* v. *Young* (1956), reversing a loyalty firing and in effect throwing out Eisenhower's 1953 order which authorized summary dismissal of civil service employees in "non-sensitive" positions, requiring instead that such employees be acted against only through normal civil service procedures rather than through the loyalty program; and *Pennsylvania* v. *Nelson* (1956), reversing a Pennsylvania sedition conviction and declaring that federal legislation had superseded all state legislation which punished sedition against the U.S.

The climax of the Court's assault on McCarthyism came in 1957. In *Jencks* v. *U.S.*, the court reversed the perjury conviction of a labor leader for falsely taking the Taft-Hartley non-communist oath, on the grounds that he had been denied the opportunity to see FBI files which contained reports on the pre-trial statements of adverse witnesses. The court held that the defense should be allowed to inspect relevant reports of pre-trial statements of witnesses in governmental hands. On June 17, 1957, which soon became known as "Red Monday," the court handed down a series of striking decisions which appeared to mark a major gain for civil liberties. In *Watkins* v. *U.S.* the court reversed a contempt citation initiated by HUAC on the grounds that the committee had failed to make clear what relevancy the questions asked of Watkins had to any valid legislative purpose. While the decision was narrowly drawn on this point, the rhetoric of Warren's decision suggested a determination to emasculate HUAC. Warren wrote that Congress had "no general authority to expose the private affairs of individuals without justification in terms of the function of the Congress" and that all inquiries must "be related to and in furtherance of a legitimate task of Congress."

The court's decision the same day in *Yates* v. *U.S.* spelled the end of federal prosecutions of CP leaders under the Smith Act. In *Yates*, the court nullified the "organize" provision of the Smith Act as it related to the CP by ruling that it referred only to the reconstitution of the CP in 1945, not to ongoing organizational activities, and that the statute of limitations under this charge had thus run out in 1948. The court also held that "advocacy" in the Smith Act must not be interpreted to mean advocacy of abstract doctrine urging the overthrow of the government but instead must involve advocacy of "action" by the "use of language reasonably and ordinarily calculated to incite persons to such action . . . Those to whom the advocacy is addressed must be urged to *do* something, rather than merely to believe in something." Since the government would now have to demonstrate that the CP was actually engaged in plotting the overthrow of the government rather than engaged in a conspiracy to read subversive books, all of the pending Smith Act cases soon collapsed either as a result of the government voluntarily dropping them or courts throwing them out.[25]

Also on June 17, 1957, the Court ordered John Stewart Service reinstated to government employment in a technical loyalty program decision, and in *Sweezy* v. *New Hampshire* reversed a contempt conviction resulting from the refusal of a Marxist professor to answer questions about his political activities posed to him by New Hampshire's attorney general. The Sweezy decision was based on grounds similar to those used in Watkins. Other decisions of the 1957 court term reversed the actions of two state bars which had refused applications from persons, partially because of their refusals to answer questions about political beliefs.

The tremendously adverse reaction which quickly developed to the Supreme Court's 1956 and 1957 decisions demonstrated the limits to the "thaw" in the domestic cold war.[26] For the most part, the Court's decisions had been rather narrowly drawn. They had not ended the loyalty program, had not barred further hearings by congressional committees into subversive activity and had not barred prosecutions under the Smith Act under certain conditions. In effect, the Court had merely held that the government could not "push the hunt for communists and security risks to the extreme of dispensing with normal procedural regularities of American law."[27]

However, the reaction of many members of Congress and other reputable elements of American society to the Court's decisions were of outrage and dark suggestions of communist influence on the court. Thus, the *Chicago Tribune* wrote, "The boys in the Kremlin may wonder why they need a fifth column in the United States so long as the Supreme Court is determined to be so helpful." The Georgia legislature in 1957 called for the impeachment of six Supreme Court justices for giving aid and comfort to the Communists. The SISS reported that, "decisions of the

Supreme Court during 1957 operated to continue the undermining of official efforts at effective anti-communist activity."[28] Strong feelings quickly built up in Congress to pass legislation to either remove certain areas related to subversive activity from the Supreme Court's jurisdiction entirely or to legislatively reverse a number of decisions in the internal security area. In both 1958 and 1959 the House passed bills which would have reversed a number of such decisions, but they were blocked in the Senate, partly as a result of parliamentary manuevering on the part of Senate majority leader Lyndon B. Johnson, and partly as a result of support which the court did receive for its positions from major segments of the press and the legal profession.

The reaction to the Supreme Court decisions of 1956 and 1957 was just one indication of the limits to relaxation of political repression in the U.S. during the second half of the 1950's. While the degree of overt repressive activity on the part of the government clearly did decline after 1954, the executive and legislative branches continued to take many actions which made it clear that radical dissent was still not welcome in America. These actions must be viewed as especially repressive in view of the fact that by 1954 most voices of dissent had long been shackled. The Communist Party and the Progressive Party were in ruins, radical strength in the labor movement had been almost completely destroyed, opposition to American cold war foreign policies was practically unheard of, and suggestions of radical alternatives to the existing political and economic structure in America were almost equally rare.

Nevertheless, until the 1957 *Yates* decision, the Eisenhower administration continued to press Smith Act cases against CP leaders. Further, as the first group of convicted CP leaders emerged from jail during the mid-1950's, the administration began to re-indict them under the membership clause of the Smith Act and began to indict other communists under this clause. By 1956, about fifteen communists had been indicted solely for Communist Party membership (until the bringing of the first of the membership indictments in 1954, CP leaders and members had been prosecuted under the Smith Act only under the organizational and advocacy clauses of the act).[29] The Eisenhower administration also continued to press for the registration of the CP, alleged "communist fronts" and two allegedly "communist infiltrated" labor unions before the SACB. Fourteen leaders of one of these unions, the International Union of Mine, Mill and Smelter Workers (a direct descendant of the old WFM), were indicted in 1956 for conspiracy to defraud the government in connection with filing false Taft-Hartley non-communist affidavits. In 1956 the Social Security administration attempted to revoke old-age benefits of CP employees based on CP wages, and in the same year Internal Revenue Service agents raided headquarters of the *Daily Worker* throughout the country, seized furniture, typewriters and newspaper records, and claimed that the CP owed back taxes of hundreds of thousands of dollars.[30]

Also in 1956, according to Justice Department revelations made in November, 1974, the FBI initiated a "counter-intelligence" program (COINTELPRO) designed to disrupt the remnants of the CP.[31] The COINTELPRO operation was far more than an ordinary surveillance or intelligence program; instead it involved active efforts by FBI agents to destroy and sow confusion inside the ranks of the CP. COINTELPRO activities against the CP including the following, according to the Justice Department revelations: 1) sending anonymous or fictional materials to CP members or groups designed to "create dissention and cause disruption"; 2) making available to news media information already public "in order to expose the aims and activities" of the CP; 3) leaking "informant-based or non-public information" to news media; 4) advising local, state and federal authorities of Party activities in order to affect adversely their credit standing or employment status; and informing, usually through anonymous communications, family and groups to which the individuals belonged of their "radical or immoral activity." According to the Justice Department, 1388 separate COINTELPRO actions were implemented against the CP before the program was allegedly terminated in 1971. As the Department noted, the CP operation became "in some respects the model" for similar operations begun against the SWP in 1961, "white hate groups" in 1964, "black nationalists" in 1967 and the "New Left" in 1968.

The COINTELPRO operation which began in 1956 was to some extent only a formalization of previous harassment of the CP which had been directed by the FBI on an *ad hoc* basis for a number of years. Thus, an August, 1956, FBI memo which signalled the formal beginning of COINTELPRO noted that in the past the FBI had "sought to capitalize on incidents involving the Party and its leaders in order to foster factionalism, bring the Communist Party and its leaders into disrepute before the American public and cause confusion and dissatisfaction among rank-and-file members of the CP." The memo indicated that the FBI would initiate plans to urge the IRS to investigate underground members of the CP who failed to file tax returns or filed under false names; to encourage the SWP to attack the CP; to block CP plans to merge with and take over another socialist group; and to have FBI informants embark on a disruptive program within the CP designed to "raise objections and doubts as to the success of any proposed plan of action by the CP leadership" and aimed at "feeding and fostering from within the internal fight currently raging" as a result of the Smith Act prosecutions and the conflict created by Soviet Premier Khruschev's denunciation of Stalin. Subsequently, the FBI furnished the IRS with the names and addresses of underground communists, FBI informants within the CP attempted to foster factionalism within the party and the FBI sent anonymous mailings critical of the CP to members who were believed to have doubts about the CP leadership.

Other techniques used by the FBI were disrupting meetings, rallies and press conferences through causing the last-minute cancellation of hall rentals, packing audiences at CP meetings with anti-communists and giving friendly reporters "embarassing questions" to ask communists. According to a letter sent by FBI Director Hoover to Attorney General William Rogers in May, 1958, the net effect of the COINTELPRO operation was to create "acrimonious debates," "suspicions," and "jealousies" within the CP, to lead to "disillusionment and defection among Party members and increased factionalism at all levels" and to cause "consternation" among party leaders who were "unable to determine whether these operations are government inspired or represent activities of dissident elements inside or outside the party." Although the precise results of FBI efforts cannot be determined, between 1957 and 1959, what was left of the CP was virtually destroyed by factional infighting. Even as the CP collapsed into a tiny sect of a few thousand members, FBI COINTELPRO activities increased and expanded. Until 1960 the only targets of COINTELPRO were party members, but beginning in that year groups allegedly under communist influence and "fellow travelers" who took positions supported by the Communists also began to be targeted. In one 1960 case the FBI tried to block a speaker allegedly sponsored by a communist-front organization from speaking on a college campus by informing newspapers of the scheduled appearance. When the president of the university was contacted by one of the newspapers, he decided to cancel the meeting. The sponsoring organization obtained a court ruling overturning the ban, and the FBI then ordered an investigation of the judge.[32]

Congressional anti-communist vigilance continued during the late 1950's. While congressional hearings into communist activity declined sharply after 1954, this can be attributed largely to the fact that the source of available subversives to be investigated had been pretty well mined. As the number of actual communists declined, the percentage of FBI informers in the party increased, and in several cases in the late 1950's FBI men unwittingly identified other FBI men as CP members before HUAC.

Hearing Days of HUAC 1954-1960[33]

1954	72
1955	43
1956	62
1957	40
1958	23
1959	28
1960	22

Doing the best it could under the circumstances, HUAC investigated the few remaining left-wing unions, various peace organizations, left-wing summer camps, suspect teachers and show business personalities, and the few remaining communists and left-wing organizations. HUAC devoted considerable time to harassing the Fund for the Republic, a civil liberties-oriented organization originally funded by the Ford Foundation. The Fund had particularly aroused the committee's ire, by, among other activities, sponsoring publication of a book which exposed the blacklist in the communications industy, and awarding $5000 to a Quaker organization in Massachusetts which had had the temerity to hire a woman as a librarian who had taken the fifth amendment before SISS in 1953 after being accused of former CP membership.[34]

Congress as a whole remained only slightly less vigilant than HUAC. In 1958, Congress required that applicants for student loans and grants under the National Defense Education Act swear that they did not belong to or support any organizations advocating the illegal overthrow of the government. In 1959, Congress included in the Landrum-Griffin act a provision which repealed the Taft-Hartley anti-communist oath and replaced it by making it a criminal offense for any person "who is or has been a member of the Communist Party" during the preceding five years to serve as an officer or employee of "any labor organization."[35]

The states joined the federal government in maintaining their anti-subversive vigilance after 1954. The Supreme Court decision in *Nelson* which declared that state laws which punished seditious activity directed against the United States government had been superseded by the Smith Act, led to the dismissal of sedition prosecutions in Michigan, Massachusetts, Kentucky and Louisiana.[36]

The heritage of the Red Scare was thoroughly exploited in the southern states in the late 1950's to discredit the burgeoning civil rights movement. Red-baiting of civil rights organizations such as the NAACP became increasingly commonplace, while in a number of cases repressive laws ostensibly designed to fight communism were applied to civil rights leaders and organizations. For example, Carl Braden was convicted of sedition in Kentucky in 1954 after a home which he had purchased in a white neighborhood had been resold to a black friend. After the home was bombed by local whites, Braden was arrested for sedition on the grounds that a book on communism had been found in his home. (This case was dismissed in 1956 under the *Nelson* ruling, but Braden was later convicted for contempt of Congress when he refused to answer questions about his political associations after being called before HUAC in 1958 as a result of a letter he wrote opposing Congressional nullification of the *Nelson* decision.)[37]

In a number of southern states, laws were passed during the late 1950's which, modelled on communist registration laws, would have required the NAACP to disclose membership lists. During the late 1950's and early 1960's, southern legislative investigating committees often investigated the NAACP and other civil rights organizations under the guise of investigating subversive activities, and southern state officials sometimes tried to suppress civil rights organizations on the basis of anti-subversive laws. In most of these cases, the Supreme Court invalidated the actions of state officials.[38] Thus, in *NAACP* v. *Alabama ex rel. Patterson* (1958), the Court threw out attempts of Alabama officials to force the registration of the NAACP and disclosure of membership lists under an Alabama law compelling foreign corporations doing business in the state to register. In *Louisiana ex rel. Gremillion* v. *NAACP* (1961), the Court held unconstitutionally vague a Louisiana law barring "non-trading" associations from operating in the state if affiliated with out-of-state "non-trading" associations "any of the officers or members of the board of directors on which are members of Communist, Communist-front or subversive organizations, as cited" by HUAC or "the United States Attorney." In *Gibson* v. *Florida Legislative Investigating Committee* (1963), the court reversed the contempt conviction of the president of the Miami branch of the NAACP who had refused to submit membership and contribution records to a state legislative committee which was investigating "communist infiltration" into various organizations. In *Dombrowski* v. *Pfister* (1965) the court threw out another Louisiana anti-communist law which had been used to justify raids and arrests against the offices and homes of the Southern Conference Educational Fund, a civil rights organization.[39]

The generally repressive atmosphere which continued to prevail in the U.S. during the late 1950's is also well illustrated by the sacrosanct position of the FBI during this period. By the late 1950's the FBI had achieved a position as a virtually autonomous, unsupervised and untouchable organization only marginally compatible with the requirements of a democratic society. The FBI not only thoroughly infiltrated, attempted to disrupt and harassed dissident organizations such as the CP, but also operated as a virtually independent political action organization. Following the Supreme Court decision in *Jencks,* the FBI organized a major campaign against the court's action, which involved sending letters to Congress, contacting third parties and attempting to influence newspaper editorial writers.[40] FBI Director J. Edgar Hoover publicly stated that there was an "urgent" need for new legislation to insure the FBI's ability to "carry out its internal security and law enforcement responsibilities."[41] The eventual outcome of FBI lobbying was congressional passage of a bill which did not significantly change the impact of the Court's decision in *Jencks,* but had the appearance of taking a slap at the Court.

The FBI also made pronouncements about American foreign policy. In January, 1960, shortly after Soviet Premier Nikita Khruschev visited the U.S., Hoover reported to the SISS that the visit had created an "atmosphere favorable to communism among Americans" and an opportunity for the CP to enhance its influence.[42] In April, 1960, William Sullivan, chief of the research section of the FBI's Intelligence Division, told the Sixth Military-Industrial Conference that American businessmen should relinquish thoughts of profitable trade with the Soviet Union, and termed Russian appeals for increased trade "clearly an attempt to appeal to American business leaders over the heads of our governmental officials."[43]

Criticism of the FBI was generally regarded in the late 1950's as something akin to lese majesty. In May, 1958, Cleveland industrialist Cyrus Eaton publicly labelled the FBI's "snooping" as highly alarming, and stated, "Hitler in his prime, through the Gestapo, never had any such spy organization as we have in this country today." As a result of these remarks, HUAC let it be known that it was going to subpoena Eaton. Although the subpoena was never served, probably because of widespread public protests, the message that criticism of the FBI was dangerous was clearly conveyed.[44]

By 1958 and 1959, the Supreme Court began to withdraw under the impact of the continuing climate of repression and the strong attacks made upon it.[45] The first signs of retreat came in two 1958 decisions: in *Beilan* v. *Board of Education* and in *Lerner* v. *Casey* the court upheld the firing of a Philadelphia school teacher for "incompetency", for refusal to answer questions of school officials about his past political affiliations, and the firing of a New York subway conductor for being a person of "doubtful trust and reliability" under the New York Security Risk Law for refusing to answer similar questions posed by city officials. These cases closely resembled the 1956 *Slochower* case which had been decided in an opposite way. However, the court was not yet in full retreat. Other 1958 decisions included *Kent* v. *Dulles* and a companion case which held that the State Department could not deny passports on the basis of political beliefs and affiliations; *Sacher* v. *U.S.*, reversing a contempt of Congress conviction by reaffirming *Watkins*; *Speiser* v. *Randall* and a companion case ruling that California's constitutional and statutory provision making the tax exemption of religious and charitable institutions dependent on swearing loyalty oaths was unconstitutional; and *Harmon* v. *Brucker*, throwing out the Army's former policy of giving other than honorable discharges for pre-service activities.

In its 1959 decisions, the court clearly signalled a major retreat which was to last until 1961. In *Barenblatt* v. *U.S.* the court upheld the contempt conviction of a college professor who had refused to answer HUAC's questions about his political affiliations in a decision which indicated a reversal of the implications of the 1957 *Watkins* and *Sweezy* decisions. Similarly, in *Uphaus* v. *Wyman*, the court upheld the contempt conviction of a New Hampshire man who had refused to surrender a guest list of a camp which New Hampshire's attorney general suspected of being a communist meeting place. In *Uphaus*, the court also made clear that the 1956 *Nelson* decision had by no means barred state action against seditious activity directed against the *states,* but only against state action based on seditious activity directed against the *federal* government. The court did in 1959 reverse a contempt of Congress conviction and one security firing on technical grounds, and in *Greene* v. *McElroy* ruled out the government's procedure of making security decisions on private employees working on government contracts without the right of confrontation and cross-examination.

In its 1960 and 1961 decisions, the Court continued to show signs of extreme caution, probably fortified by the House's passage of legislation to reverse its passport decision in *Kent* and its loyalty finding in *Greene*. In *Nelson and Globe* v. *Los Angeles* (1960), the Court upheld the firing of two Los Angeles County employees for their refusal to answer questions of a HUAC subcommittee in a case which appeared to parallel *Slochower*. In 1961 the court upheld contempt convictions in two more cases, upheld the constitutionality of the registration provisions of the 1950 Internal Security Act, upheld the constitutionality — and in the case of *Scales* v. *U.S.*, a conviction — of the membership clause of the Smith Act, and for the first time upheld a security firing in the case of a short-order cook in a privately owned cafeteria in a Naval ordinance installation. In one 1961 decision (*Konigsberg* v. *State Bar of California*), the court even upheld the exclusion on loyalty grounds of a lawyer by the California state bar, even though in 1957 the Court had overturned a previous attempt to exclude him from the bar on virtually the same grounds.

The Kennedy Years:
A New Frontier in Civil Liberties?

The Kennedy years clearly saw a significant increase in the amount of dissenting activity in American society and a general improvement in the climate for civil liberties. It was during the Kennedy administration that the student protest movement of the 1960's took root.[46]

There are a number of reasons for the reinvigoration of activism and dissent in American society, which came primarily from young people of college age — i.e. the oldest group of politically active age which did not carry around with them strong and inhibiting memories of the McCarthy years. One major reason clearly lies in the image projected by President John F. Kennedy. Whereas Eisenhower's image had been of elderly passivity, Kennedy presented an image of youthful dynamism. The major theme of Kennedy's campaign in 1960 had been that America could not "stand still" and that it was time to "get this country moving again."[47] In accepting the Democratic nomination for president, Kennedy spoke of the need for a choice between "the fresh air of progress and the stale, dank atmosphere of 'normalcy.'"[48] Aside from his rhetoric, Kennedy's personal style and appearance suggested "vigor" and movement. Thus, as Paul Murphy has suggested, "The activism of the new administration quickly became its public trademark."[49]

A second reason for the rebirth of activism in the early 1960's was that both foreign and domestic models of protest activity became apparent at about the same time. The Cuban revolution of 1959 and Fidel Castro's nose-thumbing of the U.S. demonstrated to Americans who had long contained within themselves dissatisfaction with the existing capitalist-Cold War consensus that the consensus was not unassailable; and that a "third" alternative might exist to American capitalism and Russian totalitarianism. (Also, Eisenhower's initial lies about the U-2 incident and the initial U.S. denial of responsibility for the Bay of Pigs invasion of Cuba helped to undermine students' respect for the integrity of the American government). Another foreign model was the major role which student protests played in overthrowing reactionary governments in South Korea and Turkey in 1960.[50] Closer to home, 1960 saw the development of the "sit-in" movement among blacks in the South protesting segregated eating facilities. Within a year of the first sit-in at Greensboro, North Carolina, in January, 1960, over fifty thousand blacks and whites had participated in sit-ins, and over thirty-six hundred of them went to jail. Civil rights protests in the following years spread throughout the country, and involved thousands of white supporters who gained "field" experience in the techniques of demonstrations that could later be applied to other issues.[51]

While whites could participate in the civil rights movement only in a supportive capacity, other movements began to develop around issues of education, civil liberties and peace which involved white college students in a central role. The first signs of such protests had developed during the last few years of the Eisenhower administration. In 1957 and 1958 activist student political and educational reform parties were formed at the University of California and several other universities. At about the same time, two "pre-New Left" journals, *Studies on the Left,* and *New University Thought* were founded at the Universities of Wisconsin and Chicago.[52] Beginning in about 1957, the peace movement began to develop as a somewhat influential force in American society, centering around the issues of stopping the atmospheric testing of nuclear weapons and general disarmament. The organization which formed the backbone of the movement was the National Committee for a Sane Nuclear Policy (SANE), which by 1958 had gained twenty-five thousand members.[53]

The peace movement suffered considerable harassment and redbaiting from governmental officials. For example, in 1958 government spokesmen hinted that there was a communist plot behind the efforts of pacifists to block nuclear tests in the Pacific by sailing vessels into restricted areas. In June 1960, SISS subjected Nobel Prize Laureate Linus Pauling to questioning for his role in circulating petitions protesting nuclear testing.[54] Also in 1960, as SANE was reaching the height of its influence and appeared to be on the verge of becoming a "really powerful force in American politics"[55] the organization was torn apart as a result of charges of Communist influence made by SISS chairman Sen. Thomas Dodd. As a result of Dodd's charges and subsequent SISS hearing into "Communist Infiltration in the Nuclear Test Ban Movement," SANE purged a large number of members and lost many more who resigned in protest over the purges. SANE also adopted a loyalty test, rejecting the membership of persons who adhered to "communist or other totalitarian doctrines," thus copying the ACLU.[56] Although SANE was badly shaken by the SISS affair, it did survive, and there were a number of signs that protest activity was increasing as the decade ended. In 1959, the Student Peace Union (SPU) was organized; it recruited five thousand members within a year. In May, 1960, nearly two thousand persons in New York City refused to take shelter during the annual air raid drills, and police arrested only twenty-six of them. In April, 1959, twenty-five thousand persons marched to call for integration of the Washington, D.C. public schools, and in 1960 thousands marched for peace in San Francisco, New York, and Los Angeles. An organization known as Women's Strike for Peace (WSP) developed out of an almost spontaneous protest by fifty thousand women held in the fall of 1961.[57]

As the peace movement showed signs of continuing growth, additional congressional hearings were held in an attempt to discredit it. In December, 1962, HUAC investigated "Communist Activities in the Peace Movement."[58] The hearings largely focused on WSP. Although HUAC presented bouquets to the women witnesses who appeared before it, the major aim of the hearings was to show that WSP was under communist domination and in general to try to "cast the darkest shadow possible on the entire peace movement."[59] The Kennedy administration, however, showed signs of receptivity to peace demonstrators. For example, during a February, 1962, Washington protest against nuclear weapons testing, President Kennedy sent coffee and cocoa out to the demonstrators, and, in 1961, he succeeded in getting Congressional authorization for the establishment of an Arms Control and Disarmament Agency within the federal government. In the aftermath of the 1963 nuclear test ban treaty in which the Soviet Union and the U.S. agreed to ban further atmospheric testing, the peace movement faded away or merged with the liberal wing of the Democratic Party.[60]

Aside from educational reform and peace, students also began to demonstrate increasing concern over issues related to civil liberties even before Kennedy took office. The first organized major expression of opposition to HUAC came during hearings held in May, 1960 in San Francisco.[61] HUAC had been a regular visitor to California. In 1957, a young cancer researcher committed suicide when he was subpoenaed to appear before the committee, and in 1959 the names of a number of California teachers who were about to be subpoenaed were leaked to the press in violation of HUAC's own rules, and then the hearings were never held. HUAC instead submitted its information on the teachers to local officials, and several teachers subsequently lost their jobs.

During the 1960 hearings, thousands of students protested HUAC's arrival by marching outside City Hall, where the hearings were being held, and by lining up before the doors of the hearing room in order to gain access to the public seats. On May 13, police inside City Hall turned high pressure fire hoses on students lined up outside the hearing room, and then proceeded to eject them from the building by washing, clubbing, dragging and throwing them down a flight of stairs. The police, HUAC and FBI Director Hoover maintained afterwards that the disturbances had been a communist plot and that they had begun when a student had assaulted a policeman and led a charge of students towards the hearing room. However, the student charged with leading the assault was found not guilty, and charges against about sixty other students were dismissed.

Another indication of student concern over civil liberties was a series of fights against bans on left-wing speakers on college campuses, institutionalized relics of McCarthyism which were still in force at many state-supported institutions. Thus, three thousand students boycotted classes at New York City College in 1961 to protest a ban on Communist speakers, and students at Ohio State University were denied the right to hear a number of critics of HUAC, including Communist spokesman and scholar Herbert Aptheker, before a speaker ban was lifted in 1965. The Ohio State free speech fight received national publicity when Aptheker appeared on campus and remained silent before a crowd of over twenty-five hundred persons, while faculty members read excerpts from his books, checked out of the University library, to the audience.[62]

By 1962, a long moribund student organization originally known as the Student League for Industrial Democracy (SLID), which had changed its name in 1960 to Students for a Democratic Society (SDS), was showing signs of a revival. Starting with about two hundred fifty members in 1960, SDS, which was concerned with more broadly based goals of social reform than the peace, educational, civil rights or civil liberties movements, grew to about one thousand members by 1964. In its first few years, SDS was essentially a moderate reform-oriented group. Its initial policy statement, the so-called "Port Huron Statement" of 1962, suggested working through "liberal" institutions such as the labor movement and existing political parties, and stressed a highly humanistic philosophy centered around the concept of "participatory democracy."[63]

Until about 1965, with the growth of major protests against the Vietnam War, there were *no* significant organizations dedicated to a truly fundamental challenge to the basic orientation of either the American economic or political structure or to American foreign policy. Instead, the most significant movements which did exist were "limited in nature and strictly limited to issues of individual liberties (i.e. the HUAC demonstration and the civil rights movement) or to specific policies of the administration (i.e. nuclear testing)."[64] Furthermore, aside from the civil rights movement, the number of students or others involved in active protests remained extremely small. Until the Vietnam War demonstrations of 1965, the largest protest demonstration by white students occurred when five thousand students at Ohio State University protested the faculty's rejection of a Rose Bowl invitation.[65]

While dissent during the Kennedy administration remained limited in objectives and numbers, dissent did become considerably more acceptable in American society during the Kennedy years. Aside from the image of activism and change presented by President Kennedy, however, the contribution of the Kennedy administration towards improving the climate of civil liberties cannot be said to have been a very strong one.

Part of the mythology that has grown up around John F. Kennedy and his brother Robert, the Attorney General, is that they were both avid supporters of civil liberties. Not surprisingly, this concept has been pushed most avidly by members of the Kennedy entourage, such as presidential aides Theodore Sorenson and Arthur Schlesinger, Jr. For example, Schlesinger maintains that Robert Kennedy was "concerned and responsive" to civil liberties questions and "presided over a quiet and thorough liquidation of the McCarthyite heritage." Schlesinger stresses that Robert Kennedy regarded the political operations of the CP as of "no danger," and attacked those "who in the name of fighting communism, sow seeds of suspicion and distrust by making false or irresponsible charges." He adds that Robert Kennedy argued against the denial of visas to foreigners with suspect political ideas and opposed restricting the travel of Americans to countries such as Communist China, Albania and Cuba. Schlesinger says Robert Kennedy opposed the prosecution of students who travelled to Cuba as preposterous and quotes him as saying, "Why shouldn't they go? If I were twenty-one years old, that's what I would like to do this summer."[66]

Both Schlesinger and Sorenson note that President Kennedy appointed to federal offices or honored in various ways many persons who had been targets of right-wing attacks during the previous decade.[67] Their characterization of the Kennedy administration as extremely favorable to concepts of civil liberties has been accepted virtually *in toto* by the distinguished constitutional historian Paul Murphy, in his recent volume in the "New American Nation" series, which is probably the most highly regarded collaborative history of the United States.[68]

Such an assessment of the Kennedy administration's civil liberties record is not entirely without foundation, but it is a picture viewed through extraordinarily tinted glasses. It is true that Kennedy did appoint or honor many targets of right-wing attacks. For example, J. Robert Oppenheimer, who had been denied an AEC security clearance in 1954, was honored at a White House dinner for Nobel Prize winners in 1962 and was given the AEC's 1963 Enrico Fermi award. Edward R. Murrow, one of McCarthy's prime targets in the communications industry, was appointed head of the United States Information Agency by Kennedy, and Murrow in turn appointed Reed Harris, who had resigned from the Voice of America following McCarthy's hearings in 1953, to a top ranking position. Others similarly honored or appointed included Linus Pauling, Philip Jessup, Henry Wallace, Arthur Miller, Eleanor Roosevelt and Charles Bohlen.[69]

It is also true that President Kennedy made certain symbolic gestures and statements indicating a concern for civil liberties. For example, when a reporter at a news conference branded two State Department employees "well-known security risks" Kennedy defended them; he ordered an end to Post Office seizure of foreign Communist propaganda; and he signed in 1962 a bill he had fought for as a senator repealing the anti-communist oath required for National Defense Education Act (NDEA) loans. Kennedy also pardoned the only person convicted under the membership provision of the Smith Act, Junius Scales, over the opposition of the FBI and congressional red-hunting bodies, but the courage of such an action is somewhat negated by the fact that Scales had long since repudiated the Communist Party.[70]

The Kennedy Administration also ended prosecutions of CP members under the membership clause of the Smith Act; again this must be weighed against the fact that the Supreme Court in upholding the membership provision in *Scales* v. *U.S.* (1961) and *Noto* v. *U.S.* (1961) imposed such stringent requirements to gain convictions that further prosecutions would most probably have been futile.[71]

Robert Kennedy also did make some efforts to temper anti-communist hysteria. For example, in his first interview as Attorney General, he stated he was thinking about abolishing the Justice Department's Internal Security Division, and he publicly stated that overseas communism rather than the American CP was what threatened the U.S. Robert Kennedy added that "what is almost hysteria about the activities of communists within the U.S. is misplaced apprehension."[72]

Unfortunately, there is a darker side of the Kennedy administration's record on civil liberties. For example, although Robert Kennedy is alleged to have opposed restrictions on travel to Cuba, the fact is that it was the Kennedy administration which first imposed such travel bans in February, 1961, and it was Robert Kennedy's Justice Department which prosecuted students who defied these bans in 1962 and 1963. Further, as Schlesinger admits, although supposedly both President and Robert Kennedy opposed similar bans on travel to China, Albania and other countries, somehow such restrictions never were lifted. It was not until 1967 that they were abandoned after a Federal Court declared them unconstitutional.[73]

Further, although Robert Kennedy supposedly viewed the domestic Communist Party as posing little threat, the Kennedy administration pursued a vigorous policy of prosecuting American communists. For example, the Kennedy administration continued to press efforts to force the CP and "communist front" organizations, and the allegedly "communist infiltrated" International Union of Mine, Mill and Smelter Workers (IUMMSW) to register with the SACB. The Kennedy Administration also continued to press a five-year old Taft-Hartley perjury conspiracy case against the IUMMSW.[74]

Not only did the Kennedy administration continue to press *existing* prosecutions of domestic communists, it also initiated *new* proceedings. The Kennedy administration for the first time attempted to enforce the provisions of the Internal Security Act which required CP officers to register the party when the party failed to register, and, also for the first time attempted to enforce the act's requirement that individual CP members register since the CP had been ordered to register but had failed to do so. By the end of 1965, the SACB had ordered forty-four persons to register, but the Supreme Court threw out these orders on the grounds of self-incrimination in *Albertson* v. *SACB* (1965). The SACB order that the CP register itself and a subsequent conviction of the CP for failing to register under indictments initiated by the Kennedy administration in 1961 and again by the Johnson administration in 1965 were all thrown out by federal courts on self-incrimination grounds. Efforts to force registration of "communist front" organizations and "communist infiltrated" labor unions with the SACB all had collapsed by 1966 either because the organizations involved had dissolved, the government dropped the proceedings or federal courts found the government case either could not be sustained or had grown "stale" with time. In 1963, the Justice Department brought proceedings to require an obscure organization known as the Advance Youth Organization (AYO) to register as a communist front with the SACB, the first such action brought since 1956. The total membership of AYO was less than two hundred suggesting that it hardly posed a serious threat to American security.[75]

Aside from these positively repressive actions, neither President nor Robert Kennedy made any serious attempt to challenge the basic loyalty-security apparatus — the loyalty program, the SACB, the Attorney General's list or the virtually autonomous power of the FBI in internal security matters. FBI abuses continued unchecked and with little apparent interest from the Kennedys. Despite the obvious lack of any serious threat to national security arising from the limited protest activities of the early sixties, the FBI continued an active program of infiltrating all prominent protest groups and gathering dossiers on suspect individuals.[76]

The most significant development in FBI intelligence activities during the Kennedy administration was a massive increase in surveillance activities directed at Americans involved in "pro-Castro Cuban activities." FBI surveillance of such persons had begun in November, 1960, when field offices were instructed to gather information on persons "engaged in substantial activities in furtherance of the aims and purpose of the Cuban government, in support of pro-Castro groups or organizations or in furtherance of the communist or subversive infiltration of pro-Castro groups." The chief target of FBI investigative activity was the Fair Play for Cuba Committee. At the request of the FBI, the National Security Agency provided the Bureau with intercepted international communications concerning the commercial and personal contacts between Cuba and a list of American citizens and businesses submitted to NSA by the FBI. Following the Bay of Pigs invasion of 1961 and the Cuban missile crisis of 1962, FBI intelligence activities stepped up and a special "Cuban section" was created for placing Cuban aliens on the Security Index of persons deemed "potentially dangerous" to the U.S. and therefore targetted for arrest in a time of emergency. In 1962, 11,165 persons were listed on the Security Index, including about 200 persons engaged in "pro-Castro Cuban activities or who sympathize strongly with such activities." Another 11,000 persons were listed on the Reserve Index for priority investigation during a time of emergency.[77]

In addition to its surveillance of left-wing political activity, the FBI continued its investigation of civil rights demonstrations and "other racial matters." In February, 1962, the FBI asked its field offices for information indicating "subversive" influence on Dr. Martin Luther King, Jr., leader of the Southern Christian Leadership Conference (SCLC), a non-violent civil rights group. In May, 1962, the FBI placed King on its Reserve Index, and in October, 1962, the FBI began a formal investigation of SCLC and King on the grounds that communists might be influencing SCLC. The FBI closely monitored preparations for the August 28, 1963 Civil Rights March on Washington. In October, 1963, the FBI stepped up its investigations of "communist influence on the Negro" in a memo to field offices which reported an "urgent need for imaginative and aggressive tactics to be utilized through our Counter-intelligence Program for the purpose of attempting to neutralize or disrupt the Party's activities in the Negro field."[78]

One indication of the intensity of FBI activity was that at the 1963 hearings before the SACB concerning AYO, it was revealed that among the less than two hundred members of AYO were eleven FBI informers who had been paid over $45,000 for their labors. One of the informers had been an officer of the organization and had received over $6,000 from the FBI.[79]

Although the CP was in complete disarray by the early 1960's, with a membership in the low thousands, FBI COINTELPRO activities directed against the CP increased. Robert Kennedy was informed of the FBI's anti-CP activities, including the "use of various techniques to keep the

Number of FBI COINTELPRO operations directed against the CP[80]

1957	35
1958	51
1959	65
1960	115
1961	184
1962	147
1963	128

party off balance and disillusion individual communists" in a letter from FBI Director Hoover in January, 1961.[81] In 1961, the FBI initiated a new COINTELPRO directed against the Socialist Workers Party (SWP); apparently Robert Kennedy was not informed about this program. Before the program was supposedly terminated in 1971, the FBI approved and implemented forty-six separate disruptive COINTELPRO operations against the SWP; in addition from 1960 to 1966, the FBI conducted over ninety burglaries of SWP offices, and photographed over eight thousand pages of SWP files, including financial records and personal letters.[82]

The FBI memo written by Hoover which began the SWP COINTELPRO operation in 1961 nowhere claimed that the SWP had been engaged in illegal activities; instead, Hoover wrote, in justifying the program that:

> The Socialist Workers Party (SWP) has, over the past several years, been openly espousing its line on a local and national basis through running candidates for public office and strongly directing and/or supporting such causes as Castro's Cuba and integration problems arising in the south. . . . One of the purposes of this program would be to alert the public to the fact that the SWP is not just another socialist group but follows the revolutionary principles of Marx, Lenin and Engels, as interpreted by Leon Trotsky.[83]

Many of the FBI's SWP COINTELPRO activities in the early 1960's were designed to sabotage SWP electoral activities. Thus, the FBI forged letters in attempts to disrupt SWP campaigns for local office in San Francisco in 1961 and 1963, sent derogatory material to New York news media in 1963 and 1965 to discredit SWP candidates there, distributed leaflets attacking an SWP candidate for the U.S. Senate in New Jersey in 1964, and sent an anonymous letter to the President of the Denver school board in 1965 in an effort to prevent a local SWP candidate from being elected to the board. Other SWP COINTELPRO efforts in the early 1960's included anonymously calling SWP headquarters in New York in 1962 to falsely allege that the FBI had obtained SWP documents from a party member who had turned informer, and convincing the New Jersey Division of Alcoholic Beverage Control in 1962 to raid and break up a SWP meeting at a mountain camp on the grounds of liquor violations.[84]

Robert Kennedy was particularly negligent in his lackadaisical supervision of and acquiescence to FBI wiretapping demands. This is not especially surprising since from the beginning of his tenure as Attorney General, he had repeatedly urged the legalization of wiretapping. Upon entering office, Robert Kennedy failed to ask for a list of wiretaps in progress, and once in office he never established any criteria for approval of taps, never kept any record of the taps he had approved, never reviewed the utility of existing taps and apparently never once turned down an FBI wiretap request based on national security grounds. Robert Kennedy approved wiretaps on two newsmen in connection with news leaks; on an organization simply because it was believed to be under communist influence; on Black Nationalist leader Malcom X because, the FBI reported, Malcolm X was planning to form a new group which would be "more aggressive"; and on three Agriculture Department employees, the clerk of the House Agriculture Committee, a lawyer and a registered agent of a foreign country in connection with alleged illegal activities by a foreign country regarding a sugar quota bill which the Kennedy administration was trying to push through Congress. According to an FBI memo, political intelligence developed as a result of the latter series of wiretaps "contributed heavily" to the Administration's success in getting its bill passed. FBI burglaries of dissident groups and break-ins designed to install "bugs" continued during the Kennedy administration. Between 1960 and 1963, there were at least 16 break-ins to install microphones in cases involving "internal security, intelligence and counter-intelligence." Although the FBI informed the Justice Department about the "bugging" break-ins, Justice Department officials did not know about the "black bag job" burglaries designed to obtain sensitive information, such as those used against the SWP. Altogether, the FBI installed about 600 wiretaps and 270 "bugs" during the Kennedy administration.[85]

The most important case thus far revealed in which Kennedy approved wiretaps resulted from an FBI request to tap the phone of civil rights leader Martin Luther King, on the grounds that King was being influenced by communists. The FBI wiretap request, which was approved by Kennedy in October, 1963, asked for permission to tap King's phone at his current or "any future address" and on the SCLC office or any later address where it might move. FBI surveillance of King eventually grew to over twenty separate wiretaps and bugs on King's home, offices and hotels, which produced thousands of hours of tapes on King's activities, but no evidence that King posed any danger to the national security or was linked to communism. In December, 1963, top FBI officials secretly decided to use the information it could gather about King to "discredit" and "neutralize" him as an "effective Negro leader." The taps and bugs were only a small part of what became a concerted FBI effort to harass King, which lasted until King's assassination in 1968. The FBI investigated King's tax returns and financial affairs, tried to prevent his meetings with world leaders and Pope Paul VI, tried to discourage colleges from giving King honorary degrees, attempted to block funding of King's projects and tried to discredit King with the press, religious leaders, Congressmen and executive branch officials. In 1964 the FBI mailed King a tape derived from its electronic surveillance with a letter which was interpreted by King and his aides as a suggestion to commit suicide or face public release of the tape. After King's assassination in 1968 the FBI tried to head off proposals that a national holiday be named for him.[86]

Perhaps in return for his cooperation, the FBI furnished Robert Kennedy with numerous items of politically useful information derived from its intelligence operations. Among these were information about plans of civil rights leaders, on Martin Luther King's personal life, on a woman who claimed she had been engaged to marry President Kennedy, and information derived from "bugging" a Congressman's hotel room in connection with the sugar quota lobby investigation.[87]

The FBI and the Justice Department were not the only governmental agencies which harassed dissenters during the Kennedy Administration. Upon the direct request of President and Robert Kennedy, the Internal Revenue Service in 1961 and 1963 launched special investigations of "extremist" right and left-wing groups. As a result of the investigations, the tax-exempt status of six organizations was revoked. The special IRS investigations of extremist groups was terminated in 1966.[88] Meanwhile, in Congress, HUAC continued to investigate dissenters, although HUAC hearings were at their lowest ebb since 1946-47. While most hearings made "meagre fare" as the organizations investigated had "a handful of members, little money, short lives and no influence,"[89] this in itself is significant since it shows that even during a period when there was an extreme dearth of organizations in fundamental opposition to the basic tenets of American society, they still did not escape harassment. Thus, HUAC held hearings into obscure organizations like the Fund for Social Analysis (a group which funded Marxist research), and the National Assembly for Democratic Rights, an organization formed to protest the Supreme Court's 1961 decision upholding the constitutionality of the registration provisions of the Internal Security Act. The pickings were so slim that some groups, like the Fair Play for Cuba Committee were investigated by both HUAC and SISS. In January, 1963, SISC subpoenaed seven officials and directors of the Pacifica Foundation after Pacifica-sponsored radio stations broadcast interviews with two ex-FBI agents who criticized the Bureau. These hearings met such strong public opposition that they were soon discontinued.[90]

Congress as a whole also remained ever vigilant for any signs of subversion. In repealing the NDEA oath requirement in 1962, Congress made it a criminal offense for any member of a Communist organization under final order to register with the SACB to apply for or use any federal scholarship or fellowship funds, and granted the Office of Education and the National Science Foundation authority to revoke any fellowship or stipend awarded to graduate students or researchers when such action was determined to be "in the best interest of the United States."[91] After President Kennedy in 1961 ordered an end to Post Office confiscation of foreign communist propaganda, Congress quickly passed a law requiring the Post Office to detain such material unless the addressee specifically requested that such mail be delivered (the Supreme Court declared this law unconstitutional in *Lamont* v. *Postmaster General* [1965]). Such legislation, of course, required the compilation of a list of persons who wished to receive such material, one copy of which reportedly was obtained by HUAC.[92]

In May, 1961, the House, with Robert Kennedy's approval, passed legislation to make on-going organizational work for the Communist Party a crime, in effect reversing part of the Supreme Court's ruling in *Yates*. The House also passed a bill to place on a statutory basis a loyalty program for seamen and longshoremen that otherwise rested on the authority of a presidential executive order. Also under Robert Kennedy's prodding, the House approved a bill which would have extended the 1917 sedition act (in effect in peacetime ever since the Korean War due to a congressional enactment at that time providing that the law was to remain in effect "until six months after the termination of the national emergency" proclaimed by Truman in December, 1950) to cover seditious statements made by Americans *overseas* for the first time.[93]

The major governmental institution which truly supported freedom of political expression in the United States during the Kennedy administration (and with a few exceptions, throughout the 1960's), was the Supreme Court.[94] In addition to *Lamont* v. *Postmaster General* (1965), *Albertson* v. *SACB* (1965), *Louisiana ex rel. Gremillion* v. *NAACP* (1961), *Gibson* v. *Florida Legislative Investigating Committee* (1963), and *Dombrowski* v. *Pfister* (1965), discussed already, the court issued a long series of major decisions striking down repressive laws beginning in 1961. In December, 1961, the Court for the first time struck down a negative state loyalty oath, in a Florida case (*Cramp* v. *Board of Public Instruction*) which involved an oath requiring public employees to swear they had never lent "aid, support, advice, counsel or influence to the Communist Party." In subsequent decisions state loyalty oaths "began to fall like veritable flies."[95] In *Keyishian* v. *Board of Regents* (1967) the court directly reversed its 1952 decision in *Adler* upholding New York's Feinberg Law. In *U.S.* v. *Brown* (1965) the Court threw out the 1959 Landrum-Griffin bar on Communist Party members serving as union officers or employees. In *Aptheker* v. *Secretary of State* (1964) the Court threw out the denial of passports to CP members authorized in the Internal Security Act and in *U.S.* v. *Laub* (1967) it held the State Department could not bar travel to Cuba. In *U.S.* v. *Robel* (1967) the Court invalidated the provision of the Internal Security Act which made it illegal for members of groups under SACB orders to register to engage in employment in any defense facility. In *Schneider* v. *Smith* (1968) the Court invalidated the government's program for keeping subversives from employment on American merchant vessels.

A number of states joined the executive and legislative branches of the federal government in sternly fighting the communist menace during the early 1960's. In 1961, five states passed anti-communist legislation of the strongest imaginable type (four of the states completely outlawed the CP), apparently reflecting fear engendered by the Cuban revolution and political pressure generated by extreme right-wing groups such as the John Birch Society.[96] As already noted, a number of southern states used anti-communism as an excuse to harass the civil rights movement.[97]

While the actual enforcement of state anti-subversive legislation was relatively rare, it was not entirely unknown. For example, in 1963, three student members of the Young Socialist Alliance at the University of Indiana were prosecuted for sedition, partly on the basis of private conversations held in an apartment that had been surreptitiously tape-recorded by a landlord.[98] In *Stanford* v. *Texas* (1965), the Supreme Court ruled invalid a search warrant which had been issued under Texas's Suppression Act, which outlawed the CP. The warrant had authorized the seizure of all "books, records, pamphlets, cards, receipts, lists, memoranda, pictures, recordings and other written instruments" concerning the Texas C.P. Among the items seized under it were books by Jean Paul Sartre, Pope John XXIII and Supreme Court Justice Hugo Black, as well as such items as a marriage certificate and personal correspondence.[99] The Miami public schools banned Aldous Huxley's *Brave New World* and George Orwell's *1984* while a teacher in Wrenshall, Minnesota, was fired and then reinstated after having his students read *1984*.[100] In San Diego, the public schools banned the showing of two educational films on Communist China, "apparently because they showed too many smiling Chinese children."[101] Communist Party General Secretary Gus Hall was banned from speaking at five state-supported institutions in Washington State, while British biologist J.B.S. Haldane was barred from speaking at the University of North Carolina after he refused to say if he was a CP member.[102]

While such examples of state and local repression were constant reminders of the limitations on freedom of thought and speech in America during the early 1960's, the relative increase in tolerance evident on the federal level was also demonstrated in some of the states and cities, and in the private sector. For example, courts in Pennsylvania, New York, and

California, respectively, rejected attempts to deny unemployment benefits to persons fired for taking the fifth amendment before a congressional committee, refused to uphold denial of a drivers license solely for CP membership and threw out a law requiring declarations of loyalty by organizations seeking to use public school facilities. Communist speaker bans were ended at the University of California and the City University of New York. Increasing opposition to the continuation of HUAC was voiced; for example, the American Federation of Teachers and the Central Intelligence Agency-subsidized National Student Association called for HUAC's abolition, and in March, 1961, 250 leading professors issued a similar appeal. The thirteen-year old Hollywood blacklist began to crumble in 1960 when movie producer Otto Preminger announced he would give full credit to Dalton Trumbo, one of the "Hollywood Ten," for Trumbo's script-writing of "Exodus."[103]

A striking development during the Kennedy administration was the rapid growth of extreme right-wing organizations, spearheaded by the John Birch Society, and the immunity of such groups from official harassment, even though their influence was far greater than that exerted by the CP or other left-wing remnants.[104] The only exception to this general rule was the American Nazi Party, whose members were occasionally subjected by local authorities to arbitrary denials of their right to hold public meetings and demonstrations, and to wear swastikas, both during the early 60's and subsequently. After 1964, the Nazis became one of the targets of an FBI COINTELPRO operation largely directed against the revived Ku Klux Klan; FBI tactics included telling party members of the Jewish descent of a Nazi officer and anonymously informing Chicago officials of building violations at Nazi headquarters in that city, leading to the closure of the building.[105] For the most part, however, the extreme right wing was able to pursue its activities unmolested; as political scientist H. Frank Way noted in 1964, "An appeal to God, country and the free enterprise system is built-in insurance that what happened to the radical left immediately after World War II will not be the fate of the radical right."[106]

To sum up the general civil liberties picture in the U.S. during the Kennedy years, there is little doubt that a climate considerably more conducive to dissidence and activism developed during this period, and that the Kennedy administration contributed to this improved climate to some extent. However, those who received the major benefits of the Kennedy administration's largesse were those liberals who had been unfairly smeared with the communist brush during the McCarthy period and dissidents who did not really question the fundamental directions of American foreign and domestic policy (such as the peace marchers who were given coffee and cocoa). The few truly radical groups that existed or developed during this period, such as the CP, the SWP, the Fair Play for

Cuba Committee and the Advance Youth Organization, continued to suffer severe governmental reprisals, and even liberal groups such as Women's Strike for Peace and the Pacifica Foundation came under investigation by congressional committees, presumably as a warning to other groups not to get too far out of line. It was fairly, if not entirely, safe to be a *liberal* during the Kennedy years, and to this extent things had improved; but freedom of speech, travel and association still did not exist for those with a *radical* critique of American society.

11

The Vietnam War Era, 1965-1975

The Social Setting for Political Repression, 1965-1975

During the 1965-75 period (referred to hereafter as the "Vietnam War era") the United States went through a period of political repression, which, at its greatest height in 1967-71, exceeded in intensity any other time in the twentieth century with the possible exceptions of the 1917-20 and 1947-54 periods. The social setting for this intense period of political repression was a background of political turbulence, dissent and violence unmatched in American history since the Civil War.[1]

Clearly the major catalyst for these developments was the American involvement in the Vietnam War, and the growing dissatisfaction with that involvement. However, the Vietnam War and the protests against it, alone, would probably not have led political authorities to institute political repression on the level that it reached had not the war been accompanied by other factors. Among the most important of these other factors were: the worst series of racial disorders in American history, accompanied by the increasing popularity of black militancy, symbolized by the "Black Power" movement, and the rise of the Black Panthers in the late 1960's; a startling rise in violent crime, which made "law and order" the favorite program of all three presidential candidates in the 1968 election; and the growth of a "counterculture" among American youth, who expressed their disdain for American society by adopting dress, hair, drug, sex and life "styles" that outraged older, conservative and more powerful Americans.[2]

As the Vietnam War continued, protests against the war grew in both numbers and militancy, until by 1969, an influential segment of the leading anti-war organization, Students for a Democratic Society (SDS), the Weathermen, split off and openly urged the use of bombings and other similar tactics to bring about a violent, anti-capitalist revolution.[3] The emergence of Weatherman, and its analysis, which pointed to American capitalism and imperialism as the fundamental cause of the war and other major ills in American society, reflected a general trend within the anti-war movement to move from a position concerned solely with the war to a general, Marxist or pseudo-Marxist critique of American society, and to adopt an increasingly militant posture.

The fact that the growth of an increasingly strong and radical anti-war and then generally anti-establishment political movement, the development of black militancy and uprisings, the soaring crime rate, and the youth "counterculture" all occurred during the same period led to general fears that American society was (to use the title phrase of William O'Neill's book) "coming apart." Thus, as Thomas Powers writes:

> The spread of drugs and flower children throughout 1967 convinced many people that the spiritual and moral strength of the country were disintegrating. The riots which physically damaged and emotionally shocked a dozen cities that summer, and nearly destroyed Newark and Detroit, raised the possibility that the country was on the verge of an internal breakdown.[4]

It was in this atmosphere that the political repression of the Vietnam War era was initiated by the Johnson and Nixon administrations and by states and localities throughout the country.

The increasing strength and militancy of the anti-war movement are easily documented. For example, membership in SDS jumped from about ten thousand in October, 1965 to eighty thousand or more in November, 1968. The number of people turning out at major anti-war demonstrations climbed steadily, from forty thousand in Washington, D.C., in November, 1965, to three hundred thousand in New York and San Francisco in April, 1967, to about five hundred thousand in Washington, D.C. and San Francisco in November, 1969.[5] Campus demonstrations, centered around the war, but frequently embracing other issues, jumped from over 400 during the 1966-67 academic year, to over 3400 during the 1967-68 year, to 9,408 protests during the 1969-70 academic year. Demonstrations following the Cambodian invasion and the Kent State shootings of May, 1970, involved over four million students at over 1,300 colleges across the country and led 536 schools to shut down completely for at least a short period. Even high schools were affected by the protest wave of the late 1960's; during the 1968-69 academic year 20 percent of the nation's high schools were affected by protest demonstrations, and during the 1968-69 year, 60 percent of high schools were affected.[6] Another measure of the growth of protest sentiment was the sudden burgeoning of an anti-establishment "underground press," which encompassed an estimated four hundred fifty papers with a circulation of about five million at its height, including about fifty papers published for or by dissident soldiers.[7] Prosecutions by the Justice Department for draft resistance jumped from 380 during the 1965 fiscal year to over 3,300 during the 1968 fiscal year, while draft delinquencies increased from 15,600 to 31,900 between October, 1967, and October, 1969.[8]

As protests increased in number, they increased in militancy and violence. Protests before the 1968-69 academic year used increasingly militant tactics, such as sit-ins which attempted to block campus recruiters for the CIA and the military or which attempted to close down government buildings, but except for a handful of incidents there was little physical violence against persons or property, except for that inflicted *upon* protesters by police or right-wing demonstrators.[9] After 1968 however (by which time political repression was *already* well-advanced) incidents of violence increased dramatically during protests. In January, 1971, *Scanlan's Magazine* published the following figures for what it called "Guerilla Acts of Sabotage and Terrorism in the U.S." including sniping, bombings, arson, molotov cocktails and "terrorism:"

	1965	1966	1967	1968	1969	1970 (thru Sept. 7)
Government	2	3	1	11	21	47
Corporations	4	5	15	28	86	110
Homes	3	3	4	9	22	21
High Schools	4	16	19	21	90	42
Colleges	0	2	6	26	85	161
Police	3	4	11	124	168	113
Military	0	1	0	17	31	52
TOTAL	16	34	56	236	503	546

While the *Scanlan's* figures include some dubious data (for example, among the incidents they list as involving "guerilla acts of sabotage and terrorism" are fires set at schools by children), clearly they do indicate a pattern of increasing violence that is also borne out by descriptions of many campus demonstrations in the 1968-69 academic year and later. According to the FBI, property damage on college campuses reached over $3 million in 1968-69, and jumped to over $9.5 million in the 1969-70 year.[10] During, May, 1970, the month of the Kent State shootings, there were 169 incidents of bombings and arson, 95 of them associated with college campuses; in the first week of May alone, 30 ROTC buildings on campuses were burned or bombed.[11] There were 35,302 assaults on policemen in 1970 (compared to 16,793 in 1963) and during the 1968-69 fiscal year 337 persons were arrested (and 269 convicted) for attempts or threats against government officials.[12] According to FBI figures, terrorist incidents from 1971 through 1975 included 255 terrorist bombings, 122 firebombings, 45 sniping incidents, 120 shootings, 24 ambushes and 21 instances of arson; during this period 48 police officers were killed and 152 wounded in various incidents.[13]

Perhaps the most shocking form of violent protest was the massive increase in bombings, which skyrocketed after 1968. On college campuses, bombings jumped from 10 in the spring of 1968, to 41 in the fall of 1968, to 84 in the spring of 1969, and, during the 1969-70 academic year, to 174 bombings and attempts on college campuses.[14] According to the Alchohol, Tobacco and Firearms Division of the Treasury Department, between January 1, 1969 and April 15, 1970, there were 4,330 bombings, 1,475 unsuccessful bombing attempts and 35,129 threatened bombings across the nation. Of the 36 percent of total incidents that could be attributed to some cause, over half of these (over 8,200 incidents) were connected with "campus disturbances and student unrest."[15] Between July, 1970, and March, 1971, there were 812 bombings across the country, while during all of 1971, there were 2,054 incidents involving explosives and incendiary devices. Three young radicals were killed in March, 1970, when their bomb factory blew up in a New York City townhouse, and another young radical was sentenced to twenty-three years in prison after being convicted in another bombing which killed a research physicist at the University of Wisconsin.[16] The greatest concentration of bomb incidents was in California, with 1,048 bombings and attempted bombings in 1970, and 1,084 in 1971. California bombings and attempted bombings dropped sharply after 1971, falling to 538 in 1972, 363 in 1973, 529 in 1974 and 165 in the first three months of 1975.[17] Nationally, bomb incidents declined after 1971, but were increasing again by 1975. In 1974, there were 2,044 bombing incidents which killed 23 persons, injured 189 and caused property damage of $8.6 million, and in 1975, 2,053 bombing incidents killed 69, wounded about 300 and caused over $25 million in damage. Only a small percentage of these bombings were attributed specifically to terrorists, however, including about 90 in 1975 and 45 in 1974.[18]

Without question, the 1968-75 period saw a greater number of incidents of anti-government violence than any period since the Civil War. But it is important to keep several points in mind in considering the amount of violence that occurred during this period. Political repression was already well advanced by 1968, before there had been a large number of violent incidents. There were never any signs of any serious, coordinated attempt to "overthrow" the government ("Weatherman," the most violence-prone organized group, had about two to three hundred members)[19] and despite the large number of violent incidents they never amounted to more than an irritating pinprick in a country stretching over three thousand miles from ocean to ocean. There is strong evidence that FBI and other police informers were involved in creating a number of violent incidents. Finally, violence *never* was the dominant force in the protest movement — during the 1969-70 school year only about 8 percent of all campus protests involved violence, and less than 6 percent of protests involved violence following the Kent State shootings.[20]

Johnson and the Great Society

The aftermath of the assassination of John F. Kennedy seemed to confirm the apparent trend of the Kennedy years towards lessened political repression. Although Kennedy's accused assassin, Lee Harvey Oswald, was widely reported to have had Communist and other left-wing affiliations, the assassination was not followed by any signs of a "red scare." An examination of the ACLU's monthly publication, *Civil Liberties,* for 1964 and 1965 reveals that most news relevant to the subject of political repression was generated by various favorable Supreme Court and other federal court decisions. HUAC activity continued to decline; at the beginning of the 1964 congressional session, the committee actually asked for a decreased appropriation. Political deportations continued at the extremely small level which had been characteristic of the previous ten years.

Hearing Days By HUAC, 1962-1965[21]	
1962	26
1963	12
1964	16
1965	10

The period's relatively few publicly known repressive acts were very limited in scope and seemed to be more ritualistic than meaningful. For example, in 1964 Congress passed a bill requiring disloyalty-disclaimers from youths enrolling in the Job Corps. The Civil Rights Act of 1964 included a provision that members of the Communist Party or any other organization under final registration orders from the SACB were excluded from protection against employment discrimination by the Equal Employment Opportunity Commission. In the aftermath of the defection to Russia of two employees of the National Security Agency (NSA), Congress also passed in 1964 legislation granting summary dismissal power to the Secretary of Defense to fire any NSA employee without hearings or charges.[22] Arizona's Assistant Attorney General wrote the Communist Party a letter in 1964 informing them that a 1961 state law barred the CP from the ballot; he added that, "The subversive nature of your organization is even more clearly designated by the fact that you do not even include your zip code on your letters."[23]

That red-baiting and hard-line anti-communism had lost most of their political appeal seemed to be confirmed by the 1964 congressional and presidential election. Lyndon Johnson was elected president in a landslide over Republican Presidential Candidate Barry Goldwater, who had made a career of unyielding opposition to communism, and who appeared to favor a much stronger stand against communism in Vietnam. In the congressional elections, not a single congressman noted for his interest in civil liberties failed to regain his seat, including all eighteen congressmen who had voted against the most recent HUAC appropriation bill and were seeking re-election to the House.[24]

Underneath the surface of the apparent civil liberties calm in 1964, however, were the first stirrings of some of the protest activities — and subsequent repression — that would shatter the calm of American society in the second half of the 1960's. Nineteen sixty-four was the year of a serious race riot in Harlem, the first of the worst series of race riots in American history, which soon made "law and order" a major issue in the American political arena. In the aftermath of the riot, the Progressive Labor Party (PLP), a Maoist-oriented group formed in 1962 by former members of the Communist Party, was subjected to severe harassment by New York City officials. William Epton, a black PLP organizer, was prosecuted and convicted of "criminal anarchy," the first time such a charge had been brought in New York State in over forty years.[25] Thirty other PLP members were subpoenaed by a New York Grand Jury, and over ten were subsequently convicted for contempt of the grand jury.[26] The general approach of the grand jury seemed to be that the riots resulted from a PLP plot, even though an FBI report concluded that the disturbances were "a senseless attack on all constituted authority without directed purpose or object . . . systematic planning or organization."[27] While PLP agitation during the riots clearly was aimed at the fostering of disorder, there is no evidence that its actions had any serious impact on the course of the riots. Nevertheless, as one observer noted, New York authorities "tried to use PL's stupidity and addiction to violence as a crowbar to break the organization, by jailing its leaders, draining its treasury and intimidating its members," thereby succeeding only in feeding "the fanaticism of PL, driving it even further into a Marxist-Leninist fantasy world."[28]

Another sign of times to come in 1964 was a major attempt by members of SDS to organize poor people in selected cities around the country in a program known as the Economic Research and Action Project (ERAP); ERAP workers in Newark, New Jersey, were soon visited by an FBI agent, and ERAPers at various cities were "red-baited and beatnik-baited by city halls and local papers" and subjected to "countless arrests, raids, harassments, badgerings and false accusations."[29]

A third event of 1964 that portended the future was the so-called "Free Speech Movement" (FSM) at the University of California at Berkeley.[30] The FSM arose for many varied and complex reasons, but the immediate trigger for the Berkeley disorders was a repressive University regulation which banned on-campus organization and solicitation of funds for off-campus political action, a rule which in effect "suspended much of the Bill of Rights, creating an enclave where the Constitution did not obtain."[31] University President Clark Kerr later conceded:

> The University of California had the most restrictive policies (regarding) political activity of any university I've ever known, outside a dictatorship.[32]

The eventual outcome of months of turmoil at Berkeley was a student sit-in at the University's administration building which was broken up by police in the early hours of December 3, 1964, with the arrest of 814 students. During the course of the FSM protests, President Kerr twice suggested the students were under communist influence, a charge which was echoed by State Sen. Hugh Burns, chairman of California's Un-American Activities committee. In January, 1965, the University announced that student organization and solicitation for off-campus political action would henceforth be allowed on the Berkeley campus.

Finally, 1964 saw the first major stirrings of public awareness and protest over the war in Vietnam. Perhaps the first public anti-war demonstration had occurred in October, 1963 when a handful of SDS members protesting the visit to Washington of Mme. Ngo Dinh Nhu, sister-in-law of South Vietnamese dictator Ngo Dinh Nhu, were arrested for picketing outside the Washington Press Club, where Mme. Nhu had been invited to speak. In May, 1964, PLP sponsored anti-war marches and rallies in several cities — seventeen were convicted of disorderly conduct in New York although testimony at their trial indicated there had been no disorders until police attempted to disperse the rally — and sponsored the first attempt to urge resistance to the draft in the context of the Vietnam War.[33]

In 1965, the war was seriously escalated by the Johnson administration and public protests began to become more frequent and gain increasing publicity. A serious decline in the civil liberties climate quickly became evident, largely as a result of a calculated campaign by high-ranking officials in the executive branch and by the Congress to intimidate and repress dissident activity.

As early as 1964, the Johnson administration had banned all financial and commercial transactions with North Vietnam and the National Liberation Front (generally known in the West as the Viet Cong), and in February, 1965, a U.S. Customs agent seized, and then released under ACLU challenge, a Viet Cong propaganda film as it was about to be shown at the University of Cincinnati.[34] In August, 1965, in the wake of a series of highly publicized burnings of draft cards as anti-war protests, Congress passed a law making it illegal to knowingly mutilate or destroy one's draft card. This bill was passed by both houses, without hearings, within nine days of its introduction. Since failure to possess a draft card was already a violation of draft regulations, passage of the bill was clearly aimed at repressing a form of dissent which had obtained widespread media coverage. The congressional floor debate was filled with comments to the effect that draft card burners were filthy beatniks, communist stooges and traitors. The Johnson administration quickly brought charges against alleged violators of the law, and the Supreme Court, in one of the few decisions that marred an otherwise good civil liberties record from 1965 to 1970, upheld the law in *U.S. v. O'Brien* (1968).[35]

A widespread campaign was begun by top-ranking administration officials and Congressional red-hunting committees to portray the anti-war movement as a communist plot, with the inevitable overtone of possible prosecutions under anti-subversive laws. The first major effort along these lines was a staff study released by SISS on the eve of planned nation-wide anti-war protests scheduled for October 15-16, 1965. The SISS report charged that control of the anti-war movement was in the hands "of communist and extremist elements who are openly sympathetic to the Vietcong and openly hostile to the U.S. . . . This is particularly true of the national Vietnam protest movement scheduled for October 15-16."[36]

Following the protests, which attracted about one hundred thousand demonstrators, President Johnson's press secretary publicly expressed Johnson's concern that "even well-meaning demonstrators can become the victims of communist aggression" and the president's surprise that "any one citizen would feel toward his country in a way that is not consistent with the national interest." At the same time, Attorney General Nicholas Katzenbach announced that the Justice Department would investigate groups seeking to attack the draft, and stated that in groups such as SDS, "where people are saying things similar to what is being said by Peking, you are likely to find some communists involved." Katzenbach added that the government felt antidraft activity was beginning to "move in the direction of treason" and added:

> There are some communists in it and we may have to investigate. We may very well have some prosecutions.

He said the Justice Department had already uncovered some persons in SDS who were "possible" communists and that SDS was one of "many" groups under examination.[37] President Johnson was subsequently quoted as having given his "full endorsement" to the Justice Department's investigation of "possible communist infiltration of the antidraft movement," while Vice-President Humphrey announced that the "international communist movement" had "organized and masterminded" the demonstrations.[38] With such signs of official endorsement of "red" charges, newspapers began to send out stories with "the clear implication that SDS was a subversive organization."[39]

Such statements from high administration officials apparently reflected President Johnson's heartfelt conviction, which grew stronger with time, that opponents of his Vietnam policy were part of an international communist conspiracy.[40] According to Eric Goldman, who served for a period as special consultant to Johnson, the president told him in 1966 that "the Russians" were behind opposition to his war policies and were in constant touch with anti-war Senators. "The Russians think up things for the Senators to say," Goldman reports Johnson as saying. "I often know before they do what their speeches are going to say."[41] These suspicions were apparently instrumental in 1967 in leading Johnson to push the CIA into what eventually became a large-scale domestic intelligence operation in a futile attempt to discover major links between foreign communists and domestic dissidents.[42]

Shortly after the October 1965 demonstrations, citizens who wrote to the White House to express their disagreement with Johnson's Vietnam policies began to receive acknowledging letters from the Internal Security Division of the Justice Department — thereby suggesting such dissenters were being investigated for possible violation of some federal law.[43]

In March, 1966, Katzenbach announced that the Justice Department was petitioning the SACB to have the W.E.B. DuBois Clubs, a small but vocal anti-war group under strong communist influence, registered as a communist-front organization. Aside from Robert Kennedy's proceedings against AYO, this was the only time such action had been taken since 1956. Within a few hours of Katztnbach's announcement, a group of DuBois Club members were assaulted outside their Brooklyn office by residents who had previously ignored them. Police failed to protect the DuBois members from assault, but succeeded in arresting five of them. At about the same time, a bomb blew up the DuBois national headquarters in San Francisco.[44]

In August, 1966, HUAC held tumultous hearings into the anti-war movement, during which fifty witnesses and spectators were arrested for disorderly conduct. Before the hearings began the committee requested and obtained membership lists of anti-war organizations from the Universities of California and Michigan. After the hearings ended, HUAC issued a report charging that a "widespread and well-organized" effort initiated by communist groups existed in opposition to the American war effort, with a long-range goal of overthrowing the U.S. government and installing a "communist totalitarian dictatorship." As a result of HUAC's urging, the House passed in October, 1966, a bill to make it a federal crime to give assistance to forces engaged in "undeclared war" with the U.S. or to interfere with the movement of military personnel or supplies. This bill, which followed efforts by anti-war forces to raise money and blood to aid the Viet Cong and to block troop trains, was opposed by Attorney General Ramsey Clark and did not pass the Senate.[45]

Shortly before anti-war demonstrations scheduled for April 1967, HUAC issued a report which claimed that forthcoming demonstrations "may be attributed primarily to communists" and were intended to "do injury and damage to the United States and to give aid and comfort to its enemies." On the day of the demonstrations, President Johnson let it be known that the FBI was "keeping an eye" on anti-war activity, and at about the same time, Secretary of State Dean Rusk charged "the world-wide communist apparatus is working very hard" in the demonstrations.[46]

Probably the most influential and consistent red-baiter was FBI Director Hoover. Since the great days of McCarthyism, the FBI had found few communists to hunt, and Hoover leapt at the opportunity to discover a communist conspiracy in the rising signs of discontent with American society. In January, 1966, Hoover charged the CP had played an "ever-increasing role in generating opposition to the United States position in Vietnam" and that the CP and other subversive groups had "supported and participated" in most of the major anti-war demonstrations. In February, 1966, Hoover termed SDS "one of the most militant organizations" involved in anti-war protests, and charged that "communists are actively promoting and participating in the activities of this organization."[47]

In 1967, Hoover charged that "communists and subversives and extremists strive ceaselessly to precipitate racial trouble and to take advantage of racial discord in this country. Such elements were active in exploiting and aggravating the riots, for example, in Harlem, Watts, Cleveland and Chicago." He attacked the DuBois Clubs as "new blood for the vampire of international communism" and stated that the DuBois clubs "together with other so-called 'New Left' organizations such as the Students for a Democratic Society work constantly in furtherance of the aims and objectives of the Communist Party throughout the nation." In 1968, Hoover termed SDS "anarchistic and nihilistic" and reported that an SDS convention had featured a workshop on "Sabotage and Explosives." What Hoover neglected to say was that the workshop had been especially set up to draw off undercover agents so other groups could meet without having to worry about infiltration.[48]

By 1967 and 1968, the increasing tempo and popularity of protest activity, which included draft card burnings, induction refusals and massive anti-war demonstrations, led to more and sterner measures of repression.[49] Beginning in early 1967, the Treasury and Post Office departments forbade efforts to send relief to civilian war victims in North Vietnam and areas of South Vietnam controlled by communist forces, acting under the authority of the 1917 Trading With the Enemy Act, which was in force only because President Truman's declaration of a state of emergency issued in December, 1950, had never been repealed. The Treasury Department enforced its will by ordering banks not to honor checks destined for such efforts and by freezing the bank accounts of several organizations, while the Post Office Department simply refused to accept parcels bound for the forbidden areas.[50] In May, 1967, Postmaster General Lawrence O'Brien banned from the mails an issue of a magazine distributed from Peking, partially on the grounds that it encouraged Negro soldiers to "sabotage operations" in Vietnam; among the grounds cited for his authority was the 1908 "anarchist" mail ban and the 1917 Sedition Act, which was also in force due to Truman's 1950 declaration. In June, 1970 a federal court declared O'Brien's action illegal.[51]

In August, 1967, the Department of the Interior announced that picketers in front of the White House would be limited to one hundred persons, and demonstration permits might be forbidden altogether if it appeared that more than one hundred persons might seek entry to the area. Previously, the White House sidewalk, which is separated from the mansion itself by a high iron fence and several hundred yards of lawn, had accomodated thousands of demonstrators on numerous occasions without any serious security threat or interference with traffic.

On October 21, 1967, a few hours before a scheduled anti-war protest in Washington, President Johnson signed a law which had been rushed through Congress, which in essence banned all protests on Capitol Hill by making it illegal to picket, demonstrate or use loud, threatening or abusive language in the Capitol area. Both the White House and Capitol restrictions were subsequently overturned by federal courts; before the Capitol ban was reversed, demonstrators were arrested for reading lists of Vietnam War dead on the Capitol steps, and during the 1971 "Mayday" demonstrations, twelve hundred persons were arrested while peacefully listening to a speech by a Congressman on the Capitol steps.[52]

On October 21, 1967, about one hundred thousand persons marched on the Pentagon in an anti-war protest. Thousands of persons broke through lines set up by federal troops and marshalls and stayed on the Pentagon grounds beyond the expiration of the parade permit, and a small group attempted to break into the Pentagon; however, the only damage caused by demonstrators was a single window broken by a thrown rock. Troops and marshalls responded to the demonstration by widespread use of tear gas and clubs; altogether seven hundred were arrested and over one thousand persons brutally beaten.[53] Five days after the Pentagon demonstration, Selective Service Director Lewis Hershey sent a letter to all local draft boards recommending that registrants who participated in "illegal demonstrations," interfered with recruiting or otherwise violated selective service regulations be subject to reclassification and immediate induction. Hershey wrote:

> Deferments are only given when they serve the national interest. It is obvious that any action that violates the Military Selective Service Act or the Regulations or the related processes cannot be in the national interest.[54]

Hershey's directive was obviously intended to intimidate demonstrators, since one could never tell in advance what an "illegal demonstration" or the "national interest" might involve; thus the only sure way for draft-eligible men to avoid possible retaliatory induction would be to avoid all protest whatsoever. From December 1, 1967 to December 1, 1968, 537 students who turned in their draft cards lost their student deferments and were declared eligible for induction as a result of the Hershey directive. In one case, an Oklahoma SDS member was reclassified because his draft board determined that it "did not feel that your activity as a member of SDS is to the best interest of the U.S. government." The use of punitive reclassification as a weapon to intimidate war protesters who otherwise qualified for draft exemptions was declared unconstitutional by the Supreme Court in a series of cases in 1970.[55]

In December, 1967, Hershey and Attorney General Ramsey Clark issued a joint statement which seemed to back off somewhat from Hershey's directive. The statement indicated that "lawful protest activities" would not lead to reclassification, called upon local law enforcement agencies to "vigorously prosecute violations of local laws" which might occur in anti-draft demonstrations, and suggested that reclassification would occur *only* for violation of *draft regulations,* such as failure to have draft cards in one's possession. As an apparent effort to salve Hershey's feeling for apparently reversing his position that participation in "illegal demonstrations" could lead to reclassification, the Justice Department at the same time announced the formation of a special unit to speed up investigation and prosecution of violations of the draft act and "related statutes" with special attention to be paid to violations of the "counsel, aid or abet" and "obstruction of recruiting" provisions of the draft act.[56]

Shortly after this announcement, the Justice Department under the "liberal" Attorney General Clark initiated the single most repressive overt action of the Johnson administration — the indictment of William Sloane Coffin, chaplain of Yale University, nationally known pediatrician Dr. Benjamin Spock and three other anti-war leaders in January, 1968, for conspiracy to "counsel, aid and abet" violations of the draft and to interfere with administration of the draft.[57]

There is very strong circumstantial evidence that the indictment was intended as a warning to all anti-war demonstrators and spokesmen that they might very well face similar charges. All of the overt actions cited in support of the indictment were public activities, such as signing statements and making speeches against the war, along with collecting draft cards turned in by *other* persons and forwarding them to the Justice Department. During the trial, the position of the Justice Department's prosecutors was that all twenty-eight thousand signers of an anti-draft statement, all persons who voiced support or even applauded at rallies where the defendants spoke, and even newsmen who reported the defendants' speeches could be indicted as members of the conspiracy. At one point, government prosecutors stated that the publishers and booksellers of a book which printed anti-draft statements could also be indicted. When one government attorney was asked during the trial why the government had picked out these five defendants among the thousands of protesters, he made an analogy to the inability of police to catch all speeders. He stated:

> One of the reasons for enforcement of the law is deterrent to others — you can't get everybody in the speed trap, but you are going to get enough so that *everybody* knows. If it's a real bad speed trap and a danger to the safety of the community, there comes a point where maybe you will have to have enough police out there to stop *everybody* who speeds.[58]

Because the charges brought during the Coffin-Spock trial were conspiracy, making the crime consist of an alleged agreement between the conspirators, the government was under no obligation to show that any of the defendants' acts actually led anyone to resist the draft, and in fact Gen. Hershey explicitly stated that there was no evidence of such an effect.[59] The outcome of the trial was acquittal of one of the defendants and conviction of the four others, but the convictions were set aside on a technicality by a federal appeals court, with two of the defendants freed from all further prosecution on grounds of insufficient evidence and the two others remanded for possible retrial. Although the government never retried the case and thus all defendants went free, the appeals court decision made no basic challenge to the constitutionality of the government's position, thus creating a situation in which "an individual now cannot know at the time he signs petitions, expresses his opinion or joins others in a lawful demonstration, whether or not he will later be linked by that act to a criminal conspiracy."[60]

As student protests and urban riots mounted in the last year of the Johnson administration, so did the forces of repression. In December, 1967, both houses of Congress, with the support of the administration (although not of Attorney General Clark), passed legislation to revive the all-but-moribund SACB. Since the courts had essentially made it impossible for the SACB to force alleged communists or communist organizations to register, the new bill gave the SACB power to simply list by fiat groups found to be communist-action or communist-front organizations or persons found to be members of communist-action organizations. The bill provided that the SACB would expire unless a new proceeding was instituted before it by the Attorney General and a hearing conducted by the SACB before the end of 1968. Clark dutifully obliged in July, 1968, by asking the board to designate seven individuals as CP members. This proceeding was thrown out by a U.S. appeals court in 1969 in a decision which the Supreme Court refused to review, thereby rendering the SACB toothless again until President Nixon attempted to revive it once more in 1971.[61]

Nineteen sixty-eight proved to be a banner year for repression. HUAC issued a report which urged the use of the Internal Security Act's concentration camps for the "temporary imprisonment of warring guerillas" and claimed that radical and black groups were "seriously considering the possibility of instituting armed insurrection in this country." HUAC added that SDS was planning "guerilla-type operations against the government," thus anticipating the actions of a small fraction of SDS by over a year.[62]

Following the urban riots which broke out in the aftermath of the assassination of civil rights leader Martin Luther King, Congress passed in April, 1968, a provision making it illegal for any person to travel or to use any facility of interstate commerce, including the mails or telephones, with the intent to incite, organize, promote, encourage, participate in or carry on a riot, and thereafter performing or attempting to perform "any other overt act" in furtherance thereof. The bill defined a riot as an act of violence or the threat of the commission of an act of violence by one or more persons in a group of three or more persons which constituted a "clear and present danger or shall result in damage or injury to the property of any other person or to the person of any other individual."[63]

In effect, this law meant that any time a minor disturbance occurred involving three persons, if it could be shown that any person involved in the disturbance had previously made a long distance call or mailed a letter across state lines, he could be tried for a federal crime on the basis of his alleged state of mind at the time he used such facilities of interstate commerce. This law, which would be used by the Nixon administration in a number of cases, created a federal super-Smith Act, in effect outlawing not only advocacy of overthrow of the government, but advocacy of anything that might be construed as an "overt act" inciting a riot. The anti-riot law had been *opposed* by Attorney General Clark in the summer of 1967 and by President Johnson in January, 1968, but shortly thereafter Johnson reversed himself and proposed, with the support of Clark, a variant of the bill which was finally adopted. Clark did exercise restraint in administration of the law. In the aftermath of the riots at the Democratic Convention in Chicago, in August, 1968, Clark's staff reported to him that there was no basis for prosecution of demonstrators under the law, and Clark refused to bring such charges, despite strong pressure from President Johnson and others. Shortly before leaving office, Clark reiterated his determination not to prosecute the demonstrators, adding, "If the new administration does prosecute them, that will be a clear signal that a crackdown is on the way."[64]

The anti-riot law was not the only repressive legislation of 1968. In response to flag-burning demonstrations, Congress outlawed public mutilation or defacing of the flag, and in response to increased student anti-war demonstrations, a small percentage of which involved violence or law-breaking, Congress passed a bill barring federal financial aid for two years to students or teachers convicted in a local court of rioting, who were also found by their college to have disrupted school activities through such rioting. This bill was followed in subsequent months and years by a flood of similar legislation; by the 1971 fiscal year, Congress had included provisions cutting off federal funds to students or employees involved in disruptive activities in ten separate authorization or appropriation acts. Many of these provisions were extremely vague; thus any student receiving federal aid would have no way of knowing exactly what kind of activities might lead to a termination of his support. In 1969 and 1970, at least one thousand college students lost federal funds as a result of these laws. In December, 1972, a federal court declared one of these laws unconstitutionally vague as applied to a young woman who had participated in a sit-in against ROTC, and had been forced to drop out of school as a result of the aid cut-off.[65]

In June, 1968, Congress passed as part of the Omnibus Crime Control and Safe Streets Act of 1968 a provision which for the first time in American history explicitly legalized federal wiretapping and eavesdropping. Under the bill the Attorney General and state officials were authorized to apply for court warrants authorizing tapping and bugging to seek evidence of a wide range of federal offenses punishable by more than a year in jail. The bill further provided that in emergency cases involving "national security" or "organized crime" tapping and bugging could proceed without a court order for forty-eight hours. The most glaring loophole of the bill was a wholly gratuitous provision which stated that nothing in the bill or previous legislation should be construed to limit the president's power to take such measures "as he deems necessary" to protect national security information against foreign intelligence activities, to protect the nation against "actual or potential attack or other hostile acts" of a foreign power, to obtain foreign intelligence information deemed "essential" to American security, or to protect the government from overthrow "by force or other unlawful means, or against any other clear and present danger to the structure or existence of the government." The clear meaning of this provision seemed to be that in cases involving either foreign intelligence operations or domestic "subversion" tapping and bugging could proceed without court supervision.[66]

Undoubtedly the greatest repressive legacy left behind by the Johnson administration was an immense buildup in the political surveillance machinery of the federal government. Ironically, during the 1964-1966 period, before the full dimensions of racial and anti-war protests became apparent, the FBI and Johnson administration took a number of steps to tighten controls on political surveillance machinery. In 1964, Hoover banned further FBI use of "mail covers" (examining the outside of envelopes for address information) and "trash covers" (examining garbage). Johnson, before signing the 1968 law, took a strong stand against wiretapping, and in June, 1965, barred any wiretapping by government agencies without approval of the Attorney General, and authorized such approval only to collect information "essential to protecting our national security." Attorney General Nicholas Katzenbach, in March, 1965, required that the FBI gain approval in advance from the Attorney General before implementing any microphone surveillance.

Beginning in 1965, Hoover greatly restricted the use of FBI wiretaps and bugs, and in 1966 the FBI ended its twenty-six year old program of opening mail and banned further use of "black bag jobs" to obtain sensitive information during break-ins from domestic "subversive" groups.[68] However, these steps amounted only to minor reforms that did not seriously restrict FBI intelligence activities during the late 1960's. While taps and bugs decreased, the FBI still used them and had little difficulty in getting advance approval from Attorney General Nicholas Katzenbach, who assured the FBI that he would "continue to approve all" requests in the "national security" area as "I have in the past." Thus, in 1965, Katzenbach approved requests for taps on SDS, the Student Non-Violent Coordinating Committee (SNCC) and others. FBI break-ins to install bugs continued, and Katzenbach, Johnson and other officials were informed of at least some aspects of the FBI's continuing campaign to discredit Martin Luther King, but did

FBI Wiretaps and Microphone Surveillances, 1960-1974[67]

Year	Telephone Wiretaps	Microphone "Bugs"
1960	114	74
1961	140	85
1962	198	100
1963	244	83
1964	260	106
1965	233	67
1966	174	10
1967	113	0
1968	82	9
1969	123	14
1970	102	19
1971	101	16
1972	108	32
1973	123	40
1974	190	42

nothing to stop it. Altogether, the FBI installed about eight hundred wiretaps from 1964 to 1968, and about seven hundred bugs, and made over one hundred fifty "surreptitious entries" to install bugs in non-criminal intelligence investigations. Although the FBI ended its mail-opening in 1966, it continued to receive information from the CIA's mail-opening project, as it had since 1958.[69]

The FBI was encouraged to step up its domestic intelligence activities in many areas by the Johnson administration. Johnson relied on the FBI to an extraordinary degree and in extraordinary ways throughout his administration. During the 1964 election campaign, FBI agents who were sent to the Democratic National Convention, supposedly to determine the seriousness of any "danger" or "threats" to Johnson, carefully monitored the activities of fifteen different protest groups and relayed to Johnson what a Senate Intelligence Committee staff report termed "the most sensitive plans and tactics" of the Mississippi Freedom Democratic Party delegate challenge, which was the "most important single issue that might have disturbed President Johnson." An FBI memo summarizing the convention operation reported that "by means of informant coverage, by use of various confidential techniques, by infiltration of key groups through use of undercover agents, and through utilization of agents using appropriate cover as reporters, we were able to keep the White House fully appraised of all major developments during the Convention." Later a top presidential aide informed the FBI, according to an FBI document, that the "job the Bureau had done in Atlantic City was one of the finest the President had ever seen," and that because of the FBI information the "bad elements" active at the convention "were not able to be very effective."[70] During the final days of the 1964 campaign, a top Johnson assistant asked the FBI to report on all persons employed by Republican presidential challenger Barry Goldwater, and subsequently Johnson officials requested the FBI to furnish information on persons who were critical of the Warren Commission's report on the assassination of President Kennedy.[71]

FBI infiltration and disruption of dissident groups greatly increased during the Johnson administration. Under pressure from Johnson and the Justice Department, the FBI took strong measures against the revived KKK, initiating a counter-intelligence program (COINTELPRO) against "White Hate" groups in 1964 that was largely directed against the KKK, along with a few other racist groups such as the American Nazi party and the National States' Rights Party. The COINTELPRO operation was designed to "expose, disrupt and otherwise neutralize" such groups based on the FBI's similar program operated against the CP since 1956 and the SWP since 1961. The FBI program called on agents to expose the "devious maneuvers and duplicity" of the groups, to block attempts to consolidate forces or recruit new members and to "capitalize upon organizational and personal conflicts of their leadership." The FBI kept the Justice Department at least vaguely informed about its new COINTELPRO. Hoover wrote Attorney General Katzenbach in September, 1965, that the FBI was "seizing every opportunity to disrupt the activities of Klan organizations," and similar general references to the program were made in letters sent to Attorney General Ramsey Clark in 1967 and Attorney General John Mitchell in 1969.[72]

As was the case with the KKK of the 1920's, the Klan of the late 1950's and 1960's unquestionably engaged in many acts of violence, which makes it difficult to clearly identify which actions taken against the group were politically repressive rather than reasonable efforts to uphold reasonable laws. Klansmen were implicated in at least six murders of civil rights workers in 1964 and 1965, and between 1956 and 1963 at least 138 dynamitings and uncounted beatings and burnings occurred in the south which were attributable to racial hate groups such as the Klan. Many federal and state prosecutions which severely weakened the Klan in the south after 1963 do not appear to fall in the repressive category.[73]

However, many of the almost three hundred actions which the FBI admits to having initiated against "White Hate" groups under its COINTELPRO operation from 1964 until its alleged termination in 1971 clearly did amount to severe forms of political repression. FBI agents massively infiltrated the Klan, with almost two thousand informants within the organization by 1965 who amounted to about 20 percent of the total membership. FBI agents reached leadership positions in seven of the fourteen Klan groups across the country, headed one state Klan organization and even created a splinter Klan group which grew to nearly two hundred members and became involved in physical confrontations with the regular Klan organization in one state. Other techniques used were anonymous mailings to Klan members of thousands of postcards with cartoons attacking the

Klan leadership and suggesting the Klan was heavily infiltrated by the FBI, which were designed to embarass and discourage Klan members. The FBI also created a phony citizens organization entitled the Committee for Domestic Tranquility, which mailed thousands of letters to Klan members attacking the KKK leadership. The FBI also sent anonymous letters accusing Klansmen of being FBI informants, sent a letter to the wife of a Klansman suggesting her husband was committing adultery, faked a picture showing a Klansman consorting with Cuban Prime Minister Castro, cancelled motel reservations made for a Klan meeting and pressured the Veterans Administration and the Internal Revenue Service into cutting off the pension and prosecuting for income tax evasion a disabled Klan veteran. The FBI also planted phony news stories and leaked confidential information to newsmen in attempts to discredit the KKK. The FBI obtained tax information from the IRS as part of its COINTELPRO, and according to an FBI memo, used information obtained from a "black bag job" of a KKK office to "most effectively . . . disrupt the organization." In 1967, a Klansman complained that a letter which had supposedly been sent to him by another Klan group violated mail fraud statutes, without realizing that the FBI had in fact composed and sent it. When the KKK official complained to the FBI and the Post Office, the FBI solemnly told him the complaint was not within FBI jurisdiction, and then kept tabs on the Post Office and the Justice Department investigation of the matter, without informing either agency of the real origins of the letter.[74]

Perhaps the most outrageous FBI operation involving the Klan occurred in 1968, when FBI agents and local police in Meridian, Mississippi, paid two members of a Klan group $36,500 to lure two other KKK members into an attempt to bomb a Jewish businessman's home. Although police expected two males who were suspects in previous bombings in the Meridian area to show up for the bomb attempt, only one of the expected bombers showed up, along with a woman companion; waiting police shot and killed the woman and seriously wounded the man. Police who set the trap subsequently stated they expected a gun battle and never thought the bombers would be taken alive. One of the two FBI informers in the case was under a ten-year sentence in connection with the 1964 murder of three civil rights workers, and both informers were promised immunity from prosecution in several other bombing cases.[75]

Aside from the FBI operations, the Klan was also subjected to a 1965 HUAC investigation, designed to show that the Klan was composed of "crooks and freaks."[76] Although, as usual, the investigation resulted in no legislation, HUAC was able to "produce some evidence of wrongdoing, mostly petty finaglings, rarely available in the case of Communists"[77] and seven KKK witnesses were cited for contempt when they refused to turn over membership records.

FBI anti-Klan activities amounted only to a minor diversion from the FBI's favorite target — the left, including militant black movements. The Harlem disorders and subsequent racial disturbances during the 1964-66 period led the FBI, under prodding from the Johnson administration, to greatly step up its investigation of "general racial matters" which had begun during the 1950's and continued, with Justice Department support, during the Kennedy administration. In June, 1964, a month before the Harlem disorder, the FBI established a special unit to handle "the over-all problem of communist penetration with the racial movement," and in September, 1964, FBI field offices were directed to "broaden" their efforts in this area, interpreting the term "communist" in its "broadest sense" as including not only the CP but also "splinter and off-shoot groups" such as the PLP and SWP. By 1965, reporting requirements were increased to encompass *all* civil rights activity, whether involving "subversives" or not, as agents were directed to supply "complete" information regarding "planned racial activity, such as demonstrations, rallies, marches or threatened opposition to activity of this kind," including full coverage of "meetings" and "any other pertinent information concerning racial activities." In late 1966, FBI field offices were instructed to begin preparing semi-monthly summaries of "existing racial conditions in major urban areas," including descriptions of the "general programs" concerning the "racial issue" of "civil rights organizations" as well as "black nationalist," "Klan" and "hate-type" groups, with a focus on indications of "subversive or radical infiltration," identities of "leaders and individuals involved," minority community "objectives" and the "number, character and intensity of the techniques used by the minority community."[78] The twenty-five year old investigation of the NAACP was intensified. The New York FBI office used sixteen informants and confidential sources to report on NAACP activities there and reported to headquarters all of the national officers and board members of the organization, along with any FBI data on past subversive associations.[79]

Meanwhile, Hoover publicly exaggerated Communist influence in the civil rights movement, reporting, for example, in 1964 that the "communist influence" in the "Negro movement" was "vitally important" and that non-communists were "hard pressed to keep them out and minimize their influence." According to a Senate Intelligence Committee staff report, FBI records indicate that Hoover "rejected the findings of the FBI's most experienced intelligence officers on this issue, that he influenced his own subordinates to abandon their own judgement and to exaggerate Communist influence in the civil rights movement, and that these subordinates then instituted massive investigative efforts to find every possible bit of evidence of Communist links in order to substantiate the Director's preconception."[80]

As the FBI stepped up its monitoring of civil rights activity, COINTELPRO activities directed against the CP continued, with such tactics as informing the news media that the son of a CP couple had been arrested for drugs and that the wife of a CP leader had purchased a new car as an example of the "prosperity" of the CP leadership. In 1964, the FBI planted a document in the car of a leading New York CP official that made him appear an informer; subsequently the official (who had been convicted under the Smith Act and ordered to register as a Communist by the SACB) was expelled from the party. A 1965 FBI memo reporting the expulsion stated that the affair "crippled the activities of the New York State communist organization and the turmoil within the party continues to this date." The FBI created a fictional organization in 1965 entitled the Committee for Expansion of Socialist Thought in America, which purported to attack the CP from the "Marxist right." As a result of other COINTELPRO activity, an internal FBI memo stated in 1965, "many meeting places formerly used on a regular basis by the Communists have been barred from their use." An FBI paper prepared for presentation by Hoover before the House Appropriation Subcommittee in 1965 reported one COINTELPRO technique was "the most effective single blow ever dealt the organized communist movement." In October, 1966, the FBI launched Operation Hoodwink, an effort to set the CP and organized crime against each other by sending the two groups forged letters. Thus, in one case, the FBI sent a letter to a Mafia figure criticizing his labor practices and purporting to come from the CP. Frequently actions which came under the CP COINTELPRO label were directed at non-CP groups and individuals. Thus, the FBI targeted the entire Unitarian Society of Cleveland in 1964 because the minister and some members circulated a petition calling for the abolition of HUAC and because the church gave office space to a group the FBI did not like. In 1965, the FBI tried to block a City Council campaign of a lawyer who had defended Smith Act defendants. In 1966, the FBI tried to get the Texas State Alcoholic Beverage Control Commission to raid a Democratic Party fundraising affair because two Democratic candidates who would be present had participated in anti-war and anti-HUAC activities.[81]

As anti-war protests mushroomed, the FBI, under prodding from the Johnson administration, began to vastly broaden its targets and intelligence activities. In April, 1965, Johnson asked the FBI for a report on communist influence in anti-war demonstrations and met personally with Hoover to discuss the issue. According to Hoover's memo of the meeting, Johnson said he was "quite concerned over the anti-Vietnam situation that has developed in this country" and "there was no doubt in his mind" that "communists" were "behind the disturbances that have already occurred." Beginning in 1965, President Johnson asked the FBI for reports on Senators, journalists and private citizens who sent telegrams to the White House or whose names were printed in the Congressional Record as opposed to the war. Among the targets of these checks were philosopher Hannah Arendt, television newsman David Brinkley and columnist Joseph Kraft. In early 1966, a Johnson aide asked the FBI to monitor televised hearings of the Senate Foreign Relations Committee and prepare a memorandum comparing statements of Senate war critics to the "Communist Party line." In March, 1966, Johnson personally requested the FBI to "constantly keep abreast" of contacts between certain foreign officials and "Senators and Congressmen and any citizen of a prominent nature" since he felt "that much of the protest concerning his Vietnam policy, particularly the hearings in the Senate" had been "generated" by foreign officials. Subsequently the FBI began sending biweekly lists of such contacts to the White House, based at least partially on electronic surveillance of foreign embassies. In response to a 1967 White House request for information on seven anti-war Senators, the FBI provided Johnson with information on the public speeches of the Senators.[82]

After his meeting with Johnson in April, 1965, Hoover ordered intensified coverage of SDS so "that we will have proper informant coverage similar to what we have in the Ku Klux Klan and the Communist Party." Hoover's directive was soon manifested in an ostentatious program of interviewing SDS officers and supporters, along with a large scale program of infiltrating SDS chapters and the development of cooperative intelligence exchanges with campus police forces and administrators.[83] In February, 1966, FBI agents were directed to investigate all "free universities," (student-run classes offered near college campuses on a non-credit basis) because "several" such organizations had allegedly been formed by the CP and "other subversive groups." Thus, an April, 1966, FBI report on a "free university" in Detroit included a detailed study of formation, curriculum content and associates of the group. It was sent to military intelligence, the Secret Service, the State Department and the Justice Department. FBI surveillance of a public teach-in in Philadelphia in March, 1966, resulted in a forty-one page intelligence report based on coverage by thirteen informants and sources, including reports on remarks by ministers, college teachers, a college chaplain, a representative of the ACLU, members of the right-wing Young Americans for Freedom, and members of SDS, the SWP and the DuBois Club. Copies of this report were sent to military intelligence, the State Department, and the Internal Security and Civil Rights Division of the Justice Department. In May, 1966, Hoover urged FBI field offices to "intensify and expand" coverage of the anti-war movement in order to achieve "advance detection" of any "violent outbreaks."[84]

In August, 1967, the FBI added to its list of COINTELPRO targets the category of "black nationalist hate groups." The FBI memo launching the "black nationalist" program listed its purpose as intended to "expose, disrupt, misdirect, discredit or otherwise neutralize" such organizations, "their leadership, spokesmen, membership and supporters." The memo called on FBI agents to expose to "public scrutiny" the "pernicious background of such groups, their duplicity and devious maneuvers," to frustrate their efforts to "consolidate their forces or to recruit new or youthful adherants" and to take every opportunity to "exploit through counter-intelligence techniques the organizational and personal conflicts of the leadership of the groups and where possible an effort should be made to capitalize upon existing conflicts between competing black nationalist organizations." Agents were also told to consider "techniques to preclude violence-prone or rabble rouser leaders of hate groups from spreading their philosophy publicly through various mass communications media," to disrupt, ridicule or discredit such groups by use of media contacts and to "determine evidence of misappropriation of funds or other types of personal misconduct on the part of militant nationalist leaders so any practical or warranted counterintelligence may be instituted." Among the targets listed for the COINTELPRO operation were SCLC, SNCC, the Nation of Islam (Black Muslims), Stokely Carmichael, H. Rap Brown and Elijah Muhammed. Martin Luther King was officially added to the target list in March, 1968, although he had long been subjected to COINTELPRO-type tactics.[85]

Following the mammoth racial disorders in the summer of 1967 in Detroit, Newark and other cities, President Johnson announced that he had given the FBI "standing instructions" to "search for evidence on conspiracy" in connection with riots. In September, 1967, Attorney General Clark directed the FBI to

> use the maximum resources, investigative and intelligence, to collect and report all facts bearing upon the question as to whether there has been or is a scheme or conspiracy by any group of whatever size, effectiveness or affiliation to plan, promote or aggravate riot activity.

Clark also directed the FBI to expand and develop "sources or informants" in "black nationalist organizations" like SNCC as well as "other less publicized groups" in order to "determine the size and purpose of these groups and their relationships to other groups, and also to determine the whereabouts of persons who might be involved" in violations of Federal law.[86] In direct response to this pressure from Clark, the FBI expanded its COINTELPRO in early 1968, initiating a "ghetto informant" program designed to develop sources among people who lived and worked in a "ghetto area" who would report on such topics as "black extremist organizations," the names of "Afro-American type book stores" and their "owners, operators and clientele" and all indications of efforts by foreign powers to "take over" the Negro militant movement. By 1969, over four thousand "ghetto informants" had been developed by the FBI.[87] An FBI memo dated March 4, 1968, one month before the assassination of Martin Luther King, specified FBI goals in its COINTELPRO operation as including preventing the "coalition of militant black nationalist groups" since this might be a first step toward a "true black revolution"; preventing the "rise of a 'messiah'" such as King, Carmichael or Muhammed who "could unify and electrify the black nationalist movement;" preventing violence through pinpointing "potential troublemakers" and neutralizing them; discrediting militants among "responsible" blacks, the "responsible" white community, among white " 'liberals' who have vestiges of sympathy for militant black nationalists simply because they are Negroes," and "in the eyes of Negro Radicals, the followers of the movement, an area which requires 'special measures' "; and alienating youth from black nationalist organizations. The primary target for all such activities was to be "the most violent and radical groups and their leaders."[88]

By the time FBI COINTELPRO operations were supposedly terminated in April, 1971, 295 separate actions were implemented as part of the "Black Nationalist" program.[89] Perhaps indicative of the effectiveness of the program, at least in some areas, was an FBI memo sent to field offices in February, 1968, which reported that the FBI had "alerted" Philadelphia police about the activities of the Revolutionary Action Movement (RAM), a COINTELPRO target described by the FBI as "pro-Chinese Communist." The FBI memo said Philadelphia police put RAM leaders under "close scrutiny," arrested them "on every possible charge until they could no longer make bail," and as a result, RAM leaders "spent most of the summer in jail and no violence traceable to RAM took place."[90]

Aside from militant black groups, the major focus of FBI attention by 1968 was the New Left and anti-war demonstrators. By March, 1968, the FBI was routinely sending to the White House reports on anti-war demonstrations. In May, 1968, shortly after the student takeover of five buildings at Columbia University, Hoover issued a directive calling for a new COINTELPRO operation directed against the "New Left." Hoover's directive stated the purpose of the program was to "expose, disrupt and otherwise neutralize the activities of the various New Left organizations, their leadership and adherents." Specifically, FBI agents were called on to "expose" the "devious maneuvers and duplicity" of these activists through the "cooperation of reliable news media," to frustrate "every effort of these groups and individuals to consolidate their forces or to recruit new or youthful members," to give consideration "in every instance . . . to disrupting the organized activity of these groups," to miss no opportunities "to capitalize upon organizational and personal conflicts of the leadership" and to "inspire action in instances where circumstances warrant." According to an internal FBI memo, among the reasons for implementing the program was that New Left individuals were calling for "revolution in America" and "for the defeat of the United States in Vietnam," were continually and falsely alleging police brutality, did not "hesitate to utilize unlawful acts to further their so-called causes" and on many occasions "viciously and scurrilously attacked the Director and the Bureau in an attempt to hamper our investigation of it and to drive us off the college campuses." A major purpose of the program was to "neutralize the New Left and the Key Activists," who were defined as "those individuals who are the moving forces behind the New Left."[91]

By the time COINTELPRO activities were allegedly ended by the FBI in April, 1971, the New Left had been the target of about 290 disruptive actions directed against groups ranging from SDS to Antioch College, the New Mexico Free University and the Inter-University Committee for Debate on Foreign Policy. About 40 percent of all New Left COINTELPRO activity was devoted to attempting to keep targets from speaking, teaching, writing or publishing.[92]

Other new FBI directives concerning the New Left issued in 1968 called for a "comprehensive study of the whole movement," including information about "public statements, the writings and the leadership activities," sources of funds, circulation and contents of propaganda, "communist influence," attitudes towards political activities, violence, religion, race relations and education, and information on "factionalism" and "security measures." Hoover told agents that they were to report "in advance" any plans concerning "agitational activities." Agents were informed by Hoover that he would hold them "personally responsible" to insure that the FBI had adequate information on New Left Activities which could only be developed through "adequate high level informants who are in a position to obtain detailed information regarding the activities and future plans" of New Left groups and individuals. Among the disruptive tactics Hoover suggested were preparing leaflets using "the most obnoxious pictures" of New Left leaders to counteract New Left influence on campuses; instigating "personal conflicts or animosities" among New Left leaders; creating the impression that certain New Left leaders were informants; sending newspaper articles to university officials, wealthy donors, members of legislatures, and parents of New Left students to "show the depravity of New Left leaders;" alerting local police to "opportunities" to make drug arrests of New Left members; sending anonymous material about New Left faculty to university officials, legislatures and the press; exploiting hostilities between SDS and other protest groups; and using "misinformation" to "confuse and disrupt" New Left activities, such as notifying people that planned events had been cancelled or postponed.[93]

By 1968, the FBI was operating COINTELPRO actions against the CP, SWP, the New Left, White Hate groups and Black Nationalist organizations. The number of COINTELPRO activities undertaken during the Johnson administration reached new highs, although there is no evidence that the Johnson administration (or the Nixon administration) was ever

FBI COINTELPRO actions, 1964-68[95]

1964	230
1965	220
1966	240
1967	180
1968	123

informed about the New Left, SWP and Black Nationalist COINTELPROs.[94] As the FBI expanded its COINTELPRO, the Bureau also began to compile special lists of individuals whom it regarded as particularly troublesome and continually updated its Security Index list of persons to be arrested in case of a war or national emergency. In August, 1967, the FBI began compiling a Rabble Rouser Index, later renamed the Agitator Index. The list at first consisted of "racial agitators and individuals who have demonstrated a potential for fomenting racial discord." Later, the criteria broadened to include persons with a "propensity for fomenting" any disorders which affected the "internal security," including "black nationalists, white supremacists, Puerto Rican nationalists, anti-Vietnam demonstration leaders and other extremists" as well as "any person who tries to arouse people to violent action by appealing to their emotions, prejudices, et cetera; a demagogue." In January, 1968, the FBI began a Key Activists list, designed to include persons in SDS and "anti-Vietnam war groups" who were "extremely active and most vocal in their statements denouncing the United States and calling for civil disobedience and other forms of unlawful and disruptive acts." Once "key activists" were identified, FBI agents were instructed to maintain "high level informant coverage" on them, and develop information on their "sources of funds, foreign contacts and future plans." Subsequently the FBI obtained from the IRS tax information on the "key activists" and targetted them for New Left COINTELPRO actions. In March, 1968, the FBI initiated a Black Nationalist Photograph Album program, which focused on "militant black nationalists" who travelled extensively. Under this program, each FBI field office was to be provided with pictures and biographical information on targetted persons.[96]

Meanwhile, the Security Index was updated. By 1968, persons in the Black Nationalist and Anarchist category were eligible for inclusion on the emergency arrest list. The anarchist category represented an FBI adaption to the character of the New Left movement. In the past, persons usually were placed on the Security Index by virtue of their leadership or membership role in a particular organization, such as the CP or SWP. An FBI memo of April, 1968 stressed to field offices, however, that they should not neglect Security Index investigations of persons in the New Left movement whose "potential dangerousness" to the "internal security" was "clearly demonstrated by their statements, conduct and actions" simply because "no membership in a basic revolutionary organization could be established." The memo told agents that "even if a subject's membership in a subversive organization cannot be proven, his inclusion of the Security Index may often be justified because of activities which establish his anarchistic tendencies" including rejection of public pronouncements and activities which "establish his rejection of law and order and reveal him to be a potential threat to the security of the United States."[97]

In 1968, following review of emergency detention procedures by a committee headed by Attorney General Ramsey Clark, the Justice Department formally established Security Index criteria. The new criteria included "membership or participation in the activities of a basic revolutionary organization within the last five years;" leadership or active "substantial participation" within the last three years in one or more "front organizations" in furtherance of purposes which coincide with those of a "basic revolutionary organization;" and other persons "who could be expected" to seize the opportunity presented by a national emergency to commit any acts of "interference with or threat to the survival and effective operation" of national, state and local governments and the "defense effort," whether or not they were members of "basic revolutionary or front" organizations or had committed "overt acts or statements within the time limits prescribed." The FBI's policy of ignoring the provisions of the 1950 Emergency Detention provisions of the Internal Security Act for eighteen years (with Justice Department approval) was formally abandoned as a result of the 1968 study. Thus, the Justice Department noted that unlike FBI plans made under the 1948 Justice Department plan, if an emergency occurred, the Attorney General would abide by "the requirement that any person actually detained will be entitled to a hearing at which time the evidence will have to satisfy the standards of the Emergency Detention Act." Nevertheless, the Department recognized that in fact the new Security Index standards were broader than those defined in the 1950 law, but indicated this was acceptable because of the "needed flexibility and discretion at the operating level in order to carry on an effective surveillance program."[98]

The FBI was by no means the only federal agency engaged in widespread spying on domestic dissidence during the Johnson administration. CIA opening of international mail, which began in 1956 and ended in 1973, reached its greatest heights during 1966 and 1967. Although originally the CIA project had focused on opening mail which, according to the Senate Intelligence Committee "might reasonably have been expected to lead to genuine foreign intellignce or counterintelligence information," as domestic protests rose in the 1960's the CIA added many names to its "watchlists" that "were far more likely to generate essentially domestic rather than foreign intelligence information."[99] The FBI asked the CIA for information on many groups and individuals in the anti-war, civil rights and women's movements, and the CIA responded by placing on its watchlists such groups as SNCC, SDS, the American Friends Service Committee, *Ramparts* magazine and Liberation News Service.[100] The FBI was given the fruits of CIA opening of over twenty thousand letters from 1965 to 1968, which included, according to a 1966 FBI memo, information on "persons involved in the peace movements, anti-Vietnam demonstrations, women's organizations, 'teach-ins' " and "racial matters" along with data on "U.S. citizens' travel plans, including those of known subversives" and the sex lives of a variety of Americans and foreigners.[101]

The CIA also began a number of new domestic spying activities during the Vietnam War period. In February, 1967, the CIA Office of Security initiated Project MERRIMAC, which was designed to protect CIA facili-

CIA Mail Opening in New York, 1958-1973[102]

Year	Total items opened	Total items given FBI
1958	8,633	666
1959	13,299	1,964
1960	12,725	2,342
1961	14,025	3,520
1962	13,932	3,017
1963	16,748	4,167
1964	14,904	5,396
1965	13,309	4,503
1966	15,499	5,984
1967	23,617	5,863
1968	12,288	5,322
1969	9,821	5,384
1970	10,207	4,975
1971	9,018	2,701
1972	8,060	1,400
1973	2,273	642
Total	215,820	57,846

ties, personnel and operation against protest demonstrations in the Washington area. In the course of this project, CIA "assets," most of whom were construction and trades workers employed on a part-time basis, infiltrated and/or monitored about fifteen organizations in the Washington area, ranging from Women's Strike for Peace and the Washington Urban League to the Student Non-Violent Coordinating Committee and the Black Panthers. Although the program was supposedly concerned only with threats to the CIA, the dozen or so agents involved were gradually instructed to increase the scope of their reporting to include information on the general plans, associations, activities and funding of the targetted groups. In some cases, group leaders were photographed and followed home in order to identify them. The MERRIMAC program was largely terminated in 1968, since the Washington police by then were able to collect information on dissident groups. Meanwhile, the CIA Office of Security continued Project RESISTANCE, begun in December, 1967, which was a broad effort to obtain general information about radical groups across the country, especially on college campuses, supposedly to predict violence which might threaten CIA installations, recruiters or contractors, and to gather information with which to evaluate possible future CIA employees. This project largely relied on newspaper clippings, but also obtained information from the FBI, local campus officials and police. The main product of RESISTANCE was the publication of weekly Situation Reports, summarizing and analyzing past events and projecting a calendar of upcoming events which might involve violence or disruption directed against government facilities. By the time RESISTANCE was terminated in June, 1973, from six hundred to seven hundred files with twelve thousand to sixteen thousand names had been gathered.[103]

Both MERRIMAC and RESISTANCE fed information into what became the CIA's largest domestic political intelligence program, Operation CHAOS.[104] CHAOS began in August, 1967, and continued until March, 1974, as a result of pressure from President Johnson, and later, President Nixon to investigate foreign involvement in the American anti-war movement. Although the CIA repeatedly reported that foreign ties to American dissident movements were insubstantial, Johnson and Nixon refused to accept these findings and continually pressed the CIA to expand its investigations. While the focus of Operation CHAOS always remained the relationship between American dissent and foreign governments, the project also involved gathering huge amounts of information which basically involved the American protest movement itself.

During the Johnson administration, the major sources of CHAOS information were FBI reports on domestic protest, reports from CIA agents already stationed abroad, information derived from CIA opening of first class mail that had been occurring since 1956, and reports from NSA based on its monitoring of international telephone calls and cable traffic. CHAOS furnished "watchlists" of dissident groups and individuals to both NSA and the CIA mail-opening project. Altogether eleven hundred pages of material were obtained from NSA during the 1967-1974 period. Requests for information from CIA stations abroad called for reports on "illegal and subversive" contacts between domestic protesters and "foreign elements" which "might range from casual contacts based merely on mutual interest to closely controlled channels for party directives." Americans of interest were defined in 1968 as including "radical students, antiwar activists, draft resisters and deserters, black nationalists, anarchists and assorted 'New Leftists.' "[105] In many cases, the CIA gathered information on the foreign travels and activities of specific dissidents at the request of the FBI.

As a Senate staff report noted in 1976, "A major purpose of CHAOS activity in actual practice became its participation with the FBI in the Bureau's internal security work."[106] Similarly, the Rockefeller Commission on the CIA reported that the CHAOS operation "became a repository for large quantities of information on the domestic activities of

American citizens" and "much of the information was not directly related to the question of the existence of foreign connections with domestic dissidence."[107] Before CHAOS was terminated in March, 1974, files had been gathered on seventy-two hundred American citizens and about 100 organizations, and over three hundred thousand names and organizations had been entered into CIA computers in connection with the program. Among the organizations studied were SDS, Women's Strike for Peace, the Black Panther Party, Clergy and Laymen Concerned About Vietnam, and Grove Press, Inc. Grove Press was apparently studied because it had published a book by a British intelligence officer who turned out to be a Soviet agent. Included in the CIA file on Grove Press were movie critics' reviews of the film "I Am Curious Yellow," a sex-oriented movie which had been produced by the press. As a result of the CHAOS operation, the CIA generated thirty-five hundred memoranda for internal use, three thousand memos which were sent to the FBI, and about forty memos and studies which were sent to the White House and high level executive officials.

As the CIA was accelerating its domestic intelligence operations in 1967, NSA supplemented its program of general monitoring of the private international telegrams of American citizens dating from World War II (Project SHAMROCK) by targeting for telegram and telephone interception specific individuals whose names were placed on a "watch list" for intensive study.[108] This program, known as Project MINARET, concentrated on attempts to uncover possible foreign influence on American anti-war and civil rights protesters. Names for inclusion on the watchlists were furnished by the FBI, CIA, Secret Service, military intelligence agencies and NSA itself, with a cumulative total of about twelve hundred. According to a Senate Intelligence Committee staff report on MINARET, watchlist names "ranged from members of radical political groups to celebrities, to ordinary citizens involved in protests against their government" and organizations that were watchlisted included some "communist-front groups" and groups that "were nonviolent and peaceful in nature."[109] Although MINARET focussed on foreign involvement in the American protest movement, the non-selective process involved in intercepting communications led to the monitoring of huge amounts of information about completely lawful activity. According to the Senate Intelligence Committee staff report most of the intercepted communications "were of a private and personal nature, or involved rallies and demonstrations that were public knowledge," such as "communications discussing a peace concert, a correspondent's report from Southeast Asia to his magazine in New York, and a pro-Vietnam war activist's invitations to speakers for a rally."[110]

At about the same time that MINARET and CHAOS were established in 1967, Army intelligence began a large-scale domestic spying operation, allegedly to help the Army make plans for the use of troops in domestic disorders.[111] Although Army intelligence had begun collecting information on civilian political activity in connection with racial disorders in the south in the early 1960's, until 1967 such activity was essentially confined to studying areas where civil disorders were likely or had already occurred, and information on civilians was gathered from non-military sources. The turning point came in 1967, following the riots in Newark and Detroit, with the use of 130 Army intelligence agents to penetrate, report on and photograph demonstrators at the October, 1967 protest march at the Pentagon, and pressure from the White House and the Justice Department to step up intelligence operations. In 1968, the Army formally established a domestic intelligence operation focussed on "dissident elements," and the "civil rights" and "anti-Vietnam/anti-draft" movements. According to Assistant Secretary of Defense Robert Froehlke, in testimony before a Senate subcommittee in 1971, Army directives called for information collection on "any category of information related even remotely to people or organizations active in a community in which the potential for a riot or disorder was present."[112] Before the program was terminated in 1971 due to public exposure and criticism, Army intelligence had about fifteen hundred plainclothesmen assigned to collect political information about what the Senate Intelligence Committee later termed "virtually every group seeking peaceful change in the United States."[113] Index card files were gathered on more than one hundred thousand civilian protesters and on more than seven hundred sixty thousand organizations and "incidents." In addition to centralized Army intelligence files maintained at bases near Washington, D.C. local army units carried on their operations and investigations, with little central control. Thus, Fourth Army headquarters at Fort Sam Houston, Texas, had its own collection of one hundred twenty thousand file cards on "personalities of interest."

The vast majority of organizations and individuals studied by Army intelligence involved completely peaceful and lawful activity. Among the groups spied on were the ACLU, ADA, American Friends Service Committee, NAACP, KKK, Women's Strike for Peace, Urban League, *Ramparts* magazine, Anti-Defamation League of B'nai Brith, John Birch Society, Young Americans for Freedom, CP and the National Organization for Women. Files were opened on Senator Adlai Stevenson, Congressman Abner Mikva, Georgia State Senator Julian Bond, civil rights leaders Martin Luther King, Whitney Young, Jesse Jackson and Julius Hobson and anti-war leaders Joan Baez, Benjamin Spock, and William Sloane Coffin. In order to gather information, Army agents illegally monitored private radio communications, travelled and marched with anti-war demonstrators, posed as press representatives, and infiltrated organizations of suspect groups. Army intelligence both received and disseminated information to other intelligence agencies, including local police, the FBI, NSA and CIA.

Among the stranger activities of Army intelligence agents were the monitoring of protests by welfare mothers in Milwaukee; infiltration of a coalition of church youth groups and young Democrats in Colorado; attending a Halloween party for elementary school children in Washington, D.C. on the suspicion a local "dissident" might be present; monitoring classes at New York University, where a prominent civil rights leader was teaching; attending a conference of priests in Washington, D.C., held to discuss birth control; and using government money to buy liquor and marijuana in order to infiltrate a commune in Washington, D.C. during a counter-inaugural demonstration in January, 1969. Information collected and/or sought for inclusion in Army files included information on the political, financial and sexual lives of individuals and information on the leaders, plans, purposes and funding of dissident organizations. In a few cases, lower level military intelligence agents acting without authorization engaged in harassing and disruptive activities, such as giving demonstrators "misinformation" and tearing down notices of rallies and demonstrations.

The Senate Judiciary Subcommittee on Constitutional Rights, which conducted hearings into the Army program in 1971, concluded that the surveillance had been "utterly useless" to the Army in terms of providing advance information on potential civil disturbances and was "merely wasting time, money and manpower and infringing on the rights of the citizens it was supposed to be guarding." The Subcommittee added that "these vast collections of fragmentary, incorrect and irrelevant information, composed of vague conclusions and judgments and overly detailed descriptions of insignificant facts, could not be considered 'intelligence' by any sense of the word."[114]

Along with the development of a massive domestic surveillance program, the Army began to develop contingency plans for armed intervention during civil disturbances, according to documents released in August, 1975.[115] The plans, known as "Garden Plot," called for centralized Army intervention in coordination with local and state government and police authorities in the event of civil disorders fostered by "dissident elements," including "civil rights movements," "anti-Vietnam-anti-draft movements," and "subversive conspiratorial aspects." Under the plan, beginning in 1968 and continuing for at least two years, two brigades (up to forty-eight hundred men) of troops were kept on twelve hour standby alert at all times in case of civil disorders. Under the plan, two "paper war" exercises, involving sketching "scenarios" of civil disturbances and practicing — on paper — responses to them, were carried out on the national level in 1969 and 1970, and six paper operations dubbed "Cable Splicer" were carried out in Western states between 1968 and 1974. In California, these exercises involved cooperation with the governor, the national guard, the highway patrol, the police of Los Angeles and other California cities and high-ranking utility executives. Exercises carried out at the national level were originally named "Quiet Town," but were renamed "Gram Metric" on orders from the National Security Council, which contended the original name was too descriptive of the exercise's goal. According to some reports circulating in 1975, the Army also drew up plans for imposing martial law in the country. While none of the documents released in August, 1975, confirmed this, some of the documents that were released were censored and other documents were not released at all.

Faced with a flood of intelligence information coming in from the FBI, CIA, NSA, Army intelligence and other sources, Attorney General Clark, in December, 1967, established an Interdivisional Information Unit (IDIU) within the Justice Department to coordinate "all information" relating to organizations and individuals, "who may play a role, whether purposefully or not, either in instigating or spreading civil disorders, or in preventing or checking them."[116] IDIU soon began collecting, computerizing and disseminating information on dissident activities, using a computer system which could generate lists of all "members or affiliates" of an organization, their location and travel, "all incidents" relating to "specific issues" and "all information" on a "planned specific demonstration." By 1970, the IDIU computer was receiving over forty thousand "intelligence reports" a year concerning "civil disorders and campus disturbances" from a wide variety of intelligence agencies and was producing a daily morning and evening report on disturbances across the country. The computer generated a list of over ten thousand "anti-war activists and other dissidents" which was furnished to the CIA for use in Operation CHAOS, and, during the Nixon administration, to the IRS for use in targeting political dissidents for income tax investigations. Among the persons and groups included in the IDIU computer by 1971 were farm labor organizer Caesar Chavez, former *New York Times* film critic Bosley Crowther, black entertainer Sammy Davis, Jr., investigative reporter Seymour Hersh, the NAACP, the Urban League and the United Farm Workers of California. Other persons listed included an individual described as "a bearded militant who writes and recites poetry" and a "student at Merritt College and a member of the Peace and Freedom Party as of mid-1968."

The 1968 presidential campaign reflected the increasing pressures developing for repression. All three presidential candidates — Richard Nixon, George Wallace and Hubert Humphrey — made "law and order" a major theme of their campaign. By 1968 increasing racial disorders, anti-war demonstrations, leaping crime rates, and the growth of a "counter-cultural" movement among the young, featuring bizarre styles of hair and clothing and widespread use of drugs had all become lumped together in the minds of many Americans as a general threat to peace and stability. Nixon and vice-presidential candidate Spiro Agnew sought to take full advantage of this atmosphere. As journalist Theodore White noted, the entire Nixon campaign was based on the theory that "the nation had had its fill of turbulence, bloodshed, killing, violence and adventure," and offered "no promises to the nation beyond law-and-order."[117] Meanwhile, behind the scenes, President Johnson directed the FBI to place Mrs. Anna Chennault, a prominent Republican, under surveillance, and to check the long distance telephone records of Agnew, in connection with his fears that the South Vietnamese were in contact with Nixon supporters in an attempt "to sabotage his peace negotiations in the hope that Nixon would win the election and then take a harder line towards North Vietnam."[118]

The "Law and Order" Nixon Administration

When the Nixon administration entered office in January, 1969, it inherited from the Johnson administration a formidable apparatus to effect a program of political repression — a massive intelligence program conducted by the FBI, army intelligence, the CIA and other governmental agencies; new federal laws which permitted federal aid cut-offs to unruly college students, facilitated federal prosecution of virtually anyone who was involved in a disturbance involving three or more persons who had recently mailed a letter, crossed, or made a telephone call across state lines, and which appeared to authorize both court-ordered and warrantless wiretapping of domestic "subversives," selective service regulations providing for the punitive drafting of dissident males; and the precedent of a major conspiracy prosecution against leaders of the anti-war movement. The Nixon administration took full advantage of these precedents and opportunities, and went beyond them to massively increase political repression during its tenure in office. The downfall of the Nixon administration, culminating in the first presidential resignation in American history, essentially flowed from its application of the techniques of political repression which had been used for decades against so-called "fringe" or "extremist" groups to one of the major "respectable" political parties — the Democratic Party.

Political repression during the Nixon years reached heights that had not been known in American history for twenty years. Historian Henry Steele Commager wrote in an article which appeared in *Look* magazine in July, 1970:

> Not since the days when Sen. Joseph McCarthy bestrode the political stage, have we experienced anything like the current offensive against the exercise of freedom in America. If repression is not yet as blatant or as flamboyant as it was during the McCarthy years, it is in many respects more pervasive and more formidable.[119]

In December, 1974, the *Los Angeles Times* matter-of-factly noted in a front page story that recent revelations of CIA spying on and FBI disruption of the activities of dissident groups, of special procedures undertaken by the Internal Revenue Service to deal with "extremists," and of the activities associated with the Watergate scandal raised "serious questions about whether the nation was headed towards a police state under Mr. Nixon."[120]

The political repression of the Nixon administration was essentially the result of the confluence of two factors: the continued growth (at least until 1970) of the strongest and most broadly based radical movement in American history since the great depression; and the character of the top leadership of the Nixon administration, which collectively had a mind-set more hostile to basic concepts of civil liberty than any administration in American history.[121] The Nixon White House was gripped by a "siege" mentality, the feeling that as President Nixon stated in a private conversation that was tape recorded and released in connection with the Watergate investigation, "Nobody is a friend of ours. Let's face it!"[122] Not only was the White House surrounded by enemies, in the Nixon view, but those enemies were engaged in a type of sinister plot, against whom any measures were justified. In another tape-recorded White House conversation, Nixon said to his counsel, John Dean:

> I want the most comprehensive notes on those who tried to do us in (in the 1972 election). They didn't have to do it. If we had had a close election and they were playing the other side I would understand this. No — they were doing this quite deliberately and they are asking for it and they are going to get it. . . . We have not used the Bureau (FBI) and we have not used the Justice Department but things are going to change now.[123]

The public rhetoric of the Nixon administration was as repressive in tone as the private utterances. Nixon termed protesting students "bums" and warned, "We have the power to strike back if need be and to prevail" if they did not exercise what he deemed as sufficient restraint.[124] Vice-President Agnew assailed dissenters in a series of highly publicized vitriolic speeches during the first year of the Nixon administration. Referring to what he said was a "glib, activist element who would tell us our values are lies," he suggested that "we can . . . afford to separate them from our society — with no more regret that we should feel over discarding rotten apples from a barrel."[125] White House Chief of Staff Robert Haldeman referred to Democratic critics of Nixon's Vietnam policies as "consciously aiding and abetting the enemy," (the constitutional definition of treason) while chief White House domestic advisor John Erlichman referred to protests "as part of an apparent campaign to force upon the President a foreign policy favorable to the North Vietnamese and their allies."[126] Assistant Attorney General Richard Kleindeinst (later Attorney General) explained there would be no need to suspend constitutional provisions if dissent seemed to be getting out of hand, since:

> There is enough play at the joints of our existing criminal law — enough flexibility — so that if we really felt that we had to pick up the leaders of a violent uprising we could. We would find some things to charge them with, and we would be able to hold them that way for a while.[127]

The repressive measures of the Nixon administration were not limited to private and public rhetoric but were manifested in many actions. Repression under the Nixon administration took three major forms: 1) a massive expansion of covert domestic surveillance of political dissidents such as SDS, black militants and other "traditional" targets of intelligence activity, carried out by "established" intelligence agencies such as the FBI, CIA, Army Intelligence and the Internal Revenue Service, together with active attempts to harass and disrupt such groups, at least on the part of the FBI; 2) a major overt (i.e. public) program of harassment directed against the "opposition," featuring a series of shaky conspiracy trials against radical leaders, the conversion of the grand jury into an agency to harass and gather information about radical groups, an attempt to intimidate the "liberal" news media, and harassment and illegal arrests of anti-war demonstrators; and 3) the creation of secret White House-controlled intelligence and operations units which brought to bear against the Democratic Party techniques of wiretapping, burglary and disruption which had been used for years against "extremist" organizations.

Domestic Surveillance By Established Agencies

A massive expansion of political surveillance operations by established intelligence agencies occurred during the Nixon administration. In most cases the groundwork for such expansion had been laid by the Johnson administration. According to a report on American intelligence agencies published by a private research group in 1975, domestic intelligence operations during the late 1960's and early 1970's kept over one quarter of a million Americans under "active surveillance," while "hundreds of thousands more had information about their lawful political activity included in intelligence agency files" and "thousands of organizations composed of individuals exercising their rights of association and political protest" were investigated.[128] The Senate Intelligence Committee reached similar conclusions in a 1976 report based on a study of American domestic intelligence activities since the 1930's, with a concentration on the Vietnam War era, when, it noted, such activities had reached their "greatest extent." The Committee reported that domestic intelligence agencies had investigated a "vast number of American citizens and domestic organizations," many of whom "were not suspected of criminal activity," and that intelligence agencies had "regularly collected information about personal and political activities irrelevant to any legitimate governmental interest." By using informants, wiretaps, "bugs," mail openings and burglaries, the Committee reported, intelligence agencies collected "vast amounts" of information about hundreds of thousands of Americans, including "intimate details of citizens' lives and about their participation in legal and peaceful political activites." The Commttee reported that intelligence activities had "infringed on a broad scale" the privacy and freedom of the targets of intelligence activities, and that their effects had extended "far beyond the citizens directly affected . . . to untold numbers of other Americans who may be intimidated." In some cases, the Committee said, segments of the government had adopted tactics unworthy of a democracy and occasionally reminiscent of the tactics of totalitarian regimes." The Committee stated that "virtually every element of our society has been subjected to excessive government-ordered intelligence inquiries" and "opposition to government policy or the expressing of controversial views was frequently considered sufficient for collecting data on Americans." The "ultimate responsibility" for intelligence abuses, the Committee stated, rested on high ranking government officials who for decades had shown a "pattern of reckless disregard of activities that threatened our Constitutional system."[129]

THE FBI

The FBI remained the leading domestic intelligence agency, and its role in surveilling and disrupting radical organizations expanded considerably during the Nixon administration. The scope of FBI operations was revealed by a number of unusual developments during the 1971-76 period, including a burglary and subsequent publication of FBI documents stolen from an FBI field office in Media, Pennsylvania in March, 1971; published accounts by former FBI agents, especially those of Robert Wall, who resigned from the FBI in 1970 after serving in the political intelligence branch of the Washington, D.C. office for three years; FBI revelations made in response to Freedom of Information Act lawsuits and lawsuits filed by victims of FBI surveillance and disruption; a survey of FBI domestic intelligence operations released by the General Accounting Office in 1976; and documents and studies concerning the FBI published by the Senate Select Committee on Intelligence in 1975 and 1976. The complete truth about FBI operations will probably never be known, since allegedly "personal" files maintained by J. Edgar Hoover were destroyed upon his death in 1972.[130]

The sum total of the revelations of 1971-76 indicated an FBI spying and disruption operation, focussed especially on the New Left, black militant, and anti-war movements, of astounding scope and illegality. According to F. A. O. Schwartz, chief counsel to the Senate Intelligence Committee, FBI surveillance of the New Left amounted to a "wholly comprehensive listing of everything these people thought or did on any subject you can imagine their having a concern with."[131] Recent studies of the FBI during the late 1960's and early 1970's have concluded that "there seems no limit to the politically active organizations or persons" who may become targets of FBI intelligence,[132] that the FBI was "monitoring all forms of political dissent,"[133] that the attitude of top administration and FBI officials was that "in a country in ferment, the FBI could and should, know everything that might someday be useful in some undefined manner,"[134] and that the FBI's interest and attention extended to

> virtually all politically active persons who do not operate within the confines of the two major parties, to all organizations who take a militant or strong dissenting position, to all groups who are considered by the Bureau potentially disruptive and to all persons associated with these.[135]

By 1971, the FBI had an estimated two thousand agents assigned to political intelligence operations, and they in turn supervised about seven thousand "ghetto informants" and seventeen hundred "regular" domestic intelligence informants, and received information from another fourteen hundred "confidential sources" such as bankers, telephone company employees and landlords not on the FBI payroll. Between 1955 and 1975, the FBI investigated seven hundred forty thousand "subversive matters" and one hundred ninety thousand "extremist matters."[136] Although the statutory basis of the "subversive" investigations was the possibility that the targets might be likely to overthrow the U.S. government, not a single prosecution for planning or advocating such activity resulted from the over five hundred thousand "subversive" investigations carried out from 1960 to 1974. A General Accounting Office study of almost one thousand FBI domestic intelligence investigations carried out in 1974 estimated that of the total 17,528 such investigations in 1974, only 1.3 percent led to prosecutions and convictions for violations of *any* laws and that advance knowledge of any activity — legal or illegal — was obtained in only about 2 percent of the cases. In most cases where advance knowledge was obtained it concerned activities such as speeches, demonstrations and meetings.[137]

During the Nixon administration, the Justice Department and the White House pressed the FBI to increase its intelligence capacity. Thus, in March, 1969, the Internal Security Division (ISD) of the Justice Department informed the FBI that it was considering conducting a grand jury investigation of "some future serious campus disorder" with a view towards prosecution under the Anti-Riot Act, the Smith Act or various statutes dealing with seditious conspiracy and insurrection. Therefore, the ISD asked the FBI to "secure in advance the names of any persons planning activities which fall within the proscription" of such statutes. The ISD also asked the FBI to "furnish us with the names of any individuals who appear at more than one campus either before, during or after any active disorder or riot." In February, 1970, the White House asked the FBI for information on the "income sources of revolutionary groups."[138]

The FBI responded to increasing White House pressure, the increasing use of violence in protests and its own inclinations by pressing its agents to report more information. Thus, in May, 1969, Hoover asked agents to report on "each public appearance by Black and New Left extremists," with a "particular effort" to be made to "obtain recordings of or reliable witnesses to inflammatory speeches or statements made which may subsequently become subject to criminal proceedings." In April, 1970, the FBI instructed all field offices to investigate all persons living in communes, which the Bureau defined "as a group of individuals residing in one location who practice communal living, i.e. they share income and adhere to the philosophy of a Marxist-Leninist-Maoist oriented revolution." All members of such communes were to be investigated for possible inclusion on the Security Index.[139] In September, 1970, FBI field officers were authorized to use eighteen to twenty-one year old informants for the first time and were instructed to "immediately institute an aggressive policy of developing new productive informants who can infiltrate the ranks of terrorist organizations, their collectives, communes and staffs of their underground newspapers." In October, 1970, FBI officials called on agents to report on "every Black Student Union and similar group, regardless of their past or present involvement in disorders," along with investigations of "all individuals" belonging to SDS and "militant New Left campus organizations" to determine "whether they have a propensity for violence." All persons investigated were to be considered for potential inclusion on the Security Index.[140] In December, 1970, the FBI began a "Key Black Extremist" program, designed to pinpoint "black extremists who are either key leaders or activists and are particularly extreme, agitative, anti-government and vocal in their calls for terrorism and violence." All such individuals were to be placed in the top priority arrest category of the Security Index, and agents were instructed to study "all aspects" of their finances, obtain "suitable handwriting specimens," obtain records of "inflammatory statements made which may subsequently become subject to criminal proceedings," investigate any possible violations of Federal laws, pay particular attention to travel plans and financial arrangements for travel, and give "continuing consideration" to developing means to "neutralize the effectiveness" of such persons.[141]

The FBI continued to expand its activities in 1971, opening up investigations of the New University Conference, a group of dissident college professors and graduate students, and of Vietnam Veterans Against the War (VVAW). The VVAW investigation was begun largely because the Bureau feared the group "may be a target" for infiltration by "subversive groups." In May, 1972, FBI agents were warned against "incomplete and nonspecific reporting" on demonstrations which failed to include such information as "number of protesters present, identities of organizations and identities of speakers and leading activists."[142]

FBI agents and informants responded to the pressure from headquarters with an astounding output of intelligence information which reported the minutest details of the political and personal lives of thousands of completely peaceful and lawful individuals and organizations. Thus, FBI agents in the Washington, D.C., area investigated high school students who protested about the quality of their food, and kept a Smithsonian Institution program held on Frederick Douglass in connection with Black History week under surveillance. A high school student was investigated because he had attended the trial of a "subversive," a married couple were investigated because they had gone to a New Left party, and a fourteen year old boy and his father were investigated when it was discovered that the boy had attended an East German youth camp. The FBI maintained a life-time profile of an antiwar activist whose only criminal offense had been a $5 breach of the peace fine in 1954, and had an extensive file on Julian Bond, a black member of the Georgia legislature, which included reports on his public speeches and activities. The FBI investigated "Earth Day" programs in Washington, D.C. in April, 1970, and reported on a public speech of Sen. Edmund Muskie. A file of eighteen thousand pages was maintained on anti-war activist Tom Hayden. The FBI investigated a public meeting of opponents of the Anti-Ballistic Missile (ABM) System in 1969 and of a group that supported amnesty for Vietnam War veterans in 1974.[143]

Meetings of Women's Liberation groups were infiltrated and extensively reported on. Thus, one informant's report included the information that "approximately eight females were participating," that one of the women "kept going in and out of the meeting to attend her small child" and that "other rather hippie-type individuals" were coming and going. Another report on a women's liberation meeting indicated that each woman "stated why she had come to the meeting and how she felt oppressed sexually or otherwise."[144] Another informant reported that at numerous New Left meetings in the Boston area participants were "sitting around the table or a living room completely in the nude," that the participants, "both male and female, live and sleep together regularly" and that it was "not unusual to have these people take up residence with a different partner after a six or seven month period." The informant added that "certain individuals have been known to wear the same clothes for an estimated period of weeks and in some instances for months."[145]

Frequently such reports were disseminated by the FBI to numerous other intelligence agencies. Thus, the report on the 1969 anti-ABM meeting was sent to the White House, CIA, State Department, three military intelligence agencies, Secret Service, IDIU, the Attorney General, Deputy Attorney General, and the Internal Security and Civil Rights Divisions of the Justice Department.[146]

The FBI supplemented its agent and informant coverage of dissidents with continued use of wiretaps and bugs. Altogether the FBI placed over 700 wiretaps and 160 bugs between 1969 and 1974, using "surreptitious entries" to install bugs in ninety-one cases between 1969 and 1975 involving "internal security, intelligence and counterintelligence." Among the groups subjected to electronic surveillance were the Black Panthers (the subject of six separate taps by March, 1971), and a variety of individuals and groups associated with "racial extremism," New Left and domestic protest groups, groups dedicated to "strategic sabotage" and groups associated with the "Weatherman" faction of SDS.[147] Attorney General John Mitchell approved wiretaps against three groups planning an anti-war demonstration in Washington in November, 1969, with the major justification provided by the FBI that the demonstration "could possibly attract the largest number of demonstrators ever to assemble in Washington, D.C.," and "the large number is cause for major concern should violence of any type break out."

Another wiretap was approved by Mitchell in 1970 on the basis of an FBI request which stated that the group was attempting to "develop strong ties with the cafeteria, maintenance and other workers on campus" and wanted to "go into industry and factories . . . and take the radical politics they learned on campus and spread them among factory workers." As the result of this tap the FBI obtained the identities of almost fifteen hundred persons who were in touch with the group over a six-month period.[148]

Attorney General Mitchell publicly asserted in June, 1969, that the president had the constitutional power to authorize electronic surveillance without court order "concerning domestic organizations which seek to attack and subvert the government by unlawful means."[149]

Similar positions had been taken by American presidents since Franklin Roosevelt, but never before had this position been asserted publicly, and never before had a federal law (the 1968 Omnibus Crime Act) existed which specifically authorized electronic surveillance *with* court orders. Mitchell's position was rejected by a unanimous Supreme Court in *United States* v. *U.S. District Court* (1972) which held the administration must obtain court orders when seeking electronic surveillance against "domestic" radicals (the court specifically did not rule on the propriety of warrantless tapping in cases involving foreign threats to the national security).[150]

In many court cases, the Nixon administration dropped prosecution rather than disclose electronic surveillance records, including the prosecution of Black Panther leader David Hilliard, for allegedly threatening Nixon's life; the prosecution of Leslie Bacon, an anti-war activist, for perjury before a grand jury and conspiracy to firebomb a bank; and the prosecutions of twelve Weathermen indicted under the 1968 Anti-Riot Act in connection with violent demonstrations in Chicago in October, 1968, and of fifteen Weathermen for conspiracy to bomb military and police installations. Before the latter case was dismissed, the government did turn over wiretap records of SDS headquarters in Chicago for nine months in 1969 and 1970, amounting to overhearings of twelve thousand calls. In a number of cases, grand jury subpoenas of radicals were dismissed when the government refused to answer allegations of warrantless wiretapping.[151]

The inevitable result of the Nixon administration's position on wiretapping and the information about various wiretaps which was made public was a widespread fear of wiretapping that made the telephone a virtually useless piece of equipment for the transmission of sensitive information for thousands of Americans during the Nixon administration. Charles Goodell, who served in the Senate until 1970, has written that his Senate phone was tapped and states that in the fall of 1971 a conservative Senator called Goodell from his home, only to say, "You know I can't *talk* on this phone." In 1971, Democratic House Majority Leader Hale Boggs and Sen. Joseph Montoya charged the FBI was tapping the phones of Congressmen; Boggs added, "There is hardly a member of the House who is not fearful of using his telephone." Rep. Emmanuel Cellar, chairman of the House Judiciary Committee, said in April, 1971, that while he had no proof that any congressman's phone was being tapped that fear of being overheard inhibited congressmen in their conversations. In August, 1972, Democratic Vice-Presidential candidate Sergeant Shriver claimed a wiretap had been placed on the phone of his law partner.[152] Sanford J. Ungar, in his 1972 history of the "Pentagon Papers" controversy, writes that, "many employees of the *Washington Post* have long suspected that their home telephones and perhaps even extensions at the newspaper are tapped."[153] In October, 1973, Supreme Court Justice William O. Douglas stated in a Court opinion that he was "morally certain" that the conference room of the Court had been "bugged."[154]

Along with "bugs," wiretaps and informers, the FBI continued to maintain lists of persons to be considered for immediate arrest in time of emergency. Although Congress repealed the Emergency Detention Provisions of the Internal Security Act of 1950 in 1971, which provided the only legal basis for the collection of such lists, the FBI simply renamed its "Security Index" the "Administrative Index" (ADEX) on the theory that in an emergency a President could ask Congress to reinstate the authority and such a list would again be necessary. Attorney General Mitchell approved the FBI's decision to keep an "administrative index" on the grounds that the authority to create a list "compiled and maintained to assist the Bureau in making readily retrievable and available the results of its investigations into subversive materials and related matters is not prohibited by repeal of the Emergency Detention Act."[155] While the FBI did not tell Mitchell explicitly that the ADEX would also serve as an emergency arrest list in asking for his approval, according to a Senate Intelligence Committee staff report, there was "informal" Justice Department knowledge of the real purpose of the list.[156]

When the Security Index became the ADEX in 1971, the Bureau included in the new list the Reserve Index, dating from the 1950's, which included persons who would be subject to "priority investigation" after Security Index arrests occurred. The Reserve Index became the lowest-priority category of the ADEX, described as consisting of "teachers, writers, lawyers, etc" who did not actively participate in subversive activity "but who were nevertheless influential in espousing their respective ideologies." The minimal criteria for inclusion on the ADEX was that an individual be "in a position to influence others to engage in acts inimical to the national defense or furnish financial aid or other assistance to revolutionary elements because of their sympathy, associations, or ideology." In September, 1972, the ADEX was reduced from 15,259 names to 4,786, under stricter criteria limiting names to persons who "have shown a willingness and capability of engaging" in acts "which would result in interference with or a threat to the survival and effective operation of national, state or local government." These persons were perceived as including all who posed "an actual danger now." In June, 1973, the ADEX became "strictly an administrative device" that should play no part "in investigative decisions or policies," which suggests that, officially at least, the FBI retained a completely useless list. The ADEX still contained 1,300 names when it was completely abolished shortly after the FBI admitted its existence in October, 1975.[157]

While FBI intelligence gathering through the use of informants and electronic surveillance were at least indirectly disruptive in that they allowed the administration to know the plans of dissidents in advance, the FBI also was involved in directly disruptive tactics through the COINTELPRO operation and the use, or at least toleration of, *agents provocateur*. The COINTELPRO activities increased along with other FBI activities, hitting their peak since the beginning of the program in 1969. COINTELPRO actions, which frequently involved forged or anonymous letters, included attempts to disrupt marriages, to stir factionalism within and between dissident groups, to have dissidents fired from jobs and ousted by landlords, to prevent protesters from speaking and protest groups from forming, to have derogatory material planted in the press or among acquaintances of targets, to interfere with peaceful demonstrations

FBI COINTELPRO Operations, 1969-1971[158]	
1969	280
1970	180
1971 (through April)	40

and deny facilities for meetings and conferences, to cause funding cut-offs to dissident groups, to prevent the distribution of literature and to get local police to arrest targets for alleged criminal law violations.[159]

According to the Senate Intelligence Committee, FBI COINTELPRO activities "often risked and sometimes caused serious emotional, economic or physical damage" and involved violations of "federal and state statutes prohibiting mail fraud, wire fraud, incitement to violence, sending obscene materials through the mail and extortion."[160] A Committee staff report termed COINTELPRO a "sophisticated vigilante operation aimed squarely at preventing the exercise of First Amendment rights of speech and association" that demonstrated the Bureau's feeling that the FBI "has a role in maintaining the existing social order, and that its efforts should be aimed toward combatting those who threaten that order."[161] One top FBI official told the Senate Committee that FBI leaders "never gave a thought" to the constitutionality of COINTELPRO, while another high-ranking FBI official, who had been in charge of the FBI's internal Inspection Division, said, "There was no instruction to me . . . that the Inspector should be on the alert to see that constitutional values are being protected."[162]

COINTELPRO operations directed against the SWP in the late 1960's and early 1970's included attempts to have SWP members, including at least five teachers, fired from their jobs by writing anonymous letters or covertly supplying information to employers; distribution of phony rightwing newspapers on college campuses attacking the SWP; and mailing anonymous abusive letters in attempts to sabotage political campaigns of SWP members and to foster unrest within the party. In other SWP incidents, a sixteen year old girl was investigated after sending a letter to the SWP seeking information for a school assignment, the FBI tried to have the Boy Scouts remove a scoutmaster because his wife was an SWP member, and FBI agents tried to discourage attendance at an SWP-sponsored vacation school by anonymously disseminating information that latrines at the campsite for the school were unlighted and that there was no electricity in the cabins.[163]

In other COINTELPRO actions, the FBI tried in several cases to disrupt New Left and black militant groups by writing letters to the spouses of activists suggesting that their partners had been engaged in extramarital relations. In one such case, an FBI agent claimed credit for breaking up a marriage. In two cases FBI agents attempted to disrupt attempts by activist groups to provide housing for out-of-town demonstrators by obtaining housing forms and filling them out with false names and addresses of persons purporting to be willing to provide housing. Informants were used to stir factionalism within dissident groups in a number of cases. Thus in one 1968 incident in Los Angeles an FBI informant suggested that the head of one faction of SDS was using group funds to support a drug habit and that another leader had previously embezzled funds. The Los Angeles FBI office reported that "as a result of actions taken by this informant, there have been fist fights and acts of name calling at several of the recent SDS meetings." In San Diego in 1969, an FBI informant falsely suggested that a draft counsellor was an FBI informant, leading to his complete ostracization by his colleagues. In a 1970 San Diego incident, an informant suggested that a group leader "may be either a bisexual or a homosexual."[164] In addition to anonymously mailing reprints of published material — thus the FBI flooded Jewish members of the CP with clippings on Soviet mistreatment of Jews — the FBI sometimes manufactured its own propaganda to ridicule protesters. In 1969, the New York field office produced a flyer with pictures of four New Left leaders, which was billed as a "pick the fag" contest, promising prizes including "five hundred rolls of red toilet tissue, each sheet bearing the picture of Chairman Mao in living color!"[165]

Other COINTELPRO activity, according to reports published by the *New York Times* in the summer of 1976, based on information supplied by sources close to the FBI and the Justice Department, included physical assaults on dissidents, the disabling and burning of cars owned by radicals, the stealing of mail from mailboxes of dissidents, widespread installation of illegal wiretaps and bugs, and, in at least one case, the kidnapping of a militant in an attempt to disrupt his activities and intimidate him.[166] While there is no way of measuring precisely the impact of COINTELPRO upon the New Left, one indicator is the claim made in an internal FBI document written in 1971 that more than half of the seventy-three persons placed on the "Key Activist" list of New Left leaders since its inception in 1968 had become subjects of "some type of prosecutive action" by federal or local officials.[167]

Whether or not COINTELPRO really ended in April, 1971, as the FBI claims, appears very doubtful. The FBI memo cancelling the program stated that in "exceptional circumstances" FBI field offices could still make counterintelligence recommendations to headquarters which would be considered on an "individual basis." According to a Senate Intelligence Committee staff report published in May, 1976, there have been at least three COINTELPRO-type actions since April, 1971; further, the staff report noted, the boundary between COINTELPRO and "aggressive investigation" can be "extremely thin."[168] FBI Director Clarence Kelly admitted in June, 1976, that despite former Director J. Edgar Hoover's order in 1966 banning FBI burglaries in cases involving domestic dissidents, that a "limited number" of such burglaries occurred in 1972 and 1973. According to press accounts, most of these burglaries occurred in the New York City area as part of a search for fugitive members of the terrorist Weatherman underground. According to high level FBI and Justice Department sources quoted in the news accounts, such burglaries also occurred in other cities and were directed against other targets. They numbered in the "hundreds" and they resumed before 1972 and continued until 1975 or 1976, according to these sources.[169]

In other incidents the FBI received material stolen by FBI informants who had infiltrated dissident groups. Thus, one informant who penetrated the VVAW provided the FBI with mailing lists and documents related to legal defense matters, while another informer stole correspondence from two groups he infiltrated for the FBI, used the $10,000 paid him by the FBI to finance a photographic studio, then sold the pictures to leftwing publications and turned the negatives over to the FBI. FBI documents released in a court suit in the summer of 1976 revealed that one informant who had infiltrated the youth organization of the SWP in Denver stole material on at least five separate occasions in 1973, and broke into the SWP Denver office in July, 1976, and carried out four cartons of documents, several of which later turned up in FBI files. Other FBI documents revealed in the court suit disclosed that the FBI received the fruits of documents that were removed from other SWP offices on at least eight occasions in the first half of 1975, and that at least twice in 1975 FBI agents searched through SWP trash and removed papers, despite previous FBI assurances that "trash covers" had ended in 1966.[170] In many other cases during the Vietnam War era, dissident individuals and groups reported thefts of financial and organizational records in incidents that suggested FBI involvement. Such burglaries were reported at six regional offices of SDS during the spring of 1972, and about fifteen break-ins were reported at the offices of lawyers who were defending radical clients.[171]

Perhaps the most incredible evidence concerning FBI involvement in political repression during the Vietnam War era is the overwhelming indication that many FBI informants acted as *agents provocateur,* either with or without the knowledge of their FBI supervising agents. Subtle pressure towards *agent provocateur* activity inevitably exists in an informant type of situation, since the informant knows that if he can incite a group to illegality and then report on the planned illegality, he will be immune from prosecution, yet will be regarded by his supervisors as reporting crucial information and will be regarded by the group he infiltrated, if indeed it has inclinations toward illegality, as one of them. On the other hand, an informer who can report no movement toward illegality is likely to be regarded as dispensable by an intelligence agency, and therefore risks losing his job. These inherent pressures toward *agent provocateur* activity were fostered by the FBI's carelessness in its selection of informers. Thus, in September, 1975, a woman who tried to assassinate President Gerald Ford turned out to be a former FBI informer.[172] FBI documents released in a court suit in July, 1976, revealed that another FBI informer had been retained by the bureau and given a salary raise even though the FBI knew that during the period he was an informer he had confessed to an extortion charge, committed numerous burglaries unrelated to his FBI work and had been hospitalized for a month for psychiatric treatment. This informer was rated as "excellent" by FBI internal inspectors in January, 1974, one month after he turned over to the FBI material stolen from a youth affiliate of the SWP.[173]

Probably the most incredible provocation incident involved an FBI and Seattle police informer, Alfred Burnett, who lured Larry Eugene Ward into planting a bomb at a Seattle real estate office on the morning of May 15, 1970, by paying Ward $75, providing him with the bomb and giving him transportation to the bombing scene. Ward, a twenty-two year old veteran who had been twice wounded and decorated three times for service in Vietnam, was shot and killed by waiting Seattle police as he allegedly fled after the bombing attempt, although he was unarmed, on foot and boxed in by police cars.[174]

Burnett, the FBI informer, was a twice-convicted felon who had been released from jail as a result of FBI statements to the Seattle police that he could provide valuable information on a wave of bombings in the Seattle area that had brought pressure on Seattle and FBI officials. When Burnett told the FBI that a bombing would occur at the Hardcastle Realty Co. in Seattle on the morning of May 15, the FBI relayed the information to Seattle police who prepared for the bombing. However, according to Burnett's later statements, he was unable to recruit the man he had originally hoped to have set the bomb, a former Black Panther named Davis, so he convinced Ward to plant the bomb at the last moment in return for $75. Burnett said he distinctly told the FBI that the bomber was Ward instead of Davis and that Ward was unarmed, but Seattle police maintain that their messages from the FBI did not state Ward was unarmed.

Burnett said later, "The police wanted a bomber and I got one for them. I didn't know Larry Ward would be killed." Seattle Police Intelligence Chief John Williams blamed the FBI, stating, "As far as I can tell Ward was a relatively decent kid. Somebody set this whole thing up. It wasn't the police department." Subsequently Seattle's mayor publicly advocated killing convicted bombers before a Senate committee, and citing the Ward case, noted the incidence of bombings in Seattle had declined since the slaying. He added, "I suspect killing a person involved in a bombing . . . might be somewhat of a deterrent."[175]

Another major provocation case involved Howard Berry Godfrey, an FBI informer who testified before a grand jury and in court that he had helped to organize the Secret Army Organization (SAO), an armed right-wing vigilante terrorist group that harassed San Diego area radicals in 1971 and 1972. Godfrey testified that the FBI had paid all of his expenses, including membership dues and the costs of supplying weapons, explosives and propaganda for the SAO. He stated that he had ridden along with an SAO member when the latter had fired a shot into a house occupied by young leftists that shattered the elbow of a young woman, and that he provided the explosives and training used by another SAO member to bomb a "pornographic" movie theater. Court testimony by Godfrey's former FBI supervisor in San Diego confirmed that he was an FBI informer and revealed that after Godfrey had turned over the gun used in the shooting to the FBI supervisor, that the latter had withheld the gun and his knowledge of those responsible for the shooting from San Diego police for six months. According to statements made out of court by Godfrey and confirmed by police and other sources, the SAO and Godfrey had engaged in a wide variety of other terroristic activities in San Diego, including burglarizing offices and stealing records of activist groups, firebombing and vandalizing cars, issuing death threats, and breaking into and destroying thousands of dollars of equipment and newspapers owned by local left-wing newspapers.

The SAO also produced a poster demanding the arrest of President Nixon for "treason" during his visit to China in 1972. Although Godfrey was never prosecuted, his testimony led to the convictions of several SAO members, and jail sentences for two of them, on charges ranging from attempted murder to illegal possession of explosives. Following widespread publicity about the Godfrey case in early 1976, FBI Director Clarence Kelly confirmed that Godfrey had been a paid FBI informant but denied that the FBI had funded the SAO or condoned any illegal activities.[176]

Probably the most-well known *agent provocateur* was Thomas

Tongyai, known as Tommy the Traveler. Tongyai, who was paid both by the FBI and local police, spent over two years travelling among colleges in western New York State urging students to kill police, make bombs and blow up buildings. He supplied students with radical speakers, literature and films, tried to organize an SDS chapter at Hobart College, organized SDS conferences in Rochester and urged students to participate in the Weatherman "Days of Rage" in Chicago in October, 1969. Tongyai constantly talked of violence, carried a grenade in his car, showed students how to use an M-1 rifle and offered advice on how to carry out bombings. After some students at Hobart College apparently took his advice and bombed the Hobart ROTC building, and Tongyai's cover was exposed, the local sheriff commented, "There's a lot of difference between showing how to build a bomb and building one." As a result of disturbances connected with Tongyai's activities on the Hobart campus, nine students and faculty faced criminal charges, but Tongyai was cleared by a local grand jury and went on to become a policeman in Pennsylvania. Tongyai explained, "The best cover for an undercover agent who wanted to get on campus was portraying the part of a radical extremist, which I did."[177]

Horace L. Packer, an FBI informer who was the chief government witness in the Seattle Eight conspiracy case,[178] testified that he was under FBI instructions to "do anything to protect my credibility." He testified that while infiltrating SDS and Weatherman at the University of Washington he supplied campus radicals with drugs, weapons and materials used for preparing molotov cocktails. Packer even admitted he supplied and the FBI paid for paint used to spray the Federal courthouse in Seattle during a demonstration in February, 1970 — a key element in the charge of conspiracy to damage federal property which was one of the major charges in the case. Packer also testified that he used drugs, including "acid, speed, mescaline" and cocaine while acting as an informer, that he "smoked dope all the time," that he had been arrested several times during campus demonstrations, and that he had violated the conditions of a suspended sentence he had received for participating in a Weatherman assault on ROTC facilities at the University of Washington.[179]

Defendants in the so-called "Camden Twenty-eight" case were acquitted in May, 1972, although they had been caught in the act of attempting to destroy Selective Service files in August, 1971, in Camden, New Jersey, by over eighty FBI agents, after the judge instructed the jury to acquit if they felt government participation in setting up the crime had gone to "intolerable lengths" that were "offensive to the basic standards of decency and shocking to the universal sense of justice." The key government witness in the case, Robert W. Hardy, an FBI informer, testified during the trial that he had provided 90 percent of the burglary tools and much of the expertise for the break-in and that the plot could not have been carried out without him.[180]

In May, 1973, the *New York Times* reported that private and governmental sources had confirmed what was already suspected among radical circles — that Larry G. Grantwohl, one of the most militant Weathermen, had acted as an FBI informant and *agent provocateur*. Grantwohl had been widely known among the Weathermen for his skill in making bombs and fuses as well as his habit of carrying a revolver and a straight razor; sources told the *Times* that he had also given lessons in bombmaking to Weathermen and participated in the bombing of a public school near Cincinnati in 1969. Grantwohl was one of fifteen Weathermen indicted in June, 1970 for conspiracy to bomb police and military installations in four cities, but the charges against him were later dropped. At last report, he was writing a book entitled *The Bombers: I Was a Weatherman for the FBI*.[181]

William Divale, an FBI informer who later published a book entitled *I Lived Inside the Campus Revolution*, functioned as one of the leading radicals in southern California from 1965 until he surfaced in 1969 during an attempt by the Justice Department to revive the SACB by proving that some of Divale's associates were *real* communists.[182] At various times Divale served as chairman of the UCLA and Central Los Angeles W.E.B. DuBois Club, on the DuBois Los Angeles and Southern California councils, on the Communist Party Southern California Youth Commission and as chairman of the CP Southern California Education Commission. Divale's self-confessed provocative activities included the writing of pamphlets stressing police brutality in the aftermath of the 1965 Watts riot in Los Angeles, an unsuccessful attempt to organize an SDS chapter at Pasadena City College (PCC), the organization of numerous protests at UCLA and PCC, participation at lie-downs in the Los Angeles produce market in an attempt to prevent trucks from unloading non-union grapes, and the spraying of revolutionary slogans on building walls with red paint. Divale wrote, "I was a leader, not merely a follower," and for his leadership abilities, he reports, the FBI paid him almost $15,000.[183]

Boyd Douglass, the FBI informer who was the major government witness at the Berrigan conspiracy trial,[184] played a similar role on the campus of Bucknell University. Aside from his role in smuggling letters back and forth between the imprisoned Phillip Berrigan and Sister Elizabeth McAlister, thus providing the only link between the two key alleged conspirators, Douglas functioned as an active, militant radical during his generous leaves from prison to study at Bucknell. His apartment became a meeting ground for members of the Catholic resistance, and he personally recruited students into protest activity, arranged for Bucknell students and faculty to meet with war resisters, and set up meetings at which anti-war speakers came to Bucknell. Douglass offered to provide a gun which could not be traced for use in an alleged kidnapping plot and passed on to one of the alleged conspirators explosives manuals he had obtained from an FBI agent. While the government presented Douglass as a highly believable witness in court, his personal background included desertion from the army, two attempts at suicide, and numerous arrests and convictions on various charges including passing bad checks, impersonating an army officer and assaulting an FBI agent. A government physician had concluded that he was a "sociopath and a pathological liar" while his father stated, "He has told me so many lies practically all his life that I can't believe nothing he tells me." Douglass was paid over $9,000 by the FBI.[185]

Another campus *agent provocateur* was Charles Grimm, who functioned as a local police and FBI informant on the campus of the University of Alabama at Tuscaloosa. Among his activities were the burning of Dressler Hall on the campus on May 7, 1970 (at the direction of the FBI, he said), the throwing of three molotov cocktails into a street on May 14, 1970 and the throwing of objects at police officers on the campus on May 18, 1970.[186]

THE CIA

The CIA joined the FBI in expanding its political intelligence operations during the Nixon administration. The Nixon White House continually pressed the CIA for more information on ties between the domestic protest movement and foreign elements, and the CIA responded by expanding its Operation CHAOS, begun in 1967. Thus, White House aide Tom Huston asked the CIA in June, 1969, for a new report on "foreign Communist support of revolutionary protest movements in the U.S.," adding that " 'support' should be liberally construed to include all activities by foreign Communists designed to encourage or assist" American protesters.[187]

In 1969, the CHAOS project, which until then had basically relied on the reports of the FBI and other intelligence agencies and of CIA agents regularly stationed abroad, began to recruit its own agents to go abroad and report on any foreign connections with American dissident groups. The CIA recruited some of these agents from domestic dissident groups and others were instructed to associate with such groups in the U.S. before going abroad. The CHAOS project was also, beginning in 1969, furnished with reports from another project within the CIA which also instructed its agents to infiltrate American dissident groups in the U.S. before going abroad for foreign intelligence purposes. Altogether, CHAOS was able to draw on about fifty agents from the two programs, and gathered huge quantities of information on purely domestic aspects of the protest movement. One of the agents became an officer in one domestic group, and another became involved as an advisor in a U.S. Congressional campaign and furnished CHAOS with reports on behind the scenes activities in the campaign. Among the overseas activities of CIA agents which fed into CHAOS, according to CIA documents revealed in July, 1976, were burglaries, wiretapping and bugging directed against American dissidents who were living or traveling abroad. Another source of information for CHAOS was the CIA's Domestic Contract Service (DCS), which beginning in 1969 furnished the CIA with reports from its own agents and local police officials gathered in response to CHAOS requests for information gathered in connection with the DCS function of collecting "foreign intelligence" information from cooperating Americans who travelled abroad or who had contacts with foreign businesses and governments.[188] CHAOS also called on NSA to supply even the most "innocuous" information it could gather by intercepting foreign communications of Americans involved in "civil disorders, radical student or youth activities, racial militant activities, radical antiwar activities, draft evasion/deserter support activities, or in radical related media activities."[189]

At its peak during the Nixon administration, the CHAOS office at CIA headquarters included over fifty agents and was furnishing the FBI with over one thousand reports a month, reporting on such topics as the activities of political dissidents on college campuses, the movement of American **dissenters abroad** and the activities of foreign visitors to American protest groups. The CIA revealed in 1975 that among the persons included in its files were seventy-five congressmen; among the items revealed by Congresswoman Bella Abzug as being in her CIA file were copies of letters written to the Soviet Union in connection with her law firm and reports of her public political activities in the U.S. dating from 1951, including her appearance before HUAC as a lawyer in 1953.[190]

The CHAOS project was gradually wound down after 1972, and was terminated in March, 1974, apparently as a result of the decline in domestic protest activity and the new atmosphere created by the Watergate scandal. In terminating the program, CIA Director William Colby told CIA stations abroad in March, 1974, that thereafter the CIA would focus "clearly on the foreign organizations and individuals involved" with "domestic matters" and "only incidentally on their American contacts." However, CIA agents were still permitted to report any information obtained as a "byproduct" of their activities "which makes Americans abroad suspect for security or counterintelligence reasons."[191]

CIA mail-opening, begun in 1956, continued until February, 1973. From 1969 to 1973, the CIA opened about forty thousand letters and forwarded the contents of about fifteen thousand letters to the FBI, which in March, 1972, asked the CIA for information on communist and New Left organizations and individuals, "Cubans and pro-Castro individuals," "protest and peace organizations," and members of "Marxist-Leninist subversive and extremist groups," such as SDS, the Black Panthers, Weathermen and the Progressive Labor Party.[192] The program was ended when Chief Postal Inspector William Cotter, who knew about the mail-opening as a result of his previous CIA position, refused to permit continuation of the operation without obtaining "higher level" approval. By the time the mail-opening project ended, the CIA had opened two hundred fifteen thousand letters since 1956, indexed one and one-half million names derived from the letters in its computers, and, according to the Senate Intelligence Committee had monitored "communications of domestic dissidents of all types."[193]

THE NSA

The National Security Administration continued its SHAMROCK program of intercepting international telegrams dating from World War II, and continued its MINARET program begun in 1967 of targetting domestic dissidents furnished to NSA by other intelligence agencies for particular attention. Between 1969 and 1973, NSA disseminated about two thousand reports based on MINARET watchlists to other agencies. At the height of MINARET in early 1973, NSA was targetting six hundred Americans. MINARET was terminated by NSA in October, 1973, after Attorney General Elliot Richardson advised NSA the program was of "questionable legality" in light of the 1972 Supreme Court decision outlawing warrantless electronic surveillance in cases involving "domestic" threats to the national security. However, the Richardson directive only barred NSA from *specific* monitoring of domestic intelligence targets, and thus did not ban NSA from continuing its SHAMROCK program of general monitoring of *all* international telegrams. SHAMROCK was officially ended in May, 1975, when NSA ceased obtaining copies of international telegrams. From the inception of the program during World War II, NSA had intercepted millions of telegrams sent to, from or through the United States, at an estimated rate of one hundred fifty thousand per month in the last years of the program.[194]

The ending of SHAMROCK did not mean an end to NSA monitoring of international communications, however. NSA technical capabilities allow it to intercept any communications sent through the air, which includes virtually all long distance telephone and telegraph communications. NSA continues to monitor international communications, and continues to pick up messages involving American citizens. The only difference the termination of MINARET and SHAMROCK have made is that NSA no longer *targets* communications of Americans, and, as of August, 1975 does not monitor telephone circuits with one terminal in the U.S. without the approval of top-level NSA personnel. According to the Senate Intelligence Committee, NSA guidelines also provide for discarding intercepted messages without a "foreign intelligence" component, and when messages involving Americans are retained and disseminated to other agencies, "in practically all cases the name of an American citizen, group or organization is deleted by NSA." Nevertheless, NSA's "pursuit of international communications does result in the incidental interception and dissemination of communications which the American sender or receiver expected to be kept private."[195]

ARMY INTELLIGENCE

Army intelligence continued to increase its operations under the Nixon administration. In April, 1969, Army intelligence developed a plan calling for "the identification of all personalities involved, or expected to become involved, in protest activities." A particular target for Army intelligence was organizers of coffeehouses and underground newspapers who tried to recruit military personnel for protest activities. During 1969 and 1970, the Army conducted investigations of seventeen coffeehouses and fifty-eight underground papers. Following press exposure of Army intelligence activities in 1970 and the scheduling of Senate hearings into the program in 1971, the Defense Department announced in March, 1971, that it was banning the collection of information on persons and organizations "unaffiliated" with the military except where "essential" to the military mission, and destroying all material previously gathered not falling within this category.[196]

However, the Nixon administration strenuously opposed any legislative or judicial restrictions on Army intelligence during Senate hearings and in response to a court suit seeking to enjoin the Army. Assistant Attorney General William Rehnquist told the Senate Judiciary Subcommittee on Constitutional Rights that the President inherently possessed virtually unlimited powers to maintain surveillance of anyone who *might* violate the law, stated the administration would "vigorously oppose" *any* legislative or judicial supervision of its surveillance of American citizens and maintained that even if the executive branch collected and disseminated derogatory information about individuals unrelated to law breaking it would not violate any constitutional rights. The Supreme Court turned back a challenge to Army surveillance in *Laird* v. *Tatum* (1972) on the grounds that the plaintiffs in the suit had failed to present sufficient evidence of any specific harm or threat of future harm arising from the Army's activity. The deciding vote in the five-to-four decision was cast by newly appointed Justice William Rehnquist, who ignored the judicial tradition of not voting in cases where there had been previous personal involvement.[197]

The official termination of the Army civilian surveillance program in March, 1971, did not end all such Army activities or lead to the destruction of all of the files gathered. Army intelligence units in many areas simply turned their files over to local or state police, and the Army discovered in 1975 that thousands of files that should have been destroyed were still being maintained by the Army. Senate hearings held in 1974 also indicated that the Air Force and Naval Intelligence had conducted domestic intelligence operations and were retaining files in apparent violation of the 1971 directive.[198]

Military collection of information about civilians continued under the provision of March, 1971, Defense Department termination directive, which allowed collection of information "about activities threatening defense military and civilian personnel and defense activities and installations," such as "subversion of the loyalty, discipline or morale of Department of Defense military or civil personnel by actively encouraging disruption of law, disobedience of lawful orders or regulations, or disruptions of military activities." Under this provision, Navy and Air Force intelligence conducted at least five investigations of civilian groups between March, 1971 and March, 1975. Thus, Naval intelligence agents infiltrated anti-war groups in San Diego in 1971 and 1972, allegedly to protect "Naval personnel, property and functions" against threatened sabotage and disruption. Although directed against organizations with military personnel among their members or who were organizing anti-war activities near Naval facilities, the program became a general investigation of the targeted groups, including the collection of information about their financial and political connections.

Aside from the loophole permitting military intelligence investigations of civilians allegedly posing "threats" to the military, the Defense Department directive of March, 1971, does not apply outside the United States, even to American civilians. Thus, in 1972 the Army investigated "Americans in Berlin for McGovern," and in 1976 the Army was still authorized to open mail and wiretap American civilians living in West Berlin.[199] The March, 1971, directive also explicitly provided that top Defense Department officials could authorize collection of information about civilians if such activity was deemed "essential" to the military. According to the Senate Intelligence Committee, the terms of the directive "are so ambiguous that future surveillance activities in the civilian community might be undertaken consistent" with it. While the Committee reported that on the whole implementation of the directive had been "vigorous and effective," with only "rare and relatively minor" exceptions it warned that limitations on military surveillance "remain only in the form of an internal regulation, which can be rescinded or amended by the Secretary of Defense."[200]

THE IRS

The Internal Revenue Service was used in a massive scale for political purposes during the Nixon administration in an attempt to harass and disrupt political dissidents. Between 1968 and 1974, the IRS gave to the FBI confidential tax information on 120 leaders of the anti-war and militant black movements, as part of the FBI's COINTELPRO activity. According to a February, 1969, FBI memo, the Bureau also succeeded in getting the IRS to inquire into many of these cases, anticipating that the inquiry "will cause these individuals considerable consternation, possibly jail sentences eventually" and would help the FBI achieve its objective of obtaining "prosecution of any kind" in order to "remove them from the movement."[201] The IRS also furnished the FBI with a list of contributors to SDS developed in connection with an IRS audit of SDS. The IRS also passed the list on to the White House.

In July, 1969, the IRS established the Special Services Staff (SSS) to "coordinate activities in all Compliance Divisions involving ideological, militant, subversive, radical and similar type organizations; to collect basic intelligence data and to insure that the requirements of the Internal Revenue Code concerning such organizations have been complied with." One SSS memo listed among the targets of the project persons travelling to Cuba, Algeria and North Vietnam, and persons who "organize and attend rock festivals which attract youth and narcotics."[202] The SSS unit was created by IRS in response to pressure from the White House and a Senate Subcommittee which had been reviewing IRS files on activist organizations, including the Black Panthers. The purpose of the program was clearly to cause extraordinary attention to be paid by IRS to groups selected on political criteria. Thus, the head of SSS, in various memos, referred to the project as hopefully leading to "enforcement actions needed to help control an insidious threat to the internal security of this country" and expressed the feeling that "enforcement against flagrant law violators would have some salutary effect in this overall battle against persons bent on destruction of this government."[203]

Names of individuals and organizations to be subjected to SSS scrutiny were obtained from the Inter-Divisional Information Unit (IDIU) of the Justice Department, and from the FBI, which, according to an internal memo, hoped SSS would "deal a blow to dissident elements."[204] The FBI lists included twenty-three hundred organizations categorized as "old" and "new" left and "right wing," plus a list of all known "underground" newspapers and their editors. The IDIU list included over ten thousand names, including persons the Justice Department felt could be of *assistance* in quelling civil disturbances; since SSS did not know that such persons were included on the list it indiscriminately established files on such persons.

Altogether, SSS established files on 2,873 organizations and 8,585 individuals, checked about five thousand of the files against tax records, and referred 225 persons and organizations to field offices for audit, collection or intelligence action. The overwhelming majority of the groups on whom files were kept were liberal and left-wing groups, including organizations associated with Women's Liberation, the Black Panther Party, the National Council of Churches, ADA, the Urban League, the American Library Association, the Ford Foundation, the ACLU, the Playboy Foundation, the American Jewish Congress, the National Education Association, Common Cause, the *New York Review of Books* and *Rolling Stone,* a "counterculture" newspaper. Among individuals investigated were New York City Mayor John Lindsay, U.S. Senators Charles Goodell and Ernest Gruening, columnist Joseph

Alsop, comedian Godfrey Cambridge, singers James Brown and Joan Baez, and actress Shirley MacLaine. The end result of the SSS project, which was terminated after newspaper publicity in 1973, was that the IRS assessed a total of $622,000, of which $500,000 was attributable to four cases.

Instances of political pressure put on the IRS by the White House to punish specific people not held in favor by the Nixon administration were revealed during various proceedings associated with the Watergate scandal.[205] In September, 1972, White House Counsel John Dean personally turned over to IRS Commissioner Johnny Walters a list of 575 members of Democratic Presidential candidate George McGovern's staff and contributors and told Walters that White House chief domestic advisor John Erlichman wanted the IRS to determine what type of information could be developed concerning the individuals. Dean testified that when the IRS sat on the request, he again raised the subject with Walters, to no avail, at the express direction of President Nixon. White House officials later succeeded in having the IRS initiate tax audits on a *Newsday* reporter who had written a critical article on Nixon's personal friend, Charles "Bebe" Rebozo, and on Democratic National Committee Chairman Lawrence O'Brien. According to Walters, when the IRS audit of O'Brien, conducted two months before the 1972 election date, proved unsatisfactory to Erlichman, Erlichman told Walters, "I'm goddamn tired of your footdragging tactics."[206] Under White House pressure, the IRS turned over tax information to presidential aides in a number of other cases.

For a short period in 1970, several local offices of another unit of the IRS, the Alcohol, Tobacco and Firearms Unit, embarked, according to Secretary of the Treasury David Kennedy, on a program of "determining the advisability of the use of library records as an investigative technique to assist in quelling bombings." During the course of this program, which was terminated following national publicity in July, 1970, IRS agents visited twenty-seven libraries in the Atlanta area to "determine the feasibility of utilizing libraries as an investigative technique to determine the availability of books on explosives, and whether the names of the borrowers of such books could be obtained if needed in connection with an investigation of a suspect or suspects in a specific bombing." In addition, three libraries in other parts of the country were visited, in two cases to determine if specific suspects had checked out books on explosives. During two of these thirty visits, names of library borrowers were obtained and copied.[207]

OTHER FEDERAL AGENCIES

In addition to the FBI, the CIA, the NSA, army intelligence and the IRS, more than ten other federal agencies were involved in political intelligence gathering, some of which relied primarily on other agencies to forward information to them and lacked their own investigative staffs.[208] The best-known of these other agencies is the Secret Service, which revealed in 1975 that it had forty-seven thousand names on file as potential threats to the President or others under its protection, and that it was keeping three hundred persons considered "extremely dangerous" under surveillance.[209] Secret Service guidelines called for the collection of information on potential assassins and those making violent threats or plans against high government officials, on persons who threatened, planned or attempted to "embarass" such officials or "insist upon contacting high government officials for the purpose of redressing imaginary grievances" and on "anti-American or anti-U.S. government demonstrations" and "civil disturbances." Among persons included in Secret Service files in 1972 were civil rights leaders Ralph Abernathy, Coretta King and Roy Wilkins, Congressman Walter Fauntroy, anti-war leader Benjamin Spock and organizations such as the John Birch Society and the NAACP. Among the more unusual activities of the Secret Service during the Nixon administration were the wiretapping of the phone of Nixon's brother, Donald, allegedly for fear "unsavory" characters might seek to embarass the President through Donald Nixon; the barring of anti-war protesters from attending a public rally at Charlotte, North Carolina in October, 1971, at which Nixon was to appear; and the confiscating and burning of ninety thousand issues of a publication in 1973 because it had a reproduction of a five-dollar bill with a portrait of Nixon. In May, 1976, the Secret Service revealed in response to a lawsuit that its agents had covertly photographed speakers and tape-recorded proceedings at the 1971 convention of the Young Socialist Alliance, (YSA) the youth groups of the SWP, and had reported the names of YSA officers and one hundred persons attending the convention. This revelation suggests that Secret Service intelligence operations are far greater than have thus far been disclosed.

Among the other federal agencies gathering intelligence files were the Customs Bureau of the Treasury Department; the Intelligence Division of the Post Office, the Civil Service Commission, which employed seventeen clerks to read and clip from radical publications, and, according to a CSC publication in 1971, maintained "approximately 2.5 million index cards containing information related to communist and other subversive activities" in *addition* to files on ten million citizens who had sought federal employment since 1939;[210] the Immigration and Naturalization Service; the passport division of the State Department (with a reported list of two hundred forty thousand names of persons of "questionable citizenship" by 1975);[211] the Department of Justice Community Relations Service; and civil rights and poverty projects sponsored by the Department of Health, Education and Welfare and the now-defunct Office of Economic Opportunity.

THE HUSTON PLAN

Despite the huge quantity of political intelligence flowing into the executive branch, the Nixon administration was dissatisfied with both the quality and coordination of intelligence information. President Nixon was particularly dissatisfied with the inability of the intelligence community to come up with evidence showing strong foreign links with the domestic protest movement, while elements within the intelligence community were especially dissatisfied with the FBI's halt to the use of burglaries and lessened use of electronic surveillance dating from the mid-1960's, with FBI Director Hoover's refusal to use informants younger than twenty-one, and with Hoover's cut-off of formal liasion with other intelligence agencies in the spring of 1970. On July 14, 1970, Nixon approved a plan (the so-called Huston plan) designed to remedy these dissatisfactions, which resulted from a series of meetings among top officials of the CIA, FBI, NSA and Defense Intelligence Agency (DIA) to whom Nixon's feelings had been conveyed, both personally and through his representative, Tom Charles Huston.[212]

The Huston Plan approved by Nixon proposed a broadening of NSA coverage of communications to include coverage of the "communications of U.S. citizens using international facilities;" intensified "electronic surveillance and penetration" of "individuals and groups" who "pose a major threat to the internal security;" an end to restrictions on the use of mail covers (copying down information from the outsides of envelopes, halted by the FBI in 1964), plus opening of mail "on selected targets of priority foreign intelligence and internal security interest;" use of "surreptitious entry" (i.e. burglaries) against "urgent and high priority internal security targets;" and relaxation of restrictions on "development of campus sources" to allow "expanded coverage of violence-prone campus and student related groups" along with increased CIA coverage of "American students (and others) traveling or living abroad." The Huston Plan also proposed creating an interagency committee to coordinate domestic intelligence.

Nixon approved the plan on Huston's advice although Huston wrote to Nixon that the use of "surreptitious entries" and mail-opening would be illegal. Ironically, the report of the intelligence agencies that ultimately led to approval of the plan misled Nixon by informing him that mail-opening was not occuring (although the CIA was opening mail) and suggesting that NSA was not monitoring international communications of Americans (which it was). Nixon countermanded his approval of the plan on July 28, 1970 as a result of strong protests from Hoover and Attorney General John Mitchell. Despite Nixon's final decision not to approve the plan, the CIA continued to open mail and NSA continued to monitor international communications of Americans. The FBI stepped up its domestic intelligence operations, including authorizing the use of eighteen to twenty-one year old informants in 1970 and the resumption of mail covers in 1971. In December, 1970, an Interagency Evaluation Committee (IEC), with a strong resemblance to the interagency committee suggested in the Huston Plan was established, but it did little aside from prepare about thirty studies on domestic dissent before it was dissolved in July, 1973, shortly after the Huston Plan was exposed in the Watergate hearings. In 1971 a White House intelligence unit, the so-called "Plumbers," burglarized the offices of the psychiatrist of Daniel Ellsberg, then under indictment in the "Pentagon Papers" case. In 1972, agents of the Committee to Re-Elect the President, a Republican organization under the supervision of top presidential advisors, burglarized and wiretapped the offices of the Democratic National Committee during the election campaign. By 1972, the FBI had resumed the use of burglaries against domestic "subversive" targets.[213]

In effect, every recommendation of the Huston Plan was eventually carried out, although not in a coordinated way. A Senate Intelligence Committee staff report noted in 1976:

> The Huston Plan provides a tragic commentary on the state of American democracy in the summer of 1970. Tom Charles Huston, the top White House advisor for internal security affairs, advised the President of the United States, in effect, to authorize the violation of the Constitution and specific federal statutes. . . . Nixon accepted the advice and gave his approval to the unlawful intelligence plan. . . . Throughout the episode, some of the intelligence agencies concealed projects from the White House . . . and, after the President took back his authority from the intelligence plan, certain agencies continued to implement the provisions anyway.[214]

Public, Overt Repression

All of the Nixon administration actions discussed thus far were essentially *sub rosa*, i.e. they were actions primarily directed towards secretly gaining intelligence on and disrupting radical organizations and were publicized only as the result of leaks from ex-government agents, from the "surfacing" of informers or forced government responses at court trials, or from the Media burglarly. They did not involve public and overt types of repression, i.e. actions which are clearly designed to publicly demonstrate that the government is out to "get" people and organizations holding certain types of views. However, in the Nixon administration massive *sub rosa* repression went hand in hand with massive overt, public repression.

There were four major types of repressive public policies carried out: a series of often extremely shaky conspiracy prosecutions against radical leaders; the use of grand juries as instruments to gather political intelligence and harass radicals; attempts to harass and intimidate the "liberal" press; and attempts to harass anti-administration demonstrators.

CONSPIRACY PROSECUTIONS

The Nixon administration instituted an extraordinary series of conspiracy trials against anti-war leaders — in fact, together with the Spock-Coffin trial of the Johnson administration, the Nixon administration prosecuted virtually every prominent anti-war leader. What was perhaps the most extraordinary thing about the prosecutions was that the major charges brought either all collapsed during the judicial process, or the cases were thrown out due to illegal government activities or refusal to disclose records of illegal wiretapping. The outcome was the same whether the government was trying sensational nationally publicized cases like the "Chicago Eight" and the "Gainesville Eight," or obscure cases like the "Kansas City Four" and the "Evanston Four."[215] By the fall of 1974, the Justice Department was so puzzled by its failures that it set up a special task force to study why it was doing so poorly in cases with political overtones; the task force concluded that the main problem was that somehow defense lawyers were able to select jurors sympathetic to their clients or "willing to be convinced of government misconduct."[216] While the prosecutions failed in one sense — historian William Manchester termed them "an unparalled series of judicial disasters for the government"[217] .— they succeeded sensationally in another. Namely, they succeeded in tying up huge amounts of time, money and energy that the anti-war and radical movements could have used to expand rather than expend on protracted and costly defense struggles.

The first major conspiracy trial, the so-called Chicago Conspiracy or Chicago Eight trial,[218] resulted from indictments handed down in March, 1969 of eight anti-war leaders under the 1968 Anti-Riot Act for conspiring to cross state lines with intent to incite a riot. Six of the defendants were also individually charged with crossing state lines with intent to incite a riot, and two were additionally charged with teaching and demonstrating the use of incendiary devices. The charges stemmed from the disorders at the 1968 Democratic National Convention in Chicago, which a government study commission (the so-called Walker Commission) clearly suggested resulted primarily from the refusal of Chicago authorities to grant demonstrators permits and from subsequent brutal and indiscriminate attacks by Chicago police on demonstrators, the vast majority of whom were intent on peaceful protest.[219] Although President Johnson's last attorney general, Ramsey Clark, refused to authorize prosecution of any demonstrators under the Anti-Riot Act, and instead initiated proceedings against Chicago policemen before a Chicago grand jury, the new attorney general, John Mitchell, asked the grand jury to also proceed against demonstration leaders. On March 20, 1969, the Chicago grand jury returned indictments against eight Chicago policemen under civil rights statutes, and against eight demonstrators, six of whom were highly visible radical leaders, including pacifist David Dellenger, Black Panther Party Chairman Bobby Seale, SDS leaders Tom Hayden and Rennie Davis and "Yippie" (a phrase usually shorthanded as "radicalized hippie") leaders Jerry Rubin and Abbie Hoffman. No indictments were returned against Chicago city or police officials, whom the Walker commission had suggested bore the greatest blame for the disorders.

The eight policemen were quickly acquitted. Seale's case was severed in mid-trial (and never retried) when Federal Judge Julius Hoffman found him in contempt of court and summarily sentenced him to an unprecedented four years in prison, as a result of repeated outbursts by Seale following Judge Hoffman's refusal to either allow Seale to defend himself or to have the services of a lawyer of his own choosing. After a tumultuous trial[220] — which at one point featured Seale tied to a chair with a gag in his mouth — the remaining seven defendants were found innocent of the conspiracy charge, the two charged with teaching the use of incendiary devices were acquitted, and the other five were found guilty of crossing state lines with intent to incite a riot.[221] Judge Hoffman, whose disgust and contempt for the defendants was scarcely concealed throughout the trial, sentenced the five to maximum terms of five years in jail and $5,000 fines, and then added 175 contempt sentences ranging from two and a half months to over four years against all seven defendants and two of their lawyers. Many of the contempt sentences were based on the flimsiest possible grounds; for example Dellenger was sentenced to six months for calling the judge "Mr." Hoffman, and Davis was sentenced to twenty-nine days for applauding at one point and laughing at another.

Eventually both the contempt and substantive convictions were overturned by the Ninth Circuit Court of Appeals, in the latter case on the grounds that Hoffman had displayed a "deprecatory and often antagonistic attitude toward the defense." The government never retried the substantive charges, but did retry 38 of the 175 contempt charges in 1973, five years after the incidents leading to the original indictments. Three defendants and one lawyer were found guilty of a total of 13 charges of contempt in the new trial, but the trial judge refused to impose any sentence, stating that Hoffman had been guilty of "condemnatious conduct" and had "from the beginning of the trial telegraphed to the jury his contempt for the defendants."[222]

The next major conspiracy case initiated by the Nixon administration involved charges brought in 1971 against the Rev. Phillip Berrigan and seven others, most of whom were prominent in the Catholic anti-war movement, on charges of a conspiracy to raid draft boards, blow up heating tunnels in Washington, D.C., and kidnap presidential aide Henry Kissinger.[223] Additionally, Father Berrigan and two others were charged in connection with smuggling letters out of the prison where Berrigan was serving time for a draft board raid, and two defendants were charged with attempting to send a letter threatening to kidnap Kissinger.

Most of the defendants in the case had publicly acknowledged participating in draft board raids (the indictment was worded so that a guilty finding in this regard could lead to a guilty finding for the entire conspiracy charge), but the evidence in support of the two major charges — the bombing and kidnapping plot — was extraordinarily weak, relying almost entirely on the testimony of an informer who had been certified by a government psychiatrist as a "sociopath and pathological liar."[224] The only evidence aside from his testimony consisted essentially of what one news account characterized as "desultory dinner-table conversation and incidental gossip in love letters."[225]

Evidence for the existence of a plot at more than a fantasy level was so thin that in the fall of 1970 Justice Department officials had concluded the case was insufficient to present to a grand jury. However, on November 27, 1970, FBI Director Hoover publicly charged before a Congressional committee that a plot existed to blow up Washington tunnels and kidnap Kissinger, and specifically named Berrigan, along with his brother Daniel, who was never indicted in the case. Hoover's extraordinary action, amounting in effect to the bringing of criminal charges without any judical process, appears to have been the major factor leading the Justice Department to seek an indictment.[226] Although the defense in the trial did not present a single witness, the outcome of the proceeding was a jury deadlock ten to two for acquittal on all charges save the letter smuggling counts. Subsequently a federal court of appeals overturned convictions on six of the seven counts of smuggling letters since all but one of the letters had been smuggled out by the government informer while he was acting under the orders of the prison warden.[227] When in the end Berrigan went to jail on the one remaining count, he became the only person in American history to ever go to jail (or even be prosecuted) on such a charge.[228]

The third major conspiracy prosecution brought by the Nixon administration was the so-called "Pentagon Papers" case.[229] It involved a fifteen count indictment against Daniel Ellsberg and Anthony Russo charging conspiracy to defraud the government of its "lawful function of witholding classified information from the public;" converting, embezzling or stealing the "Pentagon Papers" (a multi-volume study of American policy in Vietnam from 1950 to 1967 compiled by the Defense Department from 1967 to 1969); and giving documents related to the national defense to a person not entitled to receive them (a charge made under the Espionage Act of 1917, a war-time statute which was in force because President Truman's declaration of a state of "national emergency" made in 1950 in connection with the Korean War had never been revoked).[230] Ellsberg was subject to up to 155 years and Russo up to 35 years under the indictment, which superseded an earlier indictment which had charged only Ellsburg and would have brought a maximum of 20 years in jail.

The charges in the "Pentagon Papers" case were unique in the history of American justice. They had stemmed from the leaking of the "papers" and their subsequent publication in the *New York Times* and other papers in mid-1971, when they were three years old, divulged no information about secret military plans or preparation and involved primarily disclosures of diplomatic and political decisions reached by an administration no longer in office. Although the Pentagon Papers did show that "the American people had been systematically misled by their elected and appointed leaders,"[231] they seemed to pose no threat to vital national security secrets. In fact, the government prosecutor in the case argued that under the Espionage Act it was necessary only to show that the papers pertained to the "national defense" and not that they "be vitally important or that their disclosure would be injurious to the United States." The wording of the government indictment relating to the Espionage Act charged only that the defendants had given national defense documents to persons "not entitled to receive them," a startling departure from past such prosecutions which had attempted to show, as the statute specified, that the defendant had acted "with intent or reason to believe that the information to be obtained is to be used to the injury of the United States or to the advantage of any foreign nation."[232] Further, while Russo and Ellsburg were charged with conspiring to defraud the government of its "lawful" function of witholding classified information, no statute existed authorizing the classification system of the government, which was based entirely on presidential executive orders.

The Pentagon Papers trial was marked by a series of virtually unbelievable instances of government misconduct, including attempts by the government to suppress internal memoranda and studies casting doubt on the national security significance of the papers,[233] an apparent government denial of any use of wiretaps and then an admission that Ellsburg and someone connected with the defense had both been overheard on taps directed against other persons, and the secret offer of the directorship of the FBI to presiding Judge Matthew Byrne by White House Domestic Advisor John Erlichmann in the middle of the trial. The most sensational revelation was that persons associated with the White House Special Investigations Unit (the so-called "Plumbers") an organization set up within the White House at the direction of President Nixon to end news "leaks," had burglarized the office of Ellsburg's psychiatrist after the indictment had been handed down in 1971. White House papers released in the course of the Watergate investigation revealed that the purpose of the burglary was to obtain information which could be used to create a "negative press image" about Ellsburg in an attempt to, as White House Counsel Charles Colson said, to "plumber" Howard Hunt in one telephone conversation, "put this bastard into one hell of a situation and discredit the New Left."[234] With the final straw the government's temporary inability to uncover its wiretap records on Ellsburg, Judge Byrne ordered a mistrial and dismissed the case in April, 1973.

The fourth major conspiracy case brought by the Nixon administration, the so-called "Gainesville conspiracy" or "Gainesville Eight"[235] case (named after the Florida trial site), involved charges against eight members and supporters of the Vietnam Veterans Against the War (VVAW) for conspiring to disrupt the Republican National Convention of 1972 by organizing assaults on various buildings in the Miami area with devices ranging from "'fried' marbles, ball bearings, 'cherry' bombs, and smoke bombs" to "wrist rocket slingshots . . . cross bows" and automatic weapons and incendiary devices. The VVAW had been planning to demonstrate (peacefully, they said) at both 1972 conventions in Miami. The timing of the grand jury hearings which led to the indictment — in Tallahassee, five hundred miles from Miami — made it impossible to hold demonstrations at the Democratic convention, while the jailing of four VVAW members for a month without bail for refusing to answer grand jury questions (Supreme Court Justice William O. Douglas finally intervened to order bail) and the arraignment of the eight persons indicted on the last day of the Republican Convention eliminated plans to demonstrate then.

Although some of the government witnesses claimed to have heard VVAW members talk about using a variety of weapons, including anti-tank weapons and bazookas, to disrupt the convention, the only weapons introduced as evidence were slingshots. The key government witness was William Lemmer, an FBI informer who had been Arkansas VVAW coordinator. Lemmer had recently been held for a sanity hearing by his wife, had told a Congressional committee that the Army had threatened him with a psychiatric discharge and had recently been released by police after they had confiscated a loaded rifle and pistol and a doctor had recommended that he see a psychiatrist. His wife released one letter which indicated Lemmer blamed the VVAW for a breakup in his marriage; it included the statement that if he came to "get" the veterans it would not be noisily but in "tennis shoes" and with "a length of piano wire."[236] The defense called but a single witness in the case, following which the jury acquitted all of the defendants after deliberating three and one-half hours.

In addition to the above cases, the Nixon administration brought a number of other conspiracy prosecutions against anti-war leaders that for various reasons drew considerably less attention. A number of cases, notably two conspiracy prosecutions against the Weathermen, were dropped with little publicity because of government reluctance to disclose records of illegal wiretaps (in some cases little publicity also resulted from the fact that the cases were dropped after 1972, when anti-radical hysteria had calmed down with the weakening of the radical movement).[237]

One other case which did go to trial was the so-called "Seattle Eight" trial, held in December, 1970, involving charges against eight leaders of the "Seattle Liberation Front" (SLF), for conspiracy to damage federal property, and additional charges against five defendants under the 1968 Anti-Riot Law.[238] The SLF was, publicly at least, a moderate group which had been formed as an alternative to Weatherman, and which had devoted itself mostly to community organizing, especially among Seattle's poor and unemployed. Perhaps not coincidentally, the Seattle indictment was the only major federal indictment aimed at a particular regional movement, and the radical movement in Seattle was one of the strongest in the country (perhaps reflecting the heritage of the general strike of 1919 and the IWW movement in the Pacific Northwest).

The charges in the case grew out of an SLF-sponsored demonstration in February, 1970, which ended up with window-breaking and paint-spraying of the federal courthouse in Seattle. Although the demonstration — called to protest the contempt sentences in the Chicago conspiracy case — had been planned only ten days before it occurred, four of the defendants were charged with crossing states lines the previous December with intent to incite a riot; another defendant (a visiting philosophy professor at the University of Washington) was charged with using interstate telephone lines with intent to incite a riot as the result of a long-distance call placed a week before the demonstration.

The Seattle trial was marked, in the words of one observer, by "harassment" by the judge, and constant interruption of the proceedings by defendants "with comments, denials, questions and occasionally what polite society regards as obscenities, but what passes for vocabulary in the informal street culture."[239] The judge, George H. Boldt, declared a mistrial when the defendants protested his refusal to give any kind of shelter in the entire courtroom building to spectators who were waiting outside in the rain to gain entrance to the trial. He then sentenced five defendants to a year in jail for contempt and two to six months for contempt (one defendant had gone underground and never shown up), based on the "totality" of their behavior during the trial and their actions during a courtroom brawl which broke out during the contempt proceedings.

Judge Boldt then denied release on bail until appeals could be heard, and continued to deny bail even after an appeals court had ordered him to grant it. Subsequently the appeals court again ordered release on bail — successfully, this time — overturned the contempt citations and recommended that another judge rehear the contempt cases. When the cases were reheard a year later, the seven defendants pleaded no contest to the contempt charges — apparently mostly out of exhaustion — and were sent to jail for periods ranging from thirty days to five months. The government never retried the original charges and dismissed the case in March, 1973. In the meantime, the once-thriving radical movement in Seattle had been made a shambles.[240]

REPRESSIVE GRAND JURIES[241]

The conversion of the grand jury system into a major instrument for harassing and intimidating political radicals was another overt repressive technique used extensively by the Nixon administration. Beginning in 1970, federal grand juries throughout the country were convened for what clearly were general "fishing expeditions," coordinated by the Internal Security Division of the Justice Department, into the activities of radical and anti-war groups.

Between 1970 and January, 1973, over one hundred grand juries in thirty-six states and eighty-four cities looked into dissident activities, and over one thousand persons were subpoenaed to appear before such bodies. About four hundred indictments resulted from these proceedings, which in many cases seemed to be more of a general political intelligence operation than a normal grand jury investigation of specific crimes. In the case of twenty-five people subpoenaed before a Harrisburg, Pennsylvania, grand jury in April, 1971, the only apparent basis for the subpoenas was the fact that they had all been mentioned in the smuggled prison letters of the Berrigan conspiracy case.

According to William Olson, head of the Internal Security Division for a period during the Nixon administration:

> In many cases you go into an investigative grand jury with only a suspicion that criminal laws have been violated. And sometimes as the grand jury progresses you get bits and pieces. And sometimes they fit in not with what you started out to investigate, but with other crimes, not necessarily in the same jurisdiction.[242]

Witnesses appearing before these grand juries were forced to testify in secret and without the presence of legal assistance in the grand jury room, and under threat of contempt and jail sentences. Under a 1970 federal law which was frequently invoked during these proceedings, witnesses could be granted "use" immunity under which a witness' words could not be used to prosecute him but under which prosecution could occur if the government could independently develop the same information — until the passage of this law, which was upheld by the Supreme Court in 1972, the government had to grant total immunity from prosecution in order to compel testimony. Witnesses were asked detailed questions about their personal beliefs and associations and about their general knowledge of radical and anti-war activities. Questions asked at these grand jury sessions included the following:

> Tell the grand jury every place you went after you returned to your apartment from Cuba, every city you visited, with whom and by what means of transportation you travelled and who you visited at all of the places after you left your apartment in Ann Arbor, Michigan, in May of 1970.

> I want you to describe for the grand jury every occasion during the year 1970, when you have been in contact with, attended meetings which were conducted by or attended by, or been any place when any individual spoke whom you knew to be associated with or affiliated with Students for a Democratic Society, the Weathermen, the Communist Party, or any other organization advocating revolutionary overthrow of the United States, describing for the grand jury when these incidents occurred, where they occurred, who was present and what was said by all persons there and what you did at the time that you were in these meetings, groups, associations or conversations.
>
> I want you to tell the grand jury over the last two years every telephone number which you have had at a place where you resided, or every telephone number at a place where you have had access to the use of that telephone.[243]

In several cases, grand juries interrogated witnesses with regard to alleged crimes in which indictments had already been handed down, indicating that one of the purposes of the investigations was to bolster indictments which did not have enough evidence behind them to sustain convictions. One such grand jury session in connection with the "Pentagon Papers" case led to the subpoenaing of a wide range of anti-war scholars, journalists and lawyers in the Boston area, and the jailing of Professor Samuel Popkin of Harvard for his refusal to reveal what he contended were confidential sources developed in connection with his scholarly research.[244] In a number of cases, the government dropped subpoenas against witnesses who demanded to know the extent to which government wiretapping might be involved in questions asked of them, but court challenges to other aspects of these grand jury proceedings were consistently rejected, including challenges brought on first and fourth amendment grounds, on the right of privacy or on the alleged irrelevancy of the questions asked. In January, 1974, for example, the Supreme Court, in *U.S. v. Calandra* ruled that grand jury witnesses had to answer questions even if they were based on illegal searches and seizures.[245] Refusal to testify under grants of immunity led to the jailing of about thirty perons for contempt during the 1971-73 period, leading one critic of the Nixon administration's use of the grand jury to comment, "The grand jury has become an effective means by which the government can jail politically suspect persons without having to go through the time and expense of a trial."[246] Other students of the grand jury process concluded that the Nixon administration was turning grand juries into part of a general political intelligence apparatus and "as a means, by compelling testimony through grants of immunity, of laundering evidence that has already been illegally obtained (through burglaries and wiretaps)."[247]

INTIMIDATION OF THE PRESS

Another facet of the Nixon administration's policy of overt political repression was an attempt to intimidate the "liberal" press, especially the three major television networks and the *New York Times* and the *Washington Post,* the two most influential anti-war papers.[248] This campaign began in late 1969, as the anti-war movement was continuing to grow. In October, 1969, presidential aide Jeb Magruder sent a memorandum to White House Chief of Staff H. R. Haldeman recommending that various governmental agencies, including the IRS, the anti-trust division of the Justice Department and the Federal Communications Commission (FCC) be used to control criticism from the news media.[249] Shortly thereafter, on November 13, 1969, Vice-President Agnew criticized television news commentators for their "instant analysis and querulous criticism" of a recent speech by President Nixon, and suggested the need to increase control of the "concentration of power" held in the hands of a "tiny and closed fraternity of privileged men, elected by no one, and enjoying a monopoly sanctioned and licensed by the government." The next day it was revealed that Nixon's newly appointed FCC chairman, Dean Burch, had requested transcripts of network commentaries following the Nixon address Agnew had referred to. A week later, Agnew turned his fire on the *New York Times* and the *Washington Post,* and White House Communications Director Herb Klein warned that if TV networks and newspapers "fail to examine" the problems "you have today . . . you do invite the government to come in."[250]

At about the same time as Agnew's attacks, the Nixon administration began a massive program of subpoenaing the files and unused films and photographs of reporters who had been assigned to cover radical groups such as the Weathermen and the Black Panthers, thus seeking to make reporters in effect government informers, and establishing a situation in which radical groups would seek out news coverage only at the risk that anything they revealed to the news media would become subsequently accessible to the government upon demand. Such government subpoenas were upheld by the Supreme Court in the 1972 case of *U.S.* v. *Caldwell,* wherein the court ruled five to four that Earl Caldwell, a *New York Times* reporter assigned to cover the Black Panthers, did not have the right to refuse to reveal his sources to a grand jury. Caldwell subsequently burned all of his records on the Black Panthers rather than risk compromising his relationship to the group. The key vote in the Supreme Court decision was cast by William Rehnquist, who had participated in the subpoenaing of press representatives as assistant attorney general immediately before he was appointed to the court.[251]

Following the Caldwell decision, dozens of newsmen who refused to reveal subpoenaed information or to disclose their sources found themselves threatened with jail terms, and some eventually were imprisoned. CBS and NBC television alone received fifty-two subpoenas between January, 1969 and July, 1971. Rising protests from the news media led the Justice Department to draw up guidelines for further use of subpoenas, and the rate of their use declined after 1970.[252]

In June, 1971, the Nixon administration's assault on freedom of the press reached a new level, when for the first time in American history the federal government sought to enjoin in advance the publication of material in the news media, in the celebrated "Pentagon Papers" case.[253] The attempt to bar publication of the "Pentagon Papers" was ultimately rejected by the Supreme Court in a six to three decision (*New York Times Co. v. U.S.*), but in the meantime the *New York Times*, the *Washington Post*, the *Boston Globe* and the *St. Louis Post Dispatch* were all temporarily banned by federal courts from publishing the "papers." The Supreme Court decision, which cost the *New York Times* $150,000 in legal fees, was a weak reed for freedom of the press, since only two justices held that the First Amendment barred prior restraint under any circumstances, while seven justices indicated prior restraint could be justified under certain conditions. Subsequently, after the Beacon Press of the Unitarian-Universalist Church published the "Pentagon Papers," the Justice Department subpoenaed all of the church's bank records — not those of Beacon Press only — including copies of every check written and deposited between June 1 and October 15, 1971. Following disclosure of this action, donations to the church declined, and church president Robert West stated that nearly everywhere he had spoken about the government action he had been asked, "If I buy a copy of the Pentagon Papers, am I subject to investigation? Will a file be opened on me?"[254]

By 1971, effects of the Nixon administration's attack on the press were evident throughout the news media. According to one study of the Nixon administration and the press, "The administration substantially succeeded in making the press more timid," and news media began to neglect stories unfavorable to Nixon and to "scrape for the 'good news' favored by the administration."[255] One survey of the effect of the administration's pressure on the press issued in 1971 concluded that there had been a "subtle tendency — almost impossible to document or measure — of the press itself to pull back; to consider the controversiality of its actions before it takes them, and then, in some cases, not to take these actions — to engage in self-censorship."[256] Thus, one newscaster, responsible for deciding the content of a local station's news program, stated:

> It's a matter of deciding that a project you want to undertake and that you *would* have undertaken before, just might not be worth the trouble to undertake now. It's the worst form of censorship, I think. It literally chills me when I think about and see it, and I have been seeing it.[257]

According to a leading account of the Watergate scandal, most of the press shied away from investigating the Watergate break-in before the 1972 election "in large part because the administration's three year campaign of intimidation had succeeded beyond its wildest expectations."[258]

The administration added to the pressure in April, 1972 when the anti-trust division of the Justice Department filed suit against the three major TV networks. Although the origins of the suit are not clear, both CBS and ABC charged in response that the Nixon administration was retaliating against the networks for their news coverage. CBS White House Correspondent Dan Rather stated in an affidavit that he had been "quietly and privately threatened" by White House press secretary Ron Ziegler, domestic affairs advisor John Erlichman and counsel Charles Colson. CBS President Frank Stanton said Colson had phoned him in November, 1972, and warned that unless CBS substantially changed its news treatment that things would get "much worse" for CBS and that the White House would bring CBS to its "knees" financially.[259] In December, 1972, White House Telecommunications Director Clay Whitehead warned local television stations that they might lose their licenses if they failed to correct "ideological plugola" allegedly supplied to them in network broadcasts. In October, 1973, White House speechwriter Pat Buchanon stated that "every legal and constitutional means" should be taken to "break the power of the networks."[260]

Following the Watergate break-in, the main focus of White House wrath became the *Washington Post,* which covered and uncovered the story far more than any other paper. The White House Press office unleashed what one reporter termed "perhaps the most ferocious attack in American history" on the credibility of the *Post* and resorted to such petty tactics as excluding sixty-eight year old *Post* social events reporter Dorothy McCardle from covering White House gatherings. Behind the scenes, in September, 1972, President Nixon told White House Counsel John Dean that the Post would have "damnable, damnable problems" as the result of its Watergate coverage, and specifically referred to broadcasting stations owned by the *Post.* Three and a half months later, the only challenges filed in the country before the FCC against the renewal of licenses for any TV stations in the country were filed against two *Post*-owned stations in Florida. Prominent political supporters of Nixon turned out to be involved in the challenges.[261]

HARASSMENT OF DEMONSTRATORS

In addition to the bringing of conspiracy prosecutions against radical leaders, the transformation of the grand jury into a political intelligence agency and the attempt to intimidate the liberal press, the Nixon administration also embarked on a number of other overt repressive actions. Anti-war demonstrations were particular targets of wrath of the Nixon administration, and strenuous efforts were made to discourage, harass, and in some cases illegally arrest demonstrators. This was particularly true of the administration's handling of the November, 1969 "Moratorium" and the May, 1971 "Mayday" demonstrations in Washington, D.C.

Although anti-war demonstrations in October, 1969, had drawn over two hundred thousand protesters across the nation and no serious incidents of any kind occurred, Justice Department and FBI officials preceded the planned November, 1969 "Moratorium" with numerous suggestions that violence and bloodshed would dominate the demonstrations, and that communists were in control.[262] In preparation for the demonstration, the Nixon administration announced publicly that over forty thousand troops and police would be on hand or on alert, and for the first time since the 1932 Bonus March, machine guns were set up on the steps of the Capitol building. Justice Department officials at first refused to grant parade permits, while FBI agents visited bus companies which had agreed to bring demonstrators to Washington and "hinted broadly about communists, violence, subpoenas and the possibility of damage to buses."[263]

On November 13, the first day of the demonstrations, 186 persons were arrested while peacefully praying on the public concourse of the Pentagon. Their convictions were subsequently overturned by a federal court of appeals which noted that the government had discriminatorily enforced the regulation barring disorderly conduct on government property under which the arrests had been made.[264] During the major demonstration held on November 15, over two hundred fifty thousand persons marched in the largest political demonstration in American history, without significant incident. The only incidents of violence during the three days of demonstrations were minor — a clash between tear gas throwing police, who attempted to break up an unauthorized march, and rock throwing and window-breaking militants on the evening of November 14; and the breaking of about eight windows at the Justice Department by a crowd on November 15, following the main demonstration, broken up with the massive use of tear gas which affected thousands of innocent passerby. A total of about 160 arrests were made during the entire demonstrations, aside from the Pentagon Prayer arrests.

Although Washington, D.C. officials praised the conduct of the demonstrators, Justice Department officials afterwards characterized the demonstration as dominated by violence and threatened prosecutions under the Anti-Riot Act. FBI officials subsequently obtained bank records of persons who had written checks to cover the costs of bus transportation to the demonstration from New York.[265]

The climax of the Nixon administration's hostility to anti-war demonstrations came in response to the so-called "Mayday" demonstrations of May 3-5, 1971.[266] Mayday organizers had openly called for demonstrations to block rush-hour traffic in Washington and "stop the government." Washington police supplemented by Army and National Guard troops, and operating under instructions from top Nixon administration officials, responded to demonstrators who illegally attempted to block streets and bridges with automobiles, trash cans and their own bodies with a program of massive, indiscriminate and clearly illegal arrests. On May 3, seventy-two hundred persons were arrested, the largest total in any single day in American history, with the possible exception of the

Palmer Raids. In the course of making the arrests, police abandoned all normal arrest procedures, including recording the names and alleged misdeeds of the arrestees. Hundreds of innocent bystanders, including journalists and government employees on their way to work, were scooped up in the police dragnet, and then held in overcrowded jail cells or in a hastily erected outdoor stockade. In subsequent days, another sixty-two hundred persons were arrested, including twelve hundred arrested while peacefully listening to a speech on the Capitol steps on May 5. President Nixon subsequently praised Washington police for a "magnificent job" and Attorney General John Mitchell urged local police to follow the example. Deputy Attorney General Richard Kleindeinst announced that police procedures had been justified under the doctrine of "'qualified' martial law," a constitutional doctrine which was previously unknown, but which had the virtue, as the Washington ACLU branch pointed out, of imposing "the conditions of martial law in fact" while avoiding a "formal proclamation with its legal requirements."[267]

In the aftermath of the Mayday arrests, thousands of cases were thrown out of court or dismissed by government prosecutors. A total of about 625 persons pled no contest or guilty, while 122 were convicted after pleading not guilty and 1000 persons forfeited bail, out of the 13,400 arrested. In September, 1974, a federal district judge ordered all no contest and guilty pleas be invalidated unless the government could prove they were not coerced, and ordered all arrest records stemming from the Mayday demonstrations destroyed. Another court decision declared unconstitutional the 1967 law banning demonstrations on the capitol grounds, thereby invalidating the May 5 arrests. In January, 1975, a federal district court jury awarded twelve million dollars to those arrested on the Capitol grounds, including damages for violation of first and fourth amendment rights, for false imprisonment, for cruel and unusual punishment and for malicious prosecution.[268]

In July, 1975, U.S. district court Judge Joseph C. Waddy issued a sweeping opinion which found massive civil rights violations and unnecessary police violence during every major demonstration in Washington, D.C. since 1969, and ordered the erasure of illegal arrest records for the 1969-1975 period.[269]

Another overt repressive measure taken by the Nixon administration was an attempt to revive the SACB, moribund since a 1969 federal court decision had declared unconstitutional the attempt by Congress and the Johnson administration to revive it in 1968.[270] In July, 1971 Nixon issued an executive order which expanded the classes of organizations whose members could be barred from federal employment on loyalty grounds, and simultaneously issued an executive order giving the SACB the power to update the Attorney General's list of subversive organizations (unchanged since the mid 1950's) in order to determine which groups fell within the new loyalty directive. The SACB was to hold hearings on organizations before placing groups on the list in compliance with the Supreme Court's decision in *McGrath*.[271] However, since the SACB had been originally established and its power defined in the 1950 Internal Security Act, Congress deleted all funds for the SACB in October, 1972, on the grounds that the executive order was usurping congressional authority. Subsequently, the Nixon administration abolished the SACB in 1973, by dropping it from the budget, and in June, 1974 Nixon abolished the Attorney General's list by executive order, and ordered federal agencies not to use, publish or circulate it in any way.[272]

Although the political repression of the Nixon period was overwhelmingly an executive branch-initiated program (unlike the 1950-54 period when the legislative branch led the way), Congressional red-hunting committees were not silent during the Nixon administration. Thus, in 1969 the Senate Permanent Subcommittee on Investigations issued subpoenas to a number of leading universities, seeking information on persons and groups allegedly involved in campus disorders, including the names of all officers and faculty advisors of all campus organizations, and records identifying all persons who took part in the Columbia sit-in and building occupation of 1968.[273] Domestic subversion and disorders were studied in 1969 and 1970 by the Investigations Subcommittee, along with the Senate and House Internal Security Committees (the latter having changed its name from the House Un-American Activities Committee). The hearings of the Investigations Subcommittee into the finances of the Black Panther Party in 1969 appear to have been instrumental in the decision of the IRS to give special attention to "extremist" organizations. In 1970, HISC asked 179 schools to report the names and dates of appearances of all guest lecturers on their campuses between September, 1968 and May, 1970, along with the names of the groups sponsoring the speakers and the amounts and sources of payments to the speakers. Although a federal district judge barred HISC from printing the list of "radical" speakers subsequently compiled, the committee did so anyway. In 1971, HISC subpoenaed officials of and held hearings into leading anti-war groups such as the New Mobilization Committee to End the War in Vietnam and the Progressive Labor Party (PLP). In May, 1975, the Supreme Court upheld in *Eastland* v. *U.S. Servicemen's Fund* subpoenas issued by SISS and HISC for the bank records of several anti-war groups, including the *Servicemen's Fund*, which had financed underground newspapers and coffee houses near military bases, and PLP.[274]

Covert Repression Directed by the White House

The covert and overt forms of political repression during the Nixon administration discussed thus far were massive in scope, yet they (with the possible exception of IRS activities) essentially simply expanded precedent that had been well-established by previous administrations. A third facet of political repression during the Nixon years marked a sharp departure from past types of repression in two ways. The Nixon administration set up and administered from within the White House and the White House-controlled Committee for Re-Election of the President in 1972 (CRP) its own political surveillance and operations network, instead of relying on the traditional agencies. Further, the Nixon administration, operating through this network, applied to a "mainstream" party — the Democratic Party — techniques of wiretapping, burglary, massive political intelligence operations and harassment that had previously been reserved for "extremist" groups. The discovery of these two aspects of Nixonian political repression ultimately led to the President's resignation.

The tendency of the Nixon White House to develop its own intelligence and operations apparatus and to apply these techniques to the Democratic Party were evident early in the administration. Beginning in 1969, two former New York City policemen, John Caulfield and Anthony Ulasewicz, were hired for the purpose of obtaining sensitive political information.[275] Ulasewicz later testified his job was to uncover "political dirt" on leading Democratic contenders for the presidency in 1972, including Senators Edward Kennedy and Edmund Muskie. He also investigated a number of other people annoying to the White House, including Richard M. Dixon, a comedian who made a living imitating the President. In June, 1969, Caulfield, at the request of White House Domestic Affairs Advisor John Erlichman arranged for a wiretap to be placed on the phone of columnist Joseph Kraft, and in the fall of 1970, again at Erlichman's request, Caulfield monitored a wiretap which the Secret Service had placed on Nixon's brother, Donald. Caulfield's other duties included investigating tax-exempt organizations which displeased the Nixon administration.[276]

Beginning in May, 1969, President Nixon ordered the FBI to wiretap seventeen persons, including four newsmen, allegedly in connection with news leaks which jeopardized national security information.[277] The taps were maintained outside of normal FBI channels and violated Justice Department guidelines for wiretaps conducted without judicial warrants. Two of the wiretaps were maintained on the phones of former National Security Council employees after they left government employment and were working in the campaign of Democratic presidential contender Edmund Muskie. The House Judiciary Committee concluded during its 1974 impeachment investigation that the wiretaps did not concern national security but were installed "for political purposes, in the President's interest and on his behalf."[278] The tapping program was terminated in February, 1971. In July, 1971, Nixon ordered that records of the taps be moved from FBI headquarters to the White House apparently out of fear that FBI Director Hoover would use his knowledge of the taps to blackmail Nixon into retaining Hoover.

Beginning in the spring of 1971, White House officials prepared scores of list of "enemies" and "opponents" of the Nixon administration.[279] An August, 1971, memorandum from White House Counsel John Dean indicates that the purpose of the lists was to facilitate use of the "available federal machinery to screw our political enemies" in such areas as "grant availability, federal contracts, litigation, prosecution, etc." One "enemies" list containing the names of over five hundred McGovern supporters was turned over to the IRS by Dean in September, 1972, with the request that IRS determine what information could be developed on the individuals. Another "enemies" list contained the names of over two hundred prominent Democratic politicians and supporters, along with academics, journalists, and celebrities, including football star Joe Namath, actors Gregory Peck and Paul Newman, one Nobel and four Pulitzer Prize winners, the President of Yale University and the Dean of the Harvard Law School. Another list included one person who had donated $1 to the Muskie campaign, along with all one hundred persons who had taken part in a dinner tribute to union leader Victor Reuther.

In July, 1971, following publication of the "Pentagon Papers," the White House established a "special investigations unit," later known as the "Plumbers," under the supervision of Erlichman, allegedly for the purpose of stopping news leaks.[280] The "plumbers" subsequently obtained from the CIA (with White House assistance) a psychological profile of Daniel Ellsburg, who was indicted in the "Pentagon Papers" case, and broke into the office of Ellsburg's psychiatrist in an attempt to develop material which could be used to discredit him.

In the autumn of 1971, White House Chief of Staff Robert Haldeman approved the hiring of Donald Segretti as part of a plan to develop "political intelligence and covert activities" for the 1972 presidential campaign.[281] From September, 1971, until March, 1972, Segretti recruited twenty-two persons to infiltrate and disrupt the Democratic primaries, and was paid over $45,000 in salaries and expenses by Nixon's personal lawyer, Herbert Kalmbach. Officials of the Committee for the Re-Election of the President (CRP) simultaneously hired about five other agents who infiltrated the campaigns of Democratic candidates. The focus of the activities of the twenty-five to thirty Republican agents was to weaken the candidacy of Sen. Edmund Muskie, who in early 1971 was running ahead of Nixon in public opinion polls, and to foster splits within the Democratic Party and prevent the party from uniting on one candidate. In many cases, the Republican agents distributed phony campaign material or purchased phony advertisements designed to discredit or embarass Democratic candidates and cause dissension within the Democratic Party. For example, flyers were distributed misrepresenting the position of Democratic candidates and falsely promising food and liquor at Democratic meetings. In one case a phony press release prepared on the stationary of presidential hopeful Hubert Humphrey claimed that another presidential candidate had previously been confined to an insane asylum; in another case a counterfeit letter prepared on Muskie stationary charged that two other candidates had been involved in sexual improprieties. In a number of cases anonymous material was prepared attacking or embarassing to various candidates, and then Republican agents informed newspapers or other candidates that the material had been prepared by one of the other presidential hopefuls. The Senate Watergate Committee later concluded that these tactics "helped to leave the Democratic Party bitterly divided at the close of the Presidential primaries."[282]

Beginning in April, 1972, CRP funds were used to finance a political intelligence operation which involved two break-ins and attempts to wiretap the Democratic National Committee. During the second break-in, on June 17, 1972, the burglars were caught, leading to the so-called "Watergate" scandal. A score of prominent CRP and Republican officials, including White House aides Dean, Haldeman and Erlichman, and former Attorney General and campaign director John Mitchell were convicted and sentenced to jail in connection with the break-in and subsequent attempt to "cover up" ties between the burglars and the CRP.[283]

In July, 1974, the House Judiciary Committee recommended that President Nixon be impeached. One of the three proposed articles of impeachment charged that Nixon had

> repeatedly engaged in conduct violating the constitutional rights of citizens, impairing the due and proper administration of justice and the conduct of lawful inquiries, or contravening the laws governing agencies of the executive branch and the purposes of these agencies.

Among the specific charges made in the article were that Nixon had misused the IRS, the FBI, the Secret Service and other executive personnel "in violation of or disregard of the constitutional rights of citizens" by directing that investigations be made for purposes "unrelated to national security, the enforcement of laws or any other lawful function of his office" and had authorized and permitted a "secret investigative unit" to function within the White House which "engaged in covert and unlawful activities and attempted to prejudice the constitutional right of an accused to a fair trial."[284] In essence, this was a charge that the President had engaged in unacceptable types of political repression.

On August 8, 1974, President Richard M. Nixon announced that he would resign, following the revelation that in June, 1972, he had directed the CIA to head off an FBI investigation which might trace the Watergate break-in to the CRP.

In the end, what destroyed the Nixon administration was its attempt to use the same techniques of political repression against the Democratic Party that had long been utilized — and at least generally known about, with little perceptible protest — against "radical" and "extremist" groups. As Noam Chomsky, a leading academic who became a major spokesman for the anti-war movement stated bitterly:

> Plainly what CREEP (a designation sometimes used for CRP) was doing to the Democrats is insignificant in comparison with the bi-partisan at-

tack on the Communist Party in the post war period, or, to take a less familiar case, the campaign against the Socialist Workers Party. . . . Serious civil rights and anti-war groups have regularly discovered government provocateurs among their most militant members. Judicial and other harassment of dissidents and their organizations has been common practice, whoever happens to be in office. . . . Watergate is, indeed a deviation from past practice, not so much in scale or in principle as in the choice of targets. The targets now include the rich and respectable, spokesmen for official ideology, men who are expected to share power, to design social policy and to mold popular opinion. Such men are not fair game for persecution at the hands of the state.[285]

State and Local Repression, 1965-75

The upsurge in political repression on the federal level beginning in about 1965 was matched by a similar trend on the state and local levels. One of the major developments in states and localities during the late 1960's and early 1970's, as on the federal level, was an enormous increase in political surveillance. According to one journalistic estimate, by January, 1972, more than five hundred municipalities had political intelligence divisions, generally known as "Red Squads," attached to their police operations.[286] Another journalistic account estimated that about forty-six hundred agents were assigned to local police intelligence work.[287] In addition to the local "Red Squads," many states including Texas, Oklahoma, Massachusetts and New Jersey, had their own intelligence operations. Indicative of the growth of such forces during the Vietnam War period are published accounts indicating that the Los Angeles intelligence division jumped from 84 men in 1969 to 167 in 1970; the Detroit force, formed in 1961, grew to 70 by 1968; and the New York squad jumped from 123 in 1968 to 361 in 1972. By 1969, in the Chicago area alone, over 1,000 agents from city, county, state and federal intelligence agencies were reported working on political intelligence assignments.[288] Illinois State Police Superintendant James T. McGuire reported, "I've never seen anything like the intensity of the current investigations in all my years in law enforcement."[289] Both Chicago and Philadelphia reportedly had more agents assigned to political intelligence than to organized crime.[290]

Most of these intelligence agencies carried out activities similar to those of the FBI, except on a local operational scale, including the building of massive intelligence files, the overt surveillance and photographing of political demonstrations, and the infiltration — and in some cases, provocation — of dissident groups. At its height, the New York City intelligence operation had files on 1.2 million persons and on one hundred twenty-five thousand organizations; these files were ordered cut back to 240,000 names and twenty-five thousand organizations in early 1973 after it was revealed that the CIA had trained fourteen New York City police officers in how to organize intelligence files. Los Angeles police officials announced in April, 1975, that they were destroying about two million files on fifty-five thousand persons that went all the way back to the days of the IWW in the 1920's; they also stated they had decided to keep files on another twenty-five hundred persons.[291]

The head of Philadelphia's anti-subversive squad boasted on nationwide TV in 1970 that his unit had files on eighteen thousand persons and six hundred organizations, while Oklahoma's intelligence agency revealed in an application for federal funding that it had files on six thousand political dissidents and on eight hundred six organizations.[292]

The criteria that many of these local and state intelligence operations used in order to determine who should be placed under surveillance were frequently so vague that virtually any political protest activity could be and often was included. Thus, the commander of the New Orleans intelligence division testified in court that his men attended and took pictures at all public events at which views they considered "controversial" were expressed.[293] An assistant to the city manager of Albuquerque, New Mexico, stated that undercover agents were assigned to the University of New Mexico campus whenever "feeling is developing" over a campus or national political issue.[294] The head of Chicago's intelligence unit stated that his squad maintained surveillance over "any organization that could create problems for the city or the country."[295] A representative of the Philadelphia red squad reported coverage of "all meetings, rallies, lectures, marches, sit-ins, laydowns, fasts, vigils or any other type of demonstration that has ominous overtones."[296] The Massachusett Division of Subversive Activities (abolished by the state legislature in late 1971) reported in 1969 that it kept a file of "peace groups, civil rights and other such groups, where, due to the enthusiasm, they might have a tendency to adopt or show a policy of advocating the commission of acts of force or violence to deny other persons their rights under the constitution."[297]

As the result of the publication of a Chicago grand jury report in November, 1975, the activities of Chicago police intelligence have been more carefully studied than any other local or state intelligence squad. The grand jury concluded that Chicago police intelligence operations had "assaulted the fundamental freedoms of speech, association, press and religion, as well as the constitutional right to privacy of hundreds of individuals" and had nothing to show for "their intensive efforts except a substantial waste of time and money."[298] The grand jury said it was "shocked by the limited education and lack of training" of intelligence officers, and reported that Chicago police intelligence reports contained "unwarranted, unsupported and erroneous characterizations, assumptions, and conclusions." The jury reported that beginning in 1969 the police "launched a massive intelligence campaign" against Chicago community groups, none of which advocated violence or exhibited any history of violence. The "true motivation" for spying on community groups was political, the jury reported, noting that all of the groups investigated "at one time or another were critical of the policies of the Mayor of Chicago."

As part of the investigation, the jury reported that Chicago police attended public meetings called by the target groups, penetrated private planning sessions of the organizations and attempted to assume leadership roles. The grand jury also noted that the police maintained "extensive intelligence files" on certain "elected officials who were critical of the local political power structure." According to press accounts, among the names contained in Chicago intelligence files were those of Republican mayoral candidate John Hoellen, State Senators Robert Mann and Richard Newhouse, Sears Roebuck & Company Chairman Arthur Woods, University of Notre Dame President Theodore Hesburgh and former football star Gayle Sayers. One Chicago police official maintained, "The names of prominent people ended up in police files because they were in, at, near, or in the presence of somebody under police surveillance, be he a commie, hood, or some other subversive."[299]

Among the fruits of other state and local intelligence organizations were the following:

- Houston police gathered information on many prominent citizens, including Congressmen Bob Casey and Barbara C. Jordan, U.S. District Judge Woodrow Seal, local ministers, judges and businessmen and local state and federal officials. Baltimore police had files on local newsmen and political officials, including Congressman Parren J. Mitchell and State Senator Clarence Mitchell. Seattle police had similar files on scores of prominent citizens, including U.S. Attorney Stan Pitkin.[300]

- The Texas Department of Public Safety opened an investigation of an airline pilot who had publicly opposed the construction of a nuclear power station near Dallas on environmental and safety grounds. An Alabama state agency, the Alabama Commission to Preserve the Peace, spied on faculty members and students at two state universities and kept tabs on some black public officials, civil rights groups and persons it considered "hippies."[301]

- The New York State police maintained extensive noncriminal intelligence records on hundreds of thousands of public officials, private citizens and organizations. Among those who were subjects of files were New York City Mayor John Lindsay, Congressmen Herman Badillo, Shirley Chisholm, Charles B. Rangel and Benjamin Rosenthal, members of the New York legislature, actor Dustin Hoffman, cartoonist Jules Feiffer, anthropologist Ashley Montagu and Women's rights leaders Gloria Steinem and Betty Friedan.[302]

State and local intelligence units cooperated closely with the FBI and other intelligence gathering organizations. Thus, the commander of the New Orleans Red-Squad stated that the contents of his files were passed on to "every conceivable authority that might have an interest in causing any prosecution or further investigation of the persons."[303] The Massachusetts State unit reported that it cooperated with the FBI, HISC, the Immigration and Naturalization Service, Army Intelligence, the SACB, CSC, the Department of Defense, the Treasury Department and other branches of the Massachusetts State government. The New York City unit indicated that it shared its files with thirty-two other agencies ranging from the FBI and IRS on the federal level to the Board of Education and the Waterfront Commission on the local level.[304] The Chicago Grand Jury reported that the security and confidentiality of Chicago intelligence files were "non-existent" and that "nearly anyone remotely connected with any public office had almost unlimited access to the information."[305]

In many cases, information from "Red Squad" files were disseminated in highly unusual ways. Between 1964 and 1968 the Massachusetts state agency made 11,312 "security name checks" of persons on file for the benefit of corporations and private agencies. In cities in Massachusetts and California, political intelligence information was leaked to newsmen for the purpose of damaging the campaigns of persons running for public office. Los Angeles files on the political opponents of two city councilmen were made available to the councilmen by police; other Los Angeles files on liberal and political organizations which were administering federal grants were transmitted to Los Angeles congressmen in hopes of getting the funds cut off.[306]

In a number of cases, local police intelligence agents played crucial roles in radical groups. Thus, a Texas state police agent was elected chairman of the University of Texas SDS, and the co-chairman of an SDS group in Columbia, South Carolina, described as "probably the best liked and most trusted person in the movement in South Carolina," turned out to be an agent for the South Carolina Law Enforcement Division.[307] The Chicago Grand Jury reported that after one police intelligence agent became the president of a community group he had been assigned to infiltrate the organization began to "experience a loss of membership and was soon in financial difficulty."[308]

In some cases, local police intelligence agents actively attempted to harass, disrupt or provoke dissident groups. Numerous cases have been documented for the Chicago area. Thus, one Chicago police agent led an SDS sit-in and participated in a Weatherman action which ended in his expulsion from Northeastern Illinois State College for throwing the college president off a stage.[309] Another Chicago undercover agent admitted in a 1970 case that he had supplied money and purchased chemicals used to produce explosives, and that he had burglarized the Chicago apartment of a cousin of a Weatherman defendant. Subsequently the material which had been burglarized was suppressed in court as illegally seized, but the victim of the burglary was later questioned about some of the same material before a grand jury.[310] In October, 1975, charges against seven Chicago defendants accused of attacking police officers were dropped by the prosecution because the disorder leading to the charges was caused by an infiltrator attacking a police sergeant.[311]

Chicago newspapers reported in April, 1975, that Chicago police and Army Intelligence had cooperated to finance and direct right-wing terrorist activities against political dissidents in northern Illinois from 1969 to 1971.[312] The Chicago Grand Jury report of November, 1975, indicated that the Chicago police and Army Intelligence had frustrated its investigation by destroying evidence and refusing to cooperate, but that Chicago police officers had testified that they "believed it their duty" to burglarize offices and to "disrupt the activities of organizations by destroying mailing lists, lists of financial contributors, office equipment and even by stealing money." One Chicago police officer testified that he had become the president of an organization he infiltrated and urged members to commit acts of violence. According to the Grand Jury, the officer specifically urged members of the group to shoot police officers and "demonstrated the most strategic placement of snipers in downtown Chicago which would make possible the highest number of casualties."[313]

Cases in which police intelligence officers acted as *agents provocateur* in cities other than Chicago included the following.

- Oakland Policemen Robert Wheeler testified during the "Oakland Seven" conspiracy trial that he had been in charge of communication at demonstrations at the Oakland Induction Center that led to the trial, and that he had provided organizers with walkie-talkie equipment. Another Oakland policeman, Bruce Coleman, testified that he had volunteered to provide firecrackers for use against the police and that his job as an undercover agent had included explaining demonstration tactics to an SDS meeting.[314]
- Miami police admitted that one of their undercover agents offered to help one of the defendants in the "Gainesville Eight"[315] trial purchase machine guns. Major Adam Klimkowski, commander of the Miami police Special Investigation Section, stated, "We were hoping for the overt act necessary to produce a charge of conspiracy."[316]
- Two of the four persons who closed the University gates at Ohio State University in Columbus, in April, 1970, later turned out to be undercover agents of the Ohio State Highway Patrol. The closing of the gates touched off disorders which led to the dispatch of the Ohio National Guard to the campus and the shooting of many students by police.[317]
- In a 1969 Los Angeles case in which two men were charged with transferring hand grenades without filling out federal registration forms, it turned out that a Los Angeles policeman had supplied the grenades involved.[318]

State and local political repression during the Vietnam War era was by no means restricted to surveillance and covert operations. Local police and state national guard also were involved in numerous instances of excessive use of force, including a number of killings, against both peaceful and not-so-peaceful demonstrators.[319] The frequently excessive violence displayed by these law officials undoubtedly was partially a reflection of the widely-held belief among police officials, fostered by the FBI, that anti-war demonstrators were either communists or under communist influence. Aside from the repeated public statements to this effect by FBI Director Hoover, the FBI transmitted its view of protesters as part of a communist conspiracy through its regular program of seminars, briefing and training of local police.[320] A government study commission reported in 1969 that police viewed "students, other anti-war protesters and blacks as a danger to our political system" and that their "response to mass protest has resulted in steady escalation of conflict, hostility and violence." According to one study of the police forces of five major cities, the police were "coming to see themselves as the political force by which radicalism, student demonstrations and black power can be blocked."[321]

The most notorious episode of excessive police violence occurred during the 1968 Chicago demonstrations during the Democratic National Convention. Subjected to obscene catcalls from many demonstrators and, from a small minority, showers of rocks and sticks, Chicago police responded with what a government study panel (the "Walker Commission") termed "unrestrained and indiscriminate" violence which at times, "can only be called a police riot."[322] The Walker commission commented:

> The violence was made all the more shocking by the fact that it was often inflicted upon persons who had broken no law, disobeyed no order, made no threat. These included peaceful demonstrators, onlookers, and large numbers of residents who were simply passing through, or happened to live in, the areas where confrontations were occurring.[323]

Over one thousand civilians suffered injuries at the hands of the Chicago police during the week of the convention — over five times the reported injuries to police. Indicative of the indiscriminate — or perhaps the planned — nature of the police violence was the fact that over sixty-five of the three hundred newsmen assigned to cover the convention demonstrations suffered injuries at the hands of the police.

While the 1968 convention disorders in Chicago attracted the most press attention, similar police behavior was a frequent accompaniment of demonstrations during the Vietnam War period. In June, 1967, Los Angeles police attacked peaceful demonstrators gathered in front of a hotel where President Johnson was speaking, clubbing and beating men and women, elderly persons, children and invalids, pulling people out of cars in the area and beating them, and destroying demonstrators' placards. About two hundred people were injured and forty had to be hospitalized.[324] Demonstrators who attempted to close down the Oakland, California, induction center by surrounding the building on October 17, 1967, "were warned by police to move, and then were assaulted. No other word applies. . . . Demonstrators, reporters and bystanders were clubbed indiscriminately, and attempts to resist goaded the police to inevitable excess."[325] Following the police assault, many demonstrators showed up at the Oakland center on October 20, 1967, dressed in motorcycle helmets and carrying shields, and responded to police attacks by barricading streets with motor vehicles, trees and garbage cans.[326]

On October 18, 1967, during a sit-in which obstructed a corridor in a building at the University of Wisconsin in an attempt to block campus recruitment by the Dow Chemical Company, Madison and University police attacked students with fists and nightsticks after they were pushed out of the building when they tried to enter. When the students emerged from the building, some bleeding and bruised, and some dragged out by the police, onlookers outside the building tried to obstruct the police. Students threw rocks and bricks, and police responded with tear gas and mace. Seven police and sixty-five students were treated at hospitals for injuries resulting from the melee.[327] Following blockages of traffic during a demonstration protesting a speech by Secretary of State Dean Rusk in New York in November, 1967, mounted police forced one group of demonstrators back against a ledge, while a line of police standing on the ledge attacked the crowd from the rear. On December 8, 1967, New York police ordered a crowd to disperse from a demonstration in front of a federal office building, and when the crowd refused, trapped the demonstrators in front of an iron fence and attacked with clubs.[328]

In January, 1968, after a few demonstrators gathered outside a San Francisco hotel where Secretary Rusk was speaking threw objects, police indiscriminately attacked with clubs.[329] In March, 1968, New York police suddenly attacked a "Yippie" demonstration at Grand Central Station, indiscriminately clubbing protesters. A month later, New York police made a similar attack on demonstrators at Washington Square.[330] During April, and May, 1968, New York police beat demonstrators, faculty and onlookers with nightsticks, blackjacks, fists and handcuffs, and threw some students and dragged others down steps by their hair, while breaking up student sit-ins at Columbia University.[331] Daniel Bell, the noted sociologist who was not regarded as sympathetic by most protesters, wrote that during the first "bust" in April, that the "police simply ran wild."[332] The blue-ribbon commission appointed by Columbia University to investigate the disorders concluded that during the second "bust" in May, "police engaged in acts of individual and group brutality for which a layman can see no justification unless it be that the way to restore order in a riot is to terrorize civilians."[333]

In April, 1968, Chicago police suddenly and brutally attacked a peaceful demonstration held to protest the war.[334] In June, 1968, police in Berkeley, California attacked a peaceful crowd listening to speeches in support of the French student strike with tear gas, riot batons, sticks and stones. During a weeklong rampage, police used tear gas against private residences, beat crowds leaving movie theatres, gassed first aid stations, broke into a church and smashed cameras of newspaper photographers. Thirty-seven persons were treated for injuries at local hospitals.[335]

An official police investigation of the disturbances reported that "the most common observation was that the police appeared to have 'gone berserk' or 'lost their cool' or otherwise acted in a nonrational way."[336] In December, 1969, peaceful demonstrators gathered outside a hotel in New York to protest President Nixon's appearance were attacked by fist and club-swinging police. In one incident, a number of people were pulled out of a van by police, beaten and arrested, apparently because the driver made a "V" for peace sign, and called out "This is what Richard Nixon's fascist police are going to be like, and don't you forget it."[337]

As student protests escalated, so did the response of local police and state officials, and the indiscriminate shooting of protesters became increasingly common. The first fatality occurred during disorders at Jackson State College in Mississippi in May, 1967, when police fired shotguns at a group of persons advancing on a police barricade, killing one student and wounding two others.[338] In February, 1968, three students were killed and twenty-eight others injured when South Carolina State highway patrolmen fired on them without warning as they were peacefully demonstrating against a segregated bowling alley near South Carolina State College at Orangeburg. Many of the students were shot while lying on the ground; the nine highway patrolmen responsible for the shooting were acquitted and promoted.[339]

In May, 1969, students at Berkeley, California marched on a vacant lot owned by the University of California which they had transformed into a park and which the University had sealed off with an eight foot fence to prevent further unauthorized use of the land. During a week of disorders which followed, police banned peaceful marches, made mass arrests and met protesters, (who were in some cases armed with rocks and bottles) with massive and indiscriminate use of tear gas, shot guns, clubs and bayonets. One person was killed by police fire, another permanently blinded, and about two hundred persons were injured by police gunfire and clubs. At one point, police sprayed the campus with tear gas from a helicopter, thereby gassing classrooms, the University hospital and a recreation area nearly a mile from the campus where women and children were swimming.[340] During the disorders, California Governor Ronald Reagan, who had been elected in 1966 on a platform of "cracking down" on student protesters, proclaimed, "If it's a blood bath they want, let it be now."[341] *Newsweek* commented on the so-called "People's Park" disorders, that the Berkeley police

> had gone on a riot, displaying a lawless brutality equal to that of Chicago, along with weapons and techniques that even the authorities in Chicago did not dare employ: the firing of buckshot at fleeing crowds and unarmed bystanders and the gassing — at times for no reason at all — of entire streets and portions of a college campus.[342]

During the "People's Park" disorders, more casualties occurred than were reported from all of France during the 1968 student and worker protests. Ten deputies and two former deputies were later indicted under federal statutes for shooting demonstrators and bystanders with intent to impose summary punishment. "People's Park" remained a vacant lot in 1976.[343]

Another student was shot and killed by police in May, 1969, at North Carolina Agricultural and Mechanical College.[344] During the so-called "Days of Rage" sponsored by the militant Weatherman faction of SDS in Chicago in October, 1969, one of the first clear instances in which demonstrators initiated violence without provocation, police shot eight demonstrators, and in two cases police squad cars ran at full speed into running crowds.[345] During disorders at the University of California at Santa Barbara in February, 1970, during which students burned a branch of the Bank of America, one student was killed and two were wounded by police gunfire, and hundreds more were injured by police and national guardsmen.[346] In March, 1970, twelve students were shot and fifty-seven injured by police in Buffalo. In April, 1970, about twenty students were wounded, most of them from shotgun fire, during a clash with national guardsmen at Ohio State University.[347]

In the most-well known shooting incident, Ohio national guardsmen shot and killed four students and wounded nine after breaking up a peaceful demonstration at Kent State University on May 4, 1970. Although the official position of the guard was that the lives of guardsmen were in imminent danger from rock-throwing students, only one guardsman was injured enough to require hospitalization, and the nearest of the students killed and wounded was twenty yards away from the guardsmen. Most of the students were shot in the side or in the back. Subsequently a county grand jury absolved the guard, while indicting twenty-five students, ex-students and faculty members on felony charges. Eventually three of those indicted were found guilty or pleaded guilty to minor charges, while one student was acquitted and the other charges were dismissed for lack of evidence.[348]

While the Kent State shootings attracted enormous national attention, the aftermath on the Kent campus was virtually ignored by the national press. During the ten days immediately following the shootings, while the campus was closed, police ransacked every room among Kent State's thirty-one dormitories, without warrants, in search of weapons; they found a total of two hunting weapons, sixty knives, three slingshots, several BB guns and a yellow button which stated, "Dare to struggle, dare to win." Student Body President Craig Morgan, who was among those indicted by the grand jury, and who succeeded in having the charges quashed, was arrested again in May, 1971 at a commemorative demonstration; he subsequently won, along with two others, $5,000 in a malicious prosecution suit. In April, 1972, Reinhold Mohr was arrested by Kent city police for possession of illegal weapons after members of the Kent State VVAW chapter told police he had offered to provide them with a submachine gun and a rocket-propelled grenade launcher. The city police later released Mohr, who had been arrested carrying the weapons, when it was revealed that he was a university undercover agent planted in the VVAW to spy on its members. The university suspended Mohr but he was reinstated by the state civil service agency after the campus police chief testified he was only following orders.[349]

Although a government study commission reported in May, 1971, that the shooting by the Ohio Guard had been "unnecessary, unwarranted and inexcusable," Attorney General John Mitchell refused to convene a federal grand jury to investigate the incident following the refusal of Ohio officials to bring charges. However, in 1974, during the "Watergate" revelations, Attorney General Elliot Richardson convened a federal grand jury which indicted eight guardsmen for conspiracy to violate the civil rights of the students. In November, 1974, Federal Judge Frank Battisti ordered a directed verdict of acquittal on the grounds that the government failed to prove the guardsmen had intentionally set out to violate the students' rights. In August, 1975, a jury returned a verdict of "not guilty" in a civil suit filed by parents of the dead students and by the wounded students against Ohio officials and national guardsmen in connection with the Kent State shootings.[350]

The Kent State shooting was not the last killing of protesters. On May 14, 1970, Jackson City, Mississippi, police and Mississippi state highway patrolmen fired into a dormitory and a crowd of students during student disorders, killing two and wounding twelve. A county grand jury cleared the police, stating that when people engaged "in civil disorders and riots, they must expect to be injured or killed when law enforcement officers are required to reestablish order."[351]

In July, 1970, two students were killed by police at Lawrence, Kansas, and one killed at the University of Wisconsin in Milwaukee.[352] In August, 1970, Los Angeles police attacked a crowd of over twenty thousand Mexican-American anti-war demonstrators with tear gas and nightsticks after a disturbance broke out at a liquor store a block away from the demonstration; during the rioting that followed a newspaper reporter was killed when he was struck in the head by a tear gas projectile fired by a deputy sheriff.[353] In November, 1972, two students were shot to death by deputy sheriffs at Southern University in New Orleans. Subsequently, a special commission established by the Louisiana state attorney general concluded there was "no justification for the shootings."[354]

While police brutality and shootings were perhaps the most visible and physically damaging forms of state and local repression during the Vietnam War era — and for that reason the most likely to receive national press coverage — political dissidents during this period faced many other types of harassment and persecution. Frequently, political repression on the state and local level took bizarre forms. In 1966, the Georgia state legislature became the first such body to refuse to seat an elected representative for political reasons since 1940, when it excluded Julian Bond, director of communications for the Student Nonviolent Coordinating Committee (SNCC), after Bond had endorsed a SNCC statement expressing support for draft resisters. In December, 1966, the Supreme Court ruled unanimously that the Georgia legislature had acted in violation of the first amendment by its action, and ordered Bond seated.[355]

In September, 1969, a red flag law was used to arrest a demonstration leader in Detroit.[356] In 1971, a Pittsburgh store owner was charged under a 1974 blasphemy statute for displaying a poster depicting the face of Christ with the text:

> Wanted: for sedition, criminal anarchy, vagrancy, and conspiracy to overthrow the established government. Dresses poorly; said to be carpenter by trade; ill-nourished; associated with common working people, unemployed and bums. Alien; said to be a Jew.[357]

This prosecution was subsequently dropped.

There were numerous cases in which political dissidents were arrested, and in some cases sentenced to extraordinarily harsh terms, on drug charges, leading to general suspicions among the Left of selective law enforcement or even planting of drugs for the purpose of making arrests.[358] John Sinclair, leader of the radical White Panther Party in Michigan, was sentenced to nine and one-half years in jail for smoking marijuana in the presence of two undercover police agents, while Lee Otis Johnson, a black militant and anti-war organizer at Texas Southern University was sentenced to thirty years for giving a marijuana cigarette to an undercover agent. After long imprisonments, both of these sentences were overturned on appeal.[359] Martin Sostre, the owner of a left-wing bookstore in Buffalo, was sentenced to thirty to forty-one years for possession and sale of heroin in 1968 shortly after charges of arson and riot brought against him in connection with riots in the Buffalo ghetto in 1967 were dropped. Sostre's defenders have presented persuasive evidence that the drugs were planted on him by arresting officers.[360] According to Frank Donner, the ACLU expert on political surveillance, writing in 1971, "The pot bust has become a punitive sanction against political dissent and the threat of prosecution is a favorite method of 'hooking' student informers."[361]

An extraordinary number of prosecutions were begun in states and localities during the Vietnam War era for violations of flag desecration statutes. These cases generally involved prosecutions of persons who in some way altered a flag or displayed it in an unorthodox manner, such as replacing the field of stars with a "peace symbol" or sewing a flag to clothing. The ACLU reported in May, 1971, that it had "easily" one hundred flag cases under consideration.[362] Convictions under flag desecration statutes were overturned, or acquittals were obtained, often on technical grounds, in Hawaii, Minnesota, New York, Colorado, Washington State, New Hampshire, Pennsylvania and California before the Supreme

Court ruled on the issue in three 1974 cases.[363] In March, 1974, the court ruled unconstitutionally vague a Massachusetts law which barred "contemptuous" treatment of the flag in a case in which a nineteen-year-old had been sentenced to a year in jail for walking down the street with a small flag sewn to the seat of his pants. In July, 1974, the court ruled against New York in a case where members of two anti-war groups had been prosecuted for displaying buttons with a peace symbol imposed on the flag. The court ruled unconstitutionally vague in this case New York's law which barred the placement of any "word, figure, design or any advertisement" upon the flag.[364] In *Spence* v. *Washington* (1974) the court overruled a Washington State conviction, under a law similar to the New York statute, for placing a large peace symbol on a flag which was flown out of the window of an apartment. The court decision in this case was based on first amendment grounds.[365]

Despite these rulings, flag prosecutions continued. Thus, in August, 1974, a juvenile court judge in Ohio ordered two teen-age girls to apologize, to attend flag ceremonies for a week, to observe a curfew for six months, and to not communicate with each other in any way for a year, for burning an American flag. In June, 1975, a New Hampshire federal judge upheld a conviction resulting from a case in which a man had sewn a flag to his jacket, even though New Hampshire had repealed the law involved in the meantime. As a result, the man involved faced a $300 fine and four months in jail.[366]

Another series of prosecutions were initiated purely for the use of offensive speech, under disorderly conduct and related laws, and under criminal syndicalism laws which had been unused since the McCarthy days. Beginning with the criminal anarchy prosecution of William Epton in New York in 1964,[367] prosecutions under criminal syndicalism and related statutes were brought in California, Kentucky, Georgia, Mississippi, Arkansas and Ohio.[368] Most of these prosecutions involved so-called "Black Power" advocates whose speeches were alleged to have touched off disorders, but this was not always the case. For example, three anti-poverty workers were arrested for criminal syndicalism in Kentucky in 1967, apparently on the basis of their possession of anti-war literature.[369] In a 1968 Ohio case a leader of the Ku Klux Klan was sentenced to one to ten years for a speech suggesting that "revengeance" might have to be taken "if our President, our Congress, our Supreme Court, continues to suppress the white, Caucasion race."[370] In 1974, a professor at the University of Arkansas was convicted under that state's criminal anarchy law (as well as under a law barring communists from state employment), apparently solely for his admitted membership in the Maoist-oriented Progressive Labor Party.[371] State prosecutions were invalidated when state and federal courts threw out criminal syndicalism laws in Mississippi, Georgia, California and Kentucky. In the Ohio Ku Klux Klan case, *Brandenberg* v. *Ohio* (1969), the Supreme Court overturned the conviction, ruling that states could not forbid advocacy of force or law violation except where such advocacy "is directed to inciting or producing imminent lawless action and is likely to incite and produce such action."[372]

In addition to the criminal syndicalism cases, there appear to have been numerous cases of prosecution under disorderly conduct and related statutes as a result of the utterance of "offensive" language by protesters, judging from the number of such cases reaching the Supreme Court. The Court overturned or remanded with clear instruction to lower courts to overturn six such cases from 1971 to 1974.[373] Thus, in *Cohen v. California* (1971) the Court overturned the conviction of a man who had been tried under a California disturbing-the-peace statute for wearing a jacket bearing the words, "Fuck the Draft," in a Los Angeles Courthouse corridor, although no evidence was presented that any disturbance resulted from his action. In *Hess v. Indiana* (1973) the court reversed on *Brandenberg* grounds the disorderly conduct conviction of a student who had proclaimed "We'll take the fucking street" during an anti-war demonstration after police had moved one hundred demonstrators out of a street they were blocking.[374] In *Lewis v. New Orleans* (1974) the court reversed on grounds of vagueness a conviction under a breach of the speech statute of a woman who had addressed police officers who were arresting her son as "G-d- f——g police."[375] Despite these decisions, in May, 1975, a Cincinnati judge sentenced a nineteen-year-old to thirty days in the workhouse or one day on a pig farm for calling a police officer a "pig," under a disorderly conduct statute.[376]

In addition to speech and flag prosecutions, local authorities in many areas made a practice of general harassment of individuals who "looked" like anti-establishment protesters, particularly those who wore long hair or otherwise looked like "hippies." In the summer of 1967 Philadelphia banned from and arrested "hippies" who congregated in Rittenhouse Square, while police in Denver, in July, 1968, and in New Orleans and Atlanta in the summer of 1970 made wholesale arrests of "hippies" and "street people" under loitering and similar statutes. The American Civil Liberties Union reported in 1973 that "hippies" and "longhairs" were subject to a much higher likelihood of search or harassment while crossing the international border in the state of Washington and while travelling the New Jersey turnpike.[377]

While most of the flag, speech and "hippie" arrests and harassments appear to have been almost random in nature, local police applied a concentrated program of political repression on three elements of the anti-war movement: members of SDS, persons associated with "underground" newspapers, and persons associated with coffeehouses which sought to attract off-base members of the military.

SDS members were the most visible white dissidents and were subjected to not only covert surveillance and infiltration but also petty harassment by local police and, in some cases, open surveillance clearly designed to intimidate. Repression was probably worst in Chicago, the site of

SDS national headquarters. In addition to conducting open surveillance of SDS, Chicago police arbitrarily arrested at least ten persons assigned to the headquarters "for simply driving to the office" during the summer of 1967. In May, 1969 Chicago police and firemen appeared at the office, in response, they declared, to reports of a shooting and a fire in the office. When SDS officials told them there was no shooting or fire, an agreement was reached to the effect that the fire chief alone could inspect the premises. However, a group of firemen attempted to enter the office, and when SDS staff members resisted, police joined in the fray. Five SDS staffers were arrested and held on $1,000 bail on charges of "battery on an officer," "interfering with a fireman" and "inciting mob action."[378] During the 1969 SDS convention in Chicago, Chicago police assigned over five hundred men to "undercover" work. Many of them clustered outside the convention area, taking pictures of everyone in the area. When SDS members complained, one police official told them, "This is America; people can take pictures without fear of harassment."[379]

Radicals who attempted to operate coffeehouses catering to off-base military were another favorite target for local political repression. Coffeehouse organizers at Muldraugh, Kentucky, near Fort Knox, were denied business and health permits by local authorities, and then ordered to close down as a "nuisance" by the local police chief. When the coffeehouse obtained a temporary restraining order from a federal judge in order to remain open, the Meade County grand jury subpoenaed and questioned six of the organizers and then indicted them under public nuisance and sanitation laws.[380] Organizers who opened a coffeehouse near Fort Sill, Oklahoma were arrested for trespassing on government property and sentenced to six months in jail and $500 fines, because, a federal judge stated, "acts of lowering the morale of the troops at Fort Sill are a serious matter."[381] Coffeehouse organizers near Fort Dix, New Jersey, were repeatedly stopped for alleged traffic violations, and state troopers photographed cars and persons in front of the coffeehouse and took down license numbers of cars parked in the lot.[382]

Coffee house organizers and patrons in Columbia, South Carolina, near Fort Jackson, were subjected to two years of relentless surveillance by uniformed and undercover city, county, state and military police. In early 1970, the Richland County Grand Jury issued an indictment charging that the coffeehouse operators were "keeping and maintaining a public nuisance." The day after the indictment was handed down, the coffeehouse staff was arrested and the house was closed and padlocked by police, acting under a court order. Three of the coffee house operators were subsequently sentenced to six years in prison. In the previous eighty years, only ten similar charges had been entered in Richland County, with the longest sentence ever handed down eighteen months. Subsequent national protests were so strong that the local prosecutor agreed to reduce punishment to a year of probation and a suspended sentence. The coffeehouse never reopened and the local movement disappeared.[383]

Workers on "underground" newspapers across the country were especial targets of local police repression. Scores of underground press workers were arrested for drugs, vagrancy, littering, obscenity and a variety of other charges.[384] Shortly after the *San Diego Street Journal* published an expose on a leading local businessmen in the fall of 1969, San Diego police searched the offices without a warrant, arrested more than twenty street vendors for "obstructing the sidewalk" under an ordinance subsequently declared unconstitutional by a municipal court, and then arrested street vendors for littering.[385] (During this same period, the offices of the *Street Journal* were broken into twice and over $4,000 of equipment was stolen; these activities were carried out by an FBI informer and a right-wing terrorist group which he organized.) In October, 1968, Dallas police raided the offices of *Dallas Notes* with a search warrant allowing them to look for "pornographic materials" and carried out over two tons of material, including four typewriters, credit cards and costume jewelry, leaving behind a shambled office strewn with papers and torn-out electrical wiring. Police charged the editor of the *Dallas Notes* with "possession of pornography," a charge thrown out by federal court. Subsequently he was re-arrested for obscenity — a charge which was again thrown out — and then for instigating a riot, a charge which resulted in a three year jail sentence.[386]

Police in Jackson, Mississippi rented a house directly behind the office of the *Kudzu* in order to maintain twenty-four hour surveillance. Subsequently one staff member was detained by police for dropping a cigarette butt in a gutter, and staff members were arrested for possession of marijuana following a search of their office made by eight police with drawn guns. The charge was later dropped for lack of evidence.[387] Street vendors for the *New Orleans Nola Express* were repeatedly arrested for peddling without a license and vagrancy. Federal Judge Herbert Christenberry concluded that the evidence "overwhelmingly established a policy of the police to arrest persons selling underground newspapers under the guise that they were impeding pedestrian traffic" and issued an injunction enjoining the city from further interference with *Nola Express* vendors.[388] Other arrests for obscenity or interference with street vendors were reported in Berkeley, San Francisco, New York, Los Angeles, Atlanta, Milwaukee, Philadelphia, Indianapolis, and throughout the Washington, D.C. metropolitan area. In Montgomery County, Maryland, one man was arrested for *possessing* a copy of an underground paper.[389]

Repression on the Campus

University campuses were the center of anti-war and anti-establishment protest throughout the Vietnam War era, and it is not surprising that many "special" measures were taken by state, local and campus authorities to repress on-campus dissent. While most of these measures were taken directly or indirectly by university authorities, they acted, in many cases, under strong pressure from local, and, especially, state political leaders. Shortly after the Columbia sit-in of April, 1968, state legislatures were flooded with proposals to outlaw various radical organizations and to withold funds from unruly students or insufficiently tough administrators. More than one hundred such bills were introduced in California alone. During the 1969 and 1970 legislative sessions, thirty-two states passed a total of nearly eighty laws dealing with campus unrest. Many of these laws required the withdrawal of financial aid from students committing crimes or violating campus rules. Laws passed in four states demanded the immediate expulsion of students who violated campus rules, and two states required the firing of faculty members who violated such rules. Statutes passed in twelve states demanded the criminal prosecution of persons involved in sit-ins and building takeovers. The strongest and most comprehensive measures were passed in those states where the most extensive and violent campus protests occurred, such as California, New York, Wisconsin and Ohio.[390]

Most of these laws simply imposed *additional* penalties on already unlawful conduct, in effect making students at public colleges or students receiving public financial aid subject to penalties above and beyond what any other person would normally be subject to under disorderly conduct or similar statutes. Further, many of the bills were so vaguely worded that the only clear message they conveyed was that *any* type of protest activity, legal or not, *might* lead to severe penalties, and therefore the only safe course was not to protest at all. The President's Commission on Campus Unrest, headed by former Pennsylvania Governor William Scranton, termed the state laws "anti-student and anti-university laws that range from the unnecessary and ill-directed to the purely vindictive."[391] Analyzing similar federal laws, the Commission said:

> Few of the provisions already enacted clearly define the conditions and conduct that justify withdrawing an individual's financial aid. Each creates substantial administrative difficulties, and the interplay of inconsistent provisions, sometimes applicable to the same student, makes it almost impossible to establish workable guidelines. In many cases it is unclear whether the termination of financial assistance is automatic (upon conviction of a crime, for example) or at discretion of the institution. Due process requirements under these statutes, and the duration of the ineligibility they impose, are insufficiently defined. The statutes discriminate against students who receive federal aid because they have no effect on those, often from wealthy families, who do not.[392]

A New Mexico state court threw out in 1969 that state's law, passed a few months earlier, which banned "wrongful" use of public property, on the grounds of vagueness. The law had been used to arrest six students who were sitting on the porch of the University president's home during a protest. In 1971, a Pennsylvania court threw out a statute which required every college in the country, as a condition of having its students receive Pennsylvania state aid, to agree to report the names of all students dismissed from college or arrested for participating in disturbances. In 1973, a federal court declared unconstitutionally vague Illinois' law, which revoked all state aid for students who participated "in any disorderly disturbance or course of conduct directed against the administration of policies" of any state-supported college. The Illinois law had been used by the chancellor of the University of Illinois to order aid revoked from thirty-nine students who had been arrested following a demonstration, even though they had been subsequently cleared by separate University disciplinary proceedings.[393]

In addition to the special campus legislation, state officials made their displeasure with student demonstrators known to university officials in other ways. State officials, such as California Gov. Ronald Reagan, exercised an extraordinary interest in the details of curriculum and faculty appointments at universities where disruptions had occurred, and in "some states, appropriations for higher education were delayed or denied; in others funds were diverted from major universities and colleges to community colleges where there have been fewer protests."[394] In one state, according to the Scranton Commission, a state university considered "soft" on protesters was the only college denied an increased legislative appropriation; in another state the legislature singled out by name a "soft" dean as ineligible to receive any salary.[395]

The Illinois State Senate passed a special resolution "urging" the University of Illinois not to "recognize" (a term meaning only the use of University meeting rooms and not implying endorsement) a campus branch of the W.E.B. DuBois Clubs shortly after the University Board of Trustees had decided to grant recognition (a decision normally made routinely by the University bureaucracy). Shortly afterwards the Board of Trustees reversed itself and banned the DuBois Club.[396]

In most cases University administrators were not so obtuse as to require such special and overt prodding. As student protests increased in number and violence, colleges increasingly called in local police and national guardsmen, with the inevitable resultant charges of police brutality, which as the Scranton Commission conceded "too often" were true.[397] During the 1968-69 school year, police or guardsmen were called to at least 127 campuses; during the May, 1970, disorders following the Cambodia invasion and the Kent State shootings, guardsmen intervened on twenty-four occasions on 21 campuses in sixteen states.[398] According to the Scranton Commission:

> During a number of recent campus disorders, the Guard has been sent onto campuses prematurely. Sometimes this has been the result of inade-

quate information, planning and coordination. On other occasions, political considerations appear to have contributed to the decision.[399]

Arrests and expulsions of students skyrocketed during the late 1960's. In the spring of 1968, over eleven hundred persons were arrested during campus disorders; in the fall of 1968, over twelve hundred; in the spring of 1969, over four thousand. About three hundred students were expelled or suspended in the spring of 1968; in the spring of 1969 the figure climbed to over one thousand.[400] Certainly not all — perhaps not even most — of these arrests and expulsions or suspensions can be categorized as political repression; undoubtedly in many or most cases serious violations of reasonable laws and/or university regulations occurred. But many of these proceedings involved such large numbers of persons that it is difficult to believe that individual guilt or innocence was carefully considered. For example, during May, 1970, disturbances, Illinois national guardsmen rounded up and arrested over one hundred students on the University of Illinois "quad;" eight hundred ninety-one students were arrested at Mississippi Valley State in February, 1970. Altogether eighteen hundred protesters were arrested during the May 1 through 15, 1970 period.[401]

Increasingly serious charges were brought as protests increased. Thus, one member of the Progressive Labor Party at Harvard was charged with "assault" and given a year in jail for grabbing a dean by the arm, seven Voorhees College students got eighteen to twenty-four month sentences for "rioting" in connection with a building takeover, and three students at San Fernando Valley State received one to twenty-five year terms for conspiracy, false imprisonment and kidnapping for holding administrators temporarily captive during a building seizure.[402]

University administrators used a variety of other weapons in addition to calling in police forces or expelling students in response to rising student protests. At several campuses, court injunctions were obtained to block student sit-ins and building seizures. According to one legal analysis, "too often" the temporary restraining orders obtained from courts in the injunctive process

> are vague or overly broad on their face and thus represent sweeping restrictions on the constitutional rights of other students not directly involved in the confrontation. For these students, the order acts as a system of prior restraints upon their rights to assembly and free speech.[403]

At a number of campuses, radical organizations were completely outlawed. Thus, the W.E.B. Dubois Club was banned at Indiana University as well as the University of Illinois, and by the spring of 1969 SDS had been banned at more than ten publicly supported universities. In *Healy* v. *James* (1972) the Supreme Court declared the banning of SDS at Central Connecticut State College illegal as it was apparently based on no evidence other than the college's dislike of SDS philosophy.[404] Attempts were also made at some publicly supported colleges to ban or interfere with "underground" newspapers. Thus, the *Philadelphia Free Press* was banned from campuses of Pennsylvania State University.[405] In *Papish v. the Board of Curators of the University of Missouri* (1973) the Supreme Court overturned the expulsion of a graduate student who had distributed an underground paper which had on its front page a picture of a policeman raping the Statue of Liberty and the Goddess of Justice, and which contained an article entitled "M--f-- acquitted." The court ruled that "the mere dissemination of ideas — no matter how offensive to good taste — on a state university campus may not be shut off in the name alone of 'conventions of decency.' "[406]

An additional weapon used by University administrators was the firing of left-wing instructors, which reached a level during the 1965-75 period unmatched since the McCarthy days. Among the more notable firings were the following.

- At San Francisco State, months of violent confrontations between students and police (during which seven hundred arrests were made) were set off when Glenn Dumke, Chancellor of the State College system, went over the head of the college president and ordered the suspension of George Murray, an English instructor and Black Panther "Minister of Education," for allegedly advocating that minority students arm themselves for self-protection. Also at San Francisco State, two other professors were fired for their political views, and two were denied tenure, one for his role in the student strike protesting Murray's suspension, and one apparently for his role in hiring Murray originally.[407]

- Staughton Lynd, a widely published expert in American colonial history who travelled to North Vietnam in defiance of the State Department in 1966, was denied employment by the Board of Governors of State Colleges and Universities in Illinois, after being approved for hiring at Chicago State College by the faculty and the college administration. Earlier Lynd had been approved for hiring by the faculties of Northern Illinois University and the University of Illinois at Chicago Circle, but his appointment was blocked by administrators. The Board of Governors announced it was making its decision because Lynd's trip to North Vietnam "goes beyond mere dissent." Subsequently, as a result of nationwide publicity, Chicago State did hire Lynd for a one-year position, but at the end of the year, Lynd was unable to find a tenured position and left academia.[408]

- The Board of Regents of the University of California fired Angela Davis from UCLA because of her Communist Party membership. Although California courts ruled the firing unconstitutional, the Board of Regents refused to reinstate her on the grounds that some of her speeches had been "so extreme . . . and so obviously false" that she was unfit. This decision was made although all appropriate UCLA officials and a special blue-ribbon faculty committee appointed at the request of the regents had supported her.[409]

- Michael Parenti, a political science professor at the University of

Vermont, active in anti-war demonstrations, was denied renewal of his contract by the University Board of Trustees despite unanimous recommendations from his department, his dean and the University administration. Subsequently the trustees issued a statement noting that it did not question Parenti's "professional competence" but that his "professional conduct" had not been acceptable. The chairman of the Trustees explained, "We are required to protect the image of the University." Subsequently Vermont settled a court suit initated by Parenti for $175,000 in damages for an undisclosed sum.[410]

- Peter Bohmer, a radical economics professor at San Diego State College, was ordered fired by the personal intervention of State College Chancellor Dumke, following charges that he discriminated in his grading practices against conservative students, although Bohmer had been cleared of the charges by three separate investigations, and was supported by his department and the San Diego State president.[411]

- Morris Starsky, a philosophy professor at Arizona State University, active in the Socialist Workers Party and one of the most important anti-war leaders in Arizona, was fired in connection with his anti-war activities by the Arizona Board of Regents in 1970, despite support from two faculty committees and the University president. Subsequently, two federal courts ruled the firing was politically motivated and unconstitutional, and it was revealed that the FBI, as part of its SWP COINTELPRO activities, had written an anonymous letter attacking Starsky to one of the faculty committees reviewing his case.[412]

Less publicized political firings occurred at the City University of New York, the University of Connecticut, Oklahoma State University, Indiana State, the University of Wisconsin at Milwaukee, and West Chester State College in Pennsylvania.[413]

Joint Federal-Local Repression of the Black Panthers

The organization which suffered the most from political repression during the Vietnam War era was probably the Black Panthers.[414] The Panthers represented everything that conservative, white American elites feared the most. Not only were they black, but they espoused the need for a Marxist revolution, frequently brandished guns, and loudly proclaimed the right to use violence to defend themselves against attack in language that, to most Americans, was frightening and violated all the rules of polite middle class behavior.

Thus, Panther Minister of Education Eldridge Cleaver, who ran for president on the ticket of the short-lived Peace and Freedom Party in 1968, declared in one of his campaign speeches:

> To all the pigs of the power structure, I say 'Fuck you!' . . . To the pig power structure of Babylon: If you brutalize the people, if you murder the people, then the people have a right to kill you. We want to erase your way of life from the planet Earth and create a world in which people can

live in peace. Someone asked me what my first act will be if I'm elected president and move into the White House. . . . I'll burn the mother fucker down.[415]

While the fact that the Panthers were black unquestionably added to the repression they faced, it was essentially their political ideology and rhetoric that led to that repression, i.e. the Panthers were victims of "political" repression rather than mere racial discrimination.[416]

The Panthers first attracted public attention by strolling into the California capitol building at Sacramento, twenty strong, in May, 1967, carrying loaded rifles and shotguns to protest consideration of a bill forbidding the carrying of loaded weapons within incorporated areas — an action which was perfectly legal at the time. The proposed bill was introduced (and later passed) precisely to deal with the Panthers' habit of carrying loaded weapons in Oakland, California, where the organization was founded, as part of a program which, the Panthers said, was designed to prevent police abuse of blacks. Basking in the publicity which the Sacramento incident and subsequent clashes with police in the Oakland area brought them, the Panthers began to organize chapters across the country. By October, 1968, "healthy and functioning size" chapters were in operation in New York, Chicago, Los Angeles, Denver and Omaha, as well as the San Francisco Bay area. In New York City, nearly eight hundred members were recruited in June, 1968 alone.[417] In the fall of 1968, the Panthers had a membership of over two thousand, and claimed a readership of one hundred thousand for their weekly newspaper, and the party's "fame and influence had grown greatly."[418] At its peak in 1969, before repression began to decimate the party, the Panthers had an estimated membership of five thousand.[419]

As the Panthers expanded in strength, scope and influence, so did police and FBI repression, especially after the election and inauguration of Richard Nixon as president. While most police actions against the Panthers were taken by local authorities, the FBI and the Justice Department encouraged local police and supplied them with intelligence for use against the Panthers, and the FBI engaged in widespread infiltration and attempts to disrupt them. In November, 1968, shortly after Nixon's election, FBI Director J. Edgar Hoover sent instructions to fourteen FBI offices directing agents to "fully capitalize" upon differences between the Panthers and a rival black militant group, United Slaves (US), and to "exploit all avenues of creating further dissension in the ranks of the BPP" including the proposal of "imaginative and hard-hitting counterintelligence measures aimed at crippling the BPP (Black Panther Party)." Subsequently, the Panthers became the main target of the FBI's "Black Nationalist" COINTELPRO begun in 1967; of the total of 295 actions taken as part of the program, 233 were directed against the Panthers between 1968 and early 1971.[420]

The FBI's anti-Panther COINTELPRO actions were the most vicious and intense of the entire COINTELPRO operation. FBI agents in San Diego and Los Angeles attempted to whip up bitter strife and warfare between the Panthers and US, even though they knew their actions might lead to violence and death, by mailing anonymous letters and cartoons to Panthers ridiculing them which the FBI believed the Panthers would blame on US. Four Panthers were killed by US members in 1969 and there were numerous beatings and shootings. According to a Senate Intelligence Committee staff report, "Although individual incidents in this dispute cannot be directly traced to efforts by the FBI, FBI officials were clearly aware of the violent nature of the dispute, engaged in actions which they hoped would prolong and intensify the dispute, and proudly claimed credit for violent clashes between the rival factions."[421] Thus, in September, 1969, the San Diego FBI office reported in connection with the Panther-US dispute:

> Shootings, beatings and a high degree of unrest continues to prevail in the ghetto area of southeast San Diego. Although no specific counterintelligence action can be credited with contributing to the overall situation, it is felt that a substantial amount of the unrest is directly attributable to this program (COINTELPRO).[422]

Other FBI tactics directed against the Panthers included using informers and anonymous or forged letters and phone calls to falsely suggest that certain Panthers were police informers, even though the FBI believed that Panthers had murdered members that it suspected of being informers. After the San Diego FBI office placed anonymous calls to Panther leaders naming other members as informants, reinforced by rumors spread by an FBI informant within the BPP, the field office boasted that one of the accused members fled San Diego in fear of his life. Other FBI tactics included attempting to get landlords to oust Panther members and offices from their buildings; attempting to break up the marriages of Panthers; trying to foster discord between the Panthers and supporting groups, especially SDS; targeting for COINTELPRO actions persons who spoke in support of or gave money to the Panthers; spreading rumors that individual Panthers were immoral; attempting to cripple the Panther newspaper and block Panther leaders from speaking in public; and disseminating derogatory information about the Panthers to the press. One major target of the FBI was the Panther's free Breakfast for Children program. Churches that allowed the Panthers to use their facilities for the program were targetted; thus anonymous complaining letters and phone calls were placed to a church in San Diego that was a serving place for the program (a month later the priest involved was transferred).[423]

The FBI extensively wiretapped the Panthers and established special Panther squads at all local FBI offices where Panthers were active. These FBI squads and other federal agencies supplied information to local police and encouraged them to bring charges against and raid Panther groups.[424] Thus, in San Diego, the FBI encouraged police to arrest Panthers for traffic violations and drug charges, and furnished information that "sex orgies" were occurring "on almost a nightly basis" at the local Panther headquarters. A 1970 FBI memo stated:

> As a result of our efforts, the Black Panther Party in San Diego is no more. It has been completely done away with.[425]

FBI agents in the Chicago area also repeatedly prodded police to raid Panther homes and headquarters, and supplied information which led to a police raid in December, 1969, during which two Panthers were shot and killed.

The FBI was not the only federal agency which set out to destroy the Panthers. Shortly after John Mitchell became Attorney General, the Justice Department created a "Special Panther Unit" to coordinate investigations, and five Department attorneys were sent to San Francisco to supervise a special grand jury which was convened to investigate the Panthers for possible violations of the Smith and Anti-Riot Acts. The San Francisco U.S. Attorney commented, "Whatever they say they're doing, they're out to get the Black Panthers."[426] The grand jury subpoenaed records and original manuscripts of the Panther newspaper, as well as films, records and correspondence of "establishment" news media relating to their coverage of the Panthers. In February, 1970, Seattle's mayor publicly announced that he had turned down the request of a unit of the IRS for city aid in an "information gathering" raid on Panther offices there because he opposed "Gestapo-type raids against anyone."[427] The rhetoric of the Nixon administration was clearly designed to encourage local police action, also. Thus, J. Edgar Hoover termed the Panthers "the greatest threat to the internal security of the country," Vice-President Agnew called the organization a "completely irresponsible, anarchistic group of criminals" and Jerris Leonard, the head of the Civil Rights Division of the Justice Department, termed the Panthers a "bunch of hoodlums" and stated, "We've got to get them."[428]

Repression of the Panthers by local police reached its peak shortly after the Nixon administration took office. From April to December, 1969, police raided Panther headquarters in San Francisco, Chicago, Salt Lake City, Indianapolis, Denver, San Diego, Sacramento and Los Angeles, including four separate raids in Chicago, two in San Diego, and two in Los Angeles. Frequently Panthers were arrested during these raids on charges such as illegal use of sound equipment, harboring fugitives, possessing stolen goods and flight to avoid prosecution, and later released. In September, 1969, alone, police across the nation arrested Panthers in forty-six separate incidents ranging from traffic violations to attempted murder.[429]

Police raids frequently involved severe damage to Panther headquarters. Thus, during a raid at Sacramento in June, 1969, in search of an alleged sniper who was never found, police sprayed the building with tear gas, shot up the walls, broke typewriters and destroyed bulk food which the Panthers were distributing free to ghetto children. Sacramento Mayor Richard Marriot said he was "shocked and horrified" by the "shambles" he reported police had left behind. During raids on Panther headquarters in Philadelphia in September, 1970, police ransacked the office, ripped out plumbing and chopped up and carted away furniture. Six Panthers were led into the street, placed against a wall and stripped as Police Chief Frank Rizzo boasted to newsmen, "Imagine the big Black Panthers with their pants down."[430]

Many of the scores of local police-Panther gunfights which occurred during the 1967-69 period are awash in contradictory claims, with the Panthers and the police each charging the other opened fire first or was in some way responsible for initiating violence. During this period, ten Panthers and two police were killed and another twenty police and about ten Panthers were wounded in gunfights. Six of the Panthers killed were shot by police who had already been wounded, according to an investigation of the shootouts by journalist Edward Jay Epstein.[431]

If there was ever any question about whether or not the Panthers were the victims of political repression, it was settled by an extraordinary experiment conducted in the summer of 1969, when a group of fifteen students at California State College, Los Angeles, placed bumper stickers depicting a menacing picture of a panther with large "Black Panther" lettering on the rear bumpers of their cars. Although none of the fifteen students had been cited for a "moving" traffic violation in the preceding year, the participants received a total of thirty-three traffic citations in seventeen days, and in five cases were subjected to thorough police searches of their cars. When the investigator announced the end of the study on the eighteenth day, the remaining drivers "expressed relief, and went straight to their cars to remove the stickers."[432]

Police repression of the Panthers has been most carefully documented for Chicago as the result of investigations into a police raid on a Panther apartment there on December 4, 1969, which resulted in the death of of two Panthers and the wounding of four others.[433] Subsequent investigations revealed a long background of conflict between police and Panthers in Chicago. By early 1969, according to the FBI, the Panthers had about twenty-five to thirty members in Chicago. The Panthers were gaining increasing publicity and expanding their operations, especially the free breakfast program, an attempt to provide free medicine for black families and an attempt to form a coalition with black "gangs" in Chicago. By the end of May, 1969, there had been ninety-five arrests of Panthers in Chicago. On June 4, FBI and local police raided Panther headquarters, allegedly seeking a wanted fugitive. Although they did not find the fugitive, eight Panthers were arrested and later released on charges of harboring a fugitive. FBI agents confiscated property, money and documents, including a list of Panther contributors, during the raid. On June 8, Chicago police stopped a car full of Panthers for a traffic violation and subsequently charged the occupants with possession of explosives and narcotics, charges which were later dropped. On June 19 and July 8, Panthers were arrested in Chicago for selling the party newspaper. On July 16, two police were wounded and a Panther was killed in a shootout. Charges against another Panther for attempted murder were later dropped. On July 30, a Panther was arrested for a traffic violation and another five were arrested for possession of marijuana; these charges were later dropped. On July 31, five police and three Panthers were wounded in a gun battle near Panther headquarters. Panthers and street witnesses reported the police had fired first and then tried to set fire to the Panther office. Charges against the three Panthers were later dropped. Police raided Panther headquarters again on October 4, responding, police said, to reports of "sniper fire." The Panthers claimed that police had tried to set the office on fire and had ransacked the office and ruined food and medical supplies. Charges against six Panthers for attempted murder were subsequently dropped. On November 13, one Panther and two police were killed in a gun-fight.

The climax of police repression of the Chicago Panthers came during the December 4, 1969 raid, conducted by fourteen police, armed with twenty-seven firearms, including five shotguns and a submachine gun, in the middle of the night. Following the raid, in which two Panthers died and four were wounded, the police claimed that the Panthers had opened fire first and that there had been scores of shots fired by the Panthers. Subsequently, a special federal grand jury found that between eighty-three and ninety-nine shots had been fired by police, but only one shot could be identified as coming from a Panther weapon. The grand jury concluded that the investigation of the raid made by the Chicago police laboratory, which had backed up the police version, was "so seriously deficient that it suggests purposeful malfeasance"[434] (Chicago police who were questioned by the police investigators, it turned out, had been supplied both with the questions they would be asked *and* the answers they should give in advance). Informed in advance of the grand jury report, the state dropped charges against seven Panthers who had survived the raid for attempted murder, armed violence, unlawful possession of weapons and unlawful use of weapons. As a result of the federal grand jury report, a special Cook County grand jury was convened and indicted Cook County State's Attorney Edward Hanrahan, who had organized the raid, an assistant State's attorney, and twelve policemen for "conspiracy to obstruct justice" in connection with the aftermath of the raid. On November 1, 1972, Chicago Judge Phillip Romitti ordered these charges dismissed following presentation of the government's case. It was later revealed that the man serving as a bodyguard for one of the slain Panthers and as chief of Panther security was an FBI informant who had provided information crucial to the raid, including a floor plan of the apartment. In mid-1976, a forty-seven million dollar civil suit filed by Panthers who survived the raid and the parents of the two slain Panthers was being tried in a Chicago federal court, with defendants including the FBI, Chicago police, the FBI informant and Hanrahan.[435]

In addition to police raids and harassment arrests of Panthers, there were a number of cause celebre trials of Black Panthers during the Vietnam war period. In one of the most publicized cases, Black Panther founder Huey Newton was tried for murder in connection with the shooting death of an Oakland policeman in October, 1967. Newton was convicted in his first trial for voluntary manslaughter, but the verdict was overturned on a technicality after Newton had served twenty-two months of a fifteen year sentence. Newton was released after two later trials ended in hung juries. Black Panther Chairman Bobby Seale was charged along with the seven other Chicago Conspiracy defendants, although he had only the most tangential connection with the Chicago demonstrations, having flown in at the last moment as a substitute speaker, given two speeches and left. (The charges against Seale were later dropped when the government refused to disclose wiretap evidence.) Before the Chicago trial began, Seale was arrested in connection with the alleged torture-slaying of a New Haven Panther. The main witness against Seale was a former Panther whom Seale had expelled from the party and whose medical records included two psychiatric findings that he was mentally defective. Although Seale denied the charges, two New Haven Panthers did plead guilty to charges of second degree murder and conspiracy to kidnap resulting in death in the same case. The jury in the trial was ready to acquit Seale but one or two jurors refused to vote for acquittal unless a woman who was on trial at the same time was convicted. The judge ordered both cases dismissed when the jury reported itself hopelessly deadlocked.[436]

In May, 1971, the so-called "Panther Twenty-one" were acquitted in New York City of charges of having conspired to bomb department stores, blow up police stations and murder policemen; a number of the defendants had been held in jail for over two years under $100,000 bails. In August, 1969, three Black Panthers were arrested while riding in a car with a New York City undercover agent, Wilbert Thomas, and charged with a variety of offenses including conspiracy to rob a hotel, attempted murder of a policeman and illegal possession of weapons. During the trial, it developed that Thomas had supplied the car, had drawn a map of the hotel — the only tangible evidence tying the Panthers to the alleged robbery scheme — and had offered to supply guns. The Panthers were eventually convicted only on a technical weapons charge, based on the fact that a shotgun, which the Panthers said had been planted by Thomas, was found in the car.[437]

By the end of 1969, the Black Panther Party had been severely damaged by arrests, trials, shootouts and police and FBI harassment which had jailed, killed or exiled most of the top leadership of the party.[438] Nevertheless, in March, 1970, the FBI initiated what the Senate Intelligence Committee has labelled a "concerted program" to drive a permanent wedge between two factions in the party, one supporting Eldridge Cleaver, (who had fled the United States when his parole on a 1958 assault conviction was revoked following his alleged involvement in a gunfight with Oakland police in 1968) and the other supporting Newton, then still in jail.[439] In the following months, the FBI sent Panthers scores of forged and anonymous letters, some on bogus facsimiles of Panther stationary, designed to whip up hatred between Cleaver and Newton and their followers. In January, 1971, FBI headquarters, referring to the violent split which had ripped apart what was left of the Panthers, urged field offices to "further aggravate" the "present chaotic situation" within the party; subsequently FBI disruption attempts intensified. In February, 1971, the San Francisco field office reported that due to FBI efforts, the fortunes of the Panthers "are at a low ebb." In March, 1971, FBI headquarters called a halt to the program since "the differences between Newton and Cleaver now appear to be irreconcilable." By then, the Panthers were finished as an effective or influential force.[440]

The Significance of Political Repression in the Vietnam War Era

Because covert, as well as overt, poltical repression reached massive levels during the Vietnam War era, in attempting to assess the significance of political repression during this period, it is necessary to answer two questions. Did *overt* political repression, such as conspiracy prosecutions, excessive use of police force and overt surveillance, significantly deter people from speaking out, demonstrating and joining protest organizations, or significantly hamper the operation of protest groups by driving away members, jailing members or causing major diversions of resources? Did *covert* political repression, as manifested in surveillance, disruption and *agent provocateur* activities, such as those involved in the FBI's COINTELPRO operation, significantly disrupt and discredit protest organizations and thereby make the organizations less attractive to others and/or cause internal bickering and factionalization?

With respect to the Black Panthers, the answers to both of these questions clearly is yes. The ability of the Panthers to recruit new members and to function effectively were unquestionably severely hampered by political repression that represented, in the words of a Senate Intelligence Committee staff report, an attempt to "destroy" them.[441] Police and FBI operations against the Panthers were so intense that after 1968 the Panthers were forced to devote most of their limited resources to trying to stay out of jail. Recent revelations have also made it clear that the FBI contributed heavily to the split that destroyed what was left of the Party in 1970 and 1971.[442]

There is also good reason to believe that the very intensity of the repression faced by the group drove the Panthers into greater extremism and thus made repression appear more "justified." Thus, Gary Marx writes that the increasingly revolutionary and violent stance of the Panthers

> was certainly a response in part to their internal ideology and the characteristics and wishes of members. But it is as certain that the killing of Panthers by police; raids of questioned legality on their offices; extensive surveillance and use of undercover agents; denials of basic civic liberties — such as the right to make political speeches and distribute their literature; excessive stops for traffic offenses; general harassment; and their stigmatization by national political leaders had an important effect on their subsequent ideology and behavior and helped, to some extent, make true the original police assessment of them as a violent revolutionary group.[443]

With respect to white protest organizations, the weight of the evidence indicates that the answer to part of the first question is no and the answer to another part of the first question is yes; the answer to the second question is "quite possibly," but there is not sufficient evidence presently available to make an intelligent assessment.

Certainly overt political repression did have the effect of deterring *some* people from protest activities, and unquestionably the purpose of such repression was partially to create such a deterrent effect. For this reason, the government prosecutor in the Spock-Coffin conspiracy trial referred to the possibility of coming to "a point where maybe you will have to have enough police out there to stop *everybody*." There is some clear evidence that the fear of becoming subject to political repression did deter some people, although such evidence is always very difficult to obtain and inevitably rather slender. Thus, Steven Kelman, a Harvard undergraduate who opposed the 1969 SDS strike and who was affiliated with the Socialist Party's miniscule youth group, the Young People's Socialist Alliance (YPSL) writes that:

> students could put in long and hard hours of work, sleeping on floors and eating peanut butter and jelly, for Gene McCarthy, secure in the knowledge that they were signing their names to nothing that might end up with the FBI and damage their future career. I could name dozens of Harvard students who would join the YPSL but for fear of the effect it might have on their future careers.[444]

According to a *Washington Post* story about police photography published in August, 1971, "Countless numbers of times . . . citizens have complained in person, in writing or by telephone that they find the presence of police photographers offensive and intimidating to their intentions to protest peacefully and lawfully."[445]

According to Malcolm Moos, president of the University of Minnesota, after army surveillance at the University became known, fear of being under surveillance hung like a "deadly mist" over the campus.[446] Former presidential science advisor, and then provost-elect at MIT Jerome Weisner stated in 1971 before a Senate subcommittee:

> Many, many students are afraid to participate in political activities of various kinds which might attract them because of their concern about the consequences of having a record of such activities appear in a central file. They fear that at some future date, it might possibly cost them a job or at least make their clearance for a job more difficult to obtain.[447]

The 1970 Report of the White House Conference on Youth reported a feeling among youth of an "abrogation and diminuation of civil rights" and concern over a "chilling effect that has resulted in a feeling of fear and intimidation among the youth, minorities and a significant number of people in this nation and members of both houses" of Congress because of "political surveillance of citizens who express themselves by engaging in protesting public policies."[448] Rutgers law professor Frank Askin reported in 1972, "Many members of Congress admit privately that the dossiers maintained by the FBI and other national security agencies are a principal factor in the reluctance of their colleagues to challenge the practices and budgets of the FBI and the House Internal Security Committee."[449] Kirkpatrick Sale, in his book *SDS*, writes that "as summary expulsions and other forms of university discipline became more commonplace, (SDS) chapters found it increasingly difficult to attract large numbers of liberal students to campus demonstrations" and that by the fall of 1968 "no one could be sure any longer about being able to make a political/moral point without getting thrown out of school, beaten into a hospital or packed off to jail."[450]

Despite this evidence, there is much greater evidence to suggest that political repression did *not* significantly deter protest activities. Protests *increased* even as political repression increased, at least until 1970 or 1971. Further, the reaction to specific incidents of political repression such as the Spock-Coffin indictment, the Chicago Conspiracy indictment, the Kent State Shootings and the "Pentagon Papers" affair, was almost invariably to *increase* dissent. Contemporary observers frequently commented on the great amount of dissent that continued throughout the Vietnam War era. Thus, constitutional law expert George Anastaplo wrote in 1973:

> The truly significant thing in recent years has not been the attempt of the current administration to suppress criticism, but rather the marked inability of the administration to do so effectively.[451]

Constitutional law professor Gerald Gunther of Stanford commented in June, 1971:

> The critical test of freedom is how many people are willing to speak out and voice criticism of government policy — and right now we are having a one hell of a lot of it, loud and clear.[452]

If political repression did not succeed in intimidating dissenters, the question arises: why not? The answer is essentially that by the time repression reached major overt proportions, with the inauguration of the Nixon administration, the government had already been severely discredited in legitimacy and the major cause around which repression had ultimately been focused — support of the war in Vietnam — no longer even had the majority support of the American people. The Nixon administration came into office faced with this problem because the Johnson administration, partly in order to conceal from the American people its increasing involvement in Vietnam, failed to foster a true wartime hysteria, and thus "discouraged formation of the patriotic myopia that often prevails in a fully mobilized country."[453] Partly because of this approach and partly because the task was so monumental, the Johnson administration failed to really "sell" the war to the American people. The development of the so-called "credibility gap," created when the Johnson administration's predictions that the war would soon end repeatedly failed to be fulfilled, further undercut the legitimacy of the war effort, and ultimately the legitimacy of the American government in the eyes of large numbers of citizens.[454] As early as February, 1968, a majority of Americans with an opinion felt that the country "made a mistake sending troops to fight in Vietnam."[455] Most importantly, large and influential sections of the American intellectual, journalistic and even governmental (in the Congress) elites refused to support American war policies after early 1968 and thus the American public was constantly exposed to two sides of an issue, instead of the one-sided viewpoints expressed during World War I and the Cold War.[456] Further, during the Johnson administration, while covert political repression was expanding rapidly, *overt* political repression was fairly spotty. The brutality at the 1967 Pentagon Demonstration was an exception; most of the yearly anti-war demonstrations held in Washington during the Johnson administration were permitted without much fuss; the Spock trial was the only prosecution brought during a period when counselling persons to avoid the draft was not an especially rare occurrence; and the Johnson administration refused to prosecute demonstrators in the Chicago convention disorders.

The result of all of these factors — the spotty repression of the Johnson administration, the lack of passionate — or even majority — support for the war, and the existence of influential elites who openly opposed the war created a situation in which the Nixon administration faced massive opposition when it tried to repress dissent, creating as many new opponents as it frightened away protestors every time it took a new repressive step. In many ways, the reaction of the American people to Nixonian repression was similar to the reaction of the American people in 1932 to the Bonus Army affair — it simply took away further legitimacy from an already discredited government. It is only in this context that it is possible to understand the inability of the Nixon administration to get juries and courts to convict in the long series of political prosecutions it brought, an outcome that would have been absolutely inconceivable in the 1917-20 or 1947-54 periods. Even a fairly conservative Supreme Court, with four out of nine justices appointed by Nixon, had a rather good record in blocking political repression. Particularly notable were the decisions in the warrantless national security wiretaps case, the "Pentagon Papers" case, cases involving flag and offensive speech prosecutions, the banning of a campus SDS chapter and the expulsion of a student who had distributed "underground" newspapers.[457]

While overt political repression thus did not significantly deter persons from speaking out, demonstrating or joining protest groups, there is clear evidence that the series of criminal prosecutions aganst antiwar leaders did have a debilitating effect. The Seattle Eight conspiracy trial appears to have wrecked a growing protest movement in the Seattle area, and other trials tied up important protest leaders for long periods of time, and enormous amounts of money, time and energy that could have been devoted to building the movement. For example, the defense in the Ellsburg case alone cost one million dollars.[458] According to Kirpatrick Sale, "as arrests and jailings mounted, (SDS) chapter resources, both of money and time, tended more and more to be concentrated on raising bail and providing legal defenses." He adds:

> Repression proved to be ultimately very debilitating for SDS both nationally and locally, exacerbating the paranoid style, wearing down individuals and eating into groups, tying up people in courts, exhausting both finances and energy, forcing chapters to give up some confrontational tactics, sending leaders into jail and exile, and over the whole organization casting the dark realization of what the stakes are in even an infant, proto-revolution. But its effect was gradual and diffuse, like a slow poison . . . the thousands of young leftists harassed, arrested, beaten, shot and jailed by (mid-1970) needed no . . . convincing that repression, at least in its initial stages existed in the United States. . . . Even if the organizations of the left had been stable and powerful, even if they had been prepared for the intensity of the government's reaction, even if they had been psychologically set for a government willing to go to war against its own people, even then they would have had a difficult time holding together, advancing the Movement, pushing out new ideas, broadening the left. But they were not, and the repression in these years took a doubly heavy toll.[459]

Similarly, the *Los Angeles Times*, in a September, 1975 story on the demise of the radical movement, reported that the movement's internal problems "might not have destroyed the movement" but they were "exploited, exaggerated by the government's planned program of sabotage and disruption" and that "conspiracy trials, which the government invariably lost, sapped the movement's leadership, funds and morale."[460]

The answer to the question of whether *covert* political repression helped to significantly disrupt and discredit protest organizations is difficult to discuss intelligently. On the surface, the disintegration of the protest movement that occurred after 1970[461] appears to have resulted from three factors: the "winding down of the war" and the ending of the draft, the first a major and the second a subsidiary issue in the protest movement; the confusion and organizational chaos caused in mid-1969 when SDS split into three factional groups; and the discrediting caused to the movement by its apparent increasingly open advocacy and use of violence, especially with the emergence of "Weatherman" in 1969. Clearly political repression did not have anything to do with the first reason but the second and third reasons may well have been partly encouraged or caused by government informants and *agent provocateurs*. There is simply no way to know without obtaining the files of the FBI and other government intelligence agencies, but in the light of recent revelations it would be foolish to discount this possibility. The existence of at least some *agent provocateurs* has been well established, and although this certainly does not mean that all violence can be attributed to government agents, it does cast grave doubt over the question of who did create at least major aspects of the violence which occurred. With regard to the split of SDS into factional groups, there is certainly no hard evidence to indicate the FBI or other governmental bodies were highly involved in this, but the 1968 New Left COINTELPRO directive did order FBI agents to sow internal confusion and disruption within New Left organizations, and there is clear evidence that such activities were actually undertaken by FBI and other government operatives.

While an assessment of the impact of covert *agent provocateur* and disruptive activities of government agents awaits the release of further evidence from government files, it is clear that the general knowledge of massive government infiltration and surveillance that existed within the protest movement did cause problems. The government was well aware of the disruptions and fears that such knowledge could cause. Thus, one former FBI officer, when asked why the FBI did nothing to dispel widespread fears of wiretapping, stated:

> It's very nice to know that the people you're chasing are afraid to use telephones. In fact that's one reason why in chasing the Communist Party we didn't have to use many taps. They were scared to use telephones.[462]

One of the "Media" papers stolen from an FBI office revealed that a conference of FBI agents concerned with the New Left had reached a "pretty general consensus that more interviews" with protesters "are in order for plenty of reasons, chief of which are it will enhance the paranoia endemic in these circles and will further serve to get the point across there is an FBI agent behind every mailbox."[463]

The most careful study of the New Left which has appeared, Kirkpatrick Sale's *SDS*, concludes that covert surveillance and the knowledge of such activities within SDS had a significant effect on the organization:

> In practically no instance were chapters prepared to deal with phone-tapping, daily surveillance, police infiltration. . . . As infiltration grew, fear and

suspicion began to infest formerly easygoing organizations and the early SDS spirit of openness and honesty suffered the pall of secrecy and incipient paranoia.[464]

Aside from the "provable" effects of political repression on the protest movement, there is a certain significance to the fact that during the Vietnam War era, repression increasingly took on a covert character. Although there was much overt repression — certainly more physical violence against protesters, for example, than during the 1947-54 period, and indeed since the 1930's — the dominant character of repression during this period was massive, secret and essentially completely judicially unrestrained surveillance, penetration, disruption and provocation activity by government agents. In a sense this increasing "subtlety" in repression simply furthered a trend which can be seen developing throughout modern American history if repression is compared for the 1870-1900, 1917-20, 1947-54 and 1965-73 periods. During the 1870-1900 period, the dominant form of repression was brutal and highly public — arrests, beatings and shootings of workers on the streets. During the 1917-20 period, the dominant form of repression was arrests emanating from police raids on specific targets, with considerably less violence, at least from public officials (as opposed to vigilante groups). During the 1947-54 period, the dominant form of repression was job firings and congressional hearings; there were relatively few arrests and virtually no violence, and also no normal legal protections for the accused during the firing and hearing processes. During the Vietnam War era, repression was frequently not even visible and therefore completely insusceptible to effective legal attack. Thus, as Gary Marx notes, "The latent reason (or at least consequence) for using [undercover] agents may be to harass, control and combat those who, while not technically violating any laws, hold political views and have life-styles that are at odds with the dominant society."[465] While surveillance activity is secret enough to avoid effective legal countermeasures, it is important to note that the general *existence* of such activity is publicized enough to foster intimidation and disruption. Thus, as Frank Donner notes:

> Surveillance is an especially attractive weapon in a democracy with explicit constitutional limitations on invasions of free expression, because its sanctions are submerged. It is "only" an investigation of the "facts," we are told; it neither enjoins nor punishes political expression and activities. Yet it can hardly be denied that the self-censorship which it stimulates is far more damaging than many express statutory or administrative restraints. It yields a maximum return of repression for a minimum investment of official power. . . . The recruitment of informers is *intended* as a restraint on free expression, a curb on movements for change. . . . In the overwhelming majority of cases, it is not the information furnished by the spy which makes him a Bureau (FBI) asset but the fact that he is there — an intruder who intimidates and demoralizes his targets. This coercive aim explains the curious dualism in American infiltration practice; while the identity of the individual informer is concealed, the fact that there is a widespread network of informers in the American left is widely publicized.[466]

The documentation of the widespread use of *agents provocateur* in the Vietnam War era in particular (as well as revelations of CIA involvement in foreign coups and assassination plots) points strongly to the question which Gary Marx raises in an article on *agents provocateur,* namely "whether public events are what they appear to be."[467] It is difficult in this connection not to recall that in George Orwell's *1984,* the government not only represses the opposition, but also creates and maintains it, and by controlling what information is made public completely shapes the world view of its subjects. The American government does not *appear* to have reached this stage yet, but the warning signs apparent in the 1965-75 period are too strong and clear for the danger to be shrugged off.

The Prospects for Political Freedom in the U.S.: Fall, 1976

In some respects, the prospects for political freedom in the United States in the fall of 1976 look brighter than they have in many years. The withdrawal of American troops from Vietnam beginning in 1969 and the termination of American troop involvement in the war in 1973, the disintegration of the domestic protest movement after 1970, and especially, the revelations associated with the Watergate scandal in 1973 and 1974 have created a public climate increasingly hostile to political repression.

As early as 1971, Congress began to demonstrate a mood considerably different from that shown during the late 1960's, when the Anti-Riot and Federal Aid ban bills were passed. In February and March, 1971, Sen. Samuel Ervin's Subcommittee on Constitutional Rights held hearings into Army surveillance that led to the Army's promise to cease such activities. In 1971, both houses of Congress passed legislation to repeal the "emergency detention" provisions of the Internal Security Act of 1950, which explicitly barred the executive branch from exercising emergency detention procedures in the future without express Congressional consent. In 1972, Congress blocked President Nixon's attempt to revive the SACB, an action which eventually led Nixon to abolish the SACB in 1973 and the Attorney General's list of subversive organizations in June, 1974. Congressional hearings in 1973 and 1974 led to President Nixon's resignation in connection with abuses of presidential power in the Watergate affair.[468]

In January, 1975, the House abolished the House Internal Security Committee (formerly HUAC) and voted to transfer its jurisdiction and files to the House Judiciary Committee, thus ending thirty-seven years of the committee's existence as an autonomous body. In March, 1976, the House defeated an attempt to earmark Judiciary Committee funds in order to reactivate the Internal Security Committee.[469] In 1975 and early 1976, congressional committees in both houses investigated intelligence agency abuses. In May, 1976, following the Senate Intelligence Committee's issuance of blistering report on such abuses, the Senate voted 72 to 22 to create a permanent committee to monitor the intelligence agencies. The committee was given exclusive jurisdiction within the Senate over the activities and funding of the CIA, shared oversight of the FBI with the Senate Judiciary Committee, and shared oversight over the defense intelligence agencies, including the NSA, with the Senate Armed Services Committee. In establishing the intelligence committee, the Senate requested all intelligence agencies to keep the committee "fully and currently informed with respect to intelligence activities, including any significant anticipated activities." While the committee was not given any veto over planned intelligence activities which it learned about, it was empowered to ask the Senate to allow it to publish information given to it in secret, thus presumably torpedoing any secret intelligence activity the committee disapproved of.[470]

The death of J. Edgar Hoover in 1973, the resignation of President Nixon in 1974, and the general mood of heightened awareness of civil liberties issues resulting from the Watergate scandal clearly affected the executive branch also. An unparalleled series of disclosures of FBI activities, including the COINTELPRO operation and FBI mail-openings and burglaries of domestic groups, began in 1973. In 1975, NSA monitoring of private international communications of American citizens was revealed, along with previously unknown aspects of CIA domestic operations, including the reading of private mail and penetration of domestic protest groups.[471] Among the FBI revelations was confirmation of what had long been "felt" in Washington: that FBI Director J. Edgar Hoover had maintained secret files containing derogatory information on presidents, executive branch officers and Congressmen, and that Hoover had "improperly disseminated" some of this information. According to Attorney General Edward Levi and Justice Department spokesmen, Presidents Kennedy, Johnson and Nixon had in a "small number of instances . . . misused" the FBI to gather "political intelligence information" on political opponents, including congressmen who were "opposed to and critical of" their policies.[472] According to a recent book on Watergate, "any president who might be tempted" to fire Hoover "would be deterred by the knowledge that Hoover had enough dirt on most public figures" including enough "highly derogatory information on the sex lives, drinking habits and other indiscretions of these people" to "tar their reputations irredeemingly, if not put them in jail." Further, Hoover "made sure that Nixon — like other Presidents before him — knew of his store of information by sharing some of the juicier tidbits with him from time to time."[473] According to a recent study of the FBI, Hoover's files included "allegations about the extramarital affairs of President Roosevelt and his wife Eleanor, the inside story about an undersecretary of state believed to be a homosexual . . . incidents from Richard Nixon's years as Vice-President and the early escapades of John F. Kennedy." Included in the files were information on every congressman, including material "to indicate whether he could be counted as a Bureau 'friend'."[474]

Other revelations made in the wake of Watergate and Hoover's death concerned the extent of FBI autonomy. A spokesman for the General Accounting Office, an agency supposed to oversee all other government agencies, revealed in December, 1974 that it was investigating the FBI for the first time since 1908, since although, "we always believed we had the authority to conduct an investigation into FBI activities . . . the late FBI chief J. Edgar Hoover just wouldn't approve of it."[475] Dean Rusk, Secretary of State under Kennedy and Johnson, testified in September, 1974:

> It is hard to exaggerate that Mr. Hoover in effect took orders only from himself, sometimes from an attorney-general, usually from a president, and that was it.[476]

An internal White House memorandum that was released in the course of the Watergate investigations contained a statement by White House aide Tom Huston that "at some point, Hoover has to be told who is President."[477]

According to official statements, abuses of federal agencies in the intelligence field ended during the 1971-75 period. Thus, the FBI stated that its COINTELPRO operations ended in 1971, the Army claimed to have halted its domestic surveillance activities in 1971, the CIA stated it ended its domestic infiltration and intelligence activities and its mail interception operation in 1973 and 1974, and NSA claimed to have halted its targetted interception of overseas cable and telephone calls by Americans by 1975.[478] Attorney General Levi claimed in the summer of 1975 that no warrantless wiretaps or bugs were then being directed against "American citizens and none will be authorized by me except in cases where the target . . . is an agent or a collaborator of a foreign power," a position clearly full of loopholes but representing an advance from the position of the Nixon administration. In March, 1976, the Ford administration asked Congress for legislation which would require Federal court warrants for bugging and wiretapping in foreign intelligence and national security matters, even involving foreign powers or foreign agents, and restricting such surveillance against American citizens to persons involved in espionage, terrorism or sabotage. These guidelines would eliminate electronic surveillance for general intelligence gathering in cases involving domestic "subversives" and would seemingly eliminate the right claimed by American presidents since 1940 to tap and bug without court warrants in certain types of "national security" cases, especially those involving foreign powers or agents. However the proposed legislation included a provision which stated that nothing in the bill would limit the President's "inherent constitutional power" to order electronic surveillance in national security cases beyond the legislation's scope, a phrase seemingly at odds with the intent of the proposal.[479]

In December, 1975, Levi announced the creation of a watchdog agency within the Justice Department to oversee investigations into alleged misconduct by FBI and other Justice Department employees.[480] In March, 1976, Levi put into effect a set of guidelines to regulate

FBI domestic intelligence operations, which provided that the FBI could conduct investigations only on individuals or groups involved in violence or illegality, or on groups or individuals that "will" become involved in violence or law-breaking with the intent of overthrowing the government, interfering with the activities of foreign governments or their representatives or "substantially impairing — for the purpose of influencing the United States Government policies or decisions" the Federal government, state governments or interstate commerce. A proposed provision allowing FBI agents to take "nonviolent emergency measures" that could include "disrupting plans for using force or violence" by dissident groups was deleted after members of Congress complained this might lead to another COINTELPRO, but Levi said there still "may be situations of great human peril in which the FBI might seek to take steps to prevent enormous violence from taking place." In April, 1976, Levi appointed a committee of three lawyers, two of whom did not work for the Justice Department, to monitor the FBI's compliance with the new guidelines, evaluate their effectiveness and make suggestions for improvements.[481] Clearly, these guidelines contained many potential loopholes, especially the clause which authorized investigations of groups or individuals who "will" break the law, since this phrase would either require an ability to forecast the future or authorize investigations of virtually anybody. Nevertheless, an FBI actually operating in good faith under these guidelines would clearly be under far more control that it had been when operating only under the whims of J. Edgar Hoover and American presidents. One early sign that the guidelines may have a substantial impact on FBI policy came in September, 1976, when Levi ordered an end to the FBI's thirty-eight-year investigation of the Socialist Workers Party on the ground that the investigation could not be justified under the guidelines. Levi's order terminated FBI spying which had amassed eight million file entries on the SWP, involved over three hundred informers from 1960 to 1976, and included the use of burglaries, wiretaps, overt and covert surveillance and COINTELPRO activities designed to disrupt the party (which according to the SWP never had more than twenty-five hundred members). During the almost forty years of FBI investigation, the only prosecution of SWP members was the 1941 Smith Act prosecution of eighteen SWP leaders, which then Attorney General Francis Biddle later conceded had been an error.[481a]

In February, 1976 President Ford announced a general ban on the CIA and other intelligence agencies (aside from the FBI, which was covered under Levi's regulations) from using electronic or physical surveillance or infiltration to collect information on the domestic activities of Americans. The CIA was specifically barred from electronic eavesdropping inside the U.S., and the NSA was barred from intercepting any "communication which is made from, or is intended by the sender to be received in, the United States." What were termed "limited exceptions" would allow intelligence gathering, including the use of physical surveillance, on Americans who are present or former employees of intelligence agencies, persons who come into contact with such people, persons being considered for employment by the intelligence agencies, intelligence agency contractors, persons or activities "that pose a clear threat to intelligence agency facilities or personnel," or persons "reasonably believed to be acting on behalf of a foreign power or engaging in international terrorist or narcotics activities or activities threatening the national security." NSA was specifically authorized to monitor overseas communications of Americans to gather "information concerning corporations or other commercial organizations which constitute foreign intelligence or counterintelligence."[482] Enough loopholes are included in these provisions to raise serious questions (the entire CIA domestic spying operation of the Vietnam War era arose out of concern that domestic protesters were "acting on behalf of a foreign power") but the existence and publication of the guidelines at least reflected an increased awareness of the potential for abuses of American civil liberties by the White House.

Along with the shift in attitudes (and apparently in activities) in the legislative and executive branches, a general public atmosphere was created, largely due to Watergate, which was much more supportive of civil liberties issues after 1973 than it had been in the previous five to eight years. Thus, Alan Westin, editor of the ACLU publication, *Civil Liberties Review*, exulted in early 1974, "Watergate has put Americans in a mood distinctly favorable to political liberty."[483] Public opinion polls taken in late 1973 showed that, unlike 1967, when surveys showed that homosexuals, black militants, student demonstrators and atheists were regarded by over 50 percent as "dangerous or harmful to the country," instead "government officials who try to use official intelligence agencies for political advantage" were placed in that category by 88 percent and a majority no longer viewed any of the 1967 groups as a menace.[484] While in 1970, majorities or pluralities had favored banning meetings called to "denounce the president" and requiring that all protest meetings be reviewed in advance by authorities to make sure the demonstration was not "urging overthrow of the system," by 1973, poll results had reversed. At the same time, polls showed that 75 percent of Americans felt that "wire-tapping and spying under the excuse of national security is a serious threat to people's privacy."[485] Pollster Louis Harris, summing up some of these data, concluded, "it is evident that many of the acts of those who took steps to monitor and curb . . . . radical and deviant activity are viewed by most Americans as more harmful to the country than the objects of (Nixon) administration concern."[486]

Despite these signs favorable to political freedom, there were other more ominous signs. FBI Director Clarence Kelley, at various times during the 1973-1976 period, defended the COINTELPRO operations of the FBI and said Congress should authorize such tactics for future emergency use; opposed proposed Congressional prohibitions on surreptitious entries, mail opening or inspection of private papers without a court order based on evidence a crime had been or was about to be committed; urged expanded use of wiretapping, at the same time other administration officials were requesting increasing Congressional restrictions on tapping; repeatedly warned about the danger of terrorists and of communist-directed espionage; opposed increased Congressional oversight of the FBI; and warned that excessive concern for individual rights was jeopardizing American national security and that Americans "must be willing to surrender a small measure of our liberties to preserve the great bulk of them."[487] Kelly also stated that the FBI was continuing to compile "personal behavior" information, including sex and drinking habits, on reporters and government officials, including Congressmen.[488] Appearing before a House subcommittee in November, 1974, Kelly refused to promise that he would not reinstitute COINTELPRO activities, stating only that he would not "abridge" the rights of any citizen without prior approval of the attorney general "unless in balance there would be a feeling on my part that it would perhaps be a good idea."[489] Kelly finally apologized for the first time for FBI abuses under the Hoover regime in May, 1976, following a series of devastating indictments of FBI activities issued by the Senate Intelligence Committee. Kelly said there had been "abuses of power" and that some FBI activities "were clearly wrong and quite indefensible" and must "never" be repeated. Kelly added that the FBI "never again will occupy a unique position that permitted improper activity without accountability." Yet in the same speech in which these remarks were made, Kelly said that "neither the American people nor the cause of civil liberty" would benefit if the FBI retired "a bit from the battlefront" and abdicated "some of its investigative powers."[490]

Although the federal government has not successfully prosecuted a single case under internal security statutes since 1957, in 1976 the FBI was still maintaining five hundred thousand files under the category "subversive matters." According to the Senate Intelligence Committee, these files include "massive amounts of irrelevant and trivial information," including information gained through warrantless electronic surveillance, mail opening and burglaries.[491] The committee also reported that as of June, 1975, the FBI still had on its payroll fifteen hundred domestic intelligence informants and was budgeting for fiscal 1976 more than twice as much for domestic intelligence investigations ($7.4 million) than for organized crime informants. In addition to domestic intelligence informants on the FBI payroll, the FBI also was using 1,254 "confidential sources" such as "bankers, telephone company employees, and landlords" to provide similar information.[492]

In May, 1975, the Justice Department asserted that it had the right to break into homes without a warrant in "foreign espionage and intelligence" cases; subsequently the Senate Intelligence Committee revealed that the FBI was in fact conducting "surreptitious entries" in such cases to implant microphone surveillance instruments. Attorney General Levi revealed in June, 1975, that warrantless taps and bugs authorized by the Justice Department, supposedly only against "foreign targets," were at a seven-year high in 1974.[493]

In June, 1975, CIA Director William Colby revealed that the CIA had files on seventy-five Congressmen, and bluntly told members of a House subcommittee that members of Congress were not "immune" from CIA surveillance during travels abroad if they came "in contact with some group that was a legitimate" CIA target. Colby maintained that the CIA was no longer involved in domestic intelligence gathering, but added that the domestic files gathered in Operation CHAOS "are not massive when a quarter of a million people are demonstrating in front of the White House." The Senate Intelligence Committee revealed in May, 1976, that the CIA was still maintaining files derived from its seventeen-year-long program of illegally opening international mail.[494]

Aside from the loopholes contained in virtually all of the restrictions on domestic intelligence gathering announced by executive branch agencies during the 1971-1976 period — loopholes which have clearly allowed or will allow the military, the NSA and the CIA to collect domestic intelligence under certain circumstances and will allow the FBI to conduct investigations when it thinks people "will" break the law — the most fundamental threat of political repression is that all of these restrictions are based entirely on executive orders or internal directives and thus can be changed in the same manner. Although the permanent Senate committee created to oversee the intelligence agencies in May, 1976, indicated that it will attempt to write into law such restrictions, in the meantime American intelligence agencies can write their own rules. As one spokeswoman for a civil liberties research organization noted, "All that the executive branch has offered the nation to stand as a bulwark between a history of abuses of secret powers and a future possibility of their return is the facile assertion that Watergate has somehow turned all American officials into automatically honorable men who can again be trusted with vast power."[495] In September, 1976, a federal grand jury was investigating FBI burglaries in the early 1970's amidst speculation that former or present FBI officials would be indicted. However, up till then, not a single official or employee of any American intelligence agency had been prosecuted for any of the vast array of abuses that occurred during the Vietnam War era, including burglaries, mail openings, and illegal electronic surveillance.

Signs of danger to political freedom in 1976 were also evident from the Supreme Court and the Congress. While the Court issued few decisions directly related to political dissent during 1975-1976, the general trend of the Court's rulings was distinctly unfavorable towards dissenters. Thus, in March, 1976, the Court ruled that the armed services could ban political candidates and demonstrators from military bases. In April, 1976, the court inexplicably refused to review a lower court ruling upholding convictions of three persons under an Illinois law banning desecration of the flag, resulting from a flag burning incident, although in three similar cases in 1974 the Court had overruled convictions.[496]

In the Congress, while HISC was dead by 1976, SISS continued to publish irresponsible reports suggesting that political dissidents were "subversive." Thus, in May, 1976, SISS issued a report, based on two days of hearings which featured only two witnesses, that termed the People's Bicentennial Commission (a group presenting an "alternative" interpretation of the American revolution) a group of "political extremists" seeking to exploit the bicentennial of American independence "for the purpose of overthrowing our free society."[497]

In mid-1976, the Congress was considering a proposed revision of the criminal code, which included provisions the *Los Angeles Times* termed the most "sweeping assault" against democratic self-government "since the Alien and Sedition" acts.[498] Among the provisions of the code revision were an attempt to rejuvenate the Smith Act by circumventing the Supreme Court's decision in *Yates*[499] by punishing advocacy which "incites others to engage in conduct which . . . at some future time would facilitate the "overthrow" of the government" or active membership in "an organization which has as a purpose" such "incitement." The revision also included a provision which authorizes the mass arrest of demonstrators within sight or sound of the President by declaring them to be trespassers upon a "Temporary Residence of the President." Other provisions would create for the first time in American history an "official secrets act" by outlawing knowingly communicating national defense information or any classified information to any person "not authorized to receive it," regardless of motivation or the nature of the information. Further, the *possession* or publication of government documents by persons not authorized to possess or publish the information would also be made a criminal offense.[500]

Even as Congress was considering the criminal code revision, in February, 1976 President Ford proposed that Congress pass a special bill providing criminal and civil penalties for all federal agencies and contractors who released classified information to unauthorized persons. According to some interpretations, such a bill would have made illegal news "leaks" that disclosed CIA domestic spying and plots to assassinate foreign officials, NSA interceptions of international communications of Americans and information associated with the Watergate scandal. Ford also asked Congress to expand governmental power to open mail, currently permitted only in criminal investigations with a court warrant, to also allow obtaining a court warrant to open mail in cases where the government could show "probable cause to believe that the sender or recipient is an agent of a foreign power who is engaged in spying, sabotage or terrorism," in order to obtain "vitally needed foreign intelligence information."[501]

Aside from these specific threats to political liberties in 1976, the more general threat posed by increasingly sophisticated technology continued to grow. During the 1965-75 period, the government intercepted private mail, tapped telephones and obtained bank records of dissenters, thus allowing it to trace virtually all communications and transactions of protesters. Disclosures by congressional committees and government agencies have indicated that at least seventy-nine federal government agencies maintain eight thousand record systems which contain over 3 billion records on individuals, including 279.6 million mental health records, 916.4 million profiles on alcoholism and drug addiction, and over 1.2 billion financial records.[502] According to Arthur R. Miller, a computer specialist in the University of Michigan law school, laser technology now makes it feasible to store a 20-page dossier on every American on a piece of tape less than five thousand feet long; in 1971, Miller warned that the United States is "on the pathway toward a dossier dictatorship."[503] In August, 1975, Senator Frank Church, then chairman of the Senate Intelligence Committee, warned that American intelligence capabilities developed to cope with "potential enemies" could "at any time" be

> turned around on the American people, and no American would have any privacy left, such is the capacity to monitor everything, telephone conversations, telegrams, it doesn't matter. There would be no place to hide. If this government ever became a tyranny, . . . the technological capacity that the intelligence community has given the government could enable it to impose total tyranny and there would be no way to fight back because the most careful effort to combine together in resistance to the government, no matter how privately it was done, is within the reach of the government to know.[504]

Whatever the truth presently is concerning the activities of American intelligence agencies, the fear of surveillance remains and continues to inhibit the political activities of American citizens. Thus, one Washington reporter who has written a book on the FBI wrote in April, 1976:

> For all the assurances that the FBI and the CIA have changed, that they are no longer misbehaving, many people remain skeptical. They are still not sure whether they are getting the truth. Washington reporters working on sensitive stories still retreat to pay phones for their most delicate calls, and controversial politicians worry about the privacy of files in their offices and homes. . . . Some executive branch officials agree that it is always a good idea to be careful — one never knows to what lengths the spies of the Soviets, the Chinese, and other potentially hostile foreign powers might go. But it was not these spies whom the journalists, senators and congressmen feared; it was the ones who work for their own government.[505]

Conclusion

It is a dangerous task to attempt to reach meaningful and valid generalizations about over one hundred years of the history of a country. However, it is a task which must be undertaken, unless history, in Shakespeare's words, is to be regarded as a "tale told by an idiot, full of sound and fury, signifying nothing." Whether or not, as philosopher George Santayana suggests, those who learn from history will *not* be condemned to repeat it is another question, but certainly if no attempt to make generalizations is made, we will not even learn from it. There are many generalizations which can be reached concerning political repression in the United States from 1870 to the present. In this chapter, two subjects will be concentrated on: the significance of political repression for American society and politics, and those factors which explain why repression has repeatedly risen and fallen over time.

This chapter is designed to draw on the history of political repression which constitutes the central portion of this book, without repeating the historical material contained therein. Readers who wish to refresh their memories about particular historical developments briefly referred to in this chapter should consult the historical material referred to by page number in the notes to this chapter.

The Significance of Political Repression

Political repression has been an important and neglected factor in shaping major aspects of American political development since 1870. This does not mean that political repression *alone* explains these aspects. Nor does this suggest that political repression in modern American history has had the character of repression in Nazi Germany or Stalinist Russia, or even that political repression in the U.S. has been "worse" than in most countries, only that it has influenced *American* development in important ways.

One continuing limiting factor on the strength of political repression in the U.S. is that American society has unquestionably had a strong moral and legal tradition of support for civil liberties and the right to dissent, *side-by-side* with traditions of xenophobia, conformity, nativism, and insecurity about the meaning of such terms as "loyalty" and "American" which have fed repression. Ralph Miliband, one of the few Western social scientists to pay serious attention to the role political repression has played in Western industrialied societies, writes:

> It is a dangerous confusion to believe and claim that, because "bourgeois freedoms" are inadequate and constantly threatened by erosion, they are therefore of no consequence. For all its immense limitations, there is a wide gulf between "bourgeois democracy" and the various forms of conservative authoritarianism, most notably Fascism, which have provided the alternative type of political regime for advanced capitalism.[1]

Having thus qualified the remainder of this section, a review of modern American history shows that political repression has *contributed significantly* to the following.

- The failure of the labor movement as a whole to achieve major power until the 1930's.
- The destruction of radical labor movements.
- The destruction of radical political movements.
- The continuing self-censorship which Americans have imposed upon their own exercise of basic political freedoms.

The Hindering of the Labor Movement

Political repression of American labor from 1870 until the mid-1930's was massive and continuous, and played a significant role in delaying labor's emergence as a major power. Until the passage of the Wagner Act, an enormous institutionalized mechanism devoted to the suppression of the labor movement was tolerated and/or implemented by political authorities: governmental officials tolerated company towns, private police, private armies and private arsenals with attendant denials of basic political freedoms to millions of workers, supplied local police, state militia and federal troops, and used techniques of harassment, mass arrests and court injunctions to repress the labor movement. In many cases, the apparatus of repression operated unspectacularly and on a day-to-day basis; in other cases the apparatus operated in an intense and spectacular way, especially when called upon to put down strikes. Both the day-to-day forms of repression, such as the banning or harassment of attempts at labor organizing, and the more spectacular forms, such as mass arrests and use of injunctions and troops to break strikes, had profound, if not precisely measureable, effects on the development of the American labor movement.[2]

Perhaps the clearest single indication of the importance of repression, specifically in terms of the failure of government to protect labor's political civil liberties, is the spectacular upsurge of labor strength in the 1930's, when labor became a "specially protected client of the federal government."[3] Similar spectacular gains had come when conservative labor's rights were given special governmental protection during World War I; those gains vanished in the 1920's when the government resumed its repressive policy.[4]

Political repression was harshest towards labor struggles which affected key sectors of the economy whose capture by labor would have meant spectacular breakthroughs. Thus, political repression was especially massive, harsh and repetitive in important strikes affecting railroads, steel, textiles, mining, lumber and agriculture.[5] Repression was often particularly intense during strikes at especially crucial plants and industrial areas. Examples include repression at Homestead in 1892, site of the largest and most modern steel plant in the country; at Lawrence, Massachusetts in 1912, a key center for woolen worsted products and home of the largest firm in the industry; at Patterson, New Jersey, in 1913, the nation's leading silk production center; at the Durst ranch in Wheatland, California, in 1913, the largest agricultural employer in the state; at Virginia, Minnesota in 1916-17, during a strike at the largest white pine mill in the world; during the 1917 strikes in key lumber and copper areas; during the 1919 steel strike, where repression centered in the crucial western Pennsylvania steel areas; during the 1929 Gastonia, North Carolina strike, at the largest textile mill in the world; and during the 1931 strike in Danville, Virginia, site of the largest textile firm in the South.[6]

In many cases, repression was of crucial importance in breaking major strikes, and therefore of great importance in shaping American labor history. The two single most important strikes in American labor history from 1890 to 1930 were the Pullman strike of 1894 and the Steel Strike of 1919. Both were broken to a large extent by political repression, and their failures had immense consequences for American labor history. The crushing of the Pullman strike destroyed the American Railway Union, the largest union in American labor history; the ARU was also the first important industrial union, and had gained a stronghold in the most important American industry in the country.[7] By 1919, the steel industry had replaced railroads as the single most important industry, and the crushing of the steel strike had similar implications.[8] A victory in either one of these strikes alone might well have led to a massive labor breakthrough and the establishment of labor as a major power in American society twenty to forty years before it achieved such a position, and at a time when the labor movement as a whole was considerably more radical than it had become by the mid-1930's.

Other major strikes or important organizational campaigns either broken by or drastically altered by repression include the Coeur d'Alene strikes of 1892 and 1899, the WFM campaign in Colorado in 1903-1904, the Patterson and Calumet strikes of 1913, the southern coal and lumber strikes of 1908 and 1912-13, the Mesabi strike of 1916, the 1917 copper and lumber strikes, the textile strikes of 1926-1931, the California agricultural strikes of the 1930's, and the Little Steel Strike of 1937.[9] Repression did not always succeed — the 1912 Lawrence strike and the 1934 strikes in San Francisco, Toledo and Minneapolis-St. Paul are evidence of that.[10] But political repression did hinder labor enough to be *one* of the major forces which shaped the labor movement and barred it from significant power until the passage of the Wagner Act, "perhaps the most important civil liberties statute ever passed by Congress."[11]

The absence of a strong labor movement in American history until the 1930's had innumerable side effects and ramifications, which were clearly exemplified during the 1920's. As a result of the weakening of the labor movement (and radical movements) during the repression of 1919 and the 1920's, business ruled virtually unchecked during the decade, gaining disproportionate benefits from the period's prosperity. One of the major causes of the Great Depression was that American workers simply did not have enough money to purchase the goods the economy was capable of producing. If the labor movement had been stronger in the 1920's, American workers might have gained higher wage levels, and the Depression might have been avoided or greatly alleviated.[12]

The Destruction of Radical Labor

Political repression proved a major hindrance to the labor movement as a whole, but it was especially concentrated and consistent, and had especially pernicious effects, with regard to the most radical elements of the labor movement. Four major radical union movements gained significant influence in modern American labor history, and all four were literally smashed by political repression or severely adversely affected by it, at the peak of their strengths.

The first such union was the communist-anarchist movement, which had achieved major influence in the Chicago labor movement by 1886. The communist-anarchists were wiped out in the aftermath of the Haymarket affair, which featured the hanging of four of their leaders without any reasonable proof of their involvement in the bombing.[13] The second important radical union was the Western Federation of Miners, a socialist-oriented industrial union which by the early twentieth century had about fifty thousand members and had become the most important labor organization in the west. The WFM was physically decimated by arbitrary arrests and deportations in the 1903-1904 Colorado labor war.[14]

The third major radical labor movement, the Industrial Workers of the World, had a membership of over one hundred thousand and major strength among farm, lumber and copper workers by 1917. The IWW, an industrial union open to all workers, openly demanded an end to the capitalist system. The IWW was at its peak of strength in 1917 and showing signs of increasing stability and determination when it was completely disrupted by World War I government raids and conspiracy prosecutions which led to the jailing of the entire top IWW leadership. Remnants of the IWW which survived the war-time repression continued to suffer severe repression in the few major strikes they led after the war — in California in 1923-24, in Colorado in 1927, and in Washington State in 1933. Given the constant and vicious repression faced by the IWW, the impassioned debate among scholars as to whether the IWW was a real labor union or simply a revolutionary propaganda outfit is somewhat irrelevant; as William Preston notes, "Perhaps the answer would be to describe the IWW as a defense organization."[15] Indeed, the entire history to the IWW is simply a history of political repression, from the Steunenberg trial, to Goldfield, the free speech fights, Lawrence, Wheatland, Patterson, Grabow, Everett, World War I and Centralia.[16]

The fourth major radical union movement was the Communist Party. Literally every major strike the Communist Party was involved in (except during the reformist periods of 1935-39 and 1941-45) met intense repression. Among these were the Passaic, New Bedford and Gastonia strikes of 1926-1929, the California agricultural strikes of 1930-1935, the Harlan County strike of 1933 and the North American Aviation Strike of 1941.[17] After World War II, when the CP resumed its radical line it retained major strength in the CIO, including control of over 20 percent of all CIO unions. Beginning in 1947, the CP unions and their leaders faced deportation proceedings, Congressional investigations, and numerous criminal prosecutions. The 1947 Taft-Hartley requirement that all union officers swear non-Communist oaths to qualify for Wagner Act benefits, the 1954 Communist Control Act provisions removing Wagner Act benefits from "communist-infiltrated" organizations, and the 1958 Landrum-Griffin ban on CP members serving as union officers were all designed to completely destroy CP strength among American workers. Combined with CIO ousters (under strong government pressure) of CP-dominated unions, these measures decimated communist influence in the American labor movement.[18]

The "mainstream" labor movement came under special attack when it showed signs of becoming radical. The peaks of political repression of labor — 1877, 1886, 1894 and 1919 — occurred when the labor movement as a whole appeared to be moving in disturbingly radical directions. In each case, the effect of repression was to curb the labor movement as a whole and/or to prod labor leaders to adopt more conservative policies. Repression of the violent and spontaneous 1877 railroad strikes, combined with the effects of the 1873-1877 depression, largely destroyed the post-Civil War labor movement.[19] After the labor movement recovered in the early 1880's, the Haymarket affair of 1886 and the repression associated with it helped to destroy the leading element of the labor revival, the Knights of Labor, which was viewed as a radical threat. The demise of the Knights and the impact of the Haymarket repression helped to bring the more conservative American Federation of Labor to the fore, and in general led the labor movement to adopt a much more conservative posture in the late 1880's.[20] The revival of labor in the 1890's, signs of increasing radicalism in the AFL and the threat of the emergence of a major industrial union in the railroad industry, the American Railway Union, was cut short by the repression of the 1892-96 period, and especially by the smashing of the Pullman strike. Signs of AFL flirtation with socialism and political action ended shortly after the Pullman disaster.[21] The 1919 Red Scare repression, especially of the coal and steel strikes, again scared the AFL's leadership away from the increasingly radical position American workers had been moving toward and reinforced the conservative direction of the AFL.[22] The psychological aftermath of the 1919 repression and the intense repression of labor during the 1920's kept the radical labor movement virtually paralyzed for ten years and reinforced the AFL's conservative inclinations. By the time the Wagner Act was passed, the historical heritage of the repression of radical labor insured that the surviving labor movement was safely conservative.[23]

Even Phillip Taft and Selig Perlman, two labor historians associated with the Commons-Perlman school of historiography, which has celebrated the conservative approach of the AFL as accurately reflecting the lack of class consciousness among American workers, have conceded that repression helped to drive the AFL away from a more radical approach:

> A succession of "tests" of the reaction of the American community to proposals of revolutionary change in the institution of private property, . . . had invariably evoked the same disastrous result. Thus the Chicago anarchists, . . . were made to feel the ferocious self-defense of a gigantically growing and self-satisfied community against those who would import the methods and aspirations of Russia and of Spain. Later, in the Pullman Strike of 1894, the labor movement saw how the courts, the Federal Executive and the ruling forces in the country could be counted on to act as one in crushing any real or fancied industrial rebellion. From this experience — for according to Gompers, the Haymarket bomb in Chicago in 1886 defeated the national eight-hour movement of that year — the leaders of the American Federation of Labor concluded that under no circumstances could labor afford to arouse the fears of the public for the safety of private property as a basic institution.[24]

The single most influential figure in the shaping of American labor history, Samuel Gompers, preached a form of accommodation with business, relegating labor to a permanent subordinate role, which bore remarkable resemblance to the accomodationist philosophy being taught simultaneously to black Americans by Booker T. Washington. As Christopher Lasch notes, Washington

> engineered a retreat from reform in favor of the same "practical," immediate and seemingly more realistic objectives toward which Gompers had steered the main body of the labor movement. Like Gompers, Washington spoke the language of the American business culture and tried to assure businessmen that recognition of the rights of minorities posed no threat to the status quo.[25]

Similarly, Robert Wiebe writes that AFL leaders, "somewhat after the fashion of Booker T. Washington, wooed doubters by appearing to ask so little that no decent citizen could deny them."[26]

No serious scholar would suggest that Washington really *wanted* black Americans to remain permanently subordinate to whites. Yet most scholars have interpreted American labor history to suggest that labor's subordination to business was perfectly acceptable to most workers, rather than exploring the possibility that repression and fear forced labor to be conservative, to avoid suffering the same fate as the Chicago anarchists, the WFM, the IWW, and the CP unions. In William Preston's pungent phrase, "These facile generalizations about working class attitudes smell like the labor history version of plantation paternalism."[27]

Two incidents in American labor history particularly reflect the ultimate American "solution" to the labor problem. During World War I, the federal government formed an alliance with the "safe" AFL against the IWW, granting the AFL concessions while destroying the IWW.[28] From 1947-1954, the federal government attempted to destroy CP influence in the unions. By the time the 1954 Communist Control Act was passed, the government was assured enough of the safeness of the AFL and CIO to exempt all unions associated with them from the punitive provisions of the act.[29] The American solution to the labor problem, then, was destruction of radical unions and acceptance of conservative unions — *after* their immunity from radical infection had been clearly demonstrated.

There is no way of demonstrating what would have happened had the WFM, the IWW and the CP union not been repressed, but their strengths cannot be lightly dismissed. We will never know if radical unions *might have* flourished in the U.S. without political repression; but we do know that every time they *did* flourish they were destroyed or severely damaged by political repression. To suggest radical labor *could not* have developed strength because it *did not*, without exploring all of the reasons why it did not, would be similar to concluding that trees could not grow in a particular area without bothering to notice that when trees did grow, someone invariably stripped off their bark.

The Failure of Radical Political Movements

There have been three major radical political movements in modern American history: the Socialist Party, the Communist Party, and the "New Left." Each was severely damaged by political repression during its peak of influence.

The Socialist Party reached its peak of electoral support during World War I due to its anti-war stand. During the war, the party suffered intense political repression in the form of arrests of party leaders, post office bans on SPA publications, and physical attacks on party members by police and vigilantes. The wartime repression completely destroyed about 30 percent of party local organizations, and drastically changed the geographical, ethnic and ideological balance of the party. The effects of the World War I repression, together with the 1919 split in the SPA, which the repression contributed to by weakening the center wing of the party, effectively destroyed the SPA; the party never recovered from these twin blows.[30]

The Communist Party became the dominant radical party after the 1919 split, taking away from the SPA most of its membership. The CP was severely and repeatedly repressed throughout its existence, in strikes, electoral campaigns, and simply attempting to survive, except when it supported government policies (1935-1939 and 1941-1945). Peaks in CP influence, when it was in opposition to the government, came in 1919, 1929-1935, 1939-1941, and 1945-1955; in each of the periods the party faced especially severe repression. Repression in 1919, characterized by raids and mass arrests, deportations and criminal syndicalism prosecutions was so severe that it decimated the newlyborn CP and drove it underground. Party membership essentially collapsed; those who remained constituted the party's most extreme wing, those most conspiratorially inclined and isolated from American life and most inclined to be guided ideologically by Soviet Russia. With the Stalinization of the party in the twenties, these characteristics became firmly embedded in the party and were to hamper it throughout its existence.[31] During 1929-1935, the CP showed strong signs of recovery, and subsequently met repression greater than any it had faced since 1919. Meetings were regularly broken up, and members were deported and prosecuted for criminal syndicalism. Organizational activity among the unemployed, agricultural workers, and other laborers was met with severe repression.[32]

When the CP adopted the "popular front" line in 1935, repression eased. However, when the party showed signs of increasing strength, and especially after the Nazi-Soviet alliance and adoption of a new "line" in 1939, repression against it increased again. CP members were barred from federal relief funds and federal employment. The CP was a major target of the 1940 Smith Act, the first peacetime sedition act since 1798. During the 1940 elections, the CP was barred from the ballot in fifteen states. During 1939-1941, the party was investigated by Congress and three state legislatures.[33]

The Russian-American alliance during World War II temporarily lessened repressive actions against the CP, but with the beginning of the Cold War and a switch in the CP "line," repression was resumed. Federal and state legislative investigations, deportations, sedition prosecutions, state and federal loyalty programs, the Attorney General's list of subversive activities, and federal and state anti-Communist legislation, including the complete outlawing of the party in some states, virtually decimated the CP and drove it underground for the second time in its history. It is symbolic of the intensity of post-World War II repression that the FBI's COINTELPRO operation designed to destroy the CP was begun in 1956, when the party was already in shreds.[34]

American repression of the CP after World War II was matched among other major democratic states only in West Germany, where the Communist Party was much stronger and which was closer geographically to the Soviet Union. Thus, given the threat posed, the American repression of the CP exceeded that of any other democratic nation.[35] England, weaker economically and militarily than the U.S., and closer physically to the Soviet Union, had a CP of approximately the same strength as the United States after World War II. Yet England "appeared to be favored by a climate of political tolerance."[36] According to Herbert Hyman's comparative study of civil liberties in two countries, the difference was caused by the much greater scope of official legislative and executive actions in the U.S., which legitimized attacks on civil liberties.

Following the demise of the CP, the New Left became the dominant radical movement during the Vietnam War era. Overt repression, especially conspiracy prosecutions of New Left leaders and harassing arrests and raids of the militant Black Panthers, led to considerable diversion of radical political activity from offensive to defensive struggles, but the most characteristic form of repression during this period was massive, covert surveillance and disruption and discrediting activity by governmental agents. The impact of such covert activity, which included the use of *agents provocateur,* burglaries and attempts by government agents to foster discord and disruption within the protest movement, is difficult to measure precisely. However, it is safe to conclude that such covert political repression, in combination with overt repression, played a very major role in destroying the Black Panthers, and, in combination with other factors, helped to bring about the downfall of the New Left.[37]

Repression not only harmed specific parties — it destroyed the continuity of American radical movements. The 1917-1920 and 1947-1954 repressive periods left a void during the twenties and fifties which necessitated the rebuilding of organizational structures when events in 1929 and the late 1960's led to greatly increased dissent. It is impossible to say exactly what difference an existing organizational base would have made, but certainly it would have accelerated and strengthened the radicalization of the thirties and sixties. Sociologist T. B. Bottomore states that Marxist or socialist movements failed to gain major influence in the United States during the Great Depression "above all" because

> there was no socialist movement which provided a real alternative to the New Deal. The situation was entirely different in most of the European countries. There large working class parties existed, already socialist if not Marxist in doctrine. The revival of Marxist thought was more profound and had a greater effect.[38]

Bottomore also attributes the "conformist state of mind" that dominated the fifties at least partly to the "absence of any important left-wing social movements" as well as the "defensiveness of intellectuals under the pressure of McCarthyism."[39] Similarly, Christopher Lasch attributes the weakness of radical thought in America following 1920 and 1950 to the fact that intellectuals had no mass movement they could relate to, leading to the "isolation of intellectuals from the rest of society."[40]

The Self-Censorship of American Citizens

The effects of political repression are not easy to pin down with any precision, since its real effects are not always its overt manifestations, such as the breaking of a strike or the shooting of a dissenter. The most important yet least measurable results of political repression are that it prevents people from doing things or even thinking things. In this sense the whole effect of political repression is much greater than the sum of its parts. Political repression has been a constant and intrusive presence in American political life during the 1870-1975 period, a presence that virtually all politically active and dissenting Americans are aware of, and which inevitably has affected their political behavior in small and large ways. Just as political repression has frequently been a rational response by political authorities to increasing threats to their power, self-censorship by American citizens has been a rational response to political repression, reflecting the fact that there have historically been major limitations on political freedoms, even in the "land of the free."

One of the most startling aspects of American political life is the virtual exclusion of socialism from any serious consideration as a possible solution to American economic or other problems. The mere charge of "socialism" or "communism" has been repeatedly used in American history to hinder the development of scores of reform movements and proposals, by serving the function of blocking off any further thought about them. For example, in the 1870-1900 period, cries of "communism" were used to attack the labor movement, proposals for railroad regulations, and limitations on working hours and farmers' pleas for reforms. During the 1920's, labor, the ACLU, the Progressive Party and scores of reform proposals were similarly attacked. In the 1930's, the label "communism" was used to attack the Roosevelt administration, the labor movement and proposals for direct relief, agricultural reforms, deficit financing, the TVA and pure food and drug legislation. The "red" tag was used from 1947 to 1954 to attack medicare, the Progressive Party, and scores of individuals and ideas. During the 1960's, the anti-war movement suffered similar attacks.[41]

The exclusion of socialism as a serious consideration cannot be attributed solely to such attacks and political repression, since many Americans are hostile to socialism or communism for other reasons. However, the long history of political repression directed against communist and socialist groups has unquestionably inhibited many Americans from thinking about or investigating such topics. The fear of being investigated by the FBI, wiretapped, hauled before legislative committees, deported or prosecuted for sedition has not been unrealistic. When political authorities punish people for association with certain movements and parties, people are acting quite rationally in being afraid to associate with such groups. And when the government itself issues "red baiting" statements against such groups at the same time that repressive activities are carried out against them, such statements become an element of repression themselves. Thus, Truman publicly linked the Progressive Party with the Communists during the period of the first Smith Act prosecutions, and repeated red-baiting attacks by governmental officials against the anti-Vietnam War movements were accompanied by conspiracy prosecutions, grand jury investigations and a massive surveillance program.[42]

Such attacks and prosecutions cause even highly critical groups to tone down their policies. For example, a former SDS President stated in 1965 that because certain ideas could be too easily associated with communism "and thence dismissed, indeed pilloried, along with their advocates . . . it is safer to stick, at least in our public faces, with liberal issues and the campaigns for marginal reforms."[43]

This sort of self-censorship has results that go beyond negating constitutional political freedoms. The unwillingness of Americans to seriously consider socialist solutions may mean that American society can never solve some of its problems. As Ralph Milliband writes:

> The fact that governments accept without question the capitalist context in which they operate is of absolutely fundamental importance. . . . The general commitment deeply colors the specific response, and affects not only the solution envisaged for the particular problem perceived, but the mode of perception itself; indeed, ideological commitment may and often does prevent perception at all, and makes impossible not only prescription for the disease, but its location.[44]

The self-censorship which political repression has imposed upon many American citizens has colored all of modern American history to some extent, but its effects can be seen most clearly in those periods which followed the most intense instances of repression. The 1920's and the 1950's were dominated by complacency about American problems, a lack of vigorous political debate, a dearth of new ideas about social problems and an extraordinary lack of dissent with regard to governmental policies. By any measure, these two decades stand out as the least productive and creative in modern American political history. Both of these decades also followed periods of intense repression that decimated the major organizations which had served as vehicles of radical thought and dissent and created a general atmosphere in which Americans did not feel "safe" in expressing dissenting political ideas.[45]

Because there were no significant efforts in these decades to deal with or discuss major social and political problems, such problems developed to a much greater degree than they might have otherwise and presented American society with grave crises in the following decades. The partial link between the destruction of the labor and radical movements in 1917-20 and the Great Depression has already been discussed.[46] During the 1950's dissent was again stifled. The existence of the poor and the deterioration of American cities were ignored during the 1950's and then suddenly discovered when the political climate changed in the early 1960's. There was virtually no debate on American foreign policy during the 1950-1965 period among the general public, and, more importantly, American foreign policy-makers themselves were afraid to freely debate foreign policy alternatives as a result of the long-range effects of the repression of the 1947-54 period. Experts in the State Department who had correctly predicted Mao Tse-Tung's success were fired, stripping the department of its best expertise on the Far East. Those who remained in the department were afraid to show any signs of "softness" towards communism. Officials in the White House, including every president from Truman to Nixon, felt forced to avoid looking "soft," even if that meant sending troops to foreign countries that had no clear relationship to American security and using the CIA to overthrow governments that posed only a domestic political threat to presidents who dreaded being accused of "losing" a country to communism. It is impossible to state precisely how great a part such considerations played in the twenty-five year American involvement in Vietnam, but they were unquestionably involved.[47]

Variables Associated with Changing Levels of Political Repression

A review of modern American history indicates that political repression has increased and decreased at various times, rather than staying at any one constant level. For example, from 1870-1929, "peaks" of political repression were reached, approximately, in 1877, 1886, 1894, 1908, and 1917-1920, while levels tended to increase immediately before and decrease immediately after all of these years.[48] Given the tendency of levels of political repression to repeatedly rise and fall, it seems likely that changes in certain variables may help to explain these increases and decreases.

The evidence of modern American history suggests that five variables consistently affect the level of political repression. The most important, and the *only* variable which *must* change for levels of political repression to change, is the attitude of policy-making authorities with regard to political dissidents. In order for political repression to increase, political authorities must decide to take actions that will increase it; in order for political repression to decrease, political authorities must decide to take actions that will decrease it. These actions manifest a shift in attitude on the part of political authorities, and this shift is the only variable which, by itself, can change the level of political repression.

There are other variables which do not in themselves directly affect levels of political repression, but are influential in changing the attitudes of political authorities. In modern American history, increased strain and tension in society and increased dissent (which frequently, but not always, occur together) have been the most important causes of political authorities increasing political repression; decreased strain and tension and decreased dissent have been the most important causes of political authorities decreasing political repression. Two other variables have played a somewhat less important role, largely limited to either spurring on or reining in political authorities already embarked on a policy of political repression. The existence of elements in society which can easily be made scapegoats, and lack of opposition to repression by key elites facilitates an expansion of repressive policies, while the lack of suitable scapegoats and significant opposition to repression by key elites hinders the expansion and continuation of politically repressive policies. (By key elites, what is meant are politically influential persons who do not make governmental policy, such as lower-level governmental officials, intellectuals, journalists, lawyers, businessmen, and, since 1935, labor leaders.)

Even if a change in the attitudes of the political authorities occurs without *any* change in the other variables, the level of political repression will change. However, such changes are *unlikely* to occur without change among at least some of the other variables, except in more totalitarian societies. The control exerted by Hitler and Stalin allowed them to increase or decrease political repression virtually on their political whims, with little regard for such factors as any signs of increasing strain or dissenting "threats" to the society, or the reactions of other persons. It follows that the more authoritarian democratic regimes become, the less will the attitudes of political authorities be affected or constrained by any factors external to themselves.

The level of strain and dissent in the society, the presence or absence of suitable target groups and the attitudes toward repression of key elites are all factors likely to affect the attitude of political authorities in more democratic societies. These factors are independent variables and can either reinforce or counteract each other in their impact on political authorities. Changes in the level of political repression will be most likely to occur if *all* of the variables change *markedly* in the same direction. If the variables move in different directions or exhibit little change a major change in repressive policies will be much less likely. Thus, a high level of strain and dissent will tend to increase the anxiety of political authorities and incline them towards a policy of repression, and the existence of suitable target groups and the lack of opposition to repression by key elites will tend to make adoption of a strongly repressive policy politically feasible and successful. Conversely, a low level of strain and dissent will tend to lower anxieties of political authorities and make a resort to political repression unlikely, and the lack of suitable target groups and strong opposition to repression from key elites would make the adoption of such policies politically costly and less likely to succeed. In the first set of circumstances political authorities would be likely to institute strongly repressive measures, while in the second set of circumstances adoption of a policy of intense repression would be unlikely. Intermediate levels of repression are likely to occur when the variables go in different directions; for example, where levels of strain and dissent are high, but the government is discredited, is unable to successfully pin the blame for society's troubles on a scapegoat group and faces strong opposition from key elites when repressive policies are adopted.

The Shifting Attitude of Political Authorities

The level of political repression changes only when the attitude of political authorities changes. Decisions affecting the level of political repression are made as a matter of *choice* by policy making authorities; political repression does not *have* to occur. As Otto Kircheimer notes, any regime confronted with an opposition group

> has a number of choices, running the gamut from genuine toleration to total supression. The decision against toleration and the . . . implementation of repressive measures are a matter of *choice*.[49]

The changing attitude of political authorities has been involved in all cases discussed in this book when the level of political repression has changed, but one of the clearest examples of how such a change in attitudes can occur without significant change on the other variables was the shift in attitudes on the federal level when Franklin D. Roosevelt took power in 1932. Herbert Hoover had been moving in an increasingly repressive direction as the Great Depression worsened and political protest increased. However, when Roosevelt became president, the federal government demonstrated greater tolerance towards dissent and emphasized reform rather than repression to deal with the increasing dissatisfaction in American society.[50] One veteran symbolized the changing atmosphere when he said of Mrs. Roosevelt's greeting the 1933 bonus army, "Hoover sent the army, Roosevelt sent his wife."[51]

Other cases of changing attitudes of political authorities usually also reflect changing external developments, but in each case the final decision with regard to political repression remained a matter of choice by political authorities. Thus, Franklin Roosevelt's tolerance for dissent strongly diminished under the impact of the increasing strain imposed on American society by the foreign policy crisis associated with the coming of World War II and the increasing strength of dissident elements that Roosevelt regarded as "subversive." After 1938, political repression in the U.S. greatly increased, reflecting to a large extent the changing attitudes of Roosevelt. During the war itself, at a time of great strain in American society (but little dissent), when support for the civil liberties of anti-war groups was virtually nil and when Japanese-Americans and pro-Nazis served as excellent scapegoats, Roosevelt again displayed his repressive capabilities.[52] Other examples, showing a clear relationship between a change in a president's attitude and increasing levels of political repression occurred during periods of increased strain and considerable dissent in the 1947-1950 period as Truman implemented such policies as the loyalty program, Smith Act prosecutions, and political deportations, and during the Vietnam War, when Johnson's increasing intolerance towards dissent led to a massive build-up in domestic surveillance activities.[53]

Conversely, the relative tolerance towards diversity exhibited by the Kennedy administration clearly helped to foster increased dissent and lessened repression during the 1960-1963 period, although this tolerance did not extend to "hard core" radicals.[54] Perhaps the clearest example of a president's changed attitude leading to lessened political repression was Eisenhower's decision in March, 1954, to stop appeasing McCarthy and take the offensive against him. This decision was probably the most important single action in stopping the worst excesses of "McCarthyism."[55] In both of these cases, the level of tension and dissent in American society was considerably less than at the height of the cold war, the major scapegoat (the Communist Party) had been virtually annihilated by repression already, and influential elites were expressing increased opposition to political repression.

As these examples suggest, the President is the single "political authority" whose attitude has been the most important with regard to political repression, at least since World War I. American politics generally has seen a shift in power from the private sector to the public sector, within the public sector from state and local government to the federal government, and within the federal government to the executive branch. All of these general shifts in American political power have been reflected in developments relevant to political repression. During the late nineteenth century, most political repression resulted from governmental tolerance of violations of the political liberties of dissenters by private parties; when government intervened directly it was when private forces were unable to contain strikes and demonstrations, and almost invariably emanated from the state and local level. The federal government became involved only when state and local resources were exhausted, as in the 1877 and 1894 railroad strikes.[56] In the twentieth century, governmental repression became increasingly overt and direct, reflecting the general tendency of government to increase its activities. The turning point was the passage of restrictive immigration legislation, sedition and criminal anarchy and syndicalism acts during the 1900-1920 period, and the increasing use of court injunctions in labor disputes.[57] With the major exception of World War I, most direct governmental repression continued to originate on the state and local level until the approach of World War II.[58] Since about 1940, the federal government has clearly taken the lead in setting the general tone with regard to political repression, with state and local repression tending to follow the federal lead. Especially significant events indicating this trend were the passage of the Hatch Act in 1939 and the Smith Act in 1940, the virtual federalization of repression during World War II, the initiation of the loyalty program and Smith Act prosecutions in 1947-1948, the passage of the Internal Security and the Communist Control Acts in 1950 and 1954, the congressional anti-subversive investigations of the 1947-54 period, and the vast expansion of federal internal security surveillance operations.[59] This shift in power from the state and local to the federal government with regard to political repression reflected a similar shift in political power generally.

Another general tendency which has been reflected with regard to political repression has been a shift in power from the legislative to executive branch. During the 1917-20, 1939-1945 and 1947-54 periods of intense repression spearheaded by the federal government, Congress and the executive branch both played important roles. Thus, Congress authorized most World War I Federal repression with the Espionage and Sedition Acts, supported repression during the 1939-1945 period with the Hatch and Smith Acts, and played a major role in fostering repression during the 1947-1954 period through legislative investigations and the Internal Security and Communist Control Acts.[60] Although there clearly was congressional pressure for repression during the Vietnam War era, also, the actions of the Johnson and Nixon administrations in vastly expanding domestic surveillance activities and initiating dubious prosecutions of political dissidents reflected executive domination and initiation of repression to a greater degree than in previous periods in American history. One of the important tools Johnson and Nixon were able to use in repressive as well as other types of activities was the ability to take actions that remained secret outside of a small group in the executive branch, including the initiation of CIA and Army domestic surveillance, and a vast expansion of FBI activities.[61]

While presidential dominance in political repression has grown along with general presidential power especially in *recent* years, the evidence of American history since World War I suggests that severe political repression will not occur without the clear tolerance or active encouragement of the president (Wilson, 1917-20; Hoover, 1929-32; Franklin Roosevelt, 1939-45; Truman, 1947-53; Eisenhower, 1953-54; Johnson, 1967-68; Nixon, 1969-73).[62] Conversely, active opposition to repression by a president can drastically modify the characteristics of the repression (Roosevelt, 1933; Eisenhower, 1954).[63] There has been no significant difference between "liberal" and "conservative" presidents in carrying out repressive policies. Since World War I, American presidents with relatively non-repressive records have included Calvin Coolidge, a conservative, and John F. Kennedy, a liberal, while the most repressive presidents have included liberals Woodrow Wilson, Franklin Roosevelt, Harry Truman and Lyndon Johnson, along with conservative Richard Nixon.

Although the president is the most important political authority with regard to influencing the level of repression, he is not the only person with influence. On the federal level, Congress and the courts, especially the Supreme Court, can exercise significant influence on the level of political repression if they choose to.

When all three branches of the federal government are united upon a policy of severe repression, repression reaches unusually high levels. Thus, during the 1917-20 and 1947-54 periods, all three branches of the federal government pursued policies of repression, and these periods were among the most repressive in modern American history.[64] During the 1957-58 and Vietnam War periods, the Supreme Court clearly hindered repressive efforts, and after 1971 Congress helped to hinder repression initiated by the Nixon administration.[65]

While the federal government has taken the lead in setting a repressive or non-repressive atmosphere since World War II, state and local governments still play important roles. State and local governments have normally followed the federal lead during periods of repression, as in World War I, 1947-54, and the Vietnam War era and have thus added to the repressive atmosphere established in Washington.[66] However, state and local governments can undermine federal efforts. During the Great Depression, (before federal dominance with regard to political repression had been clearly established), a number of state governments undermined attempts by the Hoover administration to create a repressive atmosphere and later attempts by the Roosevelt administration to shift the emphasis from repression to reform.[67] Clearly repression will be more intense when political authorities on all levels of government are united. During the 1917-20 and 1947-54 periods, the united efforts of federal, state and local governments played a significant role in fostering two of the most repressive periods in modern American history.

The *reasons* political authorities have chosen to resort to political repression in modern American history (as opposed to the *conditions* that facilitate or hinder making such choices which are discussed below) can be grouped into four analytically distinct, if sometimes temporarily inseparable, classes. A resort to political repression can simply reflect a basic lack of sympathy with principles of civil liberty that can be manifested under certain circumstances with few costs. A resort to political repression can reflect a genuine fear that the political opposition will otherwise pose a real threat to governmental power or policies. Political repression can be resorted to essentially as a means of solving a crisis in societal integration. Political repression can also be fostered to bring personal political benefits to the repressors.

The harassment of pro-fascist forces during World War II by the Roosevelt administration is a clear example of political repression reflecting a lack of sympathy for civil liberties. The anti-war opposition was virtually negligible and had minimal power or influence, yet it was subjected to an intense campaign of political repression. While the wartime atmosphere insured that implementing such repression had few political costs to the Roosevelt administration, due to the lack of support for the civil liberties of dissidents, it also brought few political gains. It was not needed to bring about war-time unity, since that already existed. Political repression during World War II largely reflected the fact that President Roosevelt was "never more than vaguely interested in civil liberties"[68] and had no compunctions about resorting to repression when the costs were minimal. (On the other hand, Roosevelt reversed Hoover's repressive policies towards the left because he perceived that such policies were political liabilities during the early years of the Depression.) While the World War II example is perhaps the clearest case of a link between a fundamental lack of support for civil liberties and the implementation of political repression, there are many others which reflect this together with some of the other motives listed above. Thus, Lyndon Johnson resorted to political repression partly because he (accurately) viewed anti-war sentiment as a threat to his power and policies, but also because, as Eric Goldman has commented, Johnson "did not really believe" in the right to dissent, "or to put the matter more precisely, he believed in the right but did not believe it should be exercised."[69] The fear that political opposition will threaten governmental power or policies has been involved in most instances of American political repression. The response of the business-government alliance to the rise of the labor movement, Wilson's repression of anti-war opposition, the Great Red Scare of 1919, Truman's repressive actions against foreign policy critics and Johnson and Nixon's repression of anti-war opposition were all reflections of this fear. The more radical the opposition involved (e.g. the IWW, WFM, SPA, SWP and New Left), the more threatening it has appeared to political authorities, and the greater their fears and repressive response has been.

Solving crises in societal integration has been a common motivation in leading political authorities to adopt policies of political repression. General fears that society was "coming apart" are evident in many crises that eventuated in political repression: the depressions and labor outbursts of 1873-1877, 1884-1886, and 1892-1896; the political and labor upheaval of 1919 and the 1930's; and the intense crisis of the Vietnam War era. In such circumstances, political repression, by focussing the fears of a society on a suitable scapegoat, can be used to reintegrate a society. Such efforts can be particularly effective if the repression is directed against a group that can be linked to foreign threat or foreign "isms," as was done perhaps most successfully during the 1919 Red Scare.[70]

Finally hopes for personal political benefit has frequently motivated political repressors, especially during periods of high societal strain when suitable scapegoats are available. An early case was the anti-IWW campaign of Washington State newspaperman Albert Johnson, which led to a Congressional career. Other cases include Attorney General Palmer, Richard Nixon, Joseph McCarthy, and Ronald Reagan.[71] Unquestionably some of these men were sincere but they were also well aware of the political pot of gold at the end of the subversive-hunting rainbow. Thus, during the 1950-1954 period, the Communist Party posed no serious threat to anything, but anti-communism was a potent and beneficial political stance. As Otto Kircheimer writes, the Communist party became a

> political football for politicians and party machines at the local or state level. The legislative fight around the 1954 Communist Control Act, for example, revealed clearly that the legislators' decisions were not based on preferences for one or the other course of action, or on the merits or demerits of either; they were determined by the need to outdo the other fellow in vociferously rabid anti-Communism.[72]

Strain and Tension in Society

Increased strain and tension in American history has frequently been associated with increased levels of political repression. Factors which have regularly led to both increased strain and tension and to an increased repressive response on the part of political authorities have been severe economic problems, such as depressions (1873-78, 1884-86, 1893-97, 1907-08, 1913-16, 1929-32) and strike waves (1886, 1894, 1919, 1934); participation in wars (1917-18, 1941-45, 1950-54, 1965-73), or severe foreign policy crises which appeared to threaten war (1938-41, 1947-50); and the spread of political philosophies abroad that were viewed as threatening by political authorities (the Paris Commune in 1871, the Russian Revolution of 1917, the spread of Nazism in Europe after 1935, the spread of communism in Europe after 1945, the Chinese Revolution of 1949).[73]

That a war or severe foreign policy crisis can facilitate domestic repression has long been noted by political observers. For example, James Madison wrote to Thomas Jefferson in 1798, during the Alien and Sedition crisis (in which the Federalist administration took advantage of a war scare with France to repress the opposition Republicans), "Perhaps it is a universal truth that the loss of liberty at home is to be charged to the provisions against dangers, real or pretended, from abroad."[74] Similarly, Alexis de Toqueville wrote in the nineteenth century:

> No protracted war can fail to endanger the freedom of a democratic country. War must invariably and immeasureably increase the powers of civil government. It must almost compulsorarily concentrate the direction of all men and the management of all things in the hands of the administration. If it leads not to despotism by sudden violence, it prepares men for it more gently by their habits. All those who seek to destroy the liberties of a democratic nation ought to know that war is the surest and shortest means to accomplish it.[75]

The ending of those events which have led to increased strain and tension, i.e., the ending of depressions (1878, 1886, 1897, 1908) and strike waves (1887, 1895, 1920); the ending of foreign wars (1945, 1954, 1974) or an end to the spread of threatening philosophies abroad (an apparent stop to the spread of communism in 1920 and in the mid-1950's) will tend to facilitate a lessened repressive response by political authorities.[76]

Events which create severe strain in society facilitate a repressive response by political authorities for a number of reasons. Perhaps most important is that the authorities view such events as posing particularly troublesome threats to their legitimacy and authority. The "stakes" are rarely higher for political authorities than in their handling of severe economic disturbances or of severe foreign policy crises and wars. Political authorities, acting in such situations, feel particularly vulnerable to attack, and therefore are inclined to move against dissent much more rapidly than in non-crisis situations. Since the consequences of widespread public perceptions that the administration has made major errors in crisis situations are so great (i.e. Hoover's election defeat in 1932, Johnson's forced withdrawal in 1968), the political authorities tend to attempt to curb any discussion or protests that suggest errors have been made or any major signs of dissent that appear to pose a serious threat to existing power relationships. Particularly in foreign policy crises in the twentieth century, American presidents have frequently adopted the position that their policies are so clearly and evidently "right" that other opinions are simply "wrong" and cannot be tolerated, or else can only result from some conspiratorial and subversive relationship between domestic dissenters and foreign enemy powers (Wilson in World War I, Roosevelt in World War II, Truman during the "Cold War," Johnson and Nixon during the Vietnam War).[77]

A crisis that leads to increased strain and tension in society is frequently linked with other developments that facilitate a repressive response from political authorities. Frequently economic difficulties and foreign wars result not only in increased strain and tension in the society but also lead to increased dissent. This tends to create not only additional fears in the minds of political authorities about threats to their power, but also frequently creates general fears in the population about society "coming apart." Under such conditions of increased strain and tension coupled with increased dissent and seeming societal disintegration, political authorities may seek to use repressive techniques to reunify the society, at least around the issue of hatred for dissenters. Under such conditions, searches are especially likely to be made for suitable scapegoats. As Walter Metzger points out:

> The fear of conspiracy usually flourishes in times of societal anxiety. When men face social problems too new for settled habits to control and too complex for current knowledge to explain, they will ascribe them to the work of outside agents — to the jealousy and malice of the gods, or to the intrigues of hostile strangers.[78]

A crisis atmosphere is also frequently accompanied by a banding together of key elite groups and their increased willingness, or even eagerness, to support repressive policies.

Under these conditions of societal crisis, increased dissent, a search for scapegoats and a collapse of support for civil liberties among key elites, ambitious politicians searching for an issue to bring them to public prominence may come to the fore as a result of their repressive proposals and actions (i.e. A. Mitchell Palmer). Also under these conditions, a basic lack of sympathy for civil liberties on the part of political authorities is particularly likely to be manifested, since the costs will be so few. Thus, the repressive actions taken against the IWW and SPA during World War I might have been much more difficult to achieve under calmer times.

Although frequently linked to other factors that tend to facilitate repression, the existence of societal strain and tension acts as an independent variable in increasing the likelihood of repressive policies, and is not *always* linked with these other factors. For example, dissent actually decreased after Pearl Harbor and from 1947 to 1954, yet repression increased under the crisis conditions of the society.[79] During the Great Depression and the Vietnam War, many key elites felt reform and not repression was needed, and attempts to find scapegoats proved rather unsuccessful because the target groups of repressors encompassed large and influential segments of the population. Nevertheless, political authorities on the federal level during the Hoover, Johnson, and Nixon administration increased levels of repression in response to the general state of crisis in American society.[80] The existence of a crisis atmosphere, in short, is an independent variable that *tends* to facilitate repression and *tends* to be linked to other factors that facilitate repression; but these relationships do not always hold true and therefore each factor must be analyzed independently.

Dissent

Periods of increased repression have followed periods of increased dissent often during modern American history. Examples include the repressive periods centered around 1873-1878, 1884-1886, 1892-1894, the "war" against the WFM in Colorado in 1903-1904, the 1908 anarchist scare, anti-IWW and anti-labor repression during the 1912-1917 period, the 1917-1920 period, the repression initiated by the Hoover administration during 1929-1932 and the repression during the Vietnam War era. Decreased repression has generally followed decreased dissent; for example, following 1877, 1886, 1894, 1919, 1954, and the end of the Vietnam War.[81]

The major reason for this relationship is that increased dissent is viewed as a threat to the power and policies of the political authorities; once dissent reaches a certain level, the threat has often been viewed as so great that civil liberties must be sacrificed to the maintainence of power. Thus, repression has often increased markedly following some clear display of increasing influence or some major success by dissenting groups, i.e. *after* the rapidly increasing influence of the anarchists in the Chicago labor movement and the Knights of Labor had been manifested in 1885-86; *after* the success of the American Railway Union in the 1893 strike against the Great Northern Railroad; *after* rapid gains by the WFM in

Colorado and the West in 1903-04; *after* SPA election gains in 1917; *after* tremendous IWW organizational gains during the 1915-17 period; *after* the Seattle general strike and increasing evidence of growing radical influence in 1919; *after* CP gains among the unemployed, agricultural workers, and other laborers during the Great Depression; *after* signs of increasing strength by the Progressive Party in 1947-1948; *after* major gains by the anti-war movement during the Vietnam War.[82] Political repression is often triggered by increased dissent generally, and especially by clear evidence that dissenters are becoming successful.

Increased dissent is frequently linked temporally with other factors likely to increase repressive levels — societal crises such as unpopular wars and depressions that increase strain, a collapse of support for civil liberties by key elites, and a search for suitable "scapegoats" on whom the blame can be pinned. Under these conditions, political authorities are likely to be motivated not only by fear of a direct threat to their power in implementing repression, but also by the other motivating factors — repression as a means of bringing the society "together," the political rewards obtainable, and the opportunity to implement repressive policies at small cost.

Although dissent acts as an independent factor in facilitating repression, increased dissent is not invariably linked with increased repression. Thus, the increased dissent of the Kennedy years did not result in increased repression until it was accompanied by the major crisis brought on by the Vietnam War and civil disorders at home, along with the development of a deviant "counterculture" that served at least as a somewhat, if not entirely, satisfactory scapegoat group.[83] Further, increased dissent is not always a factor when repression increases, since dissent decreased yet repression increased during World War II and 1947-1954.

Just as increased dissent often leads to increased repression, decreased dissent *usually* leads to decreased repression. This decreased dissent may have two very different causes. Dissent may decrease because sources of strain have decreased (i.e. a depression or unpopular war has ended) and political dissidents have been satisfied. Dissent may also decrease because repression has succeeded and dissidents have been silenced, as after the 1917-20 and 1947-54 periods.[84] In both instances, decreased dissent results in decreased repression, but the reasons for the decrease in dissent are very different. (Conversely, a lack of repression may either reflect a tolerant government or a lack of dissenters to repress. One recalls the incident in which a Soviet dissident was told by a policeman who was arresting him in Red Square, "You fool, if you had kept your mouth shut, you could have lived peacefully."[85])

It is difficult to predict, without knowing the exact historical situation, what effect an *increase* in the level of political repression will have upon the level of dissent. When the government has the support of the vast majority of the politically active, influential and articulate segments of the population, as during World War I, World War II and the Cold War, increased repression will usually succeed in curbing dissent, since the minority dissenters will have little support from outside their own groups. On the other hand, when the government is discredited, and dissent is widespread even among influential segments of the population, increased repression may lead to an increased delegitimization of the political authorities and increased dissent. This was the case during the Hoover period of the Great Depression, with the repression of the Bonus Army serving mostly to further discredit the Hoover administration.[86] Similarly, during the Vietnam War, increased repression further delegitimized a government which had already been severely discredited, and dissent increased. This accounts for the extraordinary string of defeats the Nixon administration suffered in the courts in comparison with governmental successes during World War I and the Cold War.[87]

Target Groups

In American society, some groups have had certain "strange" characteristics which have made them easy targets and easy scapegoats for real or imagined social ills. This "strangeness" has included such characteristics as unusual dress, hair and personal life styles (the Vietnam War era); borrowing ideas from "foreign" sources (the communist and socialist movements, and, allegedly, the labor movement); having a heavy immigrant component (again, the communist, socialist, and labor movements); or simply being remote from centers of power, numerically weak, or rejecting generally held ideas (most of the dissenters discussed in this study). The American experience suggests that the more dissenters can identify with the "mainstream," the less likely political authorities are to institute or expand political repression. However, the existence or absence of suitable target groups largely acts to hinder or facilitate political authorities already embarked on a policy of repression in a context of societal crisis and/or increased dissent. Rarely, if ever, does the mere existence of a suitable scapegoat group outside of such a context lead to any significant change in the level of political repression. In modern American history, the only instance that even comes close to such an occurrence was the anarchist scare of 1901-03. Even in this case, there was a "crisis" set off by the assassination of McKinley, while the briefness and mildness of the scare were precisely because there was no significant increase in dissent during this period and no general societal crisis.[88] In other words, the mere existence of a handful of anarchists could not sustain a prolonged or intense period of political repression by itself.

In the proper context, "suitable" targets do facilitate repression because political authorities perceive the political benefits are likely to be high, the reintegration benefits substantial, and the policy likely to be successful, when the "strange" and "deviant" are persecuted, especially since such groups are unlikely to have much support among influential segments of the society. On the other hand, the persecution of mainstream, entrenched groups is likely to meet powerful resistance from elites, lead to increased devisiveness in the society, backfire politically and fail to succeed in stifling dissent. Thus, attempts to make scapegoats out of radicals, the unemployed, and labor during the Great Depression failed to make significant headway, because increasing numbers of influential elements of American society regarded conservative and business elements who sought to foster repression as the real villains and identified with the proposed targets of repression. The tremendous resistance to repression which developed clearly helped to impose limits on the repressors.[89] Sen. McCarthy found that he had chosen "unsuitable" targets when he attempted to investigate the CIA and American clergymen; what finally ruined him was his attack on the U.S. Army, a target which could hardly have been more "unsuitable."[90] The Johnson and Nixon administrations met opposition when their repression of the anti-war movement meant attacking a group with growing middle-class and intellectual support.[91] It seems very likely that the strong resistance to repression in the Vietnam War era which resulted both helped to greatly limit the degree of repression which did occur, and was responsible for the fact that much of the repression was covert rather than overt. Nixon was forced to resign when it became known that he had covertly used the techniques of political repression traditionally directed only against "extremist" groups against the Democratic Party, an eminently "unsuitable" target group for such tactics.[92]

Repression has been most successful, both in terms of political benefits for the repressors and severe hampering of the repressed, when the targets have been most "suitable." Examples include the labor movement (until it became "mainstream"); the communist-anarchist and anarchist movements; the IWW, SPA and CP; and pro-fascist groups during World War II. Although at times many of these groups showed signs of increasing strength and influence, they never really captured the allegiance of a large or powerful percentage of the population. Most were associated in the public mind with "foreign" ideologies or memberships, and were considered personally "bizarre" in various ways. Radical groups with many alien members have been particularly susceptible to successful repression, since as Geoffrey Perrett notes, aliens are "easily identified, are numerically weak, have no great political leverage, have few powerful friends, are split into scores of fragments and are often at odds with one another.[93] Migrant labor has repeatedly suffered severe repression for similar reasons.[94]

The weakness of these groups made them successful targets for political repression, and the success of the repression made it difficult for them to grow strong. The failure of repression against stronger groups (the labor movement during the 1930's and the anti-war movement during the 1960's) necessitated that at least the most popular of their demands be granted (e.g. the Wagner Act and the various jobs and relief programs of the New Deal, the end of the draft and the end of the Vietnam War in the 1960's). This enabled the political authorities to isolate and later repress the truly "suitable" target groups (e.g. the fate of the communists *after* the depression and World War II, the fate of the more radical elements during late 1960's and the early 1970's).

Political repression in any society is limited by the fact that the usefulness of essential groups must not be destroyed. Thus, when the 1919 Red Scare showed signs of hampering industrial production and when McCarthyism showed signs of destroying the effectiveness of the Army, major elite groups began to impose controls on the repression.[95] Similarly, during World War II Japanese-Americans living on the west coast were relatively few and were dispensable, but Japanese-Americans living in Hawaii were essential to the economy and so were not rounded up.[96] As Geoffrey Perrett notes:

> A scapegoat is definitionally someone who can be dispensed with. Otherwise his sacrifice becomes our sacrifice.[97]

Eugene Walter notes that for a terrorristic regime to function "the victims in the process of terror must be expendable," "terror must be balanced by working incentives that induce co-operation," (e.g. jail for the IWW, but benefits for the AFL) and "cooperative relationships must survive the effect of the terror" since "if the impact of the terror destroys the network of relationships that supports collective activities and political interactions, the entire cooperative system will break down."[98]

Groups which have repeatedly been the targets of political repression in modern American history have been mainly on the political left. The only major exception to this tendency has been the repression suffered by the pro-fascist right during World War II, and the repression suffered by the Ku Klux Klan in the 1920's and 1960's. However, repression suffered by the KKK was inextricably involved with governmental investigations and prosecutions for very real killings, bombings and beatings,[99] while the political left repeatedly suffered severe and continuous repression simply for speech and organizational activities. The only clear parallel to repression suffered by the left as a matter of course for speech was the repression of the pro-Nazi right during World War II.[100] The historical lesson is that the extreme right that does not engage in overt violence is safe from repression no matter what it says and believes except in time of war, while the extreme left can expect to suffer repression simply for speech. Thus, the non-violent radical right flourished unhindered during the 1920's and 1950's, while the remaining tatters of the non-violent left suffered repression whenever they emerged publicly. Clearly, the non-violent right is essentially immune from repression for the same reason that the non-violent left is repeatedly subjected to repression: namely, conservative forces control American government and society. The ideas of the extreme right — anti-communism, free enterprise philosophy, superpatriotism — are also the ideas of the powerful elements in American society, admittedly somewhat vulgarized, while the ideas of the extreme left pose a threat to these elements by their very utterance. Thus the left suffers for the expression of ideas only, while the right is immune unless actually posing a threat to law and order, or unless opposing governmental policies in time of war, when the evidence of twentieth century American history suggests that any group is going to suffer severe repression no matter what its ideological orientation.

As America has become increasingly concerned about international affairs, the targets of repression have increasingly become groups dissenting over foreign policy. Until World War II, America's focus was essentially inward, and a basic fear of governmental officials was of lower-class uprisings and the major target of repression was the labor movement. After the labor movement was tamed and accepted as a respectable partner in American society, America's perspective turned increasingly outward, and the basic fear of governmental officials became internal dissenting elements aligned with foreign foes, and the major target of repression became foreign policy critics during periods of international war and tension. This trend in targets of repression shows again the integral link between the nature of American political repression and general trends in American society and politics.

Opposition by Key Elites

Lack of opposition to repression by key elites tends to make it more likely that political authorities will implement or expand policies of repression; opposition to repression by such elites tends to hinder or limit the implementation of repressive policies. Like the existence or absence of suitable target groups, the opposition or lack of opposition by key elites to repression largely acts to hinder or facilitate political authorities already embarked on a policy of repression in a context of societal crisis and/or increased dissent. There do not appear to be any cases in American history where a decision to implement repressive policies was largely based on lack of opposition to repression by elites. However, there is considerable historical evidence which suggests that when key elites do not support political liberties for dissident groups (1873-1900, 1917-20, World War II, 1947-54) that repression tends to expand and to be quite severe.[101] The 1919 Red Scare and the McCarthy period ended shortly after key elites increasingly opposed the continuation or expansion of repressive policies, however, and the implementation of repressive policies during the Great Depression and the Vietnam War period were greatly limited by strong opposition to such policies by key elites.[102] The absence or presence of "suitable" target groups historically has been linked with opposition or lack of opposition to repression by key elites, but these variables can be analyzed separately. Thus, some "suitable" radical remnants continued to exist in 1920 and 1954, but key elites shifted their position from tolerance or support of repression to opposition to repression, and these shifts appear to have been quite influential in imposing limits on the repression.

Opposition to political repression by key elites hinders the implementation or expansion of repressive policies because political authorities frequently gauge their political strength by the amount of support they receive from such elites, since the "mass" is generally regarded as inarticulate or unintelligeable, and lacks the political or financial resources to express itself. In a society which retains democratic features, political authorities cannot govern effectively without a certain level of political support, and in some cases policies simply cannot be implemented without the support of influential elites. Thus, for political authorities to ignore signs of strong opposition to important policies by influential elites will mean either political paralysis or eventual electoral repudiation. The major importance of elite opinion is to potentially impose barriers on the imposition of repressive policies when conditions otherwise make their implementation likely.

There is little reason to believe that "mass," as opposed to elite public opinion, has had significant influence on political authorities. Public opinion polls have repeatedly demonstrated a lack of majority public support for the right of political dissent from the time of the first polls taken on this question in 1936 to the present, during times of war, peace, crisis, non-crisis, weak dissent, and strong dissent. Public opinion has generally grown less tolerant of dissent during periods of intense repression, and more tolerant of dissent during periods of relative tolerance, but there is no reason to believe that this causes the general political atmosphere rather than reflecting it. Further, while periods of political repression have alternated with periods of greater tolerance, public opinion on the right of dissent appears to have been steadily growing more negative. Thus, Hazel Erksine, in a review of public opinion polls dealing with freedom of speech from 1936 to 1970, concluded:

> Before 1950, a maximum of 49 percent would have allowed an extremist to speak freely. During the 1950's permissiveness toward radicals never climbed above 29 percent. Since 1960 only two in ten would accord free expression to any extreme point of view.[103]

Perhaps the clearest evidence that "mass" public opinion has little relation to the level of political repression is poll data indicating that during the height of McCarthyism few Americans were highly concerned by the Communist "menace." A survey of almost five thousand Americans taken during Army-McCarthy hearings in the spring of 1954 found that less than one percent expressed concern about the threat of communism when asked "What kind of things do you worry about?" When a follow-up question, "Are there other problems you worry or are concerned about, especially political or world problems?" was asked, only about six percent referred to the Communist threat. Samuel Stouffer, the survey director, concluded that these and other responses demonstrate that the Communist threat (as well as the threat to civil liberties) was not a matter of "burning preoccupation" among the American public during this period.[104] In William Spinrad's words, "whatever widespread pro-McCarthyite sentiment existed represented only that of an applauding audience rather than a pressuring public."[105] Political repression, in short, is created and fostered by elites, not masses.

> The people are largely passive and approving. The active participation of the people in the process of repression is not even necessary. Their approval and non-interference is enough to permit elites to promote and administer repression. If fascism came to America it would not require popular participation — merely popular non-opposition.[106]

Closing Words

Writing a book, and particularly a book that originated as a Ph.D. dissertation, is inevitably to some extent a purely academic exercise. But the preservation of political freedom is not an academic exercise. That a book such as this can be openly published is a clear sign that the United States remains a country that has more political freedom than most countries in the world. But that it was necessary to write this book is a reflection that that freedom is gravely endangered. Since the research for this book began, Chile, Uruguay and India, three countries with long histories of political democracy, have become totalitarian states. If the trends of the last fifty years in the United States continue, it will not be possible to publish a book such as this in another fifty years.

The first step towards solving a problem is recognizing that it exists. One of the most poignant expressions of this idea, with relation to political repression, was made by Senator Philip Hart, following revelations of FBI misconduct before the Senate Intelligence Committee in 1975. Senator Hart said:

> As I'm sure others have, I have been told for years by, among others, some of my own family, that this is exactly what the Bureau was doing all of the time, and in my great wisdom and high office, I assured them that . . . it just wasn't true, it couldn't happen. . . . The trick now, . . . is for this committee to be able to figure out how to persuade the people of this country that indeed it did go on. And how shall we insure that it will never happen again? But it will happen repeatedly unless we can bring ourselves to understand and accept that it did go on.[107]

The United States has received repeated warnings during the past century, and especially in the last few decades, that it is headed for totalitarianism; the warnings have been as clear as a large highway sign would be informing a driver on a freeway that he was about to head over a cliff. The fate of political freedom in the United States rests on whether the warnings are heeded, or whether the country continues to head in the direction of the totalitarian abyss.

Notes

All sources are given a complete citation when they are first listed. After the first citation, works are usually cited only by author's name. When one author has written more than one work (or if more than one person with the same last name is cited), a brief title is also included in later citations. All works cited in more than one chapter are also listed with a full citation in the bibliography. The following abbreviations are used in the notes:

ACLUAR	American Civil Liberties Union, *Annual Report*
AHR	*American Historical Review*
APSR	*American Political Science Review*
AW	*Arizona and the West*
CL	*Civil Liberties*
CLR	*Civil Liberties Review*
HIR	*Impeachment of Richard M. Nixon, President of the United States; The Final Report of the Committee of the Judiciary, House of Representatives* (New York: Bantam, 1975).
HS	U.S., Bureau of the Census, *Historical Statistics of the United States, Colonial Times to 1957.*
INS	U.S., Immigration and Naturalization Service, *Annual Report.*
ISS	U.S., Legislative Reference Service, *Internal Security and Subversion*, 89th Congress, 1st Session.
JAH	*Journal of American History*
JW	*Journal of the West*
LAT	*Los Angeles Times*
LH	*Labor History*
MH	*Minnesota History*
NYT	*New York Times*
OH	*Ohio History*
PHR	*Pacific Historical Review*
PNQ	*Pacific Northwest Quarterly*
PSQ	*Political Science Quarterly*
SDET	*San Diego Evening Tribune*
SDU	*San Diego Union*
SICH	U.S., Senate, Select Committee to Study Governmental Operations With Respect to Intelligence Activities, *Hearings on the Federal Bureau of Investigation*, 94th Congress, 1st session.
SICFR	U.S., Senate, *Final Report of the Select Committee to Study Governmental Operations with Respect to Intelligence Operations, Book II: Intelligence Activities and the Rights of Americans,* Report No. 94-755, 94th Congress, 2nd session, April 26, 1976.
SICSR	U.S., Senate, *Final Report of the Select Committee to Study Governmental Operations with Respect to Intelligence Activities, Book III: Supplementary Detailed Staff Reports on Intelligence Activities and the Rights of Americans,* Report No. 94-755, 94th Congress, 2nd session, April 23, 1976.
SWR	*The Senate Watergate Report* (New York: Bantam, 1975)
WMH	*Wisconsin Magazine of History*

INTRODUCTION

1. For an excellent short discussion of this subject, see Thomas I. Emerson, *Towards A General Theory of the First Amendment* (New York: Vintage, 1967), pp. 3-15.
2. There is a three-fold justification for drawing the line at 1870: 1) limits simply have to be drawn somewhere, and one hundred years of history is enough; 2) 1870 falls within the period traditionally regarded as a major breaking point in American history because of the conclusion of the Civil War and the tremendous growth of the modern-day American industrial apparatus, and the creation of the modern labor force in the years following the Civil War; and 3) from the author's perspective, political repression took a quantum leap upwards in terms of its significance and consistency after 1870. All discussion of Reconstruction-related events are excluded from this study, although Reconstruction was not terminated until 1877.
3. *The American Political Tradition* (New York: Vintage, 1948), p. viii.
4. *Political Oppositions in Western Democracies* (New Haven: Yale University Press, 1968), pp. xiii-xiv.
5. Thus, David M. Potter in *People of Plenty* (Chicago: University of Chicago Press, 1954) suggests that the alleged notorious unresponsiveness of American workers to concepts of class warfare can be accounted for by the fact that the United States has traditionally been a prosperous country and "has had a greater measure of social equality and social mobility than any highly developed society in human history" (p. 95). Although America has never been a classless society, Potter states, the myth of equality has had enough reality component to it to retain "a most tenacious hold" on the minds of American workers and thus divert them from class struggle ideologies (p. 97). Daniel Boorstin, in *The Genius of American Politics* (Chicago: University of Chicago Press, 1953), similarly accounts for the lack of serious ideological debate in American history; since America "was the land of dreams-come true," Boorstin states, there was no need for Americans to devote their time to idle ideological speculation and American political theory amounted to "givenness," the belief that "values in America are in some way or other automatically defined: given by certain facts of geography or history" (pp. 8-9, 171). Louis Hartz, in *The Liberal Tradition in America* (New York: Harcourt, Brace, 1955), accounts for the lack of strong opposition to what he views as the dominant American philosophy of private property and liberal democracy in terms of America's lack of a feudal past and the resultant absence of an inherited tradition of class separation and conflict. The absence of feudal restrictions on land holding and on class mobility led virtually everyone to develop the mentality of an "independent entrepreneur," Hartz argues, and created a social climate in which the mass of the people were "bound to be capitalistic" and "capitalism, with its spirit disseminated widely, is bound to be democratic" (pp. 22, 89). Another influential argument explaining the lack of a strong American radical tradition, associated with historian Frederick Jackson Turner, is that the availability of cheap land in the west created a "safety valve" which defused radical discontent among eastern workers by providing an escape when eastern conditions became unsatisfactory (see Richard Hofstadter and Seymour Lipset, eds., *Turner and the Sociology of the Frontier* [New York: Basic Books, 1968], pp. 6-7; and Ray Billington, ed., *The Frontier Thesis* [New York: Holt, Rinehart & Winston, 1966], p. 5). The alleged flexibility of American political institutions is another argument frequently advanced to explain the lack of a strong radical tradition in the United States. Thus, William E. Hesseltine, in *Third Party Movements in the United States* (Princeton: D. Van Nostrand, 1962), argues that the two major parties have disarmed dissenters by stealing the programs of third parties.
6. "Consensus" historiography, in the words of a leading scholar of American historiography, John Higham, emphasized "consensus and continuity" in American history and "thus softened the outlines and flattened the crises of American history.... In functioning as a conservative frame of reference, the consensus approach gave us a bland history, in which conflict was muted, in which the classic issues of social justice were underplayed, in which the elements of spontaneity, effervescence and violence in American life got little sympathy or attention" (*Writing History* [Bloomington: Indiana University Press, 1972], p. 146]. On consensus historiography, see Higham, "The Cult of the 'American Consensus': Homogenizing Our History," *The Shaping of Twentieth Century America*, eds. Richard M. Abrams and Lawrence W. Levine (Bos-

ton: Little, Brown, 1971), pp. 699-709; Higham, *History* (Englewood Cliffs, New Jersey: Prentice-Hall, 1965), pp. 221-24; Richard Hofstadter, *The Progressive Historians* (New York: Vintage, 1970), pp. 437-66. Consensus historiography was at its height during the height of the Cold War at a time when, as Higham notes, "in an age of unceasing international peril" American historians "could hardly avoid a somewhat conservative view of their country's history" (*History*, p. 221). During the late 1960's and early 1970's, an increasing number of young historians launched attacks on the consensus school, but they have as yet failed to dethrone it and have produced no consistent or distinctive approach to American history" other than a "hostility to liberalism" (Higham, Writing American History, pp. 167-68). For an example of a virulent attack on consensus historians, see Norman Pollack, "Fear of Man: Populism, Authoritarianism and the Historian," *Agricultural History*, 39 (April, 1965), pp. 59-67. For a critical analysis of anti-consensus historians, see Irwin Unger, "The 'New Left' and American Historiography," *AHR*, 72 (July, 1967), pp. 1237-263. Collections of articles by anti-consensus historians can be found in Barton J. Bernstein, ed., *Towards A New Past: Dissenting Essays in American History* (New York: Vintage, 1969) and in Irwin Ungar, ed., *Beyond Liberalism: The New Left Views American History* (Waltham, Massachusetts: Xerox, 1971).

7. *Private Power and American Democracy* (New York: Vintage, 1970), p. 25.
8. *Political Oppositions*, pp. 38-45, 65.
9. Belmont, California: Wadsworth, 1972, p. 199.
10. For example, see Everett Kassalow, *Trade Unions and Industrial Relations* (New York: Random House, 1969) pp. 6-14; H. M. Gitelman, "Perspectives on American Industrial Relations," *Business History Review*, 47 (Spring, 1973), p. 5; Seymour Lipset, *The First New Nation* (Garden City New York: Doubleday, 1967), pp. 195-96; James Holt, "The Trade Unions and Socialism in the United States," *Journal of American Studies*, 7 (December, 1973), p. 321.
11. *Trade Unions*, p. 14.
12. *History of Labour in the United States*, 4 volumes (New York: MacMillan, 1918-1935) 1, pp. 4-6, 17. See the discussion of Commons in Mark Perlman, *Labor Union Theories in America* (Evanston, Illinois: Row, Peterson & Co., 1958), p. 190.
13. New York: MacMillan, 1928, pp. 162-69. See the discussion of Perlman in Mark Perlman, *Labor Union Theories*, pp. 190-210.
14. Robert H. Zeiger, "Workers and Scholars: Recent Trends in American Labor Historiography," *LH*, 13 (Spring, 1972), p. 265. See also Thomas Kreuger, "American Labor Historiography Old and New: A Review Essay," *Journal of Social History*, 4 (Spring, 1971) pp. 277-85; and John Laslett, *Labor and the Left: A Study of Socialist and Radical Influences in the American Labor Movement, 1881-1924* (New York: Basic Books, 1970), p. 304. For summaries of mainstream American labor historiography, see Henry Pelling *American Labor Unions* (Chicago: University of Chicago Press, 1960), pp. 221-24; Marc Karson, *American Labor Unions and Politics* (Boston: Beacon Press, 1965), pp. 286-306; and Phillip Taft, "Labor History and the Labor Movement Today, *LH*, 7 (Winter, 1966), pp. 70-77. William D. Dick, *Labor and Socialism in America: The Gompers Era* (Port Washington, New York: Kennikat, 1972) stresses the role of American Federation of Labor President Samuel Gompers in guiding the AFL along conservative lines, a slight modification, but not a departure, from mainstream labor historiography.
15. Reprinted and translated as "American Capitalism's Economic Rewards," *Failure of a Dream? Essays in the History of American Socialism*, John Laslett and Seymour Lipset, eds. (Garden City: Doubleday, 1974), p. 599.
16. *The Socialist Party of America* (Chicago: Quadrangle, 1967), p. 263. Many of the articles included in the source cited in the preceding footnote stress these themes. Two major books on the Socialist Party stress internal factionalism as the key factor in the party's failure; see James Weinstein, *The Decline of Socialism in America, 1912-1925* (New York: Vintage, 1969); and Ira Kipnis, *The American Socialist Movement, 1897-1912* (New York: Monthly Review, 1972).
17. *Marxian Socialism in the United States* (Princeton: Princeton University Press, 1967), pp. viii, x.
18. Irving Howe and Lewis Coser, *The American Communist Party* (New York: Praeger, 1962); Theodore Draper, *American Communism and Soviet Russia* (New

York: Viking, 1960); and David Shannon *The Decline of the American Communist Party* (New York: Harcourt, Brace, 1959).

19. *The Theory of Collective Behavior* (New York: The Free Press, 1971), p. 17.

20. Consensus historians rarely point out that political repression during the American Revolution was so severe that a higher percentage of dissidents (i.e. Tories) fled from the colonies during the Revolution than fled from France during the French Revolution — and the Americans (unlike the French) never returned to their country. Thus, as historian Robert Palmer points out, "The 'American consensus' rests in some degree on the elimination from the national consciousness, as well as from the country, of a once important and relatively numerous element of dissent" (*The Age of the Democratic Revolution, I* [Princeton: Princeton University Press, 1969], p. 190).

21. *Governing Without Consensus* (Boston: Beacon Press, 1972), pp. 32-33, 37, 41 (sentence order rearranged).

22. *Political Oppositions*, pp. xvi, 390-92.

23. "Shall This Be All? U.S. Historians Versus William D. Haywood, et al," *LH*, 12 (Summer, 1971) p. 440. For a similar comment, see Holt, p. 326.

24. This is also true of standard reference source. Thus the *International Encyclopedia of the Social Sciences* has no entry under "political repression" and no relevant entry under "repression." Standard English dictionaries also have no listing, although it is possible to put together a definition from the definitions of "political" and "repression." Thus, *Webster's New Collegiate Dictionary* (1973) offers a definition of "political" as "of or relating to government" and offers under "repress," to "put down by force" or to "prevent the natural or normal expression, activity or development of." This would seem to suggest that it is political repression for government agents (firemen) to "put down by force" or prevent the "natural development" of fires.

25. For examples of the casual use of "repression," "coercion," and "suppression," see Robert Dahl, *Regimes and Oppositions* (New Haven: Yale University Press, 1973), pp. 13-18; Lyford P. Edwards, *The Natural History of Revolutions* (Chicago: University of Chicago Press, 1928), pp. 34-35; Harry Eckstein, "On the Etiology of Internal Wars," *History and Theory*, 4 (1965), p. 154; William Gamson, *Power and Discontent* (Homewood, Illinois: Dorsey, 1968), pp. 191-92; Joseph LaPalombara and Myron Weiner, eds., *Political Parties and Political Development* (Princeton: Princeton University Press, 1969), p. 34; Gabriel Kolko, *The Roots of American Foreign Policy* (Boston, Beacon, 1969), p. 8; Dahl, *Political Oppositions*, pp. xiv-xvi; Rose, *Governing*, pp. 26, 32-33, 37, 41.

26. *The Seamy Side of Democracy: Repression in America*, (New York: David McKay, 1973), p. 6. Another recent book which focusses on repression, Murray Levin's *Political Hysteria in America: The Democratic Capacity for Repression* (New York: Basic Books, 1971), never attempts to define either "political hysteria" or "repression."

27. *Seamy Side*, p. 169.

28. *Governing*, p. 31.

29. Rose, *Governing*, p. 31. This discussion draws heavily upon Rose, *Governing*. See also the discussion in Otto Kircheimer, *Political Justice* (Princeton: Princeton University Press, 1969), pp. 25-172, especially pp. 46-53; and in Stephen Schafer, *Political Criminals* (New York: MacMillan, 1974), pp. 19-29.

30. *Governing*, p. 29.

31. *Toward A General Theory*, p. 61.

32. *Behemoth: The Structure and Practice of National Socialism, 1933-1944*, (New York: Harper & Row, 1963), p. 440.

33. For a brief discussion of what such due process standards would include, see Ivo D. Duchachek, *Right and Liberties in the World Today: Constitutional Promises and Reality* (Santa Barbara, California: ABC-Clio Press, 1973), pp. 133-53; and Henry J. Abraham, *Freedom and the Court*, (New York: Oxford University Press, 1972), pp. 111-12.

34. Kircheimer, p. 29.

35. Emerson, *Toward A General Theory*, p. 87; *LAT*, March 25, 1975.

36. Louis Joughin and Edmund M. Morgan, *The Legacy of Sacco and Vanzetti* (Chicago: Quadrangle, 1964).

37. Richard H. Frost, *The Mooney Case* (Stanford: Stanford University, 1968).

38. Melvin Dubofsky, *We Shall Be All: A History of the Industrial Workers of the*

World (Chicago: Quadrangle, 1969), pp. 96-105, 248, 254-55; Jack Nelson and Ronald J. Ostrow, *The FBI and the Berrigans* (New York: Coward, McCann & Geoghegan, 1972).
  39. Ivo K. Fierabend, Rosalind L. Fierabend and Betty A. Nesvold, "Social Change and Political Violence: Gross National Patterns," *Violence in America*, eds. Hugh D. Graham, Ted R. Gurr (New York: Bantam, 1969), p. 661.
  40. Dahl, *Political Oppositions*, p. xiii.
  41. *LAT*, February 5, 1975.
  42. *Rights and Liberties*, p. 174.
  43. *The Fear of Conspiracy: Images of Un-American Subversion from the Revolution to the Present* (Ithaca: Cornell University, 1971), p. xiii.
  44. H. C. Peterson and Gilbert C. Fite, *Opponents of War, 1917-1918* (Seattle, University of Washington Press, 1957), p. 352.

CHAPTER ONE

  1. Philip Taft and Philip Ross, "American Labor Violence: Its Causes, Character and Outcome," *Violence*, eds. Graham and Gurr, p. 281. Taft and Ross do not appear to have made any serious comparative study of this subject; therefore their comment should be read as indicating the high level of violence in *American* labor history rather than as a definitive comparative statement.
  2. Taft and Ross, p. 380.
  3. See Taft and Ross, pp. 281-395; Gitelman, "Perspectives;" Richard Hofstadter and Michael Wallace, eds., *American Violence: A Documentary History* (New York: Vintage, 1971), pp. 18-20; Michael Wallace, "The Uses of Violence in American History," *The American Scholar*, 40 (Winter, 1970-1971), pp. 90-94; Alphonso Pinkney, *The American Way of Violence* (New York: Vintage, 1972), pp. 27-32.
  4. "Sometimes, of course, the police were provoked by strikers. . . . But sometimes — the Lawrence strike (1912) and the Memorial Day Massacre (1937) are among the best known examples of commonplace events — the police just ran amok and wantonly assaulted strikers without provocation or justification" (Gitelman, p. 19).
  5. Hofstadter and Wallace, p. 19.
  6. Lewis Lorwin, *The American Federation of Labor* (Washington, D.C.: The Brookings Institution, 1933), p. 355.
  7. "Reflections on the History of the French and American Labor Movements" *Journal of Economic History*, 17 (March, 1957), p. 37.
  8. Quoted in Arthur M. Ross and Paul T. Hartman, *Changing Patterns of Industrial Conflict* (New York: John Wiley, 1960), p. 165.
  9. Vernon H. Jensen, *Heritage of Conflict* (Ithaca: Cornell University Press, 1950), pp. 38-53; Taft and Ross, pp. 301-02.
  10. See C. Vann Woodward, *Reunion and Reaction* (Garden City, New York: Doubleday, 1956).
  11. Sidney Fine, *Laissez Faire and the General Welfare State* (Ann Arbor: University of Michigan Press, 1964), p. 64; Arthur A. Ekirch, Jr., *The Decline of American Liberalism* (New York: Atheneum, 1969), p. 128; Thomas C. Cochran and William Miller, *The Age of Industrial Enterprise* (New York: Harper & Row, 1961), p. 108.
  12. Cochran and Miller, pp. 132-33; Russel B. Nye, *Midwestern Progressive Politics* (New York: Harper & Row, 1965), p. 36; Fred A. Shannon, *The Centennial Years* (Garden City: Doubleday, 1969), p. 24.
  13. Ronald M. Gephart, "Politicians, Soldiers and Strikes: The Reorganization of the Nebraska Militia and the Omaha Strike of 1882," *Nebraska History*, 46 (June, 1965), p. 96. Generally on this topic see C. Vann Woodward, *Origins of the New South* (Baton Rouge, Louisiana State University Press, 1951), pp. 1-142; and Horace Samuel Merrill, *Bourbon Democracy of the Middle West* (Seattle: University of Washington Press, 1967).
  14. Quoted in Eric Goldman, *Rendezvous with Destiny* (New York: Vintage, 1955), p. 33.
  15. Harold U. Faulkner, *Politics, Reform and Expansion* (New York: Harper & Row, 1963), p. 159.

16. John D. Hicks, *The Populist Revolt* (Lincoln: University of Nebraska Press, 1961), p. 60; Nye, p. 39.
17. Cochran and Miller, pp. 131-32.
18. Shannon, *Centennial*, p. 109; Nye, p. 27.
19. *From Slavery to Freedom* (New York: Vintage, 1969), p. 315.
20. John P. Roche, *Quest for the Dream* (New York: MacMillan, 1963), p. 17.
21. Quoted in Cochran and Miller, p. 163.
22. *Dynamite!* (New York: Vintage, 1931), p. 23.
23. Ray Ginger, *Age of Excess* (New York: MacMillan, 1965), p. 36.
24. Cochran and Miller, p. 163.
25. Quoted in Nye, p. 30.
26. John M. Blum, *The Promise of America* (Baltimore: Penguin, 1967), p. 42.
27. Roche, *Quest*, p. 20.
28. Quoted in Walter P. Metzger, *Academic Freedom in the Age of the University* (New York: Columbia Press, 1961), p. 141.
29. Roche, *Quest*, pp. 18-20; Samuel E. Morrison, Henry Steele Commager and William E. Leuchtenburg, *The Growth of the American Republic*, II (New York: Oxford University Press, 1969), pp. 85-86; Irving Bernstein, *The Lean Years* (Baltimore: Penguin, 1966), pp. 205-06; Henry David, *The History of the Haymarket Affair* (New York: Collier, 1963), pp. 41-45; Fine, *Laissez Faire*, pp. 149-51, 159-60; Cochran and Miller, pp. 169-70.
30. John R. Roche, "Entrepreneurial Liberty and the Fourteenth Amendment," *LH*, 4 (Winter, 1963) pp. 8, 31.
31. Robert V. Bruce, *1877: Year of Violence* (Chicago: Quadrangle, 1970), p. 15.
32. Quoted in Herbert G. Gutman, "Industrial Workers Struggle for Power," *Underside of American History*, II, ed. Thomas R. Frazier (New York: Harcourt, Brace, 1974), p. 51.
33. Blum, *Promise*, p. 57; Faulkner, *Politics*, p. 91; John A. Garraty, *The New Commonwealth* (New York: Harper & Row, 1968), p. 129; Foster Rhea Dulles, *Labor in America* (New York: Crowell, 1966), p. 165; Cochran and Miller, pp. 261-64; Bruce, p. 23.
34. Bruce, p. 234.
35. Shannon, *Centennial*, pp. 210-11.
36. Quoted in Bruce, p. 26.
37. Jerold S. Auerbach, "The Depression Decade," *The Pulse of Freedom*, ed. Alan Reitman (New York: Norton, 1975), pp. 73, 78.
38. On the company town, see James R. Allen, *The Company Town in the American West* (Norman: University of Oklahoma Press, 1966); Stanley Buder, *Pullman* (New York: Oxford University Press, 1967); Liston Pope, *Millhands and Preachers* (New Haven: Yale University Press, 1942); Bernice L. Webb, "Company Town — Louisiana Style," *Louisiana History*, 9 (Fall, 1968), pp. 325-39; Samuel Yellin, *American Labor Struggles* (New York: Monad, 1974), pp. 295-96; Woodward, *Origins*, p. 420; Jerold S. Auerbach, *Labor and Liberty: The LaFollette Committee and the New Deal* (Indianapolis: Bobbs-Merrill, 1966), pp. 14-16, 20-22, 105-07; Jensen, *Heritage*, pp. 274-77.
39. Allen, p. 106.
40. Taft and Ross, pp. 317, 383; Paul T. Murphy, *The Meaning of Freedom of Speech* (Westport, Connecticut: Greenwood, 1972), p. 72.
41. Auerbach, *Labor*, p. 115.
42. Bernstein, *Lean*, p. 153.
43. Pope, p. 155.
44. Unfortunately there are no precise figures available either on the number of workers who lived in such towns or on the percentage of the total work force involved. The most extensive study of the company town, Allen's work cited in footnote 38, above, lists almost two hundred such towns in eleven western states, but does not give complete population data. Judging from the data he does give, most of these towns appear to have employed two hundred-three hundred workers, suggesting that in the west at any one time such towns employed fifty thousand workers. If one takes into consideration the spouses and children of these workers, the fact that many workers at one time or another worked in the same town, the occurrence of such towns in other parts of the country and the fact that some company towns were considerably

Notes   (Ch. 1) 44-78   581

larger (Pullman, Illinois, for example had a population of eight thousand six hundred in 1885 [Buder, p. 89]), to state that "millions" were affected by such arrangements seems reasonable.

45. Auerbach, *Labor,* p. 15.
46. James Weinstein, *The Corporate Ideal in the Liberal State* (Boston: Beacon, 1969), pp. 210-11.
47. Auerbach, *Labor,* p. 105.
48. On private police, see Bernstein, *Lean,* pp. 151, 475; Auerbach, *Labor,* pp. 100-06; Leonard Whipple, *The Story of Civil Liberty in the United States* (New York: Vanguard, 1927), pp. 216-20; Taft and Ross, *passim;* Frost, pp. 25-29.
49. Auerbach, *Labor,* pp. 105-06.
50. Quoted in Whipple, p. 217.
51. Russell R. Elliott, *Radical Labor in the Nevada Mining Booms, 1900-1920* (Carson City: University of Nevada Press, 1961), pp. 57-58. See Taft and Ross, *passim,* for many accounts in which private police shot strikers.
52. Leon Wolff, *Lockout: The Story of the Homestead Strike of 1892* (New York: Harper & Row, 1965), p. 69.
53. "Perspectives," p. 21.
54. Auerbach, *Labor,* p. 101.
55. Auerbach, *Labor,* p. 101.
56. On labor spies, see Auerbach, *Labor,* pp. 97-99; Leo Huberman, *The Labor Spy Racket* (New York: Modern Age, 1937).
57. Auerbach, *Labor,* p. 99.
58. Auerbach, *Labor,* p. 105.
59. David, p. 56.
60. Auerbach, *Labor,* p. 105.
61. Wallace, p. 92; Roche, *Quest,* p. 19.
62. Harriet L. Herring, "The Industrial Worker," *Culture in the South,* W. T. Couch, ed. (Chapel Hill: University of North Carolina Press, 1935), p. 369.
63. Sidney Lens, *The Labor Wars* (Garden City: Doubleday, 1974), p. 243.
64. Bernstein, *Lean,* p. 152.
65. P. Shalloo, *Private Police* (Philadelphia: American Academy of Political and Social Sciences, 1933), quoted in Taft and Ross, p. 317.
66. Sterling Spero and Abram L. Harris, *The Black Worker* (New York: Atheneum, 1969), pp. 235-37.
67. Barton C. Hacker, "The United States Army as a National Police Force," *Military Affairs,* 33 (April, 1969), p. 259; Wolfe, p. 120; Taft and Ross, *passim.*
68. Hacker, p. 259.
69. William H. Riker, *Soldiers of the States* (Washington, D.C.: Public Affairs Press, 1957), pp. 44-55; Martha Detrick, *The National Guard in Politics* (Cambridge: Harvard University Press, 1965), pp. 17-20.
70. Alan Hynding, "The Coal Miners of Washington Territory: Labor Troubles in 1880-1890," *AW,* 12 (Autumn, 1970), pp. 229-30.
71. Hacker, p. 259.
72. William J. Gaboury, "From Statehouse to Bull Pen: Idaho Populism and the Coeur d'Alene Troubles of the 1890's," *PNQ,* 58 (January, 1967), pp. 14-22; Jensen, *Heritage,* pp. 25-37, 72-87; Taft and Ross, p. 323; Bernstein, *Lean,* pp. 18,204; Lens, p. 318.
73. Commons, II, p. 441.
74. John E. Haynes, "Revolt of the 'Timber Beasts': The IWW Lumber Strike in Minnesota," *MH,* 42 (Spring, 1971), pp. 171-73.
75. James R. Mock, *Censorship 1917* (Princeton: Princeton University Press, 1941), p. 229.
76. Quoted in Whipple, pp. 227-28.
77. Jerry M. Cooper, "The Wisconsin National Guard in the Milwaukee Riots of 1886," *WMH,* 55 (Autumn, 1971), pp. 31-48; John Higham, *Strangers in the Land* (New York: Atheneum, 1970), pp. 89-90; Yellin, pp. 205-50; Donald J. McClurg, "The Colorado Coal Strike of 1927," *LH,* 4 (Winter, 1966), pp. 68-92; Donald F. Sofchalk, "The Chicago Memorial Day Incident," *LH,* 6 (Winter, 1965), pp. 3-43.
78. Gaboury, "From Statehouse;" Jensen, *Heritage,* pp. 25-37, 72-87, 356; A. C.

Hutson, Jr., "The Coal Miners Insurrection of 1891 in Anderson County, Tennessee," *East Tennessee Historical Society's Proceedings*, 7 (1935), pp. 105-15; Ray Ginger, *Eugene V. Debs* (New York: Collier, 1962), pp. 95-96; Eugene O. Porter, "The Colorado Coal Strike of 1913," *The Historian*, 12 (Autumn, 1949), pp. 3-27.

79. Bruce, pp. 53-54.
80. Paul T. Bechtol, "The 1880 Labor Dispute in Leadville," *Colorado Magazine*, 47 (Fall, 1970), p. 325. See also Jensen, *Heritage*, pp. 19-24.
81. Gephart, pp. 89-120; William Ivy Hair, *Bourbonism and Agrarian Protest* (Baton Rouge: Lousiana State University Press, 1969), pp. 172-74.
82. Taft and Ross, p. 297.
83. Russell R. Elliott, "Labor Troubles in the Mining Camp at Goldfield, Nevada," *PHR*, 19 (November, 1950), pp. 368-83; Taft and Ross, pp. 338-39.
84. Joseph Rayback, *A History of American Labor* (New York: The Free Press, 1966), pp. 91-92. Benjamin Taylor and Fred Whitney, *Labor Relations Law* (Englewood Cliffs, New Jersey: Prentice-Hall, 1971), pp. 13-23.
85. *Beyond Equality: Labor and the Radical Republicans, 1862-1872* (New York: Vintage, 1967), p. 147.
86. Bruce, pp. 308, 311; Shannon, *Centennial*, pp. 223-24; David, pp. 51-53; Donald L. McMurry, "The Legal Ancestry of the Pullman Strike Injunctions," *Industrial and Labor Relations Review*, 14 (January, 1961), pp. 263-68.
87. David, p. 54; Commons, II, pp. 441-45, 503.
88. Commons, II, p. 504.
89. Philip S. Foner, *History of the Labor Movement in the United States* (Four vols.; New York: International, 1947-1965), II, p. 25.
90. David, pp. 443-44.
91. On the growth of the labor injunction, see Felix Frankfurter and Nathan Greene, *The Labor Injunction* (New York: MacMillan, 1930); McMurray, "Legal;" Taylor and Whitney, pp. 25-41, 69-99; Charles O. Gregory, *Labor and the Law* (New York: Norton, 1961), pp. 83-104.
92. For discussion of these cases, see the appropriate index entries in Taylor and Whitney, *Labor*; and Gregory, *Labor*.
93. Bernstein, *Lean*, p. 200.
94. Frankfurter and Greene, p. 52.
95. Bernstein, *Lean*, pp. 194-96.
96. Frankfurter and Greene, p. 53.
97. Bernstein, *Lean*, p. 196.

CHAPTER TWO

1. This analysis draws heavily on the following: Robert Wiebe, *The Search for Order* (New York: Hill & Wang, 1967); Ginger, *Age*; Faulkner, *Politics*; Garraty, *New Commonwealth*; Cochran and Miller, pp. 129-80; Richard Hofstadter, *The Age of Reform* (New York: Vintage, 1955); John G. Sproat, *"The Best Men": Liberal Reformers in the Gilded Age* (New York: Oxford University Press, 1971).
2. Wiebe, *Search*, p. 76.
3. Gutman, "Industrial Workers," p. 14.
4. *"The Best Men,"* pp. 227, 235, 277.
5. George L. Cherry, "Metropolitan Press Reaction to the Paris Commune," *Mid-America*, 32 (1950), pp. 3-12; Samuel Reznick, "Distress, Relief and Discontent in the U.S. During the Depression of 1873-1878," *Journal of Political Economy*, 58 (December, 1950), pp. 494-512; Herbert Gutman, "The Failure of the Movement by the Unemployed for Public Works in 1873," *PSQ*, 80 (June, 1965), pp. 254-75; Bruce, pp. 226-28; Higham, *Strangers*, pp. 30-31; Nye, p. 52; Garraty, *New Commonwealth*, p. 313.
6. Reznick, "Distress," p. 511.
7. Samuel Bernstein, "American Labor and the Paris Commune," *Science and Society*, 15 (Spring, 1951), p. 161.
8. Russell Fraser, "John Peter Altgeld," *American Radicals*, ed. Harvey Goldberg (New York: Modern Reader, 1969), p. 129.

9. Robert D. Ward and William W. Rogers, *Labor Revolt in Alabama* (University: University of Alabama Press, 1965), p. 20. It became standard practice as early as the 1870's for reformers to preface their remarks by disclaiming any belief in communism. Thus, when Boston reformer William G. Moody proposed some reforms to a Congressional committee in 1878 he felt it necessary to emphasize his program was "neither socialism nor communism" (Reznick, "Distress," p. 508).

10. Joseph J. Holmes, "Red Baiting as Used Against Striking Workingmen in the United States, 1871-1920," *Studies in History and Society*, 5 (Spring, 1974), p. 1.

11. On the labor movement after the Civil War, see Montgomery, *Beyond Equality;* Rayback, pp. 114-42; Dulles, pp. 95-122; Gerald N. Grob, *Workers and Utopia* (Chicago: Quadrangle, 1969), pp. 11-33; Norman J. Ware, *The Labor Movement in the United States, 1860-1895* (New York: Vintage, 1929), pp. 1-21; Foner, I, pp. 370-433.

12. Grob, *Workers*, p. 14.

13. Montgomery, pp. 326-34 (quotation, p. 330).

14. Rayback, p. 119.

15. Solon J. Buck, *The Granger Movement* (Cambridge: Harvard University Press, 1913); Nye, pp. 44-58; Theodore Saloutos, *Farmer Movements in the South* (Lincoln: University of Nebraska, 1960), pp. 31-43.

16. Morris Hillquit, *History of Socialism in the United States* (New York: Dover, 1971), pp. 135-92; Howard H. Quint, *The Forging of American Socialism* (Indianapolis: Bobbs-Merrill, 1964), pp. 3-15; Bernstein, "American Labor," pp. 144-62; Bell, *Marxian Socialism*, pp. 19-24; Foner, I, pp. 409-17, 445-53; Lillian Symes and Travers Clement, *Rebel America* (Boston: Beacon, 1972), pp. 117-19.

17. Gutman, "Failure;" Herbert G. Gutman, "The Tompkins Square Riot in New York City," *LH*, 6 (Winter, 1965), pp. 44-70; Gutman, "Industrial Workers," pp. 29-31; Reznick, "Distress."

18. Gutman, "Failure," p. 254.

19. Gutman, "Failure," p. 273.

20. Bruce, pp. 20-22; Nathan Fine, *Farmer and Labor Parties in the U.S., 1828-1928* (New York: Rand School of Social Science, 1928), p. 108.

21. Dulles, pp. 114-16; David T. Burbank, *Reign of the Rabble: The Saint Louis General Strike of 1877* (New York: Augustus M. Kelly, 1966), p. 5; Edgar Bernhard, et al., *Pursuit of Freedom: A History of Civil Liberty in Illinois* (Chicago: Chicago Civil Liberties Committee, 1942, p. 155; Foner, I, p. 455.

22. Gutman, "Tompkins Square;" Gutman, "Failure," pp. 261-62.

23. Gutman, "Tompkins Square," p. 148.

24. Gutman, "Industrial Workers," pp. 18, 31-32: Ware, p. 33; Bruce, p. 120; Foner, I, pp. 459-60; Sidney H. Kessler, "The Negro in Labor Strikes," *Midwest Journal*, 6 (Summer, 1954), p. 25.

25. It was characteristic of the smaller cities and towns during the late nineteenth century that social distance between classes was much smaller than in larger cities, and in many cases corporate power and industrial ideology had not yet penetrated. Similar support of strikers was evident in many small-town strikes during this period. Thus, during a coal lockout at Braidwood, Illinois, in 1874, local officials swore in strikers as special deputies, and local police and judicial officials clearly discriminated against strikebreakers, thereby helping miners to win the dispute (Herbert Gutman, "Trouble in the Railroads in 1973-1874," *LH*, 2 [Spring, 1961], pp. 2-235; Gutman, "Industrial Workers," pp. 20-22).

26. *Centennial Years*, p. 213. On the Molly Maguires, see Wayne Broehl, *The Molly Maguires* (New York: Vintage, 1968); Shannon, *Centennial*, pp. 212-15; Lens, pp. 11-35; Harold W. Aurand, *From the Molly Maguires to the United Mine Workers* (Philadelphia: Temple University, 1971), pp. 96-114.

27. Broehl, *passim;* Rayback, p. 133.

28. *History*, p. 133.

29. Broehl, pp. 349-50.

30. Broehl, pp. 359-60.

31. Aurand, p. 25.

32. On the 1877 strikes, see Bruce, *1877;* Lens, pp. 36-62; Shannon, *Centennial*, pp. 219-24; Yellin, pp. 10-37; Bennett M. Rich, *The President and Civil Disorders* (Washington, D.C.: Brookings Institution, 1941), pp. 80-86; Burbank, *Reign;* Jeremy Brecher, *Strike!* (San Francisco: Straight Arrow, 1972), pp. 1-24.

33. Bruce, p. 183.
34. Burbank, *Reign*, p. 122.
35. On St. Louis, see Burbank, *Reign*. On Philadelphia, see Mackey, "Law and Order, 1877: Philadelphia's Response to the Railroad Riots," *Pennsylvania Magazine of History and Biography*, 96 (April, 1972), pp. 183-202.
36. See Bruce, *passim;* Burbank, *Reign, passim;* Reznick, "Distress," pp. 509-10; Higham, *Strangers*, p. 31; Gerald Grob, "The Railroad Strikes of 1877," *Midwest Journal*, 6 (Winter, 1954-1955), pp. 16-33; Holmes, pp. 2-3.
37. Grob, "Railroad Strikes," p. 20.
38. Grob, "Railroad Strikes," p. 24.
39. *History*, p. 135.
40. Rayback, p. 135; Dulles, p. 122; Yellin, p. 36; Garraty, *New Commonwealth*, p. 160; Shannon, *Centennial*, p. 219; Bruce, pp. 307-08; Burbank, *Reign*, pp. 173-87; Reznick, "Distress," p. 510; Gephart, p. 103; Cooper, pp. 32-33.
41. Arthur A. Ekirch, "The American Liberal Tradition and Military Affairs," *Bayonets in the Streets*, ed. Robin Higham (Lawrence: University Press of Kansas, 1969), p. 146.
42. Reznick, "Distress," p. 507; Rayback, p. 130.
43. Quoted in Barbara Solomon, *Ancestors and Immigrants* (Chicago: University of Chicago, 1972), p. 99.
44. Quoted in Grob, *Workers*, p. 36.
45. Grob, "Railroad Strikers," pp. 29-33.
46. Quoted in Solomon, p. 53.
47. Quoted in Cochran and Miller, p. 271.
48. Rush Welter, *Popular Education and Democratic Thought in America* (New York: Columbia University Press, 1965), pp. 208-09.
49. Maldwyn Jones, *American Immigration* (Chicago: University of Chicago Press, 1960), pp. 250-51.
50. For examples, see p. 16, above: Ware, pp. 92, 196; David, p. 54.
51. Samuel Reznick, "Patterns of Thought and Action in an American Depression, 1882-1886," *AHR*, (January, 1956), pp. 284-307.
52. Reznick, "Patterns," p. 287.
53. Higham, *Strangers*, pp. 46-54.
54. On the Knights of Labor, see Ware, *Labor;* Grob, *Workers*, pp. 34-137.
55. Ware, p. 66.
56. *HS*, p. 99.
57. Dulles, p. 141; Rayback, p. 163; Ware, p. 311.
58. Ware, pp. xi-xvi. On the Knights and blacks, see Spero and Harris, pp. 40-48.
59. Ware, p. xvi.
60. Symes and Clement, p. 165.
61. The best source on the IWPA is David, *The History of the Haymarket Affair*.
62. David, pp. 95-96.
63. Bell, *Marxian Socialism*, p. 26; Quint, *Forging*, pp. 23, 25.
64. David, p. 102.
65. On the IWPA in Chicago, see David, pp. 101-38, Bell, *Marxian Socialism*, p. 26; Rayback, p. 166; Ware, pp. 313-14.
66. David, p. 132.
67. Brecher, p. 31.
68. Commons, II, pp. 373-74.
69. On the Gould strike, see Shannon, *Centennial*, pp. 228-29, Brecher, pp. 32-36; Ware, pp. 146-69; McMurry, "Legal Ancestry," pp. 238-39.
70. Rayback, p. 166; Garraty, *New Commonwealth*, p. 166; David, p. 116.
71. Wiebe, *Search*, pp. 77-78.
72. Cooper, "Wisconsin National Guard."
73. Cooper, p. 44.
74. On Haymarket, see David, *History;* Lens, pp. 63-75; Yellin, pp. 39-71; Brecher, pp. 36-71; Ware, pp. 299-313; Ray Ginger, *Altgeld's America, 1890-1905* (Chicago: Quadrangle, 1965), pp. 35-60.
75. David, p. 161.
76. John P. Altgeld, "Reasons for Pardoning Fielden, Neebe and Schwab," *The Chicago Haymarket Riot*, ed. Bernard R. Kogan (Boston: D.C. Heath, 1959), p. 107.

77. David, p. 294.
78. David, p. 190.
79. Burbank, *Reign*, p. 200; James M. Morris, "No Haymarket For Cincinnati," *OH*, 83 (Winter, 1974), pp. 17-32.
80. David, p. 191.
81. David, p. 192.
82. Jason Epstein, *The Great Conspiracy Trial* (New York: Vintage, 1971), especially pp. 1-16. The sole evidence against one of the 1886 defendants (Oscar Neebe) was that he owned stock in an anarchist paper; appeared in the offices of the paper on the day after the bombing; belonged to the IWPA; had remarked on the evening before the bombing, in connection with the McCormick shooting, that "it's a shame the police act that way, but maybe the time comes when it gives the other way — that they (the workers) get a chance too;" and was found to have two guns, a sword and a red flag when his house was searched without a warrant (David, p. 204).
83. *Centennial*, p. 236.
84. Yellin, p. 63. Increasing protests over the trial and sentences eventually led to the commutation of two death sentences to life imprisonment. One of the five condemned committed suicide in jail, while the other four were hung on November 11, 1887, after the Illinois and U.S. Supreme Courts refused to intervene. In 1893, Illinois Governor John Peter Altgeld pardoned the three remaining prisoners, declaring that the jury had been biased and much of the state's evidence fabricated.
85. Higham, *Strangers*, p. 54; Jones, pp. 252-53.
86. Rayback, p. 168.
87. Dulles, p. 122; Higham, *Strangers*, pp. 54-55; David, pp. 178-89; Holmes, pp. 3-4.
88. David, p. 436.
89. Higham, *Strangers*, pp. 55, 58.
90. Commons, II, pp. 441, 503-04, 508; David, pp. 443-44; Foner, II pp. 116-17; Rayback, p. 169; Bernhard, p. 179; Wiebe, *Search*, p. 79; Chester Destler, *American Radicalism, 1865-1901* (Chicago: Quadrangle, 1966), p. 101.
91. Michael A. Gordon, "The Labor Boycott in New York City, 1880-1886," *LH*, 16 (Spring, 1975), p. 225.
92. Gordon, pp. 225-28. A New York City grand jury described the boycott as a "hydra-headed monster, dragging its loathsome length across this continent, sucking the very lifeblood from our trade and commerce."
93. Riker, pp. 47, 54-55.
94. Bell, *Marxian Socialism*, p. 26; Burbank, *Reign*, p. 199; Yellin, p. 71; Shannon, *Centennial*, p. 240; David, pp. 399-404, 436-40.
95. Dick, p. 16, and Ware, p. 316, suggest the Haymarket affair and public reaction to it strongly hurt the Knights, while David, pp. 442-43, and Grob, *Workers*, p. 137, discount this as a major reason for the decline of the Knights.
96. David, p. 342.
97. David, p. 343; Ware, p. 318.
98. *Marxian Socialism*, pp. 39-40.
99. Ware, p. 182; David, p. 447.
100. Quoted in Garraty, *New Commonwealth*, p. 170.
101. Garraty, *New Commonwealth*, p. 168.
102. David, pp. 342-43.
103. Ware, p. 66.
104. *HS*, p. 99.
105. Arnold M. Paul, *Conservative Crisis and the Rule of Law* (New York: Harper & Row, 1969), p. 35.
106. Woodward, *Origins*, pp. 229-30; Frederick Myers, "The Knights of Labor in the South," *Southern Economic Journal*, 6 (1939-1940), pp. 479-87; George B. Tindall, *South Carolina Negroes* (Baton Rouge: Louisiana State University Press, 1966), pp. 115-17; Hair, pp. 176-85; Kessler, pp. 27-33; Hofstadter and Wallace, pp. 139-41.
107. Ginger, *Age*, pp. 132-33; Shannon, *Centennial*, pp. 229-233; McMurry, "Legal Ancestry," pp. 239-243.
108. Ginger, Commons, II, pp. 474-78; Wolff, p. 69; Irving Bernstein, *Turbulent Years* (Boston: Houghton Mifflin, 1971), p. 432.

109. *HS*, p. 99.
110. Quoted in Wolff, p. 26.
111. Wolff, p. 70.
112. Higham, *Strangers*, p. 89.
113. Wolff, *Lockout!*, gives the best account of the Homestead strike. For shorter accounts, see Brecher, pp. 53-63; Lens, pp. 76-88; Yellin, pp. 72-100.
114. Wolff, p. 164.
115. On Coeur d'Alene, see Gaboury, "From Statehouse;" Jensen, *Heritage*, pp. 25-37; Dubofsky, *We Shall*, pp. 28-35; Lens, pp. 129-32; Brecher, pp. 63-64; Ginger, *Debs*, pp. 102-03.
116. Commons, II, p. 498; Ginger, *Debs*, pp. 95-96.
117. Hutson, "Coal Miners," pp. 105-15; A. C. Hutson, Jr., "The Overthrow of the Convict Lease System in Tennessee," *East Tennessee Historical Society's Proceedings*, 8 (1936), pp. 82-103.
118. Roger W. Shugg, "The New Orleans General Strike of 1892," *Louisiana Historical Quarterly*, 21 (April, 1938), pp. 547-60.
119. Paul, p. 109; Homer Cummings and Carl McFarland, *Federal Justice* (New York: MacMillan, 1937) pp. 437-38.
120. Shugg, p. 559.
121. On the populists, see Hicks, *Populist Revolt*; Nye, pp. 56-111; Saloutos, pp. 69-152; Woodward, *Origins*, pp. 188-204, 235-290.
122. Hicks, *Populist*, pp. 239-240.
123. Woodward, *Origins*, p. 258.
124. Wiebe, *Search*, p. 95. On 1892 repression see also Woodward, *Origins*, pp. 259-62; Hicks, *Populist*, pp. 253-54.
125. Quint, *Forging*, p. 79.
126. On the nationalist clubs and Christian socialism, see Quint, *Forging*, pp. 72-141; Samuel P. Hays, *The Response to Industrialism, 1885-1914* (Chicago: University of Chicago, 1957), pp. 41-42; Wolff, p. 12.
127. Samuel Reznick, "Unemployment, Unrest and Relief in the United States During the Depression of 1893-1897," *Journal of Political Economy*, 61 (August, 1953), p. 329.
128. Reznick, "Unemployment," p. 332. See also, on the 1893 depression, Donald L. McMurry, *Coxey's Army* (Seattle: University of Washington Press, 1968), pp. 3-20; Faulkner, *Politics*, pp. 88, 142-63.
129. Wolff, p. 187; Richard Drinnon, *Rebel in Paradise: A Biography of Emma Goldman* (Boston: Beacon, 1970), pp. 50-51; Dulles, p. 168.
130. David, p. 439; Drinnon, pp. 55-61; James Joll, *The Anarchists* (New York: Grosset & Dunlap, 1966), pp. 130-37.
131. David, pp. 412-16; Ginger, *Altgeld's America*, pp. 86-87.
132. Commons, II, pp. 509-12; Grob, *Workers*, pp. 176-78.
133. Ward and Rogers, *Labor Revolt*; Woodward, *Origins*, pp. 266-68; Reznick, "Unemployment," p. 334; *HS*, p. 99.
134. Almont Lindsay, *The Pullman Strike* (Chicago: University of Chicago, 1964), pp. 14-16, 258; Charles A. Peckham, "The Ohio National Guard and Its Police Duties, 1894," *OH*, 83 (Winter, 1974), pp. 51-67.
135. Jensen, *Heritage*, pp. 38-53.
136. Wiebe, *Search*, pp. 77-89; Paul, *passim*; Ginger, *Age*, p. 97; Goldman, *Rendezvous*, p. 43; Higham, *Strangers*, pp. 68-105; Hofstadter, *Age*, p. 165.
137. Wiebe, *Search*, p. 58.
138. Wiebe, *Search*, p. 57; Hays, p. 42; Higham, *Strangers*, p. 75; Merle Curti, *The Roots of Loyalty* (New York: Atheneum, 1968), pp. 189-94.
139. Higham, *Strangers*, pp. 77-87.
140. Metzger, pp. 151-60. There were a series of other academic freedom cases during the 1892-1900 period, at least six of which ended in firings, but most of them involved private universities and therefore were not cases of "political repression" as defined herein. The University of Wisconsin remained leery of radicalism; thus, in 1910, Edward A. Ross, a prominent reform economist who had been fired earlier by Stanford University for political reason was reprimanded by the Wisconsin Board of Regents for announcing to his class that anarchist leader Emma Goldman would give a public lecture in Madison (Metzger, pp. 146-49, 155).

141. The best source on the "unemployed armies" is McMurry, *Coxey's Army*. See also Faulkner, *Politics*, pp. 164-69; Lindsay, pp. 13-14; Rich, pp. 88-9; Paul, pp. 128-29.
142. The best source on the strike is Lindsay, *Pullman Strike*. See also Buder, *Pullman;* Yellin, pp. 101-36; Lens, pp. 89-126; Brecher, pp. 78-96; Ginger, *Debs,* pp. 106-99; Ginger, *Altgeld's America,* pp. 142-67; Paul, pp. 131-58.
143. Quoted in Ginger, *Debs,* pp. 144-45.
144. Lindsay, p. 275.
145. Bernhard, p. 182.
146. Yellin, p. 131.
147. Lindsay, p. 260.
148. Lindsay, p. 168.
149. Lindsay, p. 262.
150. Ginger, *Debs,* p. 149.
151. Ginger, *Debs,* p. 197.
152. Lindsay, p. 137.
153. Lindsay, p. 323.
154. Commons, II, pp. 510-11.
155. Rayback, p. 198.
156. Ginger, *Debs,* p. 198.
157. Quoted in Symes and Clement, p. 137.
158. Quoted in Thomas R. Brooks, *Toil and Trouble: A History of American Labor* (New York: Delta, 1964), p. 83.
159. Quoted in Bernard Mandel, *Samuel Gompers* (Yellow Springs, Ohio: Antioch Press, 1963), pp. 122-23.
160. Ginger, *Debs,* p. 165.
161. Ginger, *Debs,* p. 198.
162. Quint, *Forging,* p. 71.
163. "Organized Labor and the Immigrant in New York City," *LH,* 2 (Spring, 1961), p. 184.
164. Quoted in Michael Rogin, "Voluntarism: The Political Functions of an Antipolitical Doctrine," *Industrial and Labor Relations Review,* 15 (July, 1962), p. 524 (emphasis added).
165. See Faulkner, *Politics,* pp. 187-279; Goldman, *Rendezvous,* pp. 49-57; Higham, *Strangers,* pp. 103-10.
166. *HS,* p. 99.
167. *HS,* p. 99.
168. See Paul, *Conservative Crisis.*
169. Quoted in Paul, pp. 204-05.
170. See Paul W. Glad, *McKinnley, Bryan and the People* (Philadelphia: Lippincott, 1964).
171. Faulkner, *Politics,* p. 193.
172. Faulkner, *Politics,* p. 208.
173. *Midwestern Progressive Politics,* p. 117.
174. Wiebe, *Search,* p. 105.
175. Harold U. Faulkner, *The Decline of Laissez-Faire* (New York: Harper & Row, 1968), p. 7.
176. *Strangers,* p. 107.
177. See Ginger, *Age,* pp. 188-94; E. Berkeley Tompkins, *Anti-Imperialism in the United States* (Philadelphia: University of Pennsylvania Press, 1970), pp. 46, 66-67, 71, 125).
178. Ginger, *Debs,* p. 219; Drinnon, pp. 226-27.
179. Tompkins, pp. 206-10; Frank Friedel, "Dissent in the Spanish-American War and the Phillipine Insurrection," *Dissent in Three American Wars* (Cambridge: Harvard University Press, 1970), pp. 84-85; Daniel B. Schirmer, *Repuplic or Empire: American Resistance to the Phillipine War* (Cambridge: Schenkman, 1972), pp. 152-56; Howard H. Quint, "American Socialists and the Spanish-American War," *American Quarterly,* 10 (Summer, 1958), pp. 131-41; Drinnon, p. 226.

CHAPTER THREE

1. *Politics,* pp. 278-79. For similar comments, see Higham, *Strangers,* pp. 107-08; Jones, p. 261; George E. Mowry, *The Era of Theodore Roosevelt* (New York: Harper & Row, 1962), p. 2; William Preston, Jr., *Aliens and Dissenters* (New York: Harper & Row, 1966), p. 29. Oscar Handlin. *The American People in the Twentieth Century* (Boston: Beacon, 1963), pp. 4-5.
2. *Response,* p. 84. See also Nye, p. 30.
3. The following analysis draw heavily on Hofstadter, *Age,* pp. 235-41; Richard M. Abrams, "The Failure of Progressivism," *Shaping,* eds. Abrams and Levine, pp. 207-24; John N. Ingham, "A Strike in the Progressive Era," *Pennsylvania History,* 90 (July, 1966), pp. 353, 376; Goldman, *Rendezvous,* pp. 55-64; Fine, *Laissez Faire,* pp. 275-76, 382-84; Michael P. Rogin, *The Intellectuals and McCarthy* (Cambridge: MIT Press, 1970), p. 206; George Mowry, *The California Progressives* (Chicago: Quadrangle, 1963), pp. 99-102, 143-47; Cochran and Miller, pp. 274-80, 296; Henry F. Pringle, *Theodore Roosevelt* (New York: Harcourt, Brace, 1956), pp. 258-59; Mowry, *Era,* pp. 99-103; Stanley Shapiro, "The Great War and Reform: Liberals and Labor, 1917-1919," *LH,* 12 (Spring, 1971), pp. 323-44; Hays, pp. 84-86; Robert H. Wiebe, *Businessmen and Reform* (Chicago: Quadrangle, 1968), pp. 157-78.
4. Abrams, p. 210.
5. Quoted in Ginger, *Age,* p. 299.
6. Wiebe, *Businessmen,* p. 157.
7. Preston, "Shall This Be All?" p. 440. See also Paul Murphy, "Sources and Nature of Intolerance in the Twenties," *JAH,* 51 (June, 1964), p. 6.
8. Faulkner, *Decline,* pp. 36, 251-53; Cochran and Miller, p. 235.
9. Abrams, p. 221.
10. Otis Pease, *The Progressive Years* (New York: George Braziller, 1962), p. 6.
11. Cochran and Miller, pp. 231, 280.
12. Joll, pp. 129-38, 141, 176; David, p. 437.
13. On the McKinley anarchist scare, see Sidney Fine, "Anarchism and the Assassination of McKinley," *AHR,* 9 (July, 1955), pp. 777-99; Higham, *Strangers,* p. 111; Drinnon, pp. 69-73; Charles Lewarne, "The Anarchist Colony at Home, Washington, 1901-1902," *AW,* 14 (Summer, 1972), pp. 155-69. On anarchist strength in the early twentieth century, see Robert J. Goldstein, "The Anarchist Scare of 1908: A Sign of Tensions in the Progressive Era," *American Studies,* 15 (Fall, 1974), p. 58.
14. *Strangers,* p. 111.
15. Preston, *Aliens,* p. 31. Roosevelt asked for the exclusion and deportation of alien anarchists who advocated assassination; the creation of a literacy requirement for immigrants to "decrease the sum of ignorance so potent in producing the envy, suspicion, malignant passion and hatred of order out of which anarchist sentiment inevitably springs;" and the establishment of a "certain standard of economic fitness" to bar cheap labor that gave birth to "pestilential social conditions in our great cities, where anarchist organizations have their greatest possibility of growth."
16. Preston, *Aliens,* p. 32.
17. Fine, "Anarchism," pp. 793-94; Lewarne, "Anarchist," p. 167.
18. Whipple, p. 304; Fine, "Anarchism," p. 798; Higham, *Strangers,* p. 113.
19. Preston, *Aliens,* p. 33; *INS,* 1956, p. 95.
20. This development was made much more obvious by the pattern of repression which developed during World War I (see Chapter Four, below). As Paul L. Murphy has noted, "Prior to the Wilson administrations's massive war-time program of conscription, espionage legislation, sedition laws, censorship and deliberate surveillance of the mails and frequent repression of critics of the government, federal authorities, reading the Bill of Rights fairly literally, had not passed laws restricting freedom of speech, press, assembly or religion . . . . they had left social control of deviant activities in the hands of states and local communities. . . . World War I brought the spector of something new ("Communities in Conflict," *Pulse,* ed. Reitman, p. 24).
21. On the WFM see George C. Suggs, Jr., *Colorado's War on Militant Unionism: James H. Peabody and the Western Miners* (Detroit: Wayne State University Press, 1972); Melvyn Dubofsky, "Origins of Western Working Class Radicalism," *LH,* 7 (Spring, 1966), pp. 131-55; Dubofsky, *We Shall,* pp. 19-80; Jensen, *Heritage,* pp. 54-219.

22. Joseph R. Conlin, *Big Bill Haywood and the Radical Union Movement*, (Syracuse: Syracuse University Press, 1969), p. 37.
23. Wiebe, *Search*, p. 38.
24. Jensen, *Heritage*, pp. 58-59; Melvyn Dubofsky, "The Leadville Strike of 1896-1897," *Mid-America*, 48 (April, 1966), pp. 99-118.
25. Jensen, *Heritage*, p. 67.
26. On the 1899 Coeur d'Alene strike, see Gaboury, pp. 18-22; Jensen, *Heritage*, pp. 72-87; Dubofsky, *We Shall*, pp. 29-37.
27. Dubofsky, "Origins," p. 152.
28. Suggs, *Colorado's War*, pp. 20-22; Carl Hein, "William Haywood and the Syndiaclist Faith," *American Radicals*, ed. Goldberg, pp. 182-83.
29. George C. Suggs, "Prelude to Industrial Warfare: The Colorado City Strike," *Colorado Magazine*, 44 (Summer, 1967), p. 248.
30. On the Colorado "labor war" of 1903-04, see Suggs, *Colorado's War*; Suggs, "Prelude;" George C. Suggs, "Strike Breaking in Colorado: Governor James H. Peabody and the Telluride Strike, 1903-1904," *JW*, 5 (October, 1966), pp. 455-75; Jensen, *Heritage*, pp. 118-59; Dubofsky, *We Shall*, pp. 43-54; Lens, pp. 127-155; Laslett, *Labor*, p. 260.
31. Jensen, *Heritage*, pp. 130-31; Lens, p. 148.
32. Suggs, "Prelude," p. 262.
33. *Colorado's War*, pp. 11-12, 189, 191-92.
34. See the documents reprinted in Joyce L. Kornbluh, ed., *Rebel Voices: An I.W.W. Anthology* (Ann Arbor: University of Michigan Press, 1964), pp. 12-13. In addition to this book, the best sources on the IWW are Dubofsky, *We Shall;* Foner, IV; Patrick Renshaw, *The Wobblies* (Garden City, New York: Doubleday, 1968); and Joseph R. Conlin, *Bread and Roses Too: Studies of the Wobblies* (Westport, Connecticut: Greenwood, 1969). The classic, but outdated, account is Paul Brissenden, *The I.W.W.: A Study of American Syndicalism* (New York: Columbia University Press, 1920).
35. On the Steunenberg affair, see Jensen, pp. 192-218; Dubofsky, *We Shall*, pp. 96-105; Conlin, Big Bill Haywood, pp. 59-80; David H. Grover, *Debaters and Dynamiters* (Corvallis: Oregon State University Press, 1964).
36. Ginger, *Debs*, p. 264.
37. Ginger, *Debs*, p. 268.
38. Jensen, *Heritage*, pp. 134-35.
39. Rayback, pp. 240-43; Laslett, *Labor*, pp. 263-66.
40. Conlin, *Big Bill Haywood*, p. 80.
41. Jensen, *Heritage*, pp. 236-44; Dubofsky, *We Shall*, p. 105.
42. See Weinstein, *Corporate Ideal*, pp. 3-40 and *passim*.
43. Yellin, pp. 137-70.
44. Selig Perlman, quoted in Faulkner, *Decline*, p. 295.
45. Dulles, p. 193.
46. Commons, II, p. 524; Dulles, p. 186.
47. Mowry, *Era*, p. 11.
48. On the San Francisco strike and its aftermath, see Walter Bean, *Boss Reuf's San Francisco* (Berkeley: University of California Press, 1968); Mowry, *California*, pp. 23-38, Foner, III, pp. 287-96; Commons, III, pp. 71-81.
49. Commons, III, p. 74.
50. Foner, III, p. 50; Commons, III, pp. 328-29.
51. Porter, "Colorado," pp. 3-4.
52. Foner, III, p. 400.
53. Allan K. Powell, "The 'Foreign Element' and the 1903-1904 Carbon County Coal Miners Strike," *Utah Historical Quarterly*, 43 (Spring, 1975), pp. 135-54.
54. Taft and Ross, pp. 312, 318.
55. Dulles, pp. 393-99.
56. Foner, III, pp. 39, 309.
57. Taft and Ross, pp. 310-11; Bernhard, pp. 184-86; Rayback, pp. 316-17.
58. Mowry, *California*, pp. 48-50.
59. Mowry, *Era*, pp. 216-22; Faulkner, *Decline*, pp. 30, 420.
60. Wiebe, *Search*, p. 201; Goldstein, pp. 59-60.
61. On Goldfield, see Elliot, "Labor Troubles," pp. 369-83; Dubofsky, *We Shall*, pp. 120-25; Jensen, *Heritage*, pp. 219-35.

62. Brooks, p. 109. On the 1907-1908 labor decisions and the AFL response, see Karson, pp. 50-53; Bernstein, *Lean*, pp. 197-200; Faulkner, *Decline*, pp. 298-99.
63. Rayback, p. 223.
64. This material and the material in the next three paragraphs is taken from the author's article, "The Anarchist Scare of 1908," which is based on the primary sources cited therein.
65. Woodward, *Origin*, p. 363; Spero and Harris, pp. 357-58.
66. Graham Adams, Jr., *The Age of Industrial Violence, 1910-1915* (New York: Columbia University Press, 1966), pp. 101-11 (quotation, p. 107); Faulkner, *Decline*, p. 312.
67. On McKee's Rock, see Ingham, pp. 353-77; Dubofsky, *We Shall*, pp. 199-209; Robert L. Tyler, "The IWW and the West," *American Quarterly*, 12 (Summer, 1960), pp. 179-80.
68. Wiebe, *Search*, pp. 208-11.
69. Faulkner, *Decline*, pp. 30-32.
70. Weinstein, *Decline*, pp. 84-85, 93, 103, 116-17; Harry W. Laidler, *History of Socialism* (New York: Crowell, 1968), pp. 587-88.
71. Shannon, *Socialist Party*, pp. 1-42; Bell, *Marxian Socialism*, p. 79.
72. Especially Bell, *Marxian Socialism*, pp. 79-71, 90-97; and Kipnis, pp. 418-29.
73. "Socialism's Hidden Heritage: Scholarship Reinforces Political Mythology," *For a New America: Essays in History and Politics From 'Studies on the Left' 1959-1967*, eds. James Weinstein and David W. Eakins, (New York: Vintage, 1970), p. 234. See also Weinstein, *Decline*, pp. 27-118; and James Weinstein, "The Problems of the Socialist Party Before World War One," *Failure*, eds. Laslett and Lipset, pp. 300-40.
74. Laslett, *Labor*, p. 302, takes strong exception to this statement, based on rather limited data, while Dick, pp. 68-78, strongly supports it. See also p 83, below.
75. Quest, p. 53. On the IWW, see the sources cited in footnote 34 of this chapter.
76. Brissenden, p. 251.
77. Eldridge F. Dowell, *A History of Criminal Syndicalism Legislation in the United States* (New York: De Capo, 1969), p. 36.
78. Brissenden, p. 4.
79. Quoted in Joyce Kornbluh, "The Industrial Workers of the World," in Gibbs Smith, *Labor Martyr: Joe Hill* (New York: Grosset & Dunlap, 1969), pp. 9-10.
80. Weinstein, *Decline*, pp. 31, 36, 40-41; Karson, pp. 130-31.
81. John S. Smith, "Organized Labor and Government in the Wilson Era, 1913-1921: Some Conclusions," *LH*, 3 (Fall, 1962), pp. 265-86; Dulles, p. 205; Karson, pp. 42-89; Faulkner, *Decline*, pp. 309-16.
82. "Organized Labor," p. 270.
83. Higham, *Strangers* p. 177.
84. On the Bethlehem strike, see Adams, pp. 188-94; Ingram, p. 375; Taft and Ross, p. 316; David Brody, *Steelworkers in America* (New York: Harper & Row, 1969), p. 121.
85. Adams, p. 191.
86. Adams, p. 194.
87. Adams, pp. 114-18; Taft and Ross, pp. 314-15; Wallace, p. 92.
88. Kipnis, p. 348.
89. On the 1910 union drive in Los Angeles and the *Times* bombing, see Kipnis, pp. 348-56; Mowry, *California*, pp. 47-56; Adams, pp. 1-20.
90. Adams, p. 27.
91. On the free speech fights, see Dubofsky, *We Shall*, pp. 173-97; Kornbluh, *Rebel*, pp. 94-126; Robert Tyler, *Rebels of the Woods: The IWW in the Pacific Northwest* (Eugene: University of Oregon Press, 1967), pp. 33-43; Conlin, *Bread*, pp. 70-78; Foner, IV, pp. 172-213. On the free speech fight in Fresno, see Ronald Genini, "Industrial Workers of the World and their Fresno Free Speech Fight, 1910-1911," *California Historical Quarterly*, 53 (Summer, 1974), pp. 100-113; on Aberdeen, Charles Lewarne, "The Aberdeen, Washington, Free Speech Fight of 1911-1912," *PNQ*, 66 (January, 1975), pp. 1-12; on San Diego, Grace L. Miller, "The IWW Free Speech Fight: San Diego, 1912," *Southern California Quarterly*, 54 (Fall, 1972), pp. 211-228; and Rosalie Shanks, "The IWW Free Speech Movement: San Diego, 1912," *San Diego Historical Quarterly*, 19 (Winter, 1973), pp. 25-33; on Minot, Charles J. Haug,

"The Industrial Workers of the World in North Dakota, 1913-1917," *North Dakota Quarterly*, 39 (Winter, 1971), pp. 87-92.

92. Shanks, p. 29.

93. Miller, p. 227.

94. On the BTW, the IWW in Louisiana and the Grabow and Merryville affairs, see Merl E. Reed, "Lumberjacks and Longshoremen: The IWW in Louisiana," *LH*, 13 (Winter, 1972), pp. 41-59; Merl E. Reed, "The IWW and Individual Freedom in Louisiana, 1913," *Louisiana History*, 10 (Winter, 1969), pp. 61-69; Grady McWhiney, "Louisiana Socialists in the Early Twentieth Century," *Journal of Southern History*, 20 (August, 1954), pp. 325-35; Dubofsky, *We Shall*, pp. 211-19.

95. Julian F. Jaffe, *Crusade Against Radicalism: New York During the Red Scare, 1914-1924* (Port Washington, New York: Kennigat, 1972), p. 28; Tyler, *Rebels*, pp. 56-60; Kornbluh, *Rebel*, p. 252; Higham, *Strangers*, pp. 177-78 (quotation, p. 178).

96. Preston, *Aliens*, pp. 67-73; Michael Bassett, "The Socialist Party Dilemma, 1912-1914," *Mid-America*, 47 (October, 1965), p. 254; Foner, IV, p. 132.

97. On the Lawrence strike and subsequent developments, see Dubofsky, *We Shall*, pp. 227-62; Yellin, pp. 171-204; Kornbluh, *Rebel*, pp. 158-96; Conlin, *Big Bill Haywood*, pp. 124-36.

98. Preston, *Aliens*, pp. 44-45; Dubofsky, *We Shall*, pp. 258-59.

99. Dubofsky, *We Shall*, pp. 194-95.

100. On the 1912 strikes see Philip Newman, "The First IWW Invasion of New Jersey," *Proceedings of the New Jersey Historical Society*, 58 (1940), pp. 268-83; Michael H. Ebner, "The Passaic Strike of 1912 and the Two IWWs," *LH*, 11 (Fall, 1970), pp. 452-66. On the 1913 Patterson strike, see Dubofsky, *We Shall*, pp. 263-86; Adams, pp. 75-99; Kornbluh, *Rebel*, pp. 197-226; Morris Schonbach, *Radicals and Visionaries: A History of Dissent in New Jersey* (Princeton: Van Nostrand, pp. 62-65.

101. Adams, p. 82.

102. Dubofsky, p. 278.

103. Quoted in Foner, IV, pp. 370-71.

104. Dubofsky, *We Shall*, pp. 285-87; Tyler, *Rebels*, p. 60; Foner, IV, pp. 224-25, 373-90.

105. On Wheatland, see Woodrow C. Whitten, "The Wheatland Episode," *PHR*, 17 (February, 1948), pp. 37-42; Adams, pp. 196-97; Dubofsky, *We Shall*, pp. 294-300; Kornbluh, *Rebel*, pp. 228-29; Foner, IV, pp. 258-80; Stuart Jamieson, *Labor Unionism in American Agriculture* (Washington, D.C.: Government Printing Office, 1954), pp. 60-62.

106. On the West Virginia conflicts of 1912-1913, see David A. Corbin, "*The Socialist and Labor Star*: Strike and Suppression in West Virginia, 1912-1913," *West Virginia History*, 34 (January, 1973), pp. 168-86; Weinstein, *Decline*, p. 34; Taft and Ross, pp. 329-30.

107. Corbin, pp. 173-73.

108. On Calumet, see William Beck, "Law and Order During the 1913 Copper Strike," *Michigan History*, 54 (Winter, 1970), pp. 275-92; Jensen, *Heritage*, pp. 272-88.

109. Jensen, *Heritage*, p. 288.

110. On the 1913-1914 Colorado events and the "Ludlow Massacre," see Yellin, pp. 205-50; Porter, "Colorado," pp. 3-27; Adams, pp. 146-75; Weinstein, *Corporate Ideal*, pp. 191-98; Allen, pp. 57-65.

111. Yellin, p. 237; Shannon, *Socialist Party*, p. 60.

112. *HS*, p. 73; Faulkner, *Decline*, pp. 31-35.

113. Foner, IV, pp. 435-61; Mowry, *California*, pp. 198-99; Smith, *Labor Martyr*, pp. 124-25; Bernhard, pp. 156-57.

114. Carey McWilliams, *Factories in the Fields* (Santa Barbara, California: Peregrine Publishers, 1971), p. 165.

115. Jaffe, pp. 38-40; Foner, IV, pp. 442-48.

116. Tyler, *Rebels*, pp. 50-52: Norman H. Clark, *Mill Town: A Social History of Everett, Washington* (Seattle: University of Washington Press, 1970), pp. 136-37; Smith, *Labor Martyr*, p. 119; Foner, IV, pp. 209-10, 456-58.

117. On the 1914-1916 anarchist scare, see Frost, pp. 45-51; Drinnon, pp. 175-76; Jaffe, pp. 43-44; Zechariah Chafee, *Free Speech in the United States* (New York:

Atheneum, 1969), p. 156; Francis Russell, *Tragedy in Dedham: The Story of the Sacco-Vanzetti Case* (New York: McGraw-Hill, 1971), p. 80.

118. Higham, *Strangers*, p. 183.
119. Higham, *Strangers*, pp. 183-93; Preston, *Aliens*, pp. 73-85.
120. Chaffee, *Free Speech*, pp. 585, 593; Dowell, p. 14.
121. Arnon Gutfeld, "The Levine Affair: A Case Study in Academic Freedom," PHR, 39 (February, 1970), p. 28.
122. Preston, *Aliens*, pp. 59-61; Dubofsky, *We Shall*, pp. 299-300.
123. Taft and Ross, pp. 326-27.
124. Mowry, *California*, pp. 198-99; Frost, pp. 56-61.
125. Dubofsky, *We Shall*, pp. 301-07.
126. Bernhard, pp. 187-88.
127. Philip Taft, "The IWW in the Grain Belt," LH, 1 (Winter, 1960), p. 64; Haug, "IWW in North Dakota, 1913-1917," pp. 93-99; Cletus E. Daniel, "Wobblies on the Farm: The IWW in the Yakima Valley," PNQ, 65 (October, 1974), p. 167.
128. Schonbach, p. 68; Taft and Ross, p. 327.
129. Taft and Ross, p. 326; Brody, *Steelworkers*, pp. 181-83; Kornbluh, *Rebel*, p. 292.
130. On the Mesabi strike, see Neil Betten, "Riot, Revolution and Repression in the Iron Range Strike of 1916," MH, 41 (Summer, 1968), pp. 82-93; Dubofsky, *We Shall*, pp. 321-22.
131. Betten, p. 92.
132. Haynes, pp. 163-75.
133. On the Hill case, see Smith, *Labor Martyr: Joe Hill*; Dubofsky, *We Shall*, pp. 308-13; Kornbluh, *Rebel*, pp. 127-57; Philip S. Foner, *The Case of Joe Hill* (New York: International, 1965).
134. On the Mooney case, see Frost, *The Mooney Case;* Albert Gunns, "The Mooney-Billings Case," PNQ, 60 (October, 1969), pp. 216-220.
135. On the Everett "massacre," see Clark, *Mill Town;* Norman H. Clark, "Everett 1916, and After," PNQ, 57 (April, 1966), pp. 57-72; Kornbluh, *Rebel*, p. 98; Dubofsky, *We Shall*, pp. 337-42.
136. For example, Dulles, p. 219; Faulkner, *Decline*, p. 307; Symes and Clement, pp. 273-74.
137. Brissenden, p. 354.
138. On the AWO and the IWW rejuvenation, see Taft, "IWW," pp. 53-67; Haug, "IWW in North Dakota, 1913-1917," pp. 93-102; Renshaw, pp. 133-42; Kornbluh, *Rebel*, pp. 230-32; Dubofsky, *We Shall*, pp. 317-18, 343-46; Preston, *Aliens*, pp. 91-99.
139. Taft, "IWW," p. 64.
140. Taft, "IWW," p. 55.
141. On the NPL, see Robert L. Morlan, *Political Prairie Fire: The NonPartisan League, 1915-1922* (Minneapolis: University of Minnesota Press, 1955); Nye, pp. 289-94; Theodore Saloutos and John D. Hicks, *Twentieth Century Populism* (Lincoln: University of Nebraska Press, 1951), pp. 149-218.
142. Saloutos and Hicks, p. 185.
143. Arthur S. Link, *Woodrow Wilson and the Progressive Era* (New York: Harper & Row, 1963), pp. 174-79.
144. Don Whitehead, *The FBI Story* (New York: Pocket Books, 1958), pp. 29-34; Higham, *Strangers*, pp. 195-98.
145. Higham, *Strangers*, p. 197.
146. Frederick C. Luebke, *Bonds of Loyalty: German Americans and World War One* (Dekalb: Northern Illinois University Press, 1974), p. 134.
147. Harry N. Scheiber, *The Wilson Administration and Civil Liberties, 1917-1921* (Ithaca: Cornell University Press, 1960), pp. 3-13; Higham, *Strangers*, pp. 198-200; Luebke, pp. 142-46, 169-78.
148. Higham, *Strangers*, p. 100; Schieber, pp. 4-5.
149. Scheiber, p. 6.
150. John Blum, "Nativism, Anti-Radicalism and the Foreign Scare, 1917-1920," *Midwest Journal*, 3 (Winter, 1950-1951), p. 48.
151. Luebke, pp. 169-71.
152. Scheiber, pp. 8-9.

153. Preston, *Aliens*, pp. 73-85; Higham, *Strangers*, pp. 202-04.
154. Scheiber, p. 13.
155. Mock, p. 42.
156. Brissenden, pp. 383-84; Hugh T. Lovin, "The Red Scare in Idaho, 1916-1918," *Idaho Yesterdays*, 17 (Fall, 1973), p. 6; Robert C. Sims, "Idaho's Criminal Syndicalism Act," *LH*, 15 (Fall, 1974), pp. 511-12.
157. Cummings and McPharland, pp. 416-17; Preston, *Aliens*, p. 105.

CHAPTER FOUR

1. For example, see Preston W. Slosson, *The Great Crusade* (Chicago: Quadrangle, 1971), p. 29; William J. Breen, "The North Carolina Council of Defense During World War I," *North Carolina Historical Review*, 50 (January, 1973), p. 1.
2. The scope of the CPI's activities were to be unmatched "until the rise of totalitarian dictatorships after the war" (Ekirch, *Decline*, p. 215). In addition to whipping up hatred for all things German, the CPI declared that the war was a "crusade not merely to re-win the tomb of Christ, but to bring back to earth the rule of right, the peace, goodwill to men and gentleness he taught" (William E. Leuchtenburg, *Perils of Prosperity* [Chicago: University of Chicago Press, 1958], p. 46. In a pinch the CPI could also be counted on to perform partisan political services for the Wilson administration. Seward W. Livermore, *Woodrow Wilson and the War Congress, 1916-1918* [Seattle: University of Washington Press, 1968], pp. 114, 290).
3. Thomas A. Bailey, *Woodrow Wilson and the Lost Peace* (Chicago: Quadrangle, 1963), p. 15.
4. Slosson, p. 28.
5. Philip A. Taft, "The Federal Trials of the IWW," *LH*, 3 (Winter, 1962), p. 58; Taft, "IWW," p. 62.
6. Fine, *Farmer*, pp. 310-14; Weinstein, *Decline*, p. 127.
7. Bell, *Marxian Socialism*, p. 102.
8. Bell, *Marxian Socialism*, p. 102.
9. Weinstein, *Decline*, pp. 145-59; James Weinstein, "Anti-War Sentiment and the Socialist Party," *PSQ*, 74 (June, 1959), pp. 215-39; Bell, *Marxian Socialism*, p. 103; Shannon, *Socialist Party*, pp. 104-05.
10. Morlan, pp. 110-12, 151-52; Livermore, pp. 153-54; Carol Jensen, "Loyalty as Political Weapon: The 1918 Campaign in Minnesota," *MH*, 43 (Summer, 1972), pp. 46-47.
11. Frank L. Grubbs, *The Struggle for Labor Loyalty: Gompers, the AFL and the Pacifists, 1917-1920* (Durham, North Carolina: Duke University Press, 1968), pp. 29, 50-51; Ginger, *Debs*, p. 362; Charles Chatfield, *For Peace and Justice: Pacifism in America, 1914-1941* (Boston: Beacon, 1973), pp. 27-28.
12. Ronald Radosh, *American Labor and Foreign Policy* (New York: Vintage, 1970), p. 57.
13. Weinstein, *Decline*, p. 136; Peterson and Fite, p. 234; Livermore, p. 41.
14. Weinstein, *Decline*, pp. 138, 160. See also Radosh, pp. 56-57; Grubbs, *Struggle*, passim; Peterson and Fite, passim.
15. Roche, *Quest*, p. 36; Chaffee, *Free Speech*, pp. 105-06; Elizabeth Stevenson, *The American 1920's* (New York: MacMillan, 1970), p. 38; Mock, p. 5.
16. Robert E. Cushman, "The Impact of the War on the Constitution," *The Impact of the War on America* (Ithaca: Cornell University Press, 1942), p. 21.
17. Scheiber, p. 17.
18. Scheiber, pp. 22-23, 27.
19. Peterson and Fite, p. 14.
20. See Scheiber, pp. 17-20; Peterson and Fite, pp. 15-17; Mock, pp. 48-50; Chafee, *Free Speech*, pp. 38-39.
21. See Scheiber, pp. 22-26; Peterson and Fite, pp. 208-21; Mock, pp. 53-54; Chafee, *Free Speech*, pp. 39-42.
22. Cummings and McPharland, p. 418.

23. Scheiber, pp. 14, 45; Mock, pp. 195-96; Luebke, pp. 248-49, 255-56.
24. Peterson and Fite, pp. 139-41; Chafee, *Free Speech*, p. 184.
25. Scheiber, pp. 14-15; Harold M. Hyman, *To Try Men's Souls* (Berkeley: University of California Press, 1960), pp. 268-70.
26. Scheiber, pp. 14-15.
27. Scheiber, p. 20. See also Peterson and Fite, p. 98; Luebke, pp. 241-43.
28. Luebke, pp. 242, 271-73; Mock, pp. 141-42; Scheiber, p. 34.
29. Preston, *Aliens*, pp. 181-91; Donald Johnson, *The Challenge to American Freedoms* (Lexington: University of Kentucky Press, 1963), p. 125.
30. Chafee, *Free Speech*, p. 100. See also Mock, pp. 26-27.
31. Preston, *Aliens*, p. 105.
32. Hyman, *To Try*, p. 271.
33. Preston, *Aliens*, pp. 115-16, 156, 161; Joan M. Jensen, *The Price of Vigilance* (Chicago: Rand McNally, 1968), pp. 118-24, 224-32; Ginger, *Debs*, p. 386; Hyman, *Soldiers and Spruce: Origins of the Loyal Legion of Loggers & Lumbermen* (Los Angeles: University of California Institute of Industrial Relations, 1963), pp. 84, 98; Johnson, *Challenge*, pp. 34, 80; Arnon Gutfeld, "The Ves Hall Case, Judge Bourquin and the Sedition Act of 1918," *PHR*, 37 (May, 1968), p. 175; Dubofsky, *We Shall*, pp. 453-54.
34. On the APL, the best source is Jensen, *Price of Vigilance*. See also Hyman, *To Try*, pp. 272-97; Cummings and McPharland, pp. 421-22; Scheiber, p. 43; Whitehead, p. 39.
35. Jensen, *Price*, pp. 185, 187.
36. Hyman, *To Try*, p. 275.
37. Jensen, *Price*, p. 48.
38. *Quest*, p. 44.
39. Jensen, *Price*, pp. 191-218; Peterson and Fite, pp. 231-34; Scheiber, p. 48; Max Lowenthal, *The Federal Bureau of Investigation* (New York: Harcourt, Brace, 1950), pp. 26-35.
40. Peterson and Fite, p. 233.
41. Scheiber, p. 48.
42. Preston, *Aliens*, pp. 152-207.
43. Johnson, *Challenge*, pp. 17-55; Peterson and Fite, pp. 121-38, 259-64; Mock, p. 5; Chatfield, *For Peace*, pp. 57-58, 68-87; Jensen, *Price*, pp. 83-85; Burt Noggle, *Into the Twenties: The United States from Armistice to Normalcy* (Urbana: University of Illinois Press, 1974), quotation, p. 92.
44. Scheiber, pp. 46-49.
45. Jensen, *Price*, p. 224.
46. Johnson, *Challenge*, p. 69.
47. Scheiber, pp. 45-49; Chafee, *Free Speech*, pp. 60-69; Jensen, *Price*, p. 261.
48. Goldman, *Rendezvous*, p. 197; Carl Swisher, "Civil Liberties in War Time," *PSQ*, 55 (September, 1940), p. 329; Ekrich, *Decline*, p. 217; Arthur Schlesinger, Jr., *Politics of Upheaval* (Boston: Houghton Mifflin, 1966), p. 45; Luebke, pp. 247, 310-11.
49. Mock, pp. 179-91; Peterson and Fite, p. 36.
50. Weinstein, *Corporate Ideal*, pp. 237-38.
51. Chafee, *Free Speech*, pp. 97-100; Mock, pp. 131-52; Peterson and Fite, pp. 93-101; Donald Johnson, "Wilson, Burleson and Censorship in the First World War," *Journal of Southern History*, 28 (February, 1962), pp. 45-58; O. A. Hilton, Freedom of Press in Wartime, 1917-1919," *Southwestern Social Science Quarterly*, 28 (March, 1948), pp. 346-61; Scheiber, p. 32.
52. Hilton, "Freedom of Press," p. 353.
53. Drinnon, pp. 184-99; Franklin, p. 476; C. Vann Woodward, *Tom Watson* (New York: Oxford University Press, 1963), pp. 451-58; Weinstein, *Decline*, pp. 137-38; David Manwaring, *Render Unto Caesar* (Chicago: University of Chicago, 1962), pp. 29-30.
54. Scheiber, p. 32.
55. Livermore, pp. 70-78; Mock, pp. 138-39.
56. Benjamin G. Rader, "The Montana Lumber Strike of 1917," *PHR*, 38 (May,

1967), p. 189. See also, on the lumber strike, Dubofsky, *We Shall*, pp. 360-65; Tyler, *Rebels*, pp. 90-154; Kornbluh, *Rebel*, pp. 253-55; and Hyman, *Soldiers, passim*.

57. On the copper strikes, see Meyer H. Fishbein, "The President's Mediation Commission and the Arizona Copper Strike, 1917," *Southwestern Social Science Quarterly*, 30 (December, 1949), pp. 175-82; Arnon Gutfeld, "The Speculator Disaster in 1917," *AW*, 11 (Spring, 1969), pp. 27-38; Arnon Gutfeld, "The Murder of Frank Little," *LH*, 10 (Spring, 1969), pp. 177-92; John H. Lindquist, "The Jerome Deportation of 1917," *AW*, (Autumn, 1969), pp. 233-46; John H. Lindquist and James Fraser, "Sociological Interpretation of the Bisbee Deportation," *PHR*, 37 (November, 1968), pp. 401-22; Philip Taft, "The Bisbee Deportation," *LH*, 13 (Winter, 1972), pp. 3-40; Dubofsky, *We Shall*, pp. 366-75; Kornbluh, *Rebel*, pp. 293-96.

58. Preston, *Aliens*, p. 108.

59. Preston, *Aliens*, pp. 88-117; Tyler, *Rebels*, pp. 130-37; Rader, pp. 205-07; Dubofsky, *We Shall*, pp. 402-03, 451.

60. On the Loyal Legion, the best source is Hyman, *Soldiers and Spruce: Origins of the Loyal Legion of Loggers of Loggers & Lumbermen*. See also Robert L. Tyler, "The United States Government as Union Organizer: The Loyal Legion of Loggers Lumbermen," *Mississippi Valley Historical Review*, 47 (December, 1960), pp. 434-51.

61. Hyman, *Soldiers*, p. 226.

62. Hyman, *Soldiers*, p. 305.

63. On the IWW raids and subsequent indictments, see Dubofsky, *We Shall*, pp. 404-10; 423-44; Tyler, *Rebels*, pp. 123-24; Conlin, *Big Bill Haywood*, p. 178; Taft, "Federal Trials;" Jensen, *Price*, pp. 64-76; Preston, *Aliens*, pp. 118-51; Rayback, p. 282; Karson, pp. 206-07; Clayton R. Koppes, "The Kansas Trial of the IWW," *LH*, 16 (Summer, 1975), pp. 338-58; Woodrow C. Whitten, *Criminal Syndicalism and the Law in California, 1919-1927* (Philadelphia: American Philosophical Society, 1969), pp. 19-21.

64. Dubofsky, *We Shall*, p. 406.

65. Clayton R. Koppes, "The Industrial Workers of the World and County Jail Reform in Kansas, 1915-1920," *Kansas Historical Quarterly*, 16 (Spring, 1975), p. 70.

66. Koppes, "Kansas Trial," p. 347.

67. Dubofsky, *We Shall*, pp. 438-41; Whitten, *Criminal Syndicalism*, pp. 19-21.

68. Robert Tyler, "Rebels of the Woods," *Oregon Historical Quarterly*, 55 (March, 1954), p. 25; Preston, *Aliens*, pp. 88-89; Dubofsky, *We Shall*, pp. 348-58; Peterson and Fite, p. 50.

69. On the trials, see Taft, "Federal Trials;" Preston, *Aliens*, pp. 118-51; Dubofsky, *We Shall*, pp. 423-44; Peterson and Fite, pp. 235-47; Johnson, *Challenge*, pp. 88-106; Koppes, "Kansas Trial."

70. Preston, *Aliens*, pp. 143-49; Peterson and Fite, pp. 236-37; Taft, "Federal Trials," p. 70; Dubofsky, *We Shall*, pp. 431-32. Similarly repressive tactics had been used by the federal government to hamper the defense in the Goldman-Berkman trial for conspiracy to obstruct the draft (Drinnon, p. 196).

71. Fine, *Farmer*, p. 318; Weinstein, *Decline*, p. 145; Johnson, "Wilson," p. 49; Peterson and Fite, pp. 30-32, 36-38, 47, 96-98; Richard A. Falk, "Socialist Party of Ohio — War and Free Speech," *OH*, 78 (Spring, 1969), p. 109.

72. Bell, *Marxian Socialism*, p. 103; Weinstein, *Decline*, p. 236; Michael Bassett, "The American Socialist Party and the War, 1917-1918," *Australian Journal of Politics*, 11 (December, 1965), pp. 277-82.

73. Fine, *Farmer*, pp. 318-19; Peterson and Fite, pp. 164-66, 184-86, 248-55; Ginger, *Debs*, pp. 372-95; Weinstein, *Decline*, pp. 160-61; Falk, pp. 110-13.

74. Scheiber, p. 32; Shannon, *Socialist Party*, p. 110.

75. Garin Burbank, "The Disruption and Decline of the Oklahoma Socialist Party," *Journal of American Studies*, 7 (August, 1973), p. 175.

76. Shannon, *Socialist Party*, pp. 105-09; Peterson and Fite, pp. 40-42; Sherry Warwick, "Radical Labor in Oklahoma: The Working Class Union," *Chronicles of Oklahoma*, 52 (Summer, 1974), pp. 180-95. See Burbank, "Disruption," for a study arguing that the Oklahoma SPA was the "victim of political repression sanctioned by national authority" and that the Democratic Party of Oklahoma, by attempting to tar the state SPA with the accusation of disloyalty "was not waging an irrational battle against

political phantasms any more than the national Democratic administration was irrational in jailing Eugene Debs and banning Socialist newspapers from the mail," since the Oklahoma SPA was a "formidable social movement" which "challenged their political and economic dominance in local affairs" (pp. 133, 150).

77. Bassett, "American Socialist Party," pp. 288-91; Shannon, *Socialist Party*, p. 121.
78. Radosh, pp. 118-20; Merle Fainsod, *International Socialism and the World War* (Garden City, New York: Doubleday, 1969), pp. 183-90.
79. *International Socialism*, p. 190.
80. Chatfield, *For Peace*, pp. 60-61.
81. Grubbs, *Struggle, passim*; Peterson and Fite, pp. 74-80; Chatfield, *For Peace*, pp. 59-60.
82. The best source on the AFL-Wilson alliance is Simeon Larson, *Labor and Foreign Policy: Gompers, the AFL and the First World War* (Rutherford, New Jersey: Fairleigh Dickinson University, 1975). See also Grubbs, *Struggle, passim*; Radosh, pp. 7-286; Karson, pp. 90-116; Rayback, pp. 273-75; Dulles, pp. 224-28; Brody, *Steelworkers*, pp. 202-13.
83. Larson, p. 29.
84. Larson, pp. 21, 24.
85. Radosh, p. 9.
86. Grubbs, *Struggle*, p. 16.
87. Larson, p. 84.
88. Karson, p. 95.
89. Larson, pp. 25, 27.
90. Karson, p. 100.
91. George Soule, *Prosperity Decade* (New York: Rinehart & Co. 1947), p. 333.
92. Larson, pp. 114, 123.
93. Grubbs, *Struggle*, pp. 91, 102-03; Larson, p. 126.
94. Radosh, p. 17.
95. Karson, p. 14; see also Grubbs, *Struggle*, pp. 66, 10.
96. John Laslett, "Socialism and the American Labor Movement: Some New Reflections," *LH*, 8 (Spring, 1967), p. 151.
97. Laslett, *Labor*, pp. 38, 45.
98. Radosh, p. 18.
99. Radosh, p. 18.
100. Rayback, p. 275; Taft, "Federal Trials," p. 73; Dubofsky, *We Shall*, p. 401; Dulles, p. 226; Kornbluh, p. 316; Whitten, *Criminal Syndicalism*, pp. 15, 19; Hyman, *Soldiers*, pp. 48, 63; Brecher, p. 103.
101. Preston, *Aliens*, p. 129; Larson, pp. 148-49.
102. Soule, p. 333; Peterson and Fite, p. 100.
103. Dubofsky, *We Shall*, pp. 415-19; Hyman, *Soldiers*, pp. 67-69.
104. Larson, p. 143.
105. See Grubbs, *Struggle, passim*; Larson, pp. 136-53; Radosh, pp. 58-71; Weinstein, *Corporate Ideal*, pp. 240-43; Karson, p. 103.
106. Shannon, *Socialist Party*, p. 117. The AALD was also used as a government front in attempts to influence foreign labor movements to support American foreign policy, thus presaging CIA use of the AFL-CIO during the Cold War (Grubbs, *Struggle*, pp. 119-20; Larson, pp. 150-52; Radosh, pp. 431-39).
107. Harold Nelson, ed., *Freedom of the Press from Hamilton to the Warren Court* (Indianapolis: Bobbs-Merrill, 1967), p. 308.
108. See Luebke, *Bonds of Loyalty: German Americans and World War I*.
109. On local repression of the IWW, see Tyler, *Rebels*, pp. 116-54; Dubofsky, *We Shall*, pp. 376-98; Preston, *Aliens*, pp. 88-118; Kornbluh, *Rebel*, pp. 316-25; James A. Robinson, *Anti-Sedition Legislation and Loyalty Investigations in Oklahoma* (Norman: University of Oklahoma Bureau of Government Research, 1956), pp. 1-7; Whitten, *Criminal Syndicalism*, pp. 15-21; Peterson and Fite; pp. 43-61, 167-80; Nelson, pp. 317-18; Lindquist, "Jerome Deportation;" Lindquist and Fraser, "Sociological Interpretation."
110. Nelson, p. 317.
111. Mock, p. 35.

112. Peterson and Fite, pp. 172-74; Robinson, p. 3.
113. Whitten, *Criminal Syndicalism*, p. 20.
114. Taft, "Bisbee;" Lindquist, "Jerome Deportation;" Lindquist and Fraser, "Sociological Interpretation."
115. Sims, pp. 516, 520; Charles J. Haug, "The Industrial Workers of the World in North Dakota, 1918-1925," *North Dakota Quarterly*, (Summer, 1973), pp. 6-7.
116. Herbert Shapiro, "The Herbert Bigelow Case: A Test of Free Speech in Wartime," *OH*, 81 (Spring, 1972), pp. 108-21.
117. For local repression of the SPA, see Weinstein, *Decline*, pp. 119-76; Shannon, *Socialist Party*, pp. 106-13; Fine, *Farmer*, pp. 317-20; Bassett, "American Socialist," pp. 277-91; Peterson and Fite, pp. 43-60, 157-66.
118. Weinstein, *Decline*, pp. 143, 200; Peterson and Fite, p. 32; Fine, *Farmer*, pp. 317-20.
119. Peterson and Fite, pp. 74-80; Arthur W. Thurner, "The Mayor, the Governor and the People's Council," *Journal of the Illinois State Historical Society*, 65 (Summer, 1973), pp. 125-43; Grubb, *Struggle, passim;* Chatfield, *For Peace*, p. 28; Kenneth E. Hendrickson, "The Socialists of Reading, Pennsylvania, and World War I," *Pennsylvania History*, 36 (October, 1969), p. 441; William E. Nicholas, "World War I and Academic Dissent in Texas," *AW*, 14 (Autumn, 1972), p. 221.
120. George B. Tindall, *The Emergence of the New South* (Baton Rouge: Louisiana State University Press, 1967), p. 50; Robinson, p. 41; Nelson, pp. 308-20.
121. Chafee, *Free Speech*, pp. 578-97; Mock, pp. 24-25; Dowell, *passim;* Jaffe, pp. 105-08; Gutfeld, "Ves Hall," p. 173-74.
122. Chafee, *Free Speech*, p. 51.
123. Robinson, p. 4; Rader, p. 205; Tyler, *Rebels*, p. 149; Murphy, *Meaning*, p. 43.
124. Lovin, "Red Scare, p. 11.
125. Rader, pp. 206-07.
126. Sims, p. 512.
127. Robert Mowitz, "Michigan," *The States and Subversion*, ed. Walter Gellhorn (Ithaca: Cornell University Press, 1952), p. 186.
128. On the councils, see Slosson, p. 54; Breen, "North Carolina;" O. A. Hilton, "The Minnesota Public Safety Commission in World War I, 1917-1919," *Oklahoma Agricultural and Mechnical College, Arts and Sciences Bulletin*, 47 (May 15, 1951), pp. 1-44; O. A. Hilton, "The Oklahoma Council of Defense and the First World War," *Chronicles of Oklahoma*, 20 (March, 1942), pp. 18-42; O. A. Hilton, "Public Opinion and Civil Liberties in Wartime, 1917-1919," *Southwestern Social Sciences Quarterly*, 28 (December, 1947), pp. 202-07; Livermore, pp. 42-43; Hyman, *Soldiers*, pp. 41-57-59, 78, 82; Charles S. Johnson, "Two Montana Newspapers — The Butte Bulletin and the Helena Independent and the Montana Council of Defense, 1917-1921," (Unpublished B. A. thesis, University of Montana, 1970). The same forces that dominated the APL and the state councils also dominated local draft boards and frequently used them for repressive purposes. While the privileged were often able to buy draft exemptions, troublesome workers were quickly drafted by selective service boards that were controlled by businessmen (Livermore, p. 196; Brody, *Steelworkers*, p. 201; Hyman, *Soldiers*, pp. 107, 307-08). There were various links of one sort or another between the APL, military intelligence, the state councils, draft boards, the Justice Department and private business interests (Hyman, *Soldiers*, pp. 78, 84, 107, 128, 283, 286, 307-09).
129. Breen, pp. 10, 24-30; Livermore, pp. 44, 215; Jensen, "Loyalty," p. 54; Saloutos and Hicks, p. 189; Hilton, "Freedom of the Press," p. 353; Johnson, "Two Montana Newspapers."
130. Hilton, "Public Opinion," pp. 202, 207; Hilton, "Minnesota Public Safety Commission," pp. 13-14; Hilton, "Oklahoma Council," p. 33; Robinson, p. 5; Hyman, *Soldiers*, pp. 61, 77; Johnson, "Two Montana Newspapers," p. 8; Livermore, pp. 201, 287; Metzger, p. 223; Hugh T. Lovin, "World War Vigilantes in Idaho, 1917-1918," *Idaho Yesterdays*, 18 (Fall, 1974), p. 8; Haug, "IWW in North Dakota, 1918-1925," p. 9.
131. Betten, "Riot;" Haynes "Revolt;" Morlan, *Political Prairie Fire*.
132. On the situation in Minnesota, see Hilton, "Minnesota Public Safety Commis-

sion;" Morland, pp. 150-82; Jensen, "Loyalty;" Mock, p. 33; Peterson and Fite, pp. 155-56, 189-93.
133. Jensen, "Loyalty;" Morlan, pp. 152-77, 193-200; Nelson, pp. 318-20.
134. Morlan, p. 200.
135. Robert N. Manley, "The Nebraska State Council of Defense and the NPL,"
136. Douglas Bakken, "The NPL in Nebraska, 1917-1920," *North Dakota History,* 39 (Spring, 1972), pp. 25-31.
Nebraska History, 43 (December, 1962), pp. 235, 243.
137. Manley, p. 250.
138. Saloutos and Hicks, pp. 188-90; Hilton, "Minnesota Public Safety Commission," p. 28; Peterson and Fite, pp. 187-88; Morlan, pp. 173-79, 204-06; Lovin, "Red Scare," pp. 11-13.
139. For a discussion of the decline of the NPL, see Morlan, pp. 226-335; Saloutos and Hicks, pp. 185-218; Nye, pp. 292-95.
140. Nye, pp. 292-95.
141. Dubofsky, *We Shall,* p. 444.
142. Rayback, p. 290. For the story of the decline of the IWW, see Dubofsky, *We Shall,* pp. 423-68; Kornbluh, *Rebel,* pp. 316-25; Conlin, *Bread,* pp. 141-50; John S. Gambs, *Decline of the IWW* (New York: Columbia University Press, 1932).
143. Roche, *Quest,* p. 52; Soule, p. 189.
144. Bassett, "American Socialist," p. 290.
145. Shannon, *Socialist Party,* p. 104.
146. "Decline of American Radicalism in the Twentieth Century," *For A New America,* eds. Weinstein and Eakins, p. 210.
147. Kolko, "Decline," p. 210.
148. Shannon, *Socialist Party,* pp. 116-22; Weinstein, *Decline,* pp. 161-62, 182-83; Noggle, pp. 90-91.
149. Weinstein, *Decline,* pp. 169-70; Hendrickson, "Socialists of Reading;" Robert C. Reinders, "Daniel W. Hoan and the Milwaukee Socialist Party During the First World War," *WMH,* 36 (Autumn, 1952), pp. 48-55.
150. Weinstein, *Decline,* p. 170.
151. Fine, "Anarchism," p. 799.
152. Shannon, *Socialist Party,* pp. 100-02.
153. Metger, p. 230.
154. Shannon, *Socialist Party,* p. 101; Blum, "Nativism," p. 49; Preston, *Aliens,* pp. 142-49; Stevenson, pp. 41-43; Chatfield, *For Peace,* p. 29; Johnson, *Challenge,* pp. 20-24; Wiebe, *Search,* p. 292.
155. Gutfeld, "Ves Hall;" Chafee, *Free Speech,* pp. 60, 70, 74-79; Scheiber, p. 43; Conlin, *Bread,* p. 142; Swisher, p. 330; Roche, *Quest,* p. 47; Drinnon, p. 193; Paul L. Murphy, *The Constitution in Crisis Times* (New York: Harper & Row, 1972), p. 13.

CHAPTER FIVE

1. See Robert K. Murray, *Red Scare: A Study in National Hysteria, 1919-1920* (New York: McGraw-Hill, 1964); Stanley Coben *A. Mitchell Palmer: Politician* (New York: Columbia University Press, 1963), pp. 196-245; Stanley Coben, "A Study in Nativism: The American Red Scare of 1919-1920," *Twentieth Century America,* eds. Barton J. Bernstein and Allen J. Matusow (New York: Harcourt, Brace, 1969), pp. 90-109; Blum, "Nativism;" Leuchtenburg, *Perils,* pp. 66-83.
2. Rayback, pp. 282-83; Dubofsky, *We Shall,* p. 443; Scheiber, pp. 46-48; Coben, *Palmer,* pp. 200-01; Preston, *Aliens,* pp. 186-207; Johnson, *Challenge,* pp. 48-53; Robert Ward, "The Origins and Activities of the National Security League, 1914-1919," *Mississippi Valley Historical Review,* 47 (June, 1960), p. 63; Noggle, pp. 93-99; Jensen, *Price,* pp. 238-56, 267-69.
3. On SPA growth and the subsequent split, see Weinstein, *Decline,* pp. 177-233; Shannon, *Socialist Party,* pp. 126-49; Theodore Draper, *The Roots of American Communism* (New York: Viking, 1963), pp. 50-196; Howe and Coser, pp. 27-49; Bell, *Marxian Socialism,* pp. 99, 108-12; Murray, *Red Scare,* pp. 33-56.
4. Noggle, p. 8.

5. Noggle, pp. 31-45; Shapiro, "Great War;" Murphy, *Meaning*, p. 32; Draper, *Roots*, p. 139; Robert Friedheim, *The Seattle General Strike* (Seattle: University of Washington Press, 1964), pp. 12, 20; Philip L. Cook, "Red Scare in Denver," *Colorado Magazine*, 43 (1966), p. 310; Murray, *Red Scare*, p. 94; Ralph E. Shaffer, "Formation of the California Communist Labor Party," *PHR*, 36 (February, 1967), p. 65; Ray T. Wortman, "An IWW Document of the 1919 Rossford Strike," *Northwest Ohio Quarterly*, 43 (Summer, 1971), pp. 37-42.

6. Leuchtenburg, *Perils*, p. 70; Karson, p. 114; Murray, *Red Scare*, pp. 7-9; Shapiro, "Great War," pp. 327-29, 333-37; Dick, pp. 147-49; David Brody, *Labor in Crisis: The Steel Strike of 1919* (Philadelphia: Lippincott, 1965), pp. 72-77.

7. Shapiro, "Great War," p. 336.

8. Karson, p. 115; Dick, p. 149.

9. Arthur M. Schlesinger, Jr., *The Crisis of the Old Order* (Boston: Houghton Mifflin, 1957), p. 40.

10. Murphy, *Meaning*, pp. 61-62; Dick, pp. 156, 161; Murray, *Red Scare*, pp. 110, 117-18; Whitten, *Criminal Syndicalism*, p. 34; Frost, pp. 330-31; Brody, *Labor*, p. 130 (Fitzpatrick quotation); Weinstein, *Decline*, pp. 222-23.

11. Frost, pp. 320-22, 330; Murray, *Red Scare*, p. 9; Draper, *Roots*, p. 197; Coben, *Palmer*, p. 173; Brody, *Labor*, p. 129; Brecher, pp. 115-18; Soule, pp. 190-91.

12. Murray, *Red Scare*, pp. 58, 87, 108 and *passim;* Dulles, p. 230; Levin, *passim.*

13. "The First World War and American Democracy," *War as A Social Institution*, eds. J. A. Clarkson and T. C. Cochran (New York: Columbia University Press, 1941), p. 171.

14. Bailey, *Woodrow Wilson and the Lost Peace;* Thomas A. Bailey, *Woodrow Wilson and the Great Betrayal* (Chicago: Quadrangle, 1963); Arthur J. Waskow, *From Race Riot to Sit-in* (Garden City, New York: Doubleday, 1966); Murray, *Red Scare*, pp. 5-7; Friedheim, pp. 7-8; Soule, pp. 81-84; Wesley M. Bagby, *The Road to Normalcy: The Presidential Campaign and Election of 1920* (Baltimore: Johns Hopkins University Press, 1968), p. 22; Brody, *Labor*, p. 80.

15. David Mitchell, *1919: Red Mirage* (New York: MacMillan, 1970); Howe and Coser, p. 26; Draper, *Roots*, p. 133; Murray, *Red Scare*, pp. 40-45.

16. Friedheim, pp. 23-51.

17. Friedheim, *The Seattle General Strike*, gives the best account of the strike. For shorter accounts, see Murray, *Red Scare*, pp. 58-66; Brecher, 104-14; and William Crook, *Communism and the General Strike* (Hamden, Connecticut: Shoe String Press, 1960).

18. Murray, *Red Scare*, pp. 68-73.

19. Murray, *Red Scare*, pp. 73-77; Jaffe, pp. 90-91; Draper, *Roots*, p. 195; Whitten, *Criminal Syndicalism*, p. 27; Coben, *Palmer*, p. 204; Stephen M. Millett, "Charles R. Ruthenberg: The Development of an American Communist, 1909-1927," *OH*, 81 (Summer, 1972), p. 202.

20. Murray, *Red Scare*, p. 77.

21. Murray, *Red Scare*, pp. 77-81; Coben, *Palmer*, pp. 192-216; Jaffe, pp. 92-94.

22. Friedheim, pp. 8-9, 151; Tyler, *Rebels*, p. 150; Murphy, *Meaning*, p. 47.

23. Tyler, *Rebels*, pp. 151-52.

24. Kurt Wetzel, "The Defeat of Bill Dunne: An Episode in the Montana Red Scare," *PNQ*, 64 (January, 1973), pp. 15-18.

25. Whitten, *Criminal Syndicalism*, pp. 21-41; Nelson Van Valen, "The Bosheviki and the Orange Growers," *PHR*, 22 (August, 1953), pp. 39-50.

26. Jaffe, pp. 77-87, 110-15. In February, 1919, the University of Montana created a minor cause celebre by suspending Professor Louis Levine for insubordination and unprofessional conduct prejudicial to the welfare of the University. Levine's crime had been publication of a monograph critical of Montana's tax structure. After Levine's firing, the Montana Senate inaugurated an investigation of the University, but reported there was no truth to the charge that socialism was being taught there. Levine was reinstated by the Montana Board of Education in April, 1919, following widespread local and national criticism of the firing, and subsequently became well known as an author and economist under the name Lewis Lorwin (Gutfeld, "The Levine Affair"). In July, 1919, a professor of Germanic languages was fired by the University of Texas

following a public controversy resulting from charges that he had propagandized for the German Kaiser by reprinting the German national anthem in elementary school German grammar textbooks and by comparing the German federal union to American federalism and maintaining the German Kaiser was responsible to Germany's parliament. At about the same time, Rice University fired a professor after the mayor of Houston announced an investigation of an address the professor had given to a Sunday school class (Nicholas, pp. 221-28).

27. On the Lusk Committee, see Jaffe, pp. 119-42; Murray, *Red Scare*, pp. 98-102; and Lawrence Chamberlain, *Loyalty and Legislative Action: A Survey of Activity by the New York State Legislature* (Ithaca: Cornell University Press, 1951), pp. 9-49.

28. Dowell, p. 14; Murray, *Red Scare*, pp. 231-34.

29. Dowell, p. 87.

30. Friedheim, p. 150; Coben, "Study," p. 102; Whitten, *Criminal Syndicalism*, pp. 22, 24; Murray, *Red Scare*, pp. 68-69.

31. August R. Ogden, *The Dies Committee* (Washington, D.C.: Catholic University, Press, 1945), pp. 14-17; Robert K. Carr, *The House Committee on Un-American Activities* (Ithaca: Cornell University Press, 1952), p. 11; Jaffe, pp. 119-20; Lowenthal, pp. 36-66; Murray, *Red Scare*, pp. 94-98; Hendrickson, p. 447; Johnson, *Challenge*, p. 126.

32. Noggle, pp. 46-82; David Burner, "1919: Prelude to Normalcy," *Change and Continuity in Twentieth Century America*, eds. John Braeman, et al. (Columbus: Ohio State University, 1965), pp. 7-24.

33. Chafee, *Free Speech*, pp. 80- 97; Murphy, *Constitution*, pp. 23-28; As Chafee points out, according to the court's decision, "it was a criminal falsehood to say that we entered the war to save the Morgan loans" while during the 1934 Nye Committee hearings "it was almost a crime to say that we did *not* enter the war to save the Morgan loans " (p. 95).

34. Murray, *Red Scare*, p. 80; Murphy, *Meaning*, p. 68; Frost, pp. 332-33; Coben, *Palmer*, pp. 208-12; Robert Warth, "The Palmer Raids," *South Atlantic Quarterly*, 48 (January, 1949), pp. 1-23.

35. Jensen, *Price*, pp. 257-75.

36. Coben, *Palmer*, p. 212 (quotation). On the July 4 fiasco, see also Murray, *Red Scare*, pp. 115-17; Frost, pp. 333-35.

37. Murray, *Red Scare*, pp. 193-94; Lowenthal, pp. 83-143; Frost, p. 335; Jensen, *Price*, p. 275.

38. Murphy, *Meaning*, pp. 68-69.

39. Coben, *Palmer*, p. 207.

40. Murray, *Red Scare*, p. 193.

41. Murray, *Red Scare*, pp. 178-80; Jaffee, pp. 95-96; Franklin, pp. 480-83; Waskow, pp. 58-59, 78-79, 188-90; Stanley Coben, "The Failure of the Melting Pot," *Underside of American History*, II, ed. Thomas R. Frazier (New York: Harcourt, Brace, 1974), p. 164; William Cohen, "Riots, Racism and Hysteria: The Response of Federal Investigators to the Race Riots of 1919," *Massachusetts Review*, 13 (Summer, 1972), pp. 373-400.

42. Waskow, pp. 189-90.

43. Cohen, p. 398.

44. Waskow, pp. 121-74; Tindall, *Emergence*, pp. 152-54; Franklin, p. 483.

45. James E. Fickle, "Management Looks at the 'Labor Problem': The Southern Pine Industry During World War I and the Postwar Era," *Journal of Southern History*, 40 (February, 1940), pp. 68-69; F. Ray Marshall, *Labor in the South* (Cambridge: Harvard University Press, 1967), pp. 99-100.

46. Murray, *Red Scare*, pp. 122-34; Leuchtenburg, *Perils*, p. 73.

47. Murray, *Red Scare*, p. 127.

48. Murray, *Red Scare*, pp. 132, 160; Scheiber, pp. 55-57; Crook, "Red Scare," p. 312; Stevenson, pp. 65-66. Hanson became such a popular figure because of his role in the Seattle strike that he shortly thereafter resigned as mayor to tour the country to speak about the communist danger. He subsequently earned $38,000 for his efforts in seven months, compared to his annual salary as mayor of $7500. Hanson later became a candidate for president, but was never seriously considered. President

Wilson added considerably to the hysteria arising from the police strike, terming it a "crime against civilization." Subsequently, when Coolidge defeated his Democratic opponent in the November elections, Wilson, himself a Democrat, congratulated Coolidge for a victory for "law and order," and declared, "When that is the issue, all Americans stand together." Wilson also fueled the Red Scare in his statements made during his 1919 speaking tour across the nation in support of the League of Nation. He suggested that opposition to the League was a Bolshevik plot and repeatedly suggested that there was a danger of revolution in the U.S. Thus, he asserted the "poison of disorder, the poison of revolt, the poison of chaos," had worked their way "into the veins of this free people" and stated "organized propaganda" against the Versailles Treaty "proceeded from exactly the same sources . . . which threatened this country here and there with disloyalty."

49. Jensen, *Price*, p. 276.
50. *Labor*, p. 7.
51. For accounts of the strike, see Brody, *Labor in Crisis: The Steel Strike of 1919*; Brody, *Steelworkers*, pp. 135-52; Yellin, pp. 251-91; Lens, pp. 228-56; Jensen, *Price*, pp. 278-80; Soule, pp. 191-94.
52. Lens, p. 248; Murray, *Red Scare*, p. 147.
53. Yellin, p. 275.
54. Brecher, p. 123.
55. Dulles, p. 223.
56. Handlin, p. 144.
57. Murray, *Red Scare*, p. 156.
58. Murray, *Red Scare*, pp. 153-63; Waskow, p. 8; Coben, *Palmer*, pp. 177-84.
59. Coben, *Palmer*, pp. 176-77, 185-85.
60. Laslett, *Labor*, p. 129.
61. Coben, "Study," p. 101.
62. Murray, *Red Scare*, p. 17.
63. Murray, *Red Scare*, pp. 164, 173-77.
64. Higham, *Strangers*, p. 227; Coben, "Study," p. 103.
65. Murray, *Red Scare*, pp. 195-96; Coben, *Palmer*, pp. 214-15.
66. Coben, *Palmer*, p. 215.
67. Murray, *Red Scare*, pp. 196-7; Coben, *Palmer*, pp. 219-21; Warth, pp. 5-6; Jaffe, pp. 179-81.
68. Edward J. Muzik, "Victor L. Berger: Congress and the Red Scare," *WMH*, 47 (Summer, 1964), pp. 309-15.
69. Murray, *Red Scare*, p. 198; Coben, *Palmer*, pp. 221-22; Warth, p. 7; Chafee, *Free Speech*, pp. 247-60. Palmer devoted over half of his report to Emma Goldman. Flynn and Hoover personally observed the departure of the *Buford* (Drinnon, pp. 212-14, 222).
70. Jaffe, pp. 132-34, 198-215; Chamberlain, p. 35; Draper, *Roots*, p. 203.
71. Shannon, *Socialist Party*, p. 125.
72. Robert L. Tyler, "Violence at Centralia," *PNQ*, 45 (October, 1954), pp. 116-24; John M. McClelland, Jr., "Terror on Tower Avenue," *PNQ*, 57 (April, 1966), pp. 65-72; Dubofsky, *We Shall*, pp. 455-56; Rayback, p. 289; Murray, *Red Scare*, pp. 185-86; Daniel, p. 167. Eventually eleven Wobblies were tried for the incident in a courtroom packed with Legionaires and with federal troops stationed on the courthouse lawn. Two defense witnesses were arrested for perjury during the trial, and the judge ruled out arguments based on self-defense. Seven defendants were sentenced to twenty-five to forty years in prison, with the last not released until 1939. No attempt was made to find the lynchers of Everest.
73. Sims, pp. 523-24.
74. Crook, "*Red Scare*," pp. 214-16; Shaffer, pp. 59-78; Whitten, *Criminal Syndicalism*, pp. 38-40, 66.
75. Whitten, *Criminal Syndicalism*, p. 38.
76. On the Palmer raids, see Murray, *Red Scare*, pp. 210-17; Coben, *Palmer*, pp. 222-29; Warth, pp. 1-23; Preston, *Aliens*, pp. 217-21; Lowenthal, pp. 147-236; Chafee, *Free Speech*, pp. 204-15.
77. Coben, *Palmer*, p. 228.

78. Stevenson, p. 61.
79. Howe and Coser, p. 51; Jaffe, p. 189.
80. Warth, pp. 16-17.
81. Coben, *Palmer*, p. 241.
82. Murray, *Red Scare*, pp. 229-30; Chafee, *Free Speech*, pp. 247-69; Muzik, p. 318.
83. Warth, p. 14; Murray, *Red Scare*, pp. 216, 234-35; Howe and Coser, pp. 58-59; Bernhard, pp. 87-89. Police who raided a technnical school in Chicago showed particular interest in papers covered with algaebraic formulas, which were suspected of being mysterious ciphers. During the trial of the top CLP leaders in Chicago, the state's attorney told the jury that if a verdict of not guilty were returned, "Tear from your parks and your cemeteries he busts in marble and bronze of Lincoln and Washington, and put in their places the busts of Lenin and Trotsky; take from your churches the Christs on the cross and put Judas there." He concluded with a recitation of *all* of the stanzas of the national anthem (Howe and Coser, pp. 58-59).
84. Thomas E. Vadney, "The Politics of Repression: A Case Study of tthe Red Scare in New York," *New York History*, 49 (January, 1968), pp. 56-74; Melvin Urofsky, "A Note on the Expulsion of the Five Socialists," *New York History*, 47 (January, 1966), pp. 41-49; Jaffe, pp. 143-68; Chafee, *Free Speech*, pp. 269-82; Murray, *Red Scare*, pp. 235-38.
85. Coben, *Palmer*, p. 184-86.
86. Preston, *Aliens*, pp. 244-45.
87. Kornbluh, *Rebel*, p. 296; Crook, "Red Scare," pp. 323-26; Carey McWilliams, *North From Mexico* (New York: Greenwood, 1968), p. 174.
88. Murray, *Red Scare*, p. 250; Preston, *Aliens*, p. 228.
89. Preston, *Aliens*, p. 228.
90. Murray, *Red Scare*, pp. 219-22.
91. Levin, p. 195.
92. Murray, *Red Scare*, p. 219; Davis, *Fear*, p. 226.
93. Murray, *Red Scare*, *passim*; Jaffe, pp. 141, 220; Chamberlain, pp. 46-47.
94. Warth, p. 12; Johnson, *Challenge*, pp. 149-52; Murphy, *Meaning*, pp. 88-89; Coben, *Palmer*, pp. 242-44; Murray, *Red Scare*, pp. 245-46; Higham, *Strangers*, pp. 232-33; Whitten *Criminal Syndicalism*, p. 48; Woodrow C. Whitten, "The Trial of Charlotte Anita Whitney," *PHR*, 15 (September, 1946), pp. 286-94.
95. Hyman, *Soldiers*, *passim*; Dubofsky, *We Shall*, pp. 416-19.
96. Weinstein, *Corporate Ideal*, p. 243.
97. Murray, *Red Scare*, p. 255; Coben, *Palmer*, p. 239.
98. Murray, *Red Scare*, p. 250; Chafee, *Free Speech*, p. 227.
99. Murray, *Red Scare*, p. 250; Murphy, *Constitution*, p. 30; Johnson, **Challenge**, p. 163; Justice Department infiltration of the communist parties was so great that Department officials had instructed their agents to arrange meetings of the CP and CLP for January 2 to facilitate the raids. In at least one case, a department agent had become a district party leader, and in general agents assumed the roles of agitators "of the wildest types" (Chafee, *Free Speech*, p. 217).
100. Vadney, pp. 61-72; Chafee, *Free Speech*, p. 275; Murphy, *Constitution*, pp. 87-88; Murray, *Red Scare*, pp. 242-44; Bagby, p. 37.
101. Murray, *Red Scare*, pp. 247-49; Coben, *Palmer*, pp. 213-14; Preston, *Aliens*, pp. 224-26.
102. Lowenthal, pp. 73-74; Fred J. Cook, *The FBI Nobody Knows* (New York: Pyramid, 1965), pp. 108-14.
103. Murray, *Red Scare*, pp. 252-54; Coben, *Palmer*, pp. 235-36; Jaffe, p. 222.
104. Howe and Coser, p. 26; Murray, *Red Scare*, p. 81; Leuchtenburg, *Perils*, p. 81; Coben, "Study," p. 108.
105. *Search*, p. 290.
106. Robert K. Murray, *The Harding Era* (Minneapolis: University of Minnesota Press, 1969), p. 89. On the 1920 election, see Bagby, *The Road to Normalcy: The Presidential Campaign and Election of 1920*.
107. Shannon, *Socialist Party*, p. 163; Draper, *Roots*, pp. 158, 190, 206-07; Whitehead, p. 61.
108. *Into the Twenties*, p. 115.
109. Howe and Coser, pp. 52-64; Draper, *Roots*, pp. 197-395; Theodore Draper,

American Communism and Soviet Russia (New York: Viking, 1960).

CHAPTER SIX

1. On the twenties, see John D. Hicks, *Republican Ascendency* (New York: Harper & Row, 1963); Schlesinger, *Crisis;* Robert K. Murray, *The Politics of Normalcy: Governmental Theory and Practice in the Harding-Coolidge Era* (New York: Norton, 1973); Frederick Lewis Allen, *Only Yesterday* (New York: Bantam, 1959); Stevenson, *The American 1920's*. For economic history, see Soule, *Prosperity Decade*. The best work on labor is Bernstein, *Lean Years*. On civil liberties, the best work is Murphy, *The Meaning of Freedom of Speech*.
2. Murphy, *Meaning*, p. 122.
3. *Midwestern Progressive Politics*, p. 320.
4. Quoted in Schlesinger, *Crisis*, p. 45.
5. *Red Scare*, p. 264.
6. See Murphy, *Meaning*, pp. 184-219; Higham, *Strangers*, pp. 234-99; David M. Chalmers, *Hooded Americanism: The History of the Ku Klux Klan* (Chicago: Quadrangle, 1968); Roche, *Quest*, pp. 103-29.
7. Higham, *Strangers*, pp. 300-30; Jones, pp. 272-77.
8. Bernstein, *Lean*, pp. 146-50.
9. Chalmers, *Hooded Americanism;* Higham, *Strangers*, pp. 285-99.
10. Hicks, *Republican*, pp. 155-56; Michael Parenti, *The Anti-Communist Impulse* (New York: Random House, 1969), p. 67; Oscar T. Barck, Jr., and Nelson M. Blake, *Since 1900* (New York: MacMillan, 1952), p. 342.
11. The best source on the case remains Joughin and Morgan, *The Legacy of Sacco and Vanzetti*. See Russell, *Tragedy in Dedham*, for the viewpoint that Sacco was guilty and Vanzetti, at the least, was an "accessory after the fact" (p. xxii).
12. Russell, p. 6.
13. Joughin and Morgan, p. 255.
14. Joughin and Morgan, pp. 272-97, 311-12.
15. *Lean Years*, p. 144.
16. Quoted in Leuchtenburg, *Perils*, p. 144.
17. Quoted in Schlesinger, *Crisis*, p. 61.
18. Stevenson, p. 131.
19. See Leuchtenburg, *Perils*, pp. 97-103, 188-93, 245-47; Cochran and Miller, pp. 345-48; Stevenson, pp. 86, 129-31; Eckirch, *Decline*, pp. 257-59; Schlesinger, *Crisis*, pp. 61-65; Soule, pp. 131-42.
20. Soule, p. 297.
21. Harold Wilensky, *The Welfare State and Equality* (Berkeley: University of California Press, 1974), pp. 73-74.
22. Noggle, p. 169.
23. Leuchtenburg, *Perils*, p. 202.
24. Curti, *Roots*, pp. 234-35.
25. Soule, pp. 113, 123, 222, 284, 317, 325, 333; Leuchtenburg, *Perils*, pp. 193-94; Walter Johnson, *1600 Pennsylvania Avenue* (Boston: Little, Brown, 1963), pp. 7-8; Schlesinger, *Crisis*, pp. 65-66, 111; Bernstein, *Lean*, pp. 58-59, 63-65, 71.
26. Schlesinger, *Crisis*, p. 160.
27. Murphy, *Meaning*, p. 172.
28. *ACLUAR*, 1927-1928, pp. 3-4.
29. Schieber, pp. 35-36; Johnson, "Wilson," pp. 57-58. On the amnesty campaign see Taft, "Federal Trials," pp. 81-91; Ginger, *Debs*, pp. 425-35; Johnson, *Challenge*, pp. 181-93; Murphy, *Meaning*, pp. 134-37; Preston, *Aliens*, pp. 257-67. The prisoners were slowly released from 1921 to 1923, depending on the domestic political situation and the amount of public pressure brought to bear upon the administration. Thus, Eugene Debs was released in 1921 in one of the first executive commutations, in order to "stop the discussion which had a tendency to unsettle situations" because there was so much popular support for his release. On the other hand, commutations were held up in 1922, for fear of encouraging radicals during a strike wave (Preston, *Aliens*, pp. 259, 263). In some cases, prisoners were released only if they agreed to deportation,

and some Wobblies were arrested for deportation purposes when they served out their terms. A number of prisoners were released only if they agreed to remain law-abiding, and to in no way encourage further law breaking. This condition further weakened what was left of the IWW, since it created a major split within the organization among remaining IWW prisoners and unjailed Wobblies as to whether or not this condition should be accepted (Dubofsky, *We Shall,* pp. 461-62; Preston, *Aliens,* pp. 257-67). Preston concludes that the Justice Department's amnesty program "depended not on the sufficiency or fairness of the punishment but on the amount of social unrest, strikes, the supposed imminence of revolution and the readiness of the prisoners to reorient their views" and that Coolidge's unconditional commutation of the last prisoners in 1923 reflected the "official" recognition that many men were serving terms on little or no evidence" (*Aliens,* p. 271). Another indication of declining hysteria was a drastic decline in the number of articles in popular periodicals dealing with communism and bolshevism. Over five articles per thousand indexed in *Reader's Guide* dealt with this subject from 1919-1921; less than two per thousand from 1922-1924 (Murphy, *Meaning,* p. 317).

30. Jaffe, p. 213; Bernhard, pp. 88-89; Whitten, "Trial," p. 286; David R. Colburn, "Governor Alfred E. Smith and the Red Scare, 1919-1920," *PSQ,* 80 (September, 1973), p. 443.

31. Chafee, *Free Speech,* p. 41; Vadney, pp. 71-72; Jaffe, pp. 164-65, 138-39; Muzik, p. 318; Leuchtenburg, *Perils,* pp. 130-31; *ACLUAR,* 1923, p. 5; Dowell, p. 137; Whitten, *Criminal Syndicalism,* p. 58; Draper, *Roots,* pp. 372, 390; Tyler, *Rebels,* pp. 152-53; Robinson, p. 13; Howe and Coser, p. 176; Murphy, "Communities in Conflict," *Pulse,* ed. Reitman, pp. 28-64. The Lusk Laws, passed by the New York legislature in 1921 outlawed the Socialist Party, required all teachers to take a loyalty oath, gave the Board of Regents power to license most private schools and appropriated $100,000 so the state attorney general could continue to ferret out and prosecute sedition, disloyalty and criminal anarchy.

32. *INS,* 1956, p. 95. These data are taken from the listing of aliens deported for being"subversive or anarchistic" under the Anarchist Exclusion Act of 1903 and subsequent immigration laws providing for deportation based solely on the holding of objectionable opinions.

33. *ACLUAR,* 1923-1929. This tabulation is based on data in the ACLU *Annual Reports* indicating incarceration for violation of state criminal syndicalism laws and similar offenses. The overwhelming number of those jailed under such offenses were in California.

34. Preston, *Aliens,* pp. 236-37.

35. The immigration laws still provided means for dealing with alien radicals. Throughout the 1920's, the Immigration Bureau and federal courts denied naturalization to IWW members on grounds they could not be attached to the principles of the Constitution. An attempt to denaturalize an IWW member failed when the defendant proved he had been a citizen for five years before he joined the IWW, thus indicating no lack of attachment to the constitution at the time of his naturalization. Count Karolyi, who had been the first president of the Hungarian Republic, was admitted to the U.S. only on condition that he pledge not to give "political speeches" in 1925, while an English communist member of Parliament was denied entry to the country for the purpose of attending the Inter-Parliamentary Union Conference (Preston, *Aliens,* pp. 268-71; Murphy, "Communities in Conflict," p. 58).

36. Hyman, *Soldiers,* p. 340. See also Preston, *Aliens,* pp. 243-46.

37. Murphy, *Meaning,* p. 191.

38. Murphy, *Meaning,* pp. 192-94; Chatfield, *For Peace,* pp. 156-59; Murphy, "Sources," pp. 72-73.

39. Joughin and Morgan, pp. 216-18; Murphy, "Sources," p. 72.

40. Hyman, *To Try,* p. 323.

41. Lowenthal, pp. 292-94.

42. Murphy, *Meaning,* p. 188.

43. Quoted in Lowenthal, pp. 270-71; and Johnson, *Challenge,* pp. 172-73.

44. Johnson, *Challenge,* p. 165.

45. Murphy, *Meaning,* pp. 184-88; Lowenthal, pp. 269-300; Cook, *FBI,* pp. 116-41; Johnson, *Challenge,* pp. 165-75; Preston, *Aliens,* p. 242-43; Waskow, p. 194; Murphy, "Communities in Conflict," pp. 143-46.

46. Sanford J. Ungar, *FBI: An Uncensored Look Behind the Walls* (Boston: Little, Brown, 1976), p. 45.
47. Murray, *Politics*, p. 121.
48. Ungar, *FBI*, p. 45.
49. Lowenthal, p. 298.
50. Preston, *Aliens*, p. 243.
51. *SICH*, pp. 554-55.
52. Lowenthal, p. 299.
53. Johnson, *Challenge*, pp. 174-75.
54. *SICH*, p. 556.
55. Jensen, *Price*, p. 288.
56. Chafee, *Free Speech*, pp. 284-354; Murphy, *Constitution*, pp. 82-88.
57. Murray, *Red Scare*, p. 272.
58. *ACLUAR*, 1923-1929, *passim*.
59. Draper, *Roots*, pp. 227-36; Howe and Coser, pp. 63-64; Draper, *American Commuunism*, *passim*. Although Fraina eventually became an avid anti-communist, the government attempted to deport him in 1952 amidst a wave of political deportations initiated by President Truman. Fraina died of a cerebral hemmorrhage before the proceedings were concluded — in his favor (Draper, *Roots*, pp. 301-02).
60. Howe and Coser, pp. 99-103; Draper, *Roots*, pp. 363-75.
61. Ginger, *Debs*, p. 454; *ACLUAR*, 1927-1928, p. 32.
62. Howe and Coser, p. 176.
63. Howe and Coser, p. 176.
64. David L. Sterling, "The 'Naive Liberal,' the 'Devious Communist' and the Johnson Case," *OH*, 78 (Spring, 1969), pp. 182, 195.
65. Shannon, *Socialist Party*, pp. 182, 195.
66. *ACLUAR*, 1923, p. 18; 1927-1928, p. 33.
67. Weinstein, *Decline*, pp. 235-39, 272-74.
68. Weinstein, *Decline*, pp. 238-39.
69. See Kenneth C. MacKay, *The Progressive Movement of 1924* (New York: Columbia University Press, 1947). Weinstein, *Decline*, pp. 272-323, is useful on the question of participation in the movement by the SPA and radical farm and labor groups.
70. MacKay, p. 12. See also Arthur S. Link, "What Happened to the Progressive Movement in the 1920's?" *AHR*, 64 (July, 1959), pp. 833-51, for an argument along these lines.
71. MacKay, p. 111.
72. Schlesinger, *Crisis*, p. 60.
73. MacKay, p. 164.
74. MacKay, pp. 170-71.
75. Weinstein, *Decline*, p. 324.
76. Murphy, *Meaning*, pp. 107-11; Schlesinger, *Crisis*, pp. 143-52; Leuchtenburg, *Perils*, pp. 122-25.
77. Allen, *Only Yesterday*, p. 43.
78. Leuchtenburg, *Perils*, p. 83.
79. See Bessie Louise Pierce, *Civic Attitudes in American School Textbooks* (New York: Arno Press, 1971), *passim*; Bessie Louise Pierce, *Public Opinion and the Teaching of History* (New York: De Capo, 1970), *passim*; David E. Bunting, *Liberty and Learning: The Activities of the ACLU in Behalf of Freedom of Education* (Washington, D.C.: American Council on Public Affairs, 1942), p. 59 and *passim*; Murphy, *Meaning*, pp. 126-27, 208-12; Cochran and Miller, pp. 332-39; Curti, *Roots*, pp. 237-38; *ACLUAR*, 1926, p. 21; 1928-1929, p. 23.
80. Bunting, pp. 91-98.
81. Philip G. Altbach and Patti M. Peterson, "Before Berkeley: Historical Perspectives on American Student Activism," *The New Pilgrims: Youth Protest in Transition*, eds. Philip G. Altbach and Robert S. Laufer (New York: David McKay, 1972), p. 17.
82. Patti M. Peterson, "Student Organizations and the Anti-War Movement in America, 1900-1960," *Peace Movements in America*, ed. Charles Chatfield (New York: Schocken, 1973), p. 121.
83. Chatfield, *For Peace*, pp. 153-54, 157.
84. See the sources cited in footnote six of this chapter.
85. On the Klan, see Chalmers, *Hooded Americanism*; Kenneth T. Jackson, *The Ku*

Klux Klan in the City (New York: Oxford University Press, 1970); Higham, *Strangers,* pp. 285-99; Seymour Martin Lipset and Earl Raab, *The Politics of Unreason: Right-Wing Extremism in America, 1790-1970* (New York: Harper & Row, 1973), pp. 116-45.

86. Jackson, p. xii.
87. Jackson, p. 242.
88. Jackson, pp. 38, 57, 79, 110, 130, 151, 186, 190-91; Chalmers, pp. 48, 121, 125, 142, 148, 184, 195, 223.
89. Chalmers, p. 221.
90. Jackson, pp. 69, 87, 95, 102, 151, 171, 182, 190-9; Chalmers, pp. 48, 121, 143, 149, 154, 184, 199, 250, 254, 271.
91. Chalmers, pp. 49-55; Higham, *Strangers,* p. 298.
92. Bernstein, *Lean,* pp. 131, 195-200, 407.
93. See the appropriate index entries for discussion of these cases in Bernstein, *Lean;* and Gregory, *Labor.* See also Stanley I. Kutler, "Labor, the Clayton Act and the Supreme Court," *LH,* 3 (Winter, 1962), pp. 19-38.
94. Bernstein, *Lean,* p. 213.
95. Murphy, *Constitution,* p. 67.
96. Riker, p. 65; Taft and Ross, pp. 338-46.
97. *HS,* p. 99.
98. *HS,* p. 99.
99. *HS,* p. 99.
100. Wolfe, p. 120.
101. On the situation in California, see Whitten, *Criminal Syndicalism,* pp. 52-66; George Kirchwey, *A Survey of the Workings of the Criminal Syndicalism Law of California* (Los Angeles: California Committee, ACLU, 1926); Martin Zanger, "Politics of Confrontation: Upton Sinclair and the Launching of the ACLU in Southern California," *PHR,* 38 (November, 1969), pp. 383-406; Chafee, *Free Speech,* pp. 326-32; Dubofsky, *We Shall,* pp. 474-75.
102. Haug, "IWW in North Dakota, 1918-1925," pp. 16-17; Tyler, *Rebels,* pp. 152-53; Sims, p. 525; Dowell, pp. 96, 131; Robinson, p. 13. The Oklahoma convictions were overturned on appeal in 1925 and there were no further prosecutions in the state during the twenties. Oregon prosecutions ceased after a hung jury in a 1923 case. Prosecutions in the state of Washington ceased in 1923 after fifty-two jailings for criminal syndicalism. In Idaho, prosecutions ceased after the Idaho Supreme Court ruled in January, 1924, that work slowdowns and nonviolent, noncriminal acts could not be construed as constituting sabotage under that state's criminal syndicalism law. Following this decision, Idaho's legislature amended its law to include in the definition of criminal syndicalism "work done in an improper manner, slack work, waste of property or loitering at work," but no charges were ever brought under the amended definition.
103. McClung, pp. 68-92; Charles J. Bayard, "The 1927-1928 Colorado Coal Strike," *PHR,* 32 (August, 1963), pp. 235-50; Bernstein, *Lean,* p. 142; Kornbluh, *Rebel,* p. 353.
104. On Passaic, see Howe and Coser, pp. 239-43; Murphy, *Meaning,* pp. 153-56; Bernard K. Johnpoll, *Pacifists Progress: Norman Thomas and the Decline of American Socialism* (Chicago: Quadrangle, 1970), p. 48; Schonbach, pp. 75-77.
105. Howe and Coser, pp. 245-52; Bernstein, *Lean,* p. 203.
106. Howe and Coser, pp. 243-45.
107. The best account of Gastonia remains Pope, *Millhands and Preachers.* See also, Bernstein *Lean,* pp. 20-28; Howe and Coser, pp. 257-62; Tindall, *Emergence,* pp. 343-47; Yellin, pp. 306-16.
108. The second trial of the Gastonia defendants was marked by repeated references to their religious and political beliefs. In his closing arguments to the jury, the prosecutor asked, "Do you believe in the flag of your country, floating in the breeze, kissing the sunlight, singing the song of freedom? Do you believe in North Carolina? Do you believe in good roads? . . . Gastonia — into which the union organizers came, fiends incarnate, stripped of their hoofs and horns, . . . They came into peaceful, contented Gastonia, with its flowers, birds and churches . . . sweeping like a cyclone and tornado to sink damnable fangs into the heart and lifeblood of my community" (quoted in Pope, p. 303).
109. On the railroad strike, see Murphy, *Meaning,* pp. 159-63; Cummings and McPharland, pp. 457-59; Dulles, pp. 239-40; Bernstein, *Lean,* pp. 211-12; Soule, pp. 202-

04; Lowenthal, pp. 282-88; Taft and Ross, pp. 340-43; Soule, pp. 202-04; Murray, *Harding*, pp. 238-58.

109a. Commons, IV, pp. 494-96.

110. Murphy, "Communities in Conflict," p. 35. On West Virginia, see Murphy, "Communities in Conflict," pp. 35-38; Murphy, *Meaning*, pp. 138-42; Brecher, pp. 135-38; Commons, IV, pp. 494-96.

111. Taft and Ross, pp. 338-39; Murphy, *Meaning*, p. 146.

112. Bernstein, *Lean*, pp. 129-31.

113. Murphy, *Meaning*, p. 147.

114. Spero and Harris, pp. 235-37.

115. Charles Wollenberg, "Huelga, 1928 Style: The Imperial Valley Cantaloupe Workers' Strike," *PHR*, 38 (February, 1969), pp. 45-58.

116. Bernstein, *Lean*, p. 97.

117. Murphy, *Meaning*, pp. 114-15, 339-40.

118. On Elizabethton and Marion, see Bernstein, *Lean*, pp. 13-20, 29-32; Tindall, *Emergence*, pp. 341-43, 347-50; Yellin, pp. 300-06, 316-21.

CHAPTER SEVEN

1. Bernstein, *Lean*, pp. 434, 436.

2. *Hitting Home: The Great Depression in Town and Country* (Chicago: Quadrangle, 1970), pp. 16, 22. For other examples, see Alex Baskin, "The Ford Hunger March — 1932," *LH*, 13 (Summer, 1972), pp. 333, 359; Schlesinger, *Crisis*, p. 252; Frederick Lewis Allen, *Since Yesterday* (New York: Bantam, 1961), p. 66; Harris G. Warren, *Herbert Hoover and the Great Depression* (New York: Norton, 1967), pp. 224-238.

3. *ACLUAR*, 1932-1933, p. 3.

4. "Radicalism in the Great Depression," *Essays in Radicalism in America*, ed. Leon Blair (Austin: University of Texas Press, 1972), p. 103.

5. Garraty, "Radicalism," p. 103.

6. Shannon, *Socialist Party*, pp. 204-06.

7. Howe and Coser, pp. 175-235.

8. Frances Fox Piven and Richard A. Cloward, *Regulating the Poor* (New York: Vintage, 1972), p. 61.

9. Rayback, p. 317.

10. Bernard Karsh and Philip L. Garmen, "The Impact of the Political Left," *Labor and the New Deal*, eds. Milton Derber and Edwin Young (Madison: University of Wisconsin Press, 1957), p. 96.

11. Karsh and Garmen, *Labor*, p. 96.

12. *The Great Depression* (Englewood Cliffs, New Jersey: Prentice-Hall, 1960), p. 111.

13. Sternsher, p. 14.

14. Adamic, p. 445; Schlesinger, *Crisis*, p. 3; Caroline Bird, *The Invisible Scar* (New York: Pocket Books, 1967), p. 25.

15. Tindall, *Emergence*, pp. 385-86.

16. Bird, pp. 84-85; Robert Bendiner, *Just Around the Corner* (New York: Dutton, 1968), pp. 52, 57.

17. See Donald J. Lisio, *The President and Protest: Hoover, Conspiracy and the Bonus Riot* (Columbia: University of Missouri Press, 1974).

18. Bernstein, *Lean*, pp. 305-06, 387-88; *ACLUAR*, 1931-1932, pp. 9, 29-30; 1932-1933, pp. 11-13, 35-6; Baskin, p. 342. Altogether almost thirty thousand aliens, many of whom Secretary of Labor Doak described as "Reds," were deported in 1931, in what amounted to the most wholesale violation of civil liberties in the U.S. since the Palmer Raids. According to a 1936 report to Congress by the Commissioner of Immigration, the "Doak Raids" were characterized by arrests without warrants, illegal raids on peaceful assemblies and forced detention of those present, both alien and citizen, and detention of aliens in jail for many months under unreasonable bails until hearings could be held. In one notorious incident, federal and local police surrounded the downtown plaza in Los Angeles on February 26, 1931, and detained over four hundred persons, of whom less than ten were eventually held for deportation. In the Los Angeles area between February and April, 1931, a total of three thousand to four

thousand persons were rounded up, but only 389 deportations and voluntary departures resulted. As many as seventy-five thousand Mexican-Americans are believed to have fled the Los Angeles area for other parts of the U.S. as a result of the round-ups. See Bernhard, pp. 116-17; Bernstein, *Lean,* p. 305; Abraham Hoffman, "Stimulus to Repatriation: The 1931 Federal Deportation Drive and the Los Angeles Mexican Community," PHR, 42 (May, 1973), pp. 205-19.

19. INS, 1956, pp. 95-96. See footnote 32, Chapter Six.
20. *ACLUAR,* 1930-1931, p. 23, 1931-1932, p. 32.
21. Preston, *Aliens,* pp. 271-72.
22. Dowell, p. 107.
23. Schlesinger, *Crisis,* p. 256.
24. Murphy, *Meaning,* p. 221; Lisio, pp. 56-62 and *passim.*
25. Schlesinger, *Crisis,* p. 306; Robert A. Divine, *American Immigration Policy, 1924-1952* (New Haven: Yale University Press, 1957), p. 104.
26. Bernstein, *Lean,* pp. 429-32; Schlesinger, *Crisis,* pp. 219-20; Lisio, pp. 58-61.
27. The best source on the Bonus Army is Lisio, *President and Protest.* Other useful sources include Roger Daniels, *The Bonus March* (Westport, Connecticut: Greenwood, 1971); Rich, pp. 168-75; Bernstein, *Lean,* pp. 437-55; Warren, pp. 224-36; Schlesinger, *Crisis,* pp. 356-65.
28. Lisio, pp. 155, 192; Daniels, *Bonus,* p. 160.
29. Daniels, *Bonus,* p. 159.
30. Schlesinger, *Crisis,* p. 256; Bird, p. 90.
31. Schlesinger, *Crisis,* pp. 448-49; Warren, pp. 239-40.
32. Schlesinger, *Crisis,* pp. 434, 437; James M. Burns, *Roosevelt: The Lion and The Fox* (New York: Harcourt, Brace, 1956), p. 143; Johnson, *1600,* p. 37.
33. Chafee, *Free Speech,* pp. 190-91.
34. Carr, pp. 12-13.
35. Walter Goodman, *The Committee* (Baltimore: Penguin, 1969), p. 6.
36. Murphy, *Meaning,* p. 232.
37. Goodman, p. 7.
38. *ACLUAR,* 1930-1931, pp. 3-4.
39. Ogden, p. 26.
40. Ogden, pp. 26-32.
41. *ACLUAR,* 1929-1930, p. 3.
42. Jerold S. Auerbach, "The Depression Decade," *Pulse,* ed. Reitman, p. 67. See tables on this page and page 177.
43. *ACLUAR,* 1930-1931, p. 5.
44. Dowell, p. 119; Dan T. Carter, *Scottsboro: A Tragedy of the American South* (New York: Oxford University Press, 1971), p. 122; Sternsher, p. 24.
45. Daniels, *Bonus,* p. 110.
46. *ACLUAR,* 1930-1931, p. 15; 1931-1932, p. 20; 1932-1933, p. 11.
47. *ACLUAR,* 1930-1931, pp. 14, 20; 1932-1933, p. 6; Frost, p. 417.
48. *ACLUAR,* 1930-1933, *passim;* Bernhard, pp. 158-63; Bernstein, *Lean,* pp. 426-28; Baskin, p. 339; Schlesinger, *Crisis,* pp. 166-67; Piven and Cloward, p. 64; Daniel J. Leab, "'United We Eat': The Creation and Organization of the Unemployed Councils in 1930," *LH,* 8 (Fall, 1967), pp. 306-07.
49. William Manchester, *The Glory and the Dream* (New York: Bantam, 1975), pp. 55-56.
50. Leab, p. 307.
51. Manchester, p. 56.
52. Bernstein, *Lean,* p. 428; Hofstadter and Wallace, pp. 172-4.
53. Baskin, pp. 324-60.
54. Bernhard, p. 163; *ACLUAR,* 1931-1932, p. 14.
55. *ACLUAR,* 1932-1933, p. 43.
56. Bernhard, p. 159.
57. Wilson Record, *The Negro and the Communist Party* (New York: Atheneum, 1971), p. 94.
58. Fund for the Republic, *Digest of the Public Record of Communism in the United States* (New York: Fund for the Republic, 1955), p. 315.
59. Fund for the Republic, *Digest,* pp. 31-36.

Notes (Ch. 7) 60-92   609

60. James R. Prickett, "Communists and the Automobile Industry in Detroit Before 1935," *Michigan History*, 57 (Fall, 1973), p. 191.
61. *ACLUAR*, 1929-1930, p. 20.
62. Jamieson, p. 265.
63. On the CP campaign in the south, see Howe and Coser, p. 212; Tindall, *Emergence*, pp. 377-85; Carter, *passim*; John Moore, "Communists and Fascists in a Southern City: Atlanta, 1930," *South Atlantic Quarterly*, 67 (Summer, 1968), pp. 437-54.
64. Dowell, p. 107.
65. Carter, pp. 177, 259 and *passim*; Jamieson, p. 293; Tindall, *Emergence*, p. 378; Thomas A. Kreuger, *And Promises to Keep: The Southern Conference on Human Welfare* (Nashville: Vanderbilt University, 1967), pp. 1-10.
66. On the ASU, see Carter, pp. 124-29, 175-78; Jamieson, pp. 292-97; Tindall, *Emergence*, pp. 379-80.
67. On Harlan County, see Tony Bubka, "The Harlan County Coal Strike of 1931," *LH*, 11 (Winter, 1970), pp. 41-57; Lawrence Grauman, Jr., "'That little Ugly Running Sore': Some Observations on the Participation of American Writers in the Investigations of Conditions in the Harlan and Bill County, Kentucky, Coal Fields, in 1931-1932," *Filson Club Historical Quarterly*, 36 (1962), pp. 340-54; Tindall, *Emergence*, pp. 383-86; Bernstein, *Lean*, pp. 377-81; Murphy, *Meaning*, pp. 239-44.
68. Jamieson, p. 39.
69. Jamieson, pp. 80-86; McWilliams, *Factories*, pp. 212-15.
70. Tindall, *Emergence*, pp. 375-77; Bernstein, *Lean*, pp. 33-40.
71. Jamieson, pp. 240-41.
72. John L. Shover, "The Communist Party and the Midwest Farm Crisis of 1933," *JAH*, 51 (September, 1964), pp. 258, 265; William E. Leuchtenburg, *Franklin D. Roosevelt and the New Deal* (New York: Harper & Row, 1963), pp. 25-26.
73. Bernstein, *Lean*, pp. 411, 421-25; Bird, p. 24; Frost, p. 402; Dulles, pp. 262-63.
74. Bernstein, *Lean*, pp. 215-18; Chafee, *Free Speech*, pp. 362-66; Carter, p. 161.
75. Bernstein, *Lean*, pp. 391-415; Rayback, pp. 319-20.
76. Richard L. Watson, Jr., "The Defeat of Judge Parker," *JAH*, (September, 1963), pp. 213-34.
77. Bernstein, *Lean*, pp. 411-12.
78. Bernstein, *Lean*, p. 410; Carter, p. 103.
79. Moore, p. 442; Hofstadter and Wallace, p. 172; Bernstein, *Lean*, pp. 428, 434; Leuchtenburg, *Roosevelt*, p. 24; Tyler, *Rebels*, p. 220; Bernhard, pp. 158-63; Murphy, *Meaning*, p. 233-34; Sternsher, pp. 34-35; Schlesinger, *Crisis*, p. 252; Piven and Cloward, pp. 66-72.
80. Robert Goldston, *The Great Depression* (Greenwich, Connecticut: Fawcett, 1968), p. 64.
81. Leuchtenburg, *Roosevelt*, p. 22.
82. Bird, p. 81.
83. Derter Perkins, *The New Age of Franklin Roosevelt* (Chicago: University of Chicago, 1957), pp. 7-9; Leuchtenburg, *Roosevelt*, pp. 41-42; Arthur M. Schlesinger, Jr. *The Coming of the New Deal* (Boston: Houghton Mifflin, 1958), pp. 1-23; Burns, *Roosevelt: Lion*, pp. 163-82.
84. Frost, pp. 439-41; Schlesinger, *Crisis*, pp. 440-41; Bird, p. 99; Schlesinger, *Coming*, pp. 14-15 (quotation, p. 15); Preston, *Aliens*, p. 272; *ACLUAR*, 1933-1934, pp. 6-7; Drinnon, pp. 275-80; Lisio, pp. 57-58, 291-94.
85. Schlesinger, *Crisis*, p. 7.
86. Burns, *Roosevelt: Lion*, pp. 228-29.
87. Schlesinger, *Politics*, pp. 584, 638-39.
88. Bernstein, *Turbulent*, pp. 25-35.
89. Auerbach, *Labor*, pp. 211-12.
90. Bernstein, *Turbulent*, pp. 318-51, 648, 788; Dulles, pp. 264-76; Rayback, pp. 327-45; Broadus Mitchell, *Depression Decade: From New Era Through New Deal, 1929-1941* (New York: Harper & Row, 1969), pp. 277-83.
91. Auerbach, *Labor*, *passim*, quotation p. 204; see also Jerold S. Auerbach, "The LaFollette Committee: Labor and Civil Liberties in the New Deal," *JAH*, 51 (December, 1964), pp. 435-59.
92. Carter, p. 322; Chafee, *Free Speech*, pp. 384-98.

93. Bernstein, *Turbulent,* pp. 635-81.
94. Auerbach, *Labor,* p. 211.
95. On the Friends of the New Germany and its troubles, see Sander A. Diamond, *The Nazi Movement in the United States* (Ithaca: Cornell University Press, 1974), pp. 128-201; Leland V. Bell, *In Hitler's Shadow: The Anatomy of American Nazism* (Port Washington, New York: Kennikat, 1973), pp. 7-18; Geoffrey S. Smith, *To Save A Nation: American Countersubversives, the New Deal and the Coming of World War II* (New York: Basic Books, 1973), p. 90.
96. On the committee hearings, see Ogden, pp. 32-27; Goodman, pp. 10-12; Carr, pp. 13-14; Earl Latham, *The Communist Conspiracy in Washington* (New York: Atheneum, 1969), pp. 34-38; Diamond, pp. 157-59, 167-69, 175-76.
97. Diamond, p. 158.
98. Whitehead, pp. 193-94; *SICH,* pp. 558-59.
99. Schlesinger, *Coming,* pp. 40, 118, 264, 293, 311, 326, 337; Bernstein, *Turbulent,* p. 332; Bird, p. 136; Tindall, *Emergence,* pp. 611, 617.
100. Schlesinger, *Coming,* pp. 457-59.
101. Schlesinger, *Coming,* pp. 460, 463, 472-74.
102. Schlesinger, *Politics,* p. 86.
103. Schlesinger, *Politics,* pp. 86-87.
104. Whitehead, p. 190; *SICH,* p. 561.
105. Whitehead, p. 190.
106. *INS,* 1956, pp. 95-96. See footnote 32, Chapter Six.
107. Charles P. Larrowe, *Harry Bridges: The Rise and Fall of Radical Labor* (New York: Lawrence Hill, 1972), pp. 104, 106.
108. Drinnon, pp. 228-29.
109. *ACLUAR,* 1934-1935, pp. 6, 36-37.
110. Schlesinger, *Politics,* pp. 93-94; Chafee, *Free Speech,* pp. 446-54, quotation, p. 454.
111. M. S. Venkatarami, "Norman Thomas, Arkansas Sharecroppers and the Roosevelt Agricultural Policies, 1933-1937," *Mississippi Valley Historical Review,* 47 (September, 1960), pp. 225-46.
112. Schlesinger, *Politics,* p. 91.
113. D. R. Nissen, "Federal Anti-Communist Legislation From 1931-1941," (Unpublished M. A. Thesis, University of Illinois, 1959), pp. 18-22.
114. Schlesinger, *Politics,* p. 502.
115. Schlesinger, *Politics,* pp. 518-19, 526, 544, 553, 606, 619, 624-25, 629; Burns, *Roosevelt: Lion,* p. 242.
116. Schlesinger, *Politics,* p. 606.
117. Schlesinger, *Politics,* p. 623.
118. Schlesinger, *Politics,* p. 625.
119. Schlesinger, *Politics,* p. 620.
120. Schlesinger, *Politics,* p. 622.
121. Bernstein, *Turbulent,* pp. 37-216, quotation, p. 45.
122. Lens, p. 318.
123. Schlesinger, *Coming,* p. 396.
124. *HS,* p. 99.
125. *HS,* p. 99.
126. Wolfe, p. 120; *ACLUAR,* 1935-1936, p. 18; 1937-1938, p. 27.
127. Tindall, *Emergence,* pp. 505-39; Kreuger, *And Promises,* pp. 1-10, quotation, p. 5; Auerbach, *Labor,* pp. 94-96; Jerre Mangione, *The Dream and the Deal: The Federal Writers Project* (New York: Avon, 1972), pp. 44-45.
128. Tindall, *Emergence,* pp. 509-12; Bernstein, *Turbulent* pp. 298-315; Lens, pp. 304-06; Brecher, pp. 168-77.
129. Auerbach, *Labor,* pp. 107, 115-20, quotation, p. 116; Tindall, *Emergence,* pp. 528-29.
130. Taft and Ross, pp. 348-58.
131. *Labor Unionism,* p. 39.
132. Jamieson, pp. 39-40.
133. On the agricultural situation in California, see Jamieson, pp. 86-105; Bernstein,

Turbulent, pp. 153-60; McWilliams, *Factories*, pp. 211-304; Clarke Chambers, *California Farm Organizations* (Berkeley: University of California, 1952), pp. 31-53, 70-81, 108-14; Charles Wollenberg, "Race and Class in Rural California: The El Monte Berry Strike of 1933," *California Historical Quarterly*, 51 (Summer, 1972), pp. 156-64.

134. Quoted in Jamieson, pp. 99, 103.
135. McWilliams, *Factories*, p. 212.
136. Bernstein, *Turbulent*, p. 159.
137. Jamieson, p. 17.
138. Jamieson, p. 104.
139. Jamieson, pp. 103-4.
140. *Turbulent*, p. 160.
141. Bernstein, *Turbulent*, p. 166.
142. Bernstein, *Turbulent*, p. 168.
143. Bernstein, *Turbulent*, pp. 168-70; Jamieson, pp. 113-15; Chambers, pp. 33-34, 108-09.
144. Chambers, p. 109.
145. Jamieson, p. 41; Chambers, p. 110.
146. Chambers, p. 110.
147. Chambers, p. 111.
148. McWilliams, *Factories*, pp. 240-43.
149. McWilliams, *North*, p. 192.
150. Jamieson, p. 126.
151. Jamieson, p. 140.
152. McWilliams, *Factories*, pp. 254-59.
153. Jamieson, pp. 151, 167, 171-72; McWilliams, *Factories*, pp. 259-60, 313; Chambers, pp. 71-72.
154. Auerbach, *Labor*, pp. 177-96 (quotation, p. 187).
155. Daniel, p. 167.
156. Daniel, pp. 173, 175. In addition to Daniel, "Wobblies on the Farm: The IWW in the Yakima Valley," see Jamieson, pp. 437-39; Tyler, *Rebels*, pp. 223-24.
157. Jamieson, pp. 359-60.
158. William D. Rowley, "The Loup City Riot of 1934: Main Street Versus the 'Far-Out' Left," *Nebraska History*, 47 (September, 1966), pp. 295-327.
159. Jamieson, pp. 376-79, 454, 387-88.
160. Jamieson, p. 209.
161. Jamieson, pp. 219, 280.
162. Jamieson, p. 209.
163. On the STFU, see Donald H. Grubbs, *Cry from the Cotton: The Southern Tenant Farmers' Union and the New Deal*, (Chapel Hill: University of North Carolina, 1971); Tindall, *Emergence*, pp. 409-21; Venkatarami, pp. 225-46; Jerold S. Auerbach, "Southern Tenant Farmers: Socialist Critics of the New Deal," *LH*, 7 (Winter, 1966), p. 349; Jamieson, pp. 306-22; William H. Cobb and Donald H. Grubbs, "Arkansas' Commonwealth College and the Southern Tenant Farmers' Union," *Arkansas Historical Quarterly*, 25 (Winter, 1966), pp. 284-311.
164. Quoted in Tindall, *Emergence*, p. 412.
165. Quoted in Venkatarami, p. 234.
166. Helen Z. Papanikolas, "Unionism, Communism and the Great Depression: The Carbon County Coal Strike of 1933," *Utah Historical Quarterly*, 41 (Summer, 1973), pp. 254-300.
167 In the north repression during the textile strike centered in Rhode Island, where the governor viewed the dispute as a communist insurrection. At Saylesville and Woonsocket, state troops opened fire on crowds of militant strikers, killing four and wounding about ten (Brecher, pp. 173-74). A number of 1934 strikes that have received relatively little attention involved considerable violence on the part of labor. Thus, Milwaukee streetcar workers sabotaged dozens of street cars, striking hackies in Philadelphia burned a hundred taxicabs and New York cabdrivers drove most of the city's fifteen thousand cabs off the streets (Leuchtenburg, *Roosevelt*, p. 111).
168. On the San Francisco general strike, see Bernstein, *Turbulent*, pp. 252-98 (quotation, p. 297); Larrowe, pp. 13-94; Lens, pp. 283-304; Brecher, pp. 252-98; Yellin, pp. 327-58; Crook, *Communism*, p. 107-48.

169. On the Auto-lite strike, see Bernstein, *Turbulent Years*, pp. 218-29; Lens, pp. 307-10.
170. On Minneapolis, see Bernstein, *Turbulent*, pp. 229-52; Schlesinger, *Coming*, pp. 385-89; Brecher, pp. 161-66; Lens, 310-17.
171. Bernstein, *Turbulent*, p. 231.
172. Brecher, p. 165.
173. Taft and Ross, pp. 356-58.
174. Crook, *Communism*, pp. 149-53; Taft and Ross, p. 357.
175. McWilliams, *North*, p. 195.
176. Tyler, *Rebels*, pp. 225-26.
177. Bernstein, *Turbulent*, pp. 432-634; Lens, pp. 339-75; Brecher, pp. 177-216.
178. Wolfe, p. 120.
179. Leuchtenburg, *Roosevelt*, p. 241.
180. Sidney Fine, "The General Motors Strike: A Re-Examination," *AHR*, 70 (April, 1965), pp. 651-713; J. Woodford Howard, Jr., "Frank Murphy and the Sitdown Strikes of 1937," *LH*. 1 (Spring, 1960), pp. 103-40; Bernstein, *Turbulent*, pp. 499-571.
181. Bernstein, *Turbulent*, p. 740.
182. Bernstein, *Turbulent*, pp. 741-48.
183. Bernstein, *Turbulent*, pp. 432-98.
184. Bernstein, *Turbulent*, p. 473.
185. On the little steel strike see Auerbach, *Labor*, pp. 131-41; Bernstein, *Turbulent*, pp. 473-98.
186. Auerbach, *Labor*, p. 137.
187. Donald S. McPherson, "The 'Little Steel' Strike of 1937 in Johnstown, Pennsylvania," *Pennsylvania History*, 39 (April, 1972), pp. 219-38 (quotations, pp. 230, 236).
188. On the Memorial Day Massacre, see Sofchalk, "The Chicago Memorial Day Incident;" Bernstein, *Turbulent*, pp. 485-90; Auerbach, *Labor*, pp. 121-30.
189. Sofchalk, p. 25.
190. *ACLUAR*, 1935-1936, p. 5.
191. *ACLUAR*, 1933-1938, *passim*.
192. Bernhard, p. 78.
193. Schlesinger, *Politics*, p. 88; Bernhard, pp. 76-78; Durward Long, "Wisconsin: Changing Styles of Administrative Response," *Protest!* eds. Julian Foster and Durward Long (New York: Morrow, 1970), p. 247; Cobb and Grubbs, p. 298; Chamberlain, pp. 55-56.
194. Auerbach, "Depression Decade," *Pulse*, ed. Reitman, p. 69.
195. Smith, *To Save*, p. 68; Max Heirich and Sam Kaplan, "Yesterday's Discord," *The Berkeley Student Revolt*, eds. Seymour M. Lipset and Sheldon Wolin (Garden City: Doubleday, 1965), p. 13.
196. Heirich and Kaplan, *Berkeley*, eds. Lipset and Wolin, pp. 12-13; Peterson, p. 125; Manwaring, pp. 56-80.
197. *ACLUAR*, 1934-1935, pp. 13-14; Dowell, pp. 14-16; Mowitz, p. 190.
198. *ACLUAR*, 1937-1938, 1938-1939, *passim;* Metzger, pp. 223-24.
199. Kreuger, *And Promises*, p. 73; Philip M. Stern, *The Oppenheimer Case* (New York: Harper & Row, 1969), pp. 17-18; Howe and Coser, pp. 319-96.
200. Schlesinger, *Politics*, pp. 42-68.
201. Charles E. Larson, "The EPIC Campaign of 1934," *PHR*, 27 (May, 1958), pp. 127-47; Schlesinger, *Politics*, pp. 112-21.
202. Schlesinger, *Politics*, pp. 117-18.
203. Schlesinger, *Politics*, p. 107; Leuchtenburg, *Roosevelt*, pp. 95-96.
204. Leuchtenburg, *Roosevelt*, p. 117.
205. Altbach and Peterson, pp. 19-23; Chatfield, *For Peace*, pp. 259-60; Schlesinger, *Politics*, p. 156.
206. Auerbach, *Labor, passim*.
207. Howard K. Beale, *A History of Freedom of Teaching in American Schools* (New York: Scribners, 1941), p. 267.
208. Leuchtenburg, *Roosevelt*, pp. 143-66.
209. Schlesinger, *Politics*, p. 94.
210. Schlesinger, *Politics*, pp. 325-26.

211. Howe and Coser, pp. 319-96.

212. Latham, p. 19.

213. The question of how great an influence the CP exerted during the "popular front" period of 1935-1939 has been a subject of lively debate. Eugene Lyons, in his book *The Red Decade*, first published in 1941 and reprinted in 1970 by Arlington House of New Rochelle, New York, first made the phrase "red decade" popular as a description suggesting pervasive communist influence. Granville Hicks, in his article, "How Red Was the Red Decade?" (Harpers, July, 1953), attempted to rebut Lyons. Other perspectives on the question of communist influence in the thirties are contained in Howe and Coser, pp. 319-96; Frank Warren, *Liberals and Communism* (Bloomington: Indiana University Press, 1966) and Murray Kempton, *Part of Our Time: Some Monuments and Ruins of the Thirties* (New York: Delta, 1967).

214. Brecher, p. 216; Lens, p. 329. See generally Ronald Radosh, "The Corporate Ideology of American Labor Leaders from Gompers to Hillman," *For a New America*, eds. Weinstein and Eakins, pp. 125-52.

215. Dulles, p. 296.

CHAPTER EIGHT

1. *ACLUAR*, 1938-1939, p. 52.

2. On the development of anti-New Deal and anti-labor sentiment in 1937-1938 and increasing tensions related to European developments, see James T. Patterson, *Congressional Conservatism and the New Deal* (Lexington: University of Kentucky Press, 1967); Leuchtenburg, *Roosevelt*, pp. 231-325; Latham, p. 7; Sofchalk, pp. 34-43. On the growth of the Bund, see Diamond, pp. 202-304; Bell, *In Hitler's Shadow*, pp. 19-92; Leland V. Bell, "The Failure of Nazism in America: The German American Bund, 1936-1941," *PSQ*, 85 (December, 1970), pp. 319-86. The best source on the Dies Committee is Ogden, *The Dies Committee*. On CP growth, see Howe and Coser, pp. 319-86. On the "War of the Worlds" panic, see Hadley Cantril, *The Invasion from Mars: A Study in the Psychology of Panic* (Princeton: Princeton University Press, 1940).

3. *ACLUAR*, 1939-1940, p. 4.

4. Quoted in Ogden, p. 43.

5. On the background to the Dies Committee, see Ogden, pp. 38-45; Goodman, pp. 12-23.

6. On the growth of the Bund and growing public hostility to it, see Diamond, pp. 202-304; Bell, *In Hitler's Shadow*, pp. 19-92; Smith, To Save, pp. 87-100.

7. On the Dies committee and the Bund, see Ogden, *passim*; Goodman, pp. 63-64, 114-15; Diamond, pp. 308-12, 323-24, 332-33.

8. See Howard, "Frank Murphy," pp. 134-35; Frost, p. 482; Ogden, pp. 74-84.

9. Ogden, pp. 92-93.

10. Quoted in Davis, *Fear*, p. 283; and in Richard Polenberg, "Franklin Roosevelt and Civil Liberties: The Case of the Dies Committee," *The Historian*, 30 (February, 1968), p. 166.

11. Thomas I. Emerson and David M. Helfeld, "Loyalty Among Government Employees," *Yale Law Journal*, 58 (December, 1948), p. 10; Ogden, pp. 152-63; Goodman, pp. 69-75.

12. Emerson and Helfeld, pp. 11-12.

13. Emerson and Helfeld, pp. 9, 11.

14. Ogden, p. 63.

15. On the Federal Theatre, see Jane D. Matthews, *The Federal Theatre, 1935-1939* (Princeton: Princeton University Press, 1967); on the Federal Writers Project, see Mangione, *The Dream and the Deal: The Federal Writers Project*.

16. Ogden, p. 36. In reply to the question, Hallie Flanagan, director of the Theatre Project, stated, "Put it in the record, that he was the greatest dramatist in the period of Shakespeare, immediately preceding Shakespeare."

17. Mangione, p. 306.

18. Mangione, p. 319.

19. *The Politics of Fear* (Lexington: University of Kentucky Press, 1970), p. 32.
20. Mangione, p. 321.
21. Nissen, p. 26.
22. Nissen, p. 35; Donald S. Howard, *The Works Progress Administration and Federal Relief Policy* (New York: Russell Sage Foundation, 1943), p. 225; Mangione, pp. 321-26.
23. Nissen, pp. 36-38.
24. Swisher, p. 337; Chafee, *Free Speech,* p. 464.
25. Arthur S. Link and William B. Catton, *American Epoch,* III (New York: Alfred A. Knopf, 1967), p. 484.
26. Howard, *Works Progress,* p. 320; Nissen, p. 38.
27. Swisher, p. 340.
28. Larrowe, pp. 221-22.
29. Auerbach, *Labor,* pp. 198-203.
30. Eleanor Bontecue, *The Federal Loyalty-Security Program* (Ithaca: Cornell University Press, 1953), p. 12.
31. Chafee, *Free Speech,* pp. 439-90; Nissen, pp. 41-59.
32. Quoted in Chafee, *Free Speech,* p. 446.
33. Goodman, p. 106.
34. Nissen, p. 24; Chafee, *Free Speech,* p. 461.
35. Nissen, pp. 65-69.
36. Nissen, pp. 29-33.
37. Bontecue, p. 166.
38. Nissen, p. 69.
39. Howard, *Works Progress,* p. 120.
40. Dulles, pp. 330-31; Richard Polenberg, *War and Society* (Philadelphia: Lippincott, 1972), p. 166.
41. Carr, p. 251.
42. Carey McWilliams, *Witch Hunt* (Boston: Little, Brown, 1950), p. 243.
43. Goodman, p. 105.
44. SICH, pp. 563-67.
45. SICH, pp. 567-70.
46. SICH, pp. 570-77; Frank J. Donner, "Hoover's Legacy," *The Nation* (June 1, 1974), pp. 678-80; Jerry J. Berman and Morton H. Halperin, eds., *The Abuses of the Intelligence Agencies* (Washington, D.C.: Center for National Security Studies, 1975), pp. 16-17.
47. SICH, pp. 409-11.
48. Whitehead, p. 205.
49. Ungar, *FBI,* p. 103.
50. SICH, pp. 412-15.
51. Nissen, pp. 26-27.
52. Howe and Coser, p. 400.
53. Howe and Coser, pp. 400-01.
54. Lowenthal, pp. 317-18; Cook, *FBI,* pp. 243-46.
55. Cook, *FBI,* pp. 234-41; Whitehead, pp. 205-13; Lowenthal, pp. 319-20.
56. The complete text of Roosevelt's memorandum is printed in Christine M. Marwick, "Warrantless National Security Wiretaps," *First Principles,* 1 (October, 1975), pp. 6-7. See also Frank Donner, "Electronic Surveillance," *CLR,* 2 (October, 1975), pp. 17-20; Victor Navasky and Nathan Lewin, Electronic Surveillance,"*Investigating the FBI,* eds. Pat Watters and Stephen Gillers, (New York: Ballantine, 1974), p. 291.
57. Berman and Halperin, p. 7.
58. SIFER, p. 6.
59. Cook, *FBI,* p. 241; Whitehead, p. 217.
60. Lowenthal, pp. 356-62.
61. SICH, pp. 452-54, 471-72.
62. Whitehead, pp. 336-37.
63. James M. Burns, *Roosevelt: The Soldier of Freedom,* 1940-1945 (New York: Harcourt, Brace, 1970), pp. 3-4.
64. Emerson and Helfeld, pp. 14-15.

65. Ralph S. Brown, *Loyalty and Security* (New Haven: Yale University Press, 1958), p. 326; *ACLUAR*, 1940-1941, p. 37; Polenberg, "Roosevelt," pp. 172-73.
66. *LAT*, February 25, 1975.
67. Smith, *To Save*, p. 140.
68. Smith, *To Save*, pp. 170, 172, 176.
69. Larrowe, pp. 146-237.
70. Bontecue, p. 166; Whitehead, p. 434.
71. Robert E. Cushman, "The Purge of Federal Employees Accused of Disloyalty," Public Administration Review, 3 (Autumn, 1943), pp. 297-317.
72. On the North American Aviation strike, see Rich, pp. 177-87; Burns, *Roosevelt: Soldier*, pp. 117-18; Alan Barth, *The Loyalty of Free Men* (New York: Pocket Books, 1952), p. 41; Bernstein, *Turbulent*, pp. 765-66; Howe and Coser, pp. 397-98.
73. Howe and Coser, p. 398.
74. On the SWP raid and trial, see Thomas L. Pahl, "G-String Conspiracy, Political Reprisal or Armed Revolt? The Minnesota Trotskyite Trial," *LH*, 8 (Winter, 1967), pp. 30-52; Thomas L. Pahl, "The Dilemma of a Civil Libertarian: Francis Biddle and the Smith Act," *The Journal of Minnesota Academy of Science*, 34 (1967), pp. 161-63; Bernstein, *Turbulent Years*, pp. 780-82.
75. Bernstein, *Turbulent*, p. 781; Pahl, "G-String Conspiracy," p. 37.
76. Pahl, "G-String Conspiracy," p. 51. Acting Attorney General Francis Biddle, who authorized the prosecutions, later claimed that he acted in hopes that the Supreme Court would declare the Smith Act unconstitutional, a procedure that seems to have unnecessarily played with the lives of twenty-nine men. Biddle wrote later that he regretted the prosecutions and admitted that "by no conceivable stretch of a liberal imagination" could the SWP have been said to constitute a "clear and present danger" to the government, since there had been "no substantial overt act outside of talk and threats, openly expressed in the time honored Marxist lingo" (*In Brief Authority* [Garden City: Doubleday, 1962] p. 152).
77. *SICSR*, pp. 376-77.
78. *SICSR*, pp. 412-44.
79. *SICSR*, pp. 415-17.
80. *SICSR*, pp. 255, 301, 315, 353-71, 413-19, 636-77.
81. C. Herman Pritchett, *The Roosevelt Court* (Chicago: Quadrangle, 1969), pp. 96, 221.
82. Chamberlain, pp. 59-70.
83. Chamberlain, p. 77.
84. Chamberlain, p. 125.
85. Chamberlain, p. 154.
86. Chamberlain, p. 163.
87. Vern Countryman, *Un-American Activities in the State of Washington* (Ithaca: Cornell University Press, 1951), pp. 7-10.
88. Edward Barrett, Jr., *The Tenney Committee: Legislative Investigation of Subversive Activities in California* (Ithaca: Cornell University Press, 1951), pp. 3-9; David P. Gardner, *The California Oath Controversy*, (Berkeley: University of California, 1967), p. 276.
89. Robinson, pp. 20-31.
90. Robinson, p. 24.
91. Robinson, p. 26.
92. Robinson, p. 29.
93. Robinson, p. 30.
94. *ACLUAR*, 1938-1939, p. 32; Tindall, *Emergence*, p. 634.
95. *ACLUAR*, 1940-1941, pp. 3-4, 19-20, 26, 34-35; Goeffrey Perrett, *Days of Sadness, Years of Triumph* (Baltimore: Penguin, 1974), p. 91.
96. On local and state repression of the Bund, see Diamond, pp. 208, 291, 307-08, 317, 329-36, 343-46; Bell, *In Hitler's Shadow*, pp. 93-98, 102-06; Schonbach, pp. 89-99.
97. Bell, *In Hitler's Shadow*, p. 105.
98. Bell, *In Hitler's Shadow*, p. 104.
99. *American People*, p. 195.
100. Bell, "Failure of Nazism,'" p. 597. The Bund was not the only right-wing organization facing state and local repression during this period. In 1939, New York City

officials began a general policy of arresting members of the pro-facist Christian Front and other "similar hatred-breeding and discriminatory groups" who sought to speak publicly. Over 230 arrests and 101 convictions of "rabble rousers" were obtained by October, 1939. Joseph E. McWilliams, a candidate for Congress, was convicted of disorderly conduct and sent to jail for seventy-five days as a result of anti-Semetic speeches given in New York during the 1940 campaign. William Dudley Pelley leader of the pro-fascist Silver Shirts, was frequently in trouble with North Carolina authorities. He was put on five years probation in 1935 as a result of apparently valid charges involving manipulation of funds in connection with his press, and was sought by North Carolina authorities in 1939 on the grounds that he had violated his probation by publishing pro-Nazi materials. After a North Carolina judge denounced Pelley's "unpatriotic propaganda and practices" and ordered his arrest, police raided his headquarters and confiscated his files. Pelley eventually surrendered to Asheville officials in October, 1941. In the meantime the Silver Shirts and Pelley had been investigated by the Dies Committee (Gustavus Myers, *History of Bigotry in the United States* [New York: Capricorn, 1960], pp. 337, 406, 414; Smith *To Save*, pp. 64-65, 134, 139, 145-56, 160-61, 181).

101. *ACLUAR*, 1940-1941, p. 21. These laws are quoted in ISS, a compilation of "anti-subversive laws" listed by state. For individual states, see Barrett, *Tenney*, p. 8; Robinson, p. 37; Bernhard, p. 91; Clark Byse, "A Report on the Pennsylvania Loyalty Act," *University of Pennsylvania Law Review*, 101 (1952-1953), pp. 536-37; Mowitz, p. 199.

102. Dulles, pp. 327-31; Rayback, p. 365; Wolfe, p. 120; Taft and Ross, pp. 361-65.

103. Gerald A. Rose, "The Westwood Lumber Strike," *LH*, 13 (Spring, 1972), pp. 174-99.

104. Rose, "Westwood," p. 189.

105. Rose, "Westwood," p. 193.

106. Louis Cantor, "A Prologue to the Protest Movement: The Missouri Sharecroppers Roadside Demonstration of 1939," *JAH*, 55 (March, 1969), p. 814.

107. Cantor, p. 816.

108. Harold W. Horowitz, "Report on the Los Angeles City and County Loyalty Programs," *Stanford Law Review*, 5 (1953), pp. 233-34; *ACLUAR*, 1939-1940, p. 33; Perrett, p. 159.

109. Manwaring, pp. 163-86.

110. *ACLUAR*, 1940-1941, p. 27.

111. *ACLUAR*, 1940-1941, pp. 27-29.

112. U.S. News and World Report, *Communism and the New Left* (Washington, D.C.: U.S. News and World Report, 1970), p. 137.

113. Perrett, pp. 102-03, 150.

114. Rayback, p. 370; Perrett, p. 102.

115. Perrett, pp. 94, 99-101.

116. Perrett, pp. 107-08.

117. Perrett, pp. 112, 114-15.

118. On the ACLU controversy, see *ACLUAR*, 1940-1941, pp. 48-49; Corliss Lamont, ed., *The Trial of Elizabeth Gurley Flynn by the American Civil Liberties Union* (New York: Modern Reader, 1968); Auerbach, "Depression Decade," pp. 91-102.

119. Auerbach, "Depression Decade," p. 102.

120. *Quest*, p. 184. According to Clinton Rossiter (*Constitutional Dictatorship* [Princeton: Princeton University Press, 1948], p. 65), the government's civil liberties record "would have been well-nigh perfect" save for the Japanese-American affair. For other examples of this approach, see Link and Catton, p. 539; Nelson, pp. xxxxix; John W. Caughey, *In Clear and Present Danger* (Chicago: University of Chicago Press, 1958), p. 2; Davis, *Fear*, pp. 264-65; Ekirch, *Decline*, p. 307; Handlin, pp. 213-15; Goodman, p. 156; Johnson, *1600*, pp. 156-57; Murphy, *Meaning*, p. 280; Robert E. Cushman, "Civil Liberties," *APSR*, 37 (February, 1943), pp. 49-50; Hyman, *To Try*, pp. 329, 332.

121. *ACLUAR*, 1943-1944, p. 5.

122. For examples, see *ACLUAR*, 1941-1942, p. 3; Cushman, "Impact," p. 16; Cushman, "Civil Liberties," pp. 49-50; Ekirch, *Decline*, p. 307; Goodman, pp. 107, 137; Roche, *Quest*, pp. 186-87; Link and Catton, p. 537 (quotation).

123. *ACLUAR*, 1942-1943, p. 3.

124. Hyman, *To Try*, pp. 327-28.
125. Biddle, *In Brief*, pp. 111-12.
126. Cushman, "Impact," pp. 14, 20. See also Whitehead, pp. 228-29; Bernhard, p. 141; Cook, *FBI*, p. 256; Swisher, p. 345.
127. Murphy, *Constitution*, p. 225.
128. Cushman, "Civil Liberties," p. 53.
129. On the treatment of enemy aliens, see Allan R. Bosworth, *America's Concentration Camps* (New York: Bantam, 1968), pp. 37-38; Eugene V. Rostow "The Japanese American Cases — A Disaster," *Shaping*, eds. Abrams and Levine, pp. 461-62; Polenberg, *War*, pp. 42-43; Cushman, "Civil Liberties," pp. 52-53; Link and Catton, p. 539; Whitehead, pp. 219-21; Jones, pp. 302-03.
130. Fred I. Israel, "Military Justice in Hawaii, 1941-1944," *The Diversity of Modern America*, eds. David Burner (New York: Appleton Century Crofts, 1970), p. 237.
131. Israel, p. 238.
132. Burns, *Roosevelt: Soldier*, pp. 209-10.
133. Burns, *Roosevelt: Soldier*, pp. 209-10, 214-15; Polenberg, *War*, pp. 43, 134; *ACLUAR*, 1941-1942, pp. 3-5; Biddle, *In Brief*, pp. 237-38; Perrett, pp. 211, 222.
134. *ACLUAR*, 1942-1943, p. 36; Polenberg, *War*, pp. 45-47; Myers, pp. 432-33; Kreuger, *And Promises*, p. 101; Perrett, pp. 226-28.
135. Quoted in Polenberg, *War*, pp. 45-46.
136. *ACLUAR*, 1942-1943, p. 34.
137. *In Brief*, pp. 237-38.
138. Quoted in Polenberg, *War*, p. 45.
139. On the Japanese American deportations and incarcerations, see Bosworth, *America's Concentration Camps;* Jacobus tenBroek, Edward N. Barnhart and Floyd Matson, *Prejudice, War and the Constitution* (Berkeley: University of California, 1968); Dorothy S. Thomas and Richard Nishimoto, *The Spoilage* (Berkeley: University of California Press, 1969); Rostow, "The Japanese-American Cases;" Polenberg, *War*, pp. 61-72.
140. Quoted in tenBroek, p. 110.
141. Quoted in Polenberg, *War*, pp. 62-63.
142. A. Russell Buchanon, *The United States and World War II* (New York: Harper & Row, 1964), II, p. 326.
143. *ACLUAR*, 1942-1943, p. 31; 1943-1944, p. 39.
144. *ACLUAR*, 1941-1945, *passim;* Cushman, "Civil Liberties," p. 50.
145. Perrett, p. 218.
146. Perrett, p. 250.
147. Myers, pp. 430-35; Polenberg, *War*, p. 47; *ACLUAR*, 1941-1942, p. 42; 1942-1943, pp. 45-46; 1943-1944, p. 35.
148. On the sedition case, see Edwin Corwin, *Total War and the Constitution* (New York: Alfred A. Knopf, 1947), pp. 110-16; Polenberg, *War*, p. 48; *ACLUAR*, 1943-1944, pp. 31-32; Biddle, *In Brief*, pp. 241-43; Perrett, pp. 360-62.
149. Perrett, p. 361; Corwin, p. 114.
150. Burns, *Roosevelt: Soldier*, p. 453.
151. Corwin, p. 115.
152. Biddle, *In Brief*, p. 243.
153. "Shadows of War and Fear," *Pulse*, ed. Reitman, p. 114.
154. Pritchett, *Roosevelt*, p. 119.
155. Pritchett, *Roosevelt*, pp. 117-18.
156. Polenberg, *War*, p. 101; *ACLUAR*, 1941-1942, p. 29; 1943-1944, pp. 20, 31.
157. Barrett, *Tenney*, pp. 28-29; *ACLUAR*, 1941-1942, pp. 30, 39; 1944-1945, p. 25.
158. Myers, pp. 341-42; Bell, "Failure," p. 599.
159. Myers, pp. 352-59.
160. Biddle, *In Brief*, pp. 243-48. In his book, Biddle says, "It was time to take action against this troublesome priest," a phrase disturbingly similar to King Henry's plea uttered before his aides murdered Thomas à Becket.
161. Myers, p. 340; Cushman, "Civil Liberties," p. 54.
162. Pritchett, *Roosevelt*, p. 401; Polenberg, *War*, pp. 440-41.
163. Pritchett, *Roosevelt*, pp. 119-20.
164. *ACLUAR*, 1943-1944, p. 41; 1944-1945, p. 52.
165. Diamond, pp. 346-49.

166. *In Brief,* pp. 297-307.
166a. Murphy, *Constitution,* p. 232.
166b. Pritchett, *Roosevelt,* p. 119; Buchanan, pp. 326-27.
167. Myers, pp. 340-43; Schonbach, pp. 98-100; Bell, "Failure," p. 599; *ACLUAR,* 1941-1942, p. 30.
168. *SICFR,* pp. 61-62; *SICSR,* 301, 353-71; *SICH,* pp. 357-59; *LAT,* July 15, September 26, 1975; Berman and Halperin, pp. 21-22.
169. *SICSR,* pp. 421-22.
170. *SICSR,* p. 765; *SICFR,* p. 34.
171. On the treatment of CO's, see Lawrence Wittner, *Rebels Against War: The American Peace Movement, 1941-1960* (New York: Columbia University Press, 1970), pp. 41-42, 70-92; Perrett, pp. 359-60.
172. Polenberg, *War,* pp. 21-22; Rayback, p. 376.
173. Quoted in Polenberg, *War,* p. 178.
174. Polenberg, *War,* pp. 177-83.
175. Stern, pp. 48-51.
176. Polenberg, *War,* p. 122; Burns, *Roosevelt: Soldier,* p. 510.
177. Rayback, pp. 378-83; Dulles, p. 335; Brecher, pp. 221-26; Polenberg, *War,* pp. 155-61.
178. Polenberg, *War,* p. 158.
179. Quoted in Brecher, p. 223.
180. Brecher, pp. 224-26; Rayback, pp. 381-83; Polenberg, *War,* pp. 166-75.
181. Emerson and Helfeld, p. 17.
182. Cushman, "Purge," pp. 308-10; Emerson and Helfeld, pp. 64-65; Bontecue, pp. 16-17.
183. Emerson and Helfeld, p. 77.
184. Cushman, "Purge," pp. 310-15; Polenberg, *War,* pp. 50-51; Bontecue, pp. 18-20.
185. Bontecue, pp. 166-67; Ogden, p. 270; Barth, *Loyalty,* p. 111.
186. Emerson and Helfeld, pp. 55-56; Hyman, *To Try,* pp. 329-32.
187. Ogden, p. 260.
188. Goodman, pp. 131-34.
189. On the Pickens affair and subsequent developments, see Frederick L. Schuman, "'Bill of Attainder' in the Seventy-Eighth Congress," *APSR,* 37 (October, 1943), pp. 819-29; Cushman, "Purge," pp. 297-308; Goodman, pp. 139-52.
190. Goodman, p. 149.
191. "Purge," p. 305.
192. Pritchett, *Roosevelt,* p. 117.
193. Pritchett, *Roosevelt,* pp. 96-99, 222; Manwaring, p. 208.
194. Reprinted in John C. Wahlke, ed., *Loyalty in a Democratic State* (Boston: D.C. Heath, 1952), p. 34.
195. Pritchett, *Roosevelt,* pp. 156-58, 225.
196. See the discussion in Rostow, "The Japanese American Cases."
197. Quoted in Rostow, p. 460.
198. Clinton Rossiter, *The Supreme Court and the Commander in Chief* (Ithaca: Cornell University Press, 1951), p. 54.
199. Wittner, pp. 37-38, 56-57.
200. Barrett, *Tenney,* pp. 25-30, 121-33.
201. Schonbach, p. 99.
202. *ACLUAR,* 1941-1942, p. 30; 1942-1943, p. 36; Francis Biddle, *The Fear of Freedom* (Garden City: Doubleday, 1951), pp. 23-24; Barrett, *Tenney,* p. 297; *ISS,* p. 133.
203. *ACLUAR,* 1941-1942, p. 36.
204. Thomas I. Emerson, *The System of Freedom of Expression* (New York: Vintage, 1970), p. 67.
205. Manwaring, pp. 165-86.
206. Manwaring, pp. 177-81, 185-86.
207. Manwaring, p. 187.
208. *Days,* p. 358.
209. Perrett, pp. 357-58.
210. *Days,* p. 358.

CHAPTER NINE

1. *ACLUAR*, 1944-1945, p. 11.
2. *ACLUAR*, 1945-1946, pp. 5-8.
3. *ACLUAR*, 1946-1947, p. 4.
4. Polenberg, *War*, pp. 39-40; Pope, pp. 304-06; Chamberlain, pp. 77-78; Barrett, *Tenney*, pp. 7-8.
5. Carr, p. 251.
6. McWilliams, *Witch Hunt*, p. 243; Goodman, p. 139.
7. John Lewis Gaddis, *The United States and the Origins of the Cold War* (New York: Columbia University Press, 1972), p. 33.
8. Howe and Coser, p. 427.
9. Burns, *Roosevelt: Soldier*, p. 416.
10. Howe and Coser, p. 432.
11. Wittner, pp. 115-20; Gaddis, pp. 33-42; Howe and Coser, pp. 432-34.
12. Shannon, *Decline*, pp. 3-8; Howe and Coser, pp. 419-28; Joseph R. Starobin, *American Communism in Crisis* (Cambridge: Harvard University Press, 1972), p. 250.
13. Howe and Coser, pp. 419, 425; Shannon, *Decline*, pp. 3-4.
14. Goodman, pp. 158-59; Burns, *Roosevelt: Soldier*, pp. 525, 529; Polenberg, *War*, p. 208; Gaddis, pp. 57-60.
15. Gaddis, p. 59; Burns, *Roosevelt: Soldier*, p. 529.
16. Goodman, pp. 160-61; Link and Catton, p. 569.
17. Brecher, pp. 226-30; Taft and Ross, p. 366; Rayback, pp. 389-95.
18. Cabell Phillips, *The Truman Presidency* (Baltimore: Penguin, 1969), pp. 113-18.
19. Rayback, pp. 392-95; Dulles, p. 356.
20. Rayback, pp. 393-94; Dulles, p. 357.
21. Rayback, p. 396.
22. Rayback, p. 396; Dulles, p. 356.
23. Emerson, *System*, p. 164.
24. Rayback, pp. 397-400, 409-10; Dulles, pp. 356-59.
25. Quoted in Harold W. Chase, *Security and Liberty: The Problem of Native Communists, 1947-1955* (Garden City, New York: Doubleday, 1955), p.56.
26. Starobin, pp. 158, 169; Howe and Coser, p. 466; Chase, p. 60.
27. Chase, p. 60.
28. Eric Goldman, *The Crucial Decade — and After, 1945-1960* (New York: Vintage, 1960), pp. 25-26.
29. Gaddis, p. 154.
30. Burns, *Roosevelt: Soldier*, p. 582.
31. Goodman, p. 168.
32. Bontecue, p. 23; Emerson and Helfeld, p. 18.
33. Goodman, pp. 167-89; Carr, pp. 19-36.
34. Goodman, p. 173; Carr, p. 33.
35. On the *Amerasia* affair, see E. J. Kahn, Jr., *The China Hands* (New York: Viking, 1975), pp. 165-72; Latham, pp. 203-15; Cook, *FBI*, pp. 265-71; Griffith, *Politics*, pp. 35-38.
36. Griffith, *Politics*, p. 38; Brown, p. 22; Stern, p. 95.
37. Phillips, pp. 358-39; Richard M. Freeland, *The Truman Doctrine and the Origins of McCarthyism* (New York: Schocken, 1974), pp. 121-23; Marwick, "Warrantless," p. 7; Donner, "Electronic Surveillance," pp. 20-21; *SICSR*, p. 430.
38. Barth, *Loyalty*, pp. 164-75; Donner, "Electronic Surveillance," p. 22; Thomas I. Emerson, "The FBI as a Political Police," *Investigating*, eds, Watters and Gillers, pp. 227, 230.
39. Ungar, *FBI*, pp. 126-27.
40. Emerson and Helfeld, p. 18.
41. Emerson and Helfeld, p. 17; Bontecue, p. 22.
42. Peter H. Irons, "American Business and the Origins of McCarthyism: The Cold War Crusade of the United States Chamber of Commerce," *The Specter: Original Essays on the Cold War and the Origins of McCarthyism*, eds. Robert Griffith and Athan Theoharis (New York: New Viewpoints, 1974), pp. 72-89; Stern, p. 95.

43. *The Truman Era* (New York: Vintage, 1973), p. xxiv.
44. Donald F. Crosby, "The Politics of Religion: American Catholics and the Anti-Communist Impulse," and Ronald Lora, "A View from the Right: Conservative Intellectuals, the Cold War and McCarthy," *The Spectre,* eds. Griffith and Theoharis, pp. 18-72.
45. On the 1946 campaign, see Griffith, *Politics,* p. 11; Stern, pp. 95-96; Latham, p. 365; Countryman, *Un-American,* pp. 10-11; Johnson, *1600,* p. 226.
46. Earl Mazo and Stephen Hess, *Nixon* (New York: Popular Library, 1968), pp. 39-40.
47. McWilliams, *Witch Hunt,* p. 141.
48. Griffith, *Politics,* p. 11.
49. Carr, pp. 37-38.
50. Griffiths, *Politics,* p. 38.
51. On the general development of American foreign policy during this period, see Gaddis, pp. 63-316. For public opinion polls, see Athan Theoharis, *Seeds of Repression: Harry S. Truman and the Origins of McCarthyism* (Chicago: Quadrangle, 1971), pp. 194-205. For adverse reaction to the "Iron Curtain" speech, see Goldman, *Crucial,* p. 38; Gaddis, p. 309; Herbert Agar, *The Price of Power* (Chicago: University of Chicago Press, 1957), p. 59.
52. See Curtis MacDougall, *Gideon's Army* (New York: Marzani and Munsell, 1965), pp. 22-127; Karl M. Schmidt, *Henry A. Wallace, Quixotic Crusader* (Syracuse: Syracuse University Press, 1960), pp. 1-30.
53. Shannon, *Decline,* pp. 13-110; Freeland, pp. 35-43.
54. Thomas G. Paterson, "Introduction: American Critics of the Cold War and Their Alternatives," *Cold War Critics,* ed. Thomas G. Paterson (Chicago: Quadrangle, 1971), p. 4.
55. Paterson, pp. 3-15.
56. Freeland, pp. 58-68.
57. Freeland, pp. 135-43.
58. Quoted in Freeland, p. 140.
59. Joseph Jones, *Fifteen Weeks* (New York: Harcourt, Brace, 1955), pp. 186-87.
60. Freeland, p. 135.
61. Freeland, pp. 58-69.
62. Quoted in Goldman, *Crucial,* p. 59.
63. This thesis is elucidated in Freeland, *The Truman Doctrine and the Origins of McCarthyism.*
64. On the temporary commission, see Theoharis, *Seeds,* pp. 103-04 (includes quotations); Alan D. Harper, *The Politics of Loyalty: The White House and the Communist Issue, 1946-1952* (Westport, Connecticut: Greenwood, 1969), pp. 27-42; Freeland, pp. 123-43.
65. Starobin, p. 111.
66. Freeland, p. 115.
67. Pertinent sections of the loyalty order are reproduced in Henry Commager, ed., *Documents of American History, II* (New York: Appleton Century Crofts, 1962), pp. 527-31. On the loyalty program, see Bontecue, *The Federal Loyalty-Security Program;* Brown, *Loyalty and Security;* Emerson and Helfeld, "Loyalty Among Government Employees;" Harper, *Politics of Loyalty;* Barth, *Loyalty of Free Men;* Walter Gellhorn, *Security, Loyalty and Science* (Ithaca: Cornell University Press, 1950); Bert Andrews, *Washington Witchhunt* (New York: Random House, 1948); Stern, *The Oppenheimer Case;* Wahlke, ed. *Loyalty in a Democratic State.*
68. As the Truman program affecting all governmental employees took effect, "sensitive" agencies such as the State Department and the armed forces which had previously been given power by Congress to summarily remove employees, were authorized to continue to operate under separate standards and procedures. Thus, in October, 1947, the State Department issued regulations providing for the immediate firing of any employee deemed to constitute a "security risk." Among the factors which the regulations provided could be considered in determining whether or not an employee was a security risk were support or association of literally any kind with groups seeking to unconstitutionally alter the form of the U.S. government, as well as "written evidences or oral expressions by speeches or otherwise, of political, economic and social views."

By December, 1950, there were at least fourteen cases of employees cleared of charges concerning their "loyalty" but found nevertheless to be untrustworthy on "security" grounds, suggesting that they could not be trusted with access to sensitive information, although there was no evidence of overt disloyalty (Emerson and Helfeld, pp. 33-35; Bontecue, pp. 48-51).

69. Quoted in Emerson, *System*, p. 215.
70. Bontecue, p. 30.
71. Cases in which accused applicants or employees were able to learn the identity of their accusers demonstrate the grave danger that not disclosing such information created. For example, in one case, one charge was that a Jewish employee was a regular reader of the *Daily Worker* (the CP newspaper). The informant turned out to be a janitor who was a naturalized German citizen of allegedly pro-Nazi sentiments. Under oath at a loyalty hearing, he said he had only found the newspaper in the accused's garbage pail "once or twice" in the course of two years (Emerson and Helfeld, p. 106). In at least three cases, accused employees were able to discredit their accusers by identifying them and demonstrating that the accusers were of unbalanced minds; in one of these cases, the informant had been hospitalized for paranoid delusions of being persecuted by communists (Bontecue, p. 32; Biddle, *Fear*, pp. 232-33).
72. Bontecue, p. 72.
73. Brown, p. 35; Bontecue, p. 87; Stern, p. 485; Gellhorn, *Security*, pp. 152-53.
74. Emerson and Helfeld, pp. 72, 74; L. A. Nikoloric, "The Government Loyalty Program," *Loyalty*, ed. Wahlke, p. 55; Bontecue, pp. 139, 141; Stern, p. 486.
75. Barth, *Loyalty*, p. 130.
76. Elmer Davis, *But We Were Born Free* (New York: Permabooks, 1956), p. 5; Gellhorn, *Security*, p. 152.
77. Bontecue, pp. 101-56.
78. Brown, pp. 489-97.
79. Phillips, p. 364; Bontecue, p. 106.
80. Barth, *Loyalty*, p. 135.
81. Emerson and Helfeld, p. 133.
82. Emerson and Helfeld, p. 20.
83. *The Committee*, p. 195.
84. Gaddis, p. 351.
85. MacDougall, pp. 147-71; Starobin, p. 158; Shannon, *Decline*, p. 143; Irwin Ross, *The Loneliest Campaign: The Truman Victory of 1948* (New York: Signet, 1969), pp. 141-48.
86. MacDougall, pp. 184, 193-94, 227, 249, 299, 315-16, 322.
87. Ross, pp. 68-69; MacDougall, pp. 323-24.
88. MacDougall, p. 312.
89. MacDougall, pp. 435-62, *passim*.
90. Freeland, pp. 144-50, 239-42; Goodman, pp. 190-225; Carr, pp. 37-79.
91. Freeland, pp. 149-50.
92. I. F. Stone, *The Haunted Fifties* (New York: Vintage, 1969), p. 26.
93. Freeland, pp. 146-49 (quotation, p. 146); Goodman, p. 196.
94. Goodman, pp. 207-25; Carr, pp. 52-78; Robert Vaughn, *Only Victims: A Study of Show Business Blacklisting* (New York: G. P. Putnam's Sons, 1972), pp. 75-117.
95. Carr, p. 59.
96. Goodman, p. 209; Howard Zinn, *Post-War America, 1945-1971* (Indianapolis: Bobbs-Merrill, 1973), pp. 164-65.
97. Goodman, p. 211.
98. Goodman, p. 225.
99. Carr, pp. 23, 31, 80, 166.
100. Carr, p. 251.
101. Andrews, pp. 1-77; Freeland, pp. 202-04.
102. On the Attorney General's list, see Freeland, pp. 208-16; Bontecue, pp. 157-204; Barth, *Loyalty*, pp. 103-17; Gellhorn, *Security*, pp. 134-43; Thomas I. Emerson, David Haber and Norman Dorsen, *Political and Civil Rights in the United States* (Boston: Little, Brown, 1967), pp. 386-88; Fund for The Republic, *Digest*, pp. 77-78.
103. Barth, *Loyalty*, p. 111.

104. Theoharis, *Seeds*, pp. 106-07; Athan Theoharis, "The Escalation of the Loyalty Program," *Politics and Policies of the Truman Administration*, ed. Barton J. Bernstein (Chicago: Quadrangle, 1970), p. 264.
105. Bontecue, pp. 181-84, 188-91.
106. Freeland, pp. 207-10; Gellhorn, *Security*, pp. 136-39.
107. *Truman Doctrine*, pp. 210-11.
108. Freeland, p. 212.
109. Gelhorn, *Security*, p. 139; Robert E. Cushman, *Civil Liberties in the United States* (Ithaca: Cornell University Press, 1956), pp. 173-74; Fund for the Republic, *Digest*, pp. 77-78; Freeland, pp. 209, 215; Bontecue, pp. 176-78.
110. "Loyalty," p. 82.
111. Freeland, pp. 209-09; Bontecue, pp. 176, 184-88; Countryman, *Un-American*, pp. 32-33; Shannon, *Decline*, pp. 83-85; Wilson Record, *Race and Radicalism: The Communist Party and the NAACP in Conflict* (Ithaca: Cornell University Press, 1964), pp. 138, 150.
112. Shannon, *Decline*, p. 84.
113. John N. Thomas, *The Institute of Pacific Relations* (Seattle: University of Washington, 1974), pp. 51, 62-63.
114. Freeland, pp. 215-16.
115. Bontecue, p. 204.
116. *Loyalty*, p. 110.
117. Freeland, pp. 224-25; MacDougall, pp. 398-99.
118. Edwin P. Hoyt, *Paul Robeson* (Cleveland: World Publishing, 1967), pp. 205-16.
119. Freeland, pp. 217-19, 292-98; Chase, p. 68; Goodman, p. 207.
120. SICH, pp. 416-26.
121. See above, p. 248.
122. Freeland, p. 236; Ross, pp. 31-32; Phillips, p. 198.
123. MacDougall, pp. 325, 337-38, 341; Freeland, pp. 264, 286.
124. MacDougall, p. 684; Harper, p. 77.
125. MacDougall, p. 690.
126. MacDougall, pp. 215-19, 295-96, 362-69, 392-95, 401-07, 423-24, 446-49, 479-80, 638-39, 702-718, 785-92, 843-44; Schmidt, pp. 136, 306, 219-21; Athan Theoharis, "The Rhetoric of Politics: Foreign Policy, Internal Security and Domestic Politics in the Truman Era," *Politics and Policies of the Truman Administration*, ed. Bernstein, p. 221.
127. MacDougall, p. 791.
128. *Gideon's Army*, p. 403.
129. MacDougall, p. 391.
130. This and the next paragraph are based largely on MacDougall, *Gideon's Army*; Schmidt, *Wallace*; Ross, *Loneliest Campaign*; Howe and Coser, pp. 470-78; Shannon, *Decline*, pp. 164-82.
131. H. H. Wilson, "Introduction" to MacDougall, p. x.
132. Schmidt, p. 316.
133. Paterson, p. 14. An important new book which supports the general argument contained herein concerning the Wallace campaign, Richard J. Walton, *Henry Wallace, Harry Truman and the Cold War* (New York: Viking, 1976), was published too late for incorporation into the manuscript.
134. Emerson and Helfeld, pp. 20-21; Freeland, pp. 202-04; Andrews, pp. 74-77; Griffith, *Politics*, pp. 40-41.
135. On the Condon affair, see Goodman, pp. 231-38; Carr, pp. 131-53.
136. Goodman, p. 241; Barth, *Loyalty*, p. 211.
137. Ross, pp. 159-60, 183; Emerson and Helfeld, pp. 21-26; Goodman, pp. 244-60.
138. Cook, *FBI*, p. 86.
139. Ross, p. 192, Emerson and Helfeld, pp. 24-25; Harper, p. 76.
140. Goodman, p. 269; Alistair Cooke, *A Generation on Trial* (Baltimore: Penguin, 1968), p. 91; Carr, p. 128.
141. On the Hiss case, see Cooke, *A Generation on Trial;* Cook, *FBI*, pp. 286-312; Goodman, pp. 252-69.
142. Mazo and Hess, p. 58.

143. *Newsweek,* March 29, 1976.
144. Griffith, *Politics,* p. 47; Barth, *Loyalty,* pp. 164-75; Allen J. Matusow, ed., *Joseph R. McCarthy* (Englewood Cliffs, New Jersey: Prentice-Hall, 1970), p. 9.
145. Griffith, *Politics,* pp. 46-47; Tang Tsou, *America's Failure in China,* II (Chicago: University of Chicago, 1967), p. 528.
146. McWilliams, *Witch Hunt,* pp. 82-96; Gellhorn, *Security,* pp. 186-200.
147. Starobin, pp. 209-10; Countryman, *Un-American,* p. 378; McWilliams, *Witch Hunt,* pp. 190-91.
148. Larrowe, pp. 276, 299-300, 337.
149. Brown, pp. 64-70; Chase, p. 61; Gellhorn, *Security,* pp. 101-10. Gellhorn points that the armed services had conducted a limited screening operation of private employees before 1949, but the program appears to have been vastly expanded in late 1949.
150. Carr, p. 169.
151. Carr, pp. 168-86; Goodman, pp. 272-82; Stern, pp. 130-31.
152. Matusow, pp. 8-9.
153. Goldman, *Crucial,* p. 134.
154. Goldman, *Crucial,* p. 135-36; Matusow, pp. 8-9.
155. Goldman, *Crucial,* p. 137.
156. Matusow, p. 9.
157. Griffith, *Politics,* p. 48.
158. Harper, p. 128; Richard H. Rovere, *Senator Joe McCarthy* (Cleveland: Meridian Books, 1960), p. 135.
159. Rovere, pp. 135-36.
160. Harper, p. 133.
161. Mazo and Hess, pp. 128-29; Griffith, *Politics,* pp. 52-114.
162. Harper, p. 138; Griffith, *Politics,* pp. 88, 100-06; Walter and Miriam Schneir, *Invitation to an Inquest: Reopening the Rosenberg 'Atom Spy' Case* (Baltimore: Penguin, 1973), pp. 76-89; Walter Gellhorn, "A General View," *States,* ed. Gellhorn, pp. 358-92.
163. Griffith, *Politics,* pp. 117-22; Harper, pp. 149-61; Richard Longaker, "Emergency Detention: The Generation Gap, 1950-1971," *Western Political Quarterly,* 27 (September, 1974), pp. 395-408; William R. Tanner and Robert Griffith, "Legislative Politics and 'McCarthyism': The Internal Security Act of 1950," *Specter,* eds. Griffith and Theoharis, pp. 172-89.
164. A short summary of the Internal Security Act can be found in Chase, pp. 27-32, 68-70.
165. *SICH,* pp. 416-27.
166. *SICH,* pp. 659-62; *SICFR,* pp. 55-56.
167. Longaker "Emergency," pp. 399-400.
168. As a result of this program, about three thousand eight hundred of the maritime labor force were denied clearance by the end of 1955, about half of whom were seaman, who were thus totally barred from practicing their profession on American ships. The procedures followed by the Coast Guard in implementing the program were particularly obnoxious, with charges generally limited to stereotyped accusations of communism and hearings held at which the Coast Guard presented no evidence or witnesses. These procedures were found so inadequate that in 1956 a federal district court ordered the Coast Guard to give adequate notice of specific charges and invalidated all suspended licenses until new procedures were instituted. In 1968, the Supreme Court invalidated the entire program in *Schneider* v. *Smith,* ruling that the Magnusson Act failed to contain any provisions which authorized the government to "probe the reading habits, political philosophy, beliefs and attitudes on social and economic issues of prospective seamen on our mershant vessels" (Brown, pp. 71-73; Emerson, *System,* pp. 36-7, 190-91).
169. Bontecue, pp. 290-92.
170. Griffith, *Politics,* pp. 115-16; Phillips, p. 374.
171. Ronald J. Caridi, *The Korean War and American Politics: The Republican Party as a Case Study* (Philadelphia: University of Pennsylvania Press, 1968), pp. 97-100.
172. Mazo and Hess, p. 72; Griffith, *Politics,* pp. 122-23; Richard M. Fried, "Electoral Politics and McCarthyism: The 1950 Campaign," *Specter,* eds. Griffith and Theoharis.
173. Fried, "Electoral Politics;" Harper, pp. 171-72; Griffith, *Politics,* pp. 125-26;

Countryman, *Un-American,* p. 328; Donald J. Kemper, *Decade of Fear: Senator Hennings and Civil Liberties* (Columbia: University of Missouri Press, 1965), pp. 27-32.
174. Fried, "Electoral Politics," p. 222.
175. Griffith, *Politics,* pp. 131-87; Rovere, pp. 119-80; Goodman, pp. 297-320; Schneir and Schneir, pp. 119-74.
176. The most influential treatment along these lines is Walter and Miriam Schneir, *Invitation to an Inquest.*
177. Schneir and Schneir, p. 170.
178. Herbert S. Parmet, *Eisenhower and the American Crusades* (New York: MacMillan, 1972), p. 259.
179. *LAT,* November 24, 1975.
180. *New Republic,* February 14, 1976.
181. Parmet, pp. 92-97; Mazo and Hess, pp. 76-89.
182. Stern, pp. 196-97; Parmet, pp. 127-33; Mazo and Hess, pp. 91-125; Griffith, *Politics,* pp 188-95.
183. Griffith, *Politics,* p. 195.
184. Griffith, *Politics,* p. 58; Harper, pp. 128-29, 138, 145; Richard Longaker, *The President and Civil Liberties* (Ithaca: Cornell University Press, 1961), p. 60.
185. Griffith, *Politics,* pp. 88-89; Fred J. Cook, *The Nightmare Decade: The Life and Times of Senator Joe McCarthy* (New York: Random House, 1971), pp. 259-61.
186. Lowenthal, pp. 448, 450-51.
187. Phillips, p. 376; Griffith, *Politics,* pp. 146-51.
188. Harper, pp. 174-82.
189. Harper, pp. 222-23.
190. Harper, pp. 223-24.
191. Longaker, *President* pp. 60-61; Cook, *Nightmare,* p. 347; Harper, p. 220.
192. Cook, *Nightmare,* pp. 346-47.
193. Theoharis, *Seeds,* p. 137.
194. Theoharis, *Seeds,* pp. 136, 141-42.
195. Tanner and Griffith, p. 187.
196. Bontecue, pp. 69-72; Chase, p. 42; Griffith, *Politics,* p. 141.
197. Leonard B. Boudin, "The Right to Travel," *The Rights of Americans,* ed. Norman Dorsen (New York: Vintage, 1972), pp. 384-87; Chase, p. 31; Cushman, *Civil Liberties,* pp. 209-10.
198. Barth, *Loyalty,* p. 6.
199. Brown, p. 175.
200. On the 1952 Immigration Act, see Chase, pp. 70-73; Emerson, Haber and Dorsen, pp. 320-28.
201. Stone, *Haunted,* pp. 30-35.
202. C. Herman Pritchett, *Civil Liberties and the Vinson Court* (Chicago: University of Chicago, 1954), pp. 100-14; Murphy, *Constitution,* pp. 305-06.
203. Pritchett, *Civil Liberties,* pp. 305-06; Murphy, *Constitution,* p. 306.
204. *Civil Liberties,* pp. 101-02.
205. Caughey, *In Clear,* p. 95.
206. *INS,* 1956, pp. 96-97; see Chapter 6, footnote 32.
207. Emerson, *System,* pp. 150-51; Longacker, *President,* pp. 84-85; Caughey, *In Clear,* pp. 181-82.
208. Chase, pp. 7, 30; Emerson, *System,* p. 133; Robert Mollan, "Smith Act Prosecutions: The Effects of the *Dennis* and *Yates* Decisions," University of Pittsburgh Law Review, 1126 (June, 1965), pp. 707-10; Carr, p. 10.
209. Brown, pp. 365-70.
210. John W. Spanier, *The Truman-MacArthur Controversy and the Korean War,* (New York: Norton, 1965), p. 134; Tsou, pp. 558-62.
211. Johnson, *1600,* p. 246.
212. Latham, p. 305; Griffith, *Politics,* p. 87.
213. Chase, pp. 47-48; Brown, pp. 77-81; Parmet, pp. 254-55.
214. Alonzo Hamby, "The Vital Center, the Fair Deal and the Quest for a Liberal Political Economy," *AHR,* 77 (June, 1972) p. 674.
215. Hamby, p. 674; Harper, p. 252.
216. For example, Agar, pp. 153-56; Johnson, *1600,* pp. 287-95.
217. Johnson, *1600,* p. 292.

218. *Eisenhower*, p. 267.
219. Parmet, p. 164; Davis, *But We Were Born Free*, pp. 17-18.
220. Agar, p. 152.
221. Parmet, pp. 233-34.
222. Brown, pp. 367-68; Kahn, pp. 247-56; Ross Terrill, "When America 'Lost' China: The Case of John Carter Vincent," *The Atlantic* (April, 1968), pp. 78-86; Griffith, *Politics*, pp. 133-35; Parmet, pp. 234-36.
223. Parmet, pp. 237-40; Griffith, *Politics*, p. 199.
224. On the VOA and IIA hearings, see Latham, pp. 323-49; Goldman, *Crucial*, pp. 252-53; Griffith, *Politics*, pp. 212-16; Alan Barth, *Government by Investigation* (New York: Viking, 1955), pp. 45-57.
225. Latham, p. 326.
226. Latham, pp. 332, 338.
227. On June 14, 1953, Eisenhower seemingly rebuked McCarthy by telling a Dartmouth College audience, "Don't join the book burners." However, despite the fact that communications to the White House applauded his statement by better than ten to one, Eisenhower told a press conference three days later that he had not ordered any policy changes and that if the State Department was "banning a book which is an open appeal to everybody in these foreign countries to be communist, then I would say that falls outside of the limits in which I was speaking, and they can do as they please to get rid of them." Later, when told that Dashiell Hammett's detective stories were among the books that had been discarded, Eisenhower said he wouldn't have done that (Goldman, *Crucial*, pp. 253-55; Parmet, pp. 262-63).
228. Griffith, *Politics*, p. 217; Barth, *Government*, pp. 58-59; Telford Taylor, *Grand Inquest: The Story of Congressional Investigations* (New York: Ballantine, 1961), pp. 133-43.
229. Stone, *Haunted*, p. 35.
230. INS, 1956, p. 97. See Chapter six, footnote 32.
231. Chase, pp. 45-57; Brown, pp. 31-34; Parmet, pp. 256-57.
232. Kemper, p. 81.
233. Kahn, pp. 257-61; John Finney, "The Long Trial of John Paton Davies," *New York Times Magazine* (August 31, 1969), pp. 9ff; Brown, pp. 368-69.
234. Kahn, p. 33.
235. Kemper, p. 82; Johnson, *1600*, p. 289; Parmet, p. 382; Latham, p. 369.
236. Johnson, *1600*, p. 290.
237. Mollan, pp. 709-10; Emerson, Haber and Dorsen, pp. 193-94.
238. Nelson Rockefeller, *Report to the President by the Commission on CIA Activities Within the United States* (New York: Manor, 1975), pp. 101-15; SICSR, pp. 565-635.
239. Rockefeller, pp. 105-06, 115.
240. Ungar, *FBI*, pp. 445-46.
241. Donner, "Electronic Surveillance," pp. 20-22.
242. Griffith, *Politics*, p. 292; Chase, pp. 33-34.
243. The 1954 Act is summarized in Chase, pp. 32-33, 62-63.
244. Emerson, *System*, p. 150.
245. On the labor provisions of the Communist Control Act, see Brown, p. 76; Chase, p. 63. On subsequent legal actions taken by the Eisenhower administration, see F. S. O'Brien, "The 'Communist-Dominated' Unions in the United States Since 1950," *LH*, 12 (Summer, 1971), pp. 184-209.
246. See Stern, *The Oppenheimer Case*; Parmet, pp. 342-44, 385-87.
247. *First Principles*, 1 (January, 1976), p. 1.
248. Griffith, *Politics*, pp. 201-03; Parmet, pp. 241-46.
249. Latham, pp. 348-49; Barth, *Government*, pp. 53-57.
250. Parmet, pp. 64-65; Griffith, *Politics*, pp. 229-32.
251. Parmet, pp. 265-66; Griffith, *Politics*, pp. 231-32; Mazo and Hess, p. 134.
252. On the general subject of congressional investigations of "subversion," see Taylor, *Grand Inquest*; and Barth, *Government By Investigation*.
253. Goodman, pp. 500-10.
254. Griffith, *Politics*, p. 328. These figures include multiple investigations by the same committees.
255. Chase, pp. 34-35.

256. Carr, p. 273; Barth, *Government*, pp. 22, 81.
257. Barth, *Government*, p. 85.
258. Goodman, pp. 325-52.
259. Goodman, p. 330.
260. Goodman, p. 332; Brown, pp. 100-02.
261. Taylor, p. 12.
262. Barth, *Government*, p. 160.
263. On HUAC during this period, see Carr, *The House Committee on Un-American Activities;* Goodman, pp. 167-366; Frank J. Donner, *The Un-Americans* (New York: Ballantine, 1961); Carl Beck, *Contempt of Congress* (New Orleans: Phauser Press, 1959).
264. Carr, p. 280; Donner, *Un-Americans*, p. 64.
265. Donner, *Un-Americans*, p. 61.
266. Donner, *Un-Americans*, pp. 40-41.
267. Donner, *Un-Americans*, pp. 142-47.
268. Cushman, *Civil Liberties*, p. 199; Donner, pp. 163-66, 294-96.
269. Carr, pp. 259-60.
270. Goodman, p. 200; Carr, p. 269.
271. Cushman, *Civil Liberties*, p. 200.
272. On communist informers, see Herbert Packer, *Ex-Communist Witnesses* (Stanford: Stanford University Press, 1962).
273. Chase, p. 7; Cook, *FBI*, p. 44.
274. Zechariah Chafee, "Thirty-Five Years with Freedom of Speech," *Freedom*, ed. Nelson, p. 338.
275. Lowenthal, p. 459.
276. Emerson, Haber and Dorsen, p. 392.
277. Davis, *But We Were Born Free*, p. 49.
278. *Truman*, p. 191.
279. Donner, *Un-Americans*, pp. 147, 154; Parmet, p. 255; Brown, p. 80; Mangione, pp. 298-301; Griffith, *Politics*, p. 83; Countryman, *Un-American*, pp. 286-331; Mollan, p. 715; Caughey, *In Clear*, pp. 180-81; Emerson, Haber and Dorsen, pp. 172-73, 392-3.
280. The best study of this general subject is Gellhorn, *The States and Subversion*. See also William Prendergast, "State Legislatures and Communism: The Current Scene," APSR, 44 (September, 1950), pp. 556-74. On particular states, see Barrett, *The Tenney Committee* (California); Countryman, *Un-American Activities in the State of Washington;* Chamberlain, *Loyalty and Legislative Action* (New York); and Robinson, *Anti-Sedition Legislation and Loyalty Investigations in Oklahoma*.
281. Robert Griffith, "American Politics and the Origins of 'McCarthyism'," *Specter*, eds. Griffith and Theoharis, p. 15.
282. ISS lists and categories all state laws dealing with "internal security and subversion" by state but does not give the dates the various laws were passed. To construct this table it was necessary to look up the laws listed in the statute books of each state in order to determine the date of passage. All state laws which are quoted in the following pages are excerpted and cited in full in this source.
283. Kathleen L. Barber, "The Legal Status of the Communist Party: 1965," *Journal of Public Law*, 15 (1965), p. 103; Robinson, pp. 42-44; Edward L. Barrett, Jr., "California," William Prendergast, "Maryland," Mowitz, "Michigan," all in *States*, ed. Cellhorn, pp. 51, 155-56, 202.
284. *Civil Liberties*, p. 201.
285. Brown, p. 104; Henry Steele Commager, *Freedom, Loyalty, Dissent* (New York: Oxford University Press, 1954), p. 83; Gellhorn, "General View," *States*, ed. Gellhorn, p. 369; Taylor, p. 12; Chamberlain, pp. 192-93.
286. Chamberlain, pp. 197-98.
287. Prendergast, "Maryland," pp. 140-83; Brown, p. 103; Gellhorn, "General View," p. 361.
288. Chase, p. 2.
289. Brown, pp. viii, 18; Cushman, *Civil Liberties*, p. 174; Kemper, p. 117; Stern, p. 474; Caughey, "McCarthyism Rampant," *Pulse*, ed. Reitman, p. 170.
290. Prendergast, "State Legislatures," p. 561.
291. Caughey, *In Clear*, p. 11; Brown, p. 15; Glenn Abernathy, *The Right of As-*

sembly and Association (Columbia: University of South Carolina Press, 1961), p. 207.
292. Caughey, "McCarthyism Rampant," pp. 169-71.
293. Hymen, *To Try*, p. 338. For an exhaustive account of loyalty oaths required of teachers, see Joseph E. Bryson, *Legality of Loyalty Oath and Non-Oath Requirements for Public School Teachers* (Asheville, North Carolina: Miller Printing, 1963).
294. Prendergast, "Maryland;" Mowitz, "Michigan," both in *States*, ed. Gellhorn, pp. 166, 206; Robinson, p. 48.
295. Countryman, *Un-American*, p. 161; Barrett, *Tenney*, p. 42; Biddle, *Fear*, p. 143.
296. See, respectively, Countryman,*Un-American Activities in the State of Washington;* Barrett, *The Tenney Committee;* and E. Houston Harsha, "The Broyles Commission," *States*, ed. Gellhorn, pp. 54-139.
297. Countryman, *Un-American*, p. 150.
298. Barrett, *Tenney*, p. 45.
299. Barrett, *Tenney*, pp. 68, 75.
300. Countryman, *Un-American*, p. 159; Barrett, *Tenney*, p. 20.
301. Barrett, *Tenney*, p. 340.
302. Ingrid W. Scobie, "Jack B. Tenney and the 'Parasitic Menace': Anti-Communist Legislation in California, 1940-1949," *PHR*, 43 (May, 1974), p. 190.
303. Countryman, *Un-American*, pp. 186-285; Barth, *Loyalty*, pp. 228-31; McWilliams, *Witch Hunt*, pp. 139-70.
304. Barrett, *Tenney*, p. 175.
305. Gardner, *The California Oath Controversy;* John W. Caughey, "Farewell to California's 'Loyalty' Oath," *PHR*, 38 (May, 1969), pp. 123-28.
306. Chafee, "Thirty Five Years," *Freedom*, ed. Nelson, pp. 333-34.
307. On the Oklahoma investigation, see Robinson, pp. 31-35; McWilliams, *Witch Hunt*, pp. 339-40; Gellhorn, "General View," pp. 366-67.
308. Robinson, pp. 21, 33-34.
309. See Harsha, "Broyles Commission."
310. Harsha, p. 66.
311. Harsha, p. 89.
312. Harsha, p. 97.
313. Harsha, p. 103.
314. Harsha, p. 139.
315. Harsha, p. 127.
316. Countryman, *Un-American*, pp. 163-85, 329.
317. Robinson, p. 42.
318. Robinson, pp. 43, 45.
319. Harsha, p. 135; Barrett, *Tenney*, p. 314.
320. Barrett, "California," p. 48.
321. Barrett, "California," p. 51.
322. Barrett, "California," pp. 49-51; Gardner, pp. 146-205.
323. Horowitz, pp. 233-46; Schneir and Schneir, p. 81; Gellhorn, "General View," pp. 383-85.
324. The Birmingham and local repressive ordinances are reprinted in Fund for the Republic, *Digest*, pp. 455-72. See also Emerson, Haber and Dorsen, pp. 209-10; and Robert Cushman, "Local Government and Loyalty Problems," *The American City* (December, 1951), p. 169.
325. Biddle, *Fear*, p. 31.
326. Emerson, Haber and Dorsen, pp. 209-10; Caughey, *In Clear*, p. 4; Robert MacIver, *Academic Freedom in Our Time* (New York: Columbia University Press, 1955), pp. 35, 43.
327. Commager, *Freedom, Loyalty*, p. 21; MacDougall, p. 408; James Aronson, *The Press and the Cold War* (Boston: Beacon, 1973), p. 152; Manchester, p. 581; MacIver, p. 35; Goldman, *Crucial*, pp. 238-59; Wittner, p. 219; Stefan Kanfer, *A Journal of the Plague Years* (New York: Atheneum, 1973), p. 151.
328. Caughey, *In Clear*, p. 11; Brown, p. 9; Hoyt, p. 151; Manchester, p. 582; Kanfer, p. 150; Henry S. Commager, *Freedom and Order* (Cleveland: World Publishing, 1966), p. 103; Robinson, pp. 39-40; Robin Brooks, "Domestic Violence and America's Wars," *Violence*, eds. Graham and Gurr, pp. 542, 549.
329. MacDougall, p. 401.

330. On Peekskill, see Hoyt, pp. 184-92; Abernathy, pp. 43-49; Hofstadter and Wallace, pp. 365-69.
331. Hofstadter and Wallace, p. 365.
332. Caughey, "McCarthyism Rampant," pp. 172-73.
333. Brown, p. 122; McWilliams, *Witch Hunt,* p. 195; Goodman, p. 239.
334. On the blacklists in the communications industries, see Merle Miller, *The Judges and the Judged: The Report on Blacklisting in Radio and Television* (Garden City: Doubleday, 1952); Kanfer, *A Journal of the Plague Years;* Brown, pp. 157-63; Millard Lampell, "I Think I Ought to Mention I Was Blacklisted," *Thirty Years of Treason,* ed. Eric Bentley (New York: Viking, 1973), pp. 700-08; Goodman, p. 378.
335. Les K. Adler, "The Politics of Culture: Hollywood and the Cold War," *Specter,* ed. Griffith and Theoharis, p. 249.
336. Adler, p. 259.
337. Wittner, p. 217.
338. Brown, pp. 146-50; Hoyt, pp. 209-10; Aronson, pp. 60, 82, 133-36, 140-46; Ross Y. Koen, *The China Lobby in America* (New York: Harper & Row, 1974), pp. 130-31; Thomas, pp. 126-27.
339. Barth, *Government,* p. 172; Goodman, pp. 327-28.
340. Goodman, pp. 325-32; "Academic Freedom and Tenure in the Quest for National Security," AAUP Bulletin, 42 (Spring, 1956), pp. 49-107, discusses many of the most important cases. For a general discussion of the problem, see MacIver, *Academic Freedom in our Time.*
341. Barth, *Government,* p. 171.
342. Harsha, p. 81.
343. McWilliams, *Witch Hunt,* pp. 214-18; "Academic Freedom and Tenure in the Quest for National Security," pp. 70-71.
344. Commager, *Freedom Loyalty, p.* 20; Kemper, p. 45; Cook, *Nightmare,* pp. 340-41. For a general discussion of the reluctance of lawyers to defend political dissidents during the McCarthy period, see Milnor Alexander, "The Right to Counsel for the Politically Unpopular," *Law in Transition Quarterly,* 22 (1962), pp. 19-45; Jonathan D. Casper, "Lawyers and Loyalty-Security Litigation," *Law and Society Review,* 3 (1969); Jonathan D. Casper, *The Politics of Civil Liberties* (New York: Harper & Row, 1972), pp. 75-79.
345. Brown, pp. 109-16.
346. Brown, pp. 115-16; Goodman, pp. 313-14; Murphy, *Constitution,* p. 175.
347. Shannon, *Decline,* p. 45; Howe and Coser, p. 457; O'Brien, "Communist," p. 185; Chase, pp. 61-62.
348. Chase, p. 34.
349. David Oshinsky, "The CIO and the Communists," *Specter,* eds. Griffith and Theoharis, p. 139.
350. O'Brien, "Communist," pp. 184-88; Oshinsky, pp. 116-51.
351. Oshinsky, p. 150.
352. O'Brien, "Communist," p. 205.
353. Rayback, p. 408.
354. Brown, p. 141; Chase, p. 64; O'Brien, "Communist," pp. 425-26; Rayback, pp. 425-26.
355. See MacDougall, *passim.*
356. Griffith, *Politics,* pp. 120-21; Tanner and Griffith, p. 183.
357. Tanner and Griffith, p. 184.
358. Griffith, Politics, *passim;* Barber, p. 102.
359. Griffith, *Politics,* pp. 120, 294.
360. Byse, pp. 507-08.
361. Prendergast, "Maryland," p. 155.
362. Barrett, *Tenney,* pp. 307-08.
363. Mary S. McAuliffe, "The Politics of Civil Liberties: The ACLU During the McCarthy Years," *Specter,* eds. Griffith and Theoharis, pp. 163-70.
364. See Pritchett, *Civil Liberties Under the Vinson Court.*
365. *Congress,* p. 77.
366. For discussion of these cases, see the appropriate index entries in Pritchett, *Civil Liberties;* Murphy, *Constitution;* Emerson, *System;* and Abraham, *Freedom.*
367. Shannon, *Decline,* p. 93; Chase, p. 7.

368. *American Communist Party*, p. 483.
369. Shannon, *Decline*, pp. 88, 218.
370. See Shannon, *Decline*, pp. 191-203, 227-48; Howe and Coser, pp. 478-90; Starobin, pp. 3-7, 195-205, 220-223.
371. *Decline*, p. 227.
372. *American Communism*, pp. 221-22.
373. Howe and Coser, pp. 483-84.
374. Shannon, *Decline*, p. 366.
375. Countryman, *Un-American*, pp. 150-52.
376. Wittner, pp. 151-239 (quotation, p. 222).
377. Gellhorn, *Security*, pp. 161-62.
378. McWilliams, *Witch Hunt*, p. 338.
379. On the effects of the Cold War atmosphere on science, see Gellhorn, *Security, Loyalty and Science;* Walter Gellhorn, "Security, Secrecy and the Advancement of Science," *Civil Liberties Under Attack*, ed. Clair Wilcox (Philadelphia: University of Pennsylvania Press, 1951), pp. 85-106; Barth, *Loyalty*, pp. 185-211; Stern, pp. 434-39.
380. Gellhorn, *Security*, pp. 93-94.
381. Stern, p. 285.
382. *Security*, p. 232.
383. Thomas, p. 34. On the IPR, see Thomas, *The Institute of Pacific Relations;* Koen, pp. 132-55; Latham, pp. 296-314.
384. Thomas, p. 129.
385. Thomas, p. 128.
386. Thomas, pp. 112-13,156-59; Thomas C. Reeves, *Freedom and the Foundation: The Fund for The Republic in the Era of McCarthyism* (New York: Alfred A. Knopf, 1969), p. 108.
387. See Reeves, *Freedom and the Foundation*.
388. *Loyalty*, pp. 36, 181, 195, 487-88.
389. Shannon, *Decline*, p. 361.
390. Cook, *Nightmare*, p. 17.
391. Brown, pp. 183-86; Stern, pp. 439-40; 481.
392. Miller, *Judges*, p. 144; *Chicago Sun-Times*, May 30, 1974; LAT, September 21, 1975; April 29, 1976.
393. Brown, pp. 183-86; Beck, p. 14.
394. Cook, *Nightmare*, pp. 547-48.
395. William Spinrad, *Civil Liberties*, (Chicago: Quadrangle, 1970), pp. 121-22.
396. *Loyalty*, pp. 188-89.
397. Goodman, p. 415.
398. Countryman, *Un-American*, p. 241.
399. Frank Askin, "Surveillance: The Social Science Perspective," *Columbia Human Rights Law Review*, 4 (1972), p. 87.
400. Marie Jahoda and Stuart W. Cook, "Security Measures and Freedom of Thought," *Yale Law Journal*, 61 (March, 1952).
401. Cook, *Nightmare*, p. 17.
402. Lampbell, p. 707.
403. Stone, *Truman*, pp. 100-01.
404. Bentley, pp. 604-05.
405. Brown, p. 191.
406. Cook, *Nightmare*, p. 20.
407. Jahoda and Cook, pp. 303-04, 318.
408. Jahoda and Cook, pp. 307-08, 314.
409. Jahoda and Cook, pp. 304, 308.
410. Charlotte A. and Herbert Kaufman, "Some Problems of Treatment Arising from the Federal Loyalty and Security Program," *American Journal of Orthopsychiatry*, 25 (October, 1953), p. 824.
411. Paul Chodoff, "Loyalty Programs and Mental Health in the Washington Area," *Psychiatry*, 16 (November, 1953), p. 399.
412. Phillips, p. 364; Barth, *Loyalty*, p. 132; Bontecue, p. 156.
413. *Federal*, pp. 155-56.
414. Biddle, *Fear*, p. 226; Stern, p. 473.
415. Paul Lazarsfeld and Wagner Thielens, Jr., *The Academic Mind* (Glencoe,

Illinois: Free Press, 1958). A summary appears in Joseph Lyford, "Social Science Teachers and the 'Difficult Years,'" *AAUP Bulletin,* 43 (December, 1957), pp. 636-45.

416. This figure is misleadingly low, since "conservative respondents" who "often remarked that they didn't need to be cautious because their thinking was in tune with the opinion prevailing in the community" are included (p. 87). In other words, those who agreed with repressive policies did not feel repressed!

417. Samuel A. Stouffer, *Communism, Conformity and Civil Liberties* (New York: Wiley, 1966), pp. 78, 80.

418. Massimo Teodori, eds., *The New Left: A Documentary History* (Indianapolis: Bobbs-Merrill, 1969), p. 9.

419. Jack Newfield, *A Prophetic Minority* (New York: Signet, 1967), p. 26.

420. Newfield, p. 28.

421. Cook, *Nightmare,* p. 19.

422. Kirkpatrick Sale, *SDS* (New York: Vintage, 1974), p. 692.

423. Teodori, p. 10.

424. James V. Compton, *Anti-Communism in American Life Since the Second World War* (St. Charles Missouri: Forum Press, 1973), p. 11; Brown, p. 190.

425. Robert Sklar, "Introduction," *Truman,* Stone, p. ix.

426. Wittner, p. 221.

427. *Witch Hunt,* p. 323; Caughey, "McCarthyism Rampant," pp. 164-65.

428. Caughey, "McCarthyism Rampant," p. 165; Arnold M. Rose, *The Power Structure* (New York: Oxford University Press, 1967), pp. 407, 444-45; Fred W. Friendly, *Due to Circumstances Beyond Our Control* (New York: Vintage, 1968), pp. 89, 91; Chase, p. 2.

429. *Freedom, Loyalty,* pp. 141-42.

430. Parmet, p. 576.

431. *In Clear,* p. 120.

432. Ekirch, *Decline,* p. 321; Parenti, *Anti-Communist,* p. 81.

433. *Roots of War* (Baltimore: Penguin, 1972), p. 175.

434. *Coming Apart: An Informal History of America in the 1960's* (New York: Quadrangle/New York Times, 1971), p. 46.

435. George Kahin and John W. Lewis, *The United States in Vietnam* (New York: Delta, 1967), pp. 157-59.

436. Brown, pp. 198, 365-70; Commager, *Freedom, Loyalty,* pp. 27-30; Cook, *Nightmare,* pp. 549-52; David Halberstam, *The Best and the Brightest* (New York: Random House, 1972), pp. 111-15, 323-27, 379-91.

437. Commager, *Freedom, Loyalty,* pp. 29-30.

438. Cook, *Nightmare,* p. 551.

439. Kahn, p. 7.

440. Koen, pp. 213-14.

441. Richard C. Kagen, "Introduction," *China Lobby,* Koen, p. xii.

442. *LAT,* March 6, 1975.

443. Halberstam, p. 189.

444. "How Could Vietnam Happen: An Autopsy," *Shaping,* eds. Abrams and Levine, pp. 683, 685.

445. *Papers on the War* (New York: Pocket Books, 1972), p. 91.

446. Kahin and Lewis, pp. 30-31; Halberstam, p. 120; Ellsburg, pp. 82-88. See above, p. 333.

447. Parmet, p. 357.

448. Parmet, pp. 374-75, 392.

449. *Kennedy* (New York: Bantam, 1966), p. 343.

450. *A Thousand Days* (New York: Fawcett, 1967), p. 317.

451. *A Thousand Days,* p. 446.

452. *Best,* p. 103.

453. New York Times, *The Pentagon Papers* (New York: Bantam, 1971), p. 150.

454. Quoted in Ellsberg, p. 100.

455. Quoted in *LAT,* April 13, 1975.

456. Halberstam, p. 298.

457. New York Times, *Pentagon Papers,* p. 426.

458. Ernest R. May, "Vietnam Fades as a Political Issue," *LAT,* April 13, 1975;

Jerome Slater, *Intervention and Negotiation: The United States and the Dominican Revolution* (New York: 1970), pp. 199-200.
459. Slater, p. 199.
460. Slater, pp. 31-32.
461. Ellsberg, p. 102.
462. Sanford J. Ungar, *The Papers and the Papers: An Account of the Legal and Political Battles Over the Pentagon Papers* (New York: Dutton, 1975), pp. 79, 126.
463. LAT, December 7, 1975.
464. Halberstam, p. 343.
465. "Legacies of the Cold War," *The Price of Liberty*, ed. Alan Reitman (New York: Norton, 1968), p. 60.
466. Caughey, *In Clear*, p. 134.
467. Spinrad, pp. 106-07. Robert M. Hutchins, Chancellor of the University of Chicago, said in 1949, "The miasma of thought-control that is now spreading over the country is the greatest menace to the United States since Hitler" (Harsha, p. 99).
468. *National Security and Individual Freedom* (Cambridge: Harvard University Press, 1955), p. 22.
469. "Freedom and Authority in the Amphibial State," *Midwest Journal of Political Science*, 1 (May, 1957), p. 41.
470. Quoted in C. Herman Pritchett, *Political Offenders and the Warren Court* (New York: Russell and Russell, 1967), pp. 19-20.
471. "Thirty-five Years," *Freedom*, ed. Nelson, p. 330.
472. Longaker, "Emergency," p. 402.
473. *Shadow and Substance* (London: Collier, 1969), p. 45.
474. Barth, *Loyalty*, p. 11.
475. Stern, pp. 479-83.
476. Millis, p. 66.
477. Stern, p. 475.
478. *Champaign-Urbana (Illinois) Courier*, January 9, April 15, 1974.
479. *SICFR*, pp. 38-67; *SICSR*, pp. 427-69.
480. *SICFR*, p. 48.
481. *SICFR*, p. 47.
482. *SICFR*, p. 175.
483. *SICFR*, pp. 46-47.
484. *SICFR*, pp. 319, 450-54.
485. *SICFR*, pp. 51-52.
486. *SICFR*, p. 40.

CHAPTER TEN

1. Rogin, *Intellectuals*, p. 232; Cook, *Nightmare*, pp. 461-62.
2. On the Army-McCarthy affair, see Griffith, *Politics*, pp. 244-69; Parmet, pp. 345-53, 272-75; Cook, *Nightmare*, pp. 463-519; Rovere, pp. 205-22.
3. Griffith, *Politics*, p. 248.
4. Griffith, *Politics*, p. 273.
5. Parmet, p. 353.
6. Griffith, *Politics*, p. 261.
7. Parmet, pp. 351, 374.
8. Griffith, *Politics*, pp. 264, 271, 279, 281.
9. Griffith, *Politics*, p. 264.
10. Griffith, *Politics*, pp. 264-65.
11. Griffith, *Politics*, p. 263.
12. Parmet, p. 382.
13. Brown, pp. 359-60; Griffith, *Politics*, pp. 305-06; Parmet, pp. 381-82.
14. *Reeves*, pp. 96-97; Caughey, *In Clear*, p. 179; Kemper, pp. 94-95.
15. Kemper, pp. 96-98; Caughey, *In Clear*, pp. 180-1.
16. Kemper, pp. 99-100; Reeves, pp. 131, 213.
17. Kemper, pp. 94, 111; Reeves, p. 131.

18. Link and Catton, pp. 730, 799-801; Griffith, *Politics*, p. 318; Wittner, p. 255.
19. For derivation of this table see Chapter Nine, footnote 282.
20. *INS*, 1972, p. 82. See Chapter Six, footnote 32.
21. Kemper, pp. 121, 127-28; Reeves, p. 203.
22. Stone, *Haunted*, p. 86.
23. Longaker, "Emergency," p. 400.
24. On the Warren Court, see Pritchett, *The Political Offender and the Warren Court*. For specific cases discussed below, see appropriate index entries in this book and in the sources cited in Chapter Nine, footnote 366.
25. Mollan, pp. 714-17,725-40.
26. See Walter F. Murphy, *Congress and the Court* (Chicago: University of Chicago Press, 1965).
27. Murphy, *Congress*, p. 111.
28. Murphy, *Congress*, pp. 97, 113, 172.
29. Mollan, pp. 717-20.
30. Emerson, Haber and Dorsen, pp. 172-73, 193-96; Shannon, *Decline*, pp. 72, 279. O'Brien "Communist," pp. 198-99, 203-04; Murray Kempton, *America Comes of Middle Age* (New York: Viking, 1972), pp. 7-12.
31. Department of Justice Press Release, November 18, 1974.
32. *SICH*, pp. 372-76, 408, 601, 819-20; *SICSR*, pp. 16-17, 28-29, 64-72; Howe and Coser, pp. 490-99, 555-71.
33. Goodman, pp. 508-18.
34. Goodman, pp. 367-434; Reeves, *passim*.
35. Barber, pp. 106, 109; Emerson, *System*, p. 171.
36. Emerson, Haber and Dorsen, p. 217.
37. Ronald L. Goldfarb, *The Contempt Power* (Garden City, New York: Doubleday, 1971), pp. 188-90.
38. These cases are discussed under the appropriate index entries in Emerson, *System*; Murphy, *Constitution*; and Abraham, *Freedom*.
39. In 1962, two workers for the Student Non-Violent Coordinating Committee (SNCC) were charged in Louisiana for criminal anarchy; the charges were later dropped. In 1963, four civil rights workers were charged with "inciting to insurrection" in Georgia, which carried the death penalty. A three-judge federal court later declared the statute involved unconstitutional and the four were released (Howard Zinn, *SNCC* [Boston: Beacon, 1965], pp. 17-74, 183).
40. Murphy, *Congress*, pp. 127-53.
41. Murphy, *Congress*, p. 141.
42. Parmet, p. 551.
43. Parmet, pp. 291-92.
44. Goodman, pp. 418-19; Cook, *FBI*, pp. 48-49.
45. The following cases are discussed in the sources cited in footnote 38 of this chapter.
46. See generally Newfield, *A Prophetic Minority*; Paul Jacobs and Saul Landau, *The New Radicals* (New York: Vintage, 1966); Teodori, *The New Left*; James P. O'Brien, "The Development of the New Left," *New Pilgrims*, ed. Altbach and Laufer, pp. 32-45; Jerome H. Skolnick, *The Politics of Protest* (New York; Ballantine, 1969), pp. 87-91; Sale, *SDS*, pp. 15-95.
47. Theodore H. White, *The Making of the President, 1960* (New York: Pocket Books, 1960), p. 307; Sorenson, p. 201.
48. Sorenson, p. 189.
49. *Constitution*, p. 354.
50. Teodori, pp. 21-22; Newfield, p. 30.
51. Zinn, *SNCC*.
52. Teodori, p. 477; Jacobs and Landau, pp. 10, 323.
53. Wittner, pp. 241-44.
54. Wittner, pp. 241, 249.
55. Nathan Glazer, quoted in Wittner, p. 258.
56. Wittner, pp. 258-61; Goodman, p. 441.
57. Wittner, pp. 265-67, 270, 273, 276.
58. Goodman, pp. 437-43.
59. Goodman, p. 438.

Notes (Ch. 10) 60-98 633

60. Sale, p. 46; Wittner, pp. 277-78.
61. On the San Francisco demonstrations, see Goodman, pp. 424-32; David Horowitz, *Student* (New York: Ballantine, 1962), pp. 67-105; David Horowitz and Fred Haines, "Black Friday," *Violence in America*, ed. Thomas Rose (New York: Vintage, 1970), pp. 240-56.
62. Sale, pp. 125-26; Jacobs and Landau, p. 326; Newfield, p. 29; James S. Turner, "Ohio State," *Protest!* ed. Foster and Long, pp. 351-58.
63. Sale, pp. 15-95; Jacobs and Landau, pp. 27-41.
64. Teodori, p. 20.
65. O'Brien, "Development," p. 34.
66. *A Thousand Days*, pp. 341-43.
67. Sorenson, pp. 286, 374; Schlesinger, *Thousand Days*, p. 628.
68. *Constitution*, p. 373.
69. Stern, pp. 454-55; Friendly, pp. 54-58, 67; Sorenson, pp. 286, 374.
70. Schlesinger, *Thousand Days*, pp. 628, 642; Emerson, *System*, p. 150; Barber, p. 106; Victor S. Navasky, *Kennedy Justice* (New York: Atheneum, 1971), pp. 42-43.
71. Mollan, pp. 740-47; Emerson, Haber and Dorsen, pp. 153-55.
72. Navasky, pp. 41-42; William W. Turner, *Hoover's FBI*, (New York: Dell, 1971), p. 183.
73. Jacobs and Landau, p. 325; Boudin, p. 390; Schlesinger, *Thousand Days*, pp. 342-43.
74. O'Brien, "Communist," pp. 198-99; Emerson, Haber and Dorsen, pp. 189, 194-96.
75. Frank Donner, "Political Informers," *Investigating*, eds. Watters and Gillers, p. 326; Turner, p. 188.
76. Navasky, pp. 44-48.
77. *SICSR*, pp. 465-68, 744-45.
78. *SICSR*, pp. 84-88, 105-11.
79. John Elliff, "Scope and Basis of FBI Data Collection," *Investigating*, ed. Watters and Gillers, p. 248; Turner, *Hoover's FBI*, pp. 188-90; Cook, *FBI*, pp. 380-81; Donner, "Political Informers," p. 326.
80. *SICH*, p. 408.
81. *SICH*, pp. 821-26.
82. FBI documents disclosed in 1976 revealed that the FBI's New York office recommended commendations and cash incentive awards for a team of six FBI agents who had carried out fifteen burglaries directed against the SWP in 1964 and 1965. The documents stated that the burglars had obtained "extremely valuable information" about the SWP, including data on membership, finances, and activities. Department of Justice Press Release, November 18, 1974; Lat, March 29, July 29, 1976; NYT, June 28, July 29, 1976; SICSR, p. 363.
83. Aryeh Neier, *Dossiers: The Secret Files They Keep on You* (New York: Stein & Day), pp. 149-50.
84. *LAT*, April 8, November 12, 1975; *SDET*, March 19, 1975; Berman and Helperin, pp. 26-30. The SWP has published a collection of FBI documents relating to COINTELPRO obtained in a court suit filed in 1974 in Cathy Perkus, ed., *COINTELPRO: The FBI's Secret War on Political Freedom* (New York: Monad, 1975).
85. Navasky, pp. 74-86, 152-74; *SICFR*, pp. 60-64, 233-34.
86. *SICSR*, pp. 79-181; *SICFR*, pp. 219-23.
87. *SICFR*, pp. 52-53, 60-61; *SICSR*, pp. 92-93.
88. Berman and Halperin, p. 88.
89. Goodman, p. 435.
90. Goodman, pp. 435-52; Cook, *FBI*, pp. 49-50; Turner, 134-36.
91. *CL*, November, 1962.
92. Emerson, *System*, pp. 150-52; *CL*, April, 1965.
93. *CL*, June, 1961; May, 1963.
94. For discussion of these cases, see appropriate index entries in the sources cited in this chapter, footnote 38.
95. Abraham, p. 166.
96. Quoted under lists of statutes by state in *ISS*.
97. See above, pp. 409-10.
98. *CL*, November, 1963; April, 1965.

99. *CL*, March, 1965.
100. *CL*, May, 1960; November, 1961; February, 1962.
101. *CL*, September, 1961.
102. *CL*, June, 1962; October, 1963.
103. *CL*, February, April, October, 1960; March, May, October, November, 1961; February, 1962; October, 1963.
104. On the growth of the right wing during the early 1960's, see Daniel Bell, ed., *The Radical Right* (Garden City: Doubleday, 1964); Arnold Forster and Benjamin R. Epstein, *Danger on the Right* (New York: Random House, 1964); Lipset and Raab, pp. 248-337; George Thayer, *The Farther Shores of Politics* (New York: Simon and Schuster, 1968), pp. 13-299.
105. H. Frank Way, *Liberty in the Balance* (New York: McGraw-Hill, 1964), pp. 64-66; Thayer, pp. 13-33; *Newsweek*, August 25, 1975; *CL*, October, 1966; April, October, 1972; January, March, 1973, May, 1975.
106. *Liberty*, p. 66.

CHAPTER ELEVEN

1. Writing in 1971, the presidentially-appointed Scranton Commission stated, "The crisis on American campuses has no parallel in the history of the nation. This crisis has roots in divisions of American society as deep as any since the Civil War. The divisions are reflected in violent acts and harsh rhetoric; and in the enmity of those Americans who see themselves as occupying the opposing camps. Campus unrest reflects and increases a more profound crisis in the nation as a whole" (William Scranton, *Report of the President's Commission on Student Unrest* [New York: Avon, 1971, p. 1]).
2. Elaboration on these points would take this study too far afield. However, some useful sources would include the following. On the 1960's generally, O'Neill, *Coming Apart: An Informal History of America in the 1960's*. On black militancy, Zinn, *SNCC*; Gene Marine, *The Black Panthers* (New York: Signet, 1969); Otto Kerner, *Report of the National Advisory Commission on Civil Disorders* (New York: Bantam, 1968). On the crime problem and the mood of the country during the 1968 election, Richard Harris, *The Fear of Crime* (New York: Praeger, 1960); Ramsay Clark, *Crime in America* (New York: Pocket Books, 1971); Theodore H. White, *The Making of the President, 1968* (New York: Pocket Books, 1970).
3. On the growth of the "New Left," see Sale, *SDS*; Newfield, *A Prophetic Minority*; Jacobs and Landau, *The New Radicals*; Teodori, *The New Left*; Foster and Long, eds., *Protest!*; O'Brien, "The Development of the New Left;" Seymour M. Lipset and Sheldon S. Wolin, eds., *The Berkeley Student Revolt* (Garden City, New York: Doubleday, 1965); and Thomas Power, *The War at Home* (New York: Grossman, 1973). On Weatherman, see Harold Jacobs, ed., *Weatherman* (San Francisco?: Ramparts, 1970); Thomas Powers, *Diana: The Making of a Terrorist* (New York: Bantam, 1971); and Stuart Daniels, "The Weatherman," *Government and Opposition*, 9 (Autumn, 1974), pp. 430-59.
4. *War*, p. 217.
5. Sale, pp. 242, 335, 664; Paul Hoffman, *Moratorium: An American Protest* (New York: Tower, 1970), pp. 181-82, 192.
6. Sale, pp. 305, 445, 485, 512, 632, 636-37.
7. Robert J. Glessing, *The Underground Press in America* (Bloomington: Indiana University Press, 1971), pp. 6, 10.
8. Michael Ferber and Staughton Lynd, *The Resistance* (Boston: Beacon, 1971), pp. 281-84.
9. Sale, p. 446; Skolnick, pp. 66-67, 245-48.
10. Department of Justice Press Release, November 18, 1974.
11. Sale, p. 637.
12. Sale, p. 633; Manchester, p. 1198.
13. *LAT*, January 14, 1976.
14. Sale, pp. 427, 503, 632.
15. Sale, p. 632; Scranton, p. 38; Rockefeller, p. 290.
16. *LAT*, June 1, 1975; Manchester, pp. 1199, 1212.

17. Roger Lewis, *Outlaws of America* (Baltimore: Penguin, 1972), p. 175.
18. *SDET*, January 1, 23, 1976; *LAT*, January 14, 1976; *NYT*, February 15, 1976.
19. Sale, p. 630.
20. Sale, pp. 632-33, 636.
21. Goodman, pp. 520-22.
22. *CL*, January, 1965; Goodman, pp. 407-08, 412.
23. *CL*, March, 1964.
24. Theodore White, *The Making of the President, 1964* (New York: Signet, 1966); Powers, *War*, pp. 1-17; O'Neill, pp. 107-21; *CL*, January, 1965.
25. Paul Harris, "Black Power Advocacy: Criminal Anarchy or Free Speech," *California Law Review*, 56 (1968), pp. 702-40; Newfield, p. 121.
26. Newfield, pp. 112-21; Sale, pp. 135-36; John T. Elliff, *Crime, Dissent and the Attorney General* (Beverly Hills: Sage, 1971), pp. 86-89.
27. Newfield, p. 120.
28. Newfield, p. 121.
29. Sale, p. 134.
30. On the Free Speech Movement, see Lipset and Wolins, eds., *The Berkeley Student Revolt*; Sheldon S. Wolin and John H. Schaar, *The Berkeley Rebellion and Beyond* (New York: *New York Review of Books*, 1970); Sale, pp. 162-67; Powers, *War*, pp. 30-34.
31. Powers, *War*, p. 31.
32. Wolin and Schaar, p. 70.
33. Sale, pp. 119-21; *CL*, December, 1966; July, 1967.
34. *CL*, September, 1965; Elliff, *Crime*, p. 167.
35. Lawrence R. Velvel, "Freedom of Speech and the Draft Card Burning Cases," *Kansas Law Review*, 16 (January, 1968), pp. 149-79; "Note: Constitutional Law — Freedom of Speech — Desecration of National Symbols as Protected Political Expression," *Michigan Law Review*, 66 (March, 1968), pp. 1054-55. As Velvel notes, "The only real difference between the burning law and the possession regulation is that the latter does not happen to have been specifically designed to stifle a particular form of protest" (p. 173).
36. Ted Finman and Stewart MacAulay, "Freedom to Dissent: The Vietnam Protests and the Worlds of Public Officials," *Wisconsin Law Review*, 1966 (Summer, 1966), pp. 676-77.
37. Finman and MacCaulay, pp. 675-76; Sale, p. 230; Eliff, *Crime*, pp. 159-60.
38. Emerson, *System*, p. 91; Parenti, *Anti-Communist Impulse*, p. 13.
39. Sale, p. 230.
40. Halberstam, pp. 453, 623-24.
41. *The Tragedy of Lyndon Johnson* (New York: Dell, 1974), p. 592. Goldman comments that Johnson "did not really believe" in the right to dissent, "or to put the matter more precisely, he believed in the right but did not believe that it should be exercised" (p. 490).
42. See below, pp. 454-57.
43. *CL*, January, 1966; Commager, *Freedom and Order*, p. viii.
44. Finman and MacAulay, p. 633; Newfield, p. 156; Ed Cray, *The Enemy in the Streets* (Garden City: Doubleday, 1972), p. 223; Paul Chevigny, *Police Power* (New York: Vintage, 1969), pp. 170-73.
45. Goodman, pp. 473-81; Davis, *Fear*, p. 358.
46. Goodman, p. 483; Emerson, *System*, p. 91; Parenti, *Anti-Communist Impulse*, p. 13.
47. Finman and MacAulay, p. 676; Sale, p. 275.
48. Epstein, p. 40; Turner, pp. 185-86; Sale, p. 456; Powers, *Diana*, pp. 63-64.
49. On the growth of the protest movement, see Sale, pp. 203-455.
50. *CL*, May, 1968; Elliff, *Crime*, p. 167.
51. *CL*, May, 1968; July, 1970.
52. *CL*, December, 1967; August, 1969; January, 1973; October, 1974.
53. Sale, pp. 383-86; Powers, *War*, pp. 239-42; Committee of the Professions, "Pentagon: War and Protest," *Violence*, ed. Rose, pp. 257-68.
54. Jessica Mitford, *Trial of Dr. Spock* (New York: Vintage, 1970), pp. 53-54.
55. *CL*, June, 1969, March, 1970; Sale, p. 407.

56. Mitford, pp. 55-56.
57. On the Spock-Coffin case, see Mitford, *Trial of Dr. Spock;* Charles Goodell, *Political Prisoners in America* (New York: Random House, 1973), pp. 220-26; Paul Lauter and Florence Howe, "Notes on a Political Trial," *Trials of the Resistance* (New York: Vintage, 1970), pp. 74-105.
58. Mitford, pp. 65-70-1, 191.
59. Mitford, p. 67.
60. Goodell, p. 226.
61. Emerson, *System,* pp. 146-47; Abraham, pp. 174-75.
62. Emerson, *System,* p. 145; Sale, p. 443.
63. On the anti-riot act, see Richard Harris, *Justice* (New York: Avon, 1970), p. 169; Emerson, *System,* pp. 408-09; Epstein, pp. 38-53.
64. Epstein, pp. 43-49; Harris, *Justice,* pp. 63-65. The Anti-Riot Act is perhaps the most potentially repressive law on the federal statute books today. Its particular utility — and danger — is that it can be applied in the future to whatever group happens to become unpopular. Thus, the bill was originally designed to hamper black militants, but was quickly applied to anti-war activists. As Otto Kircheimer notes in discussing repressive legislation generally, "A blueprint has been made available and specifications will be inserted if and when required" (*Political Justice,* p. 44).
65. Harris, *Justice,* pp. 176-77; Scranton, pp. 221-22; Sale, pp. 444, 645, *NYT,* December 29, 1972.
66. Harris, *Fear; SICSR,* pp. 288-89.
67. *SICSR,* p. 301.
68. Navasky and Lewin, p. 300; Harris, *Fear,* pp. 50, 110; Harris, *Justice,* p. 122; Marwick, "Electronic Surveillance," p. 8; Donner, "Electronic Surveillance," p. 29; *SICSR,* pp. 68-69; *SICFR,* pp. 110-11.
69. *SICFR,* pp. 105, 110; *SICSR,* pp. 146-54, 301.
70. *SICH,* pp. 480, 495, 508-09; Ungar, *FBI,* pp. 288-89.
71. *SICH,* pp. 476-77.
72. *SICH,* pp. 378-83, 602-04; *SICSR,* pp. 66-69, 470-75; Goodman, pp. 466-67; Department of Justice Press Release, November 18, 1974.
73. Chalmers, pp. 344-96; Thayer, pp. 85-106; Don Whitehead, *Attack on Terror: The FBI Against the Ku Klux Klan in Mississippi* (New York: Funk and Wagnalls, 1970).
74. Department of Justice Press Release, November 18, 1974; *LAT,* August 16, November 30, December 3, 1975; *SDU,* August 17, 1975; *SDET,* August 16, December 3, 1975; *Newsweek,* August 25, December 1, 1975; Berman and Helperin, pp. 27-30; *SICH,* pp. 403-05, 513-27; *SICSR,* pp. 251, 847.
75. *LAT,* February 13, 1975; Whitehead, *Attack,* pp. 289-301.
76. Goodman, p. 469.
77. Goodman, p. 469.
78. *SICSR,* pp. 139, 475-84; *SICFR,* pp. 71, 83.
79. *SICSR,* p. 483.
80. *SICSR,* p. 480 (quotation); Elliff, *Crime,* pp. 84-86.
81. *SICH,* pp. 18-19, 763-65; Berman and Halperin, p. 28; *LAT,* May 24, 1975; *SICSR,* pp. 46, 59, 72; *SICFR,* pp. 214, 240-48; Frank J. Donner, "Let Him Wear a Wolf's Head: What the FBI Did to William Albertson," *CLR,* 3 (April/May, 1976), pp. 12-22.
82. *SICH,* pp. 476-79, 638-40, 718-20; *SICFR,* pp. 119-20, 227-30; *SICSR,* pp. 483-89.
83. *SICSR,* p. 485; Sale, pp. 275-76, 328-29, 407, 499-500.
84. *SICSR,* pp. 249, 487-90.
85. *SICH,* pp. 383-85; *SICSR,* pp. 179-80.
86. *SICFR,* pp. 83-84; *SICSR,* pp. 491-93.
87. *SICFR,* p. 75; *SICSR,* pp. 252-55.
88. *SICH,* pp. 386-92; *SICFR,* pp. 87-88.
89. *SICSR,* p. 188.
90. *SICSR,* p. 220.
91. Department of Justice Press Release, November 18, 1974; *SICH,* pp. 393-95; *SICSR,* pp. 516-17.
92. *SICFR,* pp. 214-15.
93. *SICH,* pp. 669-675, 684-85; *SICSR,* p. 506.

94. *SICFR*, p. 281.
95. *SICH*, p. 601.
96. *SICSR*, pp. 510-12, 516-18.
97. *SICSR*, p. 514.
98. *SICSR*, pp. 515-16; see above, pp. 312, 323-24.
99. *SICSR*, p. 573.
100. *SICSR*, pp. 574, 631.
101. U.S., Senate, *Hearings Before the Select Committee to Study Governmental Operations with Respect to Intelligence Activities, Volume Four; Mail Opening*, 94th Congress, First Session, pp. 246-48.
102. *SICSR*, p. 632.
103. *SICSR*, pp. 721-26; Rockefeller, pp. 151-59.
104. Rockefeller, pp. 130-50; *SICSR*, pp. 681-732.
105. *SICSR*, pp. 692, 694.
106. *SICSR*, p. 716.
107. Rockefeller, p. 149.
108. *SICSR*, pp. 743-52.
109. *SICSR*, pp. 749-50.
110. *SICSR*, p. 750.
111. On Army Intelligence, see Christopher Pyle, "CONUS Intelligence: The Army Watches Civilian Politics," *Blowing the Whistle*, ed. Charles Peters and Taylor Branch (New York: Praeger, 1972); Christopher Pyle, "Spies Without Masters: The Army Still Watches Civilian Politics," *CLR*, 1 (Summer, 1974), pp. 38-49; Nick Egleson, "The Surveillance Apparatus," *State Secrets: Police Surveillance in America* (New York: Holt, Rinehart & Winston, 1974), 1 7-16; U.S., Senate, Subcommittee on Constitutional Rights, *Army Surveillance of Civilians: A Documentary Analysis*, 92nd Congress, 1st Session, 1971; Berman and Halperin, pp. 50-62; *SICSR*, pp. 785-834.
112. *SICFR*, p. 167.
113. *SICFR*, p. 799.
114. U.S., Senate, Subcommittee on Constitutional Rights, *Army Surveillance*, p. 97.
115. *LAT*, August 26, 1975.
116. *SICH*, p. 534; Rockefeller, pp. 117-21; SICSR, pp. 495-505.
117. *Making, 1968*, p. 301.
118. *SICH*, pp. 483-84.
119. Commager, "Is Freedom Dying in America?" *Look*, July 14, 1970.
120. December 23, 1974.
121. On the general atmosphere which characterized the Nixon administration, see J. Anthony Lukas, *Nightmare: The Underside of the Nixon Years* (New York: Viking, 1976); Jonnathan Schell, *The Time of Illusion* (New York: Knopf, 1976); Rowland Evans and Robert D. Novak, *Nixon in the White House* (New York: Vintage, 1971); Theodore H. White, *Breach of Faith: The Fall of Richard Nixon* (New York: Atheneum, 1975); Dan Rather and Gary P. Gates, *The Palace Guard* (New York: Warner, 1975).
122. *The White House Transcripts* (New York: Bantam, 1974), p. 108.
123. *White House Transcripts*, p. 63.
124. Harris, *Justice*, p. 176.
125. Jules Witcover, *White Knight: The Rise of Spiro Agnew* (New York: Random House, 1972), p. 309.
126. New York Times, *The Watergate Hearings*, (New York: Bantam, 1973), p. 500; Goodell, pp. 170-71.
127. Goodell, p. 186.
128. Berman and Halperin, p. 2.
129. *SICFR*, pp. 3, 6-7, 165, 169, 267.
130. Among the more important sources on the FBI during the Vietnam War are the following *SICH, SICFR; SICSR*, pp. 1-677; Ungar, *FBI*; Berman and Halperin, pp. 14-50; Frank Donner, "Theory and Practice of American Political Intelligence," *New York Review of Books*, April 22, 1971; Emerson, "FBI," Elliff, "Scope," Donner, "Political Informers," and Robert Wall, "Why I Got Out of It," all in *Investigating the FBI*, eds. Watters and Gillers; Turner, *Hoover's FBI*; Cowan, et al., *State Secrets*; Robert Wall, "Special Agents for the FBI," *New York Review of Books*, January 27, 1972; Department of Justice Press Release, November 18, 1974; *LAT*, April 8, October

6, September 25, November 12, 19, 1975; *SDET,* March 19, June 25, 1975; *NYT,* November 19, 1975; *Newsweek,* December 1, 1975; Perkus, ed. *COINTELPRO.*
131. *SICH,* p. 15.
132. Elliff, *Crime,* p. 234.
133. Ungar, *FBI,* p. 140.
134. *SICFR,* p. 70.
135. Emerson, "FBI," p. 228.
136. Donner, "Theory and Practice," p. 27; *SICSR,* pp. 228, 260; *SICFR,* p. 167.
137. *SICFR,* pp. 6, 19; *LAT,* September 25, 1975, February 24, 1976.
138. *SICSR,* pp. 508, 522.
139. *SICH,* p. 693; *SICSR,* pp. 509-10, 518.
140. *SICSR,* pp. 525-28; *SICH,* pp. 700-02; Cowan, et al, *State Secrets,* pp. 195-96.
141. *SICSR,* pp. 530-31.
142. *SICSR,* p. 534; *SICH,* p. 682.
143. Wall, "Why I Got Out of It," pp. 342-45; *LAT,* September 25, 1975; Turner, *Hoover's FBI,* p. 192; Emerson, "FBI," p. 227; *SDET,* September 5, 1975, May 22, 1976; Elliff, "Scope," p. 241; *SICSR,* pp. 245-47.
144. Cowan, et al., *State Secrets,* p. 157.
145. *SICSR,* p. 24.
146. *SICFR,* pp. 357-58.
147. *SICSR,* pp. 301, 319-20; *SICFR,* p. 110.
148. *SICSR,* pp. 338-39.
149. Epstein, pp. 108-13; Harvey Silverglade, "The 1970's: A Decade of Repression," *With Justice for Some,* eds. Bruce Wasserstein and Mark J. Green, (Boston: Beacon, 1972) pp. 371-72.
150. *NYT,* June 20, 1972.
151. Hoffman, pp. 195, 200; *Chicago SunTimes,* August 5, 1972; *NYT,* November 2, 1972, October 16, 1973, January 4, 1974; Athan Theoharis, "Will Congress Stop the Snooping?" *The Nation,* February 2, 1974, pp. 410-41.
152. Goodell, pp. 7, 261; *Chicago Sun-Times,* April 26, 1971; August 20, 1972; Turner, *Hoover's FBI,* p. 102.
153. Ungar, *The Papers and the Papers,* p. 133.
154. *Champaign-Urbana Courier,* October 15, 1973.
155. *SICSR,* pp. 542-48.
156. *SICSR,* p. 548.
157. *SICSR,* pp. 546-47, 551-52, 557; *LAT,* October 23, 1975.
158. *SICH,* p. 601.
159. Department of Justice Press Release, November 18, 1974; *SICSR,* pp. 3-77.
160. *SICFR,* pp. 139, 216.
161. *SICSR,* pp. 3, 7.
162. *SICSR,* pp. 11, 64.
163. Perkus, *COINTELPRO; LAT,* April 8, October 6, November 12, 1975; *SDET,* March 19, June 25, 1975; Neier, pp. 146-48.
164. *SICSR,* pp. 31, 45-46; *SICFR,* p. 15.
165. *SICSR,* p. 38.
166. *NYT,* June 25, July 11, August 22, 1976.
167. *SICSR,* p. 533.
168. *SICSR,* p. 13.
169. *LAT,* July 1, 1976 *NYT,* July 1, 9, August 3, 22, 28, September 5, 29, October 21, 1976.
170. *NYT,* June 27, August 1, 1976; *LAT,* August 1, 4, 8, 9, 1976; Donner, "Theory and Practice," p. 30. *SICSR,* pp. 237-38. In September, 1976, a Denver grand jury indicated the FBI informant in connection with the July, 1976 SWP burglary (*NYT,* September 24, 1976).
171. See NYT, August 9, 1974; *Champaign-Urbana Courier,* September 10, 1973; Frank J. Donner and Richard I. Lavine, "Kangaroo Grand Juries," *The Nation,* November 29, 1973, p. 529; Powers, *Diana,* p. 83; Sale, pp. 552-53; Lukas, pp. 37, 196, Ungar, *FBI,* p. 478.
172. *LAT,* September 25, 1975. Generally on the subjects of *agents provocateur,* see Paul Chevigny, *Cops and Rebels* (New York: Pantheon, 1972) and Gary T. Marx, "Thoughts on a Neglected Category of Social Movement Participant: *The Agent Pro-*

vocateur," *American Journal of Sociology,* 80 (September, 1974), pp. 402-42.

173. *LAT,* August 1, 8, 1976; *NYT,* August 1, 1976; *International Herald-Tribune,* August 3, 1976. This informer is the same person indicted by the Denver grand jury in September 1976, in connection with burglarizing an SWP office (see footnote 170, above, and the accompanying text).

174. For discussion of the Ward incident, see *Chicago Sun-Times,* May 30, 1971; Chevigny, *Cops,* pp. 258-59; Donner, "Hoover's Legacy," p. 693.

175. *Chicago Sun-Times,* May 30, 1971; Donner, "Hoover's Legacy," p. 693; Pinkney, p. 198.

176. *SDU,* May 26, August 6, September 14, 1972, January 11-18, 1976; *NYT,* January 24, 1975; *New York Review of Books,* March 18, 1976; *LAT,* January 26, 1976.

177. Frank Donner, "The Agent Provocateur as Folk Hero," *CL,* September, 1971; Chevigny, Cops, pp. 250-51.

178. See pp. 492-93, below.

179. *Seattle Times,* December 7, 1970; *NYT,* December 6, 8, 1970.

180. *NYT,* May 21, August 9, 1973.

181. *NYT,* May 20, 1973; Jacobs, pp. 464-70.

182. See p. 441, above.

183. *I Lived Inside the Campus Revolution* (New York: Barnes & Noble, 1970).

184. See pp. 488-89, below.

185. See Nelson and Ostrow, *The FBI and The Berrigans,* especially pp. 142, 169, 266; and *NYT,* March 23, 1972.

186. Chevigny, *Cops,* pp. 251-52; *CL,* July, 1973.

187. *SICSR,* p. 699.

188. *SICSR,* pp. 699-705; Rockefeller, pp. 130-50.

189. *SICSR,* pp. 720, 751.

190. *NYT,* June 26, 1975; *LAT,* March 6, 1975.

191. *SICSR,* p. 707.

192. *SICSR,* p. 630.

193. *SICFR,* p. 108.

194. *SICSR,* pp. 743-52.

195. *SICSR,* pp. 741-42.

196. *SICSR,* pp. 789, 806.

197. Goodell, pp. 267-68; Ira Glasser, "The Constitution and the Courts," *What Nixon is Doing to Us,* eds. Alan Gartner, Colin Greer and Frank Riesman (New York: Harper & Row, 1973), p. 174.

198. *SICSR,* pp. 823, 831; Berman and Halperin, pp. 63-65.

199. *SICSR,* pp. 815-22, 827; *SDET,* November 26, 27, 1975; Halperin and Berman, pp. 65-68;*NYT,* May 15, 1976.

200. *SICSR,* pp. 828, 832.

201. *SICSR,* pp. 850-1.

202. Berman and Halperin, p. 90; *Chicago Daily News,* August 6, 1973. On the SSS, see Berman and Halperin, pp. 90-92; *SICSR.* pp. 876-90; *LAT,* November 18, 1974, January 26, March 22, October 3, 1975; *SDU,* October 3, 1975; *SDET,* October 3, 1975.

203. *SICSR,* pp. 881-82, 885.

204. *SICSR,* p. 884.

205. *SWR,* pp. 213-19; *HIR,* pp. 207-11; Lukas, pp. 24-26; Berman and Halperin, pp. 89-90.

206. Lukas, p. 26.

207. Judith F. Krug and James A. Harvey, *American Libraries* (October, 1970), pp. 843-45.

208. Donner, "Theory and Practice," p. 27; Egleson, "Surveillance Apparatus," *State Secrets,* Cowan, et al., pp. 5-7.

209. On the Secret Service, see Berman and Halperin, pp. 80-83; *LAT,* March 14, 1975; *SDET,* May 24, 1976.

210. Associated Press Dispatch in Daily Illini (Champaign, Illinois), March 24, 1971. The supervisor of the CSC operation, while talking to a reporter, waved his hand toward a pile of publications and said, "That's what we check. It's full of subversive material. Note the Commie art. Picasso and others all tied into communism."

211. *LAT*, January 8, 1975.
212. On the Huston Plan, see Rockefeller, pp. 119-28; *SICSR*, pp. 921-86; Lukas, pp. 31-36; Berman and Halperin, pp. 149-53; Ungar, *FBI*, pp. 471-82. Huston Plan documents are reprinted in *The Watergate Hearings*, pp. 748-59.
213. *SICSR*, pp. 974-80; see pp. 472, 478-79, 502-03.
214. *SICSR*, p. 981.
215. Manchester, p. 1208.
216. *SDET*, May 19, 1975.
217. *Glory*, p. 1208.
218. On the Chicago conspiracy trial, see Epstein, *The Great Conspiracy Trial*. Excerpts from the trial record can be found in Mark Levine, et al. eds., *The Tales of Hoffman* (New York: Bantam. 1970).
219. Daniel Walker, *Rights in Conflict* (New York: Bantam, 1968).
220. The testimony of the prosecution featured a string of about 30 police undercover agents and infiltrators.
221. After the trial was over, government prosecutor Thomas Foran admitted that on the night of the worst violence, August 28, 1968, "the police moved in and got even for what they had been taking from the demonstrators for three days. After that the police felt great. They were smiling and waving and you could see that it was a great psychological thing for them" (Epstein, p. 297).
222. *Champaign-Urbana (Illinois) News Gazette*, November 22, 1972; *NYT*, December 7, 1973.
223. On the Berrigan case, see Nelson and Ostrow, *The FBI and the Berrigans*.
224. See pp. 476-77, above.
225. *Chicago Sun-Times*, February 18, 1973.
226. See Frank Donner and Eugene Cerruti, "The Grand Jury Network," *The Nation*, January 3, 1972, pp. 11-12.
227. *NYT*, June 28, 1973.
228. Nelson and Ostrow, p. 197.
229. On the Pentagon Papers case, see Peter Schrag, *Test of Loyalty* (New York: Simon and Schuster, 1974); and Ungar, *The Papers and the Papers*.
230. *CL*, January, 1965.
231. Schrag, p. 166.
232. Tom Wicker, "The Iron Curtain," *NYT*, November 19, 1972.
233. Schrag, pp. 260-72. Notes taken by White House domestic affairs advisor John Erlichmann at a meeting in the White House in July, 1971, included a notation to the effect that Secretary of Defense Melvin Laird had informed the White House that 98 percent of the Pentagon Papers could have been declassified. A tape-recorded conversation of July 24, 1971, quotes President Nixon as stating with regard to a published report about classified disarmament information, "This does affect the national security — this particular one. This isn't like the Pentagon Papers" (*NYT*, July 23, 1973).
234. Barry Sussman, *The Great Coverup: Nixon and the Scandal of Watergate* (New York: Signet, 1974), p. 214. On the attempt to discredit Ellsberg, see *SWR*, pp. 64-71, 196-202. In the course of the "plumbers" investigation of Ellsberg, two "psychiatric profiles" of Ellsberg were obtained from the CIA, along with technical assistance such as disguises and false identification which were used in connection with the burglary. On June 3, 1974, Colson pleaded guilty to obstructing justice by engaging in a scheme to prepare, obtain and leak derogatory information about Ellsberg. On July 12, 1974, Erlichman and plumbers G. Gordon Liddy, Bernard Barker and Eugenid Martinez were convicted of conspiracy to violate Ellsberg's civil rights in connection with the burglary. Erlichman was also found guilty of three counts of perjury.
235. See Fred Cook, "Justice in Gainesville," *The Nation*, October 1, 1973; *NYT*, September 1, 1973; *Newsweek*, August 20, 1973; Donner and Lavine, pp. 530-31.
236. Cook, "Justice," p. 301.
237. See above, p. 468.
238. See generally, Bernard Weiner, "What, Another Conspiracy?" *The Nation*, November 2, 1970; and Bernard Weiner, "The Orderly Perversion of Justice," *The Nation*, February 1, 1971. See also the sources cited in footnote 179 of this chapter.
239. Weiner, "Orderly," p. 146.

240. *Seattle Times,* February 23, 1972; *Washington Post,* March 29, 1972; *NYT,* March 27, 1973.

241. See generally on this topic, Donner and Cerruti, "The Grand Jury Network;" Donner and Lavine, "Kangaroo Grand Juries;" David J. Fine, "Federal Grand Jury Investigations of Political Dissidents," *Harvard Civil Rights — Civil Liberties Law Review,* 7 (1972), pp. 432-77; Goodell, pp. 233-54; Glasser, "Constitution," pp. 175-78; James R. Bendat, "A Disturbing Shift in the Grand Jury's Role," *LAT,* October 2, 1974; Paul Cowan, "Inquisition in the Courtroom," *State Secrets,* Cowan et al., pp. 86-104; Ungar, *FBI,* pp. 280-90; Judy Mead, "Grand Juries," *First Principles,* 2 September, 1976).

242. Cowan, "Inquisition," p. 94. The figure of 400 indictments has been published in a variety of sources cited in the preceding footnote. A column by Jack Anderson in the *San Diego Evening Tribune* of June 11, 1976, also cited this figure, and added that only 10% of the 400 indictments led to convictions. Judy Mead, in her article cited in the preceding note, also reported the 400 indictment figure, and stated that only 15% of the indictments had led to convictions or please to lesser charges. In response to a letter from the author of the present book, Guy Goodwin, a lawyer with the Criminal Division of the Justice Department, who formerly had been in charge of the grand juries as head of the special litigation section of the now-abolished Internal Security Division of the Justice Department, denied the accuracy of thse figures and the charges of political intimidation with regard to the purpose of the grand juries. In a letter to the author dated October 1, 1976, Goodwin stated that "approximately one hundred" indictments had resulted from the grand juries and that "approximately seventy-five percent of these cases resulted in convictions." Goodwin maintained that "Contrary to some published reports, the use of the federal grand jury was properly limited solely to the investigation of criminal conduct in those federal districts in which there was proper venue after receipt from Federal investigative agencies of evidence that such criminal conduct had ocurred. The federal grand jury was never utilized for any other purpose and information elicited in its investigation of criminal conduct was not disseminated for other uses." The present author stands by his interpretation.

243. Donner and Cerruti, pp. 6-7; Glasser, "Constitution," pp. 177-78.

244. Donner and Lavine, pp. 522-24.

245. *LAT,* October 2, 1974.

246. Bendat, *LAT,* October 2, 1974. In one case, five witnesses who refused to testify before a Phoenix grand jury served five months in jail for contempt (until the grand jury expired) and upon their release were issued subpoenas from a new grand jury. Faced with the possibility of perpetual jail, they agreed to testify (Donner and Cerruti, p. 7).

247. Donner and Lavine, p. 528.

248. For general comments on Nixon and the press, see Theodore H. White, *The Making of the President, 1972* (New York: Atheneum, 1973), pp. 261-86; William E. Porter, *Assault on the Media: The Nixon Years* (Ann Arbor: University of Michigan Press, 1976).

249. Porter, *Assault,* pp. 244-49.

250. Witcover, pp. 311-15; Fred Powledge, *The Engineering of Restraint* (Washington, D.C.: Public Affairs Press, 1971), p. 43; Porter, *Assault,* pp. 42-57.

251. Powledge, pp. 11-14; Nat Hentoff, "Subverting the First Amendment," *What Nixon,* eds. Gartner, Greer and Riessman, pp. 218-22.

252. Powledge, p. 45; *CL,* December, 1972; *Newsweek,* October 16, 1972.

253. See Ungar, *The Papers and the Papers;* Abraham, pp. 156-58; and Porter, *Assault,* pp. 81-110.

254. Hentoff, pp. 222-23.

255. Ungar, *Papers,* p. 117.

256. Powledge, p. 7.

257. Powledge, p. 8. In March, 1970, Nixon's eldest daughter, Tricia, told a newsman that Agnew's effect on the news media, "helping it to reform itself" had been "amazing. . . . I think they've taken a second look. You can't underestimate the power of fear," (Cook, *Nightmare,* pp. 577-78).

258. Lukas, p. 275.

259. *Newsweek,* April 24, 1972; *NYT,* December 22, 1973; Porter, *Assault,* pp. 154-59.

260. *Newsweek,* November 12, 1973; Porter, *Assault,* pp. 251, 300-04.
261. *Champaign-Urbana Courier,* August 8, 1973; Sussman, pp. 102, 135-37.
262. On the November moratorium, see Hoffman, *Moratorium;* Elliff, *Crime,* pp. 211-23.
263. Hoffman, p. 145.
264. *CL,* July, 1972.
265. Neier, p. 146.
266. On Mayday, see Glasser, pp. 161-63; Cray, pp. 234-35; Sussman, pp. 210-12; Lewis Chester, at al., *Watergate: The Full Inside Story* (New York: Ballantine, 1973), pp. 33-35; Lukas, pp. 9-11.
267. Quoted in Glasser, p. 162.
268. Cray, p. 235; *CL,* November, 1974; *LAT,* January 17, 1975.
269. *LAT,* July 31, 1975.
270. See pp. 441, above.
271. See p. 369, above.
272. Donner, "Hoover's Legacy," p. 686; *CL,* July, 1972; *Champaign-Urbana Courier,* June 2, 5, 1974. Between the issuance of the Nixon order and the Congressional action of October, 1972, the SACB investigated 233 groups left over from the old Attorney General's list, only to find they were all defunct (or at least were no longer at previous mailing addresses, since the "investigation" apparently consisted of sending letters to the organizations). When the SACB expired in 1973, it had spent over $7 million since 1950 without ever succeeding in making any person or group register with the Attorney General (*St. Louis Post-Dispatch,* February 25, 1973).
273. Glasser, pp. 172-3.
274. *CL,* August, 1969; November, December, 1970; January, March, July, 1971; Frank J. Donner, "Political Intelligence: Cameras, Informers and Files," *CLR,* I (Summer, 1974), p. 25; ACLU, *Academic Freedom and Civil Liberties of Students in Colleges and Universities* (New York: ACLU, nd), p. 25; *LAT,* October 16, 1974, May 28, 1975.
275. See generally *SWR,* pp. 182-88, 192-96, 216-18, 226-27; Chester, pp. 53-55; Lukas, pp. 13-17, 64-65, 107-08.
276. The Secret Service refused to testify before the Senate Watergate Committee about the Donald Nixon wiretap, claiming it was within the "protective function" of the Secret Service and therefore privileged. Nixon publicly stated that the purpose of the tap was to monitor conversations with his brother in which persons might try to exert "improper influence." The House Judiciary Committee concluded that the Secret Service has "no legal jurisdiction to wiretap for such purposes" (*SWR,* pp. 187-88; *HIR,* p. 220). Caulfield told the Senate Watergate Committee that White House Special Counsel Charles Colson wanted him to burglarize the Brookings Institution to determine if the organization had obtained a copy of the Pentagon Papers in the summer of 1971. According to Caulfield, Colson suggested to him that the Brookings Institution be firebombed, and that the "fire regulations in the District of Columbia could be changed to have the FBI respond and obtain the file in question." Caulfield said he reported this to White House Counsel John Dean. Dean said he took the suggestion seriously enough to fly immediately from Washington to the Western White House at San Clemente, California, where Dean said he convinced Erlichman to call Colson and cancel the idea. In the meantime, Ulasewicz visited the Brookings Institution in order to determine the physical layout of the building (Lukas, pp. 89-90).
277. See *HIR,* pp. 51-52, 212-18, 222-28; Chester, pp. 25-27, 49-50; Lukas pp. 41-46.
278. *HIR,* p. 218.
279. *SWR,* pp. 58-64, 210-14; Chester, pp. 79-85; Lukas, pp. 12-13, 18-22.
280. *SWR,* pp. 64-70, 196-202; Chester, pp. 63-72; Sussman, pp. 212-30; Lukas, pp. 68-108.
281. See *SWR,* pp. 247-310; Chester, pp. 110-12; Lukas, pp. 150-68.
282. *SWR,* p. 309.
283. See Chester, pp. 132-62; Sussman, pp. 1-13, 41-110; *HIR,* pp. 51-199; Lukas, pp. 169-209; *SWR,* pp. 51-53, 74-88.
284. Reprinted in *HIR,* p. 3-8.
285. "Watergate: A Skeptical View," *New York Review of Books,* September 20,

1973, p. 3.

286. Transcript, "Surveillance: Who's Watching," broadcast by National Educational Television, January 31, 1972, p. 2.

287. Egleson, p. 16.

288. See *CL*, December, 1968; February, 1969; September, 1974; Donner, "Theory and Practice," pp. 28-29.

289. Harris, *Justice*, p. 126.

290. Donner, "Theory and Practice," p. 28.

291. Egleson, p. 21; *LAT*, April 11, 1975.

292. Donner, "Political Intelligence," p. 21; *CL*, October, 1970.

293. *CL*, July, 1970.

294. *NYT*, March 29, 1971.

295. Donner, "Theory and Practice," p. 36.

296. Donner, "Theory and Practice, p. 30.

297. Donner, "Theory and Practice," p. 28.

298. "Improper Police Intelligence Activities: A Report by the Extended March, 1975, Cook County Grand Jury," *First Principles*, I (January, 1976), pp. 3-11.

299. *Newsweek*, April 7, 1975; *Chicago Tribune*, March 23, 1975; *LAT*, November 11, 1975.

300. *LAT*, January 7, 18, 1975; *Baltimore Sun*, December 31, 1974; *SDET*, December 25, 1975.

301. *LAT*, September 24, 1975; *SDU*, May 17, 1976.

302. *LAT*, November 7, 1975; *NYT*, May 9, 1976.

303. Donner, "Theory and Practice," p. 31.

304. Donner, "Theory and Practice," p. 38; Egleson, p. 20.

305. "Improper Police Intelligence Activities," p. 6.

306. Neier, p. 146; *CL*, February, 1969.

307. Sale, p. 408; Barbara Herbert, "Jack Weatherford," *State Secrets*, Cowan, et al., p. 227.

308. "Improper Police Intelligence Activities," p. 7.

309. Donner, "Theory and Practice," p. 33; Levine, pp. 60-61.

310. Transcript, "Surveillance: Who's Watching," pp. 708; Donner and Lavine, p. 529.

311. *SDET*, October 16, 1975.

312. *Chicago Sun-Times*, April 13, 1975; *LAT*, April 13, 1975.

313. "Improper Police Intelligence Activities," p. 9.

314. Emma Rothschild, "Notes from a Political Trial," *Trials of the Resistance*, pp. 114-15.

315. See p. 491, above.

316. *NYT*, August 9, 1973.

317. *NYT*, October 31, 1970.

318. Chevigny, *Cops*, pp. 259-60.

319. A study published in 1969 comparing American police with police in Western European democracies concluded that in general American police practices offer a "startling contrast to the European picture of minimal police force," but that, "If the American police are prone to use violent and repressive tactics, American society offers them the means and the climate to do so. No other democratic nation compares to the United States in the acceptance and even glorification of violence as a way to solve problems" (George E. Berkley, *The Democratic Policeman* [Boston: Beacon, 1969], pp. 111, 197). In addition to overt physical violence against demonstrators, police repression during the Vietnam War era sometimes took the form of failing to protect demonstrators against vigilantes. Thus, in October, 1965, during an incident at the Oakland-Berkeley, California city line, Oakland police failed to interfere with a motorcycle gang which violently attacked an anti-war march. Eventually, Berkeley police moved in and arrested six of the attackers. In March, 1966, Boston police looked on while four draft card burners were savagely beaten on the steps of a courthouse by twenty-five high school students. In March, 1966, New York City police stood by while vigilantes attacked members of the anti-war DuBois Club, then arrested several club members who had been assaulted. In perhaps the most notorious of these episodes,

New York City police failed to interfere when "hard hat" construction workers went on a rampage on May 8, 1970, beating student war protesters with helmets, pliars and wrenches, invading a hall to force the raising of a flag from half staff to full staff, and invading Pace College and beating students there. Peter I. Brennan, president of the two hundred thousand member building and trades construction council, said the union leadership had nothing to do with the attack but condoned it as resulting from men being "fed up with the violence by anti-war demonstrators, by those who spit on the American flag and deserted it." Subsequently the construction workers' "hard hat" became a symbol of patriotism and Brennan organized nationwide demonstrations by construction workers in support of American foreign policy. On May 26, 1970, President Nixon called Brennan and other union leaders to the White House and accepted a "hard hat" from Brennan. Subsequently Brennan was appointed Secretary of Labor by Nixon (Skolnick, p. 360; Newfield, p. 157; MacAulay and Finman, p. 673; Cray, p. 223; Chevigny, *Police*, pp. 170-73; Fred J. Cook, "Hard Hats: The Rampaging Patriots," *Annual Editions: Readings in Government '72* [Guilford, Connecticut: Dushkin, 1972], pp. 14-20).

320. Skolnick, pp. 261-65; Rodney Stark, *Police Riots* (Belmont, California: Wadsworth, 1972), pp. 110-13, 163-66.
321. Skolnick, pp. 282, 289.
322. Walker, pp. 1, 5.
323. Walker, p. 1.
324. Cray, pp. 228-33; Skolnick, p. 247; Stark, pp. 23-32; *CL*, November, 1967.
325. Powers, *War*, p. 236. See also Rothschild, pp. 108-09; Sale, p. 375; Skolnick, p. 60; Ferber and Lynd, pp. 142-43.
326. As a result of the Oakland disorders, seven demonstration leaders were indicted for conspiring to commit misdemeanors, a charge which is a felony in California. The Alameda County district attorney explained, "Technically, a hundred or even a thousand of the demonstrators could have been indicted for their actions, but we simply don't have enough courts so we have to take the most militant leaders." The Oakland Seven were acquitted following a three-month trial (Rothschild, pp. 106-34, quotation, p. 318).
327. Sale, pp. 371-73; Long, "Wisconsin," *Protest!*, eds. Foster and Long, pp. 257-59.
328. Powers, *War*, pp. 244, 249.
329. Stark, p. 6; Skolnick, p. 360; *CL*, February, 1969.
330. Stark, p. 6; Skolnick, p. 347.
331. Pinkney, pp. 130-41; Cray, pp. 226-28; Daniel Bell, "Columbia and the New Left," *Black Power and the Student Rebellion*, eds. James McEvoy and Abraham Miller, (Belmont, California: Wadsworth, 1969), pp. 31-73.
332. Bell, "Columbia," p. 52.
333. *Crisis at Columbia* (New York: Vintage, 1968), p. 182.
334. Stark, pp. 4-5; Skolnick, pp. 247-48; *CL*, September, 1968.
335. Stark, pp. 32-54.
336. Stark, pp. 53-54.
337. Peggy Kerry, "The Scene in the Streets," *Government Lawlessness in America*, eds. Theodore Becker and Vernon G. Murray, (New York: Oxford University Press, 1971), pp. 59-68, quotation, p. 66.
338. Scranton, p. 416.
339. Pinkney, p. 178; Clark, p. 157.
340. Pinkney, p. 163; Harris, *Justice*, p. 176; Stark, pp. 6-7; Grover Lewis, "Prisoners of War in Sunny California," *Government Lawlessness*, eds. Becker and Murray, pp. 133-38; Wolin and Schaar, pp. 73-95.
341. *Newsweek*, January 6, 1975.
342. Quoted in Harris, *Justice*, p. 176.
343. Hofstadter and Wallace, p. 8; Elliff, *Crime*, pp. 203-04.
344. Sale, p. 641.
345. Sale, p. 608; Tom Thomas, "The Second Battle of Chicago," *Weatherman*, ed. Jacobs, p. 203.
346. Sale, p. 632; Pinkney, p. 194. Subsequently, the Santa Barbara County Sheriff's Department fired a police captain who had been involved in the riots, charging that he had dropped tear gas on demonstrators from helicopters in violation of Federal aviation regulations, had slapped handcuffed prisoners and had shown up at several

clashes with demonstrators wearing a filigreed Spanish sword and medieval spike-studded brass ball. In December, 1974, a federal judge ordered the arrest records of over six hundred persons arrested during a series of 1970 riots at the University of California at Santa Barbara erased, thereby officially eliminating the original arrests (*Newsweek*, November 29, 1971; *LAT*, December 10, 1974).

347. Sale, p. 632; *NYT*, October 31, 1970.
348. Scranton, pp. 233-410; *Chicago Sun-Times*, December 26, 1971.
349. *CL*, April, 1973; April, 1975; I. F. Stone, *The Killings at Kent State* (New York: Vintage, 1971), p. 124.
350. Scranton, p. 289; *CL*, April, 1975; *Newsweek*, November 25, 1974; *LAT*, October 21, 1974; August 28, 1975.
351. Scranton, pp. 411-65, quotation, p. 458.
352. Sale, p. 641.
353. *LAT*, September 1, 1975.
354. *Champaign-Urbana Courier*, July 12, 1973; *Newsweek*, November 27, 1972.
355. Emerson, *System*, pp. 68-69.
356. Powers, *Diana*, p. 114.
357. *CL*, September, 1971.
358. Lewis, p. 48; Laurence Leamer, *The Paper Revolutionaries: The Rise of the Underground Press* (New York: Simon and Schuster, 1972), p. 143.
359. Goodell, pp. 199-206.
360. Sostre remained in prison until he was released on parole in February, 1976, despite the recantation of the chief witness against him and the suspension and indictment on drug charges of the chief police witness against him. Subjected to searches of a type declared unconstitutional in a court case brought by Sostre against New York state, Sostre was charged with assaulting prison officers when he resisted the continued use of such searches after the court decision (Goodell, p. 196; Vincent Copeland, *The Crime of Martin Sostre* [New York: McGraw-Hill, 1970]; Amnesty International, *Report on Torture* [New York: Farrar, Straus and Giroux, 1975], p. 193; *NYT*, February 15, 1976).
361. "Theory and Practice," p. 37.
362. *CL*, May, 1971.
363. *CL*, February, 1967; September, October, 1970; February, May, 1971.
364. *NYT*, July 9, 1974.
365. Gerald Gunther and Noel T. Dowling, *Constitutional Law and Individual Rights, 1974 Supplement* (Mineola, New York: Foundation Press, 1974), pp. 307-14.
366. *NYT*, August 3, 1974; *SDET*, June 13, 1975.
367. See p. 434, above.
368. Harris, "Black Power," pp. 702; Emerson, *System*, pp. 755-56.
369. *CL*, October, 1967.
370. Emerson, *System*, p. 156.
371. Gene Lyons, "Letter from the Land of Opportunity," *New York Review of Books*, May 30, 1974, pp. 33-36.
372. Emerson, *System*, pp. 155-56.
373. Most of these cases are discussed in Haig Bosmajian, "Chief Justice Warren Burger and Freedom of Speech," *The Midwest Quarterly*, 15 (Winter, 1974), pp. 135-38; and William R. Thomas, *The Burger Court and Civil Liberties* (Brunswick, Ohio: King's Court, 1976), pp. 97-108.
374. Gunther and Dowling, pp. 277-78.
375. Gunther and Dowling, pp. 320-22.
376. *LAT*, May 30, 1975.
377. *CL*, September, 1967; September, 1968; January, April, 1973; Leamer, pp. 153-56.
378. Sale, p. 348.
379. Sale, pp. 532-33.
380. Ben A. Franklin, "Post Town Upset by Antiwar G.I.'s" *Government Lawlessness*, eds. Becker and Murray, pp. 329-31.
381. Jensen, *Price*, p. 305.
382. *CL*, October, 1969.
383. Goodell, pp. 187-93.

384. Leamer, pp. 125-27; Glessing, pp. 37, 67, 88-89, 103; John Burks, "The Underground Press," *The Age of Paranoia,* ed. Rolling Stone (New York: Pocket Books, 1972), pp. 21, 56-57; *CL,* October, 1969; *Wall Street Journal,* July 7, 1969.
385. Leamer, pp. 131-35; *Time,* March 23, 1970.
386. Leamer, pp. 138-41; Burks, pp. 55-56; *Wall Street Journal,* July 7, 1969.
387. Leamer, pp. 141-46.
388. Leamer, pp. 146-53.
389. *CL,* October, 1969; Glessing, p. 88; Burks, pp. 56-57.
390. Sale, pp. 443, 547; Scranton, p. 40; Bruce Wasserstein, "The Courts and the Campus," *With Justice For Some,* eds. Bruce Wasserstein and Mark J. Green (Boston: Beacon, 1972), p. 41; "Campus Confrontation: Resolution by Injunction," *Columbia Journal of Law and Social Problems,* 6, (1970), pp. 30-48; Mona G Jacqueny, *Radicalism on Campus, 1969-1971: Backlash in Law Enforcement and in the Universities* (New York: Philosophical Library, 1972), pp. 71-72.
391. Scranton, p. 147.
392. Scranton, pp. 221-22.
393. *Champaign-Urbana Courier,* December 14, 1973; *CL,* August, 1969; October, 1970; September, 1971.
394. Scranton, pp. 41-42.
395. Scranton, p. 126.
396. *Chicago Sun-Times,* February 16, March 15, 1967.
397. Scranton, p. 37.
398. Sale, p. 550; Scranton, p. 174.
399. Scranton, p. 179.
400. Sale, pp. 501, 550.
401. *Daily Illini* (Champaign, Illinois), January 13, 1973; Sale, pp. 61, 637.
402. Sale, p. 500.
403. "Campus Confrontation: Resolution by Injunction," p. 18.
404. *National Observer,* October 2, 1966; Sale, pp. 501, 551; *Tampa Tribune,* March 26, 1972.
405. Glessing, p. 37.
406. Basmajian, pp. 138-39. In addition to cases at the college level, there were scores of cases around the country involving censorship of high school newspapers and retaliation against high school students who worked on such papers. Thus, the chairman of the Montgomery County, Maryland, school board banned distribution of the *Washington Free Press* in county high schools because "it advocates revolution and makes disparaging remarks about the CIA and the police," while a high school senior in Seattle was suspended from school as the result of anti-war editorials he wrote as editor of the student paper. In one high school case, *Tinker v. Des Moines Board of Education* (1969) the Supreme Court ruled unconstitutional the expulsion of high school children in Des Moines for their wearing of black armbands to protest the war. The court ruled the school could bar protests only if they materially and substantially interfered with school operations (Mark J. Green, "The Law of the Young," *With Justice for Some* eds. Wasserstein and Green, pp. 5-6; Jean Strouse, *Up Against the Law: The Legal Rights of People Under 21* [New York: Signet, 1970], pp. 21-45; Michael Nussbaum, *Student Legal Rights: What They Are and How to Protect Them* [New York: Harper & Row, 1970], pp. 85-100; Michael Dorman, *Under 21: A Young People's Guide to Legal Rights* [New York: Dell, 1971], pp. 23-55.
407. James McEvoy and Abraham Miller, "The Crisis at San Francisco State," *Campus Power Struggles,* ed. Howard S. Becker (Chicago: Aldine, 1970), pp. 57-58; Sale, pp. 518-19.
408. *NYT,* July 18, October 20, 1967; August 9, 1968.
409. Miss Davis was subsequently acquitted of charges of criminal conspiracy, kidnapping and murder in connections with allegations that she had supplied guns that were used in a courtroom shootout that led to the deaths of four persons in California in 1970 (*Chicago Sun-Times,* February 27, 1972; Manchester, pp. 1201-1205).
410. *The Chronicle of Higher Education,* February 14, 1972; *Champaign-Urbana Courier,* April 2, 1974.
411. *SDU,* May 9, 1972; *New York Review of Books,* March 18, 1976. A week after his firing, Bohmer received an award for outstanding teaching from San Diego State (*SDU,* May 17, 1972).

412. *LAT*, January 30, April 8, 1975; Thomas F. Hoult, *The March to the Right* (Cambridge: Schenkman, 1972).
413. Sale, p. 551; Michael Miles, "The Triumph of Reaction," *Change: The Magazine of Higher Learning*, 4 (Winter, 1972-1973), pp. 30-36; *SDET*, June 17, 1975.
414. On the Panthers, see Marine, *The Black Panthers;* and Don A. Schanche, *The Panther Paradox* (New York: Paperback Library, 1971).
415. Schanche, pp. 82-83.
416. See Pinkney, p. 120; O'Neill, pp. 187-88; Michael J. Arlen, *An American Verdict* (Garden City: Doubleday, 1974), pp. 94-98.
417. Marine, pp. 180-81.
418. Epstein, p. 64.
419. Cray, p. 195.
420. *SICSR*, p. 188; *SICH*, pp. 406-07.
421. *SICSR*, p. 188.
422. *SICSR*, pp. 192-93.
423. *SICSR*, pp. 46-49, 198-200, 208-220.
424. *SICSR*, pp. 220-23, 319; Arlen, pp. 129-30; Elliff, *Crime*, pp. 123-48; Unger, *FBI*, pp. 464-66.
425. *LAT*, January 4, 5, 1976; *SDU*, January 4, 5, 1976.
426. Elliff, *Crime*, p. 140.
427. Cray, p. 200.
428. O'Neill, p. 187; Cray, p. 207; Epstein, p. 95.
429. Cray, pp. 195-207; Pinkney, pp. 119-24; Donner, "Hoover's Legacy," p. 683.
430. Cray, p. 198, 200-01.
431. "The Panthers and the Police," *New Yorker*, February 13, 1971, pp. 45ff. See also, Arlen, pp. 99-102; Cray, p. 201.
432. F. K. Heussenstamm, "Bumper Stickers and the Cops," *Transaction*, 8 (February, 1971), pp. 32-33.
433. On the Chicago raid of December 4, 1969 and preceding and following developments, see Arlen, *An American Verdict;* and Commission of Inquiry Into the Black Panthers and the Police, *Search and Destroy* (New York: Metropolitan Applied Research Center, 1973).
434. Arlen, p. 59.
435. Ungar, *FBI*, pp. 465-66; *LAT*, January, 16, February 7, 1976.
436. Gilbert Moore, *A Special Rage* (New York: Harper & Row, 1972); Goodell, p. 115.
437. Murray Kempton, *The Briar Patch* (New York: Dutton, 1973); Chevigny, *Cops and Rebels*.
438. Pinkney, p. 121; O'Neill, p. 187; Cray, p. 207.
439. *SICSR*, p. 200.
440. *SICSR*, pp. 205-07.
441. *SICSR*, p. 187.
442. See above, pp. 529-30.
443. "Thoughts," p. 438.
444. *Push Comes to Shove* (Boston: Houghton Mifflin, 1970), pp. 186-87.
445. August 5, 1971.
446. Frank Askin, "Surveillance: The Social Science Perspective," *Columbia Human Rights Law Review*, 4 (1972), p. 83.
447. Askin, p. 83.
448. Askin, pp. 78-79.
449. Askin, p. 85.
450. *SDS*, p. 503.
451. *Chicago Sun-Times*, July 8, 1973.
452. *Champaign-Urbana News-Gazette*, June 6, 1971.
453. Skolnick, p. 37.
454. Skolnick, pp. 35-42, offers an analysis along these lines.
455. Skolnick, p. 44.
456. See Skolnick, p. 43; Powers, *The War at Home*.
457. See pp. 468, 487-93, 496, 514-16, 521-22.
458. Schrag, p. 19.
459. *SDS*, pp. 503, 553.
460. September 22, 1975.

461. On the collapse of the movement, see Sale, *SDS*, pp. 600-657; John P. Diggins, *The American Left in the Twentieth Century* (New York: Harcourt, Brace, 1973), pp. 176.
462. Navasky and Lewin, p. 283.
463. Donner, "Theory and Practice," p. 31.
464. *SDS*, p. 503.
465. "Thoughts," p. 434.
466. "Political Informers," pp. 318-19; see also Marx, pp. 428-29.
467. "Thoughts," p. 438.
468. See 480, 499-500, 503 above, Longaker, "Emergency Detention," pp. 395-408.
469. *LAT*, January 15, 1975, March 30, 1976. In 1971, Massachusetts and Oklahoma abolished state anti-subversive units. In 1975, the California legislature abolished its legislative Subcommittee on Un-American Activities, the successor to the "Tenney Committee" of the McCarthy period, and Alabama abolished its Commission to Preserve the Peace, which had gathered files on dissident groups (*CL*, April, 1971; *Boston Globe*, December 8, 1971; *LAT*, April 8, 1975; *SDU*, May 17, 1976).
470. *NYT*, May 20, 1976; *SDU*, May 23, 1976; *LAT*, May 30, 1976.
471. See pp. 463-84, above.
472. *LAT*, March 1, 1975; *Newsweek*, March 10, 1975.
473. Lukas, p. 35.
474. Ungar, *FBI*, pp. 269-70, 286-87.
475. *LAT*, December 22, 1974.
476. *LAT*, September 29, 1974.
477. *SWR*, p. 55.
478. See pp. 463-84, above.
479. *LAT*, June 26, 1975, March 24, 30, 1976; *NYT*, June 26, 1975.
480. *LAT*, December 10, 1975.
481. *LAT*, December 12, 1975, March 9, 11, 1976; *NYT*, March 9, 1976; *SDET*, March 9, 11, April 7, 1976.
481a. FBI documents revealed in a SWP court suit in October 1976 revealed that despite Lev's order, FBI Director Clarence Kelly directed FBI agents in September 1976 to continue investigating SWP members who had engaged in activities indicating they are "likely to use force or violence in violation of a federal law," although investigations of the SWP as such could be terminated. Subsequently, Kelly instructed agents to continue such investigations only in accordance with the Attorney General's guidelines, which required that all field offices report investigations to FBI headquarters for referral to the Justice Department for a determination if they should be continued. NYT, September 15, 1976; *Washington Post*, October 8, 1976. For a summary of the thirty-eight year FBI campaign against the SWP, see David Atkins, "The SWP and the FBI," First Principles, 2 (September, 1976), and Political Rights Defense Fund, *The Nation's Press Views the Landmark Suit that is Uncovering FBI and CIA Crimes* (New York: 1976). In September, 1976, FBI Director Clarence Kelly told the Senate Intelligence Committee that the number of American citizens and organizations under investigation because of their political beliefs had declined from 21,414 to 626 over the previous three years. However, Kelly did not make clear how many investigations were dropped because of the new critria and how many were dropped as a result of the lessening of radical and dissenting activity. Thus, Kelly said the FBI "began closing thousands of investigations" when the Vietnam War ended, i.e. before the new Justice Department guidelines were implemented. Further confusion was added when Kelly said the reduction in cases investigated had been made possible "largely because we have discontinued investigation of rank and file members" of organizations in favor of focusing on the activities of the groups as a whole, their leadership and those members who have indicated their willingness "to use force or violence in violation of Federal law." Kelly also indicated that investigations of some radical and revolutionary groups who allegedly threatened the national security focused on the need to investigate their intentions in order to prevent hostile acts before they occur and such cases were "beyond the pale" of normal criminal investigations since the need to learn of planned behavior "somewhat submerges the need to prosecute." In October, 1976, the FBI indicated in a court suit that over 20 of its undercover informers had broken off contact with the bureau in the previous three months out of fear that their identities might become public. *NYT*, September 23, October 25, 1976.

482. *LAT*, February 18, 19, 1976; *SDET*, February 18, 1976; Christine Marwick, "Reforming the Intelligence Agencies," *First Principles*, 1 (March, 1976), pp. 3-13; Morton Halperin, "The Fraud Plan," *First Principles*, 1 (March, 1976), pp. 15-16.
483. "From the Editor," *CLR*, 1 (Winter/Spring, 1974), p. 4.
484. "From the Editor," *CLR*, 1 (Winter/Spring, 1974), p. 4.
485. *Champaign-Urbana (Illinois) Courier*, October 25, December 7, 1973.
486. *Champaign-Urbana Courier*, October 1, 1973.
487. *Champaign-Urbana Courier*, January 13, 1974; *LAT*, November 20, 1974, January 14, February 12, March 22, 1976; *SDU*, June 27, 1975, January 12, 13, 14, 1976; *SDET*, August 9, 1975; Ungar, *FBI*, p. 603. On the FBI under Kelly, see Ungar, *FBI*, pp. 565-604.
488. *LAT*, June 15, 1975.
489. *LAT*, November 21, 1974.
490. *SDU*, May 23, 1976.
491. *SICFR*, pp. 6, 263-64.
492. *SICSR*, pp. 228-29; *SICFR*, p. 8.
493. *LAT*, May 20, June 25, 1975.
494. *LAT*, June 26, 1975; *NYT*, June 26, 1975; *SICSR*, p. 561.
495. Christine Marwick, "Using Civil Litigation to Protect Constitutional Rights," *First Principles*, I (April, 1976), p. 3. On loopholes in restrictions on the intelligence agencies, see pp. 539-41, above.
496. *LAT*, March 25, 1976; *NYT*, April 27, 1976.
497. *Los Angeles Herald Examiner*, May 8, 1976.
498. *LAT*, May 18, 1976.
499. See p. 405, above.
500. *LAT*, July 6, 1975; Richard Griley, "Nixon's Official Secrets Act," *The Nation*, March 2, 1974, pp. 265-68; Milton Viorst, "Nixon's Revenge," *Harpers*, February, 1976, pp. 20-24.
501. *LAT*, February 18, 19, 1976.
502. *NYT*, June 10, 1974; *SDU*, September 28, 1975; Ungar, *FBI*, p. 619.
503. *The Assault on Privacy* (New York: Signet, 1972), p. 26; Duchacek, p. 98.
504. *LAT*, August 18, 1975; *SDET*, August 18, 1975. Duchacek, (p. 97) writes: "In his *1984* George Orwell described the ultimate horrors of the Thought Police and their ubiquitous instrument of surveillance, the telescreen; 'You had to live — did live, from habit that became instinct — in the assumption that every sound you made was overheard and, except in darkness, every movement scrutinized.' Already by the 1960's infra-red techniques permitted a room to be watched and photographed from an adjoining room [in darkness]."
505. Sanford J. Ungar, "The Intelligence Tangle," *The Atlantic*, April 1976, p. 42.

CONCLUSION

1. *The State in Capitalist Society* (New York: Basic Books, 1969), pp. 266-67.
2. See above, pp. 3-19.
3. Richard Rubenstein, *Rebels in Eden: Mass Political Violence in the United States* (Boston: Little, Brown, 1970), p. 91.
4. See above, pp. 121-25, 183-191, 211-12, 228-29.
5. For repression during railroad strikes, see above, pp. 30-32, 36, 44, 47, 53-7, 188-89, 290; on steel strikes, see pp. 45-46, 84-85, 151-53, 229-31; on textile strikes, see pp. 88-90, 187-88, 191, 206, 219-20; on mining strikes, see pp. 28-30, 46-47, 51, 70-72, 75-77, 79, 91-93, 95-96, 115-16, 126, 153, 186, 189-90, 205-06, 220, 226, 228, 290; on lumber strikes, see pp. 87-88, 96, 115-16, 228, 260; on agricultural strikes, see pp. 87-88, 96, 115-16, 228, 260; on agricultural strikes, see pp. 43-44, 90-91, 95, 150-51, 205-06, 220-26.
6. See above, pp. 45-46, 88-91, 96, 151-53, 187-88, 206.
7. See above, pp. 53-57.
8. See above, pp. 151-53.
9. See above, pp. 46-47, 71-73, 79, 87-88, 95-96, 115-16, 187-88, 191, 206, 220-24, 229-31.

10. See above, pp. 87-88, 226-28.
11. Auerbach, *Labor*, pp. 211-12.
12. See above, pp. 169-71.
13. See above, pp. 38-42.
14. See above, pp. 71-72.
15. "Shall This Be All?" p. 444.
16. See above, pp. 73-74, 77, 86-90, 97-98, 115-19, 155-56.
17. See above, pp. 187-88, 205-06, 220-24, 252.
18. See above, pp. 289-91, 312, 318, 364-66, 406, 409.
19. See above, pp. 30-33.
20. See above, pp. 34-44.
21. See above, pp. 44-60.
22. See above, pp. 141-43, 151-53, 190-91.
23. See above, pp. 183-91, 236.
24. Commons, IV, p. 5.
25. *The Agony of the American Left*, (New York: Vintage, 1969), p. 18.
26. *Search*, p. 125.
27. "Shall This Be All?" p. 440.
28. See above, pp. 121-25.
29. See above, pp. 289-91, 312, 318, 364-66, 406, 409.
30. See above, pp. 106, 119-21, 126-27, 132-33.
31. See above, pp. 154-63.
32. See above, pp. 201-06, 218-22, 226.
33. See above, pp. 240-61.
34. See above, pp. 288-371, *passim*.
35. Kircheimer, pp. 135, 155-58.
36. Herbert H. Hyman, "England and America: Climates of Tolerance and Intolerance," *The Radical Right*, ed. Bell, p. 269.
37. See above, pp. 530-37.
38. *Critics of Society: Radical Thought in North America* (New York: Vintage, 1969), p. 48.
39. *Critics*, p. 67.
40. *Agony*, pp. 43, 58-59.
41. See above, pp. 24-25, 167-68, 179-81, 214, 383-84, 435-38.
42. See above, pp. 312-13, 435-60.
43. *Teodori*, pp. 222-23.
44. *State*, p. 72.
45. See above, pp. 167-71, 369-91.
46. See above, p. 550.
47. See above, pp. 385-91.
48. See above, pp. 23-191, *passim*.
49. *Political Justice*, p. 419.
50. See above, pp. 197-201, 209-13.
51. Schlesinger, *Coming*, p. 15.
52. See above, pp. 247-55, 262-77.
53. See above, pp. 298-319, 435-60.
54. See above, pp. 412-26.
55. See above, pp. 399-401.
56. See above, pp. 30-32, 53-57.
57. See above, pp. 18-19, 67-70, 108-10, 127-28, 145-47.
58. See above, pp. 23-236, *passim*.
59. See above, pp. 244-45, 262-83, 299-305, 312-13, 321-24, 340-41, 443-60, 463-486.
60. See above, pp. 108-09, 244-45, 321-23, 340, 343-48.
61. See above, pp. 435-504.
62. See above, pp. 107-21, 197-201, 247-55, 264-76, 299-343, 443-486.
63. See above, pp. 209-13, 399-401.
64. See above, pp. 107-25, 134, 144-59, 299-349, 368-69.
65. See above, pp. 404-06, 534, 537-38.
66. See above, pp. 125-31, 348-60, 504-30.
67. See above, pp. 206-09, 217-33.
68. Perrett, p. 220.

69. Goldman, *Tragedy,* p. 490.
70. See above, pp. 139-58.
71. See above, pp. 88, 154-59, 295, 319-21, 511-12.
72. *Political Justice,* pp. 157-58.
73. On the relationship between economic depressions and repression, see above, pp. 26-27, 34, 50, 77, 93, 195-209; on strike waves, see pp. 36-38, 51-56, 143, 226; on the effect of participation in war, see pp. 105-35, 262-83, 321, 429; on the effect of severe foreign policy crises, see pp. 99-101, 239-262, 287-320; on the effect on the spread of threatening ideologies abroad, see pp. 24-25, 143-44, 239-40, 317.
74. Harry Howe Ranson, "Can American Democracy Survive the Cold War?" (Garden City, New York: Doubleday, 1964), p. xv.
75. Quoted in *LAT,* May 4, 1975.
76. See pages cited in footnote 73, above.
77. See above, pp. 107, 250-51, 266, 298, 312, 448-49, 462-63.
78. *Academic Freedom,* p. 177.
79. See above, pp. 263-84, 360-69.
80. See above, pp. 206-09, 533-34.
81. See above, pp. 32-34, 41-44; 58-60, 171-73, 399-405, 537-41.
82. See above, pp. 34-42, 53-57, 70-74, 98-99, 105-06, 139-45, 201-06, 306, 312-14, 430.
83. See above, p. 429.
84. See above, pp. 167-71, 381-91.
85. Duchacek, p. 77.
86. See above, p. 209.
87. See above, pp. 532-34.
88. See above, pp. 66-70.
89. See above, pp. 206-09, 233-36.
90. See above, pp. 342-43, 399-401.
91. See above, pp. 533-34.
92. See above, pp. 500-04.
93. *Days of Sadness,* p. 89.
94. See above, pp. 206, 220-226.
95. See above, pp. 159, 399-401.
96. See above, pp. 264-65.
97. *Days of Sadness,* p. 230.
98. *Terror and Resistance* (New York: Oxford University Press, 1972), pp. 341-42.
99. See pp. 181-82, 445.
100. See above, pp. 268-73.
101. See above, pp. 23-24, 134-35, 159, 265-66, 360-69.
102. See above, pp. 159-60, 206-09, 233-36, 399-401, 533-34.
103. *SICFR,* pp. 2-3.

Bibliography

This bibliography includes only sources which are cited in two or more chapters of this book. Since all sources are given a complete citation in the notes when they are first referred to, any source *not* listed here can be found in the chapter notes. This bibliography does not necessarily include all of the most important sources used for this book, and inclusion in this bibliography does not necessarily mean the source is especially important. The criteria for inclusion in the bibliography was simply citation in more than one chapter, so that the reader who is searching for a complete citation of a source will be able to find it either here or after a search of the notes from no more than one chapter.

Abraham, Henry J. *Freedom and the Court.* New York: Oxford University Press, 1972.
Abrams, Richard M., and Lawrence Levine, eds. *The Shaping of Twentieth Century America.* Boston: Little, Brown, 1971.
Adamic, Louis. *Dynamite!* New York: Vintage, 1931.
Adams, Graham, Jr. *The Age of Industrial Violence, 1910-1915.* New York: Columbia University Press, 1966.
Allen, James R. *The Company Town in the American West.* Norman: University of Oklahoma Press, 1966.
Altbach, Phillip G., and Robert S. Laufer, eds. *The New Pilgrims: Youth Protest in Transition.* New York: David McKay, 1972.
Altbach, Phillip G., and Patti M. Peterson. "Before Berkeley: Historical Perspectives on American Student Activism," in Altbach and Laufer, *New Pilgrims.*
Askin, Frank. "Surveillance: The Social Science." *Columbia Human Rights Law Review,* 4 (1972).
Auerbach, Jerold S. "The Depression Decade," in Reitman, *Pulse of Freedom.*
Auerbach, Jerold S. *Labor and Liberty: The LaFollette Committee and the New Deal.* Indianapolis: Bobbs-Merrill, 1966.
Bailey, Thomas A. *Woodrow Wilson and the Lost Peace.* Chicago: Quadrangle, 1963.
Barber, Kathleen L. "The Legal Status of the Communist Party: 1965," *Journal of Public Law,* 15 (1965).

Barrett, Edward, Jr. *The Tenney Committee: Legislative Investigations of Subversive Activities in California*. Ithaca: Cornell University Press, 1951.
Barthe, Alan. *The Loyalty of Free Men*. New York: Pocket Books, 1952.
Baskin, Alex. "The Ford Hunger March—1932," *Labor History*, 13 (Summer, 1972).
Bell, Daniel. *Marxian Socialism in the United States*. Princeton: Princeton University Press, 1967.
Berman, Jerry J., and Morton H. Halperin, eds. *The Abuses of the Intelligence Agencies*. Washington, D.C.: Center for National Security Studies, 1975.
Bernhard, Edgar, et al. *Pursuit of Freedom: A History of Civil Liberty in Illinois*. Chicago: Chicago Civil Liberties Committee, 1942.
Bernstein, Irving. *The Lean Years*. Baltimore: Penguin, 1966.
Bernstein, Irving. *The Turbulent Years*. Boston: Houghton Mifflin, 1971.
Betten, Neil. "Riot, Revolution and Repression in the Iron Range Strike of 1916," *Minnesota History*, 41 (Summer, 1968).
Biddle, Francis. *The Fear of Freedom*. Garden City, New York: Doubleday, 1951.
Blum, John. "Nativism, Anti-Radicalism and the Foreign Scare," *Midwest Journal*, 3 (Winter, 1950-1951).
Bontecue, Eleanor. *The Federal Loyalty-Security Program*. Ithaca: Cornell University Press, 1953.
Boudin, Leonard B. "The Right to Travel," in Norman Dorsen, ed., *The Rights of Americans* (New York: Vintage, 1972).
Brecher, Jeremy. *Strike!* San Francisco: Straight Arrow, 1972.
Brody, David. *Steelworkers in America*. New York: Harper and Row, 1969.
Brooks, Thomas R. *Toil and Trouble: A History of American Labor*. New York: Delta, 1964.
Brown, Ralph S. *Loyalty and Security*. New Haven: Yale University Press, 1958.
Bruce, Robert V. *1877: Year of Violence*. Chicago: Quadrangle, 1970.
Buder, Stanley. *Pullman*. New York: Oxford University Press, 1967.
Burns, James M. *Roosevelt: The Soldier of Freedom, 1940-1945*. New York: Harcourt, Brace, 1970.
Byse, Clark. "A Report on the Pennsylvania Loyalty Act," *University of Pennsylvania Law Review*, 101 (1952-1953).
Carr, Robert K. *The House Committee on Un-American Activities*. Ithaca: Cornell University Press, 1952.
Caughey, John W. *In Clear and Present Danger*. Chicago: University of Chicago Press, 1958.
Chafee, Zechariah. *Free Speech in the United States*. New York: Atheneum, 1969.
Chalmers, David M. *Hooded Americanism: The History of the Ku Klux Klan*. Chicago: Quadrangle, 1968.
Chamberlain, Lawrence. *Loyalty and Legislative Action: A Survey of Activity by the New York State Legislature*. Ithaca: Cornell University Press, 1951.
Chatfield, Charles. *For Peace and Justice: Pacifism in America, 1914-1941* (Boston: Beacon, 1973), pp. 27-28.
Chevigny, Paul. *Cops and Rebels*. New York: Pantheon, 1972.
Cochran, Thomas C., and William Miller. *The Age of Industrial Enterprise*. New York: Harper & Row, 1965.
Commager, Henry Steele. *Freedom and Order*. Cleveland: World Publishing, 1966.
Commons, John R., et al. *History of Labour in the United States*. New York: MacMillan, four volumes, 1918-1935.
Conlin, Joseph R. *Bread and Roses, Too*. Westport, Connecticut: Greenwood, Syracuse University Press, 1969.

Conlin, Joseph R. *Bread and Roses, Too*. Westport, Connecticcut: Greenwood, 1969.
Cook, Fred J. *The FBI Nobody Knows*. New York: Pyramid, 1965.
Cook, Fred J. *The Nightmare Decade: The Life and Times of Senator Joe McCarthy*. New York Random House, 1971.
Countryman, Vern. *Un-American Activities in the State of Washington*. Ithaca: Cornell University Press, 1951.
Crook, William. *Communism and the General Strike*. Hamden, Connecticut: Shoe String Press, 1960.
Cummings, Homer, and Carl McFarland. *Federal Justice*. New York: MacMillan, 1937.
Curti, Merle. *The Roots of Loyalty*. New York: Atheneum, 1968.
Cushman, Robert E. "The Impact of the War on the Constitution," in *The Impact of the War on America*. Ithaca: Cornell University Press, 1942.
Daniel, Cletus E. "Wobblies on the Farm: The IWW in the Yakima Valley," *Pacific Northwest Quarterly*, 65 (October, 1974).
David, Henry. *The History of the Haymarket Affair*. New York: Collier, 1963.
Davis, David Brion, ed. *The Fear of Conspiracy: Images of Un-American Subversion from the Revolution to the Present*. Ithaca: Cornell University Press, 1971.
Diamond, Sander A. *The Nazi Movement in the United States*. Ithaca: Cornell University Press, 1974.
Dick, William M. *Labor and Socialism in America: The Gompers Era*. Port Washington, New York: Kennikat, 1972.
Donner, Frank. "Electronic Surveillance," *Civil Liberties Review*, 2 (October, 1975).
Donner, Frank. "Hoover's Legacy," *The Nation*, June 1, 1974.
Donner, Frank. "Political Informers," in Watters and Gillers, *Investigating*.
Donner, Frank. "Theory and Practice of American Political Intelligence," *New York Review of Books*, April 22, 1971.
Dowell, Eldridge F. *A History of Criminal Syndicalism Legislation in the United States*. New York: DeCapo, 1969.
Draper, Theodore. *American Communism and Soviet Russia*. New York: Viking, 1960.
Draper, Theodore. *The Roots of American Communism*. New York: Viking, 1963.
Drinnon, Richard. *Rebel in Paradise: A Biography of Emma Goldman*. Boston: Beacon, 1970.
Dubofsky, Melvin. *We Shall Be All: A History of the Industrial Workers of the World*. Chicago: Quadrangle, 1969.
Duchacek, Ivo D. *Rights and Liberties in the World Today: Constitutional Promises and Reality*. Santa Barbara, California: ABC-Clio Press, 1973.
Dulles, Foster Rhea. *Labor in America*. New York: Crowell, 1966.
Ekrich, Arthur, Jr. *The Decline of American Liberalism*. New York: Atheneum, 1969.
Elliff, John. "Scope and Basis of FBI Data Collection," in Watters and Gillers, *Investigating*.
Elliott, Russell R. "Labor Troubles in the Mining Camp at Goldfield, Nevada," *Pacific Historical Review*, 19 (November, 1950).
Epstein, Jason. *The Great Conspiracy Trial*. New York: Vintage, 1971.
Emerson, Thomas I., and David M. Helfeld. "Loyalty Among Government Employees," *Yale Law Journal*, 58 (December, 1948).
Emerson, Thomas I., David Haber and Norman Dorsen. *Political and Civil Rights in the United States*. Boston: Little-Brown, 1967.
Emerson, Thomas I. *The System of Freedom of Expression*. New York: Vintage,

1970.
Emerson, Thomas I. *Towards a General Theory of the First Amendment.* New York: Vintage, 1967.
Faulkner, Harold U. *The Decline of Laissez-Faire.* New York: Harper & Row, 1968.
Faulkner, Harold U. *Politics, Reform and Expansion.* New York: Harper & Row, 1963.
Fine, Nathan. *Farmer and Labor Parties in the United States, 1828-1928.* New York: Rand School of Social Science, 1928.
Fine, Sidney. "Anarchism and the Assassination of McKinley," *American Historical Review,* 9 (July, 1955).
Fine, Sidney. *Laissez-Faire and the General Welfare State.* Ann Arbor: University of Michigan Press, 1964.
Foner, Philip S. *History of the Labor Movement in the United States.* New York: International Publishers, four volumes, 1947-1965.
Foster, Julian, and Durward Long. *Protest!* New York: Morrow, 1970.
Franklin, John Hope. *From Slavery to Freedom.* New York: Vintage, 1969.
Freeland, Richard M. *The Truman Doctrine and the Origins of McCarthyism.* New York: Schocken, 1974.
Friedheim, Robert. *The Seattle General Strike.* Seattle: University of Washington Press, 1964.
Friendly, Fred W. *Due to Circumstances Beyond Our Control.* New York: Vintage, 1968.
Frost, Richard H. *The Mooney Case.* Stanford, California: Stanford University Press, 1968.
Fund for the Republic. *Digest of the Public Record of Communism in the United States.* New York: Fund for the Republic, 1955.
Gaboury, William J. "From Statehouse to Bull Pen: Idaho Populism and the Coeur d'Alene Troubles of the 1890's," *Pacific Northwest Quarterly,* 58 (January, 1967).
Gardner, David P. *The California Oath Controversy.* Berkeley: University of California, 1967.
Garraty, John A. *The New Commonwealth.* New York: Harper & Row, 1968.
Gellhorn, Walter, ed. *The States and Subversion.* Ithaca: Cornell University Press, 1952.
Gephart, Ronald M. "Politicians, Soldiers and Strikes: The Reorganization of the Nebraska Militia and the Omaha Strike of 1882," *Nebraska History,* 46 (June, 1965).
Ginger, Ray. *Age of Excess.* New York: MacMillan, 1965.
Ginger, Ray. *Eugene V. Debs.* New York: Collier, 1962.
Gitelman, H. M. "Perspectives on American Industrial Relations," *Business History Review,* 47 (Spring, 1973).
Goldman, Eric. *Rendez-vous with Destiny.* New York Vintage, 1955.
Goodman, Walter. *The Committee.* Baltimore: Penguin, 1969.
Graham, Hugh D. and Ted R. Gurr, eds. *Violence in America.* New York: Bantam, 1969.
Gregory, Charles O. *Labor and the Law.* New York: Norton, 1961.
Griffith, Robert. *The Politics of Fear.* Lexington: University of Kentucky Press, 1970.
Griffith, Robert and Athan Theoharis, eds. *The Spectre: Original Essays on the Cold War and the Origins of McCarthyism.* New York: New Viewpoints, 1974.
Gutfeld, Arnold. "The Levine Affair: A Case Study in Academic Freedom," *Pacific Historical Review,* 39 (February, 1970).

Bibliography 657

Halberstam, David. *The Best and the Brightest*. New York: Random House, 1972.
Handlin, Oscar. *The American People in the Twentieth Century*. Boston: Beacon Press, 1963.
Haug, Charles J. "The Industrial Workers of the World in North Dakota, 1918-1925," *North Dakota Quarterly*, (Summer, 1973).
Haynes, John E. "Revolt of the 'Timber Beasts': The IWW Lumber Strike in Minnesota," *Minnesota History*, 42 (Spring, 1971).
Hays, Samuel P. *The Response to Industrialism*. Chicago: University of Chicago Press, 1957.
Hendrickson, Kenneth E. "The Socialists of Reading, Pennsylvania and World War I," *Pennsylvania History*, 36 (October, 1969).
Hicks, John D. *The Populist Revolt*. Lincoln: University of Nebraska Press, 1961.
Higham, John. *Strangers in the Land*. New York: Atheneum, 1970.
Hofstadter, Richard. *The Age of Reform*. New York: Vintage, 1955.
Hofstadter, Richard and Michael Wallace, eds. *American Violence: A Documentary History*. New York: Vintage, 1971.
Horowitz, Harold W. "Report on the Los Angeles City and County Loyalty Programs," *Stanford Law Review*, 5 (1953).
Howe, Irving and Lewis Coser. *The American Communist Party*. New York: Praeger, 1962.
Hutson, A. C., Jr. "The Coal Miners Insurrection of 1891 in Anderson County, Tennessee," *East Tennessee Historical Society's Proceedings*, 7 (1935)
Hyman, Harold M. *Soldiers and Spruce: Origins of the Loyal Legion of Loggers and Lumbermen*. Los Angeles: University of California Institute of Industrial Relations, 1963.
Hyman, Harold M. *To Try Men's Souls*. Berkeley: University of California Press, 1960.
Jacobs, Paul and Saul Landau. *The New Radicals*. New York: Vintage, 1966.
Jaffe, Julian F. *Crusade Against Radicalism: New York During the Red Scare, 1914-1924*. Port Washington, N.Y.: Kennikat, 1972.
Jamieson, Stuart. *Labor Unionism in American Agriculture*. Washington, D.C.: Government Printing Office, 1954.
Jensen, Joan M. *The Price of Vigilance*. Chicago: Rand McNally, 1968.
Jensen, Vernon H. *Heritage of Conflict*. Ithaca: Cornell University Press, 1950.
Johnson, Donald. *The Challenge of American Freedoms*. Lexington: University of Kentucky Press, 1963.
Johnson, Walter, *1600 Pennsylvania Avenue*. Boston: Little Brown, 1963.
Joll, James. *The Anarchists*. New York: Grosset & Dunlap, 1966.
Jones, Maldwyn. *American Immigration*. Chicago: University of Chicago Press, 1960.
Joughlin, Louis and Edmund M. Morgan. *The Legacy of Sacco and Vanzetti*. Chicago: Quadrangle, 1964.
Karson, Marc. *American Labor Unions and Politics*. Boston: Beacon Press, 1965.
Kemper, Donald J. *Decade of Fear: Senator Hennings and Civil Liberties*. Columbia: University of Missouri, 1965.
Kipnis, Ira. *The American Socialist Movement, 1897-1912*. New York: Monthly Review.
Kirchheimer, Otto. *Political Justice*. Princeton: Princeton University Press, 1969.
Kreuger, Thomas A. *And Promises to Keep: The Southern Conference on Human Welfare*. Nashville: Vanderbilt University, 1967.
Kornbluh, Joyce L., ed. *Rebel Voices: An I.W.W. Anthology*. Ann Arbor: University of Michigan Press, 1964.
Larrowe, Charles P. *Harry Bridges: The Rise and Fall of Radical Labor*. New York: Lawrence Hill, 1972.

Laslett, John. *Labor and the Left: A Study of Socialist and Radical Influences in the American Labor Movement*. New York: Basic Books, 1970.
Latham, Earl. *The Communist Conspiracy in Washington*. New York: Atheneum, 1969.
Lens, Sidney. *The Labor Wars*. Garden City, N.Y.: Doubleday, 1974.
Leubke, Frederick C. *Bonds of Loyalty: German Americans and World War One*. Dekalb: Northern Illinois University Press, 1974.
Leuchtenburg, William E. *Franklin D. Roosevelt and the New Deal*. New York: Harper & Row, 1963.
Leuchtenburg, William E. *The Perils of Prosperity*. Chicago: University of Chicago Press, 1958.
Levin, Murry. *Political Hysteria in America: The Democratic Capacity for Repression*. New York: Basic Books, 1971.
Lindsay, Almont. *The Pullman Strike*. Chicago: University of Chicago Press, 1964.
Lipset, Seymour M. and John Lasslet, eds. *Failure of a Dream? Essays in the History of American Socialism*. Garden City: Doubleday, 1974.
Lipset, Seymour M. and Earl Raab. *The Politics of Unreason: Right-Wing Extremism in America, 1790-1970*. New York: Harper & Row, 1973.
Longaker, Richard. "Emergency Detention: The Generation Gap, 1950-1971," *Western Political Quarterly*, 27 (September, 1974).
Lovin, Hugh. "The Red Scare in Idaho, 1916-1918," *Idaho Yesterdays*, 17 (Fall, 1973).
Lowenthal, Max. *The Federal Bureau of Investigation*. New York: Harcourt Brace, 1950.
Manchester, William. *The Glory and the Dream*. New York: Bantam, 1975.
Manwaring, David. *Render Unto Caesar*. Chicago: University of Chicago Press, 1962.
Mangione, Jerre. *The Dream and the Deal: The Federal Writers Project*. New York: Avon, 1972.
Marwick, Christine M. "Warrantless National Security Wiretaps," *First Principles*, 1 (October, 1975).
McClurg, Donald J. "The Colorado Coal Strike of 1927," *Labor History*, 4 (Winter, 1966).
McMurry, Donald L. *Coxey's Army*. Seattle: University of Washington Press, 1968.
McMurry, Donald L. "The Legal Ancestry of the Pullman Strike Injunctions," *Industrial and Labor Relations Review*, 14 (January, 1961).
McWilliams, Carey. *Factories in the Fields*. Santa Barbara, California: Peregrine, 1971.
McWilliams, Carey. *North from Mexico*. New York: Greenwood, 1968.
McWilliams, Carey. *Witchhunt*, Boston: Little, Brown, 1950.
Metzger, Walter P. *Academic Freedom in the Age of the University*. New York: Columbia University Press, 1961.
Mock, James R. *Censorship, 1917*. Princeton: Princeton University Press, 1941.
Mollan, Robert. "Smith Act Prosecutions: The Effects of the *Dennis* and *Yates* Decisions," *University of Pittsburgh Law Review*, 26 (June, 1965).
Montgomery, David. *Beyond Equality: Labor and the Radical Republicans, 1862-1872*. New York: Vintage, 1967.
Morlan, Robert L. *Political Prairie Fire: The Non-Partisan League, 1915-1922*. Minneapolis: University of Minnesota Press, 1955.
Mowitz, Robert. "Michigan," in Gellhorn, *States*.
Murphy, Paul L. "Communities in Conflict," in Reitman, *Pulse*.
Murphy, Paul L. *The Constitution in Crisis Times*. New York: Harper & Row, 1972.

Murphy, Paul L. *The Meaning of Freedom of Speech.* Westport, Connecticut: Greenwood, 1972.
Murphy, Paul L. "Sources and Nature of Intolerance in the Twenties," *Journal of American History,* 51 (June, 1964).
Murray, Robert K. *The Harding Era.* Minneapolis: University of Minnesota Press, 1969.
Murray, Robert K. *Red Scare: A Study in National Hysteria, 1919-1920.* New York: McGraw-Hill, 1964.
Muzik, Edward J. "Victor L. Berger: Congress and the Red Scare," *Wisconsin Magazine of History,* 47 (Summer, 1964).
Navasky, Victor, and Nathan Lewin. "Electronic Surveillance," in Watters and Gillers, *Investigating.*
Nelson, Jack, and Ronald J. Ostrow. *The FBI and the Berrigans.* New York: Coward, McCann & Geoghegan, 1972.
Nelson, Harold, ed. *Freedom of the Press from Hamilton to the Warren Court.* Indianapolis: Bobbs-Merrill, 1967.
Newfield, Jack. *A Prophetic Minority.* New York: Signet, 1967.
Noggle, Earl. *Into the Twenties: The United States from Armistice to Normalcy.* Urbana: University of Illinois Press, 1974.
Nissen, D. R. "Federal Anti-Communist Legislation from 1931-1941." Unpublished M.A. Thesis, University of Illinois, 1959.
Nye, Russel B. *Midwestern Progressive Politics.* New York: Harper & Row, 1965.
O'Brien, F. S. "The 'Communist-Dominated' Unions in the United States Since 1950," *Labor History,* 12 (Summer, 1971).
O'Brien, James P. "The Development of the New Left," in Altbach and Laufer, *New Pilgrims.*
Ogden, August R. *The Dies Committee.* Washington, D.C.: Catholic University Press, 1945.
Parenti, Michael. *The Anti-Communist Impulse.* New York: Random House, 1969.
Parmet, Herbert S. *Eisenhower and the American Crusades.* New York: MacMillan, 1972.
Perrett, Geoffrey. *Days of Sadness, Years of Triumph.* Baltimore: Penguin, 1974.
Perkus, Cathy, ed. *COINTELPRO: The FBI's Secret War on Political Freedom.* New York: Monad, 1975.
Pinkney, Alphonso. *The American Way of Violence.* New York: Vintage, 1972.
Polenberg, Richard. *War and Society.* Philadelphia: Lippincott, 1972.
Pope, Liston. *Millhands and Preachers.* New Haven, Connecticut: Yale University Press, 1942.
Porter, Eugene O. "The Colorado Coal Strike of 1913," *The Historian,* 12 (Autumn, 1949).
Preston, William, Jr. *Aliens and Dissenters.* New York: Harper & Row, 1966.
Preston, William, Jr. "Shall This Be All? U.S. Historians Versus William D. Haywood, et al," *Labor History,* 12 (Summer, 1971).
Pritchett, C. Herman. *The Political Offender and the Warren Court.* New York: Russell and Russell.
Rayback, Joseph. *A History of American Labor.* New York: The Free Press, 1966.
Reeves, Thomas C. *Freedom and the Foundation: The Fund for the Republic in the Era of McCarthyism.* New York: Alfred A. Knopf, 1969.
Rich, Bennett M. *The President and Civil Disorders.* Washington, D.C.: The Brookings Institution, 1941.
Riker, William H. *Soldiers of the States.* Washington, D.C.: Public Affairs Press, 1957.

Robinson, James A. *Anti-Sedition Legislation and Loyalty Investigations in Oklahoma*. Norman: University of Oklahoma Bureau of Government Research, 1956.
Roche, John P. *Quest for the Dream*. New York: MacMillan, 1963.
Rockefeller, Nelson. *Report to the President by the Commission on CIA Activities Within the United States*. New York: Manor, 1975.
Rogin, Michael P. *The Intellectuals and McCarthy*. Cambridge, Mass.: MIT Press, 1970.
Rose, Richard. *Governing Without Consensus*. Boston: Beacon Press, 1972.
Russell, Francis. *Tragedy in Dedham: The Story of the Sacco-Vanzetti Case*. New York: McGraw-Hill, 1971.
Sale, Kirkpatrick. *SDS*. New York: Vintage, 1974.
Saloutos, Theodore and John D. Hicks. *Twentieth Century Populism*. Lincoln: University of Nebraska Press, 1951.
Scheiber, Harry N. *The Wilson Administration and Civil Liberties*. Ithaca: Cornell University Press, 1960.
Schlesinger, Arthur M., Jr. *The Crisis of the Old Order*. Boston: Houghton-Mifflin, 1957.
Schlesinger, Arthur M., Jr. *The Politics of Upheaval*. Boston: Houghton-Mifflin, 1966.
Schlesinger, Arthur M., Jr. *A Thousand Days*. New York: Fawcett, 1967.
Schonbach, Morris. *Radicals and Visionaries: A History of Dissent in New Jersey*. Princeton: Van Nostrand, 1964.
Shannon, David. *The Decline of the American Communist Party*. New York: Harcourt, Brace, 1959.
Shannon, David. *The Socialist Party of America*. Chicago: Quadrangle, 1967.
Shannon, Fred. *The Centennial Years*. Garden City, N.Y.: Doubleday, 1969.
Shapiro, Stanley. "The Great War and Reform: Liberals and Labor, 1917-1919," *Labor History*, 12 (Spring, 1971).
Sims, Robert C. "Idaho's Criminal Syndicalism Act," *Labor History*, 15 (Fall, 1974).
Skolnick, Jerome H. *The Politics of Protest*. New York: Ballantine, 1969.
Smith, Geoffrey S. *To Save a Nation: American Countersubversives, the New Deal and the Coming of World War II*. New York: Basic Books, 1973.
Smith, Gibbs. *Labor Martyr: Joe Hill*. New York: Grosset and Dunlop, 1969.
Sofchalk, Donald F. "The Chicago Memorial Day Incident," *Labor History*, 6 (Winter, 1965).
Soule, George. *Prosperity Decade*. New York: Rinehart & Co., 1947.
Spinrad, William. *Civil Liberties*. Chicago: Quadrangle, 1970.
Stern, Phillip. *The Oppenheimer Case*. New York: Harper & Row, 1969.
Stevenson, Elizabeth. *The American 1920's*. New York: MacMillan, 1970.
Stone, I. F. *The Haunted Fifties*. New York: Vintage, 1969.
Suggs, George C., Jr. *Colorado's War on Militant Unionism: James H. Peabody and the Western Federation of Miners*. Detroit: Wayne State University Press, 1972.
Swisher, Carl. "Civil Liberties in War Time," *Political Science Quarterly*, 55 (September, 1940).
Symes, Lillian and Travers Clement. *Rebel America*. Boston: Beacon, 1972.
Taft, Philip and Philip Ross. "American Labor Violence: Its Causes, Character and Outcome," in Graham and Gurr, *Violence*.
Taft, Philip. "The IWW in the Grain Belt," *Labor History*, 1 (Winter, 1960).
Taft, Philip. "The Federal Trials of the IWW," *Labor History*, 3 (Winter, 1962).
Teodori, Massimo, ed. *The New Left: A Documentary History*. Indianapolis: Bobbs-Merrill, 1969.

Thayer, George. *The Farther Shores of Politics.* New York: Simon & Schuster, 1968.
Tindall, George B. *The Emergence of the New South.* Baton Rouge: Louisiana State University, 1967.
Tyler, Robert. *Rebels of the Woods: The IWW in the Pacific Northwest.* Eugene: University of Oregon Press, 1967.
Turner, William W. *Hoover's FBI.* New York: Dell, 1971.
Ungar, Sanford. *The FBI: An Uncensored Look Behind the Walls.* Boston: Little, Brown, 1976.
Ungar, Sanford. *The Papers and the Papers: An Account of the Legal and Political Battles over the Pentagon Papers.* New York: Dutton, 1975.
Vadney, Thomas E. "The Politics of Repression: A Case Study of the Red Scare in New York," *New York History,* 49 (January, 1968).
Wahlke, John C., ed. *Loyalty in a Democratic State.* Boston: D. C. Health, 1952.
Wallace, Michael. "The Uses of Violence in American History," *American Scholar* 40 (Winter, 1970-1971).
Watters, Pat, and Stephen Gillers, eds. *Investigating the FBI.* New York: Ballantine, 1974.
Waskow, Arthur. *From Race Riot to Sit-in.* Garden City, N.Y.: Doubleday, 1966.
Weinstein, James. "Anti-War Sentiment and the Socialist Party," *Poltical Science Quarterly,* 74 (June, 1959).
Weinstein, James. *The Corporate Ideal in the Liberal State.* Boston: Beacon, 1969.
Weinstein, James. *The Decline of Socialism in America, 1912-1925.* New York: Vintage, 1969.
Whitehead, Don. *The FBI Story.* New York: Pocket Books, 1958.
Whipple, Leonard. *The Story of Civil Liberty in the United States.* New York: Vanguard, 1927.
Whitten, Woodrow C. Criminal Syndicalism and the Law in California, 1919-1927. Philadelphia: American Philosophical Society, 1969.
Whitten, Woodrow C. "The Wheatland Episode," *Pacific Historical Review,* 17 (February, 1948).
Wiebe, Robert. *The Search for Order.* New York: Hill & Wang, 1967.
Wittner, Lawrence. *Rebels Against War: The American Peace Movement, 1941-1960.* New York: Columbia University Press, 1970.
Wolfe, Alan. *The Seamy Side of Democracy: Repression in America.* New York: David McKay, 1973.
Wolff, Leon. *Lockout: The Story of the Homestead Strike of 1892.* New York: Harper & Row, 1965.
Woodward, C. Vann. *Origins of the New South.* Baton Rouge: Louisiana State University Press, 1951.
Yellin, Samuel. *American Labor Struggles.* New York: Monad, 1974.
Zinn, Howard. *SNCC.* Boston: Beacon, 1965.

Index

All cities and counties mentioned in the book are indexed in alphabetical order under the state they are included within. All strikes are listed in chronological order under the category "strikes." All Supreme Court decisions are listed in chronological order under the category "Supreme Court." Congressional and state legislative investigative committees are listed under the categories "congressional investigating committees" and "state legislative investigating committees." Actions of individual state legislatures are listed by state in the category "state legislatures." Themes discussed in the conclusison of the book are listed under sub-categories of the topic "Political Repression." Major trials are listed under the topic "Trials." All colleges and universities are listed alphabetically under "Colleges and Universities." Unions organized on a trade, industrial or regional basis are listed alphabetically under "unions."

Abzug, Bella, 340, 478.
Academic freedom, threats to, in 1890's, 52; in Progressive Era, 94, 97; in World War I, 127, 129-30; in 1919 Red Scare, 147; in 1920's, 180-81; in Great Depression, 232; in Truman-McCarthy period, 362-63; in Vietnam War era, 518-23. See Firings, of teachers; Students; Expulsions; Colleges and Universities.
Acheson, Dean, 319-20, 325, 328, 335.
Adamic, Louis, 7.
Adams, Brooks, 7.
Addams, Jane, 134, 147-48.
Adler, Larry, 375-76.
Adomian, Len, 376.
Advance Youth Organization (AYD), 418, 426, 437.
Agents provocateur, 40, 73, 93, 110, 117, 159, 160, 211, 218, 249, 432, 473-77, 507-08, 512-13, 529, 535, 537.
Agnew, Spiro, 460-62, 495, 526.
Agricultural labor, 90-1, 85, 146, 150-51,
158, 190, 196, 205-06, 220-24, 570.
Alabama, 25, 51, 79, 87, 205, 207, 219, 351-52, 410, 506; Bessemer, 205, 219, 358; Birmingham, 202-03, 205, 219, 313, 358-59; Chambers Co., 219; Mobile, 186; Montgomery, 205.
Alien and Sedition Acts (1798), x, 67, 103, 212, 565.
Alien Enemies Act (1798), 103, 264, 272.
Alien Registration Act (1940). See Smith Act; Immigration Legislation, 1940.
Altgeld, John Peter, 38, 51.
Amerasia affair, 292-95, 330.
America First, 251, 253, 261.
American Association for the Advancement of Science, 315, 361.
American Alliance for Labor and Democracy (AALD), 124, 159.
American Association of University Professors (AAUP), 134, 361.
American Bar Association (ABA), 233, 363-64.

American Civil Liberties Union (ACLU), in World War I, 110, 112, 114, 125; in 1919 Red Scare, 147-48; in 1920's, 172-73, 175-76, 181, 191; in Great Depression, 195, 201, 231, 233, 235; in World War II period, 239-40, 261-63, 266, 268-69, 278; in Truman-McCarthy period, 287, 359, 361, 366, 368; in 1954-1964 period, 414; in Vietnam War era, 433, 435, 458, 482, 514, 516.

Americans for Democratic Action (ADA), 313, 314, 366, 400, 458, 482.

Americans Friends Service Committee (AFSC), 454, 458.

American League for Peace and Democracy (ALPD), 241-42.

American Legion, 155-56, 168, 209, 254, 257, 283, 329.

American Federation of Labor (AFL), xvi, xviii, 10; in 1870-1900 period, 42-6, 48, 51, 54, 56-9; in Progressive Era, 63-4, 70-1; 74-5, 78, 82-6, 88; and World War I, 115-16, 121-26, 134; and 1919 Red Scare, 139, 141-45; 151-53, 159; and 1920's, 174, 179-80, 185, 187, 190-91; and Great Depression, 197, 206, 208, 221, 226, 235-36; and World War II, 243, 252, 259, 260-61, 276; and Truman-McCarthy period, 341, 364-65; and effects of repression upon, 57-59, 153, 190-91, 551-53.

American Nazi Party, 425, 445.

American Protective League (APL), 110-112, 116, 129, 140, 149, 264.

American Review of Soviet Medicine, 371-72.

Anarchist Exclusion Act (1903). See Immigration Legislation, 1903.

Anarchists, in 1880's, 41-43; in 1890's, 44, 50-51; in Progressive Era, 64, 66, 101; and scare of 1901-1903, 66-70; and scare of 1907-09, 76-80; and scare of 1914-16, 93-94; and World War I, 110, 114, 134; and Red Scare of 1919, 155, 168-69; and 1920's, 174; as scapegoat, 570. See International Working Peoples Association.

Anarchist scares. See Scares, anarchist.

Anderson, George W. 135, 160.

Anti-Riot Act (1968), 442-43, 465, 468, 487, 492, 498, 526.

Arizona, 81, 115-16, 158, 175, 181, 184, 324, 433; Ash Fork, 125; Bisbee, 125-26; Choloride, 125; Galconde, 125; Jerome, 125-26; Kingman, 125; Mineral, 25; Ray, 125; Tucson, 125.

Arkansas, 107, 127, 216, 232, 257, 515; Phillips Co., 150-51, Marked Tree, 225.

Armed forces. See Federal troops; National guard; Military intelligence.

Army-McCarthy affair, 399-40, 570-71, 573.

Arrests of dissidents, as repressive technique, 14-16; in 1870's, 28, 31-32, 57; in 1880's, 37-9, 41, 44; in 1890's, 47-8, 50-3, 56, 71; in Progressive Era, 78-80, 85-98; in World War I, 109, 112-119, 125-26, 128, 131; in 1919 Red Scare, 145-48, 151-53, 156-58, 168; in 1920's, 169, 177-78, 180, 186-91; in Great Depression, 200, 202-06, 208, 218-28, 230, 232; in World War II period, 258-61, 275, 282-83; in Truman-McCarthy Period, 313, 359-60; in 1954-1964 period, 413-14; in Vietnam War era, 430, 432, 435, 437, 439, 451, 498, 512, 515-18, 520-22, 526-29.

Askin, Frank, 532.

Assassinations and attempts, 66-67, 78, 48, 432, 473.

Associated Farmers (AF), 222-24.

Atomic Energy Commission (AEC), 295, 315, 318-19, 324, 341, 364.

Auerbach, Jerold, 9, 262.

Aurand, Harold, 30.

Bacon, Leslie, 468.
Baez, Joan, 458, 483.
Baker, Newton D., 112, 150.
Baldwin, Roger, 147-48, 175-76.
Ballot exclusion laws. See Exclusions, from ballot.
Barnett, Richard, 384.
Barth, Alan, 303-04, 311.
Beal, Fred, 287.
Beard, Charles and Mary, 8.
Belfrage, Cedric, 331.
Bell, Daniel, xiii, 42, 510.
Bellamy, Edward, 50, 81.
Bentley, Elizabeth, 293, 316, 347.
Berger, Victor, 19-20, 140, 155, 157, 172.
Berkman, Alexander, 50, 167, 114, 134, 155.
Bernstein, Irving, 169, 222.
Berrigan, Philip, 476, 488. See Trials, Berrigan conspiracy.
Biddle, Francis, 248, 253-43, 263-66, 269, 271-72, 277-78, 280, 540.
Bielski, A. Bruce, 148.
Bigelow, Herbert, 126.
Billings, Warren K., 97-256.
Black Panther Party (BPP), 429, 455, 457, 467-68, 482, 495, 500, 522-30; effects of repression upon, 530-31, 555.
Blacks. See Black Panther Party; National Association for the Advancement of Colored People; Civil Rights Movement; Racial Disorders.

Bohmer, Peter, 501.
Bohlen, Charles, 342, 417.
Bombings, 78, 85, 93-5, 97, 99, 117, 145, 149, 161, 169, 431-32, 445-46, 473-76.
Bond, Julian, 458, 467, 514.
Bontecue, Eleanor, 380.
Bonus Expeditionary Force (Bonus Army, BEF), 197-200, 202, 209-10, 498, 534, 469.
Bourne, Randolph, 134.
Bourquin, George M., 135, 159.
Boyce, Edward, 71.
Boycotts, 41, 44, 53-54, 76-78, 153-54, 290.
Bottomore, T. B., 555-56.
Braden, Carl, 409.
Bridges, Harry, 215, 245, 251, 272, 318, 341.
Brody, David, 152.
Browder, Earl, 249, 262, 287-88.
Brown, H. Rap, 450.
Brown, Ralph S., 374, 376.
Brownell, Herbert, 337, 339, 340, 364, 400, 403.
Bryan, William Jennings, 6, 59-60, 64.
Budenz, Louis, 347.
Bunche, Ralph, 333, 347.
Bureau of Investigation. See Federal Bureau of Investigation.
Burglaries of dissident groups, 111, 175-76, 272, 292, 294, 396, 420-31, 443, 445, 472-73, 477, 485-86, 490, 502, 507, 538, 540-43.
Burleson, Albert, 114, 119, 172.
Burnett, Alfred, 473-74.
Burns, William, 85, 74-715.
Business domination, after Civil War, 5-9; in 1920's, 169-71, 550.
Butler, Nicholas Murray, 215, 262.

Cain, Harry, 402.
California, 6, 7, 81, 85, 89, 97, 107, 117, 118, 132, 140, 145-47, 156, 159, 161, 172, 181, 185-86, 196, 202, 206, 210, 220-24, 232-34, 242, 256, 259, 267, 270, 281-82, 288, 295, 305, 313, 324-25, 350, 352, 411-12, 414, 424, 432, 459, 476, 507, 514, 515, 519-20; Berkeley, 81, 510-11, 518; Burbank, 359; Fresno, 86, 182; Imperial Valley, 190, 206, 222; Kern Co., 221, 223; Los Angeles, 55, 76, 79, 85, 93, 145, 156, 182, 185, 202-04, 223, 252, 260, 264, 346, 353, 358-59, 362, 368, 414, 459, 471, 476, 504, 507-09, 513, 516, 518, 524-26; Los Angeles County, 352, 358-59, 412; Oakland, 53, 156, 359, 508-10, 524, 530; Orange Co., 223; Sacramento, 55, 93, 146, 524, 526-27; Salinas Valley, 223; San Diego, 86-87, 90, 424, 471, 474, 481, 518, 524-26; San Francisco, 37, 75, 79; 94, 97, 117, 121, 126, 207, 215-16, 226-27, 339, 414-15, 420, 430, 437, 510, 518, 524, 526; San Joaquin Valley, 221-22; Santa Clara Co., 206, Santa Rosa, 227; Stockton, 95, 223; Tulare Co., 221; Westwood, 260; Wheatland, 90-91.
Canada, 5, 274, 293-95.
Cantrell, D. C., 355.
Canwell, Albert, 295, 353.
Case Bill (1947), 290.
Carmichael, Stokely, 450.
Castro, Fidel, 388, 413, 419, 446, 478.
Caughey, John, 384.
Chafee, Zechariah, 159, 397.
Chambers, Whittaker, 293, 316, 317.
Chaplin, Charles, 331.
Christensen, Parley P., 179.
Christian Front, 249.
Christian Mobilizers, 253.
Central Intelligence Agency (CIA), 339-40, 342, 390, 394, 436-37, 444, 454-58, 460-61, 463, 467, 477-79, 485, 502-04, 537-41, 543-44, 558, 562, 570.
Church, Frank, 340, 545.
Civil Rights Movement, 395, 409-10, 413, 418, 424, 445-47.
Civil Service Commission (CSC), 109, 250, 266-67, 277-78, 308, 338, 484, 507.
Civil War, 3, 6, 17.
Clark, Ramsey, 437, 439-42, 445, 450, 454, 460, 487.
Clark, Tom, 294, 298-99, 306-07, 316, 318.
Clayton Act (1914), 84, 183-84.
Cleaver, Eldridge, 523, 530.
Cleveland, Grover, 6-7, 56.
Clubb, Oliver E., 386.
Cochran, Thomas and William Miller, 66.
Coffeehouses, anti-war, 480, 520, 517-18.
Coffin, William Sloane, 440, 458, 487.
Coal and Iron Police (Pennsylvania), 13, 29-30, 85, 190.
Coben, Stanley, 150.
COINTELPRO, 407, 452-3, 470-72, 481, 538-39, 540-42; against Communist Party, 407-08, 419-20, 447-48, 471; against Socialist Workers Party, 420-21, 471, 523, 540; against right-wing "hate groups," 425, 445-46; against "black nationalists," 449-51, 471, 524-26, 530; against "New Left," 451-52, 471, 535.
Colby, William, 478, 543.
Colleges and universities. U. of Alabama, 477; Antioch, 452; Arizona State, 523; U. of Arkansas, 515; Brown, 332; Bucknell, 476; U. of California, Berk-

eley, 232-33, 256, 262, 275, 313, 319, 352, 354-55, 358, 363, 413, 425, 434-35, 457, 511; U. of California, Santa Barbara, 512; California State College, Los Angeles, 527; Central Connecticut State, 521; U. of Chicago, 232, 262, 356, 413; Chicago State, 522; U. of Connecticut, 313, 435, 523; U. of Colorado, 363; Columbia, 262, 336, 451, 500, 510, 519; Commonwealth C. 232, 257-58; Harvard, 262, 340, 521, 531; Hobart, 475; Hunter, 382; U. of Illinois, Champaign-Urbana, 180, 202, 520-21; U. of Illinois, Chicago Circle, 522; U. of Indiana, 424, 521; Indiana State, 313; Iowa, State University of, 313; Jackson State, 511, 513; U. of Kansas City, 363; Kent State, 430-32, 512-13, 520, 532; U. of Michigan, 262, 313, 363, 437; U. of Minnesota, 131, 233, 375, 532; Mississippi Valley State, 521; U. of Missouri, 313, 522; U. of Nebraska, 130; U. of New Mexico, 505; New York City Municipal, 147, 256, 363, 404, 415, 425, 523; New York U., 459; U. of North Carolina, 318, 404; North Carolina Agricultural and Mechanical, 512; Northeastern Illinois State, 507; Northern Illinois, 522; Ohio State 180-81, 363, 415-16, 508, 512; U. of Oklahoma, 256-57, 355, 363; Oklahoma Agricultural and Mechanical, 357; Oklahoma State, 523; Oregon State, 363; Pasadena City, 478; Pennsylvania State, 522; Princeton, 262; Queens, 382; Roosevelt, 356; Rutgers, 363; San Diego State, 363, 523; San Fernando Valley State, 521; San Francisco State, 522; South Carolina State, 511; Southern Illinois, 363; Southern U., 513; Southwestern C., 127; U. of Texas, 127, 352, 507; Texas Southern, 514; U. of Utah, 97; U. of Vermont, 363, 523; U. of Virginia, 127, 233; Voorhees C., 521; U. of Washington, 354, 356, 362-63, 371, 377, 475, 492; Wayne State, 363; Wellesley, 174; West Chester State, 523; Western Washington, 256; U. of Wisconsin, Madison, 52, 232, 413, 432, 510; U. of Wisconsin, Milwaukee, 513, 523.
Colorado, 28, 55, 72-74, 92, 127, 131, 181, 207, 251, 313, 459, 514; Colorado Springs, 72; Cripple Creek, 5, 51, 70, 72; Denver, 37, 78, 141, 156, 158, 178, 420, 472, 516, 524, 526; El Paso Co., 51; Idaho Springs, 72; Leadville, 70-71; Ludlow, 92-93; Pueblo, 152, 156; Telluride, 71-72.
Comintern, 144, 172, 174, 246, 288.

Commager, Henry Steele, 383, 461.
Commission on Industrial Relations, 11, 15, 90, 96, 212.
Committee on Public Information (CPI), 105, 107, 129.
Committee for the Re-Election of the President (CRP), 486, 501-04.
Commons, John R., xii, 552.
Commonwealth v. *Hunt* (1842), 17.
Commune of Paris, 24-28, 30, 32, 37, 41, 144.
Communism, fear of. See Scares; Red-Baiting; Nativism.
Communism, traditional explanations for failure in U.S., xiii.
Communist Control Act (1954), 340-41, 366-67, 551, 553, 562, 564.
Communist Labor Party (CLP), 156, 160-162, 172, 174.
Communist Party (CP), xvii, xix, 68-69, 551, 553, 561, 565, 568, 570; and Red Scare of 1919, 141, 155-58, 160-63; and 1920's, 169, 172-75, 177-78, 186-88; and Great Depression, 195-208, 210, 212, 214-15, 219, 221-22, 226-27, 231-33, 235-36; and World War II period, 239-42, 245-51, 253-62, 264, 271-72; 279; and Truman-McCarthy period, 287-89, 291, 293-94, 296-99, 302-04, 307, 309, 310, 312-18, 321-23, 330-32, 339-40, 345-46, 348-51, 354-55, 358, 360-65, 367-71, 376, 382; and 1954-1964, 404-10, 423-25; and Vietnam War Era, 433-34, 438, 441, 447-48, 458, 494, 504, 522, 535; effects of repression upon, 161-63, 369-71, 551, 554-55, 561.
Communist scares. See Scares.
Communications industry, effects of repression upon, during Truman-McCarthy period, 361-62; during Nixon Administration, 495-97.
Company towns, 10-11, 13, 23, 29, 212, 260.
Condon, Edward U., 315.
Condon, Robert L., 401.
Congress, 6, 550, 554; in 1870-1900 period, 41, 43, 56; in Progressive Era, 67, 79, 88, 94, 100-01; and World War I, 105, 107-10; and 1919 Red Scare, 149-51, 158; and 1920's, 170, 174-76, 180; and Great Depression, 198, 200, 207-08, 213-14, 216-17, 233-34; and World War II period, 240, 243-46, 251-52, 254-55, 259, 275-80; and Truman-McCarthy period, 290, 292, 295, 296, 298, 305-07, 309, 318-19, 321, 323-24, 338, 340, 343-46, 351, 366, 385, 394; and 1954-1956 period, 403-06, 409-10, 414, 421-23; and Vietnam War era, 433, 435, 439,

Index 667

441-42, 469, 499, 500, 532-33, 537-41, 543-44.
Congressional investigating committees, Fish committee, 201, 204, 209, 213; House Committee on Un-American Activities (HUAC), later House Internal Security Committee, known from 1938-1945 as Dies Committee, 240-44, 247, 257-59, 261, 277, 288-89, 292, 296, 300, 306-08, 313, 315-17, 319, 321, 326, 343-46, 353, 356, 361, 363-64, 368, 374-48, 404, 408-12, 414-16, 422-23, 425, 433, 437, 441, 446, 448, 478, 500, 506, 532, 537, 544; House Civil Service Committee, 292, 295, 299; LaFollette Committee, 11, 12, 212, 217, 220, 223-24, 229-30, 233; McCormack-Dickstein Committee, 213-14; Overman Committee, 148; Reece Committee, 374; Senate Intelligence Committee, 176, 253, 274, 324, 395-96, 444, 447, 454, 457-58, 463-64, 469-70, 472, 479, 481, 486, 525, 530, 537, 542-43, 545, 574; Senate Internal Security Subcommittee (SISS), 326, 333, 343-44, 363, 373, 376, 402, 405-06, 408, 410, 413-14, 422, 436, 500, 544; Tydings Committee, 321, 327-28, 377; Senate Judiciary Subcommittee on Constitutional Rights, 459, 480; other committees, 214, 244, 213-16, 321, 343, 500, 503-04, 538.
Congress of Industrial Organizations (CIO), 212, 229-30, 236, 252, 276, 291, 341; and communist influence, 233, 236, 241, 243, 359, 260-61, 289, 319, 364-65, 551, 553.
Congress of Industrial Organizations Political Action Committee (CIO-PAC), 289, 295.
Connecticut, 326; Darien, 180; Hartford, 155, 310; New Haven, 529; Southberg, 258; Waterbury, 76.
Conner, Eugene "Bull," 313.
Conscientious objectors, and World War I, 112-13, 140; and World War II, 274-75.
Consensus approach to American history, x-xiv.
Conspiracy doctrine, and labor movement, 17-19, 23, 28, 32, 34, 39-40, 41, 48, 56, 76; and political radicals—see Trials; Smith Act; Sedition laws; Criminal Syndicalism laws; Criminal Anarchy laws.
Coolidge, Calvin, 151, 168, 170, 172, 174, 178-79, 562.
Copeland, Aaron, 334.
Coplon, Judith, 294, 317.
Coser, Lewis, 369-70.
Cotter, Cornelius P., 392.

Coughlin, Charles, 259, 268, 271.
Council on National Defense (CND), 84, 122, 129.
Courts, and dissidents. See Arrests; Conspiracy Doctrine; Trials; Labor Injunctions; Supreme Court.
Coxey, Jacob S., 53, 93.
Coxey's Army, 53, 93.
Creel, George, 107, 113-14, 121, 124.
Crime waves, 1919, 143; during Vietnam War era, 429-30.
Criminal anarchy laws and prosecutions, 68-70, 90, 147, 155, 163, 186-87, 205, 225, 244, 258, 434, 515.
Criminal syndicalism laws and prosecutions, 69, 101, 127-28, 146-47, 152, 156, 163, 172-73, 175, 177-78, 185-86, 198, 202-06, 212, 222, 224, 226, 231, 244, 256-57, 322, 350, 515.
Crouch, Paul, 348.
Cuba, 388, 413, 416-17, 419, 424, 478, 482.
Cushman, Robert, 280, 351.
Cvetic, Matthew, 345, 347.
Czolgosz, Leon F., 66-67.

Dahl, Robert, x-xi, xiv.
Dassin, Jules, 375.
Daugherty, Harry, 174-75, 188.
Daughters of the American Revolution (DAR), 52, 174, 233, 288.
David, Henry, 39.
Davies, John Paton, 329, 338.
Davis, Angela, 522.
Davis, David B., xi.
Davis, Rennie, 488.
Dean, John, 462, 483, 497, 503.
Debs, Eugene, 54, 56, 69, 73, 81, 119, 174, 179.
Defense Department, 245, 267-68, 318-19, 235, 387, 480-81, 459, 507.
See Federal troops; Military intelligence.
Delaware, 178-232; Wilmington, 53.
Dellenger, David, 488.
Democratic Party, 6, 48-49, 59, 100, 113, 208, 217, 289, 296-8, 314, 321, 327-28, 367, 384, 401, 461, 463, 501-04, 570.
Democratic theory, ix.
Demonstrations, protesting unemployment, 26-27, 52-53, 77, 93, 196, 198, 200, 203-04, 231; protesting war in Vietnam, 430, 435-39, 497-99.
Denaturalization proceedings, for politically repressive reasons, 79, 110, 241, 246, 249, 271-72, 337.
Dennis, Eugene, 204.
Dennis, Lawrence, 269.
Deportations, of aliens for politically re-

pressive resasons, 68, 79, 110, 112, 140, 147, 152, 154, 155, 158, 160, 169, 172-73, 190-91, 197, 201, 215-16, 226, 228, 233, 245, 251, 271-72, 311-12, 331-32, 337, 360, 369, 402-04, 433; of strikers from strike areas, 72, 75, 87, 97, 125-26, 146, 178, 185-86, 206, 225, 260.

Depressions, and fostering of political repression, 23, 575; of 1873, 24, 26-28, 33, 551, 564-65; of 1880's, 34, 564-65; of 1893, 44, 50, 564-65; of 1907, 77, 80-81, 565; of 1910-1911, 80; of 1914, 81, 93-94, 98, 565; of 1929 (Great Depression), 171, 195-236, 550, 558, 560, 563-65, 568-70, 572.

Deputization of private police and private employees, 13, 28, 37, 76, 87-88, 91-92, 95-97, 152, 219, 223, 227-28, 230.

DeSola, Ralph, 347.
DeTouqueville, Alexander, 565.
Dewey, Thomas, 289, 315, 319.
Dickstein, Samuel, 213, 240. See Congressional investigating committees, McCormack-Dickstein Committee.
Dies, Martin, 240-43, 277-79, 288-89. See Congressional investigating Committees, House Committee on Un-American Activities.
Dilling, Elizabeth, 215, 269.
Dissent. See Political Repression, variables of affecting intensity of.
Divale, William, 476.
Dodd, Thomas, 414.
Dominican Republic, 389-90.
Donner, Frank, 514, 536.
Douglass, Boyd, 476-77.
Douglass, Paul, 366, 396.
Douglass, William O. 396, 469, 491.
Draft, opposition to, in World War I, 107; in Vietnam War, 430, 435-36; repressive use of, 116, 252, 275-76, 290, 439-40.
Draft card burnings, 435; outlawing of, 435.
Draper, Paul, 375-76.
Drug arrests, 514.
Dubofsky, Melvyn, 58.
DuBois Clubs, 437, 438, 520.
Duchacek, Ivo, xxi.
Dulles, Foster Rhea, 153, 336.
Dulles, John Foster, 334, 336, 386, 388.
Dunne, William F., 146.
Dye, Thomas R., xi.
Eastman, Max, 126.
Eaton, Cyrus, 411.
Eight-hour day agitation, 25-26, 35, 37-40, 43, 45, 72, 116, 122.

Einstein, Albert, 297, 383.
Eisenhower, Dwight D., 309, 327, 331-34, 337-43, 365-67, 388, 396, 399-400, 402, 404, 406, 412-13, 561-62.
Elaine Massacre (1919), 150-51.
Elections, of 1892, 49, of 1896, 59, of 1917, 106; of 1920, 161, 178-79; of 1924, 178-79; of 1928, 178; of 1932, 200; of 1934, 234; of 1936, 210, 216-17, 228, 231; of 1938, 242; of 1940, 242; of 1944, 289; of 1946, 290, 295, 297, 299; of 1948, 315-16, 319; of 1950, 321, 325-26; of 1952, 327; of 1954, 401; of 1960, 412; of 1964, 433, 444-45; of 1968, 429, 460-61, 509; of 1972, 486, 491, 502-04.
Ellsberg, Daniel, 387, 486, 489-91, 502, 554.
Ely, Richard T. 52.
Enemy aliens, treatment during World War I, 108-09, 140; during World War II, 264.
Emergency detention, Justice Department and FBI plans for, 248, 254, 293, 312, 322-24, 366, 393, 403, 418, 441, 453-54, 465-66, 469-70, 537.
Emerson, Thomas, xvii, 304, 310.
Epton, William, 434, 515.
Erlichman, John, 462, 483, 490, 497, 501-02.
Erskine, Hazel, 573.
Espionage Act (1917) and prosecutions, 69, 103, 113-14, 117, 121, 128, 135, 140, 146, 149, 155, 172-73, 244, 264, 268-69, 270, 293, 317, 319-21, 340, 348, 489-90, 562.
Ettor, Joseph, 89.
Europe, ix, xi, xii, 12, 24, 33, 41, 50-51, 66, 139, 143-44, 161, 239-40, 296, 298.
Everest, Wesley, 156.
Exclusions, for political reasons, from appearing on the ballot, 232, 256, 258, 259, 282, 348-50, 394, 433; from entrance to the bar, 412; from federal employment, 244-46, 266-67, 322, 341; from federal fellowships, 423, 442, 519; from juries, 345; from the House of Representatives, 155, 157; from state legislatures, 157, 160, 256, 513-14; from state employment, 245, 259; from public housing, 310; from tax exemptions, 322; from union office, 341; from state welfare benefits, 282, 310, 345; from federal welfare benefits, 244-45; from city employment, 260; from attending school, 283, 330-31; from veterans benefits, 310; from passports, 322, 341; from merchant marine employment, 324; from immi-

gration and naturalization, 68, 88, 245-46, 311, 322-23. See Loyalty programs; Internal Security Act; Communist Control Act; Immigration Laws.
Expulsions and suspensisons of students, 181, 232, 262, 283, 330-31, 521.
Fainsod, Merle, 120.
Fair Play for Cuba Committee, 419, 422, 425.
Fairbank, John K., 362.
Farmer, militancy, 24-26, 44, 48-50, 201, 224. See Non-Partisan League.
Farmer-Labor Party, 1920, 179; 1924, 179.
Fast, Howard, 303, 336, 362.
Faulkner, Harold, 64.
Federal Bureau of Investigation, and World War I, 140; and 1919 Red Scare, 148-50, 162; and 1920's, 174-77; and Great Depression, 200, 213-15; and World War II era, 241, 246-54, 259, 263-64, 272-73, 276, 278, 282; and Truman-McCarthy period, 288, 292-95, 299-300, 306-07, 312, 317, 319, 323-24, 326-27, 333, 335, 339-40, 342, 345-47, 375, 382, 394-96; and 1954-1964, 407-08, 410-11, 417-22; and Vietnam War era, 430, 432, 434, 437, 438, 443-58, 460-78, 481-82, 485-86, 490-91, 497-98, 501, 503-04, 506-08, 518, 523, 524-32, 535, 538-43, 562, 574. See also Hoover, J. Edgar; Burglaries; Microphone Bugs; Wiretapping; *Agents Provacateurs;* COINTELPRO.
Federal Communications Commission (FCC), 495, 497.
Federal government. See Political repression, federal role in; also see entries for individual presidents; for Congress; House; Senate; Congressional Investigating Committees; Supreme Court; individual executive departments and intelligence agencies; and Federal troops.
Federal Theatre Project, 242-43.
Federal troops, 14, 16; and 1870-1900, 31, 47, 51, 53, 55-56, 71; and Progressive Era, 77, 79, 101, and World War I, 110-11, 115-16; and 1919 Red Scare, 144-45, 147, 151-53, 158-59, 161; and 1920's, 169, 189-90; and Great Depression, 198-200; and World War II period, 252, 268, 276; since World War II, 276, 439, 498.
Federal Writers Project, 243-44.
Fieffer, Jules, 382, 506.
Firings, for political reasons, of federal employees, 279-80, 295, 335, 338-39, 374-75; of state and local government employees 182, 352, 362-63, 375; of teachers, 97, 127, 131, 147, 180, 187, 256, 258, 281, 344, 354-55, 411, 414; of private employees, 345, 361, 375. See Loyalty programs.
First International, 25-26.
Fish Committee. See Congressional Investigating Committees.
Flag desecration statutes and prosecutions, 72, 114, 203, 442, 514, 544.
Flynn, Elizabeth Gurley, 262.
Flynn, William J., 149-50.
Florida, 81, 114, 259, 281, 324, 351; Gainesville, 491; Jacksonville, 358-59; Miami, 358-59, 410, 424, 491, 508; Tallahassee, 491; Tampa, 205.
Ford, Gerald, 390, 473, 539-40, 544.
Ford, Richard, 90-91.
Ford Foundation, 340, 374, 409, 482.
Foreign Agents Registration Act (1938) and prosecutions, 244, 249, 250, 272, 332.
Foreign policy, effect of Truman-McCarthy repression in stifling new initiatives, 384-90, 558; crises in, fostering repression, 565.
Foreign subversion, fear of. See Nativism.
Foreman, Carl, 375.
Foster, William Z., 178.
Fraina, Louis, 177-78.
France, 4.
Frankfurter, Felix, 159.
Franklin, John Hope, 7.
Free Speech Movement, 434-35.
Free Speech fights. See Industrial Workers of the World.
Freeland, Richard, 309.
French Revolution, 24, 144.
Frick, Henry, 44-45, 50, 229.
Friends of Progress, 270, 282.
Friends of the New Germany, 213-14, 239, 241.
Fulbright, William, 390, 399.
Fund for the Republic, 373-74, 409.

Gaddis, John Lewis, 285.
Galileo, **ix-x**.
Garmen, Francis P., 149-50, 158.
Garraty, John A., 195.
Gellhorn, Walter, 372-73.
General Intelligence Division (GID) of Federal Bureau of Investigation, 149-50, 158-59, 176, 248.
Georgia, 94, 107, 182, 202, 204, 208, 212, 219, 351, 513-15; Atlanta, 483, 516, 518; Macon, 219.
German-American Bund, 239-41, 246-47, 250-51, 253, 256, 258-60, 266, 269, 270-72, 278, 282.
German-Americans, and World War I, 81, 99-100, 108-10, 114, 125; and

Great Depression, 213-14; and World War II, 253, 259, 264.
Germany, 99, 105, 107, 120, 143-44, 161, 213-14, 240-41, 244, 246, 252, 259, 284, 271, 287-88.
Ginger, Ray, 56.
Giovannitti, Arturo, 89.
Gitelman, H. M., 12.
Gitlow, Benjamin, 172.
Glassford, Pelham, 198, 222.
Godfrey, Howard Berry, 474.
Goldman, Emma, 51, 60, 79, 94, 134, 114, 155, 210, 216.
Goldman, Eric, 436, 564.
Goldwater, Barry, 433, 445.
Gompers, Samuel, **xiv**, 57-58, 74, 78, effects of repression upon, 83-85, 552-53.
Gompers v. Buck's Stove and Range, 78.
Goodell, Charles, 468, 482.
Goodman, Walter, 305.
Gould, Jay, 35, 37, 42.
Grand juries, use of for political intelligence by Nixon administration, 493-94.
Grangers, 26, 48, 81.
Grantwohl, Larry G., 476.
Great Britain, 58, 107, 113, 274, 298, 555.
Green Corn Rebellion, 120.
Gregory, Thomas, 107-08, 112-13, 140.
Griffith, Robert, 243.
Grimm, Charles, 477.
Grottkau, Paul, 38.

Halberstam, David, 388, 390.
Haldeman, Robert, 462, 495, 502-03.
Handlin, Oscar, 53, 259.
Hanrahan, Edward, 528-29.
Hardy, Robert W., 475.
Harris, Reed, 336, 417.
Harris, Roy, 334.
Hanson, Ole, 144-45, 151.
Harding, Warren, 160-61, 172, 174, 188-89.
Hart, Philip, 574.
Hartz, Louis, **xi**.
Hatch Act (1939), 244, 250, 259, 278-79, 562.
Hawaii, 264-65, 281, 318, 339, 383, 514, 571.
Hayden, Tom, 467, 488.
Hayes, Rutherford B., 31.
Haymarket affair, 17-18, 34, 37-42, 44, 51, 52, 67, 82, 94, 290, 550-52; see International Working People's Association.
Hays, Samuel, 64.
Haywood, William, 72-74.
Hearst press, 215-16, 231, 234-35.
Helfeld, David, 304, 310.

Hershey, Lewis, 252, 275, 439-41.
Hewitt, George, 348.
Higham, John, 60, 67.
Hill, Joe, 96-97.
Hilliard, David, 468.
Hilquit, Morris, 119.
Hiss, Alger, 316-17, 319-20, 326, 329, 335, 368, 376.
Hoan, Daniel W., 133.
Hoffa, Jimmy, 252-53.
Hoffman, Abbie, 488.
Hoffman, Julius, 488.
Hofstadter, Richard, x, 4.
Holliday, Judy, 377.
Hollywood ten, 306-07.
Hoover, Herbert, 195, 197-201, 206, 209-10, 562-64, 566-67, 569.
Hoover, J. Edgar, and 1919 Red Scare, 149-50, 156; and 1920's, 158, 160, 175-76; and Great Depression, 210, 215; and World War II period, 247-50, 253-54; 264; and Truman-McCarthy period, 293, 298, 307, 329, 332, 340, 344, 346, 351, 396; and 1954-1964, 408, 410, 415, 420; and Vietnam War era, 436-38, 443, 445, 447-49, 451-52, 464, 472, 485, 489, 501, 508, 524, 526, 538-40, 542. See Federal Bureau of Investigation.
House of Representatives, 140, 155, 157, 160, 172, 201, 208, 312-14, 216, 240, 244-48, 275, 279-80, 288-89, 315-16, 321, 325, 346, 406, 412, 423, 437, 537.
Howe, Irving, 369-70.
Humphrey, Hubert H., 340, 366, 367, 436, 460, 502.
House Committee on Un-American Activities. See Congressional investigating committees.
House Internal Security Committee. See Congressional investigating committees.
Huston, Tom Charles, 477, 485-86, 539.
Huston Plan, 485-86.
Hutchins, Robert M., 231, 356, 374.
Hyman, Herbert, 555.

Ickes, Harold, 26, 242, 265.
Idaho, 81, 101, 115, 126, 131, 156, 186, 225, 228; Caldwell, 72; Clearwater Co., 126; Coeur d'Alene, 46-47, 71; Latah Co., 126; Nampa, 128; Pocatello, 128.
Illinois, 16, 18, 76, 85, 128, 172, 182, 202, 230, 232, 259, 282, 313, 325, 520; Champaign-Urbana, 202; Chicago, 12-13, 15, 27, 30-32, 34, 36-42, 51, 54-56, 66-67, 76-79, 85, 94-95, 106, 111, 117-119, 127, 157, 169, 182, 188, 197, 203-04, 208, 230-31, 259, 262, 318, 428, 442, 468, 475, 487-88, 504-

12, 516-17, 524, 526-29, 533; Collinsville, 125; Cook Co., 306; East St. Louis, 37, 40; Herrin, 4, 190; Lewiston, 258; Melrose Park, 204; Moline, 106; Pullman, 10, 53; Peoria, 359; Rock Island, 106; Spring Valley, 51, 64; Staunton, 126; Virden, 5.
Immigration laws and proceedings thereunder, of 1882, 33; of 1903 (Anarchist Exclusion Act), 67-70, 88: of 1917, 69, 100, 110; of 1918, 69, 110, 147, 154; of 1920, 69, 158; of 1924, 168; of 1940 (Alien Registration Act, Smith Act), 69, 245; of 1950 (Internal Security Act), 322-23, 331; of 1952 (Walter-McCarren Act), 69, 331); proposed laws of 1913 and 1915, 94.
Income, maldistribution of, 8-9, 65-66, 170-71.
Indiana, 11, 16, 28, 85, 106, 127, 181, 232, 282, 351-52, 359; Connorsville, 261; Gary, 152, 214; Hammond, 55; Indianapolis, 27, 31, 182, 359, 518, 526; La Porte, 53; Muncie, 77; Terre Haute, 228.
Inflation, in 1919, 139, 143; post-World War II, 291.
Industrial accidents, 66.
Industrial Workers of the World (IWW), xiii - xv, 15-16, 65, 68, 84, 95, 97, 236, 553, 564, 567-68, 571; founding of and early activity, 73-74, 77, 80-81; growth in Progressive Era, 82-83, 98-99; and attitude towards violence, 82-83; and free speech fights in Progressive Era, 82, 86-87, 93, 96-97; strikes during Progressive Era, 86-91, 95-96; and immigration laws, 94, 88, 101, 10, 112, 118, 140, 147; and Justice Department investigations before World War I, 89, 94; growth during World War I, 105-06, 140; repression by federal government during World War I, 110, 113, 115-19, 121, 123-25, 134, 140; repression by states and localities during World War I, 125-27, 130; during 1919 Red Scare, 146-48, 155-56, 158, 160-62; in 1920's and afterwards, 173-74, 185-86, 224, 228, 322, 492, 505; effects of repression upon, 132, 139, 550-51; as scapegoat group, 570.
Institute for Pacific Relations (IPR), 310, 373-74.
Intelligence agencies. See Federal Bureau of Investigation, Central Intelligence Agency, National Security Agency, Internal Revenue Service, Justice Department, Military Intelligence, Red Squads.

Inter-Divisional Information Unit, of Justice Department, 460, 467, 482.
Internal Revenue Service (IRS), 234, 373-74, 401, 406-07, 422, 446, 453, 460, 463, 481-83, 495, 500, 502-03, 507, 526.
Internal Security Act (1950) and prosecutions, 321-24, 328, 329, 331-32, 339, 346, 348, 350-51, 366, 392-94, 403-04, 412, 418, 423-24, 454, 469, 500, 507, 562. See Emergency Detention; Subversive Activities Control Board.
Internal Security Division, of Justice Department, 417, 437, 465, 593.
International Information Administration, 335-36, 342.
International communications, interception of. See National Security Agency.
International Working Peoples Association (IWPA), 34, 36-42, 70, 82, 550, 552, 553, 567.
Interstate Commerce Act (1887), 44, 56.
Interworld Church Movement, 153, 212.
Iowa, 6, 131, 133; Council Bluffs, 208; Des Moines, 93; Sioux City, 93.
Isaacson, Leo, 311-12.
Italian-Americans, and World War II, 253, 264.

Jacobs, Melville, 377.
Jackson, Robert, 249, 252, 263-64, 281.
Jamieson, Stuart, 4-5, 221.
Japanese-Americans, and World War II, 260, 262, 264-68, 272, 281, 324, 571.
Jefferson, Thomas, 114, 565.
Jehovah's Witnesses, and World War I, 115; and expulsions for refusing to salute flag, 232; and World War II repression, 354-55, 261, 267, 274, 280, 282-83.
Jenner, William, 325, 327, 337.
Jessup, Philip, 328, 371, 417.
John Birch Society, 424-25, 458, 484.
Johnson, Albert, 88, 564.
Johnson, Hiram, 87, 90, 167.
Johnson, Lee Otis, 514.
Johnson, Lyndon Baines, 389-90, 406, 418, 430, 433, 435-37, 439, 441-45, 447-50, 452, 454, 456, 460-61, 463, 487, 499, 509, 533, 538, 561-62, 564-65, 567, 570.
Johnson, Manning, 333, 347-48.
Josephson, Matthew, 196.
Justice Department, in Progressive Era, 89, 94; in World War I, 101, 110-13, 115, 117-18, 121, 124, 126, 135; in 1919 Red Scare, 148-50, 152, 154, 158, 160-61; in 1920's, 169, 173-77, 189; in Great Depression, 198, 213;

in World War II period, 241, 247-48, 251, 253, 254, 264, 265, 269, 271, 278-79, 293; in Truman-McCarthy period, 293, 306-07, 309, 312, 319, 323-24, 326, 329, 333, 346, 348, 369; in 1954-1964, 402, 407, 417-18; in Vietnam War era, 430, 436, 440, 445-47, 449, 454, 458, 460, 462, 465, 467, 469, 476, 484, 487, 489, 495-98, 501, 526, 539-40, 542-43. See Federal Bureau of Investigation, Internal Security Division, Inter-Divisional Information Unit, listings under individual Attorney Generals.
Kaghan, Theodore, 336.
Kane, Francis F., 159.
Kansas, 117, 140, 182; Ft. Leavenworth, 274; Kansas City, 93; Lawrence, 513.
Katzenbach, Nicholas, 436-37, 443-445.
Kelley, Clarence, 472, 474, 541-42.
Kelly's Army, 93.
Kennedy, Edward, 240, 501.
Kennedy, John F., 384, 388-89, 412, 414, 416, 422-23, 425, 432, 445, 447, 538, 561, 568.
Kennedy, Robert F., 416-23, 437.
Kentucky, 28, 196, 202, 281, 409, 515; Ft. Knox, 517; Harlan Co., 10, 13, 205-06, 220; Louisville, 30, 53, 182; Meade Co., 517; Muldraugh, 517; Newport, 126.
Killings and shootings, in incidents involving dissidents and political authorities, 3-4, 11-12, 15-16; in 1870's, 31; in 1880's, 37-38, 40, 43-44; in 1890's, 45-47, 51, 55-56, 71; in Progressive Era, 75-77, 80, 84-85, 87, 89-92, 94-96, 98; in 1919 Red Scare, 145, 150-52, 156, 158; in 1920's, 186, 188, 189, 190-91; in Great Depression, 199, 203-06, 218-22, 225-28, 230-31, 260; in Truman-McCarthy period, 287; in Vietnam War era, 430-31, 446, 473-74, 508, 511-13, 525-29. See Violence.
King, Martin Luther, 340, 418, 421-22, 441-443-44, 450, 458.
Kircheimer, Otto, 560, 565.
Kissinger, Henry, 390, 488-89.
Kleindeinst, Richard, 462, 499.
Knights of Labor, 34-37, 42-44, 70, 105, 551, 567.
Kolko, Gabriel, 132.
Korean War, 320-21, 325-26, 333, 348, 357-60, 365, 374, 387, 402, 423.
Kraft, Joseph, 448, 501.
Ku Klux Klan (KKK), 168, 181-82, 258, 445-46, 458, 515, 571.
Kuhn, Fritz, 241, 258, 259, 271-72.
Kunze, William, 269-70.
Labor, Department of, 160, 198, 216.
Labor injunctions, as repressive technique, 17-19; in 1870-1900 period, 23, 34, 37, 44, 46-48, 54-56; in Progressive Era, 75-77, 85, 88, 91; in 1919 Red Scare, 153; in 1920's, 179, 183, 188-89, 191; in Great Depression, 206-08; in Truman-McCarthy period, 290.
Labor movement. Changing government responses to, xvii; traditional explanation for lack of radicalism in xi, xiv, techniques used to repress, 9-19. Growth of, after Civil War, 25-26; in 1880's, 34-35; in 1890's, 44-45, 49-51; in Progressive Era, 74-75, 83-84; in World War I, 122-24; in Great Depression, 211-12, 217-18, 228-29; in World War II, 276. Militant and radical elements within, in 1870's, 25-26, 32; in 1880's, 34-38; in 1890's, 51-56; in Progressive Era, 70-73, 77, 81-84; in 1919 Red Scare, 139-43, 151-53. Effects of repression in halting general growth of labor movement and stifling radical and militant elements, 547-53; in 1870's, 33-34; in 1880's, 42-43; in 1890's, 56-59; in 1904-1910, 76; in World War I, 132; in 1919 Red Scare, 153, 161; in 1920's, 190-91. See individual labor movements and unions.
Ladejinsky, Wolf, 401-02.
LaFollette, Philip, 234.
LaFollette, Robert, 140, 179-80, 212.
LaFollette Committee. See Congressional investigating committees.
LaGuardia, Fiorello, 258, 297.
Lampell, Millard, 377.
Landrum-Griffin Act (1959), 409, 423, 551.
Lasch, Christopher, 552, 556.
Lasser, David, 246, 279.
Lattimore, Owen, 333, 347, 362, 401.
Lazarsfeld, Paul, 380-81.
Legal profession, and Truman-McCarthy period, 363-64.
Levi, Edward, 538-40, 543.
Lewis, John L., 276, 290.
Link, Arthur, 244.
Lippmann, Walter, 261, 297, 384.
Little, Frank, 117.
Long, Huey, 234.
Lorwin, Val R., 4.
Los Angeles Times, 85.
Louisiana, 37, 43, 51, 28, 87, 114, 125, 182, 234, 252, 349, 351, 409-10; Bogalusa, 151; Grabow, 87; Merryville, 187-88; New Orleans, 48, 76, 205, 339, 505, 506, 516, 518; Thibodaux, 44.
Lovett, Robert Morss, 279-80.
Loyal Legion of Loggers and Lumbermen, 116.
Loyalty oaths, 180, 232, 318, 348-52, 355, 357-58, 368-69; 394, 409, 411, 417, 423, 433.

Loyalty programs, federal, 78, 109-11, 244, 250-51, 266-67, 277-80, 289, 239-94, 299-305, 308, 318-19, 322, 324-25, 328-30, 335, 337-39, 341-42, 351, 371, 374, 376, 379-80, 392-94, 401-04, 412, 499, 562; state and local, 180, 348-50, 358-59. See Firings, from federal, state and local governments.
Loyalty Review Board (LRB), 300, 302, 304, 330, 332, 335.
Lusk Committee. See state legislative investigating committees, New York.
Lynd, Staughton, 522.

MacArthur, Douglas, 199, 270, 309, 327, 333, 387.
MacDougall, Curtis, 313.
Magnusson Act (1950), 324.
Mail, opening of, 111, 250, 254, 273, 294, 339-40, 394-96, 443-44, 454-56, 478, 481, 485, 538-39, 541, 543-44.
Mails, suppression of the, 79, 94, 103, 109, 114-21, 156, 197-98, 210, 250-51, 332, 392, 417, 423, 438.
Maine, 107, 219.
Malcolm X, 421.
Manchester, William, 487.
Mankind United, 270.
March, Frederick and Mrs. 294, 353, 375.
Marcuse, Herbert, xviii.
Marshall, George C., 309, 327, 335.
Martial law, 11, 14, 47-48, 71, 72, 75, 77, 88, 91-92, 95, 145, 152, 182, 189, 219, 224, 228, 230, 252, 264-65, 268, 281, 460.
Martin, Joseph, 296, 305, 327.
Marx, Gary, 531, 536, 537.
Marx, Karl, 26, 41.
Marxist parties. See International Working Peoples Association; Workingman's Party of the U.S.; Communist Party; Communist Labor Party; Socialist Workers Party.
Maryland, 13, 31, 53, 325, 350-52; Baltimore, 31, 506; Bethesda, 372; Cumberland, 31, 358; Montgomery Co., 518.
Masks, laws barring wearing of, 182.
Massachusetts, 168-69, 180, 224, 351, 409, 504-07, 515; Boston, 17, 27, 77, 93, 145, 169, 178, 182, 204, 467, 494; Dedham, 169; Fall River, 27; Ipswich, 95; Lawrence, 88-89; Lynn, 157; Milford, 94; New Bedford, 187; S. Braintree, 168.
Matthews, J. B., 342, 356.
Matthews, Jane, 243.

Matusow, Harvey, 402, 348.
May Day, riots of 1919, 145; demonstration of 1971, 439, 498-99.
Mazzei, Joseph, 348.

McCarren, Patrick, 322, 333.
McCarthy, Joseph R., xviii, 100, 244, 295, 320, 321, 325-30, 334-37, 339, 341-45, 348, 362, 367, 377, 399, 412, 515, 522, 561, 564, 570, 572-73.
McConnell, Grant, xi.
McGovern, George, 481, 483, 502.
McGranery, James P., 329, 331.
McGrath, J. Howard, 312, 329, 332, 346.
McGrath, Earl J., 318, 346.
McKinley, William, 59, 66-67.
McLeod, Scott, 335.
McNamara, James, 85-86.
McNamara, John J., 85-86.
McPharland, James, 29, 73.
McWilliams, Carey, 383.
Memorial Day Massacre (1937), 230-31.
Metzger, Walter, 566.
Michigan, 28, 55, 128, 133, 178, 182, 202, 230, 232, 350, 351, 409, 534; Battle Creek, 55; Bridgman, 178; Calumet, 91; Dearborn, 203, 208; Detroit, 26-27, 77, 93, 145, 155-57, 203, 207-08, 212, 249, 271, 352, 359, 430, 449-50, 458, 504, 514; Flint, 204, 229, 345; Hancock, 92; Houghton Co., 91; Lansing, 202; Monroe, 230; Paine, 91; River Rouge, 125.
Microphone bugging, 111, 254, 272-73, 293, 340, 342, 395-96, 421, 442-44, 467, 477, 539, 542-43.
Miliband, Ralph, 548, 557.
Military intelligence, in World War I, 110, 112, 116, 140; in 1919 Red Scare, 148-52, 158, 160; in 1920's, 173-74, 177; in Great Depression, 199-200, 202, 215; in World War II period, 247-48, 272-75; in Truman-McCarthy period, 300; in Vietnam War era, 449, 457-61, 463, 467, 481-81, 485, 506, 528, 532, 537, 539, 543.
Militia, see National Guard.
Millis, Walter, 391.
Minnesota, 6, 15, 81, 99, 106, 119, 127, 128, 130-31, 133, 234, 242, 514; Bemidji, 125; Mesabi Range, 95-96; Minneapolis, 82, 99, 125, 133, 182, 227-28, 252-53; Moorhead, 186; New Ulm, 131; Virginia, 86; Wrenshall, 424.
Mississippi, 197, 219, 282, 351, 511, 515; Jackson, 518; Meridian, 446.
Missouri, 55, 260, 326; Fulton, 296; St. Louis, 26-27, 30-31, 77, 203-04.
Mitchell, John, 445, 467, 469, 485, 487, 499, 503, 513, 526.
Mohawk Valley Formula, 229-30.
Molly Maguires, 24-25, 28-30, 33, 40, 73.
Montana, 6, 81, 94, 115-16, 118, 127-28, 131, 146-47, 159, 350; Butte, 81, 95, 110, 115, 117, 130, 141, 146, 158, 159; Duluth, 128; Kalispell, 128.

Montgomery, David, 17.
Mooney, Tom, 96-97, 117, 142, 143, 149, 202, 210, 256.
Most, Johann, 36, 39, 67.
Movie industry, effect of Truman-McCarthyism upon, 361-62.
Mowitz, Robert J., 128.
Mowry, George, 143.
Moyer, Charles, 72-74, 92.
Muck, Carl, 109.
Muhammed, Elijah, 395, 450.
Mundt-Nixon Bill. See Internal Security Act.
Murphy, Frank, 207, 229, 242.
Murphy, Paul, 412, 416.
Murray, George, 522.
Murray, Philip, 261, 312-13, 365.
Murray, Robert, 167.
Murrow, Edward R., 399, 417.
Muskie, Edmund, 467, 501-02.

The Nation, 141, 219, 265-66, 382.
Nation of Islam (Black Muslims), 395, 450.
National Association for the Advancement of Colored People (NAACP), 175, 253-54, 395-96, 409-10, 447, 458, 460, 484.
National Civic Federation (NCF), 63, 74, 83, 106.
National Committee on American-Soviet Friendship (NCASF), 309-10.
National Defense Education Act (NDEA, 1958), 409, 417, 423.
National Education Association (NEA), 33, 261, 318, 362, 482.
National Guard, 5, 13-16; in 1870's, 28, 31-32, 34; in 1880's, 37, 39, 41, 43-44; in 1890's, 45-48, 51, 55-56, 70; in Progressive Era, 72, 75-77, 79, 88, 90-92, 95; in World War I, 126; in 1919 Red Scare, 149, 151-52, 161; in 1920's, 169, 182, 184-88, 190-91; in Great Depression, 205-07, 218-20, 224-30; in World War II period, 260; in Truman-McCarthy period, 289; in Vietnam War era, 459, 508, 512, 520-21.
National Industrial Recovery Act (NIRA, 1933), 211.
National Labor Party, 142.
National Labor Union, 25-26.
National Labor Relations Board (NLRB), 211, 217, 231, 291, 341. See Wagner Act.
National Lawyers Guild (NLG), 233, 364.
National Security Administration (NSA), 273-74, 419, 433, 456-58, 460, 478-79, 485, 538-41, 543-44.

National Security League, 140, 148.
National States Rights Party, 445.
National University Conference, 466.
Nationalist Clubs, 50.
Nationality Act (1940), 246.
Nathan, Otto, 330.
Nativism, in 1870's, 24-28, 32-33; in 1880's, 34, 40-41; in 1890's, 52; in Progressive Era, 94, 100; in 1919 Red Scare, 154-58; in 1920's, 167-68; in World War II period, 245. See German-Americans; Italian-Americans; Japanese-Americans; Communist Party; Red-Baiting.
Nazism, groups favoring, 213-15, 239-40, 245, 254, 256, 259, 425. See Friends of the New Germany, German-American Bund, American Nazi Party.
Nazi-Soviet Non-Aggression Pact (1939), 240, 262, 289, 554.
Nebraska, 117, 224, 240; Fairbury, 125; Lincoln, 125; Omaha, 16, 524.
Neuman, Franz, xviii.
Nevada, 81; Ely, 11-12; Goldfield, 77.
New Hampshire, 351, 405, 411, 514-15.
New Jersey, 67, 119, 157, 202, 224-25, 258-59, 282, 294, 420, 504, 516; Atlantic City, 182, 444; Bayonne, 95; Bridgeton, 114; Camden, 178, 328, 475; Ft. Monmouth, 337; Franklin, 126; Garfield, 89, 187; Haledon, 90; Harrison, 182; Jersey City, 233, 359; Metuchen, 95; Newark, 67, 430, 434, 450, 458; Passaic, 89, 187; Patterson, 66, 76, 79.
New Left, growth of, 429-31; targetted by FBI, 451-54; effects of repression upon, 530-37. See Students for a Democratic Society; Black Panther Party.
New Mexico, 67, 519; Albuquerque, 505; Gallup, 125, 228, Grant Co., 360; Raton, 55.
New Republic, 118, 122, 134, 141, 219, 261.
New York State, 28, 50, 67-68, 106, 146-47, 151, 160, 172, 182, 232, 255-56, 258-59, 310, 326, 351, 352, 359, 369, 404, 424, 438, 448, 475, 506, 514, 515, 519; Albany, 31; Brooklyn, 178, 249, 360; Buffalo, 30, 47, 67, 106, 512, 514; Little Falls, 88; New York City, 26-28, 36, 41, 51, 67, 77-79, 85, 92-94, 100, 106, 112, 145-48, 154, 161, 169, 175, 181-82, 187, 201, 203, 213, 232-33, 255-56, 289, 294, 339, 351, 360, 362, 411, 414, 420, 430, 432, 434-35, 437, 447, 504, 507, 510, 511, 518, 524, 529; Peekskill, 360; Rochester, 79, 359, 475; Schenectady, 81, 364; Tarrytown, 92.

Index   675

New York Times, 109, 361-62, 490, 495-96.
Newton, Huey, 529-30.
Nixon, Donald, 484, 501.
Nixon, Richard M., 295, 317, 320, 321, 325, 327, 338, 340, 342-43, 390, 399, 401, 430, 441-42, 452, 456, 460-65, 468, 474, 477, 481, 483, 485-88, 493-99, 501-03, 511, 524, 526, 533-34, 537-39, 558, 562-64, 566-67, 569-70.
Non-Partisan League (NPL), 98-99, 105-06, 125, 130-31, 134, 174; effects of World War I repression upon, 131-32, 139, 161.
Norris-LaGuardia Act (1932), 19, 258, 290.
North Carolina, 207, 219, 270, 287; Charlotte, 484; Durham, 313; Gastonia, 187-88, 287; Greensboro, 413.
North Dakota, 99, 126, 130, 132, 186, 207; Fargo, 126, 186; Minot, 87.
Nottingham Program, 141-42.
Nye, Russell, 59, 132, 167.

Ober Act (1949), 351, 357, 359, 367-68.
O'Brien, John Lord, 203, 392.
O'Brien, Lawrence, 438, 483.
Ohio, 28, 81, 106, 119, 127, 190, 202, 224, 230, 351-52, 359, 515, 519; Akron, 90, 202; Canton, 11, 230; Cleveland, 28, 119, 127, 145, 182, 289, 448; Cincinnatti, 26-27, 39, 126, 359, 476, 516; Columbus, 30, 360, 508; Dayton, 82, 106; East Youngstown, 95; Hocking Valley, 28; Martins Ferry, 178; Massillon, 53, 230; Springfield, 182; Youngstown, 152, 230.
Oklahoma, 81, 117, 119, 121, 128, 182, 186, 256-57, 324, 350, 352, 504-05; Ft. Sill, 517; Oklahoma City, 257, 359-60; Sapul, 359; Tulsa, 126, 182.
Olney, Richard, 54, 57.
Omnibus Crime Control and Safe Streets Act (1968), 442-43, 468.
O'Neill, William, 385, 430.
Oppenheimer, Frank, 375.
Oppenheimer, Robert, 341-42, 372-73, 375, 402, 416-17.
Orchard, Harry, 73.
Oregon, 93, 115-16, 146-47, 172, 180-81, 198, 267, 202, 212, 233; Albany, 93; Portland, 128, 186, 202; Woodburn, 93.
Overman, Lee, 148.
Overman Committee. See Congressional Investigating Committees.

Pacifica Foundation, 422-426.
Pacifists, in 1920's, 181; in 1930's, 234; in Truman-McCarthy period, 371; in 1954-1964, 413-14. See Conscientious objectors.
Packer, Horace L., 475.
Paine, Thomas, 303, 359.
Palmer, A. Mitchell, 145, 149, 150, 153-61, 245, 248, 250, 564, 567.
Palmer Raids, 144, 154-58, 160, 162, 172, 370, 499.
Panic of 1907, 80-81.
Pardons and commutations for political offenses, 98, 172, 210, 287-88.
Parenti, Michael, 522-23.
Parmet, Herbert, 326, 334.
Parsons, Albert, 39.
Passport denials and restrictions for political reasons, 111, 120, 311, 330, 392, 393, 411, 423-24. See Travel, political restrictions on.
Patterson, Leonard, 334, 347.
Pauling, Linus, 330, 396, 413, 417.
Peabody, James, 72.
Pelly, William Dudley, 270-71.
Pennsylvania, 28-31, 45, 67, 106, 152, 172, 190, 202, 207, 230, 233, 258, 282, 324, 345, 349, 351, 404, 424, 514, 520; Alleghany, 53; Braddock, 95; Cheswick, 169; Duquesne, 10; Harrisburg, 30, 493; Homestead, 45-46; Johnstown, 230; McKees Rock, 80; McKeesport, 358-59; Media, 464; Old Forge, 178; Philadelphia, 27-28, 31-32, 77-79, 119, 127, 203, 276, 411, 449, 451, 504-05, 516, 518, 527; Pittsburgh, 28, 30-31, 37, 67, 148, 152, 345, 514; Pittston, 15; Rankin, 95; Reading, 31, 33; South Bethlehem, 84; Susquehanna Depot, 28.
People's Bicentennial Commission, 544.
People's Council of America for Peace and Democracy, 106-07, 121, 124-25, 127, 130.
Perlman, Selig, xii-xiii, 552.
Perrett, Geoffrey, 284, 570-71.
Peterson, H. C., and Gilbert C. Fite, 118.
Picasso, Pablo, 331.
Pinkerton Detectives, 12, 29, 38, 45-46, 73.
Police, and dissidents, 13-14; in 1870's, 26-8, 31; in 1880's, 37-42; in 1890's, 45, 53; in Progressive Era, 66, 75-80, 84-85, 87-90, 92-98; in World War I, 111-12, 117, 125-26; in 1919 Red Scare, 144-47, 149-52, 155-56; in 1920's, 169, 177-78, 180, 185-88; in Great Depression, 198-206, 208, 218-30; in World War II period, 258, 260-61, 282; in Truman-McCarthy period, 313, 359-60; in 1954-1964 period, 415; in Vietnam War era, 435, 437, 446, 451, 456, 487, 499, 509-13, 516-18,

520, 524, 526-30.
Political Intelligence. See individual intelligence agencies.
Political Repression. Definition of, xvi-xxi neglect of possible importance by American social scientists, ix-xvi; in U.S., compared to other countries, xxi, 547-48; factors limiting intensity in U.S., 547-48; changing techniques of in American history, 536; why directed largely against political left in American history; as reflection of general trends in American society, 561-62, 570.

Federal role in, 561-63; in 1870-1900 period, 23-24, 52-56; in Progressive Era, 67-70, 77-79, 89, 99-101; in World War I, 107-25; in 1919 Red Scare, 140, 147-50, 154-58; in 1920's 172-77, 180, 188-89; in Great Depression, 197-201, 213-16; in World War II period, 240-55, 263-81; in Truman-McCarthy period, 290-348; in 1954-1964, 399-424; in Vietnam War era, 432, 435-504, 523-30, 537-45; importance of Congress' role, 562-63; importance of Supreme Court's role, 562-63. State and local role in, 561-63; in 1870's, 26-32; in 1880's, 37-44; in 1890's, 45-55; in Progressive Era, 67-68, 70-73, 75-76, 77-80, 84-99, 101; in World War I, 125-31; in 1919 Red Scare, 144-47, 151-53, 155-58; in 1920's, 169, 173, 178, 180, 182, 185-91; in Great Depression, 201-206, 218-33; in World War II period, 255-62, 281-83; in Truman-McCarthy period, 348-60; in 1954-1964, 409-10, 424-25; in Vietnam War era, 434-35, 504-30.

Significance in American history, ix-x, 547-58. Effects on labor movement, 547-53; effects on radical labor, 550-53; effects on radical political movements, 553-56; effects in fostering self-censorship, 556-58.
Variables affecting intensity of, xvi, 55, 74, *Attitudes of political authorities*, 558-65. *Levels of tension and strain in society*, xv, 559-60, 565-67, 568; growth of strain and tension, in 1870's, 24-32; in 1880's, 34-42; in 1890's, 44-56; in Progressive Era, 64-66, 76-78, 80-84, 86, 93-94, 96-101; in 1919 Red Scare 139-45; in Great Depression 195-97; in World War II period, 289-93, 316-21; in Vietnam War period, 429-32, 434-35; lessened strain and tension, in 1870's, 32-33; in 1880's, 42-43; in 1890's, 58-60; after World War I, 140; after 1919 Red Scare, 159-61; in 1920's, 171-73; in 1954-1965, 401-405; in Vietnam War era, 537-41; strain and tension as reflection of depressions, 565; of strike waves, 565; of wars, 565, 572; of foreign policy crises threatening war, 565; of spreading threatening foreign ideologies, 565.
Levels of dissent, **xv,** 559-60, 566-69. Attitudes of key elites, **xv,** 559-60, 566, 568-570, 572-74; supportive of repression, in 1870's, 23-28, 30, 32-33; in 1880's, 34-35, 37, 39-41; in 1890's, 48-52, 56; in Progressive Era, 64, 71-72, 77, 80, 84, 89; in World War I, 134-35; in 1919 Red Scare, 139, 141-45, 151-53, 161; in 1920's, 167-71, 173-80; in Great Depression, 196-97, 215, 234; in World War II period, 241, 261-62, 265-66; in Truman-McCarthy period, 295, 360-69; in 1954-1964, 405-06; opposition to repression, in 1919 Red Scare, 159-60, in Great Depression, 206-09, 235; in Truman-McCarthy period, 313; in 1954-1964, 400-01; in Vietnam War era, 533, *Target groups, suitability of,* xv, 559-60, 566, 568-72.

Reasons for resort to, 563-65, 566-67, 568-70, 572; reasons for failure of, in Great Depression, 206-09, 233-36; in Vietnam era, 533-34; long-term effects of in 1919 Red Scare, 167-71; in Truman-McCarthy period, 369-96; impact on American foreign policy, 385-91.
Populists, 48-49, 51-53, 59-60, 71, 81, 105, 132.
Post, Louis, 134, 160.
Post Office, 110, 113, 115, 145, 438, 446, 484. See mail, opening of; mails, suppression of.
Pound, Roscoe, 159, 160.
Powderly, Terence, 35, 42.
Powers, Thomas, 430.
Preparedness movement, 97-100.
Press, suppression of for political reasons, in 1880's, 39; in Progressive Era, 67, 72, 79, 80, 86, 90-91, 94-95; in World War I, 103, 109, 114-15; in 1919 Red Scare, 147, 156, 158-59; in 1920's, 172, 182, 189; in Great Depression, 198, 206, 210; in World War II, 268-69, 271-72.
Preston, William, xiv, 65, 269, 551, 553.
Preventive law, development of during Truman-McCarthy period, 391-93.
Pritchett, C. Herman, 331-32.
Private police, espionage and arsenals, as repressive technique, 11-12; in 1870-1900 period, 23, 29-30, 37, 44-45; in

Progressive Era, 85, 87, 95, 97-98; in 1920's, 174-75, 189; in Great Depression, 211-12, 218-19, 229-30.
Progressive Citizens of America (PCA), 306, 311.
Progressive Labor Party (PLP), 434-35, 447, 478, 500, 515, 521.
Progressive Party, 1912, 179; 1924, 179-80; 1948, 306, 311-14, 319, 382, 406, 568.

Racial disorders, of 1919, 143, 150-51; of Vietnam War era, 429-30, 434, 438, 441, 446-47, 450, 458, 514.
Radicalism. Growth of, in 1870's, 25-26; in 1880's, 34-37; in 1890's, 48-51; in Progressive Era, 81-84, 98-100; in World War I, 105-07, 140, 143; in Great Depression, 96, 234-35; in Truman-McCarthy period, 288-89, 296-98, 305-06; in Vietnam War era, 429-32. Effects of repression in hampering, in 1870's, 33-34; in 1880's, 41-42; in 1890's, 56-59; in World War I, 131-34; in 1919 Red Scare, 159-63; in 1920's, 169-72; in Truman-McCarthy period, 314, 369-71; in Vietnam War era, 530-37; in American history from 1870-1976, 550-56. Traditional explanations for failure of in U.S., x, xiv.
Railroads, power of after Civil War, 6-7.
Ramparts, 454, 458.
Rapp-Coudert Committee. See State legislative investigating committees, New York.
Rayback, Joseph, 29, 32.
Reagan, Ronald, 511, 520, 564.
Recessions, 1886, 25; 1913, 81, 93; 1918, 43; 1937, 239.
Reconstruction, desires for after World War I, 141.
Record, Wilson, 205.
Red flag laws and prosecutions, 94, 145, 147, 207, 232, 514.
Red-baiting, 556; in 1870's, 25-28, 30, 32-33; in 1880's, 41; in 1890's, 59; in World War I, 143; in 1919 Red Scare, 148, 151-53; in 1920's, 168, 174, 179, 190; in Great Depression, 199-201, 214-17, 235; in World War II period, 260; in Truman-McCarthy period, 383-84; in 1954-1964, 409-10; in Vietnam War era, 435-38, 447.
Red Channels, 361.
Red Jacket injunction, 183, 208.
Red Scares. See Scares.
Red squads, 504-08.
Registration, laws requiring of political dissidents, 182, 270, 282, 315, 322-23, 340, 348-50, 358, 409. See Internal Security Act; Subversive Activities Control Board.
Rehnquist, William, 480, 495.
Republican Party, 6, 49, 59, 113, 167, 170, 173, 179, 216-17, 234, 289, 293, 295-96, 298-99, 305, 315-16, 319-21, 325-27, 333-34, 400-01.
Revolutionary Action Movement (RAM), 451.
Rhode Island, Pawtucket, 76; Providence, 359.
Richelieu, Cardinal, xxiii.
Robeson, Paul, 311, 359-60, 362.
Roche, John, 8, 111, 262, 393.
Rockefeller Commission on CIA, 339-40, 456-57.
Rockefeller Foundation, 340, 374.
Rockefeller, John D., 92-93.
Roosevelt, Eleanor, 210, 215, 233, 242, 251, 292, 306, 396, 417, 560.
Roosevelt, Franklin D., 5, 176, 200, 209-17, 288-29, 234-36, 239, 341-42, 245, 247-54, 259, 262-72, 275, 277-78, 280-82, 287-89, 291, 294, 296-98, 305-06, 309, 318, 325, 468, 538, 560, 562, 564, 566.
Roosevelt, Theodore, 5, 40, 65, 67, 73-74, 77.
Rose, Richard, xiv-xvii
Rosenberg, Julius and Ethel, 326-27. See Trials, Rosenberg Case.
Rossister, Clinton, 281.
Rostow, Eugene, 281.
Rubin, Jerry, 488.
Rusk, Dean, 333, 388, 390-91, 437, 510, 539.
Russia, xxii, 107, 112, 120-21, 141-44, 148, 162, 167, 200-01, 210, 240, 252, 257, 264, 273, 287-89, 291-93, 296-97, 317, 320, 334, 402, 414.
Russo, Anthony, 489-90.
Ruthenberg, Charles E., 119, 163, 178.

Sane Nuclear Policy, National Committee for a (SANE), 413-14.
Sacco, Nicola, 94. See Trials, Sacco-Vanzetti.
Sale, Kirkpatrick, 532, 534, 535.
Salsedo, Andrea, 161.
Scares. Red Scare of 1873-1878, 24-34; communist-anarchist-labor scare of 1886, 34-44; communist-anarchist-labor scare of 1892-1896, 44-60; anarchist-labor scare of 1892-1896, 44-60; anarchist scare of 1901-1903, 66-70; anarchist-labor scare of 1907-1909, 76-80; anarchist scare of 1914-1916, 93-94; red scare of 1919-1920, 63, 128, 139-63, 167-68, 552, 554, 564; re scare of 1934-1935, 213-17.

678   Political Repression in Modern America

Schaack, Michael J., 39.
Schine, G. David, 336, 399.
Schlesinger, Arthur, Jr., 215, 288, 416-17.
Schneiderman, William, 249, 271.
Scientific research, effect of Truman-McCarthyism upon, 372-73.
Scottsboro case, 205, 207, 212.
Scranton Commission, 519-20.
Seale, Bobby, 488, 529.
Secret Service, 198, 200, 449, 200, 449, 457, 467, 484, 501, 503.
Seeger, Pete, 361.
Selective Service Act (1940), 245-46, 262.
Senate, U.S., 7, 112, 140, 148, 152, 154-55, 157, 159, 174-75, 190, 197, 199, 208, 211, 216, 245, 275, 280, 321, 325, 347, 367, 299-400, 402, 406, 437, 480, 557-58.
Service, John Stewart, 292-93, 302, 330, 333, 338, 405.
Sedition laws and prosecutions, 69, 101, 103, 113-14, 119, 121, 127-28, 131, 146-47, 155-59, 172, 173, 258-59, 261, 263-64, 266, 268-71, 282, 345, 348-50, 409, 423-24, 562.
Shannon, David, xiii, 132, 196, 370.
Shannon, Fred, 29, 39.
Sherman Anti-Trust Act (1890), 8, 19, 48, 56, 59, 78, 84, 183-84.
Silver Shirts, 241, 269-71.
Sinatra, Frank, 292, 353.
Sinclair, John, 514.
Sinclair, Upton, 188, 253, 303.
Slacker raids, 111.
Smelser, Neil, xiv.
Smith, Alfred E., 160, 172, 216.
Smith, Gerald L. K., 217, 269.
Smith, J. Malcolm, 392.
Smith, John S., 84.
Smith Act (Alien Registration Act, 1940) and prosecutions, 69, 245, 251-52, 263, 269, 312-13, 317, 322-33, 339-40, 346-47, 351, 363-64, 368-69, 375, 392-94, 404-07, 412, 417, 448, 465, 526, 540, 544, 554, 557, 562.
Smith-Connally Act (1943), 277, 290.
Smoot-Hawley Tariff (1930), 200.
Social Democratic Party, 81. See Socialist Party of America.
Socialist Labor Party (SLP), 26, 36, 48, 105.
Socialist Party of America (SPA), xiii, 54, 69, 74, 79, 85-86, 88-91, 531, 564, 567-68, 570; growth in Progressive Era, 80-83; and labor, 83, 123, 153; opposition to World War I, 105-06, 110; repression of during World War I, 110-11, 113, 119-21, 125-27, 140; strength remaining after World War I, 133-34; growth in 1919, 140-41; split in 1919, 141, 153; in 1919 Red Scare, 145-47, 155, 157, 160-62; in 1920's and after, 172, 174, 177-79, 180, 196, 235; effects of repression upon, 132-33, 553-54.
Socialist Workers Party (SWP), 252-53, 254, 264, 268, 407, 420-21, 425, 447, 471-73, 564.
Socrates, x.
Sombart, Werner, xiii.
Sorenson, Theodore, 388, 416.
Sostre, Martin, 514.
South Carolina, 43, 107, 219, 507; Calhoun Falls, 313; Charleston, 313; Columbia, 517; Ft. Jackson, 517; Greenville, 205; Orangeburg, 511; Richland Co., 517.
Southern Christian Leadership Conference (SCLC), 419, 421, 450.
South Dakota, 119, 127, 131, 133; Aberdeen, 86, 125; Yankton Co., 125.
Southern Conference Educational Fund, 410.
Southern Conference on Human Welfare, 265.
Southern Tenant Farmers Union (STFU), 225-26, 260.
Spanish-American War, 60, 64.
Spinrad, William, 574.
Spock, Benjamin, 440, 458, 484, 487.
Sproat, John G., 24.
Starobin, Joseph, 370.
Starksy, Morris, 523.
State and local councils of defense during World War I, 129-31; Connecticut, 129; Idaho, 130; Iowa, 130; Minnesota, 129-31; Montana, 129-30; Nebraska, 130-31; Nevada, 130; North Carolina, 129; North Dakota, 130; Oklahoma, 129; Oregon, 129; South Dakota, 129; Wisconsin, 129-30.
State legislative investigating committees, 353-56, 409-10. Arkansas, 232, 259; Arizona, 353; California (Tenney Committee), 256, 259, 282, 288, 353-55, 357, 435; Colorado, 357; Florida, 410; Illinois (Broyles Commission), 257, 353, 355-57, 363; New York (Lusk, McNaboe, Rapp-Coudert Committees), 147, 150, 155, 157, 236, 255-56, 258-59, 288; Oklahoma, 257, 355; Washington (Canwell Committee), 348, 353-54, 357, 371; Wisconsin, 232.
State legislatures, in 1870's, 17-18; in 1880's, 41; in Progressive Era, 68, 94; World War I, 127-28; 1919 Red Scare, 147; 1920's, 180, 182; Great Depression, 232; World War II period, 258-60; Truman-McCarthy period, 348-53; 1954-1964, 402-03, 409-10, 424; Viet-

nam War era, 519. Alabama, 351-52; Arizona, 182; Arkansas, 232; California, 182, 232, 256, 259, 270, 282, 350, 357-58, 367, 519; Delaware, 232, 350; Florida, 259, 359, 351; Georgia, 351, 513-14; Idaho, 101; Illinois, 182, 282, 357, 520; Indiana, 232, 351; Louisiana, 282, 349, 351; Maryland, 351, 367; Massachusetts, 180, 351; Michigan, 182, 232, 350-51; Minnesota, 128; Mississippi, 282, 351; Montana, 127, 351; New Hampshire, 351; New York, 68, 147, 157, 160, 172, 182, 255, 351, 519; Ohio, 351, 519; Oklahoma, 256-67, 350, 357; Oregon, 146, 180, 233; Tennessee, 232, 351; Texas, 350-52; Washington, 146, 233, 256, 295, 351, 357; Wisconsin, 180, 519.

State Department, 176, 215, 247, 295, 302, 308, 311, 315-16, 319-21, 325, 329-31, 333, 335, 338, 385-87, 392, 401, 411, 417, 424, 449, 467, 522, 558.

Steele, Walter, 243, 307.
Sternsher, Bernard, 195.
Steunenberg, Frank, 29, 63-74, 77, 82, 85.
Stevens, Robert, 337, 343, 399.
Stockholm Conference, 120-21.
Stone, Harlan F., 175-76.
Stone, I. F., 295, 347, 362.
Stouffer, Samuel, 381, 573.
Strikebreakers, 28, 38, 44, 46-47, 51, 70, 80, 91, 95, 98, 187, 190, 218, 226-28.
Student Non-Violent Coordinating Committee (SNCC), 443, 450, 454-55, 514.
Students for a Democratic Society (SDS), 415, 429-30, 434-36, 438-39, 441, 443, 449, 452-54, 457, 463, 468, 471, 473, 378, 381, 394, 407-08, 516-17, 521, 525, 531, 534-36. See Weatherman.
Strikes, data on, 34, 45, 59, 143, 184-85, 218, 219-30, 290-91; waves of: 1868-1872, 25-26; 1886, 36-37, 565; 1894, 44, 51, 565; 1919, 143, 565; 1934, 226, 565; 1937, 228-29; 1946, 289. Chronological list of: New York City eight-hour day (1872), 26; Philadelphia weavers (1973-1874), 28; New York cigar workers (1973-74), 28; Pittsburgh printers (1870's), 28; Cleveland coal (1870's), 28; railroad, 1873-74), 28; railroad strikes of 1877, 16, 24, 28, 30-34, 40, 69, 551, 561; Leadville mining (1880), 16; Omaha Smelting (1880, 1882), 16; Union Pacific (1884), 35; Gould railroad system (1885), 35 (1886), 37; eight-hour day strikes of 1886, 36-41; McCormack strike (1886), 38; Louisiana agricultural (1887), 43; Burlington (1888), 44; Pennsylvania coal and coke (1890, 1891), 15, 45; New York Central (1891), 45; Homestead (1892), 45-46, 50, 57, 549; Coeur d'Alene (1892), 46-47, 57, 70, 549; Buffalo Railroad (1892), 47, 57; Anderson County, Tennessee Coal (1891-92), 48; Great Northern (1894), 18, 44, 51-59, 69, 139, 151, 549, 552, 561; Coeur d'Alene (1899), 71, 549; Telluride mining (1901), 71; San Francisco teamsters (1901), 75; Coal strike of 1902, 74-75; Paterson silk (1902), 76; New Orleans street car (1903), 76; Colorado coal strikes of 1903-04, 72-73, 75, 549-50; Carbon Co., Utah Coal (1903), 75-76; Chicago typographers (1905), 76; Chicago teamsters (1905), 76; Goldfield miners (1907-08), 16, 77; Muncie street car (1908), 77; Alabama coal (1908), 79; New York garment workers (1909), 79; McKees Rock steel (1909), 80; Bethlehem steel (1910), 84; New York cloakmakers (1910), 85; Chicago garment workers, (1910), 85; Los Angeles strikes of 1910, 85; Lawrence textile (1912), 81-82, 88-89, 98, 549-50; Louisiana lumber (1912), 87-88, 549; Seattle tailors (1912), 88; Washington sawmills (1912), 88; Paterson textile (1912), 89 (1913), 89-90, 98, 549; Passaic textile (1912), 89; Garfield textile (1912), 89; Akron rubber (1913), 90; Coos Bay loggers, (1913), 90; Detroit auto (1913), 90; West Virginia Coal (1912-1913), 91; Calumet copper (1913-14), 91; Colorado coal (1914), 15, 16, 92; Chicago clothing (1915), 95; Bayonne oil (1915), 95; Mesabi iron ore (1916), 95-96, 549; Virginia, Minnesota, lumber (1916-1917) 65, 549; World War I copper and lumber, 115, 124, 549; Seattle General (1919), 144-46, 148, 153, 568; Southern California citrus (1919), 146; Boston police (1919), 151, 153; 1919 steel, 10, 151-53, 158, 212, 549, 552; 1919 coal, 153, 158, 552; 1920 railroad, 157-58; Butte miners (1920), 158; Denver street car (1920), 158; Arizona cotton (1920), 158; 1922 railroad, 174, 188-89, 208; 1922 coal, 16, 190, 192; Hetch-Hetchy (1922), 185; San Pedro dock (1923), 185-86; Passaic textile (1926), 187, 551; New York garment (1926), 187; New York fur (1926), 187; Colorado coal (1927), 15-16, 186, 551; New Bedford textile (1928), 187, 551; Imperial Valley agricultural

(1928) 190; Gastonia textile (1929), 187, 549, 551; Elizabethton textile (1929), 191; Marion textile (1929), 191; Harlan Co. coal (931), 205-06, 551; Danville textile (1931), 206; Colorado beet workers (1932), 206; California agricultural (1930-32), 206, 551; California agricultural (1933-1934), 222-23, 551; Yakima agricultural (1933), 224; San Francisco general (934), 215-16, 226-27, 550; Toledo electrical (1934), 227, 550; Minneapolis truckers (1934), 227-28, 252, 550; cotton textile (1934), 219-20; Terre Haute general (1935), 228; Gallup coal (1935), 228; Idaho loggers (1936), 228; Arkansas cotton (1936), 225; little steel (1937), 15, 229-31; California agricultural (1935-1938), 223-25; other agricultural (1933-1938), 224-25; 1937 auto sit-in (228-29, 239); 1941 coal, 246-47; North American Aviation (1941), 252, 260; 1943 coal, 276; Philadelphia transit (1944), 276; oil workers (1945), 290; packinghouse workers (1946), 290; 1946 railroad, 290; 1946 coal, 290.

Students, and dissent, in 1920's, 181; in Great Depression, 231-32; in Truman-McCarthy period, 381-82; in 1954-1964 period, 413, 415; in Vietnam War era, 430-32, 434-35, 518-23.

Subversive Activities Control Board (SACB), 322, 332, 339, 340-41, 346, 348, 393-94, 402, 406, 418, 423, 424, 433, 437, 441, 448, 476, 499-500, 507, 537.

Subversive organizations. Attorney General's list of, 300, 308-10, 313, 346, 350, 369, 371, 392-94, 499-500, 537; Federal World War II list of, 304, 318; House Committee on Un-American Activities list of, 346; New York list of, 351, 369; Maryland list of, 351.

Supreme Court, 3, 18-19, 47, 68, 77, 119, 135, 148-49, 151, 159, 172, 176, 179, 207, 211, 212, 217, 239-40, 249, 254-55, 267-68, 270, 272, 280, 282-83, 287, 290, 311, 318, 331, 332, 348, 355, 368-69, 393-94, 404-06, 410-11, 412, 423-24, 439, 441, 493, 514-15, 534, 543-44. Major decisions in chronological order: In *Re Debs* (1895), 18, 56, 59; *U.S. v. E. C. Knight Co.* (1895), 57; *Pollack v. Farmers Loan and Trust Co.*, (1895), 59; *In Re Lennon* (1897), 18; *Lawlor v. Loewe* (1908), 8, 77-78; *Hitchman Coal and Coke v. Mitchell*, (1917), 18-19, 183; *Schenck v. U.S.* (1919), 177; *Duplex Printing Co. v. Deering* (1921), 18, 183; *American Steel Foundries vv. Tri-City Central Trades Council* (1921), 18, 184; *Truax v. Corrigan* (1921), 184; *Coronado* cases (125), 19, 184; *Bedford Cut Stone v. Journeyman* (1927), 184; *Herndon v. Lowry* (1937), 212; *DeJonge v. Oregon* (1937), 212; *Hague v. CIO* (1939), 233; *Kessler v. Strecker* (1939), 245; *Thornhill v. Alabama* (1940), .254-55; *Minersville School District v. Gobitis* (1940), 255, 261; *Cox v. New Hampshire* (1941), 255; *Milkwagon Drivers Union v. Meadowmoor Dairies* (1941), 255; *Chaplinsky v. New Hampshire* (1942), 280; *Jones v. Opelika* (1942, 1943), 280; *West Virginia State Board of Education v. Barnette* (1943), 280, 283; *Schneiderman v. U.S.* (1943), 271, 280; *Hartzel v. U.S.* (1944), 280; *Baumgartner v. U.S.* (1944), 271, 280; *Korematsu v. U.S.* (1944), 281; *Ex Parte Endo* (1944), 281; *Thomas v. Collins* (1945), 281; *Duncan v. Kokonomoku* (1946), 281; *Bailey v. Richardson* (1950), 368; *American Communications Association v. Douds* (1950), 368; *Dennis v. U.S.* (1951), 368, 393; *Gerende v. Board of Supervisors of Elections of Baltimore* (1951), 368; *Garner v. Board of Public Works of Los Angeles* (1951), 368; *Joint Anti-Fascist Refugee Committee v. McGrath* (1952), 369; *Adler v. Board of Education* (1952), 369; *Weiman v. Updegraff* (1952), 369; *Shaughnessy v. U.S. ex rel Mezei* (1953), 331-32; *Barsky v. Board* (1954), 404; *Galvan v. Press* (1954), 404; *Peters v. Hobby* (1955), 404; *Sclochower v. Board* (1956), 404, 411, 412; *Cole v. Young* (1956), 404; *Pennsylvania v. Nelson* (1956), 404, 409, 411; *Pencks v. U.S.* (1957), 404, 410; *Watkins v. U.S.* (1957), 404-05, 411; *Yates v. U.S.* (1957), 405-06, 423, 544; *Sweezy v. New Hampshire* (1957), 405, 411; *NAACP v. Alabama ex rel Patterson* (1958), 410; *Beilan v. Board of Education* (1958), 411; *Lerner v. Casey* (1958), 411; *Kent v. Dulles* (1958), 411; *Sacher v. U.S.* (1958), 411; *Speiser v. Randall* (1958), 411; *Harmon v. Brucker* (1958), 411; *Barenblatt v. U.S.* (1959), 411; *Uphaus v. Wyman* (1959), 411; *Greene v. McElroy* (1959), 412; *Nelson and Globe v. Los Angeles* (1960), 412; *Scales v. U.S.* (1961), 412, 417; *Noto v. U.S.* (1961), 417; *Konigsberg v. State Bar of California* (1961), 412; *Cramp v. Board of Public Instruction* (1961), 423; *Louisiana ex rel Gremillion v. NAACP* (1961), 410, 423; *Gibson v. Florida Legislative Investigating Committee* (1963), 410, 423; *Aptheker v. Secretary of State* (1964), 423-24; *Dombrowski v. Pfister* (1965), 410, 423; *Lamont v. Postmaster General* (1965), 423; *U.S. v. Brown* (1965), 423; *Stanford v. Texas* (1965), 424; *Keyishian v. Board of Regents* (1967), 423; *U.S. v. Laub* (1967), 424; *U.S. v. Robel* (1967), 424; *Schneider v. Smith* (1968), 424; *U.S. v. O'Brien* (1968), 435; *Brandenberg v. Ohio* (1969), 515-16; *Cohen v. California* (1971), 516; *New York Times v. U.S.* (1971), 496; *U.S. v. Caldwell* (1972), 495; *Tatum v. Laird* (1972), 480; *U.S. v. U.S. District Court* (1972), 468; *Healy v. James* (1972), 521; *Hess v. Indiana* (1973), 516; *Papish v. the Board of Curators of the University of Missouri* (1973), 522; *U.S. v. Calandra* (1974), 494; *Spence v. Washington* (1974), 515; *Lewis v. New Orleans* (1974), 516; *Eastland v. U.S. Servicemen's Fund* (1975), 500.

Taft, William Howard, 65, 89, 183.
Taft-Hartley Act (1947) and prosecutions under, 290-91, 341, 364, 366, 368, 404, 406, 409, 418, 551.
Technology, threat to political freedom of, 542-43.
Tennessee, 232, 351; Chattanooga, 205, 233; Coal Creek, 47; Elizabethton, 191; Knoxville, 359; Memphis, 182, 202.
Tenney, Jack, 353, 357. See State Legislative Investigating Committees, California.
Texas, 37, 81, 131, 135, 181-82, 198, 281, 350-52, 504, 506-07; Dallas, 182, 204, 506, 518; El Paso, 53; Houston, 359, 500.
Thomas, J. Parnell, 242, 292, 307, 316, 345.
Thomas, Norman, 187, 225, 297, 382.
Thompson, James, 386.
Threats to President's life, 101, 109, 484.
Tompkins Square Riot (1874), 27, 57.
Tongyai, Thomas (Tommy the Traveler), 475.
Trading with the Enemy Act (1917), 109, 438.
Travel, political restrictions on, 417, 424, 522. See Passports.
Treasury Department, 110, 310, 328, 437-38, 483-84, 507.
Trials. Berrigan conspiracy, 476-77, 488-89, 493; Chicago conspiracy, 487-88, 492, 529, 532; Judith Coplon, 317; Ettor-Giovannitti, 89; Gainesville conspiracy, 491, 608; Alger Hiss, 316-17, 319; Joe Hill, 96-97; Haymarket anarchists, 39-40; Industrial Workers of the World War I conspiracy, 117-18, 146; 1910 *Los Angeles Times* bombing, 85-86; Molly Maguires, 29; Tom Mooney, 97; Pentagon Papers, 469, 486, 489-90, 491, 494, 496, 502, 532, 534; Rosenberg, 320-21, 326, 362, 368; Sacco-Vanzetti, 73, 96, 168-69; Seattle Conspiracy, 492-93; Spock-Coffin, 440-41; Steunenberg, 73-74.
Truman, Harry S., 168, 248, 278, 289-90, 293-94, 296-301, 304-09, 311-12, 314-22, 324, 326-35, 337-38, 343, 348-49, 366, 371, 387, 392, 396, 402, 423, 438, 489, 557-58, 562, 564, 566.
Truman Doctrine, 297-99, 305.
Tydings Committee. See Congressional Investigating Committees.

Underground press, 430, 480, 482, 500, 518, 522.
Uniforms, laws barring wearing of, 258-59.
Unions. Agricultural Workers Organization (AWO), 98; Amalgamated Association of Iron, Steel and Tin Workers (AAISTW), 45-46; Amalgamated Clothing Workers (ACW), 83, 95, 123; Amalgamated Machinists Union, 84; Amalgamated Trades and Labor Assembly (Chicago), 36; American Railway Union (ARU), 53-58, 70, 549, 552, 567; Brewery Workers, 81, 123; Brotherhood of Railway Trainmen, 57; Brotherhood of Timber Workers (BTW), 87-88; California State Federation of Labor, 124, 142; Cannery and Agricultural Workers Union (CAIWU), 221-22; Central Labor Union (Milwaukee), 38; Chicago Central Labor Union, 36; Chicago Federation of Labor, 142; Chicago Typographical Union, 76; Cigarmakers, 43, 83; Carpenters, 45, 83; Fur Workers, 249; Illinois State Federation of Labor, 43, 83; International Association of Bridge and Structural Iron Workers (IABSIW), 85; International Association of Machinists (IAM), 81, 83, 123; International Ladies Garment Workers Union, (ILGWU), 79, 81; International Seafarers Union (ISU), 189; International Woodworkers Association (IWA), 260; International Union of Mine, Mill and Smelter Workers (IUMMSW), 406, 418; National Miners Association, 28; National Miners Union (NMU), 205-06, 226; National Maritime Union, 312; New York Federation of Labor, 160; Ohio Federation of Labor, 142; Pennsylvania of Labor, 83, 148; Railroad brotherhoods, 54, 57, 74, 141-42, 153, 174, 179, 188-89; Teamsters, 75, 252-53;

United Electrical Workers, 364-65; United Farm Workers, 460; United Mine Workers (UMW), 51, 74-75, 78-79, 81, 84, 87, 91-92, 142, 153, 183, 186, 189-90, 205, 218, 220, 226; United Textile Workers (UTW), 187, 276; Western Federation of Miners WFM), 70-75, 91, 550, 564, 567; Western Labor Union, 71; Workingman's Amalgamated Council (New Orleans), 48; Workingman's Benevolent Association (WBA), 29.
Union of Russian Workers, 146, 154-55.
United Nations, 328, 333.
United Slaves (US), 524-25.
Urban League, 150, 455, 458, 460, 482.
Utah, 81, 97; Carbon Co., 75, 226; Ogden, 55; Salt Lake City, 93, 96, 182, 526.

Viereck, George Sylvester, 272.
Vietnam War, xxii, 361, 384, 386-91, 415-16, 429-30, 433, 435-38, 448-49, 451, 453-55, 463, 482, 489, 533, 535, 537, 557-58, 561-64, 566-72.
Vietnam Veterans Against the War (VVAW), 466, 472, 491, 513.
Violence, in incidents involving dissidents and political authorities. In labor disputes, 3-4, 11, 15. In 1870's, 26-31; in 1880's, 37-38, 40; in 1890's, 46-47, 51, 54, 70-75; in Progressive Era, 75-77, 79-80, 84-98; in World War I, 116; in 1919 Red Scare, 145, 150-52, 158; in 1920's, 169, 186-88; in Great Depression, 198-99, 203-05, 211, 219-28, 230; in World War II period, 260-61, 283; in Truman-McCarthy period, 313, 360; in 1954-1964 period, 415; in Vietnam War era, 430-32, 439, 487, 492, 498, 508-13, 520, 522, 535.
Violations of law by companies in labor disputes, 15-16, 46-47, 71, 77, 87, 91-92.
Virginia, 51; Danville, 206; Richmond, 203.
Voice of America, 334-36.
Voorhis Act (1940), 246.
Wagner Act (1935), 3, 5, 9-10, 63, 211-12, 214, 218, 220, 230, 233, 235-36, 247, 260, 291, 548, 550, 551-52, 571.
Waite, David, 5, 51, 55, 70.
Wallace, George, 390, 460.
Wallace, Henry, 216, 279, 294, 296-97, 305-06, 308, 311-14, 316, 356, 366, 377, 417.
Walker Commission, 487, 509.
War Department. See Defense Department.
Warren, Earl, 367, 357, 404.
Washington state, 81, 115-16, 119, 131-32, 146-47, 155-56, 173, 233, 256, 267 295, 326, 349, 351, 424, 514-16; Centralia, 155-56; Everett, 93, 97-98; Home, 67; Pasco, 180; Seattle, 77, 141, 144-45, 147, 157, 203, 208, 473, 475, 492-93, 506, 534; Spokane, 86, 128; Tacoma, 356; Yakima, 95, 224-25.
Washington, D.C., 52-53, 93, 127, 141, 169, 180, 198-200, 210, 216, 233, 288, 352, 372, 379, 414, 430, 435, 438-39, 455, 459, 466, 467, 488, 498-99, 518.
Washington, Booker T., 552-53.
Washington Post, 78, 313, 361, 469, 495-97.
Watergate scandal, 175, 461-63, 478, 486, 496-97, 501-04, 513, 537-38, 541, 543, 544.
Watson, Goodwin, 279-80.
Watson, Tom, 94, 114-15.
Way, H. Frank, 425.
Weatherman, 429, 432, 467-68, 472, 475-76, 478, 491-92, 494, 507, 512, 535.
Weinstein, Allen, 317, 326.
Weinstein, James, 81.
West Virginia, 119, 183, 189, 258; Logan Co., 189; Martinsburg, 31; Mingo Co., 189; Wheeling, 53.
Wheeler, Burton K., 130, 135, 146, 174, 175, 251.
Whitney, Charlotte Anita, 159, 172.
Wiebe, Robert, 80, 161, 553.
Williams, Roger, xiv.
Wilson, William B., 112, 147-48, 155, 160.
Wilson, Woodrow, 5, 6, 83, 94, 97.
Wiretapping, 111, 175-76, 249-50, 254, 273, 294, 317, 342, 395, 421, 442-44, 467-69, 477, 481, 484, 490-91, 494, 501-02, 525, 529, 539, 540, 542-43.
Wirt, William A., 214.
Wisconsin, 133, 180, 225, 232, 234, 295, 327, 515; Milwaukee, 26, 37-38, 40, 81-82, 119, 127, 133, 249, 458, 518.
Wolfe, Alan, xvi.
Women's Strike for Peace (WSP), 414, 426, 455, 457-58.
Workingman's Party of the U.S. (WPUS), 26, 30-31.
Works Progress Administration (WPA), 242, 244, 246.
Worker, Daily and *Sunday*, 370, 406.
World War I, xiv, xxii, 10, 63-64, 69, 99, 105-35, 139, 141, 143-44, 160-61, 198, 210, 212, 263, 269, 291, 549-50, 553, 554, 561-63, 566-67, 569.
World War II, 69, 105, 253, 240, 248, 262-84, 287-88, 291, 294, 308, 316, 319, 324, 360, 364, 371, 373, 457, 551, 554-55, 560-64, 566, 568-72.
Wrong-thinking, attack on during Truman-McCarthy period, 391-92.
Wyoming, 178.

Yorty, Samuel, 256.
Young People's Socialist League, 119, 531.
Young Socialist Alliance (YSA), 424, 484.

Zeigler, L. Harmon, xi.